University Casebook Series

December, 1982

ACCOUNTING AND THE LAW, Fourth Edition (1978), with Problems Pamphlet (Successor to Dohr, Phillips, Thompson & Warren)

George C. Thompson, Professor, Columbia University Graduate School of Business.
Robert Whitman, Professor of Law, University of Connecticut.
Ellis L. Phillips, Jr., Member of the New York Bar.
William C. Warren, Professor of Law Emeritus, Columbia University.

ACCOUNTING FOR LAWYERS, MATERIALS ON (1980)

David R. Herwitz, Professor of Law, Harvard University.

ADMINISTRATIVE LAW, Seventh Edition (1979), with 1983 Problems Supplement (Supplement edited in association with Paul R. Verkuil, Dean and Professor of Law, Tulane University)

Walter Gellhorn, University Professor Emeritus, Columbia University.
Clark Byse, Professor of Law, Harvard University.
Peter L. Strauss, Professor of Law, Columbia University.

ADMIRALTY, Second Edition (1978), with Statute and Rule Supplement

Jo Desha Lucas, Professor of Law, University of Chicago.

ADVOCACY, see also Lawyering Process

AGENCY, see also Enterprise Organization

AGENCY—PARTNERSHIPS, Third Edition (1982)

Abridgement from Conard, Knauss & Siegel's Enterprise Organization, Third Edition.

ANTITRUST AND REGULATORY ALTERNATIVES (1977), Fifth Edition

Louis B. Schwartz, Professor of Law, University of Pennsylvania.
John J. Flynn, Professor of Law, University of Utah.

ANTITRUST SUPPLEMENT—SELECTED STATUTES AND RELATED MATERIALS (1977)

John J. Flynn, Professor of Law, University of Utah.

BUSINESS ORGANIZATION, see also Enterprise Organization

BUSINESS PLANNING (1966), with 1982 Supplement

David R. Herwitz, Professor of Law, Harvard University.

BUSINESS TORTS (1972)

Milton Handler, Professor of Law Emeritus, Columbia University.

CHILDREN IN THE LEGAL SYSTEM (1983)

Walter Wadlington, Professor of Law, University of Virginia.
Charles H. Whitebread, Professor of Law, University of Southern California.
Samuel Davis, Professor of Law, University of Georgia.

UNIVERSITY CASEBOOK SERIES—Continued

CIVIL PROCEDURE, see Procedure

CLINIC, see also Lawyering Process

COMMERCIAL AND CONSUMER TRANSACTIONS, Second Edition (1978)

William D. Warren, Dean of the School of Law, University of California, Los Angeles.
William E. Hogan, Professor of Law, Cornell University.
Robert L. Jordan, Professor of Law, University of California, Los Angeles.

COMMERCIAL LAW, CASES & MATERIALS ON, Third Edition (1976), with 1982 Supplement

E. Allan Farnsworth, Professor of Law, Columbia University.
John Honnold, Professor of Law, University of Pennsylvania.

COMMERCIAL PAPER, Second Edition (1976)

E. Allan Farnsworth, Professor of Law, Columbia University.

COMMERCIAL PAPER AND BANK DEPOSITS AND COLLECTIONS (1967), with Statutory Supplement

William D. Hawkland, Professor of Law, University of Illinois.

COMMERCIAL TRANSACTIONS—Principles and Policies (1982)

Alan Schwartz, Professor of Law, University of Southern California.
Robert E. Scott, Professor of Law, University of Virginia.

COMPARATIVE LAW, Fourth Edition (1980)

Rudolf B. Schlesinger, Professor of Law, Hastings College of the Law.

COMPETITIVE PROCESS, LEGAL REGULATION OF THE, Second Edition (1979), with Statutory Supplement and 1982 Case Supplement

Edmund W. Kitch, Professor of Law, University of Chicago.
Harvey S. Perlman, Professor of Law, University of Virginia.

CONFLICT OF LAWS, Seventh Edition (1978), with 1982 Supplement

Willis L. M. Reese, Professor of Law, Columbia University,
Maurice Rosenberg, Professor of Law, Columbia University.

CONSTITUTIONAL LAW, Sixth Edition (1981), with 1982 Supplement

Edward L. Barrett, Jr., Professor of Law, University of California, Davis.
William Cohen, Professor of Law, Stanford University.

CONSTITUTIONAL LAW: THE STRUCTURE OF GOVERNMENT (Reprinted from CONSTITUTIONAL LAW, Sixth Edition), with 1982 Supplement

Edward L. Barrett, Jr., Professor of Law, University of California, Davis.
William Cohen, Professor of Law, Stanford University.

CONSTITUTIONAL LAW, CIVIL LIBERTY AND INDIVIDUAL RIGHTS, Second Edition (1982)

William Cohen, Professor of Law, Stanford Law School.
John Kaplan, Professor of Law, Stanford Law School.

CONSTITUTIONAL LAW, Tenth Edition (1980), with 1982 Supplement

Gerald Gunther, Professor of Law, Stanford University.

CONSTITUTIONAL LAW, INDIVIDUAL RIGHTS IN, Third Edition (1981), with 1982 Supplement (Reprinted from CONSTITUTIONAL LAW, Tenth Edition)

Gerald Gunther, Professor of Law, Stanford University.

UNIVERSITY CASEBOOK SERIES—Continued

CONTRACT LAW AND ITS APPLICATION, Second Edition (1977)

The late Addison Mueller, Professor of Law, University of California, Los Angeles.
Arthur I. Rosett, Professor of Law, University of California, Los Angeles.

CONTRACT LAW, STUDIES IN, Second Edition (1977)

Edward J. Murphy, Professor of Law, University of Notre Dame.
Richard E. Speidel, Professor of Law, University of Virginia.

CONTRACTS, Fourth Edition (1982)

John P. Dawson, Professor of Law Emeritus, Harvard University.
William Burnett Harvey, Professor of Law and Political Science, Boston University.
Stanley D. Henderson, Professor of Law, University of Virginia.

CONTRACTS, Third Edition (1980), with Statutory Supplement

E. Allan Farnsworth, Professor of Law, Columbia University.
William F. Young, Professor of Law, Columbia University.

CONTRACTS, Second Edition (1978), with Statutory and Administrative Law Supplement (1978)

Ian R. Macneil, Professor of Law, Cornell University.

COPYRIGHT, PATENTS AND TRADEMARKS, see also Competitive Process

COPYRIGHT, PATENT, TRADEMARK AND RELATED STATE DOCTRINES, Second Edition (1981), with Problem Supplement and Statutory Supplement

Paul Goldstein, Professor of Law, Stanford University.

COPYRIGHT, Unfair Competition, and Other Topics Bearing on the Protection of Literary, Musical, and Artistic Works, Third Edition (1978)

Benjamin Kaplan, Professor of Law Emeritus, Harvard University,
Ralph S. Brown, Jr., Professor of Law, Yale University.

CORPORATE FINANCE, Second Edition (1979), with 1982 New Developments Supplement

Victor Brudney, Professor of Law, Harvard University.
Marvin A. Chirelstein, Professor of Law, Yale University.

CORPORATE READJUSTMENTS AND REORGANIZATIONS (1976)

Walter J. Blum, Professor of Law, University of Chicago.
Stanley A. Kaplan, Professor of Law, University of Chicago.

CORPORATION LAW, BASIC, Second Edition (1979), with Documentary Supplement

Detlev F. Vagts, Professor of Law, Harvard University.

CORPORATIONS, see also Enterprise Organization

CORPORATIONS, Fifth Edition—Unabridged (1980)

William L. Cary, Professor of Law, Columbia University.
Melvin Aron Eisenberg, Professor of Law, University of California, Berkeley.

CORPORATIONS, Fifth Edition—Abridged (1980)

William L. Cary, Professor of Law, Columbia University.
Melvin Aron Eisenberg, Professor of Law, University of California, Berkeley.

CORPORATIONS, Second Edition (1982)

Alfred F. Conard, Professor of Law, University of Michigan.
Robert N. Knauss, Dean of the Law School, University of Houston.
Stanley Siegel, Professor of Law, University of California, Los Angeles.

CORPORATIONS, THE LAW OF: WHAT CORPORATE LAWYERS DO (1976)

Jan G. Deutsch, Professor of Law, Yale University.
Joseph J. Bianco, Professor of Law, Yeshiva University.

CORPORATIONS COURSE GAME PLAN (1975)

David R. Herwitz, Professor of Law, Harvard University.

CORRECTIONS, SEE SENTENCING

CREDIT TRANSACTIONS AND CONSUMER PROTECTION (1976)

John Honnold, Professor of Law, University of Pennsylvania.

CREDITORS' RIGHTS, see also Debtor-Creditor Law

CRIMINAL JUSTICE, THE ADMINISTRATION OF, Second Edition (1969)

Francis C. Sullivan, Professor of Law, Louisiana State University.
Paul Hardin III, Professor of Law, Duke University.
John Huston, Professor of Law, University of Washington.
Frank R. Lacy, Professor of Law, University of Oregon.
Daniel E. Murray, Professor of Law, University of Miami.
George W. Pugh, Professor of Law, Louisiana State University.

CRIMINAL JUSTICE ADMINISTRATION, Second Edition (1982)

Frank W. Miller, Professor of Law, Washington University.
Robert O. Dawson, Professor of Law, University of Texas.
George E. Dix, Professor of Law, University of Texas.
Raymond I. Parnas, Professor of Law, University of California, Davis.

CRIMINAL LAW, Second Edition (1979)

Fred E. Inbau, Professor of Law Emeritus, Northwestern University.
James R. Thompson, Professor of Law Emeritus, Northwestern University.
Andre A. Moenssens, Professor of Law, University of Richmond.

CRIMINAL LAW (1982)

Peter W. Low, Professor of Law, University of Virginia.
John C. Jeffries, Jr., Professor of Law, University of Virginia.
Richard C. Bonnie, Professor of Law, University of Virginia.

CRIMINAL LAW, Third Edition (1980)

Lloyd L. Weinreb, Professor of Law, Harvard University.

CRIMINAL LAW AND PROCEDURE, Fifth Edition (1977)

Rollin M. Perkins, Professor of Law Emeritus, University of California, Hastings
College of the Law.
Ronald N. Boyce, Professor of Law, University of Utah.

CRIMINAL PROCEDURE, Second Edition (1980), with 1982 Supplement

Fred E. Inbau, Professor of Law Emeritus, Northwestern University.
James R. Thompson, Professor of Law Emeritus, Northwestern University.
James B. Haddad, Professor of Law, Northwestern University.
James B. Zagel, Chief, Criminal Justice Division, Office of Attorney General of
Illinois.
Gary L. Starkman, Assistant U. S. Attorney, Northern District of Illinois.

UNIVERSITY CASEBOOK SERIES—Continued

CRIMINAL PROCEDURE, CONSTITUTIONAL (1977), with 1980 Supplement

James E. Scarboro, Professor of Law, University of Colorado.
James B. White, Professor of Law, University of Chicago.

CRIMINAL PROCESS, Third Edition (1978), with 1982 Supplement

Lloyd L. Weinreb, Professor of Law, Harvard University.

DAMAGES, Second Edition (1952)

Charles T. McCormick, late Professor of Law, University of Texas.
William F. Fritz, late Professor of Law, University of Texas.

DEBTOR–CREDITOR LAW, Second Edition (1981), with Statutory Supplement

William D. Warren, Dean of the School of Law, University of California, Los Angeles.
William E. Hogan, Professor of Law, New York University.

DECEDENTS' ESTATES (1971)

Max Rheinstein, late Professor of Law Emeritus, University of Chicago.
Mary Ann Glendon, Professor of Law, Boston College.

DECEDENTS' ESTATES AND TRUSTS, Sixth Edition (1982)

John Ritchie, Emeritus Dean and Wigmore Professor of Law, Northwestern University.
Neill H. Alford, Jr., Professor of Law, University of Virginia.
Richard W. Effland, Professor of Law, Arizona State University.

DECEDENTS' ESTATES AND TRUSTS (1968)

Howard R. Williams, Professor of Law, Stanford University.

DOMESTIC RELATIONS, see also Family Law

DOMESTIC RELATIONS, Third Edition (1978), with 1980 Supplement

Walter Wadlington, Professor of Law, University of Virginia.
Monrad G. Paulsen, Dean of the Law School, Yeshiva University.

ELECTRONIC MASS MEDIA, Second Edition (1979)

William K. Jones, Professor of Law, Columbia University.

EMPLOYMENT DISCRIMINATION (1983)

Joel W. Friedman, Professor of Law, Tulane University.
George M. Strickler, Professor of Law, Tulane University.

ENERGY LAW (1983)

Donald N. Zillman, Professor of Law, University of Utah.
Laurence Lattman, Dean of Mines and Engineering, University of Utah.

ENTERPRISE ORGANIZATION, Third Edition (1982), with 1982 Corporation and Partnership Statutes, Rules and Forms Supplement

Alfred F. Conard, Professor of Law, University of Michigan.
Robert L. Knauss, Dean of the Law School, University of Houston.
Stanley Siegel, Professor of Law, University of California, Los Angeles.

ENVIRONMENTAL POLICY LAW (1982)

Thomas J. Schoenbaum, Professor of Law, Tulane University.

EQUITY, see also Remedies

UNIVERSITY CASEBOOK SERIES—Continued

EQUITY, RESTITUTION AND DAMAGES, Second Edition (1974)

Robert Childres, late Professor of Law, Northwestern University.
William F. Johnson, Jr., Professor of Law, New York University.

ESTATE PLANNING, Second Edition (1982), with Documentary Supplement

David Westfall, Professor of Law, Harvard University.

ETHICS, see Legal Profession, and Professional Responsibility

ETHICS AND PROFESSIONAL RESPONSIBILITY (1981) (Reprinted from THE LAWYERING PROCESS)

Gary Bellow, Professor of Law, Harvard University.
Bea Moulton, Legal Services Corporation.

EVIDENCE, Fourth Edition (1981)

David W. Louisell, late Professor of Law, University of California, Berkeley.
John Kaplan, Professor of Law, Stanford University.
Jon R. Waltz, Professor of Law, Northwestern University.

EVIDENCE (1968)

Francis C. Sullivan, Professor of Law, Louisiana State University.
Paul Hardin, III, Professor of Law, Duke University.

EVIDENCE, Seventh Edition (1983) with Rules and Statute Supplement (1981)

Jack B. Weinstein, Chief Judge, United States District Court.
John H. Mansfield, Professor of Law, Harvard University.
Norman Abrams, Professor of Law, University of California, Los Angeles.
Margaret Berger, Professor of Law, Brooklyn Law School.

FAMILY LAW, see also Domestic Relations

FAMILY LAW (1978), with 1983 Supplement

Judith C. Areen, Professor of Law, Georgetown University.

FAMILY LAW AND CHILDREN IN THE LEGAL SYSTEM, STATUTORY MATERIALS (1981)

Walter Wadlington, Professor of Law, University of Virginia.

FEDERAL COURTS, Seventh Edition (1982)

Charles T. McCormick, late Professor of Law, University of Texas.
James H. Chadbourn, Professor of Law, Harvard University.
Charles Alan Wright, Professor of Law, University of Texas.

FEDERAL COURTS AND THE FEDERAL SYSTEM, Hart and Wechsler's Second Edition (1973), with 1981 Supplement

Paul M. Bator, Professor of Law, Harvard University.
Paul J. Mishkin, Professor of Law, University of California, Berkeley.
David L. Shapiro, Professor of Law, Harvard University.
Herbert Wechsler, Professor of Law, Columbia University.

FEDERAL PUBLIC LAND AND RESOURCES LAW (1981)

George C. Coggins, Professor of Law, University of Kansas.
Charles F. Wilkinson, Professor of Law, University of Oregon.

FEDERAL RULES OF CIVIL PROCEDURE, 1982 Edition

FEDERAL TAXATION, see Taxation

UNIVERSITY CASEBOOK SERIES—Continued

FOOD AND DRUG LAW (1980), with Statutory Supplement

Richard A. Merrill, Dean of the School of Law, University of Virginia.
Peter Barton Hutt, Esq.

FUTURE INTERESTS (1958)

Philip Mechem, late Professor of Law Emeritus, University of Pennsylvania.

FUTURE INTERESTS (1970)

Howard R. Williams, Professor of Law, Stanford University.

FUTURE INTERESTS AND ESTATE PLANNING (1961), with 1962 Supplement

W. Barton Leach, late Professor of Law, Harvard University.
James K. Logan, formerly Dean of the Law School, University of Kansas.

GOVERNMENT CONTRACTS, FEDERAL (1975), with 1980 Supplement

John W. Whelan, Professor of Law, Hastings College of the Law.
Robert S. Pasley, Professor of Law Emeritus, Cornell University.

INJUNCTIONS (1972)

Owen M. Fiss, Professor of Law, Yale University.

INSTITUTIONAL INVESTORS, 1978

David L. Ratner, Professor of Law, Cornell University.

INSURANCE (1971)

William F. Young, Professor of Law, Columbia University.

INTERNATIONAL LAW, see also Transnational Legal Problems and United Nations Law

INTERNATIONAL LAW IN CONTEMPORARY PERSPECTIVE (1981), with Essay Supplement

Myres S. McDougal, Professor of Law, Yale University.
W. Michael Reisman, Professor of Law, Yale University.

INTERNATIONAL LEGAL SYSTEM, Second Edition (1981), with Documentary Supplement

Joseph Modeste Sweeney, Professor of Law, Tulane University.
Covey T. Oliver, Professor of Law, University of Pennsylvania.
Noyes E. Leech, Professor of Law, University of Pennsylvania.

INTERNATIONAL TRADE AND INVESTMENT, REGULATION OF (1970)

Carl H. Fulda, late Professor of Law, University of Texas.
Warren F. Schwartz, Professor of Law, University of Virginia.

INTRODUCTION TO LAW, see also Legal Method, On Law in Courts, and Dynamics of American Law

INTRODUCTION TO THE STUDY OF LAW (1970)

E. Wayne Thode, late Professor of Law, University of Utah.
Leon Lebowitz, Professor of Law, University of Texas.
Lester J. Mazor, Professor of Law, University of Utah.

JUDICIAL CODE and Rules of Procedure in the Federal Courts with Excerpts from the Criminal Code, 1981 Edition

Henry M. Hart, Jr., late Professor of Law, Harvard University.
Herbert Wechsler, Professor of Law, Columbia University.

UNIVERSITY CASEBOOK SERIES—Continued

JURISPRUDENCE (Temporary Edition Hardbound) (1949)

Lon L. Fuller, Professor of Law Emeritus, Harvard University.

JUVENILE, see also Children

JUVENILE JUSTICE PROCESS, Second Edition (1976), with 1980 Supplement

Frank W. Miller, Professor of Law, Washington University.
Robert O. Dawson, Professor of Law, University of Texas.
George E. Dix, Professor of Law, University of Texas.
Raymond I. Parnas, Professor of Law, University of California, Davis.

LABOR LAW, Ninth Edition (1981), with Statutory Supplement

Archibald Cox, Professor of Law, Harvard University.
Derek C. Bok, President, Harvard University.
Robert A. Gorman, Professor of Law, University of Pennsylvania.

LABOR LAW, Second Edition (1982), with Statutory Supplement

Clyde W. Summers, Professor of Law, University of Pennsylvania.
Harry H. Wellington, Dean of the Law School, Yale University.
Alan Hyde, Professor of Law, Rutgers University.

LAND FINANCING, Second Edition (1977)

Norman Penney, Professor of Law, Cornell University.
Richard F. Broude, Member of the California Bar.

LAW AND MEDICINE (1980)

Walter Wadlington, Professor of Law and Professor of Legal Medicine, University
of Virginia.
Jon R. Waltz, Professor of Law, Northwestern University.
Roger B. Dworkin, Professor of Law, Indiana University, and Professor of Bio-
medical History, University of Washington.

LAW, LANGUAGE AND ETHICS (1972)

William R. Bishin, Professor of Law, University of Southern California.
Christopher D. Stone, Professor of Law, University of Southern California.

**LAWYERING PROCESS (1978), with Civil Problem Supplement and Criminal
Problem Supplement**

Gary Bellow, Professor of Law, Harvard University.
Bea Moulton, Professor of Law, Arizona State University.

LEGAL METHOD (1980)

Harry W. Jones, Professor of Law Emeritus, Columbia University.
John M. Kernochan, Professor of Law, Columbia University.
Arthur W. Murphy, Professor of Law, Columbia University.

LEGAL METHODS (1969)

Robert N. Covington, Professor of Law, Vanderbilt University.
E. Blythe Stason, late Professor of Law, Vanderbilt University.
John W. Wade, Professor of Law, Vanderbilt University.
Elliott E. Cheatham, late Professor of Law, Vanderbilt University.
Theodore A. Smedley, Professor of Law, Vanderbilt University.

LEGAL PROFESSION (1970)

Samuel D. Thurman, Dean of the College of Law, University of Utah.
Ellis L. Phillips, Jr., Professor of Law, Columbia University.
Elliott E. Cheatham, late Professor of Law, Vanderbilt University.

UNIVERSITY CASEBOOK SERIES—Continued

LEGISLATION, Fourth Edition (1982) (by Fordham)

Horace E. Read, late Vice President, Dalhousie University.
John W. MacDonald, Professor of Law Emeritus, Cornell Law School.
Jefferson B. Fordham, Professor of Law, University of Utah.
William J. Pierce, Professor of Law, University of Michigan.

LEGISLATIVE AND ADMINISTRATIVE PROCESSES, Second Edition (1981)

Hans A. Linde, Judge, Supreme Court of Oregon.
George Bunn, Professor of Law, University of Wisconsin.
Fredericka Paff, Professor of Law, University of Wisconsin.
W. Lawrence Church, Professor of Law, University of Wisconsin.

LOCAL GOVERNMENT LAW, Revised Edition (1975)

Jefferson B. Fordham, Professor of Law, University of Utah.

MASS MEDIA LAW, Second Edition (1982)

Marc A. Franklin, Professor of Law, Stanford University.

MENTAL HEALTH PROCESS, Second Edition (1976), with 1981 Supplement

Frank W. Miller, Professor of Law, Washington University.
Robert O. Dawson, Professor of Law, University of Texas.
George E. Dix, Professor of Law, University of Texas.
Raymond I. Parnas, Professor of Law, University of California, Davis.

MUNICIPAL CORPORATIONS, see Local Government Law

NEGOTIABLE INSTRUMENTS, see Commercial Paper

NEGOTIATION (1981) (Reprinted from THE LAWYERING PROCESS)

Gary Bellow, Professor of Law, Harvard Law School.
Bea Moulton, Legal Services Corporation.

NEW YORK PRACTICE, Fourth Edition (1978)

Herbert Peterfreund, Professor of Law, New York University.
Joseph M. McLaughlin, Dean of the Law School, Fordham University.

OIL AND GAS, Fourth Edition (1979)

Howard R. Williams, Professor of Law, Stanford University.
Richard C. Maxwell, Professor of Law, University of California, Los Angeles.
Charles J. Meyers, Dean of the Law School, Stanford University.

ON LAW IN COURTS (1965)

Paul J. Mishkin, Professor of Law, University of California, Berkeley.
Clarence Morris, Professor of Law Emeritus, University of Pennsylvania.

PERSPECTIVES ON THE LAWYER AS PLANNER (Reprint of Chapters One through Five of Planning by Lawyers) (1978)

Louis M. Brown, Professor of Law, University of Southern California.
Edward A. Dauer, Professor of Law, Yale University.

PLANNING BY LAWYERS, MATERIALS ON A NONADVERSARIAL LEGAL PROCESS (1978)

Louis M. Brown, Professor of Law, University of Southern California.
Edward A. Dauer, Professor of Law, Yale University.

PLEADING AND PROCEDURE, see Procedure, Civil

UNIVERSITY CASEBOOK SERIES—Continued

POLICE FUNCTION, Third Edition (1982)

> Reprint of Chapters 1–10 of Miller, Dawson, Dix and Parnas' Criminal Justice Administration, Second Edition.

PREPARING AND PRESENTING THE CASE (1981) (Reprinted from THE LAWYERING PROCESS)

> Gary Bellow, Professor of Law, Harvard Law School.
> Bea Moulton, Legal Services Corporation.

PREVENTIVE LAW, see also Planning by Lawyers

PROCEDURE—CIVIL PROCEDURE, Second Edition (1974), with 1979 Supplement

> James H. Chadbourn, Professor of Law, Harvard University.
> A. Leo Levin, Professor of Law, University of Pennsylvania.
> Philip Shuchman, Professor of Law, University of Connecticut.

PROCEDURE—CIVIL PROCEDURE, Fourth Edition (1978), with 1982 Supplement

> Richard H. Field, late Professor of Law, Harvard University.
> Benjamin Kaplan, Professor of Law Emeritus, Harvard University.
> Kevin M. Clermont, Professor of Law, Cornell University.

PROCEDURE—CIVIL PROCEDURE, Third Edition (1976), with 1982 Supplement

> Maurice Rosenberg, Professor of Law, Columbia University.
> Jack B. Weinstein, Professor of Law, Columbia University.
> Hans Smit, Professor of Law, Columbia University.
> Harold L. Korn, Professor of Law, Columbia University.

PROCEDURE—PLEADING AND PROCEDURE: State and Federal, Fourth Edition (1979), with 1982 Supplement

> David W. Louisell, late Professor of Law, University of California, Berkeley.
> Geoffrey C. Hazard, Jr., Professor of Law, Yale University.

PROCEDURE—FEDERAL RULES OF CIVIL PROCEDURE, 1982 Edition

PRODUCTS LIABILITY (1980)

> Marshall S. Shapo, Professor of Law, Northwestern University.

PRODUCTS LIABILITY AND SAFETY (1980), with Statutory Supplement

> W. Page Keeton, Professor of Law, University of Texas.
> David G. Owen, Professor of Law, University of South Carolina.
> John E. Montgomery, Professor of Law, University of South Carolina.

PROFESSIONAL RESPONSIBILITY, Second Edition (1981), with Selected National Standards Supplement

> Thomas D. Morgan, Dean of the Law School, Emory University.
> Ronald D. Rotunda, Professor of Law, University of Illinois.

PROPERTY, Fourth Edition (1978)

> John E. Cribbet, Dean of the Law School, University of Illinois.
> Corwin W. Johnson, Professor of Law, University of Texas.

PROPERTY—PERSONAL (1953)

> S. Kenneth Skolfield, late Professor of Law Emeritus, Boston University.

UNIVERSITY CASEBOOK SERIES—Continued

PROPERTY—PERSONAL, Third Edition (1954)

Everett Fraser, late Dean of the Law School Emeritus, University of Minnesota. Third Edition by Charles W. Taintor, late Professor of Law, University of Pittsburgh.

PROPERTY—INTRODUCTION, TO REAL PROPERTY, Third Edition (1954)

Everett Fraser, late Dean of the Law School Emeritus, University of Minnesota.

PROPERTY—REAL AND PERSONAL, Combined Edition (1954)

Everett Fraser, late Dean of the Law School Emeritus, University of Minnesota. Third Edition of Personal Property by Charles W. Taintor, late Professor of Law, University of Pittsburgh.

PROPERTY—REAL PROPERTY AND CONVEYANCING (1954)

Edward E. Bade, late Professor of Law, University of Minnesota.

PROPERTY—FUNDAMENTALS OF MODERN REAL PROPERTY, Second Edition (1982)

Edward H. Rabin, Professor of Law, University of California, Davis.

PROPERTY—PROBLEMS IN REAL PROPERTY (Pamphlet) (1969)

Edward H. Rabin, Professor of Law, University of California, Davis.

PROSECUTION AND ADJUDICATION, Second Edition (1982)

Reprint of Chapters 11–26 of Miller, Dawson, Dix and Parnas' Criminal Justice Administration, Second Edition.

PUBLIC REGULATION OF DANGEROUS PRODUCTS (paperback) (1980)

Marshall S. Shapo, Professor of Law, Northwestern University.

PUBLIC UTILITY LAW, see Free Enterprise, also Regulated Industries

REAL ESTATE PLANNING (1980), with 1980 Problems, Statutes and New Materials Supplement

Norton L. Steuben, Professor of Law, University of Colorado.

REAL ESTATE TRANSACTIONS (1980), with Statute, Form and Problem Supplement

Paul Goldstein, Professor of Law, Stanford University.

RECEIVERSHIP AND CORPORATE REORGANIZATION, see Creditors' Rights

REGULATED INDUSTRIES, Second Edition, 1976

William K. Jones, Professor of Law, Columbia University.

REMEDIES (1982)

Edward D. Re, Chief Judge, U. S. Court of International Trade.

RESTITUTION, Second Edition (1966)

John W. Wade, Professor of Law, Vanderbilt University.

SALES (1980)

Marion W. Benfield, Jr., Professor of Law, University of Illinois. William D. Hawkland, Chancellor, Louisiana State University Law Center.

SALES AND SALES FINANCING, Fourth Edition (1976), with 1982 Supplement

John Honnold, Professor of Law, University of Pennsylvania.

UNIVERSITY CASEBOOK SERIES—Continued

SALES LAW AND THE CONTRACTING PROCESS (1982)

Reprint of Chapters 1–10 of Schwartz and Scott's Commercial Transactions.

SECURITIES REGULATION, Fifth Edition (1982), with 1982 Selected Statutes, Rules and Forms Supplement

Richard W. Jennings, Professor of Law, University of California, Berkeley.
Harold Marsh, Jr., Member of the California Bar.

SECURITIES REGULATION (1982), with 1983 Supplement

Larry D. Soderquist, Professor of Law, Vanderbilt University.

SENTENCING AND THE CORRECTIONAL PROCESS, Second Edition (1976)

Frank W. Miller, Professor of Law, Washington University.
Robert O. Dawson, Professor of Law, University of Texas.
George E. Dix, Professor of Law, University of Texas.
Raymond I. Parnas, Professor of Law, University of California, Davis.

SOCIAL WELFARE AND THE INDIVIDUAL (1971)

Robert J. Levy, Professor of Law, University of Minnesota.
Thomas P. Lewis, Dean of the College of Law, University of Kentucky.
Peter W. Martin, Professor of Law, Cornell University.

TAX, POLICY ANALYSIS OF THE FEDERAL INCOME (1976)

William A. Klein, Professor of Law, University of California, Los Angeles.

TAXATION, FEDERAL INCOME (1976), with 1982 Supplement

Erwin N. Griswold, Dean Emeritus, Harvard Law School.
Michael J. Graetz, Professor of Law, University of Virginia.

TAXATION, FEDERAL INCOME, Fourth Edition (1982)

James J. Freeland, Professor of Law, University of Florida.
Stephen A. Lind, Professor of Law, University of Florida.
Richard B. Stephens, Professor of Law Emeritus, University of Florida.

TAXATION, FEDERAL INCOME, Volume I, Personal Income Taxation (1972), with 1982 Supplement; Volume II, Taxation of Partnerships and Corporations, Second Edition (1980)

Stanley S. Surrey, Professor of Law, Harvard University.
William C. Warren, Professor of Law Emeritus, Columbia University.
Paul R. McDaniel, Professor of Law, Boston College Law School.
Hugh J. Ault, Professor of Law, Boston College Law School.

TAXATION, FEDERAL WEALTH TRANSFER, Second Edition (1982)

Stanley S. Surrey, Professor of Law, Harvard University.
William C. Warren, Professor of Law Emeritus, Columbia University.
Paul R. McDaniel, Professor of Law, Boston College Law School.
Harry L. Gutman, Instructor, Harvard Law School and Boston College Law School.

TAXATION OF INDIVIDUALS, PARTNERSHIPS AND CORPORATIONS, PROBLEMS in the (1978)

Norton L. Steuben, Professor of Law, University of Colorado.
William J. Turnier, Professor of Law, University of North Carolina.

TAXES AND FINANCE—STATE AND LOCAL (1974)

Oliver Oldman, Professor of Law, Harvard University.
Ferdinand P. Schoettle, Professor of Law, University of Minnesota.

TORT LAW AND ALTERNATIVES: INJURIES AND REMEDIES, Second Edition (1979)

Marc A. Franklin, Professor of Law, Stanford University.

UNIVERSITY CASEBOOK SERIES—Continued

TORTS, Seventh Edition (1982)

William L. Prosser, late Professor of Law, University of California, Hastings College.
John W. Wade, Professor of Law, Vanderbilt University.
Victor E. Schwartz, Professor of Law, American University.

TORTS, Third Edition (1976)

Harry Shulman, late Dean of the Law School, Yale University.
Fleming James, Jr., Professor of Law Emeritus, Yale University.
Oscar S. Gray, Professor of Law, University of Maryland.

TRADE REGULATION (1975), with 1979 Supplement

Milton Handler, Professor of Law Emeritus, Columbia University.
Harlan M. Blake, Professor of Law, Columbia University.
Robert Pitofsky, Professor of Law, Georgetown University.
Harvey J. Goldschmid, Professor of Law, Columbia University.

TRADE REGULATION, see Antitrust

TRANSNATIONAL LEGAL PROBLEMS, Second Edition (1976) with 1982 Case and Documentary Supplement

Henry J. Steiner, Professor of Law, Harvard University.
Detlev F. Vagts, Professor of Law, Harvard University.

TRIAL, see also Evidence, Making the Record, Lawyering Process and Preparing and Presenting the Case

TRIAL ADVOCACY (1968)

A. Leo Levin, Professor of Law, University of Pennsylvania.
Harold Cramer, of the Pennsylvania Bar.
Maurice Rosenberg, Professor of Law, Columbia University, Consultant.

TRUSTS, Fifth Edition (1978)

George G. Bogert, late Professor of Law Emeritus, University of Chicago.
Dallin H. Oaks, President, Brigham Young University.

TRUSTS AND SUCCESSION (Palmer's), Third Edition (1978)

Richard V. Wellman, Professor of Law, University of Georgia.
Lawrence W. Waggoner, Professor of Law, University of Michigan.
Olin L. Browder, Jr., Professor of Law, University of Michigan.

UNFAIR COMPETITION, see Competitive Process and Business Torts

UNITED NATIONS IN ACTION (1968)

Louis B. Sohn, Professor of Law, Harvard University.

UNITED NATIONS LAW, Second Edition (1967), with Documentary Supplement (1968)

Louis B. Sohn, Professor of Law, Harvard University.

WATER RESOURCE MANAGEMENT, Second Edition (1980), with 1983 Supplement

Charles J. Meyers, Dean of the Law School, Stanford University.
A. Dan Tarlock, Professor of Law, Indiana Unversity.

WILLS AND ADMINISTRATION, Fifth Edition (1961)

Philip Mechem, late Professor of Law, University of Pennsylvania.
Thomas E. Atkinson, late Professor of Law, New York University.

WORLD LAW, see United Nations Law

FREE ENTERPRISE

AND

ECONOMIC ORGANIZATION: ANTITRUST

By

LOUIS B. SCHWARTZ
Benjamin Franklin Professor of Law
University of Pennsylvania

JOHN J. FLYNN
Professor of Law
University of Utah

and

HARRY FIRST
Professor of Law
New York University

SIXTH EDITION

Mineola, New York
THE FOUNDATION PRESS, INC.
1983

Library of Congress Cataloging in Publication Data

Schwartz, Louis B.
    Free enterprise and economic organization.

    (University casebook series)
    Fifth ed. published as: Antitrust and regulatory
alternatives. 1977.
    Includes bibliographical references and index.
    1. Antitrust law—United States—Cases.
2. Industrial laws and legislation—United States—
Cases. I. Flynn, John J. II. First, Harry, 1945–
III. Title. IV. Series.
KF1648.S3 1983   343.73'072   83–8859
                 347.30372

ISBN 0–88277–120–5

PREFACE

The first edition of this casebook appeared in 1952 under the title *Free Enterprise and Economic Organization;* the Fifth Edition appeared in 1977 with the title *Antitrust and Regulatory Alternatives.* The Sixth Edition appears with a new variation of its original title, and a new format. This Edition separates antitrust and government regulation into two distinct, but related, volumes. The change reflects the fact that law school curricula normally provide for separate courses in the two areas; separate books will better serve curricular needs. A second volume, *Free Enterprise and Economic Organization: Government Regulation,* will be available for courses focusing solely on regulation. For those fortunate enough to teach an integrated course, the two volumes can be used simultaneously to explore and compare these different approaches to government control of business behavior.

The developments in both antitrust and government regulation since the Fifth Edition have been dramatic. Entire industries have been moved toward the "free market" sector by total or partial deregulation (e.g., airlines and motor carriers), and the courts have expanded the coverage of the antitrust laws to examine practices previously thought exempt (e.g., the conduct of municipalities, professions, labor unions). At the same time, however, courts and enforcement agencies have become more critical of many traditional antitrust concepts. This critical view had led to the reinvigoration of antitrust's "Rule of Reason"; to a more willing embrace of large firm conduct; to a greater tolerance of mergers; to an expansion of the monopoly rights of those who seek or exploit patents.

The Sixth Edition places these new developments in the context of what has come before. Like previous editions, the Sixth Edition is intended to present a comprehensive approach to antitrust, reflecting the many sources of wisdom which have enriched antitrust policy. History, psychology, politics, the felt needs of the times—along with common sense—all contribute to the evolution of antitrust policy and our understanding of it.

Economic "science" is viewed in this book as illuminating issues, but not decisive of policy. Familiarity with an economics vocabulary is essential for today's antitrust lawyer. But economics concerns itself with what can be quantified, whereas non-quantifiable values properly loom large in decisions regarding concentration of economic power, "unjust" discrimination, or "unfair" business practices. Economic models help us to understand by, in a sense, artificially simplifying situations. There is always the danger that the gap between the model and reality, as well as the magnetic influence that equations and graphs exercise over minds floundering in uncertainty, will impair rather than improve decision-making.

Is this a "casebook"? Not in any sense that Langdell would recognize. He assembled collections of judicial decisions as data to be plotted on a legal chart so as to derive the curve or equation that truly expressed "the law". Judicial opinions are reprinted in this book with quite different objectives: (i) to describe the way various businesses are in fact organized; (ii) to summarize conflicting arguments in major and continuing controversies; (iii) to illustrate a court's use of the history of legislative and judicial doctrines; and (iv) to expose assumptions about the values underlying the way we organize our economic life. Many cases are reported in brief digests rather than full reproduction of the opinions. The purpose is to familiarize students with leading decisions that are part of the intellectual working capital of practitioners and scholars, and to impart knowledge of the law not in arid and forgettable abstractions, but in the rich and memorable settings of struggles over power and money in real-life circumstances. Consistent with that purpose and to facilitate easy reading, we have omitted string citations in reproducing opinions.

A new method of instruction is implied by a collection of materials such as this. The conventional "case method" or "socratic" instruction must be modified. Complex opinions in antitrust, patent, labor, and related areas are certainly not intended to be handled with the invariable law classroom sequence: "State the facts of the case. What is the question? the rule? the reason for the decision? Is this decision logically consistent with X v. Y?" The facts are often too long and complicated for useful student summary in class; classroom discussion must proceed on the assumption that the case has been closely read. Talk is operational, such as one might hear in a law firm conference, a government office, a congressional commitee: How might the enterprise achieve its goals despite this decision? What legislation is needed to close a gap in the system of social control, revealed by a decision or by economic analysis? What reforms will this trade association have to carry out now? What sort of evidence should be marshalled in defense of a merger like this? How must patent and copyright law be changed to deal with new technologies like electronic data processing or cable television?

The student is in any event conceived to be "reading" the subject in the English university sense, i.e., pursuing an education by independent study of the materials. By no means will all the materials in the book be reviewed in class, and the classroom confrontation is in principle between equally informed people reacting to central or critical aspects of a body of information. Whole chapters and sections may be assigned for outside reading, not merely because there are not enough class hours, but because second and third year law students must begin practicing one of the professional skills—self-education from documents. The detailed Table of Contents summarizes the book's organization and evolution for both teacher and student.

The common theme of all the branches of law dealt with in this volume is the necessity of reconciling individual economic freedom with a variety of demands for private or official restraint of that freedom. The juxtaposition of these different demands, which are invariably advanced in the name of the general welfare, provides the student with an opportunity to develop his capacity to distinguish, in the complex language of traditional and modern antitrust analysis, in judicial and administrative opinions, in the reports of legislative committees, in the demands of the politically powerful, in the propaganda of giant corporation, giant union, or giant government, those "untrue Pretences of publick Good" against which the British Statute of Monopolies inveighed more than three centuries ago.

LOUIS B. SCHWARTZ
JOHN J. FLYNN
HARRY FIRST

May, 1983

*

ACKNOWLEDGMENTS

Responsibility for the Sixth Edition devolved upon us, although Louis Schwartz served as constant adviser and made many suggestions. Anyone familiar with the previous editions will readily observe that they are the organizational and substantive foundation for this book. Our intellectual debt could not be plainer.

We record our gratitude to those whose assistance was indispensable to the preparation of this volume: From Utah, Margaret "Peggy" Owens and Steven Hofer; from New York, Charles Y. Caldwell III, James Durling, Sharon Tilove, and Margery Weinstein. We acknowledge a special debt to Ms. Owens, a graduate of the University of Utah, for her insights and industry in preparing the manuscript, and to Ms. Carole Sparkes and Ms. Barbara McFarlane whose contributions went far beyond the secretarial. This project was funded, in part, by the New York University Law School Research Program.

J J F
H F

*

SUMMARY OF CONTENTS

TABLE OF CONTENTS

TABLE OF CONTENTS

B. MONOPOLY UNDER THE SHERMAN ACT—Continued

TABLE OF CONTENTS

TABLE OF CONTENTS

TABLE OF CONTENTS

E. TYING ARRANGEMENTS—Continued

THE LEGAL MONOPOLIES

CHAPTER 9. PATENT AND COPYRIGHT

*

TABLE OF STATUTES

References are to pages where the text of important statutes has been reproduced or where the substance thereof is stated.

*

TABLE OF CASES

The principal cases are in italic type. Cases discussed in notes and footnotes are in roman type. References are to Pages.

1

FREE ENTERPRISE

AND

ECONOMIC ORGANIZATION: ANTITRUST

*

Chapter 1

INTRODUCTION TO ANTITRUST LEGISLATION

A. ANTECEDENTS

THE STATUTE OF MONOPOLIES
Condensed from 21 Jac. 1, c. 3 (1623).

Forasmuch as your most excellent Majesty, in your royal judgment, and of your blessed disposition to the weal and quiet of your subjects, did in the year of our Lord God one thousand six hundred and ten publish in print to the whole realm and to all posterity that all monopolies are contrary to your Majesty's laws; and whereas nevertheless upon misinformations and untrue pretences of publick good, many such grants have been unduly obtained, and unlawfully put in execution, for avoiding whereof, and preventing of the like in time to come, be it declared and enacted that:

I. All monopolies and all commissions, grants, licenses, charters and letters patents heretofore made or granted, or hereafter to be made or granted, to any person or persons, bodies politick or corporate whatsoever, of or for the sole buying, selling, making, working or using of any thing within this realm, or of any other monopolies, or of power to give license or toleration to do, use or exercise any thing against any law. . . . are contrary to the laws of this realm, and so are and shall be utterly void.

II. All monopolies ought to be and shall be forever hereafter examined, heard, tried and determined by and according to the common laws of this realm and not otherwise.

IV. If any person at any time shall be hindered, grieved, disturbed, or disquieted, or his goods or chattels any way seized, attached, distrained, taken, carried away or detained by occasion or pretext of any monopoly, he shall recover three times so much as the damages that he sustained by means or occasion of being so hindered, etc.

VI. Provided that any declaration before mentioned shall not extend to any letters patents and grants of privilege for the term of fourteen years or under, hereafter to be made, of the sole working or making of any manner of new manufactures within this realm, to the true and first inventor or inventors of such manufactures, which others at the time of the making of such letters patents and grants shall not use, so as also they be not contrary to the law, nor mischievous to the state, by raising prices of commodities at home, or hurt of trade, or generally inconvenient.

IX. Provided also that this act shall not extend or be prejudicial . . . unto any corporations, companies or fellowships of

1

any art, trade, occupation or mystery, or to any companies or societies of merchants within this realm erected for the maintenance,
enlargement, or ordering of any trade of merchandise.

X and XII.   Provided also that this act shall not extend to any
letters patents or grants of privilege concerning printing, the dig-
ging, making or compounding of saltpeter or gunpowder, or the
making of ordnance or shot, nor to any grants, letters patents or
commissions for the keeping of any taverne or selling of wines to
be drunk in the mansion house or other place in the tenure or occupation of the party so selling.

NOTES AND QUERIES

(1) *Royal Monopolies.* The Statute was directed against legal monopolies created by act of the sovereign. Cf. *The Case of Monopolies (Darcy v.
Allein),*[1] in which the common law was used to deny enforcement of a royal
patent granting Darcy the exclusive right to import and manufacture playing
cards, on the ground that it was an unlawful restriction of access to a common trade, notwithstanding plaintiff's argument that reduction of gambling
was a legitimate public purpose which the monarch might further in this
way. Monopoly was regarded as entailing similar evils, viz., higher prices,
poorer product, and restriction of freedom to work and trade, regardless of
whether control was obtained by royal grant or private manipulation. If
these evils were serious enough to preclude the government from conferring
exclusive privileges, the community was not likely to tolerate the securing or
exercise of such control by self-appointed monopolists. It is not surprising,
therefore, that hostility to royal grants should merge with antipathy against
private restraint of trade in forming the antitrust tradition.[2]

(2) *Common Law of Restraint of Trade; Birth of the "Rule of Reason"
for "Ancillary" Restraints.*[3] *Mitchel v. Reynolds,* 1 P. Williams 181, 24
Eng.Rep. 347 (K.B. 1711). Reynolds, a baker, sold out to Mitchel, assigned
his five year lease, and gave bond not to compete within the parish during
that term. When Mitchel sued upon the bond, the judges of King's Bench
found the problem very troublesome. The case was reargued several times,
but at last they gave judgment for Mitchel on the ground that under the
circumstances shown this sort of agreement "may be useful and beneficial
as to prevent a town from being overstocked". Or it might enable an "old
man" to get more money for his shop upon retirement and so "procure to
himself a livelihood, which he might probably have lost." At the very least,
said the judges, society should not tolerate an obvious wrong to the buyer,
who has been tricked into paying something beyond the value of the physical
property for the seller's agreement not to compete, merely because there is a
bare possibility that the seller may have disabled himself from earning a living.

1. 11 Coke 84b, 77 Eng.Rep. 1260
(K.B. 1602). See Letwin, The English
Common Law Concerning Monopolies, 21
U.Chi.L.Rev. 355 (1954); Davies, Further
Light on the Case of Monopolies, 48 L.
Q.Rev. 394 (1932).

2. See Standard Oil Co. of New
Jersey v. United States, 221 U.S. 1, 51 et
seq., 31 S.Ct. 502, 512 et seq., 55 L.Ed.
619 (1911), tracing the development of
the concept of unlawful monopoly from

the Statute of Monopolies and common
law conspiracy.

3. See United States v. Addyston Pipe
& Steel Co., 85 F. 271 (6th Cir. 1898) infra p. 328; Restatement of Contracts,
Sections 515, 516 (American Law Institute, 1932); Goldschmid, Antitrust's Neglected Stepchild: A Proposal For Dealing With Restrictive Covenants Under
Federal Law, 73 Colum.L.Rev. 1193
(1973).

As far back as *Dyer's Case*[4] in 1415, a private contract, by which one subject bound himself to another to refrain from practicing his trade in a particular village for a brief period, had evoked from the bench the wrathful comment:

> The obligation is void because the condition is against the common law, and by God, if the plaintiff were here he should go to prison till he paid a fine to the King.

But in the Eighteenth Century a new era was being born. Economic and political initiative was passing from landowners to businessmen, and businessmen's ideas of propriety and justice inevitably replaced earlier conceptions of the inviolable freedom and inescapable obligation to work at one's trade. It may be assumed that by 1711 it was as commonplace for a tradesman to sell his shop, giving an agreement not to compete with the buyer, as it was outrageous in 1415. Mitchel's was, of course, not the first of such transactions, not even the first to be noted in the reports.[5] A practice must get itself accepted before an adequate rationale can be stated.

When the rationale of restraint of trade offered by *Mitchel v. Reynolds* is examined closely, it becomes apparent that the decision is not so much a product of reason as a response to the tremendous germinal forces of the new capitalism. It is true, of course, that society does not wish to encourage frauds on buyers of businesses. But it would be no judicial novelty to allow such losses to go unremedied if a more important social objective were at stake. We do not enforce gambling or other illegal contracts, despite resulting hardships, because we wish to discourage the making of such contracts. They result in idleness and other evils. Although our gambling laws have not notably diminished gambling, it may be assumed that businessmen would not long continue to pay for unenforceable contracts to refrain from competing.

Is there a community interest in putting sanctions behind contracts such as Mitchel's? How will consumers of bread benefit by keeping the old baker from reengaging in trade? Can they be hurt by "overstocking"? What evidence of overstocking is there other than the contract itself? Reynolds must have been confident that the parish had room for two bakers, or at least that the townspeople would prefer his baking to Mitchel's. Assuming that too much confection can be harmful, is it wise to leave the matter up to two bargaining bakers, or should the town council make a determination as to how much is too much? And should the matter then be left open for reconsideration in case Mitchel proves inadequate? Should the town forearm itself against the putative evil of "overstocking," by refusing to let *any* new bakery be established unless the city authorities are satisfied that public convenience or necessity will be served?

Is the decision justifiable as a kindness to old bakers, a primitive form of social security and old age insurance? It is plainly not limited to the elderly or needy. The ailing old man is least likely to reengage in business. It is the successful entrepreneur who has built up "good will" who can get a premium for his promise not to reengage in business and against whom vendees will need to invoke judicial sanctions. Besides, should a social security program be inaugurated at the expense of the citizenry for the benefit of retiring businessmen, the group most likely to have accumulated private savings?

---

4. Y.B. 2 Hen. V, vol. 5, pl. 26 (1415).   5. See Carpenter, Validity of Contracts Not to Compete, 76 U.Pa.L.Rev. 244 (1928).

But is it fair to suggest that such contracts cost the citizens money? If Baker A had $1000 worth of fixtures and Baker B paid him $1000 for that plus another $1000 for A's promise not to compete, making B's total investment $2000, will B be able to sell as cheaply as A? If his costs are somewhat higher, as for example if he borrows money and pays interest, must he either raise his prices or accept a lower profit than A did? Has the community any interest in the latter alternative? Suppose that consumers do have to pay a little more; if the value of businesses can be generally inflated by this means so that businessmen have extra funds to invest in new ventures and experiments, won't the community be better off in the long run?

Such thoughts go far beyond *Mitchel v. Reynolds.* Justice Parker was careful to hedge the new doctrine: all such agreements were "presumptively" invalid, i.e., the burden of proof of reasonableness was upon the party asserting validity of the restraint; no restraint would be tolerated unless "ancillary" to some principal transaction; the restraint must be geographically limited—"general" restraints were bad as wholly incapacitating the covenantor; the court would not uphold any part of an excessive restraint. To be avoided were "the great abuses these voluntary restraints are liable to; as for instance, from corporations who are perpetually laboring for exclusive advantages in trade, and to reduce it into as few hands as possible."

Here, nevertheless, was laid the basis for that "rule of reason" upon which the following centuries constructed an elaborate jurisprudence sustaining not only restrictive provisions in contracts of employment and sale having minimal public significance, but arguably also vast schemes for private regulation of trade.

(3) *World-wide Ancillary Restraints and Fictional Justifications. Nordenfelt v. Maxim Nordenfelt Guns and Ammunition Co.*, [1894] App. Cas. 535. A corporation was organized to acquire the business and patents of Thorsten Nordenfelt, inventor of various improvements in arms and ammunition. Nordenfelt was paid the equivalent of well over a million dollars and was given a five year contract as managing director of the company. He agreed that he would not, during the term of twenty-five years from the date of the incorporation of the company, engage in manufacturing guns or ammunition or in any business competing or liable to compete in any way with that of the company.

The company was then amalgamated with another munitions firm, the Maxim Company, to form The Maxim Nordenfelt Guns and Ammunition Co. When Nordenfelt's connection with that company terminated, the British courts enjoined him from reentering the munitions business at home or abroad. The world-wide scope of the restrictive covenant was upheld, despite the condemnation of "general" restraints in *Mitchel v. Reynolds:*

> When once it is admitted that whether the covenant be general or particular the question of its validity is alike determined by the consideration whether it exceeds what is necessary for the protection of the covenantee, the distinction between general and particular restraints ceases to be a distinction in point of law . . . it is to the advantage of the public that there should be free scope for the sale of the goodwill of a business.

There is evidence in the opinions that the judges believed they were responding to British imperial policy not "to encourage unfettered competition in the sale of arms of precision to tribes who may become her antagonists in warfare". What the judges seemed not to have realized is that they were simply underwriting that policy as made by private traders; i.e., the courts would have had no basis for this casual intervention on behalf of supposed British defense interests if the parties had not made a contract. Moreover, the decision excluded Nordenfelt from the British arms market as well, where his competition might have reduced the cost and improved the quality of British armament. The Court gave short shrift to his argument that the restrictive covenant was void because it included within its scope businesses in which the company was not engaged at the date of the contract; the injunction was simply limited to guns and ammunition.

(4) *Presumption of Validity; Divisibility of Illegal Restraint to Preserve the Legal Portion. Oregon Steam Navigation Co. v. Winsor,* 87 U.S. 64, 22 L.Ed. 315 (1873), may be taken as representative of American jurisprudence in the heyday of *laissez faire.* In 1864 the California Steam Navigation Co., which conducted steamship operations in California waters, sold the steamer New World to the Oregon Steam Navigation Co., which operated on the Columbia River, Ore. The vendee covenanted that the ship would not be used in California waters for ten years. In 1867 the ship was resold to Winsor, then operating on the Puget Sound, Washington. Winsor covenanted that the ship would not be used in either California or Oregon waters for 10 years. In 1868, however, he began operating out of San Francisco. The Supreme Court held 6–3 that Winsor was liable for breach of his covenant. Exclusion from entire states did not make the restraint "general"; the United States was deemed to be an economic unit and the restraint was no broader geographically than necessary for the protection of the vendors. The transaction "had no tendency to destroy the usefulness of the steamer, and did not deprive the country of any industrial agency. . . . The presumption [was] that the arrangement was mutually beneficial to both companies, and that it promoted the general interests of commerce on the Pacific coast." Although Winsor's covenant was excessive temporarily, insofar as it extended beyond the original ten year exclusion from California, "the line of division between the period which [was] properly covered by the restriction and that which [was] not so, [was] clearly defined and easily drawn . . . ."

Did the California Steam Navigation Co. sell any business or goodwill in Columbia River transportation? Is it reasonable to assume that Winsor would not have transferred his operations from Puget Sound to San Francisco Bay unless the demand for steamship accommodations was greater at San Francisco? How does it promote the "general" interests of commerce on the Pacific coast to exclude him? What specific interests benefited from the Court's enforcement of the contract; what interests suffered? Supposing that it might have been desirable on national-interest grounds to keep the New World operating in Puget Sound, did the Court's decision require it? Should the resolution of such a question be left to the discretion of steamship companies, as settled in their private contracts? Should it be left to the courts to make national steamship policy? Are they equipped procedurally for the task; will they hear shippers, passengers, interested governmental agencies? Should the principles which govern the validity of an agreement not to compete, made by a baker selling out his shop, govern the division of routes among steamship lines or the contract of a doctor not to practice his profession? [6] Should the differences in policy be worked out under a rule of law sustaining "reasonable" restraints, or should more specific rules be evolved?

How will it affect the scope of restrictive covenants drawn by lawyers if they know that only the "excessive" portion will be invalidated in case of

6. See Dodd, Contracts Not to Practice Medicine, 23 B.U.L.Rev. 305 (1943).

litigation, provided that the geographic or temporal line between the legal and the illegal can be "easily drawn" by the court?

THORELLI, THE FEDERAL ANTITRUST POLICY—
ORIGINATION OF AN AMERICAN TRADITION 51–53 (1955) [7]

. . . There were mainly three aspects of the old English common law concerning restrictions of trade. One referred to the related crimes of forestalling, engrossing and regrating, signifying attempts in one way or the other to "corner" the local markets by interfering with the ordinary distributive processes, especially with regard to "necessities of life." Although they had grown obsolete in their original sense in the 17th and 18th centuries, these doctrines were still occasionally applied until further use of them was prohibited in 1844. Since then, as indeed in numerous earlier cases, restrictions of the corner type have been attacked by the use of the doctrine of restraint of trade in its modern, extended sense. While reaffirmed in several American jurisdictions as late as in the early 19th century, the law against forestalling, engrossing and regrating never acquired principal significance in the United States.

The second aspect concerned public grants of monopoly. It seems that such grants explicitly sanctioned by Parliament were never questioned by the courts. But "letters patent" from the King, representing encroachments on the privilege, or freedom, of the subject to engage in trade, were widely challenged. Such a monopoly was apt to be contested particularly when the public good or service for which it was supposed to be the reward was in no proportion to the public evils ensuing from its operation. Thus, the courts withheld their sanction from a considerable number of letters patent at the end of the 16th and in the first half of the 17th century. The presumption remained, however, that grants of monopoly in recognition of innovations in trade or manufacture were in the public interest and were to be sanctioned. This was the origin of the modern patent system. These policies in regard to patents of monopoly were reaffirmed by Parliament in the famous Statute of Monopolies of 1623, which represents the formal culmination of English opposition to restrictions on trade. To some extent similar policies were applied to the guild monopolies in the 17th century, but with less noticeable results, primarily due to the fact that in this field most old and established privileges, irrespective of origin, were recognized by the courts. Opposition to all grants of monopolistic privilege, not explicitly sanctioned by popular representatives, developed even further in the colonies in the new world and became an established part of the American tradition.

The third aspect related to contracts "in restraint of trade." This concept at the old common law covered only covenants not to compete which were a minor part of, or ancillary to, a major agreement such as the sale of a business. As the geographical and occupational mo-

7. Quotation is by permission of the copyright owner, The Johns Hopkins Press.

bility of labor grew, the original unqualified rule against such stipulations was gradually relaxed. In modern times it is not believed that such agreements generally represent a serious encroachment on competition. Simply stated, the rule, in the United States as well as in England, is that such a restraint is "reasonable" if it is not larger—more extensive—than the necessary protection of the parties requires and not obviously injurious to the interests of the public (which even in this field has been considered somewhat more sensitive to possible monopolistic abuse by American courts than British). This was the limited application of the original "rule of reason." . . .

In the 17th century the courts began to apply the old doctrine of criminal conspiracy to combinations to restrain or monopolize trade. This practice reached its climax in 18th century England. From the middle of the last century it was no longer used in this sense there. The doctrine of "conspiracy to monopolize" was transplanted to the United States, but it was not widely used as a criminal law concept. Its main application was in the field of torts, and it was used rather synonymously with "combination in restraint of trade" to characterize concerted efforts to restrict competition.

Finally, what may be regarded as a strictly American development was the invalidation, in the last half of the 19th century, of a number of corporate combinations and consolidations and so-called trusts, formed with the main purpose of eliminating or restricting competition. Such arrangements were usually invalidated either because the participating corporations had acted beyond their charter powers, action *ultra vires*, or by application of the doctrines against restraints of trade and monopolies. Sometimes both these grounds were used. Generally speaking, the common law experience in this part of the field was fairly limited at the time the Sherman Act was passed, however.

It must be remembered that, principally, all these doctrines and concepts were applied by state, and not by federal, courts. There was no federal common law, at least not in this field. With the growing integration of the economic life of the nation this was bound to prove a serious handicap in the development of public policy regarding restraints on trade, since the growth of the common law was not entirely uniform in all the states.

But there was at least one more serious weakness which was bound to make the common law an insufficient device in the conscious effort to maintain a workable degree of competition and safeguard a fair opportunity for the newcomer—gradually becoming an American policy—in an era increasingly characterized by mass production and big business. That was the lack of coordinated and aggressive public prosecution and, not least, the lack of adequate penalties. The vast majority of cases at common law were private suits between parties to restrictive arrangements. That most courts were unwilling to enforce such agreements in restraint of trade no doubt deterred many businessmen from making them; it is equally clear that it did not deter a good many others.

The state of the common law at the end of the century demanded federal action.

B. BASIC ANTITRUST LEGISLATION

THE SHERMAN ANTITRUST ACT OF 1890
15 U.S.C.A. §§ 1–6.

Sec. 1. Every contract, combination in the form of trust or otherwise, or conspiracy, in restraint of trade or commerce among the several States, or with foreign nations, is declared to be illegal. Every person who shall make any contract or engage in any combination or conspiracy hereby declared to be illegal shall be deemed guilty of a felony, and, on conviction thereof, shall be punished by fine not exceeding one million dollars if a corporation, or, if any other person, one hundred thousand dollars, or by imprisonment not exceeding three years, or by both said punishments, in the discretion of the court.

Sec. 2. Every person who shall monopolize, or attempt to monopolize, or combine or conspire with any other person or persons, to monopolize any part of the trade or commerce among the several States, or with foreign nations, shall be deemed guilty of a felony, and, on conviction thereof, shall be punished by fine not exceeding one million dollars if a corporation, or, if any other person, one hundred thousand dollars, or by imprisonment not exceeding three years, or by both said punishments, in the discretion of the court.

. . .

Sec. 4. The several district courts of the United States are invested with jurisdiction to prevent and restrain violations of [this Act;] and it shall be the duty of the several United States attorneys, in their respective districts, under the direction of the Attorney General, to institute proceedings in equity to prevent and restrain such violations. . . .

. . .

CLAYTON ACT PROVISIONS AS TO SUITS BY PERSONS INJURED
15 U.S.C.A. §§ 15–16.

Sec. 4. Any person who shall be injured in his business or property by reason of anything forbidden in the antitrust laws may sue therefor in any district court of the United States in the district in which the defendant resides or is found or has an agent, without respect to the amount in controversy, and shall recover threefold the damages by him sustained, and the costs of suit, including a reasonable attorney's fee.

Sec. 4B. Any action to enforce any cause of action [hereunder] shall be forever barred unless commenced within four years after the cause of action accrued. . . .[8]

8. Section 4B applies only to suits for money damages. The equitable defense of laches applies to private actions for injunctive relief, see International Telephone & Telegraph Corp. v. General Telephone & Electronics Corp., 518 F.2d 913 (9th Cir. 1975) (four-year period is guideline); courts have been unwilling to apply

Sec. 5(a). **A final judgment or decree heretofore or hereafter rendered in any civil or criminal proceeding brought by or on behalf of the United States under the antitrust laws to the effect that a defendant has violated said laws shall be prima facie evidence against such defendant in any action or proceeding brought by any other party against such defendant . . . as to all matters respecting which said judgment or decree would be an estoppel as between the parties thereto:** *Provided,* **That this section shall not apply to consent judgments or decrees entered before any testimony has been taken. Nothing contained in this section shall be construed to impose any limitation on the application of collateral estoppel . . . .**

Sec. 5(i). **Whenever any civil or criminal proceeding is instituted by the United States . . . the running of the statute of limitations in respect of every private or State right of action arising under said laws and based in whole or in part on any matter complained of in said proceeding shall be suspended during the pendency thereof and for one year thereafter. . . .**[9]

FEDERAL TRADE COMMISSION ACT, ANTITRUST JURISDICTION OF THE COMMISSION

15 U.S.C.A. § 45.

Sec. 5(a)(1). **Unfair methods of competition in or affecting commerce, and unfair . . . acts or practices in or affecting commerce, are hereby declared unlawful.**

. . .

Sec. 5(b). **Whenever the Commission shall have reason to believe that any such person, partnership, or corporation has been or is using any unfair method of competition or unfair . . . act or practice in or affecting commerce . . . it shall issue . . . a complaint . . . containing a notice of a hearing. . . . If up-**

the defense to government injunctive suits. See United States v. Pennsalt Chemicals Corp., 262 F.Supp. 101 (E.D. Pa.1967).

Sherman Act criminal prosecutions are governed by the five year federal statute of limitations applicable to all non-capital offenses. 18 U.S.C.A. § 3282. This period can be stretched, however, by expansive definitions of what acts constitute the conspiracy. See United States v. Inryco, Inc., 642 F.2d 290 (9th Cir. 1981), certiorari dismissed 454 U.S. 1167, 102 S.Ct. 1045, 71 L.Ed.2d 324 (1982).

9. On tolling the statute of limitations, see Zenith Radio Corp. v. Hazeltine Research, Inc., 401 U.S. 321, 91 S.Ct. 795, 28 L.Ed.2d 77 (1971). The statute is tolled by pendency of a Federal Trade Commission proceeding based on the antitrust laws, Minnesota Mining & Mfg. Co. v. New Jersey Wood Finishing Co., 381 U.S. 311, 85 S.Ct. 1473, 14 L.Ed.2d 405 (1965); but not by government intervention in an administrative hearing held on a private party's complaint and in which the government did not "complain of" any substantive antitrust violation. Greyhound Corp. v. Mt. Hood Stages, Inc., 437 U.S. 322, 98 S.Ct. 2370, 57 L.Ed. 2d 239 (1978). The issues raised by the private complaint need not be identical with those presented in the governmental proceeding. Leh v. General Petroleum Corp., 382 U.S. 54, 86 S.Ct. 203, 15 L.Ed. 2d 134 (1965). A nonstatutory equitable doctrine suspends the statute of limitation so long as the offenders "fraudulently conceal" the cause of action from the victim. General Electric Co. v. City of San Antonio, 334 F.2d 480 (5th Cir. 1964); Atlantic City Elec. Co. v. General Electric Co., 312 F.2d 236 (2d Cir. 1962). But cf. Moviecolor Ltd. v. Eastman Kodak Co., 288 F.2d 80 (2d Cir. 1961); Philco Corp. v. Radio Corp. of America, 186 F.Supp. 155 (E.D.Pa.1960), as to difficulties in proving concealment or "economic coercion" to refrain from filing suit.

on such hearing the Commission shall be of the opinion that the method of competition or the act or practice in question is prohibited by [this Act,] it . . . shall issue . . . an order . . . to cease and desist from using such method of competition or such act or practice.

NOTES

(1) *Bibliography.* The major standard reference works for analysis of the antitrust laws today are Areeda & Turner, Antitrust Law: An Analysis of Antitrust Principles and Their Application (5 vols.) (1978, 1980), and Sullivan, Handbook of the Law of Antitrust (1977). Systematic exposition of the antitrust laws will also be found in Gellhorn, Antitrust Law and Economics in a Nutshell (2d ed. 1981) and Neale & Goyder, The Antitrust Laws of the U.S.A. (3d ed. 1980).

Important critiques and economic studies include: Adams, The Structure of American Industry (5th ed. 1977); Bain, Industrial Organization (1959); Blair, Economic Concentration: Structure, Behavior and Public Policy (1972); Bork, The Antitrust Paradox: A Policy At War With Itself (1978); Caves, American Industry: Structure, Conduct, Performance (4th ed. 1977); Dirlam and Kahn, Fair Competition (1954); Goldschmid, Mann, Weston, eds., Industrial Concentration: The New Learning (1974); Kaysen and Turner, Antitrust Policy: An Economic and Legal Analysis (1959); Lynch, The Concentration of Economic Power (1946); Machlup, The Political Economy of Monopoly (1952); Massel, Competition and Monopoly: Legal and Economic Issues (1962); McGee, In Defense of Industrial Concentration (1971), interestingly reviewed in Brodley, Massive Industrial Size, Classical Economics, and the Search for Humanistic Value, 24 Stan.L.Rev. 1155 (1972); Mueller, A Primer on Monopoly and Competition (1970); Nader Report (Green, Moore, Wasserstein), The Closed Enterprise System (1972); Posner, Antitrust Law: An Economic Perspective (1976); Scherer, Industrial Market Structure and Economic Performance (2d ed. 1980); Stocking, Workable Competition and Antitrust Policy (1961); Whitney, Antitrust Policies: American Experience in Twenty Industries (Twentieth Century Fund 1958).

Other interesting books dealing with organization of the economy include: Barber, The American Corporation (1970); Barnet & Muller, Global Reach: The Power of Multinational Corporations (1974); Friedman, Capitalism and Freedom (1962); Galbraith, American Capitalism—The Concept of Countervailing Power (1952); Means (ed.), The Roots of Inflation (1975); Schumacher, Small is Beautiful (1973); Schumpeter, Capitalism, Socialism and Democracy (3d ed. 1950); Solo, The Political Authority and The Market System (1974).

Presidential and Congressional investigations have produced a number of important studies of the antitrust laws.[10] The most intensive is the one undertaken by the Temporary National Economic Committee. This Committee was established by Joint Resolution of Congress on June 16, 1938, in response to a message from President Franklin D. Roosevelt. It consisted of three members of the Senate, three members of the House and representa-

---

10. Among the more significant Congressional hearings in recent years are the following conducted by the Subcommittee on Antitrust and Monopoly of the Committee on the Judiciary United States Senate: Administered Prices (29 vols., 1957–1963); Economic Concentration (11 vols., 1964–1969); The Failing Newspaper Act (8 vols., 1967–1969); The Insurance Industry (20 vols., 1958–1971); The Industrial Reorganization Act (9 vols. published 1973–1977).

tives of the following executive departments and agencies: Justice, Treasury, Labor, Commerce, Securities and Exchange Commission, and Federal Trade Commission. The Committee was directed to investigate the concentration of economic power, its causes, its effects on competition, prices, level of trade, employment, profits and consumption. It spent over $1,000,000 and took more than 17,000 printed pages of testimony from leaders of every phase of business, government experts and others. Committee staff members wrote 43 monographs on specific economic problems.[11] The work of the T.N.E.C. is summarized in Lynch, The Concentration of Economic Power (1946).

In 1953, President Eisenhower, responding to complaints of harsh and arbitrary enforcement of the antitrust laws, authorized the creation of a National Committee to Study the Antitrust Laws. It consisted of approximately 60 lawyers and economists, regarded as experts in the field. The Committee published its report in 1955. Although a number of the recommended changes in legislation or administration evoked sharp dissent within and without the Committee,[12] the report was a useful review of legal and economic issues in the antitrust field. The Report has been updated by the American Bar Association's Section of Antitrust Law under the title Antitrust Developments 1955–1968; Antitrust Law Developments (Second), published in 1983, brings the material to date, discussing the most significant points of antitrust law.

There have been three recent presidential task force reports on antitrust policy: The White House Task Force on Antitrust Policy (Neal, Chairman) submitted to President Johnson on July 5, 1968, but not published until May 27, 1969, in a Special Supplement to Antitrust & Trade Reg. Rep. No. 411; President Nixon's Task Force on Productivity and Competition (Stigler, Chairman) published in Antitrust & Trade Reg. Rep. No. 413, June 10, 1969, 115 Cong. Rec. 15,932–42 (1969); and the National Commission for the Review of Antitrust Law and Procedure (NCRALP), established by President Carter to focus primarily on the problems (both substantive and procedural) of complex antitrust litigation and on antitrust exemptions, whose Report is published in a Special Supplement to Antitrust & Trade Reg. Rep. No. 897, Jan. 18, 1979.

Current antitrust developments are reported in Antitrust & Trade Regulation Report (ATRR), published by The Bureau of National Affairs, Inc., and the Trade Regulation Reporter, published by Commerce Clearing House, Inc. European antitrust developments are covered on a regular basis in Common Market Reports, published by Commerce Clearing House, and in the Common Market Law Review.

11. E.g., Measurement of the Social Performance of Business (No. 7), Taxation of Corporate Enterprise (No. 9), Relative Efficiency of Large, Medium-Sized and Small Business (No. 13), Antitrust in Action (No. 16), Trade Association Survey (No. 22), Economic Power and Political Pressures (No. 26), Life Insurance Companies (No. 28), Patents and Free Enterprise (No. 31), Economic Standards of Government Price Control (No. 32), Saving, Investment and National Income (No. 38), Control of Petroleum Industry by Major Oil Companies (No. 39), The Motion Picture Industry (No. 43).

12. See Report of the Attorney General's National Committee to Study the Antitrust Laws (1955) and Schwartz Dissent, 1 Antitrust Bull. 37 (1955), also printed in Hearings of the Antitrust Subcommittee of the House Judiciary Committee, 84th Cong., 1st Sess., Ser. 3, pt. 1, 247–264 (1955). Symposia reviewing the work of the National Committee to Study the Antitrust Laws appeared in 24 G.Wash.U.L.Rev. 1 (1955); 53 Mich.L. Rev. 1033 (1955); 50 Nw.U.L.Rev. 305 (1955); 104 U.Pa.L.Rev. 145 (1955).

(2) *Relation Between Sections 1 and 2 of the Sherman Act: Restraining and Monopolizing Trade.* Sections 1 and 2 obviously differ in being directed respectively against "restraint" and "monopolizing," and in the necessity of proving collaboration between two or more persons in order to make out a violation of Section 1, while a single person may violate Section 2.[13] Although "restraint" is broad enough to include monopolization,[14] it also reaches lesser controls over the business of the collaborators or others. On the other hand, inasmuch as Section 2 speaks of attempt and conspiracy to monopolize, it too reaches activity which falls short of achieving monopoly power, provided that the activity is accompanied by the specific intent to monopolize.[15] Thus, Section 2 can be regarded as supplementing Section 1: Section 1 forbidding particular categories of agreements because of their known tendency to produce the evils of monopoly, while Section 2 outlaws any practice or arrangement, including those which might ordinarily be unobjectionable in themselves, if engaged in with the required unlawful purpose.[16] The relationship between the two sections is further complicated by the persistence of a doubt whether the Sherman Act reaches "monopoly without abuse"; i.e., it is possible to read Section 2 and the cases thereunder as directed only against a type of anti-social *activity* described by the verb "monopolize", and not against a particular *structure* of industry which economists might call "monopoly" or "oligopoly", and which could conceivably occur without evil purpose or reprehensible behavior.[17]

(3) *"Rule of Reason" and "Per Se" Illegality.* So much has been written on this subject[18] and so much of the case material in this book deals with specific application of these contrasting principles, that it is worthwhile here only to alert the student to the main issues in this central controversy of antitrust law. Section 1 of the Sherman Act prohibited "every" contract or combination in restraint of trade; but it was obvious that Congress could not have intended to forbid certain common business arrangements which do, as a practical matter, restrict the commercial freedom of the participants, e.g.,

---

13. See Symposium, The Antitrust Laws and Single-Firm Conduct, 30 Law and Cont.Prob. 461 et seq. (1965).

14. See United States v. Socony-Vacuum Oil Co., 310 U.S. 150, 226, 60 S.Ct. 811, 846, 84 L.Ed. 1129 (1940) ("The two sections overlap in the sense that a monopoly under Section 2 is a species of restraint of trade under Section 1"); United States v. Aluminum Co. of America, 148 F.2d 416 (2d Cir. 1945) ("[price-fixing] contracts are only steps toward that entire control which monopoly confers: they are really partial monopolies"). One situation where the distinction between the two sections becomes crucial is when a defendant is indicted in separate counts (and given separate punishments) for a conspiracy in restraint of trade, monopolization, and conspiracy to monopolize, all arising out of the same conduct. The Supreme Court upheld such an indictment against a double jeopardy claim in United States v. American Tobacco Co., 328 U.S. 781, 66 S.Ct. 1125, 90 L.Ed. 1575 (1946).

15. See pp. 157 – 180, infra.

16. See Standard Oil Co. of New Jersey v. United States, 221 U.S. 1, 60–61, 31 S.Ct. 502, 55 L.Ed. 619 (1911).

17. The problem is reviewed in Levi, A Two Level Anti-Monopoly Law, 47 Nw. U.L.Rev. 567 (1952), and Rostow, Monopoly Under the Sherman Act: Power or Purpose? 43 Ill.L.Rev. 745 (1949); Johnston and Stevens, Monopoly or Monopolization—A Reply to Professor Rostow, 44 Ill.L.Rev. 269 (1949).

18. Representative of the literature emphasizing desirability of the "rule of reason": Oppenheim, Federal Antitrust Legislation—Guideposts to a Revised National Antitrust Policy, 50 Mich.L.Rev. 1139 (1952); Adelman, Effective Competition and the Antitrust Laws, 61 Harv.L. Rev. 1289 (1948). Representative of the opposing point of view: Stocking, The Rule of Reason, Workable Competition, and Monopoly, 64 Yale L.J. 1107 (1955); Adams, The "Rule of Reason": Workable Competition or Workable Monopoly? 63 Yale L.J. 348 (1954); Kahn, A Legal and Economic Appraisal of the "New" Sherman and Clayton Acts, 63 Yale L.J. 293 (1954).

partnership agreements which preclude individual partners from engaging in competition with the firm, contracts for sale of a business with an ancillary covenant by the seller not to compete. Accordingly, it devolved upon the courts to determine which restraints were unreasonable and therefore illegal. The explicit declaration to this effect, in *Standard Oil Co. v. United States*,[19] established a "rule of reason" under the Sherman Act. On the other hand, it was recognized from the beginning that certain kinds of restraints, e.g., combinations to fix prices, were so patently inconsistent with a free competitive system that no considerations of reasonableness could, consistently with congressional intent, be accepted in justification. Such restraints are said to be illegal or unreasonable "per se."

The perennial dispute is over the proper spheres of rule of reason and per se, i.e., whether the categories of per se violation should be extended or circumscribed. Among the opposing contentions are these: Per se rules are absolute and inflexible, leaving no possibility of adaptation to peculiar circumstances of a particular business or to special requirements of trade in foreign commerce or in sections of the economy vital to national defense. They are also too often applied indiscriminately, outlawing private business agreements which not only are unlikely to have any adverse economic effects, but which may actually allow the parties to operate more efficiently. On the other hand, it is argued that per se rules are legitimately applied to a number of business practices which experience has shown are so likely to have anticompetitive effects, and so unlikely to have any redeeming qualities, that the benefits of a "no-trial" rule far outweigh its costs. Further, every business has "peculiar" conditions; the exploration of elaborate, but ultimately inconclusive, justifications would only lead to lengthier, and more expensive, antitrust litigation. Finally, per se rules are easier for business people to understand, eliminating *pro tanto* the vagueness which is one of the principal complaints against the antitrust laws. On one point all agree, however—per se rules make it easier for the government (and private plaintiffs) to win antitrust cases.

(4) *Jurisdictional Scope of the Antitrust Laws.* The Sherman Act applies to restraints of "trade or commerce" "among the several States" "or with foreign nations." The phrase "trade or commerce" has not been given close exposition by the Supreme Court, but the Sherman Act has been held applicable to a wide variety of activities. Coverage has readily been extended to, e.g., the production, distribution, and exhibition of motion pictures, to real estate brokerage, to gathering and distribution of news, to medical services to members of a non-profit health cooperative (in the District of Columbia where federal power is plenary and has been fully exercised, see Sherman Act Section 3), and to insurance underwriting.[20] Professional baseball enjoys an antitrust immunity under old and discredited decisions that what

19. 221 U.S. 1, 59–60, 31 S.Ct. 502, 515, 55 L.Ed. 619 (1911). See discussion in Report of the Attorney General's National Committee to study the Antitrust Laws (1955) 5–12. In an earlier decision the Supreme Court had indicated that Congress intended to forbid "every" restraint of trade. See United States v. Trans-Missouri Freight Association, 166 U.S. 290, 17 S.Ct. 540, 41 L.Ed. 1007 (1897). An attack upon the constitutionality of the Sherman Act, grounded on the vagueness of the "rule of reason," was defeated in Nash v. United States, 229 U.S. 373, 33 S.Ct. 780, 57 L.Ed. 1232 (1913).

20. See review of the cases in United States v. Shubert, 348 U.S. 222, 226, 75 S.Ct. 277, 280, 99 L.Ed. 279 (1955). The decision as to insurance, United States v. South-Eastern Underwriters Association, 322 U.S. 533, 64 S.Ct. 1162, 88 L.Ed. 1440 (1944), was partially nullified by the McCarran-Ferguson Act, making the antitrust laws applicable to the insurance business only "to the extent that such business is not regulated by State law." 15 U.S.C.A. §§ 1012, 1013.

was involved in "sport" was neither commerce nor commerce that was inter-state.[21] In *Flood v. Kuhn*, 407 U.S. 258, 92 S.Ct. 2099, 32 L.Ed.2d 728 (1972), the Supreme Court declined to abandon the old decisions as to base-ball, but recognized that professional sports including baseball were busi-nesses engaged in interstate commerce. The Court characterized the exemp-tion of baseball from antitrust as an "anomoly" and "aberration," immunized only by *stare decisis* and because Congress "by its positive inactions, has allowed those decisions to stand for so long." 407 U.S. at 283–84. Other professional sports have been subjected to the federal antitrust laws.[22]

"Among the several States" relates to Congressional power to regulate interstate commerce. Despite the importance of this jurisdictional limit, for constitutional policy and individual case decisions, the present materials deal summarily with this area. It is enough to note that Congress intended to exercise its Constitutional power to the fullest in the Sherman Act. Thus, as the Supreme Court has expanded the concept of "interstate commerce" in decisions sustaining federal legislation in new social and economic fields, it has become easier to convict private groups of usurping the congressional power to regulate such commerce, by monopoly or restraint in violation of the Sherman Act.[23] As Justice Jackson stated, in *United States v. Women's Sportswear Manufacturing Association*, 336 U.S. 460, 464, 69 S.Ct. 714, 716, 93 L.Ed. 805 (1949):

> The source of the restraint may be intrastate, as the making of a con-tract or combination usually is; the application of the restraint may be intrastate, as it often is; but neither matters if the necessary effect is to stifle or restrain commerce among the states. If it is interstate commerce that feels the pinch, it does not matter how local the opera-tion which applies the squeeze.[24]

21. Federal Baseball Club v. National League, 259 U.S. 200, 42 S.Ct. 465, 66 L.Ed. 898, 26 A.L.R. 357 (1922), reaf-firmed, Toolson v. New York Yankees, 346 U.S. 356, 74 S.Ct. 78, 98 L.Ed. 64 (1953).

22. Radovich v. National Football League, 352 U.S. 445, 77 S.Ct. 390, 1 L.Ed.2d 456 (1957); United States v. In-ternational Boxing Club, 348 U.S. 236, 75 S.Ct. 259, 99 L.Ed. 290 (1955). See Noll (ed.), Government and The Sports Busi-ness (1974); Jacobs & Winter, Antitrust Principles and Collective Bargaining By Athletes: Of Superstars in Peonage, 81 Yale L.J. 1 (1971).

23. Compare United States v. E.C. Knight Co., 156 U.S. 1, 15 S.Ct. 249, 39 L.Ed. 325 (1895) (acquisition of stock con-trol of 98% of the sugar refining industry held to relate solely to local manufactur-ing activities despite importation of raw materials and interstate shipment of product) with Mandeville Island Farms, Inc. v. American Crystal Sugar Co., 334 U.S. 219, 68 S.Ct. 996, 92 L.Ed. 1328 (1948) (effect on interstate commerce of local agreements fixing the farm price of sugar makes Sherman Act applicable).

24. Recent cases affirming the broad reach of this "affecting commerce" juris-diction include McLain v. Real Estate Board of New Orleans, Inc., 444 U.S. 232, 100 S.Ct. 502, 62 L.Ed.2d 441 (1980) (fix-ing commissions on residential real estate may affect demand for interstate financ-ing and title insurance); Hospital Build-ing Co. v. Trustees of the Rex Hospital, 425 U.S. 738, 96 S.Ct. 1848, 48 L.Ed.2d 338 (1976) (expenditure of hospital funds for medicines and supplies, insurance, and out-of-state financing for building construction sufficient to sustain Sher-man Act complaint); Tennessee v. High-land Memorial Cemetery, 489 F.Supp. 65 (E.D.Tenn.1980) (refusal of four ceme-teries to bury people on Sundays has suf-ficient effect on commerce). See also United States v. Employing Plasterers' Association of Chicago, 347 U.S. 186, 74 S.Ct. 452, 98 L.Ed. 618 (1954); Moore v. Mead's Fine Bread Co., 348 U.S. 115, 75 S.Ct. 148, 99 L.Ed. 145 (1954).

The Federal Trade Commission Act was amended in 1975, and the Clayton Act in 1980, to reach activities "affecting commerce." The latter amendment al-tered the Supreme Court's narrower in-terpretation in United States v. American Building Maintenance, Inc., 422 U.S. 271, 95 S.Ct. 2150, 45 L.Ed.2d 177 (1975), and was intended to make the jurisdictional

Are there any activities which have a financial impact but should not be viewed as "trade or commerce"? Should the Sherman Act, for example, be applicable to restrictions on membership in a Dental Association? to amateur athletics? to the law school accreditation activities of the American Bar Association and the Association of American Law Schools? to the United Way? [25] What policies should guide a court in deciding whether to apply the Sherman Act? To what extent should courts take account (as they have on occasion) of a defendant's "noncommercial" purpose,[26] or the policies of free speech and petition embodied in the First Amendment? [27] Although there is a general tendency to apply the Sherman Act broadly, the tension between applying the antitrust principle of competition and giving weight to other public policies has been a constant one in the development of the antitrust laws. (See also Note (10), infra p. 31).

Most states also have statutes directed against monopoly, restraint of trade, unfair trade practices and a variety of related consumer protection laws.[28] Many states have constitutional provisions dealing with trusts and monopolies and many state antitrust provisions antedate federal legislation.[29] A few states—notably California, New York, Texas and Wisconsin—have engaged in substantial enforcement over a long period of time. Under the Crime Control Act of 1976 Congress appropriated $21 million in "seed money" for distribution to the States to strengthen their antitrust enforcement.[30] The result was a marked increase in enforcement activity on the state and local level.[31] Whether this activity will now continue without federal fund-

reach of the Sherman, FTC, and Clayton Acts the same. See H.R. Rep. No. 871, 96th Cong., 2d Sess., reprinted in 1980 U.S. Code Cong. & Admin. News 2732. The Robinson-Patman Act, dealing with price discrimination, reaches only activities "in commerce." See Gulf Oil Corp. v. Copp Paving Co., Inc., 419 U.S. 186, 95 S.Ct. 392, 42 L.Ed.2d 378 (1974).

25. See, e.g., Boddicker v. Arizona State Dental Association, 549 F.2d 626 (9th Cir. 1977) (tying membership in two associations) (held: yes), certiorari denied 434 U.S. 825, 98 S.Ct. 73, 54 L.Ed.2d 83; Hennessey v. National Collegiate Athletic Association, 564 F.2d 1136 (5th Cir. 1973) (NCAA coaches rule) (held: yes); Associated In-Group Donors v. United Way, Inc., ATRR No. 860, April 20, 1978, p. D–4 (Cal.Super.Ct.) (settlement of suit); First, Competition In the Legal Education Industry (II): An Antitrust Analysis, 54 N.Y.U.L. Rev. 1049 (1979) (law schools).

26. See, e.g., Marjorie Webster Junior College, Inc. v. Middle States Association of Colleges & Secondary Schools, Inc., 432 F.2d 650 (D.C.Cir. 1970), certiorari denied 400 U.S. 965, 91 S.Ct. 367, 27 L.Ed.2d 384 (Sherman Act does not apply to school accreditation activities done with a noncommercial purpose).

27. See, e.g., Eastern Railroad Presidents Conference v. Noerr Motor Freight, Inc., 365 U.S. 127, 81 S.Ct. 523, 5 L.Ed.2d 464 (1961) (Sherman Act does not apply to lobbying); Missouri v. NOW, Inc., 620 F.2d 1301 (8th Cir. 1980), certiorari denied 449 U.S. 842, 101 S.Ct. 122, 66 L.Ed.2d 49 (Sherman Act does not apply to boycott used in political arena to influence legislation). See generally, First, Private Interest and Public Control: Government Action, The First Amendment and the Sherman Act, 1975 Utah L.Rev. 9.

28. State antitrust laws are collected in 4 CCH Trade Reg. Rep. ¶ 30,000 et seq. The National Conference of Commissioners on Uniform State Laws has Proposed a "Uniform State Antitrust Act", which has been approved by the ABA House of Delegates, see 4 CCH Trade Reg. Rep. ¶ 30,101. The Act has been strongly criticized, and has been adopted in only one State and then with considerable revision. See Stone, Reviving State Antitrust Enforcement: The Problems with Putting New Wine in Old Wineskins, 4 J.Corp.L. 547, 620–25 (1979).

29. See Flynn, Federalism & State Antitrust Regulation (1964); CCH Trade Reg.Service, Vol. 2.

30. See Stone, supra note 28, at 591.

31. See Stone, supra note 28, at 610–16; "Antitrust Enforcement in 45 States Seen Expanding Sharply With Federal Grants," Wall St. Journal, Oct. 17, 1979, p. 4.

ing, and in the wake of some unfavorable state court decisions,[32] remains to be seen.[33]

The phrase "or with foreign nations" extends the Sherman Act to United States foreign commerce, i.e., activities which affect United States imports or exports. This may lead to the application of the Sherman Act to conduct outside the United States, thereby giving rise to considerable controversy, and several courts have held that, in addition to finding an effect on United States foreign commerce, the court must assess whether there should be an extraterritorial extension of United States jurisdiction "as a matter of international comity and fairness." [34] Recognition of such a limit on the Sherman Act's jurisdictional scope came at the same time that antitrust litigants sought to apply the Act in a number of highly-publicized international situations (e.g. international price-fixing of uranium and ocean shipping).[35] This litigation provoked a number of countries to enact legislation which attempts to protect their home firms from United States antitrust laws—"blocking" statutes to prevent document production and "claw back" statutes to recover the "penal" (two-thirds) portion of a treble-damage award.[36]

Application of United States antitrust legislation to foreign commerce presents problems beyond the jurisdictional. The "act of State" and "sovereign compulsion" doctrines recognize a defense for restraints of trade either imposed under foreign government supervision or compelled by a foreign sovereign.[37] More than comity may be involved here. Protection of United

32. See, e.g., People v. Roth, 52 N.Y.2d 440, 438 N.Y.S.2d 737, 420 N.E.2d 929 (1981) (N.Y. State antitrust law does not apply to medical profession).

33. See ATRR No. 1027, Aug. 13, 1981, pp. D–1 – D–8 (reporting state response to diminished funding). See generally Flynn, Trends in Federal Antitrust Doctrine Suggesting Future Directions for State Antitrust Enforcement, 4 J. Corp.Law 479 (1979); Rubin, Rethinking State Antitrust Enforcement, 26 U.Fla.L. Rev. 653 (1974). A good primer for state antitrust enforcers is Fellmeth & Papageorge, A Treatise on State Antitrust Law and Enforcement: With Models and Forms, printed in ATRR No. 892, Dec. 7, 1978 (Spec.Supp.). For a summary of 1981 state antitrust expenditures, see ATRR No. 1009, April 9, 1981, p. D–1.

34. Timberlane Lumber Co. v. Bank of America National Trust and Savings Association, 549 F.2d 597 (9th Cir. 1976). See also Mannington Mills, Inc. v. Congoleum Corp., 595 F.2d 1287 (3d Cir. 1979). But see Pacific Seafarers, Inc. v. Pacific Far East Line Inc., 404 F.2d 804 (D.C.Cir. 1968), certiorari denied 393 U.S. 1093, 89 S.Ct. 872, 21 L.Ed.2d 784 (U.S. ships carrying AID cargo between Asian ports subject to Sherman Act); United States v. Aluminum Co. of America, 148 F.2d 416 (2d Cir. 1945) (test is effect on United States foreign commerce).

35. See, e.g., United Nuclear Corp. v. General Atomic Co., 96 N.M. 155, 629 P.2d 231, 1980–81 Trade Cas. ¶ 63,639

(1980) (giving background of uranium litigation, in context of default judgment for failure to produce documents regarding international uranium cartel), certiorari denied 451 U.S. 901, 101 S.Ct. 1966, 68 L.Ed.2d 289 (1981); ATRR No. 935, Oct. 18, 1979, pp. A16–A18 (discussing foreign reaction to proceedings against non-American shipping and uranium companies). After vigorously resisting efforts of American litigants to obtain documents from Canada relating to uranium price-fixing, Canada is now considering prosecuting Canadian uranium companies under Canadian antitrust laws. See "Canada May Prosecute Uranium Firms It Encouraged to Participate in Cartel," Wall St. Journal, June 24, 1981, p. 46.

36. See generally Gordon, Extraterritorial Application of United States Economic Laws: Britain Draws the Line, 14 Int'l Law. 15 (1980); Note, Foreign Nondisclosure Laws and Domestic Discovery Orders, 88 Yale L.J. 612 (1979); Hawk, U.S. Common Market and Antitrust (1979), ch. 4.

37. See Hunt v. Mobil Oil Corp., 550 F.2d 68 (2d Cir. 1977) (nationalization of oil business by Libya is an "act of State"); Timberlane Lumber Co. v. Bank of America National Trust and Savings Association, 549 F.2d 597 (9th Cir. 1976) (acts of Honduran Courts do not constitute "acts of State"); Interamerican Refining Corp. v. Texaco Maracaibo, Inc., 307 F.Supp. 1291 (D.Del.1970) (accepting sovereign compulsion defense). See generally Note, Rehabilitation and Exonera-

States' business may be implicated. Trading in a foreign country may require acceptance of that country's restrictive policies; or the foreign government may have imposed the restrictions to satisfy United States' protectionist trade policies (e.g., Japanese restrictions on automobile exports to the United States).[38] Indeed, concern for making certain that United States firms can compete abroad has led to calls for dramatic curtailment of the Sherman Act.[39] The Department of Justice, in an effort to quiet such fears, issued an Antitrust Guide for International Operations in 1977, giving concrete examples of its enforcement views in a number of international situations.

Congress responded to a number of these concerns by enacting the Export Trading Company Act of 1982. Title III of this Act provides a specific antitrust immunity for certain export activities via a certification process. Title IV is the Foreign Trade Antitrust Improvements Act of 1982. It directly amends the Sherman Act, by providing that the Sherman Act does not apply to conduct involving trade with foreign nations (other than import trade into the United States) unless that conduct has a "direct, substantial, and reasonably foreseeable effect" on (1) domestic commerce, (2) import trade, or (3) export trade of exporters engaged in such trade in the United States.[40] Although this statute should provide greater antitrust freedom for United States manufacturers to combine for the purpose of exporting products, it is unclear whether the statute will reduce the frictions arising out of the application of the Sherman Act to foreign activity which affects United States markets.

(5) *Public Enforcement by the Department of Justice.* The Antitrust Division of the Department of Justice enforces the Sherman and Clayton Acts, and often acts as an "advocate for competition" in proceedings before federal regulatory agencies.[41] The establishment of public enforcement of the antitrust laws was a significant contribution of the Sherman Act; at

---

tion of the Act of State Doctrine, 12 N.Y. U.J. Int'l L. & Pol. 599 (1980); Note, Sherman Act Jurisdiction and the Acts of Foreign Sovereigns, 77 Colum.L.Rev. 1247 (1977); Note, Development of the Defense of Sovereign Compulsion, 69 Mich.L.Rev. 888 (1971). The Foreign Sovereign Immunities Act, 28 U.S.C.A. §§ 1602–11, codifies a general immunity for foreign sovereigns but specifically excepts commercial acts from its grant of immunity. See Timberg, Sovereign Immunity and Act of State, 55 Tex.L.Rev. 1 (1976).

38. See 5 CCH Trade Reg. Rep. ¶ 50, 427, reporting letter of February 18, 1981, from Attorney General Smith to U.S. Trade Representative Brock describing how United States negotiators should structure the agreement to restrict imports of Japanese automobiles so as to avoid the risk of private antitrust litigation. See also Consumers Union of United States v. Rogers, 352 F.Supp. 1319 (D.D.C.1973) (agreements to restrict steel imports by British Steel Corp. and Japanese and western European companies, negotiated by Secretary of State at President's direction, not exempt from Sher-

man Act), statement vacated on appeal sub nom. Consumers Union of United States v. Kissinger, 506 F.2d 136 (D.C. Cir. 1974) (no antitrust exemption claimed by defendants), certiorari denied 421 U.S. 1004, 95 S.Ct. 2406, 44 L.Ed.2d 673 (1975).

39. Cf. Thurow, "Let's Abolish the Antitrust Laws," N.Y. Times, Oct. 19, 1980, Bus. Sec. p. 2F ("futility and obsolescence" of antitrust laws apparent from a number of vantage points, including competition in international trade; urges more cooperation among firms in U.S. to allow "nationally based cartels" to fight for international markets).

40. See Pub.L.No. 97–290, 96 Stat. 1233 (1982). Title IV also amends section 5 of the Federal Trade Commission Act. This legislation, and the general problems of applying the Sherman Act to international trade, are explored infra ch. 7, sec. E.

41. For a study of the Division, see Weaver, Decision to Prosecute: Organization and Public Policy in the Antitrust Division (1974).

common law "restraints of trade" were policed in private litigation. The Department has jurisdiction to enforce the law by criminal prosecution and proceedings in equity.[42]

With respect to criminal enforcement, historically prison sentences have rarely been imposed and fines have not been large enough to constitute a real deterrent.[43] This may be changing. In 1974 Congress reaffirmed its commitment to enforcement of antitrust policy through criminal sanctions, making violations of the Sherman Act felonies rather than misdemeanors, increasing potential jail sentences from one to three years, and raising fines from a maximum of $50,000 to a maximum of $100,000 for individuals and $1,000,000 for corporations.[44] The Department of Justice has also been increasingly attentive to the use of the criminal sanction. During the 1970's it brought a significant number of criminal cases and argued vigorously for the imposition of actual jail sentences.[45] As a result, by the end of the 1970's courts were imposing a record level of fines and actual jail time for antitrust violators.[46]

42. The Department can also sue for actual (single) damages sustained by the United States as a result of antitrust violations. 15 U.S.C.A. § 15a.

43. See Flynn, Criminal Sanctions Under State and Federal Antitrust Laws, 45 Tex.L.Rev. 1301 (1967); Kramer, Criminal Prosecutions for Violations of the Sherman Act: In Search of a Policy, 48 Geo.L.J. 530 (1960); Posner, A Statistical Study of Antitrust Enforcement, 13 J. Law & Econ. 365 (1970); Max, Statement on S. 1284, 1 Hearings, The Antitrust Improvements Act of 1975, pp. 371–386, Senate Subcomm. on Antitrust and Monopoly, 94th Cong. 1st Sess. (1975). Sutherland, White Collar Crime 46–51 (1949), argued that infrequent provision of criminal penalties in legislation against business people and infrequent resort to available criminal provisions reflect official "fear and admiration" of business people and lack of organization among consumers and other victims, as well as a general trend away from penal sanctions.

44. The Antitrust Procedures and Penalties Act, Public Law 93–528, 88 Stat. 1706, amending 15 U.S.C.A. §§ 1 and 2.

45. See Department of Justice Guidelines for Sentencing Recommendations in Felony Cases under the Sherman Act, ATRR No. 803, Feb. 24, 1977, p. F–1; appearance of Assistant Attorney General Baker of the Antitrust Division to argue for imprisonment in U.S. v. Alton Box Board Co., No. 76 CR 199 (N.D.Ill. Nov. 30, 1976); and the sentencing of 15 executives to jail for periods up to 60 days. ATRR No. 792, Dec. 7, 1976, p. A–11 and transcript of sentencing hearing at p. D–1. See also "Stiff Penalties for Price

Fixing Levied by Court," Wall St. J., Feb. 6, 1978, p. 8 (reporting letter to sentencing judge from Assistant Attorney General Shenefield urging jail terms; judge rejects "good character" in sentencing—those who reaped public esteem during years of secret price fixing must pay for their crime). A claim of cruel and unusual punishment was rejected in United States v. Prince, 515 F.2d 564 (5th Cir. 1976), where defendants sought to withdraw a plea after being surprised by a prison sentence on a plea of nolo contendere.

But compare the observation of another executive indicted for price fixing: "When you're doing $30 million a year and stand to gain $3 million by fixing prices, a $30,000 fine doesn't mean much. Face it, most of us would be willing to spend 30 days in jail to make a few extra million dollars." Business Week, p. 48, June 2, 1975. See Breit and Elzinga, Antitrust Penalties and Attitudes Toward Risk: An Economic Analysis, 86 Harv.L. Rev. 693 (1973); Kadish, Some Observations on The Use of Criminal Sanctions In Enforcing Economic Regulations, 30 Univ.Chi.L.Rev. 423 (1963). For a discussion of the propriety (and utility) of sentencing corporate executives to giving speeches about their participation in a price-fixing conspiracy, see Renfrew, The Paper Label Sentences: An Evaluation, 86 Yale L.J. 590 (1977), and accompanying critical articles.

46. For Antitrust Division workload statistics for 1969–1979, giving numbers of cases brought and penalties imposed, see ATRR No. 949, Jan. 31, 1980, p. F–1. In 1980 the Division brought 55 criminal prosecutions, nearly double that of 1979. ATRR No. 989, Nov. 13, 1980, p. A–9.

Some believe that criminal sanctions are inappropriate for violation of the antitrust laws. They believe that antitrust violations are not morally reprehensible, often being the result of competitive pressures and industry custom, occurring in an environment where business people are uncertain as to what conduct the law prohibits.[47] It is argued that an equity decree altering the business situation provides more constructive relief.[48] The Clayton Act of 1914 did not provide criminal penalties for violation of its special provisions against price discrimination, tying, exclusive dealing, and mergers.[49] Historically, the Division has brought more civil than criminal suits.

In exercising its prosecutorial discretion the Division had for many years performed a quasi-administrative function under the "railroad release" procedure, which gave inquiring counsel a tentative official opinion that proposed activity was not objectionable under the antitrust laws. Since the Attorney General is authorized to give legal advice only to the President and the executive departments, the "railroad release" letter did not go so far as to declare that a contemplated transaction would be lawful. Instead, the Department merely waived conditionally its right to institute criminal proceedings. This procedure, which has no statutory basis, has now been broadened to apply to all enforcement. Re-named the "Business Review Procedure," it is formalized in 28 C.F.R. § 50.6. In response to criticism concerning secrecy of the process, the procedure was amended in 1974 to provide for public access under stated circumstances to the request for and issuance of a Business Review Letter. Notice of many of the Letters issued is summarized in 5 CCH Trade Reg.Rep. ¶ 50,194. Denial of a requested clearance for a course of action does not necessarily mean the Division will challenge a subsequent following of the course of action; nor does issuance of a Departmental "Clearance" bind a court in subsequent litigation attacking the practice.[50]

47. See "Paving Firms Accused of Rigging Road Bids on Southeast Projects," Wall St. J., May 29, 1981, p. 1 (bid-rigging a "way of life" for 30 years; people did business "the way their fathers did" and didn't worry about things like the antitrust laws). But see "Price-Fixing Charges Rise in Paper Industry Despite Convictions," Wall St. J., May 4, 1978, p. 1 (paper industry executive testifies that at one meeting discussing prices an associate said " 'If they send us to jail, we will at least have enough to make a ball team—a baseball team.' ")

48. See Report of the Attorney General's National Committee to Study the Antitrust Laws (1955) 349–52, which, *inter alia*, quotes a statement of Department of Justice policy confining criminal prosecution to price fixing and other violations which are wilful or predatory.

49. Criminal enforcement has procedural as well as substantive significance, because it allows the Government to use the grand jury process to subpoena witnesses and documents. In civil cases, however, the Antitrust Division has statutory authorization to obtain information through "civil investigative demands." See Antitrust Civil Process Act of 1962, 15 U.S.C.A. § 1310 et seq. The demands

can be enforced only through court action. 15 U.S.C.A. §§ 1311–1314. In re Gold Bond Stamp Co., 221 F.Supp. 391 (D.C.Minn.1963) aff'd 325 F.2d 1018 (8th Cir. 1964), deals with the question of adequate specificity of the demand to forestall "fishing expeditions". See Siegel, The Antitrust Civil Process Act: The Attorney General's Pre-Action Key to Company Files, 10 Vill.L.Rev. 413 (1965). The Hart-Scott-Rodino Antitrust Improvements Act of 1976 amended the Antitrust Civil Process Act to permit the taking of oral testimony as well as the demanding of written documents; to do so with regard to potential as well as past or present violations; and to permit the demanding of documents or the taking of testimony from third parties as well as those who are the target of the investigation. 15 U.S.C.A. § 1312. The Antitrust Procedural Improvements Act of 1980 further amended the Act, allowing the Department to obtain the "products of discovery" produced in private litigation and "adversarial" administrative proceedings. Id.

50. See Blue Cross v. Virginia, 211 Va. 180, 191–92, 176 S.E.2d 439, 446 (1970) (approval through the Business Review Procedure given no weight in de-

(6) *Public Enforcement by the Federal Trade Commission.* The Federal Trade Commission also enforces the antitrust laws. Congress established the FTC in 1914, giving it jurisdiction (in Section 5 of the Federal Trade Commission Act) to halt "unfair methods of competition." [51] Virtually simultaneously, Congress passed the Clayton Act, dealing with price-discrimination, tying and exclusive supply agreements, mergers, and interlocking directorates; enforcement was given to both the Justice Department and the Federal Trade Commission. The two statutes reflected popular belief that the Sherman Act had failed to prevent improper business behavior. Congress was particularly alarmed over the Supreme Court's adoption of the "rule of reason" in 1911 (see Note (3), supra), believing that the courts were thereby usurping legislative power. The specificity of the Clayton Act, plus a newly created administrative agency with broad authority to end what one Senator described as "unjust, inequitable or dishonest competition," were thought to be adequate remedy.[52]

The FTC's antitrust jurisdiction is not identical with that of the Department of Justice. Neither the Clayton Act nor Section 5 of the FTC Act have penal provisions, and Congress did not give the FTC jurisdiction to enforce the Sherman Act. Despite the lack of direct Sherman Act authority, however, courts have interpreted "unfair methods of competition" to include any practice which would violate the Sherman Act. Courts have also held that Section 5 reaches practices which violate the "spirit" or "policies" of the Sherman and Clayton Acts, even though they do not violate the letter of the Acts. Finally, in the broadest interpretation of the Commission's Section 5 authority, the Supreme Court has held that the Commission may enjoin practices which affect consumers "unfairly" regardless of the effect on competition. This final proposition, establishing the Commission's "unfairness" jurisdiction, permits the Commission to act "like a court of equity" and consider "public values" beyond those of the antitrust laws.[53] The limits of this jurisdiction have not been tested in the courts.[54]

termining illegality under state and federal antitrust laws of a cost-plus prescription price-fixing program). For a case in which the Department of Justice denied advanced clearance, but thereafter declined to proceed against the transaction, see report of General Electric Company's acquisition of an electrical appliance firm, Wall St. J., April 14, 1965.

51. Section 5 also prohibits "unfair or deceptive acts or practices," which is the statutory authority for the Commission's consumer protection role. Other important sections of the FTC Act are: Section 6, authorizing the Commission to investigate and compile information concerning the "organization, business conduct, practices and management of any person, partnership or corporation"; require the filing of reports; investigate compliance with court orders issued against antitrust violators; investigate alleged violations of the antitrust laws upon direction of the Congress or the President; and investigate "trade conditions" in and with foreign nations; Section 7, providing an interesting but never used authority for courts to refer cases to the FTC as a

"master in chancery" for aid in framing a remedy in equity suits brought by the Attorney General to enforce the antitrust laws. See 45 U.S.C.A. §§ 46, 47.

52. For a legislative history of the Federal Trade Commission and Clayton Acts, along with a study of the FTC's beginning years, see Henderson, The Federal Trade Commission (1924).

53. Federal Trade Commission v. Sperry & Hutchinson Co., 405 U.S. 233, 244, 92 S.Ct. 898, 905, 31 L.Ed.2d 170, 179 (1972).

54. In Sperry & Hutchinson the Court, in a footnote, cited with approval an F.T.C. statement of those factors the Commission relied upon in establishing a practice as unfair:

(1) Whether the practice, without necessarily having been previously considered unlawful, offends public policy as it has been established by statutes, the common law, or otherwise—whether, in other words, it is within at least the penumbra of some common law, statutory or other established concept of unfairness;

The FTC, as an independent regulatory agency, has often been a highly visible political target. In the late 1960's it was broadly criticized as ineffective.[55] President Nixon's subsequent appointments of more activist Chairmen reinvigorated the Commission, and Congress added to the Commission's jurisdictional and rule-making powers in the 1975 Magnuson-Moss Act.[56] The Commission then instituted a number of rulemaking proceedings to deal with perceived abuses in a variety of areas (e.g., the funeral and used car industries) and pursued a novel "shared monopoly" theory in Section 5 suits against the oil industry and the makers of ready-to-eat breakfast cereals. By the end of the 1970's, however, the Commission was viewed by many in Congress as an agency out of control, engaged in over-regulation of business affairs. The result was the Federal Trade Commission Improvements Act of 1980 which, although it does not cut back the Commission's authority as far as some sought, does restrict Commission activities. It also allows a Congressional veto of proposed FTC rules if both Houses adopt a concurrent resolution to that effect within 90 days after the rule is submitted to Congress for review.[57]

Legislative oversight of the FTC has continued since 1980. In addition, the head of the Antitrust Division and the Director of OMB under President Reagan have indicated that they favor eliminating the FTC's antitrust jurisdiction. (Should we have competition or monopoly in antitrust enforcement? [58]) In this climate it is likely that the FTC will become a far more cautious enforcement agency.

(7) *Private Enforcement.* Section 4 of the Clayton Act gives private parties the right to sue antitrust violators for three times the damages caused

(2) Whether it is immoral, unethical, oppressive, or unscrupulous;

(3) Whether it causes substantial injury to consumers (or competitors or other businessmen).

405 U.S. at 244 n. 5, 92 S.Ct. at 904, 31 L.Ed.2d at 179.

Loescher, Corporate Giantism, Degradation of the Plane of Competition, and Countervailance, 8 J.Econ.Issues 329 (1974), argues that all cost savings which a firm derives from neglecting the safety of its products or employees or from harming the environment give it an unfair competitive advantage over its more ethical rivals, and so might be reached under § 5 of the FTC Act. The Commission, in a letter to Senators Ford and Danforth explaining how it intends to enforce its unfairness mandate, has stated that it will not use the "unethical" factor noted in *S&H*. The Senators were members of the Subcommittee which planned to hold hearings on the FTC's unfairness jurisdiction. The letter is printed in 5 Trade Reg.Rep. (CCH) ¶ 50,421 (Dec. 17, 1980).

55. See Cox, Fellmeth & Schulz, "The Nader Report" On the Federal Trade Commission (1969); Report of the ABA Commission to Study the Federal Trade Commission (1969). Two more recent studies of the FTC are Katzman, Regulatory Bureaucracy: the Federal Trade Commission and Antitrust Policy (1980); and Stone, Economic Regulation And The Public Interest: The Federal Trade Commission in Theory and Practice (1977).

56. See 15 U.S.C.A. §§ 45, 57a.

57. See Pub.L. No. 96–252, 94 Stat. 374 (1980). Congressional hostility to the FTC may explain Congress' refusal, in the 1980 Amendment to Section 5(a) of the Clayton Act, to extend collateral estoppel doctrines to FTC adjudications. See n. 84, infra.

58. The FTC and the Department of Justice have generally shared enforcement rather than competing for cases, with each tending to specialize (sometimes by industry, sometimes by types of legal theories or particular statutes). A formal liaison procedure to divide case responsibilities between the agencies has existed since 1948, and is detailed in Antitrust Division Manual VII–1 to –6 (1979). There are occasions, however, where one agency will act after the other has declined. See ATRR No. 522, July 20, 1971, p. A–16 (FTC issues complaint against Warner-Lambert's acquisition of Parke-Davis after Justice Department, despite staff recommendation, fails to do so). The FTC subsequently found anticompetitive effects in five product lines and ordered partial divestiture. See 88 F.T.C. 503 (1976).

by the violation, plus attorney's fees.[59]   Although this private right of action was originally established in 1890 in the Sherman Act, its full impact has come to be felt only in recent years.   Since the mid-1960's private antitrust litigation has increased dramatically, with major corporations being sued and bringing suit.[60]   The increase has been fueled, in part, by an increasing awareness by counsel of the antitrust laws, a rise in federal antitrust prosecutions (which alert private litigants to potential suits), and by the perception of a favorable judicial climate for antitrust plaintiffs.   Awards and settlements have been substantial, to say the least: $1.8 billion awarded by the jury in *MCI Communications Co. v. AT&T* (but reversed, in part, on appeal, and remanded for a new trial on damages); $87 million awarded by the jury in *Berkey Photo v. Eastman Kodak* (but reduced to $990,000 on appeal); $300 million settlement in a class action against corrugated container manufacturers; $218 million settlement in a class action against folding carton manufacturers (with a $13.5 million fee award to plaintiffs' counsel); $195 million settlement in a class action against the makers of broad spectrum antibiotic drugs.[61]

   This recent surge in private antitrust litigation has uncovered a wide variety of difficult problems which relate specifically to the right of a private litigant to sue and recover damages.   The courts (and Congress) have not yet fully solved many of them.   Note is made here of the most significant issues relating specifically to private antitrust litigation; the remainder of the materials in this book will focus more on the general substantive issues of antitrust law.

   "Standing" issues have been a major obstacle to plaintiffs seeking damages.   Courts have denied recovery, for example, when injury was "remote," rather than "direct"; or when the plaintiff was outside the "target area" of the violation.[62]   The Supreme Court has held that a plaintiff is not entitled to recover simply by showing that the defendant's conduct caused it injury.   A plaintiff must also prove that it suffered *"antitrust* injury"—"injury of the

59.   Governments can also sue for monetary injury.   The federal government can sue for single (actual) damages. States may sue for treble damages.   See Georgia v. Evans, 316 U.S. 159, 62 S.Ct 972, 86 L.Ed. 1346 (1942)).   Pfizer, Inc. v. Government of India, 434 U.S. 308, 98 S.Ct. 584, 54 L.Ed.2d 563 (1978), held that foreign governments, otherwise entitled to sue in United States courts, could sue for treble damages.   In 1982 Congress amended section 4 of the Clayton Act to allow foreign governments to sue only for actual damages, except that treble damages may still be obtained in certain cases.   See Pub.L.No. 97–393, 96 Stat. 1964 (1982).

60.   Private antitrust case filings have increased from 228 in 1960 to 1,457 in 1980.   Filings for each year between 1971 and 1980 have exceeded 1,100 per year;   the highest was 1,611 in 1977.   See 1980 Annual Rep. of Dir. Admin. Off. of U.S. Cts. at 63.   Filings declined to 1,292 in 1981.   See 43 ATRR 61 (1982).   See also "More Firms Are Filing Antitrust Lawsuits Against Competitors," Wall St. Journal, Dec. 29, 1976, p. 1.

61.   Further information on awards in private cases can be found in 1 Hearings, The Antitrust Improvements Act of 1975, p. 385 (Statement, Peter Max), Sen. Subc. Antitrust & Monop., 94th Cong., 1st Sess. (1975).

62.   See, e.g., Billy Baxter, Inc. v. Coca-Cola Co., 431 F.2d 183 (2d Cir. 1970) (franchisor denied standing to sue for alleged conspiracy to foreclose franchisees from the market), certiorari denied 401 U.S. 923, 91 S.Ct. 877, 27 L.Ed.2d 826 (1971); Loeb v. Eastman Kodak Co., 183 F. 704 (3d Cir. 1910) (denying standing to shareholder).   See also Chrysler Corp. v. Fedders Corp., 643 F.2d 1229 (6th Cir. 1981) ("zone of interests" test for standing), certiorari denied 454 U.S. 893, 102 S.Ct. 388, 70 L.Ed.2d 207.   The various standing tests are reviewed and analyzed in, e.g., Berger & Bernstein, An Analytical Framework for Antitrust Standing, 86 Yale L.J. 809 (1977); Sherman, Antitrust Standing: From *Loeb* to *Malamud,* 51 N.Y.U.L.Rev. 374 (1976).

type the antitrust laws were intended to prevent and that flows from that which makes defendants' acts unlawful." [63]

A critical standing issue in recent private treble damage actions has been the right of purchasers at various levels of the distribution process to sue price-fixers for overcharges. In *Hanover Shoe Inc. v. United Shoe Machinery Corp.*, 392 U.S. 481, 88 S.Ct. 2224, 20 L.Ed.2d 1231 (1968), the Supreme Court held that when a direct-purchaser middleman sues a price-fixing manufacturer the manufacturer can not assert in defense that the plaintiff suffered little or no injury because it was able to "pass-on" (some of) the overcharge to its customers, the "indirect" purchasers. The Court rested its result, in part, on the difficulties of proving how the middleman would have priced but for the price-fixing overcharge, and the belief that indirect purchasers would lack incentive to sue because their individual injury was likely to be small.

The question then arose whether indirect purchasers would be allowed to sue at all. In *Illinois Brick Co. v. Illinois*, 431 U.S. 720, 97 S.Ct. 2061, 52 L.Ed.2d 707 (1977), the Supreme Court held no. The Court felt that double liability might occur if an indirect purchaser could recover by showing that the overcharge had been passed-on by the direct purchaser, while, at the same time, the direct purchaser could also recover for the overcharge because the defendant would be barred from demonstrating a pass-on. The Court also again voiced concern at the potential complication and uncertainty which the use of the pass-on theory would bring to treble damage actions,[64] and determined that enforcement of the antitrust laws would be better served by not attempting to apportion the overcharge among all who may have absorbed a part of it.

Foreclosing indirect purchasers from relief most directly affects antitrust suits for damages brought on behalf of consumers,[65] including suits brought by State Attorneys General as *parens patriae* on behalf of their citizens.[66] The harshness of the result in *Illinois Brick* has led some lower courts to

63. Brunswick Corp. v. Pueblo Bowl-O-Mat, 429 U.S. 477, 489, 97 S.Ct. 690, 50 L.Ed.2d 701 (1977). See Blue Shield of Virginia v. McCready, ___ U.S. ___, 102 S.Ct. 2540, 73 L.Ed.2d 149 (1982) (allowing suit by health insurance policy holder denied reimbursement for psychotherapy performed by psychologist rather than psychiatrist; denial of reimbursement "inextricably intertwined" with alleged agreement by Blue Shield and psychiatrists to exclude psychologists from the market).

64. Commentators differ as to the propriety and ease of such an inquiry. Compare Landes and Posner, Should Indirect Purchasers Have Standing to Sue Under the Antitrust Laws? An Economic Analysis of the Rule of Illinois Brick, 46 U.Chi.L.Rev. 602 (1979), and The Economics of Passing On: A Reply to Harris and Sullivan, 128 U.Pa.L.Rev. 1274 (1980), with Harris and Sullivan, Passing on the Monopoly Overcharge: A Comprehensive Policy Analysis, 128 U.Pa.L.Rev. 269 (1979), and Passing on the Monopoly Overcharge: A Response to Landes and Posner, 128 U.Pa.L.Rev. 1280 (1980).

65. As a general matter, consumers do have standing to sue for monetary damages under the antitrust laws. Reiter v. Sonotone Corp., 442 U.S. 330, 99 S.Ct. 2326, 60 L.Ed.2d 931 (1979). Class actions on behalf of consumers, however, have not been an extremely effective vehicle for the redress of antitrust injuries. See Eisen v. Carlisle & Jacquelin, 417 U.S. 156, 94 S.Ct. 2140, 40 L.Ed.2d 732 (1974); Kline v. Coldwell, Banker & Co., 508 F.2d 226 (9th Cir. 1974). But cf. Windham v. American Brands, Inc., 539 F.2d 1016 (4th Cir. 1976), certiorari denied 435 U.S. 968, 98 S.Ct. 1605, 56 L.Ed. 2d 58 (1978).

66. Such suits were authorized in the Hart-Scott-Rodino Antitrust Improvements Act of 1976, 15 U.S.C.A. § 15c–h, establishing a "class action" mechanism for the State Attorney General to recover for monetary injury suffered by "natural persons residing in such State." In Hawaii v. Standard Oil Co., 405 U.S. 251, 92 S.Ct. 885, 31 L.Ed.2d 184 (1972), the Court had held that the State cannot sue as *parens patriae* for monetary injury to the general economy of the State. But

develop exceptions to its bar of indirect purchasers, particularly in cases where the indirect purchaser buys from the direct purchaser under a cost-plus contract.[67] Nevertheless, the rationale of *Illinois Brick* has been used to deny standing in treble damage actions to persons other than indirect purchasers,[68] and legislative attempts to overrule the case have so far been unsuccessful.[69]

With respect to trials, a major problem is simply the expense of protracted proceedings, particularly with respect to discovery.[70] There is a split of authority over whether a plaintiff is constitutionally entitled to have its claims tried by a jury.[71] There has been a considerable restriction, if not outright elimination, of the equitable defenses of "pari delicto" and "unclean hands." These defenses had been employed to defeat recovery by one who

see Georgia v. Pennsylvania Railroad, 324 U.S. 439, 65 S.Ct. 716, 89 L.Ed. 1051 (1945) (state may maintain parens patriae suit for equitable relief against antitrust violations).

67. *Hanover Shoe* recognized that where the plaintiff resold the defendant's goods under a "cost-plus" contract, the defendant might be able to assert a passing-on defense. 392 U.S. at 494. *Illinois Brick* similarly recognized that the indirect purchaser in that situation might then be allowed to sue. 431 U.S. at 735–36. Some courts have expanded the cost-plus contract exception to include "functional equivalents" of such contracts. See In re Beef Industry Antitrust Litigation, 600 F.2d 1148 (5th Cir. 1979), certiorari denied 449 U.S. 905, 101 S.Ct. 280, 66 L.Ed.2d 137 (1980); cf. Eastern Air Lines, Inc. v. Atlantic Richfield Co., 609 F.2d 497 (Temp.Emer.Ct. App.1979) (emphasizing that the functional equivalent must be a pre-existing contract). But see Mid-West Paper Products Co. v. Continental Group, Inc., 596 F.2d 573 (3d Cir. 1979) (to come within the cost-plus exception, indirect purchaser must prove pre-existing, fixed-quantity, cost-plus contracts at every level in the distribution chain, demonstrating that the indirect purchaser plaintiffs have absorbed the illegal ovecharge entirely). See also Note, A Door in the Illinois Brick Wall: A Functional Equivalent to the Cost-Plus Contract Exception, 33 Vand.L.Rev. 481 (1980). An "ownership or control" exception has been applied where the direct purchaser is controlled by the violator-supplier, e.g., a wholly-owned subsidiary or a franchisee of a supplier. See Royal Printing Co. v. Kimberly-Clark Corp., 621 F.2d 323 (9th Cir. 1980); Note, Scaling the Illinois Brick Wall: The Future of Indirect Purchasers in Antitrust Litigation, 63 Cornell L.Rev. 309, 327–29 (1978). An indirect purchaser alleging a "vertical" restraint (e.g., an agreement between a manufacturer and distributor to fix the distributor's resale price) may be treated

as a direct purchaser. See Florida Power Corp. v. Granlund, 78 F.R.D. 441 (M.D. Fla.1978); 63 Cornell L.Rev. 309, 327–29.

68. See, e.g., Reading Industries, Inc. v. Kennecott Copper Corp., 631 F.2d 10 (2d Cir. 1980) (*Illinois Brick's* concern for speculative economic assumptions about the marketplace supports rejection of claim based on attenuated theory of causality where no overcharge was alleged); In re Folding Carton Antitrust Litigation, 88 F.R.D. 211 (N.D.Ill.1980) (*Illinois Brick's* concern for burdensome proof problems forecloses standing of direct purchasers from non-defendant suppliers).

69. See Senate Comm. on the Judiciary, Report to Accompany S. 300, S.Rep. No. 96–239, 96th Cong., 1st Sess. 61 (1979); Restoring Effective Enforcement of the Antitrust Laws: Hearings on H.R. 2060 and H.R. 2204 and Other Proposals Before the Subcomm. on Monopolies and Commercial Law of the House Comm. on the Judiciary, 96th Cong., 1st Sess. 44–79 (1979); Effective Enforcement of the Antitrust Laws: Hearings on H.R. 8359B Before the Subcomm. on Monopolies and Commercial Law of the House Comm. on the Judiciary, 95th Cong., 1st Sess. 23–71 (1978); Fair and Effective Enforcement of the Antitrust Laws: Hearings on S. 1874 Before the Senate Comm. on the Judiciary, 95th Cong., 1st Sess. 92–96, 101–23 (1978).

70. These problems are explored in the Report of the National Commission For the Review of the Antitrust Laws at 11–12 (1979).

71. Compare In re Japanese Electronic Products Antitrust Litigation, 631 F.2d 1069 (3d Cir. 1980) (in a complex case, due process for the defendant may override plaintiff's jury trial right, but only in "exceptional cases") with U.S. Financial Securities Antitrust Litigation, 609 F.2d 411 (9th Cir. 1979) (seventh amendment applies without regard to complexity), certiorari denied 446 U.S. 929, 100 S.Ct. 1866, 64 L.Ed.2d 281 (1980).

was a willing participant in the unlawful scheme.   The leading case is *Perma Life Mufflers, Inc. v. International Parts Corp.*, 392 U.S. 134, 88 S.Ct. 1981, 20 L.Ed.2d 982 (1968), where, it may be noted, the suit was by a small franchised dealer against his powerful supplier, raising some question as to equality of bargaining power and the "willingness" with which the franchisee accepted the anticompetitive restraints contemplated by the franchise contract.   Judicial inclination to make antitrust violations expensive, by permitting recovery of the statutory treble damages even where plaintiff was himself a party to the anticompetitive conspiracy, has not carried so far as to provide an antitrust *defense* to a buyer in a suit to recover the purchase price of goods bought pursuant to their common scheme to raise the price of those goods.[72]   As will appear in later chapters, an antitrust defense will often be effective where the suit more directly seeks to effectuate a monopolistic arrangement, e.g., to enforce patent rights beyond the lawful scope of the monopoly grant of the patent.

Proof of damages also presents difficult problems of theory and measurement.   Particularly outside the price-fixing area, significant problems remain in terms of theorizing how a defendant's antitrust violation hurt the plaintiff.[73]   With respect to computing the amount of damages, the Supreme Court in *Bigelow v. RKO Radio Pictures*, 327 U.S. 251, 264, 66 S.Ct. 574, 579–80, 90 L.Ed. 652, 660 (1946), stressed that a defendant wrongdoer could not insist upon specific and certain proof of the injury it had itself inflicted. Nevertheless, "even where the defendant by his own wrong has prevented a more precise computation, the jury may not render a verdict based on speculation or guesswork."   Juries are allowed to act upon " 'probable and inferential, as well as direct and positive proof,' " and thus evidence of a decline in prices or profits "not shown to be attributable to other causes" may be adequate to allow a fact finder to infer damages.[74]   This still leaves a defendant free to show that the plaintiff's injury flows from its own business ineptitude, rather than any anticompetitive conduct by the defendant; this tactic is often successful.[75]

Settlements and judgments for money damages also raise a number of problems.   Settlements, as agreements, are themselves subject to potential antitrust challenge by third parties.[76]   Another problem, which has attracted

72.   Kelly v. Kosuga, 358 U.S. 516, 79 S.Ct. 429, 3 L.Ed.2d 475 (1959).   Compare Kaiser Steel Corp. v. Mullins, 455 U.S. 72, 102 S.Ct. 851, 70 L.Ed.2d 833 (1982) (in suit for nonpayment of contributions to union health and retirement funds, allows defense that contractual clause requiring payment was part of illegal boycott of non-union coal, in violation of Sherman Act; enforcing promise to pay "would command conduct that assertedly renders the promise an illegal undertaking").

73.   See, e.g., J. Truett Payne Co., Inc. v. Chrysler Motors Corp., 451 U.S. 557, 101 S.Ct. 1923, 68 L.Ed.2d 442 (1981) (victim of price-discrimination); Berkey Photo, Inc. v. Eastman Kodak Co., 603 F.2d 263 (2d Cir. 1979) (victim of monopolist's overcharge), certiorari denied 444 U.S. 1093, 100 S.Ct. 1061, 62 L.Ed.2d 783 (1980); Purex Corp. v. Procter & Gamble Co., 596 F.2d 881 (9th Cir. 1979) (competitor in market where defendant made an

illegal acquisition); Areeda, Antitrust Violations Without Damage Recoveries, 89 Harv.L.Rev. 1127 (1976).

74.   Zenith Radio Corp. v. Hazeltine Research, Inc., 395 U.S. 100, 123–24, 89 S.Ct. 1562, 1576–77, 23 L.Ed.2d 129 (1969).   See also Story Parchment Co. v. Patterson Paper Co., 282 U.S. 555, 51 S.Ct. 248, 75 L.Ed. 544 (1931).

75.   See, e.g., Van Dyk Research Corp. v. Xerox Corp., 631 F.2d 251 (3d Cir. 1980), certiorari denied 452 U.S. 905, 101 S.Ct. 3029, 69 L.Ed.2d 405 (1981).

76.   See Duplan Corp. v. Deering Milliken, Inc., 444 F.Supp. 648 (D.S.C. 1977) (settlement of patent infringement litigation gave parties power to fix prices), aff'd 594 F.2d 979 (4th Cir. 1979), certiorari denied 444 U.S. 1015, 100 S.Ct. 666, 62 L.Ed.2d 645 (1980); In re New Mexico Natural Gas Antitrust Litigation, ATRR No. 946, Jan. 10, 1980, p. A–18 (alleging settlements of state litigation and their

much attention recently, is the question whether a defendant who pays money to a plaintiff can obtain contribution from co-defendants (or unsued co-conspirators). After lower courts split on the issue, the Supreme Court held that joint and several liability obtains; in light of the specific remedial provisions of the antitrust laws, Congress did not give the courts broad common law power to fashion new relief provisions.[77] The Court's parting comment that this "complex issue" is "a matter for Congress" will likely give impetus to Congressional efforts already underway to provide contribution in certain cases.[78]

Finally, there is the overall policy question of private enforcement. Treble damage liability has been criticized as excessive (or is it inadequate, given the risks of discovery and successful prosecution?); some suggest it benefits lawyers more than consumers.[79] The Supreme Court has frequently pointed out that the private suit makes a plaintiff into a "private Attorney General" awarded treble damages as an incentive to enforce the antitrust laws. This augments the thin resources of the federal enforcement agencies; but it also dilutes control of antitrust policy and may lead to antitrust decisions contrary to official views. Should recovery be reduced to single-damages? Should the Antitrust Division intervene in "bad" cases to urge the court to decide for the defendant? [80] Should the private right to enforce the antimerger provisions of the Clayton Act be eliminated so as to end its tactical use by takeover targets, whose management seeks either to increase the amount of the takeover bid or to kill the deal and thereby retain their jobs? [81]

(8) *The Relation Between Government Litigation, Consent Judgments, and Private Recovery of Damages.* Prior to 1980, Section 5(a) of the Clay-

implementation were part of conspiracy to raise prices).

77. Texas Industries, Inc. v. Radcliff Materials, Inc., 451 U.S. 630, 101 S.Ct. 2061, 68 L.Ed.2d 500 (1981). For earlier decisions, compare Wilson P. Abraham Construction Corp. v. Texas Industries, Inc., 604 F.2d 897 (5th Cir. 1979), with Professional Beauty Supply, Inc. v. National Beauty Supply, Inc., 594 F.2d 1179 (8th Cir. 1979). See generally Easterbrook, Landes & Posner, Contribution Among Antitrust Defendants: A Legal and Economic Analysis, 23 J. Law & Econ. 331 (1980); Note, Contribution and Antitrust Policy, 78 Mich.L.Rev. 892 (1980).

78. See S. 995, 97th Cong., 1st Sess. (1981); H.R. 1242, 97th Cong., 1st Sess. (1981); S. 1468, 96th Cong., 1st Sess. (1979).

79. See "Hassles Greet Customers Due Retail Refunds," Wall St. J., June 9, 1981, p. 35 (54,000 eligible for refunds for price-fixing by major department stores between 1968 and 1974; one-third of settlement goes for attorneys fees and administrative costs; "I think the only people who make money on these cases are the lawyers who bring them," says general counsel for Saks.)

80. See "Justice Antitrust Chief Pledges Amicus Actions," Nat'l L.J., May

25, 1981, p. 2 (in "dramatic departure" from past policy, Department will file amicus briefs on behalf of defendants in effort to reverse case law holding vertical restraints illegal; head of Antitrust Division quoted as seeking to overturn "rules that economically ignorant judges decided were a good idea" and making certain that judges "do not impose rules that create inefficiencies").

81. These suits usually seek to enjoin a proposed merger, rather than requesting money damages. Equitable relief is generally available "against threatened loss or damage by violation of the antitrust laws," under Section 16 of the Clayton Act, 15 U.S.C.A. § 26. See Flynn, A Survey of Injunctive Relief Under State and Federal Antitrust Laws, 1967 Utah L.Rev. 344. Divestiture of an illegally acquired company, however, has not been ordered in private litigation. See International Telephone and Telegraph Corp. v. General Telephone and Electric Corp., 518 F.2d 913 (9th Cir. 1975) (Congress did not intend to allow divestiture). But cf. NBO Industries Treadway Co., Inc. v. Brunswick Corp., 523 F.2d 262 (3d Cir. 1975) (divestiture might be allowed in appropriate case), certiorari denied 429 U.S. 1090, 97 S.Ct. 1099, 51 L.Ed.2d 535 (1977).

ton Act (supra p. 9) made a "final judgment or decree" against a defendant in any civil or criminal case brought by the United States under the antitrust laws *prima facie* evidence of the same violations in subsequent treble damage litigation against the same defendant. In response to the view that such language might foreclose the broader application of collateral estoppel to issues fully litigated against a defendant in an earlier antitrust proceeding, Congress amended the statute in 1980 to provide that 5(a) does not limit the use of this doctrine. The legislative history of this amendment indicates that Congress intended as much preclusion as common law notions of collateral estoppel would allow. Thus, modern developments in collateral estoppel now apply in antitrust suits as they would in any other action; [82] the *prima facie* effect clause remains available where collateral estoppel is not.

Section 5(a) also contains a proviso that "consent judgments or decrees" entered before any testimony has been taken" are not to be given even *prima facie* effect. The "consent judgments or decrees" referred to are *nolo contendere* pleas entered in government criminal antitrust cases [83] and "consent decrees" entered in government civil cases.[84] Government criminal cases are often resolved by pleas of *nolo contendere;* the majority of government civil cases are settled by the entry of "consent decrees." A *nolo* plea is generally held to admit all well-pleaded facts, without contesting guilt, and is inadmissible in subsequent civil litigation over liability for the criminal conduct.[85] Consent decrees are negotiated settlements of civil cases which are entered by the court where the complaint was filed, as a final judgment with the effect of an injunction.

Prior to 1975, consent decree negotiations were generally secret; third parties affected by the decree had little opportunity or right to participate in formulating the decree; and the Department exercised wide discretion not effectively subject to judicial scrutiny, in making such settlements.[86] Revelations during the "Watergate" episode, questions raised during the confir-

82. See H.R.Rep. No. 874, 96th Cong., 2d Sess., reprinted in 1980 U.S. Code Cong. & Adm. News 2752; Parklane Hosiery v. Shore, 439 U.S. 322, 99 S.Ct. 645, 58 L.Ed.2d 552 (1979) (allowing offensive nonmutual collateral estoppel).

83. Note, The Admissibility and Scope of Guilty Pleas in Antitrust Treble Damages, 71 Yale L.J. 684 (1962).

84. Despite earlier doubts, the *prima facie* effect clause has been extended to administrative judgments of the Federal Trade Commission. See Farmington Dowel Products Co. v. Forster Manufacturing Co., 421 F.2d 61 (1st Cir. 1970); Purex Corp. v. Procter & Gamble Co., 453 F.2d 288 (9th Cir. 1971). The Commission has developed procedures for settling complaints "before any testimony" has been taken, which include an "Assurance Of Voluntary Compliance" in the pre-complaint stage and "Consent Orders to Cease and Desist" in the post-complaint stage. See 3 CCH Trade Reg.Rep. ¶¶ 9591, 9595. The 1980 amendment to the Clayton Act, however, specifically refuses to extend collateral estoppel effect to FTC findings. See 15 U.S.C.A. § 16(a).

85. For a study of the purpose and use of the *nolo* plea in antitrust cases, see Clabault & Burton, Sherman Act Indictments 1955–1965 (1966). The Justice Department has had a formal policy against consenting to the entry of *nolo* pleas since at least 1953; current policy is to consent only where the Assistant Attorney General in charge of the Antitrust Division concludes that the circumstances are "so unusual" that acceptance would be "in the public interest." See United States Department of Justice, Principles of Federal Prosecution 33 (1980). Whatever position the Department takes, however, a judge is still free to accept or reject the plea.

86. See Flynn, Consent Decrees in Antitrust Enforcement, 53 Iowa L.Rev. 983 (1968). On third party participation in government antitrust enforcement, see Buxbaum, Public Participation in the Enforcement of the Antitrust Laws, 59 Calif.L.Rev. 1113 (1971). On public participation in administrative proceedings generally, see Comment, Public Participation in Federal Administrative Proceedings, 120 U.Pa.L.Rev. 702 (1972).

mation hearings of Attorney General Kleindienst, and the subsequent misdemeanor conviction of Kleindienst for misleading the Judiciary Committee about pressures applied to the Justice Department in settling three merger cases against I.T.T. provided important impetus for passage of legislation substantially reforming the consent decree process.[87] The Antitrust Procedures and Penalties Act of 1974 [88] amended Section 5 of the Clayton Act to require: publication of proposed consent decrees, along with a "competitive impact statement" describing the alleged antitrust violation and the anticipated competitive effect of the relief proposed; a court proceeding, at which third parties may appear, to determine whether entry of the consent judgment is "in the public interest"; and a court filing by all defendants describing any written or oral communications with "any officer or employee of the United States" (other than communications solely between record counsel and Justice Department officials) relevant to the proposed decree. The proceedings of the district court in reviewing the proposed decree and the competitive impact statement are made inadmissible in subsequent antitrust litigation.

Although these amendments have opened the consent decree process to public scrutiny and third party objections,[89] a district court has yet to determine that a proposed decree is not "in the public interest." [90] This does not indicate the amendments have had no impact; the continued willingness to accept consent decrees may simply reflect the increased evidence available to a court, particularly the competitive impact statement. The amendments have also increased the information available to private treble damage litigants (making public the documents and materials the Government found determinative in formulating the decree), and have affected proceedings modifying or interpreting previously entered consent decrees, although technically addressing only the procedure for entering a consent decree.[91]

---

87. See Note, The I.T.T. Dividend: Reform of Department of Justice Consent Decree Procedures, 73 Colum.L.Rev. 594 (1973). In United States v. I.T.T. Corp., 349 F.Supp. 22 (D.Conn.1972), aff'd per curiam sub nom., Nader v. United States, 410 U.S. 919, 93 S.Ct. 1363, 35 L.Ed.2d 582 (1973), the consent decree discretion of the Department of Justice was held to be non-reviewable even upon allegations of "fraud on the court" with respect to the considerations that influenced the Department in settling the I.T.T. cases.

88. Pub.L. 93–528, 88 Stat. 1706, amending 15 U.S.C.A. § 16. For the legislative history of the Act see 1974 U.S. Code Cong. & Adm.News p. 6535 et seq.

89. Intervention in consent decree proceedings was generally denied in prior cases. City of New York v. United States, 397 U.S. 248, 90 S.Ct. 1105 (1970) (affirming denial of New York's attempt to intervene to challenge the adequacy of the proposed consent decree against the major auto manufacturers charged with collusive delay in introducing anti-pollution devices); Sam Fox Publishing Co. v. United States, 366 U.S. 683, 81 S.Ct. 1309, 6 L.Ed.2d 604 (1961). But cf. Cascade Natural Gas Corp. v. El Paso Natu-

ral Gas Co., 386 U.S. 129, 87 S.Ct. 932, 17 L.Ed.2d 814 (1967); Utah Public Service Commission v. El Paso Natural Gas Co., 395 U.S. 464, 89 S.Ct. 1860, 23 L.Ed.2d 474 (1969) (setting aside consent decree to permit intervention by Cascade and the State of California; Department of Justice denounced as "knuckling under"). The amended procedure still gives the court discretion to limit the participation of third parties. See United States v. Associated Milk Producers, Inc., 394 F.Supp. 29 (W.D.Mo.1975), aff'd, 534 F.2d 113 (8th Cir.), certiorari denied sub nom. National Farmers' Organization, Inc. v. United States, 429 U.S. 940, 97 S.Ct. 355, 50 L.Ed.2d 309 (1976).

90. But cf. United States v. American Telephone & Telegraph, 552 F.Supp. 131 (D.D.C.1982) (approving proposed consent decree as in the public interest, but only if the litigants agreed to changes in the decree specified by the court), affirmed sub nom. Maryland v. United States, ___ U.S. ___m, 103 S.Ct. 1240, ___ L.Ed.2d ___ 1983).

91. See Note, Construction and Modification of Antitrust Consent Decrees: New Approaches After the Antitrust Procedures and Penalties Act of 1974, 77 Colum.L.Rev. 296 (1977).

Despite these changes in settlement procedures, significant questions remain. The *prima facie* effect clause of Section 5(a), and now the use of offensive collateral estoppel, provide strong incentives for a defendant to settle. Should the antitrust laws continue to provide settlement incentives? Some contend that this strengthens enforcement by allowing the government to achieve much success without the cost of protracted litigation. Others argue that enforcement is weakened because the government too frequently gives up important relief to which it will be entitled after litigation, so as to secure a settlement (government enforcers resolutely deny this charge). Other issues include: To what extent should consent decrees affirmatively regulate the business of a defendant? [92] Should consent decrees be limited in duration or remain in effect until otherwise modified? [93] Should private parties be given standing to enforce consent decrees? [94] On the criminal side, should *nolo contendere* pleas be made admissible in subsequent treble damage litigation? [95]

(9) *Antitrust in Other Countries.* Since World War II, and particularly in the last decade, there has been a remarkable development of antitrust-type legislation and enforcement outside the United States. As business has become increasingly multi-national, this area has become more important. Counsel have become ever more likely to encounter antitrust restraints imposed by several jurisdictions; government antitrust enforcement agencies have become increasingly interested in the approaches taken by their counterparts in other countries (particularly the United States, recognized as the antitrust "leader"), as well as concerned about conflicting national policies.[96] Only brief mention can be made here of these foreign antitrust efforts.[97]

2. Some consent decrees contain extensive regulatory provisions. See Ergo, ASCAP and The Antitrust Laws, 1959 Duke L.J. 258; Note, An Experiment In Preventive Anti-Trust: Judicial Regulation of The Motion Picture Exhibition Market Under The Paramount Decrees, 74 Yale L.J. 1040 (1965).

93. Although the consent decree has traditionally been a permanent injunction, see, e.g., United States v. Armour & Co., 402 U.S. 673, 91 S.Ct. 1752, 29 L.Ed. 2d 256 (1971) (1920 meat packers decree), there is an increasing reliance on "duration clauses" which provide for automatic expiration after a specified period. The Antitrust Division's current standard form provides for a 10 year period. See Antitrust Division Manual IV–75 (1979). See also, e.g., United States v. Bechtel Corp, 1979–1 Trade Cas. ¶ 62,429 (N.D. Cal.1979) (20 year decree); United States v. Everest & Jennings International, 1979–1 Trade Cas. ¶ 62,508 (C.D.Cal.1979) (10 year decree).

94. See Sullivan, Enforcement of Government Antitrust Decrees by Private Parties: Third Party Beneficiary Rights and Intervenor Status, 123 U.Pa.L.Rev. 822 (1975). The proposed Antitrust Consent Decree Enforcement Act of 1981 would give individuals the right to petition the Attorney General to enforce a decree. See H.R. 1966, 97th Cong., 1st Sess. (1981).

95. See S. 1284, Title VI, 94th Cong., 1st Sess. (1975), a bill which would make nolo pleas *prima facie* evidence in subsequent civil actions "as to all matters in the indictment necessary to sustain a judgment of conviction upon a jury verdict that the defendant was guilty of the offense charged in the indictment."

96. See, e.g., ATRR No. 955, Jan. 1, 1981, p. A–6 (European Community enforcement official reported reluctant to formally cooperate with United States in gathering information, given existence of criminal penalties in U.S. law).

97. A general review of foreign antitrust legislation is found in Fugate, Foreign Commerce and the Antitrust Laws (1973), ch. 16. Hawk, United States, Common Market and International Antitrust: A Comparative Guide (1979), provides a recent up-date with emphasis on the Common Market. See also Atwood & Brewster, Antitrust and American Business Abroad (2d Ed. 1981) (2 vols.); Competition Law In Western Europe and the USA (1977, with updated supplements). The Organisation for Economic Cooperation and Development (OECD), a group of sixteen countries and three multi-country trade groups, publishes a guide to members' views on antitrust controls, titled "Comparative Summary of Legislations on Restrictive Business Practices"; the most recent was published in 1978. Current activities may be followed in

Perhaps most important in economic terms are Articles 85 and 86 of the Treaty of Rome. Signed in 1957, the Treaty established the European Economic Community (EEC), which now consists of France, West Germany, Luxembourg, the Netherlands, Denmark, Ireland, Belgium, Italy, Greece, and the United Kingdom. Article 85 corresponds generally to Section 1 of the Sherman Act; it differs by specifically naming prohibited trade practices (e.g., price-fixing, division of markets), requiring notification to the EC Commission (the Common Market enforcement arm) of restrictive agreements, and providing for a general exemption similar to the "rule of reason." Article 86 prohibits the abuse of a "dominant position," specifically mentioning some types of abusive practices; it is somewhat analogous to Section 2 of the Sherman Act. There are no specific provisions outlawing mergers or monopolies. Under the Treaty of Rome, Articles 85 and 86 are also part of the national law of member States. Although EC Commission enforcement has not traditionally been vigorous, recent imposition of a nearly $10 million fine for an agreement to prevent imports into France of high fidelity equipment may signal a new "get tough" policy.[98]

A number of major industrial countries also have antitrust legislation. Modern antitrust legislation in the United Kingdom, for example, was first adopted in 1948; subsequent amendments in 1956, 1973, and 1976 strengthened the provisions and enforcement mechanisms.[99] West Germany enacted antitrust legislation in 1957; amendments in 1973 placed greater controls on mergers and pricing policies.[1] Japan (contrary to popular belief) also has antitrust legislation, originally enacted in 1947 at the urging of American occupation authorities. Although subsequent economic development in Japan stressed a close relationship between business leaders and the Ministry of International Trade and Industry (MITI)—featuring "administrative guidance" from the MITI to control price, output, and investment—recent price-fixing by the MITI and the Japanese oil industry led to the first criminal charge and conviction for price-fixing in Japanese history. Japanese antitrust law was also strengthened by amendments in 1977, which, inter alia, increased monetary penalties for violations.[2]

CCH Common Market Reporter and CCH Euromarket News.

98. See Pioneer Hi-Fi Equipment, [1980] CCH Comm.Mkt.Rep. ¶ 10,185 (Comm'n 1979).

99. Sources on British law include the following: Everton, Trade Winds: An Introduction to the U.K.'s Law of Competition (1978); Korah, Competition Law of Britain and The Common Market (1975); Wilberforce, Campbell, & Elles, The Law of Restrictive Trade Practices and Monopolies (2d ed. 1966 & Supp. 1973); Hunter, Competition and the Law (1966); Stevens and Yamey, The Restrictive Practices Court (1965). See also "UK Government Considers Imposition of Criminal Sanctions For Price Fixing," ATRR No. 1000, Feb. 5, 1981, pp. A–12 – A–13 (notes dissatisfaction with current system for handling price-fixing agreements; Director of Office of Fair Trading opposes criminal penalties, however, fearing it might make detection more difficult because informers would be less likely to come forward).

1. See Riesenkampff & Gerber, German Merger Controls: The Role of Company Assurances, 22 Antitrust Bull. 889 (1977); "Bonn's Antitrust Agency Fights Bigness, But Actual Breakup of Firms Is Doubted," Wall St. J., Aug. 21, 1980, p. 46 (head of Federal Cartel Office condemns executive of Hoescht chemical firm for conduct bordering on price-fixing; hopes for legislation breaking up giant conglomerates and outlawing large mergers; " 'He's using the Cartel Office to build a political reputation,' " complains one manufacturer).

2. See Note, Trustbusting in Japan: Cartels and Business Cooperation, 94 Harv.L.Rev. 1064 (1981) (contains references to other authorities on Japanese antitrust law). The executives in the oil price-fixing case were fined and sentenced to prison terms which were suspended pending two-year probation. Id. at 1078 n. 79. The author of this Note concludes: "That the Japanese are themselves questioning the way their economy has been managed suggests that Ameri-

As a general matter, antitrust statutes in foreign countries are the product of economies which have taken a more tolerant view toward industry cartels than has the United States. They thus tend to favor more of a "rule of reason" approach. It may be, however, that their greater interest in antitrust-type enforcement, combined with an apparent trend in the United States to a greater use of the rule of reason (and less antitrust enforcement?), will result in an increasing similarity in the approach to competition issues in non-Communist countries.

(10) *Regulatory Alternatives.* Standing in apparent contrast to the antitrust laws are a number of statutes premised on the legislative judgment that in certain industries continuous government regulation will more effectively control business behavior than marketplace competition. These statutes often require government review or approval of certain critical business decisions, such as entry, expansion, rates, and/or conditions of service. They have their antecedents in common law duties imposed upon those engaged in so-called public or common callings to render, without discrimination, reasonably adequate service at a reasonable price. Although it is not entirely clear how a trade became a common calling, this group came to include, *inter alia*, innkeepers, carriers, ferrymen, and even surgeons.[3] Later, direct legislative action strengthened these common law duties. As early as 1820, for example, Congress allowed the District of Columbia to regulate the rates at private wharves and to set the price of chimney sweeping.[4] During this period, another early method of regulation came in the form of state grants of franchises for turnpikes and canals, which often specified maximum rates.[5]

Government regulation was relatively unimportant until the economy became increasingly industrialized after the Civil War.[6] By the 1870's, a number of states had passed legislation regulating railroad and grain warehouse rates. The Supreme Court upheld the constitutionality of such legislation in *Munn v. Illinois*, decided in 1876, giving the States broad power to regulate business "clothed with a public interest." [7] By 1886, railroads were regulated in thirty states and territories.[8] By 1889, the Supreme Court had been called upon to decide the validity of state or local regulation of rates or entry in the lighting, water, and railroad industries.[9] Thus, by the time the Sherman Act was passed in 1890 the "public utilities" field had already become

cans should think twice before imitating their collusive business practices." Id. at 1065. For a history of the adoption of antitrust laws in Japan, and a description of Japanese market structure and inter-firm relationships, see Hadley, Antitrust In Japan (1970). See also "Japan vs. Japan: Only the Strong Survive," Wall St. J., Jan. 26, 1981, p. 16 (describing vigorous domestic Japanese competition in, e.g., audio equipment, automobiles, and steel).

3. Compare Wyman, The Law of the Public Callings As A Solution of the Trust Problem, 17 Harv.L.Rev. 156, 157–66 (1904) (public callings were "virtual monopolies") with Burdick, The Origin of the Peculiar Duties of Public Service Companies, 11 Colum.L.Rev. 514, 522–24 (1911) (anyone who held himself out to serve all was conceived of as assuming a public or common calling).

4. Act of May 15, 1820, ch. 104, § 7, 3 Stat. 587.

5. See Glaeser, Outlines of Public Utility Economics 197–200 (1927).

6. See, e.g., Fainsod, Gordon & Palamountain, Government and the American Economy 242–43 (3d ed. 1959).

7. 94 U.S. 113, 126, 24 L.Ed. 77 (1876). See also Peik v. Chicago & North Western Railroad Co., 94 U.S. 164, 24 L.Ed. 97 (1876) (railroads); Chicago, B & O Railroad v. Iowa, 94 U.S. 155, 24 L.Ed. 94 (1876) (railroads).

8. See S. Rep. No. 46, 49th Cong., 1st Sess. 65 (1886).

9. See Georgia Railroad & Banking Co. v. Smith, 128 U.S. 174, 9 S.Ct. 47, 32 L.Ed. 377 (1888); New Orleans Gas-Light Co. v. Louisiana Light and Heat Producing and Manufacturing Co., 115 U.S. 650, 6 S.Ct. 252, 29 L.Ed. 516 (1885); Spring

an important area of economic life in which legislative action had moved beyond the bounds of *laissez faire.*

The oldest of the federal regulatory agencies is the Interstate Commerce Commission, established in 1887. The major focus of the original legislation was to end discriminatory practices by the railroads, both with respect to rates and services, although it also forbade "unjust and unreasonable" rates and agreements among otherwise competing railroads to pool freights or revenues on some predetermined basis. Later amendments gave the Commission the power to set rates for railroads, as well as the power to control railroad expansion and discontinuance.

This legislation is important not only because it helped establish the pattern for federal regulation, but also because it raises the question whether such government regulation serves public or private interests. A number of writers contend that railroad regulation was undertaken not to protect the helpless Midwestern farmers, but to protect Eastern merchant shippers, or independent oil producers who wanted to stop the railroads from giving low rates to Standard Oil, or even to protect the railroads themselves from "excessive" competition and potentially overzealous state regulation.[10]

Major regulated industries have included surface transportation (rail and motor carriers), air transportation, communications (telephone, radio and television broadcasting), and energy (electricity and natural gas). The major federal regulatory agencies involved are the Interstate Commerce Commission (given its additional jurisdiction over motor carriers in 1935), the Civil Aeronautics Board (created in 1938 to control entry and rates of air carriers, but will cease functioning in 1985), the Federal Communications Commission (created in 1934 to regulate communications common carriers, e.g., telegraph and telephone companies, and radio broadcasters), and the Federal Energy Regulatory Commission (a/k/a "FERC," the successor to the Federal Power Commission, with jurisdiction over interstate sales of electric energy under the Federal Power Act of 1935, and over producers and wholesalers of natural gas under the Natural Gas Act of 1938). A number of these industries are also regulated on the state level.

No industry is either totally regulated or totally "unregulated." The commonplace pattern is a mixture of regulation and antitrust, the former often imposed under a statute which still leaves some room for application of the latter. The question of the proper (or intended) scope for the antitrust laws in such industries has been an important issue in antitrust litigation from the very beginning;[11] in recent years it has received even more attention as private litigants have turned more frequently to the antitrust laws to redress economic harm and as the Department of Justice has more vigorously pursued a policy of bringing competition to the regulated sector of the economy.

When interpreting regulatory statutes which provide an antitrust exemption, courts frequently affirm that exemptions from the antitrust laws are

Valley Water Works v. Schottler, 110 U.S. 347, 4 S.Ct. 48, 28 L.Ed. 173 (1884).

10. Compare, e.g., Benson, Merchants, Farmers & Railroads: Railroad Regulation and New York Politics, 1850–1887 (1955); Kolko, Railroads and Regulation: 1877–1916 (1965); MacAvoy, The Economic Effects of Regulation: The Trunk-Line Railroad Cartels and the

Interstate Commerce Commission Before 1900 (1965); Tarbell, The History of the Standard Oil Company (1904) with Buck, The Granger Movement: 1870–1880 (1913); Sharfman, The Interstate Commerce Commission (1931).

11. See United States v. Trans-Missouri Freight Association, 166 U.S. 290, 17 S.Ct. 540, 41 L.Ed. 1007 (1897).

not to be lightly implied.[12]   Nevertheless, there have been many occasions when, either through the administrative law doctrine of "primary jurisdiction" or through interpretation of legislative history, the courts have immunized anticompetitive conduct not specifically exempted but with which a federal regulatory agency was involved.[13]   An analogous result has been achieved for some State regulation through the creation of the "state action" defense, giving an immunity where the challenged restraint is " 'clearly articulated and affirmatively expressed as state policy' " and " 'actively supervised' by the State itself." [14]

Court interpretation of statutory antitrust exemptions, and the scope accorded non-statutory immunity doctrines, is often influenced by then-current attitudes toward the efficacy of government regulation versus a free market subject to the antitrust laws.   The trend today is away from regulation. Congressional deregulation of the trucking and airline industries is solid evidence that the balance struck in past years between the two systems is not immutable.   Perhaps more significantly, however, current deregulation efforts raise the question whether we are moving toward more vigorous antitrust enforcement, or whether we are moving toward another option often favored in our economic history—no government intervention at all.[15]

C. IDEOLOGY, ECONOMICS, AND THE GOALS OF ANTITRUST

THORELLI, THE FEDERAL ANTITRUST POLICY— ORGANIZATION OF AN AMERICAN TRADITION

226–227, 564–568 (1955).[16]

[Senator] Sherman's views were typical . . . [of] the vast majority of congressmen [who] were sincere proponents of a private enterprise system founded on the principle of "full and free competition."   Most of the legislators sponsoring bills or participating in debates with speeches relating to the principal issues involved made vigorous statements to this effect.   But, generally speaking, little need was felt to attempt penetrating analyses of the underlying economic theory or to support the prevalent belief by extended argument—the members of Congress proclaimed "the norm of a free competition too self-evident to be debated, too obvious to be asserted." The two or three odd attacks that were made on competition as the mainspring of American progress and prosperity were given no atten-

12. United States v. Philadelphia National Bank, 374 U.S. 321, 351, 83 S.Ct. 1715, 1734, 10 L.Ed.2d 915 (1963); California v. Federal Power Commission, 369 U.S. 482, 82 S.Ct. 901, 8 L.Ed.2d 54 (1962); United States v. Borden Co., 308 U.S. 188, 60 S.Ct. 182, 84 L.Ed. 181 (1939).

13. See pp. 800–810, infra.

14. California Retail Liquor Dealers Association v. Midcal Aluminum, Inc., 445 U.S. 97, 100 S.Ct. 937, 63 L.Ed.2d 233 (1980). See Chapter 7, infra.

15. The issues involved in entry and rate regulation, and current deregulatory efforts, are explored more fully in Schwartz, Flynn & First, Free Enterprise and Economic Organization: Government Regulation (6th Ed. 1983).

16. Quotation is by permission of the copyright owner, The Johns Hopkins Press. See also Letwin, Law and Economic Policy: The Evolution of the Sherman Antitrust Act (1965).

tion, and those who launched the attacks in the end voted for the passage of the Sherman Act.

Congress believed in competition. It believed, moreover, that competition was the normal way of life in business. Competition was *the* "life of trade" in spite of the challenging trust and combination movement. As a general rule, business operated best when left alone. The government's natural role in the system of free private enterprise was that of a patrolman policing the highways of commerce. It is the duty of the modern patrolman to keep the road open for all and everyone and to prevent highway robbery, speeding, the running of red lights and other violations that will endanger and hence, in the end, slow down the overall movement of the traffic. Translated into the terms of commerce this means that occupations were to be kept open to all who wished to try their luck, that the individual was to be protected in his "common right" to choose his calling and that hindrances to equal opportunity were to be eliminated. Government intervention should remove obstacles to the free flow of commerce, not itself become an additional obstacle.

There can be no doubt that the Congress felt that the ultimate beneficiary in this whole process was the consumer, enjoying a continuous increase in production and commodity quality at progressively lowered prices. The immediate beneficiary legislators had in mind, however, was in all probability the small business proprietor or tradesman whose opportunities were to be safeguarded from the dangers emanating from those recently-evolving elements of business that seemed so strange, gigantic, ruthless and awe-inspiring. This is one reason why it was natural to adopt the old doctrines of the common law, doctrines whose meaning had been established largely in cases brought by business or professional people dissatisfied with the behavior of competitors. Perhaps we are even justified in saying that the Sherman Act is not to be viewed exclusively as an expression of economic policy. In safeguarding rights of the "common man" in business "equal" to those of the evolving more "ruthless" and impersonal forms of enterprise the Sherman Act embodies what is to be characterized as an eminently "social" purpose. A moderate limitation of the freedom of contract was expected to yield a maximization of the freedom of enterprise. Sherman himself, furthermore, expressed the idea probably in the minds of many of his colleagues that the legislation contemplated constituted an important means of achieving freedom from corruption and maintaining freedom of independent thinking in political life, a treasured cornerstone of democratic government.

Not much time was wasted in Congress on the display of the merits of competition. For purposes of legislation it was more important to get a clear picture of the evil to be remedied, the obstacles to free trade that were to be eliminated. Bills and debates present a kaleidoscopic picture of definitions of trusts, monopolies and combinations in restraint of trade, as well as attacks on those institutions and the elements of society that had been responsible for their recent growth and multiplication. However great variation there was as to details, we find in its midst a general idea of the problem to be coped with, which, while vague, probably was not more dimly conceived than in many other instances in which legislation has since become imperative. The aim of Congress, to rid commerce of monopolies and restraints of trade, was explicitly set forth in the Sherman Act. It had been set forth in substantially the same terms in numerous bills and a multitude of speeches. . . .

[T]he Sherman Act . . . [was not] the result of a momentary flurry of public opinion and legislative activity. Some of its roots—all closely intertwined—may be traced back several centuries, while others became more clearly distinguishable only after the Civil War. Among the latter group of background factors were those lending immediate urgency to the trust problem at the time the Sherman Act was passed. They were all intimately connected with the material development of the nation. . . . Landmarks are the shift, completed by the end of the war, of economic, social and political supremacy from the agrarian and states'-rights South to the industrial and nationalist North, magnificent railroad expansion plagued by bribery, stockwatering, discrimination and extortion, the emergence of several new industries and the beginnings of mass production in others, the increased significance of overhead costs and the disruption of traditional patterns of commercial ethics and industrial organization and, amidst it all, protracted agricultural depression and agrarian discontent. Unable to stabilize competition at a plane at once civilized and "workable," businessmen in these years of industrial turmoil either resorted to cut-throat warfare and predatory practices or went to the opposite extreme of forming restrictive agreements, pools or trusts. Yet a great many of them found neither one of these expedients satisfactory over the long pull, and the great mass of small or independent operators who were unable or unwilling to avail themselves of such means were naturally hostile to the monopolistic machinations following in their wake. Economic power in the Golden Era of industrial expansion too often tended to be used in the interest of the favored few rather than that of the public.

A number of changes in the social structure of the nation—with or without reason—added to the distrust of industrial combinations and big business. Thus, for instance, what superficially at least appeared to be a growing inequality in the distribution of wealth not infrequently was blamed on monopolies and economic privilege. The fact that the captains of industry and most members of the financial community resided in the northeastern tier of states gave rise to the cry of irresponsible and anonymous "absentee" management and ownership among the harassed farmers of the South and West. The closing of the frontier was interpreted by many as heralding the end of pioneer individualism and opportunity. Meanwhile, the increasing mechanization of industry accelerated the growth of the army of wage earners, who were more reluctant in the United States than anywhere else to accept the idea that this process would tend to decrease the opportunity of individual advancement and enterprise in that sector of the economy. The great majority of the nation's work-ingmen continued to identify themselves with the "middle-class" of small business proprietors and independent farmers and shared in their frustration at the seeming conflict between the American Dream of equal opportunity and unlimited possibilities for the able and energetic on the one hand and the new realities of life on the other. It was apparently a rather common notion that not only the cherished freedom of enterprise but also political democracy itself was being endangered by the workings of mighty business combina-tions.

It is immensely difficult to attempt to present a reasonably well-balanced summary view of the general climate of socio-economic thinking and intellectual opinion in which the antitrust policy was con-ceived. The principle embodied in the Sherman Act is fairly simple, but the ideological background of the law is broad and complex. For the present only a few strategic elements will be emphasized. One of the reasons why it is almost impossible to present an integrated pic-ture of this body of thought—on which, for want of a better term, we shall place the label *economic egalitarianism*—is that its component parts are all borrowed goods. It may even be doubted whether under close examination they would be found fully compatible. But then complete integration is rare even in what are popularly thought of as "homogeneous" philosophical systems.

The elements composing this late nineteenth century American ec-onomic egalitarianism are widely different as to their age and origi-nal setting. On the one hand certain common law traditions from time immemorial may be distinguished, on the other certain aspects of such barely digested post-bellum novelties as "Social Darwinism" and the "New School of Economics" are encountered. Economic the-ory supplied some of the basic materials; others were derived from a theory of biological evolution, ideas of Christian behavior, age-old op-position to privilege and ecologically conditioned conceptions of the American way of life. The most obvious factor of note in this com-plex is undoubtedly to be found in the teachings of classical econom-ics. The treatises in political economy most widely read in this coun-try during the period from 1865 to 1890 were in all probability those of Adam Smith and John Stuart Mill. In addition, the influential na-tive classicist school, represented by such names as Francis Wayland, Amasa Walker, Arthur L. Perry, Julian M. Sturtevant and Lyman Atwater, followed rather closely in the footsteps of the British pio-neers and Frederic Bastiat. College teaching in economics was very definitely dominated by classicism. The attitude of classicist writers toward the practical problems of monopoly was generally one of lais-sez-faire, or at least it was not very action-oriented. Some claimed that the economy was self-correcting; such abuses as might develop would soon be eliminated. A few were silent on the issue, because they failed to recognize it or felt that it was unimportant or perhaps that it could not be mastered within the framework of their theories. Others believed that potential competition was a force preventing any accumulation of monopolistic power worthy of the name. Also, publicity was not infrequently referred to as a corrective device by scholars of the day. Toward the end of the period stray representatives of classicist thinking had begun grappling with the peculiarities of the public utility industries. It was soon to be found, however, that to deal constructively with problems of monopoly in this or any other field classicism itself needed to be rejuvenated. Thus while economic egalitarianism found support for its fundamental belief in the individual as master of his own destiny and in competition as the servomechanism of economic life in classicism, that school furnished no positive guidance in the creation of antitrust legislation.

Max Weber, R.H. Tawney, Henry F. May and others have demonstrated that there was of old a vague but immensely important affinity between Protestantism on the one hand and laissez-faire individualism and glorification of private property and industriousness on the other. May even goes so far as to suggest that the prevalent social philosophy in ante-bellum America may be labeled clerical laissez faire. After the war the religious outlook on socio-economic problems became much more differentiated. While the old ideas lingered on among a great part of the clergy and the church-going public, two other fundamentally opposed trains of Christian social thought also developed. One of these started from the tenet that "godliness is in league with riches" and ended up as an element in the Gospel of Wealth whose foremost prophet was Andrew Carnegie. The other one led to the Social Gospel and, beyond that, Christian Socialism. Most influential, perhaps, of the Social Gospellers, Washington Gladden preached that the object of the Christian scheme of ethics was to counteract injuries wrought by the survival of the fittest. Man was master of his own destiny only when in Christian cooperation with his equals. Clearly there was in 1890 no unified Christian or Protestant socio-economic thought whose influence could be brought to bear on the trust problem, except perhaps the all-Christian abhorrence of irresponsible worldly power wielded in the interest of the few rather than the many. Without accepting the laissez-faire implications of traditional Protestant socio-economic thought, economic egalitarianism struck a middle way between the dichotomy of the Gospel of Wealth and the Social Gospel. It would not adopt either the doctrine of stewardship by the chosen few or the wholesale substitution of cooperation for competition.

With similar oversimplification it may be said that economic egalitarianism chose the middle way between Social Darwinism on the one hand and the New School of Economics on the other. The logical outcome of survival-of-the-fittest thinking applied to economic life in the manner suggested by Herbert Spencer and William Graham Sumner was monopoly. Sumner had nothing but contempt for the antitrust movement which was merely trying to place artificial obstacles in the way of natural evolution. Conversely, he strenuously opposed such "legislative monopolies" as those thriving under the tariff and interstate commerce laws. That the tenets of evolutionism lent themselves to broad intepretation is indicated by the facility with which economic survivalism was incorporated in the Gospel of Wealth. The significance of Social Darwinism to economic egalitarianism was mainly indirect in that evolutionism was widely interpreted as supporting popular beliefs in competition and individual initiative. Fundamentally, however, its accord with conventional economic thinking was more apparent than real, and its influence on the formation of opinion on the trust problem was essentially confusing. . . .

The most powerful factor in economic egalitarianism was also the most subtle. This factor was a composite of Anglo-Saxon and native American traditions. It would lead far beyond the scope of this work to trace in detail its origins or even its structure in 1890. Concepts of the "natural rights" of the free individual, and among them the right to choose and pursue freely his own enterprise or calling subject only to such restrictions as might be necessary in the interest of society as a whole, reach far back into medieval English history. So does distrust of overwhelming privately-wielded power and the tendency to oppose all manner of exclusive privilege. The hostility to privilege became even stronger on this side of the Atlantic than in Britain as many emigrants had left the mother country in frustration with its inequalities and as colonialism grew progressively unpopular. It is significant that the Boston Tea Party took place at the expense of a hated monopoly. The tremendous importance of the frontier in the history of American ideas is well-known to everyone. Its spiritual climate was one of intense individualism and radicalism at once. Would-be monopolists could not expect sympathetic treatment in the land of the pioneer. Neither could they hope for much tolerance from that late nineteenth century hero in fact and fiction, the poor and honest man struggling to make a way for himself. Their machinations were also in direct conflict with a deeply rooted belief in competition as a stimulus to individual and social progress and in the merits of open markets and equal access to natural resources as means of securing a fair distribution of good and profits.

Thus it was in full accord with basic notions in American thought when, especially in post-bellum times, widespread antagonism was aroused by the apparent aggrandizement of the few at the expense of the many taking place in a number of fields. In several instances, it was believed by many, this growth of unwarranted privilege could be traced back to governmental measures, among them especially land grant, monetary and tariff policies and to a less extent patent legislation. Irresponsible railroad and gas magnates thrived on land grants and right of way and eastern capitalists on "sound" currency, while the trusts were often held to feed on favors derived from the tariff and patent laws. But it was also a common view that trusts, pools and combinations were being formed on an unprecedented scale and were increasingly abusing the rights and interests of the common man, irrespective of such artificial inducements. In the minds of the farmers of the South and West and many other Americans all these varieties of privilege and power, whether self-assumed or governmentally accorded, represented mere variations on a theme which may be summarized in one word, monopoly.

BORK, THE ANTITRUST PARADOX

50–51, 54–55, 57, 61 (1978).*

Antitrust policy cannot be made rational until we are able to give a firm answer to one question: What is the point of the law—what are its goals? Everything else follows from the answer we give. Is the antitrust judge to be guided by one value or by several? If by several, how is he to decide cases where a conflict in values arises? Only when the issue of goals has been settled is it possible to frame a coherent body of substantive rules. . . .

A multiplicity of policy goals in the law seems desirable to some commentators, though they do not address the question of whether the goals contradict one another and how such contradictions are to be resolved in deciding specific cases. Other commentators appear to think the question of goals essentially unsolvable, one of those ultimate value choices about which men can never be expected to agree. . . . These are positions I wish to dispute. The antitrust laws, as they now stand, have only one legitimate goal, and that goal can be derived as rigorously as any theorem in economics. . . .

(1) The only legitimate goal of American antitrust law is the maximization of consumer welfare; therefore,

(2) "Competition," for purposes of antitrust analysis, must be understood as a term of art signifying any state of affairs in which consumer welfare cannot be increased by judicial decree.

. . .

[E]xamples of the theory of the "social and political purposes of antitrust," are, to put the matter kindly, a jumble of half-digested notions and mythologies. The vocabulary of the tradition is an attractive one, being, as Professors Carl Kaysen and Donald Turner have remarked, loosely Jeffersonian. Insofar as there can be said to be a theory behind the tradition, it is that efficiency should sometimes be curbed because of the social and political health supposedly engendered by the preservation of a sturdy, independent yeomanry in the business world. Thus, the Supreme Court attributed to Congress a policy of protecting "viable, small, locally owned businesses" even if that resulted in "occasional higher costs and prices." Added to this is a generous admixture of uncritical sentimentality about the "little guy"—though why the small corporation is "littler" than a consumer no one has troubled to explain.

The ideas are dubious on their merits. There is no persuasive evidence that a middle-level corporate executive is socially or politically a less desirable creature than he would be if he ran his own business. . . . Our national experience suggests, in fact, that misuse of the political process, dependence upon government favor, and a marked distaste for competition are as characteristic of politically potent

* From THE ANTITRUST PARADOX: A POLICY AT WAR WITH ITSELF, by Robert H. Bork, copyright (c) 1978 by   Basic Books, Inc., New York. Reprinted by permission of the publisher.

small-business, farm, and labor groups as they are of large corporations. Fragmentation for its own sake confers no clear gain, and it makes economic processes more costly. . . .

The bare language of the Sherman Act conveys little, though there are surely traces of policy in the fact . . . that Section 2 outlaws not the condition of monopoly but only the process of monopolizing. A policy of rivalry for its own sake, and in spite of the costs of industrial fragmentation, would outlaw monopoly no matter how gained. The statute's focus upon the process by which monopoly is achieved suggests a different value premise. . . .

"Competition" may be read as a shorthand expression, a term of art, designating any state of affairs in which consumer welfare cannot be increased by moving to an alternative state of affairs through judicial decree. Conversely, "monopoly" and "restraint of trade" would be terms of art for situations in which consumer welfare could be so improved, and to "monopolize" or engage in "unfair competition" would be to use practices inimical to consumer welfare.

We are compelled, I think, to accept this definition of "competition" . . . . Surely, on the face of it, this meaning is consistent with everyday speech. When we talk of the desirability of competition we ordinarily have in mind such things as low prices, innovation, choice among differing products—all things we think of as being good for consumers. Our understanding of the benefits of competition for consumers is somewhat inaccurate, but that does not affect the fact that this is usually the primary value we have in mind. Very likely this is the primary value Congress had in mind when it used the word. Moreover, because "competition" as a shorthand expression for consumer welfare enables us to employ basic economic theory, it avoids the pitfalls inherent in the other definitions surveyed. [O]nly this reading is consistent with other indicia of congressional intent and with the requirements of the judicial function.

NOTES

(1) *Our Point of View.* The question whether the antitrust laws should serve only the goal of economic "efficiency" (as Bork argues), or should encompass a broader range of objectives (as Thorelli argues they were intended to), is a fundamental one in antitrust jurisprudence. This debate has been carried on with some frequency by antitrust lawyers, professors, and economists.[17] The authors of this casebook strongly believe that the antitrust laws were intended to achieve goals beyond economic efficiency and are skeptical of the claim that economic efficiency is as clear or as achievable a

17. Good examples of this debate are: Dirlam & Kahn, Fair Competition: The Law and Economics of Antitrust Policy (1954); Bork, Bowman, Blake, and Jones, The Goals of Antitrust: A Dialogue on Policy, 65 Colum.L.Rev. 363 (1965); Antitrust Jurisprudence: A Symposium on the Economic, Political, and Social Goals of Antitrust Policy, 125 U.Pa.L.Rev. 1182 (1977); Pitofsky, The Political Content of Antitrust, 127 U.Pa.L.Rev. 1051 (1979); Fox, The Modernization of Antitrust: A New Equilibrium, 66 Cornell L.Rev. 1140 (1981). See also Hearings, Symposium on the Social and Political Effects of Economic Concentration, Subcomm. on Antitrust & Monopoly, Jud.Comm., 92d Cong., 2d Sess. (1972).

policy goal as its proponents claim.[18] Students are urged to bring to their reading a critical eye: To what extent have the courts pursued other than efficiency values in deciding antitrust cases, and how articulate have they been in defining them? Does close to a century of antitrust "common law" development show the wisdom of pursuing broader goals, or does it show that we would be better off had the courts served only the cause of efficiency? What is there about today's political culture which makes the claim for efficiency appear to be compelling? How are courts today responding to this claim?

(2) *What You Need to Know About Economic Theory.* The proponents of efficiency have at their disposal a powerful analytical tool to describe and predict the behavior of business firms (and to prescribe the efficient solutions to be sought through antitrust policy)—microeconomic theory. Microeconomics studies the decisions of consumers, firms, and industries to determine how resources are allocated, what goods and services are produced, and to whom they are distributed. Anyone who wishes to participate in the antitrust field must be able to use the language and basic concepts of microeconomics. This Note is intended to provide these basics: [19]

The "consumer" is the purchaser of goods and services from a producer. The model of the consumer constructed by economists posits a rational individual who knows his or her preferences and who, constrained by a budget, chooses among substitutable goods or services so as to maximize satisfaction. Satisfying the preferences of consumers is thought to be the prime goal of the productive system.

The "firm" is the unit that produces a good or service for sale. The model of the firm in microeconomic theory posits that each firm has profit maximization as its goal; that it is subject to a production function, based on current technology, that indicates the relationships between available inputs and the outputs they can be used to produce; and that this production function will combine inputs in a way which will minimize production costs for a given level of output.

Groups of firms selling competing products form industries. Economists studying industrial organization have theorized that certain structural characteristics of an industry are critically important for understanding and predicting the behavior of firms within that industry. One of these factors is "seller concentration"—the number of sellers in a market and their respective market shares. A second critical factor is "barriers to new entry"—the long-term advantages of established sellers in an industry over potential entrant sellers. Barriers to entry have been thought to include factors such as high capital costs to enter an industry, patents required to produce products, and trademarks or other marketing tools which serve to differentiate a particular seller's product. Economists theorize that there are links between certain market structures, the conduct of firms within a market (e.g., pricing and research), and the performance of these firms (in terms of efficiency, full employment, equitable distribution of income, and progressiveness).

18. See, e.g., Schwartz, "Justice" and other Non-Economic Goals of Antitrust, 127 U.Pa.L.Rev. 1076 (1979); Flynn, The Use of Economic Models, If Any, in Antitrust Litigation, 12 Sw.L.Rev. (1980); First, Book Review [Posner, Antitrust Law: An Economic Perspective], 52 N.Y. U.L.Rev. 947 (1977).

19. More detailed explanations can be found in a number of sources. See, e.g., Sullivan, Handbook of the Law of Antitrust 797–806 (1977); Gellhorn, Antitrust Law Economics In A Nutshell 41–83 (2d ed. 1981); Scherer, Industrial Market Structure and Economic Performance 3–21 (2d ed. 1980).

The most widely accepted examples of such links occur in the polar examples of "perfect competition" and "monopoly." A perfectly competitive market is one which has numerous sellers, each of whose participation is so small that it perceives itself as being unable to affect the product's price. A monopolized market is one which has only one seller. (The intermediate case is "oligopoly"—a market in which there are fewer than many and more than one, and in which sellers perceive their pricing decisions as being interdependent with their competitors.) According to widely accepted theory, firms in perfectly competitive markets will be "efficient." They will produce goods at the lowest possible cost ("productive efficiency") and will devote enough resources to production so that they end up producing the total amount that society desires of the goods in question ("allocative efficiency"). By contrast, monopoly firms will not allocate resources efficiently (although some economists believe that profit-maximizing monopolists will be productively efficient); they will restrict output (and raise price), producing less of the monopolized good than society would prefer. Consequently, resources which society would prefer to have used in the monopolized industry are diverted into some other industry whose product is less desired. Production could be rearranged in a way which would make all consumers better off. This "allocative inefficiency"—the failure to allocate our resources in a way which will produce that bundle of goods and services we most prefer—harms society and is the heart of the economic theorist's case against monopoly, and favoring competition. Thus, economic theory suggests that consumer welfare will be increased by having an economy which produces goods and services in competitive markets, rather than in monopolized markets, because that will enable us to satisfy more of our preferences.

In addition to the concepts and terminology set out above, students should also be familiar with the following:

"Elasticity"—This word can be attached to a number of different economic concepts, but the one most frequently encountered in this volume is "cross-price elasticity of demand." This is simply a measurement of the percentage change in the quantity demanded of one product due to a percentage change in the price charged for another. A high cross-price elasticity shows that with a small change in the price of one product consumers will greatly increase their demand for another; a low cross-price elasticity shows that there will be a small change in the quantity demanded. Cross-price elasticity can be observed when products are substitutes (e.g., butter and margarine). People also talk of demand as being "elastic" or "inelastic." This is merely another way of saying that demand is highly sensitive to price (elastic), or highly insensitive to price (inelastic). Whenever you see the word elastic, think "responsive."

"Marginal and average"—These two words can also be used with a number of economic concepts, but in this volume they will most frequently be attached to the word "cost." Marginal simply means "extra"; average, of course, means the total of something divided by the number of units. Thus, "marginal cost" is the extra cost associated with producing an extra unit of output; "average cost" is the total cost of all units produced divided by the number of units produced. Remember that "average" is only an arithmetical idea (e.g., the "average family with 2.2 children" does not exist). On the other hand, a "marginal" something is supposed to exist in the real world; one can locate the commodity whose marginal cost one is attempting to measure.

Finally, it is important to understand what supply and demand curves represent, what they generally look like, and the relation between price and output.　A supply curve is a pictorial representation of the quantity of output a producer will supply as the sales price per unit changes; this curve is most conveniently viewed as upward-sloping (i.e., as the price per unit increases, producers will increase output because the higher prices will now cover the costs of goods which had been uneconomical to produce at the lower prices).　A demand curve is a pictorial representation of the quantity of goods demanded by consumers as the price per unit changes; this curve is generally downward-sloping (i.e., as the price decreases, consumers demand more because consumers are generally observed to want more of a product as it becomes cheaper).　For any one commodity, the point at which the producers' aggregate supply curve and the consumers' aggregate demand curve intersect is the "equilibrium" point—buyers and sellers will be satisfied with the quantity produced and the price charged, and no further changes will occur.

As many of the cases in this volume will show, producers are often *not* satisfied with the price they can "get" in the market and will often seek to raise that price (e.g., by agreeing with competitors that everyone should charge a higher price).　It is important to see, however, that producers will not achieve the results they seek simply by raising the price.　By definition, at a higher price producers are willing to produce more of the commodity and consumers now want less.　The result, then, is likely to be a surplus of the commodity on the market, which surplus will eventually force the price down as sellers seek some way to dispose of it.　If the price increase is to truly be effective, output must also be restricted.　This interrelationship between price and output is critical to understanding the conduct of firms which seek to raise price.

(3) *Doubts About Received Economic Theory as a Guide to Antitrust Policy.*　The theories sketched in the preceding Note have hardly gone uncriticized.　Two categories of critics are important to the antitrust area.

First are those critics who contend that the microeconomic theorist's models of consumer and firm behavior are so unrealistic in today's economy as to be useless for arriving at antitrust policy.[20]　Managers of modern firms do not profit-maximize, even assuming they could possess all the information necessary to arrive at an optimal decision.　Rather, they might maximize sales subject to a minimum profit constraint, or pursue a variety of goals such as salary, security, or professional excellence subject to the constraint of a minimum level of reported profits.　Nor are consumers the rational satisfaction maximizers of classical economic theory; preference may be maintained out of habit or addiction, rather than out of rational choice based on knowledge of all the alternatives.　Nor do markets bear any resemblance to the theorist's requirements for perfect competition.　Rather, real markets feature firms of varying strength, government intervention, rapidly changing technology, and shifting consumer preferences.　The static world of fixed supply and demand curves, with an equilibrium point, bears no relation to the dynamics of a modern industrial economy.

Critics of microeconomic theory as a guide for antitrust policy also point to the problem of the "second best." [21]　The theory of the second best sug-

---

20.　A sample of these critics would include: Baumol, Business Behavior, Value and Growth (1959); Williamson, The Economics of Discretionary Behavior: Managerial Objectives in a Theory of the Firm (1963); Scitovsky, The Joyless Economy: An Inquiry Into Human Satisfaction and Consumer Dissatisfaction (1976).　These arguments are also explored in some greater depth in Scherer, supra n. 19, at 29–41.

21.　For discussions of the theory of the second best, and its implications for

gests that making a monopolized market into a competitive one might not necessarily improve the allocation of resources in society. Suppose, for example, that oil and natural gas are both being sold at a monopoly price. To drop only the price of natural gas to a "competitive" level might very well lead to over-consumption of natural gas in relation to oil and over-allocation of resources to natural gas. In such a situation, society might have been better off not disturbing the existing equilibrium. The "second best" policy might have been to leave both monopolies untouched, rather than optimizing piecemeal.

The second category of critics focus on industrial organization theory and the view that there are links between market structure, conduct, and performance.[22] These critics, too, see a more complicated world. Industries do not exist in neat boxes. Rather, the marketplace is made up of a continuum of substitute products produced by actual or potential rivals. Not only is this structure loose rather than rigid. We are also unable to predict how firms behave, or are likely to behave in the future, simply from looking at the shape of a market. Indeed, just as bad environment is too facile an explanation for crime, so too is the "bad environment" of a concentrated market inadequate to account for firm behavior. Bad conduct is only likely if a "cartel" (a group of competitors, formed to limit competition among themselves) consciously agrees to engage in anticompetitive behavior. Finally, critics of industrial organization theory often conclude that no matter what the industry structure may be, the problems of successfully engaging in noncompetitive behavior are great and the long-term gains are likely to be low or non-existent.

Of course, judges (like lawyers and law professors) often hold their own views of economic theory and reality, even though these views may not be clearly acknowledged. This, again, calls for the reader to exercise care in reading the coming cases: What economic theories is a court applying? Does a Judge or Justice fall into one of the two groups of critics mentioned above? Has the academic criticism of an economic theory espoused by one of the litigants reached the court in a way which affects its decision? If a judge is skeptical, what view of the world have the litigants offered as a substitute for the models and predictions of economic theory?

(4) *Beyond Economics.* Students should not assume that economics is the only social science discipline which may prove helpful to formulating antitrust policy and litigating antitrust cases. To the extent that judges become dissatisfied with economic models they may very well be persuaded to use other disciplines. One potentially emerging source for antitrust is found in literature regarding strategic planning models, developed in professional schools of business administration to assist managers in solving problems. Some of the important components of these models are: the product life cycle (picturing a product as going through the stages of introduction, growth, maturity, and decline); market segmentation (the attempt to position a product in the market so as to serve some smaller group of consumers within that product market, thereby minimizing competition from substitutes); the product portfolio matrix (a method to enable managers of multi-product

antitrust policy, see, e.g., Sullivan, Book Review, 75 Colum.L.Rev. 1214, 1219–21 (1975); Scherer, supra n. 19, at 27–29; 1 Kahn, The Economics of Regulation 69–70 (1970).

22. Many of the arguments over industrial organization theory are canvassed in Goldschmid, Mann & Weston, Industrial Concentration: The New Learning (1974). See also Posner, Antitrust Law: An Economic Perspective (1976); Bock, An Antitrust Blueprint for the 1980's, 55 N.Y.U.L.Rev. 574 (1980).

firms to allocate corporate resources among the various divisions); the experience curve (the theory that direct and indirect costs can be expected to decline as experience increases through a product's life cycle). As these business management theories become more widely known among antitrust practitioners, litigants may very well attempt to use them to explain why otherwise anticompetitive behavior should be benignly viewed. Similarly, creative antitrust lawyers might attempt to mine the discipline of philosophy to support antitrust value judgments; history to demonstrate how particular antitrust policies have actually worked; sociology to demonstrate the community effects of certain forms of enterprises; psychology to illuminate consumer behavior; political science to evaluate the extent to which business practices enable an industry to become a "private government." That many of these disciplines have not been of dramatic usefulness in the past for antitrust decision making does not mean that future theoretical developments will not bring them to center stage.[23]

D.　SOME ETHICAL PROBLEMS IN ANTITRUST LAWYERING

COUNSELING IN ANTICIPATION OF ANTITRUST PROSECUTION

Excerpt from Davis, A Trial Lawyer's Viewpoint, 30 Wisc.Bar Bull. 46, 52–5 (1957).

Establishment Of A System For The Preparation And Maintenance Of Records With Respect To The Factors, From Time to Time, Motivating The Establishment And Administration Of Price, Sales And Distribution Policies.

The problem of keeping records has both defensive and offensive aspects. The evidence relied upon by the Government in antitrust cases consists predominantly of letters and memoranda written by the defendants or their competitors contemporaneously with the alleged commission of the offenses charged. Defensively, it is important to minimize the availability of any such letters and memoranda which may be damaging. The best and safest way to accomplish this result is to see that they are not written, or if written, that they promptly be repudiated by those in authority. The best insurance against their being written lies in the effective carrying out of an education program. This is also the best assurance that a superior will recognize and correct the antitrust implications of any unfortunate and unauthorized letters that a subordinate may write.

The following extracts from actual letters or memoranda, which have confronted us in antitrust cases, will illustrate the program.

The following exchange was between a Branch Manager and the Home Office:

---

23. The basics of business strategy theories, and some of the potential implications they hold for antitrust policy, are explored in Morrison & Craswell, Papers On Business Strategy And Antitrust (Federal Trade Commission 1980). For further discussion of the potential that other social science disciplines might hold for antitrust, see Sullivan, Economics and More Humanistic Disciplines: What Are The Sources of Wisdom for Antitrust?, 125 U.Pa.L.Rev. 1214 (1977).

Branch Manager to Home Office:

> I have been communicating with some of our competitors with reference to the prices for the City of Atlanta. We have *agreed,* temporarily, to hold the price up at the standard level. We hope these same prices apply to the City of Knoxville.

Home Office reply:

> The prices in Knoxville territory are open and beyond control. We contacted our competitors to see if they would hold to the prices, the same as they did in Atlanta territory, but they stated that A would not stay in line and for everyone to go to their own price. Knoxville is *one of the very few places* where prices are wild.

Properly educated, the Branch Manager would never have written such a letter or made such an agreement, and the Home Office would not have compounded his efforts.

The following was from a Pacific Coast representative to the Home Office:

> We held a meeting on the Pacific Coast attended by representatives of A, B and C, at which uniform prices were established. We are not keeping a copy of this letter and are sending this to your home, and would suggest that you destroy same after you have read it.

Unfortunately, the letter never got home, but appeared in the company's offical files when they were subpoenaed by the Government.

As we all know, Government representatives frequently entertain the bizarre notion that trade association meetings are held only for the purpose of fixing prices. Perhaps letters such as the following have contributed to that view:

> Did Jones tell you anything regarding the Association meeting in New York and any information as to whether or not the new price structure was approved?

One of our clients, holding a valuable patent, was recently charged with agreeing with three customer licensees not to grant licenses to any competitor of the licensees. My vigorous denial of the charge was somewhat undercut when the Government came up with the following, written by one of my client's officers.

> We have enjoyed for many years a monopoly based upon patent protection. This has discouraged any competition which might have arisen. I pointed out that we had shared this position of monopoly to our mutual advantage with the well established manufacturers, such as A, B and C. We have all benefited because it has served to keep cheap and unworthy competition out of the field.

My defense, that uniformity of price in a certain industry was simply the result of legitimate price leadership, suffered a similar body blow from the following document written by a principal supplier to the industry:

> We have been disturbed about the recent increased prices agreed upon by the manufacturers . . .. The manufacturers are probably not within their legal rights in fixing prices. There is a subterfuge which one of them explained to me by which it is legal for one company to arrive at prices and then disclose those prices to other companies.

The foregoing letters were all written by representatives of long established, successful business corporations. No stronger argument for the need of a program of education should be required.

On the defensive side I do not recommend that any client attempt to strip its files in order to avoid antitrust prosecution. Laying aside any question of moral values, such an effort at prophylaxis simply is ineffective. In this day of multiple carbon copies you can be almost sure not only that all the copies in your client's possession cannot be located and destroyed, but, almost invariably, copies of the same letter will be found in the files of others. Recently, the Government was proceeding against Companies A and B. It was charged that A and B, with other competitors, held monthly meetings to discuss prices and agree on sales quotas. Company A, which I did not represent, had attempted to purify its files by stripping. The Government produced the following letter from the files of a nonindicted co-conspirator:

> We had our meeting with the representatives of A today. I was requested to write you and might incidentally say there is no copy of this letter in my file. *The A representatives have been instructed to clean out their files and destroy all copies of the reports of the monthly meetings which have been held.* We will continue to hold monthly meetings to discuss prices and the A people will attend and make longhand notes, but will not accept copies of price reports or send them on to the Home Office. I will send you copies of the monthly price reports and I suggest you show them to X (A's Sales Manager). In this way, if we are ever called on the stand, we can tell anyone who asks us that we do not give A reports concerning the amount of business we give to other companies. Please destroy this letter after you have read it.

The damaging effect of such a letter upon the defense of A Company needs no elaboration on my part.

Records can also provide substantial offensive aid in antitrust litigation. One of the difficulties in conceiving the strategy and planning the tactics for the trial of an antitrust suit is that, so often, we are limited to proof of the negative. Because of the lack of helpful records, our efforts must usually be confined, in effect, to saying to the Government "We didn't do it" as to every charge made. How much better would be our position were we in position to say and prove that "Certainly we did it. We made a unilateral decision and here are the reasons which motivated it."

We are all familiar with the emphasis which the Government places on concerted action among competitors with regard to such matters as identical prices, simultaneous price moves, use of basing point systems and rigid maintenance of similar distribution channels. We also know that, as a matter of fact, many of these phenomena result not from any agreement among competitors, but, rather, are compelled by the economics of the product or the market. Usually, however, we are devoid of any method of proving it.

Too frequently the only answer which our clients are able to give us in such situations is that "This is the way it always has been done. It was done this way when I came to the company and has never been changed, etc." A better answer must be found and, I believe, can be provided, where the facts warrant, by the keeping of proper records.

The key to legality or illegality, in situations of the type suggested, is whether the corporate action complained of was taken unilaterally or as the result of an express or implied agreement with competitors. Frequently, but not always, uniformity of action by competitors is economically unavoidable. But if no unilateral study of the facts is made by the client, with a decision reached as the result thereof, the conclusion of the Government and the courts that, since "actions speak louder than words," uniformity of action among competitors is the result of agreement, is understandable.

It is not impossible for those responsible for the establishment of the client's prices, sales and distribution policies to make a study of such policies and to determine, if their observance be continued, what are the reasons therefor. It has occurred that such a study disclosed the client's ability profitably to change such policies. No matter what result obtains, if a record be made of the fact that the study was unilaterally made and of the conclusions reached as a result thereof, the trial lawyer will be in much better position to attack against the Government's claims rather than merely to deny their validity.

The very fact that study and decision has been unilaterally made, negatives the existence of any agreement among competitors. The minutes of a meeting of the policy-making officials of one of our clients, made contemporaneously with a price move, will serve to illustrate. Our client A was a producer of a multiple line of accessories, in a market in which corporation B was historically the price leader. Prices were, for the most part, uniform, and price moves occurred after the announcement of price changes by B. The minutes were as follows:

> The purpose of the meeting was to discuss what action we should take in view of the 2½ per cent reduction in price of item X made by B. While there have been reductions in the price of scrap, coal and oil since our last price change, there have been offsetting material price increases, with the result that a price reduction at this time is not warranted. However, our business is such, particularly with item X, that if we expect to get our share of the business we will have to follow competition insofar as price is concerned. It was decided that we would do this.

A full discussion was had as to whether, in view of the price reduction in item X, we should follow by making a price reduction in our other accessories. It was decided that we should give careful consideration to the fact that in June our labor contract comes up for negotiation, and while we are hopeful that no wage demands will be made, nevertheless there is every indication that requests will be made for fringe issues. Another point of discussion was whether we would be more or less forced to make a price reduction in the event Big Steel should do so.

It was finally concluded that a price reduction in our other accessories at this time would not develop any business for reasons enumerated in the minutes.

These minutes were supplemented with detailed data as to labor and material costs, sales curves, and the like.

Such a record serves not only to provide a contemporaneous record showing unilateral action, but also is most helpful in refreshing the minds of live witnesses so as to permit them to testify in detail instead of in glittering generalities about the reasons which motivated the corporate action under question.

NOTES AND QUERIES

(1) *Document Destruction and Litigation Risks.* The destruction of documents under subpoena, and perhaps even prior to subpoena if there is knowledge that the information is about to be sought in a pending proceeding, is criminal obstruction of justice.[24] Compare *United States v. I.B.M. Corp.,*[25] where the Government sought production of documents and a computerized data base index of documents discovered in a private antitrust suit against I.B.M. by Control Data Corporation (C.D.C.). C.D.C. had employed a staff of 60 persons to process, copy and index 27 million I.B.M. documents in preparation for its antitrust case against I.B.M.[26] C.D.C.'s compilation and index of documents were destroyed upon settlement of its case with I.B.M. The trial court, in the Government case against I.B.M., ordered production of the C.D.C. material by I.B.M. Upon I.B.M.'s refusal to produce, the District Court held I.B.M. in civil contempt and imposed a *daily* penalty of $150,000 for each day I.B.M. failed to comply with the discovery order.

(2) *Litigation Tactics for the Defense.* What do you think of the following litigation strategy (reported in Antitrust and Trade Reg.Rep. No. 792, Dec. 12, 1976, p. A–2)?

James T. Halverson, former chief of the FTC's Bureau of Competition and now with a New York law firm, recommended the strategies of International Business Machines Corporation as a good example of what can be done by a company in dealing with antitrust litigation.

---

24. See Beckstrom, Destruction of Documents with Federal Antitrust Significance, 61 Nw.U.L.Rev. 687 (1966); United States v. Walasek, 527 F.2d 676 (3d Cir. 1975) (conviction and five day sentence for extensive document destruction upon service of a grand jury subpoena for information relating to padding of bills by Western Union subsidiary).

25. 60 F.R.D. 658 (S.D.N.Y.1973) appeal dismissed en banc, 480 F.2d 293 (2d Cir.) appeal dismissed 416 U.S. 976, 94 S.Ct. 2378, 40 L.Ed.2d 755 (1974); civil contempt appeal dismissed 493 F.2d 112 (2d Cir. 1973), certiorari denied 416 U.S. 985, 94 S.Ct. 2409, 40 L.Ed.2d 774 (1974).

26. For a summary of the procedural difficulties of the I.B.M. case, see 786 ATRR pp. AA–10—AA–16 (Oct. 26, 1976).

In monopolization suits, Halverson recommended that a defendant take exhaustive discovery, particularly if it has an advantage over the plaintiff in terms of resources. He also suggested that a defendant concentrate on the plaintiff's market definition problems. As an example, he pointed to IBM's government-wide discovery on use of computers. Halverson also suggested that any defendant show the plaintiff that it is not costless to sue. Thus, a defendant should counterclaim. He again noted IBM's tactical ploys and referred to Telex v. IBM, 510 F.2d 894 (CA10 1975), cert. dismissed 423 U.S. 802, 96 S.Ct. 8, 46 L.Ed.2d 244, in which IBM's counterclaim against Telex was the only thing left after appeal. In the end, he said, IBM's counterclaim made Telex "give up" on the case.

Halverson bluntly suggested that private plaintiffs look at their pocketbooks rather than the so-called "public interest," so defendants should make plaintiffs worry about their pocketbooks. He also suggested that if more than one private suit is filed, the defendant should get the weak suit to trial first. "Money is what it's all about," according to Halverson, who suggested that if a defendant perceives exposure, then it should offer the plaintiff just enough to start the process of negotiation toward a settlement. Once the offer is there and the plaintiff's board of directors has seen months of attorneys' fees and corporate disruption, the plaintiff's board will work in the defendant's favor and nudge its lawyers toward a compromise.

In settling a class action, Halverson advised corporate defendants to realistically assess single actual damages and then start negotiations at a substantially lower level. However, he warned that a late settling defendant finds itself faced with a difficult plaintiffs' counsel fortified by the money paid by defendants who settled early. Halverson also warned that under the Hart-Scott-Rodino Antitrust Improvements Act of 1976, corporate defendants that settle a private non-class action may then find themselves named in parens patriae suits filed by state attorneys general.

In settling a Government suit for alleged monopolization, Halverson advised corporate attorneys to make certain that the Government gets enough documents and data so that personnel on the Government team will turn over several times during the law suit. He also stressed that the Government is seeking to satisfy the "public interest" and thus will have trouble in formulating any remedy that will satisfy industry competitors, potential competitors, Congress, and the general public. This need to satisfy everyone may compel the Government to litigate. In any event, settlement must be approached only after extensive discovery and significant amounts of document production aimed at casting doubt on the Government's market definition. . . .

Where a defendant is faced with Government and private actions at the same time, Halverson again suggested IBM's tactics as a good model. For instance, while saying there is no hard and fast rule, he stated that IBM knew that Control Data Corporation was in better control of facts in its suit than the Government was, and thus early settlement was sought and obtained from Control Data by IBM. However, where there are criminal indictments for price fixing, the Government may have a better view of the facts, Halverson suggested, and it may be advisable to settle with the Government first. In sum, he stated, settle strong cases and try the weak cases, always while delaying the Government.

(3) *Compliance Programs; Antitrust Counsel as Educator.* Counsel's responsibility to keep corporate clients out of trouble must incorporate "antitrust audits" and training programs for sales and managerial personnel. See Van Cise, Understanding the Antitrust Laws (1976 ed.) Ch. VII Planning for Compliance. The following quotation is from another work by the same author.[27]

27. Van Cise, The Federal Antitrust
Laws 56–7 (3d ed. 1975).

The corporate management which has formulated its antitrust decisions and has in good faith taken steps to ensure their implementation also considers how it can and should record this program. All too frequently a hostile investigator discovers half-truths in written form and the defendant—to present the complete verity—must hastily improvise its proofs through witnesses who are suspect because they are interested: "Where such testimony is in conflict with contemporaneous documents we can give it little weight . . . ."[28]

The most elementary procedure for recording a compliance program is to see to it that the corporation makes its record of compliance before, rather than after, it is investigated. The contemporaneous evidence of the events and underlying considerations leading up to and immediately following a significant corporate decision should be put in writing and so be preserved. Thus, when a company acquires another corporation, it is essential that written evidence of the reasons for the acquisition, and of the absence of any attendant injury to competition, be marshaled. Also, if following a major decision of a corporation some competitor drops out of the commercial struggle, without being pushed, it is a sound precaution to collect promptly all readily accessible written evidence which establishes the true reasons for that failure.

A supplemental form of recording a compliance program relates to the proper handling of the occasional colorful prose of irresponsible employees. Inevitably, in the operations of any large corporation, some imaginative correspondent will flatly contradict, and thereby tend to undermine, the most conservative program of antitrust compliance, thereby inviting a judicial ruling that such "writings made contemporaneously with events as they were occurring . . . give ample evidence of 'an ever present manifestation of conscious wrongdoing.' "

In such an event, it is advisable not to destroy these picturesque writings. The mere destruction of such writings, unless explained, may give rise to an inference of wrongful conduct. Instead, it is best to answer the colorful document in writing, point by point, and to place both the original and the answer in the company's files. If the matter is sufficiently serious, the corporation might also follow through by doing some affirmative corporate act directly disproving the unlawful assertions of the unauthorized writer.

The importance of accurate records in a program of antitrust compliance cannot be stressed too strongly. In most of the transactions in which a corporate executive wishes to engage, his intent usually conforms to the intent of the antitrust laws. The mechanics for implementing this intent, however, are not always planned in a manner to make manifest this lawful purpose. If the executive will only consult his counsel sufficiently in advance of a proposed major transaction, the step-by-step negotiation and formalization of the original lawful purpose can be so guided and recorded that his actions similarly will be in accord with the requirements of these laws, and the supporting evidence of his antitrust compliance will be available if needed later on. A stitch of antitrust advice in time may well save the subsequent payment of an antitrust fine.

(4) *Litigation Tactics for the Private Plaintiff.* Plaintiffs' attorneys, as well as defendants' attorneys, encounter ethical problems. For example, it is not uncommon in private litigation for a plaintiff's lawyer to uncover documents indicating *per se* violations of the antitrust laws by the defendants. If the violations are of the sort that would normally be prosecuted criminally, is plaintiff's attorney obliged to inform the government?[29] May the

28. United States v. United States Gypsum Co., 333 U.S. 364, 396, 68 S.Ct. 525, 542, 92 L.Ed. 746, 766 (1948), rehearing denied 333 U.S. 869, 68 S.Ct. 788, 92 L.Ed. 1147.

29. See A.B.A. Code of Professional Responsibility, EC 4-5: "A lawyer should not use information acquired in the course of the representation of a client to the disadvantage of the client.

plaintiff's attorney indicate an intention to turn the documents over to the government unless the case is settled? [30] May defendant's attorney agree to a settlement conditioned upon the plaintiff and his attorney turning over the incriminating documents with an unspoken understanding that they will remain silent about the content of the documents? [31] May counsel for plaintiff, acting on a contingent fee basis, incur large investigating expenses and expend thousands of hours of professional time without infringing on the professional standard [32] that frowns on lawyers acquiring interests in their clients' cases? How should a lawyer deal with the conflict arising from his incentive to settle a case and collect a certain fee promptly (especially if he is not too demanding in the matter of damages for his client) as opposed to the client's possibly larger recovery if the case goes on to litigation?

Consider " 'Fine Paper' Fee Objectors Claim Support for Charges," Legal Times of Washington, Nov. 2, 1981, p. 6: [33]

> A massive audit filed on behalf of a group of class members in the fine paper antitrust litigation has found "affirmative support" for earlier charges, made by widely respected plaintiffs' lawyer Harold E. Kohn, that his co-counsel conspired to overstaff and overbill that major class action.

> The New York firm of Weil, Gotshal & Manges has submitted the 522-page report and its 1,200 pages of exhibits and appendices to U.S. District Judge Joseph L. McGlynn Jr. of Philadelphia, who presided over the litigation (MDL No. 323). The case against 15 defendants was settled for a principal sum of $50 million. The judge's task is to decide how much of the settlement fund ($62 million with interest) is to be paid out in attorneys' fees.

> The first charges of excess arose out of the plaintiffs' own camp (see Legal Times, June 15, 1981, p. I). Kohn, of Kohn, Savett, Marion & Graf (Philadelphia), balked last spring when requests of 33 fee petitioners in the case combined totaled $20 million. He argued for a cap of about half that amount. His executive committee co-chairman, Granvil I. Specks of Specks & Goldberg (Chicago), and other lawyers managing the case charged Kohn's own fee request was excessive; Kohn responded with specific claims of excess in half the petitions filed, accusing those lawyers of creating "busy work" for themselves at the expense of class members.

> Among the members of this fine paper class were 15 powerful corporations who became concerned about the level of fees being sought. These corporations hired Weil, Gotshal to argue that fee requests covering 160 attorneys for

. . ." Disciplinary Rule 4–101(c) of the CPR authorizes but does not require the lawyer to reveal "the intention of his client to commit a crime and the information necessary to prevent the crime."

30. See A.B.A. Code of Professional Responsibility, Disciplinary Rule 7–105: "A lawyer shall not present, participate in presenting, or threaten to present criminal charges solely to obtain an advantage in a civil matter."

31. See A.B.A. Code of Professional Responsibility, Canon 7: "A lawyer should represent a client zealously within the bounds of the law", and accompanying "ethical considerations."

32. See A.B.A. Code of Professional Responsibility, EC 5–7: ". . . undesirable for the lawyer . . . to become financially interested in the outcome of the litigation [but] a reasonable contingent fee is permissible in civil cases because it may be the only means by which a layman can obtain the services of a lawyer of his choice." EC 5–8 discourages "monetary advances . . . by the lawyer to his client," but declares it "not improper" to advance litigation expenses which "may be the only way a client can enforce his cause of action."

33. Reprinted by permission of *Legal Times.* See also " 'Fine Paper' Lawyer Saw Dream Become Nightmare," Legal Times of Wash., Dec. 7, 1981, p. 9 (describing affidavit in which one plaintiff's attorney claimed he had been told to "get" hours reviewing documents); "Rift Scarred Plaintiffs' Antitrust Effort," id. (describing disagreement over handling of case among plaintiffs' attorneys).

the class, claiming 70,000 hours of attorney time and 25,000 paralegal hours, should be drastically reduced.

Specks Takes Issue

Plaintiffs' lawyers are to file responses to the Weil, Gotshal report by Nov. 12. Specks, in an interview last week, heatedly took issue with the Weil, Gotshal findings, just as he and lawyers aligned with him have denied Kohn's charges against them.

The Weil, Gotshal report, primarily the responsibility of partners Ira M. Millstein and Dennis J. Block, laid out and analyzed scores of documents that were said to support Kohn's allegations. At many points, though, the report cautioned that a final determination of the accuracy of the allegations would have to await the responses of all the lawyers involved.

The report proceeded along two fronts. First, it analyzed key phases of activity throughout the case, pinpointing alleged instances of duplication and excessive time or staffing. Second, it analyzed each of the 33 petitions, recommending major cuts in virtually all of them, including Kohn's request for $1.9 million but coming down with particular harshness on Specks', whose $4.3 million request was the largest in the case.

The Kohn allegations that served as Weil, Gotshal's starting point focused on what Kohn saw as a patronage system that began at the outset of the litigation. Certain firms, he said, formed blocks to control votes on organization and strategy. Firms got voting rights by filing numerous separate complaints or by being added as new co-counsel on complaints already filed by other lawyers. The votes elected the lead counsel and executive committee members, and those lawyers were responsible for handing out committee and other work assignments—to themselves and attorneys who voted for them, Kohn charged.

Weil, Gotshal traced much of the alleged excess to failings in the plaintiffs' management approach. The report, though it did so in cautious grays and seldom in black and white, painted a picture of lawyers jumping on a bandwagon because they saw a potential for high fees, then running the case primarily with an eye to ensuring their own workload. The report reiterates the view that economy and efficiency were sacrificed as a result. And it finds support for Kohn's charge that cases were filed to create voting blocks among the management group, to control the organization and work assignments.

Too Many Lawyers

At the first formal organizational meeting, Weil, Gotshal said, "The goal apparently was to see how many firms could become involved and obtain compensation from the class, not how few." That pattern was continued throughout the case, according to the report.

A major theme of the report is the contention that far more lawyers were involved than were necessary or could be efficiently coordinated. One office supply company had five co-counsel, Weil, Gotshal noted, one of them reputedly added simply as a favor for Specks. A number of counsel hung their hats on class representatives that when the case was concluded, didn't file claims to share in the settlement fund. Weil, Gotshal concluded that counsel were filing simply "to get into the case."

The auditors also pointed, with emphasis, to five Minneapolis firms that got involved only when the case was well under way and a major round of settlements totaling $30 million had been negotiated. The case was run by two co-chairmen, an additional three "co-lead counsel," 12 executive committee members, and as Weil, Gotshal put it, "a multitude of committees and subcommittees . . . for virtually every task in the case, no matter now minute." Discovery was handled by a discovery committee with 15 subcommittees, one for each defendant.

The result of this structure, according to Weil, Gotshal, was "extensive, time-consuming coordination of efforts, duplication of work, repetition of instructions, etc. Meetings of a dozen or more attorneys from executive committee members' firms were common since each member firm apparently believed that it took a dozen or more attorneys to make decisions. Other committee meetings likewise were attended by a half-dozen or more attorneys since instructions had to be given to each firm which was 'actively participating' in the case by handling the discovery of a single defendant."

Bad Faith Filings

Weil, Gotshal also found support for what it said were "perhaps the most troublesome of all of the matters raised in these proceedings"—Kohn's charges that fee petitions of certain firms were not filed in good faith. "Certain counsel appear to have worked backward," Weil, Gotshal said, picking a fee they wanted and then proceeding to justify it without regard to the reasonable value of their services on behalf of the class. "The documents further indicate that when Mr. Kohn objected, certain counsel raised their total request still further, to compensate for anticipated reductions by this Court, and even tried to get Mr. Kohn to raise his fees."

Specks last week responded to some of the themes in the Weil, Gotshal report, terming them "libelous." He emphasized the risk and expense that the plaintiffs' group faced, arguing that a small group of law firms could never have afforded to undertake the matter. The plaintiffs started from scratch, Specks noted; unlike most cases, there was no preceding grand jury indictment paving the way. And they faced 15 defendants with substantial resources. "As a practical matter, given the logistics of these cases that are so large and so complex, it's absolutely essential that there be a number of plaintiffs' firms participating in the case," he said.

Specks expressed conviction that the record would show no more than a "minuscule" amount of unnecessary or duplicative time was spent. He also said allegations of conspiracy to control the case and run up excessive fees were not supported by the documents cited in the Weil, Gotshal report.

(5) *Sanctions for Attorney Abuse in the Litigation Process.* Concern over the boundaries of permissible attorney conduct in antitrust litigation has increased in recent years. Well-publicized cases in which parties to a suit and/or their counsel have been reprimanded include: *Litton Systems, Inc. v. American Telephone & Telegraph,*[34] where the winning plaintiff, Litton, was deprived of all costs and attorneys' fees to which it otherwise would have been entitled. This sanction was imposed as punishment for the "gross negligence" and "intentional misrepresentation" of Litton's counsel in responding to discovery orders and requests. *Berkey Photo, Inc. v. Eastman Kodak Co.,*[35] in which Mahlon F. Perkins, Jr., a lawyer for Kodak, incorrectly claimed that he had destroyed certain documents which had been furnished to an economic expert during a pretrial deposition. Perkins later pleaded guilty to criminal contempt, admitting that he made a false statement and submitted a false affidavit to the trial judge; he also resigned from his law firm following publicity of his actions.[36] *Wm. T. Thompson Co. v. General Nutrition Corp.,* in which a special master appointed by the district court imposed heavy fines on the defendant, G.N.C., as well as its two law firms for "wholesale destruction of documents." Also cited were the defendant's failure to disclose material information and the inaccurate

34. 1981–2 Trade Cas. ¶ 64,306 (S.D. N.Y.1981).

35. 603 F.2d 263 (2d Cir. 1979), certiorari denied 444 U.S. 1093, 100 S.Ct. 1061, 62 L.Ed.2d 783 (1980).

36. See "Kodak Counsel in Berkey Suit Guilty of Criminal Contempt," N.Y. L.J., Sept. 22, 1978, p. 1.

representations made to the special master and to plaintiff's attorneys. Although G.N.C.'s counsel is appealing, the sanctions, if upheld, "could cost [G.N.C.] the underlying antitrust case—and the forfeiture would give the plaintiff . . . treble damages." [37]

Attorney conduct in the litigation process is not, however, a concern only of the judiciary. For instance, in 1979, the National Commission for the Review of Antitrust Laws and Procedures (NCRALP) issued a Report to President Carter which made recommendations to curb "wasteful or abusive" discovery practices in order to "increase the efficiency of discovery procedures" in complex cases.[38] Suggestions included a reduction of discovery of "tangential, immaterial" matters by the courts handling such cases, and amendments to Rule 26 of the Federal Rules of Civil Procedure narrowing the scope of discovery and authorizing courts, on their own initiative, to issue protective orders to parties faced with unreasonable discovery demands.[39] The Commission also concluded that sanctions against dilatory and abusive behavior [40] are sometimes necessary and "can be an important and integral part of the process of expediting complex cases. . . ." [41] The Report recommended that judges be more willing to impose appropriate sanctions, and that these sanctions be used "systematically to ensure that other litigation management techniques. . . . are effective." [42] The Commission suggested, e.g., an amendment to Rule 37 of the Federal Rules of Civil Procedure to authorize sanctions for discovery delays caused by excessive and uncooperative conduct, and changes to the A.B.A.'s Disciplinary Rule 7–102, and corresponding state rules, to emphasize the affirmative obligation of an attorney to litigate expeditiously. Also proposed was an amendment to the antitrust laws to mandate an award of prejudgment interest (interest on the amount of plaintiff's actual damages from the date the complaint was served) in all but unusual cases.[43] By issuing these and other recommendations, the Commission hoped that dilatory and abusive conduct would not be tolerated, and thus lawyers would "take more seriously their responsibility to the system of justice, not just to their clients." [44] Congress responded in 1980 by amending the Clayton Act to give courts discretion to award prejudgment interest in antitrust cases.[45]

(6) *Problem.* You are counsel to Client Company. Its president complains to you that Competitor Corp. is using a discount system that is illlegally discriminatory under the Robinson-Patman amendment of the Clayton Act in that it grants non-cost-justified discounts to quantity buyers. Client proposes to respond to the competition with similar discounts, but is troubled by the fact that you have previously advised, in accordance with the law as formulated in a well-known Supreme Court case, that the defense of good faith meeting of competition is not available when the entrepreneur knows that

---

37. As reported in "Growth of a Coast Law Firm," N.Y. Times, Sept. 14, 1982, p. D1.

38. National Commission for the Review of Antitrust Laws and Procedures, Report to the President and Attorney General, January 22, 1979, p. 41.

39. Id. at 41–51.

40. Examples of dilatory and abusive conduct cited by the Commission included filing meritless claims, defenses, or counter-claims; making excessive discovery demands; providing unresponsive answers; producing masses of insignificant, nonresponsive information; mishandling documents; and disrupting depositions. See id. at 82.

41. Id. at 81.

42. Id.

43. See Id. at 81–91.

44. Id. at 83.

45. 15 U.S.C.A. §§ 15, 15a, 15c(a)(2). For legislative history, see 1980 U.S.Code Cong. & Ad.News, p. 2767.

the pricing system which he proposes to meet is illegal. Faced with the Client's exigencies and dissatisfaction, you reflect as follows:

"Why don't I tell Client that there is very little risk that his defensive adoption of Competitor's pricing practices will be prosecuted by the government or lead to significant damage recovery by the persons discriminated against? He'll be just as happy with that as if I told him the law was on his side.

"Perhaps that would be encouraging violation of the law. But the Department of Justice in a recent report has virtually called for repeal of the Robinson-Patman Act, and official enforcement has sharply declined. Many economists and lawyers think that the Act restrains price competition and is inconsistent, therefore, with the Sherman Act and public welfare. There is some chance, although not much, that the new Supreme Court would take a more generous view of the defense of meeting competition. It can hardly be immoral to violate or counsel the violation of law under these circumstances.

"The notion that Client should complain to the Federal Trade Commission rather than respond in a business way to the competitive threat is unrealistic: the Commission would either do nothing or do it far too late. The Commission might be stirred into a general investigation of the industry, including Client, by Competitor's countercomplaints; and Client's skirts are not entirely clean. We could seek an injunction in court; but that not only involves some risk of opening up an uncomfortably wider investigation, it also would probably end in a consent decree calling for the abandonment of discriminatory pricing—a decree which, paradoxically, comes perilously close to an illegal agreement among competitors to stabilize prices.

"Does not my professional duty to my client demand that I tell him precisely the legal situation he faces, including the actualities of near non-enforcement?"

Are you "counseling the violation of law?" Suppose the client asks you, "What will happen if I go ahead and meet the price?" Is the issue any different? If not, the attorney must choose between "counseling violation" and saying to a client, "I won't tell you." [46]

46. See Flynn, Professional Ethics and the Lawyer's Duty to Self, 1976 Wash. U.L.Q. 429.

MARKET STRUCTURE

Chapter 2

MONOPOLY, OLIGOPOLY, AND CONCENTRATION

A. SIGNIFICANCE OF SIZE OF FIRM AND CONCENTRATION OF ECONOMIC POWER

Laws should be designed and interpreted to promote the general welfare. To the extent that antitrust and other laws limit or encourage the development of very large concerns, those laws should ideally be based on some concensus as to the benefit or disadvantage to the community which follows from concentration of the important business of the nation in relatively few giant firms. Are big firms more efficient? Are they bigger than justified on technological grounds? Are the big getting bigger, so that fewer and fewer firms dominate an ever larger proportion of the economy? Do they dominate the government as well as the economy? From the material in this section it will quickly become apparent that there is the sharpest disagreement among economists and others on all these questions. When men of unquestionable professional qualifications and integrity can counsel opposite courses of action, it is possible to conclude that their disagreement is not in the realm of "science", but in the realm of faith or political philosophy; i.e., the crucial propositions cannot be proved or disproved with available knowledge and techniques, but are accepted or rejected as a result of a myriad of influences of heredity, training, interest and the like.

Findings regarding "efficiency" or "market performance" are especially to be received with caution, for here value judgments, assumptions and hypotheses, rather than measurement, dominate consciously or unconsciously the "scientific" process. It is difficult enough to decide what basis to use in measuring size—e.g., total assets, assets devoted to the particular kind of business, annual sales, percentage of sales in a given "market", profits, number of employees—but at least there is fair agreement on the general notion of size, and the measurements can easily be stated in numbers. Measuring efficiency of an institution like the modern corporation is quite another matter. Comparing the economic efficiency of firms is not like comparing the mechanical efficiency of machines. For the machines it is enough to determine the ratio of energy expended to work accomplished. But what is "efficiency" in an economic organization?

57

Some might say that the most efficient business corporation is the one that earns the most money per dollar of investment. But this is obviously a stockholders' point of view. From the point of view of employees the most efficient corporation might be one that pays the best wages, while still maintaining its commercial position and providing a reasonable return to investors, not by any means the maximum profit contemplated by a stockholders' standard of efficiency. Customers and consumers might put still a different content into the concept of efficiency: the most efficient firm would be one that, after making reasonable provision for employees (perhaps not as high as the union is in a position to demand) and for investors, makes only a modest profit because it spends much money on research to improve its product and sells at lower prices. Environmentalists might consider the firm which produces a socially needed product with minimum damage to the environment as the most efficient firm, despite the effects on unit costs, employment or profits. Which is most "efficient" from the social point of view that should presumably guide law and governmental policy? Note that the answer requires consideration of the *kinds* of costs incurred by the corporation as well as the aggregate of its costs or "energy input." The answer also turns in part on a judgment as to the best way to distribute among various interested groups the benefits derived from simple mechanical efficiency.

Analogous issues arise in appraising and comparing political institutions. In terms of quantifiable factors of efficiency, a federal democratic system where governmental power is in the hands of the electorate and is divided between state and nation would appear to be highly inefficient. Political systems where power is more centralized, e.g., dictatorship, appear to be efficient if we define efficiency to include only those factors which are quantifiable.[1] Consider the criticism of decision-making during the Vietnam War where American "efficiency" was measured in terms of "body counts", number of "pacified" villages and tons of bombs dropped:

The first step is to measure whatever can be easily measured. This is okay as far as it goes. The second step is to disregard that which can't be measured or give it an arbitrary quantitative value. This is artificial and misleading. The third step is to presume that what can't be measured easily really isn't very important. This is blindness. The fourth step is to say that what can't be easily measured really doesn't exist. This is suicide.[2]

Is it possible to include other and nonquantifiable factors in the concept of efficiency and still have consistent and predictable legal standards to guide decision-making concerning industry structure and behavior?[3]

1. See Brandeis, The Curse of Bigness, note (5), p. 77 infra.

2. Quoted in A. Smith, The Last Days of Cowboy Capitalism, The Atlantic Monthly, Sept. 1972 at 43.

3. See generally, Symposium on Efficiency as a Legal Concern, 8 Hofstra L.Rev. 485, et seq. (1980).

If the concept of efficiency is to be a useful guide to law and policy, it must somehow take account of quality as well as quantity. Large moving picture producers may make more or grander films on a basis satisfactory to many, while smaller producers cater to a more selective audience with films of greater artistic merit. How is this to be reflected in comparing efficiencies? In gauging efficiency in the newspaper business is output to be measured in dollars of profit or columns of print without regard to content? Similar questions must be asked in relation to the business of radio and television broadcasting. The problem is not limited to the fields of art, nor are the foregoing queries meant to imply that intangible factors overlooked in crude measures of efficiency always favor the small units. For example some of the material set out below indicates that small firms frequently have very low costs. What if such firms achieve low cost by skimping at critical but hidden points in the product and by sloughing off service or guarantee obligations?

The foregoing discussion does not mean that lawyers and lawmakers may disregard the products of investigation and thinking by economists.[4] This material, with all its contradictions, is illuminating even though not determinative. One can hold a position with more assurance if one can refer to supporting evidence, however vulnerable, and if opposing evidence does not catch one by surprise. The advocate of today must arm himself as best as may be from the arsenal of social science no matter what he may think about the data, because he is almost certain to have such weapons used against him. Where, in other ages, religion or philosophy provided the premises of decision, today nothing carries more persuasive power than that which passes under the name of science. At the very least one inconclusive "scientific" demonstration or chart must be countered by another. But familiarity with conflicting positions, carefully articulated by persons trained in describing and measuring economic phenomena, can serve the lawyer more constructively. In democratic societies, as perhaps in all societies in varying degrees, legislation and adjudication tend to incorporate some concessions to powerful opposing interests and views. Thus the judge, the legislator, and the attorney, able to handle the inconclusive data of social science with the proper combination of comprehension, receptivity and skepticism, will be more effective in devising formulas acceptable to the community and its higher tribunals.

4. On the other hand, a prominent American legal historian has recently observed: "I have the strong feeling that the economic analysis of law has 'peaked out' as the latest fad in legal scholarship and that it will soon be treated like the writings of Lasswell and McDougal. Future legal historians will need to exercise their imaginations to figure out why so many people could have taken most of this stuff so seriously." Horwitz, Law And Economics: Science or Politics?, 8 Hof.L.Rev. 905 (1980).

1. MEASURING CONCENTRATION

STRUCTURE–PERFORMANCE RELATIONSHIPS AND ANTITRUST POLICY

Excerpt From F.M. Scherer, Industrial Concentration and the Market System 128–136 (ABA Antitrust Sec. 1979).[5]

The Structure-Conduct-Performance Paradigm

Since the 1930s economists have with increasing frequency used a simple paradigm to analyze the functioning of markets. What it says in brief is that the *structure* of the market significantly affects the *conduct* of buyers and especially sellers in such activities as price-setting and product policy, and that their conduct in turn determines the ultimate economic *performance*—good, bad, or indifferent—of the market. [See pp. 41, 45, supra.] At first this structure-conduct-performance (SCP) paradigm was not much more than a hatrack upon which one could hang facts in organizing a full-scale industry study. Later it became linked to diverse theoretical models of how markets function, and many of these models were quite complex. But still more importantly, because economics is a field of inquiry that deals, at least ideally, with observable and measurable quantities, the SCP paradigm served as both impetus and foundation for statistical studies relating conduct or performance variables to structure—the latter typically measured in terms of such indices as the four-firm seller concentration ratio, the market shares of individual leading firms, and the fraction of industry output contributed by a plant deemed large enough to realize all appreciable production scale economies.

Statistical analysis is peculiarly well suited for testing the SCP paradigm, for statistics deal in tendencies, not certainties. The most frequently articulated (but not the only) prediction of the paradigm is that high seller concentration leads in various ways to a greater elevation of prices above unit costs and hence to higher profit returns. I know of no economist who holds that this relationship is applicable for every industry at every moment in time. Rather, it is believed to be a statistical tendency—prevailing on the average over a large sample of cases, like (but perhaps stronger than) the tendency for lung cancer to be contracted more frequently by heavy smokers.

5. Reprinted by permission of the copyright holder, Section of Antitrust Law, American Bar Association in 46 Antitrust Law Journal 864–72 (1977). For other recent studies of economic concentration, see: E. Herman, Corporate Control, Corporate Power (1981); J. Blair, Economic Concentration: Structure, Behavior and Public Policy (1972); F.T.C. Economic Report, The Quality of Data As A Factor in Analyses of Structure—Performance Relationships (1971); H. Goldschmid, M. Mann, & J. Weston (Eds.), Industrial Concentration: The New Learning (1974); F. Scherer, Industrial Market Structure and Economic Performance (2d Ed. 1980); W. Shepherd, The Treatment of Market Power (1975); Symposium, Private Sources of Market Share Data and Their Utility to Antitrust Lawyers, 47 Antitrust L.J. 1035 (1978).

One can argue at length over whether on balance the many statistical tests conducted thus far support the concentration-profits prediction, and to the extent that they do, how strong the tendency is. . . . [I]t seems to me that much of the past debate has been empty because most of the statistical work has used abominable data. At the heart of this difficulty is the fact that our structure indices relate for the most part to more or less narrowly defined industries, whereas much of America's business is done by corporations whose published profitability figures are for broad aggregations of meaningfully defined industries. It is a well-established statistical law that when there are unsystematic errors of measurement or matching in the variables one is relating, true relationships between the variables will tend to be obscured. Given the severe measurement and matching problems faced, it is hardly surprising that most SCP studies show only weak relationships. To me, a telling point is that the relatively few studies using data of high quality—e.g., from confidential "inside" sources—show much stronger links between structure and profitability than most of the analyses using inferior data. The only way to resolve the continuing debate over the strength of these links is not to emit still more hot air over what we have learned from characteristically bad data, but to obtain the best data possible for a broad spectrum of industries and put them to an acid test. . . .

What forces me to tarry even briefly is the crucial question: in which direction does the chain of causation between concentration and profitability run? One version of the conventional wisdom—the one from which structural antitrust draws greatest support—holds that high concentration implies the monopolistic power to elevate prices, which in turn means high profits. An alternative view with rather different implications is that concentrated industries are concentrated because a firm must have a sizeable market share to realize all economies of scale, and the enterprises dominating such industries exhibit above-normal profits because they take maximum advantage of those scale economies and are therefore more efficient than smaller fringe rivals or potential entrants (who, if they do enter, would most likely come in at an inefficiently small scale). Thus, one explanation stresses monopoly power—something we don't want; the other efficiency—something we presumably do want. My own view is that real-world relationships embody a complex admixture of these and other causal chains. Only with high-quality data will we be able to disentangle with some precision the relative importance of the diverse causes and their interactions. But note one point that is too frequently overlooked. Suppose the leading four firms in a concentrated industry do realize scale economies and therefore have lower unit costs than smaller rivals. Why should all four enjoy above-normal profits commensurate with their cost advantage? Why don't they expand output and compete on a price basis among themselves until they earn only "normal" profits? For them to retain the benefits of their superior efficiency, rather than passing the savings along to consumers in the form of lower prices, there must be some element of discretionary control over prices—that is, some degree of monopoly power. Thus, even when economies of scale and high concentration coincide, monopoly power cannot be ruled out as a contributor—to be sure, interacting with other factors—to the persistence of elevated prices and profits.

NOTES AND QUERIES

(1) *Conflicting Views on the Trend and Extent of Concentration.* The debate over the adequacy and reliability of specific data is matched by a debate over how the data which is available should be correlated with which indices of economic performance. There is dispute over the historical trends in economic concentration. One study suggests that "monopoly made rapid headway in the United States during the latter part of the nineteenth century," but that "there is nothing to support the view that it continued to do so during the twentieth."[6]

On the other hand, according to a Report on Concentration in American Industry, Subcommittee on Antitrust and Monopoly of the Senate Judiciary Committee, 85th Cong., 1st Sess. (1957) Table 1, the 50 largest firms increased their share of the total value added by manufacturing from 17% to 23% between 1947 and 1954. The share of the market held by the top four companies had risen from 36% to 50% in the electric appliance industry, from 15% to 25% in the paper industry, and from 45% to 54% in steel. The share of the four top petroleum refiners had declined from 37% to 33%.[7]

Aggregate concentration—the share of assets held by 100, 200, etc. firms—is shown in the following Table. Are the trends cause for concern?

6. Wilcox, Public Policies Toward Business 837 (1955).

7. An economist for the United States Chamber of Commerce criticized the report, asserting, for example, that the steel figures took no account of Ford Motor Company's annual two million tons of steel production, that exports, imports, and second hand markets were ignored, that 1954–1957 was unrepresentative, that the underlying data taken from Census records aggregated within single categories a huge variety of unrelated products. He conceded that the cost of what he would regard as a persuasive study was "prohibitive". (Wall St.J., p. 9 (July 11, 1957)). Barber, in "The American Corporation" (1970), pp. 20–21, stated that:

   Hyperconcentration in business is by no means a new phenomenon, but it has shown a steady tendency to become tighter during the postwar period. At the end of World War II the 100 largest manufacturing companies accounted for 23 percent of the total value added by manufacture. Some thought their position would deteriorate as new companies came on the scene and new products were put on the market. But this did not happen. Steadily the top 100's share rose, so that their present share exceeds 33 percent, nearly half again as large as the sizable position they occupied twenty years ago. In terms of assets the commanding position of the country's biggest enterprises is even more clearly evident. The 200 largest manufacturing corporations now control almost 60 percent of all manufacturing assets, up from less than 50 percent only twenty years ago.

CUMULATIVE SHARE OF CORPORATE MANUFACTURING
ASSETS HELD BY 1,000 LARGEST CORPORATIONS
1941—1964—1968—1979 [8]

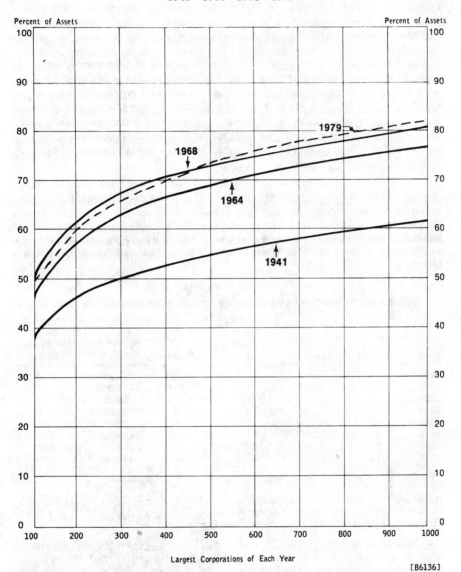

[B6136]

8. Staff Report to the Federal Trade Commission, Economic Report on Corporate Mergers, Figure 3–2, 167 (1969); Figures for 1979 compiled from Statistical Abstract of the United States, No.

This measurement of aggregate concentration deals with *manufacturing* only, and measures only concentration of *assets*. Concentration might be measured also with reference to number of employees, value of output, value added (i.e. output less value of input), etc. To what extent can such aggregate measurements provide a premise for legal policy making in antitrust? [9] Studies of concentration in the *financial* sector of the economy show that institutional investors (pension plans, investment companies, insurance companies, trust funds, foundations, etc.) had total assets of $957.6 billion in 1972.[10] Their ownership of New York Stock Exchange listed stock exceeded 45%. One study estimated that by the year 2000 total institutional stock holdings would account for 55.2% of the market value for all stocks.[11] Stock ownership by the major institutional investors appears to be heavily concentrated in the top 200 industrial firms with, for example, 43.1% of the stock of I.B.M. held by 81 institutional investors in 1969.[12] What implications do these facts raise for antitrust policy? [13]

955,569 (1980). The same information, linked to individual firm size, has been compiled by Willard F. Mueller as follows:

Number of Manufacturing Corporations with Assets Exceeding $250 Million and $1 Billion, and Share of Total Assets of Corporations Engaged Primarily in Manufacturing, 1909–1972

(Assets in Millions)

	Firms with Assets Over $1 Billion			Firms with Assets Over $250 Million		
Year	Number	Assets	Share of Total Corporation Assets	Number	Assets	Share of Total Corporation Assets
1909	1	1,822	a	3	2,480	a
1919	1	2,366	a	16	7,900	a
1929	2	5,378	8%	31	18,390	27%
1935	3	5,132	9%	25	14,882	26%
1948	12	20,107	17%	59	39,692	33%
1959	24	61,207	27%	127	115,357	50%
1969	87	229,461	46%	293	330,592	66%
1972	115	321,158	52%	350	435,708	70%

a Total asset data for all manufacturing corporations not available.

Reprinted by permission of the publisher, from The Antitrust Dilemma, by James A. Dalton and Stanford L. Levin (Lexington, Mass.: Lexington Books, D. C. Heath and Company, Copyright 1974, D. C. Heath and Company).

9. See Mintz & Cohen, America Inc.; Who Owns and Operates the United States (1971); Hacker (ed.), The Corporation Take-Over (1964); Nader & Green (eds.), Corporate Power in America (1973). As to multinational firms, see p. 86 infra.

10. Blumberg, The Megacorporation In American Society: The Scope of Corporate Power 94–5 (1975).

11. Soldofsky, Institutional Holdings of Common Stock 1900–2000: History, Projection, Interpretation, Michigan Business Studies 18, #3 (1971).

12. Blumberg, supra note 10 at 98. See also, Committee Report, Corporate Ownership and Control, Subcommittee on Reports, Accounting and Management, U. S. Senate Committee on Government Operations, 94th Cong., 1st Sess. (1975).

13. An outstanding recent analysis of financial control of large corporations, E. Herman, Corporate Control, Corporate Power, p. 161 (1981), concludes:

Financial power in the 1970s appears to constitute a strongly conservative force, accommodating and serving the dominant nonfinancial elements in the community. It does not dominate the large corporation, but what influence it has tends to press for actions that will enhance creditworthiness and profit

While aggregate concentration ratios and trends may provide some estimate of overall economic concentration, measurements of concentration by *specific markets* is more directly related to questions of competition and monopoly.   Economic theory suggests that when a high percentage of a particular industry's sales, employment, or value added, are concentrated in a few firms—a situation known as "oligopoly"—"rivals behave more like monopolists than competitors." [14]   Concentration ratios are usually stated in terms of the percentage share of the market held by the top 4, 8, 20 or more firms in the market.   Kaysen and Turner, Antitrust Policy: An Economic and Legal Analysis (1959), regarded a concentration of one third sales in the eight largest sellers as prima facie excessive because "in the majority of markets with which we are familiar, a small number of firms with larger shares of the market [makes] it likely that they will recognize the interaction of their own behavior and their rivals' response in determining the values of the market variables."   Where the first eight firms have 50% or more and the first 20 firms have 75% or more, the oligopolistic response was said to be "extremely likely." (pp. 27–28).   They proposed an antitrust policy that would give priority to attacks on concentration in large industries, where the public effect is greater, and in investment goods, because the evil effects of noncompetitive pricing at preconsumer levels are amplified at later stages.

growth.   Its natural tendency is to affiliate with "profit machines" and managements that know how to guide them and then to give them free reign.   If these managements see the future as requiring a stream of acquisitions, financial institutions will compete to finance them.   Institutional passivity in voting behavior tends to reinforce management control of the large corporation; its support of customer merger strategies, to which the largest firms are essentially immune as victims, seems to reinforce tendencies toward concentration, but as an accommodation process rather than as one involving active initiation.

14.   Mueller, A Primer on Monopoly and Competition, p. 30 (1970).   For critique and defense of methods used to measure industrial concentration see, materials cited supra note 5.

The following chart depicts the degree of sales concentration in certain major industries:

SELECTED INDUSTRIES RANKING AMONG HIGHEST   IN FIRST-4 COMPANY VALUE-ADDED CONCENTRATION RATIO [15]

(1972)
(Percentage Share of Market Held by Top Firms)

	0	25	50	75	100	
ELECTRON TUBES						(94)
HARD SURFACE FLOOR COVERINGS						(93)
FLAT GLASS						(92)
AUTOMOBILES						(92)
CEREAL FOODS						(91)
ELECTRIC LAMPS						(91)
CHEWING GUM						(89)
REFRIGERATORS AND FREEZERS						(89)
SEWING MACHINES						(89)
CIGARETTES						(84)
CHOCOLATE AND COCOA PRODUCTS						(83)
PRIMARY ALUMINUM						(83)
GYPSUM PRODUCTS						(81)
PHOTOGRAPHIC EQUIPMENT						(79)
BLENDED AND PREPARED FLOUR						(76)
CALCULATING AND ACCOUNTING MACHINES						(74)

[C6306]

15. Compiled from Jack Farkas and Deborah S. Weinberger, The Relativity of Concentration Observations, Table 9a, 16 (1978). "A first-4 company value-added concentration ratio is defined as the percent of total industry value-added accounted for by the four largest companies in the industry, in terms of value of shipments." Id., at 10. "Value of shipments is defined by the Bureau of the Census as the total selling value of the products, after discounts and allowances and excluding freight and excise taxes, plus the full economic value of all products transferred from one establishment to another." Id., at 9.

(2) *Other Measures of Concentration and Competitiveness.* The Federal Trade Commission has reported concentration on a capital asset basis as well as on the basis of sales, considering as "extreme" concentration any situation where the three largest firms control more than 60% of the "net capital assets" in the industry.[16] An alternative to concentration data as an index of the "workability of competition" is to measure the frequency of changes of rank among the top firms. Such changes suggest ease of entry into the business and the capacity of smaller firms to challenge the market leaders by lowering prices or improving product.[17]

The statistical basis for measuring concentration can itself be misleading. The traditional measurement of the market share of the top four firms (known as the "CR4" measure), derived from the historical accident of the way in which the Census Bureau collects manufacturing data, can be misleading because it does not reflect the relationship of the top firms to each other or to the rest of the market. Among the alternative methods for measuring concentration [18] is the Herfindahl-Hirschman index (also called the "H index").[19] Under this system, individual market shares (expressed in decimals, i.e., a 50% market share is expressed as .50) are squared (.50 x .50 = .25) and the sum of the squared market shares of every firm in the industry equals the H index. A pure monopoly would have an H index of 1.0. The information given by the H index compared to the CR4 method of measurement has been demonstrated as follows: [20]

[The CR4 method of measuring concentration in two industries.]

TABLE 1

Firms	Industry A	Industry B
1	40.1%	12.5%
2	3.3	12.5
3	3.3	12.5
4	3.3	12.5
5	2.0	5.0
All Others	48.0	45.0
Total	100.0	100.0

Both Industry A and Industry B have a CR4 of 50 percent, but no one would expect firms to behave identically in both industries. The biggest firm in Industry A has a market share over three times as large as the largest firm in Industry B. It is likely, ceteris paribus, that Industry A's market behavior would be less competitive than Industry B's where the four market leaders are all of equal size.

Moreover, the CR4 statistic tells us nothing about the remaining firms which could be acting as a disciplining force on the market leaders in either industry. For example, in Industry A there could be at least twen-

16. The Concentration of Productive Facilities 947 (Federal Trade Commission, 1949). See Kaplan, Big Enterprise in a Competitive System 120 (1964).

17. Joskow, Structural Indicia: Rank-Shift Analysis as a Supplement to Concentration Ratios, 42 Rev.Econ. & Stat. 113 (1960); Kaplan, Big Enterprise in a Competitive System, chap. 7 (1964).

18. For an analysis of the different methods for measuring concentration,

see F.M. Scherer, Industrial Market Structure and Economic Performance 56-80 (2d Ed. 1980).

19. See Hirschman, The Paternity of an Index, 54 Am.Econ.Rev. 761 (1964).

20. Pelster & Stangle, New Antitrust Chief and Herfindahl Index, New York L.J., pp. 1, 5 (March 17, 1981). See also, Miller, The H.-H. Index as a Market Structure Variable, 27 Antitrust Bull. 593 (1982).

ty-four additional firms with a 2 percent market share. (Chances are the number of firms would be much greater). In Industry B, without knowing anything additional, there could be another nine firms with a market share of 5 percent.

Thus, if one knew nothing other than the CR4s of these two industries (or refused to consider anything else), wrong decisions could be made.

[The H index method of measuring concentration in the same two industries.]

TABLE 2

Firm	Square of Market Share Industry A	Industry B
1	.1608	.0156
2	.0011	.0156
3	.0011	.0156
4	.0011	.0156
5	.0004	.0025
All Others	.0096	.0225
Total H index	.1741	.0874

Here we see the same industries as in Table 1, but with market shares represented as squares. Thus, Firm 1 in Industry A is shown with its market share of .401 squared to yield .1608. The summation of all of these squared shares is the Herfindahl index.

This example shows the virtue of the H index in that for two industries of equal CR4, much more information is conveyed about the size distribution of sellers by the H index. Indeed, the H index tells us that, all else being equal, competition in Industry A might be presumed to be about half as intensive as in Industry B.

Another useful property of the Herfindahl index is that its inverse or reciprocal yields the so-called "numbers equivalent." This observation, first made by Professor Adelman of M.I.T., means that 1.0 divided by the H index equals the theoretical number of equal-sized firms that would be found in the industry.[21] In our example above, the numbers equivalent value for Industry A is 5.7 firms (1 divided by .174), and for Industry B is 11.4 firms (1 divided by .0874). Again, all else being equal, it is predicted that Industry B would function more competitively than Industry A because the "theoretical" number of equal-size firms would be twice as large, thereby lessening the opportunity for collusion.

Among the criticisms of the H index method for measuring concentration is the absence of the necessary market share information for all firms in an industry to use the index with confidence. See generally, Symposium, 1982 Merger Guidelines, 71 Cal.L.Rev. 280 (1983).

21. Citing M. Adelman, Comment on the H Concentration Measure As A Number Equivalent, 51 Rev. of Econ. & Stat. 99–101 (Feb. 1969).

(3) *Significance of Corporate Size In Comparison with the Size of Governmental Units.*

BILLIONAIRE INSTITUTIONS—MANUFACTURING VERSUS
GOVERNMENTAL INSTITUTIONS, RANKED
ACCORDING TO OVERALL SIZE[22]

1979 Industrial Organization or Political Unit	Revenues Amount (Millions)	Rank	Employees Number	Rank[23]	Assets Amount (Millions)
Federal Government	465,900	1	2,875,872	1	454,500[24]
EXXON	79,107	2	169,096	17	49,490
GENERAL MOTORS	66,311	3	853,000	4	32,216
MOBIL OIL	44,721	4	213,500	15	27,506
FORD MOTOR	43,514	5	494,579	7	23,525
California	41,560	6	1,108,000	2	
TEXACO	38,350	7	65,814	22	22,992
New York	35,174	8	952,000	3	
STANDARD OIL OF CALIF.	29,948	9	39,676	28	18,103
GULF OIL	23,910	10	57,600	23	17,265
INTERNATIONAL BUSINESS MACHINES	22,863	11	337,119	14	24,530
GENERAL ELECTRIC	22,461	12	405,000	11	16,645
STANDARD OIL OF IND.	18,610	13	52,282	22	17,150
INTERNATIONAL TEL. & TEL.	17,197	14	368,000	12	15,091
ATLANTIC RICHFIELD	16,234	15	50,341	25	13,833
New York City	15,971	16	NA		
Pennsylvania	15,625	17	472,000	8	
Texas	15,421	18	667,000	5	
Illinois	15,299	19	506,000	6	
Michigan	14,482	20	448,000	10	
SHELL OIL	14,431	21	36,384	29	16,127
UNITED STATES STEEL	12,929	22	171,654	16	11,030
CONOCO	12,648	23	40,502	26	9,311
E.I. du PONT de NEMOURS	12,572	24	134,200	19	8,940
Ohio	12,509	25	469,000	9	
CHRYSLER	12,002	26	133,811	20	6,653
TENNECO	11,209	27	107,000	21	11,631
WESTERN ELECTRIC	10,964	28	168,000	18	7,128
New Jersey	10,811	29	364,000	13	
SUN	10,666	30	40,065	27	7,461

Is the significance of such figures emotive and political, or rationally related to legislative or judicial issues? When Secretary of Defense Charles E. Wilson, of President Eisenhower's cabinet, in a famous political *gaffe*, de-

22. Compiled from Statistical Abstract of the United States (1980); The 500 Largest Industrial Companies, Fortune Magazine 274–301 (May 1980). This listing does not include large non-manufacturing economic institutions such as banks or insurance companies. For such a ranking see The Fortune Directory of the Fifty Largest . . . Commercial Banking Companies, Life-Insurance Companies, Fortune Magazine 156–171 (July 16, 1979).

23. Ranked in terms of this table only.

24. Government assets figure not updated since 1972. Statistical Abstract of the United States (1979).

clared that "What's good for General Motors is good for the country," was
there not some truth in his statement? Does such a proposition approach
truth as the number of Americans working for GM, investing in GM, dependent on GM for supplies, etc., rises towards 100%?

2. CONCENTRATION, SIZE, AND EFFICIENCY

Views on the relationship of firm size and efficiency range across
a spectrum from the position that large firms or concentrated industries are almost never the product of efficiency or efficient in their
operations to the view that "any size a firm attains by internal
growth is necessarily an expression of its efficiency." [25] The debate
has been and is likely to remain a central and hotly contested issue of
antitrust policy. Claims that "empirical research" has conclusively
resolved the issue one way or another are particularly suspect. They
are more likely the rigid deductive conclusions of a particular ideology, rather than fruitful potential insights for the legal process to begin formulation of policy. The following view of concentration,
which should be compared with Scherer's view immediately thereafter, reflects the traditional catalogue of assumptions about the consequences for a competitive process where economic concentration
prevails in an industry.

JOHN M. BLAIR, ECONOMIC CONCENTRATION: STRUCTURE, BEHAVIOR AND PUBLIC POLICY

523–524 (1972).[26]

Under classical theory the criticism of monopoly was that it prevents an optimal allocation of resources. That concentration prevents not only an optimal allocation but an optimal use of resources
can be shown from an empirical examination of its specific effects.
Although interacting with one another, these effects can be classified
under a number of groupings.

There is, first, what may be termed the *efficiency* effect, which
happens also to be a cause of structural change. Because they have
customarily been treated as causes, this type of effect was examined
in . . . [prior chapters] of this work. Under today's conditions
one of the effects of concentration, as compared to a more competitive, or polyopolistic, economy, would appear to be higher costs, particularly those arising from managerial diseconomies. A corollary effect would appear to be a slower rate of invention, and possibly also,
a slower rate of innovation.

Another grouping is what might be referred to as the *price behavioral* effects. In . . . [prior chapters] it was found that rising
concentration was accompanied by decreasing depression price flexibility; that prices of concentrated industries declined less than those
of unconcentrated industries during the 1929–32 depression; that in

---

25. R. Bork, The Antitrust Paradox
192 (1978).

26. J.M. Blair, Economic Concentration: Structure, Behavior and Public Poli-

cy, p. 523–24. Copyright © 1972 Har-
court Brace Jovanovich. Used by
permission.

the recessions of 1953–54 and 1957–58 prices of concentrated industries tended to behave perversely by rising; that in upturns they
have regularly risen less rapidly than prices in unconcentrated industries; but that in the postwar era their long-term increase has been
considerably greater than that of unconcentrated industries.

A further result concerns the distribution of income—the *income
effect*. This effect can be examined through an analysis of the relationship of concentration to margins (above direct costs) and to profits.

Concentration can also have an adverse effect on the rate of *production* (and thus employment), particularly if during a downswing it
makes possible the clearing of the market by a greater curtailment in
output and a lesser reduction in price than would obtain under competition.

Finally, the perverse price flexibility of concentrated industries
during recessions not only frustrates efforts to arrest inflation by a
policy of monetary and fiscal restrictions but makes a bad situation
worse, leading inexorably to the direct control of prices by the state.

This chapter will be concerned with the *income, production*, and
policy effects of concentration.

If concentration makes for prices which, in relation to costs, remain for extended periods significantly above the level that would
prevail under competition, the result will tend to be a redistribution
of income favoring recipients with higher savings and lower consumption patterns of income use.

F.M. SCHERER, INDUSTRIAL MARKET STRUCTURE AND ECONOMIC PERFORMANCE
470–471 (2d Ed. 1980).[27]

The most that can be said with reasonable confidence is that the
social costs directly ascribable to monopoly power are modest. It is
appropriate to inquire why this is so. . . . First, a large fraction
of the American economy—perhaps as much as half—consists of industries whose structures, although seldom atomistically competitive,
include enough sellers to sustain a vigorous, workable species of competition as long as outright collusion is neither tolerated nor encouraged by the government. Second, many of the industries with
oligopolistic structures possess little or no collective power to hold
prices substantially above costs for extended periods because barriers
to new entry are modest. Obversely, pricing performance is *least*
satisfactory in those concentrated industries sealed off by very high
scale economy, product differentiation, resource control, or patent
barriers to entry. Third, high long-run price elasticities of demand
reflecting the threat of product substitution frequently discourage
maximum exploitation of short-run monopoly power, even when new
entry with a perfect substitute is blockaded. This constraint has be-

27. F.M. Scherer, Industrial Market
Structure and Economic Performance, p.
470–71 (2d Ed. 1980). Copyright © 1980
Houghton Mifflin Company. Used by
permission.

come increasingly important with industrial firms' growing sophistication in harnessing science to create new and superior synthetic materials. Uncertainty enhances the effect as professional managers strive to protect their market positions against feared but indistinct future threats by avoiding pricing strategies that encourage substitution through innovation. Fourth, the exercise of power by large buyers may countervail the pricing power of sellers, preventing the pyramiding of price distortions through a chain of vertical transactions and often (but not always) transmitting the savings to consumers. Finally, public policy has played a role. Except in some "special case" industries, the United States has since the late 1930s maintained a fairly vigorous antitrust program, striking down restrictive agreements, punishing abuses of monopoly power, preventing the consolidation of power, and raising legal and financial obstacles in the path of countless monopolistic arrangements.

NOTES

(1) *Efficiency Effects of Firm Size and Concentration.* Some attempts have been made to measure the efficiency effects of firm size by comparing the costs and rate of return on invested capital of firms of varying size. One study [28] concluded:

Individual Company-Cost Tests

In but 1 of the 59 individual company-cost tests did the largest company have the lowest cost. In 21 of these 59 tests, a company classified as medium-sized had the lowest cost. In 37 of these 59 tests, a company classified as small had the lowest cost. Of particular significance is the fact that in these 59 tests, on the average, over one-third of the companies in every array had costs lower than that of the largest company.

Tests for Groups of Companies

In only 1 of the 11 tests derived from the tables showing average costs of companies, grouped according to size, did the group containing the largest companies have the lowest average cost shown for any group. In 10 of the 11 tests the group containing companies generally classified as medium-sized had the lowest average cost shown for any group.

Individual Plant-Cost Tests

In the 53 individual plant-cost tests, the largest plant had the lowest cost in only 2 tests. A large plant, although not the largest, had the lowest cost in 4 tests. In 21 of the 53 tests, plants classified as medium-sized had the lowest cost. In 26 of the 53 tests, plants classified as small had the lowest costs. In these 53 tests, over one-third of the plants in

28. Relative Efficiency of Large, Medium-Sized, and Small Business.

Monograph No. 13 (T.N.E.C.1941). See also, Edmunds, Organizational Size and Efficiency in the U. S., 26 Antitrust Bull. 507 (1981) ("The rate of earnings on assets declines with increasing organizational size for every class size and industry group, according to data for all corporations in the United States . . . .")

each cost array had on the average lower costs than that of the largest plant.

Tests for Groups of Plants

In every one of the five tests for groups of plants, the group containing the plants classified as medium-sized had the lowest average cost shown for any group.

Tests Based on Table of Rates of Return on Invested Capital Earned by Individual Companies

In the 84 tests made for the rates of return on invested capital earned by individual companies in 18 industries, the largest company showed in the highest rate of return only 12 times. In 2 of the 84 tests a large company, although not the largest, showed the highest rate of return. In 57 of the 84 tests a company classified as medium-sized showed the highest rate of return. In 13 of the tests a company classified as small showed the highest rate of return. On the average about one-third of the total number of companies in each test showed higher rates of return than the largest company. In the 233 combined tests, large size, whether represented by a corporation, a plant, a group of corporations, or a group of plants, showed the lowest cost or the highest rate of return on invested capital in only 25 tests. In these combined tests, medium size made the best showing in 128 tests and small size in 80 tests. Thus, large size was most efficient, as efficiency is here measured, in approximately 11 percent of the total tests, medium size was most efficient in approximately 55 percent of the tests, and small size was most efficient in approximately 34 percent of the tests.

More recent evidence of a relationship between concentration and efficiency may be gleaned from the invasion of Japanese imports into American markets long dominated by a few domestic firms, including the camera, color TV, plain paper copier, and auto markets. Contrary to the popular belief that Japanese success is due to a cartelized domestic market orchestrated by central government planning for exports —"Japan Inc."—the Wall Street Journal reported:

> There's a lot of talk these days about Japan Inc. Both American and European businessmen seem to think that Japanese companies can penetrate export markets so easily because they enjoy comfortable, cartelized markets at home—under the guidance of the Ministry of International Trade and Industry (MITI).

> Nothing, however, could be further from the truth. In many industries, MITI policy used to shield Japanese companies from import competition—though in recent years, trade barriers have been tumbling rapidly. But the Japanese government has rarely been able to protect Japanese companies from *other Japanese companies*. And in almost every industry where Japanese companies have done well in export markets, they have honed their teeth in fierce domestic competition.

. . .

> In autos, Toyota and Nissan (Datsun) battle monthly for first place in domestic car registrations. There is no clear-cut victory for either of them, while in most other countries the auto industry is rolling toward monopoly. Here again, neither Nissan nor Toyota can breathe even for a

second, because the second-tier companies such as Mitsubishi, Toyo Ko-gyo (Mazda), Honda and Fuji (Subaru) are also formidable in terms of technological capabilities and cost competitiveness. One of the principal reasons for the surge of Japanese auto exports is that many Japanese carmakers, especially Honda and Fuji, have found it easier to sell in over-seas markets than in Japan.

. . .

In contrast to these highly competitive industries, Japanese companies do not do so well on world markets in industries such as cosmetics, brew-ery and construction machinery and pianos where one firm accounts for more than 50% of the Japanese market. In these industries, the leading company can generate attractive profits at home and need not challenge the risky and difficult markets overseas.

. . .

In short, it is the need for survival that is driving Japanese businesses to export, and certainly not the warm domestic climate. And to under-stand why Japanese companies do so well on world markets, it's impor-tant to recognize that they have built up their competitive strengths in perhaps the world's most competitive domestic marketplace.[29]

On the other hand, central planning by Japan's Ministry of International Trade and Industry (MITI) through long term government decisions to fi-nance or not to finance particular industries unites and channels Japan's competitive effort. One observer has characterized the results as follows: "Think of Japan as running a kind of National Football League inside the country; that is, it encourages intense competition among the teams but the league itself is a monopoly. It keeps the league closed to new entry from outside, or even within Japan.

There are severe barriers to entry in the Japanese market. But such as it is, the market is intensely competitive: the Steelers versus the Oilers ver-sus the Patriots, and so forth." [30]

(2) *Economic Cost of Concentration.* The cost of monopoly has been estimated at about 6% of the Gross National Product, or in the neighborhood of $20 to $26 billion per year between 1956 and 1961; but the range of esti-mates is wide: from 1% to 8%. A study group sponsored by Ralph Nader, in a 1971 report entitled "The Closed Enterprise System," set the cost of mo-nopoly at $48 to $60 billion a year.

"Stagflation", the phenomenon of simultaneous high unemployment and inflation, has been attributed to the domination of many basic industries by oligopolies. Follow-the-leader pricing or "administered pricing" is believed to occur in such industries, so that firms are able to raise prices even in the

29. Ohmae, Japan vs. Japan: Only The Strong Survive, Wall St.J., Jan. 26, 1981 p. 16. See also, Note, Trustbusting in Japan: Cartels and Government-Busi-ness Cooperation, 94 Harv.L.Rev. 1064 (1981) (tracing the evolution of Japanese antitrust policy since World War II and analyzing recent cases strengthening an-titrust enforcement in Japan). For a fas-cinating historical perspective on the evolution of Japanese economic policy, see F.T.C. Bureau of Competition—Of-fice of Special Projects, National Compe-tition Policy, Chaps. 1 & 6 (1981).

30. See T. McCraw, Comparison of Antitrust and Regulation in the United States and Japan, Post-War, in National Competition Policy, F.T.C. Study, supra note 29, at 34. See also Sease & Lehner, Japanese Steelmakers Thrive With the Aid of Government Policy, Wall St.J., p. 1 (April 10, 1981) (tracing MITI's activities in directing and channeling steel industry policy to maximize competitive advan-tages). See also G.C. Allen, The Japa-nese Economy (1982) (a perceptive analy-sis by a life-long observer of the Japanese economy).

face of falling demand in order to maintain pre-determined profit levels. The coexistence of rising inflation, high unemployment, and excess plant capacity—a condition inconsistent with the competitive model of the economy—is regarded by some as a cost of oligopolistic domination of basic industries.[31]

(3) *Concentration and Innovation.* Adams and Dirlam, Big Steel, Invention, and Innovation, 80 Q.J.Econ. 167 (1966), examined, in the context of the steel industry, the Schumpeter hypothesis that a degree of monopoly is required to finance and organize massive innovation: Adams and Dirlam noted that the three major revolutions in steel-making—the Bessemer, Siemens-Martin (open-hearth), and basic oxygen processes—were not the products of American research or giant corporate research projects. Each was the product of research and development by relatively tiny foreign firms and large U.S. steel firms only implemented the new technology many years after small competitors had adopted it. Adams and Dirlam concluded it is "reasonable to assume that innovation is sponsored by firms in inverse order of size" and that had large steel companies implemented the new technologies sooner their earnings would have been substantially higher and costs lower. They conclude their study by observing:

> Until the steel industry restates its accounts to reflect the efficiencies that have been possible for at least the past fifteen years, little credence should be given to its plaintive pleas for higher prices or profits.
>
> Finally, there is another implication to our study of the steel industry's curious inversion of the source of innovation. It has often been assumed that, if homogenous oligopolies do not compete in price, their leading members compete in innovating—and that the public benefits as much as, if not more than, it would by price competition. Yet the oxygen converter history reveals the steel oligopoly as failing to compete in strategic innovations. What benefits, then, remain for large size in steel? [32]

A more comprehensive study called the "Jewkes study" [33] found 16 of the 61 significant inventions studied attributable to organized research by large corporations. Most of the 16 were in the chemical industry, while those inventions not attributable to large corporate research were the product of work by individuals "with limited resources or backing" or were by individuals connected with academic institutions where they were "free to follow their own ideas without hindrance." [34]

31. For further studies of the economic cost of concentration, see H. Goldschmid, M. Mann, & J. Weston (Eds.), Industrial Concentration: The New Learning 16 (1974); J. Blair, Economic Concentration: Structure, Behavior and Public Policy (1972); Scherer, Industrial Market Structure and Economic Performance (2d Ed. 1980); Qualls, Market Structure and Price Behavior in U.S. Manufacturing 1967–72 (a staff study of the FTC Bureau of Economics indicating that price increases were no greater in concentrated than in unconcentrated industries); Kammerschen, An Estimation of the Welfare Losses from Monopoly in the American Economy, Western Economic Journal, Summer 1966, p. 233. The Post-Keynesian school of economic theorizing asserts that pricing decisions in concentrated markets are not made in terms of supply and demand, but concentrated firms are able to use their discretion over price to fix prices in terms of their needs for investment capital. See P. Kenyon, "Pricing" in A. Eichner (ed.) A Guide to Post-Keynesian Economics 34 (1979).

32. See also Bowman, Towards Less Monopoly, 101 U.Pa.L.Rev. 577 (1953); "Mini-Mill Steelmakers No Longer Very Small, Outperform Big Ones", Wall St. J., Jan. 12, 1981 p. 1 (use of scrap and modern techniques to make specialized end products cheaper than large firms).

33. J. Jewkes, D. Sawyers, R. Stillerman, The Sources of Invention (Rev. Ed.1969).

34. Id. at 82.

Blair attributes the relatively poor innovation performance of large corporations to a "matrix of factors." "[T]hey include the desire to protect the investment in an older technology, indifference to technological advance, underestimation of the demand for new products, neglect of the inventor, misdirection of research, incompatibility between organization and creativity, and the military's built-in resistance to change." [35]

Scherer's study of the issue led him to four "summary observations": "First, concentration is much higher and leading firm sizes are much larger in many markets than they need be to support the most vigorous rate of progress. Second, in some atomistic industries concentration is too low and representative firm sizes are too small for ambitious research and innovation efforts to thrive. . . . Third, some of the most strikingly profitable monopoly positions are the result, not the cause, of successful innovation attended by strong patent protection. . . . Fourth, our knowledge is too limited to predict confidently whether the rate of technical progress could be accelerated significantly by structural reforms—i.e., by forcing the deconcentration of highly concentrated industries and permitting a movement toward concentration of atomistic industries." [36]

Since World War II, well over 50% of total research and development (R & D) outlays have come from the federal government. There is considerable controversy as to the relationship of concentration to R & D expenditures by private firms or government financing of private research.[37] Qualitative measurements of new inventions are difficult to extract from statistical measurements of gross R & D expenditures. In particular, the statistics fail to distinguish between significant scientific and technological advances and trivial innovations for marketing advantage. It may be impossible ever to determine whether concentration retards or promotes innovation or whether innovation causes or promotes concentration.

Historical and philosophical studies suggest that truly revolutionary discoveries are the product of minds free of the preconceptions of the day, capable of new insights into the "reality" of the existing order.[38] While it may be unrealistic and romantic to assume that most creative inventors are lonely figures battling in poverty against entrenched interests, it may be equally unrealistic to assume that genius is found only in large lavishly subsidized laboratories managed by corporate bureaucrats.

(4) *Bain, Barriers to New Competition 110–112 (1956).* "The largest several plants in an industry . . . are typically somewhat larger than the estimated optimal size of plant; on the average such plants may be from less than double to five times the estimated optimal size. . . . But generally, plant concentration plays a minor role, and multiplant development of firms a major role, in the over-all picture of concentration by firms. . . . Thus in 11 of 20 industries the existing degree of concentration by firms as measured by the average size of the largest 4 firms is significantly greater than

---

35. J.M. Blair, Economic Concentration: Structure, Behavior and Public Policy 228 (1972).

36. F.M. Scherer, Industrial Market Structure and Economic Performance 473 (2d Ed. 1980). Copyright © 1980 Houghton Mifflin Company. Used by permission.

37. For a summary of recent studies see Markham, Concentration: A Stimulus or Retardant to Innovation?, in H. Goldschmid, M. Mann & J. Weston, (Eds.), Industrial Concentration: The New Learning 247 (1974).

38. See Kuhn, The Structure of Scientific Revolutions (2d ed. 1970).

required for these firms to have only one optimal plant per submarket.
. . . " [39]

(5) *Brandeis, The Curse of Bigness.* The following is quoted from Justice Douglas, dissenting in *United States v. Columbia Steel Co.*[40]

The only argument that has been seriously advanced in favor of private monopoly is that competition involves waste, while the monopoly prevents waste and leads to efficiency. This argument is essentially unsound. The wastes of competition are negligible. The economies of monopoly are superficial and delusive. The efficiency of monopoly is at the best temporary.

Undoubtedly competition involves waste. What human activity does not? The wastes of democracy are among the greatest obvious wastes, but we have compensations in democracy which far outweigh that waste and make it more efficient than absolutism. So it is with competition. The waste is relatively insignificant. There are wastes of competition which do not develop, but kill. These the law can and should eliminate, by regulating competition.

It is true that the unit in business may be too small to be efficient. It is also true that the unit may be too large to be efficient, and this is no uncommon incident of monopoly.

. . . No monopoly in private industry in America has yet been attained by efficiency alone. No business has been so superior to its competitors in the processes of manufacture or of distribution as to enable it to control the market solely by reason of its superiority.

The Steel Trust, while apparently free from the coarser forms of suppressing competition, acquired control of the market not through greater efficiency, but by buying up existing plants and particularly ore supplies at fabulous prices, and by controlling strategic transportation systems.

But the efficiency of monopolies, even if established, would not justify their existence unless the community should reap benefit from the efficiency; experience teaches us that whenever trusts have efficiency, their fruits have been absorbed almost wholly by the trusts themselves. From such efficiency as they have developed the community has gained substantially nothing. For instance: . . . The Steel Trust, a corporation of reputed efficiency. The high prices maintained by it in the industry are matters of common knowledge. In less than ten years it accumulated for its shareholders or paid out as dividends on stock representing merely water, over $650,000,000.

(6) *Business Performance as an Issue in Antitrust Cases.* For opposing views of leading economists on the issue whether "business performance" of an enterprise should be evaluated in determining whether it has

---

39. See also Stigler, The Economies of Scale, 1 J.Law & Econ. 54 (1958). Roberts, Some Aspects of Motor Carrier Costs: Firm Size, Efficiency, and Financial Health, 32 Land Econ. 228 (1956), analyzes operating data of large and small carriers and concludes that characteristics of the route and traffic, rather than absolute size, determine operating efficiency; many small operators had the lowest costs. Stelzer, Technological Progress and Market Structure, 23 So.Econ. J. 63 (1956), attributes the low rate of technological progress in the cotton textile industry to a state of underconcentration which precluded high profits needed to finance research.

Downie, The Competitive Process (London, 1958) offers an ingenious statistical demonstration of the efficacy of competition in rapid dispersion of the benefits of innovation.

40. 334 U.S. 495, 534, n. 1, 68 S.Ct. 1107, 1127, n. 1, 92 L.Ed. 1533, 1557, n. 1 (1948).

violated the antitrust laws, see Mason, The Current Status of the Monopoly
Problem in the United States, 62 Harv.L.Rev. 1265 (1949) and Kahn, Standards for Antitrust Policy, 67 Harv.L.Rev. 28 (1953). In measuring business
performance Mason would take account of rate of technological advance,
progressive reduction of costs and prices, low investment in relation to output, modest profits, emphasis on product improvement rather than high pressure sales effort. He acknowledges that such tests would be "extremely
difficult" to administer in a court of law. Posner, A Program for the Antitrust Division, 38 U.Chi.L.Rev. 500 (1971), calls for an enforcement policy
dominated by economists, who would apply "cost-benefit" analyses to the
selection of fruitful enforcement lines. He would not, however, make good
performance a litigable issue, and criticizes such a proposal in Williamson,
Economies as an Antitrust Defense: The Welfare Tradeoffs, 58 Am.Econ.
Rev. 18 (1968), as "quite impractical in the present state of economic knowledge."

Mueller, The New Antitrust: A Structural Approach, 12 Vill.L.Rev. 764,
773 (1967) adds:

> Perhaps the ultimate difficulty with the "performance" standard, howev-
> er, is that it has no workable *remedy* to offer when it finds "unworkable"
> competition. Having denied the existence of a causal relation between
> structure and performance, it cannot logically prescribe divestiture. And
> if it prescribes an injunctive remedy, it is then faced with the problem of
> framing a command that will effectively say to the firms in an industry,
> "Be efficient," or "Be progressive."

(7) *Voluntary Decentralization of Large Firms to Avoid Diseconomies
of Excessive Size.* Occasionally large firms take action to counter diseconomies
mies of excessive size and centralization of authority.[41] A pamphlet circulated by Gulf Oil Corporation and generally intended to prove that the petroleum industry is not excessively concentrated included a section entitled
"Away From Monopoly," describing how, as a result of losses sustained in
the Great Depression of the 1930's, cost analyses were instituted. It was
discovered that the companies were performing "literally dozens of different
kinds of operations . . . for themselves extending all the way across the
integrated organization from geophysical surveys on the one end to service
stations at the other" at a higher cost than would have been charged by
independent contractors. As a result the policy of full integration was said
to be "undergoing extensive alterations." [42] In 1955 the Pennsylvania Rail-

41. For an interesting account of decentralization and the principle of "federalism" in corporate organization, with
particular reference to the General Motors Corporation, see Drucker, Concept
of the Corporation (1946) and The New
Society (1949). See also Bigness and
Concentration of Power—A Case Study
of General Motors Corporation, Staff Report of the Subcommittee on Antitrust
and Monopoly, Senate Committee on the
Judiciary, 84th Cong., 1st Sess. (1956).

Cf. Jewkes, The Nationalization of Industry, 20 U. of Chi.L.Rev. 615 (1953),
which examines and rejects the claim
that nationalization in England resulted
in economies of scale: "The constant emphasis upon decentralization in the na-
tionalized industries is, in itself, proof
that size is now normally to be consid-

ered a liability rather than an asset.
This undoubtedly explains why each successive scheme for nationalization has resulted in a less centralized, less formal
system of organization than the one before, culminating in the scheme for iron
and steel in which ninety-two firms were
to be owned by the state but, for operation, were to be only loosely linked by a
small central organization, and were to
retain their own names, directors and
specialized types of production. Whether, in fact, decentralization is a universal
cure-all for the obvious administrative
weaknesses of the public boards is dubious."

42. Thompson, The Industry Nobody
Really Knows (Gulf Oil Corp. 1956), p.
17.

road announced an administrative reorganization of its system into 9 separate regions, each with a regional manager who would be autonomous except for overall system coordination and authority. The president of the railroad was quoted as follows:

> We believe the new regions will be appropriate in size for modern operation and greater concentration of responsibility and effort at the "grass roots," which we hope to achieve. Each of the new regions will be about the size of a smaller railroad. Therefore, by putting a complete management staff in charge of each region we expect to gain the close supervision of service typical of a smaller railroad. On the other hand, by strengthening the system organization at headquarters with staff officers in charge of policy for each phase of our business, we expect to capitalize on the advantages of our larger size.[43]

The New York Times reported "restrained optimism" among American officials that Germany would not reestablish the I.G. Farben empire which had been broken up during the Allied occupation. The basis of the optimism was a memorandum found in the Farben files showing that "the company's directors themselves had come to the conclusion that Farben was too large and complex to be managed efficiently." [44]

On the other hand, a leading economist has declared:

> Unfortunately, the voluntary division of very large enterprises never happens and apparently never even receives serious consideration. The biases inside management, at least those inside top management, are all against it. The president and the directors like the prestige of directing a very large enterprise. The closest approach to voluntary break-up is the creation of semi-independent organizations inside the big organization, as has been done by General Motors.[45]

3. FACTORS OTHER THAN PRODUCTIVE EFFICIENCY AFFECTING THE RELATIVE PERFORMANCE OF LARGE AND SMALL FIRMS

Factors other than inherent ability to provide better products at minimum cost may distort measurements of relative efficiency of large and small firms. Political influence, for example, may be used to secure legislation or other favorable government action. Almost every act of government has a differential impact on large and small enterprises: taxation, tariffs, standards and specifications for products which the government will buy for itself or permit to be sold in interstate commerce, regulation of transportation rates, or of consumer credit, restrictions on the right to go into certain businesses or to expand operations are only a few examples.[46] A sales tax may

43. Wall St.J., Sept. 29, 1955, p. 2. See also, "Some Firms Fight Ills Of Bigness by Keeping Employee Units Small", Wall St.J., Feb. 5, 1982, p. 1.

44. N. Y. Times, Jan. 15, 1955, p. 6.

45. Slichter, Big Business: When Is It Too Big? N. Y. Times Sunday Magazine, March 20, 1955, p. 13, at p. 34. See also Kaysen and Turner, Antitrust Policy: An Economic and Legal Analysis (1959), Chap. 3, marshalling evidence against superiority of management of the largest corporations.

46. See The Organization and Procedures of the Federal Regulatory Commissions and Agencies and Their Effect on Small Business, H.Rep.No.2967, 84th Cong., 2d Sess. (Select Committee on Small Business, 1956); Adams and Gray, Monopoly in America: the Government as Promoter (1955); Adams and Hendry, Trucking Mergers, Concentration, and Small Business, An Analysis of Interstate Commerce Commission Policy, 1950–56, Committee Print of a Report prepared for the Senate Committee on Small Business, 85th Cong., 1st Sess.

favor vertically integrated firms where it applies not only to purchases by ultimate consumers but also to sales of raw materials or other goods to processors and resellers.[47] Ownership of transport facilities provides the integrated firm transportation at cost while independent shippers may be required to pay the higher non-competitive rates, fixed by public authority for the stated purpose of maintaining the transportation system as a whole. The government provides subsidies for constructing and operating private ships for international transportation, and for the rehabilitation of the privately owned railroad system, all involving enterprises of large size.[48]

Loan guarantees are given to giant defense contractors and a large auto maker. Local communities with power to issue tax-exempt bonds frequently did so for the purpose of providing cheap capital facilities to large corporations and enticing them to establish plants in the locality. In a reaffirmation of the old adage about many ways to skin a cat, corporations have turned to other devices for bargaining special advantages from local governments. Tax exempt industrial revenue bonds, intended for urban renewal and economic rehabilitation of blighted areas, have been widely used to finance such ventures as shopping centers, fast-food outlets and ski resorts. The 1980 loss in tax revenue due to the sale of such bonds is estimated to be $1 billion.[49] General Motors has taken the urban renewal tactic for corporate welfare one step further, by enlisting the eminent domain powers of the City of Detroit to condemn a residential neighborhood for a new Cadillac plant. Condemnation of the homeowners' property for transfer to a private manufacturing company to construct a manufacturing plant was found not to violate a State constitutional prohibition against taking private property for private use. The Michigan Court held any benefit to General Motors was "incidental" to the benefit to Detroit in alleviating unemployment.[50]

Such influences do not always operate to favor Big Business. This may be seen in the history of discriminatory taxation against chain stores,[51] and in some features of the antitrust legislation itself, e.g., provisions of the Robinson-Patman Act which tend to preserve middlemen despite possible cost savings from direct dealing between producer and retailer.[52]

(1957) (Commission following a "double standard" favoring large firms).

47. Cf. Gray v. Powell, 314 U.S. 402, 62 S.Ct. 326, 86 L.Ed. 301 (1941) (tax on coal produced and sold in violation of certain wage and price controls, exemption for coal consumed by the producer); see Stocking and Watkins, Cartels in Action 176 n. 10 (1946), referring to the sales tax as a factor in the movement toward vertical integration in the German steel industry.

48. See, for example, the Transportation Act of 1958, providing government guarantees for railroad borrowing up to $500,000,000. 72 Stat. 568, 49 U.S.C.A. § 1231 et seq.

49. See "UAW Protests Toyota Dealer's Bid For Helping Hand From The Public," Wall St.J., April 23, 1981, p. 25.

50. Poletown Neighborhood Council v. Detroit, 410 Mich. 616, 304 N.W.2d 455 (1981).

51. See Liggett Co. v. Lee, 288 U.S. 517, 53 S.Ct. 481, 77 L.Ed. 929 (1933).

52. See p. 872 infra. Other legislation authorizes government procurement agencies to pay higher prices to small producers in certain circumstances.

Illegal practices may also account for some difference in the performance of large and small enterprises. As attested by the long record of successful prosecutions against large enterprises, monopolistic practices unfairly handicap smaller rivals.[53] On the other hand, some observers believe that business practices of larger corporations are more likely to conform to public interest standards:

> The fact that a concern is larger than any of its rivals means that most of its policies and activities are conspicuous and must stand up under the scrutiny of competitors, suppliers, customers and Government officials.

> This scrutiny is not a perfect restraint, but it does mean that the business standards of the very largest concerns are likely to be superior to those of most small enterprises. Hence, in the present state of our limited knowledge about business practices one is probably justified in arguing that bigness in business makes on the whole for better ethical practices, better treatment of customers, employes and suppliers, than smallness in business.[54]

Even lawful commercial practices may operate to the advantage of large business units without any clear or necessary relation to efficiency. For example, national advertising by press, radio and television, a method of molding consumer preferences, is effectively available only to large firms. From one point of view, this can be regarded as merely an aspect of superior efficiency in marketing. Advertising that would consist of information to the public about the product, its price, and its merits would, indeed, be a proper part of competition for markets. But it is obvious that much advertising goes far beyond this limited informational objective. Repetition of the brand name or association of the product with such attractive irrelevancies as beautiful women, famous personages, or an intriguing jingle are calculated to create an automatic favorable response. One need not determine whether advertising of this sort is, all things considered, desirable or undesirable. For the present purposes it is enough to note one of its consequences: that commercial rivalry between the big national advertiser and those not large enough to use this selling technique ceases to be an even contest of who can make and sell most cheaply what the consumer wants or generate different consumer wants by mass advertising. One of the competitors now has the power to manipulate the consumers' preferences. It is impossible to determine

53. For illustrations of the insistence of big buyers on illegal discrimination, see United States v. General Motors Corp., 226 F.2d 735 (3d Cir. 1955) (kickback of freight rates by Baltimore and Ohio Railroad made through the railroad's acquisition of a plant site for resale to GM at a loss of $171,329.28); United States v. New York Great A. & P. Tea Co., 173 F.2d 79 (7th Cir. 1949) (A. &

P.'s insistence not merely on low prices to itself, but on higher prices to its rivals); Interstate Circuit, Inc. v. United States, 306 U.S. 208, 59 S.Ct. 467, 83 L.Ed. 610 (1939) (imposition of disadvantages on competing movie exhibitors).

54. Slichter, Big Business: When Is It Too Big?, N. Y. Times Magazine, March 20, 1955, p. 13.

the impact of this factor on the comparative performance of large and small firms.[55]

Size itself, even though initially acquired lawfully and by superior efficiency, confers continuing advantages over others, advantages not necessarily identifiable with efficiency. As the firm's hold on its market approaches the point of dominance or monopoly, it becomes increasingly able to dictate prices both to its customers and to its suppliers. With a wider profit margin it becomes possible for the firm to finance its own expansion without passing the scrutiny of banks and investors. Consumers thus provide capital without cost to the monopolistic firm, freeing it of a cost which others must bear. This in turn makes the dominant company a more attractive investment when it does require additional outside financing. Its interest rates will be lower; its stock will sell for higher prices.

CONGLOMERATE BIGNESS AS A SOURCE OF POWER

Excerpt from an article by Corwin Edwards in Business Concentration and Price Policy (National Bureau of Economic Research 1955) pp. 331, 335-7.[56]

Closely associated with differences in financial strength is a difference between the attitudes of large concerns toward one another and their attitudes toward smaller business enterprises. A large concern usually must show a regard for the strength of other large concerns by circumspection in its dealings with them, whereas such caution is usually unnecessary in dealing with small enterprises. The interests of great enterprises are likely to touch at many points, and it would be possible for each to mobilize at any one of these points a considerable aggregate of resources. The anticipated gain to such a concern from unmitigated competitive attack upon another large enterprise at one point of contact is likely to be slight as compared with the possible loss from retaliatory action by that enterprise at many other points of contact. There is an awareness that if competition against the large rival goes so far as to be seriously troublesome, the logic of the situation may call for conversion of the warfare into total war. Hence there is an incentive to live and let live, to cultivate a cooperative spirit, and to recognize priorities of interest in the hope of reciprocal recognition. Those attitudes support such policies as refraining from sale in a large company's home market below whatever price that company may have established there; refraining from entering into the production of a commodity which a large company has developed; not contesting the patent claims of a large company even

55. Bain, Barriers to New Competition 142 (1956): "Product differentiation is of at least the same general order of importance as an impediment to entry as are economies of large-scale production and distribution." Cf. Turner, Conglomerate Mergers and Section 7 of the Clayton Act, 78 Harv.L.Rev. 1313, 1332 (1965), deprecating economies in promotional costs as a factor favorable to mergers.

56. Quoted by permission of the author and the publisher, Princeton Univ. Press. See also Blake, Conglomerate Mergers and the Antitrust Laws, 73 Colum.L.Rev. 555 (1973); Adams, Market Structure and Corporate Power: The Horizontal Dominance Hypothesis Reconsidered, 74 Colum.L.Rev. 1276 (1974); Stocking and Mueller, Business Reciprocity and the Size of Firms, 30 U.Chi.Bus.J. 73 (1957).

when they are believed to be invalid; abstaining from an effort to win away the important customers of a large rival; and sometimes refusing to accept such customers even when they take the initiative.

Similar policies by a large company toward a small one are seldom encountered. The small concern's business is limited geographically, or in the commodities it covers, or in the classes of customers with which it is concerned, or in some other way; and the large company can seldom be seriously injured by aggressive tactics which the small one may undertake, or by retaliatory or disciplinary tactics which may be employed against it by the small company. The large company is in a position to hurt without being hurt. The attitude of the small company may range from eager deference to defiant independence; but, whatever its quality, it will take the policies of the large concern into account. The attitude of the large company may range from generosity through indifference to peremptory exercise of authority; but, whatever its quality, the policies underlying it will not be substantially modified by the probable course of action of small companies except in cases in which the small companies act in concert.

This aspect of the power of large concerns becomes more conspicuous as the diversity of operations becomes greater, that is, as the likelihood that the large concern has monopoly power in any particular market becomes less. When the large company spreads across many products throughout a wide geographical area and covers a series of stages in production and distribution, its opportunities for multiple contacts with other large concerns are at their greatest, and the advantage to be derived from an effort to get the best of another large company at a particular point is least evident. Similarly, such a company has the maximum chance to discipline or destroy any particular small company by a localized attack without serious inconvenience to itself, and has the minimum vulnerability to attack from a single small company. Monopoly prosecutions under the antitrust laws have contained frequent evidence of the use of local price-cutting by large nationwide companies to discipline localized competitors; but the opportunity to use such tactics usually depended, not upon monopolization of the national or regional market, but upon a difference in the resources and geographic spread of the aggressor and the victim. In recent decades, the antimonopoly agencies and the legislative bodies have received many complaints from specialized producers or distributors who assert that their business has been seriously injured by price reductions on their specialty that have been made by diversified business enterprises using the specialty as a loss leader. The diversified concern employing loss leader tactics often appeared to have no significant degree of monopoly power.

Differentials in size rather than in monopoly power are the source of such advantages. The large concern has a special status, even though it may operate in an industry so large that its percentage of the total market is small. The small enterprise lacks these advantages even though it may operate in an industry so small that it has a practical monopoly from which it derives other types of advantages. The consideration of the large company for other large companies and its authority over small companies can be seen in dealings with suppliers, distributors, and competitors alike, in each of the fields of operation in which the large concern is substantially engaged. If a concern as large as DuPont sells various products for which its share of the market ranges from 100 per cent to 5 per cent, it may monopolize some of these products and not others; but even where it sells only a small part of the total supply, the fact that the seller is very large is likely to be a source of significant power.

NOTES

(1) *Report of the Attorney General's National Committee to Study the Antitrust Laws* (1955) p. 326:

Effective competition may be affected not only by the total number of sellers; their relative size and strength must also be considered. This does not mean that close equality of size among the various firms is essential for workable competition to exist, but only that the rivalry should not depend entirely upon sellers who are so weak or inefficient as to exist by sufferance. For such firms are not independent, and are not properly counted among the number of effectively competitive sellers. And as the number of independent sellers reaches unity, the market obviously reaches monopoly. The presence in any market of a unit much stronger than the others is a factor to be closely examined for its bearing on the workably competitive character of that market, and on the issue of whether any firm in fact exists only by sufferance, but by itself is not indicative of the absence of workable competition.

Where the number of sellers is large, each one of them faces an impersonal market with a market price which he can take or leave. He can do little to affect total supply or to raise the market price.

When sellers are few, each producing a significant share of total market supply, each seller is aware of the fact that any substantial change in his price or his production will have an appreciable effect upon total market supply and market price, and will tend to elicit responsive changes in the prices and outputs of his rivals. Hence there is a mutual awareness rather than an impersonal market relationship. Where such a market is isolated from competitive pressures, the possibility of successful collusion is greater, to detect it is harder, and its rewards may be more immediate and tempting. Hence there is need for vigilance in scrutinizing such industries, without prejudging whether in fact any type of conspiracy exists. When sellers are few, even in the absence of conspiracy, the market itself may not show many of the characteristics of effective competition, and in fact may not be effectively competitive in the economic sense.

(2) *Slichter, Big Business: When Is It Too Big?* The New York Times Magazine, March 20, 1955, pp. 13, 30:

. . . Even the traditional view that competition would be seriously impaired whenever production is concentrated among a relatively few firms has been disproved by experience. Where competitors are few there is usually a vigorous struggle for larger shares of the market and some competitors succeed in growing much faster than their rivals, as is attested by the rapid growth of Dow Chemical, Inland Steel, Ford Motors, Gulf Oil, Phillips Petroleum, and many others.

The reason that concentration of production among a few big rivals usually stimulates competition rather than weakens it is obvious. Consumer tastes and preferences are unpredictable. When each of a few firms has a large share of the business, a shift of consumer preferences can cause disastrous losses to some firms, as the Chrysler Corporation discovered a year ago when its models failed to meet the public taste. Under these circumstances the safest course of action for each competitor is to study the tastes of consumers continuously and to endeavor constantly to improve his product and his service—or the service of his dealers.

Hence, the concentration of production among a few large rivals strongly stimulates efforts of the several firms to improve their products and service. And since no one in a small group likes to be the first to raise prices, the concentration of production among a few large firms tends to protect consumers against rising prices. . . .

4. NON-ECONOMIC VALUES AND THE SIGNIFICANCE OF CONCENTRATION

Difficult as it is to measure the relative efficiency of large and small business, it is even more difficult to measure the non-economic consequences of business concentration. It is said that when business becomes concentrated in relatively few hands, the owners and managers tend to acquire a dangerous degree of political power as well. The combination of political and economic power, which otherwise might act as checks upon each other, leads to an anti-democratic authoritarianism.[57] This appeared to be the official thesis of the victorious allies in World War II, especially the United States; and they embarked upon a program of deconcentration and decartelization in occupied Germany and Japan. In regard to the relation between enterprise freedom and civil liberty, consider the report from Moscow concerning an appeal by a group of Soviet intellectual leaders to Communist party officials. The group listed among its libertarian goals: freedom of information, amnesty for political prisoners, independence of prosecutors and courts, elimination of internal passports, and "organization of industrial companies with a high degree of independence in planning, production processes, sales and supplies, finances and personnel."[58]

It is noteworthy that European Socialist parties have generally been indifferent or opposed to deconcentration, favoring as they do a more or less thorough unification of political and economic responsibilities, nationalization of key industries, and central planning.[59]

57. Schwartz, Institutional Size and Individual Liberty: Authoritarian Aspects of Bigness, 55 Nw.U.L.Rev. 4 (1960); Edwards, Big Business and the Policy of Competition (1956) especially pp. 1–6, 131–2.

58. Phila.Evening Bull., April 3, 1970, p. 8.

59. See generally Report on Foreign Legislation Concerning Monopoly and Cartel Practices of the Subcommittee on Monopoly of the Select Committee on Small Business, U. S. Senate, 82d Cong., 2d Sess. (1952).

From the point of view of such a program, the amalgamation of private businesses into relatively few units with ever increasing government supervision simplifies and facilitates the ultimate socialization. Some American political economists who are very far from being socialists also welcome or are reconciled to high concentration on the ground that giant businesses, finding themselves under constant scrutiny of courts, administrative agencies, legislative committees, and public opinion, no longer function like ordinary private institutions but develop a sense of responsibility for public welfare, and become quasi-political bodies.[60]

Another school of thought dismisses most non-economic concerns about concentration of large firms as baseless or argues whatever non-economic concerns exist because of concentration should not be accounted for through antitrust policy.[61]   Antitrust policy, it is claimed, should only occupy itself with the maximization of "economic efficiency" as defined by the abstract models peculiar to the school of thought making the argument.   Aside from scholarly and persuasive arguments to the contrary,[62] a deeper jurisprudential issue persists within this significant debate about the underlying assumptions formulating the scope and direction of the antitrust laws.   That question is whether the analysis of factual disputes arising under any law can ever escape recourse to political, social and moral values in determining which laws are relevant, what the laws found relevant mean, and what result ought to follow when the facts and law interact to induce a conclusion.[63]   Or, as Felix Cohen asserted, is every legal question unavoidably a moral one? [64]

NOTES AND QUERIES

(1) *Multinational Corporations.*   The phenomenon of world-wide business organizations has been attracting increased attention.[65]   The striking

60.   See Berle, The Twentieth Century Capitalist Revolution (1954); Berle, The Future of Democratic Capitalism (1950); Lilienthal, Big Business, A New Era (1953).

61.   See R. Bork, The Antitrust Paradox (1978); R. Posner, Antitrust Law: An Economic Perspective (1976); Brozen, The Concentration-Collusion Doctrine, in ABA, Industrial Concentration and the Market System, 90 (1979).

62.   See Pitofsky, The Political Content of Antitrust, 127 U.Pa.L.Rev. 1051 (1979); Schwartz, "Justice" and Other Non-Economic Goals of Antitrust, 127 U.Pa.L.Rev. 1076 (1979); Symposium, Antitrust Jurisprudence: A Symposium On The Economic, Political and Social Goals of Antitrust Policy, 125 U.Pa.L. Rev. 1182 (1977).

63.   See Flynn, The Role of Economic Analysis In Antitrust Litigation, 12 S.W.

U.L.Rev. 334 (1980); Leff, Economic Analysis of Law: Some Realism About Nominalism, 60 Va.L.Rev. 451 (1974); Wiles, Ideology, Methodology, and Neoclassical Economics, 2 J. P. Keynesian Econ. 155 (1979).

64.   F. Cohen, The Ethical Basis of Legal Criticism (1959).

65.   See Barnet and Muller, Global Reach (1974); Vernon, Sovereignty at Bay (1971); Kindelberger, The International Corporation (1970); Barber, The American Corporation, Part V—The Internationalization of Business (1970); Vagts, The Multinational Enterprise, 83 Harv.L.Rev. 739 (1970); Tariff Commission Report to the Senate Finance Committee, Feb. 1973, on Implications of Multinational Firms for World Trade and Investment.

character and scale of these operations is made manifest in the following excerpt from Barber, The American Corporation (1970):

ITT tells much of the story in its own words, proclaiming that "well over half of [its] worldwide research and development in telecommunications and electronics is done in Europe by Europeans." The company, generally thought of as "American," embraces over 150 associated firms, employing 300,000 people (more than half "foreign"), and carries on research, manufacturing, sales or service in fifty-seven countries, with sales outlets in sixty-two more. A company with world commitments, such as ITT, not only dramatizes the multinational dimensions of contemporary business, but underscores the need to treat such a firm in international terms. To pretend that ITT is just an American firm, or that Unilever is just a British enterprise, or that Shell is Dutch is absurd—a fiction good neither for these firms' own long-term interests or for the citizens of any of the several countries whose economies are affected by their operations.

Today all of the functional characteristics of modern business have become transnational, subsuming nations and demanding suitable institutional and legal treatment. Yet as almost always seems to be the case, legal policy is several decades behind the evolution of business and technology. . . .

International business activities form a veritable web of interconnections. To show what this can mean, contemplate something seemingly as simple as a supertanker that hauls crude oil from the Middle East to a refinery in Belgium. Built in Japan on behalf of a group of California investors, it is financed by a syndicate of New York banks and is chartered on a long-term basis to a Dutch oil company. The ship itself flies a Panamanian flag, is manned by a Hong Kong-Chinese crew under a German master, and is insured by Lloyds of London. What is "the" nationality of such a ship—American, Dutch, Panamanian? The question itself is naive and there can really be no answer, for the ship is in essence nothing but a piece of floating international property—stateless, in one sense, or multinational, in another. It typifies the character of contemporary business.

Business organizations of that character easily evade American and other national laws relating to the structure and commercial activities of national units. If American antitrust laws forbid a cartel between European and American automobile manufacturers, approximately the same trade results might be achieved by intra-enterprise decision: the American parent of the European subsidiary simply decides against exporting its European products to the United States. Within the limits of oligopoly power to coordinate policies of entire industries, such decisions would be more effective than a tariff in keeping European cars out of the American market or American cars out of the European market. Headquarters of the multinational corporation will also determine whether third markets are to be supplied from "home" or elsewhere. Efforts in any one nation to "cool" the economy by instituting deflationary controls on credit will be difficult to enforce against corporate decisions to provide capital from intra-enterprise resources outside the country. Restraints on export of dollars, imposed to regulate balance of payments and international monetary exchange rates, lose their force when the international firm can build up a dollar balance abroad simply by refraining from repatriating its profits on foreign operations. Taxes and welfare burdens in one nation may be evaded by corporate choice to transfer operations elsewhere.

The gap in political control of multinational firms is analogous to one that prevailed in the United States when corporate enterprise had grown beyond the control of any one state while the federal government lagged in assuming and exercising national power. Pressures begin to be felt for the creation of international political controls, the beginnings of which can be seen in the European Community. On the other hand, it is well to recall that generations of pressure within the United States for a national law of incorporation of business enterprise has failed to achieve results, as giant enterprise conserves its power under the banner of "states' rights." There are those who see the brightest prospects for world peace in the relatively uninhibited knitting together of world economic interests by cadres of "denationalized" managers of multinational firms. Others see a new imperialism of the economically developed nations integrating their economic power to maintain dominance over the underdeveloped.

(2) *Quality of Life; Racial Discrimination; Integrity of the Individual.* One of the nonpecuniary gains that goes with monopolistic power is said to be "the indulgence of one's tastes in the kind of people with whom one prefers to associate." The links between economic concentration and a social structure which excludes minorities from positions of power and prestige are often suggested [66] but seldom quantified.[67] There is some evidence that monopolistic enterprises discriminate against Blacks more frequently than competitive ones.[68] Some also claim that the large corporation, by necessity or by virtue of its size, demands conformity to the goals of the enterprise and submerges individualism to that end. Consider:

> The big corporations offer good pay, security, and good prospects for advancement. But what is more—and this is not clearly understood— they offer a way of life. In return for the relatively good pay, job security and job opportunity which the big corporations afford, the employee is expected to give not only his talents and devotion, but also his conformity. A typical training pamphlet of the General Electric Corporation, which came to my attention recently, advised all professional employees, as part of their basic code of conduct, to avoid taking an interest in "controversial" questions.

> And there is some evidence that many college students who aspire to work for these corporations are taking this advice in advance. Some members of some faculties in some colleges and universities have suggested this attitude as the correct one for those who want to "get on" in the great bureaucracies which have grown up in the corporate world.

> In these new bureaucracies, there have developed the same faults and failings which usually characterize collectivist bureaucracies—the modeling of thought as well as action on the attitude of the "boss," the pressure for conformity, the red tape, the centralization of authority, and the reluctance to go out on a limb or take a chance. The engineers, the scientists and technologists, the lawyers, the statisticians, the public relations experts, the advertising experts, the merchandisers . . . all those working for Big Business and making up the corporate bureaucracies, are

66. Baltzell, The Protestant Establishment 135, 206, 315 (1964).

67. For an important effort to measure some of the social and political effects of big business, see F.T.C., The Economics of Firm Size, Market Structure and Social Performance (1980) (Conference papers on discretionary power, wealth and income distribution, community welfare, political influence, and worker satisfaction).

68. See Shepherd, Market Power and Racial Discrimination in White Collar Employment, 14 Antitrust Bull. 141 (1969); A. Kahn, 1 The Economics of Regulation 29–30 (1970).

being pressed into a single mold. The individual is supposed to disappear, becoming instead a unit on a "team" and a cog in a wheel. The individual is induced to fuse his identity into that of the corporation. He becomes what William H. Whyte has called "The Organization Man." [69]

The supermarket tomato—pallid, tough, tasteless, odorless, artificially reddened but not ripened—has been seen as the product of hyperorganization: large scale mechanized agribusiness and retail distribution through enterprises so large, so depersonalized, so governed by techniques of refrigeration and display, as to be incapable of handling the real thing:

> So the very quality for which people supposedly buy fresh tomatoes is precisely what an advanced system of research, growing and distribution has succeeded in filtering out as economically unimportant. And, instead of the simple fragrant, tender, juicy and glorious-tasting fruit we once knew, we see stacks of transparent sealed boxes containing sets of three or four pinkish globes . . . each of them embalmed in a thin coat of wax for cosmetic effect, and all uniformly dry, mealy, and insipid. [Whiteside, Tomatoes, The New Yorker, Jan. 24, 1977, at p. 61]

Whiteside ascertained that the Florida commercial tomato had been bred to resist an impact of 13.4 miles an hour, as compared with the standard of 5 m.p.h. for auto bumpers.

The plight of workers in large corporate bureaucracies or in large manufacturing plants may be cushioned however, by the often-noted correlations between higher wages and plant size, higher wages and larger firm size, and higher wages and concentration.[70] One study of the correlation between wage rates and industry concentration found a uniform decrease in wages from the largest to the smallest firm. This led the author to conclude:

> The finding of higher wages in the larger firms has implications for those concerned with antitrust and with small business policy. An increase in the share of small business in production obtained by antitrust measures against large firms or subsidies to small firms is likely to result in higher paid workers being displaced by lower paid workers. The findings here suggest that antitrust and small business programs may not be in the economic interests of the working classes, except to the extent they realize benefits as consumers.[71]

(3) *Governmental Deference to the Large Firm.* Adams and Hendry, reviewing decisions of the Interstate Commerce Commission affecting large and small trucking concerns, concluded that the large concerns were treated more favorably:

> It is as though the Commission, faced with a large, powerful, and obviously thriving enterprise, is reluctant to take any step which might bring fundamental change in its operations. Faced with obvious success, the

69. Lehman, The Plight of the Individual in a Big Business Economy, Address at the City College of New York (April 2, 1957). For case studies of pressures to conform leading individuals to commit illegal and unethical acts on behalf of the corporation, see R. Heilbroner, In The Name of Profit (1972); M. Mintz & J. Cohen, Power, Inc. (1976); J. P. Wright, On A Clear Day You Can See General Motors, Chap. 4 (1979). For case studies of individuals who resisted conforming, see R. Nader, P. Petkas & K. Blackwell, Whistle Blowing (1972).

70. F.T.C., The Economics of Firm Size, Market Structure and Social Performance, 326–383 (1980).

71. Miller, Large Firms Are Good for Their Workers: Manufacturing Wages as a Function of Firm Size and Concentration, 26 Antitrust Bulletin, 285, 145 (1981), © Copyright, Federal Legal Publications, Inc., 157 Chambers Street, New York, NY 10007.

Commission shrinks from following the logic of its convictions—from applying the spirit of the act it administers. To order drastic change in the affairs of smaller firms seems to offer less of an obstacle—perhaps the fear of mistakes is less if the magnitude of the possible error is smaller. Whatever the reason, the very existence of a large firm—its presence as a "going concern"—seems to protect it against any thoroughgoing change in its position or operating methods.[72]

Governments regularly "bail out" giant failing enterprises, thus affording them a form of insurance against bankruptcy. The community and the taxpayers thereby assume some of the normal risks of capitalists. The extension of substantial loan guarantees to Chrysler in an attempt to avoid the failure of a large employer and widespread losses to the financial community, suggests some firms may have become so large or regionally significant that society can not afford failure of the firm. On the other hand, can society afford the costs of propping up firms no longer able to compete? Does it make a difference what factors are causing the firm's difficulty? Mismanagement? Competition by foreign firms? An unforeseen rise in oil prices? Should a distinction be drawn between the failure of a large auto manufacturer and that of a large railroad (Penn-Central) or a city (New York City)?

Charles R. Ross, a former member of the Federal Power Commission, suggested a further reason for governmental deference to large firms in describing the process of his appointment to and experience on the Commission:

> As any veteran of regulation knows only too well, economic power and political power are indivisible. The latter is an indispensable product of the former. The larger the corporation, the greater the political leverage. The greater the diversity in interests of the corporation, the larger the number of prospective appointments to regulatory commissions that must be influenced.

> I cannot believe that I would have been reappointed to the Federal Power Commission finally in 1965, after sweating it out for a year or so, if Vermont had been the scene of extensive oil and gas operations, or if Vermont were controlled by a large regional utility system. Fortunately for me, Senator Aiken and Senator Prouty were perfectly free men and thus senatorial approval was forthcoming.

> . . . When my appointment came up—it was due to come up in June of 1964 . . ., a local trade publication, an oil and gas publication, said President Johnson's first act in the energy field was to see that Commissioner Ross would not be appointed. This was in November of 1963, and it was not until March of 1965 that President Johnson announced that I would be reappointed.

> The appointment is only the beginning. It is ironic, however, that if a State regulator has stepped on a few toes in trying to regulate and is being considered for appointment to a Federal agency, he is more than likely to be blackballed.

> In any case, when I appeared before the Senate Commerce Committee for appointment, one question was asked: "What do you know about the oil and gas business?" And I said: "I do not know anything." And I have heard since that that was probably the thing that allowed me to slide through without too much controversy.

72. Report for the Select Committee on Small Business, U.S. Senate, 85th Cong., 1st Sess. (1957) p. 6.

Once on the scene, the regulator is confronted by sweet-talking executives, tough, hard-hitting lawyers and experts . . .. The doors of exclusive clubs are opened to the innocent regulators. The lure of life in the lap of luxury with minions to anticipate every desire . . . becomes not just a dream but an actuality if one does not get too smart. On the other hand, if one does get too smart, it is back to the farm for our country bumpkin. The flattery, the press releases, the respect afforded an official regardless of performance, the cocktail parties, the utility and regulatory conventions at which comradeship between regulator and regulated is the No. 1 business, all combine to work imperceptively and irresistibly toward prolonging "Life on the Potomac" both during and after the period of regulatory appointment. The average intelligent regulator knows only too well how easy life may be, even if he goes home, if he has played ball. The prospect of important legal clients, the thoughts of large political donations and the realization that you can be the establishment's No. 1 boy back home or a part of the big scene here in Washington insure the "right decision" or, if not, at the very least the industry lawyer starts off with the dice loaded in his favor.[73]

(4) *Political Power, Corruption and Corporate Size.* In a society where government economic decisions can have a significant impact and the electoral success of political candidates is heavily dependent on campaign fundraising, large corporations commanding substantial sums of discretionary income exert a growing influence on the political process. Recent events of questionable corporate financial influence in political events have been summarized as follows:

Historians may well record the 1970s as the period when the political power of large corporations was unmasked, making it an issue of great political debate. First came revelations of improper domestic political conduct. International Telephone and Telegraph employed its considerable power in a well-orchestrated drive to receive a favorable antitrust consent decree. The Watergate investigations uncovered numerous illegal political contributions by large corporations. In April 1974, Mr. George M. Steinbrenner, chairman of the board of American Shipbuilding Corporation and owner of the New York Yankees, became the first corporate executive ever indicted on felony charges in connection with illegal corporate political contributions. The numerous disclosures of domestic corporate misconduct in political affairs soon were overshadowed by evidence of massive corporate bribery and political interventions in the affairs of other nations. The ITT efforts to overthrow the Allende government in Chile have been documented by the Senate Foreign Relations Committee. United Brands admitted it made a $1.3 million payment to an official of the Honduras government to reduce that country's banana tax; it subsequently admitted making payments of $750,000 to officials of the Italian government.

Northrop Corporation paid $30 million in agents' fees to influence sales of its aircraft to foreign countries. Of this, $450,000 was paid to two Saudi Arabian generals. It subsequently told the Securities Exchange Commission (SEC) it made improper commission payments to five countries. Gulf Oil disbursed $4 million to the ruling political party in South Korea; $110,000 to the President of Bolivia; and $350,000 to his political party. The SEC has charged Gulf with falsifying financial re-

---

73. Symposium on the Economic, Social and Political Effects of Economic Concentration, pp. 256–57, Subcommittee on Antitrust & Monopoly, Sen. Judiciary Comm., 92d Cong. 2d Sess. 1972.

ports to conceal $10.3 million in contributions to politicians at home and abroad from 1960–1972. Tenneco, Inc., the huge conglomerate, admitted it made payments to state and local officials in the United States as well as payments to foreign "consultants" to acquire "properties or materials from foreign governments."

Lockheed Aircraft Corporation paid huge amounts to foreign officials and political organizations to influence aircraft sales to foreign governments. In Saudi Arabia, alone, it has paid or committed $106 million in "commissions" since 1970, millions of which were funneled to Saudi officials through numbered accounts in Liechtenstein and Geneva. It subsequently disclosed making large bribes to government officials in Japan and Italy. It admitted making a $1.1 million payment to a "high Dutch official" whom the Dutch government identified as Prince Bernhard, husband of Queen Juliana. Lockheed's political clout in America had previously been demonstrated by its success in getting the Congress to guarantee a $195 million loan to Lockheed.

Perhaps no observer of the large modern corporation was surprised that America's largest industrial corporation apparently is also one of the top corporate contributors to foreign elections. During the last 10 years, Exxon Corp. has contributed more than $59 million to various political parties in Italy, alone. Inexplicably, Exxon even contributed $86,000 to the Italian Communist party. It also has admitted making political contributions in Canada and one other country, as well as payments in three unnamed countries to government officials and officials of government-owned companies.

America's second-largest industrial corporation, General Motors (GM), also joined the ranks of large corporations making political contributions abroad, although the contributions disclosed to date have been modest when compared to Exxon's. General Motors officers admitted giving contributions in the "five-figure" bracket to each of Canada's two major political parties in that country's latest elections. General Motors also made $250,000 in political contributions in Korea as well as $225,000 to the South Korean National Defense Fund, a quasi-government group that raises funds for national defense from "voluntary contributions." A stockholder proposal calling on GM to "affirm the non-partisanship of the corporation" was defeated, with 95.8 per cent of the votes cast against the motion.

Nor are these isolated cases of corporate bribery and illegal political activities at home and abroad. At least six drug companies have disclosed making bribes abroad. By early 1976, the SEC had received about 30 "corporate confessions" of wrongdoing and, according to one SEC official, "the number is climbing so rapidly no one has time to count." [74]

(5) *Queries.* If most people prefer the security of working for large corporations and are relatively indifferent to the alleged political, social, and other dangers of a highly centralized economy, should not the law encourage centralization? Is it demonstrable that centralization of political or economic power is hostile to progress in art, science, or philosophy? Consider the

74. Reprinted with permission of Macmillan Publishing Co., Inc. from The Structure of American Industry, 5th Edition, by Walter Adams, Ed., article "Conglomerates: A Nonindustry" by W. Mueller, 442, 458–60 Copyright © 1977 by Macmillan Publishing Co., Inc. See also, Salamon & Siegfried, "The Relationship Between Economic Structures and Political Power", in T. Duchesneau (Ed.), Competition in the U.S. Energy Industry, 381 (1975); Siegfried, Market Structure and the Effect of Political Influence, 3 Industrial Organizational Rev. 1 (1975).

roles played by princely or plutocratic patrons in ancient Greece, Renais-
sance Italy, Elizabethan England, Eighteenth Century France, and in latter-
day America with its philanthropic foundations (Ford, Rockefeller, Carnegie,
Guggenheim, Mellon) derived from giant industrial empires. Are antitrust
concepts and programs incompatible with the development of the welfare
state or national economic planning because of the resistance of antitrust to
centralization of economic decision-making? [75]

Why base political power and the vote, in theory at least, in the individual
voter? Is this any longer realistic or responsible when almost 50% of those
eligible to vote chose not to vote in the 1980 presidential election? Does it
make more sense for large corporations and other significant interest groups
(i.e., labor unions, trade associations, churches, N.A.A.C.P., etc.) to run our
political affairs by electing office holders and relegate individuals to exercise
their political rights in and through the interest groups they choose to join?
Is this the reality of modern political life anyway, despite its departure from
the ideals of Jeffersonian democracy?

(6) *Savings Under Capitalism and Communism.* Capitalism and communism may be regarded as alternative systems for withholding from the
worker a part of current earnings in order to augment savings, investment,
and production facilities, thus to increase the amount available for consumption later. From this point of view capitalism could be said to be mainly
relying on voluntary postponement of consumption, using the incentive of
interest rates and profit possibilities. Communism relies mainly on involuntary postponement, since wage rates and prices are set by the state. But
there are elements of involuntary saving in capitalist societies, as when monopoly or oligopoly is permitted to augment corporate profits. So also there
are elements of voluntarism in communist saving systems. From the point
of view of building up production facilities, either system may have advantages depending on the social and economic structure of a given society. Obviously voluntary saving will be more feasible and attractive in an affluent
society. Sterner measures may be unavoidable in a society where most people are so miserably poor that they can never aspire to save, to live off accumulated earnings, or to become owners or creditors of economic enterprises.
For such people also the appeal of a doctrine that appears to eliminate
"unearned income"—interests and profits, the incentives of capitalism—presumably for distribution among workers, has an understandable magnetism.
Is there a social interest in the United States, England, Italy, or Sweden in
encouraging monopoly profits that build up large accumulations of capital in
a politically painless way, if such accumulations then become subject to socialization through taxes or through the sense of public responsibility of corporate managers? Can the gigantic capitalist successes of Nineteenth Century America be attributed in part to the non-existence of antitrust laws?

---

75. See Walden, Antitrust in the Posi-
tive State, 41 Tex.L.Rev. 741 (1963) and
42 Tex.L.Rev. 602 (1964); cf. Schwartz,
Antitrust in the Age of Planning, in
Crossroads Papers (1965); G. Lodge, The
New American Ideology (1975).

B. MONOPOLY UNDER THE SHERMAN ACT

1. SUBSTANTIVE ELEMENTS OF THE OFFENSE OF MONOPOLIZATION

Section 2 of the Sherman Act,[76] on its face, appears to delineate at least three separate offenses: (1) monopolizing; (2) attempting to monopolize; or, (3) combining or conspiring to monopolize "any part of trade or commerce." In this subsection we consider the offense of monopolizing any part of trade or commerce.

It should be noted that the statute is not limited to a seller monopolizing trade, but may also include a buyer monopolizing trade or commerce. The courts have generally identified monopolization as the possession or the exercise of the power to fix prices or exclude competition. In some cases the possession of the power under the circumstances is deemed to be sufficient, in the absence of excuse or justification, to prove the offense. Other cases appear to stress the exercise of the power to fix prices or exclude competition as proof of the offense.

In either case, the identification of the power, the geographic locus of its possession or exercise, and the identity of the product or service said to be monopolized are considered legally and economically significant issues in the analysis. The broad analytical outline of proving the offense is often described as requiring: "(1) Proof of relevant product and geographic markets; (2) a showing of monopoly power . . . to fix prices or exclude competition in the markets defined; and (3) some additional element of conduct in either acquiring, exercising or maintaining monopoly power in the affirmative sense of conduct with a purpose or effect to acquire or maintain a monopoly or in the negative sense of an unexplained and unjustified possession of persistent substantial monopoly power which competition might otherwise be expected to erode." [77]

Stating the generality and exploring its meaning and consequences in a specific factual context are, of course, two different things. In the context of a particular industry how does one identify the relevant markets, both product and geographic, in which to look for monopoly power? When is it appropriate to infer monopoly power is present or is being exercised? Why is added evidence of conduct necessary to prove the offense and what facts will suffice to meet this element of the offense? How do each of the elements of the analysis interact in light of the facts unique to the case before the court?

76. Supra p. 8.

77. Flynn, Monopolization Under the Sherman Act: The Third Wave and Beyond, 26 Antitrust Bull. 1, 10–11 (1981).

All these are but introductory questions in a monopolization case. They are also questions which cannot be answered in the abstract or pinned down by rigid and static definitions divorced from the controversies in which they arise, the underlying policies of the law, or the values and skills of judges charged with answering them in specific cases.

UNITED STATES v. ALUMINUM CO. OF AMERICA

Circuit Court of Appeals of the United States, Second Circuit, 1945.
148 F.2d 416.

L. HAND, CIRCUIT JUDGE. . . . "Alcoa" is a corporation, organized under the laws of Pennsylvania on September 18, 1888; its original name, "Pittsburgh Reduction Company", was changed to its present one on January 1, 1907. It has always been engaged in the production and sale of "ingot" aluminum, and since 1895 also in the fabrication of the metal into many finished and semi-finished articles. It has proliferated into a great number of subsidiaries, created at various times between the years 1900 and 1929, as the business expanded. Aluminum is a chemical element; it is never found in a free state, being always in chemical combination with oxygen. One form of this combination is known as alumina; and for practical purposes the most available material from which alumina can be extracted is an ore called "bauxite". Aluminum was isolated as a metal more than a century ago, but not until about 1886 did it become commercially practicable to eliminate the oxygen, so that it could be exploited industrially. One, Hall, discovered a process by which this could be done in that year, and got a patent on April 2, 1889, which he assigned to "Alcoa", which thus secured a legal monopoly of the manufacture of the pure aluminum until on April 2, 1906, when this patent expired. Meanwhile Bradley had invented a process by which the smelting could be carried on without the use of external heat, as had theretofore been thought necessary; and for this improvement he too got a patent on February 2, 1892. Bradley's improvement resulted in great economy in manufacture, so that, although after April 2, 1906, anyone could manufacture aluminum by the Hall process, for practical purposes no one could compete with Bradley or with his licensees until February 2, 1909, when Bradley's patent also expired. On October 31, 1903, "Alcoa" and the assignee of the Bradley patent entered into a contract by which "Alcoa" was granted an exclusive license under that patent, in exchange for "Alcoa's" promise to sell to the assignee a stated amount of aluminum at a discount of ten per cent below "Alcoa's" published list price, and always to sell at a discount of five per cent greater than that which "Alcoa" gave to any other jobber. Thus until February 2, 1909, "Alcoa" had either a monopoly of the manufacture of "virgin" aluminum ingot, or the monopoly of a process which eliminated all competition.

The extraction of aluminum from alumina requires a very large amount of electrical energy, which is ordinarily, though not always, most cheaply obtained from water power. Beginning at least as early as 1895, "Alcoa" secured such power from several companies by contracts, containing in at least three instances, covenants binding the power companies not to sell or let power to anyone else for the manufacture of aluminum. "Alcoa"—either itself or by a subsidiary—also entered into four successive "cartels" with foreign manufacturers of aluminum by which, in exchange for certain limitations upon its import into foreign countries, it secured covenants from the foreign producers, either not to import into the United States at all, or to do so under restrictions, which in some cases involved the fixing of prices. These "cartels" and restrictive covenants and certain other practices were the subject of a suit filed by the United States against "Alcoa" on May 16, 1912, in which a decree was entered by consent on June 7, 1912, declaring several of these covenants unlawful and enjoining their performance; and also declaring invalid other restrictive covenants obtained before 1903 relating to the sale of alumina. ("Alcoa" failed at this time to inform the United States of several restrictive covenants in water-power contracts; its justification— which the judge accepted—being that they had been forgotten.) "Alcoa" did not begin to manufacture alumina on its own behalf until the expiration of a dominant patent in 1903. In that year it built a very large alumina plant at East St. Louis, where all of its alumina was made until 1939, when it opened another plant in Mobile, Alabama.

None of the foregoing facts are in dispute, and the most important question in the case is whether the monopoly in "Alcoa's" production of "virgin" ingot, secured by the two patents until 1909, and in part perpetuated between 1909 and 1912 by the unlawful practices, forbidden by the decree of 1912, continued for the ensuing twenty-eight years; and whether, if it did, it was unlawful under § 2 of the Sherman Act, 15 U.S.C.A. § 2. It is undisputed that throughout this period "Alcoa" continued to be the single producer of "virgin" ingot in the United States; and the plaintiff argues that this without more was enough to make it an unlawful monopoly. It also takes an alternative position: that in any event during this period "Alcoa" consistently pursued unlawful exclusionary practices, which made its dominant position certainly unlawful, even though it would not have been, had it been retained only by "natural growth." Finally, it asserts that many of these practices were of themselves unlawful, as contracts in restraint of trade under § 1 of the Act, 15 U.S.C.A. § 1. "Alcoa's" position is that the fact that it alone continued to make "virgin" ingot in this country did not, and does not, give it a monopoly of the market; that it was always subject to the competition of imported "virgin" ingot, and of what is called "secondary" ingot; and that even if it had not been, its monopoly would not have been retained by unlawful means, but would have been the result of a growth which the Act does not forbid, even when it results in a monopoly. We shall first consider the amount and character of this competition; next, how far it established a monopoly; and finally, if it did, whether that monopoly was unlawful under § 2 of the Act.

From 1902 onward until 1928 "Alcoa" was making ingot in Canada through a wholly owned subsidiary; so much of this as it imported into the United States it is proper to include with what it produced here. In the year 1912 the sum of these two items represented nearly ninety-one per cent of the total amount of "virgin" ingot available for sale in this country. This percentage varied year by year up to and including 1938: in 1913 it was about seventy-two per cent; in 1921 about sixty-eight per cent; in 1922 about seventy-two; with these exceptions it was always over eighty per cent of the total and for the last five years 1934–1938 inclusive it averaged over ninety per cent. The effect of such a proportion of the production upon the market we reserve for the time being, for it will be necessary first to consider the nature and uses of "secondary" ingot, the name by which the industry knows ingot made from aluminum scrap. This is of two sorts, though for our purposes it is not important to distinguish between them. One of these is the clippings and trimmings of "sheet" aluminum, when patterns are cut out of it, as a suit is cut from a bolt of cloth. The chemical composition of these is obviously the same as that of the "sheet" from which they come; and, although they are likely to accumulate dust or other dirt in the factory, this may be removed by well known processes. If a record of the original composition of the "sheet" has been preserved, this scrap may be remelted into new ingot, and used again for the same purpose. It is true that some of the witnesses—Arthur V. Davis, the chairman of the board of "Alcoa" among them—testified that at each remelting aluminum takes up some new oxygen which progressively deteriorates its quality for those uses in which purity is important; but other witnesses thought that it had become commercially feasible to remove this impurity, and the judge made no finding on the subject. Since the plaintiff has the burden of proof, we shall assume that there is no such deterioration. Nevertheless, there is an appreciable "sales resistance" even to this kind of scrap, and for some uses (airplanes and cables among them), fabricators absolutely insist upon "virgin": just why is not altogether clear. The other source of scrap is aluminum which has once been fabricated and the article, after being used, is discarded and sent to the junk heap, as for example, cooking utensils, like kettles and pans, and the pistons or crank cases of motorcars. These are made with a substantial alloy and to restore the metal to its original purity costs more than it is worth. However, if the alloy is known both in quality and amount, scrap, when remelted, can be used again for the same purpose as before. In spite of this, as in the case of clippings and trimmings, the industry will ordinarily not accept ingot so salvaged upon the same terms as "virgin." There are some seventeen companies which scavenge scrap of all sorts, clean it, remelt it, test it for its composition, make it into ingots and sell it regularly to the trade. There is in all these salvage operations some inevitable waste of actual material: not only does a certain amount of aluminum escape altogether, but in the salvaging process itself some is skimmed off as scum and thrown away. The judge found that the return of fabricated products to the market as "secondary" varied from five to twenty-five years, depending upon the article; but he did not, and no doubt could not, find how many times the cycle could be repeated before the metal was finally used up.

There are various ways of computing "Alcoa's" control of the aluminum market—as distinct from its production—depending upon what one regards as competing in that market. The judge figured its share—during the years 1929–1938, inclusive—as only about thirty-three per cent; to do so he included "secondary," and excluded that part of "Alcoa's" own production which it fabricated and did not therefore sell as ingot. If, on the other hand, "Alcoa's" total production, fabricated and sold, be included, and balanced against the sum of imported "virgin" and "secondary," its share of the market was in the neighborhood of sixty-four per cent for that period. The percentage we have already mentioned—over ninety—results only if we both include all "Alcoa's" production and exclude "secondary". That percentage is enough to constitute a monopoly; it is doubtful whether sixty or sixty-four percent would be enough; and certainly thirty-three per cent is not. Hence it is necessary to settle what he [sic] shall treat as competing in the ingot market. That part of its production which "Alcoa" itself fabricates, does not of course ever reach the market as ingot; and we recognize that it is only when a restriction of production either inevitably affects prices, or is intended to do so, that it violates § 1 of the Act. However, even though we were to assume that a monopoly is unlawful under § 2 only in case it controls prices, the ingot fabricated by "Alcoa," necessarily had a direct effect upon the ingot market. All ingot—with trifling exceptions—is used to fabricate intermediate, or end, products; and therefore all intermediate, or end, products which "Alcoa" fabricates and sells, pro tanto reduce the demand for ingot itself. The situation is the same, though reversed, as in Standard Oil Co. v. United States, 221 U.S. 1, 77, 31 S.Ct. 502, 523, 55 L.Ed. 619, where the court answered the defendants' argument that they had no control over the crude oil by saying that "as substantial power over the crude product was the inevitable result of the absolute control which existed over the refined product, the monopolization of the one carried with it the power to control the other." We cannot therefore agree that the computation of the percentage of "Alcoa's" control over the ingot market should not include the whole of its ingot production.

As to "secondary," as we have said, for certain purposes the industry will not accept it at all; but for those for which it will, the difference in price is ordinarily not very great; the judge found that it was between one and two cents a pound, hardly enough margin on which to base a monopoly. Indeed, there are times when all differential disappears, and "secondary" will actually sell at a higher price: i.e. when there is a supply available which contains just the alloy that a fabricator needs for the article which he proposes to make. Taking the industry as a whole, we can say nothing more definite than that, although "secondary" does not compete at all in some uses, (whether because of "sales resistance" only, or because of actual metallurgical inferiority), for most purposes it competes upon a substantial equality with "virgin."   On these facts the judge found that "every pound of secondary or scrap aluminum which is sold in commerce displaces a pound of virgin aluminum which otherwise would, or might have been, sold." We agree: so far as "secondary" supplies the demand of such fabricators as will accept it, it increases the amount of "virgin" which must seek sale elsewhere; and it therefore results that the supply of that part of the demand which will accept only "virgin" becomes greater in proportion as "secondary" drives away "virgin" from the demand which will accept "secondary." (This is indeed the same argument which we used a moment ago to include in the supply that part of "virgin" which "Alcoa" fabricates; it is not apparent to us why the judge did not think it applicable to that item as well.) At any given moment therefore "secondary" competes with "virgin" in the ingot market; further, it can, and probably does, set a limit or "ceiling" beyond which the price of "virgin" cannot go, for the cost of its production will in the end depend only upon the expense of scavenging and reconditioning. It might seem for this reason that in estimating "Alcoa's" control over the ingot market, we ought to include the supply of "secondary," as the judge did. Indeed, it may be thought a paradox to say that anyone has the monopoly of a market in which at all times he must meet a competition that limits his price. We shall show that it is not.

In the case of a monopoly of any commodity which does not disappear in use and which can be salvaged, the supply seeking sale at any moment will be made up of two components: (1) the part which the putative monopolist can immediately produce and sell; and (2) the part which has been, or can be, reclaimed out of what he has produced and sold in the past. By hypothesis he presently controls the first of these components; the second he has controlled in the past, although he no longer does. During the period when he did control the second, if he was aware of his interest, he was guided, not alone by its effect at that time upon the market, but by his knowledge that some part of it was likely to be reclaimed and seek the future market. That consideration will to some extent always affect his production until he decides to abandon the business, or for some other reason ceases to be concerned with the future market. Thus, in the case at bar, "Alcoa" always knew that the future supply of ingot would be made up in part of what it produced at the time, and, if it was as far-sighted as it proclaims itself, that consideration must have had its share in determining how much to produce. How accurately it could forecast the effect of present production upon the future market is another matter. Experience, no doubt, would help; but it makes no difference that it had to guess; it is enough that it had an inducement to make the best guess it could, and that it would regulate that part of the future supply, so far as it should turn out to have guessed right. The competition of "secondary" must therefore be disregarded, as soon as we consider the position of "Alcoa" over a period of years; it was as much within "Alcoa's" control as was the production of the "virgin" from which it had been derived. This can be well illustrated by the case of a lawful monopoly: e.g. a patent or a copyright. The monopolist cannot prevent those to whom he sells from reselling at whatever prices they please. Nor can he prevent their reconditioning articles worn by use, unless they in fact make a new article. At any moment his control over the market will therefore be limited by that part of what he has formerly sold, which the price he now charges may bring upon the market, as second hand or reclaimed articles. Yet no one would think of saying that for this reason the patent or the copyright did not confer a monopoly. . . .

We conclude therefore that "Alcoa's" control over the ingot market must be reckoned at over ninety per cent; that being the proportion which its production bears to imported "virgin" ingot. If the fraction which it did not supply were the produce of domestic manufacture there could be no doubt that this percentage gave it a monopoly—lawful or unlawful, as the case might be. The producer of so large a proportion of the supply has complete control within certain limits. It is true that, if by raising the price he reduces the amount which can be marketed—as always, or almost always, happens—he may invite the expansion of the small producers who will try to fill the place left open; nevertheless, not only is there an inevitable lag in this, but the large producer is in a strong position to check such competition; and, indeed, if he has retained his old plant and personnel, he can inevitably do so. There are indeed limits to his power; substitutes are available for almost all commodities, and to raise the price enough is to evoke them. Moreover, it is difficult and expensive to keep idle any part of a plant or of personnel; and any drastic contraction of the market will offer increasing temptation to the small producers to expand. But these limitations also exist when a single producer occupies the whole market: even then, his hold will depend upon his moderation in exerting his immediate power.

The case at bar is however different, because, for aught that appears there may well have been a practically unlimited supply of imports as the price of ingot rose. Assuming that there was no agreement between "Alcoa" and foreign producers not to import, they sold what could bear the handicap of the tariff and the cost of transportation. For the period of eighteen years—1920–1937—they sold at times a little above "Alcoa's" prices, at times a little under; but there was substantially no gross difference between what they received and what they would have received, had they sold uniformly at "Alcoa's" prices. While the record is silent, we may therefore assume—the plaintiff having the burden—that, had "Alcoa" raised its prices, more ingot would have been imported. Thus there is a distinction between domestic and foreign competition: the first is limited in quantity, and can increase only by an increase in plant and personnel; the second is of producers who, we must assume, produce much more than they import, and whom a rise in price will presumably induce immediately to divert to the American market what they have been selling elsewhere. It is entirely consistent with the evidence that it was the threat of greater foreign imports which kept "Alcoa's" prices where they were, and prevented it from exploiting its advantage as sole domestic producer; indeed, it is hard to resist the conclusion that potential imports did put a "ceiling" upon those prices. Nevertheless, within the limits afforded by the tariff and the cost of transportation, "Alcoa" was free to raise its prices as it chose, since it was free from domestic competition, save as it drew other metals into the market as substitutes.

Was this a monopoly within the meaning of § 2? The judge found that, over the whole half century of its existence, "Alcoa's" profits upon capital invested, after payment of income taxes, had been only about ten per cent, and, although the plaintiff puts this figure a little higher, the difference is negligible. The plaintiff does indeed challenge the propriety of computing profits upon a capital base which included past earnings that have been allowed to remain in the business; but as to that it is plainly wrong. An argument is indeed often made in the case of a public utility, that the "rate-base" should not include earnings re-invested which were greater than a fair profit upon the actual investment outstanding at the time. That argument depends, however, upon the premise that at common law—even in the absence of any commission or other authority empowered to enforce a "reasonable" rate—it is the duty of a public utility to charge no more than such a rate, and that any excess is unlawfully collected. Perhaps one might use the same argument in the case of a monopolist; but it would be a condition that one should show what part of the past earnings were extortionate, for not all that even a monopolist may earn is caput lupinum. The plaintiff made no such attempt, and its distinction between capital, "contributed by consumers" and capital, "contributed by shareholders," has no basis in law. "Alcoa's" earnings belonged to its shareholders, they were free to withdraw them and spend them, or to leave them in the business. If they chose to leave them, it was no different from contributing new capital out of their pockets. This assumed, it would be hard to say that "Alcoa" had made exorbitant profits on ingot, if it is proper to allocate the profit upon the whole business proportionately among all its products—ingot, and fabrications from ingot. A profit of ten per cent in such an industry, dependent, in part at any rate, upon continued tariff protection, and subject to the vicissitudes of new demands, to the obsolescence of plant and process—which can never be accurately gauged in advance—to the chance that substitutes may at any moment be discovered which will reduce the demand, and to the other hazards which attend all industry; a profit of ten per cent, so conditioned, could hardly be considered extortionate.

There are however, two answers to any such excuse; and the first is that the profit on ingot was not necessarily the same as the profit of the business as a whole, and that we have no means of allocating its proper share to ingot. It is true that the mill cost appears; but obviously it would be unfair to "Alcoa" to take, as the measure of its profit on ingot, the difference between selling price and mill cost; and yet we have nothing else. It may be retorted that it was for the plaintiff to prove what was the profit upon ingot in accordance with the general burden of proof. We think not. Having proved that "Alcoa" had a monopoly of the domestic ingot market, the plaintiff had gone far enough; if it was an excuse, that "Alcoa" had not abused its power, it lay upon "Alcoa" to prove that it had not. But the whole issue is irrelevant anyway, for it is no excuse for "monopolizing" a market that the monopoly has not been used to extract from the consumer more than a "fair" profit. The Act has wider purposes. Indeed, even though we disregarded all but economic considerations, it would by no means follow that such concentration of producing power is to be desired, when it has not been used extortionately. Many people believe that possession of unchallenged economic power deadens initiative, discourages thrift and depresses energy; that immunity from competition is a narcotic, and rivalry is a stimulant, to industrial progress; that the spur of constant stress is necessary to counteract an inevitable disposition to let well enough alone. Such people believe that competitors, versed in the craft as no consumer can be, will be quick to detect opportunities for saving and new shifts in production, and be eager to profit by them. In any event the mere fact that a producer, having command of the domestic market, has not been able to make more than a "fair" profit, is no evidence that a "fair" profit could not have been made at lower prices. True, it might have been thought adequate to condemn only those monopolies which could not show that they had exercised the highest possible ingenuity, had adopted every possible economy, had anticipated every conceivable improvement, stimulated every possible demand. No doubt, that would be one way of dealing with the matter, although it would imply constant scrutiny and constant supervision, such as courts are unable to provide. Be that as it may, that was not the way that Congress chose; it did not condone "good trusts" and condemn "bad" ones; it forbad all. Moreover, in so doing it was not necessarily actuated by economic motives alone. It is possible, because of its indirect social or moral effect, to prefer a system of small producers, each dependent for his success upon his own skill and character, to one in which the great mass of those engaged must accept the direction of a few. These considerations, which we have suggested only as possible purposes of the Act, we think the decisions prove to have been in fact its purposes.

It is settled, at least as to § 1, that there are some contracts restricting competition which are unlawful, no matter how beneficent they may be; no industrial exigency will justify them; they are absolutely forbidden. Chief Justice Taft said as much of contracts dividing a territory among producers, in the often quoted passage of his opinion in the Circuit Court of Appeals in United States v. Addystone Pipe & Steel Co., 6 Cir., 85 F. 271, 291. The Supreme Court unconditionally condemned all contracts fixing prices in United States v.

Trenton Potteries Co., 273 U.S. 392, 397, 398, 47 S.Ct. 377, 71 L.Ed. 700, ... Starting, however, with the authoritative premise that all contracts fixing prices are unconditionally prohibited, the only possible difference between them and a monopoly is that while a monopoly necessarily involves an equal, or even greater, power to fix prices, its mere existence might be thought not to constitute an exercise of that power. That distinction is nevertheless purely formal; it would be valid only so long as the monopoly remained wholly inert; it would disappear as soon as the monopoly began to operate; for, when it did—that is, as soon as it began to sell at all—it must sell at some price and the only price at which it could sell is a price which it itself fixed. Thereafter the power and its exercise must needs coalesce. Indeed it would be absurd to condemn such contracts unconditionally, and not to extend the condemnation to monopolies; for the contracts are only steps toward that entire control which monopoly confers: they are really partial monopolies. . . . [T]here can be no doubt that the vice of restrictive contracts and of monopoly is really one, it is the denial to commerce of the supposed protection of competition. To repeat, if the earlier stages are proscribed, when they are parts of a plan, the mere projecting of which condemns them unconditionally, the realization of the plan itself must also be proscribed.

We have been speaking only of the economic reasons which forbid monopoly; but, as we have already implied, there are others, based upon the belief that great industrial consolidations are inherently undesirable, regardless of their economic results. In the debates in Congress Senator Sherman himself in the passage quoted in the margin showed that among the purposes of Congress in 1890 was a desire to put an end to great aggregations of capital because of the helplessness of the individual before them.[78] That Congress is still of the same mind appears in the Surplus Property Act of 1944, 50 U.S. C.A.Appendix § 1611 et seq., and the Small Business Mobilization Act, 50 U.S.C.A.Appendix § 1101 et seq. Not only does § 2(d) of the first declare it to be one aim of that statute to "preserve the competitive position of small business concerns," but § 18 is given over to directions designed to "preserve and strengthen" their position. In United States v. Hutcheson, 312 U.S. 219, 61 S.Ct. 463, 85 L.Ed. 788, a later statute in pari materia was considered to throw a cross light

78. [Court's footnote.] "If the concerted powers of this combination are intrusted to a single man, it is a kingly prerogative, inconsistent with our form of government, and should be subject to the strong resistance of the State and national authorities . . . ." 21 Cong.Record, 2457.

"The popular mind is agitated with problems that may disturb social order, and among them all none is more threatening than the inequality of condition, of wealth, and opportunity that has grown within a single generation out of the concentration of capital into vast combinations to control production and trade and to break down competition. These combinations already defy or control powerful transportation corporations and reach State authorities. They reach out their Briarean arms to every part of our country. They are imported from abroad. Congress alone can deal with them, and if we are unwilling or unable there will soon be a trust for every production and a master to fix the price for every necessity of life. . . ." 21 Cong.Record, 2460. See also 21 Cong.Record, 2598.

upon the Anti-trust Acts, illuminating enough even to override an earlier ruling of the court. Throughout the history of these statutes it has been constantly assumed that one of their purposes was to perpetuate and preserve, for its own sake and in spite of possible cost, an organization of industry in small units which can effectively compete with each other. We hold that "Alcoa's" monopoly of ingot was of the kind covered by § 2.

It does not follow because "Alcoa" had such a monopoly, that it "monopolized" the ingot market: it may not have achieved monopoly; monopoly may have been thrust upon it. If it had been a combination of existing smelters which united the whole industry and controlled the production of all aluminum ingot, it would certainly have "monopolized" the market. In several decisions the Supreme Court has decreed the dissolution of such combinations, although they had engaged in no unlawful trade practices. . . . We may start therefore with the premise that to have combined ninety per cent of the producers of ingot would have been to "monopolize" the ingot market; and, so far as concerns the public interest, it can make no difference whether an existing competition is put an end to, or whether prospective competition is prevented. The Clayton Act itself speaks in that alternative: "to injure, destroy, or prevent competition." § 13(a), 15 U.S.C.A. Nevertheless, it is unquestionably true that from the very outset the courts have at least kept in reserve the possibility that the origin of a monopoly may be critical in determining its legality; and for this they had warrant in some of the congressional debates which accompanied the passage of the Act. This notion has usually been expressed by saying that size does not determine guilt; that there must be some "exclusion" of competitors; that the growth must be something else than "natural" or "normal"; that there must be a "wrongful intent," or some other specific intent; or that some "unduly" coercive means must be used. At times there has been emphasis upon the use of the active verb, "monopolize," as the judge noted in the case at bar. What engendered these compunctions is reasonably plain; persons may unwittingly find themselves in possession of a monopoly, automatically so to say: that is, without having intended either to put an end to existing competition, or to prevent competition from arising when none had existed; they may become monopolists by force of accident. Since the Act makes "monopolizing" a crime, as well as a civil wrong, it would be not only unfair, but presumably contrary to the intent of Congress, to include such instances. A market may, for example, be so limited that it is impossible to produce at all and meet the cost of production except by a plant large enough to supply the whole demand. Or there may be changes in taste or in cost which drive out all but one purveyor. A single producer may be the survivor out of a group of active competitors, merely by virtue of his superior skill, foresight and industry. In such cases a strong argument can be made that, although the result may expose the public to the evils of monopoly, the Act does not mean to condemn the resultant of those very forces which it is its prime object to foster: finis opus coronat. The successful competitor, having been urged to compete, must not be turned upon when he wins. The most extreme expression of this view is in United States v. United States Steel Corporation, 251 U.S. 417, 40 S.Ct. 293, 64 L.Ed. 343, and which Sanford, J., in part repeated in United States v. International Harvester Corporation, 274 U.S. 693, 708, 47 S.Ct. 748, 71 L.Ed. 1302. It so chances that in both instances the corporation had less than two-thirds of the production in its hands, and the language quoted was not necessary to the decision; so that even if it had not later been modified, it has not the authority of an actual decision. But, whatever authority it does have was modified by the gloss of Cardozo, J., in United States v. Swift & Co., 286 U.S. 106, p. 116, 52 S.Ct. 460, 463, 76 L.Ed. 999, when he said, "Mere size . . . is not an offense against the Sherman Act unless magnified to the point at which it amounts to a monopoly . . . but size carries with it an opportunity for abuse that is not to be ignored when the opportunity is proved to have been utilized in the past." "Alcoa's" size was "magnified" to make it a "monopoly"; indeed, it has never been anything else; and its size, not only offered it an "opportunity for abuse," but it "utilized" its size for "abuse," as can easily be shown.

It would completely misconstrue "Alcoa's" position in 1940 to hold that it was the passive beneficiary of a monopoly, following upon an involuntary elimination of competitors by automatically operative economic forces. Already in 1909, when its last lawful monopoly ended, it sought to strengthen its position by unlawful practices, and these concededly continued until 1912. In that year it had two plants in New York, at which it produced less than 42 million pounds of ingot; in 1934 it had five plants (the original two, enlarged; one in Tennessee; one in North Carolina; one in Washington), and its production had risen to about 327 million pounds, an increase of almost eightfold. Meanwhile not a pound of ingot had been produced by anyone else in the United States. This increase and this continued and undisturbed control did not fall undesigned into "Alcoa's" lap; obviously it could not have done so. It could only have resulted, as it did result, from a persistent determination to maintain the control, with which it found itself vested in 1912. There were at least one or two abortive attempts to enter the industry, but "Alcoa" effectively anticipated and forestalled all competition, and succeeded in holding the field alone. True, it stimulated demand and opened new uses for the metal, but not without making sure that it could supply what it had evoked. There is no dispute as to this; "Alcoa" avows it as evidence of the skill, energy and initiative with which it has always conducted its business; as a reason why, having won its way by fair means, it should be commended, and not dismembered. We need charge it with no moral derelictions after 1912; we may assume that all it claims for itself is true. The only question is whether it falls within the exception established in favor of those who do not seek, but cannot avoid,[*]

[*] How could Alcoa have "avoided" monopoly? What lawful activities would you have advised it to spurn in order to forestall this decision that it was an unlawful monopoly?

the control of a market. It seems to us that that question scarcely survives its statement. It was not inevitable that it should always anticipate increases in the demand for ingot and be prepared to supply them. Nothing compelled it to keep doubling and redoubling its capacity before others entered the field. It insists that it never excluded competitors; but we can think of no more effective exclusion than progressively to embrace each new opportunity as it opened, and to face every newcomer with new capacity already geared into a great organization, having the advantage of experience, trade connections and the elite of personnel. Only in case we interpret "exclusion" as limited to manoeuvres not honestly industrial, but actuated solely by a desire to prevent competition, can such a course, indefatigably pursued, be deemed not "exclusionary." So to limit it would in our judgment emasculate the Act; would permit just such consolidations as it was designed to prevent.

"Alcoa" answers that it positively assisted competitors, instead of discouraging them. That may be true as to fabricators of ingot; but what of that? They were its market for ingot, and it is charged only with a monopoly of ingot. We can find no instance of its helping prospective ingot manufacturers. . . .**

We disregard any question of "intent." Relatively early in the history of the Act—1905—Holmes, J., in Swift & Co. v. United States, supra, (196 U.S. 375, 396, 25 S.Ct. 276, 49 L.Ed. 518), explained this aspect of the Act in a passage often quoted. Although the primary evil was monopoly, the Act also covered preliminary steps, which, if continued, would lead to it. These may do no harm of themselves; but, if they are initial moves in a plan or scheme which, carried out, will result in monopoly, they are dangerous and the law will nip them in the bud. For this reason conduct falling short of monopoly, is not illegal unless it is part of a plan to monopolize, or to gain such other control of a market as is equally forbidden. To make it so, the plaintiff must prove what in the criminal law is known as a "specific in-

Cf. Du Pont decision to license Olin Industries, Inc. to produce cellophane under Du Pont's patents. The following account is from the Washington Post, No. 11, 1949, p. 1, reporting an explanation given by a Du Pont official: "During the war and since, except for a short period," he said, "there has been a shortage of cellophane. Under normal circumstances duPont would have built additional capacity. However the Department of Justice filed suit against the company, alleging that it already controlled so large a percentage of the market as to be guilty of monopoly. This being the case, we did not feel warranted in spending the stockholders' money in expansion in this field." The contract with Olin, he said, was the outcome of efforts for more than a year to find a company willing and able to invest at least the 20 million dollars considered necessary for a company to enter the field.

The government's monopoly suit failed legally, but may have won economically by causing Du Pont to forego tightening its monopoly of cellophane and licensing Olin to manufacture the product. See Waldman, The du Pont Cellophane Case Revisited: An Analysis of the Indirect Effects of Antitrust Policy on Market Structure and Performance, 25 Antitrust Bull. 805 (1980). If competition can establish itself only with the help of the existing dominant concern, does that not testify to the monopoly power of that concern?

** Does this mean that evidence of "helping" would have counted in favor of Alcoa? Is there an obligation on large companies to help their "competitors"?

tent"; an intent which goes beyond the mere intent to do the act. By far the greatest part of the fabulous record piled up in the case at bar, was concerned with proving such an intent. The plaintiff was seeking to show that many transactions, neutral on their face, were not in fact necessary to the development of "Alcoa's" business, and had no motive except to exclude others and perpetuate its hold upon the ingot market. Upon that effort success depended in case the plaintiff failed to satisfy the court that it was unnecessary under § 2 to convict "Alcoa" of practices unlawful of themselves. The plaintiff has so satisfied us, and the issue of intent ceases to have any importance; no intent is relevant except that which is relevant to any liability, criminal or civil: i.e. an intent to bring about the forbidden act. Note 59 of United States v. Socony-Vacuum Oil Co., supra, 310 U.S. 150 on page 226, 60 S.Ct. 811 on page 845, 84 L.Ed. 1129, on which "Alcoa" appears so much to rely, is in no sense to the contrary. Douglas, J., was answering the defendants' argument that, assuming that a combination had attempted to fix prices, it had never had the power to do so, for there was too much competing oil. His answer was that the plan was unlawful, even if the parties did not have the power to fix prices, provided that they intended to do so; and it was to drive home this that he contrasted the case then before the court with monopoly, where power was a necessary element. In so doing he said: "An intent and a power . . . are then necessary," which he at once followed by quoting the passage we have just mentioned from Swift & Co. v. United States, supra, 196 U.S. 375, 25 S.Ct. 276, 49 L.Ed. 518. In order to fall within § 2, the monopolist must have both the power to monopolize, and the intent to monopolize. To read the passage as demanding any "specific" intent, makes nonsense of it, for no monopolist monopolizes unconscious of what he is doing. So here, "Alcoa" meant to keep, and did keep, that complete and exclusive hold upon the ingot market with which it started. That was to "monopolize" that market, however innocently it otherwise proceeded. So far as the judgment held that it was not within § 2, it must be reversed.

II—Alcoa's Unlawful Practices

[At this point the court discussed alleged exclusionary practices of Alcoa, e.g. the purchase of Canadian waterpower sites which were about to be acquired by persons interested in aluminum production. Alcoa officers had testified that these purchases were made to provide for the company's own expanding needs and without knowledge of the purchase negotiations of other persons. The Circuit Court of Appeals refused to overrule the trial judge's ruling for the defendant on this issue of motives.

The trial court was also sustained in ruling that Alcoa's investments in and control over certain fabricating companies were not "merely manoeuvres to suppress or exclude competitors" even though Alcoa "may have hoped in this way to secure at least a friendly market for its ingot, if ingot competition should increase."

Alcoa was held to have unlawfully suppressed competition in the business of rolling ingot into sheet aluminum, by means of a "price squeeze"; i.e. by keeping the margin between the price of ingot sold to competing sheet rollers and the price at which it sold sheet so narrow that competing sheet rollers could not stay in business.

The government was defeated in its contention that Alcoa had excluded foreign competition by means of a cartel agreement with foreign producers imposing quotas upon their exports to the United States. Aluminium Limited, the Canadian "fledgling" of Alcoa was found to have violated the Sherman Act by participating in this cartel, but Alcoa was absolved of responsibility for this despite evidence that Alcoa and Limited were under the common control of the Mellon family and Arthur V. Davis (their joint interests in each company amounting to about 49%), that the companies collaborated closely, and that Alcoa would be the beneficiary of the exclusion of foreign aluminum from the American market.]

[For the remedy phase of the case, see section 4 infra].

NOTES AND QUERIES

(A) Defining the Relevant Product Market

(1) *Queries.* Let AS stand for Alcoa's domestic sales of aluminum ingot; AF Alcoa's ingot used in Alcoa's own fabricating operations; S, secondary ingot; I, imported ingot other than imports controlled by Alcoa; W, all foreign ingot production. Write the fraction which, according to Judge Hand, represented Alcoa's share of the market. What are the reasons given for including or excluding particular factors? Could the government have eliminated all doubt as to the existence of a monopoly by charging monopoly of domestic *manufacture* of virgin ingot and sales of such ingot?

(2) *Substitute Products and "Cross-Elasticity".* In *United States v. E. I. Du Pont De Nemours & Co.*, 351 U.S. 377, 76 S.Ct. 994, 100 L.Ed. 1264 (1956), the Court, by a vote of 4–3, sustained a district court judgment for the defendant in a suit charging monopolization of cellophane. The district court made a finding that the relevant market was "flexible packaging materials," including brown wrapping paper, wax paper, and aluminum foil, notwithstanding that cellophane had a combination of qualities not matched by any of these materials, and so commanded a price two or three times as high as most of these wrapping materials. Both the District and the Supreme Court were much influenced by the fact that for each possible use of cellophane there were one or more alternatives not controlled by du Pont, and that some customers would switch from cellophane to an alternative wrapping upon relatively small shift in price relationships. Defendant introduced elaborate statistical evidence of this "cross-elasticity" of demand. On the approach to delimitation of a product market, Justice Reed's opinion for the majority declared:

> Determination of the competitive market for commodities depends on how different from one another are the offered commodities in character

or use, how far buyers will go to substitute one commodity for another. For example, one can think of building materials as in commodity competition but one could hardly say that brick competed with steel or wood or cement or stone in the meaning of Sherman Act litigation; the products are too different. This is the interindustry competition emphasized by some economists. See Lilienthal, Big Business, c. 5. On the other hand, there are certain differences in the formulae for soft drinks but one can hardly say that each one is an illegal monopoly. Whatever the market may be, we hold that control of price or competition establishes the existence of monopoly power under § 2. Section 2 requires the application of a reasonable approach in determining the existence of monopoly power just as surely as did § 1. This of course does not mean that there can be a reasonable monopoly. . . . When a product is controlled by one interest, without substitutes available in the market, there is monopoly power. Because most products have possible substitutes, we cannot, as we said in Times-Picayune Pub. Co. v. United States, 345 U.S. 594, 612, 73 S.Ct. 872, 882, give "that infinite range" to the definition of substitutes. Nor is it a proper interpretation of the Sherman Act to require that products be fungible to be considered in the relevant market.

The Government argues:

> "We do not here urge that in *no* circumstances may competition of substitutes negative possession of monopolistic power over trade in a product. The decisions make it clear at the least that the courts will not consider substitutes other than those which are substantially fungible with the monopolized product and sell at substantially the same price."

But where there are market alternatives that buyers may readily use for their purposes, illegal monopoly does not exist merely because the product said to be monopolized differs from others. If it were not so, only physically identical products would be a part of the market. . . . The varying circumstances of each case determine the result. In considering what is the relevant market for determining the control of price and competition, no more definite rule can be declared than that commodities reasonably interchangeable by consumers for the same purposes make up that "part of the trade or commerce", monopolization of which may be illegal.

The dissenting opinion by Chief Justice Warren relied heavily on evidence that du Pont itself had recognized the distinctive market for cellophane by entering into a cartel and other restrictive arrangements relating to this product. Such arrangements could hardly have served their purpose if competition from other wrapping materials effectively limited du Pont's freedom in pricing:

The trial court found that

> "Du Pont has no power to set cellophane prices arbitrarily. If prices for cellophane increase in relation to prices of other flexible packaging materials it will lose business to manufacturers of such materials in varying amounts for each of du Pont cellophane's major end uses." Finding 712.

This further reveals its misconception of the antitrust laws. A monopolist seeking to maximize profits cannot raise prices "arbitrarily." Higher prices of course mean smaller sales, but they also mean higher per-unit profit. Lower prices will increase sales but reduce per-unit profit. Within these limits a monopolist has a considerable degree of latitude in determining which course to pursue in attempting to maximize profits. The trial judge thought that, if du Pont raised its price, the market would "penalize" it with smaller profits as well as lower sales. Du Pont proved him wrong. When 1947 operating earnings dropped below 26% for the first time in 10 years, it increased cellophane's price 7% and boosted its earnings in 1948. Du Pont's division manager then reported that "If an operative return of 31% is considered inadequate then an upward revision in prices will be necessary to improve the return." It is this latitude with respect to price, this broad power of choice, that the antitrust laws forbid. Du Pont's independent pricing policy and the great profits consistently yielded by that policy leave no room for doubt that it had power to control the price of cellophane. The findings of fact cited by the majority cannot affect this conclusion. For they merely demonstrate that, during the period covered by the complaint, du Pont was a "good monopolist," i.e., that it did not engage in predatory practices and that it chose to maximize profits by lowering price and expanding sales. Proof of enlightened exercise of monopoly power certainly does not refute the existence of that power.[79]

(3) *Delineating "Submarkets".* In *United States v. Grinnell Corp.*, 384 U.S. 563, 86 S.Ct. 1698, 16 L.Ed.2d 778 (1966), the Court declared that markets would be defined on the same principles under the monopolization provisions of the Sherman Act ("any part" of interstate and foreign commerce) as under the merger provisions of Section 7 of the Clayton Act ("any line" of commerce), and added: "There may be submarkets that are separate economic entities." 384 U.S. at 572. In the leading case under Section 7 of the Clayton Act, *Brown Shoe Co. v. United States*, 370 U.S. 294, 82 S.Ct. 1502, 8 L.Ed.2d 510 (1962), Chief Justice Warren, writing for the majority, stated:

> The outer boundaries of a product market are determined by the reasonable interchangeability of use or the cross-elasticity of demand between the product itself and substitutes for it. However, within this broad market, well-defined submarkets may exist which, in themselves, constitute product markets for antitrust purposes. . . . The boundaries of such a submarket may be determined by examining such practical indicia as industry or public recognition of the submarket as a separate economic entity, the product's peculiar characteristics and uses, unique production facilities, distinct customers, distinct prices, sensitivity to price changes and specialized vendors.[80]

If these tests were followed in *du Pont*, would the Court have reached the same result? Should du Pont's power be measured in submarkets where the unique characteristics of cellophane for certain end uses, i.e., packaging cigarettes, gave it 75 to 80% of the market? Is a "submarket" not a market? What, if anything, does the concept add? Is the concept simply a legal fiction to circumvent the over-inclusiveness of markets defined by the cross elasticity test? Are verbal tests for defining markets being used to identify something tangible or simply as a means for beginning an intellectual analy-

79. The du Pont case is analyzed in Waldman, The du Pont Cellophane Case Revisited: An Analysis of the Indirect Effects of Antitrust Policy on Market Structure and Performance, 25 Antitrust Bull. 805 (1980); Turner, Antitrust Policy and the Cellophane Case, 70 Harv.L.Rev.

281 (1956); Stocking and Mueller, The Cellophane Case and the New Competition, 45 Am.Econ.Rev. 29 (1955).

80. 370 U.S. at 325, 82 S.Ct. at 1523–24, 8 L.Ed.2d at 535–36.

sis of whether there has been a displacement of the competitive process in ways which impinge the policies of the statute?

(4) *Some Examples of Product Market Definitions.* In *Telex Corp. v. I.B.M. Corp.*[81] Telex claimed, *inter alia*, that I.B.M. possessed monopoly power in the basic computer (main frame) market and in the market for "peripheral devices plug-compatible" with I.B.M. computers.[82] The District Court held that peripheral devices which were plug-compatible with I.B.M. computers constituted a market distinct from similar devices which required special adapters for use with I.B.M. computers. The Court summarized the precedents for a narrow view of interchangeability, in delineating submarkets, as follows:

> [T]here may be differentiations between virgin ingot and secondary ingot; first run motion pictures and subsequent run motion pictures; promotion of championship fights and the promotion of non-championship fights; accredited central station protection services and non-accredited central protection services, local alarm services, and other on-site protection services; replacement elements for air preheaters and the air preheaters themselves; gas ranges and electric ranges; major league baseball concessions and concession services for other large spectator sporting events, including professional football, basketball or horse racing; regularly scheduled and consolidated retail delivery services for retail establishments; and non-local credit reporting, life and health insurance reporting, fire and casualty insurance reporting and personal reporting. Even products that are physically identical or fungible are not necessarily to be grouped in the same relevant market if, in fact, they are marketed to different classes of customers and are separately treated as of different commercial value by end users. . . . Inquiry should focus on the practical business realities of the marketplace and not on mere economic theory. . . . A meaningful definition for the relevant market must focus on what the buyers do and not on what the sellers do, or theoretically can do.[83]

In reversing, the Tenth Circuit found "plain error" in the District Court's definition of the product market. The Court of Appeals stressed evidence that tended to show that the cost of developing interfaces which would make peripheral equipment plug-compatible with the computers manufactured by others was sufficiently low as to require a product market definition which included peripheral devices not plug-compatible with I.B.M. The Court of Appeals emphasized elasticity of supply to define the market, rather than elasticity of demand; or, what sellers might do, rather than what buyers in fact do. Is this an appropriate test? Is it appropriate if there is a substantial cost in manufacturing interfaces or substantial buyer resistance to using them even though the cost was minimal? [84]

81. 367 F.Supp. 258 (N.D.Okl.1973), reversed 510 F.2d 894 (10th Cir. 1975), certiorari dismissed 423 U.S. 802, 96 S.Ct. 8, 46 L.Ed.2d 244 (1976).

82. "Peripheral devices" include magnetic tape drivers, electronic "memories", printout equipment and other machines which connect with the basic computer (main frame) so as to expand or alter its capabilities. A peripheral device is said to be "plug-compatible" with a basic computer (the central processing unit—"CPU") if it can simply be connected with the CPU—plugged in—without a special adapter. Note that it is within the power of the manufacturer of the CPU to incorporate some "peripheral" elements, e.g., memories, into the basic computer. How does this affect market delineation?

83. 367 F.Supp. at 337–38.

84. In its findings of fact, the District Court expressly rejected I.B.M.'s claim

Compare *Greyhound Computer Corp., Inc. v. I.B.M. Corp.*[85] Plaintiff charged I.B.M. with monopolizing the market for leasing general purpose digital computers for commercial application. Holding a jury could find such a "submarket" "sufficiently distinct in commercial reality to permit a company that dominated these submarkets to exclude competition and control prices," [86] the court first distinguished general purpose computers from the market for dedicated application computers and micro-computers, process control computers and large scientific computers. The court did so on the grounds that: "other computers are not reasonably interchangeable with general purpose commercial systems, and . . . no significant substitution in fact takes place. Other evidence indicated that computer systems manufacturers tend to specialize in but one of these types of computers, that the industry and its customers recognized these categories of computers, and that the various categories have distinct prices and sets of competitors employing different marketing techniques." [87] The court held a jury might further fractionate the "market" by finding leasing of general purpose computers a separate submarket distinct from the sale of such computers because: 1) leasing and sales serve different customer needs; and 2) the industry and its customers recognized the distinction between leasing and selling.

Are these tests appropriate for determining whether unlawful monopolization has taken place? [88] Is the problem one of describing a tangible thing or activity and place in which to quantify a percentage share possessed by a defendant? Consider the following criticism:

> There appears to be a willingness to fragment markets further in the analytical process of identifying the presence or absence of monopoly power with primary reliance placed on market tests evolved in merger

that interfaces could be easily or cheaply made. 367 F.Supp. at 338-39. See also Recent Developments, Telex v. I.B.M.: Implications for the Businessman and the Computer Manufacturer, 60 Va.L.Rev. 884, 890–91 (1974). But cf. Note, The Development of the Sherman Act Section 2 Market Share Test and Its Inapplicability to Dynamic Markets, 49 So.Cal.L.Rev. 154 (1975), criticizing the District Court market analysis in Telex.

Note that the courts have generally applied the same tests for determining product markets in monopolization cases under Section 2 and merger cases decided under Section 7 of the Clayton Act. See, e.g., United States v. Grinnell Corp., 384 U.S. 563, 573, 86 S.Ct. 1698, 1705, 16 L.Ed.2d 778, 788 (1966): "We see no reason to differentiate between 'line' of commerce in the context of the Clayton Act and 'part' of commerce for purposes of the Sherman Act." See pp. 218–19, infra. For an argument that there are reasons for drawing a distinction, see Flynn, Monopolization under the Sherman Act: The Third Wave and Beyond, 26 Antitrust Bull. 1, 26–27 (1981); Comment, Relevant Geographic Market Delineation: The Interchangeability of Standards in Cases Arising Under Section 2 of the Sherman

Act and Section 7 of the Clayton Act, 1979 Duke L.J. 1152.

85. Greyhound Computer Corp., Inc. v. International Business Machines Corp., 559 F.2d 488 (9th Cir. 1977), certiorari denied 434 U.S. 1040, 98 S.Ct. 782, 54 L.Ed. 2d 790 (1978).

86. 559 F.2d at 493.

87. Id.

88. For similar approaches fractionating market definitions in private cases alleging monopolization and attempts to monopolize, see Associated Radio Service Co. v. Page Airways, Inc., 624 F.2d 1342 (5th Cir. 1980), certiorari denied 450 U.S. 1030, 101 S.Ct. 1740, 68 L.Ed.2d 226 (1981) (sale and installation of avionic systems in Grumman Gulfstream II aircraft); Photovest Corp. v. Fotomat Corp., 606 F.2d 704 (7th Cir. 1979), certiorari denied 445 U.S. 917, 100 S.Ct. 1278, 63 L.Ed.2d 601 (1980) (photo-finishing services provided through drive-in kiosks in Marion County, Indiana, distinct from photo-finishing services provided through other outlets); SmithKline Corp. v. Eli Lilly & Co., 575 F.2d 1056 (3d Cir.), certiorari denied 439 U.S. 838, 99 S.Ct. 123, 58 L.Ed.2d 134 (1978) (antibiotic cephalosporins distinct from other antibiotics).

cases. Yet the opinions tend to use market tests as devices producing a concrete conclusion describing a physically identifiable and frozen thing in a tangible area of space. The function of defining relevant markets in monopolization litigation should be understood and used in a more subtle way. Market definitions are only the beginning of an analytical process leading to a judgment on the intangible question of whether it is appropriate to determine that a defendant's structure and/or behavior have displaced the competitive process in the context of the facts and circumstances peculiar to the case and in a way inconsistent with the goals of antitrust policy.

. . .

In determining whether industry structure or unilateral behavior displaces competition, market definitions may be helpful in organizing the analysis so that it is practical, significant, economically sensible, and manageable in the context of the judicial process. But market analysis is subservient to the broader qualitative question of whether the policy of the law has been violated, and on occasion market analysis should be dispensed with where the level of predatory behavior is obviously destructive of a competitive process. The persistence of dominance in a significant area of economic activity may also warrant a common sense conclusion that power is present in a form inconsistent with the competitive ideal and the public interest requires it be constrained or eliminated where the persistence of dominance is likely and its erosion by the market is unlikely, even though some theoretical arguments about the metaphysical concept of markets may be advanced to escape liability.

Elsewhere market definitions should be understood in a way that is analogous to the function of rule of reason analysis in Section 1 cases. Where it is not readily apparent that industry structure or behavior is consistent or inconsistent with the competitive ideal, market analysis serves as a mechanism for determining whether it is fair, just, practical, and economically sensible to isolate or fragment an area of economic activity as an area where the goals of antitrust policy can work and to make judgments about whether they are at work in light of all the facts and circumstances of the industry.[89]

(5) *Non-market Determination of Monopoly or Attempt to Monopolize.* The suggestion of Chief Justice Warren's dissent in the *DuPont* case, that a market may be limited to the product to which defendant directs his monopolistic effort, substantially ignoring substitutes as to whose competition he appears indifferent,[90] is both persuasive and troublesome. On the one hand, defendant is clearly in a unique position to judge whether he has power to price his product free, within broad limits, of constraining influence of sub-

89. Flynn, supra note 77.

90. See also Marcus, Antitrust Bugbears: Substitute Products—Oligopoly, 105 U.Pa.L.Rev. 185 (1956): It is submitted that if a thing may be restrained within the meaning of section 1 of the Sherman Act, it may be monopolized within the meaning of section 2 of the Act. If all the makers of cellophane agree to, and do, fix the price of cellophane at one cent higher than certain other packaging materials, this is both an agreement in restraint of trade and an exercise of monopoly power, whether or not there were substitute materials. If the parties to the agreement find they cannot maintain the agreement, it is hardly likely to be of long duration and both the restraint and the monopoly power will disappear. If there were an agreement among all cellophane makers to restrict the output of cellophane, here again there would be both an agreement in restraint of trade and an expression of an intent to exercise collective monopoly power.

stitutes. This is only another way of saying that the cross-elasticity is low. It seems to imply that some practices lawful under Section 1, even if engaged in by combinations of firms, may be unlawful for a single firm under Section 2 although it has not achieved and is unlikely to achieve a significant power position in a relevant market.

On the other hand, this line of reasoning leads to difficulties—and this by reference only to the intent of the defendant. There would be a quite subjective basis for distinguishing legal competition (pricing of one's own goods, selecting one's own outlets) and illegal monopolizing. It also blurs a distinction seemingly called for by the Sherman Act's differentiating between Section 1 and Section 2 offenses.

Some argue that there is need to fill a legislative gap between the collaborative offenses banned by Section 1 and "predatory" business tactics by powerful firms reachable, under conventional Section 2 interpretation, only if the firm has achieved or is within striking distance of "monopoly" in a defined market. Another way of closing the gap is embodied in cases which dispense with market analysis where the charge is attempt to monopolize.[91] This, too, would make the line between legality and illegality depend largely on "predatory intent." Others would prefer to supplement the combination offenses of Section 1 and the unilateral dominance offense of Section 2 only by administrative devices such as Section 5 of the Federal Trade Commission Act under which improper practices may be prohibited prospectively without imposing criminal or treble damage sanctions retroactively.

(6) *Structural-Behavioral and Short-Term/Long-Term Distinctions in Monopolization Litigation.* In *United States v. Corn Products Refining Co.,*[92] a 1916 opinion by Judge Hand, it was suggested that there are two broad categories or theories for proving unlawful monopolization. One approach is a structural approach where "it is the mere possession of economic power . . . capable, by its own variation in production, of changing and controlling price, which is illegal."[93] A second approach, a conduct approach, emphasizes the exercise of a power to fix prices or exclude competition by unfair or abusive practices, without much regard for the source of the power to do so.[94] The distinction and its significance for market tests have been elaborated as follows:

> Actual displacement of competition by the persistent possession or use of monopoly power, the primary concern of Section 2 of the Sherman Act, may occur through a variety of means ranging from abusive behavior, fixing prices or excluding competitors, to the structure of a firm, where structure itself is claimed to have the necessary effect of fixing prices or excluding competitors. Each type of case is analyzed pursuant to the *ALCOA* formula of proof of markets, proof of power in the markets defined and proof of conduct even though behavioral cases emphasize the conduct element of the formula and structural cases emphasize the market-power part of the formula. Thus, the same verbal test for a market

91. See p. 159 infra.

92. 234 F. 964 (S.D.N.Y.1916)

93. Id. at 1012.

94. Id. at 1012–13. For a modern version of the *Corn Products* case, involving the same defendant, see, Dimmitt Agri Industries Inc v. CPC International, Inc., 679 F.2d 516, 519 (5th Cir. 1982):

"Despite the passage of time (or perhaps because of it) the officers of Corn Products Refining, now CPC International Inc. ('CPC'), have not learned the perils of incriminating internal memoranda. Students of antitrust law may consequently be excused a feeling of déjà vu upon reading this case."

may produce different conceptualizations of a market, depending upon whether it is claimed competition has been displaced by behavioral means, structural effects or some combination of both.[95]

Professor Richard Schmalensee has stated: "[t]here are two rather different forms of monopoly power: short-run and long-run power. Although this distinction is important to economists, it often seems to be overlooked by judges deciding antitrust case law."[96] Short-run monopoly power is defined as being "equivalent to the statement that the firm's optimal price is above its marginal cost." [97] Noting that most firms have some short-run monopoly power in this sense and that antitrust enforcement should not be "concerned with all deviations from perfection but only with important deviations," Schmalensee suggests non-trivial short-run monopoly power is present where price exceeds marginal cost by an "appreciable margin." [98]

Long-run monopoly power of a type likely to be of antitrust concern is defined as power that permits a firm or group of firms to protect excess profits from competitive erosion.[99] In both the case of short-run monopoly power and long-run monopoly power, Schmalensee questions the relevance of relevant market analysis. "At best such exercises can give some information on short-run monopoly power, but better and more reliable information may be obtained through analysis of profitability. Moreover, market definition-market share exercises can shed no light at all on long-run monopoly power—the power to prevent the erosion of profits through more intense rivalry—unless one adopts a particularly limited form of the 'size is power' model, which is difficult to defend."[1] *Queries:* Is *ALCOA* a case of structural monopoly or behavioral monopoly? Is it a case of short-run or long-run monopoly power? In light of the above comments, was it necessary for Judge Hand to define the relevant product market in *ALCOA* at all? What different analytical approach might you suggest?

(7) *Monopolizing One's Own Goods?* Cases cited in the footnote [2] suggest that one may be adjudged guilty of monopolizing or attempting to monopolize by exercising the usual owner's prerogatives with respect to one's own goods, sometimes in circumstances where the product is not shown to be unique and no dominance of a broader market has been demonstrated. Does the existence of a patent, copyright, or trade mark, in a sense "lawful monopolies", sufficiently insulate the product in question so that it constitutes the market, regardless of substitutes? [3] To what extent should potential competition affect the delineation of "markets"; for example, if A is the sole

95. Flynn, supra note 77 at 27–28.

96. Schmalensee, On The Use Of Economic Models In Antitrust: The *Realemon* Case, 127 U.Pa.L.Rev. 994, 1005 (1979).

97. Id.

98. Id. at 1006.

99. Id. at 1008.

1. Id. at 1044.

2. See United States v. Klearflax Linen Looms, 63 F.Supp. 32 (D.Minn.1945); Mount Lebanon Motors, Inc. v. Chrysler Corp., 283 F.Supp. 453 (W.D.Pa.1968), affirmed 417 F.2d 622 (3d Cir. 1969); Rea v. Ford Motor Co., 355 F.Supp. 842 (E.D. Pa.1972), reversed in part, 497 F.2d 577 (3d Cir. 1974), certiorari denied 419 U.S.

868, 95 S.Ct. 126, 42 L.Ed.2d 106 (1974) on remand 406 F.Supp. 271 (D.C.Pa. 1975). Cf., Motion Pictures Patents Co. v. Universal Film Manufacturing Co., 243 U.S. 502, 37 S.Ct. 416, 61 L.Ed. 871 (1917); Eastman Kodak Co. v. Southern Photo Materials Co., 273 U.S. 359, 47 S.Ct. 400, 71 L.Ed. 684 (1927); International Salt Co., Inc. v. United States, 332 U.S. 392, 68 S.Ct. 12, 92 L.Ed. 20 (1947); In the Matter of Use of the Carterphone Device in Message Toll Telephone Service, 13 F.C.C.Rep.2d 430 (1967).

3. Compare Walker Process Equipment, Inc. v. Food Machinery & Chemical Corp., p. 1182 infra (patent); United States v. Loew's Inc., 371 U.S. 38, 83 S.Ct. 97, 9 L.Ed.2d 11 (1962) (copyright).

producer of chemical X and five other firms produce the raw material, which they could easily process as A does, does A have a monopoly? [4] Where a firm manufactures and sells complex equipment requiring maintenance and repairs, is the market for repair services of the equipment one that may be monopolized by the manufacturer? [5]

(B) Defining the Relevant Geographic Market

Since Section 2 of the Sherman Act makes it unlawful "to monopolize any part of the trade or commerce among the several States, or with foreign nations", monopoly power must be measured in a relevant geographic market as well as a relevant product market. Why did Judge Hand in the *Alcoa* case not consider the world-wide market for virgin ingot as the relevant geographic market in which to measure Alcoa's share of the market? Should Alcoa have been permitted to defend its large share of domestic production of virgin ingot on the grounds that the international market was dominated by other giant producers of virgin ingot and Alcoa's size was necessary for it to compete in the international market as well as effectively compete for the domestic market? What factors should a court consider in delineating a relevant geographic market and submarkets?

(1) In *United States v. Yellow Cab Co.*, 332 U.S. 218, 67 S.Ct. 1560, 92 L.Ed. 2010 (1947), the complaint charged Yellow Cab and Checker Cab Co. with combining and conspiring to restrain and to monopolize: (1) the sale of vehicles for use as taxicabs to the major cab companies in Chicago, Pittsburgh, New York City and Minneapolis, and (2) the business of furnishing cab services for hire in Chicago and its vicinity. In upholding the complaint as to the sale of cabs in the above named cities, the Court stated:

> Likewise irrelevant is the importance of the interstate commerce affected in relation to the entire amount of that type of commerce in the United States. The Sherman Act is concerned with more than the large, nation-wide obstacles in the channels of interstate trade. It is designed to sweep away all appreciable obstructions so that the statutory policy of free trade might be effectively achieved. As this Court stated in Indiana Farmer's Guide Pub. Co. v. Prairie Farmer Pub. Co., 293 U.S. 268, 279, 55 S.Ct. 182, 185, 79 L.Ed. 356, 361 (1934), 'The provisions of §§ 1 and 2 have both a geographical and distributive significance and apply to any part of the United States as distinguished from the whole and to any part of the classes of things forming a part of interstate commerce.' It follows that the complaint in this case is not defective for failure to allege that [Checker] has a monopoly with reference to the total number of taxicabs manufactured and sold in the United States. Its relative position in the field of cab production has no necessary relation to the ability of the appellees to conspire to monopolize or restrain, in violation of the Act, an appreciable segment of interstate cab sales. An allegation that such a segment has been or may be monopolized or restrained is sufficient. [The Court upheld dismissal of the charge of monopolizing local cab service in Chicago on the ground that the "part" of commerce involved was not interstate commerce.]

4. See Low, Ease of Entry: A Fundamental Defense in Merger Cases, 36 G.Wash.L.Rev. 515 (1968).

5. See Spectrofuge Corp. v. Beckman Instruments, Inc., 575 F.2d 256 (5th Cir.

1978), certiorari denied 440 U.S. 939, 99 S.Ct. 1289, 59 L.Ed.2d 499 (1978).

(2) *Defining Relevant Geographic Market by Examining the Defendant's Behavior and Intent.* In *Woods Exploration & Production Co., Inc. v. Alcoa*, 438 F.2d 1286 (5th Cir. 1971), owners of wells in a 4000 acre gas field in Texas charged the major producer with monopolizing the production of gas in the field. In finding the gas field an appropriate geographic market for Section 2 purposes, the Fifth Circuit stated (438 F.2d at 1304–06):

> Defendants argue that the Appling Field cannot constitute a relevant market for it is a source of supply rather than a market. This argument, however, fails to recognize that "relevant market" is simply a shorthand phrase used to describe "the arena within which the strength of competitive forces is measured," P. Areeda, Antitrust Analysis ¶ 201, at 71 (1967). It does not necessarily mean the selling place. . . .
>
> Plaintiffs do not argue that defendants possess or have attempted to possess monopoly power over the marketing of natural gas. They instead contend that defendants possess monopoly power over the extraction of gas from the Appling Field. An essential fact in the natural gas industry is that adjoining land owners usually extract gas from a common gas reservoir. Thus, if one producer can inhibit or eliminate the extraction of gas by another, the inhibitor can prolong the life of the field and enhance his own future production figures. With regard to extraction of gas—which is at the heart of plaintiffs' complaint—the Appling Field therefore is the relevant area of competition. It is the "part" of "trade or commerce" with regard to which we must measure the power to exclude competitors. . . .
>
> [I]n the present case we can look to the Appling Field and see the existence of a practice "the obvious natural effect of which was to" eliminate or thwart competitive extraction of gas from the Field by plaintiffs. Nor does it matter that this circumscribed area of competition is small, or that the effect on the public at the place of ultimate sale may be minor. . . . We therefore hold that the trial court erred in finding that the Appling Field was not a relevant market.[6]

By emphasizing the intent of a defendant or the predatory nature of the exclusionary conduct, is the court making relevant market a subsidiary consideration in order to attack unilateral predatory behavior?[7] Assume a ru-

6. See also, International Travel Arrangers, Inc. v. Western Airlines, Inc., 623 F.2d 1255 (8th Cir. 1980), certiorari denied 449 U.S. 1063, 101 S.Ct. 787, 66 L.Ed.2d 605 (airline flights from Minneapolis to Las Vegas and Hawaii relevant market); Mid-Texas Communications Systems, Inc. v. American Telephone & Telegraph Co., 615 F.2d 1372 (5th Cir. 1980) certiorari denied 449 U.S. 912, 101 S.Ct. 286, 66 L.Ed.2d 140 (telephone service for a new residential community outside Houston a relevant market).

7. See William Goldman Theatres, Inc. v. Loew's, Inc., 150 F.2d 738 (3d Cir. 1945). In Denver Petroleum Corp. v. Shell Oil Co., 306 F.Supp. 289 (D.Colo. 1969), plaintiffs alleged Shell had monopolized the purchase of crude oil and condensate in Rio Arriba County, New Mexico by refusing to transport oil other than its own in its pipeline. In rejecting Shell's argument for measuring monopoly power in a larger geographic area the court stated (306 F.Supp. at 304):

> "Defendant would have us engage in market analysis, considering the full breadth of 'economic and competitive realities,' to determine that the market structure is, if not nationwide, at least as broad as the entire Four Corners region. . . .
>
> "However, in our opinion, such analysis is unnecessary in this case and the 'relevant market' is in that sense irrelevant. We have here a practice illegal in itself, operation of the pipelines as private carriers, a purpose and the obvious natural effect of which was to exclude nonlocal competition from the crude supply which Shell badly needed. When one must 'look' for a monopoly, determining a relevant market in which

ral town has been served by two motion picture theatres for a number of years. Both theatres have been marginally profitable. Assume the owner of one theatre begins a price war, offering monthly passes below cost to all residents of the area, and has expressly stated it is her purpose to drive out the competing theatre and to substitute one first class theatre in place of two second class theatres. Actionable under the Sherman Act? [8] Would it be actionable if one theatre owner burned down the competing theatre in order to gain control of the market? In order to settle a grudge?

Geographic markets may be determined by industry or public recognition of the geographic area as a distinct arena of competition, considering such factors as cost of transportation, tariffs, and local regulations excluding competitors.[9] As with product markets, there has been a tendency to borrow from geographic market tests used in merger cases under Section 7 of the Clayton Act.[10] At least one case has rejected Section 7 tests for geographic "submarkets" on the ground that the Sherman Act is "not couched in such local and pragmatic terms," [11] despite the language of Section 2 prohibiting the monopolization of "any part" of trade or commerce.

In *Hecht v. Pro-Football, Inc.*,[12] the court reversed a lower court geographic market definition of the entire nation, in a case where the plaintiffs were seeking to establish an A.F.L. pro-football team (pre-merger of the leagues) in Washington, D.C. Hecht's access to R.F.K. Stadium, the only suitable location for pro-football in the Washington, D.C. area, was blocked by the exercise of a restrictive covenant in the lease between the stadium authority and the Washington Redskins. In finding the D.C. metropolitan region for professional football the relevant geographic and product markets, the court stated:

> The relevant geographic market is 'the area of effective competition,' the area 'in which the seller operates, and to which the purchaser can practically turn for supplies.' It is well settled that the relevant market 'need not be nationwide,' and that 'where the relevant competitive market

to look and in which to evaluate competitive effects is obviously an essential first step. But when, with an illegal practice such as is present here in mind, one can look at an area and see the existence of monopoly power, not by inference from market share, but by determining actual ability to exclude competition and control prices, there appears no real need to go further."

8. Cf. Union Leader Corp. v. Newspapers of New England, Inc., 284 F.2d 582 (1st Cir. 1960), certiorari denied 365 U.S. 833, 81 S.Ct. 747, 5 L.Ed.2d 744 (1961), rehearing denied 365 U.S. 890, 81 S.Ct. 1026, 6 L.Ed.2d 201.

9. See Lorain Journal v. United States, 342 U.S. 143, 72 S.Ct. 181, 96 L.Ed. 162 (1951); United States v. Griffith, 334 U.S. 100, 68 S.Ct. 941, 92 L.Ed. 1236 (1948); See United States v. Columbia Steel Corp., 334 U.S. 495, 68 S.Ct. 1107, 92 L.Ed. 1533 (1948), rehearing denied 334 U.S. 862, 68 S.Ct. 1525, 92 L.Ed. 1781; Gamco Inc. v. Providence Fruit &

Produce Bldg., Inc., 194 F.2d 484 (1st Cir. 1952), certiorari denied 344 U.S. 817, 73 S.Ct. 11, 97 L.Ed. 636 (wholesale fruit market building a relevant product and geographic market where retail buyers congregate there and there is easy access to shipping facilities); William Goldman Theatres, Inc. v. Loew's, Inc., 150 F.2d 738 (3d Cir. 1945), certiorari denied 334 U.S. 811, 68 S.Ct. 1016, 92 L.Ed.2d 1742 (1948) (downtown theatre district separate relevant market from suburban theatre districts).

10. See Comment, Relevant Geographic Market Delineation: The Interchangeability of Standards In Cases Arising Under Section 2 of The Sherman Act and Section 7 of The Clayton Act, 1979 Duke L.J. 1152.

11. United States v. Dairymen, Inc., 1978–1 Trade Cases ¶ 62,053 (W.D.Ky. 1978).

12. 570 F.2d 982 (D.C.Cir.1977), certiorari denied 436 U.S. 956, 98 S.Ct. 3069, 57 L.Ed.2d 1121 (1979).

covers only a small area the Sherman Act may be invoked to prevent un-reasonable restraints within that area.'   Indeed, courts have regularly identified relevant geographic markets as single cities or towns, and even portions thereof.[13]

Do you agree with this analysis? Should the geographic market delineation include competition like the Baltimore Colts playing 45 miles away? Is the function of geographic market definitions in Section 2 cases designed for less tangible purposes than measuring the metes and bounds of a physical "part" of commerce? [14]

(C) Identifying the Presence of Monopoly Power

The search for relevant product and geographic markets and the quanti-tative measurement of the share of the markets defined is often assumed to be a reliable guide to a conclusion that monopoly power is present or not present. Judge Hand's *ALCOA* test of 33%, "no"; 64%, "maybe"; and 90%, "yes", has been widely followed. But is the quantitative measurement of market share a reliable standard in all circumstances for determining wheth-er a firm possesses the power to fix prices or exclude competition? [15] Con-sider the following:

> Ever since Judge Hand's numerical test of 90% yes, 64% maybe and 33% no in *ALCOA*, courts have continued to attach great weight to percent-age share of the "market" measured at a specific point in time. In most cases, a market share in excess of 70% appears to result in a finding of monopoly power, while less than 50% market share results in a finding of no monopoly power. In the 50% to 70% range, evidence beyond market share appears to be required before a finding of monopoly power will be sustained. The commentators, as well as some courts, are unanimous in pointing out that market share—big or little—is a factor, but should not be the sole factor in determining whether or not monopoly power exists. A firm may have a large market share yet lack the ability to fix prices or exclude competitors because entry barriers are low. Conversely, a firm with a relatively small market share may still possess the power to fix prices or exclude competitors particularly where entry barriers are high, there is excess capacity and the firm is earning excessive profits. More-over, monopoly power may be inferred from factors not so directly depen-dent upon market definitions like entry barriers, excessive profits over a sustained period of time, the relative size of competitors, the actual use of economic power by predatory conduct, and a trend toward greater or lesser economic power.[16]

The search for more subtle standards from which to infer the existence or non-existence of monopoly power has included reliance upon neo-classical price theory. Within the constraints of neo-classical price theory, market power is defined as the "ability to set price above marginal cost." [17] Only

---

13. Id. at 988.

14. See Flynn, supra note 77.

15. See generally, III P. Areeda & D. Turner, Antitrust Law, Chap. 8 (1978); L. Sullivan, Antitrust, pp. 74–93 (1977).

16. Flynn, supra note 77 at 50–52. But see, Dimmitt Agri Industries, Inc. v. CPC International, Inc., 679 F.2d 516 (5th Cir. 1982) (21% market share plus preda-tory pricing; such a low market share not monopolization as a matter of law.)

17. Landes & Posner, Market Power in Antitrust Cases, 94 Harv.L.Rev. 937, 939 (1981). For critical analysis of the Landes & Posner position see Comments, Landes and Posner On Market Power:

that market power which is substantial or that which is substantial and persistent over time, is of antitrust concern. The measure of market power, under this line of analysis, is said to require an assessment of market share in light of demand and supply elasticities. Others have offered profitability as a touchstone for determining the presence of monopoly power. An excessive level of profits, particularly persistent excess profits is said to be a reliable basis from which to infer the presence of monopoly power.[18] While not offered as a conclusive test in all cases or as an easy standard to define in any case, the existence of abnormally high profits in conjunction with other indicia of monopoly power is widely thought to be at least a less arbitrary standard than a mechanical measure of market share. The absence of high profits however, does not discount the existence of monopoly power. See *Alcoa,* supra p. 101.

Underlying assumptions about the scope and purpose of the Sherman Act and the degree to which the statute "ought" to be relied upon to curb behavioral as well as structural displacements of the competitive process and eliminate short-term as well as long-term disruptions of the competitive process, generate differing assessments of the reliability of particular standards used to infer the presence of monopoly power. Further complications arise because the differences in the circumstances, reality, and context in which each case arises make the application of any single test or rigid model less than satisfactory. It is also well to remember, before one criticizes too quickly serious efforts to grapple with this most difficult, elusive and complex issue of antitrust policy, Felix Cohen's trenchant observation: "Lawyers . . . have special opportunities to learn what many logicians have not yet recognized: that truth on earth is a matter of degree, and that, whatever may be the case in Heaven, a terrestrial major league batting average above .300 is nothing to be sneezed at." [19]

(D) Monopoly Power Plus (?) Equals Unlawful Monopolization.

(1) Conduct Tests, Defenses, Burdens of Proof.

In *United States v. United Shoe Machinery Corp.,*[20] Judge Wyzanski suggested three tests to determine whether a firm with monopoly power has "monopolized" in violation of Section 2: (1) whether it had acquired or maintained a power to exclude others as a result of using an unreasonable "restraint of trade" in violation of Section 1 of the Sherman Act; (2) whether the firm uses or plans to use any exclusionary practice, even though it is not a technical restraint of trade; and (3) whether the firm has "an overwhelming share of the market" in which case it illegally monopolizes merely by doing business, whether or not it employs exclusionary practices. In the last case there is available the defense that defendant owes its monopoly to "superior skills, superior products, natural advantages (including accessibility to raw materials or markets), economic or technological efficiency, ... low margins of profit maintained permanently and without discrimination, or licenses conferred by, and used within, the limits of law (including patents on

Four Responses, 95 Harv.L.Rev. 1787 (1982).

18. See Schmalensee, supra note 96.

19. Field Theory and Judicial Logic, 59 Yale L.J. 238, 239 (1950).

20. 110 F.Supp. 295, 342 (D.C.Mass. 1953), affirmed per curiam 347 U.S. 521, 74 S.Ct. 699, 98 L.Ed. 910 (1954).

one's own inventions, or franchises granted directly to the enterprise by a public authority)."

Should the burden of proof be shifted to the defendant once the plaintiff has proved the possession of monopoly power in a relevant market? Consider the following:

> . . . Once the Government has borne the burden of proving what is the relevant market and how predominant a share of that market defendant has, it follows that there are rebuttable presumptions that defendant has monopoly power and has monopolized in violation of § 2. The Government need not prove, and in a well-conducted trial ought not to be allowed to consume time in needlessly proving, defendant's predatory tactics, if any, or defendant's pricing, or production, or selling, or leasing, or marketing, or financial policies while in this predominant role. If defendant does wish to go forward, it is free to do so and to maintain the burden of showing that its eminence is traceable to such highly respectable causes as superiority in means and methods which are "honestly industrial", as Judge Hand characterized the supposititious socially desirable monopolizer.[21]

The proposed Industrial Reorganization Act [22] would have made it unlawful for any corporation or group of corporations, by agreement or otherwise, to "possess monopoly power in any line of commerce in any section of the country or with foreign nations. . . . There shall be a rebuttable presumption that monopoly power is possessed—(1) by any corporation if the average rate of return on net worth after taxes is in excess of 15 percentum over a period of five consecutive years out of the most recent seven years preceding the filing of the complaint, or (2) if there has been no substantial price competition among two or more corporations in any line of commerce in any section of the country for a period of three consecutive years out of the most recent five years preceding the filing of the complaint, or (3) if any four or fewer corporations account for 50 percentum (or more) of sales in any line of commerce in any section of the country in any year out of the most recent three years preceding the filing of the complaint." The proposed Act provides that the presumptions are rebuttable if (1) the power is due solely to the ownership of valid patents "lawfully acquired and lawfully used", or (2) it can be proved that remedies would "result in a loss of substantial economies." Are these legal standards justified?[23] Are they workable?[24]

21. Wyzanski, J., in United States v. Grinnell Corp., 236 F.Supp. 244 (D.R.I. 1964), affirmed with modification of decree in 384 U.S. 563, 86 S.Ct. 1698, 16 L.Ed.2d 778 (1966). But cf. Clarke Marine Corp. v. Cargill, Inc., 226 F.Supp. 103 (E.D.La.1964), dismissing a treble damage suit on the ground that defendant's monopoly was attributable to "superior technical skill and effective competitive activity." The court put "a heavy burden of proof" on the plaintiff. 226 F.Supp. at 111. See, Note, Section 2 of the Sherman Act—Is A Per Se Test Feasible?, 50 Iowa L.Rev. 1196 (1965).

22. S. 1167, § 101, 93rd Cong., 1st Sess. (1973). The bill specifies seven industries for special attention by the Commission: chemical and drugs, electrical

machinery and equipment, electronic computing and communication equipment, energy, iron and steel, motor vehicles, and nonferrous metals. Id. § 203. Extensive hearings have been held on restructuring proposals in each of these industries. See Hearings, The Industrial Reorganization Act, Subcommittee on Antitrust and Monopoly, U. S. Senate Judiciary Committee (1973–76).

23. See H. Goldschmid, M. Mann & J. Weston, Industrial Concentration: The New Learning, Chap. 7 (1974); Note, The Industrial Reorganization Act: An Antitrust Proposal to Restructure The American Economy, 73 Colum.L.Rev. 635 (1973); Note, A Legislative Approach to Market Concentration: The Industrial

(2) *A Sliding Scale of Conduct Evidence?*

Judge Wyzanski's verbalization of three tests for unlawful monopolization appears to recognize implicitly that monopolization which might be declared unlawful under Section 2 falls within a broad spectrum of circumstances ranging from structural cases to behavioral ones, with many cases falling somewhere between the two ends of the spectrum. The same general formula for analyzing all cases within the spectrum (market definition, share of market, and conduct indicating one with monopoly power has "monopolized") is applied, despite differences in the facts and the means by which the goal of preserving a competitive process is claimed to be illegally impinged. As in the case of market definitions shifting and changing with the structural or behavioral thrust of a particular case, the weight and implication of conduct evidence also shifts and changes depending upon the structural or behavioral and long-term monopoly or short-term monopoly thrust of a particular case. A sliding scale for assessing conduct evidence, from the relatively innocuous to the highly predatory, appears to be at work across the structural-behavioral spectrum. While not an explicit or neatly defined scale, or a rule which can or should be applied to all cases, the predatory quality of conduct evidence necessary to prove a structural violation is significantly less in a structural case than in a behavioral case. Thus in *ALCOA*, the unexplained and persistent possession of monopoly power itself appeared to constitute a violation of the statute in the absence of excuse or justification. In cases like *United States v. Grinnell*,[25] where the defendant was charged with monopolizing accredited central station protective service (automatic electronic security and fire alarm service for subscribers through a central local office), the sources of the monopolization alleged were found to be long-standing Section 1 violations, predatory pricing campaigns against competition in local markets, and acquisitions of competing companies. Justice Fortas, in dissent, described the trial court's narrow market definitions as "tailored precisely to fit the defendant's business" and "Procrustean" [26] (a conclusion with which the trial judge later agreed).[27] The case was primarily one alleging behavioral monopolization, where the basis for claiming a displacement of the competitive process was the defendant's predatory conduct. The trial court held:

> 7.   What justifies this application of Section 2 of the Sherman Act to these defendants is not avoidance of 'the curse of bigness', or the fear that men will be converted into robots, or the dread that society will be stratified into trusts more burdensome than feudalism, or colonialism, or socialism, or communism, or some other despised polity, or a concern lest giants larger than the state itself shall lead us into tyranny or into the need of a socialistic regimen as an antidote to private despotism.

> 8.   It is even doubtful whether we can say that here we have the danger of a business becoming slothful, routinized, sleepy, or wanting in

Reorganization Act, 24 Syracuse L.Rev. 1100 (1973).

24. For a criticism of the "efficiencies" defense based on the S.E.C.'s experience with a similar defense in the Public Utility Holding Company Act of 1935, see Brodley, Industrial Concentration and Legal Feasibility: The Efficiencies Defense, IX J.Econ.Issues 365 (1975).

25. 384 U.S. 563, 86 S.Ct. 1698, 16 L.Ed.2d 778 (1966).

26. 384 U.S. at 587, 86 S.Ct. at 1712, 16 L.Ed.2d at 796.

27. Wyzanski, The Judicial View of Section 2 Litigation, 10 Sw.U.L.Rev. 45, 48 (1978).

alertness, initiative, and progressiveness, as a result of the quiet life sought and usually achieved by a monopolist.

. . .

10.   In cases like this where the Sherman Act ban against monopolizing is invoked against defendants who have secured dominance of a small industry by imposing unlawful restraints of trade and by a steady stream of acquisitions of competitive enterprises, the usual rhetoric is quite out of place.   All that is at stake here is the rooting out of a plant of minor importance in the rich forest of the American economy, not because it overshadows all of us, or even many of us, but because it represents an ultimate growth from seeds which have been declared unlawful.   Congress in Section 1 of the Sherman Act outlawed the means and in Section 2 outlawed the end achieved by those means.[28]

Narrow market tests and a finding of monopoly power were apparently justified in light of the repeated exercise of significant predatory and exclusionary conduct.[29]

Is this a justified result?   Should unilateral predatory behavior by a small firm without long-term monopoly power be potentially a violation of Section 2 of the Sherman Act if it has an effect of fixing prices or excluding competitors?   Should proof of a specific intent to fix prices or exclude competitors also be required?

(3) *Problem—"No-Conduct" Monopolization*

Assume the following bill has been proposed as added language to Section 2 of the Sherman Act.   Should the bill be adopted?[30]

Dissipation of Monopoly Power Act

An act for the purpose of supplementing Section 2 of the Sherman Act by providing for the expeditious litigation of monopolization cases brought by the United States Department of Justice or the Federal Trade Commission, for the efficient achievement of effective remedies dissipating monopoly power in significant sectors of the economy without penalty or the loss of economies of scale, and for other purposes.

Be it enacted, that Section 2 of the Sherman Act is hereby supplemented by adding the following subsection:

28.   United States v. Grinnell Corp., 236 F.Supp. 244, 258 (D.R.I.1964).

29.   A Supreme Court majority, in affirming the lower court except as to remedy, noted at the end of its opinion of the violation phase of the case: "Since the record clearly shows that this monopoly power was consciously acquired, we have no reason to reach the further position of the District Court that once monopoly power is shown to exist, the burden is on the defendants to show that their dominance is due to skill, acumen, and the like."   384 U.S. at 576, n. 7, 86 S.Ct. at 1708, n. 7, 16 L.Ed.2d at 789, n. 7.

30.   See P. Areeda & D. Turner, III Antitrust Law pp. 35–70 (1978); Report,

Nat'l Comm. for the Review of Antitrust Laws and Procedures, pp. 151–163 (1979); Dougherty, Elimination of the Conduct Requirement in Government Monopolization Cases, 48 Antitrust L.J. 869 (1979); Dougherty, Kirkwood & Hurwitz, Elimination of the Conduct Requirement in Government Monopolization Cases, 37 Wash. & Lee L.Rev. 83 (1980); Flynn, No Conduct Monopolization: An Assessment for the Lawyer and Businessman, 49 Antitrust L.J. 1255 (1980); Fox, Monopoly and Competition: Tilting the Law Towards a More Competitive Economy, 37 Wash. & Lee L.Rev. 49 (1980).

Section 2A

Every person who possesses monopoly power in any relevant market shall be subject to proceedings to be brought by the United States Department of Justice or the Federal Trade Commission. Such proceedings shall be commenced in the United States District Court for the District of Columbia. Final review of all orders, decisions, remedies and other final actions by the District Court shall be solely by writ of certiorari from the United States Supreme Court.

Upon a finding that the person possesses monopoly power, the Court shall order the parties to the proceeding to propose remedies for the dissipation and elimination of the monopoly power found. Ordinarily, dissolution, divestiture or some other form of structural relief shall be the preferred remedy. In formulating such a remedy, the Court shall attempt to create the maximum number of viable entities possible without loss of substantial economies of scale. The burden of establishing substantial economies of scale shall be on the person found to possess monopoly power.

No punishment, civil or criminal, shall attach to a finding that a person possesses monopoly power; nor shall any penalty, civil or criminal, be imposed by virtue of the remedies selected by the Court to dissipate and eliminate the power found. Nor shall prima facie effect be given the judgment of the Court pursuant to Section 5 of the Clayton Act, 15 U.S.C. § 16, or any res judicata or collateral estoppel effect be given such judgment in any other proceeding to the prejudice or injury of the person found to have monopoly power pursuant to this Section.

The *Otter Tail* case which follows illustrates the use of Section 2 of the Sherman Act to reach monopolizing *behavior* as distinguished from monopolistic *structure*. Otter Tail's monopolistic structure was lawful under the Federal Power Act, and would have been lawful even if it had embraced 100% of the business in its area. Its "predatory practices"—including even litigation against allegedly illegal encroachments on its lawful monopoly—nevertheless subjected it to Section 2.

OTTER TAIL POWER CO. v. UNITED STATES

Supreme Court of the United States, 1973.
410 U.S. 366, 93 S.Ct. 1022, 35 L.Ed.2d 359, rehearing denied 411 U.S. 910, 93 S.Ct. 1523, 36 L.Ed.2d 201, on remand 360 F.Supp. 451 (D.C.Minn.), affirmed 417 U.S. 901, 94 S.Ct. 2594, 41 L.Ed.2d 207 (1974).

[Digest] Defendant, Otter Tail Power Company sells electric power at retail in 465 towns in Minnesota, North Dakota, and South Dakota. The power industry is generally viewed as functioning at three levels, *viz.* generation of power, long distance transmission of power for sale at wholesale to retail distributors, and local or retail distribution of power. There are 510 towns in Otter Tail's service area, 465 of which Otter Tail serves at retail under municipally granted franchises of 10 to 20 years duration. Otter Tail's general policy is to acquire municipally operated retail systems within its service area. Since 1946, Otter Tail had acquired municipally owned systems in six towns. Between 1945 and 1970, there were contests in 12 towns where Otter Tail held franchises to replace the Otter Tail franchise with municipally owned systems. Three towns established municipal systems, even though they faced such obstacles as buying power at wholesale from Otter Tail, the only supplier with transmission lines capable of delivering wholesale power.

The Justice Department charged that Otter Tail attempted to monopolize and monopolized in violation of § 2 of the Sherman Act the retail distribution of power in its service areas by tactics designed to prevent communities in which its retail distribution franchise had expired from replacing it with a municipal distribution system. Among the tactics employed by Otter Tail were: (1) refusal to sell power at wholesale to proposed municipal systems in the communities where it had been retailing power; (2) refusal to "wheel" power (transmit power purchased from other sources by the municipal systems) through Otter Tail's transmission lines; (3) litigating to delay establishment of municipal systems (primarily suits questioning the validity of bonds issued by municipalities to acquire a municipal power system); and (4) contracting with potential suppliers of wholesale power, e.g., the Bureau of Reclamation and rural electric cooperatives, barring use of Otter Tail's lines for wheeling power to towns which Otter Tail had served at retail.

The Court rejected Otter Tail's claim that it was not subject to antitrust regulation by virtue of Section 202(b) of the Federal Power Act, authorizing the Federal Power Commission to compel involuntary interconnections for supplying power. Finding no express exemption, implied exemption or pervasive regulatory scheme inconsistent with antitrust policy the Court rejected Otter Tail's claim that its refusal to supply or wheel power was immune from antitrust regulation.

MR. JUSTICE DOUGLAS delivered the opinion of the Court.

. . .

The record makes abundantly clear that Otter Tail used its monopoly power in the towns in its service area to foreclose competition or gain a competitive advantage, or to destroy a competitor, all in violation of the antitrust laws. The District Court determined that Otter Tail has "a strategic dominance in the transmission of power in most of its service area" and that it used this dominance to foreclose potential entrants into the retail area from obtaining electric power from outside sources of supply. Use of monopoly power "to destroy threatened competition" is a violation of the "attempt to monopolize" clause of § 2 of the Sherman Act. So are agreements not to compete, with the aim of preserving or extending a monopoly. In Associated Press v. United States, 326 U.S. 1, 65 S.Ct. 1416, 89 L.Ed. 2013, a cooperative news association had bylaws that permitted member newspapers to bar competitors from joining the association. We held that that practice violated the Sherman Act, even though the transgressor "had not yet achieved a complete monopoly."

When a community served by Otter Tail decides not to renew Otter Tail's retail franchise when it expires, it may generate, transmit, and distribute its own electric power. . . . Interconnection with other utilities is frequently the only solution. That is what Elbow Lake in the present case did. There were no engineering factors that prevented Otter Tail from selling power at wholesale to those towns that wanted municipal plants or wheeling the power. The District Court found—and its findings are supported—that Otter Tail's refusals to sell at wholesale or to wheel were solely to prevent municipal power systems from eroding its monopolistic position.

Otter Tail relies on its wheeling contracts with the Bureau of Reclamation and with cooperatives which it says relieve it of any duty to wheel power to municipalities served at retail by Otter Tail at the time the contracts were made. The District Court held that these restrictive provisions were "in reality, territorial allocation schemes," and were *per se* violations of the Sherman Act. Like covenants were there held to "deny defendant's competitors access to the fenced-off market on the same terms as the defendant." . . . The fact that some of the restrictive provisions were contained in a contract with the Bureau of Reclamation is not material to our problem for, as the Solicitor General says, "government contracting officers do not have the power to grant immunity from the Sherman Act." Such contracts stand on their own footing and are valid or not, depending on the statutory framework within which the federal agency operates. The Solicitor General tells us that these restrictive provisions operate as a "hindrance" to the Bureau and were "agreed to by the Bureau only at Otter Tail's insistence," as the District Court found. The evidence supports that finding.

The District Court found that the litigation sponsored by Otter Tail had the purpose of delaying and preventing the establishment of municipal electric systems "with the expectation that this would preserve its predominant position in the sale and transmission of electric power in the area."[31] The District Court in discussing Eastern Railroad Presidents Conference v. Noerr Motor Freight, 365 U.S. 127, 81 S.Ct. 523, 5 L.Ed.2d 464, explained that it was applicable "only to ef-

---

31. [Court's footnote 9] After noting that the "pendency of litigation has the effect of preventing the marketing of the necessary bonds thus preventing the establishment of a municipal system," . . . the District Court went on to find:

"Most of the litigation sponsored by the defendant was carried to the highest available appellate court and although all of it was unsuccessful on the merits, the institution and maintenance of it had the effect of halting, or appreciably slowing, efforts for munici-

pal ownership. The delay thus occasioned and the large financial burden imposed on the towns' limited treasury dampened local enthusiasm for public ownership. In some instances, Otter Tail made offers to the towns to absorb the towns' costs and expenses, and enhance the quality of its service in exchange for a new franchise. Hankinson, after several years of abortive effort, accepted this type of offer and renewed defendant's franchise." . . .

forts aimed at influencing the legislative and executive branches of the government." . . . That was written before we decided California Motor Transport Co. v. Trucking Unlimited, 404 U.S. 508, 513, 92 S.Ct. 609, 613, 30 L.Ed.2d 642, where we held that the principle of *Noerr* may also apply to the use of administrative or judicial processes where the purpose to suppress competition is evidenced by repetitive lawsuits carrying the hallmark of insubstantial claims and thus is within the "mere sham" exception announced in *Noerr*. On that phase of the order, we vacate and remand for consideration in light of our intervening decision in *California Motor Transport Co.**

Otter Tail argues that, without the weapons which it used, more and more municipalities will turn to public power and Otter Tail will go downhill. The argument is a familiar one. It was made in United States v. Arnold, Schwinn & Co., 388 U.S. 365, 87 S.Ct. 1856, 18 L.Ed. 2d 1249, a civil suit under § 1 of the Sherman Act dealing with a restrictive distribution program and practices of a bicycle manufacturer. We said: "The promotion of self-interest alone does not invoke the rule of reason to immunize otherwise illegal conduct."

The same may properly be said of § 2 cases under the Sherman Act. That Act assumes that an enterprise will protect itself against loss by operating with superior service, lower costs, and improved efficiency. Otter Tail's theory collided with the Sherman Act as it sought to substitute for competition anticompetitive uses of its dominant economic power.

The fact that three municipalities which Otter Tail opposed finally got their municipal systems does not excuse Otter Tail's conduct. That fact does not condone the antitrust tactics which Otter Tail sought to impose.

. . .

Except for the provision of the order [relating to the use of litigation as a monopolistic tactic] the judgment is *Affirmed.*

[Justices Blackmun and Powell did not participate in the decision. Justices Burger, Stewart and Rehnquist concurred on remanding the issue of the use of litigation as a tactic for monopolizing in light of *California Motor Transport Co.,* but dissented from the holding that the Federal Power Act did not vest primary jurisdiction in the Federal Power Commission to regulate Otter Tail's refusals to deal and refusals to wheel].[32]

* What standard should be applied to "repetitive lawsuits carrying the hallmarks of insubstantial claims" before concluding they restrain or monopolize trade? See Hebner, Litigation As An Overt Act In Furtherance of An Attempt to Monopolize, 38 Ohio State L.J. 245 (1977); Note, Limiting The Antitrust Immunity For Concerted Attempts To Influence Courts and Adjudicatory Agencies: Analogies to Malicious Prosecution and Abuse of Process, 86 Harv.L.Rev. 715 (1973).

32. The terms and conditions upon which Otter Tail is required to wheel power continue to be litigated. See Otter Tail Power Co. v. Federal Energy Regulatory Commission, 583 F.2d 399 (8th Cir. 1978).

NOTES AND QUERIES

[handwritten margin notes: "Either 1. illegal monop or 2. att to monop"]

(1) *Use of Monopoly Power in One Market to Injure Competition in Another Market.* In *United States v. Griffith*,[33] the defendants were charged with using the power they held by virtue of operating the only or major motion picture theatres in several New Mexico, Oklahoma, and Texas towns to demand that film distributors give them exclusive first-run rentals of films, control of second-run rentals, and other preferential treatment in towns where they faced competition. In holding the defendant's conduct violated Section 2 of the Sherman Act, the Court stated:

> [M]onopoly power, whether lawfully or unlawfully acquired, may itself constitute an evil and stand condemned under § 2 even though it remains unexercised. For § 2 of the Act is aimed, inter alia, at the acquisition or retention of effective market control. . . . Hence the existence of power 'to exclude competition when it is desired to do so' is itself a violation of § 2, provided it is coupled with the purpose or intent to exercise that power. . . . It is indeed 'unreasonable, per se, to foreclose competitors from any substantial market.' . . . The anti-trust laws are as much violated by the prevention of competition as by its destruction. . . . It follows a fortiori that the use of monopoly power, however lawfully acquired, to foreclose competition, to gain a competitive advantage, or to destroy a competitor, is unlawful.

> . . .

> If monopoly power can be used to beget monopoly, the Act becomes a feeble instrument indeed. Large-scale buying is not, of course, unlawful per se. It may yield price or other lawful advantages to the buyer. It may not, however, be used to monopolize or to attempt to monopolize interstate trade or commerce. Nor, . . . may it be used to stifle competition by denying competitors less favorably situated access to the market.[34]

Cases like *Otter Tail* and *Griffith* have given rise to the generalization that use of monopoly power in one market to monopolize another market is unlawful. But, what if monopoly power in one market is exercised in ways which injure competition in a market the monopolist does not compete in? When will a monopolist's conduct in related markets be considered conduct justifying the conclusion that the monopolist is using power in its monopoly market to monopolize the related market?

The first question is often raised in cases where a monopolist refuses to deal[35] and in cases where some action or non-action by a monopolist in its market injures or distorts competition in other markets. For example, in *Official Airline Guides, Inc. v. Federal Trade Commission*[36] the defendant, publisher of the only "Bible" of all airline schedules and fares in one place, was charged with violating Section 5 of the F.T.C. Act by refusing to integrate the schedules of certificated, intrastate and commuter airlines in its publication. The effect of the defendant's refusal was to handicap intrastate and commuter airlines in competing for connecting flights with certificated

---

33. 334 U.S. 100, 68 S.Ct. 941, 92 L.Ed. 1236 (1948).

34. 334 U.S. at 107–08, 68 S.Ct. at 945–46, 92 L.Ed. at 1243–44.

35. The leading cases are summarized and analyzed in Byars v. Bluff City News Co., 609 F.2d 843 (6th Cir. 1979). See al-

so Note, Refusals To Deal By Vertically Integrated Monopolists, 87 Harv.L.Rev. 1720 (1974).

36. 630 F.2d 920 (2d Cir. 1980), certiorari denied 450 U.S. 917, 101 S.Ct. 1362, 67 L.Ed.2d 343 (1981).

carriers whose connecting flights were all listed together. Connecting flights of commuter and intrastate carriers were listed separately. The defendant's refusal to integrate the schedules was of no observable benefit to it, but did injure intrastate and commuter airlines by placing them at a competitive disadvantage for connecting flights with users of the publication, a publication that is a monopoly in its field.

The F.T.C. held the publisher was a monopolist of a "scarce resource" and as such had a legal duty to exploit that resource in a manner that creates no "unjustified or invidious distinctions among competitors seeking access to the scarce resource."[37] The Commission held the refusal to integrate schedules was "arbitrary" [38] in the sense that it resulted in "substantial injury to competition and lacks substantial business justifications" [39] and ordered the defendant to integrate the schedules of connecting flights of each class of carrier in its monopoly publication.

The Second Circuit reversed. The court distinguished those cases holding unlawful a monopolist's conduct which adversely affects related markets on the ground that the monopolists in those cases were competitors in the related markets. The court added:

> [W]e think enforcement of the FTC's order here would give the FTC too much power to substitute its own business judgment for that of the monopolist in any decision that arguably affects competition in another industry. Such a decision would permit the FTC to delve into, as the Commission itself put the extreme case, 'social, political, or personal reasons' for a monopolist's refusal to deal. . . . Professors Areeda and Turner give examples of a monopolist theater which refuses to admit men with long hair or a monopolist newspaper which refuses to publish advertising from cigarette manufacturers. . . .[40] The Commission says that neither of these examples would trigger antitrust scrutiny because there is no competition among persons who attend movies, and refusing to publish advertisements for all cigarette companies would not place any of them at a disadvantage *vis-a-vis* a competitor. . . . Nevertheless, the Commission's own example . . . of a monopolist newspaper refusing to take advertisements from a particular cigarette company because of the style of prior advertisements or the political views of its president shows just how far the Commission's opinion could lead us. What we are doing, as the Commission itself recognized, is weighing benefits to competition in the other field against the detrimental effect of allowing the Commission to pass judgment on many business decisions of the monopolist that arguably discriminate among customers in some way.

> . . .

> Only recently we said . . . : '[i]t has always been the prerogative of a manufacturer to decide with whom it will deal.' . . . We think that even a monopolist, as long as he has no purpose to restrain competition or to enhance or expand his monopoly, and does not act coercively, retains this right. Absent enlightenment from above, or clarification from Congress, this is our decision on the merits.[41]

With whom do you agree? Is the court's analysis that *all* refusals to deal by a monopolist ought not be remedied by antitrust policy conclusive on the

37. 3 Trade Reg.Rep. ¶ 21,650 (FTC 1979).

38. Id. at p. 21,815.

39. Id. at p. 21,819.

40. Citing III P. Areeda & D. Turner, Antitrust Law, pp. 270–71.

41. 630 F.2d at 927–28.

question whether some ought to be unlawful?[42]   Should Section 2 of the Sherman Act be read as imposing affirmative duties on a monopolist?   If O.A.G. had also owned a certificated carrier, presumably the F.T.C. would not be disabled from either imposing duties on the way O.A.G. organized its publication or in ordering divestiture.   Is the court unduly concerned about interfering with the liberty of a monopolist to be arbitrary?

(2) *Pricing Practices as an Exercise of Monopoly Power From One Market to Another—Predatory Pricing.*   The pricing practices of a monopolist in markets where it is the sole or primary supplier, or where the monopolist is vertically integrating or competing with firms in related but non-monopolized markets, often present difficult issues of whether the pricing is pro-competitive and a result of efficiencies or anti-competitive and the result of an illegal translation of market or monopoly power from one market to another.   Pricing practices potentially displacing the competitive process in violation of the Sherman Act can be manipulated in a number of ways by a firm with monopoly power.[43]   For example, an oil company with monopoly power over gasoline marketing in one regional market which is the result of having the only refinery in the area, might seek to monopolize an adjacent geographic market by raising prices in the monopolized market to support price cuts driving out competitors in adjacent markets.   Once competition is driven from an adjacent market, the firm can then raise prices to a monopoly level in the adjacent market.   Or, an oil company with monopoly power over local supply may vertically integrate into the retail market and begin competing at retail with independent franchised retailers it supplies with gasoline. By manipulating the wholesale transfer price, the refiner could either sell gasoline at its wholly-owned retail outlets below cost while charging its independent franchised retailers a wholesale price above cost (predatory pricing) or sell gasoline at its wholly-owned retail outlets well above cost while charging its independent franchisees a wholesale price that equals the refinery run outlet's retail price (predatory costing).   In either case, the franchised retailer will be unable to compete profitably and will be driven from the market.

Although these kinds of pricing tactics have generated considerable debate in recent litigation and in the academy, they are not recent phenomena. A 1914 article [44] commented on the pricing strategies of the "trusts" of that era as follows:

> Local price-cutting has been a frequent and familiar weapon of the trusts.   As here used the term means that an organization cuts the prices of its products to a point below the cost of production in one or more of the localities where competition exists.   The loss entailed is usually recouped by the profits from the high prices charged in those regions where competition is either insignificant or non-existent.   This method has been employed repeatedly by large and powerful organizations.   The

42.   See Flynn, Monopolization Under The Sherman Act: The Third Wave and Beyond, 26 Antitrust Bull. 1, 123–25 (1981); Note, The Monopolist's Refusal To Deal: An Argument For A Rule of Reason, 59 Texas L.Rev. 1107 (1981).

43.   "Predatory pricing behavior involves a reduction of price in the short run so as to drive competing firms out of the market or to discourage entry of new firms in an effort to gain larger profits via higher prices in the long run than would have been earned if the price reduction had not occurred."   Joskow & Klevorick, A Framework for Analyzing Predatory Pricing Policy, 89 Yale L.J. 213, 219–20 (1979).

44.   Stevens, Unfair Competition, 29 Pol.Sci.Q. 282, 284–86 (1914).   This article was cited extensively in the Senate debates over the Clayton Act and Federal Trade Commission Act, in connection with discussions of discriminatory local price-cutting as an improper competitive tactic.

ultimate outcome in such cases, with but few exceptions, has been the destruction and elimination of competition in those regions where the method has been employed.

Probably the best examples of the operation of local price-cutting are to be found in the histories of the old oil and powder trusts. In the case of the former organization, the prices charged in various localities appear to have been definitely governed by the percentage of competition to be met in each section. An examination of the tables of prices, profits and percentages of competition presented in the *Brief for the United States* in the suit against the Standard Oil Company shows that the prices and profits on oil as between various localities were roughly high or low according as the percentages of competition were low or high. On October 15, 1904, the Standard Oil Company's profits and losses on white-water illuminating oil ranged from as high as 6.48 cents per gallon profit in Albuquerque, New Mexico, with 17 per cent of competition, and 6.1 cents per gallon profit in Spokane, with no competition, to as low as 3.16 cents per gallon loss in Los Angeles with 33.4 per cent of competition and 1.35 cents per gallon loss in New Orleans with 51.2 per cent of competition.

From the consumer's standpoint it is desirable that a concern shall sell its products at as low a price as possible. But this fact does not justify local price-cutting. Any gain to the consumer under this method, in addition to causing a corresponding loss to some other consumer, is obviously of a temporary character. When the organizations against which a campaign of local price-cutting is directed are driven from the field, their business is absorbed by the price-cutting concern. Prices then resume a level at least as high as under fair competition. Frequently they reach an even higher one. Efficient or inefficient, no organization can long survive a program of local price-cutting. . . . The economic unfairness of the method lies in the destruction of efficient organizations. If the price charged for a given commodity were based upon production costs, every organization able to attain a certain degree of productive efficiency could compete. Every concern would have a reasonable chance of surviving. Only the inefficient would be eliminated. Under local price-cutting the prices made by the price-cutting organization have no relation to production costs. Productive efficiency is therefore no defence to competitors against such an attack. This quality alone will not enable them to survive. Possibly it may prolong the struggle. Yet even this may be doubted. It is not unlikely that the greater the productive efficiency of competitors, the more strenuous will be the warfare waged against them.

It may be argued with considerable force that an organization ought not be deprived of the use of local price-cutting. Assume that a large trust discovers that it is losing business in a given locality to concern "A." Because of its efficiency, "A" has been able to reduce its prices even below those of the trust. Ought not the latter then to be allowed to cut its prices in "A's" locality in order to regain its lost business? To answer this question in the affirmative, is to overlook the serious general consequences of the use of this method. Price-cutting in selected localities is too dangerous a weapon to be permitted to any organization. If allowed under extenuating circumstances like those supposed above, there is not and cannot be any guarantee that it will not be employed for other purposes, among which the chief would be to destroy all competition. In the above illustration the only method by which the trust should be permitted to regain the business lost to "A," is by a general instead of a local price-cut. Then if it cuts prices below the cost of production in

"A's" territory, it must do the same throughout the country. In such a situation every dollar lost by "A" in retaining its business would mean a thousand lost by the trust. "A" has a reasonable chance of surviving. Strong probability exists that it can endure this state of affairs for as long a period as the trust. If the trust's efficiency so increases that without loss it is able to reduce its prices throughout the country to a level below that of "A's" costs of production, then "A" may be forced to the wall. But such an elimination would not be unfair, since it is based upon the survival of the efficient.

There is widespread agreement that pricing and costing tactics by a firm with market power, particularly monopoly power, can be used to destroy competition and expand monopoly power from one market to another or to prevent competitive inroads in markets presently monopolized.[45] There is also widespread agreement that pricing practices, those of monopolists as well as competitors, can be a central expression of the vigorous operation of the very competitive process the statute seeks to preserve and foster. Finding standards for sensibly and sensitively sorting out the anticompetitive and the procompetitive pricing practice in the context of particular cases and in a way that is manageable by the judicial process, has become the central issue in several recent monopolization cases and a topic of wide-ranging academic debate.[46]

This issue has been extensively litigated in a series of private monopolization cases involving claims that I.B.M. has used its market power over mainframe computers to exclude competitors in markets for peripheral devices used in conjunction with computers through a variety of marketing and pricing tactics. The issue first surfaced in the computer cases in *Telex Corp. v. International Business Machines Corp.*,[47] where I.B.M. designated management "task forces" to plan responses to competition in selected submarkets for peripheral equipment. The District Court found that the price cuts implemented by the task forces were aimed at competition in peripheral markets from relatively small manufacturers. The court held the use of selected price cuts in markets where competitors were making inroads on I.B.M.'s dominant position constituted an "unlawful maintenance of a monopoly", even though there was no evidence that I.B.M. reduced prices below cost. The Court of Appeals reversed, holding that the Sherman Act should not be interpreted "to prohibit the adoption of legal and ordinary marketing methods already used by others in the market, or to prohibit price changes within the 'reasonable' range, up or down."[48] No standard was provided or

45. For a dissent from this proposition, see R. Bork, The Antitrust Paradox 149–55 (1978).

46. The debate is well summarized and analyzed in Joskow & Klevorick, A Framework for Analyzing Predatory Pricing Policy, 89 Yale L.J. 213 (1979); Brodley & Hay, Predatory Pricing: Competing Economic Theories and the Evolution of Legal Standards, 66 Cornell L.Rev. 738 (1981). See also, Chillicothe Sand & Gravel Co. v. Martin Marietta Corp., 615 F.2d 427 (7th Cir. 1980); William Inglis & Sons Baking Co. v. ITT Continental Baking Co., Inc., 668 F.2d 1014 (9th Cir. 1981) petition for cert. filed ___ U.S. ___, 103 S.Ct. 58, 74 L.Ed.2d 61

(1982); Transamerica Computer Co., Inc. v. International Business Machines Corp., 481 F.Supp. 965 (N.D.Cal.1979); E. I. DuPont de Nemours & Co., 3 Trade Reg.Rep. ¶ 21,770 (F.T.C.1980). A complete survey of the judicial opinions on predation may be found in Hurwitz & Kovacic, Judicial Analysis of Predation: The Emerging Trends, 35 Vanderbilt L.Rev. 63 (1982).

47. 367 F.Supp. 258 (N.D.Okl.1973), reversed 510 F.2d 894 (10th Cir. 1975), certiorari dismissed 423 U.S. 802, 96 S.Ct. 8, 46 L.Ed.2d 244 (1976).

48. 510 F.2d at 927.

suggested for determining the boundaries of a "reasonable range" up or down.

Professors Areeda and Turner suggested that the "reasonable range" be defined by reference to the models and concepts of neo-classical price-theory for defining costs of a firm.[49] Classical theory assumes that a monopolist will price at a level designed to maximize its present return by reducing output and raising prices beyond what would prevail in a competitive market. When faced with competition or threatened competition, the monopolist may cut prices in the short run to exclude competition and maintain its long run power to reduce output and raise prices. Classical theory further assumes that in a competitive market, sellers cannot dictate price but will continue to expand output so long as the revenue received from producing an additional unit of output exceeds the cost of producing it. When the added cost ("marginal cost") of producing an additional unit equals the added revenue ("marginal revenue") received from selling it, the firm will cease expanding output. By comparing the abstract models of pricing by a monopolist and pricing in a competitive market, it is assumed various concepts of cost can be relied upon to provide a standard courts may use to determine when specific pricing practices by a firm with monopoly power cross the line of pro-competitive behavior and become predatory exclusionary behavior of a monopolist.[50]

Different concepts of cost are arrived at by breaking down the kinds of costs facing a firm. "Fixed costs" (e.g., depreciation, management expenses) are incurred even if no output is produced. "Variable costs" (e.g., labor, materials, utilities) vary with output. Whether costs are classified as fixed or variable is dependent upon the level of output and time.[51] Beginning with these concepts, three different concepts of the cost per unit of production can be derived;

(1) Marginal cost: "the increment to total cost that results from producing an additional increment of output"; [52]

(2) Average variable cost: "the sum of all variable costs divided by output"; [53] and,

(3) Average cost: "the sum of fixed cost and variable cost, divided by output".[54]

Areeda and Turner proposed that prices above marginal cost (or its easier to determine surrogate, average variable cost) should be conclusively presumed to be non-predatory. Since "fixed costs" do not change with output in the short-run, the Areeda-Turner test emphasizes short-run variable costs as the dividing line between the predatory and the competitive price cut.

---

49. Predatory Pricing and Related Practices Under Section 2 of The Sherman Act, 88 Harv.L.Rev. 697 (1975).

50. The basic theory is set forth in Areeda & Turner, supra note 49 at 700–703. For general surveys of neo-classical theory see R. Posner, Economic Analysis of Law (2d Ed. 1977), relevant excerpts reprinted in T. Calvani & J. Siegfried, Economic Analysis and Antitrust Law, pp. 6–20 (1979); E. Gellhorn, Antitrust Law and Economics, pp. 41–83 (Nutshell Series 2d Ed. 1981).

51. "Virtually all costs are variable when a firm, operating at capacity, plans to double its output by constructing new plants and purchasing new equipment.

Moreover, more costs become variable as the time period increases. The variable costs . . . are those incurred in what is usually termed the 'short-run', namely, the period in which the firm cannot replace or increase plant or equipment. Conversely, in the 'long-run' the firm can vary quantities of *all* inputs (plant and equipment as well as short-run variable inputs); thus, all costs are variable over the long-run." Areeda & Turner, supra note 49 at 701.

52. Id. at 700.

53. Id.

54. Id.

Scholars have attacked the Areeda-Turner standard because of its emphasis on the short-run;[55] its static nature, which prevents an examination of the strategic aspects of the conduct in a dynamic context;[56] its emphasis on narrow efficiency goals to the exclusion of other considerations;[57] and the serious practical limitations upon implementing the proposal in the litigation process and in the context of the complexity of multi-product firms like I.B.M.[58] While the debate and controversy are too complex to rehearse here, the student of antitrust law should appreciate the difficulties inherent in relying on pricing practices to prove monopolization and the risks for maintaining a competitive process if the tests for proving predatory pricing are too arbitrary, artificial, burdensome or impractical to apply in the litigation process. Several more general questions should also be considered. To what extent should the determination of whether predatory pricing by a monopolist is taking place be made to turn upon abstract and static models of pricing behavior in perfectly competitive markets? To what extent can the determination avoid doing so? To what extent does the model selected permit an evaluation of long-term and short-term consequences of the pricing practices involved? How does one practically determine what are fixed and what are variable costs, particularly in cases where the alleged monopolist is a multi-product firm? What other evidence, in addition to the specific pricing practices involved, may be relied upon to prove or disprove a claim that a monopolist is using power from one market to monopolize another? Who should bear the burden of proving a monopolist's prices are above a particular cost standard?

These and other issues have generated increased skepticism in the courts about relying upon any single theory of when particular pricing practices should be deemed "predatory pricing." In *Transamerica Computer Co., Inc. v. International Business Machines Corp.,*[59] Judge Schnacke criticized the marginal cost standard as a "figment of the economists imagination", a standard incapable of proof, and a "defendant's paradise".[60] Instead, the

55. See Scherer, Predatory Pricing and The Sherman Act: A Comment, 89 Harv.L.Rev. 869 (1976); Areeda & Turner, Scherer on Predatory Pricing: A Reply, 89 Harv.L.Rev. 891 (1976); Scherer, Some Last Words on Predatory Pricing, 89 Harv.L.Rev. 901 (1976).

56. See Williamson, Predatory Pricing: A Strategic and Welfare Analysis, 87 Yale L.J. 284 (1977); Areeda & Turner, Williamson on Predatory Pricing, 87 Yale L.J. 1337 (1978); Williamson, Williamson on Predatory Pricing II, 88 Yale L.J. 1183 (1979). See also Spence, Entry Capacity, Investment and Oligopolistic Pricing, 8 Bell J. of Econ. 534 (1977).

57. See Dirlam, Marginal Cost Pricing Tests for Predation: Naive Welfare Economics and Public Policy, 26 Antitrust Bull. 769 (1981); Sullivan, Economics and More Humanistic Disciplines: What Are The Sources of Wisdom For Antitrust?, 125 U.Pa.L.Rev. 1214, 1225–32 (1977).

58. Joskow & Klevorick, supra note 46 at 216; Flynn, Monopolization Under the Sherman Act: The Third Wave and Beyond, 26 Antitrust Bull. 1, 73–74 (1981); Bodley & Hay, Predatory Pricing:

Competing Economic Theories and the Evolution of Legal Stanards, 66 Cornell L.Rev. 738 (1981).

59. 481 F.Supp. 965 (N.D.Cal.1979), affirmed 698 F.2d 1377 (9th Cir. 1983).

60. Id. at 994–95. The Court further criticized the Areeda & Turner proposal as follows:

"But even if their theory had merit, if all the world's economists were of one voice, and like Areeda and Turner, placed their faith in the monopolist to maximize social welfare by eliminating competitors from crowded industries through temporary provision of more and lower priced goods, the Congress and the courts have already placed their faith elsewhere. The goal of welfare maximization through proper resource allocation is to be accomplished by a system of effective competition, not by reliance on the presumed beneficence of a monopolist. . . . The economic rationale behind the act cannot be overcome by arguments that the monopolist has provided economic benefits. . . .

court drew the line of legality at average cost by adopting standards which: 1) conclusively presume prices in excess of average cost are lawful; and 2) consider prices below average cost illegal if they are "unreasonable" (not otherwise justifiable or excusable). Determining whether I.B.M.'s pricing of peripherals was in fact below average cost necessarily required complex and arbitrary cost accounting calculations allocating various elements of cost to the different peripheral products in question. In each case, the court concluded I.B.M. had not priced below average cost.

Is an average cost standard any more justified or capable of administration than a marginal cost or average variable cost standard? In view of the practical difficulties of proving prices are above or below any particular definition of cost, how realistic is it to expect predatory pricing cases effectively and efficiently to curb exercises of monopoly power? Is this an argument for adopting a no-conduct monopoly standard to deal with persistent monopoly power?

(3) *Predatory Costing.* In some circumstances, a monopolist may be in a position to exclude competitors by raising, rather than cutting, prices. For example, in *City of Mishawaka v. Indiana & Michigan Electric Co.*,[61] ten municipal power systems dependent on Indiana and Michigan (I. & M.) for their supply of power for resale in their service areas, charged I. & M. with monopolizing the sale of retail power in their service areas by a "price squeeze". The plaintiffs claimed I. & M. set the wholesale price for power to

"Areeda and Turner have made a policy judgment. The economic analysis used to justify that judgment is incomplete, and the judgment itself stands contradicted by the economic, political, and social policies of the Sherman Act."

Id. In William Inglis & Sons Baking Co. v. ITT Continental Baking Co., Inc., 668 F.2d 1014 (9th Cir. 1981), certiorari denied ___ U.S. ___, 103 S.Ct. 58, 74 L.Ed. 2d 61 (1982), a panel of the Ninth Circuit adopted tests of presumptive legality and illegality similar to those developed by Judge Schnacke in *Transamerica.* The Second Circuit, on the other hand, appears to have adopted a literal application of the Areeda-Turner test. See Northeastern Telephone Co. v. American Telephone & Telegraph Co., 651 F.2d 76 (2d Cir. 1981), certiorari denied 455 U.S. 943, 102 S.Ct. 1438, 71 L.Ed.2d 654 (1982). *Inglis,* supra, offered the following rationale for scrutinizing prices between average total cost and average variable cost (668 F.2d at 1035):

Although pricing below average total cost and above average variable cost is not inherently predatory, it does not follow, however, that such prices are never predatory. Predation exists when the justification of these prices is based, not on their effectiveness in minimizing losses, but on their tendency to eliminate rivals and create a market structure enabling the seller to recoup his losses. This is the ultimate standard, and not rigid adherence to a

particular cost-based rule, that must govern our analysis of alleged predatory pricing.

The court's original opinion continued with the following paragraph, see 1981–2 Trade Cas. ¶ 64,229, at p. 73,909; the court subsequently amended its opinion to delete it (too controversial?):

Much of the academic dispute over predatory pricing tests appears to be attributable to the view that a rigid rule is necessary and to disagreements about the effects of various rules on resource allocation. A review of the economic literature convinces us that the methods of calculating allocative effects are far from precise. For this reason alone, we should be reluctant to harness the law to the goal of allocative efficiency. A conclusive reason, however, is that the antitrust laws were designed to protect competition, not solely to improve allocative efficiency.

61. 560 F.2d 1314 (7th Cir. 1977), certiorari denied 436 U.S. 922, 98 S.Ct. 2274, 56 L.Ed.2d 765 (1981) (opinion of exclusive and primary jurisdiction issues); 616 F.2d 976 (7th Cir. 1980), certiorari denied 449 U.S. 1096, 101 S.Ct. 892, 66 L.Ed.2d 824 (1981), rehearing denied 450 U.S. 960, 101 S.Ct. 1421, 67 L.Ed.2d 385 (1981) (opinion on antitrust liability). See also Town of Massena v. Niagara Mohawk Power Corp., 1980–2 Trade Cases ¶ 63,526 (N.D.N.Y.1980).

them higher than I. & M.'s retail price to industrial customers, thereby preventing the municipals from competing with I. & M. for sales to industrial customers in their service areas except at a loss. One objective of the price squeeze was alleged to be the gradual takeover of the municipals by I. & M. squeezing them into "financial extinction". In upholding a finding that I. & M. violated Section 2 of the Sherman Act, the court relied upon I. & M.'s pricing tactics, coupled with evidence of a specific intent to exclude the municipals and take over their retail customers by intentionally maintaining the price squeeze through manipulation of federal wholesale and state retail rate filings, threatening the continuation of the municipal's wholesale power supply, and a past policy of acquiring municipal systems in its area.

What limitations should be placed on a monopoly supplier's pricing tactics, where it vertically integrates and competes at retail with retailers dependent on the monopolist for supply? Should it be assumed that the monopolist is using monopoly power from one market to monopolize another market where the monopolist sells at retail at a price equal to or below the wholesale price it charges its retail competitors? Should evidence of a specific intent to exclude be required in addition to evidence of the price squeeze?

(4) *Beyond Cost/Price Relations: The "Human Animus" Test of "Predation".* Sullivan, Antitrust Economics and Other, More Humanistic Disciplines: What Are the Sources of Wisdom for Antitrust?, 125 U.Pa.L.Rev. 1214 (1977) reviews the scholarly controversy over definition of predatory pricing, and concludes that the definitions proposed are "speculative and indeterminate:"

Courts could not deal with them. How, then, should antitrust respond? The answer may be that courts must look beyond economic theory for ways of dealing with predatory conduct. If we are going to rely on judges and jurors to discover predatory practices we cannot limit the inquiry to price-cost relationships. The traditional legal rule does not. It focuses on human animus. The predatory firm tries to inhibit others in ways independent of the predator's own ability to perform effectively in the market. Predation may involve grossly tortious conduct, like warehouse burning; a price reduction or expenditure is predatory where it has analogous qualities, when designed to impose losses on other firms in order to exclude them.

If this traditional norm is accepted there are factors to be examined in addition to price-cost relationships. A firm which seeks to drive out or exclude rivals by selling at unremunerative prices will leave human traces of that intent; the very concept is one of a human animus bent, if you please, upon a course of conduct socially disapproved. Pretrial discovery procedures are really quite efficient where focused on uncovering such things. And there is one task that judges and juries, informed through the adversary system, may really be good at. It is identifying the pernicious in human affairs. To contend that the conventional formulation of predatory conduct, which looks, in a sense, for evil, ought to be amended to one which looks solely to an effect validated by economic studies is to assume too much about the precision of applied economics and to assume too little about the value of more humanistic modes of inquiry.

Predatory conduct, though seldom obvious and often difficult to identify with certainty, does indeed occur. The fact that predatory activity is costly to the predator and that there is only an uncertain prospect of adequate supra-competitive returns after others are excluded surely must reduce the frequency of predatory forays. It hardly follows that they never occur or can be safely ignored. Man's capacity for destructive conduct has never been totally inhibited merely because he stands himself in the target area along with his would-be victim. The best course, moreover, is to leave the avenues of inquiry as open as may be. Objective data, such as that stressed by Areeda and Turner, could then be used either to attack or defend, but so also could any other evidence indicative of predatory intent. There are at least two hallmarks. First, there will be something odd, something jarring or unnatural seeming about the conduct when viewed in its industrial setting. It will not strike the informed observer as normal business conduct, as honestly industrial. Second, it will be aimed at a target, at an identifiable competitor or potential competitor, or an identifiable group of them.

Do you agree? Does Sullivan propose a standard which can guide firms in the marketplace or courts in the adjudication of antitrust cases? How would you analyze a case in which I.B.M. had been accused of announcing new products and improvements long before they will be available, with the purpose or effect of discouraging potential buyers of non-I.B.M. equipment? Should a court find such a practice in violation of Section 2?[62] Should the F.T.C. find such conduct an "unfair method of competition" under Section 5 of the F.T.C. Act?[63] What criteria should be used to adjudge the announcement premature and "predatory"?

(5) *Oligopolistic Advertising as an Instrument of Monopoly; Remedy?* In Report on the Supply of Household Detergents (1966), the British Monopolies Commission found that the advertising policies of Unilever, Ltd. and Procter & Gamble, Ltd., two dominant manufacturers of household detergents, were "for the purpose of preserving their respective monopolies" and "keeping new entrants out of the market", and that high prices had resulted from this monopolistic activity. The Commission recommended a 40% cut in marketing costs and a reduction in selling prices. It also proposed that excessive promotion costs be disallowed as business expense in the income tax returns. The Board of Trade, to which the Monopolies Commission reports, then worked out a compromise with the firms. They accepted a price-freeze on their highly advertised brands, but no reduction in price or restraint on advertising expenditures. They agreed to introduce a new line of top-quality soap and detergents at wholesale prices 20% lower than their established brands.

The annual report for 1966 of the Federal Cartel Office of West Germany commented on the problem of oligopolistic advertising, and indicated a policy of not treating dominant firms as substantially competing with each other if their rivalry manifested itself chiefly in inflated advertising costs. The consequence would be that such firms would be subject to orders against abuse of market-dominating power, under Section 22 of the German Law Against Restraints of Competition, and that they would lose the privilege of engaging in resale price maintenance under Section 16(1), which permitted resale price maintenance only if the goods compete with those of other suppliers.

Should such conduct be actionable under American antitrust laws?[64]

62. See Note, Innovation Competition: Beyond *Telex v. International Business Machines*, 28 Stan.L.Rev. 285 (1976).

63. See Note, Annual Style Change in the Automobile Industry as an Unfair Method of Competition, 80 Yale L.J. 567

(1971); Selander, Is Annual Style Change in the Automobile Industry an Unfair Method of Competition? 82 Yale L.J. 691 (1973).

64. See In the Matter of Kellogg Co., [F.T.C. Complaints and Orders 1970-73]

(6) *Intent to Monopolize; Pursuit of a "Natural Monopoly."* When the printers struck against the Gazette, the only newspaper published in Haverhill, Mass., its circulation fell 50%, and a group of Haverhill merchants besought one Loeb to publish a "shopper" in which Christmas advertising might appear. Loeb published the only newspaper in Manchester, N. H., 28 miles away. Upon favorable reception of his "shopper," he launched the Haverhill Journal. A "life-and-death struggle" followed, with various "unfair" tactics being employed on both sides, e.g., discriminatory reductions in advertising rates in favor of large advertisers who would agree to advertise exclusively in one paper; boycotting of newsdealers who handled the opposition paper; secret subsidies to some merchants to represent themselves as impartial proponents of the Journal; collaboration of the printers union with the Journal to persuade merchants to advertise exclusively in the Journal. Injunctive relief against unfair practices was granted against each party.[65] Both were absolved of monopolizing or attempting to monopolize insofar as they sought merely to remain or become the sole newspaper in what was conceded to be a "one-newspaper town":

> "It was a foregone conclusion that if successful the Journal would eventually drive the Gazette out of business, and, naturally, Union Leader [Loeb's enterprise publishing the Journal] proposed to succeed. But intending the natural consequences of acts which are in all respects lawful does not constitute the 'exclusionary intent' that is a prerequisite for finding a violation of section 2."

Newspapers of New England Inc. was a group of 30 New England newspapers that finally bought out the Gazette interests, from what appears to have been a mixture of motives: resentment of Loeb's methods; recognition that if he succeeded they too might face invasion of a competing paper in their one-newspaper towns; the prospect of a good investment if Loeb was defeated. The evidence was held insufficient to establish opposition by NNE to anything more than Loeb's methods. The prospect of such competition was held to be unreal in view of the fact that in 20 years only two newspapers had been started in New England; and the only one other than the Journal had soon failed.[66]

(7) *Monopoly by Internal Expansion?* The suggestion in the *ALCOA* case that aggressive expansion of capital facilities, without other predatory or exclusionary practices, might suffice to establish illegal monopolization was argued before the F.T.C. in E. I. DuPont de Nemours & Co.[67] The F.T.C. staff charged that DuPont was attempting to monopolize production of titanium dioxide pigments ("TiO2"), a chemical used in the manufacture of

Trade Reg. Rep. (CCH) ¶ 19,898 (F.T.C. 1972) (complaint charging four largest manufacturers of ready-to-eat cereals with illegally monopolizing the industry for thirty years through proliferation of brands and trademark advertising, artificial differentiation of products, unfair advertising and product promotion, control of shelf space, and acquisition of competitors). An administrative law judge has dismissed the case for failure of proof. See Trade Reg. Rep. (CCH) No. 507, part II (Sept. 14, 1981). An order denying appeal and dismissing the F.T.C.'s complaint was entered by the F.T.C. on Jan. 15, 1982. See 3 Trade Reg. Rep. (CCH) ¶ 21,899 (F.T.C. 1982).

65. Union Leader Corp. v. Newspapers of New England, 284 F.2d 582 (1st Cir. 1960), certiorari denied 365 U.S. 833, 81 S.Ct. 747, 5 L.Ed.2d 744 (1961).

66. Compare Scott Publishing Co. v. Columbia Basin Publishers, Inc., 293 F.2d 15 (9th Cir. 1961).

67. 3 Trade Reg. Rep. (CCH) ¶ 21,770 (F.T.C. 1980). See, also, Hiland Dairy, Inc. v. Kroger Co., 402 F.2d 968 (8th Cir. 1968), certiorari denied 395 U.S. 961, 89 S.Ct. 2096, 223 L.Ed.2d 748 (1969) (no attempt to monopolize violation by expanding milk processing plant to meet demand of 20% of the local milk market).

paint and paper to make them whiter or opaque. DuPont developed a technology for making TiO2 which used a different and low grade ore and was a more efficient continuous process. Other producers depended on rutile ore and a batch process. In 1970, a shortage of rutile ore caused costs for competing TiO2 producers to skyrocket and new environmental regulations added expensive pollution abatement costs to the production of TiO2. DuPont, with approximately 30% of the market in 1972, found itself with an exclusive TiO2 process that gave it a significant cost advantage over competitors dependent on more expensive ore, a less efficient manufacturing process, and faced with costly pollution abatement expenditures. DuPont decided to expand aggressively its plant capacity to capture new demand and increase its market share to 55% by 1985. It was alleged DuPont planned to price its TiO2 high enough to finance its expanded capacity, yet low enough to discourage rivals from expanding while refusing to license its cost-saving low grade ore technology.

The F.T.C. dismissed the complaint, finding DuPont's conduct was not unreasonably exclusionary under the circumstances and in light of DuPont's present market share. In the course of determining whether DuPont's conduct was "unreasonably exclusionary" the Commission observed:

> [T]he courts have fashioned a variety of criteria such as (a) whether the behavior amounted to ordinary marketing practices, (b) whether it was profitable or economically rational, (c) whether it resulted in improved product performance or (d) whether it would have been effective for a firm without market power. In addition, several of the decisions emphasize that the lawfulness of the practices depends on the market setting (e.g., nature of entry barriers) and the anticompetitive potential of the challenged practices. . . .

> In the present case, DuPont's conduct appears to be justified by respondent's cost superiority over its rivals, demand forecasts and scale economies. There is no evidence that DuPont's pricing or capacity strategies were unprofitable (regardless of the cost test employed) and, . . . the plant announcements do not appear to be misleading. Yet, that is not the end of our inquiry. As we have suggested, the proper test for measuring the reasonableness of DuPont's conduct takes account of overall competitive effects—pro and con—within the relevant market setting.

> Having reviewed the legal precedents and economic literature on the subject of predation, we believe that the conduct under question should be assessed generally in light of the respondent's market power, the nature of its conduct and prevailing market conditions. As the firm's market power approaches monopoly proportions, the standard for measuring the legality of the firm's behavior would more closely approximate the standard applicable to monopolists. . . . We suspect . . . that in many instances the challenged conduct can be fairly categorized as clearly legitimate competitive behavior, on the one hand, or as behavior which clearly has little or no redeeming justification, on the other hand. For the gray areas in between, we believe there is no substitute for a careful, considered look at the overall competitive effects of the practices under scrutiny.[68] In the absence of a stronger consensus among the courts and

---

68. [The Commission's footnote 38.] At a more specific level, some of the factors that appear especially pertinent to a proper rule-of-reason type analysis include: (1) the extent to which the conduct enhances efficiency or innovation, including profitability considerations; (2) the extent to which the conduct is a reaction to competitive behavior, demand shifts, new technology or other market conditions; (3) the permanence or reversibility of the challenged actions; (4) the alterna-

commentators as to the lawful parameters of monopoly or dominant firm behavior, we believe that a balancing approach, which takes due account of rational, efficiency related conduct, is best suited to the task at hand.[69]

Should evidence that DuPont was pricing TiO2 well in excess of its average cost plus a reasonable profit, while building additional capacity far in excess of present demand, suffice to prove unlawful monopolization?[70]   At what point, if ever, in DuPont's growth in TiO2 market share, should the F.T.C. order licensing of the exclusive DuPont process?   Should a monopolist ever be deprived of non-patent technological advantages contributing to the maintenance of its monopoly power?

BERKEY PHOTO, INC. v. EASTMAN KODAK CO.

United States Court of Appeals, Second Circuit, 1979.
603 F.2d 263, certiorari denied 444 U.S. 1093, 100 S.Ct. 1061, 62 L.Ed.2d 783 (1980).

I. THE FACTS

[Digest: Berkey, a firm providing photofinishing services and film and cameras for sale, filed a Section 2 treble damage action against Kodak, the dominant firm in the amateur photographic industry with 1977 sales of nearly $6 billion and pre-tax profits in excess of $1.2 billion. Kodak is vertically integrated in all phases of the industry. Kodak was Berkey's competitor in some markets (principally cameras until Berkey abandoned that market in 1978 and in color photofinishing services) and Berkey's supplier in other markets (film, photofinishing equipment, and color print paper). Although there was considerable controversy at trial over market definitions,[71] for purposes of the appeal the court settled on the nationwide markets for amateur conventional still cameras (principally the 110 and 126 instant loading cameras), conventional photographic film, photofinishing services, photofinishing equipment and color print paper. The court's description of these markets and the Kodak-Berkey relationship in them may be summarized as follows:

tives available to the firm; and (5) the effect of the conduct on entry barriers and rival firm behavior. As we have noted, however, resort to such benchmarks as whether the practices constituted "ordinary" or "typical" business behavior may be of some value, but they can hardly be expected to serve as reliable indicators of competitive effects, especially where market power is substantial and entry barriers high. Even behavior that improves efficiency or technology may still be unreasonable, since the benefits may be only incidental in relation to the adverse effects (e.g., improvements instituted merely as a temporary measure for the purpose of driving competitors out of

the market). As we have seen, increases in output, a normal and usually legitimate form of competitive behavior, may be used primarily as an exclusionary tactic.

69. 3 Trade Reg. Rep. at pp. 21,981–82.

70. See the testimony of the Staff's expert witness, Professor William G. Shepherd, reprinted in 11 Antitrust Law & Economics Rev. 103 (1979); 12 Antitrust Law & Economics Rev. 73, 93 (1980).

71. Berkey Photo, Inc. v. Eastman Kodak Co., 457 F.Supp. 404 (S.D.N.Y. 1978).

	KODAK Market Shares	BERKEY Market Shares	Relationship
Amateur Conventional Still Cameras	61% plus by Annual Unit Sales (1954–1973) 64% plus by Annual Dollar Volume	8.2% sales (1970–1977)	Competitors
Conventional Photographic Films	82% plus Annual Unit Sales 88% plus Annual Revenues	———	Supplier
Photofinishing Services[72]	95% of Pre-1954 Market 10% of market by 1976	One of the largest of 600 competing photofinishers	Competitors
Photofinishing Equipment	Not available and no monopoly claimed	———	Supplier
Color Print Paper	Decline from 94% to 60% in sales between 1968–1976 60% constant earnings on sales during the same period	———	Supplier

Berkey claimed Kodak used monopoly power in the camera, film, and color print paper markets to injure it in the camera and photofinishing markets and to cause Berkey to pay excessive prices to Kodak for film, color print paper and photofinishing equipment. Among the specific practices Berkey claimed Kodak used to injure it in violation of Section 2 was Kodak's introduction of a new and smaller cartridge loading camera (the 110 camera) and a new color film (Kodacolor II) for use in the camera. Kodak developed the camera and film together, without notice to competing camera manufacturers and photofinishers of the new film's small size ("format"), its claimed better quality, and its different (higher temperature) processing characteristics. The new camera and film were introduced in 1972 and were an instant and dramatic success. Kodak did not produce its old Kodacolor X film in a format compatible with the new 110 camera, nor for a period of 18 months did it produce its new Kodacolor II film in a format compatible with cameras other than its 110 model. Competing camera sellers found themselves disadvantaged for a time by not having camera models compatible with the new film and the new film was unavailable in other sizes compatible with different sized cameras. Competing film processors also found themselves disadvantaged for a time, because the new film could not be processed with the photofinishing chemicals and equipment used in processing Kodak's other films.

72. In United States v. Eastman Kodak Co., 1954 Trade Cases ¶ 67,920 (W.D.N.Y.1954), Kodak was enjoined by a consent decree from tying the sale of photofinishing services to the sale of film by including the price of photofinishing in the price of film.

Berkey claimed Kodak's conduct in introducing its new camera and film violated Section 2 of the Sherman Act. After a nine month jury trial, a verdict was entered against Kodak on several counts and treble damages, costs, and attorney's fees in excess of $87 million were entered in judgment against Kodak. The Court of Appeals reversed most of the judgment, affirmed some parts of the judgment and remanded several claims for further proceedings.]

CHIEF JUDGE KAUFMAN delivered the opinion of the Court.

II. SECTION 2 OF THE SHERMAN ACT

Section 2, . . . is aimed primarily not at improper conduct but at a pernicious market structure in which the concentration of power saps the salubrious influence of competition.

Indeed, there is little argument over the principle that existence of monopoly power . . . is "the primary requisite to a finding of monopolization." . . .

Because, like all power, it is laden with the possibility of abuse; because it encourages sloth rather than the active quest for excellence; and because it tends to damage the very fabric of our economy and our society, monopoly power is "inherently evil." . . . If a finding of monopoly power were all that were necessary to complete a violation of § 2, our task in this case would be considerably lightened. Kodak's control of the film and color paper markets clearly reached the level of a monopoly. And, while the issue is a much closer one, it appears that the evidence was sufficient for the jury to find that Kodak possessed such power in the camera market as well. But our inquiry into Kodak's liability cannot end there.

Despite the generally recognized evils of monopoly power, it is "well settled," that § 2 does not prohibit monopoly *simpliciter*—or, . . . "monopoly in the concrete."

Thus, while proclaiming vigorously that monopoly power is the evil at which § 2 is aimed, courts have declined to take what would have appeared to be the next logical step—declaring monopolies unlawful *per se* unless specifically authorized by law. To understand the reason for this, one must comprehend the fundamental tension— one might almost say the paradox—that is near the heart of § 2. This tension creates much of the confusion surrounding § 2. It makes the cryptic *Alcoa* opinion a litigant's wishing well, into which, it sometimes seems, one may peer and find nearly anything he wishes.

The conundrum was indicated . . . by Judge Hand, who was not able to resolve it. Hand . . . told us that it would be inherently unfair to condemn success when the Sherman Act itself mandates competition. Such a wooden rule, it was feared, might also deprive the leading firm in an industry of the incentive to exert its best efforts. Further success would yield not rewards but legal castigation. The antitrust laws would thus compel the very sloth they were intended to prevent. . . . [T]he statement in *Alcoa* that even well-behaved monopolies are forbidden by § 2 must be read carefully in context. Its rightful meaning is that, if monopoly power has been acquired or maintained through improper means, the fact that the power has not been used to extract improper benefits provides no succor to the monopolist.

But the law's hostility to monopoly power extends beyond the means of its acquisition. Even if that power has been legitimately acquired, the monopolist may not wield it to prevent or impede competition. . . . [A] firm that has achieved dominance of a market might find its control sufficient to preserve and even extend its market share by excluding or preventing competition. A variety of techniques may be employed to achieve this end—predatory pricing, lease-only policies, and exclusive buying arrangements, to list a few.

Even if the origin of the monopoly power was innocent, therefore, . . . maintaining or extending market control by the exercise of that power is sufficient to complete a violation of § 2. As we have explained, only considerations of fairness and the need to preserve proper economic incentives prevent the condemnation of § 2 from extending even to one who has gained his power by purely competitive means. . . .

The key to analysis, it must be stressed, is the concept of market power. . . . A firm that has lawfully acquired a monopoly position is not barred from taking advantage of scale economies by constructing, for example, a large and efficient factory. These benefits are a consequence of size and not an exercise of power over the market. . . .

In sum, although the principles announced by the § 2 cases often appear to conflict, this much is clear. The mere possession of monopoly power does not *ipso facto* condemn a market participant. But, to avoid the proscriptions of § 2, the firm must refrain at all times from conduct directed at smothering competition. This doctrine has two branches. Unlawfully acquired power remains anathema even when kept dormant. And it is no less true that a firm with a legitimately achieved monopoly may not wield the resulting power to tighten its hold on the market.

. . .

It is clear that a firm may not employ its market position as a lever to create—or attempt to create—a monopoly in another market. Kodak, in the period relevant to this suit, was never close to gaining control of the markets for photofinishing equipment or services and could not be held to have attempted to monopolize them. Berkey nevertheless contends that Kodak illicitly gained an advantage in these areas by leveraging its power over film and cameras. Accordingly, we must determine whether a firm violates § 2 by using its monopoly power in one market to gain a competitive advantage in another, albeit without an attempt to monopolize the second market. We hold, as did the lower court, that it does.

This conclusion appears to be an inexorable interpretation of the antitrust laws. We tolerate the existence of monopoly power, we repeat, only insofar as necessary to preserve competitive incentives and to be fair to the firm that has attained its position innocently. There is no reason to allow the exercise of such power to the detriment of competition, in either the controlled market or any other. That the competition in the leveraged market may not be destroyed but merely distorted does not make it more palatable. Social and economic effects of an extension of monopoly power militate against such conduct.

. . .

Accordingly, the use of monopoly power attained in one market to gain a competitive advantage in another is a violation of § 2, even if there has not been an attempt to monopolize the second market. It is the use of economic power that creates the liability. But, as we have indicated, a large firm does not violate § 2 simply by reaping the competitive rewards attributable to its efficient size, nor does an integrated business offend the Sherman Act whenever one of its departments benefits from association with a division possessing a monopoly in its own market. So long as we allow a firm to compete in several fields, we must expect it to seek the competitive advantages of its broad-based activity—more efficient production, greater ability to develop complementary products, reduced transaction costs, and so forth. These are gains that accrue to any integrated firm, regardless of its market share, and they cannot by themselves be considered uses of monopoly power.

. . .

III. THE 110 SYSTEM

We turn now to the events surrounding Kodak's introduction of the 110 photographic system in 1972. . . .

. . . Kodak's introduction of the 126 Instamatic in 1963 [had sparked a camera "revolution".] Ben Berkey, chairman of Berkey Photo, described the camera's cartridge-loading feature as "foolproof" and remarked that the new simple system gave the industry "a great boost." Even before the 126 was introduced, however, Kodak had set its sights on a new, smaller line of Instamatic cameras. The aim of Kodak's Project 30, or P–30, as it was often called, was a camera barely one inch thick but capable of producing photographs as clear and large as its bulkier cousins.

Kodak's desire to produce large, high-quality snapshots from a small camera created successive ripples in a number of ponds. As camera size decreases, so does the area of film exposed when the shutter is opened. Thus the negative must be substantially enlarged to produce a print, and the P–30 group was concerned that the Kodak color print film then in use, Kodacolor X, might not be equal to the task. There was fear that it was too "grainy"—that full-size photographs printed from tiny Kodacolor X negatives would have an unacceptably speckled, pebbly appearance, reflecting the extreme magnification of the small light-sensitive grains constituting the film.

The early view at P–30 had been that despite this problem Kodacolor X would prove "quite adequate" for the new format. By 1966, however, the Kodacolor Future System Committee, considering Kodak's film sales in the 126 size as well as in the format being created by Project 30, began actively to consider the possibility of developing a new type of Kodacolor film. This engendered the second set of ripples, for the committee realized that basic changes in the film would require a new photofinishing process, conducted at temperatures higher than those used in the so-called C–22 method by which prints were made from Kodacolor X. Some committee members, therefore, expressed concern about the effect that a new process might have on independent photofinishers, who developed Kodak film and were purchasers of Kodak equipment and supplies. These concerns were shared by a number of Kodak scientists, such as D. M. Zwick, who feared an "unethical" attempt to create a "deliberate . . . incompatibility with systems other than Kodacolor."[73]

Nevertheless, on May 10, 1967, the committee recommended that Kodak proceed with the development of the new film and finishing process, tentatively labeled P–118. This recommendation was adopted at a meeting of the Kodak management on September 20. Although management believed that many of the film improvements were desirable "without regard to the P–30 program," it decided that Kodak should consider marketing the new film in the P–30 size for approximately one year before introducing it in the 126 format. A firm date was not set at that time for introduction of P–118, but by 1969 Kodak decided that P–118 should be used to help launch the P–30 camera system in March 1972. This decision appears to have been influenced by the views of those Kodak officers who believed that

> [w]ithout a new film, the [camera] program is not a new advertisable system. Without the film, our splicer and processors [for the new high-temperature photofinishing process] are not required.

To meet this self-imposed deadline for P–118, Kodak was required to act in great haste. Indeed, the minutes of a Film Process Subcommittee meeting of August 29, 1969, noted that the decision for a 1972 release date required a "crash program" by all participating divi-

---

73. [Court's footnote 16.] Writing on March 9, 1967, Zwick saw "no need" for a new film, which would require a higher-temperature process: "We can make *small* improvements in Kodacolor X grain and sharpness, in a film which could go through the C–22 process." On the same day, another Kodak scientist, N. H. Groet of the Color Photography Division, wrote that he was "convinced that Project 30 could go with the presently available Kodacolor X film." Like Zwick, Groet conceded that a finer-grained film "would be most welcome for P–30," but he did not believe that major changes in Kodacolor X would be necessary. Indeed, he believed that the new finishing process being considered by the Kodacolor Future System Committee would raise hell in the photofinishing business, would do little to decrease the cost of the operation, and that the ultimate customer would not benefit.

sions. Development schedules were altered and some tests eliminated altogether. Not surprisingly, then, as the target date approached, Kodak realized that its new film was plagued by a number of difficulties.

Shortly after initial production runs began in October 1971, Kodak recognized that "several product deficiencies" would exist in the film, now called Kodacolor II, at the time of introduction. Indeed, just eight days before the joint announcement of the new camera, film, and photofinishing process, a technical committee listed eleven "presently identified" problems that could affect "the customer's ultimate quality." Not only did Kodacolor II have a significantly shorter shelf life than had been anticipated, but it also proved grainier than Kodak had originally hoped. This problem was highly significant, of course, because low graininess was suppossedly the quality that made Kodacolor II especially suitable for the Pocket Instamatic cameras.

Despite these deficiencies, Kodak proceeded with its plans for introduction of the 110 system, of which Kodacolor II had become an integral part. On March 16, 1972, amid great fanfare, the system was announced. Finally, said Kodak, there was a "little camera that takes big pictures." Kodacolor II was "a remarkable new film"— indeed, the best color negative film Kodak had ever manufactured. There had long been other small cameras, Kodak explained:

> But they weren't like these. Now there are films fine enough, and sharp enough, to give you big, sharp pictures from a very small negative.

In accord with Kodak's 1967 plan, Kodacolor II was sold only in the 110 format for eighteen months after introduction. It remains the only 110-size color print film Kodak has ever sold.

As Kodak had hoped, the 110 system proved to be a dramatic success. In 1972—the system's first year—the company sold 2,984,000 Pocket Instamatics, more than 50% of its sales in the amateur conventional still camera market. The new camera thus accounted in large part for a sharp increase in total market sales, from 6.2 million units in 1971 to 8.2 million in 1972. Rival manufacturers hastened to market their own 110 cameras, but Kodak stood alone until Argus made its first shipment of the "Carefree 110" around Christmas 1972. The next year, although Kodak's competitors sold over 800,000 110 cameras, Kodak retained a firm lead with 5.1 million. Its share of 110 sales did not fall below 50% until 1976. Meanwhile, by 1973 the 110 had taken over most of the amateur market from the 126, and three years later it accounted for nearly four-fifths of all sales.

Berkey's Keystone division was a late entrant in the 110 sweepstakes, joining the competition only in late 1973. Moreover, because of hasty design, the original models suffered from latent defects, and sales that year were a paltry 42,000. With interest in the 126 dwindling, Keystone thus suffered a net decline of 118,000 unit sales in 1973. The following year, however, it recovered strongly, in large part because improvements in its pocket cameras helped it sell 406,000 units, 7% of all 110s sold that year.

. . .

A. *Attempt to Monopolize and Monopolization of the Camera Market*

There is little doubt that the evidence supports the jury's implicit finding that Kodak had monopoly power in cameras. The principal issues presented to us regarding the effect of the 110 introduction in the camera market are whether Kodak engaged in anticompetitive conduct and, if so, whether that conduct caused injury to Berkey.

. . .

1. *Predisclosure*

Through the 1960s, Kodak followed a checkered pattern of predisclosing innovations to various segments of the industry. Its purpose on these occasions evidently was to ensure that the industry would be able to meet consumers' demand for the complementary goods and services they would need to enjoy the new Kodak products. But predisclosure would quite obviously also diminish Kodak's share of the auxiliary markets. It was therefore . . . "a matter of judgment on each and every occasion" whether predisclosure would be for or against Kodak's self-interest. . . .

. . .

Judge Frankel did not decide that Kodak should have disclosed the details of the 110 to other camera manufacturers prior to introduction. Instead, he left the matter to the jury, instructing them as follows:

> Standing alone, the fact that Kodak did not give advance warning of its new products to competitors would not entitle you to find that this conduct was exclusionary. Ordinarily a manufacturer has no duty to predisclose its new products in this fashion. It is an ordinary and acceptable business practice to keep one's new developments a secret. However, if you find that Kodak had monopoly power in cameras or in film, and if you find that this power was so great as to make it impossible for a competitor to compete with Kodak in the camera market unless it could offer products similar to Kodak's, you may decide whether in the light of other conduct you determine to be anticompetitive, Kodak's failure to predisclose was on balance an exclusionary course of conduct.

We hold that this instruction was error and that, as a matter of law, Kodak did not have a duty to predisclose information about the 110 system to competing camera manufacturers.

As Judge Frankel indicated, and as Berkey concedes, a firm may normally keep its innovations secret from its rivals as long as it wishes, forcing them to catch up on the strength of their own efforts after the new product is introduced. It is the possibility of success in the marketplace, attributable to superior performance, that provides the incentives on which the proper functioning of our competitive economy rests. If a firm that has engaged in the risks and expenses of research and development were required in all circumstances to share with its rivals the benefits of those endeavors, this incentive would very likely be vitiated.

Withholding from others advance knowledge of one's new products, therefore, ordinarily constitutes valid competitive conduct. Because, as we have already indicated, a monopolist is permitted, and indeed encouraged, by § 2 to compete aggressively on the merits, any success that it may achieve through "the process of invention and innovation" is clearly tolerated by the antitrust laws.

. . . Berkey postulates that Kodak had a duty to disclose limited types of information to certain competitors under specific circumstances. But it is difficult to comprehend how a major corporation, accustomed though it is to making business decisions with antitrust considerations in mind, could possess the omniscience to anticipate all the instances in which a jury might one day in the future retrospectively conclude that predisclosure was warranted. And it is equally difficult to discern workable guidelines that a court might set forth to aid the firm's decision. For example, how detailed must the information conveyed be? And how far must research have progressed before it is "ripe" for disclosure? These inherent uncertainties would have an inevitable chilling effect on innovation. They go far, we believe, towards explaining why no court has ever imposed the duty Berkey seeks to create here.

An antitrust plaintiff urging a predisclosure rule, therefore, bears a heavy burden in justifying his request. Berkey recognizes the weight of this burden. It contends that it has been met. Kodak is not a monolithic monopolist, acting in a single market. Rather, its camera monopoly was supported by its activity as a film manufacturer. Berkey therefore argues that by not disclosing the new format in which it was manufacturing film, Kodak unlawfully enhanced its power in the camera market. Indeed, Kodak not only participates in but monopolizes the film industry. The jury could easily have found that, when Kodak introduced a new film format, rival camera makers would be foreclosed from a substantial segment of the market until they were able to manufacture cameras in the new format. Accordingly, Berkey contended that Kodak illegitimately used its monopoly power in film to gain a competitive advantage in cameras. Thus Berkey insists that the jury was properly permitted to consider whether, on balance, the failure to predisclose the new format was exclusionary. We disagree.

We note that this aspect of Berkey's claim is in large measure independent of the fact that a new film, Kodacolor II, was introduced simultaneously with the new format. It is primarily introduction of the format itself—the size of the film and the cartridge in which it is packaged—of which Berkey complains. Indeed, at oral argument counsel for Berkey contended that predisclosure would have been required even had Kodak merely cut down Kodacolor X to fit the new 110 camera and cartridge.

We do not perceive, however, how Kodak's introduction of a new format was rendered an unlawful act of monopolization in the camera market because the firm also manufactured film to fit the cameras.

. . .

[T]he policy considerations militating against predisclosure requirements for monolithic monopolists are equally applicable here. The first firm, even a monopolist, to design a new camera format has a right to the lead time that follows from its success. The mere fact that Kodak manufactured film in the new format as well, so that its customers would not be offered worthless cameras, could not deprive it of that reward. Nor is this conclusion altered because Kodak not only participated in but dominated the film market. Kodak's ability to pioneer formats does not depend on it possessing a film monopoly. Had the firm possessed a much smaller share of the film market, it would nevertheless have been able to manufacture sufficient quantities of 110-size film—either Kodacolor X or Kodacolor II—to bring the new camera to market. It is apparent, therefore, that the ability to introduce the new format without predisclosure was solely a benefit of integration and not, without more, a use of Kodak's power in the film market to gain a competitive advantage in cameras.

. . .

Our analysis, however, must proceed beyond the conclusion that introduction of film to meet Kodak's new camera format was not in itself an exercise of the company's monopoly power in film. Berkey contends that Kodak in the past used its film monopoly to stifle format innovations by any other camera manufacturer. Accordingly, it argues that Kodak was barred from reaping the benefits of such developments without making predisclosure to allow its rivals to share from the beginning in the rewards.

There is, indeed, little doubt that the jury could have found that Kodak, by refusing to make film available on economical terms, obstructed sales of cameras in competing formats. Thus, Kodak has never supplied film to fit the Minox, a small camera that uses a cartridge similar to that of the Instamatics and that has been on the market since the 1930s, or similar cameras by Minolta and Mamiya that were also introduced before the Kodak 126. Merchants of these cameras, including Berkey, made numerous requests that Kodak sell film packaged in their formats, with or without the Kodak name. As an alternative, they asked Kodak to sell bulk film rolls large enough to permit the camera manufacturers economically to cut the film down to the appropriate size and spool it. Kodak denied all such appeals. Some of the miniature cameras did survive but, as even Kodak's own economic expert testified, its policy drastically reduced the ability of rival manufacturers to compete by introducing new camera formats.

We accept the proposition that it is improper, in the absence of a valid business policy, for a firm with monopoly power in one market to gain a competitive advantage in another by refusing to sell a rival the monopolized goods or services he needs to compete effectively in the second market. . . . It may be that Kodak violated the Sherman Act when it refused to sell Berkey bulk film for use in the Minolta camera, and Berkey might well have recovered for its loss of Minolta sales and for any additional expenses incurred because of Kodak's conduct.

But Berkey did not sue Kodak then for its refusal to sell film, and it concedes that it is not now claiming a right to damages on this basis. Rather, it contends that Kodak's past offenses created a continuing duty to disclose its new formats to competing camera manufacturers, and that its violation of that obligation supports the jury's verdict. For two reasons, however, we decline to recognize such a duty.

First, the benefits that would flow to Kodak's rivals in the camera market from such a rule bear no relationship to the injury caused them by the monopolist's refusal to sell films for their competing camera formats. There is no reason to suppose, for example, that the loss suffered by Berkey because Kodak undercut Minolta sales was at all comparable to the boon Berkey would have received had Kodak given it the opportunity to participate from the beginning in the 110 revolution. . . .

Second, it would be inappropriate to hold that Kodak should spontaneously have recognized a duty to release advance information of its new products to its competitors. It is important to note that Berkey, which no longer sells cameras, does not advance its predisclosure argument as part of a demand for equitable relief. . . .

Accordingly, if Berkey were still a camera maker, it might be able to demand that Kodak, to nullify the effect of its monopolistic obstruction of new formats for competing cameras, be required to allow its rivals to share from the start in the business created by its own changes in format. . . . But Berkey, in any event, does not demand prospective relief. Instead it asks us to condemn Kodak retrospectively, holding that it violated § 2 and so is liable for damages, because it did not decide on its own initiative to take unusual, self-abnegatory actions as a corrective for unadjudicated prior offenses. This is without justification.

· · ·

2. *Systems Selling*

[Berkey] claims that by marketing the Pocket Instamatics in a system with a widely advertised new film, Kodak gained camera sales at Berkey's expense. And, because Kodacolor II was not necessary to produce satisfactory 110 photographs and in fact suffered from several deficiencies, these gains were unlawful.

It may be conceded that, by advertising Kodacolor II as a "remarkable new film" capable of yielding "big, sharp pictures from a very small negative," Kodak sold more 110 cameras than it would have done had it merely marketed Kodacolor X in 110-size cartridges. The quality of the end product—a developed snapshot—is at least as dependent upon the characteristics of the film as upon those of the camera. It is perfectly plausible that some customers bought the Kodak 110 camera who would have purchased a competitor's camera in another format had Kodacolor II not been available and widely advertised as capable of producing "big, sharp pictures" from the tiny Pocket Instamatic. Moreover, there was also sufficient evidence for the jury to conclude that a new film was not necessary to bring the new cameras to market. . . .

But necessity is a slippery concept. . . . Even if the 110 camera would produce adequate snapshots with Kodacolor X, it would be difficult to fault Kodak for attempting to design a film that could provide better results. The attempt to develop superior products is, as we have explained, an essential element of lawful competition. Kodak could not have violated § 2 merely by introducing the 110 camera with an improved film.

. . .

When a market is dominated by a monopolist, of course, the ordinary competitive forces of supply may not be fully effective. Even a monopolist, however, must generally be responsive to the demands of customers, for if it persistently markets unappealing goods it will invite a loss of sales and an increase of competition. If a monopolist's products gain acceptance in the market, therefore, it is of no importance that a judge or jury may later regard them as inferior, so long as that success was not based on any form of coercion. Certainly the mere introduction of Kodacolor II along with the Pocket Instamatics did not coerce camera purchasers. . . .

Of course, Kodak's advertising encouraged the public to take a favorable view of both Kodacolor II and the 110 camera, but that was not improper. A monopolist is not forbidden to publicize its product unless the extent of this activity is so unwarranted by competitive exigencies as to constitute an entry barrier. . . . And in its advertising, a producer is ordinarily permitted, much like an advocate at law, to bathe his cause in the best light possible. Advertising that emphasizes a product's strengths and minimizes its weaknesses does not, at least unless it amounts to deception, constitute anticompetitive conduct violative of § 2.[74]

74. [Court's footnote 41]. There was evidence that Kodak indicated on the boxes in which Kodacolor II was sold that the film had a shelf life of 14 months, whereas in fact the film lost half its speed within three to six months. We need not decide whether this action amounted to deceptive advertising, or whether and under what circumstances such deception might amount to a violation of § 2. See 3 P. Areeda & D. Turner, supra, at 278–79. The Sherman Act is not a panacea for all evils that may infect business life. Before we would allow misrepresentation to buyers to be the basis of a competitor's treble damage action under § 2, we would at least require the plaintiff to overcome a presumption that the effect on competition of such a practice was *de minimis*. See id. Berkey, however, has failed to provide any evidence that a significant number of Kodak 110 purchasers would have, if the Kodacolor II boxes had included accurate information on the shelf life of the film, bought a Berkey camera in a pre-existing format instead.

3. *Restriction of Kodacolor II to the 110 Format*

. . . For eighteen months after the 110 system introduction, Kodacolor II was available only in the 110 format. Since Kodak was the first to have the 110s on the market, Berkey asserts it lost camera sales because consumers who wished to use the "remarkable new film" would be compelled to buy a Kodak camera. . . . The argument is that, since consumers were led to believe that Kodacolor II was superior to Kodacolor X, they were more likely to buy a Kodak 110, rather than a Berkey camera, so that the new film could be used.

. . .

But to prevail, Berkey must prove more, for injury is an element of a private treble damages action. Berkey must, therefore, demonstrate that some consumers who would have bought a Berkey camera were dissuaded from doing so because Kodacolor II was available only in the 110 format. This it has failed to establish. The record is totally devoid of evidence that Kodak or its retailers actually attempted to persuade customers to purchase the Pocket Instamatic because it was the only camera that could use Kodacolor II, or that, in fact, any consumers did choose the 110 in order to utilize the finer-grained film.

. . .

We conclude, therefore, that the jury could not find that Berkey suffered more than *de minimis* injury, if any, because Kodacolor II was limited to the 110 format. Although the antitrust laws afford latitude in permitting the factfinder to estimate "the extent of the damages" where precise calculation is impossible, they do not allow recovery where there has been no showing that plaintiff suffered cognizable injury. . . .

B. *Photofinishing and Photofinishing Equipment Markets*

The introduction of the 110 system provided the foundation . . . [for damages for] lost photofinishing profits and for overcharges on photofinishing equipment. These verdicts, moreover, were the basis for the only injunctive relief decreed below. . . .

1. *Damages*

Berkey's damages claims here are based on the fact that Kodacolor II, introduced along with the 110 camera, required the new, high-temperature C–41 finishing process instead of the C–22 process used for Kodacolor X and similar films. Thus independent photofinishers could not offer processing service for Kodacolor II— the only color print film Kodak ever offered in the 110 size—until they bought new equipment and received instruction in and supplies for C–41 processing. Moreover, Kodak did not give advance warning to the independents that the new film would be introduced, nor did it predisclose the C–41 process to other makers of photofinishing equipment.   Accordingly, CP&P [Kodak's photofinishing operation] was able to begin processing Kodacolor II several weeks before its competitors.

Furthermore, it is urged that Berkey faced greater expense in finishing Kodacolor II than did CP&P, because Kodak refused to divulge the formulae for chemicals used in the C–41 process.   Large photofinishers like Berkey preferred to buy these compounds from chemical suppliers in bulk, both to save money and to gain flexibility. But to be able to process Kodacolor II, they were forced to buy premixed "kits" from Kodak at twice the price.   Kodak, meanwhile, provided all but one of the CP&P plants with bulk chemicals.   And, because for some time Kodak was the only manufacturer of machinery capable of processing the new film, the independent photofinishers were required to purchase this equipment in order to proceed at all. The jury found that Kodak's prices were excessive and almost certainly found also that the equipment Kodak sold to the independents was vastly inferior to its product for CP&P.

· · ·

Kodak's conduct with respect to the independent photofinishers perhaps may be criticized as shoddy treatment of firms providing an essential service for Kodak products.   Indeed, largely for that reason a number of Kodak employees urged that photofinishers and equipment manufacturers be given advance warning of the C–41 process. The purpose of the Sherman Act, however, is not to maintain friendly business relations among firms in the same industry nor was it designed to keep these firms happy and gleeful.   Moreover, it is clear that Kodak did not monopolize or attempt to monopolize the photofinishing or equipment markets.   Thus, it is not liable under § 2 for the actions described above unless it gained a competitive advantage in these markets by use of the monopoly power it possessed in other segments of the industry.

It bears emphasis that only the wielding of power will support recovery in this context; advantages inuring to Kodak's photofinishing and equipment arms by virtue of membership in an integrated firm will not.   As we suggested earlier, a use of monopoly power is an action that a firm would have found substantially less effective, or even counterproductive, if it lacked market control.   Thus, the classic example of such a use is a refusal to deal in goods or services needed by a competitor in a second market.   But, a firm without control of the market that attempts this will simply drive the purchaser to take its patronage elsewhere.

· · ·

It is not clear, however, whether in bringing forth the 110 system Kodak did anything that a smaller firm with integrated capabilities but no market control might not have done.   Kodak did not use its power to shift the entire photofinishing market from C–22 to the C–41 process, for Kodacolor II was introduced only in the 110 size and at first represented a minuscule percentage of all color print photofinishing.   Indeed, the film was not marketed in other formats until eighteen months later, long after the original surprise had worn off. In sum, Kodak's ability to gain a rapidly diminishing competitive advantage with the introduction of the 110 system may have been attributable to its innovation of a new system of photography, and not to its monopoly power. On the other hand, we cannot dismiss the possibility that Kodak's monopoly power in other markets was at least a partial root of its ability to gain an advantage over its photofinishing competitors and to sell them overpriced equipment. . . .

We cannot resolve this ambiguity. The instructions to the jury did not draw with sufficient sharpness the distinction between exercises of power and the natural benefits of size and integration. Nor is the record so clear that we can say with certainty on which side of this demarcation the facts fall. . . . If the parties wish to pursue these claims to a final determination, therefore, a new trial will be necessary.

. . .

[In Part IV of its opinion, the Court considered Berkey's damage claims for monopolization of film and color paper, remanding for retrial because of erroneous rulings on damages and the admissibility of evidence prior to the statutory limitations period. In Part V of its opinion, the Court affirmed the jury's finding that Kodak violated Section 1 of the Sherman Act by requiring that Sylvania and G.E. not predisclose to competing camera manufacturers information regarding flashcube innovations on which Kodak, Sylvania, and G.E. were working. This part of the Court's opinion is reproduced infra, pp. 572–575. Part VI of the Court's opinion concerned evidentiary rulings arising out of the suppression of evidence by an attorney for Kodak in conjunction with testimony by an expert witness for Kodak. The Court found no prejudice resulted from the trial court's rulings on the matter and the attorney was disciplined in another proceeding for his conduct. See p. 54, supra. The Court of Appeals vacated the District Court's award of $5.3 million in attorneys fees in Part VII of the opinion.[75]]

NOTES AND QUERIES

(1) *Willful Maintenance of Monopoly Power v. Superior Product, Business Acumen or Historical Accident.* The Supreme Court's *Grinnell* test for conduct by a monopolist proving unlawful monopolization ("the willful acquisition or maintenance of that power as distinguished from growth or development as a consequence of superior product, business acumen or historic accident")[76] seems to suggest that willfully retaining a monopoly position was sufficient conduct by a monopolist to violate the Act subject only to proof of the three affirmative defenses. *Grinnell's* enumeration of three means by which market control can be lawfully maintained by a monopo-

75. Eighteen months after the reversal, it was reported the parties settled the litigation with Kodak paying Berkey $6,750,000. It was announced the settlement was for Berkey's claims on the flashcube conspiracy. All other claims were dropped. Wall St. J., Sept. 25, 1981, p. 33.

76. Supra p. 121.

list—superior products, business acumen, or historic accident—are not easily "distinguished" from "willful acquisition or maintenance" of a monopoly. Nor are these concepts easily defined in the abstract.

Berkey, and several other recent private treble damage cases,[77] have been confronted with giving meaning to the distinction in cases where innovations and aggressive marketing techniques are claimed to have an unlawful exclusionary effect.[78] As with pricing practices by a monopolist, innovation and marketing techniques by a monopolist can be both consistent with and an expression of healthy competition or a subtle technique for maintaining a monopoly and the long term displacement of the competitive process. How can and should the law distinguish competitive conduct from monopolizing conduct in the context of innovation and aggressive marketing? Is *Berkey* consistent with *ALCOA, United Shoe, Griffith* and *Grinnell*? Should "hard competition" by a monopolist, so long as it is not otherwise illegal or unethical, be permitted if it has "unnecessary" or "avoidable" exclusionary effects upon others even if superior products or business acumen are involved? Did the court adequately account for the long-term monopoly effects of Kodak's conduct in determining the legality of its conduct for purposes of Berkey's treble damage action?

(2) *Innovation by a Monopolist: Competitive or Monopolistic?* Schumpeter's theory of competition and innovation [79] suggests that the introduction of new products will upset the competitive equilibrium and give the innovator at least short-term monopoly gains at the expense of competitors. Thereafter, competitors will erode the gains by imitation or innovation of their own, while the original innovator will seek to solidify a temporary advantage into a permanent one of monopoly power. Schumpeter argued that in a world of large and powerful firms, innovation is the long-run basis for expanding output and lowering prices and therefore, short-run departures from perfect competition caused by innovation maximize long-run consumer welfare. Temporary monopoly profits, Schumpeter argued, are not only acceptable, but are also necessary to stimulate innovation. Legal intervention in such circumstances would be unwise except for cases where the innovator was successfully converting a short-run gain into a long-run monopoly.[80]

77. See, e.g., California Computer Products, Inc. v. International Business Machines Corp., 613 F.2d 727 (9th Cir. 1979); Transamerica Computer Co., Inc. v. International Business Machines Corp., 698 F.2d 1377 (9th Cir. 1983); Telex Corp. v. International Business Machines Corp., 367 F.Supp. 258 (N.D.Okl. 1973); reversed 510 F.2d 894 (10th Cir.), certiorari dismissed 423 U.S. 802, 96 S.Ct. 8, 46 L.Ed.2d 244 (1975); Sargent-Welch Scientific Co. v. Ventron Corp., 567 F.2d 701 (7th Cir. 1977), certiorari denied 439 U.S. 822, 99 S.Ct. 87, 58 L.Ed.2d 113 (1978).

78. For recent surveys of the litigation and trends in the litigation, see Comment, Draining the ALCOA "wishing well": The Section 2 Conduct Requirement After KODAK and CALCOMP, 48 Ford.L.Rev. 291 (1979); Comment, Antitrust Scrutiny of Monopolists' Innovations, 93 Harv.L.Rev. 408 (1979); Note, Aggressive Innovation and Antitrust Liability, 53 So.Cal.L.Rev. 1469 (1980); Note, An Economic and Legal Analysis

of Physical Tie-Ins, 89 Yale L.J. 769 (1980). In Northeastern Telephone Co. v. American Telephone & Telegraph Co., 651 F.2d 76 (2d Cir. 1981), certiorari denied 455 U.S. 943, 102 S.Ct. 1438, 71 L.Ed.2d 654 (1982), the Second Circuit gave further sanction to aggressive competition by a monopolist by reversing a $16 million judgment for the plaintiff. The Court held marginal cost to be the standard for predatory pricing and rejected claims that advertising, innovation and other marketing practices by A.T.& T. violated Section 2.

79. J. Schumpeter, The Theory of Economic Development 131–32 (1934); J. Schumpeter, Capitalism, Socialism and Democracy 105 (1939); Nelson & Winter, Forces Generating and Limiting Concentration Under Schumpeterian Competition, 9 Bell J.Econ. 524 (1978).

80. The theory and its antitrust implications in the context of cases like *Berkey*, are explored in Note, An Economic

Does Schumpeter's thesis provide a means for evaluating Kodak's conduct? Is there any significance for Schumpeter's thesis in the fact that Kodak never had less than 82% of the film market (and 61% of the camera market) for the twenty years preceding the introduction of its 110 system?[81] Was there competitive equilibrium for competing camera makers and the opportunity for them to innovate with new camera designs in view of Kodak's monopoly of the film market? What factors should be considered in determining whether introduction of Kodak's 110 system innovation was maintaining or enhancing, in the long run, Kodak's monopolies in film or cameras or both?[82]

(3) *The Significance of Developing Monopolization Doctrine in Private Treble Damage Litigation.* The vast majority of recent cases exploring the meaning of the Section 2 monopolization offense have been private cases, in contrast to the *ALCOA-United Shoe* era when most Section 2 cases were government cases. As the *Berkey* case demonstrates, the added requirements of proving standing, causation, the fact of damage and the amount of damage, as well as a violation of the law, may have a significant impact on the court's definition of the conduct element of the violation. Also, the private plaintiff will likely prove a violation by focusing on conduct that caused it measurable damages. Thus, the willingness of a court to infer that the conduct in question crosses the line from the competitive to the predatory may differ from government cases, because the private case must necessarily focus on conduct injuring a competitor and cause one to lose sight of the injury, if any, to competition.[83]

For example, Berkey's attempt to justify a predisclosure duty for the new film format because of Kodak's past anticompetitive conduct in refusing to make new film formats for competing camera manufacturers was rejected as conduct evidence Berkey could rely on only *in its particular damage claims* to prove Kodak unlawfully monopolized. The court did so because Berkey was not claiming damages for past refusals to deal in film for competing cameras but for refusal to predisclose the new 110 film in the new camera format for current competing camera sales. This result suggests there may be two types of "conduct" evidence in private damage cases: conduct evidence proving one with monopoly power has monopolized and conduct evidence proving the violation alleged caused the damage claimed. To the same effect is the court's denial of Berkey's claims for lost camera sales because of Kodak's refusal to make the new 110 film in different film sizes. It was held not sufficient for proof of damages purposes for Berkey to simply prove Kodak's refusal to make the film in other sizes promoted Kodak's camera monopoly. Berkey also was required to prove that it lost camera sales as a result of Kodak's conduct because Berkey's damage claim was for its lost camera sales as a result of injury to competition in cameras generally. Con-

and Legal Analysis of Physical Tie-Ins, 89 Yale L.J. 769 (1980).

81. "The most important [factor] . . . is the innovator's primary market share. . . ." Id. at 781.

82. See id. at 780–82. See also Ordover & Willig, An Economic Definition of Predation: Pricing and Product Innovation, 91 Yale L.J. 8 (1981) (proposing tests for predatory "systems innovation" involving the introduction of incompatible components).

83. See Flynn, Monopolization Under The Sherman Act: The Third Wave and Beyond, 26 Antitrust Bull. 1, 85–7, 110 (1981). See also GAF Corp. v. Eastman Kodak Co., 519 F.Supp. 1203 (S.D.N.Y. 1981) (applying collateral estoppel against Kodak, as a result of the *Berkey* case, on several issues of violation of the Sherman Act in a subsequent treble damage action by G.A.F.).

duct proving a violation but not proving the violation caused the particular plaintiff injury is insufficient to support a damage verdict.

These holdings, as well as the court's causation analysis on Berkey's photofinishing claims and its film and paper overcharge claims, raise the question of whether *Berkey* is a significant precedent for government Section 2 cases where the conduct element of the offense is in controversy. Would the result in *Berkey* be different if it were a government initiated case, rather than a private damage action?

2. ATTEMPT TO MONOPOLIZE

The development of the concept of "attempt to monopolize" as a distinct Section 2 violation has been limited by Justice Holmes' cryptic formulation of the offense in SWIFT & CO. v. UNITED STATES, 196 U.S. 375, 396, 25 S.Ct. 276, 279, 49 L.Ed. 518, 524 (1905):

> Where acts are not sufficient in themselves to produce a result which the law seeks to prevent—for instance, the monopoly—but require further acts in addition to the mere force of nature to bring that result to pass, an intent to bring it to pass is necessary in order to produce a dangerous probability that it will happen.

Holmes' definition was predicated upon the common law concept of criminal attempt,[84] requiring proof of specific intent plus dangerous probability of achieving the prohibited result—a result Holmes called "monopoly."

Subsequent decisions have developed three requirements for proving an attempt to monopolize: (1) proof of a relevant market; (2) proof of a specific intent to gain a monopoly of the market defined; and (3) proof of a "dangerous probability" of achieving monopoly.[85] Considerable confusion persists in lower court litigation as to the exact meaning of these standards and the appropriate weight to be accorded each. Criticism of the traditional test for attempts has increased over the past few years. Some writers question the need to prove relevant market.[86] Others would dispense with the "dangerous probability" requirement.[87] Others question the meaning and wisdom of the "specific intent" requirement.[88] Still others propose new tests which dispense with proving any of the requirements of the *Swift* test.[89] The Supreme Court has not provided definitive stan-

84. Citing Commonwealth v. Peaslee, 177 Mass. 267, 59 N.E. 55 (1901), an opinion Holmes authored while sitting on the Supreme Judicial Court of Massachusetts.

85. United States v. Empire Gas Corp., 537 F.2d 296 (8th Cir. 1976); Hiland Dairy, Inc. v. Kroger Co., 402 F.2d 968 (8th Cir. 1968), certiorari denied 395 U.S. 961, 89 S.Ct. 2096, 23 L.Ed.2d 748 (1969).

86. Note, Attempt to Monopolize Under the Sherman Act: Defendant's Market Power As A Requisite To A Prima Facie Case, 73 Colum.L.Rev. 1451 (1973); Note, Prosecutions for Attempt to Mo-

nopolize: The Relevance of the Relevant Market, 42 N.Y.U.L.Rev. 110 (1967).

87. See Cooper, Attempts and Monopolization: A Mildly Expansionary Answer To The Prophylactic Riddle of Section Two, 72 Mich.L.Rev. 375, 453 (1974).

88. See Hawk, Attempts to Monopolize—Specific Intent As Antitrust's Ghost In The Machine, 58 Cornell L.Rev. 1121 (1973).

89. Note, The Role of Attempt To Monopolize in Antitrust Regulation: An Economic and Social Justification for a New Approach, 31 Vand.L.Rev. 309 (1978); Note, Attempt To Monopolize: The Offense Redefined, 14 Utah L.Rev. 704, 715

dards of proof in attempt cases,[90] and a split has developed among lower federal courts and among antitrust commentators as to the appropriate elements of the offense.[91]

PHOTOVEST CORP. v. FOTOMAT CORP.

United States Court of Appeals, Seventh Circuit, 1979.
606 F.2d 704, certiorari denied 445 U.S. 917, 100 S.Ct. 1278, 63 L.Ed.2d 601 (1980).

[Digest: The defendant, Fotomat Corporation, is engaged in the retail sale of film processing, film, and camera related products through small drive-thru kiosks located generally in shopping center parking lots. From its inception in 1967, Fotomat intended to "blitz the industry" by preempting the sites for drive-thru kiosks nationally. To achieve this goal, Fotomat initially sold franchises to build up rapidly a national network of stores. The plaintiff, Photovest Corporation, was formed in 1968 by individuals desiring to invest in Fotomat franchises in the Marion County, Indiana area. Plaintiff agreed to purchase 15 Fotomat franchises for kiosks in the area, paying $21,000 for each franchise and agreeing to pay monthly royalties and advertising fees based on gross sales.

By 1969, Fotomat concluded that profits from company-operated kiosks were significantly greater than those derived from franchised stores. No new franchise sales were made thereafter and Fotomat began a program of converting its franchised locations to company-operated stores. Plaintiff's franchise agreements were for ten years with three optional five year renewals. Fotomat originally represented to Photovest that no Fotomat stores would generally be built within two miles of plaintiff's stores. The franchise agreement obligated plaintiffs to purchase all merchandise and services from Fotomat or approved sources and lease the kiosk from Fotomat under a five year lease. Fotomat agreed to sell all film and film processing to plaintiffs at cost and perform frequent pick up and delivery services of film for processing.

In 1973, defendant began opening company-operated stores near plaintiff's stores and by 1975 had saturated the Indianapolis area with 14 new company-operated stores. In violation of the franchise agreement, defendant failed to pass on discounts from film processors and charged plaintiff 7% to 26% above its costs for privately branded Fotomat film. By the time of trial, Photovest was incurring

(1969): "Conduct that has had, or if unchecked will have, the effect of either setting another's price or excluding a competitor and that is engaged in without legitimate business purpose is an attempt to monopolize."

90. Recent attempt cases in the Supreme Court have generally involved the use of monopoly power in one market to restrain trade or attempt to monopolize another market. See Otter Tail Power Co. v. United States, supra p. 120; Walk-

er Process Equipment, Inc. v. Food Machinery & Chemical Corp., 382 U.S. 172, 86 S.Ct. 347, 15 L.Ed.2d 247 (1965); Lorain Journal Co. v. United States, 342 U.S. 143, 72 S.Ct. 181, 96 L.Ed. 162 (1951).

91. For an exhaustive defense for retaining the *Swift* standard, see Handler & Steuer, Attempts to Monopolize and No-Fault Monopolization, 129 U.Pa.L. Rev. 125 (1980).

substantial losses as a result of Fotomat's company stores draining off business from plaintiff's stores.

The district court held Fotomat's conduct constituted an unlawful attempt to monopolize "the drive-thru retail photo processing submarket in the Indianapolis metropolitan area" and awarded Photovest $2,923,557 in damages.   The defendant, Fotomat, appealed.] Pell, Circuit Judge.

· · ·

Section 2 of the Sherman Act prohibits attempts to monopolize. Generally, a plaintiff claiming that the defendant violated this section must prove specific intent and conduct manifesting that intent to monopolize and a dangerous probability of success in a relevant market. Before discussing the specific intent and dangerous probability of success elements, we will first address the relevant market issue, one which the parties have vigorously contested.

A. *Relevant Market*

A definition of the relevant market is essential because "without a definition of that market there is no way to measure [the defendant's] ability to lessen or destroy competition."   There is some authority for the proposition that in an attempt to monopolize case, as distinguished from a monopolization case, a definition of the relevant market is not necessary.   In Lessig v. Tidewater Oil Co., 327 F.2d 459, 474–75 (9th Cir. 1964), cert. denied 377 U.S. 993, 84 S.Ct. 1920, 12 L.Ed.2d 1046, the court stated that "[w]hen the charge is attempt (or conspiracy) to monopolize, rather than monopolization, the relevant market is 'not in issue'." [92]   The great weight of authority, however, requires a definition of the relevant market. We are . . . unpersuaded by *Lessig* and thus shall proceed to analyze the relevant market in the present case.

The district court concluded that Fotomat attempted to monopolize "the drive-thru retail photo processing submarket in the Indianapolis metropolitan area." Fotomat argues that the district court erred in defining the submarket and that a proper definition of the relevant submarket is much broader and would include photo processing services offered in drugstores, supermarkets, etc. [93]   Under its broader market definition, it argues that its share of the market was

92. [Court's footnote 9.] This follows from the court's rejection of the premise that probability of actual monopolization is an essential element of proof of attempt to monopolize. The court rejected this premise on the theory that "specific intent itself is the only evidence of dangerous probability the statute requires—perhaps on the not unreasonable assumption that the actor is better able than others to judge the practical possibility of achieving his illegal objective." 327 F.2d at 474. See Knutson v. Daily Review, Inc., 548 F.2d 795, 813–14 (9th Cir. 1976),

cert. denied, 433 U.S. 910, 97 S.Ct. 2977, 53 L.Ed.2d 1094. See also Turner, Antitrust Policy and the Cellophane Case, 70 Harv.L.Rev. 281, 305 (1956).

93. [Court's footnote 10.] We note here that although delineating the scope of the relevant market entails analysis of both geographic market and product market, our analysis will address only the latter because the parties do not dispute the geographic delineation used by the district court.

insufficient as a matter of law to give rise to any probability that it could succeed in monopolizing that market.

. . .

[The Court upheld the trial court's definition of drive-thru kiosks offering photo processing services as the relevant product market. The Court did so on the grounds that Fotomat's prices were 20% to 50% higher for the service than other forms of retailing the service, the industry recognized drive-thru services as a different market, and consumers treated drive-thru services as a separate sub-market. Fotomat's growth, despite higher prices for its services, was found to indicate low cross-elasticity of demand between delivery of film processing services via drive-thru kiosks and other methods of retailing the service. The Court found these to be sufficient justifications for singling out the provision of retail film processing services through drive-thru kiosks in the Indianapolis metropolitan area as a relevant submarket for purposes of a Section 2 attempt to monopolize claim.]

B. *Specific Intent & Conduct*

Having affirmed the district court's delineation of the drive-thru submarket we turn now to the issue of whether Fotomat intended to monopolize the market. Although the case law contains some confusing dicta regarding the need to prove specific intent in an attempt to monopolize case, the Supreme Court has stated that:

> While the completed offense of monopolization under § 2 demands only a general intent to do the act, "for no monopolist monopolizes unconscious of what he is doing," a *specific intent* to destroy competition or build monopoly *is essential* to guilt *for* the *mere attempt* now charged.

Times-Picayune Publishing Co. v. United States, 345 U.S. at 626, 73 S.Ct. at 890. Although the specific intent requirement has been criticized, and the requisite proof to establish it is not well-settled, the district court found, and the record supports its finding of, the requisite intent, and Fotomat has not argued error in this regard.

Fotomat directs its argument to the district court's finding of predatory conduct and contends that either the finding is not supported by the record or that its conduct was not the sort which is proscribed by the antitrust laws. Photovest's theory, accepted by the district court, was that when Fotomat determined that owning the kiosks was more profitable than franchising them, Fotomat, among other things, saturated the market with company-owned kiosks to reduce severely the profitability of Photovest's kiosks and thereby attempted to reduce substantially the value of Photovest's kiosks so that Fotomat could buy them at a low price. Saturating the market was not the only method that Fotomat used, according to the district court, to reduce the profitability of Photovest's kiosks. It found that

Fotomat engaged in the following conduct in an intentional attempt to do so:

> concealment of discounts available from processors, retention of discounts from processors, the markup of film, the placement of company stores in such a manner as to siphon business from plaintiff, attempts to coerce plaintiff into remaining with Carhart [a Fotomat designated film processor], refusal to relocate losing stores, insistence on escalating rents and a number of miscellaneous found facts. Each of these was designed to reduce plaintiff's profits for purposes of reacquiring plaintiff's stores at the lowest possible price.

. . .

[T]he critical issue in this regard is whether this conduct, albeit destructive of Photovest's profit levels, is proscribed by § 2 of the Sherman Act. Fotomat poses the issue as whether the antitrust laws are violated by locating a store close to a competitor in the hopes of taking some customers from the competitor. It argues that the law does not proscribe such behavior because the antitrust laws specifically encourage competitive store locations and condemn competitors who allocate territories among themselves. . . .

. . . Fotomat's reasoning ignores the whole concept of predatory practices . . . . Many predatory practices promote competition in the short run, but if they are used to effect a monopoly by eliminating competition, they are illegal under the Sherman Act. The enforcement of § 2 of the Sherman Act will often result in a sacrifice of the most competitive conduct in the short run if the ultimate goal of that conduct is the establishment of monopoly power.

. . .

Fotomat also contends that the evidence of record does not support the findings that it expanded in the Indianapolis market for anticompetitive purposes. It relies in great part on the fact that the franchise agreement did not contain a provision prohibiting it from opening new stores which overlapped Photovest's franchised stores. But a party's right to sue for antitrust violations is not dependent on the existence of a contract provision prohibiting the alleged anticompetitive behavior. Moreover, the record in this case clearly supports the district court's findings regarding Fotomat's purpose in locating new stores in Indianapolis. . . . It opened new stores in close proximity to Photovest's best stores. One of Photovest's best stores was devastated by Fotomat's opening of three new stores in its immediate market area. One of these new store's sales never exceeded Fotomat's incremental breakeven point and by trial were well below it. Notwithstanding Fotomat's operations personnel recommendations to remove it, Fotomat did not close it, apparently willing to lose money in the short run hoping to reduce the profitability of Photovest's store for future buy-back. . . . A Fotomat internal memorandum written by an area manager establishes that Fotomat "anticipated" that the new store would "siphon" volume from Photovest's store. Also, it should be remembered that Fotomat's conduct regarding new store locations must be viewed along with its other behavior which in total was found in support of a § 2 violation. Otherwise lawful practices may become unlawful if they are part of an illegal scheme.

. . .

[The Court also found that Fotomat, in breach of the franchise agreement, reduced Photovest's profitability by retaining film processing discounts owed Photovest and by charging Photovest prices above its cost for private label film. Both types of conduct were found to be part of a scheme to reduce Photovest's profitability with the goal of buying back franchises at a low price and excluding Photovest from the market. Despite abandoning an earlier franchise clause requiring franchisees to buy from Fotomat-approved sources, Fotomat was also found to have coerced Photovest to continue dealing with one Carhart for photofinishing services or lose Fotomat's pick-up and delivery services. Carhart allegedly provided high cost but low quality service and the Court found this coercion was part of Fotomat's scheme to reduce Photovest's profitability.]

C. *Dangerous Probability of Success*

Having agreed with the district court's delineation of the relevant submarket, it is quite clear that there was a dangerous probability that Fotomat would succeed in monopolizing the market.[94] The only related issue worthy of discussion is whether Fotomat's control of the market via buy-back of the Photovest franchises would change the competitive dynamics of the market. Fotomat argues that since Photovest always followed Fotomat's recommended pricing, the buy-back would have no effect on the pricing of the goods or services in the relevant market. It argues that the same amount of photo processing would be done whether Photovest or Fotomat owned the Indianapolis drive-thru kiosks, and that the number of sites preempted by Fotomat stores would remain constant.

We are unpersuaded by this argument because it proceeds on the assumption that Fotomat's pricing behavior is not influenced by the existence of Photovest franchises and thus that if Fotomat succeeded in buying back all the Photovest franchises and obtaining a monopoly, it would not change its pricing policies. Antitrust analysis does not recognize as a defense the possibility that if a defendant obtains a monopoly, he might nevertheless not abuse his monopoly power to extract monopoly profits. The recognition of such a defense in an attempt to monopolize case would devastate the impact of § 2.

The fact that Photovest has always followed Fotomat's suggested prices does not suggest, as Fotomat implies, that the same prices would be charged if Fotomat succeeded in buying back all Photovest stores. The forces of competition may well be restraining Fotomat's

94. [Court's footnote 26.] Fotomat and Photovest together had 30 of the 39 drive-thru outlets at the conclusion of the trial. Fotomat's regional director estimated Fotomat's and Photovest's aggregate share of sales in 1975 at 95% of the Indianapolis drive-thru market.

recommended prices to its franchisees. The franchisees are not bound to follow these *recommended* prices. Without the restraints of competition, a monopolist often will find that it can maximize profits by selling a lower volume at higher prices than would prevail in a more competitive market. We cannot reverse the district court's finding of a § 2 violation on the ground that Fotomat may not, if given the opportunity, follow the path of many monopolists. Accordingly, we affirm the district court's conclusion that Fotomat violated § 2 of the Sherman Act.

. . .

NOTES AND QUERIES

(1) *The Ninth Circuit Approach to Attempts to Monopolize.* The *Photovest* decision is representative of the standards applied in a majority of circuits in attempt cases, except for the fact that few plaintiffs ever win on an attempt theory requiring proof of a relevant market and a dangerous probability of success in achieving a monopoly of the market defined. A different test is applied in the Ninth Circuit, one which emphasizes a conduct approach and a view that the attempt prohibition ought to be used to prohibit unilateral predatory conduct designed to fix prices or exclude competition without regard for defining a relevant market or the dangerous probability of the defendant gaining a monopoly.

The Ninth Circuit's separate path in attempt cases began with *Lessig v. Tidewater Oil Co.*[95] Lessig claimed Tidewater cancelled his service station lease and dealer contract because he refused to abide by Tidewater's demands that he resell gasoline at prices set by Tidewater and that he purchase and sell Tidewater sponsored tires, batteries and accessories (TBA). Lessig charged Tidewater's conduct constituted an unlawful attempt to monopolize, but the trial court refused to allow Lessig's Section 2 count to go to the jury and Lessig appealed. The Ninth Circuit, in an opinion by Judge Browning, held:

> . . . We think the court erred in withdrawing from the jury the charge that Tidewater attempted to monopolize in violation of Section 2 of the Sherman Act.

> The essence of monopoly is power to control prices and exclude competition, and what we have said demonstrates that there was evidence that Tidewater possessed the specific intent to acquire and exercise such power with respect to a part of commerce.

> Tidewater argues that attempt to monopolize is established only if there is proof of "dangerous probability of success, i.e., that if unchecked monopolization will result"; that this requires an evaluation of Tidewater's power in the relevant market; that the evidence on this issue was inadequate; and, such evidence as there was indicated a lack of any possibility that Tidewater could monopolize the sale of petroleum products or TBA.

> We reject the premise that probability of actual monopolization is an essential element of proof of attempt to monopolize. Of course, such a probability may be relevant circumstantial evidence of intent, but the spe-

95. 327 F.2d 459 (9th Cir. 1964), certiorari denied 377 U.S. 993, 84 S.Ct. 1920, 12 L.Ed.2d 1046.

cific intent itself is the only evidence of dangerous probability the statute requires—perhaps on the not unreasonable assumption that the actor is better able than others to judge the practical possibility of achieving his illegal objective.

When the charge is attempt (or conspiracy) to monopolize, rather than monopolization, the relevant market is "not in issue". United States v. E. I. DuPont DeNemours & Co., 351 U.S. 377, 395 n. 23, 76 S.Ct. 994, 1007–1008, n. 23, 100 L.Ed. 1264 n. 23 (1956). Section 2 prohibits attempts to monopolize "any part" of commerce, and a dominant position in the business of distributing petroleum products and TBA was not necessarily prerequisite to ability to attempt to monopolize an appreciable segment of interstate sales in such products. If the jury found that Tidewater intended to fix the price at which 2,700 independent service station operators resold gasoline, and to exclude other suppliers of petroleum products and sponsored TBA items from competing for the patronage of these operators, and took steps to accomplish that purpose, it could properly conclude that Tidewater attempted to monopolize a part of interstate commerce in violation of Section 2 of the Sherman Act.

Reversed and remanded.[96]

Queries: With which approach do you agree? Does the *Photovest* case require litigation of a behavioral case of monopolization (predatory conduct fixing prices or excluding competition) on a structural theory of liability?[97]

---

96. 327 F.2d at 474–75.

97. In Greyhound Computer Corp., Inc. v. International Business Machines Corp., 559 F.2d 488, 504 (9th Cir. 1977), certiorari denied 434 U.S. 1040, 98 S.Ct. 782, 54 L.Ed.2d 790 (1978), Judge Browning spelled out the basis for objecting to a requirement of proof of a market and a dangerous probability of obtaining a monopoly of the market defined as follows:

A prima facie case of attempt to monopolize is made out by evidence of a specific intent to monopolize 'any part' of commerce, plus anticompetitive conduct directed to the accomplishment of that unlawful purpose. . . .

If proof of an economic market, technically defined, and proof of a dangerous probability of monopolization of such a market were made essential elements of an attempt to monopolize, as a practical matter the attempt offense would cease to have independent significance. A single firm that did not control something close to 50 percent of the entire market, . . . would be free to indulge in any activity however unreasonable, predatory, destructive of competition and without legitimate business justification. Any concern not dangerously close to monopoly power could deliberately destroy its competitors with impunity. These are not abstract hypotheses. A market share approaching monopoly is not required to enable one concern seriously to impede the capacity of others to compete by use of abusive trade practices. A construction of the Sherman Act that would immunize such practices would be contrary to the purposes of the Act; it is not required by the Act's language or legislative history.

In Hunt-Wesson Foods, Inc. v. Ragu Foods, Inc., 627 F.2d 919 (9th Cir. 1980), certiorari denied 450 U.S. 921, 101 S.Ct. 1369, 67 L.Ed.2d 348 (1981), the court reversed the dismissal of a complaint which did not allege that the defendant's conduct posed a dangerous probability of establishing a monopoly over the prepared spaghetti sauce market. The court stated:

It is apparent that each situation will present different problems that mandate a flexible approach toward the 'mix' of conduct, actor, and market conditions that make up the offense. In some cases of clearly exclusionary conduct, the conduct itself, along with the exclusionary intent that can be inferred from it, poses such a danger to competition that it may be condemned regardless of the market power of the actor. . . . Such clearly exclusionary behavior, even though it poses no immediate measurable danger to the market, presents the potential for mischief. To the extent that such conduct inevitably harms competition, there is little reason to tolerate it.

On the other hand, in circumstances involving ambiguous conduct, the requisite degree of danger may not exist

Does the *Photovest* case end up with the same result as a court following the *Lessig* reasoning would reach by gerrymandering market definitions?

(2) *The Ninth Circuit Aftermath of Lessig.* Several post-*Lessig* Ninth Circuit opinions have generated a separate jurisprudence on the elements of the attempt to monopolize offense from that followed elsewhere. The legacy of *Lessig* has also provoked confusion within the Ninth Circuit as different panels of the Circuit attribute varying meanings and emphasis to the *Lessig* elements of the offense.[98] In *William Inglis & Sons Co. v. ITT Continental Baking Co., Inc.,*[99] in an opinion concurred in by Chief Judge Browning (author of the *Lessig* opinion), Judge Sneed spelled out the elements of the offense as follows:

A.   *The Elements of an Attempt Claim*

Although the law of this circuit on attempted monopolization has not been static, its current state recognizes three elements of an attempt claim under section 2 of the Sherman Act: (1) specific intent to control prices or destroy competition in some part of commerce; (2) predatory or anticompetitive conduct directed to accomplishing the unlawful purpose; and (3) a dangerous probability of success. To state these elements, however, is merely to begin the process of understanding the legal standards of conduct under an attempt claim. Each element interacts with the others in significant and unexpected ways. Because the parties dispute the nature of their interdependence, we must discuss each in some detail.
. . .

1.   *Specific Intent*

The element of specific intent appears to have had its genesis in the distinctions—and similarities—between *monopolization* and *attempted monopolization,* both of which are proscribed in separate terms by section 2. Thus, section 2 embraces not only an uncertain collection of evils termed "monopolization," but also conduct falling short of that result. By analogy to the law of criminal attempt, the requirement of specific intent is used to confine the reach of an attempt claim to conduct threatening monopolization.

Whatever its origins, the existence of specific intent may be established not only by direct evidence of unlawful design, but by circumstantial evidence, principally of illegal conduct. Too heavy a reliance on circumstantial evidence incurs the risk of reducing almost to the point of extinction the existence of the requirement. The type of conduct that will support the inference, therefore, must be carefully defined. This court has made it clear that the nature of such conduct varies with the conditions of the market and the characteristics of the defendant.

Thus, we consistently have held that the inference may be drawn from conduct that serves as the basis for a substantial claim of restraint of

in the absence of appreciable market power because market power increases the potential for harm. What may be legal for the company lacking substantial market power may be illegal for the firm with such power. And where the conduct is ambiguous, the market power of the firm may help clarify the intent of the actor.

627 F.2d at 925.

98. "The legacy of the Ninth Circuit's decision in Lessig v. Tidewater Oil Co. has, by and large, been confusion." Kaye, Attempt To Monopolize In The Ninth Circuit: The Legacy of Lessig, 12 Williamette L.J. 331, 344 (1976).

99. 668 F.2d 1014 (9th Cir. 1981), certiorari denied ___ U.S. ___, 103 S.Ct. 58, 74 L.Ed.2d 61 (1982).

trade. Several cases, for example, have explicitly equated such conduct with an unreasonable restraint of trade in violation of section 1 of the Sherman Act. Actions taken by a firm without market power may support the inference of intent if those actions are "of a kind clearly threatening to competition or clearly exclusionary." Some opinions have taken this language to refer to *per se* violations of section 1.

On the other hand, direct evidence of intent alone, without corroborating evidence of conduct, cannot sustain a claim of attempted monopolization. The necessity of corroborative conduct rests on the fact that direct evidence of intent alone can be ambiguous and misleading.[1] The law of attempted monopolization must tread a narrow pathway between rules that would inhibit honest competition and those that would allow pernicious but subtle conduct to escape antitrust scrutiny. Direct evidence of intent to vanquish a rival in an honest competitive struggle cannot help to establish an antitrust violation. It also must be shown that the defendant sought victory through unfair or predatory means. Evidence of conduct is thus indispensable.

The language and purpose of section 2 reinforces this necessity. While the prohibition of attempts to monopolize clearly encompasses actions that fall short of their intended result, it is equally clear that actual steps toward interference with the competitive process, and not boardroom ruminations, is the evil against which section 2 is directed. As Justice Holmes taught us, there is a difference, even in antitrust law, between preparation and attempt. *Swift & Co.*, supra, 196 U.S. at 402, 25 S.Ct. at 281.

2. *Dangerous Probability of Success*

The third element, dangerous probability of success, like the first, also is rooted in the relationship between the separate offenses of monopolization and attempt to monopolize. See, e. g., *Swift & Co.*, supra, 196 U.S. at 396, 25 S.Ct. at 279.[2] Although this element is generally treated as

---

1. [Court's footnote 6.]
What juries (and many judges) do not understand is that the availability of evidence of improper intent is often a function of luck and of the defendant's legal sophistication, not of the underlying reality. A firm of executives sensitized to antitrust problems will not leave any documentary trail of improper intent; one whose executives lack this sensitivity will often create rich evidence of such intent simply by the clumsy choice of words to describe innocent behavior. Especially misleading here is the inveterate tendency of sales executives to brag to their superiors about their competitive prowess, often using metaphors of coercion that are compelling evidence of predatory intent to the naive. Any doctrine that relies upon proof of intent is going to be applied erratically at best.

R. Posner, Antitrust Law—An Economic Perspective 189–90 (1976).

2. [Court's footnote 8.] The requirement of dangerous probability of success

originated in Justice Holmes' opinion in *Swift*:

> Where acts are not sufficient in themselves to produce a result which the law seeks to prevent,—for instance, the monopoly,—but require further acts in addition to the forces of nature to bring that result to pass, an intent to bring it to pass is necessary in order to produce a dangerous probability that it will happen. . . . But when that intent and the consequent dangerous probability exist, this statute, like many others, and like the common law in some cases, directs itself against that dangerous probability as well as against the completed result.

Swift & Co., supra, 196 U.S. at 396, 25 S.Ct. at 279. A careful reading of this language supports the rule of this circuit that dangerous probability of success may be inferred from proof of specific intent. Justice Holmes does not refer to dangerous probability as an independent element, but rather as the consequence of an intent to monopolize, or perhaps as "the *rationale* which underlies the legal

separate and independent, it can be inferred from evidence indicating the existence of the other two. However, the proper significance of this third element "has been controversial, even within this circuit."

Part of the uncertainty results, as already indicated, from the tendency to treat the element of dangerous probability of success and proof of market power as equivalent. Although related, they are not equivalent. Another source of uncertainty, also previously suggested, is that a dangerous probability of success has been treated as evidence of specific intent and vice versa. However, our more recent decisions make plain that the permissibility of inferring dangerous probability from proof of specific intent is conditional. That is, a dangerous probability of success may be inferred either (1) from direct evidence of specific intent plus proof of conduct directed to accomplishing the unlawful design, or (2) from evidence of conduct alone, provided the conduct is also the sort from which specific intent can be inferred.

These more recent decisions also establish that the dangerous probability of success requirement is not designed as a means of screening out cases of minimal concern to antitrust policy but is instead a way of gauging more accurately the purpose of a defendant's actions. Accordingly, the level of the probability of success appropriately may be raised by the defendant, as did Continental in this case, even if the plaintiff has made his case without direct proof of dangerous probability. Thus, if market conditions are such that a course of conduct described by the plaintiff would be unlikely to succeed in monopolizing the market, it is less likely that the defendant actually attempted to monopolize the market. Conversely, a firm with substantial market power may find it more rational to engage in a monopolistic course of conduct than would a smaller firm in a less concentrated market.

In sum, the dangerous probability of success element is always relevant in analyzing an attempt claim. The nature of its relevance, however, is a function of the state of the evidence offered in support of the other two elements necessary to proof of the claim.

3. *Conduct*

The conduct element of the attempt claim also is closely related to the other two elements. Thus, the first element, specific intent to control prices or exclude competition, may be inferred from certain types of conduct. The third element, dangerous probability of success, also is often dependent on proof of conduct. Finally, evidence of conduct is indispensable even when there is direct evidence of unlawful specific intent.

This interrelationship extends to the type and strength of proof required to establish each element. In the absence of direct and probative evidence of specific intent to monopolize, for example, a plaintiff must introduce evidence of conduct amounting to a substantial claim of restraint of trade or conduct clearly threatening to competition or clearly exclusionary.[3] Direct evidence of intent, on the other hand, may permit

requirement that there be a specific intent to monopolize before an attempt is found." L. Sullivan, Handbook of the Law of Antitrust § 51, at 137 (1977) (emphasis in original).

3. [Court's footnote 14.] As we already have noted, this description of conduct draws upon standards developed in the context of section 1 of the Sherman Act. However, section 2 of the Act encompasses a broader range of conduct. For example, unlike section 1, section 2 is not limited to concerted or contractual activity. . . . Actions taken by a single firm which attempts to monopolize may have no obvious counterparts in the case law of section 1. However, by drawing upon section 1 we have given general di-

reliance on a broader range of conduct, simply because the purpose of ambiguous conduct may be more clearly understood.[4] But, in general, conduct that will support a claim of attempted monopolization must be such that its anticipated benefits were dependent upon its tendency to discipline or eliminate competition and thereby enhance the firm's long-term ability to reap the benefits of monopoly power. Such conduct is not true competition; it makes sense only because it eliminates competition. It does not enhance the quality or attractiveness of the product, reduce its cost, or alter the demand function that all competitors confront. Its purpose is to create a monopoly by means other than fair competition.[5]

Query: What result if this analysis had been applied in the *Photovest* case, supra? In the *Lessig* case?

(3) *Distinguishing Aggressive Competition, "Unfair Competition," and Attempts to Monopolize.* Expanding the definition of the attempt to monopolize offense by dispensing with proof of market structure and power had been characterized as amounting to "an effort to create a federal common law of unfair competition. In the past, courts have repeatedly refused to use the Sherman Act in this way, instinctively recognizing that efforts to control the 'fairness' of competition must encounter immense difficulties."[6]

Do you agree? What "immense difficulties" do you perceive? Should competitors be free to compete by any means so long as they do not combine or conspire to restrain trade or achieve an overwhelming share of the market or a dangerous probability of doing so? Would you file an attempt to monopolize case against individuals alleged to have hired "torches" to burn out competing grocery stores in order to obtain a monopoly of the grocery business in North Brooklyn described by the cited newspaper account?[7] Should the antitrust laws be concerned only with promoting a form of economic Darwinism (survival of the fittest), leaving it to other state and federal laws to define the ethics and fairness of competition? See note at p. 20 supra, as to the possibly preferable use of Section 5 of the Federal Trade Commission Act to fill in gaps in antitrust law coverage of unethical business practices.

rection to the construction of section 2. Thus, we have held that the "reasonableness" standard of section 1 is to control the analysis of most conduct from which specific intent to monopolize may be inferred. . . .

4. [Court's footnote 15.] As our earlier discussion of the first two elements of the attempt claim recognizes, several cases have also suggested that the type of conduct sufficient to establish attempted monopolization may vary with the market power of the defendant. . . . This general proposition may prove accurate in particular cases, but we do not read our decisions as establishing any necessary or specific connection between a defendant's market power and the type of conduct a plaintiff must prove in support of its attempt claim. A plaintiff may show that proof of market power is relevant to an accurate understanding of a particular defendant's conduct, but the general standards for conduct that we discuss in the text must be

the ultimate touchstone. We note that the present case is not one in which it is necessary to specify the connection between market power and conduct.

5. [Court's footnote 16.] We have frequently referred to such activity as conduct "without legitimate business purpose." . . .

6. Cooper, Attempts and Monopolization: A Mildly Expansionary Answer To The Prophylactic Riddle of Section Two, 72 Mich.L.Rev. 373, 454 (1974).

7. See "10 Are Accused of Plot to Burn Stores of Rivals—Bid for Grocery Monopoly in Brooklyn Is Charged", New York Times, June 4, 1981, Col. 8, p. B–1. The article reports the defendants are charged with setting fire to seven stores with losses estimated at $10 million and that the 10 alleged conspirators were "part of a ring to monopolize the supermarket and grocery business in North Brooklyn by burning out the competition."

In private treble damage litigation, these issues frequently arise in the context of claims that some types of unfair competition rise to the level of an antitrust violation because they result in the elimination of a competitor. Some courts have upheld the claim under the *"Pick-Barth"* doctrine,[8] holding that a conspiracy to eliminate a competitor by unfair means constitutes a *per se* violation of Section 1 of the Sherman Act. Courts critical of the *Pick-Barth* rule [9] draw a distinction between laws designed to protect the competitive process and laws designed to establish a basic standard of morality or ethics by which the competitive process operates:

> On a more fundamental level, the *Pick-Barth* doctrine fails to perceive that the purposes of antitrust law and unfair competition generally conflict. The thrust of antitrust law is to prevent restraints on competition. Unfair competition is still competition and the purpose of the law of unfair competition is to impose restraints on that competition. The law of unfair competition tends to protect a business in the monopoly over the loyalty of its employees and its customer lists, while the general purpose of the antitrust laws is to promote competition by freeing from monopoly a firm's sources of labor and markets for its products. . . . .

> An instance where the result of antitrust law and unfair competition law enforcement may not conflict is when a firm with substantial market power, perhaps approaching that of a monopoly, uses unfair competition to augment its position by eliminating a rival concern from the market. But it is the elimination of the competition, by fair means or foul, that is the concern of the antitrust law, and it is only the unfair method on which the law of unfair competition focuses.

> The more modern courts examining the *Pick-Barth* rule have stated that it applies only when the defendant is a "significant existing competitor." [10]

While such cases usually arise under Section 1 of the Sherman Act, significant and substantial unfair trade practices by a firm possessing economic power and done with a purpose and effect of excluding competition have also been held to constitute an unlawful attempt to monopolize.[11]

(4) *Legislating a Definition of Attempt to Monopolize.* President Carter's National Commission for the Review of Antitrust Laws and Procedures (N.C.R.A.L.P.), concluded that the law of attempt to monopolize was "uneven", "much disputed" and "unclear".[12] Noting that the Supreme Court has declined to resolve the conflicts and ambiguity which have arisen and that the *Swift* approach has resulted in the possibility of "plainly predatory or vicious anticompetitive conduct going unchecked under the antitrust laws",[13] a majority of the Commission proposed that Congress adopt the following amendment to the Sherman Act:

8. Pick-Barth Co. v. Mitchell Woodbury Corp., 57 F.2d 96 (1st Cir. 1932), certiorari denied 286 U.S. 552, 52 S.Ct. 503, 76 L.Ed. 1288 (hiring competitor's employees and theft of customer lists); Atlantic Heel Co. v. Allied Heel Co., 284 F.2d 879 (1st Cir. 1960); Perryton Wholesale Inc. v. Pioneer Distributing Co., 353 F.2d 618 (10th Cir. 1965), certiorari denied 383 U.S. 945, 86 S.Ct. 1202, 16 L.Ed. 2d 208 (1966).

9. See Northwest Power Products, Inc. v. Omark Industries, Inc., 576 F.2d 83 (5th Cir. 1978), certiorari denied 439 U.S. 1116, 99 S.Ct. 1021, 59 L.Ed.2d 75 (1979).

10. Id. at 89.

11. Associated Radio Service Co. v. Page Airways, Inc., 624 F.2d 1342 (5th Cir. 1980), certiorari denied 450 U.S. 1030, 101 S.Ct. 1740, 68 L.Ed.2d 226 (1981).

12. 1 Report to the President and the Attorney General of the National Commission for the Review of Antitrust Laws and Procedures, 144 (1979).

13. Id. at 145.

PROPOSED COMPETITION PROTECTION ACT

Be it enacted, etc., That this Act may be cited as the Competition Protection Act of 1979.

Findings.

Sec. 2. Since the passage of the Sherman Act, the courts have not developed a consistent method for defining an attempt to monopolize. As a result of conflicting judicial approaches, the same business conduct may be held lawful in one jurisdiction and unlawful in another. Anticompetitive conduct has been held outside antitrust scrutiny by some courts solely on the grounds that such conduct did not imminently threaten the achievement of a monopoly position in a specific market. Even where conduct that is clearly and significantly anticompetitive has been involved, courts have frequently required lengthy inquiries into present and potential market positions of defendants. It is the conclusion of the Congress that a proviso to Section 2 of the Sherman Act is necessary to enable the statute, without deterring procompetitive behavior, to provide an effective remedy for conduct threatening to create a monopoly or otherwise to suppress competition.

Revision of Sherman Act Section 2.

Sec. 3. Section 2 of the Sherman Act, 15 U.S.C. § 2, is hereby amended to read as follows:

"Sec. 2. Every person who shall monopolize or attempt to monopolize, or combine or conspire with any other person or persons, to monopolize any part of the trade or commerce among the several States, or with foreign nations, shall be deemed guilty of a felony; and, on conviction thereof, shall be punished by a fine not exceeding one million dollars, if a corporation, or if any other person, one hundred thousand dollars, or by imprisonment not exceeding three years, or by both said punishments, in the discretion of the court. *Provided that, in determining whether a person has attempted to monopolize a part of trade or commerce, (1) a dangerous risk of monopoly shall be held to exist upon a showing that the conduct alleged to constitute the attempt significantly threatens competition in any relevant market, as determined after an evaluation of the defendant's intent, the defendant's present or probable market power, and the anticompetitive potential of the conduct undertaken; and (2) the fact that a defendant's prices were not below either average variable cost or marginal cost shall not be controlling, but may properly be considered, in assessing the defendant's intent and the conduct at issue.*"[14]

Queries: Would adoption of the proposal change the analysis or the result in *Photovest, Lessig* or *Inglis & Sons*? Does the proposal make clear what the Commission characterized as "uneven" and "unclear"? What is meant by conduct which "significantly threatens competition"? "In any relevant market"? "Intent"? "Present or probable market power"? "Anticompetitive potential"?[15]

14. Id. at 165–66.

15. For exhaustive studies of the controversy over the definition and application of the attempts offense, see Handler & Steuer, supra note 91; Note, supra note 89. See also, 48 Antitrust L.J. 1195 (1980); 48 Antitrust L.J. 813–842 (1980) (Comments on the N.C.R.A.L.P. proposal).

3. COMBINING OR CONSPIRING TO MONOPOLIZE

Section 2 of the Sherman Act explicitly reaches not only persons who monopolize, but also "every person who shall . . . attempt to monopolize *or* combine *or* conspire to monopolize. . . ."[16] (Emphasis added). Older court decisions made little distinction among the concepts of monopolization, combination or conspiracy to monopolize, and attempt to monopolize.[17] More modern decisions and academic debate about the implications of economic concentration have stirred interest in the development of new Section 2 theories to reach the claimed adverse competitive consequences of concentrated market structures (oligopolies).[18] While there are still few decisions on the use of the combination or conspiracy to monopolize prohibitions of Section 2 to reach the alleged monopolistic effects of parallel business behavior in concentrated industries, the debate over the necessity and propriety of using Section 2 is a perennial and heated one.

The distinction between "structural" monopolization cases (the pricing and exclusionary effects of market structure) and "behavioral" monopolization cases (the pricing and exclusionary effects of predatory exercises of power) has assumed more importance for the conspiracy and attempts offenses of Section 2 as litigants and some courts also seek to deal with predatory conduct by powerful firms whose individual dominance of a market falls short of monopoly. Does a charge of combination or conspiracy to monopolize require proof of a relevant market and defendant's possession of an overwhelming (or some lesser) share of that market? Or is it enough to prove a "combination" or "conspiracy" and a specific intent to fix prices or exclude competitors? In other words, is the essence of these offenses combining or conspiring to gain a "monopoly" or is it combining or conspiring to "monopolize"?

There are relatively few cases directly litigating the meaning of the combination and conspiracy offenses of Section 2. Where there is sufficient evidence to prove the existence of a contract or conspiracy, the case is likely to be filed under the well-developed standards of Section 1 of the Act claiming that the joint action is in "restraint of trade." Where there is little or no evidence of conspiracy, the action is likely to be filed as a Section 2 monopolization case or as an "attempt to monopolize" case.

16. 15 U.S.C. § 2.

17. See Standard Oil Co. v. United States, 221 U.S. 1, 31 S.Ct. 502, 55 L.Ed. 619 (1911); United States v. American Tobacco, 221 U.S. 106, 31 S.Ct. 632, 55 L.Ed. 663 (1911); Eastman Kodak Co. v. Southern Photo Materials Co., 273 U.S. 359, 47 S.Ct. 400, 71 L.Ed. 684 (1927).

18. See III P. Areeda & D. Turner, Antitrust Law 359–390 (1978); J. Bain, Industrial Organization (2d Ed. 1968); H. Goldschmid, M. Mann & F. Weston, (Eds.), Industrial Concentration: The New Learning (1974); F. Scherer, Industrial Market Structure and Economic Performance (2d Ed. 1980); L. Sullivan, Antitrust 331–73 (1977). See also, Weiss, The Structure-Conduct-Performance Paradigm and Antitrust, 127 U.Pa.L.Rev. 1104, 1105 (1979): "The main predictions of the structure-conduct-performance paradigm are: (1) that concentration will facilitate collusion, whether tacit or explicit, and (2) that as barriers to entry rise, the optimal cost-price margin of the leading firm or firms likewise will increase."

In this section, we briefly examine some of the relatively cryptic opinions dealing with the combination and conspiracy to monopolize offenses and proposals for developing theories under these offenses with wider application to concentrated industries and exclusionary conduct by powerful firms. While the issue must await development in subsequent chapters dealing with Section 1 of the Sherman Act,[19] one should not overlook at this point the significant questions for antitrust of the meanings of "combination" and "conspiracy" and what evidence will suffice to demonstrate the existence of a "combination" or "conspiracy" for Section 2 purposes.

AMERICAN TOBACCO CO. v. UNITED STATES

Supreme Court of the United States, 1946.
328 U.S. 781, 66 S.Ct. 1125, 90 L.Ed. 1575.

[Digest: American Tobacco Co., Liggett & Meyers Tobacco Co., R. J. Reynolds Tobacco Co. and others, were convicted and fined on four counts charging: (1) conspiracy in restraint of trade, (2) monopolization, (3) attempt to monopolize, and (4) conspiracy to monopolize trade and commerce in the purchase of tobacco and the sale of cigarettes. American, Liggett and Reynolds accounted for 68% to 75% of national cigarette production with the rest of the market shared by six small producers. The three firms had over 80% of the higher-priced cigarette market, while smaller firms were left to share the remainder of that market or to compete by manufacturing and selling cheaper blends of cigarettes—called "10 cent cigarettes."

Among the practices each of the three firms followed deterring entry, the Court singled out: massive and expensive national advertising, maintaining large inventories of cigarettes and reserving large sums of cash to prepay federal excise taxes. Each firm was also found to have refused to participate in new tobacco auction markets unless the other two firms participated in the new market; each maintained three year supplies of tobacco to insulate themselves from variations in annual supplies and prices of tobacco; and each would regularly bid up the price of tobacco they were not interested in buying to equalize the costs of smaller competitors. In addition to other common bidding practices, the defendants were each found to have made large purchases of cheaper tobaccos used to manufacture "10 cent cigarettes" about the time the cheaper cigarettes began making significant inroads in the cigarette market. Defendants offered no explanation of their intended use of the cheaper tobacco and evidence was offered by the Government that the composition of defendants' higher quality cigarettes remained unchanged following the defendants' large purchases of low grade tobacco.

Each firm maintained identical prices for cigarettes for several years and recent price changes were identical in amount. Each price change was initiated by Reynolds and immediately followed by American and Liggett. During the worst years of the Depression, when

---

19. See Chap. 4–6, infra.

tobacco prices were the lowest since 1905 and manufacturing costs were declining, defendants simultaneously raised prices for their leading brands. Thereafter, with sales of "10 cent cigarettes" increasing, defendants simultaneously dropped prices on their leading brands to maintain a 3¢ price differential with the 10¢ brands. As a result of these and other pricing tactics, sales of 10 cent cigarettes dropped from 22.78% to 6.4% of total cigarette sales between 1932 and 1933, whereupon defendants simultaneously raised prices to prior levels.

The jury found the defendants conspired to fix prices and to exclude competition and convicted all three defendants on each of the four counts. The Court rejected contentions that convictions on a Section 1 conspiracy count and a Section 2 conspiracy count, as well as conviction on a Section 2 monopolization count and a conspiracy to monopolize count, amounted to double jeopardy or a multiplicity of punishment in a single proceeding in violation of the Fifth Amendment. The Court held that a conspiracy to commit a crime is a different offense from the crime that is the object of the conspiracy. Defendants also argued that actual exclusion of competitors is necessary to the crime of monopolization. The Court answered that contention as follows:]

MR. JUSTICE BURTON delivered the opinion of the Court.

. . .

To support the verdicts it was not necessary to show power and intent to exclude *all* competitors, or to show a conspiracy to exclude *all* competitors. The requirement stated to the jury and contained in the statute was only that the offenders shall "monopolize any part of the trade or commerce among the several States, or with foreign nations." This particular conspiracy may well have derived special vitality, in the eyes of the jury, from the fact that its existence was established, not through the presentation of a formal written agreement, but through the evidence of widespread and effective conduct on the part of petitioners in relation to their existing or potential competitors.

. . .

The trial court described this combination or conspiracy as an "essential element" and "indispensable ingredient" of the offenses charged. It is therefore only in conjunction with such a combination or conspiracy that these cases will constitute a precedent.

. . .

The jury found a conspiracy to monopolize to a substantial degree the leaf market and the cigarette market. The jury's verdicts also found a power and intent on the part of the petitioners to exclude competition to a substantial extent in the tobacco industry.

. . .

The question squarely presented here by the order of this Court in allowing the writs of certiorari is whether actual exclusion of competitors is necessary to the crime of monopolization in these cases under

§ 2 of the Sherman Act. We agree with the lower courts that such actual exclusion of competitors is not necessary to that crime in these cases and that the instructions given to the jury, . . . correctly defined the crime. A correct interpretation of the statute and of the authorities makes it the crime of monopolizing, under § 2 of the Sherman Act, for parties, as in these cases, to combine or conspire to acquire or maintain the power to exclude competitors from any part of the trade or commerce among the several states or with foreign nations, provided they also have such a power that they are able, as a group, to exclude actual or potential competition from the field and provided that they have the intent and purpose to exercise that power.

It is not the form of the combination or the particular means used but the result to be achieved that the statute condemns. It is not of importance whether the means used to accomplish the unlawful objective are in themselves lawful or unlawful. Acts done to give effect to the conspiracy may be in themselves wholly innocent acts. Yet, if they are part of the sum of the acts which are relied upon to effectuate the conspiracy which the statute forbids, they come within its prohibition. No formal agreement is necessary to constitute an unlawful conspiracy. Often crimes are a matter of inference deduced from the acts of the person accused and done in pursuance of a criminal purpose. Where the conspiracy is proved, as here, from the evidence of the action taken in concert by the parties to it, it is all the more convincing proof of an intent to exercise the power of exclusion acquired through that conspiracy. The essential combination or conspiracy in violation of the Sherman Act may be found in a course of dealings or other circumstances as well as in any exchange of words. Where the circumstances are such as to warrant a jury in finding that the conspirators had a unity of purpose or a common design and understanding, or a meeting of minds in an unlawful arrangement, the conclusion that a conspiracy is established is justified. Neither proof of exertion of the power to exclude nor proof of actual exclusion of existing or potential competitors is essential to sustain a charge of monopolization under the Sherman Act.

A combination may be one in restraint of interstate trade or commerce or to monopolize a part of such trade or commerce in violation of the Sherman Act, although such restraint or monopoly may not have been actually attempted to any harmful extent. The authorities support the view that the material consideration in determining whether a monopoly exists is not that prices are raised and that competition actually is excluded but that power exists to raise prices or to exclude competition when it is desired to do so.

. . .

In the present cases, the petitioners have been found to have conspired to establish a monopoly and also to have the power and intent to establish and maintain the monopoly. To hold that they do not come within the prohibition of the Sherman Act would destroy the force of that Act. Accordingly, the instructions of the trial court under § 2 of the Act are approved and the judgment of the Circuit Court of Appeals is affirmed.

Affirmed.

(Justices Frankfurter and Rutledge concurred and Justices Reed and Jackson took no part in considering or deciding the case).

NOTES AND QUERIES

(1) *Monopoly by Consensus.* The Court in *American Tobacco* appeared to sanction a jury finding of conspiracy or combination to monopolize based upon the oligopolistic structure of the industry and the community of interest which evolved between the dominant firms in the market giving rise to parallel business behavior adversely affecting price competition and competitors. The Court stated elsewhere in *American Tobacco*: "The verdicts indicate that practices of an informal and flexible nature were adopted and that the results were so uniformly beneficial to the petitioners in protecting their common interests as against those of competitors that, entirely from circumstantial evidence, the jury found that a combination or conspiracy existed among the petitioners from 1937 to 1940, with power and intent to exclude competitors to such a substantial extent as to violate the Sherman Act. . . . ."[20]

What circumstances and conduct should give rise to a finding of combination or conspiracy to monopolize? As concentration ratios (the percentage share of the market controlled by the top 2, 4, and so on firms) increase, should less evidence of parallel business behavior be required? Should some forms of parallel business behavior be distinguished from others as appropriate evidence for inferring the existence of a combination or conspiracy in a concentrated industry?[21] Should high concentration ratios, plus poor performance of the industry, justify inferring a combination or conspiracy to monopolize from parallel business practices?[22]

(2) *Evolving Combination and Conspiracy to Monopolize Theories.* Government enforcement agencies have expressed a continuing interest in developing enforcement theories to deal with the assumed adverse effects of tight oligopolies engaging in parallel business behavior. For example, the Antitrust Division circulated a staff memo on "Shared Monopolies" in 1978[23] spelling out circumstances the Division believed "facilitated" collusive behavior in oligopolistic industries. Among the practices which might be viewed as facilitating collusive price fixing or a reduction of output, the Department

20. 328 U.S. at 793, 66 S.Ct. at 1131, 90 L.Ed. at 1585.

21. "The law is settled that proof of consciously parallel business behavior is circumstantial evidence from which an agreement, tacit or express, can be inferred but that such evidence, without more is insufficient unless the circumstances under which it occurred make the inference of rational, independent choice less attractive than that of concerted action. We recently articulated those circumstances . . . : '(1) a showing of acts by defendants in contradiction of their own economic interests . . . ; and (2) satisfactory demonstration of a motivation to enter an agreement.'"

Bogosian v. Gulf Oil Corp., 561 F.2d 434, 446 (3d Cir. 1977), certiorari denied 434 U.S. 1086, 98 S.Ct. 1280, 55 L.Ed.2d 791 (1978).

22. See L. Sullivan, Antitrust 358–64 (1977). Does it make a difference whether concentration in an industry is measured by concentration ratios (*viz.*, the market share of the top 2, 4, 8, etc. firms in the industry) or whether concentration is measured by the "H" index? See discussion of the "H" index, supra p. 67.

23. Reprinted in 874 ATRR F–1 (July 27, 1978); Trade Reg. Rep. #345, Part III (Aug. 8, 1978).

singled out information exchange mechanisms, price and product standardization systems, and devices which punish deviations from noncompetitive price levels. Despite intensive investigation of several industries by the Division, no case testing the theory has been filed to date.

The F.T.C.'s activity in the area of shared monopoly has focused on a 1972 F.T.C. complaint charging four firms with illegally monopolizing the ready-to-eat cereal market.[24] The complaint charged the firms with establishing and maintaining a noncompetitive market structure and shared monopoly for the past 30 years by various means and practices including proliferation of brands and trademarks, artificial differentiation of products, unfair methods of competition in advertising and product promotion, restrictive retail shelf space control programs, and acquisition of competitors. Four firms controlled 90% of the market in 1970 and the F.T.C. staff claimed the noncompetitive structure of the industry resulted in a $100 million "monopoly overcharge" on 1970 sales of "$740 million".[25] After nine years of maneuvering and several efforts to stop the proceedings by securing Congressional intervention on behalf of the respondents,[26] an administrative law judge dismissed the case for failure to prove a conspiracy and for lack of evidence that the respondents were realizing monopoly profits.[27]

Proposals have also been offered in Congress,[28] most notably the "Industrial Reorganization Act",[29] to deal with the problem of oligopoly. The proposed Industrial Reorganization Act would have established a Commission to enforce the Act before a specialized court and limited remedies to reorganization of firms found to have violated the Act. The proposal provided:

Sec. 101. (a) It is hereby declared to be unlawful for any corporation or two or more corporations, whether by agreement or not, to possess monopoly power in any line of commerce in any section of the country or with foreign nations.

(b) There shall be a rebuttable presumption that monopoly power is possessed—

(1) by any corporation if the average rate of return on net worth after taxes is in excess of 15 percentum over a period of five consecutive years out of the most recent seven years preceding the filing of the complaint, or

(2) if there has been no substantial price competition among two or more corporations in any line of commerce in any section of the country for a period of three consecutive years out of the most recent five years preceding the filing of the complaint, or

(3) if any four or fewer corporations account for 50 percentum (or more) of sales in any line of commerce in any section of the country in

24. In the Matter of Kellogg Co., [F.T.C. Complaints and Orders 1970–73] Trade Reg. Rep. (CCH) ¶ 19,898 (F.T.C. 1972).

25. See Low, et al., Cereals and the Law: A Case Summary, 12 Antitrust L. & Econ. Rev. #4, p. 11 (1980).

26. See, The F.T.C.'s Breakfast Cereal Case, 12 Antitrust Law & Econ. Rev. #3, p. 9 (1980).

27. In the Matter of Kellogg Co., Trade Reg. Rep. (CCH No. 507, part II,

(Sept. 14, 1981). An order denying appeal and dismissing the F.T.C.'s complaint was entered by the F.T.C. on Jan. 15, 1982. See 3 Trade Reg. Rep. (CCH) ¶ 21,899 (F.T.C. 1982).

28. Summarized and discussed in L. Sullivan, Antitrust 367–73 (1977).

29. S. 3831, 92nd Cong., 2d Sess. (1972); S. 1167, 93rd Cong., 1st Sess. (1973); S. 1959, 94th Cong., 1st Sess. (1975).

any year out of the most recent three years preceding the filing of the complaint.

In all other instances, the burden shall lie on the Industrial Reorganization Commission established under title II of this Act to prove the possession of monopoly power.

(c) A corporation shall not be required to divest monopoly power if it can show—

(1) such power is due solely to the ownership of valid patents, lawfully acquired and lawfully used, or

(2) such a divestiture would result in a loss of substantial economies.

The burden shall be upon the corporation or corporations to prove that monopoly power should not be divested pursuant to paragraphs (1) and (2) of the above subsection: *Provided, however,* That upon a showing of the possession of monopoly power pursuant to paragraph (1), the burden shall be upon the Industrial Reorganization Commission to show the invalidity, unlawful acquisition, and unlawful use of a patent or patents.

Queries: Is the proposed bill necessary in view of the *American Tobacco* case? Are the standards of the bill justified?

UNITED STATES v. CONSOLIDATED LAUNDRIES CORP.

United States Court of Appeals, Second Circuit, 1961.
291 F.2d 563.

Before SWAN, WATERMAN and MOORE, CIRCUIT JUDGES.

[Digest]. Defendants, eight corporations, two trade associations and several individuals engaged in the linen supply business in New York and New Jersey, were convicted of violating sections 1 and 2 of the Sherman Act, fined a total of $451,000, and four individual defendants were given short prison sentences. Count two of the indictment charged the defendants with a conspiracy to monopolize commerce in linen supplies by allocating customers among themselves, refusing to deal with each other's customers, injuring and obstructing non-members of the conspiracy in order to compel them to join the conspiracy or drive them out of business, and imposing penalties upon members who failed to conform to the terms of the conspiracy. The defendants moved for a new trial on the grounds that the government failed to give them access to documents necessary for their defense and, *inter alia,* because the prosecution failed to prove: "(a) a specific intent to monopolize, (b) a dangerous probability that monopolization would occur as a result of the conspiracy, and (c) the relevant market sought to be monopolized." In the course of its opinion reversing the conviction for failure of the government to give the defendants access to relevant documents, the Court expressed "views which may be helpful to the trial court" in a new trial on the defendants' substantive objections to the standards upon which they were convicted.

SWAN, CIRCUIT JUDGE: . . . As to point (a), it may well be doubted whether the evidence that the defendants agreed to protect old business by allocating customers would be sufficient, if standing alone, to prove a specific intent to monopolize rather than only an intent to restrain trade. But this evidence does not stand alone. Assuming the correctness of Judge Palmieri's findings, the defendants took concerted action to drive independent non-cooperating linen suppliers out of business. In our opinion this was sufficient to support the conclusion that defendants had the specific intent to monopolize. Also promises made to independents that they could raise prices by joining the alleged conspiracy gave further support to this conclusion. As to point (b), it will suffice to say that no authority has been called to our attention which indicates that the Government must prove a dangerous probability that monopolization will result from such a conspiracy. As to point (c), the charge here is conspiracy to monopolize, not monopolization. In a monopolization case the market must be proved. See International Boxing Club v. United States, 358 U.S. 242, 79 S.Ct. 245, 3 L.Ed.2d 270. This is because such a charge requires a showing of power to exclude competitors, and without an accurate delineation of the market, it is impossible to determine the presence or absence of this power. But where the charge is conspiracy to monopolize, the essential element is not the power, but the specific intent, to monopolize. Section 2 makes it unlawful "to conspire to monopolize 'any part' of interstate commerce, without specifying how large a part must be affected. Hence it is enough if some appreciable part of interstate commerce is the subject" of the conspiracy.

. . .

NOTES AND QUERIES

(1) *The Relevance of Relevant Markets and Size of Market Share in Combinations or Conspiracies to Monopolize.* In Turner, Antitrust Policy and the *Cellophane* Case, 70 Harv.L.Rev. 281, 304–306 (1956), Professor Turner stated:

> Each of the section 2 offenses—attempt, conspiracy, and combination to monopolize, and individual monopolizing—involves two elements: monopoly (as a goal or as a result), and purpose and intent, which is principally derived from conduct. With *Cellophane*, monopoly with respect to market definition has come to mean three different things, depending on the offense involved. The breakdown, perhaps oversimplified, is as follows:
>
> (1) *Attempts and Conspiracies.*—Monopoly is control over any appreciable amount of commerce, even though that amount is not a market in any meaningful economic sense.
>
> (2) *Combinations.*—Monopoly is control over a market from which qualitatively distinct substitutes are prima facie (and possibly conclusively) excluded.
>
> (3) *Individual Monopolizing.*—Monopoly is control over a market in which qualitatively distinct substitutes are included (either prima facie or conclusively) once it is shown that they are reasonably interchangeable.
>
> The three different meanings of monopoly are in effect different answers to this question: To what extent is monopoly power an important element in the offense, or, in other words, to what extent will monopoly

power be presumed?   In attempt and conspiracy cases the courts are almost disregarding the element of power.   In combination cases power is a recognized element, but the courts are willing to presume that control over a single product constitutes monopoly power, at least in the absence of convincing proof to the contrary.   In individual monopolization cases, power is more important; the competition of reasonably interchangeable substitutes is fully recognized, and the Government can show that control over a single product gives monopoly power, if at all, only by demonstrating a substantial margin of advantage over the substitutes.

The reasons for treating the element of monopoly differently must stem from differences in the element of conduct involved in each offense. In examining these differences, I think the attenuation of the monopoly concept in attempt and conspiracy cases can easily be justified, and so can the transition to a more careful consideration of monopoly in instances of combination.

The kind of conduct that typically establishes the requisite "specific intent" in attempt and conspiracy cases is clearly conduct which has no social or economic justification.   No benefits can be expected, at least in the long run, from predatory pricecutting, coercive refusal to sell, and similar abuses of economic power.   If defendants are attempting to drive someone out of the market by foul means rather than fair, there is ample warrant for not resorting to any refined analysis as to whether the intent is to drive everyone out or whether, having taken over all of the production of a particular commodity, the defendants would still face effective competition from substitutes.   . . .

The case of combination, as distinct from conspiracy, is somewhat different.   (While combination and conspiracy, have often loosely been used to mean the same thing, I am here speaking of combination in the form of permanent amalgamation by merger or otherwise.)   The difference is in the inferences that may fairly be drawn from the conduct.   Voluntary combination will not always give rise to an unambiguous inference of bad intent or bad results, since there is the possibility of technological or other economies which will result from the move or may have primarily motivated it.   Thus, unlike the typical attempt or conspiracy case where one may readily infer that the principal goal is aggrandizement unmerited by superiority in product or technique, the combination case requires some additional justification for paying only casual attention to definition of market.   . . .

There are still justifications, however, for adopting a definition of the market in combination cases which is narrow in that it excludes any consideration of qualitatively distinct substitutes and for condemning a combination that "monopolizes" a single product, even though in some cases it may be that substantial market power does not in fact result.   These justifications are historical and practical.   The legislative history of the Sherman Act and a spotty but recurring theme in the cases indicate a bias against large combinations and in favor of relatively small entrepreneurship.   It is possible, as Judge Hand pointed out in *Alcoa*, to prefer an economy populated by numerous individual units even at some cost in efficiency.

Do you agree?   Is the thesis also supported by the express language of the statute; *viz*, Section 2 makes it unlawful to "combine or conspire," not to "combine *and* conspire"?

(2) *Are "Combinations to Monopolize" and "Conspiracies to Monopolize" Different?* Professor Turner suggests that there is a difference between "combinations to monopolize" and "conspiracies to monopolize." What is the distinction? Is "combination" broader or narrower than "conspiracy"? In an oligopoly industry characterized by persistent high profits, follow-the-leader pricing and marketing practices, and absence of new entrants over a sustained period of time, have the members of the industry "combined" to monopolize? [30]

(3) *Conduct Proving a Specific Intent.* Professor Turner suggests that the type of conduct proving the requisite intent for conspiracy cases is "clearly conduct which has no social or economic justification."[31] Would this standard include conduct which proves a purpose to fix prices or exclude competitors but falls short of proving a specific intent to gain a monopoly in the sense of an overwhelming share of a relevant market? Should the standard relied upon by Judge Hand in *Alcoa* be sufficient in conspiracies to monopolize, i.e., "no intent is relevant except that which is relevant to any liability . . . an intent to bring about the forbiden act"?[32]

4. REMEDIES

Section 4 of the Sherman Act confers upon the federal courts jurisdiction to "prevent and restrain violations of this Act." When a court has been convinced that a violation has occurred, the question of drafting an appropriate remedial judgment arises. In cases arising under Section 2, the central issue will often be a choice between divestiture, to break up the concentration of economic power, or injunctive relief to curb predatory practices or narrow the range of "discretionary authority"[33] which can be exercised by the defendant. A court which has already found defendant guilty of a monopoly offense will accept responsibility to restore unfettered competition by its degree and to protect it against anticipatable undermining. This

---

30. Cf. Bogosian v. Gulf Oil Corp., supra note 21; Kellogg Co., supra note 27, Note, Annual Style Change In the Automobile Industry as an Unfair Method of Competition, supra note 63.

31. Compare American Football League v. National Football League, 205 F.Supp. 60, 64 (D.Md.1962), affirmed 323 F.2d 124 (4th Cir. 1963) ("[n]either rough competition nor unethical business conduct is sufficient. The requisite intent to monopolize must be present and predominant.") with Patterson v. United States, 222 F. 599, 633–34 (6th Cir. 1915) ("[w]e think it clear that there was substantial evidence to the effect that there was a conspiracy . . . . In the publications of the company and in the communications between the officers and agents having to do with competition, terms of warfare were not infrequently used, such as battle, flight, enemy, ammunition, shot, whipped, victory, and flags flying. During that time all the competitors named then in existence retired from the field").

32. See Hunt-Wesson Foods, Inc. v. Ragu Foods, Inc., 627 F.2d 919 (9th Cir. 1980), certiorari denied 450 U.S. 921, 101 S.Ct. 1369, 67 L.Ed.2d 348 (1981): "[N]o particular level of market power or 'dangerous probability of success' has to be alleged or proved in a conspiracy claim where the specific intent to monopolize is otherwise apparent from the character of the actions taken. . . . But where actions are ambiguous, the existence and extent of market power may make the inference of specific intent from conduct more or less plausible. . . . Hunt alleges that . . . [defendants] conspired to monopolize [the spaghetti sauce market] with the requisite specific intent and in addition alleges that Ragu had market power. This is sufficient to withstand a motion to dismiss." Id. at 926–27.

33. Dewey, The New Learning: One Man's View, in Industrial Concentration: The New Learning 13 (H. Goldschmid, M. Mann & J. Weston, Editors 1974). See generally, Rothschild (Ed.), Power In Economics (1971).

might call for divestiture even though the defendant does not at the time of the decree possess overwhelming power in the relevant market. Moreover, power will be appraised much more flexibly than simply by reference to market shares. Nevertheless, the courts have exercised notable, if not excessive, self-restraint in using the structural remedy of divestiture. Only where anticompetitive acquisition of rival firms has played a part in the violation, has divestiture of the illegally acquired assets been readily granted.[34] Judge Wyzanski, in UNITED STATES v. UNITED SHOE MACHINERY CORP.,[35] explained judicial hesitation to order drastic structural relief as follows:

> Judges in prescribing remedies have known their own limitations. They do not *ex officio* have economic or political training. Their prophecies as to the economic future are not guided by unusually subtle judgment. They are not so representative as other branches of the government. The recommendations they receive from government prosecutors do not always reflect the over-all approach of even the executive branch of the government, sometimes not indeed the seasoned and fairly informed judgment of the head of the Department of Justice. Hearings in court do not usually give the remote judge as sound a feeling for the realities of a situation as other procedures do. Judicial decrees must be fitted into the framework of what a busy, and none too expert, court can supervise. Above all, no matter with what authority he is invested, with what facts and opinion he is supplied, a trial judge is only one man, and should move with caution and humility.
>
> That considerations of this type have always affected anti-trust courts is plain from the history of the Standard Oil, American Tobacco and Alcoa cases. To many champions of the anti-trust laws these cases indicate judicial timidity, economic innocence, lack of conviction, or paralysis of resolution. Yet there is another way of interpreting this judicial history. In the anti-trust field the courts have been accorded, by common consent, an authority they have in no other branch of enacted law. Indeed, the only comparable examples of the power of judges is the economic role they formerly exercised under the Fourteenth Amendment, and the role they now exercise in the area of civil liberties. They would not have been given, or allowed to keep, such authority in the anti-trust field, and they would not so freely have altered from time to time the interpretation of its substantive provisions, if courts were in the habit of proceeding with the surgical ruthlessness that might commend itself to those seeking absolute assurance that there will be workable competition, and to those aiming at immediate realization of the social, political, and economic advantages of dispersal of power.

34. See, Remedies in Merger Cases, p. 322 ff. infra.

35. 110 F.Supp. 295, 347–48 (D.C. Mass.1953), affirmed 347 U.S. 521, 74 S.Ct. 699, 98 L.Ed. 910 (1954); on motion to modify the decree 266 F.Supp. 328 (D.C.Mass.1967), reversed 391 U.S. 244, 88 S.Ct. 1496, 20 L.Ed.2d 562 (1968); consent decree entered, 1969 Trade Cases ¶ 72,688 (D.Mass.1969).

Thus, the implications of an overwhelming share of market power may change where a court turns from the question of violation to the issue of prescribing "relief which will terminate the illegal monopoly, deny the defendant the fruits of its statutory violation, and insure that there remain no practices likely to result in monopolization in the future."[36]

The remedy phase of the *ALCOA* case illustrates the cross-currents of policy and the shift in approach between the violation and relief phases of the case. Final resolution of the remedy issues in *ALCOA* was further complicated by the long delay in determining which court would hear the appeal since the Supreme Court lacked a quorum of six justices to hear the original appeal. In addition the emergency created by World War II caused construction of several government-owned aluminum plants to help meet the war-time need for aluminum, thereby adding a new dimension to the structure of the market that did not exist at the time of the trial. Judge Hand took note of these developments in the remedy phase of his opinion remanding the case for further proceedings in the trial court.

UNITED STATES v. ALUMINUM CO. OF AMERICA

United States Court of Appeals, Second Circuit, 1945.
148 F.2d 416, 445–47.

L. HAND, J.

. . . Nearly five years have passed since the evidence was closed; during that time the aluminum industry, like most other industries, has been revolutionized by the nation's efforts in a great crisis. That alone would make it impossible to dispose of the action upon the basis of the record as we have it; and so both sides agree; both appeal to us to take "judicial notice" of what has taken place meanwhile, though they differ as to what should be the result. The plaintiff wishes us to enter a judgment that "Alcoa" shall be dissolved, and that we shall direct it presently to submit a plan, whose execution, however, is to be deferred until after the war. . . .

[I]t is impossible to say what will be "Alcoa's" position in the industry after the war. The plaintiff has leased to it all its new plants and the leases do not expire until 1947 and 1948, though they may be surrendered earlier. No one can now forecast in the remotest way what will be the form of the industry after the plaintiff has disposed of these plants, upon their surrender. It may be able to transfer all of them to persons who can effectively compete with "Alcoa"; it may be able to transfer some; conceivably, it may be unable to dispose of any. The measure of its success will be at least one condition upon the propriety of dissolution, and upon the form which it should take, if there is to be any. It is as idle for the plaintiff to assume that dissolution will be proper, as it is for "Alcoa" to assume that it will not be; and it would be particularly fatuous to prepare a plan now,

36. United States v. United Shoe Machinery Corp., 391 U.S. 244, 250, 88 S.Ct. 1496, 1500, 20 L.Ed.2d 562, 567 (1968).

even if we could be sure that eventually some form of dissolution will
be proper. Dissolution is not a penalty but a remedy; if the industry
will not need it for its protection, it will be a disservice to break up an
aggregation which has for so long demonstrated its efficiency.
. . . .

But there is another, and even more persuasive, reason why we
should not now adjudge a dissolution of any kind. The Surplus Property Act of 1944 provides the method by which the plaintiff's "surplus" properties shall be disposed of: "aluminum plants and facilities" among the rest, § 19(a)(1). The "Surplus Property Board,"
§ 5(a), is to "designate one or more Government agencies to act as
disposal agencies," § 10(a), and they are to "have responsibility and
authority for the disposition of such property and for the care and
handling of such property, pending its disposition," § 11(d), subject to
the Board's regulations. These "agencies" may dispose of the
properties "by sale, exchange, lease, or transfer, for cash, credit, or
other property, with or without warranty, and upon such other terms
and conditions, as the agency deems proper" § 15(a). The following,
among other "objectives," are to "regulate the orderly disposal of
surplus property": "(b) to give maximum aid in the reestablishment
of a peacetime economy of free independent private enterprise"; "(d)
to discourage monopolistic practices and to strengthen and preserve
the competitive position of small business concerns in an economy of
free enterprise"; "(p) to foster the development of new independent
enterprise"; "(r) to dispose of surplus property as promptly as feasible without fostering monopoly or restraint of trade . . .." So
far as consistent "with the usual and customary commercial practice"
preference is to be given to smaller purchasers, § 18(b); to whom,
when proper, money may be lent, § 18(f). Finally, no "disposal agency" shall even "begin negotiations" to sell a plant which has cost over
a million dollars without advising the Attorney General of "the probable terms or conditions" of the sale; and he in turn must tell the
"agency" whether "the proposed disposition will violate the antitrust
laws."[37] The act must not be read to "impair, amend, or modify"
those laws, or to "prevent their application" to purchasers of surplus
property. In view of these declarations of the purpose of Congress,
the "agency" which the Board "designates" to dispose of the plaintiff's "aluminum plants and facilities" may well believe that it cannot
do so without some plan or design for the industry as a whole, some
comprehensive model which shall, so far as practicable, re-establish
"free independent private enterprise," "discourage" monopoly,
"strengthen" small competitors, "foster" independents and not foster
"monopoly or restraint of trade." If it should find this method desirable, it would have to learn what purchasers were in the market, how
strong they were, what units they could finance and operate, and in
what position they would be to compete. In such a model or design
the "agency" would have to assign a place to "Alcoa," and that place
no one of course can now anticipate. Conceivably "Alcoa" might be

37. Similar provisions were enacted   the Federal Property and Administrative
as permanent legislation in Sec. 207 of   Services Act of 1949, 40 U.S.C.A. § 488.

left as it was; perhaps it might have to be dissolved; if dissolved, the dissolution would depend upon how the other plants were distributed. . . .[38]

UNITED STATES v. ALUMINUM CO. OF AMERICA

District Court of the United States, Southern District of New York, 1950.
91 F.Supp. 333.

[Digest of the opinion of KNOX, J.] Two important new producers of aluminum, Reynolds and Kaiser, appeared in the post World War II market as a result of government-financed construction during the war and of the program of disposal of surplus war plants after the war. But Alcoa still had 85% of the open market sales of ingot to nonintegrated producers (i.e. excluding from consideration ingot fabricated by the producing companies). In this situation the government moved for a decree divesting Alcoa of some of its production facilities in order to set up a fourth aluminum company. Alcoa countered with a motion for a declaration that, due to changed conditions, it was no longer a monopoly and that it was therefore entitled to purchase certain additional facilities from the government.

The criterion of relief is what is needed to restore effective competition. Account must be taken of the recent view of the Supreme Court that concentration of power itself, without abuse, may violate the law. Remedies have expanded beyond mere injunction against restrictive practices; and may include any provision necessary to deprive the monopolist of the fruits of his violation or to recreate conditions for effective competition. Therefore the court can take steps to reduce Alcoa's power even though it may not be presently an unlawful monopoly.

Power is to be measured not simply in terms of percentage of a market—"a shorthand expression of power"—but of total resources, including the leverage gained by vertical integration. Bu the *Columbia Steel* case [p. 209, infra] shows that the courts must also take "cognizance of the economic needs and organization of American industry", especially since there the Supreme Court did not interfere even at the preventive stage, whereas here the question is whether to take apart a long-integrated organization. The court, however, must "provide against reasonable expectation of the resumption of future unlawful conditions", and all doubts regarding remedies must be resolved in favor of the government. It must forestall, for example, even the possibility that Alcoa may have monopoly "thrust upon it" under reasonably predictable market developments:

> "In determining the extent of permissible power that is consistent with the anti-trust laws in a particular industry, the following

38. The recommended program appears in Aluminum Plants and Facilities, Report of the Surplus Property Board to Congress (1945); First Supplemental Report of War Assets Administration to Congress (1947). It was "not a plan for the industry as a whole, but merely a set of guiding principles" and was not accorded even "presumptive validity" in formulating the eventual decree against Alcoa. See United States v. Aluminum Co. of America, 91 F.Supp. 333, 354 (S.D. N.Y.1950).

factors are relevant: the number and strength of the firms in the market; their effective size from the standpoint of technological development, and from the standpoint of competition with substitute materials and foreign trade; national security interests in the maintenance of strong productive facilities, and maximum scientific research and development; together with the public interest in lowered costs and uninterrupted production." (347)

Alcoa's position in the postwar market is not to be gauged by its percentage of total sales of primary aluminum to non-integrated producers, even though primary aluminum was the very product as to which Alcoa had been adjudged a monopolist. Alcoa's 85% of that market is not a true index of its power as against Reynolds and Kaiser, because in a time of short supply, Reynolds and Kaiser voluntarily chose not to sell ingot, in order to supply their own fabricating facilities. For the same reason, Alcoa's conceded power to make the price in this "market" is discounted. (364–5)

"The integration of these producers requires market to be a broad concept, unrelated to any particular aluminum product." (357) Secondary ingot can no longer be regarded as a portion of the supply controlled by Alcoa, because during the War Alcoa's production was governed by government requisition rather than the company's forecasts of market demand; and in the post-war market Reynolds' and Kaiser's judgment, as well as Alcoa's, determines the future supply of scrap. On the basis of metal controlled and sales, including sales of fabricated products, Alcoa does approximately half the post-war aluminum business, Reynolds one quarter and Kaiser one sixth, with the latter making some apparent gains. Here is no *"prima facie"* monopoly, and therefore a detailed comparative appraisal of "resources" must be undertaken (365–402), covering plant capacity and location, raw materials owned or under contract, manufacturing costs, power supply and price, research and patent positions, affiliations. Alcoa's enormous advantage is demonstrated. Its diversification of product assures great market stability. (364) The common control of Alcoa and Aluminum Limited of Canada by a small group of stockholders and the family ties between the executive heads of the two companies are regarded as a particularly powerful resource of Alcoa and threat to other producers (although this relationship had been held legal in the original proceeding) because Limited has since succeeded in reducing its mill costs to the point where the United States is its logical market. (392–8)

(399–402): The importance of disaffiliating Limited is emphasized by the virtual certainty that the number of domestic producers cannot be increased owing to limited amounts of power, ore and financial backing for an integrated company capable of standing up to Alcoa. Accordingly, the dominant shareholders of Alcoa are ordered to dispose of their holdings in one or the other company.

(402–416): The government had pushed Alcoa into granting licenses under its patents to Reynolds and Kaiser in connection with the plant disposal program. The license agreements included provisions granting back to Alcoa non-exclusive licenses to all improvements developed by the licensees. The court orders deletion of the grant-back provisions:

"With regard to this crucial technological matter, Alcoa, by virtue of the grant-back, enjoys a marked advantage over its competitors. It will have exclusive control of its own improvements. It will also have free use of any improvements made by Reynolds or Kaiser, whereas, as between the latter two firms, only the inventing company will stand to benefit. Thus, the efforts of either Reynolds or Kaiser may serve to improve Alcoa's position, and do harm to one of the other two concerns. Moreover, because an improvement by Reynolds or Kaiser can never injure Alcoa, their major competitor, it appears to me that the smaller companies will likely be discouraged from pursuing, with fullest vigor, technological investigation in the possibilities of the future. This helps to explain, perhaps, why Alcoa's research department had 762 employees in 1949, while Reynolds and Kaiser combined had but 88." (410)

Alcoa's resistance to government pressure to grant patent licenses to Reynolds and Kaiser, so that the latter might operate the surplus plants after the war, does not establish such monopolistic intent as to justify divestiture on this ground. Since, under present law, even normal competitive activities may lead to illegal monopoly: "In order to prompt a magnification of remedies, I believe the evidence must clearly show that the monopoly was a product of abusive or predatory trade practices, which are beyond the bounds of lawful competition." (415) In this connection, the court considers as a transaction to Alcoa's credit its furnishing Reynolds and Kaiser raw materials in time of shortage, and as a discreditable transaction its refusal to relieve Reynolds of some embarrassing inventory.* The refusal was based in part on an opinion of counsel that it would be a violation of the antitrust laws for Alcoa to buy Reynolds' output.**

(416–7): The government's proposal that another integrated producer be put together from fragments carved out of Alcoa is rejected on grounds of national security and general welfare, plus the difficulty of creating a new organization capable of competing with Alcoa without further weakening Reynolds and Kaiser. The new firm would have to draw its management personnel from Alcoa to be efficient, and would either be dependent on Alcoa for research or require the dismemberment of Alcoa's research staff.

"The future development of the industry depends upon its being composed of financially sound and well-integrated organizations. One must constantly remember that aluminum products are in fierce rivalry with articles composed of other materials, and which are manufactured and sold by concerns that, in size, are fully equal to Alcoa.

* Has competition come to mean the   ** Why?
necessity of maintaining one's weaker
competitors?

Indeed, in some instances, the resources of such competing firms far exceed those of all three domestic aluminum producers.

"If the aluminum industry is to develop fully, and be able to satisfy the tremendous demands to which, in the natural course of events, it will be subjected, it must not be reduced to a state of relative impotence. On the contrary, the industry, if its present stature is to be maintained, must carry on a continuous process of encroachment upon the preserves of other industries whose products are manufactured by corporations that will not abjectly surrender the trade positions they now hold. The success of any such effort to encroach upon fields of endeavor that are now occupied by strongly entrenched competitors can be achieved only by companies that are rich in resources, and which are capable of undertaking extensive scientific and market experimentations. At the present juncture, the weakening of any aluminum producer would lessen the buoyancy of the industry as a whole. Rightly or wrongly, from an economic and social standpoint, big business in many industries is an actuality, and if such enterprises are to be subjected to effective competition, their trade rivals must be of somewhat comparable strength." (416)

Jurisdiction was retained for five years to permit the Court then to reexamine the competitive situation in the industry.[39]

NOTES AND QUERIES

(1) *Queries.* Note the difference in approach to appraisal of economic power between Judge Hand, with his percentages of the market, and Judge Knox. Does Judge Knox's opinion mean that an illegal combination of all the copper companies into one firm would not be broken up if the court believed that only a firm of that size could compete effectively with the steel and aluminum giants? Does this opinion mean that if a large organization achieves such dominance in research that national security depends upon that research, the organization must be perpetuated as a private monopoly? How were Reynolds and Kaiser supposed to survive if success in the metals field requires an organization like Alcoa's? Should the decree have ordered Alcoa to make all future inventions available to Reynolds and Kaiser at a reasonable fee, so long as its dominance in research continued?

If the significance of monopoly is the power to exclude competition or determine prices, is it possible for this power to exist to a socially undesirable degree where one organization handles less than 33% of the business? In such cases is the power likely to be the result of agreements and other restraints prohibited by Section 1? Should unlawful monopoly be defined as that degree of concentration of trade control which, independent of restraints prohibited by Section 1, gives the monopolist substantial assurance that its price and related business determinations will be followed by the trade? Is the distinction between monopoly and restraint of trade essentially a question of what judicial relief is appropriate; i.e., are dissolution and

39. The *Alcoa* case is discussed in Adams, Dissolution, Divorcement, Divestiture: The Pyrrhic Victories of Antitrust, 27 Ind.L.J. 1 (1951). The government's petition to extend the period of judicial supervision was denied in United States v. Aluminum Co. of America, 153 F.Supp. 132 (S.D.N.Y.1957) ("Kaiser and Reynolds more than maintained their competitive position in the phenomenal expansion of the industry").

divestiture appropriate where the mere size of the defendant creates a trade atmosphere inimical to economic freedom of action for other enterprisers in the field, whereas injunctions against restrictive practices suffice to remedy violations of Section 1 and "behavioral" violations of § 2? [40]

(2) *Alcoa Sequels.* The consent judgment in the *Alcoa* case, 1954 Trade Cases ¶ 67,745, required Alcoa to set aside for independent fabricators 110,000 tons annually out of proposed imports of Canadian ingot by Alcoa. Should Alcoa have been forbidden to make long term arrangements to buy ingot from Limited, its "disaffiliated" potential competitor? See "Aluminium Ltd.'s U. S. Expansion Is Antitrust Target," Wall Street Journal, Dec. 31, 1964, p. 16, for a report on the Canadian Company's proposal to buy aluminum fabricating facilities from National Distillers & Chemical Corp. The Department of Justice sought an injunction. Is Limited's vigorous expansion into the U. S. a Good Thing, resulting from its "liberation" by the *Alcoa* decree? A Bad Thing because it will favor the newly acquired subsidiary fabricator over its other American customers? [41] A Necessity, if Limited is to compete with Alcoa and other vertically integrated American producers? For more recent developments, see "Alcoa's Dominance in Aluminum Industry Wanes as Rivals Grow, Markets Get Tight," Wall Street Journal, March 25, 1982, p. 31, reporting that until 1979 Alcoa's only big competitors were Reynolds and Kaiser; that Alcoa's market share was about 60 per cent through the late 1970's; and that Alcan (formerly Aluminium Limited) with a current share of 15 per cent was *beginning* to threaten Alcoa's position. Alcoa's attempt to expand and diversify by acquisition of a relatively small manufacturer of copper cable, which competes with aluminum cable in some uses, was frustrated in *United States v. Aluminum Co. of America.*[42]

(3) *Other Divestiture Cases.* Illustrative of cases where divestiture has been decreed are: *Standard Oil Co. of New Jersey v. United States;*[43] *United States v. Paramount Pictures, Inc.* [44] (principal producers of moving pictures, having monopolized first run exhibition by preferentially cross-licensing each other's theaters, required to dispose of theater interests); *Schine Chain Theatres, Inc. v. United States* [45] (defendants operating chain of moving picture theaters used bargaining power, derived from the fact that in many towns they had the only theater, to obtain from moving pictures distributors unfair preferences over competing operators in multiple-theater towns, and subsequently bought out many of such competitors; defendants were enjoined from illegal practices and required to dispose of 50 theaters in multiple-theater towns); *United States v. United Fruit Co.*[46] (consent decree requiring defendant to organize a competitive firm which

40. See O'Connor, The Divestiture Remedy In Sherman Act 2 Cases, 13 Harv.J.Legis. 687 (1976).

41. Cf. Report on Small Business and the Aluminum Industry, Subcommittee No. 3, Select Committee on Small Business, H.Rep.No.2954, 84th Cong., 2d Sess. (1956), on the continuing difficulties experienced by small fabricating enterprises in obtaining aluminum in a period of high demand, when the Big Three integrated producers could profitably use ingot and sheet in their own fabricating operations.

42. 377 U.S. 271, 84 S.Ct. 1283, 12 L.Ed.2d 314 (1964), rehearing denied 377 U.S. 1010, 84 S.Ct. 1903, 12 L.Ed.2d 1057.

43. 221 U.S. 1, 31 S.Ct. 502, 55 L.Ed. 619 (1911); but cf. reintegration of components permitted in United States v. Standard Oil Co. of New Jersey, 47 F.2d 288 (E.D.Mo.1931) (merger of Standard Oil Co. of New York with Vacuum Oil Co. to create Socony-Vacuum, approved despite substantial competition between the firms, in view of existence of other larger competitors and absence of intent to monopolize).

44. 334 U.S. 131, 68 S.Ct. 915, 92 L.Ed. 1260 (1948).

45. 334 U.S. 110, 68 S.Ct. 947, 92 L.Ed. 1245 (1948).

46. 1958 Trade Cases ¶ 68,941 (E.D. La.1958).

would handle the equivalent of one-third of defendant's current imports of bananas; order contingent on approval of defendant's stockholders and defendant given eight years to submit a plan of compliance and four more years to put it into effect).

Among cases in which divestiture has been denied are *United States v. National Lead Co.* [47] ("no showing that four major competing units would be preferable to two"); *United States v. United Shoe Machinery Corp.*[48] ("unrealistic" to attempt to make three companies out of one monopoly firm operating in a single plant; burden on the government to propose and prove practicability of plan of dissolution; defendant divested of subsidiary monopolies in supplies; other decree provisions designed to facilitate competitors' access to United's customers); *United States v. General Electric Co.* [49] (divestiture of foreign subsidiaries denied as counter to government's declared policy to encourage American capital investment abroad; injunctive provisions adequate to relieve international trade of the restraints on American imports effectuated by defendant's participation, through these subsidiaries, in cartel arrangements to reserve the American market for itself); *United States v. New York Great Atlantic & Pacific Tea Co.*[50] (government abandons attempt to split A. & P. into 7 regional grocery chains each of which would have been among the larger grocery chains of the country).

(4) *Injunctions Simulating Divestiture.* Sometimes when divestiture is not ordered the decree will include provisions forbidding enterprises under common control from agreeing with each other to divide markets or otherwise to restrict competition among themselves.[51] How "realistic" are such orders? If an American company has an English subsidiary which produces the same article as the American firm at lower cost, is the manager of the English enterprise likely to increase exports to the United States? May the American management decline to authorize him to expand the English plant so that he can produce enough to sell in South America where the American branch is already established? May there be consultation on major issues of business policy between affiliates subject to a decree which forbids them from entering into understandings or conspiracy in restraint of trade? [52]

In *Otter Tail Power Co. v. United States*, supra, p. 124, the Court approved a district court decree which enjoined Otter Tail "from refusing to

47. 332 U.S. 319, 67 S.Ct. 1634, 91 L.Ed. 2077 (1947); cf. In the Matter of National Lead Co., 49 F.T.C. 791 (1953) (respondent supplying over 50% of nation's lead pigments, a position of "practical dominance" achieved in part by acquiring more than 50 competitors in a period of 44 years, held to have engaged in unfair methods of competition in violation of Section 5 of the Federal Trade Commission Act, and ordered not to acquire additional competitors).

48. 110 F.Supp. 295 (D.Mass.1953), affirmed per curiam 347 U.S. 521, 74 S.Ct. 699, 98 L.Ed. 910 (1954). The decree was subsequently modified to provide for divestiture, after a ten year trial period under the original decree failed to establish competitive conditions. 1969 Trade Cases ¶ 72,688 (D.Mass.) (consent decree).

49. 115 F.Supp. 835 (D.N.J.1953); but cf. United States v. Minnesota Mining &

Manufacturing Co., 92 F.Supp. 947 (D.Mass.1950); United States v. Imperial Chemical Industries, 105 F.Supp. 215 (S.D.N.Y.1952).

50. Consent Decree, 1954 Trade Cases, ¶ 67,658 (S.D.N.Y.1954); cf. criminal conviction, 173 F.2d 79 (7th Cir., 1949). For a comparable situation in which a moving picture chain which illegally abused its bargaining power to the prejudice of smaller rivals was reorganized into smaller independent chains, see United States v. Crescent Amusement Co., 323 U.S. 173, 65 S.Ct. 254, 89 L.Ed. 160 (1944).

51. E.g., Timken Roller Bearing Co. v. United States, 341 U.S. 593, 71 S.Ct. 971, 95 L.Ed. 1199 (1951).

52. Cf. discussion of relationships with foreign subsidiaries in Report of the Attorney General's National Committee to Study the Antitrust Laws 88–91 (1955).

sell power at wholesale to existing or proposed municipal electric power systems in the areas serviced by Otter Tail, from refusing to wheel electric power over the lines from the electric power suppliers to existing or proposed municipal systems in the area, from entering into or enforcing any contract which prohibits use of Otter Tail's lines to wheel electric power to municipal electric power systems, or from entering into or enforcing any contract which limits the customers to whom and the areas in which Otter Tail or any other electric power company may sell electric power." [53]   Do you believe such relief will be adequate? Should the Court consider vertical divestiture in such cases, i.e., splitting the functions of power generation, long distance transmission, and local distribution? Does the decree do this in a sense by making Otter Tail operate its long distance transmission lines as a common carrier for buyers and sellers of electric power in its service area? [54]

5. *Remedies and The "Big Case".* Lawyers oriented toward litigating the intriguing and tough substantive issues often presented by substantial monopolization cases may lose sight of what practical remedy can be achieved by the litigation if a violation is found. The lesson learned in small or routine tort cases that it does little good to bring a lawsuit if the defendant has no assets from which to satisfy a judgment (you cannot get blood out of a turnip) may be forgotten when the opportunity to bring a major or "big case" comes along. A failure to consider what remedies are practical and within the capacity and willingness of a court to implement with confidence many years after the case has been brought may result in a major victory on the question of liability turning into a defeat in the remedy phase of the case. Little or nothing is done by way of planning and proposing a remedy which is, as a practical matter, well thought out and appealing to a court fully cognizant of its responsibility. The problem becomes magnified when the time between filing the case and considering a remedy stretches into years or even decades.

Several recent "big cases" have driven home the question of the feasibility of achieving sensible remedies in litigation that is either substantively sprawling and takes years to resolve or involves a substantial and powerful firm or firms where the stakes of the litigation are very high and every means is used to resist the case.[55] In recent years, F.T.C. litigation involving the dry cereal industry has been waged for over eight years in every possible forum and by every conceivable means before being dismissed.[56] A Commission case charging several large oil companies with monopolizing the southeastern United States petroleum market has been withdrawn, in part due to the long delay in getting down to the substantive issues of the complaint.[57] Discovery battles, and litigating issues such as whether the F.T.C.

53. 410 U.S. at 368–69, 93 S.Ct., at 1025, 35 L.Ed.2d, at 363.

54. On remedy ordering regulated utility to interconnect with competitors where refusal is part of a monopolistic scheme, see MCI Telecommunications Corp. v. Federal Communications Commission, 561 F.2d 365 (D.C.Cir. 1977); on motion to compel interconnect, 580 F.2d 590 (1978); MCI Communcations Corp. v. American Telephone & Telegraph Co., 462 F.Supp. 1072 (N.D.Ill.1978).

55. See, Selection of Materials Presented to the Nat'l Comm. Rev. of Antitrust L. & P., "Complex Litigation Materials", 48 Antitrust L.J. 663–905 (1979); 48 Antitrust L.J. 1017–1215 (1979) (Staff Papers on Procedural Revisions).

56. In the Matter of Kellogg Co., Trade Reg. Rep. (CCH) No. 507, part II (Sept. 14, 1981). An order denying appeal and dismissing the F.T.C.'s complaint was entered by the F.T.C. on Jan. 15, 1982. See 3 Trade Reg. Rep. (CCH) ¶ 21,899 (F.T.C. 1982).

57. In the Matter of Exxon Corp., [F.T.C. Complaints and Orders 1973–76] Trade Reg. Rep. (CCH) ¶ 20,388 (F.T.C. 1973), dismissed Sept. 16, 1981, 3 Trade Reg. Rep. (CCH) ¶ 21,866 (F.T.C. 1981).

must file an environmental impact statement upon bringing the case,[58] prevented even a superficial skirmish over the antitrust issues of the case. Litigating the 1973 structure and operation of the industry in 1981 does not make sense if the ongoing changes in the reality of the industry makes 1981 remedies based on 1973 facts of doubtful validity.

The Justice Department and I.B.M. Corp. began waging a battle in 1969 over charges that I.B.M. monopolized various aspects of the computer industry.[59] Trial of the case began in May of 1975 and was expected to be completed sometime in 1981. A 1977 newspaper account provides a glimpse of the size of the case, two and one half years into the trial:[60]

> The trial has consumed 388 courtroom days. The transcript numbers more than 60,000 pages, equal to 200 good-sized novels. In putting the case together, the Government compiled more than 50 million documents. Fifty witnesses have been called. . . . I.B.M. has drawn up a list of 350 defense witnesses it might call. Two who were originally scheduled have died. More than 5,000 exhibits have been presented as evidence. I.B.M. figures to toss in 5,000 more.

> There have been 47 opinions, 105 memorandum endorsements, 21 pretrial orders, 12 amended pretrial orders, 32 stipulations and orders, one contempt order and one order to show cause.

> Both sides rely on computers to deal with the torrent of information. Indeed, no one knows how the case could ever be managed without computers.

Both sides expended millions of dollars in litigation, the final judgment was not expected before 1982, and, if appeals had been taken, final resolution of the case was not expected before the late 1980's—twenty years from the time the case was initiated. In early 1982, the new chief of the Reagan Administration's Antitrust Division dismissed the case, within a few months of ending the long and drawn out trial.[61]

The long-term worth of this category of "big case" is therefore open to serious question on remedy grounds alone. Whether it be the fault of the government in filing too complex a case to begin with, defendants taking advantage of every marginal opportunity for delay and obfuscation while deducting litigation expenses from their income taxes, the trial court failing to adequately control the litigation, or the inherent nature of the "big case" beast, there is a growing recognition that the remedy issue alone may make the entire exercise impractical in its present format.

Query: What solutions might you suggest to alleviate these practical problems with the "big case"? Do not bring them? Seek remedies by legislation? Better judicial control of the case? A specialized court to handle such matters? Adoption of a no-conduct monopoly standard (supra p.123) or the Industrial Reorganization Act Proposal (supra p. 176)?

(6) *Divestiture in Regulated Industries.* In the case of regulated industries, the problem of divestiture under the antitrust laws (where applicable)

58. See Mobil Oil Corp. v. Federal Trade Commission, 562 F.2d 170 (2d Cir. 1977) (impact statement not required).

59. United States v. International Business Machines Corp., Civil Action No. 69 Civ. 200 (S.D.N.Y., filed Jan. 17, 1969).

60. See "The Days and Data Pile Up at the I.B.M. Trial", N.Y. Times, Sept. 30, 1977, p. D–1, col. 8.

61. N.Y. Times, p. 1, col. 4 (Jan. 9, 1982) (asserting case was without merit). See generally, Sullivan, Monopolization: Competitive Strategies, The IBM Case, and the Transformation of Law, 60 Texas L.Rev. 587 (1982).

is complicated by two factors. The regulatory law itself is likely to confer on the regulatory agency important responsibilities respecting the structure of public utility enterprises. See discussion of primary jurisdiction at p. 800, infra. Special difficulties are presented also by the integration of core public utility operations with manufacturing and other "incidental" operations normally regarded as part of the unregulated competitive sector of the economy.

An important and controversial case of this type, one settled by a consent decree with no divestiture, was *United States v. Western Electric Co. and American Telephone and Telegraph Co.*[62] The suit, which sought to separate the regulated communications monopoly of A. T. & T. from the normally competitive manufacturing operations of Western Electric, was instituted in 1949 under a Democratic Administration and settled by consent decree without divestiture on Jan. 24, 1956[63] under a Republican Administration. The Democratically controlled Antitrust Subcommittee of the House Judiciary Committee conducted an extensive investigation of the procedures by which the decree was negotiated and the validity of the agreement to accept injunctive relief, including royalty-free licensing of patents, in lieu of divestiture.[64]

A renewed effort to restructure the Bell system by antitrust decree was initiated with the filing of a monopolization suit against A. T. & T. in 1974.[65] The lawsuit attacked the corporate interrelationship of the Bell operating companies (twenty-two regional telephone companies controlled by A. T. & T.), the Long Lines division (providing long distance communications and switching services), Western Electric (the nation's major manufacturer of communication equipment and supplies) and Bell Telephone Laboratories, Inc. (the nation's premiere research lab, financed in part by ratepayers of A. T. & T.). The gist of the complaint was the charge that A. T. & T. had monopolized the telecommunications market in the United States by restricting communication for telecommunications services through its control of the Long Lines division and the operating companies and by foreclosing competition in the sale of telecommunications equipment to the operating companies by causing Western Electric to supply substantially all of the Bell system's equipment requirements.

The trial judge, Judge Greene, strictly managed the discovery and pretrial motions in the mammoth case and opened trial of the case in January of 1981. Unlike litigation of the *I.B.M.* case,[66] the trial was moved along expeditiously by Judge Greene. Upon conclusion of the Government's case in the summer of 1981, A. T. & T. moved to dismiss under Fed.R.Civ.P. Rule 41(d) on the grounds that the Government "upon the facts and the law" had shown no right to relief. In a lengthy opinion surveying all the allegations and the Government's evidence, the court rejected the motion and held:

> The testimony and documentary evidence adduced by the government demonstrate that the Bell system has violated the antitrust laws in a number of ways over a lengthy period of time. On the three principal

62. Civ. No. 17-49 (D.N.J., Jan. 14, 1949).

63. United States v. Western Electric Co., 1956 Trade Cases ¶ 68,246 (D.N.J. 1956).

64. Hearings on American Telephone & Telegraph Co. before the Antitrust Subcommittee of the House Judiciary Committee, 85th Cong. 2d Sess., Part II–Vol. 1, Ser. No. 9 (1958).

65. United States v. American Telephone & Telegraph Co., 427 F.Supp. 57 (D.D.C.1976).

66. Before dismissal, trial of the *IBM* case had gone on for 700 trial days, accumulating 104,000 pages of transcripts and 17,000 exhibits. See 42 ATRR No. 1051, pp. 310–11 (Feb. 11, 1982).

factual issues—whether there has been proof of anticompetitive conduct with respect to the interconnection of customer owned terminal equipment . . ., the Bell system's treatment of competitors in the intercity services area [refusing access to local operating companies by competing long distance carriers] . . ., and its procurement of equipment . . .—the evidence sustains the government's basic contentions, and the burden is on defendants to refute the factual showings made in the government's case-in-chief.[67]

A. T. & T., while trial of the antitrust case was proceeding and with support from various branches of the Reagan Administration,[68] had been attempting to secure passage of legislation sanctioning the structure of A. T. & T. and allowing continued ownership of the non-regulated side of the business in a new subsidiary, nicknamed "Baby Bell." [69] Although the proposed legislation quickly passed in the Senate, opposition to the proposal developed in the House of Representatives, promising a long and drawn out struggle with an uncertain outcome.

Secret negotiations between A. T. & T. Chairman Charles L. Brown and Assistant Attorney General Baxter aimed at settling the case began late in 1981 as A. T. & T. was beginning its defense in Judge Greene's court. On January 8, 1982, the same day the Reagan Administration announced the controversial dismissal of the *I.B.M.* case and its highly controversial reversal of the long-standing policy of denying tax-exempt status for private schools and colleges which practice racial discrimination,[70] Brown and Baxter announced settlement of the A. T. & T. case.[71] The settlement, at first presented as a modification of the 1956 consent decree on file in the Federal District Court for New Jersey [72] and coupled with a motion to dismiss the pending case in Judge Greene's court in the District of Columbia,[73] proposed spinning off the 22 operating companies into independent firms, relieving A. T. & T. of the restrictions of the 1956 decree on patent licensing and entry into such fields as computers, data transmission, and anything else, and left A. T. & T. with ownership of the Long Lines Division, Western Electric, Bell

67. United States v. American Telephone & Telegraph Co., 524 F.Supp. 1336, 1381 (D.D.C.1981).

68. See "Reagan Administration Supports Bills to Deregulate The Telecommunications Market", 1019 ATRR A–21 (June 18, 1981).

69. See S. 898, 97th Cong., 1st Sess. (1981). The bill would have deregulated all but the local service aspect of the business and allowed A. T. & T. to set up a subsidiary to operate the non-regulated side of the business (Western Electric and Bell Labs). Congressional authority for Bell to retain and operate non-regulated aspects of the business would presumably have undermined the Justice Department's case against Bell or made the remedy sought (divestiture of non-regulated businesses) one that Congress had specifically authorized Bell to engage in. The Bill passed the Senate and a major lobbying effort by Bell's competitors and others blocked the bill in the House. See Schwartz, Stacked Competition and Phony Deregulation for A. T. & T.: The Proposed "Telecommunications Competition

and Deregulation Act of 1981", 3 Comm/Ent 411 (1982); Telecommunications Tiff: Bill to Deregulate Much of Bell's Phone Business and Let It Enter Data Field Goes to Senate Today," Wall St. J., Oct. 1, 1981, p. 48.

70. N. Y. Times, Jan. 9, 1982, p. 1, col. 5.

71. Id. Col. 1. See also, Wall St.J., Jan. 11, 1982, pp. 1 and 5; N. Y. Times, Jan. 11, pp. 1, D1, and D6; 1047 ATRR 82–87 (Jan. 14, 1982).

72. Supra note 63.

73. Judge Biunno of the New Jersey Federal District Court, after first signing and interpreting the decree, transferred the proposed settlement to Judge Greene's court in the District of Columbia. Judge Greene had denied the motion to dismiss the pending case and proceeded with hearings on the proposed settlement on the basis that it is a "consent decree" settling the pending case. The procedural wrangle is summarized in 1047 ATRR 83–85 (Jan. 14, 1982).

Labs and such businesses as publication of Yellow Pages. The proposed settlement called for A. T. & T. to spin off two-thirds of its assets in the form of its operating companies (estimated to be worth at least $80 billion); a move described as a "masterstroke" on A. T. & T.'s part by former F.C.C. Chairman Richard Wiley. He observed: "They gave away the future railroads of this industry, kept the moneymakers they already had, and won the right to go after anything else on the high-revenue side."[74]

The proposed decree gave A. T. & T. six months to develop a specific plan for spinning off the operating companies and eighteen months to execute the plan.[75] Some indication of the scope of the proposed divestiture and the complexity of its execution may be derived from the following chart describing the operating companies and their size as of December 31, 1980.

74. Wall Street J., Jan. 11, 1982, p. 1, col. 8. The Settlement has also been described as follows:

Once upon a time there was a divorce proceeding. The husband found a friendly judge. The two agreed that the wife didn't really need her own lawyer because the husband had everybody's best interests at heart. As the negotiations proceeded, the husband awarded himself the house, the car, the savings account, and the Oriental rugs. In exchange, the wife got the children. The wife thought this rather unfair, but dared not complain, because it took two years for the divorce to become final, and, in the meantime, her husband continued to rule the family.

AT&T's settlement with the Justice Department is, among other things, a *political* masterstroke. AT&T looks as if it is making a real sacrifice. The Administration can say it hung tough. Bell's competition is generally satisfied with the breakup. And the local phone companies aren't talking.

The January 8 consent decree lets Bell keep its very profitable Long Lines department, Western Electric, Bell Labs, and a new, unregulated high-tech subsidiary that can provide sophisticated business services, data processing, and just about anything else Bell can dream up. Bell gets out from under an earlier consent decree limiting it to telephone service and requiring it to license patents to competitors. In exchange, Bell gives up its twenty-two local phone companies, which are the most capital intensive and least remunerative part of the business.

B. Kuttner, "Ma Bell's Broken Home," The New Republic, 17 (March 17, 1982).

75. A. T. & T. has proposed a tentative plan of spinning off the operating companies into seven regional companies of roughly equal size. See "AT&T To Spin Off Its 22 Operating Subsidiaries Into 7 Regional Firms In First Step To Reorganize", Wall St. J., Feb. 22, 1982, p. 4. For a description of the complexities being encountered in working out the details of the divestiture, see "AT&T Is Pushing Plans For Dividing Its Assets By The Deadline of 1984," Wall St.J., June 25, 1982, p. 1.

BELL SYSTEM LOCAL OPERATING COMPANIES

	Assets ($millions)	Revenues ($millions)	Net Income ($millions)	Telephones (millions)
Bell Telephone of Pennsylvania	$ 4,940.6	$1,965.8	$220.3	7.97
Chesapeake & Potomac Tel. (D.C.)	793.1	375.7	383.8	1.10
Chesapeake & Potomac Tel. (Md.)	2,271.1	960.9	107.0	3.56
Chesapeake & Potomac Tel. (Va.)	2,506.5	912.0	124.4	2.98
Chesapeake & Potomac Tel. (W.Va.)	846.8	346.8	41.7	0.98
Diamond State Telephone (Del.)	366.3	144.6	19.4	0.53
Illinois Bell Telephone	5,400.5	2,405.4	256.2	8.56
Indiana Bell Telephone	1,781.5	754.0	113.5	2.67
Michigan Bell Telephone	4,377.4	1,809.3	170.0	6.34
Mountain States Telephone	6,537.1	2,689.3	319.4	7.88
New England Telephone	5,102.1	2,398.8	248.2	7.07
New Jersey Bell Telephone	4,268.2	1,905.5	237.4	6.56
New York Telephone	11,384.1	5,341.3	558.7	11.87
Northwestern Bell Telephone	4,517.3	1,815.2	219.6	5.68
Ohio Bell Telephone	3,362.9	1,495.0	151.0	5.07
Pacific Northwest Bell Telephone	4,517.3	1,385.7	157.9	3.94
Pacific Telephone	14,626.0	5,782.0	366.0	16.42
South Central Bell Telephone	9,016.4	3,579.7	483.4	10.58
Southern Bell Telephone	10,914.0	4,560.0	549.9	12.70
Southwestern Bell Telephone	14,513.6	5,843.5	644.5	16.69
Wisconsin Telephone	1,692.1	683.3	75.0	2.45

Bell of Nevada (a wholly owned subsidiary of Pacific Telephone will be reconstituted a separate company under the proposal)

Southern New England Telephone (A. T. & T. a minority shareholder—21.1% of stock; status undetermined by proposed decree.)

Cincinnati Bell (A. T. & T. a minority shareholder—29.7% of stock; status undetermined by proposed decree.)

Despite the joint motion to dismiss the pending antitrust case, Judge Greene refused to dismiss the case because he considered the settlement a settlement of the pending litigation by consent and not a modification of the prior consent decree. The settlement would therefore be subject to the requirements of public comment and a hearing under the consent decree procedures of § 5(b) of the Clayton Act.[76] Upon motion of the parties, the New Jersey case was transferred to Judge Greene's court for public comment, hearings and possible modifications.

Several criticisms of the settlement were then raised in Judge Greene's court: the divestiture of the operating companies from the Long Lines Division would result in substantially higher rates for local service because subsidies from long distance service will no longer be available (although access

---

76. 15 U.S.C. § 16(b). The parties later conceded that the Tunney Act would be followed; Judge Greene, therefore, did not rule specifically on the issue. See 43 ATRR, No. 1077, at 5–12 (Special Supp.) (D.D.C. Aug. 11, 1982). The Department's "competitive impact statement," required under the Tunney Act, is reproduced at 42 ATRR 401 (1982).

fees may be charged) to offset the cost of local service;[77] the settlement did not specify the details of the spin-off of the local companies, *viz.*, what assets will be retained by A. T. & T. and whether there will be one operating company or several;[78] A. T. & T. would retain control of the Long Lines Division with 96% of the long distance business; no provision was made for requiring licensing of new technologies developed by Bell Labs and subsidized in the past by A. T. & T. ratepayers; A. T. & T. would be free of the 1956 consent decree provisions restricting its entry into the computer and the "knowledge" industries while retaining control of a monopoly on long distance communications traffic and the resources of Bell Labs; the operating companies and their regulators were not represented in the settlement negotiations thereby leaving issues like the division of equipment and debt to be negotiated by a management likely to operate the newly reconstituted A. T. & T.; the new A. T. & T. would be allowed to retain valuable assets for its non-regulated business like the "Bell" trademark and the Yellow Pages monopoly; and, division of the best management between the divested operating companies and the reconstituted A. T. & T. was likely to favor A. T. & T.[79]

On August 11, 1982, Judge Greene issued a lengthy opinion and order approving the basic thrust of the proposed decree's divestiture of the operating companies, but also proposing several modifications in the decree under threat of resuming trial of the case, modifications subsequently accepted by both A. T. & T. and the Justice Department.[80] Asserting a right of the court to which a proposed decree is presented to determine whether the decree is in the public interest, Judge Greene conditioned his approval on the parties' acceptance of significant alterations in the decree aimed at strengthening the operating companies. The modifications: permit operating companies to provide, but not manufacture, customer equipment; transfer publication of the Yellow Pages and its $2 billion in annual revenues to the operating companies; prohibit A. T. & T. from engaging in electronic publishing over its own transmission facilities for at least seven years; require the operating companies to indicate on customer bills the availability of other long distance services; require the operating companies to give competing inter-exchange carriers the same quality and type of service given A. T. & T.; establish a 45% debt ratio for the operating companies (50% for Pacific Bell) and require the quality of the debt to be the same as that retained by A. T. & T.; and, vests authority over implementation of the decree in the Court rather than the Antitrust Division.

The longer term consequences of the restructuring of A. T. & T. will depend not only upon the impact of the final decree, but also upon the accelerating pace of technological change in the telecommunications industry. The computer and communications industries, for example, are becoming increas-

77. See "Ma Bell's Orphans: A. T. & T. Employees See Threat, Opportunity For Them In A Breakup," Wall St.J., Jan. 26, 1982, p. 1.

78. United States v. American Telegraph & Telephone Co., #555 CCH Trade Reg. Rep. Part II (D.D.C. Aug. 16, 1982); 43 ATRR No. 1077 (Special Supp.) (D.D.C. Aug. 11, 1982).

79. This issue has become a central issue in the Congressional debates following the proposed settlement and was made the subject of proposed legislation later withdrawn pending Judge Greene's decision. See 42 ATRR #1047 p. 83 (January 14, 1982); 42 ATRR #1051 p. 316 (February 11, 1982).

80. 1982–2 Trade Cases ¶ 64,900 (D.D.C.1982), affirmed ___ U.S. ___, 103 S.Ct. ___, ___ L.Ed.2d ___ (1983). Numerous private suits against A.T.&T. continue to wend their way through the courts. See, e.g., MCI Communications Corp. v. American Telegraph & Telephone Co., 1983 Trade Cases ¶ 65,137 (7th Cir. 1983); Litton Systems, Inc. v. American Telephone & Telegraph Co., 700 F.2d 785 (2d Cir. 1983).

ingly interrelated;[81] while data storage, retrieval and delivery are becoming promising new multi-billion dollar industries with the potential of creating a checkless and bookless society.[82] The settlement of complex antitrust litigation in a regulated industry is not only complicated by political considerations and the existence of regulation, but is likely to be taking place in the context of dynamic technological or other changes generating the pressures which produced the antitrust litigation in the first instance. Few can predict the consequences of removing the "dead hand" of monopoly in such circumstances, but trusting the promise of the competitive process to sort out the public interest is obviously stronger than entrusting control of the speed and direction of new technology to the self-interest of a monopolist.

(7) *Modification of Antitrust Decrees.*[83] *United States v. Swift & Co.,*[84] denied petitions to modify a 40 year old consent decree so as to permit meat packers to enter the concededly competitive grocery business despite persuasive showings of hardship and changed conditions:

. . . the continued need for the decree and the hardship suffered by the defendants are neither alternative standards for modification, either of which will suffice, as the defendants submit, nor cumulative prerequisites, both of which must be established, as the government claims. They are rather correlative elements of a single standard. As need is diminished a lesser showing of hardship will tip the scales in favor of modification, and as the defendants' suffering increases, their burden of showing decreased need is correspondingly lightened.

Compare *United States v. United Shoe Machinery Corp.,*[85] where, after a 10-year trial period contemplated by the original decree, the government was permitted to apply for divestiture upon a showing that the original injunctive relief had not restored workable competition.

It has been proposed that antitrust judgments incorporate an automatic termination date to avoid obsolete constraints and perpetual judicial supervision of businesses presumably restored to competitive status.

(8) *Foreign Law Remedies for Excessive Concentration.* The West German Law Against Restraint of Competition, which became effective Jan. 1, 1958, provides in Section 22 that "market dominating enterprises" may be required by the Cartel Authority to desist from "misuse of their market position" in specified ways. An enterprise is deemed to dominate the market if it is "without competitors or not subject to substantial competition." In determining whether market position is being misused, "all circumstances shall be considered." Under Section 23, a merger must be reported to the Cartel Authority if the combine will have over 20% of the market. If, upon a hearing, the combine is found to be a market dominating enterprise, the Authority can only act pursuant to Section 22 to prohibit abuse.[86]

81. See G. Brock, The Telecommunications Industry (1981); "I.B.M. Now Faces A. T. & T.: Overlapping of Markets Is Growing", N. Y. Times, January 11, 1982, D1.

82. See Neustadt, Skall & Hammer, The Regulation of Electronic Publishing, 33 Fed.Comm.L.J. 331 (1981).

83. See Note, Flexibility and Finality in Consent Decrees, 80 Harv.L.Rev. 1303 (1967); Kramer, Modification of Consent Decrees, 56 Mich.L.Rev. 1051 (1958).

84. 189 F.Supp. 885, 905 (N.D.Ill. 1961), affirmed 367 U.S. 909, 81 S.Ct. 1918, 6 L.Ed.2d 1249.

85. 391 U.S. 244, 88 S.Ct. 1496, 20 L.Ed.2d 562 (1968).

86. Earlier drafts of the German law required advance approval of mergers and authorized dissolution of illegal mergers. Art. 20 of Draft Law, see App. B. of Report on Foreign Legislation Concerning Monopoly and Cartel Practices, Monopoly Subcommittee of the Senate Committee on Small Business, 82d Cong. 2d Sess. (1952) p. 20; Ivo Schwartz, Anti-

Compare Article 66 of the Treaty establishing the European Coal and Steel Community.[87] It requires advance approval of "concentrations", whether effected by "merger, acquisition of shares or assets, loan, contract, or any other means of control." The High Authority approves if it finds that the transaction will not confer power:

> to influence prices, to control or restrain production or marketing, or to impair the maintenance of effective competition in a substantial part of the market for such products; or to evade the rules of competition resulting from the application of the present Treaty, particularly by establishing an artificially privileged position involving a material advantage in access to supplies or markets.

The High Authority "shall order" illegal concentrations dissolved, and "any other action which it deems appropriate to re-establish the independent operation of the enterprises or assets in question and to restore normal conditions of competition" including forced sale "on conditions preserving the legitimate interests of their proprietors", and invalidation of management acts or decisions with respect to illegally acquired properties. Although the Treaty does not confer authority to dissolve concentrations previously in existence, the High Authority is authorized to request dominant enterprises to take measures to prevent use of the position for purposes contrary to those of the Treaty. If its recommendations are disregarded, the High Authority may, in consultation with the interested government, fix prices and conditions of sale, or establish manufacturing or delivery programs to be executed by the enterprise. Concentration within the six-nation community is low by American standards, and the High Authority has been tolerant of mergers.[88]

The antitrust laws of leading industrialized nations also generally focus on conduct remedies rather than structural remedies for violations similar to structural monopolization cases under U. S. law.[89] Deconcentration of the Japanese economy after the Second World War was imposed by the occupation authority and has been described as generating a highly competitive domestic economy by the mid-1950's.[90] Actions by the Japanese government since that time have been described as gradually weakening competitive forces generated by the prior policy of permitting cartels, joint ventures and the like.[91] Recent actions by the Japanese Fair Trade Commission and amendments strengthening the Japanese Antitrust laws, including authority to order divestiture of assets by dominating corporations, may signal an upswing in antitrust enforcement in Japan.[92]

trust Legislation and Policy in Germany, 105 U.Pa.L.Rev. 617, 676 (1957). L. B. Schwartz, New Approaches to the Control of Oligopoly, 109 U.Pa.L.Rev. 31 (1960), compares foreign and American law relating to control of large firms.

87. As to the European Economic Community generally, see p. 521 infra.

88. See generally Korah, Interpretation and Application of Article 86 of the Treaty of Rome: Abuse of a Dominant Position Within the Common Market, 53 Notre Dame Law. 768 (1978); Note, Survey of Antitrust Law In The European Economic Community, 16 Santa Clara L.Rev. 535 (1976).

89. See, e.g., Markert, Control of Abuses by Market Dominating Enter-

prises Under German Antitrust Law, 11 Cornell Int.L.J. 275 (1978). The Canadian antitrust law, the Combines Investigation Act, Can.Rev.Stat. c. 314 (1952), does include authority to order divestiture. See Campbell, Canadian Combines Law: A Perspective on the Current Combines Investigation Act and Recent Case Law, 5 N.C.J.Int.Law & Comm.Reg. 57 (1980).

90. See Uekussa, Effects of the Deconcentration Measures in Japan, 22 Antitrust Bull. 687 (1977).

91. Id. at 714.

92. See Note, Trustbusting in Japan: Cartels and Government-Business Cooperation, 94 Harv.L.Rev. 1064 (1981).

GREEN, MOORE & WASSERSTEIN, THE CLOSED ENTERPRISE SYSTEM

Chap. 6: "When Winning Is Losing" pp. 179–94 (1972) [93]

Civil Injunctive Decrees

More than two-thirds of the cases that the Antitrust Division brought during the 1960s were civil suits seeking "to prevent and restrain" violations of the antitrust laws. Eighty-three percent of these were disposed of through "consent decrees"—voluntary settlements negotiated between defendants and the government and adopted by the court prior to trial. Counting consent decrees as victories, the Division's civil enforcement won/lost rate currently exceeds 90%. The figure is almost meaningless. . . . The early 1960s witnessed an unbroken string of Antitrust Division antimerger victories in the Supreme Court. Corporate antitrust counsel and dissenting Justices began to say, "The government always wins." Does it, really? The Supreme Court may declare that a merger is illegal, but the Antitrust Division must then obtain a divestiture remedy, by which is meant restoration of the *market structure* that would have existed *but for* the illegal acquisition. Do Antitrust Division divestiture decrees achieve these results? A study published in 1967 by Elzinga analyzed the outcomes in Antitrust Division and FTC antimerger decrees entered during 1955–64.[94] The relief actually obtained fell into four categories: (1) *Successful* relief was obtained when the acquired firm was fully reestablished as a viable entity under independent ownership. (2) *Sufficient* relief was obtained when the acquired firm, though fully reestablished as a viable entity, was sold to a somewhat less than independent purchaser, such as a small vertical or horizontal competitor. (3) Relief was *deficient* when the divested entity, though viable, constituted only a partial restoration of the illegally acquired assets, or where the purchaser was an obvious potential competitor. (4) *Unsuccessful* relief included (a) no relief at all, (b) no structural relief, only a ban on future acquisitions, (c) insignificant divestiture, (d) regulatory relief, (e) divestiture to a significant horizontal or vertical competitor, or (f) divestiture of a nonviable or failing firm.

Of the 39 cases in his sample, Elzinga found that 21 relief orders were unsuccessful and eight deficient. Approximately three-fourths of the cases, including 12 of 17 Antitrust Division cases, fell within the combined unsuccessful-deficient categories. . . .

The failure of structural relief is also evident when it comes to breaking up Sherman Act monopolies. Of 137 Section 2 charges filed against single firms during 1890–1969, only 24 resulted in significant divestiture of a national or large regional monopolist. And the legal proceedings consumed almost eight years on the average. Even hori-

---

93. Reprinted by permission of the copyright owner. Selected footnotes to this excerpt have been renumbered.

94. Elzinga, The Antimerger Law: Pyrrhic Victories?, 12 J.L. & Econ. 43 (1969).

zontal divestitures have seldom been structurally effective. Take the *Standard Oil* case of 1911. There, the dissolution of a national monopolist initially produced regional monopolists who were later demoted to regional oligopolists by market forces. In the famous 1945 *Alcoa* decision—which went a long way toward establishing the principle that market size alone may constitute an illegal monopoly—no divestiture at all was decreed. Instead, the Court relied upon postwar distribution of surplus aluminum, to be carried out in a manner that would create new competition for Alcoa. Kaiser and Reynolds did come into being this way, and Alcoa's market share of primary aluminum production capacity was reduced from 91% in 1941 to 38.4% in 1960. Replacing Alcoa's monopoly, however, was a vertically integrated three-firm oligopoly, which since 1945 has controlled around 90% of domestic primary and fabricated aluminum production.

The cigarette industry offers an even more salient example. By 1911 robber baron James B. Duke had gobbled up over 250 companies into the American Tobacco Trust. In that year the Supreme Court unanimously declared the monopoly illegal, but the ensuing tripartite dissolution did no more, again, than create a highly disciplined oligopoly. By 1930 R. J. Reynolds, American, and Liggett & Myers controlled 91% of the market. Various forms of inherently suspect conscious parallelism, including virtually identical prices after 1928, culminated in a criminal conviction of the tobacco oligopolists, affirmed by the Supreme Court in 1946. The government thus got a second chance to bust the tobacco trust with a follow-up civil suit.

Though a civil suit was not immediately filed, consent-decree negotiations commenced and lasted into 1949, when Attorney General Tom Clark told a Congressional committee that a civil complaint had been prepared "and will be filed very shortly." We're still waiting. . . .

Another Section 2 debacle was the 1958 *United Fruit* decree. Some monopolists have relied at least in part upon modest production efficiencies and the high capital costs of new entry to ward off competitors. But bananas? All a new firm had to do was purchase a supply from tropical growers, transport it by refrigerated ships to the United States, and market it through regular food channels. Between 1899 and 1928 United Fruit acquired 22 of its competitors. By 1946 it owned 73% of the banana boats, had tied up most of the rest of the space with exclusive dealing contracts, and controlled the Central American railroads that transported bananas to ports; in 1954 it leased or controlled 85% of the land in the Western Hemisphere tropics suitable for banana cultivation and procured 10% of its supply through exclusive dealing contracts with independent growers; United's competitors had to buy their bananas from it. Former Antitrust Division attorney Milton Kallis concluded, after investigating the banana monopoly, that United Fruit had committed every antitrust violation on the books except those involving patents.

On the day that the trial was to start, four years after the Justice Department filed its monopolization complaint, United agreed to a consent decree. After 12 pages of "don't do it again" language, the decree ordered United to spin off a new competitor with sufficient land to grow nine million stems of "average" bananas per year, about 35% of the United States banana market at the time. That was apparently so severe that United was given eight years and five months to submit a "plan" for divestiture and four years to carry it out after it was approved. The divestiture deadline was set for July 28, 1971, 17 years after the suit was filed. The purchaser turned out to be Del Monte, the world's largest producer of canned fruits and vegetables, "a potential large-scale entrant into the banana business anyway," according to a Division attorney.

The reasons for the Division's antimonopoly and antimerger failures are identical. Following an effective trial presentation on the illegality of the United Shoe Machinery Company monopoly, the government made an unsuccessful plea to break up the single-plant firm into three competitors. It was, according to Judge Wyzanski's economist-clerk Carl Kaysen, "sketchy, poorly prepared, and failed to come to grips with any of the problems involved. . . . [What was needed was] a fairly detailed plan, well-supported by evidence, not ten pages of generalizations and citations from legal authorities, supported by ten minutes of oral presentation." [95] . . . A dose of economic education from the Division would no doubt have prevented the Supreme Court's utterance in the 1947 *National Lead* case that "There is no showing that four major competing units would be preferable to two, or . . . that six would be better than four." [96]

Even the hostile opinion that divestiture is a "harsh" remedy is confined, at the Supreme Court level, to a handful of statements more than two decades old. They hardly survive the Court's structurally based merger decisions in the Sixties. Moreover, in 1969 the Supreme Court ruled that the government could reopen the 1953 *United Shoe* decree—16 years after the case was decided—and ordered the district court to assess whether its remedies had been effective against the defendant's monopoly power. As a result, United Shoe has finally been required, through divestiture, to reduce its market share to no more than 33% within two years. The Division cannot continue in the future to under-utilize its legal authority to seek "drastic" structural relief in Section 2 monopolization cases. [97]

95. Kaysen, United States v. United Shoe Machinery Corporation (Harv.Econ. Studies No. 99) p. 343 (1956). Professor Kaysen was hired as the "clerk" for the trial judge, Judge Wyzanski, for the duration of the trial. Should trial courts be provided with expert legal and economic staffs to litigate complex antitrust cases and to fashion remedies in cases where a violation is found? When such experts serve in the capacity as "clerk" to the trial judge, should litigants be given the opportunity to cross-examine the expert or have access to all advice and memoranda submitted to the trial judge by the judge's "clerk"? See Kaysen, An Economist as the Judge's Law Clerk In Sherman Act Cases, 12 A.B.A. Antitrust Sec. Rep. 43 (1958).

96. United States v. National Lead Co., 332 U.S. 319, 352, 67 S.Ct. 1634, 1650, 91 L.Ed. 2077, 2102 (1947).

97. It has been claimed that the filing of a Section 2 case itself has a substantial effect on a monopolist's behavior, improving competitive conditions in hopes of minimizing a finding of illegality in the litigation. See Waldman, The duPont Cellophane Case Revisited: An Analysis of the Indirect Effects of Antitrust Poli-

NOTES AND QUERIES

(1) *The Cost and Complexity of Structural Remedies.* On occasion, the length of time devoted to fashioning a remedy in complex cases exceeds the length of time in proving a violation. For example, the Government challenged the acquisition of the Pacific Northwest Pipeline Corporation by El Paso Natural Gas Co. in 1957. Divestiture of the illegally acquired natural gas pipeline did not take place until 17 years later, in 1974.[98] Seven years were spent in litigating jurisdictional and substantive issues, and ten years were spent in litigating the validity of a succession of divestiture plans proposed to meet a Supreme Court mandate for complete and total divestiture. It has been stated that El Paso was making 10 to 12 million dollars per yer from the illegally acquired pipeline, while also realizing the presumed benefits from the elimination of the pipeline as a potential competitor.[99] It has also been estimated that El Paso expended 15 million dollars in its battle to retain the illegally acquired pipeline. Applicants to purchase the company to be spun off spent at least $250,000 each; some spent as much as $2.5 million participating in the divestiture proceeding.[1] The successful applicant expended $1 million in the divestiture proceedings and over $2 million in setting up the new company to take over the divested assets. The printing bill alone, for printing the documents and certificates transferring the debt instruments from El Paso to the new company, was $700,000.[2] Do such cases suggest that meaningful antitrust remedies in large structural antitrust cases must be carried out in forums other than federal district courts? Should such cases be referred to the Federal Trade Commission for the fashioning of proposed remedies?[3] Should a specialized court be created to litigate such cases and impose structural remedies where the underlying cause of the violation is structural?[4] Should large firms be encouraged to restruc-

---

cy on Market Structure and Performance, 25 Antitrust Bull. 805 (1980).

98. Litigation of the case to complete divestiture involved at least eight proceedings in the Supreme Court, four of which provoked significant Supreme Court opinions. California v. Federal Power Commission, 369 U.S. 482, 82 S.Ct. 901, 8 L.Ed.2d 54 (1962); United States v. El Paso Natural Gas Co., 376 U.S. 651, 84 S.Ct. 1044, 12 L.Ed.2d 12 (1964); Cascade Natural Gas Co. v. El Paso Natural Gas Co., 386 U.S. 129, 87 S.Ct. 932, 17 L.Ed. 2d 814 (1967), on remand 291 F.Supp. 3 (D.C.Utah 1968), vacated 395 U.S. 464, 89 S.Ct. 1860, 23 L.Ed.2d 474 (1969), rehearing denied 399 U.S. 937, 90 S.Ct. 2225, 26 L.Ed.2d 809 (1970); Utah Public Service Commission v. El Paso Natural Gas Co., 395 U.S. 464, 89 S.Ct. 1860, 23 L.Ed.2d 474 (1969), rehearing denied 399 U.S. 937, 90 S.Ct. 2225, 26 L.Ed.2d 809 (1970).

99. Hearings, The Antitrust Improvements Act of 1975, U.S.Senate Subcomm. on Antitrust & Monop., Part 1, p. 432 (1975).

1. Id. at 434.

2. Id. at 435.

3. Section 7 of the F.T.C. Act, 38 Stat. 722, 15 U.S.C. § 47, provides:

"In any suit in equity brought by or under the direction of the Attorney General as provided in the antitrust Acts, the court may, upon the conclusion of the testimony therein, if it shall be then of opinion that the complainant is entitled to relief, refer said suit to the Commission, as a master in chancery, to ascertain and report an appropriate form of decree therein. The Commission shall proceed upon such notice to the parties and under such rules of procedure as the court may prescribe, and upon the coming in of such report such exceptions may be filed and such proceedings had in relation thereto as upon the report of a master in other equity causes, but the court may adopt or reject such report, in whole or in part, and enter such decree as the nature of the case may in its judgment require."

Section 7 has never been used.

4. For such a proposal see 121 Cong. Rec.S. 10731 (June 17, 1975) (Remarks of Senator Hart upon introduction of the Industrial Reorganization Act, S. 1959, 94th Cong., 1st Sess. 1975). See also, Hear-

ture themselves voluntarily by a progressive corporate income tax based upon firm size, rather than the present flat rate income tax? [5]

(2) *The Effect of the Antitrust Laws in Encouraging Large Combinations, Excerpt From Arnold, The Folklore of Capitalism* (1937). Chapter IX:

We have seen that the growth of great organizations in America occurred in the face of a religion which officially was dedicated to the preservation of the economic independence of individuals. In such a situation it was inevitable that a ceremony should be evolved which reconciled current mental pictures of what men thought society ought to be with reality. The learned mythology of the time insisted that American industry was made up of small competing concerns which, if they were not individuals, nevertheless approach that ideal. "Bigness" was regarded as a curse because it led to monopoly and interfered with the operation of the laws of supply and demand. At the same time specialized techniques made bigness essential to producing goods in large enough quantities and at a price low enough so that they could be made part of the American standard of living. In order to reconcile the ideal with the practical necessity, it became necessary to develop a procedure which constantly attacked bigness on rational legal and economic grounds, and at the same time never really interfered with combinations. Such pressures gave rise to the antitrust laws which appeared to be a complete prohibition of large combinations. The same pressures made the enforcement of the antitrust laws a pure ritual. . . . The actual result of the antitrust laws was to promote the growth of great industrial organizations by deflecting the attack on them into purely moral and ceremonial channels. The process was something like this: Since the corporation was a person, mere bigness could not make it a bad person. One cannot condemn his neighbor simply because he is big and strong. Therefore, the courts soon discovered that it was only "unreasonable" combinations which were bad, just as any court would decide that a big, strong neighbor should not be incarcerated so long as he acted reasonably. In various other ways the actual enforcement of the antitrust laws was completely emasculated by the courts, not because the courts were composed of wicked and hypocritical people, anxious to evade the law, but because such a process is inevitable when an ideal meets in head-on collision with a practical need. The process is just as unconscious as was the toleration of speak-easies in dry communities during prohibition.

. . . [A]nyone who attacked the "Trusts" could achieve the same public worship as a minister of the gospel who had the energy to attack vice. It was this that made Theodore Roosevelt a great man. Historians now point out that Theodore Roosevelt never accomplished anything with his trust busting. Of course he didn't. The crusade was not a practical one. It was part of a moral conflict and no preacher ever succeeded in abolishing any form of sin. . . . Men like Senator Borah founded political careers on the continuance of such crusades, which were entirely

ings, The Industrial Reorganization Act, U.S. Senate Subcomm. on Antitrust & Monopoly, 9 Vols. 1973—date. See also, Note, The Industrial Reorganization Act: An Antitrust Proposal To Restructure The American Economy, 73 Colum.L.Rev. 635 (1973).

5. See Simon, Antitrust and the "Size" Problem: The "Graduated" Corporate Income Tax As An Anti-Bigness Device, 6 Antitrust L. & Econ.Rev. 53 (Winter 1972–73).

futile but enormously picturesque, and which paid big dividends in terms of personal prestige. . . .

The author subsequently became Assistant Attorney General in charge of the Antitrust Division and led an unprecedented drive to enforce the antitrust laws.

(3) *Query.* Do Arnold's cynicism and the depressing record on relief against monopoly make a case for the proposed Industrial Reorganization Act p. 176 supra, or No Fault Monopolization, supra p. 123?

(4) *The Effect of the "Big Case" on Lawyers—A Comment.*

* G. Trudeau, Doonesbury, August 22, 1982, Copyright © Universal Press Syndicate, 4400 Johnson Dr., Fairway, Kansas 66205. Used by permission.

Chapter 3

MERGERS AND OTHER INTEGRATIONS

A. INTRODUCTION

Section 2 of the Sherman Act, with its proscription of monopolization, is recognizably addressed to the question of the structure of industry, although courts have recently been devoting more attention to evaluating the monopoly firm's conduct. Section 1 of the Sherman Act seems to have as its main target unlawful restrictive trade *practices*, rather than concentration of economic power, which is a structural problem. Yet Section 1 includes among the forbidden activities "combination in the form of trust or otherwise."

One of the great early Sherman Act cases split the Supreme Court five to four on whether the Act applied to the formation of a holding company to control the Great Northern and Northern Pacific railways, two vast competing transcontinental carriers. NORTHERN SECURITIES CO. v. UNITED STATES, 193 U.S. 197, 24 S.Ct. 436, 48 L.Ed. 679 (1904). The first Mr. Justice Harlan, writing for the Court, held that under these circumstances a holding company's ownership of stock in competing interstate carriers fell within the reach of federal legislative power, found the combination to be in restraint of interstate commerce, and went so far as to declare that the Sherman Act in these circumstances was "not limited to restraints . . . that are unreasonable in their nature, but embraces *all* direct *restraints* imposed by any combination . . ." 193 U.S. at 331. Mr. Justice Holmes wrote one of the dissenting opinions. Calling for strict construction of the statute, because of its penal character and to avoid constitutional doubts, he invoked common law precedents to construe the "contracts" prohibition of Section 1 as applicable to arrangements which restrain the trade *of the contracting parties*, and the "combination" prohibition as applicable only to collaborations designed to restrain trade *of other people*:

> The court below argues as if maintaining competition were the expressed object of the act. The act says nothing about competition. The prohibition [of combinations] was suggested by the trusts, the objection to which, as everyone knows, was not the union of former competitors, but the sinister power exercised or supposed to be exercised by the combination in keeping rivals out of the business and ruining those who already were in. It was the ferocious extreme of competition with others, not the cessation of competition among the partners, that was the evil feared.
>
> According to popular speech, every concern monopolizes whatever business it does, and if that business is trade between two states it

monopolizes a part of the trade among the states. Of course, the statute does not forbid that. It does not mean that all business must cease. A single railroad down a narrow valley or through a mountain gorge monopolizes all the railroad transportation through that valley or gorge. Indeed, every railroad monopolizes, in a popular sense, the trade of some area. Yet I suppose no one would say that the statute forbids a combination of men into a corporation to build and run such a railroad between the states.

I assume that the Minnesota charter of the Great Northern, and the Wisconsin charter of the Northern Pacific, both are valid. Suppose that, before either road was built, Minnesota, as part of a system of transportation between the states, had created a railroad company authorized singly to build all the lines in the states now actually built, owned, or controlled by either of the two existing companies. I take it that that charter would have been just as good as the present one, even if the statutes which we are considering had been in force. In whatever sense it would have created a monopoly, the present charter does. It would have been a large one, but the act of Congress makes no discrimination according to size. Size has nothing to do with the matter. A monopoly of "any part" of commerce among the states is unlawful. The supposed company would have owned lines that might have been competing; probably the present one does. But the act of Congress will not be construed to mean the universal disintegration of society into single men, each at war with all the rest, or even the prevention of all further combinations for a common end.

There is a natural feeling that somehow or other the statute meant to strike at combinations great enough to cause just anxiety on the part of those who love their country more than money, while it viewed such little ones as I have supposed with just indifference. This notion, it may be said, somehow breathes from the pores of the act, although it seems to be contradicted in every way by the words in detail. And it has occurred to me that it might be that when a combination reached a certain size it might have attributed to it more of the character of a monopoly merely by virtue of its size than would be attributed to a smaller one. I am quite clear that it is only in connection with monopolies that size could play any part. But my answer has been indicated already. In the first place, size, in the case of railroads, is an inevitable incident; and if it were an objection under the act, the Great Northern and the Northern Pacific already were too great and encountered the law. In the next place, in the case of railroads it is evident that the size of the combination is reached for other ends than those which would make them monopolies. The combinations are not formed for the purpose of excluding others from the field. Finally, even a small railroad will have the same tendency to exclude others from its narrow area that great ones have to exclude others from the greater one, and the statute attacks the small monopolies as well as the great. The very words of the act make such a distinction impossible in this case, and it has not been attempted in express terms.

If the charter which I have imagined above would have been good notwithstanding the monopoly, in a popular sense, which it created, one next is led to ask whether and why a combination or consolidation of existing roads, although in actual competition, into one company of exactly the same powers and extent, would be any more obnoxious to the law.

Unless I am entirely wrong in my understanding of what a "combination in restraint of trade" means, then the same monopoly may be attempted and effected by an individual, and is made equally illegal in that case by § 2. But I do not expect to hear it maintained that Mr. Morgan could be sent to prison for buying as many shares as he liked of the Great Northern and the Northern Pacific, even if he bought them both at the same time and got more than half the stock of each road.[1]

The doubts raised in the *Northern Securities* case, and the reaffirmation of the "rule of reason" in the 1911 *Standard Oil* case, contributed to the inclusion of special provisions as to intercorporate stockholding in Section 7 of the Clayton Act of 1914. Legislative concern was focused on amalgamations accomplished by purchase of stock control of competing companies. The holding company device, with its overtones of financial wizardry, had been employed in a number of highly-publicized mergers of the first decade of the 20th Century, and it was indeed a particularly effective technique. It required a smaller investment than outright purchase of assets, merely enough to buy working control. The controlling stock could be acquired without consent of the management of the acquired firm, and in secret so far as the public was concerned, so that the controlled companies continued to function as seeming competitors. Accordingly, Section 7 subjected mergers by acquisition of stock to new and more stringent standards of legality.

The courts were remarkably unreceptive to the Clayton Act innovations in merger control. In the conservative era following World War I the Supreme Court construed the Act narrowly. Given that it prohibited only stock acquisitions, the Court held the Federal Trade Commission powerless to order *asset* divestiture even when the assets acquisition was accomplished through a prior illegal stock acquisition.[2] In *International Shoe Co. v. Federal Trade Commission*, 280 U.S. 291, 50 S.Ct. 89, 74 L.Ed. 431 (1930), over the dissent of Stone, Holmes, and Brandeis, the Supreme Court interpreted Section 7's standard of legality as if it were the Sherman Act ("unduly re-

---

1. The passages quoted are from 193 U.S. at 403, 405, 406–8, 409. It was in this dissent that Holmes wrote: "Great cases like hard cases make bad law." Id. at 400. Holmes' position in this case evoked from President Theodore Roosevelt the famous irascible comment, "I could carve out of a banana a judge with more backbone than that." Bowen, Yankee From Olympus 370 (1944). Cf. Holmes' letter to Pollock, Feb. 9, 1921, 2 Holmes-Pollock Letters 63 (Howe ed. 1941) ("What the boys like about Roosevelt is that he doesn't care a damn for the law . . ."). For a fascinating description of the factual background of this case, see Letwin, Law and Economic Policy in America 182–95 (1965).

The parties never gave up. The merger of the Great Northern and Northern Pacific was finally consummated in 1960, approved by the Interstate Commerce Commission in 1967, and upheld by the Supreme Court—over the objections of the Department of Justice—in United States v. Interstate Commerce Commission, 396 U.S. 491, 90 S.Ct. 708, 24 L.Ed. 2d 700 (1970).

2. This enabled firms to avoid F.T.C. enforcement of Section 7 by simply merging their assets after an F.T.C. complaint was filed challenging the stock acquisition. See Arrow-Hart & Hegeman Electric Co. v. Federal Trade Commission, 291 U.S. 587, 54 S.Ct. 532, 78 L.Ed. 1007 (1934).

stricting competition"); freely disregarded the F.T.C.'s findings on competitive effect, substituting its own naive views relating to product and geographic boundaries of market competition; and imported into the Clayton Act justification by "good business reasons" which undermined the Sherman Act as an antimerger law. The Clayton Act did not become an effective vehicle for controlling corporate mergers until it was amended by the Celler-Kefauver Act of 1950.[3]

The antitrust provisions of the Clayton Act do not carry criminal sanctions (although the version of the Act originally passed by the House did). Civil enforcement by the Justice Department is normally in equity for injunctive relief preventing the merger or for dissolution of a consummated merger. In addition, Section 11 of the Clayton Act authorizes the Federal Trade Commission to enforce compliance with Section 7 and other sections of the Act. If, after hearing, the Commission is "of the opinion" that there has been a violation, it makes appropriate findings of fact, "which, if supported by substantial evidence, shall be conclusive," and issues an order that the violator "cease and desist" from violation. Review of a Commission decision may be had in the Court of Appeals.[4]

The term "merger" as used in this chapter includes all transactions which bring under single control enterprises that were previously independent, whether the transaction takes the form of a technical merger of one corporate identity into another, a consolidation by which a new corporation supplants two or more predecessors, an acquisition by a holding company of effective control over several previously independent businesses, a simple purchase of physical assets comprising a competitor's plant, or a joint venture whereby two competitors—without giving up their identities or presumably existing competition between them—unite their capital and efforts in forming a new enterprise for joint exploitation of a new market or for jointly carrying out certain common operations.

Merger or integration may be classified as horizontal, vertical, conglomerate, or combinations of these. It is horizontal if it brings together enterprises at the same level of operation, e.g. when one shoe manufacturer buys out another. It is vertical if it brings under common control two or more successive steps in the process of production and distribution. Thus a chain of food stores is integrating vertically if it decides to go into the business of canning foods which it sells; a manufacturer of steel integrates vertically when it buys iron mines; a department store integrates vertically if it decides to buy trucks and make its own deliveries. A merger is conglomerate if it does not fall in the previous categories; i.e., the firms combined operate in unrelated markets, e.g., a cigarette company buys control

3. For a history of judicial and administrative enforcement of the Clayton Act from 1914 to 1950, see Martin, Mergers and the Clayton Act 104–220 (1959).

4. The overlap in jurisdiction between the F.T.C. and Department of Justice is discussed at p. 21, n. 58, supra. Enforcement of Section 7 prior to its amendment in 1950 rested primarily with the F.T.C. During that time the Department of Justice brought only four suits alleging Section 7 violations; three of them also alleged Sherman Act violations. Martin, supra n. 3, at 197, 201.

of a textile producer or a chain of theaters. Most large mergers have aspects that fall into all three categories, and the boundaries of the categories are by no means clear. Is the merger of a company manufacturing glass jars and bottles with a company manufacturing cans horizontal or conglomerate? Is an electronics firm's expansion into computers vertical or conglomerate if some elements used in computers have previously been manufactured by the electronics firm?

The purpose of classifying mergers as horizontal, vertical, or conglomerate is to facilitate an appraisal of the anticompetitive potential of the consolidation. It is important to remember that the Clayton Act makes no mention of these classifications. Thus, the attempt to categorize should not be allowed to obscure the statutory question: May the effect of the acquisition be substantially to lessen competition?

The materials of this chapter are organized on the following plan. First is the *Columbia Steel* case, a failed attempt to use Section 1 of the Sherman Act to stop mergers; its very failure acted as a catalyst for the 1950 Amendments to the Clayton Act. The digest of the case illustrates the difficulties encountered in dealing with mergers under the Sherman Act, and provides information as to the organization of a basic and perennially controversial industry. The text of the Clayton Act follows at page 213, with queries designed to bring out how the drafters of the amendments to the Act sought to remedy the weaknesses illustrated in *Columbia Steel*. The excerpt from the Supreme Court's opinion in the *Brown Shoe* case summarizes the Court's analysis of the Congressional objectives in amending Section 7 of the Clayton Act. Subsequent materials are arranged by analytical category (e.g. horizontal, vertical, etc.) to illustrate how the courts have developed Section 7, and the current limitations of that statute in dealing with today's large mergers.

UNITED STATES v. COLUMBIA STEEL CO.

Supreme Court of the United States, 1948.
334 U.S. 495, 68 S.Ct. 1107, 92 L.Ed. 1533.

[Digest] This suit challenged the acquisition by the Columbia Steel Company, a subsidiary of United States Steel ("USS"), of the assets of the Consolidated Steel Corporation. Two stages of steel production were relevant: the production of rolled steel products (e.g., plates, shapes, and other unfinished steel products, which are made from ingots by means of rolling mills) and their fabrication into finished products. Two types of fabricated products were involved: fabricated plate products (e.g., welded pipes) made primarily from rolled steel plates, and fabricated structural products (e.g., bridges) made primarily from rolled steel shapes. Plate and structural fabricated products were made to specifications, unlike standard steel products made by repetitive processes (e.g., nails).

Columbia Steel was the largest producer of rolled steel in the West. It had been acquired by USS in 1930, and acted as selling agent for eastern subsidiaries of USS engaged in fabricating rolled steel. USS and subsidiaries had one-third of the nation's steel business, an investment of $1.5 billion, and annual sales in the neighborhood of $1 billion. Consolidated Steel engaged in plate and structural fabrication in plants located in California, Arizona, and Texas, and sold its products in eleven far-western states. Its assets were worth about $10 million, and its annual sales were about $20 million.

After World War II, during which Consolidated had done a large business with the government, its president Roach approached several of the big steel companies with offers to sell out. President Fairless of USS was interested, but put the matter off pending negotiations to acquire a huge government-owned rolled steel plant at Geneva, Utah, built to meet military requirements. This plant had been designed, constructed, and operated by USS under contract with the United States. It was to be disposed of pursuant to § 20 of the Surplus Property Act of 1944 [see summary at page 183 supra] so as to favor "free independent private enterprise", "discourage" monopoly, "strengthen" small competitors, "foster" independents, and not foster "monopoly and restraint of trade." Several smaller steel companies filed bids, but the USS offer of $47,500,000 for the plant which had cost $200,000,000 was well above the others. However, there was so much opposition from the Antitrust Division and other sources that USS withdrew its bid for a time. The War Assets Administration, disposal agency for the United States, solicited USS to renew its bid. Eventually the Attorney General gave the requisite approval for the sale to USS. Then the Consolidated acquisition was consummated.

The Antitrust Division sued under the Sherman Act to enjoin the acquisition of Consolidated. The Government argued that, in its vertical aspect, the acquisition foreclosed manufacturers other than USS from selling rolled steel products to an important fabricator-customer. In its horizontal aspect, the Government argued that the acquisition impaired competition and potential competition between USS and Consolidated in the sale of fabricated products. The Supreme Court affirmed the trial court's conclusion that there was no "unreasonable" lessening of competition.

With respect to the vertical aspect, USS argued that the market for rolled steel was national, and that Consolidated's purchases amounted to only one-half of one per cent of national sales. The Government argued that the figures to look at in gauging the significance of Consolidated's business were: (1) purchases of rolled steel in "Consolidated's market", i.e., the eleven western states (Consolidated bought 3%), and especially (2) purchases by fabricators in that territory who, like Consolidated, fabricated products from plates and shapes (Consolidated bought 13%). Mr. Justice Reed's opinion for the Court accepted the western states as the geographic market, but declined to restrict consideration to customers in the same class of fabricators as Consolidated, because the record suggested that rolled steel producers "can make other products interchangeably with shapes and plates"—i.e. competition would not be significantly injured by preempting sales to a particular class of customers if excluded suppliers could adapt their production to the needs of other classes of customers.

As for its horizontal aspect, the evidence was held insufficient to show unreasonable restraint of competition, although Consolidated did 11% of the fabricating business in the West, USS 13%, and Bethlehem 11%. The Court was persuaded that the "national market" was the proper basis, that the products fabricated were different and therefore not competitive, and that western fabrication was likely to expand so much that Consolidated's relative importance would decline.

In addition to considering the extent of the restraint, the Court examined the intent of the parties, and the probable impact on general welfare. President Fairless had explained the motivation of USS. It had hoped to acquire Geneva with vast capacity for producing rolled steel. It needed a "firm outlet" to achieve an integrated operation. Consolidated could be bought for less than it would cost to build an equivalent plant. The Court's opinion declared that vertical integration is not per se illegal, although there is an avowed intent that the acquired customer shall thereafter take its supplies exclusively from the parent, and that USS had only a "normal business purpose." The long history of acquisitions by USS of customers, competitors, and potential competitors was held insufficient to demonstrate monopolistic intent, especially since USS' share of the national market had declined. "Its size is impressive. Size has significance also in an appraisal of alleged violations of the Sherman Act. But the steel industry is also of impressive size and the welcome westward extension of that industry requires that the existing companies go into production there or abandon that market to other organizations." Approval by the Attorney General of the major acquisition at Geneva was regarded as indicative of national policy.

JUSTICES DOUGLAS, BLACK, MURPHY, and RUTLEDGE dissented.[5]

NOTES AND QUERIES

(1) *Queries.* If vertical integration accomplished by building additional fabricating facilities is legal, does it necessarily follow that integration by purchase of an existing fabricator must be legal? What important difference in economic consequences differentiates these two situations? How may they be differentiated under the terms of the Sherman Act?

What is the relevance of the seller's motive? Should the antitrust laws preclude sale of one's business to the highest bidder merely because the buyer is willing to pay a premium to acquire a "firm market"? What effect should be given to the fact that the owner of a small business may be selling out in exchange for stock in a big corporation in order to conserve his estate

---

5. For an interesting survey of the early history of the growth of United States Steel by merger, see Parsons & Ray, The United States Steel Consolidation: The Creation of Market Control, 18 J.Law & Econ. 181 (1975).

The play of politics and personality involved in the decision to bring the *Columbia Steel* case is described in Kramer, Of Plates and Shapes: An Antitrust Vignette, 64 Minn.L.Rev. 143 (1979).

or increase its liquidity so that inheritance taxes can be met? See Butters, Lintner, Cary, Effects of Taxation on Corporate Mergers (1951).

(2) *"Production Flexibility" vs. Actual Patterns of Trade. United States v. Bethlehem Steel Corp.,* 168 F.Supp. 576, 592 (S.D.N.Y.1958), enjoined Bethlehem's acquisition of Youngstown Sheet & Tube Co. as a violation of Section 7 of the Clayton Act. Judge Weinfeld rejected defense arguments, based on the *Columbia Steel* case, deprecating the competitive impact of the combination on the basis of "production flexibility", i.e. power of other producers to shift to new products and buyers. He accepted the Government's position, "determining lines of commerce by the peculiar characteristics and uses standard," and declared "production flexibility" in the steel industry ". . . pure theory. In practice steel producers have not been quick to shift from product to product in response to demand. Moreover, the evidence establishes that the continuing relationships between buyers and sellers in the steel industry make such shifts unlikely." The *Columbia* decision was put aside not only because it arose under the Sherman Act rather than the Clayton Act, but also because its "vitality has been questioned in the light of the passage of amended § 7." See the last paragraph of footnote 35 of the court's opinion, p. 593.

As regards geographic delimitation of the "relevant markets," the Government analysis looked both to national sales (Bethlehem and Youngstown were second and sixth respectively) and to certain regions to which both firms shipped substantial percentages of their products and which constituted "substantial and significant consuming centers." Defendants argued for a division of the country into Eastern, Mid-Continent and Western. Youngstown, it was contended, was an "effective competitor" only in the Mid-Continent sector where it had plants and Bethlehem did not. The Government demonstrated that, notwithstanding freight disadvantages, both companies shipped into each other's territories; and the court took the market as it found it, discounting defendants' explanations for the departures from what should theoretically have been natural separate markets. In addition, the court declared that regional markets, to the extent that they existed, "are so interrelated that what happens in one has a direct effect in the others and none is so separate that the buyers and sellers are not concerned with prices and supply and demand in the others." (p. 600). Also, "section of the country must be determined with respect to both buyers and sellers. The determination must be made on the basis of not only where the companies have in the past made sales, but also on the basis of where potentially they could make sales and where buyers could reasonably turn to them as alternative substantial sources of supply." (p. 599).

Judge Weinfeld rejected (168 F.Supp. at 615–618) the argument that the merger was the only way to achieve desirable expansion of capacity in the Mid-West. Cf. Affidavit of Arthur B. Homer, President of Bethlehem Steel Co., Sept. 16, 1957, in the record of the case: "Neither Bethlehem nor Youngstown, alone, will be able to provide the expansion that is envisioned as a result of the merger . . . [T]o build a new integrated steel plant in the Mid-Continent Area . . . would involve prohibitive costs per ton of new capacity and vastly greater capital resources than are available to Bethlehem and would delay almost indefinitely the provision of certain important new facilities."

On December 4, 1962, the Wall Street Journal carried the following headline on page 1: Paradox in Steel: Bethlehem's Expansion Is Trend in Industry Despite Overcapacity: Midwest Works Will Compete in Big Market Using More Metal Than It Now Makes: World's Biggest Steel Mill? On May

12, 1965, the Wall Street Journal, p. 30, headlined: Major Expansion By [Youngstown] Sheet & Tube Set Near Chicago.

SECTION 7 OF THE CLAYTON ACT OF 1914, AS AMENDED BY THE CELLER–KEFAUVER ANTI–MERGER ACT OF 1950 [6]

15 U.S.C.A. § 18.

No person engaged in commerce or in any activity affecting commerce shall acquire, directly or indirectly, the whole or any part of the stock or other share capital and no person subject to the jurisdiction of the Federal Trade Commission shall acquire the whole or any part of the assets of another person engaged also in commerce or in any activity affecting commerce, where in any line of commerce or in any activity affecting commerce in any section of the country, the effect of such acquisition may be substantially to lessen competition, or to tend to create a monopoly.

* * *

This section shall not apply to persons purchasing such stock solely for investment and not using the same by voting or otherwise to bring about, or in attempting to bring about, the substantial lessening of competition. Nor shall anything contained in this section prevent a corporation engaged in commerce or in any activity affecting commerce from causing the formation of subsidiary corporations for the actual carrying on of their immediate lawful business, or the natural and legitimate branches or extensions thereof, or from owning and holding all or a part of the stock of such subsidiary corporations, when the effect of such formation is not to substantially lessen competition.

* * *

Nothing contained in this section shall apply to transactions duly consummated pursuant to authority given by the Civil Aeronautics Board, Federal Communications Commission, Federal Power Commission, Interstate Commerce Commission, the Securities and Exchange Commission in the exercise of its jurisdiction under section 79j of this title, the United States Maritime Commission, or the Secretary of Agriculture under any statutory provision vesting such power in such Commission, Secretary, or Board.

NOTES AND QUERIES

(1) *How Does Section 7 Attempt to Remedy the Weaknesses of the Sherman Act in Relation to Mergers?* Consider the following:

(a) The effect of authorizing an administrative agency like the Federal Trade Commission to institute proceedings, hold hearings, and issue cease

---

6. As originally enacted in 1914, the first paragraph of Section 7 provided:

"That no corporation engaged in commerce shall acquire, directly or indirectly, the whole or any part of the stock or other share capital of another corporation engaged also in commerce, where the effect of such acquisition may be to substantially lessen competition between the corporation whose stock is so acquired and the corporation making the acquisition, or to restrain such commerce in any section or community, or tend to create a monopoly of any line of commerce."

and desist orders. Will it be easier or harder to prove a violation before such an agency rather than a court?

(b) What language, if any, in Section 7 allows the acquiring company to show that it had sound business reasons for the merger? Is "intent" a relevant factor under this section, or only "effect"? Does the probable effect of a transaction depend, in part, on the intent of the actors?

(c) What language, if any, entitles the acquiring company to introduce evidence that the field will remain amply competitive even if the merger goes through?

(d) Is the government required to prove that the merger impairs competition substantially or unduly? Does Section 7 eliminate the significance of the concept of "market"?

(2) *Acquisition of Non-capital Assets.* Does Section 7 apply to acquisition of part of the assets of another corporation? to all sales and purchases between competing corporations? [7]

(3) *Interlocking Directorates and Other Affiliations.* Section 8 of the Clayton Act forbids certain types of interlocking directorate or management among banks; in addition:

". . . no person at the same time shall be a director in any two or more corporations, any one of which has capital, surplus, and undivided profits aggregating more than $1,000,000, engaged in whole or in part in commerce . . . if such corporations are or shall have been theretofore, by virtue of their business and location of operation, competitors, so that the elimination of competition by agreement between them would constitute a violation of any of the provisions of any of the antitrust laws . . .."

Enforcement efforts under this and cognate provisions of regulatory acts have not proven effective.[8]

---

7. See SCM Corp. v. Xerox Corp., 645 F.2d 1195, 1210 (2d Cir. 1981), (patents are an asset), certiorari denied 455 U.S. 1016, 102 S.Ct. 1708, 72 L.Ed.2d 132 (1982); United States v. Columbia Pictures Corp., 189 F.Supp. 153, 181–83 (S.D.N.Y.1960) (exclusive exhibition rights to old feature films are an asset).

8. See, e.g., Kennecott Copper Corp. v. Curtiss-Wright Corp., 584 F.2d 1195 (2d Cir. 1978) (§ 8 does not prohibit interlocks between corporations whose independent subsidiaries are competitors); Note, Interlocking Directorates and Section 8 of the Clayton Act, 44 Albany L.Rev. 139 (1979); Sen.Subcomm. on Reports, Accounting and Management of the Comm. on Governmental Affairs, Interlocking Directorates Among the Major U. S. Corporations, S.Doc.No. 107, 95th Cong., 2nd Sess. 1 (recent study of incidence of interlocking directorates); Travers, Interlocks in Corporate Management and the Antitrust Laws, 46 Tex.L.Rev.

819 (1968); Interlocks in Corporate Management, Staff Report to the Antitrust Subcommittee of the House Committee on the Judiciary, 89th Cong., 1st Sess. (1965). But cf. United States v. Crocker National Corp., 656 F.2d 428 (9th Cir. 1981) (§ 8 prohibits interlocks between large competing banks and insurance companies, despite language that statute applies to competing corporations "other than banks"), certiorari granted sub nom., Bank America Corp. v. United States, 456 U.S. 1005, 102 S.Ct. 2294, 73 L.Ed.2d 1299 (1982). Conflicting opinions have been given by the Department of Justice and the F.T.C. as to whether United Auto Worker representatives on the boards of competing auto manufacturers would violate Section 8. Compare ATRR No. 1014, May 14, 1981, p. A–22 (F.T.C. Advisory Opinion; no violation) with 5 Trade Reg.Rep. ¶ 50,425 (Antitrust Division Business Review Letter; unable to state that Justice Department would not sue).

BROWN SHOE CO. v. UNITED STATES

Supreme Court of the United States, 1962.
370 U.S. 294, 311–23, 82 S.Ct. 1502, 1516–23, 8 L.Ed.2d 510.

MR. CHIEF JUSTICE WARREN delivered the opinion of the Court.

. . .

III. LEGISLATIVE HISTORY

This case is one of the first to come before us in which the Government's complaint is based upon allegations that the appellant has violated § 7 of the Clayton Act, as that section was amended in 1950. The amendments adopted in 1950 culminated extensive efforts over a number of years, on the parts of both the Federal Trade Commission and some members of Congress, to secure revision of a section of the antitrust laws considered by many observers to be ineffective in its then existing form. Sixteen bills to amend § 7 during the period 1943 to 1949 alone were introduced for consideration by the Congress, and full public hearings on proposed amendments were held in three separate sessions. In the light of this extensive legislative attention to the measure, and the broad, general language finally selected by Congress for the expression of its will, we think it appropriate to review the history of the amended Act in determining whether the judgment of the court below was consistent with the intent of the legislature. . . .

The dominant theme pervading congressional consideration of the 1950 amendments was a fear of what was considered to be a rising tide of economic concentration in the American economy. Apprehension in this regard was bolstered by the publication in 1948 of the Federal Trade Commission's study on corporate mergers. Statistics from this and other current studies were cited as evidence of the danger to the American economy in unchecked corporate expansions through mergers. Other considerations cited in support of the bill were the desirability of retaining "local control" over industry and the protection of small businesses. Throughout the recorded discussion may be found examples of Congress' fear not only of accelerated concentration of economic power on economic grounds, but also of the threat to other values a trend toward concentration was thought to pose.

What were some of the factors, relevant to a judgment as to the validity of a given merger, specifically discussed by Congress in redrafting § 7?

First, there is no doubt that Congress did wish to "plug the loophole" and to include within the coverage of the Act the acquisition of assets no less than the acquisition of stock.

Second, by the deletion of the "acquiring-acquired" language in the original text, it hoped to make plain that § 7 applied not only to mergers between actual competitors, but also to vertical and conglomerate mergers whose effect may tend to lessen competition in any line of commerce in any section of the country.

Third, it is apparent that a keystone in the erection of a barrier to what Congress saw was the rising tide of economic concentration, was its provision of authority for arresting mergers at a time when the trend to a lessening of competition in a line of commerce was still in its incipiency. Congress saw the process of concentration in American business as a dynamic force; it sought to assure the Federal Trade Commission and the courts the power to brake this force at its outset and before it gathered momentum.[9]

Fourth, and closely related to the third, Congress rejected, as inappropriate to the problem it sought to remedy, the application to § 7 cases of the standards for judging the legality of business combinations adopted by the courts in dealing with cases arising under the Sherman Act, and which may have been applied to some early cases arising under original § 7.[10]

Fifth, at the same time that it sought to create an effective tool for preventing all mergers having demonstrable anticompetitive effects, Congress recognized the stimulation to competition that might flow from particular mergers. When concern as to the Act's breadth was expressed, supporters of the amendments indicated that it would not impede, for example, a merger between two small companies to enable the combination to compete more effectively with larger corporations dominating the relevant market, nor a merger between a corporation which is financially healthy and a failing one which no long-

9. [Court's footnote 32; some citations omitted.] That § 7 of the Clayton Act was intended to reach incipient monopolies and trade restraints outside the scope of the Sherman Act was explicitly stated in the Senate Report on the original Act. This theme was reiterated in congressional consideration of the amendments adopted in 1950, and found expression in the final House and Senate Reports on the measure. H.R.Rep. No. 1191, 81st Cong., 1st Sess. 8 ("Acquisitions of stock or assets have a cumulative effect and control of the market . . . may be achieved not in a single acquisition but as the result of a series of acquisitions. The bill is intended to permit intervention in such a cumulative process when the effect of an acquisition may be a significant reduction in the vigor of competition." . . .

10. [Court's footnote 33; some citations omitted.] The Report of the House Judiciary Committee on H.R. 515 recommended the adoption of tests more stringent than those in the Sherman Act. A vigorous minority thought no new legislation was needed. Id., at 11–18. Between the issuance of this Report and the Committee's subsequent consideration of H.R. 2734, this Court had decided United States v. Columbia Steel Co., 334 U.S. 495, 68 S.Ct. 1107, 92 L.Ed. 1533, which some understood to indicate that existing law might be inadequate to prevent mergers that had substantially lessened competition in a section of the country, but which, nevertheless, had not risen to the level of those restraints of trade or monopoly prohibited by the Sherman Act. Numerous other statements by Congressmen and Senators and by representatives of the Federal Trade Commission, the Department of Justice and the President's Council of Economic Advisors were made to the Congress suggesting that a standard of illegality stricter than that imposed by the Sherman Act was needed. The House Judiciary Committee's 1949 Report supported this concept unanimously although five of the nine members who had dissented two years earlier in H.R.Rep. No. 596 were still serving on the Committee. The Senate Report was explicit: "The committee wish to make it clear that the bill is not intended to revert to the Sherman Act test. The intent here . . . is to cope with monopolistic tendencies in their incipiency and well before they have attained such effects as would justify a Sherman Act proceeding. . . .

er can be a vital competitive factor in the market. The deletion of the word "community" in the original Act's description of the relevant geographic market is another illustration of Congress' desire to indicate that its concern was with the adverse effects of a given merger on competition only in an economically significant "section" of the country. Taken as a whole, the legislative history illuminates congressional concern with the protection of *competition*, not *competitors*, and its desire to restrain mergers only to the extent that such combinations may tend to lessen competition.

Sixth, Congress neither adopted nor rejected specifically any particular tests for measuring the relevant markets, either as defined in terms of product or in terms of geographic locus of competition, within which the anticompetitive effects of a merger were to be judged. Nor did it adopt a definition of the word "substantially," whether in quantitative terms of sales or assets or market shares or in designated qualitative terms, by which a merger's effects on competition were to be measured.

Seventh, while providing no definite quantitative or qualitative tests by which enforcement agencies could gauge the effects of a given merger to determine whether it may "substantially" lessen competition or tend toward monopoly, Congress indicated plainly that a merger had to be functionally viewed, in the context of its particular industry. That is, whether the consolidation was to take place in an industry that was fragmented rather than concentrated, that had seen a recent trend toward domination by a few leaders or had remained fairly consistent in its distribution of market shares among the participating companies, that had experienced easy access to markets by suppliers and easy access to suppliers by buyers or had witnessed foreclosure of business, that had witnessed the ready entry of new competition or the erection of barriers to prospective entrants, all were aspects, varying in importance with the merger under consideration, which would properly be taken into account.

Eighth, Congress used the words "*may* be substantially to lessen competition" (emphasis supplied), to indicate that its concern was with probabilities, not certainties. Statutes existed for dealing with clear-cut menaces to competition; no statute was sought for dealing with ephemeral possibilities. Mergers with a probable anticompetitive effect were to be proscribed by this Act.

. . .

NOTES AND QUERIES

(1) *The Analytical Process in Section 7 Cases.* The broad standards of amended Section 7 are susceptible to a common analytical process whether a particular case be classified as horizontal, vertical or conglomerate. The tribunal or other analyst must investigate: 1) whether the statute is applicable; i.e., whether the commerce standard is met and whether an exemption is applicable because of regulatory statutes governing the industry in question; 2) how the market is defined; i.e., in what line of commerce (*product market*) and in what sections of the country (*geographic market*) will the effect

of the merger be measured; 3) whether the requisite anticompetitive effect is shown; i.e., what kind and how much evidence will prove that the effect of the acquisition "may be substantially to lessen competition or to tend to create a monopoly"; and, 4) whether there are any affirmative defenses or judicially created presumptions shifting the burden of proof in the particular circumstances.

(2) *Product and Geographic Markets.* The process for determining product and geographic markets should be familiar to the student who has already encountered these issues with respect to monopolization under Section 2 of the Sherman Act. In *United States v. Grinnell Corp.*, 384 U.S. 563, 572, 86 S.Ct. 1698, 16 L.Ed.2d 778 (1966), the Supreme Court stated that the same standards should apply under both statutes. Are there different concerns underlying the two statutes, however, which might make the application of holdings under one inappropriate for the other? How flexible are these concepts? Consider these (very flexible) cases:

United States v. Continental Can Co., 378 U.S. 441, 84 S.Ct. 1738, 12 L.Ed.2d 953 (1964). The second largest can manufacturer acquired the third largest producer of glass containers. Treating cans and bottles as a single industry, Continental ranked second with 22%, moving up to 25% with the acquisition of Hazel-Atlas. The trial court held that the government had not established a sufficient degree of interchangeability of glass and metal containers (other than in the field of beer packaging) to warrant treating the two companies as competitors in the same market. Rather, the transaction should be regarded as an expansion by Continental from one industry to another, a "conglomerate combination . . . for the purpose of establishing a diversified line of products". The Supreme Court reversed, finding a "general confrontation between metal and glass containers", a high degree of existing concentration, a long history of previous acquisitions, and a probability of "triggering" a series of similar mergers. The Court rejected the suggestion that if glass and metal containers were in the same market, plastic, paper, foil and other containers must also be considered; it admitted that there might be such a larger market, but saw within it "well-defined submarkets" relevant for antitrust purposes.

Would this transaction have impaired Continental's aggressiveness in either the metal or glass container business? Should a pro-competitive effect in one submarket be permitted to justify an anti-competitive effect in another submarket?

United States v. Pabst Brewing Co., 384 U.S. 546, 86 S.Ct. 1665, 16 L.Ed. 2d 765 (1966). Pabst was the Nation's tenth largest brewer; it acquired Blatz, the eighteenth largest. The Government alleged an effect on competition in the United States and in "various sections thereof," including Wisconsin and the three-state area of Wisconsin, Illinois, and Michigan. The Court held that the Government need only prove anticompetitive effect "somewhere" in the United States, whether throughout the country or in one or more sections. The Clayton Act "does not call for the delineation of a 'section of the country' by metes and bounds as a surveyor would lay off a plot of ground." The Court added that proof of the section of the country was "entirely subsidiary to the crucial question" of anticompetitive effect.

How can it be said that beer companies compete on a nationwide basis? Is a brewer on the East Coast likely to ship its beer to West Coast markets on a regular basis? Should the Court have examined the locations of the breweries? Can the effect on competition be accurately predicted without a clearer articulation of how to decide which firms are in competition?

(3) *Post-Brown Shoe Developments.* As the coming materials will make clear, the Government had a remarkable record of success in merger cases after *Brown Shoe*—it did not lose a case in the Supreme Court until 1974. The high-water mark of this period is *United States v. Von's Grocery Co.*, 384 U.S. 270, 86 S.Ct. 1478, 16 L.Ed.2d 555 (1966). The third largest grocery chain in Los Angeles bought out the sixth largest. Together they did 7.5% of the retail grocery business in the city. The acquisition was held illegal largely in reliance upon an observed decline in the number of single-store operators, an increase in the number of multiple-store operations, and a considerable amount of acquisition of smaller firms by the leading chains. Mr. Justice Black's opinion spoke of the purpose of the Sherman and Clayton Acts "to prevent economic concentration in the American economy by keeping a large number of small competitors in business." Justices Stewart and Harlan dissented, declaring that the Court had adopted a *per se* rule substituting a simplistic concern for numbers of competitors in place of analysis of the intensity of competition before and after the merger. Among the considerations emphasized by the dissenters were the following: Decline in single-store ownership reflects primarily technological changes, particularly the automobile and the freeway, which change the techniques of distribution without lessening competition. Remaining single stores are affiliated with purchasing cooperatives which afford them prices as favorable as the chains. The vigor of competition is attested by the fact that Safeway, the leading chain, had declined in market share from 14% to 8%. Although the aggregate share of the 20 largest chains had increased from 44% to 57% between 1948 and 1958, seven of these twenty had not even been in existence in 1948. Another demonstration of the vigor of rivalry was the constant disappearance of firms even while new ones took advantage of notable ease of entry. Von's and the acquired firm did most of their business in different sections of the city; where they overlapped their combined operations amounted to less than 1% of the trade, all done in vigorous competition with other chains and aggressive, large single-store operators.

The Court's willingness to accept the Government's views began to change in 1973 in *United States v. Falstaff Brewing* (infra pp. 269–278), in which a majority of the Court was unwilling to accept the Government's proposed construction of the Clayton Act. Two outright defeats followed in 1974, in *United States v. General Dynamics Corp.* (infra pp. 239–247) and *United States v. Marine Bancorporation, Inc.* (infra pp. 282–293); the Government has not appealed a merger case to the Supreme Court since 1975.[11]

Whether these decisions are the result of a change in philosophy by the Supreme Court, or whether the Government merely finds itself litigating cases with which the Clayton Act cannot deal, is a question which should be considered in studying the coming materials. It is also important to be aware that merger litigation has been influenced by the issuance of the Justice Department's Merger Guidelines in 1968, designed to alert business firms and their counsel of the Department's enforcement policies so that unlawful mergers could be avoided (see p. 249 infra); the passage of the Hart-Scott-Rodino Antitrust Improvements Act, providing for pre-merger notifica-

---

11. See United States v. Citizens & Southern National Bank, 412 U.S. 86, 95 S.Ct. 2099, 45 L.Ed.2d 41 (1975). In 1974 Congress amended the Expediting Act of 1903 which had provided for direct appeal in Justice Department cases from the District Court to the Supreme Court, thereby accounting for heavy Supreme Court participation in antitrust cases. Since 1974 appeals go to the court of appeals, unless the district judge, upon request, certifies the case to be "of general public importance to the administration of justice." See 15 U.S.C.A. § 29.

tion to the Justice Department and FTC so that the enforcement agencies could act prior to consummation (see pp. 324 – 325, infra); and the growth of the take-over business in an inflationary economy where corporate growth through complicated buy-out strategies seems preferable to slower growth through internal expansion (see pp. 309 – 322, infra).

B.   HORIZONTAL MERGER

UNITED STATES v. PHILADELPHIA NATIONAL BANK

Supreme Court of the United States, 1963.
374 U.S. 321, 83 S.Ct. 1715, 10 L.Ed.2d 915.

MR. JUSTICE BRENNAN delivered the opinion of the Court.

The United States, appellant here, brought this civil action in the United States District Court for the Eastern District of Pennsylvania to enjoin a proposed merger of The Philadelphia National Bank (PNB) and Girard Trust Corn Exchange Bank (Girard), appellees here. The complaint charged violations of § 1 of the Sherman Act and § 7 of the Clayton Act. From a judgment for appellees after trial the United States appealed to this Court . . .. We reverse the judgment of the District Court. We hold that the merger of appellees is forbidden by § 7 of the Clayton Act and so must be enjoined; we need not, and therefore do not, reach the further question of alleged violation of § 1 of the Sherman Act.

I.   THE FACTS AND PROCEEDINGS BELOW

A.   *The Background: Commercial Banking in the United States*

Because this is the first case which has required this Court to consider the application of the antitrust laws to the commercial banking industry, and because aspects of the industry and of the degree of governmental regulation of it will recur throughout our discussion, we deem it appropriate to begin with a brief background description. Commercial banking in this country is primarily unit banking. That is, control of commercial banking is diffused throughout a very large number of independent, local banks—13,460 of them in 1960—rather than concentrated in a handful of nationwide banks, as, for example, in England and Germany. There are, to be sure, in addition to the independent banks, some 10,000 branch banks; but branching, which is controlled largely by state law—and prohibited altogether by some States—enables a bank to extend itself only to state lines and often not that far. . . . [D]uring the decade ending in 1960 the number of commercial banks in the United States declined by 714, despite the chartering of 887 new banks and a very substantial increase in the Nation's credit needs during the period. Of the 1,601 independent banks which thus disappeared, 1,503, with combined total resources of well over $25,000,000,000, disappeared as the result of mergers.

Commercial banks are unique among financial institutions in that they alone are permitted by law to accept demand deposits. This distinctive power gives commercial banking a key role in the national economy. . . .

Banking operations are varied and complex; "commercial banking" describes a congeries of services and credit devices.[12] But among them the creation of additional money and credit, the management of the checking-account system, and the furnishing of short-term business loans would appear to be the most important. For the proper discharge of these functions is indispensable to a healthy national economy, as the role of bank failures in depression periods attests. It is therefore not surprising that commercial banking in the United States is subject to a variety of governmental controls, state and federal. Federal regulation is the more extensive, and our focus will be upon it. It extends not only to the national banks, i.e., banks chartered under federal law and supervised by the Comptroller of the Currency. For many state banks, as well as virtually all the national banks, are members of the Federal Reserve System (FRS), and more than 95% of all banks are insured by the Federal Deposit Insurance Corporation (FDIC). State member and nonmember insured banks are subject to a federal regulatory scheme almost as elaborate as that which governs the national banks.

The governmental controls of American banking are manifold. First, the Federal Reserve System, through its open-market operations, control of the rediscount rate, and modifications of reserve requirements, regulates the supply of money and credit in the economy and thereby indirectly regulates the interest rates of bank loans. This is not, however, rate regulation. The Reserve System's activities are only designed to influence the prime, i.e., minimum, bank interest rate. There is no federal control of the maximum, although all banks, state and national, are subject to state usury laws where applicable. In the range between the maximum fixed by state usury laws and the practical minimum set by federal fiscal policies (there is no law against undercutting the prime rate but bankers seldom do), bankers are free to price their loans as they choose. Moreover, charges for other banking services, such as service charges for checking privileges, are free of governmental regulation, state or federal.

12. [The following 11 footnotes are from the opinions, renumbered.] The principal banking "products" are of course various types of credit, for example: unsecured personal and business loans, mortgage loans, loans secured by securities or accounts receivable, automobile installment and consumer goods installment loans, tuition financing, bank credit cards, revolving credit funds. Banking services include: acceptance of demand deposits from individuals, corporations, governmental agencies, and other banks; acceptance of time and savings deposits; estate and trust planning and trusteeship services; lock boxes and safety-deposit boxes; account reconciliation services; foreign department services (acceptances and letters of credit); correspondent services; investment advice. It should be noted that many other institutions are in the business of supplying credit, and so more or less in competition with commercial banks, for example: mutual savings banks, savings and loan associations, credit unions, personal-finance companies, sales-finance companies, private businessmen (through the furnishing of trade credit), factors, direct-lending government agencies, the Post Office, Small Business Investment Corporations, life insurance companies.

Entry, branching, and acquisitions are covered by a network of state and federal statutes. A charter for a new bank, state or national, will not be granted unless the invested capital and management of the applicant, and its prospects for doing sufficient business to operate at a reasonable profit, give adequate protection against undue competition and possible failure. Failure to meet these standards may cause the FDIC to refuse an application for insurance and may cause the FDIC, Federal Reserve Board (FRB), and Comptroller to refuse permission to branch to insured, member, and national banks, respectively. Permission to merge, consolidate, acquire assets, or assume liabilities may be refused by the agencies on the same grounds. Furthermore, national banks appear to be subject to state geographical limitations on branching.

Banks are also subject to a number of specific provisions aimed at ensuring sound banking practices. For example, member banks of the Federal Reserve System may not pay interest on demand deposits, may not invest in common stocks or hold for their own account investment securities of any one obligor in excess of 10% of the bank's unimpaired capital and surplus and may not pay interest on time or savings deposits above the rate fixed by the FRB. The payment of interest on deposits by nonmember insured banks is also federally regulated. In the case of national banks, the 10% limit on the obligations of a single obligor includes loans as well as investment securities. Pennsylvania imposes the same limitation upon banks chartered under its laws, such as Girard.

But perhaps the most effective weapon of federal regulation of banking is the broad visitorial power of federal bank examiners. Whenever the agencies deem it necessary, they may order "a thorough examination of all the affairs of the bank," whether it be a member of the FRS or a nonmember insured bank. Such examinations are frequent and intensive. In addition, the banks are required to furnish detailed periodic reports of their operations to the supervisory agencies. In this way the agencies maintain virtually a day-to-day surveillance of the American banking system. And should they discover unsound banking practices, they are equipped with a formidable array of sanctions. If in the judgment of the FRB a member bank is making "undue use of bank credit," the Board may suspend the bank from the use of the credit facilities of the FRS. The FDIC has an even more formidable power. If it finds "unsafe or unsound practices" in the conduct of the business of any insured bank, it may terminate the bank's insured status. Such involuntary termination severs the bank's membership in the FRS, if it is a state bank, and throws it into receivership if it is a national bank. Lesser, but nevertheless drastic, sanctions include publication of the results of bank examinations. As a result of the existence of this panoply of sanctions, recommendations by the agencies concerning banking practices tend to be followed by bankers without the necessity of formal compliance proceedings. 1 Davis, Administrative Law (1958), § 4.04.

Federal supervision of banking has been called "[p]robably the outstanding example in the federal government of regulation of an entire industry through methods of supervision. . . . The system may be one of the most successful [systems of economic regulation], if not the most successful." Id., § 4.04, at 247. To the efficacy of this system we may owe, in part, the virtual disappearance of bank failures from the American economic scene.

B. *The Proposed Merger of PNB and Girard.*

The Philadelphia National Bank and Girard Trust Corn Exchange Bank are, respectively, the second and third largest of the 42 commercial banks with head offices in the Philadelphia metropolitan area, which consists of the City of Philadelphia and its three contiguous counties in Pennsylvania. The home county of both banks is the city itself; Pennsylvania law, however, permits branching into the counties contiguous to the home county, and both banks have offices throughout the four-county area. PNB, a national bank, has assets of over $1,000,000,000, making it (as of 1959) the twenty-first largest bank in the Nation. Girard a state bank is a member of the FRS and is insured by the FDIC; it has assets of about $750,000,000. Were the proposed merger to be consummated, the resulting bank would be the largest in the four-county area, with (approximately) 36% of the area banks' total assets, 36% of deposits, and 34% of net loans. It and the second largest (First Pennsylvania Bank and Trust Company, now the largest) would have between them 59% of the total assets, 58% of deposits, and 58% of the net loans, while after the merger the four largest banks in the area would have 78% of total assets, 77% of deposits, and 78% of net loans.

The present size of both PNB and Girard is in part the result of mergers. Indeed, the trend toward concentration is noticeable in the Philadelphia area generally, in which the number of commercial banks has declined from 108 in 1947 to the present 42. Since 1950, PNB has acquired nine formerly independent banks and Girard six; and these acquisitions have accounted for 59% and 85% of the respective banks' asset growth during the period, 63% and 91% of their deposit growth, and 12% and 37% of their loan growth. During this period, the seven largest banks in the area increased their combined share of the area's total commercial bank resources from about 61% to about 90%.

In November 1960 the boards of directors of the two banks approved a proposed agreement for their consolidation under the PNB charter. By the terms of the agreement, PNB's stockholders were to retain their share certificates, which would be deemed to represent an equal number of shares in the consolidated bank, while Girard's stockholders would surrender their shares in exchange for shares in the consolidated bank, receiving 1.2875 such shares for each Girard share. Such a consolidation is authorized, subject to the approval of the Comptroller of the Currency. But under the Bank Merger Act of 1960 the Comptroller may not give his approval until he has received reports from the other two banking agencies and the Attorney General respecting the probable effects of the proposed transaction on competition. All three reports advised that the proposed merger would have substantial anticompetitive effects in the Philadelphia metropolitan area. However, on February 24, 1961, the Comptroller approved the merger. No opinion was rendered at that time. But as required by § 1828(c), the Comptroller explained the basis for his decision to approve the merger in a statement to be included in his annual report to Congress. As to effect upon competition, he reasoned that "[s]ince there will remain an adequate number of alternative sources of banking service in Philadelphia, and in view of the beneficial effects of this consolidation upon international and national competition it was concluded that the over-all effect upon competition would not be unfavorable." He also stated that the consolidated bank "would be far better able to serve the convenience and needs of its community by being of material assistance to its city and state in their efforts to attract new industry and to retain existing industry." The day after the Comptroller approved the merger, the United States commenced the present action. No steps have been taken to consummate the merger pending the outcome of this litigation.

C. *The Trial and the District Court's Decision.*

The Government's case in the District Court relied chiefly on statistical evidence bearing upon market structure and on testimony by economists and bankers to the effect that, notwithstanding the intensive governmental regulation of banking, there was a substantial area for the free play of competitive forces; that concentration of commercial banking, which the proposed merger would increase, was inimical to that free play; that the principal anticompetitive effect of the merger would be felt in the area in which the banks had their offices, thus making the four-county metropolitan area the relevant geographical market; and that commercial banking was the relevant product market. The defendants, in addition to offering contrary evidence on these points, attempted to show business justifications for the merger. They conceded that both banks were economically strong and had sound management, but offered the testimony of bankers to show that the resulting bank, with its greater prestige and increased lending limit, would be better able to compete with large out-of-state (particularly New York) banks, would attract new business to Philadelphia, and in general would promote the economic development of the metropolitan area.[13]

---

13. There was evidence that Philadelphia, although it ranks fourth or fifth among the Nation's urban areas in terms of general commercial activity, ranks only ninth in terms of the size of its largest bank, and that some large business firms which have their head offices in Philadelphia must seek elsewhere to satisfy their banking needs because of the inadequate lending limits of Philadelphia's banks;

First Pennsylvania and PNB, currently the two largest banks in Philadelphia, each have a lending limit of $8,000,000. Girard's is $6,000,000.

Appellees offered testimony that the merger would enable certain economies of scale, specifically, that it would enable the formation of a more elaborate foreign department than either bank is pres-

Upon this record, the District Court held that: (1) the passage of the Bank Merger Act of 1960 did not repeal by implication the antitrust laws insofar as they may apply to bank mergers; (2) § 7 of the Clayton Act is inapplicable to bank mergers because banks are not corporations "subject to the jurisdiction of the Federal Trade Commission"; (3) but assuming that § 7 is applicable, the four-county Philadelphia metropolitan area is not the relevant geographical market because PNB and Girard actively compete with other banks for bank business throughout the greater part of the northeastern United States; (4) but even assuming that § 7 is applicable and that the four-county area is the relevant market, there is no reasonable probability that competition among commercial banks in the area will be substantially lessened as the result of the merger; (5) since the merger does not violate § 7 of the Clayton Act, *a fortiori* it does not violate § 1 of the Sherman Act; (6) the merger will benefit the Philadelphia metropolitan area economically. The District Court also ruled that for the purposes of § 7, commercial banking is a line of commerce; the appellees do not contest this ruling.

> [The opinion at this point considers defendants' arguments that the transaction was not a stock acquisition because PNB never held shares of Girard, and not an acquisition of Girard's assets within Section 7, because the assets acquisition provision is limited to corporations "subject to the jurisdiction of the Federal Trade Commission." It was urged that the statute did not purport to reach "mergers" as such, and contained no reference to asset acquisitions by corporations not subject to the FTC, as banks certainly were not. The opinion rejects this "loophole" construction as inconsistent with legislative history, which manifests a broad legislative purpose to reach every form of consolidation. The opinion then turns to the argument that the enactment of the Bank Merger Act of 1960 showed Congress' intentions as to control of mergers in this field, and constituted an implied repeal of Section 7's applicability to banks, if any.]

The Effect of the Bank Merger Act of 1960

Appellees contended below that the Bank Merger Act, by directing the banking agencies to consider competitive factors before approving mergers, immunizes approved mergers from challenge under the federal antitrust laws. We think the District Court was correct in rejecting this contention. No express immunity is conferred by the Act.[14] Repeals of the antitrust laws by implication from a regulatory statute are strongly disfavored, and have only been found

ently able to maintain. But this attempted justification, which was not mentioned by the District Court in its opinion and has not been developed with any fullness before this Court, we consider abandoned.

14. Contrast this with the express exemption provisions of, e.g., the Federal Aviation Act, 49 U.S.C. § 1384; Federal Communications Act, 47 U.S.C. §§ 221(a), 222(c)(1); Interstate Commerce Act, 49 U.S.C. §§ 5(11), 5b(9), 22; Shipping Act, 46 U.S.C. (1958 ed. Supp. III) § 814; Webb-Pomerene Act, 15 U.S.C. § 62; and the Clayton Act itself, § 7, 15 U.S.C. § 18.

in cases of plain repugnancy between the antitrust and regulatory provisions. Two recent cases, Pan American World Airways v. United States, 371 U.S. 296, 83 S.Ct. 476, 9 L.Ed.2d 325, and People of State of California v. Federal Power Comm'n, 369 U.S. 482, 82 S.Ct. 901, 8 L.Ed.2d 54, illustrate this principle. In Pan American, the Court held that because the Civil Aeronautics Board had been given broad powers to enforce the competitive standard clearly delineated by the Civil Aeronautics Act, and to immunize a variety of transactions from the operation of the antitrust laws, the Sherman Act could not be applied to facts composing the precise ingredients of a case subject to the Board's broad regulatory and remedial powers; in contrast, the banking agencies have authority neither to enforce the antitrust laws against mergers, nor to grant immunity from those laws.

In the California case, on the other hand, the Court held that the FPC's approval of a merger did not confer immunity from § 7 of the Clayton Act, even though, as in the instant case, the agency had taken the competitive factor into account in passing upon the merger application. We think California is controlling here. Although the Comptroller was required to consider effect upon competition in passing upon appellees' merger application, he was not required to give this factor any particular weight; he was not even required to (and did not) hold a hearing before approving the application; and there is no specific provision for judicial review of his decision. Plainly, the range and scope of administrative powers under the Bank Merger Act bear little resemblance to those involved in Pan American.

Nor did Congress, in passing the Bank Merger Act, embrace the view that federal regulation of banking is so comprehensive that enforcement of the antitrust laws would be either unnecessary, in light of the completeness of the regulatory structure, or disruptive of that structure. On the contrary, the legislative history of the Act seems clearly to refute any suggestion that applicability of the antitrust laws was to be affected. Both the House and Senate Committee Reports stated that the Act would not affect in any way the applicability of the antitrust laws to bank acquisitions. Moreover, bank regulation is in most respects less complete than public utility regulation, to which interstate rail and air carriers, among others, are subject. Rate regulation in the banking industry is limited and largely indirect; banks are under no duty not to discriminate in their services; and though the location of bank offices is regulated, banks may do business—place loans and solicit deposits—where they please. The fact that the banking agencies maintain a close surveillance of the industry with a view toward preventing unsound practices that might impair liquidity or lead to insolvency does not make federal banking regulation all-pervasive, although it does minimize the hazards of intense competition. Indeed, that there are so many direct public controls over unsound competitive practices in the industry refutes the argument that private controls of competition are necessary in the public interest and ought therefore to be immune from scrutiny under the antitrust laws. Cf. Kaysen and Turner, Antitrust Policy (1959), 206.

We note, finally, that the doctrine of "primary jurisdiction" is not applicable here. That doctrine requires judicial abstention in cases where protection of the integrity of a regulatory scheme dictates preliminary resort to the agency which administers the scheme. See . . . . Schwartz, Legal Restriction of Competition in the Regulated Industries: An Abdication of Judicial Responsibility, 67 Harv.L.Rev. 436, 464 (1954). Court jurisdiction is not thereby ousted, but only postponed. See . . . 3 Davis, Administrative Law (1958), 1–55. Thus, even if we were to assume the applicability of the doctrine to merger-application proceedings before the banking agencies, the present action would not be barred, for the agency proceeding was completed before the antitrust action was commenced. We recognize that the practical effect of applying the doctrine of primary jurisdiction has sometimes been to channel judicial enforcement of antitrust policy into appellate review of the agency's decision or even to preclude such enforcement entirely if the agency has the power to approve the challenged activities. Here there may be no power of judicial review of the administrative decision approving the merger, and such approval does not in any event confer immunity from the antitrust laws. Furthermore, the considerations that militate against finding a repeal of the antitrust laws by implication from the existence of a regulatory scheme also argue persuasively against attenuating, by postponing, the courts' jurisdiction to enforce those laws.

It should be unnecessary to add that in holding as we do that the Bank Merger Act of 1960 does not preclude application of § 7 of the Clayton Act to bank mergers, we deprive the later statute of none of its intended force. Congress plainly did not intend the 1960 Act to extinguish other sources of federal restraint of bank acquisitions having anticompetitive effects. For example, Congress certainly knew that bank mergers would continue subject to the Sherman Act, as well as that pure stock acquisitions by banks would continue subject to § 7 of the Clayton Act. If, in addition, bank mergers are subject to § 7, we do not see how the objectives of the 1960 Act are thereby thwarted. It is not as if the Clayton and Sherman Acts embodied approaches to antitrust policy inconsistent with or unrelated to each other. The Sherman Act, of course, forbids mergers effecting an unreasonable restraint of trade. . . . And the tests of illegality under the Sherman and Clayton Acts are complementary. "[T]he public policy announced by § 7 of the Clayton Act is to be taken into consideration in determining whether acquisition of assets . . . violates the prohibitions of the Sherman Act against unreasonable restraints." United States v. Columbia Steel Co., 334 U.S. 495, 507, n. 7, 68 S.Ct. 1107, 1114, 92 L.Ed. 1533. To be sure, not every violation of § 7, as amended, would necessarily be a violation of the Sherman Act; our point is simply that since Congress passed the 1960 Act with no intention of displacing the enforcement of the Sherman Act against bank mergers—or even of § 7 against pure stock acquisitions by banks— continued application of § 7 to bank mergers cannot be repugnant to the design of the 1960 Act. It would be anomalous to conclude that Congress, while intending the Sherman Act to remain fully applicable to bank mergers, and § 7 of the Clayton Act to remain fully applicable to pure stock acquisitions by banks, nevertheless intended § 7 to be completely inapplicable to bank mergers.

III. THE LAWFULNESS OF THE PROPOSED MERGER UNDER SECTION 7

The statutory test is whether the effect of the merger "may be substantially to lessen competition" "in any line of commerce in any section of the country." We analyzed the test in detail in Brown Shoe Co. v. United States, 370 U.S. 294, 82 S.Ct. 1502, 8 L.Ed.2d 510, and that analysis need not be repeated or extended here, for the instant case presents only a straightforward problem of application to particular facts.

We have no difficulty in determining the "line of commerce" (relevant product or services market) and "section of the country" (relevant geographical market) in which to appraise the probable competitive effects of appellees' proposed merger. We agree with the District Court that the cluster of products (various kinds of credit) and services (such as checking accounts and trust administration) denoted by the term "commercial banking" composes a distinct line of commerce. Some commercial banking products or services are so distinctive that they are entirely free of effective competition from products or services of other financial institutions; the checking account is in this category. Others enjoy such cost advantages as to be insulated within a broad range from substitutes furnished by other institutions. For example, commercial banks compete with small-loan companies in the personal-loan market; but the small-loan companies' rates are invariably much higher than the banks', in part, it seems, because the companies' working capital consists in substantial part of bank loans.[15] Finally, there are banking facilities which, although in terms of cost and price they are freely competitive with the facilities provided by other financial institutions, nevertheless enjoy a settled consumer preference, insulating them, to a marked degree, from com-

---

15. Cf. United States v. Aluminum Co. of America, 148 F.2d 416, 425 (C.A.2d Cir., 1945). In the instant case, unlike Aluminum Co., there is virtually no time lag between the banks' furnishing competing financial institutions (small-loan companies, for example) with the raw material, i.e., money, and the institutions' selling the finished product, i.e., loans; hence the instant case, compared with Aluminum Co. in this respect, is *a fortiori*. As one banker testified quite frankly in the instant case in response to the question: "Do you feel that you are in substantial competition with these institutions [personal-finance and sales-finance companies] that you lend . . . such money to for loans that you want to make?"—"Oh, no, we definitely do not. If we did, we would stop making the loans to them," (R. 298). The reason for the competitive disadvantage of most lending institutions *vis-à-vis* banks is that only banks obtain the bulk of their working capital without having to pay interest or comparable charges thereon, by virtue of their unique power to accept demand deposits. The critical area of short-term commercial credit, see pp. 1721–1722, supra, appears to be one in which banks have little effective competition, save in the case of very large companies which can meet their financing needs from retained earnings or from issuing securities or paper.

petition; this seems to be the case with savings deposits.[16] In sum, it is clear that commercial banking is a market "sufficiently inclusive to be meaningful in terms of trade realities." Crown Zellerbach Corp. v. Federal Trade Comm'n, 296 F.2d 800, 811 (C.A.9th Cir., 1961).

We part company with the District Court on the determination of the appropriate "section of the country." The proper question to be asked in this case is not where the parties to the merger do business or even where they compete, but where, within the area of competitive overlap, the effect of the merger on competition will be direct and immediate. This depends upon "the geographic structure of supplier-customer relations." Kaysen and Turner, Anti-trust Policy (1959), 102. In banking, as in most service industries, convenience of location is essential to effective competition. Individuals and corporations typically confer the bulk of their patronage on banks in their local community; they find it impractical to conduct their banking business at a distance. The factor of inconvenience localizes banking competition as effectively as high transportation costs in other industries. Therefore, since, as we recently said in a related context, the "area of effective competition in the known line of commerce must be chartered by careful selection of the market area in which the seller operates, *and to which the purchaser can practically turn for supplies*," Tampa Elec. Co. v. Nashville Coal Co., 365 U.S. 320, 327, 81 S.Ct. 623, 628, 5 L.Ed.2d 580 (emphasis supplied), the four-county area in which appellees' offices are located would seem to be the relevant geographical market. In fact, the vast bulk of appellees' business originates in the four-county area. Theoretically, we should be concerned with the possibility that bank offices on the perimeter of the area may be in effective competition with bank offices within; actually, this seems to be a factor of little significance.[17]

16. As one witness for the defendants testified:

"We have had in Philadelphia for 50 years or more the mutual savings banks offering 1/2 per cent and in some instances more than 1/2 per cent higher interest than the commercial banks. Nevertheless, the rate of increase in savings accounts in commercial banks has kept pace with and in many of the banks exceeded the rate of increase of the mutual banks paying 3 1/2 per cent. . . .

"I have made some inquiries. There are four banks on the corner of Broad and Chestnut. Three of them are commercial banks all offering 3 per cent, and one is a mutual savings bank offering 3 1/2. As far as I have been able to discover, there isn't anybody in Philadelphia who will take the trouble to walk across Broad Street to get 1/2 of 1 per cent more interest. If you ask me why, I will say I do not know. Habit, custom, personal relationships, convenience, doing all your banking under one roof appear to be factors superior to changes in the interest rate level." (R. 1388–1389.)

17. Appellees suggest not that bank offices skirting the four-county area provide meaningful alternatives to bank customers within the area, but that such alternatives are provided by large banks, from New York and elsewhere, which solicit business in the Philadelphia area. There is no evidence of the amount of business done in the area by banks with offices outside the area; it may be that such figures are unobtainable. In any event, it would seem from the local orientation of banking insofar as smaller customers are concerned, that competition from outside the area would only be important to the larger borrowers and depositors. If so, the four-county area remains a valid geographical market in which to assess the anticompetitive effect of the proposed merger upon the banking facilities available to the smaller customer—a perfectly good "line of commerce," in light of Congress' evident con-

We recognize that the area in which appellees have their offices does not delineate with perfect accuracy an appropriate "section of the country" in which to appraise the effect of the merger upon competition. Large borrowers and large depositors, the record shows, may find it practical to do a large part of their banking business outside their home community; very small borrowers and depositors may, as a practical matter, be confined to bank offices in their immediate neighborhood; and customers of intermediate size, it would appear, deal with banks within an area intermediate between these extremes. So also, some banking services are evidently more local in nature than others. But that in banking the relevant geographical market is a function of each separate customer's economic scale means simply that a workable compromise must be found: some fair intermediate delineation which avoids the indefensible extremes of drawing the market either so expansively as to make the effect of the merger upon competition seem insignificant, because only the very largest bank customers are taken into account in defining the market, or so narrowly as to place appellees in different markets, because only the smallest customers are considered. We think that the four-County Philadelphia metropolitan area, which state law apparently recognizes as a meaningful banking community in allowing Philadelphia banks to branch within it, and which would seem roughly to delineate the area in which bank customers that are neither very large nor very small find it practical to do their banking business, is a more appropriate "section of the country" in which to appraise the instant merger than any larger or smaller or different area. We are helped to this conclusion by the fact that the three federal banking agencies regard the area in which banks have their offices as an "area of effective competition." Not only did the FDIC and FRB, in the reports they submitted to the Comptroller of the Currency in connection with appellees' application for permission to merge, so hold, but the Comptroller, in his statement approving the merger, agreed: "With respect to the effect upon competition, there are three separate levels and effective areas of competition involved. These are the national level for national accounts, the regional or sectional area, and the local area of the City of Philadelphia and the immediately surrounding area."

Having determined the relevant market, we come to the ultimate question under § 7: whether the effect of the merger "may be substantially to lessen competition" in the relevant market. Clearly, this

cern, in enacting the 1950 amendments to § 7, with preserving small business. See Brown Shoe Co., supra, 370 U.S., at 315–316, 82 S.Ct., at 1518–1519, 8 L.Ed. 2d 510. As a practical matter the small businessman can only satisfy his credit needs at local banks. To be sure, there is still some artificiality in deeming the four-county area the relevant "section of the country" so far as businessmen located near the perimeter are concerned. But such fuzziness would seem inherent in any attempt to delineate the relevant geographical market. Note, 52 Colum.L. Rev. 766, 778–779, n. 77 (1952). And it is notable that outside the four-county area, appellees' business rapidly thins out. Thus, the other six counties of the Delaware Valley account for only 2% of appellees' combined individual demand deposits; 4%, demand deposits of partnerships and corporations; 7%, loans; 2%, savings deposits; 4%, business time deposits.

is not the kind of question which is susceptible of a ready and precise answer in most cases. It requires not merely an appraisal of the immediate impact of the merger upon competition, but a prediction of its impact upon competitive conditions in the future; this is what is meant when it is said that the amended § 7 was intended to arrest anticompetitive tendencies in their "incipiency." See Brown Shoe Co., supra, 370 U.S., at 317, 322, 82 S.Ct., at 1519–1520, 1522, 8 L.Ed. 2d 510. Such a prediction is sound only if it is based upon a firm understanding of the structure of the relevant market; yet the relevant economic data are both complex and elusive. See generally Bok, Section 7 of the Clayton Act and the Merging of Law and Economics, 74 Harv.L.Rev. 226 (1960). And unless businessmen can assess the legal consequences of a merger with some confidence, sound business planning is retarded. So also, we must be alert to the danger of subverting congressional intent by permitting a too-broad economic investigation. And so in any case in which it is possible, without doing violence to the congressional objective embodied in § 7, to simplify the test of illegality, the courts ought to do so in the interest of sound and practical judicial administration. This is such a case.

We noted in Brown Shoe So., supra, 370 U.S., at 315, 82 S.Ct., at 1518, 8 L.Ed.2d 510, that "[t]he dominant theme pervading congressional consideration of the 1950 amendments [to § 7] was a fear of what was considered to be a rising tide of economic concentration in the American economy." This intense congressional concern with the trend toward concentration warrants dispensing, in certain cases, with elaborate proof of market structure, market behavior, or probable anticompetitive effects. Specifically, we think that a merger which produces a firm controlling an undue percentage share of the relevant market, and results in a significant increase in the concentration of firms in that market is so inherently likely to lessen competition substantially that it must be enjoined in the absence of evidence clearly showing that the merger is not likely to have such anticompetitive effects.

Such a test lightens the burden of proving illegality only with respect to mergers whose size makes them inherently suspect in light of Congress' design in § 7 to prevent undue concentration. Furthermore, the test is fully consonant with economic theory.[18] That "[c]ompetition is likely to be greatest when there are many sellers, none of which has any significant market share," is common ground among most economists, and was undoubtedly a premise of congressional reasoning about the antimerger statute.

The merger of appellees will result in a single bank's controlling at least 30% of the commercial banking business in the four-county Philadelphia metropolitan area. Without attempting to specify the smallest market share which would still be considered to threaten un-

---

18. See Kaysen and Turner, Antitrust Policy (1959), 133; Stigler, Mergers and Preventive Antitrust Policy, 104 U. of Pa. L.Rev. 176, 182 (1955); Bok, supra, at 308–316, 328. Cf. Markham, Merger Policy Under the New Section 7: A Six-Year Appraisal, 43 Va.L.Rev. 489, 521–522 (1957).

due concentration, we are clear that 30% presents that threat.[19] Further, whereas presently the two largest banks in the area (First Pennsylvania and PNB) control between them approximately 44% of the area's commercial banking business, the two largest after the merger (PNB-Girard and First Pennsylvania) will control 59%. Plainly, we think, this increase of more than 33% in concentration must be regarded as significant.[20]

Our conclusion that these percentages raise an inference that the effect of the contemplated merger of appellees may be substantially to lessen competition is not an arbitrary one, although neither the terms of § 7 nor the legislative history suggests that any particular percentage share was deemed critical. The House Report states that the tests of illegality under amended § 7 "are intended to be similar to those which the courts have applied in interpreting the same language as used in other sections of the Clayton Act." H.R.Rep. No. 1191, 81st Cong., 1st Sess. 8. Accordingly, we have relied upon decisions under these other sections in applying § 7. In Standard Oil Co. of Cal. & Standard Stations v. United States, 337 U.S. 293, 69 S.Ct. 1051, 93 L.Ed. 1371, this Court held violative of § 3 of the Clayton Act exclusive contracts whereby the defendant company, which accounted for 23% of the sales in the relevant market and, together with six other firms, accounted for 65% of such sales, maintained control over outlets through which approximately 7% of the sales were made. In Federal Trade Comm'n v. Motion Picture Adv. Serv. Co., 344 U.S. 392, 73 S.Ct. 361, 97 L.Ed. 426, we held unlawful, under § 1 of the Sherman Act and § 5 of the Federal Trade Commission Act, rather than under § 3 of the Clayton Act, exclusive arrangements whereby the four major firms in the industry had foreclosed 75% of the relevant market; the respondent's market share, evidently, was 20%. In the instant case, by way of comparison, the four largest banks after the merger will foreclose 78% of the relevant market. And in Standard Fashion Co. v. Magrane-Houston Co., 258 U.S. 346, 42 S.Ct. 360, 66 L.Ed. 653, the Court held violative of § 3 a series of exclusive contracts whereby a single manufacturer controlled 40% of the industry's retail outlets. Doubtless these cases turned to some extent upon whether "by the nature of the market there is room for

---

19. Kaysen and Turner suggests that 20% should be the line of prima facie unlawfulness; Stigler suggests that any acquisition by a firm controlling 20% of the market after the merger is presumptively unlawful; Markham mentions 25%. Bok's principal test is increase in market concentration, and he suggests a figure of 7% or 8%. We intimate no view on the validity of such tests for we have no need to consider percentages smaller than those in the case at bar, but we note that such tests are more rigorous than is required to dispose of the instant case. Needless to say, the fact that a merger results in a less-than-30% market share, or in a less substantial increase in concentration than in the instant case, does not raise an inference that the merger is *not* violative of § 7. See, e.g., Brown Shoe Co., supra.

20. It is no answer that, among the three presently largest firms (First Pennsylvania, PNB, and Girard), there will be no increase in concentration. If this argument were valid, then once a market had become unduly concentrated, further concentration would be legally privileged. On the contrary, if concentration is already great, the importance of preventing even slight increases in concentration and so preserving the possibility of eventual deconcentration is correspondingly great.

newcomers." Federal Trade Comm'n v. Motion Picture Adv. Serv.
Co., supra, 344 U.S., at 395, 73 S.Ct., at 363, 97 L.Ed. 426. But they
remain highly suggestive in the present context, for as we noted in
Brown Shoe Co., supra, 370 U.S., at 332, n. 55, 82 S.Ct., at 1522, 8
L.Ed.2d 510, integration by merger is more suspect than integration
by contract, because of the greater permanence of the former. The
market share and market concentration figures in the contract-inte-
gration cases, taken together with scholarly opinion, support, we believe, the inference we draw in the instant case from the figures disclosed by the record.

There is nothing in the record of this case to rebut the inherently
anticompetitive tendency manifested by these percentages. There
was, to be sure, testimony by bank officers to the effect that competition among banks in Philadelphia was vigorous and would continue to
be vigorous after the merger. We think, however, that the District
Court's reliance on such evidence was misplaced. This lay evidence
on so complex an economic-legal problem as the substantiality of the
effect of this merger upon competition was entitled to little weight, in
view of the witnesses' failure to give concrete reasons for their conclusions.[21]

Of equally little value, we think, are the assurances offered by
appellees' witnesses that customers dissatisfied with the services of
the resulting bank may readily turn to the 40 other banks in the Philadelphia area. In every case short of outright monopoly, the disgrun-
tled customer has alternatives; even in tightly oligopolistic markets,
there may be small firms operating. A fundamental purpose of
amending § 7 was to arrest the trend toward concentration, the *tendency* to monopoly, before the consumer's alternatives disappeared
through merger, and that purpose would be ill-served if the law
stayed its hand until 10, or 20, or 30 more Philadelphia banks were
absorbed. This is not a fanciful eventuality, in view of the strong
trend toward mergers evident in the area; and we might note also
that entry of new competitors into the banking field is far from easy.

So also, we reject the position that commercial banking, because it
is subject to a high degree of governmental regulation, or because it
deals in the intangibles of credit and services rather than in the manufacture or sale of tangible commodities, is somehow immune from
the anticompetitive effects of undue concentration. Competition
among banks exists at every level—price, variety of credit arrangements, convenience of location, attractiveness of physical surround-
ings, credit information, investment advice, service charges, personal

21. The fact that some of the bank officers who testified represented small
banks in competition with appellees does
not substantially enhance the probative
value of their testimony. The test of a
competitive market is not only whether
small competitors flourish but also
whether consumers are well served. See
United States v. Bethlehem Steel Corp.,
168 F.Supp. 576, 588, 592 (D.C.S.D.N.Y.

1958). "[C]ongressional concern [was]
with the protection of *competition*, not
competitors." Brown Shoe Co., supra,
370 U.S., at 320, 82 S.Ct., at 1521, 8 L.Ed.
2d 510. In an oligopolistic market, small
companies may be perfectly content to
follow the high prices set by the dominant firms, yet the market may be profoundly anticompetitive.

accommodations, advertising, miscellaneous special and extra services—and it is keen; on this appellees' own witnesses were emphatic. There is no reason to think that concentration is less inimical to the free play of competition in banking than in other service industries. On the contrary, it is in all probability more inimical. For example, banks compete to fill the credit needs of businessmen. Small businessmen especially are, as a practical matter, confined to their locality for the satisfaction of their credit needs. If the number of banks in the locality is reduced, the vigor of competition for filling the marginal small business borrower's needs is likely to diminish. At the same time, his concomitantly greater difficulty in obtaining credit is likely to put him at a disadvantage *vis-à-vis* larger businesses with which he competes. In this fashion, concentration in banking accelerates concentration generally.

We turn now to three affirmative justifications, which appellees offer for the proposed merger. The first is that only through mergers can banks follow their customers to the suburbs and retain their business. This justification does not seem particularly related to the instant merger, but in any event it has no merit. There is an alternative to the merger route: the opening of new branches in the areas to which the customers have moved—so-called *de novo* branching. Appellees do not contend that they are unable to expand thus, by opening new offices rather than acquiring existing ones, and surely one premise of an antimerger statute such as § 7 is that corporate growth by internal expansion is socially preferable to growth by acquisition.

Second, it is suggested that the increased lending limit of the resulting bank will enable it to compete with the large out-of-state bank, particularly the New York banks, for very large loans. We reject this application of the concept of "countervailing power." If anticompetitive effects in one market could be justified by procompetitive consequences in another, the logical upshot would be that every firm in an industry could, without violating § 7, embark on a series of mergers that would make it in the end as large as the industry leader. For if all the commercial banks in the Philadelphia area merged into one, it would be smaller than the largest bank in New York City. This is not a case, plainly, where two small firms in a market propose to merge in order to be able to compete more successfully with the leading firms in that market. Nor is it a case in which lack of adequate banking facilities is causing hardships to individuals or businesses in the community. The present two largest banks in Philadelphia have lending limits of $8,000,000 each. The only businesses located in the Philadelphia area which find such limits inadequate are large enough readily to obtain bank credit in other cities.

This brings us to appellees' final contention, that Philadelphia needs a bank larger than it now has in order to bring business to the area and stimulate its economic development. We are clear, however, that a merger the effect of which "may be substantially to lessen competition" is not saved because, on some ultimate reckoning of social or economic debits and credits, it may be deemed beneficial. A value choice of such magnitude is beyond the ordinary limits of judicial competence, and in any event has been made for us already, by Congress when it enacted the amended § 7. Congress determined to preserve our traditionally competitive economy. It therefore proscribed anticompetitive mergers, the benign and the malignant alike, fully aware, we must assume, that some price might have to be paid.

In holding as we do that the merger of appellees would violate § 7 and must therefore be enjoined, we reject appellees' pervasive suggestion that application of the procompetitive policy of § 7 to the banking industry will have dire, although unspecified, consequences for the national economy. Concededly, PNB and Girard are healthy and strong; they are not undercapitalized or overloaned; they have no management problems; the Philadelphia area is not overbanked; ruinous competition is not in the offing. Section 7 does not mandate cutthroat competition in the banking industry, and does not exclude defenses based on dangers to liquidity or solvency, if to avert them a merger is necessary. It does require, however, that the forces of competition be allowed to operate within the broad framework of governmental regulation of the industry. The fact that banking is a highly regulated industry critical to the Nation's welfare makes the play of competition not less important but more so. At the price of some repetition, we note that if the businessman is denied credit because his banking alternatives have been eliminated by mergers, the whole edifice of an entrepreneurial system is threatened; if the costs of banking services and credit are allowed to become excessive by the absence of competitive pressures, virtually all costs, in our credit economy, will be affected; and unless competition is allowed to fulfill its role as an economic regulator in the banking industry, the result may well be even more governmental regulation. Subject to narrow qualifications, it is surely the case that competition is our fundamental national economic policy, offering as it does the only alternative to the cartelization or governmental regimentation of large portions of the economy. There is no warrant for declining to enforce it in the instant case.

The judgment of the District Court is reversed and the case remanded with direction to enter judgment enjoining the proposed merger. It is so ordered.

Reversed and remanded with direction.

MR. JUSTICE WHITE took no part in the consideration or decision of this case.

MR. JUSTICE HARLAN, whom MR. JUSTICE STEWART joins, dissenting. [This opinion marshalls legislative history to demonstrate that Congress never intended to subject bank mergers to Section 7, and continues:] The result is, of course, that the Bank Merger Act is almost completely nullified; its enactment turns out to have been an exorbitant waste of congressional time and energy. As the present case illustrates, the Attorney General's report to the designated banking agency is no longer truly advisory, for if the agency's deci-

sion is not satisfactory a § 7 suit may be commenced immediately. The bank merger's legality will then be judged solely from its competitive aspects, unencumbered by any considerations peculiar to banking. And if such a suit were deemed to lie after a bank merger has been consummated, there would then be introduced into this field, for the first time to any significant extent, the threat of divestiture of assets and all the complexities and disruption attendant upon the use of that sanction. The only vestige of the Bank Merger Act which remains is that the banking agencies will have an initial veto.
. . . .

[The memorandum opinion of JUSTICE GOLDBERG is omitted.]

NOTES AND QUERIES

(1) *Regulation of Bank Mergers and Acquisitions.* Bank mergers and acquisitions continue to be subject to regulatory as well as antitrust scrutiny.[22] The Bank Merger Act of 1966 [23] requires bank mergers to be approved in advance by the responsible banking agency, i.e., the Federal Deposit Insurance Corporation, the Federal Reserve Board, or the Comptroller of the Currency. Each agency is required to obtain reports "on the competitive factors involved" from the Attorney General and the other two agencies. Standards for agency action are set forth in subsection (5) as follows:

(5) The responsible agency shall not approve—

(A) any proposed merger transaction which would result in a monopoly, or which would be in furtherance of any combination or conspiracy to monopolize or to attempt to monopolize the business of banking in any part of the United States, or

(B) any other proposed merger transaction whose effect in any section of the country may be substantially to lessen competition, or to tend to create a monopoly, or which in any other manner would be in restraint of trade, unless it finds that the anticompetitive effects of the proposed transaction are clearly outweighed in the public interest by the probable effect of the transaction in meeting the convenience and needs of the community to be served.

In every case, the responsible agency shall take into consideration the financial and managerial resources and future prospects of the existing and proposed institutions, and the convenience and needs of the community to be served.

Even if the responsible banking agency approves a merger, the United States may still charge a violation of Section 7 of the Clayton Act. Such a suit must be brought within thirty days of approval; filing the suit automatically stays the merger. The proponents of the merger may show in defense that any anticompetitive effects are "clearly outweighed" by the "convenience and needs of the community." [24] The Bank Merger Act instructs the antitrust court, however, to review such issues "de novo." Even though the

22. Mergers and acquisitions solely involving State banks are governed by state law. Most states require the approval of a regulatory supervisor for such transactions, although standards for approval are generally either non-existent or vague. See Scott, The Patchwork Quilt: State and Federal Roles in Bank Regulation, 32 Stan.L.Rev. 687 (1980).

23. 12 U.S.C.A. § 1828(c).

24. See United States v. First City National Bank of Houston, 386 U.S. 361, 87 S.Ct. 1088, 18 L.Ed.2d 151 (1967) (citing legislative history indicating that de-

responsible banking agency may have previously made a finding as to convenience and needs when approving the merger, the court is to make its own determination, not giving " 'any special weight to the determination of the bank supervisory agency on this issue.' " [25] (This is an unusual way to treat a decision of a regulatory agency, which is normally upheld if supported by substantial evidence and not an abuse of discretion.) Bank mergers not challenged within thirty days remain subject to potential antitrust liability only under Section 2 of the Sherman Act. Acquisitions by bank holding companies are subject to the same standards, by virtue of the Bank Holding Company Act.[26]

In exercising their approval authority under the Bank Merger Act and the Bank Holding Company Act, the federal banking agencies have often used informal methods to control mergers (e.g. letters of agreement by the parties to a proposed merger, with agency approval conditioned on the promises being fulfilled over time).[27] The ultimate decision of an agency to approve or deny an application under these Acts seems to depend greatly on the agency's analysis of the likely position of the Justice Department in the particular case.[28] Estimation of the likelihood that the Justice Department will challenge a proposed merger is important, in part, because the mere filing of suit by the Antitrust Division may lead to abandonment of a proposed merger.[29] Thus, these agencies have paid close attention to the concentration ratios for horizontal mergers set out in the Antitrust Division's Merger Guidelines (see p. 249, infra), and have even followed the Division's more controversial "potential competition" theories where the merging banks are not in direct competition.[30]

(2) *Future Shock in the Banking Industry.* The banking industry described in *Philadelphia National Bank* was a highly segmented one. Legislative policy, both state and federal, has been to confine the geographic and product markets in which banks can compete. In most states, banks could not operate on a state-wide basis; interstate banking was not permitted at all.[31] "Thrift" institutions (e.g., savings and loan associations, mutual savings banks) and commercial banks were given different powers in terms of, e.g., offering checking accounts (an important point in *Philadelphia National Bank*), making commercial loans, or paying interest on time deposits (the

---

fendant banks bear burden of proving this defense by a preponderance of the evidence). For discussion of the scope of this defense, see United States v. Third National Bank in Nashville, 390 U.S. 171, 88 S.Ct. 882, 19 L.Ed.2d 1015 (1968) (banks failed to carry defense); Golden, Preparing the Convenience and Needs Defense Under the Bank Merger Act of 1966, 96 Banking L.J. 100 (1979).

25. United States v. First National Bank of Houston, 386 U.S. at 368, 87 S.Ct. at 1093 (citing remarks of Rep. Patman).

26. See 12 U.S.C.A. § 1842(c).

27. See, e.g., United States v. First National State Bancorporation, 499 F.Supp. 793 (D.N.J.1980) (Comptroller's conditional approval requiring limited divestitures before consummation of merger eliminated otherwise anticompetitive effects; Comptroller's decision up-

held despite Justice Department challenge and opposition by the other two federal regulatory agencies).

28. See Austin, The Evolution of Commercial Bank Merger Antitrust Law, 36 Bus.Law 297, 364–65 (1981).

29. See id. at 321.

30. See, e.g., Mercantile Texas Corp. v. Board of Governors, 638 F.2d 1255 (5th Cir. 1981) (Federal Reserve Board invalidated proposed merger on theory that it would eliminate "actual potential competition"; court accepts theory, but remands for further findings regarding relevant economic data). Potential competition theories are explored infra, pp. 269 – 296.

31. See McFadden Act, 12 U.S.C.A. § 36; Bank Holding Company Act (Douglas Amendment), 12 U.S.C.A. § 1842(d).

thrifts being allowed to offer a higher rate of interest).[32] The thrifts specialized in home mortgages; commercial banks offered a wider array of services. Commercial banks were forbidden from straying beyond banking services, and bank holding companies were forbidden from acquiring non-bank related corporations.[33]

This structure is now crumbling. Non-bank competitors are offering packages of financial services more attractive than bank offerings (e.g., a combined brokerage and money-market fund with check-writing and credit card privileges).[34] Inflation (and consequent high interest rates), plus competitive pressures, have forced the thrifts to pay more for funds than they are earning on low-interest home mortgages given in earlier years; this has placed many S & L's in financial jeopardy.[35] Geographical expansion is being aided both by computer technology and by novel regulatory interpretations of banking statutes.[36] The "deregulation" movement, which has gained ground in other industries, has surfaced as well in banking. State legislatures have begun to relax their branching laws.[37] On the federal level, Congress has enacted the Depository Institutions Deregulation and Monetary Control Act of 1980 (DIDA),[38] which gradually frees from control the allowable interest rates of all depository institutions, ends the checking account monopoly of commercial banks by enabling all depository institutions to offer interest-bearing demand deposit accounts ("NOW accounts"), and permits thrifts to increase the types of services they provide (e.g., credit cards, consumer loans).

These developments will bring formerly sheltered financial institutions into a new environment, posing new antitrust and policy problems. In the least there may be an impact on the definition of product and geographic

32. For pre-1980 provisions, see 12 U.S.C.A. § 1832 (checking accounts); 12 U.S.C.A. § 1464(c) (loan authority); 12 CFR §§ 217.7 (commercial bank interest rates), 526.3 (savings and loan interest rates).

33. See 12 U.S.C.A. § 1841(a). The Bank Holding Company Act of 1956, 12 U.S.C.A. §§ 1841–49, did not originally cover diversification by holding companies owning only one bank. This "loophole" was closed by amendment in 1970.

34. See "Bankers Getting Increasingly Upset About Unregulated Status of Rivals," Wall St.J., Oct. 5, 1981 (discussing "bank-type" services offered by non-bank companies, such as American Express); "Commercial Bankers Gird For New Challenge As Sears Readies Notes Sale to Public," Wall St.J., Nov. 11, 1980, p. 23 (Sears' plan to market two-to-eight-year maturity notes directly to public, in competition with certificates of deposit offered by banks and savings and loans).

35. See "Thrift Industry Regulators Cite Peril," N.Y.Times July 15, 1981, p. D1 (80% of country's S & L's experiencing operating losses; one-third "not viable" and may not survive).

36. See "Banks Likely to Widen Reach By Using Automatic Tellers," Wall St.J., Sept. 4, 1981, p. 21 (predicting

growth of "cash dispensing networks" allowing bank-card holders to make withdrawals from out of state banks); Letter from Federal Reserve Board to R. S. Miller, Jr., May 28, 1981 (formation by Chrysler Corp. of wholly-owned subsidiary, Automotive Financial Services, Inc., not covered by restrictions under Bank Holding Company Act; Automotive Services, since it would not make commercial loans, was not a "bank" even though it accepted demand deposits from Chrysler). [1981–1982 Transfer Binder] Fed.Banking Law Rep. (CCH) ¶ 98,770.

37. See Lovett and Devins, Multiple Office Banking and Market Extension Mergers, 57 N.C.L.R. 261, 263, 281–82 (1979). Pennsylvania loosened its restrictions on statewide banking in 1982; Mellon National of Pittsburgh, Pennsylvania's largest bank and the nation's fifteenth largest, subsequently agreed to acquire Girard. See Wall St.J., Aug. 3, 1982, p. 5.

38. 12 U.S.C.A. §§ 3501–3509. See Scott, "The Uncertain Course of Bank Deregulation," Regulation, at 40 (May/June 1981); Weaver and O'Malley, Depository Institutions Deregulation and Monetary Control Act of 1980: An Overview, 98 Banking L.J. 100 (1981).

markets in Section 7 bank merger cases (recall the definitions chosen in *Philadelphia National Bank*).[39] On a broader level, the current financial plight of the thrifts presents a difficult "bail-out" situation. Prevention of bank failures has been a cornerstone of regulatory policy since the Depression; but direct financial aid to failing corporations (à la Chrysler) may not be considered an attractive alternative today. A likely solution is to allow rescue by merger, and the most likely merger partners are out-of-state banks interested in geographic expansion. Should these mergers be permitted,[40] thereby introducing limited interstate banking through the back door?

The ultimate impact of current developments may well be a restructuring of the industry into a more concentrated form, with fewer firms offering a wider range of services over a larger geographic area. The distinctions between types of banks may disappear; the separation between banks and other enterprises may disappear (with banks even owning manufacturing firms). Would such an industry provide better service to consumers at lower cost? Will financing sources be less diverse? Will banks obtain excessive political power, an outcome of long-standing concern in the United States? [41]

UNITED STATES v. GENERAL DYNAMICS CORP.

Supreme Court of the United States, 1974.
415 U.S. 486, 94 S.Ct. 1186, 39 L.Ed.2d 530.

MR. JUSTICE STEWART delivered the opinion of the Court.

On September 22, 1967, the Government commenced this suit in the United States District Court for the Northern District of Illinois, challenging as violative of § 7 of the Clayton Act, 15 U.S.C. § 18, the acquisition of the stock of United Electric Coal Companies by Material Service Corp. and its successor, General Dynamics Corp. After lengthy discovery proceedings, a trial was held from March 30 to April 22, 1970, and on April 13, 1972, the District Court issued an opinion and judgment finding no violation of the Clayton Act. 341

---

39. Compare United States v. First National State Bancorporation, 499 F.Supp. 793 (D.N.J.1980) (although DIDA authorizes "thrifts" to engage in activities once reserved for commercial banks, thrifts did not yet utilize their resources to compete significantly for commercial customers in New Jersey, and therefore commercial banking was relevant line of commerce) with United States v. Crocker-Anglo National Bank, 277 F.Supp. 133, 157 (N.D.Cal.1967) (relevant product market is not only commercial banking, but includes "all institutions which compete either for the savings or investment dollar or for the extension of credit . . . .").

40. See "Citicorp Wins Bank Board Nod to Acquire S & L," Wall St.J., Aug. 17, 1982, p. 3 (first interstate acquisition of savings and loan by a bank holding company); "U. S. Clears California Federal's Merger with 4 Ailing S & Ls in Georgia and Florida," Wall St.J., Feb. 8, 1982, p. 26 (sixth interstate savings and loan merger approved by Federal Home Loan Bank Board over previous eleven months); "Bill to Aid Sick S & L's Could Eventually Lead to Interstate Banking," Wall St.J., May 21, 1981, p. 1 (FSLIC proposed bill to allow banks to enter out-of-state markets by taking over failing thrifts).

41. Compare Lovett and Devins, supra note 37 (high concentration in banking would lead to increased costs to consumers and decreased diversity of sources for financing; resulting "close-knit" banking establishments could develop "disproportionate political influence") with Carstensen, Regulating Banking in the Public Interest—The Case for an Open Approach, 57 Tex.L.Rev. 1085 (1979) (maximization of competition in banking will result in reasonable prices and insure customers of as full a choice of banks and banking services as economically possible; the right of bankers to freely engage in business is part of the fundamental American value of freedom of choice). See generally Brandeis, Other People's Money (1913).

F.Supp. 534. The Government appealed directly to this Court pursuant to the Expediting Act, 15 U.S.C. § 29, and we noted probable jurisdiction.

I

At the time of the acquisition involved here, Material Service Corp. was a large midwest producer and supplier of building materials, concrete, limestone, and coal. All of its coal production was from deep-shaft mines operated by it or its affiliate, appellee Freeman Coal Mining Corp., and production from these operations amounted to 6.9 million tons of coal in 1959 and 8.4 million tons in 1967. In 1954, Material Service began to acquire the stock of United Electric Coal Companies. United Electric at all relevant times operated only strip or open pit mines in Illinois and Kentucky; at the time of trial in 1970 a number of its mines had closed and its operations had been reduced to four mines in Illinois and none in Kentucky. In 1959, it produced 3.6 million tons of coal, and by 1967, it had increased this output to 5.7 million tons. Material Service's purchase of United Electric stock continued until 1959. At this point Material's holdings amounted to more than 34% of United Electric's outstanding shares and—all parties are now agreed on this point—Material had effective control of United Electric. The president of Freeman was elected chairman of United Electric's Executive Committee, and other changes in the corporate structure of United Electric were made at the behest of Material Service.

Some months after this takeover, Material Service was itself acquired by the appellee General Dynamics Corp. General Dynamics is a large diversified corporation, much of its revenues coming from sales of aircraft, communications, and marine products to government agencies. The trial court found that its purchase of Material Service was part of a broad diversification program aimed at expanding General Dynamics into commercial, nondefense business. As a result of the purchase of Material Service, and through it, of Freeman and United Electric, General Dynamics became the Nation's fifth largest commercial coal producer. During the early 1960's General Dynamics increased its equity in United Electric by direct purchases of United Electric stock, and by 1966 it held or controlled 66.15% of United Electric's outstanding shares. In September 1966 the Board of Directors of General Dynamics authorized a tender offer to holders of the remaining United Electric stock. This offer was successful, and United Electric shortly thereafter became a wholly-owned subsidiary of General Dynamics.

The thrust of the Government's complaint was that the acquisition of United Electric by Freeman and Material Service in 1959 violated § 7 of the Clayton Act because the takeover substantially lessened competition in the production and sale of coal in either or both of two geographical markets. It contended that a relevant "section of the country" within the meaning of § 7 was, alternatively, the State of Illinois or the Eastern Interior Coal Province Sales Area, the latter being one of four major coal distribution areas recognized by the coal industry and comprising Illinois and Indiana, and parts of Kentucky, Tennessee, Iowa, Minnesota, Wisconsin, and Missouri.

. . .

[T]he District Court found that the evidence did not support the Government's contention that the 1959 acquisition of United Electric substantially lessened competition in any product or geographic market. This conclusion was based on four determinations made in the court's opinion, 341 F.Supp., at 558–559. First, the court noted that while the number of coal producers in the Eastern Interior Coal province declined from 144 to 39 during the period of 1957–1967, this reduction "occurred not because small producers have been acquired by others, but as the inevitable result of the change in the nature of demand for coal." . . . Second, the court noted that United Electric and Freeman were "predominantly complementary in nature" since "United Electric is a strip mining company with no experience in deep mining nor likelihood of acquiring it [and] Freeman is a deep mining company with no experience or expertise in strip mining." Ibid. Third, the court found that if Commonwealth Edison, a large investor-owned public utility, were excluded, "none of the sales by United Electric in the period 1965 to 1967, the years chosen by the Government for analysis, would have or could have been competitive with Freeman, had the two companies been independent," because of relative distances from potential consumers and the resultant impact on relative competitive position. Ibid. Finally, the court found that United Electric's coal reserves were so low that its potential to compete with other coal producers in the future was far weaker than the aggregate production statistics relied on by the Government might otherwise have indicated. In particular, the court found that virtually all of United Electric's proven coal reserves were either depleted or already committed by long-term contracts with large customers, and that United Electric's power to affect the price of coal was thus severely limited and steadily diminishing. On the basis of these considerations, the court concluded: "Under these circumstances, continuation of the affiliation between United Electric and Freeman is not adverse to competition, nor would divestiture benefit competition even were this court to accept the Government's unrealistic product and geographic market definitions." Id., at 560.

II

The Government sought to prove a violation of § 7 of the Clayton Act principally through statistics showing that within certain geographic markets the coal industry was concentrated among a small number of large producers; that this concentration was increasing; and that the acquisition of United Electric would materially enlarge the market share of the acquiring company and thereby contribute to the trend toward concentration.

The concentration of the coal market in Illinois and, alternatively, in the Eastern Interior Coal Province was demonstrated by a table of the shares of the largest two, four, and 10 coal producing firms in each of these areas and for both 1957 and 1967 that revealed the following:

	Eastern Interior Coal Province		Illinois	
	1957	1967	1957	1967
Top 2 firms	29.6	48.6	97.8	52.9
Top 4 firms	43.0	62.9	54.5	75.2
Top 10 firms	65.5	91.4	84.0	98.0

These statistics, the Government argued, showed not only that the coal industry was concentrated among a small number of leading producers, but that the trend had been toward increasing concentration.[42] Furthermore, the undisputed fact that the number of coal-producing firms in Illinois decreased almost 73% during the period of 1957 to 1967 from 144 to 39 was claimed to be indicative of the same trend. The acquisition of United Electric by Freeman resulted in increased concentration of coal sales among the leading producers in the areas chosen by the Government, as shown by the following table: [43]

	1959			1967		
	Share of top 2 but for merger	Share of top 2 given merger	Percent Increase	Share of top 2 but for merger	Share of top 2 given merger	Percent Increase
Province	33.1	37.9	14.5	45.0	48.6	8.0
Illinois	36.6	44.3	22.4	44.0	52.9	20.2

42. [Court's footnote 6.] The figures demonstrating the degree of concentration in the two coal markets chosen by the Government were roughly comparable to those in United States v. Von's Grocery Co., 384 U.S. 270, 86 S.Ct. 1478, 16 L.Ed.2d 555, where the top four firms in the market controlled 24.4% of the sales, the top eight 40.9%, and the top 12 48.8%. See, id., at 281, 86 S.Ct., at 1484 (White, J., concurring). See also United States v. Pabst Brewing Co., 384 U.S. 546, 551, 86 S.Ct. 1665, 1668, 16 L.Ed.2d 765, where the top four producers of beer in Wisconsin were found to control 47.74% of the market, and the top 10 in the Nation and the local three-state area to control 45.06% and 58.93% respectively. The statistics in the present case appear to represent a less advanced state of concentration than those involved in United States v. Aluminum Co. of America, 377 U.S. 271, 279, 84 S.Ct. 1283, 1288, 12 L.Ed.2d 314, where the two largest firms held 50% of the market, and the top five and the top nine controlled, respectively, 76% and 95.7%; and in United States v. Philadelphia National Bank, 374 U.S. 321, 363, 83 S.Ct. 1715, 1741, 10 L.Ed.2d 915, where the two largest banks controlled 44% of the pre-merger market.

43. [Court's footnote 7.] The percentage increase in concentration asserted here was thus analogous to that found in Von's Grocery, supra, where the concentration among the top four, eight, and 12 firms was increased, respectively, by 18.0%, 7.6%, and 2.5% as a result of the merger invalidated there. In Philadelphia Bank, supra, the 34% increase in concentration in the two largest firms from 44% to 59% was found to be clearly significant, 374 U.S., at 365, 83 S.Ct., at 1742.

Finally, the Government's statistics indicated that the acquisition increased the share of the merged company in the Illinois and Eastern Interior Coal Province coal markets by significant degrees: [44]

	Province		Illinois	
	Rank	Share (percent)	Rank	Share (percent)
1959				
Freeman...............	2	7.6	2	15.1
United Electric	6	4.8	5	8.1
Combined..............	2	12.4	1	23.2
1967				
Freeman...............	5	6.5	2	12.9
United Electric	9	4.4	6	8.9
Combined..............	2	10.9	2	21.8

In prior decisions involving horizontal mergers between competitors, this Court has found prima facie violations of § 7 of the Clayton Act from aggregate statistics of the sort relied on by the United States in this case. . . .

The effect of adopting this approach to a determination of a "substantial" lessening of competition is to allow the Government to rest its case on a showing of even small increases of market share or market concentration in those industries or markets where concentration is already great or has been recently increasing, since "if concentration is already great, the importance of preventing even slight increases in concentration and so preserving the possibility of eventual deconcentration is correspondingly great."

While the statistical showing proffered by the Government in this case, the accuracy of which was not discredited by the District Court or contested by the appellees, would under this approach have sufficed to support a finding of "undue concentration" in the absence of other considerations, the question before us is whether the District Court was justified in finding that other pertinent factors affecting the coal industry and the business of the appellees mandated a conclusion that no substantial lessening of competition occurred or was threatened by the acquisition of United Electric. We are satisfied that the court's ultimate finding was not in error.

44. [Court's footnote 8.] The 1959 Illinois figure of 23.2% was asserted by the Government to be comparable to the 23.94% share of the Wisconsin beer market found to be significant in Pabst, supra, and the 25% share controlled by the merged company in United States v. Continental Can Co., 378 U.S. 441, 461, 84 S.Ct. 1738, 1749, 12 L.Ed.2d 953. The Province figure of 12.4% was compared with the shares held by the merged companies in Von's Grocery (7.5%), and in the Pabst national (4.49%) and three-state (11.32%) markets.

In Brown Shoe v. United States, supra, we cautioned that statistics concerning market share and concentration, while of great significance, were not conclusive indicators of anticompetitive effects:

"Congress indicated plainly that a merger had to be functionally viewed, in the context of its particular industry." 370 U.S., at 321–322, 82 S.Ct., at 1522.

"Statistics reflecting the shares of the market controlled by the industry leaders and the parties to the merger are, of course, the primary index of market power; but only a further examination of the particular market—its structure, history and probable future—can provide the appropriate setting for judging the probable anticompetitive effect of the merger." Id., at 322 n. 38, 82 S.Ct., at 1522.

In this case, the District Court assessed the evidence of the "structure, history and probable future" of the coal industry, and on the basis of this assessment found no substantial probability of anticompetitive effects from the merger.

Much of the District Court's opinion was devoted to a description of the changes that have affected the coal industry since World War II. On the basis of more than three weeks of testimony and a voluminous record, the court discerned a number of clear and significant developments in the industry. First, it found that coal had become increasingly less able to compete with other sources of energy in many segments of the energy market. Following the War the industry entirely lost its largest single purchaser of coal—the railroads—and faced increasingly stiffer competition from oil and natural gas as sources of energy for industrial and residential uses. Because of these changes in consumption patterns, coal's share of the energy resources consumed in this country fell from 78.4% in 1920 to 21.4% in 1968. The court reviewed evidence attributing this decline not only to the changing relative economies of alternative fuels and to new distribution and consumption patterns, but also to more recent concern with the effect of coal use on the environment and consequent regulation of the extent and means of such coal consumption.

Second, the court found that to a growing extent since 1954, the electric utility industry has become the mainstay of coal consumption. While electric utilities consumed only 15.76% of the coal produced nationally in 1947, their share of total consumption increased every year thereafter, and in 1968 amounted to more than 59% of all the coal consumed throughout the Nation.[45]

Third, and most significantly, the court found that to an increasing degree, nearly all coal sold to utilities is transferred under long-term requirements contracts, under which coal producers promise to meet utilities' coal consumption requirements for a fixed period of time, and at predetermined prices. The court described the mutual

45. [Court's footnote 9.] In 1968, electric utilities accounted for 59.09% of United States coal consumption, coke plants 18.20%, cement mills 1.88%, other manufacturing (including steel and rolling mills) 17.70%, and retail and miscellaneous consumers 3.14%.

benefits accruing to both producers and consumers of coal from such long-term contracts in the following terms:

> "This major investment [in electric utility equipment] can be jeopardized by a disruption in the supply of coal. Utilities are, therefore, concerned with assuring the supply of coal to such a plant over its life. In addition, utilities desire to establish in advance, as closely as possible, what fuel costs will be for the life of the plant. For these reasons, utilities typically arrange long-term contracts for all or at least a major portion of the total fuel requirements for the life of the plant. . . .

> "The long-term contractual commitments are not only required from the consumer's standpoint, but are also necessary from the viewpoint of the coal supplier. Such commitments may require the development of new mining capacity. . . . Coal producers have been reluctant to invest in new mining capacity in the absence of long-term contractual commitments for the major portion of the mine's capacity. Furthermore, such long-term contractual commitments are often required before financing for the development of new capacity can be obtained by the producer." 341 F.Supp., at 543 (footnote omitted).

These developments in the patterns of coal distribution and consumption, the District Court found, have limited the amounts of coal immediately available for "spot" purchases on the open market, since "[t]he growing practice by coal producers of expanding mine capacity only to meet long-term contractual commitments and the gradual disappearance of the small truck mines has tended to limit the production capacity available for spot sales." Ibid.

Because of these fundamental changes in the structure of the market for coal, the District Court was justified in viewing the statistics relied on by the Government as insufficient to sustain its case. Evidence of past production does not, as a matter of logic, necessarily give a proper picture of a company's future ability to compete. In most situations, of course, the unstated assumption is that a company that has maintained a certain share of a market in the recent past will be in a position to do so in the immediate future. Thus, companies that have controlled sufficiently large shares of a concentrated market are barred from merger by § 7, not because of their past acts, but because their past performances imply an ability to continue to dominate with at least equal vigor. In markets involving groceries or beer, as in Von's Grocery, supra, and Pabst, supra, statistics involving annual sales naturally indicate the power of each company to compete in the future. Evidence of the amount of annual sales is relevant as a prediction of future competitive strength, since in most markets distribution systems and brand recognition are such significant factors that one may reasonably suppose that a company which has attracted a given number of sales will retain that competitive strength.

In the coal market, as analyzed by the District Court, however, statistical evidence of coal *production* was of considerably less significance. The bulk of the coal produced is delivered under long-term requirements contracts, and such sales thus do not represent the exercise of competitive power but rather the obligation to fulfill previously negotiated contracts at a previously fixed price. The focus of competition in a given time-frame is not on the disposition of coal already produced but on the procurement of new long-term supply contracts. In this situation, a company's past ability to produce is of limited significance, since it is in a position to offer for sale neither its past production nor the bulk of the coal it is presently capable of producing, which is typically already committed under a long-term supply contract. A more significant indicator of a company's power effectively to compete with other companies lies in the state of a company's uncommitted reserves of recoverable coal. A company with relatively large supplies of coal which are not already under contract to a consumer will have a more important influence upon competition in the contemporaneous negotiation of supply contracts than a firm with small reserves, even though the latter may presently produce a greater tonnage of coal. In a market where the availability and price for coal are set by long-term contracts rather than immediate or short-term purchases and sales, reserves rather than past production are the best measure of a company's ability to compete.

The testimony and exhibits in the District Court revealed that United Electric's coal reserve prospects were "unpromising." Id., 341 F.Supp. at 559. United's relative position of strength in reserves was considerably weaker than its past and current ability to produce. While United ranked fifth among Illinois coal producers in terms of annual production, it was 10th in reserve holdings, and controlled less than 1% of the reserves held by coal producers in Illinois, Indiana, and western Kentucky. Id., at 538. Many of the reserves held by United had already been depleted, at the time of trial, forcing the closing of some of United's midwest mines.[46] Even more significantly, the District Court found that of the 52,033,304 tons of currently mineable reserves in Illinois, Indiana, and Kentucky controlled by United, only four million tons had not already been committed under long-term contracts. United was found to be facing the future with relatively depleted resources at its disposal, and with the vast majority of those resources already committed under contracts allowing no further adjustment in price. In addition the District Court found that "United Electric has neither the possibility of acquiring more [reserves] nor the ability to develop deep coal reserves," and thus was not in a position to increase its reserves to replace those already depleted or committed. Id., at 560.

Viewed in terms of present and future reserve prospects—and thus in terms of probable future ability to compete—rather than in

46. [Court's footnote 10.] The District Court found that while United Electric held six mines operating in the midwest in 1948, it had opened only three new ones since then and four had closed because of exhaustion of reserves. The court found that the evidence showed that reserves in two other mines would soon be depleted, and the respondents inform us in their briefs that these events have already occurred.

terms of past production, the District Court held that United Electric was a far less significant factor in the coal market than the Government contended or the production statistics seemed to indicate. While the company had been and remained a "highly profitable" and efficient producer of relatively large amounts of coal, its current and future power to compete for subsequent long-term contracts was severely limited by its scarce uncommitted resources. Irrespective of the company's size when viewed as a producer, its weakness as a competitor was properly analyzed by the District Court and fully substantiated that court's conclusion that its acquisition by Material Service would not "substantially . . . lessen competition . . . ."

. . .

[The dissenting opinion of Justice Douglas, in which Justices Brennan, White, and Marshall joined, is omitted.]

NOTES AND QUERIES

(1) *Avoiding the Failing Company Defense.* In the old *International Shoe* case, decided before the 1950 Amendments to the Clayton Act (discussed supra p. 207), the Supreme Court took account of the fact that the acquired company was "in failing circumstances" with "resources so depleted and the prospect of rehabilitation so remote that it faced the grave probability of a business failure with resulting loss to its stockholders and injury to the communities where its plants were operated." 280 U.S. at 301–02. This gave rise to the "failing company defense." Congressional debate over the 1950 Amendments, as recognized in *Brown Shoe* (see p. 216, supra), indicated an intent to retain the defense in cases where the acquired firm will "no longer be a vital competitive factor in the market." [47]   In *Citizen Publishing Co. v. United States*, 394 U.S. 131, 89 S.Ct. 927, 22 L.Ed.2d 148 (1969), a case involving a joint newspaper operating agreement between the Star and the allegedly failing Citizen, the Court dealt with the defense as follows:

> There is no indication that the owners of the Citizen were contemplating a liquidation. They never sought to sell the Citizen and there is no evidence that the joint operating agreement was the last straw at which the Citizen grasped.
>
> The failing company doctrine plainly cannot be applied in a merger or in any other case unless it is established that the company that acquires the failing company or brings it under dominion is the only available purchaser. For if another person or group could be interested, a unit in the competitive system would be preserved and not lost to monopoly power. So even if we assume, *arguendo*, that in 1940 the then owners of the Citizen could not long keep the enterprise afloat, no effort was made to sell the Citizen; its properties and franchise were not put in the hands of a broker; and the record is silent on what the market, if any, for the Citizen might have been.
>
> Moreover, we know from the broad experience of the business community since 1930, the year when the *International Shoe* case was decided,

47. Should Congress have retained this defense? See Posner, Antitrust Law: An Economic Perspective 20–22 (1976), arguing that Congress retained the defense out of concern for the "social costs of business failure" and that the rescue of a failing enterprise could at times be anticompetitive.

that companies reorganized through receivership, or through Chapter X or Chapter XI of the Bankruptcy Act often emerged as strong competitive companies. The prospects of reorganization of the Citizen in 1940 would have had to be dim or nonexistent to make the failing company doctrine applicable to this case.

The burden of proving that the conditions of the failing company doctrine have been satisfied is on those who seek refuge under it. That burden has not been satisfied in this case.

We confine the failing company doctrine to its present narrow scope.[48]

Would the parties in *General Dynamics* have been able to successfully assert the failing company defense, as articulated in *Citizen Publishing*? Has the majority reinvigorated the defense in another guise, making the acquired firm's financial weakness a factor to be considered in rebutting the Government's *prima facie* statistical case (turning Section 7 toward a "rule of reason" approach similar to *International Shoe*), even if it is not a total defense?[49] How can a court accurately predict how viable a competitor the acquired firm will be in the (near? distant?) future? Does the Clayton Act require accurate prediction?

(2) *A Chrysler-Ford Merger?* As reported in the Wall Street Journal on April 13, 1981, Chrysler has made a secret merger bid to Ford, which Ford has rejected: "A confidential 'white paper' that Chrysler presented Ford outlines a detailed plan under which Ford would absorb Chrysler, take over its dealer network and some of its products, cast off some Chrysler operations, and drop some of Ford's currently planned products." A later article suggests that Ford's rejection should be viewed as a "scene in an unfolding drama, not as the closing curtain." The authors of this article suggest that combining the companies could: produce a more efficient firm, with "rationalized" operations to continue each firm's strong models; provide Ford with new capital arising from Chrysler's tax losses; force the UAW to accept lower wages for its Ford employees in line with Chrysler's; allow Chrysler to shift a large part of its unfunded pension liabilities to the federal government; and generate cash through the sale of some Chrysler assets which would repay the government part of the money already loaned Chrysler. The authors conclude that the government would stand to lose a great deal more in a Chrysler liquidation and "fire sale" and that consequently the government should now intervene and encourage the deal. See

---

48. See also United States v. Third National Bank, 390 U.S. 171, 88 S.Ct. 882, 19 L.Ed.2d 1015 (1968); United States v. Greater Buffalo Press, Inc., 402 U.S. 549, 91 S.Ct. 1692, 29 L.Ed.2d 170 (1971); United States Steel Corp. v. FTC, 426 F.2d 592 (6th Cir. 1970) (possible failure of acquired company less anti-competitive than its continued existence in a giant integration; distribution of its business, in case of failure, among surviving independents is pro-competitive).

49. See Federal Trade Commission v. National Tea Co., 603 F.2d 694 (8th Cir. 1979) (under General Dynamics "other factors may discount" significance of market share; National's poor performance and imminent departure from the area shows present market share to be inaccurate reflection of future strength);

United States v. International Harvester Co., 564 F.2d 769 (7th Cir. 1977) (acquired firm's financial position properly considered for showing "weakness as a competitor"; relevant both to rebut inferences based on past market shares, and to supplement market shares in order to assess more accurately the probable anticompetitive effect). For an attempt by the F.T.C. to read the "General Dynamics defense" narrowly, see Kaiser Aluminum & Chemical Corp., 93 F.T.C. 764, 848 (1979), vacated and remanded, 652 F.2d 1324 (7th Cir. 1981) (rejecting F.T.C.'s narrow reading of General Dynamics, but noting that although the "financial weakness" of the acquired firm may be a relevant factor, it "certainly cannot be the primary justification of a merger in resistance to a § 7 proceeding").

Freeman and Bachrach, "The Case for Merging Chrysler with Ford," Wall St. Journal, May 11, 1981, p. 27.

Would the merger be lawful under Section 7? Would the failing company defense be applicable here? The *"General Dynamics"* defense? What should be the effect of Executive Branch facilitation? [50] As a policy matter is Section 7's approach to competition issues even relevant, given the complex position of modern industrial firms such as Chrysler and Ford?

(3) *Department of Justice Merger Guidelines.* The Department of Justice first issued merger Guidelines in 1968.[51] The Guidelines expressed the Department's interpretation of the case law to that time, reviewed the considerations it regarded as relevant to analyzing the legality of a merger, and described typical situations in which a merger or acquisition would "ordinarily" be challenged. These Guidelines were revised by the Department in 1982 in response to the perception that the Guidelines no longer accurately reflected current merger law and in response to the desire of the Reagan administration to make known its views on merger policy so as to "reduce the uncertainty" associated with enforcement in this area.[52]

The theme of the new Guidelines is that mergers should not be allowed which "create or enhance 'market power' ", because the use of market power to maintain prices above competitive levels transfers wealth from buyers to sellers and misallocates resources. The Guidelines state, however, that although mergers "sometimes" harm competition, mergers "generally play an important role in a free enterprise economy." Thus, the Department "seeks to avoid unnecessary interference with that larger universe of mergers that are either competitively beneficial or neutral."

The Guidelines concentrate mainly on horizontal mergers, reflecting the Administration's view that all other types of mergers are far less likely to have anticompetitive effects. A novel part of the Department's approach to horizontal mergers is its use of the Herfindahl-Hirschman Index ("HHI"; see pp. 67 – 68, supra) rather than the usual market share-concentration ratios for determining the extent of concentration in a market. The Department remains critically interested in both the extent of concentration and the increase in concentration post-merger.

The Guidelines set out different rules with regard to three levels of concentration. If the post-merger HHI is below 1000, the Department is unlikely to challenge the merger. If the post-merger HHI is above 1800, the Department is likely to challenge any merger which increases the HHI 100 points or more. (The Department indicates that an HHI of 1000 and 1800 correspond roughly to a four-firm concentration ratio of 50% and 70%; the increase in the HHI due to a merger can be quickly figured out by doubling the product of the merging firms' market shares.) The Department's view of mergers which produce an HHI between 1000 and 1800 varies depending on the increase in the HHI, and takes account of ease of entry into the market and "other factors." These "other factors" are viewed as tie-breakers; they relate to the "ease and profitability of collusion," and include the homogeneity of the product, the stability of market shares in the past, the extent to which detailed information about specific transactions or prices is readily available to competitors, and the numbers of buyers in the market.

50. Compare United States v. Socony-Vacuum Oil Co., p. 359 infra.

51. The 1968 merger Guidelines are reproduced in CCH Trade Reg.Rep. ¶ 4510. As to the Department's past occasional disregard of its Merger Guidelines, see criticism by Ralph Nader, ATRR No. 528, Aug. 31, 1971, p. A–5.

52. See Trade Reg.Rep. (CCH) ¶ 4500. The 1982 Guidelines are exhaustively critiqued in Symposium, 71 Cal.L.Rev. 281 (1983).

The Guidelines also make a significant effort to provide tests for determining the relevant product and geographic markets. The Guidelines define a market as

> a group of products and an associated geographic area such that (in the absence of new entry) a hypothetical, unregulated firm that made all the sales of those products in that area would increase its profits through a small but significant and non-transitory increase in price (above prevailing or likely future levels.)

To make this definition operational, the Department will begin with a "provisional" market of those products the merging firms' customers view as "good substitutes at prevailing prices," and will then hypothesize a price increase of 5% and ask how many buyers would likely shift to other products within one year. A similar process will be employed to determine the geographic market, beginning with the shipment patterns of the firm and its "closest competitors" and expanding outward to include sellers who could sell the product to customers within the provisional market if a hypothetical price increase of 5% were maintained for one year. These markets would stop "expanding" when the hypothetical price rise became profitable (i.e., a market would be defined in which the exercise of market power could occur). The Department also indicates that it will normally include in the market the output from facilities which "could easily and economically" be altered to produce and sell the relevant product within six months in response to a "small but significant" price increase (supply-side substitutability); durable recycled and reconditioned products; and capacity devoted to production for consumption within the firm. Finally, with respect to expanding geographic markets beyond the United States, the Department indicates it will be "somewhat more cautious" in engaging in such expansion and in assessing the likely supply response of specific foreign firms.[53]

Queries. Consider the Guidelines in light of the avowed purpose to make merger enforcement predictable. Do the Guidelines pose questions which are not readily answerable with current data?[54] Do the Guidelines adequately respond to the changes in the interpretation of Section 7 from *Philadelphia National Bank* to *General Dynamics*? Note that the Guidelines apply only to Justice Department enforcement policy;[55] neither private parties nor the courts are bound. Note also that the Guidelines still retain a heavy emphasis on market structure and economic theory. They do not

53. Compare Landes & Posner, Market Power In Antitrust Cases, 94 Harv.L. Rev. 937 (1981) (once foreign firm makes some sales within United States, entire capacity should be included in defining the market). Contra, Brennan, Mistaken Elasticities and Misleading Rules, 95 Harv.L.Rev. 1849 (1982).

54. The Antitrust Division's chief economist admitted, shortly after the Guidelines were issued, that the economic analysis envisioned by the Guidelines had been accomplished only three times by the Division. See 42 ATRR 1302 (1982). In the Justice Department's first attempt to use the 5% price-rise test to expand the geographic market beyond its provisional bounds, the district court found that the Government's survey questionnaire was not reliable enough to carry the Government's burden of proof

that the banking customers involved would have switched to a bank in another town; the court did not address the question whether adequate proof would meet the legal test for defining geographic market. See U. S. v. Virginia National Bankshares, Inc., 1982–2 Trade Cas. ¶ 64,871 (W.D.Va.1982) (oral opinion); Wertheimer, "DOJ Tries Out Its 5-Percent Geographic Market Test," Legal Times of Wash., Aug. 30, 1982, p. 17.

55. Shortly after the issuance of the Guidelines, the F.T.C. issued its own statement of enforcement policy, giving "considerable weight" to the Department's views but stressing the need to go beyond the "snapshot" of current market shares so as to get a fuller picture of market power. See 42 ATRR No. 1069 (1982).

show an abandonment of hostility to mergers. Rather, they appear to signal a "magnifying glass" approach—they look very closely at mergers, but only those mergers which fall in a very narrow range.

C. VERTICAL INTEGRATION

BROWN SHOE CO. v. UNITED STATES

Supreme Court of the United States, 1962.
370 U.S. 294, 82 S.Ct. 1502, 8 L.Ed.2d 510.

MR. CHIEF JUSTICE WARREN delivered the opinion of the Court.

I.

This suit was initiated in November 1955 when the Government filed a civil action in the United States District Court for the Eastern District of Missouri alleging that a contemplated merger between the G. R. Kinney Company, Inc. (Kinney), and the Brown Shoe Company, Inc. (Brown), through an exchange of Kinney for Brown stock, would violate § 7 of the Clayton Act. The complaint sought injunctive relief under § 15 of the Clayton Act, to restrain consummation of the merger.

A motion by the Government for a preliminary injunction *pendente lite* was denied, and the companies were permitted to merge provided, however, that their businesses be operated separately and that their assets be kept separately identifiable. The merger was then effected on May 1, 1956.

In the District Court, the Government contended that the effect of the merger of Brown—the third largest seller of shoes by dollar volume in the United States, a leading manufacturer of men's, women's, and children's shoes, and a retailer with over 1,230 owned, operated or controlled retail outlets—and Kinney—the eighth largest company, by dollar volume, among those primarily engaged in selling shoes, itself a large manufacturer of shoes, and a retailer with over 350 retail outlets—"may be substantially to lessen competition or to tend to create a monopoly" by eliminating actual or potential competition in the production of shoes for the national wholesale shoe market and in the sale of shoes at retail in the Nation, by foreclosing competition from "a market represented by Kinney's retail outlets whose annual sales exceed $42,000,000," and by enhancing Brown's competitive advantage over other producers, distributors and sellers of shoes. The Government argued that the "line of commerce" affected by this merger is "footwear," or alternatively, that the "line[s]" are "men's," "women's," and "children's" shoes, separately considered, and that the "section of the country," within which the anticompetitive effect of the merger is to be judged, is the Nation as a whole, or alternatively, each separate city or city and its immediate surrounding area in which the parties sell shoes at retail.

In the District Court, Brown contended that the merger would be shown not to endanger competition if the "line[s] of commerce" and the "section[s] of the country" were properly determined. Brown urged that not only were the age and sex of the intended customers to be considered in determining the relevant line of commerce, but that differences in grade of material, quality of workmanship, price, and customer use of shoes resulted in establishing different lines of commerce. While agreeing with the Government that, with regard to manufacturing, the relevant geographic market for assessing the effect of the merger upon competition is the country as a whole, Brown contended that with regard to retailing, the market must vary with economic reality from the central business district of a large city to a "standard metropolitan area" for a smaller community. Brown further contended that, both at the manufacturing level and at the retail level, the shoe industry enjoyed healthy competition and that the vigor of this competition would not, in any event, be diminished by the proposed merger because Kinney manufactured less than 0.5% and retailed less than 2% of the Nation's shoes.

The District Court rejected the broadest contentions of both parties. The District Court found that "there is one group of classifications which is understood and recognized by the entire industry and the public—the classification into 'men's,' 'women's,' and 'children's' shoes separately and independently." On the other hand, "[t]o classify shoes as a whole could be unfair and unjust; to classify them further would be impractical, unwarranted and unrealistic."

Realizing that "the areas of effective competition for retailing purposes cannot be fixed with mathematical precision," the District Court found that "when determined by economic reality, for retailing, a 'section of the country' is a city of 10,000 or more population and its immediate and contiguous surrounding area, regardless of name designation, and in which a Kinney store and a Brown (operated, franchise, or plan) store are located."

The District Court rejected the Government's contention that the combining of the manufacturing facilities of Brown and Kinney would substantially lessen competition in the production of men's, women's, or children's shoes for the national wholesale market. However, the District Court did find that the likely foreclosure of other manufacturers from the market represented by Kinney's retail outlets may substantially lessen competition in the manufacturers' distribution of "men's," "women's" and "children's" shoes, considered separately, throughout the Nation. The District Court also found that the merger may substantially lessen competition in retailing alone in "men's," "women's," and "children's" shoes, considered separately, in every city of 10,000 or more population and its immediate surrounding area in which both a Kinney and a Brown store are located.

Brown's contentions here differ only slightly from those made before the District Court. In order fully to understand and appraise these assertions, it is necessary to set out in some detail the District Court's findings concerning the nature of the shoe industry and the place of Brown and Kinney within that industry.

The Industry

The District Court found that although domestic shoe production was scattered among a large number of manufacturers, a small number of large companies occupied a commanding position. Thus, while the 24 largest manufacturers produced about 35% of the Nation's shoes, the top 4—International, Endicott-Johnson, Brown (including Kinney) and General Shoe—alone produced approximately 23% of the Nation's shoes or 65% of the production of the top 24.

In 1955, domestic production of nonrubber shoes was 509.2 million pairs of which about 103.6 million pairs were men's shoes, about 271 million pairs were women's shoes, and about 134.6 million pairs were children's shoes. The District Court found that men's, women's, and children's shoes are normally produced in separate factories.

The public buys these shoes through about 70,000 retail outlets, only 22,000 of which, however, derive 50% or more of their gross receipts from the sale of shoes and are classified as "shoe stores" by the Census Bureau. These 22,000 shoe stores were found generally to sell (1) men's shoes only, (2) women's shoes only, (3) women's and children's shoes, or (4) men's, women's, and children's shoes.

The District Court found a "definite trend" among shoe manufacturers to acquire retail outlets. For example, International Shoe Company had no retail outlets in 1945, but by 1956 had acquired 130; General Shoe Company had only 80 retail outlets in 1945 but had 526 by 1956; Shoe Corporation of America, in the same period, increased its retail holdings from 301 to 842; Melville Shoe Company from 536 to 947; and Endicott-Johnson from 488 to 540. Brown, itself, with no retail outlets of its own prior to 1951, had acquired 845 such outlets by 1956. Moreover, between 1950 and 1956 nine independent shoe store chains, operating 1,114 retail shoe stores, were found to have become subsidiaries of these large firms and to have ceased their independent operations.

And once the manufacturers acquired retail outlets, the District Court found there was a "definite trend" for the parent-manufacturers to supply an ever increasing percentage of the retail outlets' needs, thereby foreclosing other manufacturers from effectively competing for the retail accounts. Manufacturer-dominated stores were found to be "drying up" the available outlets for independent producers.

Another "definite trend" found to exist in the shoe industry was a decrease in the number of plants manufacturing shoes. And there appears to have been a concomitant decrease in the number of firms manufacturing shoes. In 1947, there were 1,077 independent manufacturers of shoes but by 1954 their number had decreased about 10% to 970.

Brown Shoe

Brown Shoe was found not only to have been a participant, but also a moving factor, in these industry trends. Although Brown had experimented several times with operating its own retail outlets, by 1945 it had disposed of them all. However, in 1951, Brown again began to seek retail outlets by acquiring the Nation's largest operator of leased shoe departments, Wohl Shoe Company (Wohl), which operated 250 shoe departments in department stores throughout the United States. Between 1952 and 1955 Brown made a number of smaller acquisitions: Wetherby-Kayser Shoe Company (three retail stores), Barnes & Company (two stores), Reilly Shoe Company (two leased shoe departments), Richardson Shoe Store (one store), and Wohl Shoe Company of Dallas (not connected with Wohl) (leased shoe departments in Dallas). In 1954, Brown made another major acquisition: Regal Shoe Corporation which, at the time, operated one manufacturing plant producing men's shoes and 110 retail outlets.

The acquisition of these corporations was found to lead to increased sales by Brown to the acquired companies. Thus although prior to Brown's acquisition of Wohl in 1951, Wohl bought from Brown only 12.8% of its total purchases of shoes, it subsequently increased its purchases to 21.4% in 1952 and to 32.6% in 1955. Wetherby-Kayser's purchases from Brown increased from 10.4% before acquisition to over 50% after. Regal, which had previously sold no shoes to Wohl and shoes worth only $89,000 to Brown, in 1956 sold shoes worth $265,000 to Wohl and $744,000 to Brown.

During the same period of time, Brown also acquired the stock or assets of seven companies engaged solely in shoe manufacturing. As a result, in 1955, Brown was the fourth largest shoe manufacturer in the country producing about 25.6 million pairs of shoes or about 4% of the Nation's total footwear production.

Kinney

Kinney is principally engaged in operating the largest family-style shoe store chain in the United States. At the time of trial, Kinney was found to be operating over 400 such stores in more than 270 cities. These stores were found to make about 1.2% of all national retail shoe sales by dollar volume. Moreover, in 1955 the Kinney stores sold approximately 8 million pairs of nonrubber shoes or about 1.6% of the national pairage sales of such shoes. Of these sales, approximately 1.1 million pairs were of men's shoes or about 1% of the national pairage sales of men's shoes; approximately 4.2 million pairs were of women's shoes or about 1.5% of the national pairage sales of women's shoes; and approximately 2.7 million pairs were of children's shoes or about 2% of the national pairage sales of children's shoes.

In addition to this extensive retail activity, Kinney owned and operated four plants which manufactured men's, women's, and children's shoes and whose combined output was 0.5% of the national shoe production in 1955 making Kinney the twelfth largest shoe manufacturer in the United States.

Kinney stores were found to obtain about 20% of their shoes from Kinney's own manufacturing plants. At the time of the merger, Kinney bought no shoes from Brown; however, in line with Brown's conceded reasons for acquiring Kinney, Brown had, by 1957, become the largest outside supplier of Kinney's shoes, supplying 7.9% of all Kinney's needs.

It is in this setting that the merger was considered and held to violate § 7 of the Clayton Act. The District Court ordered Brown to divest itself completely of all stock, share capital, assets or other interests it held in Kinney, to operate Kinney to the greatest degree possible as an independent concern pending complete divestiture, to refrain thereafter from acquiring or having any interest in Kinney's business or assets, and to file with the court within 90 days a plan for carrying into effect the divestiture decreed. The District Court also stated it would retain jurisdiction over the cause to enable the parties to apply for such further relief as might be necessary to enforce and apply the judgment. Prior to its submission of a divestiture plan, Brown filed a notice of appeal in the District Court. It then filed a jurisdictional statement in this Court, seeking review of the judgment below as entered.

II. JURISDICTION

[The Court held that it had jurisdiction of the appeal; the judgment below was "final" inasmuch as it directed Brown to divest itself of Kinney, notwithstanding that it also ordered the parties to submit plans of divestiture for the subsequent approval of the District Court.]

III. LEGISLATIVE HISTORY

[The Court's analysis of the legislative history of § 7 of the Clayton Act and the Celler-Kefauver Amendment of § 7 in 1950 appears at p. 215, supra.]

IV. THE VERTICAL ASPECTS OF THE MERGER

Economic arrangements between companies standing in a supplier-customer relationship are characterized as "vertical." The primary vice of a vertical merger or other arrangement tying a customer to a supplier is that, by foreclosing the competitors of either party from a segment of the market otherwise open to them, the arrangement may act as a "clog on competition," which "deprive[s] . . . rivals of a fair opportunity to compete." Every extended vertical arrangement by its very nature, for at least a time, denies to competitors of the supplier the opportunity to compete for part or all of the trade of the customer-party to the vertical arrangement. However, the Clay-

ton Act does not render unlawful all such vertical arrangements, but
forbids only those whose effect "may be substantially to lessen competition or to tend to create a monopoly" "in any line of commerce in
any section of the country." Thus, as we have previously noted,

> "[d]etermination of the relevant market is a necessary predicate
> to a finding of a violation of the Clayton Act because the threaten-
> ed monopoly must be one which will substantially lessen competi-
> tion 'within the area of effective competition.' Substantiality can
> be determined only in terms of the market affected."

The "area of effective competition" must be determined by reference
to a product market (the "line of commerce") and a geographic market (the "section of the country").

The Product Market

The outer boundaries of a product market are determined by the
reasonable interchangeability of use or the cross-elasticity of demand
between the product itself and substitutes for it. However, within
this broad market, well-defined submarkets may exist which, in themselves, constitute product markets for antitrust purposes. The
boundaries of such a submarket may be determined by examining
such practical indicia as industry or public recognition of the submarket as a separate economic entity, the product's peculiar characteristics and uses, unique production facilities, distinct customers, distinct prices, sensitivity to price changes, and specialized vendors.
Because § 7 of the Clayton Act prohibits any merger which may substantially lessen competition "in *any* line of commerce" (emphasis
supplied), it is necessary to examine the effects of a merger in each
such economically significant submarket to determine if there is a
reasonable probability that the merger will substantially lessen competition. If such a probability is found to exist, the merger is proscribed.

Applying these considerations to the present case, we conclude
that the record supports the District Court's finding that the relevant
lines of commerce are men's, women's, and children's shoes. These
product lines are recognized by the public; each line is manufactured
in separate plants; each has characteristics peculiar to itself rendering it generally noncompetitive with the others; and each is, of
course, directed toward a distinct class of customers.

Appellant, however, contends that the District Court's definitions
fail to recognize sufficiently "price/quality" and "age/sex" distinctions in shoes. Brown argues that the predominantly medium-priced
shoes which it manufactures occupy a product market different from
the predominantly low-priced shoes which Kinney sells. But agreement with that argument would be equivalent to holding that medium-priced shoes do not compete with low-priced shoes. We think the
District Court properly found the facts to be otherwise. It would be
unrealistic to accept Brown's contention that, for example, men's

shoes selling below $8.99 are in a different product market from those selling above $9.00.

This is not to say, however, that "price/quality" differences, where they exist, are unimportant in analyzing a merger; they may be of importance in determining the likely effect of a merger. But the boundaries of the relevant market must be drawn with sufficient breadth to include the competing products of each of the merging companies and to recognize competition where, in fact, competition exists. Thus we agree with the District Court that in this case a further division of product lines based on "price/quality" differences would be "unrealistic."

Brown's contention that the District Court's product market definitions should have recognized further "age/sex" distinctions raises a different problem. Brown's sharpest criticism is directed at the District Court's finding that children's shoes constituted a single line of commerce. Brown argues, for example, that "a little boy does not wear a little girl's black patent leather pump" and that "[a] male baby cannot wear a growing boy's shoes." Thus Brown argues that "infants' and babies'" shoes, "misses' and children's" shoes and "youths' and boys'" shoes should each have been considered a separate line of commerce. Assuming, *arguendo*, that little boy's shoes, for example, do have sufficient peculiar characteristics to constitute one of the markets to be used in analyzing the effects of this merger, we do not think that in this case the District Court was required to employ finer "age/sex" distinctions than those recognized by its classifications of "men's," "women's," and "children's" shoes. Further division does not aid us in analyzing the effects of this merger. Brown manufactures about the same percentage of the nation's children's shoes (5.8%) as it does of the nation's youth's and boys' shoes (6.5%), of the nation's misses' and children's shoes (6.0%) and of the nation's infants' and babies' shoes (4.9%). Similarly, Kinney sells about the same percentage of the nation's children's shoes (2%) as it does of the nation's youth's and boy's shoes (3.1%), of the nation's misses', and children's shoes (1.9%), and of the nation's infants' and babies' shoes (1.5%). Appellant can point to no advantage it would enjoy were finer divisions than those chosen by the District Court employed. Brown manufactures significant, comparable quantities of virtually every type of nonrubber men's, women's, and children's shoes, and Kinney sells such quantities of virtually every type of men's, women's, and children's shoes. Thus, whether considered separately or together, the picture of this merger is the same. We, therefore, agree with the District Court's conclusion that in the setting of this case to subdivide the shoe market further on the basis of "age/sex" distinctions would be "impractical" and "unwarranted."

The Geographic Market

We agree with the parties and the District Court that insofar as the vertical aspect of this merger is concerned, the relevant geographic market is the entire Nation. The relationships of product value, bulk, weight and consumer demand enable manufacturers to distribute their shoes on a nation-wide basis, as Brown and Kinney, in fact, do. The anticompetitive effects of the merger are to be measured within this range of distribution.

The Probable Effect of the Merger

Once the area of effective competition affected by a vertical arrangement has been defined, an analysis must be made to determine if the effect of the arrangement "may be substantially to lessen competition or tend to create a monopoly" in this market.

Since the diminution of the vigor of competition which may stem from a vertical arrangement results primarily from a foreclosure of a share of the market otherwise open to competitors, an important consideration in determining whether the effect of a vertical arrangement "may be substantially to lessen competition, or to tend to create a monopoly" is the size of the share of the market foreclosed. However, this factor will seldom be determinative. If the share of the market foreclosed is so large that it approaches monopoly proportions, the Clayton Act will, of course, have been violated; but the arrangement will also have run afoul of the Sherman Act. And the legislative history of § 7 indicates clearly that the tests for measuring the legality of any particular economic arrangement under the Clayton Act are to be less stringent than those used in applying the Sherman Act. On the other hand, foreclosure of a *de minimis* share of the market will not tend "substantially to lessen competition."

Between these extremes, in cases such as the one before us, in which the foreclosure is neither of monopoly nor *de minimis* proportions, the percentage of the market foreclosed by the vertical arrangement cannot itself be decisive. In such cases, it becomes necessary to undertake an examination of various economic and historical factors in order to determine whether the arrangement under review is of the type Congress sought to proscribe.

A most important such factor to examine is the very nature and purpose of the arrangement.[56] Congress not only indicated that "the tests of illegality [under § 7] are intended to be similar to those which the courts have applied in interpreting the same language as used in other sections of the Clayton Act," but also chose for § 7 language virtually identical to that of § 3 of the Clayton Act, 15 U.S.C. § 14, which had been interpreted by this Court to require an examination of the interdependence of the market share foreclosed by, and the economic purpose of, the vertical arrangement. Thus, for example, if a particular vertical arrangement, considered under § 3, appears to be a limited term exclusive-dealing contract, the market

---

56. [Court's footnote 48.] Although it is "unnecessary for the Government to speculate as to what is in the 'back of the minds' of those who promote the merger," H.R.Rep. No. 1191, 81st Cong., 1st Sess. 8, evidence indicating the purpose of the merging parties, where available, is an aid in predicting the probable future conduct of the parties and thus the probable effects of the merger. Swift & Co. v. United States, 196 U.S. 375, 396; United States v. Maryland & Virginia Milk Producers Assn., 167 F.Supp. 799, 804 (D.C.D.C.), aff'd, 362 U.S. 458.

foreclosure must generally be significantly greater than if the arrangement is a tying contract before the arrangement will be held to have violated the Act. The reason for this is readily discernible. The usual tying contract forces the customer to take a product or brand he does not necessarily want in order to secure one which he does desire. Because such an arrangement is inherently anticompetitive, we have held that its use by an established company is likely "substantially to lessen competition" although only a relatively small amount of commerce is affected. Thus, unless the tying device is employed by a small company in an attempt to break into a market, the use of a tying device can rarely be harmonized with the strictures of the antitrust laws, which are intended primarily to preserve and stimulate competition. On the other hand, requirement contracts are frequently negotiated at the behest of the customer who has chosen the particular supplier and his product upon the basis of competitive merit. Of course, the fact that requirement contracts are not inherently anticompetitive will not save a particular agreement if, in fact, it is likely "substantially to lessen competition or tend to create a monopoly." Yet a requirement contract may escape censure if only a small share of the market is involved, if the purpose of the agreement is to insure to the customer a sufficient supply of a commodity vital to the customer's trade or to insure to the supplier a market for his output and if there is no trend toward concentration in the industry. Similar considerations are pertinent to a judgment under § 7 of the Act.

The importance which Congress attached to economic purpose is further demonstrated by the Senate and House Reports on H.R. 2734, which evince an intention to preserve the "failing company" doctrine of International Shoe Co. v. Federal Trade Comm'n, 280 U.S. 291, 50 S.Ct. 89, 74 L.Ed. 431. Similarly, Congress foresaw that the merger of two large companies or a large and a small company might violate the Clayton Act while the merger of two small companies might not, although the share of the market foreclosed be identical, if the purpose of the small companies is to enable them in combination to compete with larger corporations dominating the market.

The present merger involved neither small companies nor failing companies. In 1955, the date of this merger, Brown was the fourth largest manufacturer in the shoe industry with sales of approximately 25 million pairs of shoes and assets of over $72,000,000 while Kinney had sales of about 8 million pairs of shoes and assets of about $18,000,000. Not only was Brown one of the leading manufacturers of men's, women's, and children's shoes, but Kinney, with over 350 retail outlets, owned and operated the largest independent chain of family shoe stores in the Nation. Thus, in this industry, no merger between a manufacturer and an independent retailer could involve a larger potential market foreclosure. Moreover, it is apparent from both past behavior of Brown and from the testimony of Brown's President, that Brown would use its ownership of Kinney to force Brown shoes into Kinney stores. Thus, in operation this vertical arrangement would be quite analogous to one involving a tying clause.

Another important factor to consider is the trend toward concentration in the industry. It is true, of course, that the statute prohibits a given merger only if the effect of *that* merger may be substantially to lessen competition. But the very wording of § 7 requires a prognosis of the probable *future* effect of the merger.

The existence of a trend toward vertical integration, which the District Court found, is well substantiated by the record. Moreover, the court found a tendency of the acquiring manufacturers to become increasingly important sources of supply for their acquired outlets. The necessary corollary of these trends is the foreclosure of independent manufacturers from markets otherwise open to them. And because these trends are not the product of accident but are rather the result of deliberate policies of Brown and other leading shoe manufacturers, account must be taken of these facts in order to predict the probable future consequences of this merger. It is against this background of continuing concentration that the present merger must be viewed.

Brown argues, however, that the shoe industry is at present composed of a large number of manufacturers and retailers, and that the industry is dynamically competitive. But remaining vigor cannot immunize a merger if the trend in that industry is toward oligopoly. It is the probable effect of the merger upon the future as well as the present which the Clayton Act commands the courts and the Commission to examine.

Moreover, as we have remarked above, not only must we consider the probable effects of the merger upon the economics of the particular markets affected but also we must consider its probable effects upon the economic way of life sought to be preserved by Congress. Congress was desirous of preventing the formation of further oligopolies with their attendant adverse effects upon local control of industry and upon small business. Where an industry was composed of numerous independent units, Congress appeared anxious to preserve this structure. The Senate Report, quoting with approval from the Federal Trade Commission's 1948 report on the merger movement, states explicitly that amended § 7 is addressed, *inter alia*, to the following problem:

"Under the Sherman Act, an acquisition is unlawful if it creates a monopoly or constitutes an attempt to monopolize. Imminent monopoly may appear when one large concern acquires another, but it is unlikely to be perceived in a small acquisition by a large enterprise. As a large concern grows through a series of such small acquisitions, its accretions of power are individually so minute as to make it difficult to use the Sherman Act tests against them. . . .

"Where several large enterprises are extending their power by successive small acquisitions, the cumulative effect of their purchases may be to convert an industry from one of intense competition among many enterprises to one in which three or four large concerns produce the entire supply." S.Rep. No. 1775, 81st

Cong., 2d Sess. 5. And see H.R.Rep. No. 1191, 81st Cong., 1st Sess. 8.

The District Court's findings, and the record facts, many of them set forth in Part I of this opinion, convince us that the shoe industry is being subjected to just such a cumulative series of vertical mergers which, if left unchecked, will be likely "substantially to lessen competition."

We reach this conclusion because the trend toward vertical integration in the shoe industry, when combined with Brown's avowed policy of forcing its own shoes upon its retail subsidiaries, seems likely to foreclose competition from a substantial share of the markets for men's, women's, and children's shoes, without producing any countervailing competitive, economic, or social advantages.

V. THE HORIZONTAL ASPECTS OF THE MERGER

[Ed. The Court held the merger illegal in respect of termination of competition between Brown and Kinney stores in many cities and metropolitan areas. Excerpts from the opinion follow.]

Congress prescribed a pragmatic, factual approach to the definition of the relevant market and not a formal, legalistic one. The geographic market selected must, therefore, both correspond to the commercial realities of the industry and be economically significant . . . it may be as small as a single metropolitan area. The fact that two merging firms have competed directly on the horizontal level in but a fraction of the geographic markets in which either has operated, does not, in itself, place their merger outside the scope of § 7. That section speaks of "any section of the country", and if anticompetitive effects of a merger are probable in "any" significant market, the merger—at least to that extent—is proscribed. . . .

The market share which companies may control by merging is one of the most important factors to be considered when determining the probable effects of the combination on effective competition in the relevant market. In an industry as fragmented as shoe retailing, the control of substantial shares of the trade in a city may have important effects on competition. If a merger achieving 5% control were now approved, we might be required to approve future merger efforts by Brown's competitors seeking similar market shares. The oligopoly Congress sought to avoid would then be furthered and it would be difficult to dissolve the combinations previously approved. Furthermore, in this fragmented industry, even if the combination controls but a small share of a particular market, the fact that this share is held by a large national chain can adversely affect competition. Testimony in the record from numerous independent retailers, based on their actual experience in the market, demonstrates that a strong, national chain of stores can insulate selected outlets from the vagaries of competition in particular locations and that the large chains can set and alter styles in footwear to an extent that renders the independents unable to maintain competitive inventories. A third significant aspect of this merger is that it creates a large national chain which is integrated with a manufacturing operation. The retail outlets of integrated companies, by eliminating wholesalers and by increasing the volume of purchases from the manufacturing division of the enterprise, can market their own brands at prices below those of competing independent retailers. Of course, some of the results of large integrated or chain operations are beneficial to consumers. Their expansion is not rendered unlawful by the mere fact that small independent stores may be adversely affected. It is competition, not competitors, which the Act protects. But we cannot fail to recognize Congress' desire to promote competition through the protection of viable, small, locally owned businesses. Congress appreciated that occasional higher costs and prices might result from the maintenance of fragmented industries and markets. It resolved these competing considerations in favor of decentralization. We must give effect to that decision.

Other factors to be considered in evaluating the probable effects of a merger in the relevant market lend additional support to the District Court's conclusion that this merger may substantially lessen competition. One such factor is the history of tendency toward concentration in the industry. As we have previously pointed out, the shoe industry has, in recent years, been a prime example of such a trend. Most combinations have been between manufacturers and retailers, as each of the larger producers has sought to capture an increasing number of assured outlets for its wares. Although these mergers have been primarily vertical in their aim and effect, to the extent that they have brought ever greater numbers of retail outlets within fewer and fewer hands, they have had an additional important impact on the horizontal plane. By the merger in this case, the largest single group of retail stores still independent of one of the large manufacturers was absorbed into an already substantial aggregation of more or less controlled retail outlets. As a result of this merger, Brown moved into second place nationally in terms of retail stores directly owned. Including the stores on its franchise plan, the merger placed under Brown's control almost 1,600 shoe outlets, or about 7.2% of the Nation's retail "shoe stores" as defined by the Census Bureau, and 2.3% of the Nation's total retail shoe outlets. We cannot avoid the mandate of Congress that tendencies toward concentration in industry are to be curbed in their incipiency, particularly when those tendencies are being accelerated through giant steps striding across a hundred cities at a time. In the light of the trends in this industry we agree with the Government and the court below that this is an appropriate place at which to call a halt.

At the same time appellant has presented no mitigating factors, such as the business failure or the inadequate resources of one of the parties that may have prevented it from maintaining its competitive position, nor a demonstrated need for combination to enable small companies to enter into a more meaningful competition with those dominating the relevant markets. On the basis of the record before us, we believe the Government sustained its burden of proof. We hold that the District Court was correct in concluding that this merger may tend to lessen competition substantially in the retail sale of men's, women's and children's shoes in the overwhelming majority of those cities and their environs in which both Brown and Kinney sell through owned or controlled outlets.

The judgment is affirmed.

[JUSTICES FRANKFURTER and WHITE did not participate in the decision. JUSTICE HARLAN dissented on the appellate jurisdiction issue, but concurred in the judgment on the merits, although he believed that shoes generally should have been taken as the line of commerce, rather than particular types of shoes, because of evidence that manufacturing facilities can be shifted "without undue difficulty" from one type of shoe to another. He rested his judgment mainly on the demonstrable probability of prejudice to independent shoe manufacturers, but disavowed reliance on any trend towards oligopoly, pointing out that "Whereas the largest four manufacturers supplied 25.9% of the Nation's needs in 1947, the largest eight supplied 31.4%, and the largest 15 supplied 36.2%, in 1955 the equivalent percentages were 22%, 27%, and 32.5%." JUSTICE CLARK'S concurring opinion expresses a preference for regarding shoes as the line of commerce and the entire country as the market.] [57]

NOTES AND QUERIES

(1) *Prior and Subsequent Vertical Merger Decisions.* The first vertical merger case brought by the government was *United States v. E. I. du Pont de Nemours & Co.*, 353 U.S. 586, 77 S.Ct. 872, 1 L.Ed.2d 1057 (1957), filed thirty-five years after the passage of the Clayton Act. The Court held that the original Section 7 (reproduced supra at p. 213, n. 6) did cover vertical mergers, despite the F.T.C.'s public position to the contrary, and that du Pont's acquisition of 23% of the stock in General Motors led to a violation of the statute. The Court held that the effect of this stock acquisition could be gauged (i) in terms of *automotive* finishes and fabrics ("peculiar characteristics and uses") rather than broader ranges of paints and textiles; (ii) substantially without regard to demonstration that GM made its purchases on the merits, often declining to buy from du Pont products other than paints and fabrics; and (iii) in the light of expression, in correspondence at the time du Pont acquired its holdings, of expectation that GM would favor du Pont as a supplier. There was evidence that du Pont higher officials arranged to be regularly informed of the extent of GM purchases, and occasionally expressed the thought that GM should look with a friendly eye on du Pont products in view of their financial affinity. The Court rejected du Pont's argument that the Government was foreclosed from suing because the acquisition occurred between 1917 and 1919, and suit was not brought until 1949. Even though the statute outlaws stock acquisition, not its holding or use, the Court held that "the Government may proceed at any time that an acquisition may be said with reasonable probability to contain a threat that it may lead to a restraint of commerce," and that the test of a violation of Section 7 is to be measured "at the time of suit." Id. at 597, 607. Does this aspect of *du Pont* give the Government *carte blanche* to upset

---

57. For a criticism of the *Brown Shoe* opinion see Peterman, The Federal Trade Commission v. Brown Shoe Company, 18 J.L. & Econ. 361 (1975).

mergers at any time—and long after—their making?   (If it does, the Government has not sought to do so, yet   . . .[58])

Vertical mergers have been attacked with somewhat greater frequency since *Brown Shoe,* but further elaboration on *Brown Shoe's* test for vertical mergers has not occurred.   The Supreme Court did consider the legality of a vertical merger in *Ford Motor Co. v. United States,* 405 U.S. 562, 92 S.Ct. 1142, 31 L.Ed.2d 492 (1972), upholding a district court finding that Ford's acquisition of the Electric Autolite Company's spark plug business violated Section 7.   The Court referred, *inter alia,* to the district court's finding that the acquisition foreclosed Ford as a purchaser of about ten percent of industry output; but the Court's analysis of this finding was not particularly probing, no doubt because the "main controversy" before the Court was over relief.   Analyses in the lower courts generally begin by determining the share of the market foreclosed, but they also examine other industry factors involved rather than adopting a straight "numbers" approach for predicting anticompetitive effect.[59]

Market foreclosure is not the only theory available for analyzing vertical mergers.   An acquiror might have been willing to integrate by internal expansion, rather than acquisition, thereby adding to competition in the market; or an acquiring firm might have such superior resources (and be willing to use them) that the acquisition will "unbalance" competition in the acquired firm's market.   These theories will be explored infra, pp. 269 – 305.

(2) *What's Wrong With Vertical Mergers?*   President Nixon's "Task Force on Productivity and Competition" reported with respect to vertical mergers: [60]

> Our task force is of one mind on the undesirability of an extensive and vigorous policy against vertical mergers: vertical integration has not been shown to be presumptively noncompetitive and the Guidelines [61] err

58. See The Backward Sweep Theory and the Oligopoly Problem, 32 Antitrust L.J. 306 (1966).

59. See, e.g., Fruehauf Corp. v. Federal Trade Commission, 603 F.2d 345 (2d Cir. 1979) (vacating F.T.C. finding that acquisition by a producer, with 15% share of concentrated market, of a purchaser of 5.8% of industry's output might lessen competition; merger would not increase barriers to entry); Ash Grove Cement Co. v. Federal Trade Commission, 577 F.2d 1368 (9th Cir. 1978) (upholding F.T.C. finding of adverse competitive effect in acquisition by cement manufacturers of firms which sold 18.3% of ready-mix concrete in market), certiorari denied 439 U.S. 982, 99 S.Ct. 571, 58 L.Ed.2d 653. Heatransfer Corp. v. Volkswagenwerk, A.G., 553 F.2d 964 (5th Cir. 1977) (acquisition of independent airconditioner manufacturer and independent distributor by automobile company led to airconditioner company's subsequent dominance of the market in violation of Section 7), certiorari denied 434 U.S. 1087, 98 S.Ct. 1282, 55 L.Ed.2d 792 (1978); Harnischfeger Corp. v. Paccar, Inc., 474 F.Supp. 1151 (E.D.Wis.1979) (sufficient market effect arising from

foreclosure of acquired firm's business, where acquiror already supplied approximately 77% of acquired firm's needs and controlled large share of concentrated market) (granting preliminary injunction); Carrier Corp. v. United Technologies Corp., 1978–2 Trade Cas. ¶ 62,393 (N.D.N.Y.), *affirmed* 1978–2 Trade Cas. ¶ 62,405 (2d Cir. 1978) (substantial foreclosure not established); United States v. Hammermill Paper Co., 429 F.Supp. 1271 (W.D.Pa.1977) (discounting share of market foreclosed because of prior sales relationship with acquired purchasers, need for seller to maintain commercial relations with independent purchasers, and ease of entry into purchasers' business).

60. See ATRR No. 413, June 10, 1969, p. X–6. Compare President Johnson's Task Force on Antitrust Policy, which proposed prohibiting all acquisitions by large firms of leading firms in any market, including vertically related markets. See ATRR No. 411, May 27, 1969, Special Supp., pp. 15–17.

61. The Guidelines referred to were those issued by the Department of Justice in 1968 setting out then-current enforcement policy. See p. 249, supra.

in so treating it. Within this area of agreement there are two positions around which the task force members cluster.

The one position asserts that many, and perhaps most, vertical mergers which do not have direct horizontal effects * are innocuous, but that in certain situations a vertical merger will have anti-competitive effects. These situations include: increases in the capital or other requirements for an integrated firm may reduce the possibility of new entry; or price discrimination may be implemented when a monopolist integrates forward or backward. A showing that an anticompetitive effect of these sorts exists is essential before a vertical merger is challenged.

The other position denies that a vertical merger has the potentiality for economic harm in the absence of horizontal effects. To some of our members, it is wholly implausible that vertical integration places entering firms at a disadvantage. A seller who fails to minimize his input and distribution costs will be undersold by his competitors: he cannot afford to sell to or buy from an affiliate if there are more efficient alternative means of supply and distribution available to his competitors (and to him). Even if the seller is a monopolist, the desire to maximize profits will lead him to seek the most efficient methods of supply and distribution, and there will be ample opportunities for nonaffiliated suppliers and outlets to compete for his patronage. Except in the case of the monopolist who cannot discriminate in price effectively without control of his outlets, vertical integration will be initiated and maintained only if and so long as it is justified by the cost savings it permits. It is not a method of extending monopoly power.

The two positions coalesce on one policy conclusion: vertical mergers should not be forbidden as a class.

Does the belief that a vertically integrated firm will readily deal with outsiders who offer lower prices depend on: unrealistic expectations about the behavior of corporate managers loyal to (and familiar with) other members of the same organization? the existence of alternative sources of supply or distribution, or the willingness of potential competitors to enter these markets? [62] In considering these questions review examples of the behavior of vertically integrated firms presented in Chapter 2, particularly *Otter Tail Power Co. v. United States*, supra p. 124, and *Berkey Photo v. Eastman Kodak*, supra p. 140. Does a strict approach toward vertical mergers help prevent monopolizing behavior "in its incipiency"?

Current theories on the reasons for vertical integration are well summarized in Kaserman, Theories of Vertical Integration, 23 Antitrust Bull. 483 (1978). He includes: saving on transaction costs and eliminating uncertainty between successive stages of production; increasing monopoly profits by

The Guidelines indicated an intention to challenge a merger between a firm which sells approximately 10% of the market and a purchasing firm which accounts for approximately 6%. The Reagan Administration's Guidelines express no direct concern over market share foreclosure with regard to vertical mergers.

* What are "horizontal effects"?

62. Cf. Trans World Airlines, Inc. v. Hughes, 332 F.2d 602 (2d Cir. 1964), certiorari granted 379 U.S. 912, 85 S.Ct. 261, 265, 13 L.Ed.2d 184, certiorari dismissed 380 U.S. 248, 85 S.Ct. 934, 13 L.Ed.2d 817, 818, affirming a $137,000,000 treble damage claim based on Howard Hughes' alleged abuse of his control over TWA, including restraint upon its purchase of jet aircraft from suppliers other than Hughes and restraint upon its securing financing on most favorable terms. The judgment was ultimately set aside on the ground that the transactions had been "approved" by the C.A.B. and were therefore exempt from the antitrust laws. Hughes Tool Co. v. Transworld Airlines Inc., 409 U.S. 363, 93 S.Ct. 647, 34 L.Ed.2d 577 (1973).

precluding purchasers from substituting for the monopolized input; the regulated monopolist seeking unregulated markets in which to "take out" some of its otherwise unrealizable monopoly profits; and using vertical integration to facilitate coordination and enforce discipline in oligopoly markets. Scherer argues that "[v]ertical integration leading to the monopolization of once-competitive industries *may* enhance monopoly power [and] raise prices . . . ." He concludes that in an oligopoly where the parties engage in strategic behavior in a dynamic context, "a good deal of skepticism is warranted in evaluating claims that monopoly power is being aggrandized through vertical integration. Yet dogmatic insistence that it cannot happen is equally unwarranted." [63]

How do these theories help us make antitrust policy toward vertical mergers?

(3) *The Efficiency Defense.* Parties proposing a merger do not generally assert (at least in public) that the merger should be consummated because it will decrease competition. Rather, they will argue that it will have beneficial effects, often in the form of operating efficiencies. To what extent should a court consider such efficiencies (what does *Brown Shoe* suggest? See also *Procter & Gamble*, infra p. 296). If, for example, a vertically integrated firm can save on distribution costs (or a horizontally integrated firm can achieve scale economies in production), should we trade that off against the increased market power the merged firm might have as a result? How could the two be "netted out"? Should consideration be given to the possibility of greater efficiencies were the parties to merge with smaller firms in the industry? Should courts (or, at least, enforcement agencies) receive evidence of efficiencies to at least tip the scales toward legality in a weak case? [64]

Beside the problems involved in measuring the "tradeoff," should we be skeptical about our ability to predict future efficiencies, or of the claims put forward by the parties advocating the merger? Consider, e.g., "Airline-Service Breakdown Presists Long After Pan Am, National Merge," Wall St. Journal, March 10, 1981, p. 37: [65]

The $400 million merger of National Airlines into Pan American World Airways in January 1980 was billed as a triumph. "The merger will create a stronger,

63. Scherer, Industrial Market Structure And Economic Performance 303, 306 (2d ed. 1980) (emphasis in original). See also Williamson, Markets and Hierarchies: Analysis and Antitrust Implications (1975), chs. 5–7 (exploring vertical integration with emphasis on minimizing transaction costs).

64. See Williamson, Economies As An Antitrust Defense Revisited, 125 U.Pa.L. Rev. 699 (1977) (arguing yes, and presenting a model for measuring the trade-off; recommends against "full-blown" use of economies defense in litigation because of operational problems). The 1982 Merger Guidelines take a skeptical view of the efficiencies defense, recognizing the difficulties of proof; the Department will not consider a specific claim except in "extraordinary cases" and then only if the case is "close."

65. Reprinted by permission of The Wall Street Journal © Dow Jones &

Company, Inc. 1981. All rights reserved. See also Daughen & Binzen, The Wreck of the Penn Central (1971); "Exxon Abandons Energy-Saving Device Cited in '79 Reliance Electric Purchase," Wall St. J., March 23, 1981, p. 14 (Exxon abandons work on energy-saving device cited as justification for $1.2 billion acquisition of Reliance Electric Co. less than two years before); "F.T.C. Cites Exxon Data on Reliance," N.Y. Times, March 24, 1981, p. D1 (internal Exxon documents indicate Reliance takeover stemmed from an acquisitions study and that the asserted justification came later); "U.S. Drops Trust Case on Exxon," N.Y. Times, Aug. 5, 1982, p. D1 (F.T.C. says Exxon "misjudged the commercial viability" of the device; lack of success diminished adverse effect on competition). See Exxon Corp., 3 Trade Reg. Rep. (CCH) ¶ 21,948 (F.T.C. July 30, 1982) (order dismissing complaint).

more efficient airline," said Pan Am, promising reduced costs and better service.

It hasn't worked out that way.

Because of continued haggling with the pilots' union, the two airlines still aren't fully integrated, preventing major cost savings. And problems associated with the merger, coupled with the sagging economy, have led to a major breakdown in Pan Am's service.

Some examples:

• Merging the reservations services of Pan Am and National produced such chaos that telephone calls from would-be travelers often haven't been answered. At one point last November, Pan Am wasn't answering a third of the calls made to its reservations numbers.

• Flight schedules were woven together too tightly, leaving little or no room for delays due to bad weather or mechanical problems. As a result, during November 40% of Pan Am's international flights and 22% of its domestic flights were seriously late.

Executive Candor

"Our service went to hell late last year," says William Seawell, chairman of Pan Am. The worst areas, he notes, were reservations, baggage delivery and on-time flight performance.

One result is that Pan Am has been losing passengers. That, coupled with high fuel prices, resulted in a $60 million operating loss in the 1980 fourth quarter, a record. Only the sale of the Pan Am building in New York City helped Pan Am produce a net profit for the period.

Mr. Seawell says the airline has mounted a major effort to restore good service, including such rudimentary things as having airplanes fly on time more often. "It's back to learning the basics, blocking and tackling," the executive says. There already is evidence that Pan Am's new program is paying off, he adds.

Initially Pan Am coveted National for its domestic system, which would complement Pan Am's international flights. A major cost advantage would be having flight crews and planes flow through from one system to another.

The Wall of China

But, as a securities analyst puts it, the pilots' union has built "a Chinese wall" between the two systems. As a result, neither flight crews nor planes from Pan Am can move onto the National system, and vice versa, resulting in millions of dollars in unnecessary costs. . . .

By Oct. 26, Pan Am did manage to integrate one function, the reservations systems of National and Pan Am. But because of the cutbacks in managers, and because employes with greater seniority were displacing those with less from their usual jobs, many weren't familiar with their tasks. National reservations clerks, accustomed to booking simple flights from Miami to New York, suddenly had to arrange trips to Abidjan and Hong Kong with connections to Pago Pago. The clerks "couldn't have been more bewildered," says a Pan Am source.

Those phone calls that were answered stretched out from five or 10 to 15 or 20 minutes as the clerks struggled to make proper reservations. Meanwhile, other potential customers were put on hold, or got a busy signal. During one November week, 154,000 calls weren't answered. "We'll never know how much revenue we lost," says William Waltrip, executive vice president of Pan Am. . . .

Pan Am still is struggling with other problems stemming from the merger. In buying National, Pan Am got four DC10s it didn't need, and it hasn't been able to sell them because of a glut of used aircraft on the market. Pan Am also has a brand new, $45 million DC10 sitting on the ground at the McDonnell Douglas plant near Los Angeles. The plane, which isn't needed now, had been ordered by National.

(4) *Protect Competitors?* The sentence "It is competition, not competitors, which the Act protects" (supra p. 262) has become an antitrust cliché, and should be memorized by the student for future use in briefs, etc. But is it correct? Did the Court mean it? (Consider the rest of the paragraph in which it appears.) Consider: [66]

> The dogma that "antitrust laws protect competition not competitors" overstates the case and ignores considerations of justice. One must amend that declaration by adding at least the following qualification: "unless individual competitors must be protected in the interests of preserving competition." A conspiracy to put a single small competitor out of business violates the Sherman Act even if there is no showing of significant impact on competition generally. In the Robinson-Patman Act, Congress explicitly extended the anti-discrimination ban to attempts to eliminate "a competitor" as well as to cases of impairment of competition. These may be regarded as instances of Congress' concern with "incipient" impairment of competition or desire to prevent transactions, trivial in themselves, which might "trigger" a series of similar transactions. But they also may be seen as a congressional concern for a non-economic goal: "justice," in the sense of fair and equal treatment of persons in like situations.

Should vertical integration be condemned despite claimed or proven economic efficiencies for the reason stated by Judge Hand in ALCOA supra p. 102): "It is possible, because of its indirect social or moral effect, to prefer a system of small producers, each dependent for his success upon his own skill and character, to one in which the great mass of those engaged must accept the direction of the few".

(5) *Special Problems of Vertical Integration in Particular Industries.* Vertical integration in the oil industry (common ownership of production, transportation, refining, and marketing) has been under attack by federal legislative proposals which would mandate: separation of oil production from refining and marketing; divorcement of all pipelines from producing companies and operation of pipelines on a common-carrier basis.[67] State legislation requiring oil producers and refiners to divest themselves of retail service stations has been enacted and upheld by the Supreme Court against constitutional challenge.[68] (Legislation has also been proposed to bar "conglomerate" diversification by oil companies, on the theory that they should use record oil profits to find more oil.[69] Are these proposals more the result

66. Schwartz, "Justice" And Other Non-Economic Goals of Antitrust, 127 U.Pa.L.Rev. 1076, 1078 (1979).

67. See "Petroleum Industry Competition Act of 1976", S. 2387, 94th Cong. 2d Sess. (1976); S.Rep. No. 94–1005, Rep. of the Senate Comm. on the Judiciary, 94th Cong., 2d Sess. (June 28, 1976). For a thorough study of the issues raised by vertical integration in the oil pipeline industry, see E. Mitchell, ed., Oil Pipelines and Public Policy (1979).

68. See Exxon Corp. v. Governor of Maryland, 437 U.S. 117, 98 S.Ct. 2207, 57 L.Ed.2d 91 (1978). See also proposed Small Business Motor Fuel Marketer

Preservation Act of 1981, S. 326, 97th Cong., 1st Sess., 127 Cong.Rec. 778 (1981) (requiring major integrated refiners to divorce themselves from direct operation of retail service stations). For a discussion of the pros and cons of divestiture in the oil industry, see Ritchie, Petroleum Dismemberment, 29 Van.L.Rev. 1131 (1976), and Adams, Vertical Divestiture of the Petroleum Majors: An Affirmative Case, 30 Vand.L.Rev. 1115 (1977).

69. See Energy Antimonopoly Act of 1979, S. 1246, 96th Cong., 1st Sess., 125 Cong.Rec. 6703 (1979) (prohibiting oil companies from acquiring other compa-

of populist ideology than economic analysis?) The major oil
gue that efficiency requires vertical integration from crude
marketing and that security of supply is essential to the eff
ing and marketing operations. The President of Mobil put

> I do not think it is in the interest of the shareholders .
> refinery and not know where you are going to put the products, or ..
> market and not know where you are going to get the products.
>
> So this is why we put refining together with marketing. Our interest is to
> be sure we can refine and market products. We want to be sure we have the
> refinery that can supply the market, and a market that can put burden on a
> refinery. Now I call that efficiency, and I call that security of supplies.[70]

Is this argument persuasive for vertical integration in the oil industry or is it
an admission that the supply levels of the industry (production and refining)
are not workably competitive? [71] Are Mobil's arguments applicable to vertical integration in production and distribution of food, clothing, television receivers and computers?

Recall the discussion of the government's efforts to divest AT & T of
some of its operations, supra pp. 191 – 197. Should the government have
sought further divestiture to eliminate vertical integration? What competitive obstacles might you expect to face Western Electric's competitors in
selling to AT & T? What competitive obstacles might you expect to face
AT & T's competitors in obtaining equipment from Western Electric?
Should the newly-created independent local telephone operating companies
be given greater freedom to vertically integrate into the design and manufacture of telephone equipment? [72]   •

D.   GEOGRAPHIC MARKET EXTENSION MERGERS

UNITED STATES v. FALSTAFF BREWING CORP.

Supreme Court of the United States, 1973.
410 U.S. 526, 93 S.Ct. 1096, 35 L.Ed.2d 475.

MR. JUSTICE WHITE delivered the opinion of the Court.

Alleging that Falstaff Brewing Corporation's acquisition of the
Narragansett Brewing Company in 1965 violated § 7 of the Clayton
Act, the United States brought this antitrust suit under the theory

nies with assets of more than $100 mil-
lion). See also "Mineral Takeovers Criticized," N.Y. Times, Mar. 16, 1981, p. D1
(" 'Don't leave anything sitting around on
a table, or we'll buy it,' said one oil company official with a laugh.")

70. 3 Hearings, "The Petroleum Industry", Subcomm. on Antitrust & Monopoly, Senate Comm. on the Judiciary,
94th Cong., 1st Sess., p. 1834 (Statement
of William P. Tavoulareas).

71. Id. at 2141 (Statement of Prof. F.
M. Scherer); Williamson, The Vertical Integration of Production: Market Failure
Considerations, 61 Am.Econ.Rev. 112
(1971).

72. See International Telephone and
Telegraph Corp. v. General Telephone &
Electronic Corp., 449 F.Supp. 1158

(D.Haw.1978), a suit attacking GTE's policy of in-house purchasing under Section
1 of the Sherman Act. GTE operating
companies annually purchased from GTE
manufacturers 7.41% of all telephone
equipment sold in the United States
(37.72% if Bell's purchases were excluded). The district court examined factors
similar to those relevant for a Clayton
Act analysis, including the extent of market foreclosure, the extent of entry barriers into the affected market, and the extent to which the policy destroyed "free
choice" by the operating companies with
respect to equipment manufactured by
competing companies. The court found a
violation of Section 1: GTE's "parent-
subsidiary dealing unreasonably restricts
the opportunities of competitors to market their products." Id. at 1182.

that potential competition in the New England beer market may be substantially lessened by the acquisition. The District Court held to the contrary, and we noted jurisdiction to determine whether the trial court applied an erroneous legal standard in so deciding. We remand to the District Court for a proper assessment of Falstaff as a potential competitor.

As stipulated by the parties, the relevant product market is the production and sale of beer, and the six New England States compose the geographic market. While beer sales in New England increased approximately 9.5% in the four years preceding the acquisition, the eight largest sellers increased their share of these sales from approximately 74% to 81.2%. In 1960, approximately 50% of the sales were made by the four largest sellers; by 1964 their share of the market was 54%; and by 1965, the year of acquisition, their share was 61.3%. The number of brewers operating plants in the geographic market decreased from 32 in 1935, to 11 in 1957, to six in 1964.[73]

Of the Nation's 10 largest brewers in 1964, only Falstaff and two others did not sell beer in New England; Falstaff was the largest of the three and had the closest brewery. In relation to the New England market, Falstaff sold its product in western Ohio, to the west and in Washington, D.C., to the south.

The acquired firm, Narragansett, was the largest seller of beer in New England at the time of its acquisition, with approximately 20% of the market; had been the largest seller for the five preceding years; had constantly expanded its brewery capacity between 1960 and 1965; and had acquired either the assets or the trademarks of several smaller brewers in and around the geographic market.

The fourth largest producer of beer in the United States at the time of acquisition, Falstaff was a regional brewer with 5.9% of the Nation's production in 1964, having grown steadily since its beginning as a brewer in 1933 through acquisition and expansion of other breweries. As of January 1965, Falstaff sold beer in 32 States, but did not sell in the Northeast, an area composed of New England and States such as New York and New Jersey; the area being the highest beer consumption region in the United States. Between 1955 and 1966, the company's net sales and net income almost doubled, and in 1964 it was planning a 10-year, $35 million program to expand its existing plants.

Falstaff met increasingly strong competition in the 1960's from four brewers who sold in all of the significant markets. National brewers possess competitive advantages since they are able to advertise on a nationwide basis, their beers have greater prestige than regional or local beers, and they are less affected by the weather or labor problems in a particular region. Thus Falstaff concluded that it must convert from "regional" to "national" status, if it was to compete effectively with the top four producers.[74] For several years Fal-

73. [Court's footnote 4.] Nationally, the number of brewers decreased from 663 in 1935 to 140 in 1965.

74. [Court's footnote 7.] In 1958, Falstaff commissioned a study of actions it should take to maximize profits. The

staff publicly expressed its desire for national distribution and after making several efforts in the early 1960's to enter the Northeast by acquisition, agreed to acquire Narragansett in 1965.

Before the acquisition was accomplished, the United States brought suit alleging that the acquisition would violate § 7 because its effect may be to substantially lessen competition in the production and sale of beer in the New England market. This contention was based on two grounds: because Falstaff was a potential entrant and because the acquisition eliminated competition that would have existed had Falstaff entered the market *de novo* or by acquisition and expansion of a smaller firm, a so-called "toe-hold" acquisition. The acquisition was completed after the Government's motions for injunctive relief were denied, and Falstaff agreed to operate Narragansett as a separate subsidiary until otherwise ordered by the court.

After a trial on the merits the District Court found that the geographic market was highly competitive; that Falstaff was desirous of becoming a national brewer by entering the Northeast; that its management was committed against *de novo* entry; and that competition had not diminished since the acquisition.[75] The District Court then held:

> "The Government's contentions that Falstaff at the time of said acquisition was a potential entrant into said New England market, and that said acquisition deprived the New England market of additional competition are not supported by the evidence. On the contrary, the credible evidence establishes beyond a reasonable doubt that the executive management of Falstaff had consistently decided not to attempt to enter said market unless it could acquire a brewery with a strong and viable distribution system such as that possessed by Narragansett. Said executives had carefully considered such possible alternatives as (1) acquisition of a small brewery on the east coast, (2) the shipping of beer from its existing breweries, the nearest of which was located in Ft. Wayne, Indiana, (3) the building of a new brewery on the east coast and other possible alternatives, but concluded that none of said alternatives would have effected a reasonable probability of a profitable entry for it in said New England market. In my considered opinion the plaintiff has failed to establish by a fair preponderance of the evidence that Falstaff was a potential competitor in said New England market at the time it acquired Narragansett. The credible evidence establishes that it was not a potential entrant into said market by any means or way other than by said acquisition. Consequently, it cannot be said that its acquisition of Narra-

study recommended, *inter alia*, that Falstaff become a national brewer by entering those areas where it was not then marketing its product, especially the Northeast, and that Falstaff should build a brewery on the east coast rather than buy.

75. [Court's footnote 11.] Over the objections of the Government, the Dis-

trict Court allowed post-acquisition evidence and noted in the opinion that the market share of Narragansett dropped from 21.5% in 1964 to 15.5% in 1969, while the shares of the two leading national brewers increased from 16.5% to 35.8%.

gansett eliminated it as a potential competitor therein." 332 F.Supp., at 972.

Also finding that the Government had failed to establish that the acquisition would result in a substantial lessening of competition, the District Court entered judgment for Falstaff and dismissed the complaint.

I

Section 7 of the Clayton Act forbids mergers in any line of commerce where the effect may be substantially to lessen competition or tend to create a monopoly. The section proscribes many mergers between competitors in a market; it also bars certain acquisitions of a market competitor by a noncompetitor, such as a merger by an entrant who threatens to dominate the market or otherwise upset market conditions to the detriment of competition. Suspect also is the acquisition by a company not competing in the market but so situated as to be a potential competitor and likely to exercise substantial influence on market behavior. Entry through merger by such a company, although its competitive conduct in the market may be the mirror image of that of the acquired company, may nevertheless violate § 7 because the entry eliminates a potential competitor exercising present influence on the market. As the Court stated in United States v. Penn-Olin Chemical Co., 378 U.S., at 174, 84 S.Ct., at 1719, "The existence of an aggressive, well equipped and well financed corporation engaged in the same or related lines of commerce waiting anxiously to enter an oligopolistic market would be a substantial incentive to competition which cannot be underestimated."

In the case before us, Falstaff was not a competitor in the New England market, nor is it contended that its merger with Narragansett represented an entry by a dominant market force. It was urged, however, that Falstaff was a potential competitor so situated that its entry by merger rather than de novo violated § 7. The District Court, however, relying heavily on testimony of Falstaff officers, concluded that the company had no intent to enter the New England market except through acquisition and that it therefore could not be considered a potential competitor in that market. Having put aside Falstaff as a potential de novo competitor, it followed for the District Court that entry by a merger would not adversely affect competition in New England.

The District Court erred as a matter of law. The error lay in the assumption that because Falstaff, as a matter of fact, would never have entered the market de novo, it could in no sense be considered a potential competitor. More specifically, the District Court failed to give separate consideration to whether Falstaff was a potential competitor in the sense that it was so positioned on the edge of the market that it exerted beneficial influence on competitive conditions in that market. . . .

The specific question with respect to this phase of the case is not what Falstaff's internal company decisions were but whether, given its financial capabilities and conditions in the New England market, it would be reasonable to consider it a potential entrant into that market. Surely, it could not be said on this record that Falstaff's general interest in the New England market was unknown; and if it would appear to rational beer merchants in New England that Falstaff might well build a new brewery to supply the northeastern market then its entry by merger becomes suspect under § 7. The District Court should therefore have appraised the economic facts about Falstaff and the New England market in order to determine whether in any realistic sense Falstaff could be said to be a potential competitor on the fringe of the market with likely influence on existing competition.[76] This does not mean that the testimony of company officials about actual intentions of the company is irrelevant or is to be looked upon with suspicion; but it does mean that theirs is not necessarily the last word in arriving at a conclusion about how Falstaff should be considered in terms of its status as a potential entrant into the market in issue.

Since it appears that the District Court entertained too narrow a view of Falstaff as a potential competitor and since it appears that the District Court's conclusion that the merger posed no probable threat to competition followed automatically from the finding that Falstaff had no intent to enter *de novo*, we remand this case for the District Court to make the proper assessment of Falstaff as a potential competitor.

II

Because we remand for proper assessment of Falstaff as an on-the-fringe potential competitor it is not necessary to reach the question of whether § 7 bars a market-extension merger by a company whose entry into the market would have no influence whatsoever on the present state of competition in the market—that is, the entrant will not be a dominant force in the market and has no current influence in the marketplace. We leave for another day the question of the applicability of § 7 to a merger that will leave competition in the marketplace exactly as it was, neither hurt nor helped, and that is challengeable under § 7 only on grounds that the company could have, but did not, enter *de novo* or through "toe-hold" acquisition and that there is less competition than there would have been had entry been in such a manner. There are traces of this view in our cases, but the Court has not squarely faced the question, if for no other reason than because there has been no necessity to consider it.

---

76. [Court's footnote 13.] . . . The Government did not produce direct evidence of how members of the New England market reacted to potential competition from Falstaff, but circumstantial evidence is the lifeblood of antitrust law, especially for § 7 which is concerned "with probabilities, not certainties," Brown Shoe Co. v. United States, 370 U.S. 294, 323, 82 S.Ct. 1502, 1522–1523, 8 L.Ed.2d 510 (1962). . . .

The judgment of the District Court dismissing the complaint against Falstaff is reversed, and the case is remanded for further proceedings consistent with this opinion.

So ordered.

Reversed and remanded.*

MR. JUSTICE BRENNAN took no part in the decision of this case. MR. JUSTICE POWELL took no part in the consideration or decision of this case.

MR. JUSTICE DOUGLAS, concurring in part.

Although I join Part I of the Court's opinion and its judgment remanding the case to the District Court for further proceedings consistent with the opinion, I offer the following observations with respect to the question which the Court does not reach.

. . .

One of the principal purposes of § 7 was to stem the " 'rising tide' of concentration in American business." When an industry or a market evidences signs of increasing competition, we cannot allow an acquisition which may "tend to accelerate concentration."

The implications of the Clayton Act, as amended by the Celler-Kefauver Act, 15 U.S.C. § 18, are much, much broader than the customary restraints of competition and the power of monopoly. Louis D. Brandeis testified in favor of the bill that became the Clayton Act in 1914. "You cannot have true American citizenship, you cannot preserve political liberty, you cannot secure American standards of living unless some degree of industrial liberty accompanies it." He went on to say in answer to George W. Perkins, who testified against the bill:

"Mr. Perkins' argument in favor of the efficiency of monopoly proceeds upon the assumption, in the first place, and mainly upon the assumption, that with increase of size comes increase of efficiency. If any general proposition could be laid down on that subject, it would, in my opinion, be the opposite. It is, of course, true that a business unit may be too small to be efficient, but it is equally true that a unit may be too large to be efficient. And the circumstances attending business today are such that the temptation is toward the creation of too large units of efficiency rather than too small. The tendency to create large units is great, not because larger units tend to greater efficiency, but because the owner of a business may make a great deal more money if he increases the volume of his business ten-fold, even if the unit profit is in the process reduced one-half. It may, therefore, be for the interest of an owner of a business who has capital, or who can obtain capital at a reasonable cost, to forfeit efficiency to a certain

---

* On remand the Government introduced no new evidence; the district court found, inter alia, that the Government had not proved the market noncompetitive and that the objective facts warranted the conclusion that Falstaff probably would not have entered *de novo* or by toehold. See 383 F.Supp. 1020 (D.R.I. 1974). The Government did not appeal.

degree, because the result to him, in profits, may be greater by reason of the volume of the business. Now, not only may that be so, but in very many cases it is so.

"And the reason why increasing the size of a business may tend to inefficiency is perfectly obvious when one stops to consider. Anyone who critically analyzes a business learns this: That success or failure of an enterprise depends usually upon one man; upon the quality of one man's judgment, and, above all things, his capacity to see what is needed and his capacity to direct others."

That is why the Celler Committee reporting in 1971 on conglomerates and other types of mergers said that "Preservation of a competitive system was seen as essential to avoid the concentration of economic power that was thought to be a threat to the nation's political and social system." Control of American business is being transferred from local communities to distant cities where men on the 54th floor with only balance sheets and profit and loss statements before them decide the fate of communities with which they have little or no relationship. As a result of mergers and other acquisitions, some States are losing major corporate headquarters and their local communities are becoming satellites of a distant corporate control. The antitrust laws favored a wide diffusion of corporate control; and that aim has been largely defeated with serious consequences. Thus a recent Wisconsin study shows that "The growth of aggregate Wisconsin employment of companies acquired by out-of-state corporations declined substantially more than that of those acquired by in-state corporations." In this connection the Celler Report states:

"The Wisconsin study found, also, that 53 percent of acquired companies after the merger had a slower rate of payroll growth. Payroll growth, notably in large firms acquired by out-of-State corporations, was depressed by mergers. Inflation in recent years has markedly raised wages and salaries. It would be reasonable to expect that payrolls in acquired companies, because of the inflation, would have advanced more than employment. In this connection, the report states: 'The fact that this frequently did not happen in companies acquired by out-of-state firms would lead one to believe that their acquirers have transferred a portion of the higher salaried employees to a location outside Wisconsin. Such transfers mean a loss of talent, retail expenditures, and personal income in the economies of Wisconsin's communities and the state.' "

The adverse influence on local affairs of out-of-state acquisitions has not gone unnoticed in our opinions. Thus "the ability of retaining 'local control' over industry and the protection of small business" was our comment in Brown Shoe Co. v. United States, 370 U.S. 294, 315–316, 82 S.Ct. 1502, 1518–1519, 8 L.Ed.2d 510 on one of the purposes of strengthening § 7 of the Clayton Act through passage of the Celler-Kefauver Act.

By reason of the antitrust laws efficiency in terms of the accounting of dollar costs and profits is not the measure of the public interest nor is growth in size where no substantial competition is curtailed.   The antitrust laws look with suspicion on the acquisition of local business units by out-of-state companies.   For then local employment is apt to suffer, local payrolls are likely to drop off, responsible entrepreneurs in counties and States are replaced by clerks.

A case in point is Goldendale in my State of Washington.   It was a thriving community—an ideal place to raise a family—until the company that owned the sawmill was bought by an out-of-state giant.   In a year or so auditors in faraway New York City, who never knew the glories of Goldendale, decided to close the local mill and truck all the logs to Yakima.   Goldendale became greatly crippled.   It is Exhibit A to the Brandeis concern which became part of the Clayton Act concern with the effects that the impact of monopoly often has on a community, as contrasted with the beneficent effect of competition.

A nation of clerks is anathema to the American antitrust dream. So is the spawning of federal regulatory agencies to police the mounting economic power.   For the path of those who want the concentration of power to develop unhindered leads predictably to socialism that is antagonistic to our system.   See Blake and Jones, The Goals of Antitrust: A Dialogue on Policy—In Defense of Antitrust, 65 Col.L.Rev. 376 (1965).

It is against this background that we must assess the acquisition by Falstaff, the largest producer of beer in the United States that did not sell in the New England market, of the leading seller in that market.

. . .   Falstaff's president testified below that Falstaff for some time had wanted to enter the New England market as part of its interest in becoming a national brewer.   And Falstaff has conceded in its brief before this Court that "given an acceptable level of profit, it has the financial capability and the interest to enter the New England beer market."   With both the interest and the capability to enter the market, Falstaff was "the most likely entrant."   FTC v. Procter & Gamble Co., supra, 386 U.S., at 580–581, 87 S.Ct., at 1231–1232. Thus, although Falstaff might not have made a *de novo* entry if it had not been allowed to acquire Narragansett, we cannot say that it would be unwilling to make such an entry *in the future* when the New England market might be ripe for an infusion of new competition.   At this point of time it is the most likely new competitor. Moreover, there can be no question that replacing the leading seller in the market, a regional brewer, with a seller with national capabilities, increased the trend toward concentration.

I conclude that there is "reasonable likelihood" that the acquisition in question "may tend to substantially lessen competition."   Accordingly, I would be inclined to reverse and direct the District Judge to enter judgment for the Government and afford appropriate relief. Nevertheless, since the Court will not reach this question and I agree with the legal principles set forth in Part I of its opinion, I join the judgment remanding the case for further proceedings.

[MR. JUSTICE MARSHALL wrote a concurring opinion, in the course of which he suggested that there are three "potential competition" theories:]

1. The Dominant Entrant.—In some situations, a firm outside the market may have overpowering resources which, if brought to bear within the market, could ultimately have a substantial anticompetitive effect. If such a firm were to acquire a company within the relevant market, it might drive other marginal companies out of business, thus creating an oligopoly, or it might raise entry barriers to such an extent that potential new entrants would be discouraged from entering the market. Such a danger is especially intense when the market is already highly concentrated or entry barriers are already unusually high before the dominant firm enters the market.

2. The Perceived Potential Entrant.—Even if the entry of a firm does not upset the competitive balance within the market, it may be that the removal of the firm from the fringe of the market has a present anticompetitive effect. In a concentrated oligopolistic market, the presence of a large potential competitor on the edge of the market, apparently ready to enter if entry barriers are lowered, may deter anticompetitive conduct within the market. From the perspective of the firms already in the market, the possibility of entry by such a lingering firm may be an important consideration in their pricing and marketing decision. When the lingering firm enters the market by acquisition, the competitive influence exerted by the firm is lost with no offsetting gain through an increase in the number of companies seeking a share of the relevant market. The result is a net decrease in competitive pressure.

3. The Actual Potential Entrant.—Since the effect of a perceived potential entrant depends upon the perception of those already in the market, it may in some cases be difficult to prove. Moreover, in a market which is already competitive, the existence of a perceived potential entrant will have no present effect at all. The entry by acquisition of such a firm may nonetheless have an anticompetitive effect by eliminating an actual potential competitor. When a firm enters the market by acquiring a strong company within the market, it merely assumes the position of that company without necessarily increasing competitive pressures. Had such a firm not entered by acquisition, it might at some point have entered *de novo.* An entry *de novo would* increase competitive pressures within the market, and an entry by acquisition eliminates the possibility that such an increase will take place in the future. Thus, even if a firm at the fringe of the market exerts no present procompetitive effect, its entry by acquisition may end for all time the promise of more effective competition at some future date.

Obviously, the anticompetitive effect of such an acquisition depends on the possibility that the firm would have entered *de novo* had it not entered by acquisition. If the company would have remained outside the market but for the possibility of entry by acquisition and if it is exerting no influence as a perceived potential entrant, then there will normally be no competitive loss when it enters by acquisition. Indeed, there may even be a competitive gain to the extent that it strengthens the market position of the acquired firm. Thus, mere entry by acquisition would not prima facie establish a firm's status as an actual potential entrant. For example, a firm, although able to enter the market by acquisition, might, because of inability to shoulder the *de novo* start-up costs, be unable to enter *de novo*. But where a powerful firm is engaging in a related line of commerce at the fringe of the relevant market, where it has a strong incentive to enter the market *de novo*, and where it has the financial capabilities to do so, we have not hesitated to ascribe to it the role of an actual potential entrant. In such cases we have held that § 7 prohibits an entry by acquisition since such an entry eliminates the possibility of future actual competition which would occur if there were an entry *de novo*.

[Justices Rehnquist and Stewart dissented.]

NOTES AND QUERIES

(1) *More Poetry Than Analysis?* Critics of an "economics-only" approach to antitrust law have often argued that microeconomics, however valid theoretically, cannot be usefully operationalized in today's complex world. Can the same argument be made of Justice Douglas' approach in *Falstaff?* Even if one agrees with the policies he espouses, how can they be made operational, particularly in view of Section 7's language focusing on "competition"? Are Douglas' views "more poetry than analysis"? [77]

(2) *"Oregon City Feels A Difference As Outsiders Move In."* New York Times, Feb. 24, 1979, p. 8: [*]

> This month the family that had owned the Blitz Weinhard Brewing Company for 123 years announced its sale to the Pabst Brewing Company of Milwaukee.

> The sale of Oregon's last brewery caused a minor ripple, but it subsided quickly, for this city, and most others of its size, has become accustomed to important local institutions' being sold to investors who live elsewhere.

> One of the unhappy voices heard here was that of William Wessinger, board chairman of Blitz Weinhard and a grandson of Henry Weinhard, who founded the brewery in 1856.

> "I just hate it," Mr. Wessinger said. "I hate the whole trend of consolidation that the country is in."

Brothers Sold Brewery

> Yet Mr. Wessinger and his brother, Fred, arranged the sale of Blitz. "The big guys have more and more leverage with their advertising dollars and big-

77. The phrase in Robert Bork's. He was describing the arguments of Walter Adams (an economist) favoring no-fault monopolization, in part to diversify social and political power. The debate was before President Carter's National Commission for the Review of Antitrust Laws and Procedures. See ATRR No. 880, Sept. 14, 1978, at A–22. What's wrong with poetry?

* © 1979 by the New York Times Company. Reprinted by permission.

order techniques," Mr. Wessinger said, adding, "It was very emotional for all of us in the family."

When World War II ended, most of Portland was owned by people who lived here. The two daily newspapers that are now merged, the radio stations, the department stores, movie theaters, hotels, lumber mills—all were then locally owned.

That has changed and, while the reasons for each sale are known and perhaps accepted, the cumulative impact is another matter.

"The biggest difference between now and the old days is in the response to community need," Oliver Larson, executive vice president of the Portland Chamber of Commerce, said. "Then, some warhorse would call a meeting of the people who decided things and it would get done. Now, they all have to contact corporate headquarters, at somewhere like Gravelswitch, Kan., and it takes forever to get an answer."

An Early Environmentalist

"You'd never find a department store manager these days worrying about cleaning up the Willamette River," Mr. Larson said.

He was referring to Harold F. Wendel, president of the department store Lipman & Wolfe from 1927 to 1967. Mr. Wendel was an environmentalist before the word was refined to its present meaning. He was chairman of the State Sanitary Authority in the 1940's and 50's when the authority forced cities and industries to clean up the Willamette River, so successfully that the salmon runs are back and swimmers use the river.

This month, however, it was announced that the name Lipmans, as the store later was known, would disappear from Portland after 99 years. Frederick & Nelson, a Marshall Field subsidiary, will take over the main store while Mervyn's, a California chain, will take over branches in the suburbs.

The most obvious, and therefore the most talked about, sales to outsiders have been in department stores and in newspapers.

One of the Newhouse newspaper chain's early acquisitions outside the New York-Pennsylvania area was The Oregonian, Portland's morning paper. Newhouse bought it in 1950, just after the owners celebrated the paper's 100th anniversary.

In the 1950's The Oregonian flourished, and the afternoon Oregon Journal sagged. After a strike against both papers in 1959, Samuel I. Newhouse acquired The Journal, which gave him a monopoly of the dailies in Oregon's major city.

The Newhouse papers here are published from the same plant, with shared printing, advertising solicitation, and circulation operations. The newsrooms are separate, but in control at the top sits Fred Stickel, who was publisher of Mr. Newhouse's Jersey Journal before coming here 11 years ago.

All four commercial television channels in Portland are owned by outside companies, too.

The ABC and NBC outlets, both of whose owners are in the Puget Sound area, have tried to provide for a degree of local control. The CBS outlet, owned for many years in part by Mr. Newhouse and by a local family, has been sold to a Denver concern.

The fourth station, KPTV, formerly the ABC outlet, became independent about 15 years ago. "Frankly, it doesn't make a bit of difference that someone away from here owns the station," said John Hansen, who has managed the station for 20 years for its owners, Chris Craft Industries. "If I owned it, I wouldn't run it much differently."

Across the street from Lipmans department store once was Meier & Frank Co., which had dominated Portland's department store trade for generations. In 1965, the May Co. acquired the store.

Chains Take Over Hotels

Once the hotels were locally owned, but now the chains—Hilton, Sheraton, Western, Marriott—have them.

There are exceptions to the trend toward outside ownership.

The banking business is becoming more local, although the largest bank, First National, is owned by an out-of-state holding company, Western Bancorp.

Recently the vice chairman of the second largest bank, Thomas S. Prideaux of U.S. National, said he made loans to national clients "only to the degree they operate in Oregon and contribute to the Oregon economy." The bank is Oregon-owned.

Local Food Chain Dominates

And food distribution is dominated here by a local chain, Fred Meyer Inc., whose founder died, at age 92, last year. But two big out-of-state chains, Safeway and Albertson's, have stores in Portland.

One of the mainstays of the Portland economy is money from the Northwest's forest industries, which now are concentrated in big companies.

"In forest products, Weyerhaeuser, Crown Zellerbach, Georgia Pacific, and U.S. Plywood gobbled up close to 50 plants in Oregon and Washington, and every purchase removed local control" said Mr. Larson of the Chamber of Commerce.

Nor is there any end to the trend in sight. As Mr. Wessinger explained his agreement to the sale of the brewery his grandfather established:

"Pabst wanted some of our brands, like Olde English Malt, which is big in New York and Georgia, and there was just one item after another that we couldn't match them on, as when they are able to buy beer cans at 26 cents a case under what we pay."

Pabst will keep the brewery open and hire the 250 employees who now work for the Wessingers, as well as Fred and Bill Wessinger, although the latter explained, "How long we last depends on what kind of job we do."

(3) *Joint Ventures and Potential Competition.* In UNITED STATES v. PENN-OLIN CHEMICAL CO., 378 U.S. 158, 84 S.Ct. 1710, 12 L.Ed.2d 775 (1964), on remand 246 F.Supp. 917 (D.C.Del.1965), affirmed 389 U.S. 308, 88 S.Ct. 502, 19 L.Ed.2d 545 (1968), the Supreme Court held that joint ventures, where two or more firms create a new enterprise to undertake a project, are governed by Section 7 where the joint venture was organized as a corporation 50% of whose stock was "acquired" by each of the joint venturers.[78] Pennsalt Chemical Corporation produced sodium chlorate at a plant located in Portland, Oregon. Olin Mathieson Chemical Corporation marketed part of Pennsalt's production in the Southeastern United States under a contract making Olin Pennsalt's marketing agent. Sodium chlorate is used in a process for bleaching pulp in the paper industry. Olin had never engaged in the commercial production of sodium chlorate, although it did own a patent on a widely used process for the bleaching of pulp which required the use of sodium chlorate. The manufacture of sodium chlorate in the southeast market

---

78. The Court rejected a "loophole" argument that the joint subsidiary was not engaged in interstate (or any) commerce at the time its stock was "acquired" by its organizers. It was sufficient that the parent firms were "in commerce" and that the subsidiary would similarly be engaged in commerce. Moreover Penn-Olin was operating in interstate commerce at the time of suit and the economic effects of an acquisition are to be measured at that point rather than at the time of acquisition. United States v. E. I. duPont deNemours & Co., 353 U.S. 586, 77 S.Ct. 872, 1 L.Ed.2d 1057 (1957).

was dominated by two firms (Hooker Chemical Corporation and American Potash & Chemical Corporation) which had 90% of the market prior to 1960.

In 1960, Pennsalt and Olin entered into a joint venture in lieu of their previous marketing agreement. The joint venture created Penn-Olin, a new corporation jointly owned by Pennsalt and Olin, which built a plant in Kentucky to manufacture sodium chlorate for the southeast market. Both Pennsalt and Olin had investigated the feasibility of independently entering the southeast market prior to forming the joint venture.

The Government brought an action under Section 7 of the Clayton Act and Section 1 of the Sherman Act seeking dissolution of the joint venture. The district court dismissed the complaint, finding no evidence of anticompetitive effect. The Supreme Court reversed, holding that the formation of a joint venture and the acquisition of the stock of the joint venture corporation brought the case within Section 7 of the Clayton Act. While acknowledging that the case differed from a typical Section 7 merger case, since the acquisition created a new competitive force in the market rather than eliminating one of the participating corporations from the market, the Court held that this factor did not exhaust the analysis required by Section 7. The Court directed the district court to weigh also the effect of the formation of the joint venture upon "potential competition." Finding that the district court limited its examination of the potential competition issue to a determination of whether *both* Olin and Pennsalt would have independently entered the southeast market, the Court held:

> We believe that the court erred in this regard. Certainly the sole test would not be the probability that *both* companies would have entered the market. Nor would the consideration be limited to the probability that one entered alone. There still remained for consideration the fact that Penn-Olin eliminated the potential competition of the corporation that might have remained at the edge of the market, continually threatening to enter. Just as a merger eliminates actual competition, this joint venture may well foreclose any prospect of competition between Olin and Pennsalt in the relevant sodium chlorate market. The difference, of course, is that the merger's foreclosure is present while the joint venture's is prospective. Nevertheless, "[p]otential competition . . . as a substitute for . . . [actual competition] may restrain producers from overcharging those to whom they sell or underpaying those from whom they buy. . . . Potential competition, insofar as the threat survives [as it would have here in the absence of Penn-Olin], may compensate in part for the imperfection characteristic of actual competition in the great majority of competitive markets." Wilcox, Competition and Monopoly in American Industry, TNEC Monograph No. 21 (1940) 7–8. . . . The existence of an aggressive, well equipped and well financed corporation engaged in the same or related lines of commerce waiting anxiously to enter an oligopolistic market would be a substantial incentive to competition which cannot be underestimated. 378 U.S. at 173–74, 84 S.Ct. at 1718–19, 12 L.Ed.2d at 787.

The Court remanded the case for findings on the "reasonable probability that either one of the corporations would have entered the market by building a plant, while the other remained a significant potential competitor." [79]

---

79. Justices Douglas and Black dissented against remanding, viewing the joint venture as a clear-cut division of markets in violation of Section 1 of the Sherman Act, as well as a violation of Section 7 of the Clayton Act. Justice White dissented without opinion. Justice Harlan dissented because he could see "no purpose to be served by this remand except to give the Government an opportunity to retrieve an antitrust case which it has lost, and properly so."

Upon remand the district court made a finding that neither firm, acting alone, would have established a plant in the southeast market, and dismissed the case. The Supreme Court affirmed the dismissal by an equally divided court.

Which of the two potential competition theories mentioned in Falstaff had the Court applied in *Penn–Olin?* Both? Note that the classification of "joint ventures" can vary, depending on the prior relations of the co-venturers (e.g., a joint venture could be "horizontal" if it eliminates direct competition between the parties), and that more than Section 7 may be available for attacking a joint venture. Problems of characterization and analysis of joint ventures are explored further, infra pp. 555 – 584.

UNITED STATES v. MARINE BANCORPORATION, INC.

Supreme Court of the United States, 1974.
418 U.S. 602, 94 S.Ct. 2856, 41 L.Ed.2d 978.

[Digest: The acquiring bank is the National Bank of Commerce (NBC), headquartered in Seattle, Washington; it is a subsidiary of Marine Bancorporation, a bank holding company. The acquired bank is Washington Trust Bank (WTB), headquartered in Spokane, Washington. As of June 30, 1972, the five largest banking organizations in Washington held 74.3% of the State's commercial bank deposits; the two largest (Seattle-First National and NBC) held 51.3%. WTB was the ninth largest in the State. The market shares in the Spokane market were (Table from Court's opinion):

DISTRIBUTION OF TOTAL DEPOSITS HELD BY BANKING ORGANIZATIONS IN THE SPOKANE METRO-POLITAN AREA, 1966–1972

(dollars in thousands)

Banking Organization	12–31–66 $	% of Total	6–30–72 $	% of Total
Washington Bancshares, Inc.*	155,885	41.1	216,340	42.1
Seattle-First National Bank	145,251	38.3	162,220	31.6
Washington Trust Bank	63,102	16.6	95,464	18.6
Sub Total	364,238	96.1	474,024	92.3
American Commercial Bank	3,552	.9	15,739	3.1
Farmers and Merchants Bank	5,593	1.5	12,558	2.5
Pacific National Bank**	5,801	1.5	11,152	2.2
Total	379,184	100.0	513,473	100.0

Note: Due to rounding, figures may not add to totals.

* Washington Bancshares, Inc., a bank holding company, owns two subsidiaries operating in Spokane, Old National Bank of Washington and First National Bank of Spokane. The deposit totals of these two banks are consolidated under the Washington Bancshares, Inc., entry in the above table.

** The bank at the bottom of the table is a branch (with two banking offices) of Pacific National Bank of Washington, which has its principal office in Seattle. This Seattle bank is in turn a subsidiary of Western Bancorporation, a multistate bank holding company with assets of approximately 14 billion dollars.

Relevant banking law was described as follows in the Court's opinion:

"Although Washington permits branching, the restrictions placed on that method of internal growth are stringent. Subject to the approval of the state supervisor of banking, Washington banks with sufficient paid-in capital may open branches in the city or town in which their headquarters are located, the unincorporated areas of the county in which their headquarters are located, and incorporated communities which have no banking office. . . . But under state law, no state-chartered bank 'shall establish or operate any branch . . . in any city or town outside the city or town in which its principal place of business is located in which any bank, trust company or national banking association regularly transacts a banking or trust business, except by taking over or acquiring an existing bank, trust company or national banking association . . . .' Since federal law subjects nationally chartered banks to the branching limitations imposed on their state counterparts, national and state banks in Washington are restricted to mergers or acquisitions in order to expand into cities and towns with pre-exisitng banking organizations.

"The ability to acquire existing banks is also limited by a provision of state law requiring that banks incorporating in Washington include in their articles of incorporation a clause forbidding a new bank from merging with or permitting its assets to be acquired by another bank for a period of at least 10 years, without the consent of the state supervisor of banking. . . . In addition, once a bank acquires or takes over one of the banks operating in a city or town other than the acquiring bank's principal place of business, it cannot branch from the acquired bank. . . . Thus, an acquiring bank that enters a new city or town containing banks other than the acquired bank is restricted to the number of bank offices obtained at the time of the acquisition. Moreover, multibank holding companies are prohibited in Washington. . . . Under state law, no corporation in Washington may own, hold, or control more than 25% of the capital stock of more than one bank. . . . Accordingly, it is not possible in Washington to achieve the rough equivalent of free branching by aggregating a number of unit banks under a bank holding company."

After the parties agreed to merge, they applied to the Comptroller of the Currency for approval pursuant to the Bank Merger Act of 1966 (see p. 236, supra). The reports required from the Attorney General, the Federal Deposit Insurance Corporation, and the Board of Governors of the Federal Reserve System on the "competitive factors involved" were all negative, primarily because of the degree of concentration in commercial banking in Washington as a whole. Nevertheless, the Comptroller approved the merger.

The Justice Department then brought suit under Section 7. It argued that the merger might substantially lessen competition: (1) by eliminating the prospect that NBC, absent acquisition of WTB, would enter Spokane *de novo* or through acquisition of a smaller bank and thus would assist in deconcentrating that market over the long run; and (2) by ending present procompetitive effects allegedly produced in Spokane by NBC's perceived presence on the fringe of the Spokane market. The Government's first theory was the primary basis upon which the case was presented to the district court.

The district court found for the defendants and the Government appealed.]

MR. JUSTICE POWELL delivered the opinion of the Court.

II. THE RELEVANT MARKETS

Determination of the relevant product and geographic markets is "a necessary predicate" to deciding whether a merger contravenes the Clayton Act. [The parties did not dispute the district court's finding that commercial banking was the relevant product market.]

Prior to trial the Government stipulated that the Spokane area is a relevant geographic market in the instant case, and there is no dispute that it is the only banking market in which WTB is a significant participant. Nevertheless, the Government contends that the entire State is also an appropriate "section of the country" in this case. It is conceded that the State is not a banking market. But the Government asserts that the State is an economically differentiated region, because its boundaries delineate an area within which Washington banks are insulated from most forms of competition by out-of-state banking organizations. The Government further argues that this merger, and others it allegedly will trigger, may lead eventually to the domination of all banking in the State by a few large banks, facing each other in a network of local, oligopolistic banking markets. This assumed eventual statewide linkage of local markets, it is argued, will enhance statewide the possibility of parallel, standardized, anticompetitive behavior. This concern for the possible statewide consequences of geographic market extension mergers by commercial banks appears to be an important reason for the Government's recent efforts to block such mergers through an application of the potential competition doctrine under § 7.

The Government's proposed reading of the "any section of the country" phrase of § 7 is at variance with this Court's § 7 cases, and we reject it. Without exception the Court has treated "section of the country" and "relevant geographic market" as identical, and it has defined the latter concept as the area in which the goods or services at issue are marketed to a significant degree by the acquired firm. E.g., *Philadelphia National Bank*, supra, 374 U.S. at 357–362, 83

S.Ct., at 1738–1741.[80]   In cases in which the acquired firm markets its products or services on a local, regional, and national basis, the Court has acknowledged the existence of more than one relevant geographic market.[81]   But in no previous § 7 case has the Court determined the legality of a merger by measuring its effects on areas where the acquired firm is not a direct competitor.   In urging that the legality of this merger be gauged on a statewide basis, the Government is suggesting that we take precisely that step, because as it concedes the section of the country in which WTB markets by far the greatest portion of its services, due to the predominantly localized character of commercial banking, is the Spokane metropolitan area.   Under the precedents, we decline the Government's invitation.   We hold that in a potential competition case like this one, the relevant geographic market or appropriate section of the country is the area in which the acquired firm is an actual, direct competitor.

Apart from the fact that the Government's statewide approach is not supported by the precedents, it is simply too speculative on this record.   There has been no persuasive showing that the effect of the merger on a statewide basis "may be substantially to lessen competition" within the meaning of § 7.   To be sure, § 7 was designed to arrest mergers "at a time when the trend to a lessening of competition in a line of commerce [is] still in its incipiency."   . . .   But it is to be remembered that § 7 deals in "probabilities," not "ephemeral possibilities."   The Government's underlying concern for a linkage or network of statewide oligopolistic banking markets is, on this record at least, considerably closer to "ephemeral possibilities" than to "probabilities."   To assume, on the basis of essentially no evidence, that the challenged merger will tend to produce a statewide linkage of oligopolies is to espouse a *per se* rule against geographic market extension mergers like the one at issue here.*   No § 7 case from this court has gone that far,[82] and we do not do so today.   For the purpose of this case, the appropriate "section of the country" and the

80. [Court's footnote 19.]   If a challenged combination takes the form of a joint venture by which two firms plan to enter a new area simultaneously, the relevant geographic market is the section of the country in which the newly formed enterprise will market its goods.   See United States v. Penn-Olin Chemical Co., 378 U.S. 158, 84 S.Ct. 1710, 12 L.Ed.2d 775 (1964).

81. [Court's footnote 20.]   See, e.g., United States v. Pabst Brewing Co., [supra. p. 218].   Some of the court's language in *Pabst* suggests that the Government may challenge a merger under § 7 without establishing any relevant geographic market.   . . .   But *Pabst* in reality held that the Government had established three relevant markets in which the acquired firm actually marketed its products—a single State, a multistate area, and the Nation as a whole.   And in that case the acquiring firm was an actual competitor of the acquired firm in all three relevant geographic markets.   Thus while *Pabst* stands for the proposition that there may be more than one relevant geographic market it did not abandon the traditional view that for purposes of § 7 "section of the country" means "relevant geographic market" and the latter concept means the area in which the relevant product is in fact marketed by the acquired firm.

* Is a rule a *"Per se"* rule if it is applied only to "geographic market extension mergers like the one at issue here"?   What does *"per se"* mean?

82. [Court's footnote 23.]   We put aside cases where an acquiring firm's market power, existing capabilities, and proposed merger partner are such that the merger would produce an enterprise likely to dominate the target market (a

"relevant geographic market" are the same—the Spokane metropolitan area.

III. POTENTIAL COMPETITION DOCTRINE

. . .The potential competition doctrine has been defined in major part by . . . United States v. Falstaff Brewing Corp., 410 U.S. 526, 93 S.Ct. 1096, 35 L.Ed.2d 475 (1973).[83] Unequivocal proof that an acquiring firm actually would have entered *de novo* but for a merger is rarely available. Thus, as *Falstaff* indicates, the principal focus of the doctrine is on the likely effects of the premerger position of the acquiring firm on the fringe of the target market. In developing and applying the doctrine, the Court has recognized that a market extension merger may be unlawful if the target market is substantially concentrated, if the acquiring firm has the characteristics, capabilities, and economic incentive to render it a perceived potential *de novo* entrant, and if the acquiring firm's premerger presence on the fringe of the target market in fact tempered oligopolistic behavior on the part of existing participants in that market. In other words, the Court has interpreted § 7 as encompassing what is commonly known as the "wings effect"—the probability that the acquiring firm prompted premerger procompetitive effects within the target market by being perceived by the existing firms in that market as likely to enter *de novo*. *Falstaff,* supra, at 531–537, 93 S.Ct., at 1100–1103. The elimination of such present procompetitive effects may render a merger unlawful under § 7.

Although the concept of perceived potential entry has been accepted in the Court's prior § 7 cases, the potential competition theory upon which the Government places principal reliance in the instant case has not. The Court has not previously resolved whether the potential competition doctrine proscribes a market extension merger solely on the ground that such a merger eliminates the prospect for long-term deconcentration of an oligopolistic market that in theory might result if the acquiring firm were forbidden to enter except through a *de novo* undertaking or through the acquisition of a small existing entrant (a so-called foothold or toehold acquisition). *Falstaff* expressly reserved this issue.

The Government's potential competition argument in the instant case proceeds in five steps. First, it argues that the potential competition doctrine applies with full force to commercial banks. Second, it submits that the Spokane commercial banking market is sufficiently concentrated to invoke that doctrine. Third, it urges us to resolve in

concept known as entrenchment). See FTC v. Procter & Gamble Co., [infra, p. 296]. There is no allegation that the instant merger would produce entrenchment in the Spokane market.

p. 264]; FTC v. Procter & Gamble Co., [infra, p. 296]; United States v. Continental Can Co., [supra, p. 218]; United States v. Penn-Olin Chemical Co., [supra, p. 280].

83. [Court's footnote 25.] See also Ford Motor Co. v. United States, [supra,

its favor the question left open in *Falstaff*. Fourth, it contends that without regard to the possibility of future deconcentration of the Spokane market, the challenged merger is illegal under established doctrine because it eliminates NBC as a perceived potential entrant. . . . We shall address those points in the order presented.

A. *Application of the Doctrine to Commercial Banks*

. . .

Although the Court's prior bank merger cases have involved combinations between actual competitors operating in the same geographic markets, an element that distinguishes them factually from this case, they nevertheless are strong precedents for the view that § 7 doctrines are applicable to commercial banking. In accord with the general principles of those cases, we hold that geographic market extension mergers by commercial banks must pass muster under the potential competition doctrine. We further hold, however, that the application of the doctrine to commercial banking must take into account the unique federal and state regulatory restraints on entry into that line of commerce. Failure to do so would produce misconceptions that go to the heart of the doctrine itself.

The Government's present position has evolved over a series of eight District Court cases, all of them decided unfavorably to its views. The conceptual difficulty with the Government's approach, and an important reason why it has been uniformly unsuccessful in the District Courts, is that it fails to accord full weight to the extensive federal and regulatory barriers to entry into commercial banking. This omission is of great importance, because ease of entry on the part of the acquiring firm is a central premise of the potential competition doctrine.

Unlike, for example, the beer industry, see *Falstaff Brewing Corp.*, supra, entry of new competitors into the commercial banking field is "wholly a matter of governmental grace . . ." and "far from easy." *Philadelphia National Bank*, supra, 374 U.S., at 367 n. 44, 83 S.Ct., at 1744. Beer manufacturers are free to base their decisions regarding entry and the scale of entry into a new geographic market on nonregulatory considerations, including their own financial capabilities, their long range goals as to markets, the cost of creating new production and distribution facilities, and above all the profit prospects in the target market. They need give no thought to public needs and convenience. No comparable freedom exists for commercial banks. . . . The regulatory barriers to entry include federal and state supervisory controls over the number of bank charters to be granted . . .. Moreover, there are state law restrictions, such as those in force in Washington, on *de novo* geographic expansion through branching and multibank holding companies. As noted earlier, Washington statutes forbid branching into cities and towns where the expanding bank does not maintain its headquarters and other banks operate, and they forbid branching from a branch in such areas. Similarly, Washington permits only one-bank holding companies. . . .

B. Structure of the Spokane Market

Since the legality of the challenged merger must be judged by its effects on the relevant product and geographic markets, commercial banking in the Spokane metropolitan area, it is imperative to determine the competitive characteristics of commercial banking in that section of the country. The potential competition doctrine has meaning only as applied to concentrated markets. That is, the doctrine comes into play only where there are dominant participants in the target market engaging in interdependent or parallel behavior and with the capacity effectively to determine price and total output of goods or services. If the target market performs as a competitive market in traditional antitrust terms, the participants in the market will have no occasion to fashion their behavior to take into account the presence of a potential entrant. The present procompetitive effects that a perceived potential entrant may produce in an oligopolistic market will already have been accomplished if the target market is performing competitively. Likewise, there would be no need for concern about the prospects of long-term deconcentration of a market which is in fact genuinely competitive.

In an effort to establish that the Spokane commercial banking market is oligopolistic, the Government relied primarily on concentration ratios indicating that three banking organizations (including WTB) control approximately 92% of total deposits in Spokane. The District Court held against the Government on this point, finding that "a highly competitive market" existed which "does not suffer from parallel or other anticompetitive practices attributable to undue market power." The court apparently gave great weight to the testimony of the banks' expert witnesses concerning the number of bank organizations and banking offices operating in the Spokane metropolitan area. The record indicates that neither the Government nor the appellees undertook any significant study of the performance, as compared to the structure, of the commercial banking market in Spokane.

We conclude that by introducing evidence of concentration ratios of the magnitude of those present here the Government established a prima facie case that the Spokane market was a candidate for the potential competition doctrine. On this aspect of the case, the burden was then upon appellees to show that the concentration ratios, which can be unreliable indicators of actual market behavior, see United States v. General Dynamics Corporation, did not accurately depict the economic characteristics of the Spokane market. In our view, appellees did not carry this burden, and the District Court erred in holding to the contrary. Appellees introduced no significant evidence of the absence of parallel behavior in the pricing or provision of commercial bank services in Spokane.

We note that it is hardly surprising that the Spokane commercial banking market is structurally concentrated. As the Government's expert witness conceded, *all* banking markets in the country are likely to be concentrated. This is so because as a country we have made the policy judgment to restrict entry into commercial banking in order to promote bank safety. Thus, most banking markets in theory will be subject to the potential competition doctrine. But the same factor that usually renders such markets concentrated and theoretical prospects for potential competition § 7 cases—regulatory barriers to new entry—will also make it difficult to establish that the doctrine invalidates a particular geographic market extension merger.

C. *Potential De Novo or Foothold Entry*

The third step in the Government's argument, resolution of the question reserved in *Falstaff*, was the primary basis on which the case was presented to the District Court and to us. The Government contends that the challenged merger violates § 7 because it eliminates the alleged likelihood that, but for the merger, NBC would enter Spokane *de novo* or through a foothold acquisition. Utilization of one of these methods of entry, it is argued, would be likely to produce deconcentration of the Spokane market over the long run or other procompetitive effects, because NBC would be required to compete vigorously to expand its initially insignificant market share.

Two essential preconditions must exist before it is possible to resolve whether the Government's theory, if proven, establishes a violation of § 7. It must be determined: (i) that in fact NBC has available feasible means for entering the Spokane market other than by acquiring WTB; and (ii) that those means offer a substantial likelihood of ultimately producing deconcentration of that market or other significant procompetitive effects. The parties are in sharp disagreement over the existence of each of these preconditions in this case. There is no dispute that NBC possesses the financial capability and incentive to enter. The controversy turns on what methods of entry are realistically possible and on the likely effect of various methods on the characteristics of the Spokane commercial banking market.

It is undisputed that under state law NBC cannot establish *de novo* branches in Spokane and that its parent holding company cannot hold more than 25% of the stock of any other bank. Entry for NBC into Spokane therefore must be by acquisition of an existing bank. The Government contends that NBC has two distinct alternatives for acquisition of banks smaller than WTB and that either alternative would be likely to benefit the Spokane commercial banking market.

First, the Government contends that NBC could arrange for the formation of a new bank (a concept known as "sponsorship"), insure that the stock for such a new bank is placed in friendly hands, and then ultimately acquire that bank. Appellees respond that this approach would violate the spirit if not the letter of state law restrictions on bank branching. They note that this method would require the issuance of either a state or a national charter, and they assert that neither state nor federal banking authorities would be likely to grant a charter for a new bank in a static, "well-banked" market like Spokane. Moreover, it is argued that such officials would be certain to refuse to do so where the purpose of the scheme was to avoid the requirements of the state branching law. Appellees further note that the stock and assets of any new state bank in Washington are inalienable for at least 10 years without approval of state banking officials, and they argue that such officials would refuse to grant approval for sale as part of a sponsorship plan.

. . . Although we note that the intricate procedure for entry by sponsorship espoused by the Government can scarcely be compared to the *de novo* entry opportunities available to unregulated enterprises such as beer producers, see *Falstaff*, supra, we will assume *arguendo* that NBC conceivably could succeed in sponsoring and then acquiring a new bank in Spokane at some indefinite time in the future. It does not follow from this assumption, however, that this method of entry would be reasonably likely to produce any significant procompetitive benefits in the Spokane commercial banking market. To the contrary, it appears likely that such a method of entry would not significantly affect that market.

State law would not allow NBC to branch from a sponsored bank after it was acquired. NBC's entry into Spokane therefore would be frozen at the level of its initial acquisition. Thus, if NBC were to enter Spokane by sponsoring and acquiring a small bank, it would be trapped into a position of operating a single branch office in a large metropolitan area with no reasonable likelihood of developing a significant share of that market. This assumed method of entry therefore would offer little realistic hope of ultimately producing deconcentration of the Spokane market. Moreover, it is unlikely that a single new bank in Spokane with a small market share, and forbidden to branch, would have any other significant procompetitive effect on that market. The Government introduced no evidence, for example, establishing that the three small banks presently in Spokane have had any meaningful effect on the economic behavior of the large Spokane banks. In sum, it blinks reality to conclude that the opportunity for entry through sponsorship, assuming its availability, is comparable to the entry alternatives open to unregulated industries such as those involved in this Court's prior potential competition cases or would be likely to produce the competitive effects of a truly unfettered method of entry. Since there is no substantial likelihood of procompetitive loss if the challenged merger is undertaken in place of the Government's sponsorship theory, we are unable to conclude that the effect of the former "may be substantially to lessen competition" within the meaning of the Clayton Act.

As a second alternate method of entry, the Government proposed that NBC could enter by a foothold acquisition of one of two small, state-chartered commercial banks that operate in the Spokane metropolitan area.[84] Appellees reply that one of those banks is located in a suburb and has no offices in the city of Spokane, that after an acquisition NBC under state law could not branch from the suburb into the city, and that such a peripheral foothold cannot be viewed as an economically feasible method of entry into the relevant market. Appellees also point out that the second small bank was chartered in 1965 and thus under state law would not have been available for acquisition until at least four years after the 1971 NBC–WTB merger agreement.

Granting the Government the benefit of the doubt that these two small banks were available merger partners for NBC, or were available at some not too distant point in time, it again does not follow that an acquisition of either would produce the long-term market-structure benefits predicted by the Government. Once NBC acquired either of these banks, it could not branch from the acquired bank. This limitation strongly suggests that NBC would not develop into a significant participant in the Spokane market, a prospect that finds support in the record. In 1964, one of the largest bank holding companies in the country, through its Seattle-based subsidiary, acquired a foothold bank with two offices in Spokane. Eight years later this bank, Pacific National Bank, held a mere 2.2% of total bank deposits in the Spokane metropolitan area, an insignificant increase over its share of the market at the date of the acquisition. An officer of this bank, called as a witness by the Government, attributed the poor showing to an inability under state law to establish further branches in Spokane.

In sum, with regard to either of its proposed alternate methods of entry, the Government has offered an unpersuasive case on the first precondition of the question reserved in *Falstaff*—that feasible alternate methods of entry in fact existed. Putting these difficulties aside, the Government simply did not establish the second precondition. It failed to demonstrate that the alternate means offer a reasonable prospect of long-term structural improvement or other benefits in the target market. In fact, insofar as competitive benefits are concerned, the Government is in the anomalous position of opposing a geographic market extension merger that will introduce a third full service banking organization to the Spokane market, where only two are now operating, in reliance on alternate means of entry that appear unlikely to have any significant procompetitive effect. Accordingly, we cannot hold for the Government on its principal potential competition theory. Indeed, since the preconditions for that theory are not present, we do not reach it, and therefore we express no view on the appropriate resolution of the question reserved in *Falstaff.*

84. [Court's footnote 44.] The third small bank in Spokane is a branch of a large nationally chartered bank in Seattle, which in turn is owned by a large holding company. There is no allegation that this small bank is a potential foothold acquisition. The Government presses its foothold-acquisition approach with considerably less vigor than its sponsorship theory, which may reflect the fact that under the former approach the total number of banking organizations in Spokane would remain the same.

We reiterate that this case concerns an industry in which new entry is extensively regulated by the State and Federal Governments.

D. Perceived Potential Entry

The Government's failure to establish that NBC has alternate methods of entry that offer a reasonable likelihood of producing procompetitive effects is determinative of the fourth step of its argument. Rational commercial bankers in Spokane, it must be assumed, are aware of the regulatory barriers that render NBC an unlikely or an insignificant potential entrant except by merger with WTB. In light of those barriers, it is improbable that NBC exerts any meaningful procompetitive influence over Spokane banks by standing "in the wings."

Moreover, the District Court found as a fact that "the threat of entry by NBC into the Spokane market by any means other than the consummation of the merger, to the extent any such threat exists, does not have any significant effect on the competitive practices of commercial banks in that market nor any significant effect on the level of competition therein." In making this finding, it appears that the District Court "appraised the economic facts" about NBC and the Spokane market "in order to determine whether in any realistic sense [NBC] could be said to be a potential competitor on the fringe of the market with likely influence on existing competition." *Falstaff*, supra. Our review of the record indicates that the court's finding was not in error. The Government's only hard evidence of any "wings effect" was a memorandum written in 1962 by an officer of NBC expressing the view that Spokane banks were likely to engage in price competition as NCB approached their market. Evidence of an expression of opinion by an officer of the acquiring bank, not an official of a bank operating in the target market, in a memorandum written a decade prior to the challenged merger does not establish a violation of § 7.

. . .

IV. CONCLUSION

In applying the doctrine of potential competition to commercial banking, courts must, as we have noted, take into account the extensive federal and state regulation of banks. Our affirmance of the District Court's judgment in this case rests primarily on state statutory barriers to *de novo* entry and to expansion following entry into a new geographic market. . . . In States that permit free branching or multibank holding companies, courts hearing cases involving such mergers should take into account all relevant factors, including the barriers to entry created by state and federal control over the issuance of new bank charters. Testimony by responsible regulatory officials that they will not grant new charters in the target market is entitled to great weight, although it is not determinative. To avoid the danger of subjecting the enforcement of the antitrust laws to the policies of a particular bank regulatory official or agency, courts should look also to the size and growth prospects of the target market, the size and number of banking organizations participating in it, and past practices of regulatory agencies in granting charters. If regulatory restraints are not determinative, courts should consider the factors that are pertinent to any potential competition case, including the economic feasibility and likelihood of *de novo* entry, the capabilities and expansion history of the acquiring firm, and the performance as well as the structural characteristics of the target market.

The judgment is affirmed.

MR. JUSTICE DOUGLAS took no part in the decision of this case.

[MR. JUSTICE WHITE, with whom MR. JUSTICE BRENNAN and MR. JUSTICE MARSHALL joined, filed a dissenting opinion, condemning the "new anti-trust majority" which "for the second time this term has chipped away at the policies of § 7 of the Clayton Act" (the first time being *United States v. General Dynamics*, supra p. 239). The dissent pointed out, inter alia, that given the opportunity NBC would "obviously" enter Spokane and that consent by banking authorities, given for the WTB acquisition, would likely have been forthcoming; that the sponsored bank method of expansion had occurred frequently in Washington; that presently existing small banks were profitable in Spokane and could have given NBC "substantial operating capacity" in Spokane; and that prior to the WTB acquisition it had been negotiating for a smaller suburban acquisition:

> "The Spokane market was highly concentrated. NBC had the resources and the desire to enter the market. There were no impenetrable legal or economic barriers to its doing so; and it is sufficiently plain from the record that absent merger with WTB, NBC could and would either have made a toehold entry or been instrumental in establishing a sponsored bank in Spokane. But NBC chose to merge with a larger bank and to deprive the market of the competition it would have offered had it entered in either of two other ways. In my opinion, this made out a sufficient *prima facie* case under § 7, which, absent effective rebuttal, entitled the United States to judgment. . . .

> "In the last analysis, one's view of this case, and the rules one devises for assessing whether this merger should be barred, turns on the policy of Clayton § 7 to bar mergers which may contribute to further concentration in the structure of American business."]

NOTES AND QUERIES

(1) *Queries.* After *Marine Bancorporation* will it be difficult for Government counsel (or a private plaintiff) to prove the elements of a potential competition case? (1) How will Government counsel show that the premerger target market was not a competitive one? If the Government relies on market share data, as defense counsel how would you rebut the inferences from this evidence? If these inferences are rebutted, what evidence could

the Government then introduce to carry its burden of proof? (2) How can the Government show that competitors in the target market "in fact" tempered anticompetitive conduct in response to the acquiring firm's presence "on the wings"? As Government counsel, what sorts of evidence would you look for? If a current competitor testifies at trial that he or she "had never been influenced" in pricing or marketing decisions by the acquiring firm's presence, what weight will such testimony likely have with the fact-finder (compare *Falstaff,* supra p. 273)? (3) What is the range of evidence relevant to the question whether an actual potential entrant "in fact" has available feasible means for entering the target market and will produce "significant procompetitive effects"? How detailed an inquiry must a court make into the acquiring firm's operating methods and financial capabilities? How can Government counsel prove with "substantial likelihood" what the target market would be like in the future with the addition of the acquiring firm? Is it harder to predict confidently what a new entrant will do in the future, than what firms already in the market will do?

Has the Court in *Marine Bancorporation* (and *General Dynamics*) abandoned its attempt to create easily administrable standards for Section 7? Is that unwise because it makes prediction by business firms more difficult? Or is the Court properly reflecting skepticism toward a simplistic market-structure view of competition, which virtually equates concentration and non-competition, and now merely telling the Government to "prove it"?

(2) *Avoiding Potential Competition Doctrines Through "Supply-Side Substitutability"?* Plaintiffs in potential competition cases following *Marine Bancorporation* have not fared well.[85] Should plaintiffs now try to reverse the usual litigation strategy over product market definition by arguing for broader markets so as to make the merger appear "horizontal"? The Federal Trade Commission attempted to do so in *Equifax, Inc. v. Federal Trade Commission,* 618 F.2d 63 (9th Cir. 1980). Equifax was engaged in the production of "mortgage reports" for customers interested in the character and financial status of prospective mortgagors. It acquired several credit bureaus which produced "credit reports," used by various consumer credit lenders, especially department stores, interested in the bill-paying habits of prospective credit customers. The FTC, while admitting that the two types of reports were "not identical and [were] differently priced," found that the reports were "substantially identical" and contained much of the same information. It based its determination that the two report types were within the same product market on the ground that a "commonality of production techniques" existed resulting in substantial elasticity on the supply side of the market. The court of appeals, however, rejected the Commission's finding, although it stated that "[i]t is well settled that cross-elasticity of supply is a valid basis for determining that two commodities should be within the same market." The court found no substantial evidence of similar techniques or

85. See, e.g., United States v. Siemens Corp., 621 F.2d 499 (2d Cir. 1980) (Government proof "inadequate" to even demonstrate likelihood of de novo entry; proof of wings effect "woefully deficient") (denying preliminary injunction); Lektro-Vend Corp. v. Vendo Corp., 500 F.Supp. 332 (N.D.Ill.1980) ("The difficulty of meeting these criteria [from *Marine Bancorporation*] has resulted in almost uniform rejection of potential competition theories in market extension cases subsequent to *Marine Bancorporation*.") (citing cases). A significant exception is Yamaha Motor Co. Ltd. v. Federal Trade Commission, 657 F.2d 971 (8th Cir. 1981), affirming the F.T.C.'s finding of a Section 7 violation based on the actual potential competition doctrine, in a joint venture between the second firm in a four-firm market and a firm not in the market.

technology, and only "insubstantial evidence" to support the finding that credit bureaus generally produced mortgage reports.

(3) *Does Section 7 Reach Mergers Which Eliminate Future Competition?* Brodley, in Potential Competition Mergers: A Structural Approach, 87 Yale L.J. 1, 42–44 (1977), argues that Congress intended Section 7 to cover future entry (footnotes omitted):

> Previous studies of the legislative history have not addressed the question of congressional intent as to potential competition. In part this may be because the words "potential competition" appear only rarely in the legislative history. The reason for this omission is that in then-current legislative usage, as reflected in several key documents, most potential competition mergers were classified as horizontal. It is here that the key to congressional intent concerning potential competition mergers must be found.

> Horizontal mergers were the object of greatest congressional concern in the deliberations over amending section 7. While the amended statute was intended to reach all mergers, horizontal acquisitions were the prime target because the contemporary "merger movement" was predominantly horizontal, and the horizontal merger most impinges upon the values Congress sought to protect. From this it appears that the judicial development of a stringent rule for horizontal mergers was singularly responsive to congressional priorities.

> The judicial and legislative views gradually diverged, however, on what constitutes a "horizontal merger." For the courts, a horizontal merger came to mean a merger between present, direct competitors. The term had a wider scope in congressional usage and included market extensions and close product extensions, as well as mergers between producers of goods that can be substitutes for each other.

> The difference in usage reflects a fundamental disagreement as to the time perspective of section 7. Congress wished to forestall concentration and to promote competitive market structures over the long run. Viewed from this longer-term perspective, the distinction between direct and potential competition blurs. Under the logic of the congressional usage, market and close product extension mergers are horizontal because, over time, potential competitors in close market proximity tend to become actual competitors. Not all potential competitors finally meet in the market place, to be sure, but as the time frame extends, the probability of such eventual competition is sufficient, according to Congress, to require a statute that reaches future events of reasonable probability.

> The narrower judicial definition of horizontal mergers reflects a shorter-term perspective. Given a sufficiently short outlook, only a merger between existing competitors (or involving a firm in the process of entry) is horizontal. . . .

> By taking a longer range view of competition the judiciary would give clearer recognition to the congressional desire not only to arrest increases in concentration, but also to promote a competitive structure in the future, for clearly Congress thought concentration to be already excessive.

(4) *Marine Bancorporation and Geographic Market Definition.* In *Marine Bancorporation* the Court held that the relevant geographic market "is the area in which the acquired firm is an actual, direct competitor." The Court remanded a companion case, *United States v. Connecticut National Bank,* 418 U.S. 656, 94 S.Ct. 2788, 41 L.Ed.2d 1016 (1974), for the trial court to pursue a localized approach to determine areas in which the merging

banks operated, despite the banks' concession that the merger should be analyzed in terms of effect on possible competition in areas not in or adjacent to current markets. To what extent are these views applicable outside potential competition cases? In horizontal cases, can the plaintiff argue for a national market if the acquired firm does not actually compete in every market across the country? In assessing foreclosure in vertical cases, must the court be confined to the geographic area where the acquired firm currently buys (or sells) its product? Lower courts after *Marine Bancorporation* do not appear to be applying such rigidly mechanical tests,[86] but *Marine Bancorporation* has rekindled litigants' interest in contesting the issue, interest which had been virtually dormant since *Pabst* (see p. 218, supra).

E. PRODUCT MARKET EXTENSION AND CONGLOMERATE MERGERS

FEDERAL TRADE COMMISSION v. PROCTER & GAMBLE CO.

Supreme Court of the United States, 1967.
386 U.S. 568, 87 S.Ct. 1224, 18 L.Ed.2d 303.

MR. JUSTICE DOUGLAS delivered the opinion of the Court.

This is a proceeding initiated by the Federal Trade Commission charging that respondent, Procter & Gamble Co., had acquired the assets of Clorox Chemical Co. in violation of § 7 of the Clayton Act. The charge was that Procter's acquisition of Clorox might substantially lessen competition or tend to create a monopoly in the production and sale of household liquid bleaches.

Following evidentiary hearings, the hearing examiner rendered his decision in which he concluded that the acquisition was unlawful and ordered divestiture. On appeal, the Commission reversed, holding that the record as then constituted was inadequate, and remanded to the examiner for additional evidentiary hearings. After the additional hearings, the examiner again held the acquisition unlawful and ordered divestiture. The Commission affirmed the examiner and ordered divestiture. The Court of Appeals for the Sixth Circuit

---

86. See, e.g., Jim Walter Corp. v. Federal Trade Commission, 625 F.2d 676 (5th Cir. 1980) (rejecting defense argument that, as a matter of law, market was 26 states in which acquired firm marketed products rather than the entire nation, as found by the F.T.C.; Government could identify area where defendant's sales have a "perceptible competitive impact" by showing, e.g., pricing interdependence among geographical areas; but F.T.C. "casual observations" inadequate to prove nationwide competition); RSR Corp. v. Federal Trade Commission, 602 F.2d 1317 (9th Cir. 1979), certiorari denied 445 U.S. 927, 100 S.Ct. 1313, 63 L.Ed.2d 760 (1980) (finding national market despite fact that high trucking costs caused producers to ship most of their product to their customers within a few hundred miles; regional pricing found to be interrelated, leading to variations in shipping distances; concentration of customers in certain geographical areas discounted because many states generate little or no demand for product); F. & M. Schaefer Corp. v. C. Schmidt & Sons, Inc., 597 F.2d 814 (2d Cir. 1979) (New York and Philadelphia metropolitan areas treated as discrete markets by beer industry and merger partners; court not required to adopt 12-state region constituting economic shipping distance); United States v. Hammermill Paper Co., 429 F.Supp. 1271 (W.D.Pa.1977) (rejecting Government contention that relevant market was where acquired customer operated; market is area in which acquiring seller and its competitors operate).

reversed and directed that the Commission's complaint be dismissed. 358 F.2d 74. We find that the Commission's findings were amply supported by the evidence, and that the Court of Appeals erred.

As indicated by the Commission in its painstaking and illuminating report, it does not particularly aid analysis to talk of this merger in conventional terms, namely, horizontal or vertical or conglomerate. This merger may most appropriately be described as a "product-extension merger," as the Commission stated. The facts are not disputed, and a summary will demonstrate the correctness of the Commission's decision.

At the time of the merger, in 1957, Clorox was the leading manufacturer in the heavily concentrated household liquid bleach industry. It is agreed that household liquid bleach is the relevant line of commerce. The product is used in the home as a germicide and disinfectant, and, more importantly, as a whitening agent in washing clothes and fabrics. It is a distinctive product with no close substitutes. Liquid bleach is a low-price, high-turnover consumer product sold mainly through grocery stores and supermarkets. The relevant geographical market is the Nation and a series of regional markets. Because of high shipping costs and low sales price, it is not feasible to ship the product more than 300 miles from its point of manufacture. Most manufacturers are limited to competition within a single region since they have but one plant. Clorox is the only firm selling nationally; it has 13 plants distributed throughout the Nation. Purex, Clorox's closest competitor in size, does not distribute its bleach in the northeast or mid-Atlantic States; in 1957, Purex's bleach was available in less than 50% of the national market.

At the time of the acquisition, Clorox was the leading manufacturer of household liquid bleach, with 48.8% of the national sales—annual sales of slightly less than $40,000,000. Its market share had been steadily increasing for the five years prior to the merger. Its nearest rival was Purex, which manufactures a number of products other than household liquid bleaches, including abrasive cleaners, toilet soap, and detergents. Purex accounted for 15.7% of the household liquid bleach market. The industry is highly concentrated; in 1957, Clorox and Purex accounted for almost 65% of the Nation's household liquid bleach sales, and, together with four other firms, for almost 80%. The remaining 20% was divided among over 200 small producers. Clorox had total assets of $12,000,000; only eight producers had assets in excess of $1,000,000 and very few had assets of more than $75,000.

In light of the territorial limitations on distribution, national figures do not give an accurate picture of Clorox's dominance in the various regions. Thus, Clorox's seven principal competitors did no business in New England, the mid-Atlantic States, or metropolitan New York. Clorox's share of the sales in those areas was 56%, 72% and 64% respectively. Even in regions where its principal competitors were active, Clorox maintained a dominant position. Except in metropolitan Chicago and the west-central States Clorox accounted for at least 39%, and often a much higher percentage, of liquid bleach sales.

Since all liquid bleach is chemically identical, advertising and sales promotion are vital. In 1957 Clorox spent almost $3,700,000 on advertising, imprinting the value of its bleach in the mind of the consumer. In addition, it spent $1,700,000 for other promotional activities. The Commission found that these heavy expenditures went far to explain why Clorox maintained so high a market share despite the fact that its brand, though chemically indistinguishable from rival brands, retailed for a price equal to or, in many instances, higher than its competitors.

Procter is a large, diversified manufacturer of low-price, high-turnover household products sold through grocery, drug, and department stores. Prior to its acquisition of Clorox, it did not produce household liquid bleach. Its 1957 sales were in excess of $1,100,000,000 from which it realized profits of more than $67,000,000; its assets were over $500,000,000. Procter has been marked by rapid growth and diversification. It has successfully developed and introduced a number of new products. Its primary activity is in the general area of soaps, detergents, and cleansers; in 1957, of total domestic sales, more than one-half (over $500,000,000) were in this field. Procter was the dominant factor in this area.

It accounted for 54.4% of all packaged detergent sales. The industry is heavily concentrated—Procter and its nearest competitors, Colgate-Palmolive and Lever Brothers, account for 80% of the market.

In the marketing of soaps, detergents, and cleansers, as in the marketing of household liquid bleach, advertising and sales promotion are vital. In 1957, Procter was the Nation's largest advertiser, spending more than $80,000,000 on advertising and an additional $47,000,000 on sales promotion. Due to its tremendous volume, Procter receives substantial discounts from the media. As a multi-product producer Procter enjoys substantial advantages in advertising and sales promotion. Thus, it can and does feature several products in its promotions, reducing the printing, mailing, and other costs for each product. It also purchases network programs on behalf of several products, enabling it to give each product network exposure at a fraction of the cost per product that a firm with only one product to advertise would incur.

Prior to the acquisition, Procter was in the course of diversifying into product lines related to its basic detergent-soap-cleanser business. Liquid bleach was a distinct possibility since packaged detergents—Procter's primary product line—and liquid bleach are used complementarily in washing clothes and fabrics, and in general household cleaning. As noted by the Commission:

> "Packaged detergents—Procter's most important product category—and household liquid bleach are used complementarily, not only in the washing of clothes and fabrics, but also in general household cleaning, since liquid bleach is a germicide and disinfec-

tant as well as a whitener. From the consumer's viewpoint, then, packaged detergents and liquid bleach are closely related products. But the area of relatedness between products of Procter and of Clorox is wider. Household cleansing agents in general, like household liquid bleach, are low-cost, high-turnover household consumer goods marketed chiefly through grocery stores and presold to the consumer by the manufacturer through mass advertising and sales promotions. Since products of both parties to the merger are sold to the same customers, at the same stores, and by the same merchandising methods, the possibility arises of significant integration at both the marketing and distribution levels."

The decision to acquire Clorox was the result of a study conducted by Procter's promotion department designed to determine the advisability of entering the liquid bleach industry. The initial report noted the ascendancy of liquid bleach in the large and expanding household bleach market, and recommended that Procter purchase Clorox rather than enter independently. Since a large investment would be needed to obtain a satisfactory market share, acquisition of the industry's leading firm was attractive. "Taking over the Clorox business . . . could be a way of achieving a dominant position in the liquid bleach market quickly, which would pay out reasonably well." The initial report predicted that Procter's "sales, distribution and manufacturing setup" could increase Clorox's share of the markets in areas where it was low. The final report confirmed the conclusions of the initial report and emphasized that Procter would make more effective use of Clorox's advertising budget and that the merger would facilitate advertising economies. A few months later, Procter acquired the assets of Clorox in the name of a wholly owned subsidiary, the Clorox Company, in exchange for Procter stock.

The Commission found that the acquisition might substantially lessen competition. The findings and reasoning of the Commission need be only briefly summarized. The Commission found that the substitution of Procter with its huge assets and advertising advantages for the already dominant Clorox would dissuade new entrants and discourage active competition from the firms already in the industry due to fear of retaliation by Procter. The Commission thought it relevant that retailers might be induced to give Clorox preferred shelf space since it would be manufactured by Procter, which also produced a number of other products marketed by the retailers. There was also the danger that Procter might underprice Clorox in order to drive out competition, and subsidize the underpricing with revenue from other products. The Commission carefully reviewed the effect of the acquisition on the structure of the industry, noting that "[t]he practical tendency of the . . . merger . . . is to transform the liquid bleach industry into an arena of big business competition only, with the few small firms that have not disappeared through merger eventually falling by the wayside, unable to compete with their giant rivals." Further, the merger would seriously diminish potential competition by eliminating Procter as a potential entrant into the industry. Prior to the merger, the Commission found,

Procter was the most likely prospective entrant, and absent the merger would have remained on the periphery, restraining Clorox from exercising its market power. If Procter had actually entered, Clorox's dominant position would have been eroded and the concentration of the industry reduced. The Commission stated that it had not placed reliance on post-acquisition evidence in holding the merger unlawful.

The Court of Appeals said that the Commission's finding of illegality had been based on "treacherous conjecture," mere possibility and suspicion. 358 F.2d 74, 83. It dismissed the fact that Clorox controlled almost 50% of the industry, that two firms controlled 65%, and that six firms controlled 80% with the observation that "[t]he fact that in addition to the six . . . producers sharing eighty per cent of the market, there were two hundred smaller producers . . . would not seem to indicate anything unhealthy about the market conditions." Id., at 80. It dismissed the finding that Procter, with its huge resources and prowess, would have more leverage than Clorox with the statement that it was Clorox which had the "know-how" in the industry, and that Clorox's finances were adequate for its purposes. Ibid. As for the possibility that Procter would use its tremendous advertising budget and volume discounts to push Clorox, the court found "it difficult to base a finding of illegality on discounts in advertising." 358 F.2d, at 81. It rejected the Commission's finding that the merger eliminated the potential competition of Procter because "[t]here was no reasonable probability that Procter would have entered the household liquid bleach market but for the merger." 358 F.2d, at 83. "There was no evidence tending to prove that Procter ever intended to enter this field on its own." 358 F.2d, at 82. Finally, "[t]here was no evidence that Procter at any time in the past engaged in predatory practices, or that it intended to do so in the future." Ibid.

The Court of Appeals also heavily relied on post-acquisition "evidence . . . to the effect that the other producers subsequent to the merger were selling more bleach for more money than ever before" (358 F.2d, at 80), and that "[t]here [had] been no significant change in Clorox's market share in the four years subsequent to the merger" (ibid.), and concluded that "[t]his evidence certainly does not prove anticompetitive effects of the merger." Id., at 82. The Court of Appeals, in our view, misapprehended the standards for its review and the standards applicable in a § 7 proceeding.

Section 7 of the Clayton Act was intended to arrest the anticompetitive effects of market power in their incipiency. The core question is whether a merger may substantially lessen competition, and necessarily requires a prediction of the merger's impact on competition, present and future. And there is certainly no requirement that the anticompetitive power manifest itself in anticompetitive action before § 7 can be called into play. If the enforcement of § 7 turned on the existence of actual anticompetitive practices, the congressional policy of thwarting such practices in their incipiency would be frustrated.

All mergers are within the reach of § 7, and all must be tested by the same standard whether they are classified as horizontal, vertical, conglomerate [87] or other. As noted by the Commission, this merger is neither horizontal, vertical, nor conglomerate. Since the products of the acquired company are complementary to those of the acquiring company and may be produced with similar facilities, marketed through the same channels and in the same manner, and advertised by the same media, the Commission aptly called this acquisition a "product-extension merger":

"By this acquisition . . . Procter has not diversified its interest in the sense of expanding into a substantially different, unfamiliar market or industry. Rather, it has entered a market which adjoins, as it were, those markets in which it is already established, and which is virtually indistinguishable from them insofar as the problems and techniques of marketing the product to the ultimate consumer are concerned. As a high official of Procter put it, commenting on the acquisition of Clorox, 'While this is a completely new business for us, taking us for the first time into the marketing of a household bleach and disinfectant, we are thoroughly at home in the field of manufacturing and marketing low priced, rapid turn-over consumer products.' "

The anticompetitive effects with which this product-extension merger is fraught can easily be seen: (1) the substitution of the powerful acquiring firm for the smaller, but already dominant, firm may substantially reduce the competitive structure of the industry by raising entry barriers and by dissuading the smaller firms from aggressively competing; (2) the acquisition eliminates the potential competition of the acquiring firm.

The liquid bleach industry was already oligopolistic before the acquisition, and price competition was certainly not as vigorous as it would have been if the industry were competitive. Clorox enjoyed a dominant position nationally, and its position approached monopoly proportions in certain areas. The existence of some 200 fringe firms certainly does not belie that fact. Nor does the fact, relied upon by the court below, that, after the merger, producers other than Clorox "were selling more bleach for more money than ever before." 358 F.2d at 80. In the same period, Clorox increased its share from 48.8% to 52%. The interjection of Procter into the market considerably changed the situation. There is every reason to assume that the smaller firms would become more cautious in competing due to their fear of retaliation by Procter. It is probable that Procter would become the price leader and that oligopoly would become more rigid.

The acquisition may also have the tendency of raising the barriers to new entry. The major competitive weapon in the successful marketing of bleach is advertising. Clorox was limited in this area by its relatively small budget and its inability to obtain substantial dis-

87. [Footnote 2 in original.] A pure conglomerate merger is one in which there are no economic relationships be- tween the acquiring and the acquired firm.

counts. By contrast, Procter's budget was much larger; and, although it would not devote its entire budget to advertising Clorox, it could divert a large potion to meet the short-term threat of a new entrant. Procter would be able to use its volume discounts to advantage in advertising Clorox. Thus, a new entrant would be much more reluctant to face the giant Procter than it would have been to face the smaller Clorox.[88]

Possible economies cannot be used as a defense to illegality. Congress was aware that some mergers which lessen competition may also result in economies but it struck the balance in favor of protecting competition. See Brown Shoe Co. v. United States, supra, 370 U.S. at 344, 82 S.Ct. 1534.

The Commission also found that the acquisition of Clorox by Procter eliminated Procter as a potential competitor. The Court of Appeals declared that this finding was not supported by evidence because there was no evidence that Procter's management had ever intended to enter the industry independently and that Procter had never attempted to enter. The evidence, however, clearly shows that Procter was the most likely entrant. Procter had recently launched a new abrasive cleaner in an industry similar to the liquid bleach industry, and had wrested leadership from a brand that had enjoyed even a larger market share than had Clorox. Procter was engaged in a vigorous program of diversifying into product lines closely related to its basic products. Liquid bleach was a natural avenue of diversification since it is complementary to Procter's products, is sold to the same customers through the same channels, and is advertised and merchandised in the same manner. Procter had substantial advantages in advertising and sales promotion, which, as we have seen, are vital to the success of liquid bleach. No manufacturer had a patent on the product or its manufacture, necessary information relating to manufacturing methods and processes were readily available, there was no shortage of raw material, and the machinery and equipment required

88. [Footnote 3 in original.] The barriers to entry have been raised both for entry by new firms and for entry into new geographical markets by established firms. The latter aspect is demonstrated by Purex's lesson in Erie, Pennsylvania. In October 1957, Purex selected Erie, Pennsylvania—where it had not sold previously—as an area in which to test the salability, under competitive conditions, of a new bleach. The leading brands in Erie were Clorox, with 52%, and the "101" brand, sold by Gardner Manufacturing Company, with 29% of the market. Purex launched an advertising and promotional campaign to obtain a broad distribution in a short time, and in five months captured 33% of the Erie market. Clorox's share dropped to 35% and 101's to 17%. Clorox responded by offering its bleach at reduced prices, and then added an offer of a $1-value ironing board cover for 50¢ with each purchase of Clorox at the reduced price. It also increased its advertising with television spots. The result was to restore Clorox's lost market share and, indeed, to increase it slightly. Purex's share fell to 7%.

Since the merger Purex has acquired the fourth largest producer of bleach, John Puhl Products Company, which owned and marketed "Fleecy White" brand in geographic markets which Purex was anxious to enter. One of the reasons for this acquisition, according to Purex's president, was that:

"Purex had been unsuccessful in expanding its market position geographically on Purex liquid bleach. The economics of the bleach business, and the strong competitive factors as illustrated by our experience in Erie, Pennsylvania, make it impossible, in our judgment, for us to expand our market on liquid bleach."

for a plant of efficient capacity were available at reasonable cost. Procter's management was experienced in producing and marketing goods similar to liquid bleach. Procter had considered the possibility of independently entering but decided against it because the acquisition of Clorox would enable Procter to capture a more commanding share of the market.

It is clear that the existence of Procter at the edge of the industry exerted considerable influence on the market. First, the market behavior of the liquid bleach industry was influenced by each firm's predictions of the market behavior of its competitors, actual and potential. Second, the barriers to entry by a firm of Procter's size and with its advantages were not significant. There is no indication that the barriers were so high that the price Procter would have to charge would be above the price that would maximize the profits of the existing firms. Third, the number of potential entrants was not so large that the elimination of one would be insignificant. Few firms would have the temerity to challenge a firm as solidly entrenched as Clorox. Fourth, Procter was found by the Commission to be the most likely entrant. These findings of the Commission were amply supported by the evidence.

The judgment of the Court of Appeals is reversed and remanded with instructions to affirm and enforce the Commission's order.[89]

MR. JUSTICE STEWART and MR. JUSTICE FORTAS took no part in the consideration or decision of this case.

[Mr. Justice Harlan wrote a concurring opinion expressing the need for "full investigation and analysis," given the inadequate state of economic knowledge about the competitive effects of conglomerate mergers. He argued, inter alia, that: it was necessary to focus on market structure to formulate administrable merger standards; although the Commission could properly regard this market as oligopolistic, defendants in conglomerate merger cases should also be free "to build their own economic cases for the proposition that the mergers will not impair competition"; that potential competition (of the "wings" variety) merely affects pricing power, but does not advance "any other social goal which Congress might be said to have favored in passing § 7"; and that "countervailing economies reasonably probable" must be weighed against adverse effects. Procter's asserted advertising economies, however, would not qualify as "real" economies in Justice Harlan's view: "Procter has merely shown that it is able to command equivalent resources at a lower dollar cost than other bleach procedures. No peculiarly efficient marketing techniques

89. See also Allis-Chalmers Mfg. Co. v. White Consolidated Industries, Inc., 414 F.2d 506 (3d Cir. 1969) cert. denied 396 U.S. 1009, 90 S.Ct. 567, 24 L.Ed.2d 501; General Foods Corp. v. Federal Trade Commission, 386 F.2d 936 (3d Cir. 1967), cert. denied 391 U.S. 919, 88 S.Ct. 1805, 20 L.Ed.2d 657; Hellman, Entrenchment Under Section 7 of the Clayton Act: An Approach for Analyzing Conglomerate Mergers, 13 Loy.Chi.L.J. 225 (1982). Procter entered the bleach market de novo in 1982. See "P & G wants to Market Bleach; Clorox Prepares for Big Fight," Wall St.J., June 24, 1982, p. 31 (reporting Clorox "may be in for the marketing fight of its life"; Clorox' market share for 1981 was 52% of liquid bleach and 60% of powdered bleach).

have been demonstrated, nor does the record show that a smaller net advertising expenditure could be expected."]

NOTE

(1) *Giant Among the Pygmies.* NBO Indus. Treadway Cos., Inc. v. Brunswick Corp., 523 F.2d 262 (3d Cir. 1975), reversed on other grounds sub nom. *Brunswick Corp. v. Pueblo Bowl-O-Mat,* 429 U.S. 477, 97 S.Ct. 690, 50 L.Ed.2d 701 (1977), was a private Section 7 action seeking damages and injunctive relief. Brunswick acquired bowling centers in New York, Colorado and New Jersey which it had supplied with bowling equipment financed by loans from Brunswick. Upon a decline in recreational bowling in the early 1960's, Brunswick decided to operate potentially profitable bowling centers which had defaulted on Brunswick loans. Between 1965 and 1975 Brunswick commenced operating 222 such bowling centers. Plaintiffs operated bowling centers in competition with Brunswick's newly acquired bowling centers and claimed that Brunswick's acquisition of the centers constituted a violation of Section 7 of the Clayton Act and deprived them of the business which they would have gained if the defaulting centers had failed.

In holding that there was sufficient evidence to go to a jury on the issue of whether Section 7 had been violated, the Court of Appeals described the risks to competition as follows:

> First, Brunswick was a major manufacturer integrating vertically forward into its customer market. Second, it was a giant entering local markets inhabited by pygmies. While both factors may have significance for purposes of Section 7, in this case the first factor standing alone is not significant. The entry of a giant into a market of pygmies certainly suggests the possibility of a lessening of horizontal retail competition. This is because such a new entrant has greater ease of entry into the market, can accomplish cost-savings by investing in new equipment, can resort to low or below cost sales to sustain itself against competition for a longer period, and can obtain more favorable credit terms.

See also *Reynolds Metals Co. v. Federal Trade Commission,* 114 U.S. App.D.C. 2, 309 F.2d 223 (1962), divesting Reynolds of Arrow, one of 8 firms engaged in converting aluminum foil into "florist foil" for the wholesale florist trade. Arrow, when acquired by Reynolds, had one third of this business, but a miniscule proportion of the larger "decorative foil" line in which florist foil might be included. Industry treatment of florist foil as a distinct market with a special class of customers and low prices sufficed to isolate this market for Section 7 purposes. As to anticompetitive impact, the court, *per* Judge (later Chief Justice) Burger, said:

> Arrow's assimilation into Reynolds' enormous capital structure and resources gave Arrow an immediate advantage over its competitors who were contending for a share of the market for florist foil. The power of the "deep pocket" or "rich parent" for one of the florist foil suppliers in a competitive group where previously no company was very large and all were relatively small opened the possibility and power to sell at prices approximating cost or below and thus to undercut and ravage the less affluent competition. The Commission is not required to establish that the Reynolds' acquisition of Arrow did in fact have anti-competitive consequences. It is sufficient if the Commission shows the acquisition had the capacity or potentiality to lessen competition. That such a potential emerged from the combination of Reynolds and Arrow was enough to

bring it within Sec. 7.   But the Commission on substantial evidence has additionally provided us with a finding of *actual* anti-competitive effect, where as an apparent consequence of retroactive price reductions for Arrow foil . . . sales of 5 of Arrow's 7 competitors had by 1957 dropped from 14% to 47% below 1955 sales.   Arrow's sales over the same period increased by 18.9%.

The necessary probability of anti-competitive effect has thus been shown.   In agreeing with the Commission, however, we do not, nor could we intimate, that the mere intrusion of "bigness" into a competitive economic community otherwise populated by commercial "pygmies" will *per se* invoke the Clayton Act.

Do you agree that competition will likely be lessened by the intrusion of a "large" firm into a market of "smaller" firms?   Isn't such an entry at least as likely to promote competition?   Should the Clayton Act stand as a barrier to the transformation of an industry "into an arena of big business competition only" (*Procter & Gamble*, supra p. 299)?   (Would you have favored a law forbidding Procter from entering the bleach business *de novo*?)   Or do the above cases simply show the courts using Section 7 to prevent monopolizing practices (e.g., predatory pricing) "in their incipiency"?   Note that these "entrenchment" or "deep pocket" theories are available in vertical as well as market extension or pure conglomerate cases; and compare the theory's articulation (the "dominant entrant") by Justice Marshall in *Falstaff*, supra p. 277.

FEDERAL TRADE COMMISSION v. CONSOLIDATED FOODS CORP.

Supreme Court of the United States, 1965.
380 U.S. 592, 85 S.Ct. 1220, 14 L.Ed.2d 95.

MR. JUSTICE DOUGLAS delivered the opinion of the Court.

The question presented involves an important construction and application of § 7 of the Clayton Act.   Consolidated Foods Corp.—which owns food processing plants and a network of wholesale and retail food stores—acquired Gentry, Inc., in 1951.   Gentry manufactures principally dehydrated onion and garlic.   The Federal Trade Commission held that the acquisition violated § 7 because it gave respondent the advantage of a mixed threat and lure of reciprocal buying in its competition for business and "the power to foreclose competition from a substantial share of the markets for dehydrated onion and garlic."   It concluded, in other words, that the effect of the acquisition "may be substantially to lessen competition" within the meaning of § 7.   The Court of Appeals, relying mainly on 10 years of post-acquisition experience, held that the Commission had failed to show a probability that the acquisition would substantially lessen competition.   329 F.2d 623.   The case is here on certiorari.

We hold at the outset that the "reciprocity" made possible by such an acquisition is one of the congeries of anticompetitive practices at which the antitrust laws are aimed.   The practice results in "an irrelevant and alien factor," intruding into the choice among competing products, creating at the least "a priority on the business at equal prices."   Reciprocal trading may ensue not from bludgeoning or coercion but from more subtle arrangements. A threatened withdrawal of orders if products of an affiliate cease being bought, or a conditioning of future purchases on the receipt of orders for products of that affiliate is an anti-competitive practice. Section 7 of the Clayton Act is concerned "with probabilities, not certainties." Reciprocity in trading as a result of an acquisition violates § 7, if the probability of a lessening of competition is shown. We turn then to that, the principal, aspect of the present case.

Consolidated is a substantial purchaser of the products of food processors who in turn purchase dehydrated onion and garlic for use in preparing and packaging their food. Gentry, which as noted is principally engaged in the manufacture of dehydrated onion and garlic, had in 1950, immediately prior to its acquisition by Consolidated, about 32% of the total sales of the dehydrated garlic and onion industry and, together with its principal competitor, Basic Vegetable Products, Inc., accounted for almost 90% of the total industry sales. The remaining 10% was divided between two other firms. By 1958, the total industry output of both products had doubled, Gentry's share rising to 35% and the combined share of Gentry and Basic remaining at about 90%.

After the acquisition Consolidated (though later disclaiming adherence to any policy of reciprocity) did undertake to assist Gentry in selling. An official of Consolidated wrote as follows to its distributing divisions:

"Oftentimes, it is a great advantage to know when you are calling on a prospect, whether or not that prospect is a supplier of someone within your own organization. Everyone believes in reciprocity providing all things are equal.

"Attached is a list of prospects for our Gentry products. We would like to have you indicate on the list whether or not you are purchasing any of your supplies from them. If so, indicate whether your purchases are relatively large, small or insignificant. . . .

. . .

"Will you please refer the list to the proper party in your organization. . . . If you have any special suggestions, as to how you could be helpful in properly presenting Gentry to any of those listed, it will be appreciated."

Food processors, who sold to Consolidated, stated they would give their onion and garlic business to Gentry for reciprocity reasons if it could meet the price and quality of its competitors' products. Typical is a letter from Armour and Co.:

"I can assure you that it is the desire of our people to reciprocate and cooperate with you in any way we can in line with good business practices, and I am sure that if our quality obstacles can be overcome, your quotations will receive favorable consideration. We value our relationship with you very highly and are disappointed that we have been unable lately to reciprocate for your fine cooperation on Armour Pantry Shelf Meats."

Some suppliers responded and gave reciprocal orders. Some who first gave generous orders later reduced them or abandoned the practice. It is impossible to recreate the precise anatomy of the market arrangements following the acquisition, though respondent offers a factual brief seeking to prove that "reciprocity" either failed or was not a major factor in the post-acquisition history.

The Commission found, however, that "merely as a result of its connection with Consolidated, and without any action on the latter's part, Gentry would have an unfair advantage over competitors enabling it to make sales that otherwise might not have been made."

And the Commission concluded:

"With two firms accounting for better than 85% of both product lines for eleven successive years, maximum concentration short of monopoly has already been achieved. If it is desirable to prevent a trend toward oligopoly, it is *a fortiori* desirable to remove, so far as possible, obstacles to the creation of genuinely competitive conditions in an oligopolistic industry. Respondents' reciprocal buying power, obtained through acquisition of Gentry, is just such an anticompetitive obstacle.

"This conclusion is buttressed by the peculiar nature of the dehydrated onion and garlic industry. In the first place, the record shows that Gentry's leading competitor, Basic Vegetable Products, Inc., has been the innovator and leader in the field. Gentry has recently made technical strides narrowing, although probably not closing, the gap between them. There is also evidence that the third firm, Puccinelli Packing Co., is not only much smaller, commanding only about 10% of each product market, but is considered by many buyers to offer an inferior product and inferior service."

The Court of Appeals, on the other hand, gave post-acquisition evidence almost conclusive weight. It pointed out that, while Gentry's share of the dehydrated onion market increased by some 7%, its share of the dehydrated garlic market decreased 12%. 329 F.2d, p. 626. It also relied on apparently unsuccessful attempts at reciprocal buying. Ibid. The Court of Appeals concluded that "Probability can best be gauged by what the past has taught." Id., p. 627.

The Court of Appeals was not in error in considering the post-acquisition evidence in this case. But we think it gave too much weight to it. No group acquiring a company with reciprocal buying opportunities is entitled to a "free trial" period. To give it such would be to distort the scheme of § 7. The "mere *possibility*" of the prohibited restraint is not enough. Probability of the proscribed evil is required, as we have noted. If the post-acquisition evidence were given conclusive weight or was allowed to override all probabilities, then acquisitions would go forward willy-nilly, the parties biding their time until reciprocity was allowed fully to bloom. It is, of course,

true that post-aquisition conduct may amount to a violation of § 7
even though there is no evidence to establish probability *in limine*.
But the force of § 7 is still in probabilities, not in what later tran-
spired. That must necessarily be the case for once the two companies are united no one knows what the fate of the acquired company
and its competitors would have been but for the merger.

Moreover, the post-acquisition evidence here tends to confirm,
rather than cast doubt upon, the probable anti-competitive effect
which the Commission found the merger would have. The Commission found that Basic's product was superior to Gentry's—as Gentry's president freely and repeatedly admitted. Yet Gentry, in a rapidly expanding market, was able to increase its share of onion sales
by 7% and to hold its losses in garlic to a 12% decrease. Thus the
Commission was surely on safe ground in reaching the following conclusion:

> "If reciprocal buying creates for Gentry a protected market,
> which others cannot penetrate despite superiority of price, quality,
> or service, competition is lessened whether or not Gentry can ex-
> pand its market share. . . . It is for this reason that we reject
> respondent's argument that the decline in its share of the garlic
> market proves the ineffectiveness of reciprocity. We do not know
> that its share would not have fallen still farther, had it not been
> for the influence of reciprocal buying. This loss of sales fails to
> refute the likelihood that Consolidated's reciprocity power, which
> it has shown a willingness to exploit to the full, will not immunize
> a substantial segment of the garlic market from normal quality,
> price, and service competition."

But the Court of Appeals ingored the Commission's findings as to
the inferiority of Gentry's product; indeed at one point it even supplanted those findings with its own conclusion that Gentry's onions
were superior:

> "Consolidated's Gentry division in the years following the ac-
> quisition, during which time it improved its onion processing
> equipment to eliminate a problem arising from the presence of
> wood splinters and *achieved a product of higher quality than
> that of its competitors*, increased its share of the rapidly ex-
> panding market by only some 7% with respect to dehydrated onion
> . . . .." 329 F.2d, at 626. (Emphasis supplied.)

But the Commission's contrary conclusion was unquestionably based
on substantial evidence, as the following excerpt from the testimony
of Gentry's president particularly indicates:

> "Q. You mentioned the fact, Dr. Prater, that Gentry had a
> reputation of being second to Basic in quality. Was one of the
> factors involved in the quality competition the wood splinter prob-
> lem?

> "A. Yes, the wood splinter problem has been a problem in the
> dehydration industry for many years. Basic exploited this exten-
> sively, and solved it by improvements in production techniques in

the use, or by the use of better methods, and by usi,
wood trays, trays of aluminum plastic glass fibers.   \
competition partially by the improvement of our produc
niques and installation of continuous conveyor dehydrato,

We do not go so far as to say that any acquisition, no matte,
small, violates § 7 if there is a probability of reciprocal buy,
Some situations may amount only to *de minimus.* But where, as
here, the acquisition is of a company that commands a substantial
share of a market, a finding of probability of reciprocal buying by the
Commission, whose expertise the Congress trusts, should be honored,
if there is substantial evidence to support it.

The evidence is in our view plainly substantial. Reciprocity was
tried over and again and it sometimes worked. The industry structure was peculiar, Basic being the leader with Gentry closing the gap.
Moreover there is evidence, as the Commissioin found, "that many
buyers have determined that their source of supply may best be protected by a policy of buying from two suppliers." When reciprocal
buying, or the inducement of it, is added, the Commission observed:

> "Buyers are likely to lean toward Basic on the ground of quali-
> ty, but, in seeking a second, protective supply channel, to pur-
> chase from Gentry in the belief that this will further their sales to
> Consolidated. Not only does Gentry thus obtain sales that might
> otherwise go to Basic or Puccinelli, but the two-firm oligopoly
> structure of the industry is strengthened and solidified and new
> entry by others is discouraged."

We conclude that there is substantial evidence to sustain that conclusion and that the order of the Commission should not have been
denied enforcement. The judgment of the Court of Appeals is accordingly reversed.

Reversed.

JUSTICES HARLAN and STEWART concurred in separate opinions.

THE DEATH OF SECTION 7?

It can be argued that Section 7 ceased functioning as an effective
antimerger statute in 1971. This is the date that the Justice Department abandoned its efforts to use the statute against conglomerate
mergers, and specifically against the International Telephone and Telegraph Company.

The effort to apply Section 7 to "pure" conglomerates began with
the election of President Richard Nixon and the confirmation of his
Assistant Attorney General for the Antitrust Division, Richard Mc-
Laren. McLaren stated at his confirmation hearings that, contrary to
the views of his Democratic predecessors,[90] he believed Section 7 applied to conglomerate mergers, and he pledged to take action to halt

90. See Turner, Conglomerate Merg-   head of the Antitrust Division from 1965
ers and Section 7 of the Clayton Act, 78   to 1968.
Harv.L.Rev. 1313 (1965). Turner was

the wave of such mergers which had taken place in recent years. Attorney General Mitchell vowed similar action.[91]

McLaren filed five conglomerate merger cases in 1969.[92] Three were against ITT, the archetype conglomerate firm. ITT had grown from the 80th largest United States corporation in 1955 to 11th largest when suit was brought. Most of its growth was through merger; between 1961 and 1970 it acquired 101 domestic corporations with combined sales of $3.8 billion. The case on which attention finally focused involved the acquisition of the Grinnell Corporation, the leading firm in the concentrated automatic fire sprinkler systems industry. The Government attempted to argue not only that the merger would have a variety of specific anticompetitive effects (e.g., reciprocity, entrenchment), but also that it would increase "aggregate" concentration, i.e., the concentration of more productive assets in the hands of fewer firms throughout the economy as a whole. The Government's theory was that an increase in aggregate concentration might substantially lessen competition in numerous (but undesignated) lines of commerce, by increasing opportunities for reciprocity and "conglomerate interdependence and forbearance" (compare the arguments later advanced in *Marine Bancorporation*, supra p. 285). The district court held, however, that Section 7 required proof of anticompetitive effects in specified markets, and that Congress did not intend to proscribe all mergers which result in economic concentration.[93] The court also rejected all the Government's other arguments relating more specifically to anticompetitive effects in the sprinkler market.

The Government perfected its appeal to the Supreme Court, but settled and dismissed the case two months later, well before the Supreme Court could pass on the merits of its theories. Apart from the questionable political pressure to settle the litigation[94] (a not-unfamil-

---

91. See ATRR No. 413, June 10, 1969, pp. A–2, X–9 (Speech to Georgia Bar Association). Republicans change—see "Tolerance on Mergers Indicated," N.Y. Times, March 20, 1981, p. D1 (Reagan Administration's designated Assistant Attorney General for antitrust testifies at confirmation hearing that he would not likely oppose mergers between firms in different industries "unless it could be shown that such combinations would diminish competition for a single product"). The Department's subsequently issued merger Guidelines make no reference to entrenchment or reciprocity theories, although they do discuss potential competition theories. The Department notes that the "conglomerate" label "adds nothing to the analysis." The Guidelines are discussed supra pp. 249 – 251.

92. See United States v. International Telephone & Telegraph Corp. (Grinnell), 324 F.Supp. 19 (D.Conn.1970), appeal dismissed 404 U.S. 801, 92 S.Ct. 20, 30 L.Ed. 2d 34 (1971); United States v. Interna-

tional Telephone and Telegraph Corp. (Canteen), 1971 Trade Cas. ¶ 73,619 (N.D. Ill.1971); United States v. International Telephone & Telegraph Corp. (Hartford), 1971 Trade Cas. ¶ 73,666 (D.Conn.1971); United States v. Ling-Temco-Vought, Inc., 315 F.Supp. 1301 (W.D.Pa.1970) (consent judgment entered); United States v. Northwest Industries, Inc., 301 F.Supp. 1066 (N.D.Ill.1969) (denying preliminary injunction).

93. See United States v. International Telephone & Telegraph Corp., 324 F.Supp. 19 (D.Conn.1970), appeal dismissed 404 U.S. 801, 92 S.Ct. 20, 30 L.Ed. 2d 34 (1971).

94. The circumstances surrounding the settlement were never satisfactorily explained. A memo by Dita Beard, an ITT lobbyist, claimed that the settlement came in return for a $400,000 contribution to the Republican Convention of 1972. See Statement of Information, Hearings before House Judiciary Comm.

iar occurrence in antitrust cases), the major damage to Government enforcement efforts came from lost opportunity. The Court which would have heard the ITT appeal—and perhaps decided it favorably—was in the process of change, but was still giving strong support to the antitrust laws.

A "new antitrust majority" (see *Marine Bancorporation,* supra p. 293) was soon in place, however. This current Supreme Court is unlikely to read Section 7 as broadly as the Government would have argued in *Grinnell;* and the old views are unlikely to be in the majority for quite some time to come.

The long-term impact of the *Grinnell* settlement was not immediately apparent. In part this was because "large merger" activity (acquired company assets greater than $10 million) peaked in 1968, and declined sharply between 1969 and 1972. It was not until 1976 that large merger activity again picked up—but this time with a vengeance.[95] In 1977 forty-one mergers involved an acquisition exceeding $100 million. In 1978 the number nearly doubled, to eighty. These trends are illustrated in the following Table: [96]

pursuant to H. Res. 803, Vol. 2955, 93d Cong., 2d Sess. 491, 614 (1974). All responsible Government officials denied this charge, and Richard Kleindienst, who was Acting Attorney General at the time of the settlement, testified before the Senate under oath that he "was not pressured." Hearings before Senate Judiciary Comm., Vol. 2205A, 92d Cong., 2d Sess. 353 (1972). The Watergate Tapes revealed, however, that President Nixon telephoned Kleindienst the day before the Government was to perfect its appeal in Grinnell and told him not to appeal. (Nixon told Kleindienst: "The IT&T thing—stay the hell out if it . . . .— my order is to drop the God damn thing. Is that clear?" Statement of Information, supra, Vol. 2954, at 347–48. Kleindienst later pleaded guilty to a misdemeanor arising out of his inaccurate testimony before the Senate; his sentence was suspended.

The tapes also indicate that Nixon told Ehrlichman to fire the Assistant Attorney General in charge of the Antitrust Division, Richard McLaren, saying that McLaren would never be a judge either.

Id. at 319. Ehrlichman agreed, but later that day Mitchell called the President and prevailed upon him to allow the Grinnell appeal to be filed (which it was); the firing of McLaren was apparently dropped. Most importantly, the tapes reveal the President's total lack of understanding of the antitrust policies which were then being followed by the Antitrust Division. Nixon ordered Ehrlichman to stop the appeal basically because he just did not want to use the antitrust laws to stop business practice: "I don't know whether ITT is bad, good, or indifferent. But there is not going to be any more antitrust actions as long as I am in this chair." Id. at 314.

95. See "Cash-Laden Firms Are In a Marrying Mood, Spurring Merger Wave," Wall St.J., Feb. 8, 1977, p. 1 ("The big merger is back.").

96. Table reprinted from Conglomerate Mergers—Their effects on Small Business and Local Communities, Comm. on Small Business, H.Doc. No. 96–393, 96th Cong., 2d Sess. 50 (1980).

TOTAL VALUE OF ANNOUNCED CORPORATE MERGERS AND ACQUISITIONS

TOTAL VOLUME
(BILLIONS OF DOLLARS)

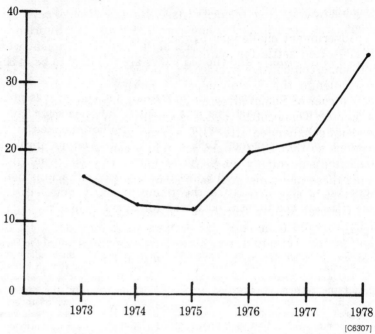

[C6307]

This new merger wave does not seem to be letting up. In 1980 there were ninety-four deals in excess of $100 million; acquisitions totalled $44.3 billion.[97] The billion-dollar deal has become virtually commonplace:[98]

LARGEST CORPORATE MERGERS AND ACQUISITIONS

Acquiring Company	Acquired Company	Value	Year	Status
DuPont	Conoco	$7.3 billion	1981	Complete
Mobil Oil	Marathon Oil	$6.5 billion	1981	Blocked
U.S. Steel	Marathon Oil	$6.4 billion	1981	Complete
Gulf Oil	Cities Service	$5.0 billion	1982	Blocked
Occidental Oil	Cities Service	$4.0 billion	1982	Complete
Standard Oil (Calif.)	Amax Inc.	$3.8 billion	1981	Failed
Shell Oil	Belridge Oil	$3.6 billion	1979	Complete
Elf Aquitaine	Texasgulf Inc.	$2.8 billion	1981	Complete
Fluor Corp.	St. Joe Minerals	$2.7 billion	1981	Complete
Kuwait Petroleum	Santa Fe	$2.6 billion	1981	Complete
Kraft Inc.	Dart Industries	$2.4 billion	1980	Complete
Freeport Minerals	McMoran Oil & Gas	$2.3 billion	1981	Complete
Sun Company	Texas Pacific Oil	$2.3 billion	1980	Complete
General Electric	Utah International	$2.17 billion	1976	Complete
Nabisco Ind.	Standard Brands	$2.0 billion	1981	Complete

97. See "Corporate Marriages Are at Record Levels," N.Y. Times, June 1, 1981, p. D1. In the first three quarters of 1981 acquisitions totalled $60.8 billion. ATRR, No. 1037, p. A–17 (1981).

98. Table, in part, from N.Y. Times, July 7, 1981, p. D4.

Acquiring Company	Acquired Company	Value	Year	Status
Standard Oil (Ohio)	Kennecott	$2.0 billion	1981	Complete
Southern Railway	Norfolk & Western	$1.7 billion	1981	Complete
Mobil Corp.	Marcor Inc.	$1.6 billion	1976	Complete
Schering Corp.	Plough Inc.	$1.6 billion	1970	Complete
Reynolds	Heublein	$1.3 billion	1982	Complete
SmithKline	Beekman	$1.0 billion	1981	Complete

Government challenges to these huge mergers—when they come at all—often settle for spin-offs of small pieces of the acquisition to end some competitive overlap.[99] For example, the F.T.C. agreed not to challenge the Sohio-Kennecott merger after British Petroleum (53% owner of Sohio) divested its 6.8% interest in Amax, a direct competitor of Kennecott;[1] G.E.'s acquisition of Utah International proceeded unchallenged after G.E. agreed to spin-off Utah's uranium operations so that G.E. would not gain a competitive advantage in the nuclear steam-supply systems market.[2] The unwillingness to challenge these mega-mergers may stem less from a lack of enforcement zeal than a lack of theory. If AT&T (the largest "utility"), Exxon, and General Motors (the first and second largest industrial corporations) merged (combined 1980 assets exceeding $194 billion), would the Clayton Act stand in the way? (Reviewing the cases, what theories would *you* argue?) Has the current Section 7 become as irrelevant to 1980's–style consolidations as the 1914 provision became to consolidations in its day?

NOTES AND QUESTIONS

(1) *Conflicting Views on Conglomerate Acquisitions.* Although there is no disagreement that huge mergers are occurring, there is strong disagreement about whether these mergers are bad. President Nixon's Task Force on Productivity and Competition, reviewing the case in 1969, saw no occasion for an antitrust attack on conglomerates "on the basis of nebulous fears about size and economic power":[3]

> A variety of legal and economic factors have contributed to the conglomerate merger movement. Relatively clear legal prohibitions on horizontal and vertical mergers, set forth in section 7 of the Clayton Act and recently articulated in the Antitrust Division's [1968] Merger Guidelines, have channeled merger activity away from these more traditional forms while leaving conglomerate mergers relatively free from antitrust restraints. Although the Merger Guidelines identify some types of conglomerate mergers as likely candidates for antitrust attack and some conglomerate mergers have been successfully attacked on antitrust grounds,

99. Note, however, that private parties may be successful in using Section 7 to obtain a preliminary injunction which fends off an unfriendly tender offer. See Mobil Corp. v. Marathon Oil Co., 669 F.2d 378 (6th Cir. 1981) (effect on retail competition in 6 states), certiorari denied 455 U.S. 982, 102 S.Ct. 1490, 71 L.Ed.2d 691 (1982).

1. "F.T.C. Won't Halt Sohio Kennecott Bid," N.Y. Times, June 3, 1981, p. D1.

2. "Justice Agency Plans No Fight Over GE Merger," Wall St.J., Oct. 4, 1976, p. 14.

3. ATRR No. 413, June 10, 1969, p. X–6. The legal and economic debate over conglomerate mergers, after the 1960's wave, is well captured in Symposium on Conglomerate Mergers and Acquisitions: Opinion & Analysis, 44 St. John's L.Rev. 3 (Special Ed. Spring 1970).

the antitrust laws leave relatively wide latitude for conglomerate mergers. This latitude reflects the fact that existing knowledge provides little basis for forecasting adverse effects on competition that support application of the merger prohibition of section 7.

The economic forces encouraging conglomerate mergers are numerous and complex, and are not easy to identify in particular cases.

These appear to include desire of owners of smaller firms to convert their holdings into more readily marketable securities; the desire of management of large firms for growth for its own sake, apart from or in addition to growth in profits; the opportunity to bring more efficient management personnel or techniques to smaller or less successful firms; the possibility of reducing costs or increasing sales by meshing product lines or processes or methods of distribution; the desire to diversify business activities and reduce risks; the possibility of using one firm's cash flows or credit in another firm with limited access to capital; the tax advantages of direct reinvestment of earnings by corporations instead of distribution to stockholders for reinvestment through the general capital market; and the opportunity for speculative gains through mergers that immediately increase the per-share earnings of the surviving firm.

Whatever the causes, it is clear that many conglomerate mergers are not explainable in terms of obvious efficiencies in integrating the production or marketing facilities of the firms involved. The merger movement has contributed to and is furthered by a specialized "merger market" in business firms as such; merger candidates and independent experts actively seek out favorable opportunities to acquire or dispose of businesses through conglomerate mergers. The existence of such a market is not a sinister symptom; it merely emphasizes the volume and complexity of merger activity and its underlying causes. Indeed, an active merger market suggests a healthy fluidity in the movement of resources and management in the economy toward their more effective utilization. The existence of such a market may serve as a significant incentive for the establishment of smaller firms. It may partially overcome imperfections in the capital market which are not readily susceptible to other effective remedies. In many cases, merger activity may replace proxy fights as an effective means for changes in corporate control.

More recent debate on (large) conglomerate mergers remains divided. As comprehensively summarized in "Conglomerate Mergers: A Study of Competition, Power and Philosophy," ATRR No. 973, July 17, 1980, pp. AA 1–AA 31: mergers may contribute "somewhat" to increases in aggregate concentration; opinions vary widely as to the motivations for conglomerate mergers, including empire building and current inflation (i.e., it is cheaper to buy firms with currently undervalued assets than to build); whatever the theory, conglomerates have not been shown to unequivocally better the performance of their acquired companies; shareholders of acquired firms benefit from these mergers; and the study of the social and political effects of such mergers, despite a number of efforts, has remained largely anecdotal.

(2) *Special Industry Problems—Publishing.* E.L. Doctorow, testimony at hearings on "Concentration in the Book-Publishing and Bookselling Industry," Subcomm. on Antitrust, Monopoly and Business Rights of Sen.Jud.Comm., Ser. No. 96–56, 96th Cong., 2d Sess. 11–13 (1980):

P.E.N. does not claim publishers are insensitive and crass by virtue of their conglomerate affiliations or that they are villains, or that they have totally sold out to commerce. . . . Our position is more basic: That apart from the

good motives or the honor or the seriousness of purpose of any particular publisher or editor, the concentration into fewer and fewer hands of the production
and distribution of literary work is by its nature constricting to free speech and
the effective exchange of ideas and the diversity of opinion. . . .

Until recent times, book publishing has been the last uncontrolled marketplace of ideas—uncontrolled by big money, uncontrolled by government regulation. It has been the place where all scholarship and discursive extended
thought, uneconomical expression of every kind—poetic, scientific, visionary,
analytical—has prevailed by virtue of publishing's having been a cottage industry—that is, one spread among many hands, the decision-making process dispersed into thousands of independent and unconnected hands.

That may no longer be true. The structure of book publishing has changed.
. . . Regardless of the good intentions of the people working in publishing
today, regardless of the enlightenment at the top levels of editorial management, the narrowing of divergent decisionmaking power into fewer corporate
organizations, either American- or foreign-owned, both at the publishing and
retailing ends of the business . . . provides the structure for a time when
enlightenment no longer prevails, when the people who have now have died or
retired, and their . . . standards of excellence infused by the capacity to be
thrilled by ideas and talent and the very quality of language in writing . . .
all that has died or retired with them. And the people who take their place no
longer come into publishing or book selling because they love books but because it is corporate life. And who may not have learned or have forgotten
what it means to publish something good solely because it is good. Or who
believe without questioning in the formulation: that which is good is that which
sells.

A certain erosion may be presumed to have already taken place. There are
signs. One is the move within the industry to replace literary awards that have
existed to recognize excellence of writing in all fields of fiction and nonfiction
with a promotional-minded award modeled on the film industry's Academy
Awards. . . .

Nobody is objecting to commerce or to making money. Publishers have always wanted to make money. [T]he best publishers of the past always knew
how to float their good books on the proceeds of their commercial books, pay
for one with the other, make money and be proud of their contribution to literature and ideas at the same time. And nothing brought more pleasure, greater
euphoria than making money from a good book. The point is that this delicate
balance of pressures within a publishing firm is upset by the conglomerate values—the need for greater and greater profits and the expectation of them over-
loads the scale in favor of commerce—depending on the particular house and
its editorial resources, faster or more slowly: the crossword-puzzle books and
cookbooks and sexual position books and how-to books and movie tie-in books
and television-celebrity books gradually occupying more of the publisher's time
and investment.

So that what we have in effect . . . is a tendency of the publishing industry to be absorbed by the entertainment industry, with all its values of pander-
ing to the lowest common denominator of public taste coming to bear. If this
is not checked we foresee the equivalent in publishing of network broadcasting—that when the publishing and distribution of books is finally in the hands
of five or seven giant corporations, we will have a condition equivalent to that
of the broadcasting industry—network publishing and network bookselling. In
this situation, where is the place for the nurturing relationship of editor and
author that after several years or several books results in a work of monumen-
tal importance to the American consciousness? Where is the incentive in network publishing for books of taste or social challenge or political boldness or
high intellect? Now one argument against the need for the intervention of
Washington into this problem is that the conglomerates in publishing will fade
away on their own when the realization dawns that publishing is such a low-
profit business and that publishing houses have as their assets not rolling stock

or real estate or big presses but people's minds—that publishing entities are built on the shaky foundation of the minds of authors and editors.

Once the terror of that realization dawns, it is said big money will fold its tent and steal away. But apart from the historical evidence that there seems no trend like this in sight, despite the concentration that has gone on in the last 20 years, retreat is undeniably one response to unprofitable investment. The other response is to take that unprofitable investment and tinker with it until it is profitable.

That is the other scenario. That discovering the idealistic and mental impediments to an efficient profit making machinery, the conglomerate management will eliminate them—change taste, simplify what is complex, find the personnel who will give them what they want, and gradually change the nature of books themselves, and create something else, almost-books, non-books, book pods. . . .

Books and what is in them have constituted the core of our verbal thought and culture. They have been the medium by which our country has maintained its historical argument with itself, in all its voices, in all the aspects of its soul. Because of that they have stood traditionally as the source of ideas and thought drawn upon and used and disseminated by the other media. A professor's painfully worked out ideas, his scholarship over the years of study, is reported in newspapers, excerpted in magazines; a novelist's work forged from the privacy of his imagination is reviewed in the papers and journals and possibly adapted for film. Traditionally all the other media have stood toward our books as extenders, popularizers, commentators—but the impulse from the book precedes all.

That core of free uneconomic expression is the source of our cultural wealth because of its central, prior, primal place. It must be left as uncontrolled, inefficient, wasteful, diverse, unstructured as possible so that our genius in the multiple witness and conscience we make as a people, can rise to our national benefit without constriction or censorship.

(3) *The "M & A" Business.* To what extent must today's merger game, with its elaborate offensive and defensive strategies, be counted as an economic cost to society, both in terms of diverting managerial resources to nonproductive uses and in terms of out-of-pocket payments to the "M & A" (Mergers & Acquisitions) industry? Consider "Merger Masters: Outside Professionals Play An Increasing Role In Corporate Takeovers," Wall St. Journal, Dec. 2, 1980, p. 1:

When Sugar Ray Leonard fought Roberto Duran for the world welterweight championship last month, sportswriters were impressed with the huge supporting casts both fighters took to New Orleans with them. There were trainers, seconds, cut-men, sparring partners, business managers, interpreters (for Duran, a Panamanian), "go-fers" and other assorted hangers-on with no apparent duties but to provide companionship for the two fighters.

Something similar seems to be taking place in the corporate arena where more and more giant companies are slugging it out in takeover brawls with hundreds of millions of dollars at stake.

When Pullman Inc. last month finally succeeded in warding off a hostile takeover attempt by McDermott Inc. by wrapping up a $646 million friendly acquisition offer from Wheelabrator-Frye Inc., it marked the end of four months of legal and strategic battling. Involved were more than a dozen law firms, as well as scores of investment bankers, accountants, proxy solicitors and public-relations professionals.

The combined fees paid by the three warring companies: $17 million. "That's obscene," concedes Wheelabrator Chairman Michael D. Dingman.

Blue Chippers on the Prowl

For comparison, when Home Insurance Co., the target of an unwanted take-over bid from Northwest Industries Inc. turned in 1968 to City Investing Co. for a rescue, the $434 million deal took only a few weeks to conclude and involved only a handful of outside experts and costs of only $6 million.

The Pullman example indicates how the game has changed from fast and dirty backroom slugfests into Cecil B. De Mille-style battle scenes with casts of thousands. No longer is it confined to the faintly disreputable so-called corporate raiders of the 1950s. Today, such blue-chippers as Inco Ltd., Mobil Corp., General Electric Co., Kennecott Corp., Exxon Corp. and Westinghouse Electric Corp. aren't too proud to take part. Their free-spending participation has transformed the once-puny takeover-advisory business into a thriving industry.

Data compiled by W.T. Grimm & Co., the Chicago merger broker, indicate that merger activity in the U.S. during this year's first half ran at a $50 billion annual rate. Investment bankers figure that is enough to generate fees of at least $750 million for the specialists who facilitate the deals—many times the level 10 years ago.

The takeover advisers' gravy train can roll regardless of whether a deal is consummated. For example, Mead Corp., the Ohio forest-products concern, escaped an unwanted takeover by Occidental Petroleum Corp. with a bitter nine-month legal defense in 1978–79. But the battle cost the combatants $15 million.

Burgeoning Law Firms

During the battle, a Washington lawyer, whose firm Occidental had hired just for studying the deal's antitrust aspects, told a seminar audience that his firm "had 75 lawyers working on the case," according to William E. Chatlos, a partner at the Wall Street proxy-solicitation firm of Georgeson & Co.

Thanks to a spate of federal and state anti-takeover laws, regulatory changes and increasing litigiousness, legal fees over the past decade have become the fastest-growing segment of takeover costs. The new business has sparked a major expansion among law firms specializing in this area and has drawn many other firms into the arena.

Consider the growth at Skadden, Arps, Slate, Meagher & Flom and at Wachtell, Lipton, Rosen & Katz, Wall Street's best-known merger-specialist law firms. In the past decade, Skadden Arps has grown to 224 lawyers from 45, and Wachtell Lipton to 65 from 18. Even century-old Sullivan & Cromwell, which didn't offer specialized merger-and-acquisition services three years ago, now has an "M & A" department employing 10 lawyers full time and an equal number part time.

Insurance Against Takeovers

Fears of takeover attempts, with all their attendant costs, have driven some companies to seek some form of advance protection. Earlier this year, Anthony Cassidy, the ingenious Lloyds of London underwriter who developed kidnap and ransom insurance, began offering tender-offer defense insurance in the U.S. The idea is to give a takeover-target company coverage of up to $5 million for the investment banking, accounting, legal, public-relations and financial-printing costs it incurs in facing up to a hostile tender offer. . . .

Claims costs of directors' liability coverage, meanwhile, are rising because of the soaring legal costs of takeover battles, according to an official at Marsh & McLennan. But he says "the business is still profitable" and drawing such big new entrants as Insurance Co. of North America and a unit of International Telephone & Telegraph Corp.'s Hartford Insurance subsidiary. Apparently they are attracted by the rich premiums involved in these policies, which range from $35,000 to over $100,000 a year for each $1 million of coverage.

Directors of a takeover target company can be caught in the crossfire when another company makes a bid for their company's shares. Under varying circumstances, either a recommendation to reject the bid or to accept it can be interpreted as contrary to the stockholders' best interests and leaves the directors subject to shareholder suits. Hence the growing number of claims under directors' liability policies.

The investment banker's fee is usually the largest single professional cost in a major takeover deal. If a transaction involves several hundred million dollars, it's reasonable to expect the banker advising the buyer to receive a $1.5 million to $3 million fee and the banker advising the seller to get a good deal more.

The seller's investment banker customarily earns a percentage of the transaction price—often about 0.5%—in a friendly deal. Contested or hostile transactions can be much more lucrative. In these, bankers representing sellers often are working under contracts that scale their fee percentage upward as the sale price exceeds certain agreed levels. Under such an agreement, First Boston Corp. earned a fee of about $6 million, or about 1% of the purchase price, for representing Pullman in the Wheelabrator deal.

Some buyers and sellers recently have noticed that investment bankers' fees most often are structured to be highest when a transaction results. This has caused some companies to worry about their bankers' objectivity in sticky situations and to turn to management consultants for a second opinion.

That's what happened late in September, when a client called in Booz, Allen & Hamilton, a large consulting firm, "at a late stage in their planning for a several hundred million dollar takeover," according to William Summers, Booz Allen executive vice president. The consulting firm concluded that the proposed transaction "didn't make sense as a business decision and they (the client) scrapped the deal," Mr. Summers says. He declines to name the client.

Disinterested Advice

John C. Kirby, senior vice president of Management Analysis Center Inc. in Cambridge, Mass., says, "We feel we can be more objective than an investment banker, since we don't have any financial reason to care whether a deal gets done or not." He adds, "We just bill our time and computer charges." The firm's takeover-advisory work, following a fourfold increase over the past five years, now accounts for 20% of its revenues.

Second opinions, of course, aren't the most common service of management consultants in takeover situations. They earn most of their fees by doing strategic studies of promising industries, screening possible acquisition targets in those industries, doing valuation studies to aid pricing decisions or developing computer software to enable clients to perform these tasks themselves if they wish.

Such services account for 20% to 25% of the revenues of Washington-based Planning Associates Inc., says Michael Kaiser, vice president. And they have helped increase the firm's staff to 200 professionals from 50, two years ago, he says. . . .

(4) *Buchwald on Merger Policy.* Appendix to Concurring Opinion of Justice Douglas, *United States v. Pabst Brewing Co.*, 384 U.S. 546, 553–55, 86 S.Ct. 1665, 1669–70, 16 L.Ed.2d 765 (1966):

Every time you pick up the newspaper you read about one company merging with another company. Of course, we have laws to protect competition in the United States, but one can't help thinking that, if the trend continues, the whole country will soon be merged into one large company.

It is 1978 and by this time every company west of the Mississippi will have merged into one giant corporation known as Samson Securities. Every company east of the Mississippi will have merged under an umbrella corporation known as the Delilah Company.

It is inevitable that one day the chairman of the board of Samson and the president of Delilah would meet and discuss merging their two companies.

"If we could get together," the president of Delilah said, "we would be able to finance your projects and you would be able to finance ours."

"Exactly what I was thinking," the chairman of Samson said.

"That's a great idea and it certainly makes everyone's life less complicated."

The men shook on it and then they sought out approval from the Anti-Trust Division of the Justice Department.

At first the head of the Anti-Trust Division indicated that he might have reservations about allowing the only two companies left in the United States to merge.

"Our department," he said, "will take a close look at this proposed merger. It is our job to further competition in private business and industry, and if we allow Samson and Delilah to merge we may be doing the consumer a disservice."

The chairman of Samson protested vigorously that merging with Delilah would not stifle competition, but would help it. "The public will be the true beneficiary of this merger," he said. "The larger we are, the more services we can perform, and the lower prices we can charge."

The president of Delilah backed him up. "In the Communist system the people don't have a choice. They must buy from the state. In our capitalistic society the people can buy from either the Samson Company or the Delilah Company."

"But if you merge," someone pointed out, "there will be only *one* company left in the United States."

"Exactly," said the president of Delilah. "Thank God for the free enterprise system."

The Anti-Trust Division of the Justice Department studied the merger for months. Finally the Attorney General made this ruling. "While we find some drawbacks to only one company being left in the United States, we feel the advantages to the public far outweigh the disadvantages.

"Therefore, we're making an exception in this case and allowing Samson and Delilah to merge.

"I would like to announce that the Samson and Delilah Company is now negotiating at the White House with the President to buy the United States. The Justice Department will naturally study this merger to see if it violates any of our strong anti-trust laws."

Art Buchwald, *Washington Post*, June 2, 1966, p. A21.

(5) *Reform Proposals.* A number of commentators have advanced proposals to reach large-firm conglomerate mergers. President Johnson's Task Force on Antitrust Policy in 1969 proposed prohibiting large firms from acquiring "a leading firm in any market." [4] Professor Blake argues that a standard of presumptive illegality based on size and without regard to market definitions and market share percentages is proper because "the antitrust laws, including section 7, have since their beginnings been directed towards . . . [a] more fundamental objective: the prevention of the destruction or erosion of the competitive system, a form of economic organization in which economic power in any form should not be permitted to limit the freedom of equally efficient smaller entrepreneurs to compete, on fair and equal terms, with larger firms or groupings of firms; and the avoidance of the political consequences of such an impairment of the traditional sys-

4. ATRR No. 411, May 27, 1969, Spec. Supp., pp. 15–17.

tem." [5]   Professor Brodley argues more narrowly for presumptive rules to deal with geographic and product market extension mergers under current Section 7, in part to take account of our "distrust of centralized power." Brodley writes: [6]

> Enforcement of an antitrust policy designed to preserve the potential for new entry into large, concentrated markets can be viewed as an attempt to limit what may be termed "discretionary economic authority" or, in positive terms, as a policy to promote diversity and diffusion of economic decisionmaking. Preventing a potential entrant from acquiring a leading firm in a significant concentrated market increases the number of decisionmaking units in the market if the potential entrant later enters de novo. The quantum of discretionary decisions made by leading firms is reduced if the potential entrant gains market share at the expense of those firms either after entry de novo or after entry through toehold acquisition.

Should we just come right out and say that "bigness *is* badness"? Presidents, Courts, and Attorneys-General usually state otherwise.[7] But is this the policy actually hidden behind the manipulation of market definitions and the acceptance of structural economic theories not empirically verified (e.g., "barriers to entry"; potential competition)?

Consider the following legislation—"The Small and Independent Business Protection Act of 1979"—proposed by Senator Kennedy. Would you vote for it? [8] If these mergers are forbidden, what will these corporations do with the cash they would otherwise use for acquisitions?

> Sec. 2.   Notwithstanding any other provision of law, no person shall merge or consolidate with any other person engaged in commerce, or acquire, directly or indirectly, such amount of the stock or other share capital of such other person as to enable such person to control such other person, or acquire, directly or indirectly, a majority of the assets of such other person, if—
>
> (a) each person has assets or sales exceeding $2,000,000,000;
>
> (b) each person has assets or sales exceeding $350,000,000; or
>
> (c) one person has assets or sales exceeding $350,000,000 and the other person has 20 per centum or more of the sales during the calendar year immediately preceding the acquisition in any significant market.
>
> Sec. 3.   (a) Except as provided in subsection (b), it shall be an affirmative defense to an offense under sections 2(b) and 2(c) that—
>
> (1) the transaction will have the preponderant effect of substantially enhancing competition;
>
> (2) the transaction will result in substantial efficiencies; or

5. Blake, Conglomerate Mergers and the Antitrust Laws, 73 Colum.L.Rev. 555, 570 (1973).

6. Brodley, Potential Competition Mergers: A Structural Synthesis, 87 Yale L.J. 1, 35 (1977).

7. See United States v. United States Steel Corp., 251 U.S. 417, 451, 40 S.Ct. 293, 299, 64 L.Ed.2d 343 (1920) ("[T]he law does not make mere size an offence . . . ."); Address of Attorney General William French Smith to District of Columbia Bar, ATRR No. 1021, July 2, 1981, p. H–2 ("We must recognize that bigness in business does not necessarily mean badness—and that success should not be automatically suspect.")

8. Using Fortune Magazine data, approximately 300 United States corporations had sales or assets exceeding $2 billion when the legislation was proposed.

(3) within one year before or after the consummation of the transaction, the parties thereto shall have divested one or more viable business units, the assets and revenues of which are equal to or greater than the assets and revenues of the smaller party to the transaction.

(b) Such affirmative defense shall not be available if one of the parties to the transaction has within one year previous to the transaction been a party to a prior transaction coming within the provisions of section 2(b) or 2(c).

Sec. 4. (a) Authority to enforce compliance with section 2 is vested in the Attorney General of the United States and the Federal Trade Commission.

(b) The Attorney General and the Federal Trade Commission shall adopt procedures by which parties to a transaction within the terms of sections 2(b) and 2(c) can ascertain the determination of the Attorney General or the Federal Trade Commission as to whether or not the transaction is within the terms of any of the affirmative defenses set forth in section 3. If the Attorney General or Commission, pursuant to such procedures, advises a party that a transaction is within the terms of any of the affirmative defenses set forth in section 3, the Attorney General and the Federal Trade Commission shall be barred by such advice in the absence of proof that the determination was based in whole or substantial part on an intentional misstatement by the party requesting such advice.

Sec. 5. Injunctive relief for private parties may be granted under the same terms and conditions as prescribed by section 16 of the Clayton Act.

DEFINITIONS

Sec. 6. (a) As used herein, "efficiencies" shall include economies of scale in manufacturing, marketing, distribution, and research and development.

(b) As used herein, "significant market" means any line of commerce in any section of the country which has annual sales of more than $100,000,000.

Sec. 7. (a) The provisions of this Act are in addition to and not in lieu of other provisions of the antitrust laws and nothing in this Act shall be deemed to authorize or make lawful anything heretofore prohibited or made illegal by other antitrust laws.

(b) This Act shall apply to all mergers or consolidations occurring after March 11, 1979.

(6) *West German Merger Wave.* The United States is not the only country experiencing a merger wave. Is international competition contributing to the desire to merge? Consider "Merger Wave Stirs Debate in Germany, But Tighter Controls Appear Unlikely," Wall St. Journal, July 6, 1980, p. 19:

> West Germany is growing increasingly concerned about a wave of mergers that keeps rolling on and on.
>
> The West German monopoly Commission said that in 1977, the latest year for which results are available, the 10 largest companies in each industrial sector averaged 43.7% of their sector's sales, up from 42.3% in 1975.
>
> That growth, the commission said, is tied to a rising number of mergers. Last year, the nation's Cartel Office was notified of 602 mergers, up from 558 in 1978.

"What we have is a slow but steady increase in economic concentration in West Germany," said Erhard Kantzenbach, chairman of a government-appointed advisory commission. "Within the 100 largest companies an increasing trend toward concentration is clear."

To change that, the commission proposed a law to enable authorities to order the disposal of holdings in concentrated sectors under certain circumstances. However, judging from industry opposition and the country's past stance toward antitrust laws, the proposal isn't expected to become law.

Industrial concentration in Germany is nothing new. During most of the past 100 years, cartels controlled the German economy, reaching a zenith when they were formalized by Adolf Hitler to help carry out his economic plans.

After World War II, Allied occupation authorities enacted a patchwork of measures to block cartels, but it wasn't until 1957 that West Germany passed an antitrust law. The right to enforce that law, however, wasn't given until 1973.

Under the law, the Cartel Office can ban a merger if it is deemed likely to create or enhance a market-dominating position, unless it can be proven to strengthen competition. But some industries have been exempt from merger control, including insurance, banking and transportation.

One hole in the law was plugged in April, when authorities amended regulations exempting small mergers from control. Under the amendment, a merger may be reviewed if both participants have sales equivalent to more than $2.3 million a year, a reduction from the earlier $28.7 million each.

However, even that change isn't expected to slow the wave of mergers. Wolfgang Kartte, the president of the cartel office, which enforces the antitrust law, said the amendment was "an accentuation but not an extension, of our control."

One proposal to boost enforcement powers was offered by the Monopoly Commission, which said the Cartel Office should have the ability to retroactively order mergers undone in certain cases.

"Things have reached a level of concentration in Germany that they wouldn't have had if our laws had been put into effect earlier," Mr. Kantzenbach said in proposing retroactive measures. "The laws were introduced too late."

However, the commission observed that the country's 100 largest companies had a 24.2% share of total industrial sales in 1978, down slightly from 24.4% in 1976, though up from 21.7% in 1972.

Noting this and the fact that the 100 companies provide 52.5% of the country's exports, the German Industry Association sharply opposed any proposed retroactive measures against industrial concentrations.

"The proposal would involve a government attack on the central nerve of German industry, which has matured in international competition," the group said. "In each case, any type of de-cartelization drastically overshoots the mark."

F.   REMEDIES IN MERGER CASES

The Supreme Court has declared that:

[C]omplete divestiture is peculiarly appropriate in cases of stock acquisitions which violate § 7. That statute is specific and narrowly directed . . . and it outlaws a particular form of economic control—stock acquisitions which tend to create a monopoly of any line of commerce. The very words of § 7 suggest that an undoing of the acquisition is a natural remedy. Divestiture or dissolution has traditionally been the remedy for Sherman Act violations whose heart is intercorporate combination and control, and it is reasonable to think immediately of the same remedy when § 7 of the Clayton Act, which particularizes the Sherman Act standard of illegality, is involved. . . . Divestiture has been called the most important of antitrust remedies. It is simple, relatively easy to administer, and sure. It should always be in the forefront of a court's mind when a violation of § 7 has been found.[9]

Litigating the remedy phase may be more complex, the controversy more bitter, and the outcome more significant than determining the guilt or innocence of the defendant.[10] There may be substantial financial or competitive incentives to delay the implementation of divestiture, and ultimate success in proving a violation may provide no more than a "Pyrrhic victory." Elzinga's study of 39 Section 7 cases indicated that the average time between acquisition and divestiture was 66 months, and that relief was "successful" in only six cases.[11] In the interim considerable "scrambling" of assets, employees, and financial operations took place. In some cases courts would order only partial divestiture or would permit piecemeal sale of the acquired firm to several buyers. Some cases were greatly complicated because the acquiring firm made additional investments in the acquired firm after the merger, raising the issue of whether a divestiture order may require the divestiture of assets in addition to those illegally acquired.[12] It has frequently proved difficult to find a suitable buyer which will not itself have Section 7 problems to operate the firm successfully and independently. Sometimes it is impossible to find any buyer at all,[13] or a trustee may be needed to operate the illegally acquired company. At times it is necessary to control the

9. United States v. E. I. duPont de Nemours & Co. (G.M.), 366 U.S. 316, 328–31, 81 S.Ct. 1243, 1251–52, 6 L.Ed.2d 318, 326–8 (1961).

10. See the description of 17 years of litigation in the El Paso case, p. 202, supra; Adams, Dissolution, Divorcement, Divestiture: The Pyrrhic Victories of Antitrust, 27 Ind.L.J. 1 (1951).

11. Elzinga, The Antimerger Law: Pyrrhic Victories, 12 J.L. & Econ. (1969) (relief "sufficient" in four cases, "deficient" in eight cases, and "unsuccessful" in 21 cases).

12. Compare Reynolds Metal Co. v. Federal Trade Commission, 309 F.2d 223, 231 (D.C.Cir.1962) (date of acquisition marks violation and limits properties to be affected by government decree; after-acquired properties considered for divestiture where they represent reinvestment of capital realized from sale of property included in an unlawful acquisition and constitute replacement of that property) with United States v. Aluminum Co. of America, 247 F.Supp. 308 (E.D.Mo.1962) (ordering divestiture of subsequently constructed property), affirmed mem., 382 U.S. 12, 86 S.Ct. 24, 15 L.Ed.2d 1.

13. See United States v. United Foam Corp., 565 F.2d 563 (9th Cir. 1977) (upholding appointment of trustee to sell properties of antitrust defendant whose behavior frustrated divestiture order). In United States v. Liquid Carbonic Corp., 121 F.Supp. 141 (E.D.N.Y.1954), modified 123 F.Supp. 653 (E.D.N.Y.), reversed 350 U.S. 869, 76 S.Ct. 114, 100 L.Ed. 769 (1955), a consent decree required defendant to dispose of two plants and appointed a trustee to carry out the sale. The terms of sale were stipulated; and provision was made for an appraisal. When the trustee was unable to dispose of the plants on the terms provided, he was discharged and the government moved for an order requiring disposition of the plants by the defendant. The company took the position that the agreed disposition having proved impractical, it should now be free to operate the plants. Held: The company would not be required to dispose at a "possible substantial loss . . . from sale under unfavorable circumstances"; but would be enjoined from operating these plants. See also "U.S. Asks Study in ITT Case on Severance of Hartford Fire Instead of Avis, Levitt," Wall St. J., Dec. 18, 1974,

post-merger business relationships of the illegally merged firms.[14] Thus, many have felt that however much the substantive tests for a violation of Section 7 have been tightened in the past two decades, the long-standing observation that "the government wins thé opinions and the defendants win the decrees" [15] has proved true in merger cases.

The major tactic for solving these relief problems has been to stop illegal mergers before they are consummated. This has led to two significant developments. One is the Merger Guidelines, first issued by the Department of Justice in 1968 and intended to give counsel a clearer indication of the Department's enforcement intentions.[16] The Guidelines are generally believed to have achieved their purpose and to have deterred some illegal mergers.[17] They were redrafted in 1982 to conform to the new Reagan Administration's views on merger enforcement.

The other major development is the enactment of a pre-merger notification statute in 1976. The idea of screening business conduct to assess legality prior to the transaction is not new; business interests had sought such legislation in the period before the enactment of the Federal Trade Commission Act in 1914.[18] The 1976 Act (Title II of the Hart-Scott-Rodino Antitrust Improvements Act) adds Section 7A to the Clayton Act.[19] It requires both parties to a merger or acquisition, or the acquiring party in the case of a tender offer, to file notification of the transaction with the F.T.C. and the Antitrust Division. The Act prohibits the acquisition of voting securities or assets for a 30-day waiting period after notification in the case of mergers and a 15-day period in the case of cash tender offers; a request for additional information by one of the Government agencies before the waiting period expires triggers an additional 20-day period (10 for cash tender offers) after compliance with the request. The notification requirement depends on (1) the size of the parties (required where a firm with sales or assets of $100 million acquires voting se-

p. 6 (detailing the difficulties in carrying out divestiture order entered three years before in settlement of ITT merger cases).

14. See, e.g., Ford Motor Co. v. United States, 405 U.S. 562, 92 S.Ct. 1142, 31 L.Ed.2d 492 (1972) (ordering Ford to purchase one-half its annual spark plug requirements from the divested plant). Compare pre-merger divestiture agreement in GE-Utah International, supra p. 313, in which Utah International's uranium operations were spun off to a new company from which G.E. was forbidden to buy.

15. Dewey, Romance and Realism in Antitrust Policy, 63 J.Pol.Econ. 93 (1955).

16. See p. 249, supra.

17. See Symposium, The Merger Guidelines, 36 Antitrust L.J. 1 (1967); 37 Antitrust L.J. 872 (1968).

18. See G. Henderson, The Federal Trade Commission 21–22 (1924); G. Kolko, The Triumph of Conservatism 174–79, 260–62 (1963).

19. 15 U.S.C.A. § 18a. The FTC by resolution in 1969 attempted to require merging firms with combined sales or assets over $250 million to notify the Commission 60 days in advance of a merger. See 1 Trade Reg. Rep. (CCH) ¶ 4540. The program was unenforceable and unsuccessful, although the Commission apparently believes it survives enactment of Hart-Scott-Rodino. See 4 CCH Trade Reg. Rep. (CCH) ¶ 42,475 (Staff interpretation of August 25, 1978). Parties are still free to "pre-clear" acquisitions through the Department of Justice's Business Review Letter (see p. 19, supra) or the F.T.C.'s Advisory Opinion process.

curities or assets of a $10 million firm); and (2) the size of the trans-
action (required where the acquiring firm would as a result of the
transaction hold 15% or more of the voting securities or assets of the
acquired firm or where the value of the acquired voting securities
and assets exceeds $15 million). Exemptions from notification in-
clude: acquisitions of bonds, mortgages, and non-voting securities,
acquisitions of limited amounts of voting securities solely for investment purposes, and transactions subject to approval by a federal regulatory agency.

The Act does not affect substantive antitrust liability; no immunity from Section 7 (or the Sherman Act) is given for non-covered transactions or for the Government's failure to act after being given pre-
merger notice. The Act does provide for expedited hearings on preliminary injunction motions, whether notification of the acquisition is
required or not, but the Act does not provide for an automatic stay if
the Government challenges a merger (compare Bank Merger Act, supra p. 236).

The Act provides that the F.T.C., with the Justice Department's
concurrence, may prescribe rules "necessary and appropriate" to carry out the purposes of the Act (including defining the terms used in
the Act). The Commission has discharged this task—in 101 triple-
column pages of the Federal Register—with a set of regulations reminiscent of the Internal Revenue Code.[20] Interpretations of these regulations have followed, along with some modifications of the initial
rules (e.g., raising the size-of-the-transaction test to exempt smaller
acquisitions).[21] The Regulations did not become effective until August 30, 1978, and thus it is still too early to be certain of their impact
on merger enforcement.[22] But neither the Act nor the Regulations
appear to have slowed the merger movement.[23]

Congress passed Hart-Scott-Rodino in large part to enable the
government to stop mergers before they were consummated. Congress did not, however, address the existing substantive law restricting the availability of preliminary injunctions to prevent a merger
from occurring before a full trial on the merits can be held. Although courts have employed differing standards in deciding whether

20. See 43 Fed.Reg. 33,450–33,557
(1978) (contains regulations and background materials). The Regulations are
codified in 16 C.F.R. §§ 800–803 (1982).

21. See 4 CCH Trade Reg. Rep. (CCH)
¶ 42,475 (staff interpretations). Proposed revisions would further decrease
the amount of required reporting. See
43 ATRR 50, 170–84 (1982) (text of proposals and data for 1981).

22. For a comprehensive guide to
Hart-Scott-Rodino, including legislative
background, see Axinn, Fogg & Stoll, Ac-
quisitions Under The Hart-Scott-Rodino
Antitrust Improvements Act (1978, with
Supplements). See also Halverson, Volk,
Pogue, & Pfunder, The Effects of Hart-
Scott-Rodino Premerger Notification Re-

quirements on Mergers, Acquisitions,
and Tender Offers, 48 Antitrust L.J. 1453
(1980); Tomlinson, Premerger Notification Under Hart-Scott-Rodino, Valuation
of Assets and Voting Securities, 26 U.C.
L.A.L.Rev. 1321 (1979); "Premerger Act
Produces More Paper, Few Ripples,"
Nat'l L.J., Oct. 8, 1979, p. 4 (reporting
few compliance problems; regulations
"have generated more paper than heat in
their first year of operation").

23. According to the F.T.C.'s Fourth
Annual Report on the operations of Hart-
Scott-Rodino, there were 1,958 transactions reported between September 1978
and November 1980; the highest monthly
total was 90 in October 1980.

to issue a preliminary injunction,[24] the most widely used test requires the Government to show (1) a reasonable probability of success in proving its case on the merits upon a final hearing, and (2) that the alleged injury to the public interest resulting from a denial of a preliminary injunction outweighs the injury to the defendants resulting from the granting of a preliminary injunction.[25] The speculative nature of showing "probable success" of proving a probable lessening of competition has led some courts to be reluctant in granting preliminary injunctions unless the plaintiff can come very close to proving a final case of violation when seeking preliminary relief.[26]

In balancing the equities in these cases, courts must choose between (i) denying the preliminary injunction and allowing the acquired firm to disappear, thereby inviting the problem of unscrambling if a violation is found; (ii) attempting to maintain the *status quo* by an order requiring the firms be kept separate in the face of the dynamic economic circumstances which caused the merger to occur; [27] or (iii) enjoining the merger or tender offer with the realization that financial obligations or shifting stock market values may preclude the parties from consummating the merger if the transaction is held up pending a long trial.[28]

Consider: (1) the relationship of the problems of effective relief to the development of stringent substantive standards of illegality; (2) the significance of pre-merger notification in allowing enforcement agencies time to develop a more substantial case for preliminary relief; (3) the standards which should govern the granting of preliminary relief in Section 7 cases; and (4) where preliminary relief is granted, the possible specificity of the court in protecting the financial, employee, technological and business integrity of the acquired firm *pendente lite* if stock or managerial control is permitted in the interim.

24. See Comment, The Goal of the New Premerger Notification Requirements: Preliminary Relief Against Anticompetitive Mergers, 1979 Duke L.J. 249 (1979).

25. See United States v. Siemens Corp., 621 F.2d 499 (2d Cir. 1980); Federal Trade Commission v. Beatrice Foods Co., 587 F.2d 1225 (D.C.Cir.1978); United States v. Tracinda Investment Corp., 464 F.Supp. 660 (C.D.Cal.1979). Compare Federal Trade Commission v. Food Town Stores, Inc., 539 F.2d 1339 (4th Cir. 1976) (Section 7 prohibits consideration of private harms in a balancing of the equities). In private litigation, the plaintiff must also demonstrate that irreparable harm will result in the absence of an injunction. See, e.g., Jackson Dairy, Inc. v. H.P. Hood & Sons, Inc., 596 F.2d 70, 72 (2d Cir. 1979); Sonesta International Hotels Corp. v. Wellington Associates, 483 F.2d 247 (2d Cir. 1973).

26. See Note, "Preliminary Preliminary" Relief Against Anticompetitive Mergers, 82 Yale L.J. 155 (1972).

27. See Federal Trade Commission v. Weyerhauser Co., 648 F.2d 739 (D.C.Cir. 1981) (lower court hold separate order reversed where it was not clear that such an order would prevent interim competitive harm; F.T.C. had shown substantial likelihood of success on the merits in a motion for a preliminary injunction).

28. See Federal Trade Commission v. Foodtown Stores, Inc., 547 F.2d 247, 248 (4th Cir. 1977) (merger abandoned following grant of preliminary relief); L. Sullivan, Handbook of the Law of Antitrust 669 n. 2 (1977) (citing cases of abandonment).

NOTES AND QUERIES

(1) *Divestiture and Hardship.   United States v. E. I. duPont De Nemours & Co.*, 366 U.S. 316, 81 S.Ct. 1243, 6 L.Ed.2d 318 (1961) supra p. 263, where duPont's long-standing acquisition of 23% of GM's stock was found to be a violation of § 7, held that the trial court had erroneously refused to order divestiture of the General Motors stock. Defendants had opposed divestiture as unnecessary to achieve the antitrust goal and harsh in its economic consequences. They urged that the antitrust goal could be achieved by allowing duPont to retain ownership without voting power; power to vote the GM shares would be "passed through" to duPont shareholders. They also argued that forced liquidation of millions of shares of General Motors stock would depress the market value of both companies, and that the involuntary distributees of the stock would have to pay burdensome capital gains taxes. Mr. Justice Brennan's opinion for the Court asserted a far-reaching responsibility of the Court to review the judgments of a single district judge as to relief, observed that "divestiture is peculiarly appropriate in cases of stock acquisitions which violate § 7 . . . a natural remedy," and concluded that a pass-through of voting rights would be ineffective to dissolve the "intercorporate community of interest". The power of duPont to sell its voteless shares and thus reestablish an important voting control in other parties would itself cause General Motors to behave circumspectly vis-a-vis duPont. Injunctive relief against various forms of duPont "influence" on GM could not be effectively policed. Since divestiture is necessary for effective relief, "economic hardship, however severe" cannot stand in the way. "Once the Government has successfully borne the considerable burden of establishing a violation of law, all doubts as to the remedy are to be resolved in its favor."

The decision was by vote of 4–3, Justices Clark and Harlan not participating, and Justices Frankfurter, Whittaker and Stewart dissenting.

(2) *Financial Consequences of the duPont Divestiture.* The Supreme Court decision requiring divestiture was announced May 22, 1961. The divestiture was carried out in three stages, July, 1962, January, 1964, and January, 1965. Prior to the first distribution of General Motors stock, Congress enacted a special provision, applicable only to this transaction, that receipt of divested stock should not be taxable as ordinary income, but as a return of capital to the duPont stockholders. Defendants' fears as to the adverse price effect of a great increase in the supply of General Motors stock proved exaggerated, at least in the opinion of investors in General Motors stock, who bid the price up from 46⅜ on May 22, 1961, to 57 on December 31, 1961, an increase of 22.9% while the Dow Jones average rose 4.1%. By December 31, 1962, after the first distribution, General Motors stock stood at 58⅛, up 25.3% from May 22, 1961, while the Dow Jones average had declined by 7.2%. Should shareholders who receive stock as a result of antitrust violations by their corporation be in a better tax position than other shareholders who receive stock distributions? Were there special equities in favor of duPont shareholders?

(3) *Treble Damage Sequel to duPont.* Minority stockholders of General Motors Corporation failed in a subsequent effort to recover treble damages from duPont, on the ground that no actual injury to General Motors had been proved. *Gottesman v. General Motors Corp.*, 436 F.2d 1205 (2d Cir. 1971). Cf. *Brunswick Corp. v. Pueblo Bowl-O-Mat*, supra p. 63.

PRICING, PRODUCTION, AND MARKETING

Chapter 4

AGREEMENTS AMONG COMPETITORS

A. INTRODUCTION

Price-fixing, production limitations, and allocation of exclusive markets by agreement among the members of a trade are interrelated phenomena. An agreement not to sell in each other's territories almost inevitably has for its purpose and effect enabling the parties to avoid competitive pricing. An agreement to maintain prices can hardly be effective unless the parties undertake to restrict their production and sales. When the Sherman Act came into force, the common law was equivocal as to the legality of such agreements. Some precedents treated these arrangements as illegal *per se*, naked restraints of trade impossible to justify as "ancillary" to some other dominant purpose. Other precedents applied a "rule of reason", inquiring whether the motive of the contracting parties was only to prevent "destructive" competition or, on the other hand, to exact extortionate profits. Some decisions distinguished between restraining trade in "necessities" and non-necessities. An agreement restricting competition between the parties might be saved from illegality by the circumstance that other sellers, not party to the agreement, remained in the field to provide some competition or potential competition.

UNITED STATES v. ADDYSTON PIPE & STEEL CO.,[1] set the course of decision under the Sherman Act. The defendants were members of an association of manufacturers of cast iron soil pipe used for sewers, culverts, etc. The association adopted a plan under which sales to specified cities were reserved for designated members. Other sales in the territory covered by the plan (most of the United States outside the Northeast) would be made at prices set by the association. Contracts were awarded to that member of the association who, in a secret association "auction", agreed to pay the highest "bonus" to the association. The bids submitted by members of the association to cities desiring to purchase pipe were then rigged so that the member designated in the secret bonus auction would be the lowest bidder, at the price set by the association. Members of the association shared in the accumulated bonuses in proportion to their production capacity. Depending upon the relation between their costs and the bid prices in

---

1. 85 F. 271 (6th Cir. 1898).

328

a given situation, some members found it more profitable to accept shares of bonus money paid by other members than to bid a higher bonus for the privilege of making and selling pipe. The United States sued to enjoin the members of the association from engaging in a combination and conspiracy in restraint of trade in violation of the Sherman Act.

Defendants filed affidavits of their managing officers, stating that the object of their association was not to raise prices beyond what was reasonable, but only to prevent ruinous competition between defendants which would have carried prices far below a reasonable level; that the bonuses charged were not exorbitant profits and additions to a reasonable price, but deductions from a reasonable price, in the nature of a penalty or burden intended to curb the natural disposition of each member to get all the business possible, and more than his due proportion; that the prices fixed by the association were always reasonable and subject to the very active competition of other pipe manufacturers; and that the reason why they sold pipe at so much cheaper rates in the Northeast than in the "pay territory" was because they were willing to sell at a loss to keep their mills going.

Judge Taft [later Republican President of the United States and thereafter Chief Justice of the Supreme Court] wrote an opinion extensively reviewing the common law precedents, from which he drew the following list of restraints which might be defended as reasonable:

> For the reasons given, then, covenants in partial restraint of trade are generally upheld as valid when they are agreements (1) by the seller of property or business not to compete with the buyer in such a way as to derogate from the value of the property or business sold; (2) by a retiring partner not to compete with the firm; (3) by a partner pending the partnership not to do anything to interfere, by competition or otherwise, with the business of the firm; (4) by the buyer of property not to use the same in competition with the business retained by the seller; and (5) by an assistant, servant, or agent not to compete with his master or employer after the expiration of his time of service.[2] Before such agreements are upheld, however, the court must find that the restraints attempted thereby are reasonably necessary (1, 2, and 3) to the enjoyment by the buyer of the property, good will, or interest in the partnership bought; or (4) to the legitimate ends of the existing partnership; or (5) to the prevention of possible injury to the business of the seller from use by the buyer of the thing sold; or (6) to protection from the danger of loss to the employer's busi-

---

2. Compare Judge Taft's formulation with Restatement of Contracts, §§ 515, 516. As to the right to restrict competitive use of property sold, see Chafee, Equitable Servitudes on Chattels, 41 Harv. L.Rev. 945 (1928). As to the use of the antitrust laws with regard to restrictive covenants in employment contracts, see Lektro-Vend Corp. v. The Vendo Co., 660 F.2d 255 (7th Cir. 1981); Wegmann v. London, 648 F.2d 1072 (5th Cir. 1981); Goldschmid, Antitrust's Neglected Stepchild: A Proposal for Dealing With Restrictive Covenants Under Federal Law, 73 Colum.L.Rev. 1193 (1973).

ness caused by the unjust use on the part of the employé of the confidential knowledge acquired in such business. . . .

Turning them to the case at hand, he continued:

Upon this review of the law and the authorities, we can have no doubt that the association of the defendants, however reasonable the prices they fixed, however great the competition they had to encounter, and however great the necessity for curbing themselves by joint agreement from committing financial suicide by ill-advised competition, was void at common law, because in restraint of trade, and tending to a monopoly. But the facts of the case do not require us to go so far as this, for they show that the attempted justification of this association on the grounds stated is without foundation.

The defendants, being manufacturers and vendors of cast-iron pipe, entered into a combination to raise the prices for pipe for all the states west and south of New York, Pennsylvania, and Virginia, constituting considerably more than three-quarters of the territory of the United States, and significantly called by the associates "pay territory." Their joint annual output was 220,000 tons. The total capacity of all the other cast-iron pipe manufacturers in the pay territory was 170,500 tons. Of this, 45,000 tons was the capacity of mills in Texas, Colorado, and Oregon, so far removed from that part of the pay territory where the demand was considerable that necessary freight rates excluded them from the possibility of competing, and 12,000 tons was the possible annual capacity of a mill at St. Louis, which was practically under the same management as that of one of the defendants' mills. Of the remainder of the mills in pay territory and outside of the combination, one was at Columbus, Ohio, two in northern Ohio, and one in Michigan. Their aggregate possible annual capacity was about one-half the usual annual output of the defendants' mills. They were, it will be observed, at the extreme northern end of the pay territory, while the defendants' mills at Cincinnati, Louisville, Chattanooga, and South Pittsburgh, and Anniston, and Bessemer, were grouped much nearer to the center of the pay territory. The freight upon cast-iron pipe amounts to a considerable percentage of the price at which manufacturers can deliver it at any great distance from the place of manufacture. Within the margin of the freight per ton which Eastern manufacturers would have to pay to deliver pipe in pay territory, the defendants, by controlling two-thirds of the output in pay territory, were practically able to fix prices. The competition of the Ohio and Michigan mills, of course somewhat affected their power in this respect in the northern part of the pay territory; but, the further south the place of delivery was to be, the more complete the monopoly over the trade which the defendants were able to exercise, within the limit already described. Much evidence is adduced upon affidavit to prove that defendants had no power arbitrarily to fix prices, and that they were always obliged to meet competition. To the extent that they could not impose prices on the public in excess of the cost price of pipe with freight from the Atlantic seaboard added, this is true; but, within that limit, they could fix prices as they chose. The most cogent evidence that they had this power is the fact, everywhere apparent in the record, that they exercised it. The details of the way in which it was maintained are somewhat obscured by the manner in which the proof was adduced in the court below, upon affidavits solely, and without the clarifying effect of cross-examination, but quite enough appears to leave no doubt of the ultimate fact. The defendants were, by their combination, therefore able to deprive the public in a large territory of the advantages otherwise accruing to them from the proximity of defendants' pipe factories, and, by keeping prices just low enough to prevent competition by Eastern manufacturers, to compel the public to pay an increase over what the price would have been, if fixed by competition between defendants, nearly equal to the advantage in freight rates enjoyed by defendants over Eastern competitors. The defendants acquired this power by voluntarily agreeing to sell only at prices fixed by their committee, and by allowing the highest bidder at the secret "auction pool" to become the lowest bidder of them at the public letting. Now, the restraint thus imposed on themselves was only partial. It did not cover the United States. There was not a complete monopoly. It was tempered by the fear of competition, and it affected only a part of the price. But this certainly does not take the contract of association out of the annulling effect of the rule against monopolies. In U.S. v. E.C. Knight Co., 156 U.S. 1, 16, 15 S.Ct. 255, Chief Justice Fuller, in speaking for the court, said:

"Again, all the authorities agree that, in order to vitiate a contract or combination, it is not essential that its results should be a complete monopoly. It is sufficient if it really tends to that end, and to deprive the public of the advantages which flow from free competition."

It has been earnestly pressed upon us that the prices at which the cast-iron pipe was sold in pay territory were reasonable. A great many affidavits of purchasers of pipe in pay territory, all drawn by the same hand or from the same model, are produced, in which the affiants say that, in their opinion, the prices at which pipe has been sold by defendants have been reasonable.* We do not think the issue an important one, because, as already stated, we do not think that at common law there is any question of reasonableness open to the courts with reference to such a contract. Its tendency was certainly to give defendants the power to charge unreasonable prices, had they chosen to do so. . . .

For the reasons given, the decree of the circuit court dismissing the bill must be reversed, with instructions to enter a de-

---

* What can account for *customers* testifying in favor of an artificially maintained higher price rather than a competitive lower price? Ideological consensus against "government interference"? Deference to a powerful supplier? Reluctance of municipal bureaucrats to acknowledge that they had overpaid?

cree for the United States perpetually enjoining the defendants from maintaining the combination in cast-iron pipe described in the bill, and substantially admitted in the answer, and from doing any business thereunder.[3]

The per se rule of *Addyston Pipe* was shaken by BOARD OF TRADE OF CHICAGO v. UNITED STATES,[4] which upheld a rule of a commodity exchange that prescribed a short period for trading in a certain category of contracts, and prohibited transactions outside trading hours at any price other than the closing bid during the trading period. Although this arrangement plainly fixed the price for a substantial part of each day, Justice Brandeis declared:

> But the legality of an agreement or regulation cannot be determined by so simple a test as whether it restrains competition. Every agreement concerning trade, every regulation of trade, restrains. To bind, to restrain, is of their very essence. The true test of legality is whether the restraint imposed is such as merely regulates and perhaps thereby promotes competition or whether it is such as may suppress or even destroy competition. To determine that question the court must ordinarily consider the facts peculiar to the business to which the restraint is applied; its condition before and after the restraint was imposed; the nature of the restraint and its effect, actual or probable. The history of the restraint, the evil believed to exist, the reason for adopting the particular remedy, the purpose or end sought to be attained, are all relevant facts. This is not because a good intention will save an otherwise objectionable regulation or the reverse; but because knowledge of intent may help the court to interpret facts and to predict consequences. The District Court erred, therefore, in striking from the answer allegations concerning the history and purpose of the call rule and in later excluding evidence on that subject. But the evidence admitted makes it clear that the rule was a reasonable regulation of business consistent with the provisions of the Antitrust Law.

Among the saving circumstances were listed: the form of the rule—a limitation on the *hours* of competitive price-making, rather than an explicit prescription of price; the use of a competitively established price as the peg price for out-of-hours trading; the limited scope of the rule, applying to only one narrow class of grain which competed with other classes of grain on the Chicago and other exchanges; the effect of the rule to favor certain smaller traders and to encourage all traders to bid and offer during the official trading period, thus maximizing the exchange's efficiency as a competitive market.

3. Affirmed, with a modification of the decree, at 175 U.S. 211, 20 S.Ct. 96, 44 L.Ed. 136 (1899). Cf. Peppin, Price-Fixing Agreements Under the Sherman Anti-Trust Law, 28 Cal.L.Rev. 297, 677 (1940). An interesting variant of the Addyston-type pool was enjoined under the California Antitrust Act in People v. Building Maintenance Contractors' Ass'n, 41 Cal.2d 719, 264 P.2d 31 (1953).

4. 246 U.S. 231, 38 S.Ct. 242, 62 L.Ed. 683 (1918).

Later cases have tended to restrict the *Board of Trade* case to its facts, especially emphasizing the function of the rule as ancillary to the maintenance of a public organized exchange.[5] UNITED STATES v. TRENTON POTTERIES,[6] revindicated the orthodox rule, in a case involving agreement among the manufacturers of 82% of all bathroom fixtures to maintain uniform prices. A criminal conviction under the Sherman Act was upheld despite the refusal of the trial judge to charge the jury in Justice Brandeis' language, above. Justice Stone writing for the Supreme Court said:

> That only those restraints upon interstate commerce which are unreasonable are prohibited by the Sherman Law was the rule laid down by the opinions of this court in the Standard Oil and Tobacco Cases. But it does not follow that agreements to fix or maintain prices are reasonable restraints and therefore permitted by the statute, merely because the prices themselves are reasonable. Reasonableness is not a concept of definite and unchanging content. Its meaning necessarily varies in the different fields of the law, because it is used as a convenient summary of the dominant considerations which control in the application of legal doctrines. Our view of what is a reasonable restraint of commerce is controlled by the recognized purpose of the Sherman Law itself. Whether this type of restraint is reasonable or not must be judged, in part at least, in the light of its effect on competition, for, whatever difference of opinion there may be among economists as to the social and economic desirability of an unrestrained competitive system, it cannot be doubted that the Sherman Law and the judicial decisions interpreting it are based upon the assumption that the public interest is best protected from the evils of monopoly and price control by the maintenance of competition. . . .

> The aim and result of every price-fixing agreement, if effective, is the elimination of one form of competition. The power to fix prices, whether reasonably exercised or not, involves power to control the market and to fix arbitrary and unreasonable prices. The reasonable price fixed today may through economic and business changes become the unreasonable price of tomorrow. Once established, it may be maintained unchanged because of the absence of competition secured by the agreement for a price reasonable when fixed. Agreements which create such potential power

---

5. Compare litigation over "bid depositories." Prime contractors make bids on large construction projects. They do so on the basis of subcontractors' bids. Sometimes after the prime contract has been awarded and the bid has become public, the winning prime contractor finds other subcontractors willing to negotiate with him to do the work for less than the original subcontractor's bid. If the practice became general, fewer subcontractors would be willing to participate in the original bid process because they would not be sure of getting the job even if they were initially the best bidders, for they might be undercut by a post-award subcontractor. May the prime contractors adopt a rule against dealing with post-award subcontractors? Cf. Mechanical Contractors Bid Depository v. Christiansen, 352 F.2d 817 (10th Cir. 1965); People v. Inland Bid Depository, 233 Cal.App.2d 851, 44 Cal.Rptr. 206 (1965).

6. 273 U.S. 392, 47 S.Ct. 377, 71 L.Ed. 700 (1927).

may well be held to be in themselves unreasonable or unlawful restraints, without the necessity of minute inquiry whether a particular price is reasonable or unreasonable as fixed and without placing on the government in enforcing the Sherman Law the burden of ascertaining from day to day whether it has become unreasonable through the mere variation of economic conditions. Moreover, in the absence of express legislation requiring it, we should hesitate to adopt a construction making the difference between legal and illegal conduct in the field of business relations depend upon so uncertain a test as whether prices are reasonable—a determination which can be satisfactorily made only after a complete survey of our economic organization and a choice between rival philosophies. Thus viewed the Sherman Law is not only a prohibition against the infliction of a particular type of public injury. It "is a limitation of rights, . . . which may be pushed to evil consequences and therefore restrained." Standard Sanitary Mfg. Co. v. United States, 226 U.S. 20, 49, 33 S.Ct. 9, 15 (57 L.Ed. 107).

. . .

Despite the clarity of the court's ruling in *Trenton Potteries*, declaring horizontal agreements fixing prices *per se* unlawful without regard to the reasonableness of the price fixed, controversy continues to this day about the nature and scope of antitrust "rules" of *per se* illegality. Are *per se* and rule of reason analysis two different categories of hard and fast legal rules or a single method of analysis relying upon evidentiary presumptions of varying levels of rebuttability to allocate burdens of proof and sort out defenses and justifications which may or may not be permissible in view of the goals of the statute? Are the rules of *per se* illegality primarily *qualitative* standards presuming displacement of the competitive process by certain means to be illegal without regard to the amount of commerce affected, or are they primarily *quantitative* standards requiring proof of a significant effect upon competition generally before the conduct will be condemned? What facts will give rise to a finding that the conduct is within or without a particular *per se* category and how far will courts go in permitting a trial of the question? Assuming conduct is identified as within a *per se* category, is there ever a defense, justification or excuse permitted for the conduct under any circumstances? Who or what may be counted as persons capable of contracting, combining, or conspiring and what kind of evidence will be judged sufficient to support a finding that two or more persons have entered a "contract", "combination", or "conspiracy" for purposes of Section 1 of the Sherman Act? Does the burden of proving a contract, combination or conspiracy unreasonably restrains trade vary depending on whether the remedy sought is a criminal penalty, civil damages or injunctive relief?

To address these and other issues, the materials in this chapter are organized primarily around the *per se* rule banning conduct identified as agreements among competitors fixing prices (horizontal price fixing). Subsequent chapters examine other rules of *per se* illegality. We examine first the distinction between *per se* and rule of reason analysis and the process by which conduct is identified as price fixing. We then take up a variety of circumstances in which courts utilize various devices in an apparent effort to mitigate the rigors of the ban on horizontal price fixing. We next examine differences in the burden of proof depending upon whether the remedy sought is civil, equitable or criminal. We conclude the section on *per se* - rule of reason analysis with an examination of whether there are any defenses, justifications or excuses permitted for conduct otherwise an unreasonable restraint of trade.

Section C of the chapter explores the closely related offenses of horizontal market divisions and production limitations. Such restraints are often part and parcel of a price fixing scheme, while also eliminating other forms of competition between the participants. In section D we turn to the question of what is meant by contract, combination or conspiracy and what is the interrelationship of the standard for proof of such agreement with the rigor of the rule of *per se* illegality for horizontal price fixing and other prohibitions of the antitrust laws? Section E examines the application of the preceding material in the unique context of trade association activities, where frequently the activities of a trade association skate the thin line between enhancing price and other competition and undermining it. The chapter concludes with a brief reference to other ways for dealing with price fixing and other horizontal restraints.

NOTES AND QUERIES

(1) *Antitrust Goals and Horizontal Price Fixing.* What are the goals of antitrust policy that are threatened by horizontal price fixing? Justice Douglas, in the famous footnote 59 (p. 358, footnote 39, infra) to the Court's opinion in *Socony Vacuum*, stated: "Whatever economic justifications particular price-fixing agreements may be thought to have, the law does not permit an inquiry into their reasonableness. They are all banned because of their actual or potential threat to the central nervous system of the economy". What is the "central nervous system" of the economy? Consider the observations of Judge Ganey, the trial judge in the famous Electrical Equipment case where 29 electrical equipment manufacturers and several executives were fined and/or given jail sentences for a long-standing conspiracy to rig bids and fix prices on the sale of heavy electrical equipment.[7] Judge Ganey stated:

> Before imposing sentence, I want to make certain observations . . . what is really at stake here is the survival of the kind of economy under which America has grown to greatness, the free enterprise system. The conduct of the corporate and individual defendants . . . has flagrantly mocked the image of that economic system of free enterprise which we profess to the country and destroyed the model which we offer today as a free world alternative to state control and eventual dictatorship.[8]

7. See generally, J. Herling, The Great Price Conspiracy: The Story of the Antitrust Violations in the Electrical Industry (1962).

8. Quoted in A. Bernhard, U.S. v. Itself: The Antitrust Convictions In the Electrical Equipment Case, Commentary in the Value Line Survey (March 13,

What is the free world alternative to state control and eventual dictatorship that is "flagrantly mocked" by a horizontal price fixing conspiracy? Consider Justice Black's widely quoted statement summarizing the philosphy underlying the Sherman Act:

'The Sherman Act was designed to be a comprehensive charter of economic liberty aimed at preserving free and unfettered competition as the rule of trade. It rests on the premise that the unrestrained interaction of competitive forces will yield the best allocation of our economic resources, the lowest prices, the highest quality and the greatest material progress, while at the same time providing an environment conducive to the preservation of our democratic political and social institutions. But even were that premise open to question, the policy unequivocally laid down by the Act is competition'.[9]

How does a horizontal price fixing agreement interfere with: The best allocation of resources? Obtaining the lowest price? Insuring the highest quality and the greatest material progress? The preservation of our democratic political and social institutions? [10]

(2) *Horizontal Price Fixing: Ideology vs. Reality.* Poetic descriptions of the commitment of our society to the ideals of "free enterprise" and "competition" have not deterred caustic observations to the contrary claimed to be based on the realities of the day rather than the mythology of a time long past.[11] For example, a commentary on Judge Ganey's remarks in sentencing the defendants in the electrical cases asserted that the free enterprise system "has not existed for a couple of hundred years"; that there is a large body of law and a long "political and economic tradition that not only permits, but even requires, control over price fluctuations"; and that enforcement of the law against price fixing in the name of preventing monopoly in many industries dominated by a few large firms would actually bring about monopoly if it were done to the letter of the law.[12] In many parts of the economy, it is claimed, large firms achieve the same result as price fixing conspiracies by follow the leader pricing. Indeed, it is argued, it may be in the firm's and the public's interest that they do so to avoid driving smaller competitors out of business, the risks of being prosecuted for monopolization, destabilizing areas of the economy, and higher prices in the long run from the waste of ruinous competition.[13] Elsewhere, it is pointed out, whole segments of the economy are removed from the competitive process by government intervention:

[B]ecause of Government intervention in the market, especially in such critical sectors as wages, agricultural prices, interest rates, and manufactured goods prices, the free economy that Judge Ganey says America professes to believe in and holds forth as a model to others is a myth. What we mean by a free economy, in reality, is a market economy in which prices are allowed to fluctuate *within socially tolerable limits.*

1961), reprinted in L. Schwartz & J. Flynn, Antitrust and Regulatory Alternatives 445 (5th Ed. 1977).

9. Northern Pacific Ry. v. United States, 356 U.S. 1, 4, 78 S.Ct. 514, 517, 2 L.Ed.2d 545, 549 (1958).

10. See Antitrust Jurisprudence: Symposium on the Economic, Political, and Social Goals of Antitrust Policy, 125 U.Pa.L.Rev. 363 (1977).

11. See, e.g., J. Galbraith, The New Industrial State (2d ed. rev. 1971); Seminar, Planning Regulation and Competition, Hearings before the Subcommittee of the Select Committee on Small Business, U.S. Senate, 90th Cong. 1st Sess. (June 29, 1967).

12. A. Bernhard, supra note 8.

13. Id.

What are socially tolerable limits?

The classical example of free prices that went beyond the socially tolerable limit and also failed to perform their function as a regulator of supply and demand is agriculture, especially during the late Twenties and Thirties. According to theory, agricultural production should have diminished from 1925 to 1932 because agricultural prices were falling during those years. But wheat, corn and other agricultural products were not produced in diminishing quantities; they were produced in increasing quantities between 1925 and 1932, not despite falling prices but *because* of falling prices. The farmer who had debts to pay and an accustomed standard of living to support, worked harder to grow *bigger* crops in order to compensate for the *lower* prices he was receiving. (The prices he paid for manufactured products, although they too declined during these years, did not fall so rapidly as farm prices, partly because of tariff protection for the manufactured goods). Now in time, the lower prices would have liquidated a large portion of the farm population and farm production. Such liquidation would have been in conformity with the law of supply and demand as it expressed itself at the time—and it might have been wise. But it might also have proven unwise in the long run, and besides, the farmer who was about to be liquidated, had no place to go. . . . Rightly or wrongly, the Government (Franklin Roosevelt's New Deal) decided in this instance rulings under the law of supply and demand were to be suspended and the liquidation of marginal farm producers enjoined. The socially tolerable limit of price fluctuation had been exceeded. To this day we have laws which regulate the tolerable limits of price fluctuation in agricultural commodities relative to other products.

We also have laws which set a minimum floor on wage rates. . . .[14]

Others claim that concentration and pricing discretion by big firms are imperative in order to meet the costly demands of modern technology, mass marketing and competition in world markets.[15] In this view, antitrust concern with price fixing is seen as a "charade" because large firms with power to fix prices unilaterally escape the prohibition on conspiratorial price fixing.[16] Still others question whether we can any longer indulge the luxury of competition in a crowded world with rapidly depleting basic resources, a growing disparity in wealth distribution, and a widening distribution of nuclear weapons capabilities in circumstances of international economic and political volatility.[17]

In addition to the skepticism one should bring to claims that ours is a "free enterprise system" and that the "unrestrained interaction of competitive forces" will yield the "greatest material progress" in all cases, it is well to question whether we can any longer afford to do so in any case. On the other hand, before one rejects a commitment to basing the organization of our economic affairs on the maintenance of a competitive process as the rule of trade, consideration should be given to what the alternatives might entail.

14. Id.

15. See Seminar, supra note 11, at 4–11 (remarks of J. K. Galbraith).

16. Id.

17. See generally, R. Heilbroner & L. Thurow, The Economic Problem, Chaps. 31–39 (6th Ed.1981).

As Churchill said of democracy: Democracy is said to be the worst form of government until the alternatives are considered.[18]

(3) *Per Se "Rules": Substantive Rules or Evidentiary Presumptions.* It has not gone unnoticed that unusual circumstances have caused courts to refuse to apply a rule of *per se* illegality in some cases in favor of a more extended inquiry into purpose and effect, or to otherwise avoid an automatic condemnation of the conduct in question by, for example, finding it a "joint venture" rather than a conspiracy, or by employing other devices of judicial legerdemain.[19] Although judicial opinions have not expressly done so, it might be useful for understanding the cases which follow to consider "rules" of *per se* illegality as evidentiary presumptions rather than unchanging substantive rules of law. It has been argued:

> We should think of both [*per se* and rule of reason analysis] as a single method of analysis for establishing or not establishing evidentiary presumptions allocating burdens of proof rather than a series of substantive rules with square corners capable of neatly dictating legal results whatever the facts, whatever the industry and whatever the circumstances. To borrow a cliché from first year law school classes, *per se* and rule of reason analysis are tools—not rules. They are methods of analysis for determining whether the statute has been violated, not rubrics to be employed as the major premise of a syllogism in deductive logic to then dictate what facts will be required or allowed to make up the minor premise. . . . [S]ome of the presumptions would be conclusive in most cases while in others the presumption would merely shift the burden of proof of justification, defense or excuse to the defendant once the particular category of conduct is shown. In still other cases there would be no presumption shifting the burden of proof, but an affirmative burden on the plaintiff to go forward with evidence proving a contract, combination, or conspiracy unreasonably restrains trade.[20]

(4) *Constitutional Constraints on Price Regulation.* The way in which pricing practices are regulated may give rise to constitutional issues ranging from separation of powers, to due process, to First Amendment questions. *United States v. L. Cohen Grocery Co.*,[21] invalidated a wartime federal statute penalizing the making of "any unjust or unreasonable rate or charge in handling or dealing in or with any necessaries." This was held to be an unconstitutional delegation to the courts of the legislative authority to define crimes:

> It leaves open . . . the widest conceivable inquiry, the scope of which no one can foresee and the result of which no one can foreshadow or adequately guard against . . . to attempt to enforce the section would be the exact equivalent of an effort to carry out a statute which in

18. W. Churchill, 18 Speeches of Winston Churchill, p. 27, Nov. 11, 1947):

"No one pretends that democracy is perfect or all wise. Indeed, it has been said that democracy is the worst form of government except all those other forms that have been tried from time to time; but there is the broad feeling in our country that the people should rule, continuously rule, and that public opinion, expressed by all constitutional means, should shape, guide, and control the actions of ministers who are their servants and not their masters."

19. See, Allison, Ambiguous Price Fixing and the Sherman Act: Simplistic Labels of Unavoidable Analysis, 16 Houston L.Rev. 761 (1979); Van Cise, The Future of Per Se In Antitrust Law, 50 Va.L. Rev. 1165 (1964).

20. Flynn, Rethinking Sherman Act Section 1 Analysis: Three Proposals for Reducing the Chaos, 49 Antitrust L.J. 1593 (1982).

21. 255 U.S. 81, 41 S.Ct. 298, 65 L.Ed. 516 (1921).

terms merely penalized and punished all acts detrimental to the public interest when unjust and unreasonable in the estimation of the court and jury.[22]

A footnote to the opinion illustrates some of the problems and the conflicts which had arisen among the district courts in the enforcement of the act; e.g., whether reasonableness of selling price should take into account original cost of the goods or the market value at the time of sale; whether a price might be unreasonably high although the seller actually lost money in the transaction; whether a loss on some items justified a higher price on others; whether a merchant's special skill and efficiency justifies a high profit to him if he sells at a price which yields the trade as a whole only a reasonable profit.[23]

United States v. National Dairy Products Corp.,[24] presented the issue of the constitutionality of section 3 of the Robinson-Patman Act, 15 U.S.C. § 13a, which makes it a crime to sell goods at "unreasonably low prices for the purpose of destroying competition or eliminating a competitor." Defendant corporation and its vice-president, Wise, were charged with violating this statute in Kansas City and six nearby local markets by intentionally selling milk below cost so as to drive competing small dairies out of business, utilizing the advantage which National Dairy possessed by reason of the fact that it operated in many different geographical localities in order to finance and subsidize a price war against its local competitors. The court refused to consider the objection of vagueness of the statute on its face, and found it constitutional "as applied," e.g., to those who intentionally sell below cost for the purpose of exterminating a small competitor. To the argument that "below cost" was itself too vague a standard for defining crime, the Court responded that whatever difficulties might arise from conflicting determinations of "cost" might be rendered "academic" if upon trial it appeared that defendants had sold below any of these costs. Besides, the required proof of predatory intent would sufficiently avert the possibility of inadvertent violation.[25] Justices Black, Stewart, and Goldberg dissented.

It is well settled that a statute may validly delegate to an administrative agency the power to review or establish public utility rates with no more specific criterion than that the rates be "just and reasonable". When the lawful price has been specified by regulation of the price control agency, compliance may be enforced by criminal prosecution.[26]

22. 225 U.S., at 89, 41 S.Ct., at 300, 65 L.Ed.2d, at 520–521.

23. See also Cline v. Frink Dairy Co., 274 U.S. 445, 47 S.Ct. 681, 71 L.Ed. 1146 (1927) (Colorado's antitrust law unconstitutional because it excepted agreements "to conduct operations at a reasonable profit in those products which can not otherwise be so marketed," a vague standard which rendered "the whole statute without a fixed standard of guilt in an adjudication affecting the liberty of the one accused"). Cf. Speegle v. Board of Fire Underwriters, 29 Cal.2d 34, 172 P.2d 867 (1946), and People v. Building Maintenance Contractors' Association, 41 Cal. 2d 719, 264 P.2d 31 (1953) (sustaining California's Cartwright Act, an antitrust statute with similar provisos, by holding the invalid provisos separable from the rest of the act).

24. 372 U.S. 29, 83 S.Ct. 594, 9 L.Ed. 2d 561 (1963), rehearing denied 372 U.S. 961, 83 S.Ct. 1011, 10 L.Ed.2d 13.

25. On the definition of "predatory pricing," see p. 133 supra. Nashville Milk Co. v. Carnation Co., 355 U.S. 373, 78 S.Ct. 352, 2 L.Ed.2d 340 (1958), held that treble damages were not recoverable for violation of section 3 of the Robinson-Patman Act because, unlike the antidiscrimination provisions of the Act, section 3 was not an amendment of the Clayton Act, and so not a part of the "antitrust laws."

26. Yakus v. United States, 321 U.S. 414, 64 S.Ct. 660, 88 L.Ed. 834 (1944) (ceiling prices must be "fair and equitable" giving due consideration to factors enumerated in the statute). On the difficulty of setting "reasonable" prices un-

The discovery of new meanings and implications of the First Amendment guarantee of freedom of speech in the economic sphere have recently established further restrictions upon government pricing regulation. In *Virginia State Board of Pharmacy v. Virginia Citizens Consumer Council, Inc.*,[27] the Court struck down a Virginia statute prohibiting prescription drug price advertising by pharmacists on freedom of speech grounds. The Court recognized for the first time that "commercial speech" is within the ambit of First Amendment freedom of speech protections and that the First Amendment encompassed a right of the recipients of commercial speech to hear the message sought to be advertised. The Court's evolving notion of First Amendment protected commercial speech and a First Amendment right "to hear" the message have been relied upon in subsequent cases to strike down state regulation banning lawyer advertising of the prices for routine legal services,[28] a ban on the expenditure of corporate funds in a state referendum on issues not directly affecting corporate interests,[29] and a regulatory prohibition against utilities including controversial political messages with mailings of customers' bills.[30] The Court's rationale for expanding First Amendment constraints upon regulation limiting advertising of prices and its recognition of corporations as "persons" for First Amendment purposes appears to be an equating of *laissez-faire* economic theory with First Amendment values. In *Virginia Board* the Court stated:

> Advertising, however tasteless and excessive it sometimes may seem, is nonetheless dissemination of information as to who is producing and selling what product, for what reason, and at what price. So long as we preserve a predominantly free enterprise economy, the allocation of our resources in large measure will be made through numerous private economic decisions. It is a matter of public interest that those decisions, in the aggregate, be intelligent and well informed. To this end, the free flow of commercial information is indispensable. . . . And if it is indispensable to the proper allocation of resources in a free enterprise system, it is also indispensable to the formation of intelligent opinions as to how that system ought to be regulated or altered. Therefore, even if the First Amendment were thought to be primarily an instrument to enlighten public decision making in a democracy, we could not say that the free flow of information does not serve that goal.[31]

Justice Rehnquist, in dissent, stated there is "nothing in the United States Constitution which requires the Virginia Legislature to hew to the teachings of Adam Smith in its legislative decisions regulating the pharmacy profession." [32]

der an official price control regime, see Symposium on Price Control in the Cold War, 19 Law & Contemp. Prob. 475 (1954); Ginsberg, Price Stabilization, 1950–1952, 100 U.Pa.L.Rev. 514 (1952); Hyman and Nathanson, Judicial Review of Price Control: The Battle of the Meat Regulations, 42 Ill.L.Rev. 584 (1947); Note, Government Regulation of Prices: A Study of Milk Control in Pennsylvania, 109 U.Pa.L.Rev. 555 (1961).

27. 425 U.S. 748, 96 S.Ct. 1817, 48 L.Ed.2d 346 (1976).

28. Bates v. State Bar of Arizona, 433 U.S. 350, 97 S.Ct. 2691, 53 L.Ed.2d 810

(1977), rehearing denied 434 U.S. 881, 98 S.Ct. 242, 54 L.Ed.2d 164.

29. First National Bank of Boston v. Bellotti, 435 U.S. 765, 98 S.Ct. 1407, 55 L.Ed.2d 707 (1978), rehearing denied 438 U.S. 907, 98 S.Ct. 3126, 57 L.Ed.2d 150.

30. Consolidated Edison Co. v. Public Service Commission, 447 U.S. 530, 100 S.Ct. 2326, 65 L.Ed.2d 319 (1980).

31. 425 U.S., at 765, 96 S.Ct., at 1827, 48 L.Ed.2d, at 360.

32. 425 U.S., at 784, 96 S.Ct., at 1836, 48 L.Ed.2d, at 372.

Query: If it is an unconstitutional infringement of free speech to prohibit price advertising, is it unconstitutional for the antitrust laws to prohibit communications fixing prices? Announcing one's prices in advance and inviting competitors to follow?

B. PER SE AND RULE OF REASON ANALYSIS OF HORIZONTAL PRICE FIXING

1. THE ANALYTICAL METHODOLOGY

APPALACHIAN COALS, INC. v. UNITED STATES

Supreme Court of the United States, 1933.
288 U.S. 344, 53 S.Ct. 471, 77 L.Ed. 825.

MR. CHIEF JUSTICE HUGHES delivered the opinion of the Court.

This suit was brought to enjoin a combination alleged to be in restraint of interstate commerce in bituminous coal and in attempted monopolization of part of that commerce, in violation of sections 1 and 2 of the Sherman Anti-Trust Act, 26 Stat. 209 (15 U.S.C.A. §§ 1, 2). The District Court, composed of three Circuit Judges, made detailed findings of fact and entered final decree granting the injunction. 1 F.Supp. 339. The case comes here on appeal. 28 U.S.C. § 380 (28 U.S.C.A. § 380).

Defendants, other than Appalachian Coals, Inc., are 137 producers of bituminous coal in eight districts (called for convenience Appalachian territory) lying in Virginia, West Virginia, Kentucky, and Tennessee. These districts, described as the Southern High Volatile Field, form part of the coal bearing area stretching from central and western Pennsylvania through eastern Ohio, western Maryland, West Virginia, southwestern Virginia, eastern Kentucky, eastern Tennessee, and northeastern Alabama. In 1929 (the last year for which complete statistics were available) the total production of bituminous coal east of the Mississippi river was 484,786,000 tons, of which defendants mined 58,011,367 tons, or 11.96 per cent. In the so-called Appalachian territory and the immediately surrounding area, the total production was 107,008,209 tons, of which defendants' production was 54.21 per cent., or 64 per cent. if the output of "captive" mines (16,455,001 tons) be deducted.[33] With a further deduction of 12,000,000 tons of coal produced in the immediately surrounding territory, which, however, is not essentially different from the particular area described in these proceedings as Appalachian territory, defendants' production in the latter region was found to amount to 74.4 per cent.

The challenged combination lies in the creation by the defendant producers of an exclusive selling agency. This agency is the defendant Appalachian Coals, Inc., which may be designated as the Compa-

33. Captive mines are those producing chiefly for the consumption of the owners, e.g., railroads, integrated steel companies.

ny. Defendant producers own all its capital stock, their holdings being in proportion to their production.* The majority of the common stock, which has exclusive voting right, is held by seventeen defendants. By uniform contracts, separately made, each defendant producer constitutes the Company an exclusive agent for the sale of all coal (with certain exceptions) which the producer mines in Appalachian territory. The Company agrees to establish standard classifications, to sell all the coal of all its principals at the best prices obtainable and, if all cannot be sold, to apportion orders upon a stated basis. The plan contemplates that prices are to be fixed by the officers of the Company at its central office, save that, upon contracts calling for future deliveries after sixty days, the Company must obtain the producer's consent. The Company is to be paid a commission of 10 per cent. of the gross selling prices f.o.b. at the mines, and guarantees accounts.** In order to preserve their existing sales outlets, the producers may designate subagents, according to an agreed form of contract, who are to sell upon the terms and prices established by the Company and are to be allowed by the Company commissions of eight per cent.† The Company has not yet begun to operate as selling agent; the contracts with it run to April 1, 1935, and from year to year thereafter unless terminated by either party on six months' notice.

The Government's contention, which the District Court sustained, is that the plan violates the Sherman Anti-Trust Act—in the view that it eliminates competition among the defendants themselves and also gives the selling agency power substantially to affect and control the price of bituminous coal in many interstate markets. On the latter point the District Court made the general finding that this elimination of competition and concerted action will affect market conditions, and have a tendency to stabilize prices and to raise prices to a higher level than would prevail under conditions of free competition. The court added that the selling agency will not have monopoly control of any market nor the power to fix monopoly prices.

Defendants insist that the primary purpose of the formation of the selling agency was to increase the sale, and thus the production, of Appalachian coal through better methods of distribution, intensive advertising and research, to achieve economies in marketing, and to eliminate abnormal, deceptive, and destructive trade practices. They disclaim any intent to restrain or monopolize interstate commerce, and in justification of their design they point to the statement of the District Court that "it is but due to defendants to say that the evi-

---

* How else might control have been distributed? What is the antitrust significance of the choice of this way of allocating control?

** What is the antitrust significance of the guarantee of credit? Will Appalachian Coals end competition in extending credit? Cf. United States v. First National Pictures, 282 U.S. 44, 51 S.Ct. 45, 75 L.Ed. 151 (1930).

† How will selling costs be reduced if old outlets and distributors are retained as "sub-agents" of Appalachian Coals, Inc.? Will these retained outlets continue to compete with each other in selling? In the price at which they sell? Will Appalachian Coals be an office from which instructions as to price issue to "sub-agents" who in other respects continue to act as representatives of the coal producers whom they formerly served?

dence in the case clearly shows that they have been acting fairly and
openly, in an attempt to organize the coal industry and to relieve the
deplorable conditions resulting from overexpansion, destructive competition, wasteful trade practices, and the inroads of competing industries." 1 F.Supp. page 341. Defendants contend that the evidence
establishes that the selling agency will not have the power to dominate or fix the price of coal in any consuming market; that the price
of coal will continue to be set in an open competitive market; and
that their plan by increasing the sale of bituminous coal from Appalachian territory will promote, rather than restrain, interstate commerce.

First. There is no question as to the test to be applied in determining the legality of the defendants' conduct. The purpose of the
Sherman Anti-Trust Act is to prevent undue restraints of interstate
commerce, to maintain its appropriate freedom in the public interest,
to afford protection from the subversive or coercive influences of monopolistic endeavor. As a charter of freedom, the act has a generality and adaptability comparable to that found to be desirable in constitutional provisions. It does not go into detailed definitions which
might either work injury to legitimate enterprise or through particu-
larization defeat its purposes by providing loopholes for escape. The
restrictions the act imposes are not mechanical or artificial. Its general phrases, interpreted to attain its fundamental objects, set up the
essential standard of reasonableness. They call for vigilance in the
detection and frustration of all efforts unduly to restrain the free
course of interstate commerce, but they do not seek to establish a
mere delusive liberty either by making impossible the normal and fair
expansion of that commerce or the adoption of reasonable measures
to protect it from injurious and destructive practices and to promote
competition upon a sound basis. The decisions establish, said this
Court in Nash v. United States, 229 U.S. 373, 376, 33 S.Ct. 780, 781,
57 L.Ed. 1232, "that only such contracts and combinations are within
the act as, by reason of intent or the inherent nature of the contemplated acts, prejudice the public interests by unduly restricting competition or unduly obstructing the course of trade." . . .

In applying this test, a close and objective scrutiny of particular
conditions and purposes is necessary in each case. Realities must
dominate the judgment. The mere fact that the parties to an agreement eliminate competition between themselves is not enough to condemn it. "The legality of an agreement or regulation cannot be determined by so simple a test, as whether it restrains competition.
Every agreement concerning trade, every regulation of trade, restrains." Chicago Board of Trade v. United States, supra. The familiar illustrations of partnerships, and enterprises fairly integrated
in the interest of the promotion of commerce, at once occur. The
question of the application of the statute is one of intent and effect,
and is not to be determined by arbitrary assumptions. It is therefore
necessary in this instance to consider the economic conditions peculiar
to the coal industry, the practices which have obtained, the nature of
defendant's plan of making sales, the reasons which led to its adop-

tion, and the probable consequences of the carrying out of that plan in relation to market prices and other matters affecting the public interest in interstate commerce in bituminous coal.

Second. The findings of the District Court, upon abundant evidence, leave no room for doubt as to the economic condition of the coal industry. That condition, as the District Court states, "for many years has been indeed deplorable." Due largely to the expansion under the stimulus of the Great War, "the bituminous mines of the country have a developed capacity exceeding 700,000,000 tons" to meet a demand "of less than 500,000,000 tons." In connection with this increase in surplus production, the consumption of coal in all the industries which are its largest users has shown a substantial relative decline. The actual decrease is partly due to the industrial condition but the relative decrease is progressing, due entirely to other causes. Coal has been losing markets to oil, natural gas and water power and has also been losing ground due to greater efficiency in the use of coal. The change has been more rapid during the last few years by reason of the developments of both oil and gas fields. The court below found that, based upon the assumption that bituminous coal would have maintained the upward trend prevailing between 1900 and 1915 in percentage of total energy supply in the United States, the total substitution between 1915 and 1930 has been equal to more than 200,000,000 tons per year. While proper allowance must be made for differences in consumption in different parts of the country, the adverse influence upon the coal industry, including the branch of it under review, of the use of substitute fuels and of improved methods is apparent.

This unfavorable condition has been aggravated by particular practices. One of these relates to what is called "distress coal." The greater part of the demand is for particular sizes of coal such as nut and slack, stove coal, egg coal, and lump coal. Any one size cannot be prepared without making several sizes. According to the finding of the court below, one of the chief problems of the industry is thus involved in the practice of producing different sizes of coal even though orders are on hand for only one size, and the necessity of marketing all sizes. Usually there are no storage facilities at the mines and the different sizes produced are placed in cars on the producer's tracks, which may become so congested that either production must be stopped or the cars must be moved regardless of demand. This leads to the practice of shipping unsold coal to billing points or on consignment to the producer or his agent in the consuming territory. If the coal is not sold by the time it reaches its destination, and is not unloaded promptly, it becomes subject to demurrage charges which may exceed the amount obtainable for the coal unless it is sold quickly. The court found that this type of "distress coal" presses on the market at all times, includes all sizes and grades, and the total amount from all causes is of substantial quantity.

"Pyramiding" of coal is another "destructive practice." It occurs when a producer authorizes several persons to sell the same coal, and they may in turn offer it for sale to other dealers. In consequence "the coal competes with itself, thereby resulting in abnormal and destructive competition which depresses the price for all coals in the market." Again, there is misrepresentation by some producers in selling one size of coal and shipping another size which they happen to have on hand. "The lack of standardization of sizes and the misrepresentation as to sizes" are found to have been injurious to the coal industry as a whole. The court added, however, that the evidence did not show the existence of any trade war or widespread fraudulent conduct. The industry also suffers through "credit losses," which are due to the lack of agencies for the collection of comprehensive data with respect to the credits that can safely be extended.

In addition to these factors, the District Court found that organized buying agencies, and large consumers purchasing substantial tonnages, "constitute unfavorable forces." "The highly organized and concentrated buying power which they control and the great abundance of coal available have contributed to make the market for coal a buyers' market for many years past."

It also appears that the "unprofitable condition" of the industry has existed particularly in the Appalachian territory where there is little local consumption as the region is not industrialized. "The great bulk of the coal there produced is sold in the highly competitive region east of the Mississippi river and north of the Ohio river under an adverse freight rate which imposes an unfavorable differential from 35 cents to 50 cents per ton." And in a graphic summary of the economic situation, the court found that "numerous producing companies have gone into bankruptcy or into the hands of receivers, many mines have been shut down, the number of days of operation per week have been greatly curtailed, wages to labor have been substantially lessened, and the states in which coal producing companies are located have found it increasingly difficult to collect taxes."

Third. The findings also fully disclose the proceedings of the defendants in formulating their plan and the reasons for its adoption. The serious economic conditions had led to discussions among coal operators and state and national officials, seeking improvement of the industry. Governors of states had held meetings with coal producers. The limits of official authority were apparent. A general meeting of producers, sales agents and attorneys was held in New York in October, 1931, a committee was appointed and various suggestions were considered. At a second general meeting in December, 1931, there was further discussion and a report which recommended the organization of regional sales agencies, and was supported by the opinion of counsel as to the legality of proposed forms of contract, was approved. Committees to present the plan to producers were constituted for eighteen producing districts including the eight districts in Appalachian territory. Meetings of the representatives of the latter districts resulted in the organization of defendant Appalachian Coals, Inc. It was agreed that a minimum of 70 per cent. and a maximum of 80 per cent. of the commercial tonnage of the territory should be secured before the plan should become effective. Approximately 73 per cent. was obtained. A resolution to fix the maximum at 90 per cent. was defeated. The maximum of 80 per cent. was adopted because a majority of the producers felt that an organization with a greater degree of control might unduly restrict competition in local markets. The minimum of 70 per cent. was fixed because it was agreed that the organization would not be effective without this degree of control. The court below also found that it was the expectation that similar agencies would be organized in other producing districts including those which were competitive with Appalachian coal, and that it was "the particular purpose of the defendants in the Appalachian territory to secure such degree of control therein as would eliminate competition among the 73 per cent. of the commercial production." But the court added: "However, the formation of Appalachian Coals was not made dependent upon the formation of other regional selling agencies and there is no evidence of a purpose, understanding or agreement among the defendants that in the event of the formation of other similar regional sales agencies there would be any understanding or agreement, direct or indirect, to divide the market territory between them or to limit production or to fix the price of coal in any market or to cooperate in any way." When, in January, 1932, the Department of Justice announced its adverse opinion, the producers outside Appalachian territory decided to hold their plans in abeyance pending the determination of the question by the courts. The District Court found that "the evidence tended to show that other selling agencies with a control of at least 70 per cent. of the production in their respective districts will be organized if the petition in this case is dismissed"; that in that event "there will result an organization in most of the districts whose coal is or may be competitive with Appalachian coal; but the testimony tends to show that there will still be substantial, active competition in the sale of coal in all markets in which Appalachian coal is sold."

Defendants refer to the statement of purposes in their published plan of organization—that it was intended to bring about "a better and more orderly marketing of the coals from the region to be served by this company (the selling agency) and better to enable the producers in this region, through the larger and more economic facilities of such selling agency, more equally to compete in the general markets for a fair share of the available coal business." The District Court found that among their purposes, defendants sought to remedy "the destructive practice of shipping coal on consignment without prior orders for the sale thereof, which results in the dumping of coal on the market irrespective of the demand"; "to eliminate the pyramiding of offers for the sale of coal"; to promote "the systematic study of the marketing and distribution of coal, the demand and the consumption and the kinds and grades of coal made and available for shipment by each producer in order to improve conditions"; to maintain an inspection and engineering department which would keep in constant contact with customers "in order to demonstrate the advantages and suitability of Appalachian coal in comparison with other competitive coals"; to promote an extensive advertising campaign which would show "the advantages of using coal as a fuel and the advantages of Appalachian coal particularly"; to provide a research department employing combustion engineers which would demonstrate "proper and efficient methods of burning coal in factories and in homes" and thus aid producers in their competition with substitute fuels; and to operate a credit department which would build up a record with respect to the "reliability of purchasers." The court also found that "defendants believe that the result of all these activities would be the more economical sale of coal, and the economies would be more fully realized as the organization of the selling agent is perfected and developed." But in view of the designation of subagents, economies in selling expenses would be attained "only after a year or so of operation."

No attempt was made to limit production. The producers decided that it could not legally be limited and, in any event, it could not be limited practically. The finding is that "it was designed that the producer should produce and the selling agent should sell as much coal as possible".* The importance of increasing sales is said to lie in the fact that the cost of production is directly related to the actual running time of the mines.

Fourth. Voluminous evidence was received with respect to the effect of defendants' plan upon market prices. As the plan has not gone into operation, there are no actual results upon which to base conclusions. The question is necessarily one of prediction. The court below found that, as between defendants themselves, competition would be eliminated. This was deemed to be the necessary consequence of a common selling agency with power to fix the prices at which it would make sales for its principals. Defendants insist that the finding is too broad and that the differences in grades of coal of the same sizes and the market demands at different times would induce competition between the coals sold by the agency "depending upon the use and the quality of the coals."

The more serious question relates to the effect of the plan upon competition between defendants and other producers. [The Court here reviews the evidence of tremendous excess coal producing capacity in the Appalachian territory not controlled by defendants, including undeveloped coal lands which could easily be brought into production by new companies.] In connection with this proof of developed and potential capacity, the "highly organized and concentrated buying power" that can be exerted must also have appropriate consideration.

Consumers testified that defendants' plan will be a benefit to the coal industry and will not restrain competition. Testimony to that

---

* Does the amount of coal which it is possible to sell depend on price? If cooperative selling raises the average price of coal, will some users shift to oil? If coal cannot be stockpiled economically or stored in significant amounts, will price maintenance require restriction of production? Will uncontrolled prices and production result in closing of some mines? Which?

effect was given by representatives of the Louisville & Nashville Railroad, the Norfolk & Western Railroad, and the Chesapeake & Ohio Railroad, "the largest railroad users of coal operating in the Appalachian region," and by representatives of large utility companies and manufacturing concerns. There was similar testimony by wholesale and retail dealers in coal. There are 130 producers of coal other than defendants in Appalachian territory who sell coal commercially. There are also "a large number of mines that have been shut down and could be opened up by the owners on short notice." Competing producers testified that the operation of the selling agency, as proposed by defendants, would not restrain competition and would not hurt their business. Producers in western Pennsylvania, Alabama, Ohio, and Illinois testified to like effect. Referring to this testimony, the court below added, "The small coal producer can, to some extent, and for the purpose of producing and marketing coal, produce coal more cheaply than many of the larger companies and is not prevented by higher cost of operation from being a competitor in the market."

The Government criticizes the "opinion testimony" introduced by defendants as relating to a competitive situation not within the experience of the witnesses, and also animadverts upon their connections and interests, but the Government did not offer testimony of opposing opinions as to the effect upon prices of the operation of the selling agency. Consumers who testified for the Government explained their dependence upon coal from Appalachian territory.

The District Court commented upon the testimony of officers of the selling agency to the effect "that the organization would not be able to fix prices in an arbitrary way but, by the elimination of certain abuses, and by better advertising and sale organization, the producers would get more in the aggregate for their coal." "Other witnesses for the defendants" said the court, "indicated that there would be some tendency to raise the price but that the degree of increase would be affected by other competitors in the coal industry and by producers of coal substitutes."

Fifth. We think that the evidence requires the following conclusions:

1. With respect to defendant's purposes, we find no warrant for determining that they were other than those they declared. Good intentions will not save a plan otherwise objectionable, but knowledge of actual intent is an aid in the interpretation of facts and prediction of consequences. Chicago Board of Trade v. United States, supra. The evidence leaves no doubt of the existence of the evils at which defendants' plan was aimed. The industry was in distress. It suffered from overexpansion and from a serious relative decline through the growing use of substitute fuels. It was afflicted by injurious practices within itself—practices which demanded correction. If evil conditions could not be entirely cured, they at least might be alleviated. The unfortunate state of the industry would not justify any attempt unduly to restrain competition or to monopolize, but the existing situation prompted defendants to make, and the statute did not

preclude them from making, an honest effort to remove abuses, to make competition fairer, and thus to promote the essential interests of commerce. The interests of producers and consumers are interlinked. When industry is grievously hurt, when producing concerns fail, when unemployment mounts and communities dependent upon profitable production are prostrated, the wells of commerce go dry. So far as actual purposes are concerned, the conclusion of the court below was amply supported that defendants were engaged in a fair and open endeavor to aid the industry in a measurable recovery from its plight. The inquiry, then, must be whether despite this objective the inherent nature of their plan was such as to create an undue restraint upon interstate commerce.

2. The question thus presented chiefly concerns the effect upon prices. The evidence as to the conditions of the production and distribution of bituminous coal, the available facilities for its transportation, the extent of developed mining capacity, and the vast potential undeveloped capacity, makes it impossible to conclude that defendants through the operation of their plan will be able to fix the price of coal in the consuming markets. The ultimate finding of the District Court is that the defendants "will not have monopoly control of any market, nor the power to fix monopoly prices"; and in its opinion the court stated that "the selling agency will not be able, we think, to fix the market price of coal." Defendants' coal will continue to be subject to active competition. In addition to the coal actually produced and seeking markets in competition with defendants' coal, enormous additional quantities will be within reach and can readily be turned into the channels of trade if an advance of price invites that course. While conditions are more favorable to the position of defendants' group in some markets than in others, we think that the proof clearly shows that, wherever their selling agency operates, it will find itself confronted by effective competition backed by virtually inexhaustive sources of supply, and will also be compelled to cope with the organized buying power of large consumers. The plan cannot be said either to contemplate or to involve the fixing of market prices.

The contention is, and the court below found, that while defendants could not fix market prices, the concerted action would "affect" them, that is, that it would have a tendency to stabilize market prices and to raise them to a higher level than would otherwise obtain. But the facts found do not establish, and the evidence fails to show, that any effect will be produced which in the circumstances of this industry will be detrimental to fair competition. A co-operative enterprise, otherwise free from objection, which carries with it no monopolistic menace, is not to be condemned as an undue restraint merely because it may effect a change in market conditions, where the change would be in mitigation of recognized evils and would not impair, but rather foster, fair competitive opportunities. Voluntary action to rescue and preserve these opportunities, and thus to aid in relieving a depressed industry and in reviving commerce by placing competition upon a sounder basis, may be more efficacious than an attempt to provide remedies through legal processes. The fact that the correction of

abuses may tend to stabilize a business, or to produce fairer price levels, does not mean that the abuse should go uncorrected or that co-operative endeavor to correct them necessarily constitutes an unreasonable restraint of trade. The intelligent conduct of commerce through the acquisition of full information of all relevant facts may properly be sought by the co-operation of those engaged in trade, although stabilization of trade and more reasonable prices may be the result. Putting an end to injurious practices, and the consequent improvement of the competitive position of a group of producers is not a less worthy aim and may be entirely consonant with the public interest, where the group must still meet effective competition in a fair market and neither seeks nor is able to effect a domination of prices.
. . .

3. The question remains whether, despite the foregoing conclusions, the fact that the defendants' plan eliminates competition between themselves is alone sufficient to condemn it. Emphasis is placed upon defendants' control of about 73 per cent. of the commercial production in Appalachian territory. But only a small percentage of that production is sold in that territory. The finding of the court below is that "these coals are mined in a region where there is very little consumption." Defendants must go elsewhere to dispose of their products, and the extent of their production is to be considered in the light of the market conditions already described. Even in Appalachian territory it appears that the developed and potential capacity of other producers will afford effective competition. Defendants insist that on the evidence adduced as to their competitive position in the consuming markets, and in the absence of proof of actual operations showing an injurious effect upon competition, either through possession or abuse of power, no valid objection could have been interposed under the Sherman Act if the defendants had eliminated competition between themselves by a complete integration of their mining properties in a single ownership. We agree that there is no ground for holding defendants' plan illegal merely because they have not integrated their properties and have chosen to maintain their independent plans, seeking not to limit but rather to facilitate production. We know of no public policy, and none is suggested by the terms of the Sherman Act, that in order to comply with the law those engaged in industry should be driven to unify their property and businesses in order to correct abuses which may be corrected by less drastic measures. Public policy might indeed be deemed to point in a different direction. If the mere size of a single, embracing entity is not enough to bring a combination in corporate form within the statutory inhibition, the mere number and extent of the production of those engaged in a co-operative endeavor to remedy evils which may exist in an industry, and to improve competitive conditions, should not be regarded as producing illegality. The argument that integration may be considered a normal expansion of business, while a combination of independent producers in a common selling agency should be treated as abnormal—that one is a legitimate enterprise and the other is not—makes but an artificial distinction. The Anti-Trust Act aims

at substance. Nothing in theory or experience indicates that the selection of a common selling agency to represent a number of producers should be deemed to be more abnormal than the formation of a huge corporation bringing various independent units into one ownership. Either may be prompted by business exigencies and the statute gives to neither a special privilege. The question in either case is whether there is an unreasonable restraint of trade or an attempt to monopolize. If there is, the combination cannot escape because it has chosen corporate form, and, if there is not, it is not to be condemned because of the absence of corporate integration. As we stated at the outset, the question under the act is not simply whether the parties have restrained competition between themselves but as to the nature and effect of that restraint.

The fact that the suit is brought under the Sherman Act does not change the principles which govern the granting of equitable relief. There must be "a definite factual showing of illegality." Standard Oil Company v. United States, 283 U.S. page 179, 51 S.Ct. 421, 427, 75 L.Ed. 926. We think that the Government has failed to show adequate grounds for an injunction in this case. We recognize, however, that the case has been tried in advance of the operation of defendants' plan, and that it has been necessary to test that plan with reference to purposes and anticipated consequences without the advantage of the demonstrations of experience. If in actual operation it should prove to be an undue restraint upon interstate commerce, if it should appear that the plan is used to the impairment of fair competitive opportunities, the decision upon the present record should not preclude the Government from seeking the remedy which would be suited to such a state of facts. We think also that in the event of future controversy arising from the actual operation of the plan the results of the labor of both parties in this litigation in presenting the voluminous evidence as to the industry, market conditions and transportation facilities and rates, should continue to be available, without the necessity of reproducing that evidence.

The decree will be reversed, and the cause will be remanded to the District Court with instructions to enter a decree dismissing the bill of complaint without prejudice and with the provision that the court shall retain jurisdiction of the cause and may set aside the decree and take further proceedings if future developments justify that course in the appropriate enforcement of the Anti-Trust Act.

It is so ordered.

MR. JUSTICE MCREYNOLDS thinks that the court below reached the proper conclusion and that its decree should be affirmed.

NOTES AND QUERIES

(1) *"Rule of Reason" Analysis. Appalachian Coals* can be viewed as a case of historical interest only, reflecting a time in the Great Depression when the Nation flirted with cartelization as a remedy for industrial plight. The case, however, can also be viewed as a model demonstration of a "rule of reason" approach to conduct which would appear to fall within a *per se*

category. To what extent did the Court's analysis weigh: (a) the peculiar characteristics of the industry; (b) the power of the participants; (c) the horizontal or vertical nature of the plan; (d) the purpose of the plan; (e) the effect of the plan; (f) public and private benefits of the plan; (g) public and private detriments of the plan; and (h) the availability of less restrictive alternatives to avoid the detriments and achieve the benefits? To what extent was the Court's evaluation of these factors influenced by underlying assumptions about the central goals of antitrust policy? Consider the Court's most recent pronouncement on the nature of a rule of reason methodology for analyzing a restraint, set forth in *National Society of Professional Engineers v. United States:* [34]

> [T]he Rule does not open the field of antitrust inquiry to any argument in favor of a challenged restraint that may fall within the realm of reason. Instead, it focuses directly on the challenged restraint's impact on competitive conditions.
>
> . . .
>
> . . . Judge (later Chief Justice) Taft so interpreted the Rule in his classic rejection of the argument that competitors may lawfully agree to sell their goods at the same price as long as the agreed upon price is reasonable. *United States v. Addyston Pipe and Steel Co.,* 85 F. 271, 282–283 (CA6 1898), aff'd, 175 U.S. 211, 20 S.Ct. 96, 44 L.Ed. 136. That case, and subsequent decisions by this Court, unequivocally foreclose an interpretation of the Rule as permitting an inquiry into the reasonableness of the prices set by private agreement.
>
> The early cases also foreclose the argument that because of the special characteristics of a particular industry, monopolistic arrangements will better promote trade and commerce than competition. That kind of argument is properly addressed to Congress and may justify an exemption from the statute for specific industries, but it is not permitted by the Rule of Reason. As the Court observed in *Standard Oil Co. v. United States,* 221 U.S. 1, 65, 31 S.Ct. 502, 517, 55 L.Ed. 619, "restraints of trade within the purview of the statute . . . [can]not be taken out of that category by indulging in general reasoning as to the expediency or nonexpediency of having made the contracts, or the wisdom or want of wisdom of the statute which prohibited their being made."
>
> The test prescribed in *Standard Oil* is whether the challenged contracts or acts "were unreasonably restrictive of competitive conditions." Unreasonableness under that test could be based either (1) on the nature or character of the contracts, or (2) on surrounding circumstances giving rise to the inference or presumption that they were intended to restrain trade and enhance prices. Under either branch of the test, the inquiry is confined to a consideration of impact on competitive conditions.
>
> In this respect the Rule of Reason has remained faithful to its origins. . . . [T]he Court has adhered to the position that the inquiry mandated by the Rule of Reason is whether the challenged agreement is one that promotes competition or one that suppresses competition. "The true test of legality is whether the restraint imposed is such as merely regulates and perhaps thereby promotes competition or whether it is such as may suppress or even destroy competition."

34. 435 U.S. 679, 98 S.Ct. 1355, 55 L.Ed.2d 637 (1978). For an excellent analysis of recent Supreme Court opinions on the *per se*-rule of reason distinction, see Redlich, The Burger Court and the Per Se Rule, 44 Albany L.Rev. 1, (1979).

There are, thus, two complementary categories of antitrust analysis. In the first category are agreements whose nature and necessary effect are so plainly anticompetitive that no elaborate study of the industry is needed to establish their illegality—they are "illegal per se;" in the second category are agreements whose competitive effect can only be evaluated by analyzing the facts peculiar to the business, the history of the restraint, and the reasons why it was imposed. In either event, the purpose of the analysis is to form a judgment about the competitive significance of the restraint; it is not to decide whether a policy favoring competition is in the public interest, or in the interest of the members of an industry. Subject to exceptions defined by statute, that policy decision has been made by the Congress.

Queries: How does one determine whether an agreement is one "whose nature and necessary effect are so plainly anticompetitive that no elaborate study is needed" without first making an elaborate study of the facts peculiar to the industry? What caused the Court to decide to make an elaborate study of the industry in *Chicago Board of Trade* and *Appalachian Coals?*

(2) *Further Queries.* The student should attempt to recreate in his imagination the conference of mine operators and their lawyers which worked out the Appalachian plan. List the difficulties of the coal business that the plan was designed to remedy. How does it remedy each? Was it expected to reduce the amount of off-sized coal produced? Was it expected to increase the amount received for such coal? What would be the effect of an increase in coal prices on the problems of excess capacity and increasing competition from other fuels? How did the lawyers propose to avoid the *Trenton Potteries* case?

Could research and promotion objectives of the industry have been pursued without the price effects of using a common selling agency?

What can be said for and against Justice Hughes' declaration that private efforts to eliminate "abuses" in the coal business by agreement among the producers were preferable to public controls?

What can be said for and against Justice Hughes' declaration that such agreements among individual producers were preferable to consolidation into a single firm? Would a consolidation of the same scope as the agreement in this case be lawful under the antitrust laws? Is it practically easier to consolidate or to effect agreements on prices and practices? Which type of integration is more likely to disintegrate?

Whose trade was restrained? Why were competitors ready to testify for the defendants? Why were coal carrying and consuming railroads ready to testify for the defendants?

What is there in Justice Hughes' opinion that would prevent a careful lawyer from counseling the coal operators to proceed with their cooperative sales plan?

(3) *Substituting Official for Unofficial Price-Fixing.* By the time the *Appalachian Coals* case was decided, the United States had embarked on the vast National Industrial Recovery Act experiment with "cooperation" in place of competition as the rule of trade. Prices were regulated by NRA Codes of Fair Competition formulated in collaboration by industry and government. Violation of a code approved by the President was a criminal offense. The Supreme Court construed Section 3(a) of the Act as authorizing the President to approve any code which in his judgment would promote "fair competition", a standard regarded by the Court as so vague as to amount to an unconstitutional delegation of legislative power to the Presi-

dent.[35] Is the authority to "promote fair competition" by restraining trade too dangerous to delegate to groups of private businessmen with or without supervision by a government agency?

UNITED STATES v. SOCONY–VACUUM OIL CO.

Supreme Court of the United States, 1940.
310 U.S. 150, 60 S.Ct. 811, 84 L.Ed. 1129.

[Digest] Defendants, major oil companies operating in the Mid-Western area, were convicted under Section 1 of the Sherman Act of conspiracy to raise and fix tank car and retail prices of gasoline by a concerted program of buying up "distress" offerings by independent refiners in the spot tank car market. Defendants sold gasoline to jobbers for distribution to retailers, and direct to retailers at a two cent a gallon margin above the jobber price. They also sold gasoline at retail through company-owned stations at $3\frac{1}{2}$ cents above the price to retailers. Standard Oil Company of Indiana was known as the price leader throughout the area; i.e. the retail price posted at its stations was generally followed by all distributors, whether independent or owned by other majors. The jobbers' long term contracts with defendants provided that the price they paid would be the current spot market price as reported in the trade journals. The theory of the prosecution was that defendants' buying program supported the spot market price, which in turn determined what their jobbers would have to pay, and further, by reason of the fixed wholesale and retail margins maintained under the leadership of Standard Oil, the retail price of gasoline. During the relevant period defendants' purchases in the spot market constituted 50% of all gasoline produced by the independent refiners.

Defendants introduced evidence that the price of crude oil had plunged, following discovery of extensive new Texas oil fields, to levels which made it unprofitable to operate less efficient wells tapping a substantial part of the then known oil reserves of the country. Such wells once shut down were hard to reestablish; "conservation" demanded their continued operation. State and federal governments adopted legislation to restrict production; but "hot" oil continued to flow in interstate commerce. Upon the enactment of the National Industrial Recovery Act in 1933, the President issued an order under § 9 of that Act prohibiting the illicit traffic. An NRA Code of Fair Competition for the petroleum industry was adopted [36] "to stabilize

---

35. Schechter Poultry Corp. v. United States, 295 U.S. 495, 55 S.Ct. 837, 79 L.Ed. 1570, 97 A.L.R. 947 (1935). The Code regime was perpetuated for bituminous coal by the Guffey Coal Act of 1935, 49 Stat. 991, and the Bituminous Coal Act of 1937, 50 Stat. 72, the latter Act being held constitutional in Sunshine Anthracite Coal Co. v. Adkins, 310 U.S. 381, 60 S.Ct. 907, 84 L.Ed. 1263 (1940). The Act expired in May 1943. The desirability of permitting the act to expire was debated in Rostow, Bituminous Coal and

the Public Interest, 50 Yale L.J. 543 (1941); Hamilton, Coal and the Economy—A Demurrer, id. at 595; Rostow, Joinder in Demurrer, id. at 613.

On proposals to solve the problems of the anthracite industry by curtailing competition, see Note, The Anthracite Coal Production Control Plan, 102 U.Pa.L.Rev. 368 (1954).

36. [Court's footnote 10.] It provided for maximum hours of work and minimum rates of pay; forbade sales below

the oil industry upon a profitable basis". Industry committees were appointed to engage in concerted buying of distress offerings by independent refiners. Each of the major companies had an independent "dancing partner" [37] assigned to it with an informal understanding that the major would buy whatever that independent could not sell at a "fair going market price". A Mechanical Subcommittee met weekly to find purchasers for new distress gasoline and to "recommend" fair market prices. Majors purchased such gasoline even when they were over-supplied themselves. With the encouragement of high federal officials, the buying program continued after NRA was held unconstitutional in 1935. Prices rose, partly as a result of these efforts but more in response to effective governmental regulation and improved business conditions.

MR. JUSTICE DOUGLAS delivered the opinion of the Court.

. . . The only essential thing in common between the instant case and the Appalachian Coals case is the presence in each of so-called demoralizing or injurious practices. The methods of dealing with them were quite divergent. In the instant case there were buying programs of distress gasoline which had as their direct purpose and aim the raising and maintenance of spot market prices and of prices to jobbers and consumers in the Mid-Western area, by the elimination of distress gasoline as a market factor. The increase in the spot market prices was to be accomplished by a well organized buying program on that market: regular ascertainment of the amounts of surplus gasoline; assignment of sellers among the buyers; regular purchases at prices which would place and keep a floor under the market. Unlike the plan in the instant case, the plan in the Appalachian Coals case was not designed to operate vis-à-vis the general consuming market and to fix the prices on that market. Furthermore, the effect, if any, of that plan on prices was not only wholly incidental but also highly conjectural. For the plan had not then been put into operation. Hence this Court expressly reserved jurisdiction in the District Court to take further proceedings if, inter alia, in "actual

cost; required integrated companies to conduct each branch of their business on a profitable basis; established, within certain limits, the parity between the price of a barrel of crude oil and a gallon of refined gasoline as 18.5 to 1; and authorized the fixing of certain minimum prices.

37. [Court's footnote 20.] Respondent R. W. McDowell, a vice president of Mid-Continent, testified as follows respecting the origin and meaning of this term:

"The phrase 'dancing partners' came up right there after Mr. Ashton had gone around the room. There were these 7 or 8 small refiners whom no one had mentioned. He said this situation reminded him of the dances that he used to go to when he was a young fellow. He said, 'here we are at a great economic ball.' He said, 'We have these major companies who have to buy gasoline and are buying gasoline, and they are the strong dancers.' And he said, 'They have asked certain people to dance with them. They are the better known independent refiners.' He said, 'Here are 7 or 8 that no one seems to know.' He said, 'They remind me of the wallflowers that always used to be present at those old country dances.' He said, 'I think it is going to be one of the jobs of this Committee to introduce some of these wallflowers to some of the strong dancers, so that everybody can dance.' And from that simile, or whatever you want to call it, the term 'dancing partner' arose."

operation" the plan proved to be "an undue restraint upon interstate commerce." And as we have seen it would per se constitute such a restraint if price-fixing were involved. . . .

Respondents seek to distinguish the Trenton Potteries case from the instant one. They assert that in that case the parties substituted an agreed-on price for one determined by competition; that the defendants there had the power and purpose to suppress the play of competition in the determination of the market price; and therefore that the controlling factor in that decision was the destrucion of market competition, not whether prices were higher or lower, reasonable or unreasonable. Respondents contend that in the instant case there was no elimination in the spot tank car market of competition which prevented the prices in that market from being made by the play of competition in sales between independent refiners and their jobber and consumer customers; that during the buying programs those prices were in fact determined by such competition; that the purchases under those programs were closely related to or dependent on the spot market prices; that there was no evidence that the purchases of distress gasoline under those programs had any effect on the competitive market price beyond that flowing from the removal of a competitive evil; and that if respondents had tried to do more than free competition from the effect of distress gasoline and to set an arbitrary noncompetitive price through their purchases, they would have been without power to do so.

But we do not deem those distinctions material.

In the first place, there was abundant evidence that the combination had the purpose to raise prices. And likewise, there was ample evidence that the buying programs at least contributed to the price rise and the stability of the spot markets, and to increases in the price of gasoline sold in the Mid-Western area during the indictment period. That other factors also may have contributed to that rise and stability of the markets is immaterial. . . .

Secondly, the fact that sales on the spot markets were still governed by some competition is of no consequence. For it is indisputable that that competition was restricted through the removal by respondents of a part of the supply which but for the buying programs would have been a factor in determining the going prices on those markets. . . .

The elimination of so-called competitive evils is no legal justification for such buying programs. The elimination of such conditions was sought primarily for its effect on the price structures. Fairer competitive prices, it is claimed, resulted when distress gasoline was removed from the market. But such defense is typical of the protestions usually made in price-fixing cases. Ruinous competition, financial disaster, evils of price cutting and the like appear throughout our history as ostensible justifications for price-fixing. If the so-called competitive abuses were to be appraised here, the reasonableness of prices would necessarily become an issue in every price-fixing case. In that event the Sherman Act would soon be emasculated; its philosophy would be supplanted by one which is wholly alien to a system of free competition; it would not be the charter of freedom which its framers intended.

The reasonableness of prices has no constancy due to the dynamic quality of the business facts underlying price structures. Those who fixed reasonable prices today would perpetuate unreasonable prices tomorrow, since those prices would not be subject to continuous administrative supervision and readjustment in light of changed conditions. Those who controlled the prices would control or effectively dominate the market. And those who were in that strategic position would have it in their power to destroy or drastically impair the competitive system. But the thrust of the rule is deeper and reaches more than monopoly power. Any combination which tampers with price structures is engaged in an unlawful activity. Even though the members of the price-fixing group were in no position to control the market, to the extent that they raised, lowered, or stabilized prices they would be directly interfering with the free play of market forces. The Act places all such schemes beyond the pale and protects that vital part of our economy against any degree of interference. Congress has not left with us the determination of whether or not particular price-fixing schemes are wise or unwise, healthy or destructive. It has not permitted the age-old cry of ruinous competition and competitive evils to be a defense to price-fixing conspiracies. It has no more allowed genuine or fancied competitive abuses as a legal justification for such schemes than it has the good intentions of the members of the combination. If such a shift is to be made, it must be done by the Congress. Certainly Congress has not left us with any such choice. Nor has the Act created or authorized the creation of any special exception in favor of the oil industry. Whatever may be its peculiar problems and characteristics, the Sherman Act, so far as price-fixing agreements are concerned, establishes one uniform rule applicable to all industries alike. There was accordingly no error in the refusal to charge that in order to convict the jury must find that the resultant prices were raised and maintained at "high, arbitrary and non-competitive levels." The charge in the indictment to that effect was surplusage.

Nor is it important that the prices paid by the combination were not fixed in the sense that they were uniform and inflexible. Price-fixing as used in the Trenton Potteries case has no such limited meaning. An agreement to pay or charge rigid, uniform prices would be an illegal agreement under the Sherman Act. But so would agreements to raise or lower prices whatever machinery for price-fixing was used. That price-fixing includes more than the mere establishment of uniform prices is clearly evident from the Trenton Potteries case itself, where this Court noted with approval Swift & Co. v. United States, 196 U.S. 375, 25 S.Ct. 276, 49 L.Ed. 518, in which a decree was affirmed which restrained a combination from "raising or lowering prices or fixing uniform prices" at which meats will be sold. Hence prices are fixed within the meaning of the Trenton Potteries case if the range within which purchases or sales will be made is agreed upon, if the prices paid or charged are to be at a certain level or on ascending or descending scales, if they are to be uniform, or if by various formulae they are related to the market prices. They are fixed because they are agreed upon. And the fact that, as here, they are fixed at the fair going market price is immaterial.[38] For purchases at or under the market are one species of price-fixing. In this case, the result was to place a floor under the market—a floor which served the function of increasing the stability and firmness of market prices. That was repeatedly characterized in this case as stabilization. But in terms of market operations stabilization is but one form of manipulation. And market manipulation in its various manifestations is implicitly an artificial stimulus applied to (or at times a brake on) market prices, a force which distorts those prices, a factor which prevents the determination of those prices by free competition alone. . . .

Under the Sherman Act a combination formed for the purpose and with the effect of raising, depressing, fixing, pegging, or stabilizing the price of a commodity in interstate or foreign commerce is illegal per se. . . . Proof that a combination was formed for the purpose of fixing prices and that it caused them to be fixed or contributed to that result is proof of the completion of a price-fixing conspiracy under § 1 of the Act.[39] The indictment in this case charged that this

---

38. But cf. General Foods Corp. v. Brannan, 170 F.2d 220 (7th Cir. 1948), holding that respondent had not been guilty of illegal manipulation of the price of rye on the Chicago Board of Trade when it purchased two million bushels from other respondents unable to meet margin calls, thus preventing this "distress" rye from depressing the market price. The Court declared that stabilization "to preserve an existing price resulting from natural forces" was not within the condemnation of the Socony-Vacuum decision, "where the price sought to be stabilized was an artificial one created by the acts of the conspirators."

39. [Court's footnote 59.] Under this indictment proof that prices in the Mid-Western area were raised as a result of the activities of the combination was essential, since sales of gasoline by respondents at the increased prices in that area were necessary in order to establish jurisdiction in the Western District of Wisconsin. Hence we have necessarily treated the case as one where exertion of the power to fix prices (i.e., the actual fixing of prices) was an ingredient of the offense. But that does not mean that both a purpose and a power to fix prices are necessary for the establishment of a conspiracy under § 1 of the Sherman Act. That would be true if power or ability to commit an offense was necessary in order to convict a person of conspiring to commit it. But it is well established that a person "may be guilty of conspiring, although incapable of committing the objective offense." United States v. Rabinowich, 238 U.S. 78, 86, 35 S.Ct. 682, 684, 59 L.Ed. 1211. And it is likewise well settled that conspiracies under the Sherman Act are not dependent on any overt act other than the act of conspiring. It is the "contract, combination . . . or conspiracy, in restraint of trade or commerce" which § 1 of the Act strikes down, whether the concerted activity be wholly nascent or abortive on the one hand, or successful on the other. And the amount of interstate or foreign trade involved is not material since § 1 of the Act brands as illegal the character of the restraint not the amount of commerce affected. In view of these considerations a conspiracy to fix prices violates § 1 of the Act though no overt act is shown, though it is not established that the conspirators had the means available for accomplishment of their objective, and though the conspiracy embraced but a part of the interstate or foreign commerce in the commodity. Whatever may have been the status of price-fixing agreements at common law the Sherman Act has a broader application to them than the common law prohibitions or sanctions. Price-fixing agreements may or may not be aimed at complete elimination of price competition. The group making those agreements may or may not have power to control the market. But the fact that the group cannot control the market prices does not

combination had that purpose and effect. And there was abundant evidence to support it. Hence the existence of power on the part of members of the combination to fix prices was but a conclusion from the finding that the buying programs caused or contributed to the rise and stability of prices.

As to knowledge or acquiescence of officers of the Federal government little need be said. The fact that Congress through utilization of the precise methods here employed could seek to reach the same objectives sought by respondents does not mean that respondents or any other group may do so without specific Congressional authority. Admittedly no approval of the buying programs was obtained under the National Industrial Recovery Act prior to its termination on June 16, 1935, (§ 2(c)) which would give immunity to respondents from prosecution under the Sherman Act. Though employees of the government may have known of those programs and winked at them or tacitly approved them, no immunity would have thereby been obtained. For Congress had specified the precise manner and method of securing immunity. None other would suffice. Otherwise national policy on such grave and important issues as this would be determined not by Congress nor by those to whom Congress had delegated authority but by virtual volunteers. The method adopted by Congress for alleviating the penalties of the Sherman Act through approval by designated public representatives [40]

necessarily mean that the agreement as to prices has no utility to the members of the combination. The effectiveness of price-fixing agreements is dependent on many factors, such as competitive tactics, position in the industry, the formula underlying price policies. Whatever economic justification particular price-fixing agreements may be thought to have, the law does not permit an inquiry into their reasonableness. They are all banned because of their actual or potential threat to the central nervous system of the economy.

The existence or exertion of power to accomplish the desired objective becomes important only in cases where the offense charged is the actual monopolizing of any part of trade or commerce in violation of § 2 of the Act, 15 U.S.C.A. § 2. An intent and a power to produce the result which the law condemns are then necessary. As stated in Swift & Co. v. United States, 196 U.S. 375, 396, 25 S.Ct. 276, 279, 49 L.Ed. 418, ". . . when that intent and the consequent dangerous probability exist, this statute, like many others, and like the common law in some cases, directs itself against that dangerous probability as well as against the completed result." But the crime under § 1 is legally distinct from that under § 2 though the two sections overlap in the sense that a monopoly under § 2 is a species of restraint of trade under § 1. Only a confusion between the nature of the offenses under those two sections would lead to the conclusion that power to fix prices was necessary for proof of a price-fixing conspiracy under § 1.

40. [Court's footnote 60.] It should be noted in this connection that the typical method adopted by Congress when it has lifted the ban of the Sherman Act is the scrutiny and approval of designated public representatives. Under the N.I.R.A. this could be done through the code machinery with the approval of the President as provided in §§ 3(a) and 5. Under § 407(8) of the Transportation Act of 1920, 41 Stat. 482, 49 U.S.C.A. § 5(8), carriers, including certain express companies, which were consolidated pursuant to any order of the Interstate Commerce Commission were relieved from the operation of the Anti-Trust laws. And see the Maloney Act (§ 15A of the Securities Exchange Act of 1934, 52 Stat. 1070, 15 U.S.C.A. § 78*o*–3) providing for the formation of associations of brokers and dealers with the approval of the Securities and Exchange Commission and establishing continuous supervision by the Commission over specified activities of such associations; and the Bituminous Coal Act of 1937, 50 Stat. 72, 15 U.S.C.A. § 828 et seq., especially §§ 4 and 12— particularly as they relate to the fixing of minimum and maximum prices by the Bituminous Coal Commission.

would be supplanted by a foreign system. But even had approval been obtained for the buying programs, that approval would not have survived the expiration in June 1935 of the Act which was the source of that approval. As we have seen, the buying program continued unabated during the balance of 1935 and far into 1936. As we said in United States v. Borden Co., 308 U.S. 188, 202, 60 S.Ct. 182, 190, 84 L.Ed. 181, "A conspiracy thus continued is in effect renewed during each day of its continuance." Hence, approval or knowledge and acquiescence of federal authorities prior to June 1935 could have no relevancy to respondents' activities subsequent thereto. The fact that the buying programs may have been consistent with the general objectives and ends sought to be obtained under the National Industrial Recovery Act is likewise irrelevant to the legality under the Sherman Act of respondents' activities either prior to or after June 1935. For as we have seen price-fixing combinations which lack Congressional sanction are illegal per se; they are not evaluated in terms of their purpose, aim or effect in the elimination of so-called competitive evils. Only in the event that they were, would such considerations have been relevant.

Accordingly we conclude that the Circuit Court of Appeals erred in reversing the judgments on this ground. *A fortiori* the position taken by respondents in their cross petition that they were entitled to directed verdicts of acquittal is untenable. . . .

Reversed.

CHIEF JUSTICE HUGHES and MR. JUSTICE MURPHY did not participate. MR. JUSTICE ROBERTS in a dissent with which MR. JUSTICE MCREYNOLDS concurred, said: ". . . concerted action to remove a harmful and destructive practice in an industry, even though such removal may have the effect of raising the price level, is not offensive to the Sherman Act if it is not intended and does not operate unreasonably to restrain interstate commerce; and such action has been held not unreasonably to restrain commerce if, as here, it involves no agreement for uniform prices but leaves the defendants free to compete with each other in the matter of price.

"No case decided by this court has held a combination illegal solely because its purpose or effect was to raise prices. The criterion of legality has always been the purpose or effect of the combination unduly to restrain commerce.

"I think Appalachian Coals, Inc., v. United States, 288 U.S. 344, 53 S.Ct. 471, 77 L.Ed. 825, a controlling authority. . . ."

NOTES AND QUERIES

(1) *The Process of Characterizing Conduct as Per Se Illegal.* The *Appalachian* and *Socony-Vacuum* cases illustrate a process sometimes called "mini-rule-of-reason" analysis. A limited preliminary analysis is made in order to determine whether comprehensive economic analysis may be dispensed with under the *per se* rule. While direct horizontal agreements to fix prices are clearly within the *per se* ban, a wide range of collaborative busi-

ness behavior may be ambiguous in respect to purpose or effect of fixing prices. For example, is the circulation of a list averaging the prices charged by auto dealers for new cars in an area price fixing or an inducement of price competition? [41] If the gasoline retailers in an area agreed to remove large and unsightly price signs at the request of a local group concerned with improving the aesthetic environment of the community, have they engaged in price fixing? [42] If the automobile manufacturers agree to engage in joint research and to defer installing new antipollution devices until they reach a consensus as to the most effective and economical technology, have they illegally restrained production or pricing? [43] Is a "mini-rule-of-reason" inquiry necessary? What additional evidence would suffice to cut off further inquiry along rule of reason lines? Should one distinguish between joint research agreements among giants and among pygmies?

(2) *Protecting Competition Versus Protection of a Competitive Process.* *Socony Vacuum*, footnote 59, appears to suggest that both joint action with a purpose to fix prices and joint action with the effect of fixing prices are unlawful, while *Appalachian Coals* appears to require a finding of both purpose and effect of fixing prices before joint action will be declared unlawful. What is the significance of the language in footnote 59: "It is the 'contract, combination . . . or conspiracy, in restraint of trade or commerce' which § 1 of the Act strikes down, whether the concerted activity be wholly nascent or abortive on the one hand, or successful on the other. And the amount of interstate or foreign trade involved is not material since § 1 of the Act brands as illegal the character of the restraint not the amount of commerce affected." In light of *Socony Vacuum*, would you argue that the essence of the § 1 offense, whether the analysis be described as *per se* or rule of reason, is joint action displacing the competitive process as the rule of trade and not the amount of competition affected by the joint action? If so, is relevant market analysis and a quantitative measurement of the amount of the market affected a necessary consideration in any § 1 case? Relevant considerations in some cases where purpose or effect are unclear? What do your conclusions say about the underlying purposes of § 1 of the Sherman Act? Is the purpose of Section 1 a mandate to competitors to compete or a prohibition upon agreements by competitors not to compete? What is the difference?

(3) *Circumventing a Per Se Prohibition on Price Fixing—The Case of the Oil Industry.* Chronic overproduction of a fungible product, with variable costs of production, frequently generates schemes within the industry involved to build a refuge from the competitive gales forcing prices down to the lowest cost producer. As *Socony-Vacuum* illustrates, the scheme need not take the form of an outright price fixing conspiracy arrived at in a smoke-filled room. Indeed, prices often cannot be fixed or stabilized in many industries absent control over production by all those capable of serving the market. By the same token, joint control of production will often lead to a stabilization of prices, if not the fixing of prices at a specific level. Agreements aimed at controlling the flow of goods or commodities into a market

41. See Plymouth Dealers' Association v. United States, 279 F.2d 128 (9th Cir. 1960).

42. Cf. United States v. Gasoline Retailers' Association, Inc., 285 F.2d 688 (7th Cir. 1961).

43. Cf. United States v. Automobile Manufacturer's Association, 307 F.Supp. 617 (C.D.Cal.1969) (consent decree prohibiting joint research on pollution controls); Comment, Antitrust Law—Environmental Law Use of Antitrust Laws As Environmental Remedy For Suppression of Pollution Control Technology, 15 B.C.Ind. & Comm.L.Rev. 813 (1974). Proposed modifications to the decree are discussed infra, p. 1032.

are often characterized, as in *Socony-Vacuum*, as horizontal price fixing agreements and *per se* violations of the Sherman Act. "Price fixing" means price stabilization, as well as fixing a specific price—high, low, or medium.

Escape from the *per se* prohibition of horizontal price fixing usually takes the form of using the powers of government to impose production or import limitations, permitting limited forms of joint action, providing subsidies, imposing tariffs, or placing a floor under prices. The history of the oil industry response to world wide overproduction, a history suggesting less than a slavish obedience to *laissez-faire* or consistency of opposition to all forms of government intervention in the "market" by the industry, illustrates well how a *per se* prohibition may be circumvented.[44] The following outlines the oil industry's response first to domestic overproduction, then overproduction from overseas, and finally, the present day development of OPEC.

(A) *Conservation and Producer-State Control of National Energy Policy.* The Interstate Compact to Conserve Oil and Gas of Feb. 16, 1935, bound the participating states to prevent various practices resulting in physical waste of petroleum resources, including "the drilling . . . or operating of a well or wells so as to bring about physical waste of oil or gas or loss in the ultimate recovery thereof." Article V provided: "It is not the purpose of this compact to authorize the states joining herein to limit production of oil or gas for the purpose of stabilizing or fixing the price thereof, or create or perpetuate monopoly, or to promote regimentation, but is limited to the purpose of conserving oil and gas and preventing avoidable waste thereof within reasonable limitations." Congress consented to this compact and to successive extensions thereof. See 77 Stat. 145 (1963). The 1955 extension directed the Department of Justice to report annually to Congress on anticompetitive practices under the compact, but Congress failed to provide funds required for an investigation of this scope.[45] The proration laws of the oil producing states provide that prospective market demand be considered in fixing the maximum production to be permitted. The Interstate Compact arrangement strikingly resembles OPEC, the international compact of petroleum exporting nations. See p. 365 infra. Are the interests of the American producer-states and the exporting nations antagonistic?

Does the Interstate Compact sanction true "conservation" measures or are the state laws, to the extent that production is kept below the "maximum efficiency rate" set by engineers, instruments of monopolistic price-fixing?[46] Low state-fixed allowables tend to discourage new drilling at the same time

44. For a more general description of the history and evolution of the oil industry see J. Blair, The Control of Oil (1976); L. Mosley, Power Play: Oil In The Middle East (1973); A. Sampson, The Seven Sisters (1975).

45. See statement of Attorney General Brownell, reported in Wall St., Sept. 6, 1956, p. 5, relating to the First Annual Report.

46. Compare Zimmerman, Conservation in the Production of Petroleum—A Study in Industrial Control (1957) with Hardwicke, Market Demand as a Factor in the Conservation of Oil, First Annual Institute on Oil and Gas Law (Southwestern Legal Foundation, 1949) 149. See

generally Rostow, A National Policy for the Oil Industry (1948); Bain, The Economics of the Pacific Coast Oil Industry (1944-7).

Gordon, Economics and the Conservation Question, 1 U.Chi.J.Law & Bus. 110 (1958), argues that some "conservation" policies amount to diverting the economy from fuel that is presently cheap to fuel that is presently more expensive, an anti-economic move with doubtful countervailing gains in the future. See also De Chazeau & Kahn, Integration and Competition in the Petroleum Industry (1959), chap. 10—Conservation, National Defense and Public Policy.

that federal tax laws purport to encourage exploration for petroleum by making substantial tax concessions in the form of artificial depletion allowances. As an engineering matter, conservation is best promoted by exploiting a given petroleum deposit as a unit, with limits on the number and spacing of wells so as to maintain maximum underground pressure. Thus, competitive drilling of wells based on individual ownership of land or oil and gas rights is curtailed on technological grounds, and owners share proportionately in the proceeds of their pooled rights. The industry has for the most part successfully opposed legislation designed to *compel* unitization.[47]

Before the advent of federal price regulation under the Natural Gas Act, state action setting minimum producer prices for natural gas was sustained on "conservation" grounds,[48] viz. that low prices caused premature abandonment of wells before all available gas had been extracted, and promoted "inferior" use of gas for industrial purposes rather than home heating and cooking. *Corporation Commission of Oklahoma v. Federal Power Commission,*[49] invalidated state price control as inconsistent with federal preemption of the field by the Natural Gas Act.

(B) *State Control of National Energy Policy; Defense? The Oil Cartel,* editorial from The Wall St.J., Feb. 21, 1957, p. 12:

President Eisenhower, Senator O'Mahoney, Secretary of the Interior Seaton, Defense Mobilizer Flemming, and the members of the House Commerce Committee ought to be much happier than they were a week ago. All of these gentlemen have been greatly concerned about the "shortage" of oil. The Government, you recall, set up an emergency committee to allow oil companies to pool resources to get oil to a Europe cut off by the Suez canal crisis. Yet only lately Mr. Eisenhower complained that enough oil wasn't forthcoming. Senator O'Mahoney blamed it all on the greedy oil companies, and the House Commerce Committee was one of several "investigating" the trouble.

Now things are looking up. This week the Texas Railroad Commission boosted the state's permissible oil production for March to a record 3.7 million barrels daily in answer to appeals from the oil companies and the Federal Government. In Washington the Texas action was called "wonderful." Mr. Flemming has quietly appealed to the state regulatory bodies in Louisiana and Oklahoma to follow this statesmanlike move and let wells in those states produce to meet the demand.

Well, the situation calls for wonder, all right, but not quite in the sense implied in the joyous cries from Washington. The wonder is that everybody should have to be so grateful to three men from Texas who comprise the "Railroad" commission. . . . If these men decide to boost oil production, then the oil companies, the general consumer and the Federal Government officials concerned can be grateful. If these men say "no," then all the others can only beg them to change their minds.

47. Cities Service Gas Co. v. Peerless Oil & Gas Co., 340 U.S. 179, 71 S.Ct. 215, 95 L.Ed. 190 (1950); cf. Williams, Conservation of Oil and Gas, 65 Harv.L.Rev. 1155, 1180 (1952) ("Price-fixing, a new movement marching under the banner of 'conservation'. . . .")

48. See Myers, Pooling and Unitization (1957), chapter VIII; Hardwicke,

Unitization Statutes: Voluntary Action or Compulsion, 24 Rocky Mountain L.Rev. 29 (1951).

49. 362 F.Supp. 522 (W.D.Okla.1973), summarily affirmed 415 U.S. 961, 94 S.Ct. 1548, 39 L.Ed.2d 863 (1974) (three judges dissenting).

This situation is possible because of a law passed by Congress a good many years ago which gave permission to the state governments to regulate production. It even permits the state agencies to cooperate with one another in a manner that hardly accords with other anti-monopoly statutes. In short, a production cartel created by government.

(C) *"Voluntary" Restriction of Oil Imports for Conservation and National Defense; Import Quotas.* A special committee of President Eisenhower's cabinet in 1957 called upon the principal oil companies voluntarily to curtail their imports in conformity with suggested quotas.[50] A number of companies protested alleged inequities in the quotas, and the Interior Department conducted public hearings on these complaints. Quotas were assigned in proportion to the volume of oil refined by each company during a selected base period in the past. Thus each company's share of imports would be fixed on a historical basis, without reference to its current sales or need for foreign crude oil. Charges that the program resembled traditional cartel plans for sharing international trade were answered by the Administration contention that the proposal did not violate the Sherman Act because the companies were to act voluntarily and individually rather than by agreement. The Wall St. J. (Aug. 1, 1957, p. 6) commented in part as follows:

> The logic of those who would put strict controls on the imports of oil, it seems to us, rests upon a strange syllogism. It runs something like this. Oil is a basic raw material, necessary in peace and absolutely essential in war. Known U.S. oil reserves are insufficient for the long future; we now see only about an eleven year supply. Therefore we must cut down on the influx of foreign oil as a defense measure. The conclusion is startling, even if all the assumptions are correct. If a raw material is in short supply at home, one might suppose that is all the more reason why we should conserve it for future use by increasing our imports now.

> Actually, the advocates of import restrictions concede as much. But they say the problem is to get more exploration for new oil at home; there won't be any exploration unless oil prices are encouragingly high; and oil prices won't be high unless we restrict cheaper foreign oil. This might be a persuasive argument if the plan was to find new wells and then cap them to save their oil for future emergencies. But that, of course, is not the idea. In practice, any hidden oil reserves will be better conserved by being left alone; the untapped oil is not going to go away.

As to the suggestion that capped domestic wells would constitute the best stockpile, consider that in 1976 an important part of the Federal Energy Ad-

---

50. Compare Lehnardt, Executive Authority and Antitrust Considerations in "Voluntary" Limits on Steel Imports, 118 U.Pa.L.Rev. 105 (1969), on the question whether the industry tail wagged the governmental dog in the arrangements by which American, Japanese, and other foreign steel producers negotiated with each other (in violation of the antitrust laws) through a State Department front.

Consumers Union v. Rogers, 352 F.Supp. 1319 (D.C.D.C.1973), held that President Nixon had no power to confer immunity from the antitrust laws upon a foreign steel cartel with which he had entered into negotiations for "voluntary" restriction of exports to America. This

declaration as to antitrust was vacated on appeal (sub nom. Consumers Union v. Kissinger, 506 F.2d 136 (D.C.Cir. 1974)) on the ground that the antitrust count had been dismissed with prejudice on plaintiff's motion in the district court, leaving only counts based on plaintiff's contention that the President had acted in violation of foreign trade legislation.

The Carter administration entered into an agreement with Japan restricting imports of Japanese television sets and giving assurance that Japanese manufacturers and exporters will not be prosecuted for antitrust violations incident to the Japanese export controls. Wall St. J., May 16, 1977, p. 7.

ministration's program was to import oil lifted out of Arabian sands and pump it into the ground again in American "salt domes."

As to the involuntary character of the "voluntary" oil import program, see *Eastern States Petroleum Corp. v. Seaton, Secretary of Interior*,[51] sustaining the government's right to deprive non-complying firms of government purchase orders. The pseudo-voluntary controls became mandatory in 1959, when the President promulgated official import quotas.[52] The legislative basis for imposition of such quotas is unclear.[53] A cabinet-level task force in the Nixon Administration reportedly agreed on scrapping the oil import quota system, replacing it with a tariff that would yield hundreds of millions of dollars to the government while introducing a modest counter-inflationary drop in the domestic price of petroleum.[54] The President later rejected the proposal.[55]

(D) *The OPEC Governmental Cartel.* The world price of petroleum was quadrupled in 1973 by an intergovernmental cartel called the Organization of Petroleum Exporting Countries (OPEC).[56] The reaction of the Nixon and Ford Administrations was "Project Independence", a program to encourage development of domestic alternatives to imported petroleum. The program relied principally on the maintenance of high oil and gas prices as an incentive for more intensive exploration and extraction, for development of costly shale oil reserves, for shifting industrial and utility users to coal, etc. Petroleum imports were to be limited by tariffs, and a minimum sales price for imported petroleum was to be set *so that any weakening in OPEC's extortion would not undermine the high-price incentive system of Project Independence!*

The Carter Administration secured passage of several major pieces of energy legislation aimed at encouraging conservation through tax and other devices. One of the laws, The Natural Gas Policy Act of 1978,[57] provides for phased-in deregulation of well-head gas pricing by 1985, with expectation that natural gas prices will gradually increase to an equivalent price per B.T.U. for oil. The price for domestically produced crude oil, in turn, was decontrolled by an Executive Order issued by President Carter aimed at increasing crude oil prices to the OPEC set world price by 1981.[58] An excess profits tax was also passed during the Carter Administration to recoup a part of the higher prices for domestic production realized by phased-in decontrol aimed at raising domestic prices to the OPEC fixed world prices.[59] It was thought that these measures would encourage conservation, stimulate domestic production of and exploration for crude, and invite innovation in the supply of alternative energy sources. Alternative programs might have: (1) fought the OPEC cartel by organizing countervailing power on the buyers' side, e.g., a national import agency; (2) put the federal government directly into the business of exploring and developing shale-oil deposits, off-shore fields, or vast domestic petroleum "reserves" earmarked for a navy that is

51. 163 F.Supp. 797 (D.D.C.1958).

52. Presid. Proc. 3279, 24 Fed.Reg. 1781 (March 12, 1959).

53. Cf. 19 U.S.C.A. § 1862.

54. Wall St. J., Oct. 24, 1969, p. 3.

55. Wall St. J., Aug. 18, 1970, p. 4. The oil import control program prior to the OPEC-created energy crisis of 1973, is brilliantly reviewed in Dam, The Implemention of Oil Import Quotas, 14 J. Law and Econ. 1 (1971).

56. See Adelman, The World Petroleum Market (1972).

57. Natural Gas Policy Act of 1978, P.L. 95–621, 92 Stat. 3351.

58. Exec. Order No. 12,153, 44 Fed. Reg. 48,949 (1979), as amended by Exec. Order No. 12,186, 44 Fed.Reg. 76,877 (1979) and Exec. Order No. 12,189, 45 Fed.Reg. 3,559 (1980).

59. Windfall Profit Tax Act (Crude Oil), P.L. 96–223, 94 Stat. 229 (1980).

converting to nuclear power; and (3) provided incentives for private investment by "safety-net" guarantees against losses attributable to a decline in the world price of petroleum, thus avoiding the inflationary effect and the bonanza profits effect of raising domestic prices to the artificial world price dictated by OPEC.

What are the possible objections to these alternatives? Is it rational to structure the world's energy economy to conform with a cartel price that is roughly 50 times the cost of producing petroleum in the Middle East? (From a world point-of-view, petroleum has never been so plentiful or low-cost as now.) Are OPEC-dictated prices justifiable as a conservation measure designed to restrain present consumption so that future generations may share in an exhaustible resource? Are they justifiable as wealth-sharing with the Third World? (The non-OPEC Third World, e.g., India, is hardest hit because it lacks domestic alternatives and is least able to meet the foreign exchange demands.) Is OPEC much different in an economic sense from the organization of American petroleum producing states pursuant to the Interstate Oil Compact?

Although the 1980's have brought tension to the ranks of OPEC and a reduction in imports as part of an overall decline in demand, foreign supply still remains vulnerable to shifts in OPEC policy and political instability in the Middle East. Domestic prices still remain high in relation to cost of production and costly innovation in alternative fuels, like production of shale oil, remain doubtful—absent massive federal subsidies—in light of the ability of OPEC to drop the world price to exclude supply from new technologies.

A massive investigation by Canadian antitrust officials, based on documents seized by government raids in 1973–74, suggests that several major international oil companies have coordinated pricing and production activity and delayed development of alternative fuels during the 60's and 70's.[60] The study charges that the activity, facilitated by joint ventures at every level of the industry and manipulation of the price of foreign oil through off-shore shell corporations, resulted in overcharges to Canadian consumers of $12.1 billion between 1958 and 1973. The study calls for extensive regulation of the industry, including vertical divestiture of pipelines and retailing, at a time when the Reagan administration is pressing for complete de-regulation of the industry in the U.S. and is following a relaxed policy toward mergers in the energy industry.

Queries: Should prices for domestic crude be allowed to rise to a cartel fixed price? How should oil prices be established when there is no necessary relationship between the costs put into the ground and the value of what is taken out? Should the government establish a federal corporation along the lines of T.V.A. to engage in the exploration for oil and gas on federal lands and offshore to establish a yardstick for the cost of producing oil and gas? If the allegations of the Canadian study referred to, supra, are substantially true and similar practices exist in the United States, what steps should the U.S. Government take? [61]

60. Report to the Restrictive Trade Practices Commission of Canada, The State of Competition In The Canadian Petroleum Industry, 7 Vols. (1981). A summary of the Report appears in Mintz, "$12.1 Billion in Oil Overcharges Seen: Canadian Probe Accuses Major Firms of Inflating Prices from '58 to '73", The Washington Post, Aug. 11, 1981, p. A–2.

61. See W. Moore, Horizontal Divestiture: Highlights on a Conference on Whether Oil Companies Should Be Prohibited From Owning Nonpetroleum Energy Resources (A.E.I. 1977); Adams, Vertical Divestiture of the Petroleum Majors: An Affirmative Case, 30 Vand.L. Rev. 1115 (1977) (outlining horizontal interlocks in foreign and domestic produc-

ARIZONA v. MARICOPA COUNTY MEDICAL SOCIETY

Supreme Court of the United States, 1982.
___ U.S. ___, 102 S.Ct. 2466, 73 L.Ed.2d 48.

JUSTICE STEVENS delivered the opinion of the Court.

The question presented is whether § 1 of the Sherman Act, 15 U.S.C. § 1, has been violated by an agreement among competing physicians setting, by majority vote, the maximum fees that they may claim in full payment for health services provided to policyholders of specified insurance plans. The United States Court of Appeals for the Ninth Circuit held that the question could not be answered without evaluating the actual purpose and effect of the agreement at a full trial. 643 F.2d 553 (1980). Because the undisputed facts disclose a violation of the statute, we granted certiorari, and now reverse.

. . .

I

The Court of Appeals, by a divided vote, affirmed the District Court's order refusing to enter partial summary judgment, but each of the three judges on the panel had a different view of the case. Judge Sneed was persuaded that "the challenged practice is not a per se violation." 643 F.2d, at 560.[62] Judge Kennedy, although concurring, cautioned that he had not found "these reimbursement schedules to be per se proper, [or] that an examination of these practices under the rule of reason at trial will not reveal the proscribed adverse effect on competition, or that this court is foreclosed at some later date, when it has more evidence, from concluding that such schedules do constitute per se violations." Ibid.[63] Judge Larson dissented, expressing the view that a *per se* rule should apply and, alternatively

tion, joint ventures, exchange agreements, interlocking directorates, etc. among the major oil companies).

62. [This and the following 11 footnotes are from the Court's opinion renumbered.] Judge Sneed explained his reluctance to apply the *per se* rule substantially as follows: The record did not indicate the actual purpose of the maximum fee arrangements or their effect on competition in the health care industry. It was not clear whether the assumptions made about typical price restraints could be carried over to that industry. Only recently had this Court applied the antitrust laws to the professions. Moreover, there already were such significant obstacles to pure competition in the industry that a court must compare the prices that obtain under the maximum fee arrangements with those that would other-

wise prevail rather than with those that would prevail under ideal competitive conditions. Furthermore, the Ninth Circuit had not applied Keifer-Stewart, supra, and Albrecht, supra, to horizontal agreements that establish maximum prices; some of the economic assumptions underlying the rule against maximum price fixing were not sound.

63. Judge Kennedy's concurring opinion concluded as follows:

"There does not now appear to be a controlling or definitive analysis of the market impact caused by the arrangements under scrutiny in this case, but trial may reveal that the arrangements are, at least in their essentials, not peculiar to the medical industry and that they should be condemned." 643 F.2d, at 560.

that a rule of reason analysis should condemn the arrangement even if a *per se* approach was not warranted. Id., at 563–569.[64]

Because the ultimate question presented by the certiorari petition is whether a partial summary judgment should have been entered by the District Court, we must assume that the respondents' version of any disputed issue of fact is correct. We therefore first review the relevant undisputed facts and then identify the factual basis for the respondents' contention that their agreements on fee schedules are not unlawful.

II

The Maricopa Foundation for Medical Care is a non-profit Arizona corporation composed of licensed doctors of medicine, osteopathy, and podiatry engaged in private practice. Approximately 1,750 doctors, representing about 70% of the practitioners in Maricopa County, are members.

The Maricopa foundation was organized in 1969 for the purpose of promoting fee-for-service medicine and to provide the community with a competitive alternative to existing health insurance plans.[65] The foundation performs three primary activities. It establishes the schedule of maximum fees that participating doctors agree to accept as payment in full for services performed for patients insured under plans approved by the foundation. It reviews the medical necessity and appropriateness of treatment provided by its members to such insured persons. It is authorized to draw checks on insurance company accounts to pay doctors for services performed for covered patients. In performing these functions, the foundation is considered an "insurance administrator" by the Director of the Arizona Department of Insurance. Its participating doctors, however, have no financial interest in the operation of the foundation.

The Pima Foundation for Medical Care, which includes about 400 member doctors, performs similar functions. For the purpose of this

64. Judge Larson stated, in part:

"Defendants formulated and dispersed relative value guides and conversion factor lists which together were used to set an upper limit on fees received from third-party payors. It is clear that these activities constituted maximum price-fixing by competitors. Disregarding any 'special industry' facts, this conduct is per se illegal. Precedent alone would mandate application of the per se standard.

"I find nothing in the nature of either the medical profession or the health care industry that would warrant their exemption from per se rules for price-fixing." Id., at 563–564 (citations omitted).

65. Most health insurance plans are of the fee-for-service type. Under the typical insurance plan, the insurer agrees with the insured to reimburse the insured for "usual, customary, and reasonable" medical charges. The third party insurer, and the insured to the extent of any excess charges, bears the economic risk that the insured will require medical treatment. An alternative to the fee-for-service type of insurance plan is illustrated by the health maintenance organizations authorized under the Health Maintenance Organization Act of 1973, 42 U.S.C. § 300e *et seq.* Under this form of pre-paid health plan, the consumer pays a fixed periodic fee to a functionally integrated group of doctors in exchange for the group's agreement to provide any medical treatment that the subscriber might need. The economic risk is thus borne by the doctors.

litigation, the parties seem to regard the activities of the two foundations as essentially the same. No challenge is made to their peer review or claim administration functions. Nor do the foundations allege that these two activities make it necessary for them to engage in
the practice of establishing maximum fee schedules.

. . .

The fee schedules limit the amount that the member doctors may
recover for services performed for patients insured under plans approved by the foundations. To obtain this approval the insurers—
including self-insured employers as well as insurance companies—
agree to pay the doctors' charges up to the scheduled amounts, and in
exchange the doctors agree to accept those amounts as payment in
full for their services. The doctors are free to charge higher fees to
uninsured patients and they also may charge any patient less than
the scheduled maxima. A patient who is insured by a foundation-
endorsed plan is guaranteed complete coverage for the full amount of
his medical bills only if he is treated by a foundation member. He is
free to go to a nonmember physician and is still covered for charges
that do not exceed the maximum fee schedule, but he must pay any
excess that the nonmember physician may charge.

The impact of the foundation fee schedules on medical fees and on
insurance premiums is a matter of dispute. The State of Arizona
contends that the periodic upward revisions of the maximum fee
schedules have the effect of stabilizing and enhancing the level of
actual charges by physicians, and that the increasing level of their
fees in turn increases insurance premiums. The foundations, on the
other hand, argue that the schedules impose a meaningful limit on
physicians charges, and that the advance agreement by the doctors to
accept the maxima enables the insurance carriers to limit and to calculate more efficiently the risks they underwrite and therefore serves
as an effective cost containment mechanism that has saved patients
and insurers millions of dollars. Although the Attorneys General of
40 different States, as well as the Solicitor General of the United
States and certain organizations representing consumers of medical
services, have filed *amicus curiae* briefs supporting the State of Arizona's position on the merits, we must assume that the respondents'
view of the genuine issues of fact is correct.

This assumption presents, but does not answer, the question
whether the Sherman Act prohibits the competing doctors from
adopting, revising, and agreeing to use a maximum fee schedule in
implementation of the insurance plans.

III

The respondents recognize that our decisions establish that price
fixing agreements are unlawful on their face. But they argue that
the *per se* rule does not govern this case because the agreements at
issue are horizontal and fix maximum prices, are among members of
a profession, are in an industry with which the judiciary has little

antitrust experience, and are alleged to have procompetitive justifications. Before we examine each of these arguments, we pause to consider the history and the meaning of the *per se* rule against price fixing agreements.

A

Section 1 of the Sherman Act of 1890 literally prohibits *every* agreement "in restraint of trade." In *United States v. Joint Traffic Assn.*, 171 U.S. 505, 19 S.Ct. 25, 43 L.Ed. 259 (1898), we recognized that Congress could not have intended a literal interpretation of the word "every"; since *Standard Oil Co. of New Jersey v. United States*, 221 U.S. 1, 31 S.Ct. 502, 55 L.Ed. 619 (1911), we have analyzed most restraints under the so-called "rule of reason." As its name suggests, the rule of reason requires the factfinder to decide whether under all the circumstances of the case the restrictive practice imposes an unreasonable restraint on competition.

The elaborate inquiry into the reasonableness of a challenged business practice entails significant costs. Litigation of the effect or purpose of a practice often is extensive and complex. Judges often lack the expert understanding of industrial market structures and behavior to determine with any confidence a practice's effect on competition. And the result of the process in any given case may provide little certainty or guidance about the legality of a practice in another context.

The costs of judging business practices under the rule of reason, however, have been reduced by the recognition of *per se* rules.[66] Once experience with a particular kind of restraint enables the Court to predict with confidence that the rule of reason will condemn it, it has applied a conclusive presumption that the restraint is unreasonable. As in every rule of general application, the match between the presumed and the actual is imperfect. For the sake of business certainty and litigation efficiency, we have tolerated the invalidation of some agreements that a fullblown inquiry might have proved to be reasonable.[67]

. . .

66. For a thoughtful and brief discussion of the costs and benefits of rule of reason versus *per se* rule analysis of price fixing agreements, see F. Scherer, Industrial Market Structure and Economic Performance 438–443 (1970). Professor Scherer's "opinion, shared by a majority of American economists concerned with antitrust policy, is that in the present legal framework the costs of implementing a rule of reason would exceed the benefits derived from considering each restrictive agreement on its merits and prohibiting only those which appear unreasonable." Id., at 440.

67. Thus, in applying the *per se* rule to invalidate the restrictive practice in

United States v. Topco Associates, Inc., 405 U.S. 596, 92 S.Ct. 1126, 31 L.Ed.2d 515 (1972), we stated that "[w]hether or not we would decide this case the same way under the rule of reason used by the District Court is irrelevant to the issue before us." Id., at 609, 92 S.Ct., at 1134. The Court made the same point in Continental T.V., Inc. v. GTE Sylvania Inc., 433 U.S. at 50, n. 16, 97 S.Ct. at 2557, n. 16:

"*Per se* rules thus require the Court to make broad generalizations about the social utility of particular commercial practices. The probability that anticompetitive consequences will result from a practice and the severity of those conse-

The application of the *per se* rule to maximum price fixing agreements in *Kiefer-Stewart Co. v. Seagram & Sons*, 340 U.S. 211, 71 S.Ct. 259, 95 L.Ed. 219 (1951), followed ineluctably from *Socony-Vacuum:*

> "For such agreements, no less than those to fix minimum prices, cripple the freedom of traders and thereby restrain their ability to sell in accordance with their own judgment. We reaffirm what we said in *United States v. Socony-Vacuum Oil Co.*, 310 U.S. 150, 223 [60 S.Ct. 811, 844, 84 L.Ed. 1129]: 'Under the Sherman Act a combination formed for the purpose and with the effect of raising, depressing, fixing, pegging, or stabilizing the price of a commodity in interstate or foreign commerce is illegal *per se.*'" Id., at 213, 60 S.Ct., at 839.

Over the objection that maximum price fixing agreements were not the "economic equivalent" of minimum price fixing agreements, *Kiefer-Stewart* was reaffirmed in *Albrecht v. Herald Co.*, 390 U.S. 145, 88 S.Ct. 869, 19 L.Ed.2d 998 (1968):

> "Maximum and minimum price fixing may have different consequences in many situations. But schemes to fix maximum prices, by substituting the perhaps erroneous judgment of a seller for the forces of the competitive market, may severely intrude upon the ability of buyers to compete and survive in that market. Competition, even in a single product, is not cast in a single mold. Maximum prices may be fixed too low for the dealer to furnish services essential to the value which goods have for the consumer or to furnish services and conveniences which consumers desire and for which they are willing to pay. Maximum price fixing may channel distribution through a few large or specifically advantaged dealers who otherwise would be subject to significant nonprice competition. Moreover, if the actual price charged under a maximum price scheme is nearly always the fixed maximum price, which is increasingly likely as the maximum price approaches the actual cost of the dealer, the scheme tends to acquire all the attributes of an arrangement fixing minimum prices." Id., at 152–153, 88 S.Ct. at 872–873 (footnote omitted).

We have not wavered in our enforcement of the *per se* rule against price fixing. Indeed, in our most recent price fixing case we summarily reversed the decision of another Ninth Circuit panel that a horizontal agreement among competitors to fix credit terms does not necessarily contravene the antitrust laws. *Catalano, Inc. v. Target Sales, Inc.*, 446 U.S. 643, 100 S.Ct. 1925, 64 L.Ed.2d 580 (1980).

B

Our decisions foreclose the argument that the agreements at issue escape *per se* condemnation because they are horizontal and fix maxi-

quences must be balanced against its procompetitive consequences. Cases that do not fit the generalization may arise, but a *per se* rule reflects the judg-ment that such cases are not sufficiently common or important to justify the time and expense necessary to identify them."

mum prices. *Kiefer-Stewart* and *Albrecht* place horizontal agree-ments to fix maximum prices on the same legal—even if not econom-ic—footing as agreements to fix minimum or uniform prices.[68] The *per se* rule "is grounded on faith in price competition as a market force [and not] on a policy of low selling prices at the price of elimi-nating competition." Rahl, Price Competition and the Price Fixing Rule—Preface and Perspective, 57 Nw.U.L.Rev. 137, 142 (1962). In this case the rule is violated by a price restraint that tends to provide the same economic rewards to all practitioners regardless of their skill, their experience, their training, or their willingness to employ innovative and difficult procedures in individual cases. Such a re-straint also may discourage entry into the market and may deter ex-perimentation and new developments by individual entrepreneurs. It may be a masquerade for an agreement to fix uniform prices, or it may in the future take on that character.

Nor does the fact that doctors—rather than nonprofessionals—are the parties to the price fixing agreements support the respondents' position. In *Goldfarb v. Virginia State Bar*, 421 U.S. 773, 788, n. 17, 95 S.Ct. 2004, 2013, n. 17, 44 L.Ed.2d 572 (1975), we stated that the "public service aspect, and other features of the professions, may re-quire that a particular practice, which could properly be viewed as a violation of the Sherman Act in another context, be treated different-ly." The price fixing agreements in this case, however, are not premised on public service or ethical norms. The respondents do not argue . . . that the quality of the professional service that their members provide is enhanced by the price restraint. The respon-dents' claim for relief from the *per se* rule is simply that the doctors' agreement not to charge certain insureds more than a fixed price fa-cilitates the successful marketing of an attractive insurance plan. But the claim that the price restraint will make it easier for custom-ers to pay does not distinguish the medical profession from any other provider of goods or services.

We are equally unpersuaded by the argument that we should not apply the *per se* rule in this case because the judiciary has little anti-trust experience in the health care industry.[69] The argument quite obviously is inconsistent with *Socony-Vacuum*. In unequivocal terms, we stated that, "[w]hatever may be its peculiar problems and characteristics, the Sherman Act, so far as price-fixing agreements

---

68. It is true that in Kiefer-Stewart, as in Albrecht, the agreement involved a vertical arrangement in which maximum resale prices were fixed. But the case al-so involved an agreement among compet-itors to impose the resale price restraint. In any event, horizontal restraints are generally less defensible than vertical re-straints. See Continental T.V., Inc. v. GTE Sylvania Inc., supra; Easterbrook, Maximum Price Fixing, 48 U.Chi.L.Rev. 886, 890, n. 20 (1981).

69. The argument should not be con-fused with the established position that a

new per se rule is not justified until the judiciary obtains considerable rule of rea-son experience with the particular type of restraint challenged. See White Mo-tor Co. v. United States, 372 U.S. 253, 83 S.Ct. 696, 9 L.Ed.2d 738 (1963). Nor is our unwillingness to examine the eco-nomic justification of this particular ap-plication of the *per se* rule against price fixing inconsistent with our reexamina-tion of the general validity of the *per se* rule rejected in Continental T.V., Inc. v. GTE Sylvania Inc., supra.

are concerned, establishes one uniform rule applicable to all industries alike." 310 U.S., at 222, 60 S.Ct., at 843. We also stated that "[t]he elimination of so-called competitive evils [in an industry] is no legal justification" for price fixing agreements, id., at 220, 60 S.Ct., at 843, yet the Court of Appeals refused to apply the *per se* rule in this case in part because the health care industry was so far removed from the competitive model.[70] Consistent with our prediction in *Socony-Vacuum*, id., the result of this reasoning was the adoption by the Court of Appeals of a legal standard based on the reasonableness of the fixed prices,[71] an inquiry we have so often condemned.[72] Finally, the argument that the *per se* rule must be rejustified for every industry that has not been subject to significant antitrust litigation ignores the rationale for *per se* rules, which in part is to avoid "the necessity for an incredibly complicated and prolonged economic investigation into the entire history of the industry involved, as well as related industries, in an effort to determine at large whether a particular restraint has been unreasonable—an inquiry so often wholly fruitless when undertaken."

The respondents' principal argument is that the *per se* rule is inapplicable because their agreements are alleged to have procompetitive justifications. The argument indicates a misunderstanding of the *per se* concept. The anticompetitive potential inherent in all price fixing agreements justifies their facial invalidation even if procompetitive

70. "The health care industry, moreover, presents a particularly difficult area. The first step to understanding is to recognize that not only is access to the medical profession very time consuming and expensive both for the applicant and society generally, but also that numerous government subventions of the costs of medical care have created both a demand and supply function for medical services that is artificially high. The present supply and demand functions of medical services in no way approximate those which would exist in a purely private competitive order. An accurate description of those functions moreover is not available. Thus, we lack baselines by which could be measured the distance between the present supply and demand functions and those which would exist under ideal competitive conditions." 643 F.2d, at 556.

71. "Perforce we must take industry as it exists, absent the challenged feature, as our baseline for measuring anticompetitive impact. The relevant inquiry becomes whether fees paid to doctors under that system would be less than those payable under the FMC maximum fee agreement. Put differently, confronted with an industry widely deviant from a reasonably free competitive model, such as agriculture, the proper inquiry is whether the practice enhances the prices charged for the services. In

simplified economic terms, the issue is whether the maximum fee arrangement better permits the attainment of the monopolist's goal, *viz.*, the matching of marginal cost to marginal revenue, or in fact obstructs that end." Id., at 556.

72. In the first price fixing case arising under the Sherman Act, the Court was required to pass on the sufficiency of the defendants' plea that they had established rates that were actually beneficial to consumers. Assuming the factual validity of the plea, the Court rejected the defense as a matter of law. United States v. Trans-Missouri Freight Assn., 166 U.S. 290, 17 S.Ct. 540, 41 L.Ed. 1007 (1897). In National Society of Professional Engineers v. United States, 435 U.S. 679, 689, 98 S.Ct. 1355, 1364, 55 L.Ed.2d 637 (1978), we referred to Judge Taft's "classic rejection of the argument that competitors may lawfully agree to sell their goods at the same price as long as the agreed-upon price is reasonable." See United States v. Addyston Pipe & Steel Co., 85 F. 271 (CA6 1898), aff'd, 175 U.S. 211, 20 S.Ct. 96, 44 L.Ed. 136 (1899). In our latest price fixing case, we reiterated the point: "It is no excuse that the prices fixed are themselves reasonable." Catalano, Inc. v. Target Sales, Inc., 446 U.S. 643, 647, 100 S.Ct. 1925, 1927, 64 L.Ed.2d 580 (1980).

justifications are offered for some. Those claims of enhanced competition are so unlikely to prove significant in any particular case that we adhere to the rule of law that is justified in its general application. Even when the respondents are given every benefit of the doubt, the limited record in this case is not inconsistent with the presumption that the respondents' agreements will not significantly enhance competition.

The respondents contend that their fee schedules are procompetitive because they make it possible to provide consumers of health care with a uniquely desirable form of insurance coverage that could not otherwise exist. The features of the foundation-endorsed insurance plans that they stress are a choice of doctors, complete insurance coverage, and lower premiums. The first two characteristics, however, are hardly unique to these plans. Since only about 70% of the doctors in the relevant market are members of either foundation, the guarantee of complete coverage only applies when an insured chooses a physician in that 70%. If he elects to go to a non-foundation doctor, he may be required to pay a portion of the doctor's fee. It is fair to presume, however, that at least 70% of the doctors in other markets charge no more than the "usual, customary, and reasonable" fee that typical insurers are willing to reimburse in full. Thus, in Maricopa and Pima Counties as well as in most parts of the country, if an insured asks his doctor if the insurance coverage is complete, presumably in about 70% of the cases the doctor will say yes and in about 30% of the cases he will say no.

It is true that a binding assurance of complete insurance coverage—as well as most of the respondents' potential for lower insurance premiums—can be obtained only if the insurer and the doctor agree in advance on the maximum fee that the doctor will accept as full payment for a particular service. Even if a fee schedule is therefore desirable, it is not necessary that the doctors do the price fixing. The record indicates that the Arizona Comprehensive Medical/Dental Program for Foster Children is administered by the Maricopa foundation pursuant to a contract under which the maximum fee schedule is prescribed by a state agency rather than by the doctors. This program and the Blue Shield plan challenged in *Group Life & Health Insurance Co. v. Royal Drug Co.*, 440 U.S. 205, 99 S.Ct. 1067, 59 L.Ed.2d 261 (1979), indicate that insurers are capable not only of fixing maximum reimbursable prices but also of obtaining binding agreements with providers guaranteeing the insured full reimbursement of a participating provider's fee. In light of these examples, it is not surprising that nothing in the record even arguably supports the conclusion that this type of insurance program could not function if the fee schedules were set in a different way.

The most that can be said for having doctors fix the maximum prices is that doctors may be able to do it more efficiently then insurers. The validity of that assumption is far from obvious, but in any event there is no reason to believe that any savings that might accrue from this arrangement would be sufficiently great to affect the competitiveness of these kinds of insurance plans. It is entirely possible that the potential or actual power of the foundations to dictate the terms of such insurance plans may more than offset the theoretical efficiencies upon which the respondents' defense ultimately rests.

C

Our adherence to the *per se* rule is grounded not only on economic prediction, judicial convenience, and business certainty, but also on a recognition of the respective roles of the Judiciary and the Congress in regulating the economy. *United States v. Topco Associates, Inc.*, supra, 405 U.S., at 611–612, 92 S.Ct., at 1135. Given its generality, our enforcement of the Sherman Act has required the Court to provide much of its substantive content. By articulating the rules of law with some clarity and by adhering to rules that are justified in their general application, however, we enhance the legislative prerogative to amend the law. The respondents' arguments against application of the *per se* rule in this case therefore are better directed to the legislature. Congress may consider the exception that we are not free to read into the statute.[73]

. . .

The judgment of the Court of Appeals is reversed.

It is so ordered.

JUSTICE BLACKMUN and JUSTICE O'CONNOR took no part in the consideration or decision of this case.

JUSTICE POWELL, with whom THE CHIEF JUSTICE and JUSTICE REHNQUIST join, dissenting.

. . .

This case comes to us on a plaintiff's motion for summary judgment after only limited discovery. Therefore, as noted above, the inferences to be drawn from the record must be viewed in the light most favorable to the respondents. This requires, as the Court acknowledges, that we consider the foundation arrangement as one that "impose[s] a meaningful limit on physicians' charges," that "enables the insurance carriers to limit and to calculate more efficiently the risks they underwrite," and that "therefore serves as an effective cost containment mechanism that has saved patients and insurers millions of dollars." The question is whether we should condemn this

73. "[Congress] can, of course, make *per se* rules inapplicable in some or all cases, and leave courts free to ramble through the wilds of economic theory in order to maintain a flexible approach." *United States v. Topco Associates, Inc.*, supra, 405 U.S., at 609, n. 10, 92 S.Ct., at 1134, n. 10. Indeed, it has exempted certain industries from the full reach of the Sherman Act. See, e.g., 7 U.S.C. §§ 291–292 (Capper-Volstead Act, agricultural cooperatives); 15 U.S.C. §§ 1011–1013 (McCarran-Ferguson Act, insurance); 49 U.S.C. § 5b (Reed-Bulwinkle Act, rail and motor carrier rate-fixing bureaus); 15 U.S.C. § 1801 (newspaper joint operating agreements).

arrangement forthwith under the Sherman Act, a law designed to *benefit* consumers.

. . .

It is settled law that once an arrangement has been labeled as "price fixing" it is to be condemned *per se*. But it is equally well settled that this characterization is not to be applied as a talisman to every arrangement that involves a literal fixing of prices. Many lawful contracts, mergers, and partnerships fix prices. But our cases require a more discerning approach. The inquiry in an antitrust case is not simply one of "determining whether two or more potential competitors have literally 'fixed' a 'price.' . . . [Rather], it is necessary to characterize the challenged conduct as falling within or without that category of behavior to which we apply the label *'per se* price fixing.' That will often, but not always, be a simple matter."

Before characterizing an arrangement as a *per se* price fixing agreement meriting condemnation, a court should determine whether it is a "naked restrain[t] of trade with no purpose except stifling of competition." Such a determination is necessary because "departure from the rule-of-reason standard must be based upon demonstrable economic effect rather than . . . upon formalistic line drawing." As part of this inquiry, a court must determine whether the procompetitive economies that the arrangement purportedly makes possible are substantial and realizable in the absence of such an agreement.

. . .

In sum, the fact that a foundation sponsored health insurance plan *literally* involves the setting of ceiling prices among competing physicians does not, of itself, justify condemning the plan as *per se* illegal. Only if it is clear from the record that the agreement among physicians is "so plainly anticompetitive that no elaborate study of [its effects] is needed to establish [its] illegality" may a court properly make a *per se* judgment. And, as our cases demonstrate, the *per se* label should not be assigned without carefully considering substantial benefits and procompetitive justifications. This is especially true when the agreement under attack is novel, as in this case.

. . .

I believe the Court's action today loses sight of the basic purposes of the Sherman Act. As we have noted, the antitrust laws are a "consumer welfare prescription." *Reiter v. Sonotone*, 442 U.S. 330, 343, 99 S.Ct. 2326, 2333, 60 L.Ed.2d 931 (1979). In its rush to condemn a novel plan about which it knows very little, the Court suggests that this end is achieved only by invalidating activities that *may* have some potential for harm. But the little that the record does show about the effect of the plan suggests that it is a means of providing medical services that in fact benefits rather that injures persons who need them.

In a complex economy, complex economic arrangements are commonplace. It is unwise for the Court, in a case as novel and important as this one, to make a final judgment in the absence of a complete record and where mandatory inferences create critical issues of fact.

WHAT SHOULD WE DO?

NOTES AND QUERIES

(1) *The Rationales for Per Se Rules: Queries:* What rationales for applying *per se* rules are set forth in *Maricopa County?* Is ease of administering a *per se* rule a sufficient ground for condemning all price-fixing arrangements? Is interference with the freedom of traders a sufficient reason for condemning maximum price-fixing?[74] What factors would provide a court with sufficient experience "to predict with confidence" that analysis under the rule of reason would generally condemn particular conduct and thereby justify applying a *per se* rule whenever the conduct is encountered? Where private conduct is perceived as the assumption of governmental power to regulate economic affairs or to define economic rights and responsibilities, should such conduct be deemed *per se* unlawful? Should the "beneficial" effect of the conduct, as the dissent argues, be considered in deciding whether to apply *per se* analysis? What benefits to consumers of medical services did the plan in *Maricopa County* offer? Should long term and short term benefits and detriments be weighed before invoking a *per se* rule or would such a process be unduly protracted and tax the economic expertise of the Court?

(2) *Maximum Price Fixing.* An article published after the Ninth Circuit opinion and before the Supreme Court decision in *Maricopa County* argued maximum price fixing agreements should be analyzed on a rule of reason basis.[75] Arguing from the neo-classical economic assumption that firms in perfectly competitive markets sell at marginal cost, the author suggested there are only two circumstances in which one should be concerned about maximum price fixing: (1) where the agreement is a "disguise for a traditional cartel" and (2) where price would exceed marginal cost without the agreement. The first, it is argued, should be unlawful; the second should not be *per se* unlawful because consumers are benefited by joint action driving prices to marginal cost or reducing marginal cost.[76] *Maricopa* is described as a case falling into the second category:

> Medical services are a textbook example of goods in which quality is uncertain, search costs are high (patients sometimes cannot search at all), purchases are infrequent, and third-party payments reduce the incentive for patients to search even when they can do so at low cost. A maximum price agreement may identify low-price sellers to the insurance companies, which may instruct the insureds to use a member of the foundation for medical care. Insurers participating in the plan will have lower costs, and the insureds will pay lower premiums. Physicians willing to accept the established maximum may join the foundation; others will not do so. The process should lead to a reduction in the cost of service, satisfying the criteria set out in the introduction to this part of the article: the maximum price agreement makes both consumers and the participating sellers better off.[77]

---

74. Cf. Union Labor Life Insurance Co. v. Pireno, __ U.S. __, 102 S.Ct. 3002, 73 L.Ed.2d 647 (1982) (involving review of chiropractor's rates, by "peer review" committee of practicing chiropractors, to determine whether number of treatments were too great and prices "unusually" high).

75. Easterbrook, Maximum Price Fixing, 48 U.Chi.L.Rev. 886 (1981).

76. Id. at 891–92.

77. Id. at 895. See also Kallstrom, Health Care Cost Control by Third Party Payors: Fee Schedules and the Sherman Act, 1978 Duke L.J. 645, 678–84 (arguing

Queries: Did the majority opinion in *Maricopa* answer this argument? Should the Court answer such an argument or is it one for Congress to answer by legislation inserting government rate regulation into a market not meeting the definition of a perfectly competitive market?

(3) *Price Stabilization.* The following internal memorandum from Assistant Attorney General Baxter to "All Attorneys Antitrust Division" and dated February 22, 1982, was forwarded to one of the authors:

> Today I encountered the most recent of a very large number of documents generated within the Division over the past year which asserted that private parties had violated Section 1 by means of an agreement which "stabilized" prices. Usually I encounter that word in a sentence which employs it conjunctively with one or more other verbs, frequently "fixed" or "raised".
>
> I suspect that this usage is derivative from the outrageous generalization of Justice Douglas in the *Scony [sic] Vacuum* case to the effect that parties commit a per se violation of Section 1 "to the extent that they raised, lowered, or stabilized prices."
>
> To suggest that all private agreements which have the effect of stabilizing prices constitute antitrust violations is idiocy of an even higher order than the suggestion that agreements lowering prices constitute such violations. That view would, for example, condemn all arrangements pertaining to futures markets.
>
> Over the months ahead, as you have occasion to employ the many items of Boiler Plate that reside in our files, I ask you to strike the word "stabilized" whenever it is used in this context. I also ask that you perform the perhaps more difficult task of excising it from your official usage.

Queries: Do you believe it appropriate to characterize Justice Douglas's statement in *Socony Vacuum* ("Under the Sherman Act a combination formed for the purpose and with the effect of raising, depressing, fixing, pegging, or stabilizing the price of a commodity . . . is illegal per se") as an "outrageous generalization"? Is it "idiocy" to suggest that all private agreements having the effect of stabilizing prices constitute antitrust violations? [78] After *Maricopa County* is it a lower level of "idiocy"—but still "idiocy"—to suggest that agreements lowering prices constitute antitrust violations?

(4) *Containment of Medical Costs, Third Party Payment, and Antitrust Policy.* Rapid and ongoing inflation in health care costs has generated widespread debate over methods to control spiraling costs. Reliance upon market forces to price hospital, doctor and prescription drug services appears not to work because most health care costs are paid by third party insurance plans—private or government operated. Patient incentives to shop for services on the basis of costs are thought to be minimal because insurers pay most of the bill and patients concerned about their well-being do not behave in accord with the economic concerns of the mythical rational maximizer—economic man. Health care providers may have few incentives to economize in a "market" where the customers' costs are covered by third party payors (Blue Cross, Medicaid, etc.) and the consumer's knowledge of

maximum price fixing by physicians should be unlawful); Note, Antitrust and Nonprofit Entities, 94 Harv.L.Rev. 802, 811–16 (1981) (similar argument).

78. See United States v. Container Corp., infra p. 396.

alternatives is limited or overwhelmed by concern for his or her immediate well-being.[79]

Maricopa County is an example of the interplay of antitrust policy and private cost control arrangements which have provoked significant antitrust litigation in recent years. In *Group Life & Health Insurance Co. v. Royal Drug Co.*,[80] the Supreme Court held an agreement between Blue Shield of Texas and three pharmacies in San Antonio for Blue Shield to reimburse the pharmacies for prescription costs and pay $2 per prescription filled for Blue Shield subscribers was not immune from antitrust scrutiny by virtue of the McCarran-Ferguson Act.[81] That Act exempts the "business of insurance" from the federal antitrust laws to the extent it is regulated by state law, except for acts of boycott, coercion or intimidation. Without passing upon the antitrust legality of the arrangement, the Court held the Blue Shield-pharmacy contracts were not the "business of insurance" and, therefore, the arrangement was not immune from antitrust scrutiny at the instance of competing pharmacies claiming they were boycotted by the arrangement.

In *Medical Arts Pharmacy of Stamford, Inc. v. Blue Cross & Blue Shield of Connecticut, Inc.*[82], the Second Circuit upheld a similar arrangement against an antitrust price fixing claim. Blue Cross offered all Connecticut pharmacies a contract which provided for reimbursement of a participating pharmacy pursuant to a formula in the contract setting prices for prescriptions filled by the pharmacy for Blue Cross subscribers. Blue Cross subscribers were free to patronize pharmacies not participating in the Blue Cross pharmacy contract and subscribers were reimbursed for their prescription expenditures by Blue Cross in an amount no greater than Blue Cross would reimburse pharmacies participating in its Prepaid Prescription Drug Agreement.

The court held the direct payment contracts with participating pharmacies "sufficiently different"[83] from the maximum price fixing struck down in *Albrecht* and *Kiefer-Stewart* (cases discussed in *Maricopa County*, supra p. 367) to preclude application of the *per se* rule against maximum price fixing, stressing the unique forces at work in the health care area,[84] particularly third party insurance payors. The court characterized the conduct as *"sui generis"*.[85] Applying a "rule of reason" analysis, the court found the plaintiff had not demonstrated an adverse effect on competition because of the contracts with participating pharmacies and therefore, the plaintiff had failed to prove a violation of the law.

Queries: Would *Medical Arts* be decided differently after the *Maricopa County* case? Is the *Maricopa County* case simply prohibiting deviations from the competitive ideal without regard to the characteristics of the industry, unless the deviation is expressly authorized by Congress? Should the Court follow this line of reasoning in areas like health care, in order to force public regulation of industries not meeting the conditions for the competitive process to work? If the Court fails to do so, is it likely that the private arrangements which might be established in the name of cost containment

---

79. See generally, C. Havighurst, Deregulating the Health Care Industry (1982); Symposium On The Antitrust Laws And The Health Services Industry, 1978 Duke L.J. 303.

80. 440 U.S. 205, 99 S.Ct. 1067, 59 L.Ed.2d 261 (1979), rehearing denied 441 U.S. 917, 99 S.Ct. 2017, 60 L.Ed.2d 389.

81. 15 U.S.C.A. §§ 1012, *et seq.*

82. 675 F.2d 502 (2d Cir. 1982).

83. Id., at 505.

84. See Note, Prepaid Prescription Drug Plans Under Antitrust Scrutiny: A Stern Challenge to Health Care Cost Containment, 75 NW.L.Rev. 506 (1980).

85. 675 F.2d at 506.

will be designed to protect private interests rather than the public interest and involve courts in complex litigation seeking to sort one from the other? Which institution is better equipped to undertake such a task? Congress or the courts? [86]

2. IDENTIFYING THE CONDUCT

BROADCAST MUSIC, INC. v. COLUMBIA BROADCASTING SYSTEM, INC.

Supreme Court of the United States, 1979.
441 U.S. 1, 99 S.Ct. 1551, 60 L.Ed.2d 1.

[Digest: Broadcast Music, Inc. (BMI) and the American Society of Composers, Authors, and Publishers (ASCAP) are organizations which license non-dramatic performances of copyrighted musical compositions. The 22,000 members of ASCAP grant the Society nonexclusive rights to license performances of their copyrighted works, collect royalties and distribute royalties in accordance with a formula. BMI, a nonprofit corporation, also operates as a copyright licensing agency in the same manner as ASCAP, representing 10,000 publishing companies and 20,000 authors and composers. ASCAP, with three million compositions, and BMI, with one million compositions, hold almost every domestic copyrighted musical composition in their repertories. Both organizations were formed to make it possible for copyright holders to license their works and receive royalties for performances of their works, rights guaranteed by the copyright law but impossible for individual composers to realize or police effectively.

CBS brought suit against both organizations challenging the practice of only granting "blanket licenses" to radio and television broadcasters. A blanket license permits the licensee to use any music in the repertory of the licensor, as often as desired, for a single license fee charged for the duration of the license. Payment is set at either a flat sum or a percentage of the network's revenue. CBS claimed the defendant's licensing practices constituted illegal price fixing under § 1 of the Sherman Act. The trial court rejected the claim that the blanket license was price fixing and a *per se* violation of the Sherman Act. The trial court further held that since direct negotiation with individual copyright owners was both available and feasible, the blanket license system was not an unreasonable restraint of trade, illegal tying, copyright misuse or monopolization. The Second Circuit

---

86. Before one leaps to the conclusion that Congress is better equipped to resolve such questions, one should consider the impact of special interest financing for Congressional election campaigns through P.A.C.s (Political Action Committees). There is evidence suggesting that the public's interest is increasingly being sacrificed to the election interests of candidates financing expensive political campaigns and the willingness of special interest groups to provide the financing in return for favorable votes on special in-terest legislation. See "Cash Politics: Special Interest Money Increasingly Influences What Congress Enacts", Wall St. J., July 26, 1982, p. 1. Among the bills cited as "circumstantial evidence" of undue P.A.C. influence is a bill proposing to exempt medical professionals from F.T.C. jurisdiction. Of the 192 House sponsors of the bill, 186 (97%) of them are recipients of campaign contributions from the American Medical Association's P.A.C.

reversed, holding that the blanket license constituted a form of price fixing illegal *per se* under § 1 of the Sherman Act. BMI and ASCAP appealed.]

MR. JUSTICE WHITE delivered the opinion of the Court.

A

To the Court of Appeals and CBS, the blanket license involves "price fixing" in the literal sense: the composers and publishing houses have joined together into an organization that sets its price for the blanket license it sells. But this is not a question simply of determining whether two or more potential competitors have literally "fixed" a "price." As generally used in the antitrust field, "price fixing" is a shorthand way of describing certain categories of business behavior to which the *per se* rule has been held applicable. The Court of Appeals' literal approach does not alone establish that this particular practice is one of those types or that it is "plainly anticompetitive" and very likely without "redeeming virtue." Literalness is overly simplistic and often overbroad. When two partners set the price of their goods or services they are literally "price fixing," but they are not *per se* in violation of the Sherman Act. Thus, it is necessary to characterize the challenged conduct as falling within or without that category of behavior to which we apply the label *"per se* price fixing." That will often, but not always, be a simple matter.

.   .   .   We have never examined a practice like this one before; indeed, the Court of Appeals recognized that "[i]n dealing with performing rights in the music industry we confront conditions both in copyright law and in antitrust law which are *sui generis.*" 562 F.2d, at 132. And though there has been rather intensive antitrust scrutiny of ASCAP and its blanket licenses, that experience hardly counsels that we should outlaw the blanket license as a *per se* restraint of trade.

B

This and other cases involving ASCAP and its licensing practices have arisen out of the efforts of the creators of copyrighted musical compositions to collect for the public performance of their works, as they are entitled to do under the Copyright Act. As already indicated, ASCAP and BMI orignated to make possible and to facilitate dealings between copyright owners and those who desire to use their music. Both organizations plainly involve concerted action in a large and active line of commerce, and it is not surprising that, as the District Court found, "[n]either ASCAP nor BMI is a stranger to antitrust litigation." 400 F.Supp., at 743.

The Department of Justice first investigated allegations of anticompetitive conduct by ASCAP over 50 years ago. A criminal complaint was filed in 1934, but the Government was granted a midtrial continuance and never returned to the courtroom. In separate complaints in 1941, the United States charged that the blanket license, which was then the only license offered by ASCAP and BMI, was an illegal restraint of trade and that arbitrary prices were being charged as a result of an illegal copyright pool. The Government sought to enjoin ASCAP's exclusive licensing powers and to require a different form of licensing by that organization. The case was settled by a consent decree that imposed tight restrictions on ASCAP's operations.[87] Following complaints relating to the television industry, successful private litigation against ASCAP by movie theaters,[88] and a Government challenge to ASCAP's arrangements with similar foreign organizations, the 1941 decree was reopened and extensively amended in 1950.[89]

Under the amended decree, which still substantially controls the activities of ASCAP, members may grant ASCAP only nonexclusive rights to license their works for public performance. Members, therefore, retain the rights individually to license public performances, along with the rights to license the use of their compositions for other purposes. ASCAP itself is forbidden to grant any license to perform one or more specified compositions in the ASCAP repertory unless both the user and the owner have requested it in writing to do so. ASCAP is required to grant to any user making written application a nonexclusive license to perform all ASCAP compositions either for a period of time or on a per program basis. ASCAP may not insist on the blanket license, and the fee for the per program license, which is to be based on the revenues for the program on which ASCAP music is played, must offer the applicant a genuine economic choice between the per program license and the more common blanket license. If ASCAP and a putative licensee are unable to agree on a fee within 60 days, the applicant may apply to the District Court for a determination of a reasonable fee, with ASCAP having the burden of proving reasonableness.[90]

The 1950 decree, as amended from time to time, continues in effect, and the blanket license continues to be the primary instrument through which ASCAP conducts its business under the decree. The courts have twice construed the decree not to require ASCAP to issue licenses for selected portions of its repertory.[91] It also remains true

87. [Court's footnote 17.] United States v. ASCAP, 1940–1943 Trade Cas. ¶ 56,104 (S.D.N.Y.1941).

88. [Court's footnote 18.] See Alden-Rochelle, Inc. v. ASCAP, 80 F.Supp. 888 (S.D.N.Y.1948); M. Witmark & Sons v. Jensen, 80 F.Supp. 843 (D.C.Minn.1948), app. dismissed sub nom. M. Witmark & Sons v. Berger Amusement Co., 177 F.2d 515 (CA 8 1949).

89. [Court's footnote 19.] United States v. ASCAP, 1950–1951 Trade Cas. ¶ 62,595 (S.D.N.Y.1950).

90. [Court's footnote 20.] BMI is in a similar situation. The original decree against BMI is reported as United States v. BMI, 1940–1943 Trade Cas. ¶ 56,096 (E.D.Wis.1941). A new consent judg-

ment was entered in 1966 following a monopolization complaint filed in 1964. United States v. BMI, 1966 Trade Cas. ¶ 71,941 (S.D.N.Y.1966). The ASCAP and BMI decrees do vary in some respects. The BMI decree does not specify that BMI may only obtain nonexclusive rights from its affiliates or that the District Court may set the fee if the parties are unable to agree. Nonetheless, the parties stipulated, and the courts below accepted, "that CBS could secure direct licenses from BMI affiliates with the same ease or difficulty, as the case may be, as from ASCAP members." 400 F.Supp., at 745.

91. [Court's footnote 21.] United States v. ASCAP (Application of Shenan-

that the decree guarantees the legal availability of direct licensing of performance rights by ASCAP members; and the District Court found, and in this respect the Court of Appeals agreed, that there are no practical impediments preventing direct dealing by the television networks if they so desire. Historically, they have not done so. . . .

Of course, a consent judgment, even one entered at the behest of the Antitrust Division, does not immunize the defendant from liability for actions, including those contemplated by the decree, that violate the rights of nonparties. But it cannot be ignored that the Federal Executive and Judiciary have carefully scrutinized ASCAP and the challenged conduct, have imposed restrictions on various of ASCAP's practices, and, by the terms of the decree, stand ready to provide further consideration, supervision and perhaps invalidation of asserted anticompetitive practices. In these circumstances, we have a unique indicator that the challenged practice may have redeeming competitive virtues and that the search for those values is not almost sure to be in vain. Thus, although CBS is not bound by the Antitrust Division's actions, the decree is a fact of economic and legal life in this industry, and the Court of Appeals should not have ignored it completely in analyzing the practice. That fact alone might not remove a naked price-fixing scheme from the ambit of the *per se* rule, but, as discussed infra, Part III, here we are uncertain whether the practice on its face has the effect, or could have been spurred by the purpose, of restraining competition among the individual composers.

. . .

III

Of course, we are no more bound than is CBS by the views of the Department of Justice, the results in the prior lower court cases, or the opinions of various experts about the merits of the blanket license. But while we must independently examine this practice, all those should caution us against too easily finding blanket licensing subject to *per se* invalidation.

A

As a preliminary matter, we are mindful that the Court of Appeals' holding would appear to be quite difficult to contain. If, as the court held, there is a *per se* antitrust violation whenever ASCAP issues a blanket license to a television network for a single fee, why would it not also be automatically illegal for ASCAP to negotiate and issue blanket licenses to individual radio or television stations or to other users who perform copyrighted music for profit? Likewise, if the present network licenses issued through ASCAP on behalf of its

doah Valley Broadcasting, Inc.), 208 F.Supp. 896 (S.D.N.Y.1962), aff'd, 331 F.2d 117 (CA 2), cert. denied, 377 U.S. 997, 84 S.Ct. 1917, 12 L.Ed.2d 1048 (1964); United States v. ASCAP (Application of National Broadcasting Co.), 1971 Trade Cas. ¶ 73,491 (S.D.N.Y.1970). See also United States v. ASCAP (Motion of Metromedia, Inc.), 341 F.2d 1003 (CA 2 1965).

members are *per se* violations, why would it not be equally illegal for the members to authorize ASCAP to issue licenses establishing various categories of uses that a network might have for copyrighted music and setting a standard fee for each described use?

Although the Court of Appeals apparently thought the blanket license could be saved in some or even many applications, it seems to us that the *per se* rule does not accommodate itself to such flexibility and that the observations of the Court of Appeals with respect to remedy tend to impeach the *per se* basis for the holding of liability.

CBS would prefer that ASCAP be authorized, indeed directed, to make all its compositions available at standard per-use rates within negotiated categories of use. But if this in itself or in conjunction with blanket licensing constitutes illegal price fixing by copyright owners, CBS urges that an injunction issue forbidding ASCAP to issue any blanket license or to negotiate any fee except on behalf of an individual member for the use of his own copyrighted work or works. Thus, we are called upon to determine that blanket licensing is unlawful across the board. We are quite sure, however, that the *per se* rule does not require any such holding.

B

In the first place, the line of commerce allegedly being restrained, the performing rights to copyrighted music, exists at all only because of the copyright laws. Those who would use copyrighted music in public performances must secure consent from the copyright owner or be liable at least for the statutory damages for each infringement and, if the conduct is willful and for the purpose of financial gain, to criminal penalties. Furthermore, nothing in the Copyright Act of 1976 indicates in the slightest that Congress intended to weaken the rights of copyright owners to control the public performance of musical compositions. Quite the contrary is true. Although the copyright law confers no rights on copyright owners to fix prices among themselves or otherwise to violate the antitrust laws, we would not expect that any market arrangements reasonably necessary to effectuate the rights that are granted would be deemed a *per se* violation of the Sherman Act. Otherwise, the commerce anticipated by the Copyright Act and protected against restraint by the Sherman Act would not exist at all or would exist only as a pale reminder of what Congress envisioned.[92]

---

92. [Court's footnote 32.] Cf. Silver v. New York Stock Exchange, 373 U.S. 341, 83 S.Ct. 1246, 10 L.Ed.2d 389 (1962).

Because a musical composition can be "consumed" by many different people at the same time and without the creator's knowledge, the "owner" has no real way to demand reimbursement for the use of his property except through the copyright laws *and* an effective way to enforce those legal rights. See Twentieth Century Music Corp. v. Aiken, 422 U.S. 151, 162, 95 S.Ct. 2040, 2047, 45 L.Ed.2d 84 (1975). It takes an organization of rather large size to monitor most or all uses and to deal with users on behalf of the composers. Moreover, it is inefficient to have too many such organizations duplicating each other's monitoring of use.

C

More generally, in characterizing this conduct under the *per se* rule,[93] our inquiry must focus on whether the effect and, here because it tends to show effect, the purpose of the practice is to threaten the proper operation of our predominantly free market economy— that is, whether the practice facially appears to be one that would always or almost always tend to restrict competition and decrease output, and in what portion of the market, or instead one designed to "increase economic efficiency and render markets more rather than less competitive."

The blanket license, as we see it, is not a "naked restraint of trade with no purpose except stifling of competition," but rather accompanies the integration of sales, monitoring, and enforcement against unauthorized copyright use. See L. Sullivan, Antitrust, § 59, at 154 (1977). As we have already indicated, ASCAP and the blanket license developed together out of the practical situation in the market place: thousands of users, thousands of copyright owners, and millions of compositions. Most users want unplanned, rapid and indemnified access to any and all of the repertory of compositions, and the owners want a reliable method of collecting for the use of their copyrights. Individual sales transactions in this industry are quite expensive, as would be individual monitoring and enforcement, especially in light of the resources of single composers. Indeed, as both the Court of Appeals and CBS recognize, the costs are prohibitive for licenses with individual radio stations, night clubs, and restaurants, and it was in that milieu that the blanket license arose.

A middleman with a blanket license was an obvious necessity if the thousands of individual negotiations, a virtual impossibility, were to be avoided. Also, individual fees for the use of individual compositions would presuppose an intricate schedule of fees and uses, as well as a difficult and expensive reporting problem for the user and policing task for the copyright owner. Historically, the market for public performance rights organized itself largely around the single-fee blanket license, which gave unlimited access to the repertory and reliable protection against infringement. When ASCAP's major and user-created competitor, BMI, came on the scene, it also turned to the blanket license.

With the advent of radio and television networks, market conditions changed, and the necessity for and advantages of a blanket license for those users may be far less obvious than is the case when the potential users are individual television or radio stations, or the thousands of other individuals and organizations performing copyrighted compositions in public. But even for television network li-

93. [Court's footnote 33.] The scrutiny occasionally required must not merely subsume the burdensome analysis required under the rule of reason, see National Society of Professional Engineers v. United States, 435 U.S. 679, 690–692, 98 S.Ct. 1335, 1364–1366, 55 L.Ed.2d 637 (1978), or else we should apply the rule of reason from the start. That is why the *per se* rule is not employed until after considerable experience with the type of challenged restraint.

censes, ASCAP reduces costs absolutely by creating a blanket license that is sold only a few, instead of thousands,[94] of times, and that obviates the need for closely monitoring the networks to see that they do not use more than they pay for.[95] ASCAP also provides the necessary resources for blanket sales and enforcement, resources unavailable to the vast majority of composers and publishing houses. Moreover, a bulk license of some type is a necessary consequence of the integration necessary to achieve these efficiencies, and a necessary consequence of an aggregate license is that its price must be established.

D

This substantial lowering of costs, which is of course potentially beneficial to both sellers and buyers, differentiates the blanket license from individual use licenses. The blanket license is composed of the individual compositions plus the aggregating service. Here, the whole is truly greater than the sum of its parts; it is, to some extent, a different product. The blanket license has certain unique characteristics: It allows the licensee immediate use of covered compositions, without the delay of prior individual negotiations[96] and great flexibility in the choice of musical material. Many consumers clearly prefer the characteristics and cost advantages of this marketable package, and even small performing rights societies that have occasionally arisen to compete with ASCAP and BMI have offered blanket licenses. Thus, to the extent the blanket license is a different product, ASCAP is not really a joint sales agency offering the individual goods of many sellers, but is a separate seller offering its blanket license, of which the individual compositions are raw material.[97] ASCAP, in short, made a market in which individual composers are inherently unable to fully effectively compete.

94. [Court's footnote 35.] The District Court found that CBS would require between 4,000 and 8,000 individual license transactions per year. 400 F.Supp., at 762.

95. [Court's footnote 36.] To operate its system for distributing the license revenues to its members, ASCAP relies primarily on the networks' records of which compositions are used.

96. [Court's footnote 37.] See Timberg, The Antitrust Aspects of Merchandising Modern Music: The ASCAP Consent Judgment of 1950, 19 Law & Contemp.Prob. 294, 297 (1954) ("The disk-jockey's itchy fingers and the bandleader's restive baton, it is said, cannot wait for contracts to be drawn with AS-CAP's individual publisher members, much less for the formal aquiescence of a characteristically unavailable composer or author"). Significantly, ASCAP deals only with nondramatic performance rights. Because of their nature, dramatic rights, such as for musicals, can be negotiated individually and well in advance of the time of performance. The same is true of various other rights, such as sheet music, recording, and synchronization, which are licensed on an individual basis.

97. [Court's footnote 40.] Moreover, because of the nature of the product—a composition can be simultaneously "consumed" by many users—composers have numerous markets and numerous incentives to produce, so the blanket license is unlikely to cause decreased output, one of the normal undesirable effects of a cartel. And since popular songs get an increased share of ASCAP's revenue distributions, composers compete even within the blanket license in terms of productivity and consumer satisfaction.

E

Finally, we have some doubt—enough to counsel against application of the *per se* rule—about the extent to which this practice threatens the "central nervous system of the economy," United States v. Socony Vacuum, 310 U.S. 150, 226 n. 59, 60 S.Ct. 811, 845, n. 59, 84 L.Ed. 1129 (1940), that is, competitive pricing as the free market's means of allocating resources. Not all arrangements among actual or potential competitors that have an impact on price are *per se* violations of the Sherman Act or even unreasonable restraints. Mergers among competitors eliminate competition, including price competition, but they are not *per se* illegal and many of them withstand attack under any existing antitrust standard. Joint ventures and other cooperative arrangements are also not usually unlawful, at least not as price-fixing schemes, where the agreement on price is necessary to market the product at all.

Here, the blanket license fee is not set by competition among individual copyright owners, and it is a fee for the use of any of the compositions covered by the license. But the blanket license cannot be wholly equated with a simple horizontal arrangement among competitors. ASCAP does set the price for its blanket license, but that license is quite different from anything any individual owner could issue. The individual composers and authors have neither agreed not to sell individually in any other market nor use the blanket license to mask price fixing in such other markets. Moreover, the substantial restraints placed on ASCAP and its members by the consent decree must not be ignored. The District Court found that there was no legal, practical, or conspiratorial impediment to CBS obtaining individual licenses; CBS, in short, had a real choice.

With this background in mind, which plainly enough indicates that over the years, and in the face of available alternatives, the blanket license has provided an acceptable mechanism for at least a large part of the market for the performing rights to copyrighted musical compositions, we cannot agree that it should automatically be declared illegal in all of its many manifestations. Rather, when attacked, it should be subjected to a more discriminating examination under the rule of reason. It may not ultimately survive that attack, but that is not the issue before us today.

. . .

The judgment of the Court of Appeals is reversed and the case is remanded to that court for further proceedings consistent with this opinion.

It is so ordered.

[Mr. Justice Stevens dissented, arguing that the record clearly established ASCAP and BMI's licensing methods violated the rule of reason. While agreeing that the blanket license was not a "species of price fixing" and *per se* unlawful, Justice Stevens argued that the practical effect of offering licensees either a blanket license or a per-program license of the entire repertory by the dominant holders of licensing authority unreasonably restrained trade. It did so because the price paid by licensees is unrelated either to the quantity or quality of the music used; licensees are required to buy more music than they can use or want; and prices "may be far higher than they would choose to spend for music in a competitive system." Characterizing the licensing systems as a "classic example of economic discrimination" and "aggregations . . . of statutory monopoly privileges," Justice Stevens concluded that the licensing practices of ASCAP and BMI are "a monopolistic restraint of trade prohibited by the Sherman Act."] [98]

NOTES AND QUERIES

(1) *Ambiguous Price Fixing—How Per Se Is the Per Se Rule?* Few direct agreements among competitors fixing prices are litigated. Most of the present-day litigation in this area is over whether the conduct in question is "price fixing" within the meaning of the *per se* prohibition or whether there is the required "contract", "combination" or "conspiracy" for Section 1 purposes. In *Catalano, Inc. v. Target Sales, Inc.,*[99] the Supreme Court held that an agreement by beer wholesalers to eliminate short term credit extended to beer retailers was *per se* unlawful price fixing. In a *per curiam* reversal of the Ninth Circuit opinion refusing to apply a *per se* test, the Court stated:

> It is virtually self evident that extending interest-free credit for a period of time is equivalent to giving a discount equal to the value of the use of the purchase price for that period of time. Thus, credit terms must be characterized as an inseparable part of the price. An agreement to terminate the practice of giving credit is thus tantamount to an agreement to eliminate discounts, and thus falls squarely within the traditional *per se* rule against price fixing. While it may be that the elimination of a practice of giving variable discounts will ultimately lead in a competitive market to corresponding decreases in the invoice price, that is surely not necessarily to be anticipated. It is more realistic to view an agreement to eliminate credit sales as extinguishing one form of competition among the sellers. In any event, when a particular concerted activity entails an obvious risk of anticompetitive impact with no apparent potentially redeeming value, the fact that a practice may turn out to be harmless in a particular set of circumstances will not prevent its being declared unlawful *per se.*

The majority of the panel of the Court of Appeals suggested, however, that a horizontal agreement to eliminate credit sales may remove a barrier to other sellers who may wish to enter the market. But in any case in which competitors are able to increase the price level or to curtail production by agreement, it could be argued that the agreement has the effect

---

98. On remand, the Second Circuit held that CBS had failed to prove that direct licensing with authors was *not* a realistic alternative to ASCAP and BMI's blanket license. The availability of the option was held to exonerate the tendency of the blanket license to unreasonably restrain trade and CBS' challenge to the blanket license was held "properly dis-

missed." CBS, Inc. v. ASCAP, 620 F.2d 930 (2d Cir. 1980); certiorari denied, 450 U.S. 970, 101 S.Ct. 1491, 67 L.Ed.2d 621, rehearing denied, 450 U.S. 1050, 101 S.Ct. 1772, 68 L.Ed.2d 247 (1981).

99. 446 U.S. 643, 100 S.Ct. 1925, 64 L.Ed.2d 580 (1980).

of making the market more attractive to potential new entrants. If that potential justifies horizontal agreements among competitors imposing one kind of voluntary restraint or another on their competitive freedom, it would seem to follow that the more successful an agreement is in raising the price level, the safer it is from antitrust attack. Nothing could be more inconsistent with our cases.

Nor can the informing function of the agreement, the increased price visibility, justify its restraint on the individual wholesaler's freedom to select his own prices and terms of sale. For, again, it is obvious that any industrywide agreement on prices will result in a more accurate understanding of the terms offered by all parties to the agreement. . . . [T]here is a plain distinction between the lawful right to publish prices and terms of sale, on the one hand, and an agreement among competitors limiting action with respect to the published prices, on the other.[1]

Considerable evidence on purpose or effect of the joint action may be required before a court will catalog the conduct under a price fixing or other *per se* label.[2] The across-the-board application of antitrust policy to most areas of the economy, many with unique characteristics or features which depart from the abstract assumptions of economic theorizing, generates a constant flow of litigation where the issue of identification of the conduct must take account of the unique characteristics of the trade of industry or the circumstances peculiar to the case before the court. While purpose or effect are generally relied upon to identify conduct like that in *Catalano* as price fixing, the court may also rely upon other factors like the characteristics of the industry, benefits or detriments of the conduct, less restrictive alternatives and the other factors normally associated with rule of reason analysis to identify the conduct as *per se* unlawful.

Distinguishing joint action which will be identified as "price fixing" for antitrust purposes was also an issue in *Arizona v. Maricopa County Medical Society*, supra p. 367. Citing *Broadcast Music*, the defendants argued their maximum price fixing fee schedules were only price fixing in a "literal sense." The Court distinguished the two cases:

The so-called "blanket license" [in *Broadcast Music*] was entirely different from the product that any one composer was able to sell by himself. Although there was little competition among individual composers for their separate compositions, the blanket license arrangement did not place any restraint on the right of any individual copyright owner to sell his own compositions separately to any buyer at any price. But a "necessary consequence" of the creation of the blanket license was that its price had to be established. We held that the delegation by the composers to ASCAP of the power to fix the price for the blanket license was not a species of the price fixing agreements categorically forbidden by the Sherman Act. The record disclosed price fixing only in a "literal sense."

This case is fundamentally different. Each of the foundations is composed of individual practitioners who compete with one another for patients. Neither the foundations nor the doctors sell insurance, and they derive no profits from the sale of health insurance policies. The members of the foundations sell medical services. Their combination in the form of the foundation does not permit them to sell any different product.

---

1. 446 U.S., at 648–650, 100 S.Ct. at 1928–29, 64 L.Ed.2d at 585–586.

2. See, Allison, Ambiguous Price Fixing and the Sherman Act: Simplistic La-

bels or Unavoidable Analysis?, 16 Houst. L.Rev. 761 (1979).

Their combination has merely permitted them to sell their services to certain customers at fixed prices and arguably to affect the prevailing market price of medical care.

The foundations are not analogous to partnerships or other joint arrangements in which persons who would otherwise be competitors pool their capital and share the risks of loss as well as the opportunities for profit. In such joint ventures, the partnership is regarded as a single firm competing with other sellers in the market. The agreement under attack is an agreement among hundreds of competing doctors concerning the price at which each will offer his own services to a substantial number of consumers. It is true that some are surgeons, some anesthesiologists, and some psychiatrists, but the doctors do not sell a package of three kinds of services. If a clinic offered complete medical coverage for a flat fee, the cooperating doctors would have the type of partnership arrangement in which a price fixing agreement among the doctors would be perfectly proper. But the fee agreements disclosed by the record in this case are among independent competing entrepreneurs. They fit squarely into the horizontal price fixing mold.[3]

Query: Do you agree that the two cases are "fundamentally different"? The dissent in *Maricopa County* argued:

In fact, however, the two agreements are similar in important respects. Each involved competitors and resulted in cooperative pricing. Each arrangement also was prompted by the need for better service to the consumers. And each arrangement apparently makes possible a new product by reaping otherwise unattainable efficiencies. The Court's effort to distinguish *Broadcast Music* thus is unconvincing.[4]

(2) *Indirect Price Fixing.* Joint tampering with other elements of competition in a particular trade or business may also come to be labeled "price fixing" where the effect of the conduct has a traceable effect on prices. For example, in *National Macaroni Manufacturer's Association v. Federal Trade Commission,*[5] manufacturers of spaghetti and macaroni agreed to use a 50-50 blend of durum and farina wheats to make their products during a period of a severe durum wheat shortage due to crop damage. Durum wheat is higher priced than farina wheats and produces a higher quality product. After the shortage ended the pact was rescinded and most manufacturers resumed making 100% durum wheat products. A subsequent recurrence of durum wheat shortages brought about a similar pact establishing a 50-50 blend a few years later and a charge by the F.T.C. that the manufacturers were engaged in price fixing. The effect of the defendant's action was to put a price lid on durum wheat prices by limiting the competition which would have taken place for a scarce commodity because of buyers bidding *up* the price. Other factors relied upon to identify the conduct as price fixing included the power of the group (70% of the U.S. spaghetti and macaroni product and sales), a reduction of demand for durum wheat in excess of the amount of shortage (there was a 5 million bushel surplus of durum wheat after 1 year of operation of the plan) and evidence of a motive by the parties to the agreement to counteract speculation by exporters of durum wheat bidding up the price in anticipation of a shortage.

3. ___ U.S., at ___, 102 S.Ct., at 2479–80, 73 L.Ed.2d, at 66–67.

4. ___ U.S., at ___, 102 S.Ct., at 2484, 73 L.Ed.2d, at 71–72. See also Medical Arts Pharmacy of Stamford, Inc. v. Blue Cross & Blue Shield of Connecticut, Inc., 675 F.2d 502 (2d Cir. 1982) (upholding maximum price agreements between Blue Cross and pharmacies for prescriptions for Blue Cross subscribers).

5. 345 F.2d 421 (7th Cir. 1965).

Other cases labeling conduct indirectly affecting prices as *per se* illegal price fixing have included agreements to refrain from posting gasoline price signs other than those on the pump,[6] agreements to refrain from distributing trading stamps,[7] and agreements to limit warranties given on products sold by members of a trade.[8] No hard and fast rules can dictate when tampering with factors other than price will be found to have such an effect on price to justify the label of "price fixing". As elsewhere in the law, the facts of antitrust cases are analyzed in light of the law, and not vice-versa.[9]

Queries: Should conspiracies by members of a trade to prevent price increases for goods or services they use in producing the product or service (a buyers' cartel) always be labeled *per se* unlawful price fixing? Assume the major law firms of the United States have become concerned about the increased cost of the legal services they provide. Part of the increase is due to rapidly increasing salaries and benefits offered new associates in the competition by law firms for law school graduates. (Top New York City beginning salaries are estimated to reach $42,000–$43,000 in 1982). Should an agreement by the major firms in New York City to "hold the line" at $40,000 be found to be a *per se* violation of the Sherman Act? What economic consequences flow from condemning this form of maximum price fixing? From permitting it? See *Maricopa County*, supra p. 367.

(3) *When Is a Fixed Price Not Price Fixing?* The *Catalano* and *BMI* cases demonstrate that it is not sufficient to know that horizontal agreements fixing prices are *per se* unlawful. While a useful standard for judging clear-cut conduct in many cases not litigated or for advising clients about a planned course of conduct, many of the cases which are litigated involve the question of whether the conduct under the circumstances is "price fixing" for Sherman Act purposes or whether it is price fixing pursuant to a "contract", "combination" or "conspiracy" under the Sherman Act.[10] Joint tampering with significant elements contributing to price levels, as in *Socony Vacuum* and *Catalano*, are labeled as *per se* unlawful price fixing. On the other hand, as subsequent cases involving trade associations will illustrate,[11] widespread sharing of industry information may or may not be considered "price fixing" depending upon an extended analysis of industry characteristics, purpose, effect, benefits, detriments and other factors normally associated with a rule of reason analysis.

The *BMI* case is also illustrative of a line of cases where the unique characteristics of the business or the unusual setting of a business relationship [12] may give a court pause before characterizing joint conduct which results in a fixed price for a specific product or service to be "price fixing" or "price fixing" that is a horizontal agreement by "competitors".

6. United States v. Gasoline Retailers' Association, Inc., 285 F.2d 688 (7th Cir. 1961).

7. Id.

8. United States v. Composition Roofers & Waterproofers Employers Association, 1979–1 Trade Cases ¶ 62,432 (E.D. N.Y.1979) (consent decree); United States v. Greater Buffalo Roofing & Sheet Metal Contractor's Association, Inc., 1977–1 Trade Cases ¶ 61,491 (W.D. N.Y.1977) (consent decree).

9. See Penne v. Greater Minneapolis Area Board of Realtors, 604 F.2d 1143 (8th Cir. 1979).

10. The issue of whether the conduct amounts to a "contract", "combination" or "conspiracy" for Sherman Act purposes is discussed infra p. 438.

11. See section D, infra p. 438.

12. See e.g., Fleer Corp. v. Topps Chewing Gum, Inc., 658 F.2d 139 (3d Cir. 1981), certiorari denied 455 U.S. 1019, 102 S.Ct. 1715, 72 L.Ed.2d 137 (1982), (joint licensing of baseball players' pictures for bubblegum baseball cards through players' union not an unreasonable restraint of trade).

For example, *Evans v. S.S. Kresge Co.*,[13] affirmed a summary judgment in favor of an antitrust defendant under the following circumstances. The Kresge department store chain leased space in or adjoining its stores to independent food retailers, and licensed them to operate under the trade name K–Mart. Taking account of the fact that there would be some overlap in stock, i.e. the landlord and tenant would be competing for some sales, Kresge required its tenant/licensees to "charge prices identical to those charged by Kresge on like items", and not to sell specified categories of goods. The Court of Appeals held that it was premature to apply a *per se* rule to a business arrangement with which the courts had had no extrinsic experience demonstrating that this was a "naked restraint [without] redeeming virtue".

Here, the relationship established by the parties demonstrates to our satisfaction that the necessary element of competition is lacking. The district court was similarly satisfied, stating as follows:

> We find that Hempfield and Kresge were not competitors. In the first place, the Kresge department stores and the Hempfield grocery supermarkets were designed to sell entirely different kinds of merchandise. That was the reason for the agreements. The fact that somewhere between 2% and 5% of merchandise sold by Hempfield was also sold by defendant's stores does not, in our view, require a finding that Hempfield and Kresge were competitors. On the contrary we believe it shows they were not. Therefore, a holding that Hempfield and Kresge competed would ignore the intensely practical business realities which underlie the antitrust laws. . . .

We grant that certain non-food items were offered for sale by both Kresge and Hempfield. On the surface, this might appear to indicate that the parties were competitors in that the proceeds of each sale went into the pocket of *either* seller Kresge *or* seller Hempfield. As we view the substance of the transaction, however, both Kresge and Hempfield presented a common front under a common name to the customer. Therefore, whether the non-food item was purchased from Kresge or from Hempfield, it was as if that item had been offered for sale by Kresge alone, but at two different locations in its K–Mart establishment. Here, the fact of non-competition is dictated by the practical business arrangement of the parties, and indeed is disclosed as their intent by uncontradicted affidavit. If for no other reason than the absence of this necessary element of "competitors", a horizontal limitation cannot be made out.

Moreover, the challenged restraint enabled Kresge to add a food component to its discount operation without causing customer confusion or threatening the low-price "K–Mart" discounting image upon which the success of K–Mart (including K–Mart Food) would depend. Therefore, far from attempting to stifle competition, the restraints had as their purpose the stimulation of business and efficiency for both the department store and the supermarket: they (the restraints) would assure that the overall operation would compete effectively in both the discount and food markets vis-a-vis other department store and food discounters. The restraints thus serve a legitimate business purpose.[14]

Queries: Were the individual copyright owners who assigned BMI or ASCAP the power to license the performance of their music and collect and

13. 544 F.2d 1184 (3d Cir. 1976), certiorari denied 433 U.S. 908, 97 S.Ct. 2973, 53 L.Ed.2d 1092 (1977).

14. 544 F.2d at 1192. See also Harold Friedman, Inc. v. Thorofare Markets, Inc., 587 F.2d 127 (3d Cir. 1978).

distribute royalties under a blanket royalty, "competitors" mutually agreeing to fix the price of products which compete with each other? Did they fix the price of individual copyrighted music or the price for a different product, *viz.*, individual copyrights sold as a package and having a different character and value as a bundle by virtue of the unique needs and characteristics of broadcasting and the legal rights granted by the copyright law? Does it make any sense to apply economic models of pricing behavior to products whose value to users or consumers bears no relation to traditional methods for establishing the cost of producing the product? Unless otherwise constrained by antitrust or other laws, are BMI and ASCAP in a position to charge what the traffic will bear? Does this suggest that the *BMI* case should have been analyzed as a § 2 monopolization case, rather than reaching for a § 1 *per se* theory of liability? Should Congress consider establishing rate regulation for situations like BMI and ASCAP? [15]

(4) *Cooperative Price Advertising by Small Retailers.* Small groceries are frequently associated in buying cooperatives and sell a common private brand of canned goods. The association may take full-page ads publicizing their price "specials", exactly as the chain stores do. When this practice, which had gone unchallenged for 30 years, was submitted to the Federal Trade Commission for an advisory opinion, the Commission majority felt bound by the per se rule against price-fixing by competitors.[16] One official in the FTC had tried to persuade the grocers' lawyer to withdraw the request for an advisory opinion, telling him: "If you ask a foolish question, you'll get a foolish answer." Commissioner Elman dissented from the Advisory Opinion stressing that the member stores were "in different neighborhoods [and] do not compete with each other in any practical sense". He also relied on an inference drawn from section 2(d) of the Robinson-Patman Act, which requires suppliers who enter into cooperative advertising arrangements with big retail chains to make proportionally equal advertising subsidies to smaller competitors; the only way in which such small sums could be effectively employed to match the big chains' advertising would be through cooperative advertising of the sort in question.

The FTC opinion evoked a storm of protest among the friends of small business in Congress. In the ensuing Congressional Committee hearing,[17] the Assistant Attorney General in charge of the Antitrust Division, who had been consulted before the FTC issued its opinion, disassociated himself from it, announcing: "It is our opinion that the action of a group of small retail business concerns in publishing cooperative advertising containing selling prices does not in and of itself constitute a violation of the Sherman Act." Do you agree?

(5) *Collective Action Against Illegal Price Discrimination. Sugar Institute, Inc. v. United States.*[18] The dominant sugar producers agreed upon a Code of Ethics providing among other things that no producer would sell sugar except at prices previously publicly announced by him. Each producer was free to announce any price without consultation with the others. It had always been the custom in the sugar trade to announce prospective price changes so that distributors could make purchases with some assurance regarding future market prices. This assurance enabled them to buy in car-

---

15. See Cirace, CBS v. ASCAP: An Economic Analysis of a Political Problem, 47 Ford.L.Rev. 277 (1978).

16. See FTC release dated April 16, 1963, reproduced in Hearings on FTC Advisory Opinion on Joint Advertisement

before the House Committee on Small Business, May 3, 1963, p. 144.

17. Id.

18. 297 U.S. 553, 56 S.Ct. 629, 80 L.Ed. 859 (1936).

load lots, a necessity in view of the narrow profit margins prevailing in the sale of sugar. Announcement of a price change by one leading producer was generally followed by all or withdrawn by the originator since sugar is a standardized commodity and no buyer would knowingly pay more for one producer's sugar than for another's. In a period of declining consumption with "excess" productive capacity, producers began to make secret concessions from their announced prices, especially to large buyers. It was to end this "unethical" practice, which in some cases at least amounted to an illegal discrimination under Section 2 of the Clayton Act, that the code provision was adopted long before the period of the NRA. The Supreme Court sustained the trial court's finding that the provision was an illegal restraint of trade in view of evidence that the effect was to help maintain higher prices than would otherwise have prevailed. Cf. *United States v. United States Gypsum Co.*, infra p. 400.

(6) *Agricultural Cooperatives.* In the United States, as elsewhere, the farmer has long enjoyed an exceptional status so far as any obligation to function as an independent, competitive producer and seller is concerned. This is attributable not only to his political power, but also to a recognition of the special circumstances of his position. Theoretically he is a capitalist, since he owns or leases his land or equipment and earns profits rather than wages. On the other hand, a very large part of the value of farm products derives from the personal labor of the small farmer, making him in this respect not unlike the wage-earner for whom unions are authorized to bargain collectively. In both cases unrestricted competition might result in personal incomes so low as to entail socially unacceptable standards of living. In both cases, also, the individual unorganized worker is seen as competing with hundreds of thousands or millions of his fellows while dealing with highly organized or monopolistic commercial enterprises, so that it seems fair and necessary to permit counter-organization. On the other hand, with the spread of large-scale corporate farming on the basis of employed labor and heavy investment in mechanical equipment, the arguments for exceptional status for the agricultural "industry" lose some of their force.[19]

Section 6 of the Clayton Act of 1914 exempted from the antitrust laws "the existence and operation of labor, agricultural, or horticultural organizations, instituted for the purposes of mutual help, and not having capital stock or conducted for profit." 15 U.S.C.A. § 17. The Capper-Volstead Act of 1922, 7 U.S.C.A. § 291, approved corporate cooperatives, authorized them to deal in products of non-members, and provided that "such associations may have marketing agencies in common." See also 15 U.S.C.A. § 521 (fishermen's marketing cooperatives). A cooperative may embrace 100% of the supply in a given market.[20] It comes into conflict with the antitrust laws only when it seeks to protect or restrict the trade of others, as by collaborating with processors to fix the price at which the latter may sell,[21] or acquires

19. See Note, Trust Busting Down on the Farm: Narrowing the Scope of Antitrust Exemptions for Agricultural Cooperatives, 61 Va.L.Rev. 341 (1975).

20. Fairdale Farms, Inc. v. Yankee Milk, Inc., 635 F.2d 1037 (2d Cir. 1980), certiorari denied 454 U.S. 818, 102 S.Ct. 98, 70 L.Ed.2d 88 (1981).

21. United States v. Borden Co., 308 U.S. 188, 60 S.Ct. 182, 84 L.Ed. 181 (1939); Otto Milk Co. v. United Dairy Farmers Association, 261 F.Supp. 381

(W.D.Pa.1966) (picketing shops handling noncoop milk.) On agricultural coops generally, see Report to the President and Attorney General of the National Commission for the Review of Antitrust Laws and Procedures, Chap. 12 (1979); Note, supra note 38; Note, Agricultural Cooperatives and the Antitrust Laws: Clayton, Capper-Volstead, and Common Sense, 44 Va.L.Rev. 63 (1958); Symposium on Agricultural Cooperatives, 27 Ind. L.J. 353 et seq. (1952), especially Part IV, p. 431, Cooperatives and the Antitrust

an independent distributor through which competitors of the coop have been marketing,[22] or carries out a program of limiting or destroying production[23] or the acquisition of monopoly power by predatory means.[24] Collaboration between two cooperatives in fixing the price at which each will sell has been held not to violate the Sherman Act, on the ground that Congress evidently intended to give cooperating farmers the power to coordinate their selling prices, and could not have intended to distinguish between farmers who organize in a single cooperative and those who prefer separate organizations.[25]

The Cooperative Marketing Act of 1926 authorized agricultural cooperatives to "acquire, exchange, interpret, and disseminate past, present, and prospective crop, market, statistical, economic, and other similar information by direct exchange . . . or through a common agent." 7 U.S.C.A. § 455. The Agricultural Marketing Agreement Act of 1937 contemplated national coordination of marketing policies through marketing agreements entered into by the Secretary of Agriculture with associations of producers, as well as with processors, handlers and others. These agreements are exempted from the antitrust laws. 7 U.S.C.A. § 608b. In relation to specified products, the Secretary may issue marketing orders imposing price control.[26] An effort to preserve some degree of competition, within this rigid system of regulation, is evident in stipulations that normally marketing orders are not to be made applicable to all areas, but should be limited to the smallest practicable regional production or marketing areas. 7 U.S.C.A. § 608c(11). But cf. *Lewes Dairy, Inc. v. Freeman*,[27] which describes the partial insulation of a regulated market area from competition of neighboring unregulated areas, by provision in the marketing order for "full regulation" of firms which sell as much as 10% of their production in the regulated area: these must pay into the "pool" a premium for *all* milk sold in liquid form, whether within or without the regulated market area.

The process of fixing prices under milk marketing orders, vesting discretion in the hands of a political appointee (the Secretary of Agriculture) without the usual procedural trappings for rate regulation by an administrative agency, has invited politicizing of the process. Well-organized political activity by cooperatives, some of them among the largest domestic corporations,[28] has been a reality for many years. A part of the Watergate scandals in-

Laws. As to the distinction between traders and farmers, for purposes of the agricultural co-op exemption, see National Broiler Marketing Association v. United States, 436 U.S. 816, 98 S.Ct. 2122, 56 L.Ed.2d 728 (1978) (exemption does not extend to co-op members which own chicks, supply feed, and assume production risks where the actual raising of the chickens is done by farmers under contract).

22. Maryland and Virginia Milk Producers Association v. United States, 362 U.S. 458, 80 S.Ct. 847, 4 L.Ed.2d 880 (1960), sustained a complaint against the Association under Section 7 of the Clayton Act and Section 2 of the Sherman Act, growing out of the acquisition of the leading dairy which persisted in buying milk from others than the Association.

23. Cf. United States v. Grower-Shipper Vegetable Association, unreported

case, N.D.Cal.Civ. 30561 (1951) (agreements among lettuce growers to disc up portion of crop) CCH Trade Reg. Serv., '48–'51 Decisions, Par. 61,339.

24. See Fairdale Farms, Inc. v. Yankee Milk, Inc., supra note 39; United States v. Dairymen, Inc., 660 F.2d 192 (6th Cir. 1981).

25. Sunkist Growers, Inc. v. Winckler & Smith Citrus Products Co., 370 U.S. 19, 82 S.Ct. 1130, 8 L.Ed.2d 305 (1962), rehearing denied 370 U.S. 965, 82 S.Ct. 1577, 8 L.Ed.2d 834; United States v. Maryland Cooperative Milk Producers, Inc., 145 F.Supp. 151 (D.C.D.C.1956).

26. See Brooks, The Pricing of Milk Under Federal Marketing Orders, 26 G.W.L.Rev. 181 (1958).

27. 401 F.2d 308 (3d Cir. 1968), certiorari denied 394 U.S. 929, 89 S.Ct. 1187, 22 L.Ed.2d 455 (1969).

28. See Note, supra n. 12.

volved the alleged exchange of campaign contributions for increases in milk prices under milk marketing orders. The effect of the process was summed up by President Nixon's advisor, John Ehrlichman. Following the meeting where the decision was made to increase price supports, Ehrlichman quipped, "Better go get a glass of milk. . . . Drink it while it's cheap."[29] It has been estimated that the increase in the price support of milk ". . . increased the cost of this essential product to the consumer by substantially more than half a billion dollars."[30]

Despite these obvious potentials for abuse, President Carter's special commission to review the antitrust laws was unable to come up with a consensus for reform of the process other than to suggest that the Secretary of Agriculture be required to consider "competitive factors" and choose the "least anticompetitive alternative" in decisions under the Agricultural Marketing Agreement Act.[31]

Queries: What recommendations would you make for changes, if any, in the process of fixing agricultural prices under marketing orders? Are there justifications for continuing exemptions from § 1 of the Sherman Act for collective action fixing or stabilizing prices by farmers and labor unions?

(7) *Queries.* Petroleum and chemical companies, among others, engage in a practice called "swapping", e.g., Petroleum Company A, having more orders in region X than it can fill at the moment, will acquire the needed supply from its competitor Petroleum Company B which has excess inventory in region X. In return B will call upon A to fill shortages that B may experience in region Y. Since prices may differ in the two regions or may change in the interval between two transactions, these competitors must negotiate about prices in their intercompany transactions. Is this unlawful under the Sherman Act? May swapping be enjoined if A and B are found to have been engaging generally in a conspiracy to restrain price competition?

May the department stores in a large city agree that the practice of pricing items at $1.98, $2.98, etc., is misleading to customers, and that they will thenceforth either sell at the even dollar figure, or else at least 15 cents below the even dollar figure?[32]

3. Sufficiency of the Evidence and Burdens of Proof

UNITED STATES v. CONTAINER CORP.

Supreme Court of the United States, 1969.
393 U.S. 333, 89 S.Ct. 510, 21 L.Ed.2d 526.

Mr. Justice Douglas delivered the opinion of the Court.

This is a civil antitrust action charging a price-fixing agreement in violation of § 1 of the Sherman Act. The District Court dismissed the complaint. The case is here on appeal.

The case as proved is unlike any other price decisions we have rendered. There was here an exchange of price information but no agreement to adhere to a price schedule as in Sugar Institute v. United States, 297 U.S. 553, 56 S.Ct. 629, 80 L.Ed. 859, or United States v. Socony-Vacuum Oil Co., 310 U.S. 150, 60 S.Ct. 811, 84 L.Ed. 1129.

29. J. Lucas, Nightmare: The Underside of the Nixon Years, 121 (1976).

30. S. Ervin, The Whole Truth: The Watergate Conspiracy 264 (1980).

31. See NCRALP Report, supra n. 14.

32. Cf. United States v. Gimbel Brothers, CCH Trade Reg. Serv., '48–'51 Decisions, Par. 61,244.

There was here an exchange of information concerning specific sales to identified customers, not a statistical report on the average cost to all members, without identifying the parties to specific transactions, as in Maple Flooring Mfrs. Assn. v. United States, 268 U.S. 563, 45 S.Ct. 578, 69 L.Ed. 1093. While there was present here, as in Cement Mfrs. Protective Assn. v. United States, 268 U.S. 588, 45 S.Ct. 586, 69 L.Ed. 1104, an exchange of prices to specific customers, there was absent the controlling circumstance, *viz.*, that cement manufacturers, to protect themselves from delivering to contractors more cement than was needed for a specific job and thus receiving a lower price, exchanged price information as a means of protecting their legal rights from fraudulent inducements to deliver more cement than needed for a specific job.

Here all that was present was a request by each defendant of its competitor for information as to the most recent price charged or quoted, whenever it needed such information and whenever it was not available from another source. Each defendant on receiving that request usually furnished the data with the expectation that it would be furnished reciprocal information when it wanted it. That concerted action is of course sufficient to establish the combination or conspiracy, the initial ingredient of a violation of § 1 of the Sherman Act.

There was of course freedom to withdraw from the agreement. But the fact remains that when a defendant requested and received price information, it was affirming its willingness to furnish such information in return.

There was to be sure an infrequency and irregularity of price exchanges between the defendants; and often the data were available from the records of the defendants or from the customers themselves. Yet the essence of the agreement was to furnish price information whenever requested.

Moreover, although the most recent price charged or quoted was sometimes fragmentary, each defendant had the manuals with which it could compute the price charged by a competitor on a specific order to a specific customer.

Further, the price quoted was the current price which a customer would need to pay in order to obtain products from the defendant furnishing the data.

The defendants account for about 90% of the shipment of corrugated containers from plants in the Southeastern United States. While containers vary as to dimensions, weight, color, and so on, they are substantially identical, no matter who produces them, when made to particular specifications. The prices paid depend on price alternatives. Suppliers when seeking new or additional business or keeping old customers, do not exceed a competitor's price. It is common for purchasers to buy from two or more suppliers concurrently. A defendant supplying a customer with containers would usually quote the same price on additional orders, unless costs had changed. Yet where a competitor was charging a particular price, a defendant would normally quote the same price or even a lower price.

The exchange of price information seemed to have the effect of keeping prices within a fairly narrow ambit. Capacity has exceeded the demand from 1955 to 1963, the period covered by the complaint, and the trend of corrugated container prices has been downward. Yet despite this excess capacity and the downward trend of prices, the industry has expanded in the Southeast from 30 manufacturers with 49 plants to 51 manufacturers with 98 plants. An abundance of raw materials and machinery makes entry into the industry easy with an investment of $50,000 to $75,000.

The result of this reciprocal exchange of prices was to stabilize prices though at a downward level. Knowledge of a competitor's price usually meant matching that price. The continuation of some price competition is not fatal to the Government's case. The limitation or reduction of price competition brings the case within the ban, for as we held in United States v. Socony-Vacuum Oil Co., supra, 310 U.S. at 224, n. 59, 60 S.Ct. at 844, interference with the setting of price by free market forces is unlawful *per se*. Price information exchanged in some markets may have no effect on a truly competitive price. But the corrugated container industry is dominated by relatively few sellers. The product is fungible and the competition for sales is price. The demand is inelastic, as buyers place orders only for immediate, short-run needs. The exchange of price data tends toward price uniformity. For a lower price does not mean a larger share of the available business but a sharing of the existing business at a lower return. Stabilizing prices as well as raising them is within the ban of § 1 of the Sherman Act. As we said in United States v. Socony-Vacuum Oil Co., supra, at 223, 60 S.Ct. at 844 "in terms of market operations stabilization is but one form of manipulation." The inferences are irresistible that the exchange of price information has had an anticompetitive effect in the industry, chilling the vigor of price competition. The agreement in the present case, though somewhat casual, is analogous to those in American Column & Lumber Co. v. United States, 257 U.S. 377, 42 S.Ct. 114, 66 L.Ed. 284, and United States v. American Linseed Oil Co., 262 U.S. 371, 43 S.Ct. 607, 67 L.Ed. 1035.[33]

Price is too critical, too sensitive a control to allow it to be used even in an informal manner to restrain competition.

Reversed.

33. [Court's footnote 3.] The *American Column* case was a sophisticated and well-supervised plan for the exchange of price information between competitors with the idea of keeping prices reasonably stable and for putting an end to cutthroat competition. There were no sanctions except financial interest and business honor. But the purpose of the plan being to increase prices, it was held to fall within the ban of the Sherman Act.

Another elaborate plan for the exchange of price data among competitors was involved in *American Linseed Oil;* and informal sanctions were used to establish "modern co-operative business methods." The arrangement was declared illegal because its "necessary tendency" was to suppress competition. 262 U.S., at 389, 43 S.Ct., at 611.

MR. JUSTICE FORTAS, concurring.

I join in the judgment and opinion of the Court. I do not understand the Court's opinion to hold that the exchange of specific information among sellers as to prices charged to individual customers,
pursuant to mutual arrangement, is a *per se* violation of the Sherman
Act.

Absent *per se* violation, proof is essential that the practice resulted in an unreasonable restraint of trade. . . . [A] practice such as
that here involved, which is adopted for the purpose of arriving at a
determination of prices to be quoted to individual customers, inevitably suggests the probability that it so materially interfered with the
operation of the price mechanism of the marketplace as to bring it
within the condemnation of this Court's decisions. Cf. Sugar Institute v. United States, 297 U.S. 553, 56 S.Ct. 629, 80 L.Ed. 859 (1936);
American Column & Lumber Co. v. United States, 257 U.S. 377, 42
S.Ct. 114, 66 L.Ed. 284 (1921).

Theoretical probability, however, is not enough unless we are to
regard mere exchange of current price information as so akin to
price-fixing by combination or conspiracy as to deserve the *per se*
classification. I am not prepared to do this, nor is it necessary here.
In this case, the probability that the exchange of specific price information led to an unlawful effect upon prices is adequately buttressed
by evidence in the record. This evidence, although not overwhelming, is sufficient in the special circumstances of this case to show an
actual effect on pricing and to compel us to hold that the court below
erred in dismissing the Government's complaint.

. . .

[MR. JUSTICE MARSHALL, in a dissenting opinion joined by JUS-
TICES HARLAN and STEWART, viewed exchange of market information
under competitive conditions as "not an evil", and found the record
insufficient to show more than a *possibility* that there had been an
anticompetitive effect in this case. Excess capacity in the industry
and ease of entry minimized any danger that price uniformity or stabilization would occur in an industry as unconcentrated as this one.
"I do not believe that the desire of a few industry witnesses to use
the information to minimize price cuts supports the conclusion that
such an agreement [to stabilize prices] was implicit. On the contrary,
the evidence establishes that the information was used by defendants
as each pleased and was actually employed for the purpose of engaging in active price competition", with much shifting of customers
from one supplier to another, and a downward trend of prices.

In the absence of evidence tending to show a "deliberate attempt
to stabilize price" or proof that the exchange of price information had
the "necessary effect of restraining price competition", the dissent
concluded that the "Government has simply not proved its case."]

UNITED STATES v. UNITED STATES GYPSUM CO.

Supreme Court of the United States, 1978.
438 U.S. 422, 98 S.Ct. 2864, 57 L.Ed.2d 854.

MR. CHIEF JUSTICE BURGER delivered the opinion of the Court.

This case presents the following questions: (a) whether intent is an element of a criminal antitrust offense; (b) whether an exchange of price information for purposes of compliance with the Robinson-Patman Act is exempt from Sherman Act scrutiny; (c) the adequacy of jury instructions on membership in and withdrawal from the alleged conspiracy . . . .

I

Gypsum board, a laminated type of wall board composed of paper, vinyl or other specially treated coverings over a gypsum core, has in the last 30 years substantially replaced wet plaster as the primary component of interior walls and ceilings in residential and commercial construction. The product is essentially fungible; differences in price, credit terms and delivery services largely dictate the purchasers' choice between competing suppliers. Overall demand, however, is governed by the level of construction activity and is only marginally affected by price fluctuations.

The gypsum board industry is highly concentrated with the number of producers ranging from nine to 15 in the period 1960–1973. The eight largest companies accounted for some 94% of the national sales with the seven "single plant producers" accounting for the remaining 6%. Most of the major producers and a large number of the single plant producers are members of the Gypsum Association which since 1930 has served as a trade association of gypsum board manufacturers.

A

Beginning in 1966, the Justice Department, as well as the Federal Trade Commission, became involved in investigations into possible antitrust violations in the gypsum board industry. . . . In late 1973, an indictment was filed in the United States District Court for the Western District of Pennsylvania charging six major manufacturers and various of their corporate officials with violations of § 1 of the Sherman Act.

The indictment charged that the defendants had engaged in a combination and conspiracy "[b]eginning sometime prior to 1960 and continuing thereafter at least until sometime in 1973," in restraint of interstate trade and commerce in the manufacture and sale of gypsum board. The alleged combination and conspiracy consisted of:

"A continuing agreement understanding and concert of action among the defendants and co-conspirators to (a) raise, fix, maintain and stabilize the prices of gypsum board; (b) fix, maintain and stabilize the terms and conditions of sale thereof; and (c) adopt and maintain uniform methods of packaging and handling such gypsum board."

The indictment proceeded to specify some 13 types of actions taken by conspirators "in formulating and effectuating" the combination and conspiracy, the most relevant of which, for our purposes, is specification (h) which alleged that the conspirators:

"telephoned or otherwise contacted one another to exchange and discuss current and future published or market prices and published or standard terms and conditions of sale and to ascertain alleged deviations therefrom.

The bill of particulars provided additional details about the continuing nature of the alleged exchanges of competitive information and the role played by such exchanges in policing adherence to the various other illegal agreements charged.

B

. . .

The focus of the Government's price fixing case at trial was inter-seller price verification—that is, the practice allegedly followed by the gypsum board manufacturers of telephoning a competing producer to determine the price currently being offered on gypsum board to a specific customer. The Government contended that these price exchanges were part of an agreement among the defendants, had the effect of stabilizing prices and policing agreed upon price increases, and were undertaken on a frequent basis until sometime in 1973. Defendants disputed both the scope and duration of the verification activities, and further maintained that those exchanges of price information which did occur were for the purposes of complying with the Robinson-Patman Act and preventing customer fraud. These purposes, in defendants' view, brought the disputed communications among competitors within a "controlling circumstance" exception to Sherman Act liability—at the extreme, precluding, as a matter of law, consideration of verification by the jury in determining defendants' guilt on the price fixing charge, and at the minimum, making the defendants' purposes in engaging in such communications a threshold factual question.

The instructions on the verification issue given by the trial judge provided that if the exchanges of price information were deemed by the jury to have been undertaken "in a good faith effort to comply with the Robinson-Patman Act," verification standing alone would not be sufficient to establish an illegal price fixing agreement. The paragraphs immediately following, however, provided that the purpose was essentially irrelevant if the jury found that the effect of verification was to raise, fix, maintain or stabilize prices. The instructions on verification closed with the observation that

"[t]he law presumes that a person intends the necessary and natural consequences of his acts. Therefore, if the effect of the ex-

changes of pricing information was to raise, fix, maintain and stabilize prices, then the parties to them are presumed, as a matter of
law, to have intended that result."

The aspects of the charge dealing with the Government's burden
in linking a particular defendant to the conspiracy, and the kinds of
evidence the jury could properly consider in determining if one or
more of the alleged conspirators had withdrawn from or abandoned
the conspiracy were also a subject of some dispute between the judge
and defense counsel. On the former, the disagreement was essentially over the proper specificity of the charge. . . . The trial judge
. . . emphasized at several points in the charge the jury's obligation to consider the evidence regarding the involvement of each defendant individually, and to find, as a precondition to liability, that
each defendant was a knowing participant in the alleged conspiracy.

. . .

C

[The description of the week long deliberation of the jury and the
trial court's exchanges with the jury foreman over an apparent deadlock of the jury are deleted. The District Court denied mistrial motions by the defense, and the jury returned guilty verdicts against the
defendants on the seventh day of its deliberations.]

D

The Court of Appeals for the Third Circuit reversed the convictions. The panel was unanimous in its rejection of the claim of pre-
indictment delay, but divided over the proper disposition of the remaining issues.

Two judges agreed that the trial judge erred in instructing the
jury that an effect on prices resulting from an agreement to exchange price information made out a Sherman Act violation regardless of whether respondents' sole purpose in engaging in such exchanges was to establish a defense to price discrimination charges.
Instead, they regarded such a purpose, if certain conditions were met,
as constituting a "controlling circumstance" which under *United
States v. Container Corp. of America*, 393 U.S. 333, 89 S.Ct. 510, 21
L.Ed.2d 526 (1969), would excuse what might otherwise constitute an
antitrust violation. . . .

One judge, in dissent, would have sustained the convictions. He
regarded the charge on verification to be consistent with *Container
Corp.*, and rejected the notion that the Robinson-Patman Act required
the exchange of price information even in the limited circumstances
identified by the majority. . . .

II

We turn first to consider the jury instructions regarding the elements of the price-fixing offense charged in the indictment. Al-

though the trial judge's instructions on the price-fixing issue are not without ambiguity, it seems reasonably clear that he regarded an effect on prices as the crucial element of the charged offense. The jury was instructed that if it found interseller verification had the effect of raising, fixing, maintaining or stabilizing the price of gypsum board, then such verification could be considered as evidence of an agreement to so affect prices. They were further charged, and it is this point which gives rise to our present concern, that "if the effect of the exchanges of pricing information was to raise, fix, maintain, and stabilize prices, then the parties to them are presumed, *as a matter of law,* to have intended that result." (Emphasis added.)

The Government characterizes this charge as entirely consistent with "this Court's long-standing rule that an agreement among sellers to exchange information on current offering prices violates Section 1 of the Sherman Act if it has either the purpose or the effect of stabilizing prices," and relies primarily on our decision in *United States v. Container Corp. of America,* 393 U.S. 333, 89 S.Ct. 510, 21 L.Ed.2d 526, a civil case, to support its position. In this view, the trial court's instructions would not be erroneous, even if interpreted, as they were by the Court of Appeals, to *direct* the jury to convict if it found that verification had an effect on prices, regardless of the purpose of the respondents. The Court of Appeals rejected the Government's "effects alone" test, holding instead that in certain limited circumstances, a purpose of complying with the Robinson-Patman Act would constitute a controlling circumstance excusing Sherman Act liability, and hence an instruction allowing the jury to ignore purpose could not be sustained.

We agree with the Court of Appeals that an effect on prices, without more, will not support a criminal conviction under the Sherman Act, but we do not base that conclusion on the existence of any conflict between the requirements of the Robinson-Patman and the Sherman Acts. Rather, we hold that a defendant's state of mind or intent is an element of a criminal antitrust offense which must be established by evidence and inferences drawn therefrom and cannot be taken from the trier of fact through reliance on a legal presumption of wrongful intent from proof of an effect on prices. Since the challenged instruction, as we read it, had this prohibited effect, it is disapproved. We are unwilling to construe the Sherman Act as mandating a regime of strict liability criminal offenses.[34]

---

34. [This and the following 8 footnotes are from the Court's opinion.] Our analysis focuses solely on the elements of a criminal offense under the antitrust laws, and leaves unchanged the general rule that a civil violation can be established by proof of either an unlawful purpose or an anticompetitive effect. See *United States v. Container Corp.,* 393 U.S., at 337; id., at 341, 89 S.Ct. at 512; id., at 514 (Marshall, J., dissenting). Of course, consideration of intent may play an important role in divining the actual nature and effect of the alleged anticompetitive conduct. See *Chicago Bd. of Trade v. United States,* 246 U.S. 231, 238, 38 S.Ct. 242, 243, 62 L.Ed. 683 (1918).

A

We start with the familiar proposition that "[t]he existence of a *mens rea* is the rule of, rather than the exception to, the principles of Anglo-American criminal jurisprudence." . . . Although Blackstone's requisite "vicious will" has been replaced by more sophisticated and less colorful characterizations of the mental state required to support criminality, see ALI Model Penal Code § 2.02 (Prop Official Draft 1962), intent generally remains an indispensable element of a criminal offense. This is as true in a sophisticated criminal antitrust case as in one involving any other criminal offense.

. . .

While strict liability offenses are not unknown to the criminal law and do not invariably offend constitutional requirements, the limited circumstances in which Congress has created and this Court has recognized such offenses attest to their generally disfavored status. . . . In the context of the Sherman Act, this generally inhospitable attitude to non-*mens rea* offenses is reinforced by an array of considerations arguing against treating antitrust violations as strict liability crimes.

B

The Sherman Act, unlike most traditional criminal statutes, does not, in clear and categorical terms, precisely identify the conduct which it proscribes. Both civil remedies and criminal sanctions are authorized with regard to the same generalized definitions of the conduct proscribed—restraints of trade or commerce and illegal monopolization—without reference to or mention of intent or state of mind. Nor has judicial elaboration of the Act always yielded the clear and definitive rules of conduct which the statute omits; instead open-ended and fact-specific standards like the "rule of reason" have been applied to broad classes of conduct falling within the purview of the Act's general provisions. Simply put, the Act has not been interpreted as if it were primarily a criminal statute; it has been construed to have a "generality and adaptability comparable to that found desirable in constitutional provisions."

. . . The 1955 Report of the Attorney General's National Committee to Study the Antitrust Laws concluded that the criminal provisions of the Act should be reserved for those circumstances where the law was relatively clear and the conduct egregious. . . . The Antitrust Division of the Justice Department took a similar though slightly more moderate position in its enforcement guidelines issued contemporaneously with the 1955 Report of the Attorney General's Committee:

> "In general, the following types of offenses are prosecuted criminally: (1) price fixing; (2) other violations of the Sherman Act where there is proof of a specific intent to restrain trade or to monopolize; (3) a less easily definable category of cases which

might generally be described as involving proof of use of predatory practices (boycotts for example) to accomplish the objective of the combination or conspiracy; (4) the fact that a defendant has previously been convicted of or adjudged to have been, violating the antitrust laws may warrant indictment for a second offense . . . . The Division feels free to seek an indictment in any case where a prospective defendant has knowledge that practices similar to those in which he is engaging have been held to be in violation of the Sherman Act in a prior suit against other persons." [35]

While not dispositive of the question now before us, the recommendations of the Attorney General's Committee and the guidelines promulgated by the Justice Department highlight the same basic concerns which are manifested in our general requirement of *mens rea* in criminal statutes and suggest that these concerns are at least equally salient in the antitrust context.

Close attention to the type of conduct regulated by the Sherman Act buttresses this conclusion. With certain exceptions for conduct regarded as *per se* illegal because of its unquestionably anticompetitive effects, see, e.g., *United States v. Socony-Vacuum Oil Co.*, 310 U.S. 150, 60 S.Ct. 811, 84 L.Ed. 1129, the behavior proscribed by the Act is often difficult to distinguish from the gray zone of socially acceptable and economically justifiable business conduct. Indeed, the type of conduct charged in the indictment in this case—the exchange of price information among competitors—is illustrative in this regard.[36] The imposition of criminal liability on a corporate official, or for that matter on a corporation directly, for engaging in such conduct which only after the fact is determined to violate the statute because of anti-competitive effects, without inquiring into the intent with which it was undertaken, holds out the distinct possibility of overdeterrence; salutary and procompetitive conduct lying close to the borderline of impermissible conduct might be shunned by businessmen who chose to be excessively cautious in the face of uncer-

35. In 1967, the Antitrust Division refined its guidelines to emphasize that criminal prosecutions should only be brought against willful violations of the law. See The President's Commission on Law Enforcement and Administration of Justice, Task Force Report: Crime and Its Impact—An Assessment 110 (1967).

36. The exchange of price data and other information among competitors does not invariably have anti-competitive effects; indeed such practices can in certain circumstances increase economic efficiency and render markets more rather than less competitive. For this reason, we have held that such exchanges of information do not constitute a *per se* violation of the Sherman Act. See, e.g., United States v. Citizens & Southern National Bank, 422 U.S. 86, 113, 95 S.Ct. 2099, 2115; 45 L.Ed.2d 41; United States v. Container Corp., 393 U.S. 333, 338, 89 S.Ct. 510, 513, 21 L.Ed.2d 526 (Fortas, J., concurring). A number of factors including most prominently the structure of the industry involved and the nature of the information exchanged are generally considered in divining the pro or anticompetitive effects of this type of interseller communication. See United States v. Container Corp., supra. See generally Sullivan, Law of Antitrust, 265–274 (1977). Exchanges of current price information, of course, have the greatest potential for generating anticompetitive effects and although not *per se* unlawful have consistently been held to violate the Sherman Act. See American Column & Lumber Co. v. United States, 257 U.S. 377, 42 S.Ct. 114, 66 L.Ed. 284 (1921); United States v. American Linseed Oil Co., 262 U.S. 371, 43 S.Ct. 607, 67 L.Ed. 1035 (1923); United States v. Container Corp., supra.

tainty regarding possible exposure to criminal punishment for even a good-faith error of judgment.[37] Further, the use of criminal sanctions in such circumstances would be difficult to square with the generally accepted functions of the criminal law. The criminal sanctions would be used not to punish conscious and calculated wrongdoing at odds with statutory proscriptions, but instead simply to *regulate* business practices regardless of the intent with which they were undertaken. While in certain cases we have imputed a regulatory purpose to Congress in choosing to employ criminal sanctions, the availability of a range of nonpenal alternatives to the criminal sanctions of the Sherman Act negates the imputation of any such purpose to Congress in the instant context.[38]

For these reasons, we conclude that the criminal offenses defined by the Sherman Act should be construed as including intent as an element.[39]

37. The possibility that those subjected to strict liability will take extraordinary care in their dealings is frequently regarded as one advantage of a rule of strict liability. See Hall, General Principles of Criminal Law 344 (1960); LaFave & Scott, Criminal Law 222–223 (1972). However, where the conduct proscribed is difficult to distinguish from conduct permitted and indeed encouraged, as in the antitrust context, the excessive caution spawned by a regime of strict liability will not necessarily redound to the public's benefit. The antitrust laws differ in this regard from, for example, laws designed to insure that adulterated food will not be sold to consumers. In the latter situation, excessive caution on the part of producers is entirely consistent with the legislative purpose. See United States v. Park, 421 U.S. 658, 671–672, 95 S.Ct. 1903, 1911, 44 L.Ed.2d 489 (1975).

38. Congress has recently increased the criminal penalties for violation of the Sherman Act. Individual violations are now treated as felonies punishable by a fine not to exceed $100,000, or by imprisonment for up to three years, or both. Corporate violators are subject to a $1 million fine. 15 U.S.C. § 1. The severity of these sanctions provides further support for our conclusion that the Sherman Act should not be construed as creating strict liability crimes. Cf. Morissette v. United States, 342 U.S. 246, 256, 72 S.Ct. 240, 246, 96 L.Ed. 288, Sayre, Public Welfare Offenses, 33 Colum.L.Rev. 55, 72 (1933) (strict liability generally inappropriate when offense punishable by im-

prisonment.) Respondents here were not prosecuted under the new penalty provisions since they were indicted prior to the December 21, 1974, effective date for the increased sanctions.

39. An accommodation of the civil and criminal provisions of the Act similar to that which we approve here was suggested by Senator Sherman in response to Senator George's argument during floor debate that the Act was primarily a penal statute to be construed narrowly in accord with traditional maxims:

"The first section, being a remedial statute, would be construed liberally with a view to promote its object. It defines a civil remedy and the courts will construe it liberally . . . . In providing a remedy the intention of the combination is immaterial.

· · ·

"The third section is a criminal statute which would be construed strictly and is difficult to be enforced. In the present state of the law it is impossible to describe in precise language, the nature and limits of the offense in terms specific enough for an indictment." 21 Cong.Rec. 2456 (1890).

Although the bill being debated by Senators George and Sherman differed in form from the Act as ultimately passed, the colloquy between them indicates that Congress was fully aware of the traditional distinctions between the elements of civil and criminal offenses and apparently did not intend to do away with them in the Act.

C

Having concluded that intent is a necessary element of a criminal antitrust violation, the task remaining is to treat the practical aspects of this requirement.[40] . . . [W]e conclude that action undertaken with knowledge of its probable consequences and having the requisite anticompetitive effects can be a sufficient predicate for a finding of criminal liability under the antitrust laws.[41]

. . .

Nothing in our analysis of the Sherman Act persuades us that this general understanding of intent should not be applied to criminal antitrust violations such as charged here. The business behavior which is likely to give rise to criminal antitrust charges is conscious behavior normally undertaken only after a full consideration of the desired results and a weighing of the costs, benefits and risks. A requirement of proof not only of this knowledge of likely effects, but also of a conscious desire to bring them to fruition or to violate the law would seem, particularly in such a context, both unnecessarily cumulative and unduly burdensome. Where carefully planned and calculated conduct is being scrutinized in the context of a criminal prosecution, the perpetrator's knowledge of the anticipated consequences is a sufficient predicate for a finding of criminal intent.

D

When viewed in terms of this standard, the jury instructions on the price-fixing charge cannot be sustained. "A conclusive presumption [of intent], which testimony could not overthrow would effectively eliminate intent as an ingredient of the offense." *Morissette*, supra, 342 U.S., at 275, 72 S.Ct., at 256. The challenged jury instruction, as we read it, had precisely this effect; the jury was told that the requisite intent followed, *as a matter of law*, from a finding that the exchange of price information had an impact on prices. Although an effect on prices may well support an inference that the defendant had knowledge of the probability of such a consequence at the time he acted, the jury must remain free to consider additional evidence before accepting or rejecting the inference. Therefore, although it would be correct to instruct the jury that it may infer intent from an effect on prices, ultimately the decision on the issue of intent

---

40. In a conspiracy, two different types of intent are generally required— the basic intent to agree, which is necessary to establish the existence of the conspiracy, and the more traditional intent to effectuate the object of the conspiracy. See LaFave and Scott, Criminal Law 464–465 (1972). Our discussion here focuses only on the second type of intent.

41. In so holding, we do not mean to suggest that conduct undertaken with the purpose of producing anticompetitive effects would not also support criminal liability, even if such effects did not come to pass. Cf. United States v. Griffith, 334 U.S. 100, 105, 68 S.Ct. 941, 944, 92 L.Ed. 1236 (1948). We hold only that this elevated standard of intent need not be established in cases where anticompetitive effects have been demonstrated; instead, proof that the defendant's conduct was undertaken with knowledge of its probable consequences will satisfy the Government's burden.

must be left to the trier of fact alone. The instruction given invaded this factfinding function.[42]

. . .

Accordingly, the judgment of the Court of Appeals is affirmed.

MR. JUSTICE STEWART joins all but Part IV of this opinion.*

MR. JUSTICE BLACKMUN took no part in the consideration or decision of this case.

[Omitted are the separate opinions of Justices Rehnquist and Stevens, concurring in part and dissenting in part, and Justice Powell, concurring in part.]

NOTES AND QUERIES

1. *The Difference Between Defining What Is Per Se Unlawful and Proving It.* The sufficiency of the evidence, both to prove the existence of an agreement and the presence of the claimed category of *per se* illegality, is an elusive and oft-confused issue. While the *Gypsum* opinion makes clear that the standard of proof where criminal penalties are sought differs from that in government equity actions like *Container*, the standards for determining when there is sufficient evidence to find a conspiratorial purpose and/or effect to fix prices are far from clear in either criminal or civil cases.[43] How much and what kind of evidence of "effect" is sufficient "effect" in civil cases? What kind of evidence will be sufficient to prove or infer purpose in criminal cases? When will an effect on prices be sufficiently apparent to infer "purpose" in the sense that the joint action was undertaken "with knowledge of its probable consequences" in a criminal case?

42. Respondents contend that "prior to the trial of this case, no court had ever held that a mere exchange of information which had a stabilizing effect on prices violated the Sherman Act, regardless of the purposes of the exchange." Respondents' Joint Brief, at 50. Retroactive application of "this judicially expanded definition of the crime" would, the argument continues, contravene the "principles of fair notice in the Due Process Clause." Ibid. While we have rejected on other grounds the "effects only" test in the context of criminal proceedings, we do not agree with respondents that the prior case law dealing with the exchange of price information required proof of a purpose to restrain competition in order to make out a Sherman Act violation.

Certainly our decision in United States v. Container Corp., 393 U.S. 333, 89 S.Ct. 510, 21 L.Ed.2d 526 (1969), is fairly read as indicating that proof of an anticompetitive effect is a sufficient predicate for liability. In that case, liability followed from proof that "the exchange of price information had an anti-competitive effect in the industry," id., at 337, 89 S.Ct., at 512, and no suggestion was made that proof of a purpose to restrain trade or

competition was also required. Thus, at least in the post-Container period, which comprises almost the entire time period at issue here, respondent's claimed lack of notice cannot be credited.

. . .

* Part IV of the opinion, discussing the validity of a defense of "controlling circumstance," *viz.*, that interseller price verification was done for the purpose of complying with the Robinson Patman Act, is considered infra p. 920.

43. See Garvey, Sherman Act and The Vicious Will: Developing Standards For Criminal Intent In Sherman Act Prosecutions, 29 Cath.U.L.Rev. 389 (1980); Symposium, Corporate Intent—Prosecutor's and Defense's Perceptions of the Practical Effects of the *Gypsum* Decision Upon the Investigation, Prosecution and Defense of Sherman Act Criminal Cases, 49 Antitrust L.J. 1099 (1980); Comment, Antitrust Liability For An Exchange of Price Information—What Happened to *Container Corporation?*, 63 Va.L.Rev. 639 (1977); Note, United States v. United States Gypsum Co., Putting A Lid on Container, 45 Brooklyn L.Rev. 417 (1979).

What standard of proof should be required in treble damage actions before a court may conclude that a violation has taken place? What standard of proof will be applied in administrative proceedings charging unlawful price fixing before the F.T.C.?

These and other issues are frequently litigated as questions of whether there is a contract, combination, or conspiracy for Sherman Act purposes, a topic considered infra section 438. At this juncture, assuming there is sufficient evidence of an agreement and a consensus that the Sherman Act prohibits agreements fixing prices in purpose or effect, the *Container* and *Gypsum* cases may profitably be viewed as cases raising an evidentiary question of the sufficiency of the evidence necessary to sustain a judgment that the defendants have in fact fixed prices, rather than simply cases of identifying the conduct as price fixing.

The distinction between substantive antitrust rules and the evidentiary standards for proving a rule is violated, as well as the resulting distinctions between varying standards of proof depending on the remedies sought, are subtle and significant ones for many modern price fixing cases. The ban on horizontal price fixing is relatively well known and few cases are litigated when the evidence of conspiracy and a purpose to fix prices is conclusive and easily shown. Instead, when cases are litigated rather than settled by consent decrees or *nolo* pleas, enforcement agencies and the courts find themselves confronted with joint activity ambiguous in its purpose or effect.[44] Whether it be the result of firms seeking to minimize price competition by skating as close to the line of openly agreeing to fix prices as possible without appearing to do so or mistakes in judgments by enforcement officials and private plaintiffs about the anti-competitive nature of pro-competitive behavior effecting prices, the typical litigated price fixing case is seldom open and shut. Considerable evidence of purpose, effect and the characteristics of the industry may be required to prove the conduct is or is not unlawful. It is at this point that the standard of proof required to prove a violation in court can be critical in drawing the line between legality and illegality.

(2) *The Standard of Proof in Post-Gypsum Criminal Cases.* In *United States v. Gillen*,[45] producers of anthracite coal were indicted for price fixing. The evidence indicated that the defendants held regular meetings at which each firm's prices were set, future price moves were planned, and price circulars listing each firm's prices were prepared. The trial court rejected an argument that there must be proof of a specific intent to fix prices, holding that "by purposely engaging in a conspiracy which necessarily and directly produces the result which the statute is designed to prevent, they are, in legal contemplation chargeable with intending that result."[46] On appeal, the Third Circuit affirmed, holding:

> Thus in price-fixing conspiracies, where the conduct is illegal per se, no inquiry has to be made on the issue of intent beyond proof that one joined or formed the conspiracy. The conduct at issue in *Gypsum* concededly was of such a nature as to warrant a further inquiry into intent. The Supreme Court's concern with those who unwittingly violate antitrust laws has no place here. Here, defendants have fixed prices, "probably the clearest violation of the antitrust laws and the one most obnox-

44. See Allison, Ambiguous Price Fixing And The Sherman Act: Simplistic Labels or Unavoidable Analysis, 16 Houst. L.Rev. 761 (1979).

45. 599 F.2d 541 (3d Cir. 1979), certiorari denied 444 U.S. 866, 100 S.Ct. 137, 62 L.Ed.2d 89 (1980).

46. 599 F.2d at 544.

ious to the underlying policy of free competition." The act of agreeing to fix prices is in itself illegal; the criminal act is the agreement.

Moreover, even if read to apply here, *Gypsum* does not require a reversal because the intent requirements will always be met in a case involving a price-fixing conspiracy. If a defendant intends to fix prices, he necessarily intends to restrain trade. In *Gypsum*, the element lacking was a finding that the defendants knew that the exchanges of price information would have the probable effect of fixing or establishing prices. In defining the standard, the Court held that knowledge that the actions will result in restraining trade is enough. Here, where their actions were nothing less than price-fixing, the violators cannot be heard to argue that they did not know that their meetings and discussions of prices would result in an unreasonable restraint of trade.[47]

The court held the evidence of the existence of a price fixing conspiracy, the defendant's knowledge of the conspiracy, and the defendant's participation in the conspiracy sufficient to uphold a guilty verdict.[48]

Query: Is the court's standard consistent with *Gypsum?* Draft a model jury instruction for use in criminal price fixing cases on the element of intent.

4. DEFENSES? JUSTIFICATIONS? EXCUSES?

While it may appear anomalous to construct seemingly inflexible rules of *per se* illegality on the one hand and then permit defenses to the rules in particular cases, it is clear that the courts have been doing just that in fact, if not expressly. Every rule of *per se* illegality has either been ignored or modified in a particular case, usually by some device of judicial legerdemain finding, for example, the conduct involved not a conspiracy, or that the agreement is not one to fix prices, that the arrangement is a "joint venture" and not a "conspiracy" to fix prices, or that even if the conduct looks like price fixing, the circumstances of the particular case or unique characteristics of the trade involved require an extended evaluation along the lines of the factors entailed in a rule of reason analysis.[49] One may rightly question just how much of a substantive "rule" of law the antitrust rules of *per se* illegality may be, when they are ignored or modified in particular cases.

On the other hand, lawyers soon learn that reality does not always conform to the assumptions and predictions of abstract rules and models of what reality ought to be and do. Unusual circumstances may require modification of the meaning and application of a specific rule in a particular case if the policies of the law are to be sensibly achieved in light of the facts and circumstances unique to a particular case. In *Broadcast Music, Inc. v. Columbia Broadcasting System,*

---

47. Id. at 545. The case is noted in 32 Hast.L.J. 499 (1980); 53 Temp.L.Q. 432 (1980); 82 W.Va.L.Rev. 371 (1979).

48. See also United States v. Cargo Service Stations, Inc., 657 F.2d 676 (5th Cir. 1981), certiorari denied 455 U.S. 1017, 102 S.Ct. 1712, 72 L.Ed.2d 135 (1982).

49. See Flynn, Rethinking Sherman Act Section 1 Analysis, Three Proposals for Reducing the Chaos, 49 Antitrust L.J. 1593 (1980); Van Cise, The Future of Per Se In Antitrust Law, 50 Va.L.Rev. 1165 (1964).

Inc.,[50] for example, the unusual plight of individual copyright holders in enforcing their legal rights justified some form of joint or collective action and the extensive government regulation of activities of ASCAP and BMI through prior antitrust consent decrees was a fact which could not be ignored in the calculus. Judging the real world by models of a world where no one lives is not only unrealistic and artificial but foolish and counterproductive. Sooner or later reality must be accounted for and given its due.

This is particularly true in antitrust law, where the broad generalities of the Sherman Act are applied to a complex economy, in a bewildering array of individual circumstances, frequently in the presence of some type of other governmental regulation or action, and in light of practical business factors unique to particular industries or trades. Several judicially constructed defenses, justifications and excuses for conduct otherwise literally violating specific antitrust rules have, of necessity, been created by the courts.[51]

Here we focus on the elusive question of whether there are any other excuses or justifications [52] ever permitted for horizontal joint activity identified as *per se* unlawful conduct. Although not expressly treated by the courts as an excuse or justification once *per se* conduct is found, it is apparent that the extended analysis occasioned by the unique circumstances or special characteristics of the business involved may be an implicit judicial recognition that there ought to be some room for consideration of justification or excuse for a restraint in a limited number of cases. Indeed, the *Chicago Board of Trade* and *Appalachian Coals* cases should be re-examined with the perspective in mind that invocation of a rule of reason analysis in a case where prices are fixed by an agreement may in fact be recognition of an excuse or justification for the conduct in some limited and unique circumstances. Reconsideration should also be given the *Broadcast Music* case [53] as one where the Court, despite its twisting and turning on the question of whether the conduct of blanket licensing should be categorized as price fixing, was implicitly recognizing that the conduct was indeed horizontal price fixing but was price fixing that was justified in light of the realities of individual copyright holders protecting their rights, the practical realities of the needs of broadcasters for ready access to a broad range of copyrighted music, the availability of a less restrictive alternative to broadcasters of individual licensing, and the existence of a consent decree regulating the activities of the licensing agencies. In such circumstances, the *per se*/rule

50. Supra p. 380.

51. See Chapter 7, infra, for an exploration of defenses related to conduct required by local, state, federal, or foreign government economic regulation.

52. In the field of torts, the concepts of excuse or justification have been abandoned in favor of the concept "privilege". Prosser defines privilege as signifying "that the defendant has acted to further an interest of such social importance that it is entitled to protection, even at the expense of damage to the plaintiff. He is allowed freedom of action because his own interests or those of the public require it, and social policy will best be served by permitting it. The boundaries of the privilege are marked out by current ideas of what will most effectively promote the general welfare." W. Prosser, Law of Torts, p. 98 (4th ed. 1971).

53. Supra p. 380.

of reason distinction appears not to be a distinction of separate categories of substantive legal rules, but evidentiary standards establishing varying levels of presumptions of legality and illegality from the nearly conclusive to the totally neutral.[54]

Elsewhere, even in some cases of conclusive presumptions (*viz.*, areas of *per se* illegality) the presumption is not absolute and may be subject to limited excuses and justifications in truly unique circumstances. For example, the Court's analysis of the *Gypsum* defendants' purported justification for exchanging price information, omitted from the excerpts of the opinion dealing with burdens of proof reprinted in part 2 of this subsection,[55] left open the possibility that in some cases there may be a "controlling circumstance" exception to liability for conduct which would otherwise constitute a *per se* section 1 violation.[56] In *Gypsum*, the defendants claimed that they exchanged price information with competitors for the sole purpose of taking advantage of the § 2(b) meeting competition defense to a charge of unlawful price discrimination under the Robinson-Patman Act.[57] The defendants argued that an exchange of price information to avoid liability under the Robinson-Patman Act should be considered a justification or excuse for engaging in joint conduct with an effect of fixing or stabilizing prices where the defendants' objective

54. See Flynn, supra note 68.

55. This part of the opinion is reproduced infra, pp. 920–922.

56. The Court viewed this issue as separate from the question of the issue of burden of proof in criminal cases because "a defendant's purpose in engaging in the prescribed conduct will not insulate him from liability unless it is deemed of sufficient merit to justify a general exception to the Sherman Act's proscriptions." The basis of the argument for a "controlling circumstance" exception was summarized by the Court as follows:

In Cement Mfrs. Protective Assn. v. United States, 268 U.S. 588, 45 S.Ct. 586, 69 L.Ed. 1104, the Court held exempt from Sherman § 1 liability an exchange of price information among competitors because the exchange of information was necessary to protect the cement manufacturers from fraudulent behavior by contractors. Over 40 years later, in United States v. Container Corp., 393 U.S. 333, 335, 89 S.Ct. 510, 511, 21 L.Ed.2d 526, Mr. Justice Douglas characterized the Cement holding in the following terms:

"While there was present here, as in Cement Mfrs. Protective Association v. United States, 268 U.S. 588, [45 S.Ct. 586, 69 L.Ed. 1104,] an exchange of prices to specific customers, there was absent the controlling circumstance, viz., that cement man-

ufacturers, to protect themselves from delivering to contractors more cement than was needed for a specific job and thus receiving a lower price, exchanged price information as a means of protecting their legal rights from fraudulent inducements to deliver more cement than needed for a specific job."

The use of the phrase "controlling circumstance" in Container implied that the exception from Sherman Act liability recognized in Cement Mfrs. was not necessarily limited to special circumstances of that case, although the exact scope of the exception remained largely undefined.

United States v. United States Gypsum Co., 438 U.S. 422, 448, 98 S.Ct. 2864, 2879, 57 L.Ed.2d 854, 876 (1978).

57. Section 2(a) of the Robinson-Patman Act, 15 U.S.C. § 13(a), makes it unlawful "to discriminate in price between different purchasers of commodities of like grade and quality . . . where the effect of such discrimination may be substantially to lessen competition or tend to create a monopoly in any line of commerce. . . ." Under Section 2(b) of the Act, it is an affirmative defense to a charge of unlawful price discrimination that the "lower price . . . was made in good faith to meet an equally low price of a competitor." 15 U.S.C. § 13(b). The Robinson-Patman Act is explored more fully in Chapter 8 infra.

was one of complying with the requirements of another law. The Court found it unnecessary to resolve the claim of a "controlling circumstance" excuse or justification by finding that a good faith belief, rather than absolute certainty, that a price concession had been offered by a competing seller was all that was required to make out the defense for Robinson-Patman Act purposes. Whether the justification or excuse of "controlling circumstance" will be recognized elsewhere remains to be seen, although there is scattered precedent supporting such an approach.[58]

The courts have also implied that rules of *per se* illegality may be mitigated in light of the unique status of the trade or business involved. The tendency is most pronounced in cases challenging the ethical rules and practices of the professions, particularly those of the legal profession. In *Goldfarb v. Virginia State Bar*[59] the court upheld an antitrust challenge to a minimum fee schedule for routine legal services adopted by the Fairfax County Bar Association and enforced by the Virginia State Bar. The Court found the fee schedule had the effect of establishing a rigid price floor for routine legal services and constituted price fixing; that the practice had the requisite effect on interstate commerce for Sherman Act jurisdiction; that the activities of learned professions are not expressly or impliedly exempt from the Sherman Act as a kind of "trade or commerce" not intended to be covered by the Act; and, that the activity in question (adoption of a minimum fee schedule fixing a minimum fee, *inter alia*, for a title search) was not exempt activity by virtue of the state action defense because the state had not required the specific conduct in question as part of its regulation of the profession. In the course of its opinion, rejecting the argument for an express or implied exemption on grounds that the practice of law is not the kind of "trade or commerce" Congress intended to regulate by the Sherman Act, the Court stated: "Whatever else it may be, the examination of a land title is a service; the exchange of such a service for money is 'commerce' in the most common usage of that word. It is no disparagement of the practice of law as a profession to acknowledge that it has this business aspect. . . ."[60] The Court's observation was qualified by the following footnote:

> The fact that a restraint operates upon a profession as distinguished from a business is, of course, relevant in determining whether that particular restraint violates the Sherman Act. It

---

58. See, e.g., Cement Manufacturer's Protective Association v. United States, 268 U.S. 588, 45 S.Ct. 586, 69 L.Ed. 1104 (1929) (joint action to prevent buyer fraud); Belliston v. Texaco, Inc., 455 F.2d 175 (10th Cir. 1972), certiorari denied 408 U.S. 928, 92 S.Ct. 2494, 33 L.Ed.2d 341 rehearing denied 409 U.S. 1001, 93 S.Ct. 306, 34 L.Ed.2d 264 (joint action to comply with the Robinson-Patman Act); Tripoli Co. v. Wella Corp., 425 F.2d 932 (3d Cir. 1970), certiorari denied 400 U.S. 831, 91 S.Ct. 62, 27 L.Ed.2d 62 (restricting re-

sale of dangerous products to consumers); Smith v. Pro Football, Inc., 593 F.2d 1173 (D.C.Cir. 1979) (validity of player draft); Harold Friedman, Inc. v. Thorofare Markets, Inc., 587 F.2d 127 (3d Cir. 1978) (agreement to exclude competitor from shopping center). See also, Boycotts, infra chap. 5.

59. 421 U.S. 773, 95 S.Ct. 2004, 44 L.Ed.2d 572 (1975).

60. Id. at 788, 95 S.Ct., at 2013, 44 L.Ed.2d, at 585.

would be unrealistic to view the practice of professions as interchangeable with other business activities, and automatically to apply to the professions antitrust concepts which originated in other areas. The public service aspect, and other features of the professions, may require that a particular practice, which could properly be viewed as a violation of the Sherman Act in another context, be treated differently. We intimate no view on any other situation than the one with which we are confronted today.[61]

An opportunity to "intimate" views about "features of the professions" justifying different treatment under the Sherman Act was presented in *Bates v. State Bar of Arizona*.[62] In *Bates*, two lawyers, operating a legal aid clinic providing low cost routine legal services for low and moderate income clients, were subjected to disciplinary proceedings by the State Bar for advertising their services and the prices for particular services. The Bar found the lawyers in violation of disciplinary rules, patterned after ABA proposed ethical rules and adopted by the Arizona Supreme Court, barring lawyer advertising and recommended a one week suspension from practice for the conduct. The Arizona Supreme Court upheld the suspension, finding the rule was adopted and enforced by a sovereign act of the State of Arizona and thereby exempt from Sherman Act liability by virtue of the state action exemption. The Arizona Court also rejected a claim that the rule violated First Amendment commercial speech rights, finding that special considerations justified state imposed limitations upon advertising by lawyers. The Supreme Court affirmed the holding on the state action defense but rejected the Arizona Court's ruling on the First Amendment issue. The Arizona disciplinary rule was found to be an impairment of the Court's evolving notion of a First Amendment protected interest in "commercial speech," first discovered in *Virginia State Board of Pharmacy v. Virginia Citizens Consumer Council*.[63] The Court, after again acknowledging that the role of professions in society may call for some wider inquiry into justifications for restraints placed on the activity of members of the profession, made an elaborate inquiry into the justifications proffered for the restraint upon "commercial speech" in the form of advertising lawyer services and fees. The justifications asserted were either found wanting or capable of remedy by a less restrictive alternative than a total ban of advertising which deprives the listener of the availability, nature and prices of products and services. Left unanswered was the degree to which the role of the professions generating activities "which could be properly viewed as a violation of the Sherman Act, in another context," would cause the Court to act differently were the Sherman Act applied to the case. The conundrum of defining the appropriate degree of self-regulation by the profes-

61. Id. at 787, n. 17, 95 S.Ct., at 2013, n. 17, 44 L.Ed.2d, at 585, n. 17.

62. 433 U.S. 350, 97 S.Ct. 2691, 53 L.Ed.2d 810 (1977), rehearing denied 434 U.S. 881, 98 S.Ct. 242, 54 L.Ed.2d 164.

63. 425 U.S. 748, 96 S.Ct. 1817, 48 L.Ed.2d 346 (1976). See discussion, supra p. 340.

sions has perhaps been expanded by the approach taken in the following decision.

NATIONAL SOCIETY OF PROFESSIONAL ENGINEERS v. UNITED STATES

Supreme Court of the United States, 1978.
435 U.S. 679, 98 S.Ct. 1355, 55 L.Ed.2d 637.

MR. JUSTICE STEVENS delivered the opinion of the Court.

This is a civil antitrust case brought by the United States to nullify an association's canon of ethics prohibiting competitive bidding by its members. The question is whether the canon may be justified under the Sherman Act, because it was adopted by members of a learned profession for the purpose of minimizing the risk that competition would produce inferior engineering work endangering the public safety. The District Court rejected this justification without making any findings on the likelihood that competition would produce the dire consequences foreseen by the association. The Court of Appeals affirmed. We granted certiorari to decide whether the District Court should have considered the factual basis for the proffered justification before rejecting it. Because we are satisfied that the asserted defense rests on a fundamental misunderstanding of the Rule of Reason frequently applied in antitrust litigation, we affirm.

I

Engineering is an important and learned profession. There are over 750,000 graduate engineers in the United States, of whom about 325,000 are registered as professional engineers. . . . They perform services in connection with the study, design, and construction of all types of improvements to real property—bridges, office buildings, airports and factories are examples. Engineering fees, amounting to well over two billion dollars each year, constitute about 5% of total construction costs. . . .

The National Society of Professional Engineers (Society) was organized in 1935 to deal with the nontechnical aspects of engineering practice, including the promotion of the professional, social, and economic interests of its members. Its present membership of 69,000 resides throughout the United States and in some foreign countries. Approximately 12,000 members are consulting engineers who offer their services to governmental, industrial, and private clients. . . .

. . . Suggested fee schedules for particular types of services in certain areas have been promulgated from time to time by various local societies. This case does not, however, involve any claim that the National Society has tried to fix specific fees, or even a specific method of calculating fees. It involves a charge that the members of the Society have unlawfully agreed to refuse to negotiate or even to discuss the question of fees until after a prospective client has selected the engineer for a particular project. Evidence of this agreement is found in § 11(c) of the Society's Code of Ethics, adopted in July 1964.[64]

The District Court found that the Society's Board of Ethical Review has uniformly interpreted the "ethical rules against competitive bidding for engineering services as prohibiting the submission of any form of price information to a prospective customer which would enable that customer to make a price comparison on engineering services." If the client requires that such information be provided, then § 11(c) imposes an obligation upon the engineering firm to withdraw from consideration for that job. The Society's Code of Ethics thus "prohibits engineers from both soliciting and submitting such price information," 389 F.Supp., at 1206, and seeks to preserve the profession's "traditional" method of selecting professional engineers. Under the traditional method, the client initially selects an engineer on the basis of background and reputation, not price.

In 1972 the Government filed its complaint against the Society alleging that members had agreed to abide by canons of ethics prohibiting the submission of competitive bids for engineering services and that, in consequence, price competition among the members had been suppressed and customers had been deprived of the benefits of free and open competition. The complaint prayed for an injunction terminating the unlawful agreement.

In its answer the Society admitted the essential facts alleged by the Government and pleaded a series of affirmative defenses, only one of which remains in issue. In that defense, the Society averred that the standard set out in the Code of Ethics was reasonable because competition among professional engineers was contrary to the public interest. It was averred that it would be cheaper and easier for an engineer "to design and specify inefficient and unnecessarily expensive structures and methods of construction." [65] Accordingly,

64. [Court's footnote 3.] That section, which remained in effect at the time of trial provided:

"Section 11—The Engineer will not compete unfairly with another engineer by attempting to obtain employment or advancement or professional engagements by competitive bidding

. . . .

"c. He shall not solicit or submit engineering proposals on the basis of competitive bidding. Competitive bidding for professional engineering services is defined as the formal or informal submission, or receipt, of verbal or written estimates of cost or proposals in terms of dollars, man days or work required, percentage of construction cost, or any other measure of compensation whereby the prospective client may compare engineering services on a price basis prior to the time that one engineer, or one engineering organization, has been selected for negotia-

tions. The disclosure of recommended fee schedules prepared by various engineering societies is not considered to constitute competitive bidding. An Engineer requested to submit a fee proposal or bid prior to the selection of an engineer or firm subject to the negotiation of a satisfactory contract, shall attempt to have the procedure changed to conform to ethical practices, but if not successful he shall withdraw from consideration for the proposed work. These principles shall be applied by the Engineer in obtaining the services of other professions."

65. [Court's footnote 7.] The entire defense pleaded in the answer reads as follows:

"18. (a) The principles and standards contained in the NSPE Code of Ethics, particularly those contained in that part of the NSPE Code of Ethics set out above, are reasonable, necessary to the public health, safety and wel-

competitive pressure to offer engineering services at the lowest possible price would adversely affect the quality of engineering. Moreover, the practice of awarding engineering contracts to the lowest bidder, regardless of quality, would be dangerous to the public health, safety, and welfare. For these reasons, the Society claimed that its Code of Ethics was not an "unreasonable restraint of interstate trade or commerce."

. . . The District Court did not . . . make any finding on the question whether, or to what extent, competition had led to inferior engineering work which, in turn, had adversely affected the public health, safety, or welfare. That inquiry was considered unnecessary because the court was convinced that the ethical prohibition against competitive bidding was "on its face a tampering with the price structure of engineering fees in violation of § 1 of the Sherman Act." 389 F.Supp., at 1200.

Although it modified the injunction entered by the District Court, the Court of Appeals affirmed its conclusion that the agreement was unlawful on its face and therefore "illegal without regard to claimed or possible benefits." 555 F.2d, at 984.

II

In *Goldfarb v. Virginia State Bar*, 421 U.S. 773, 95 S.Ct. 2004, 44 L.Ed.2d 572, the Court held that a bar association's rule prescribing minimum fees for legal services violated § 1 of the Sherman Act. In that opinion the Court noted that certain practices by members of a learned profession might survive scrutiny under the Rule of Reason even though they would be viewed as a violation of the Sherman Act in another context. The Court said:

> "The fact that a restraint operates upon a profession as distinguished from a business is, of course, relevant in determining

fare insofar as they are affected by the work of professional engineers, and serve the public interest.

"(b) Experience has demonstrated that competitive bidding for professional engineering services is inconsistent with securing for the recipients of such services the most economical projects or structures. Testing, calculating and designing the most economical and efficient structures and methods of construction is complex, difficult and expensive. It is cheaper and easier to design and specify inefficient and unnecessarily expensive structures and methods of construction. Consequently, if professional engineers are required by competitive pressures to submit bids in order to obtain employment of their services, the inevitable tendency will be to offer professional engineering services at the lowest possible price. Although this may result in some lowering of the cost of profes-

sional engineering services it will inevitably result in increasing the overall cost and decreasing the efficiency of those structures and projects which require professional engineering design and specification work.

"(c) Experience has also demonstrated that competitive bidding in most instances and situations results in an award of the work to be performed to the lowest bidder, regardless of other factors such as ability, experience, expertise, skill, capability, learning and the like, and that such awards in the case of professional engineers endanger the public health, welfare and safety.

"(d) For the aforesaid reasons, the provisions of the NSPE Code of Ethics set out above are not, in any event, in unreasonable restraint of interstate trade or commerce." Appendix at 21–22.

whether that particular restraint violates the Sherman Act. It would be unrealistic to view the practice of professions as interchangeable with other business activities, and automatically to apply to the professions antitrust concepts which originated in other areas. The public service aspect, and other features of the profession, may require that a particular practice, which could properly be viewed as a violation of the Sherman Act in another context, be treated differently. We intimate no view on any other situation than the one with which we are confronted today." Id., at 788–789, n. 17, 95 S.Ct. at 2013.

Relying heavily on this footnote, and on some of the major cases applying a Rule of Reason—principally *Mitchel v. Reynolds*, 1 P.Wms. 181, 24 Eng.Rep. 374 (1711); *Standard Oil Co. v. United States*, 221 U.S. 1, 31 S.Ct. 502, 55 L.Ed. 619; *Chicago Board of Trade v. United States*, 246 U.S. 231, 38 S.Ct. 242, 62 L.Ed. 683; and *Continental T. V., Inc. v. GTE Sylvania, Inc.*, 433 U.S. 36, 97 S.Ct. 2549, 53 L.Ed.2d 568—petitioner argues that its attempt to preserve the profession's traditional method of setting fees for engineering services is a reasonable method of forestalling the public harm which might be produced by unrestrained competitive bidding. To evaluate this argument it is necessary to identify the contours of the Rule of Reason and to discuss its application to the kind of justification asserted by petitioner.

A.   The Rule of Reason

[The Court's analysis, reprinted supra page 352, concluded that there are "two complimentary categories of antitrust analysis." A *per se* category of "agreements whose nature and necessary effect are so plainly anticompetitive that no elaborate study of the industry is needed to establish their illegality"; and a rule of reason category of "agreements whose competitive effect can only be evaluated by analyzing the facts peculiar to the business, the history of the restraint and why it was imposed." In both cases, the Court held, "the purpose of the analysis is to form a judgment about the competitive significance of the restraint; it is not to decide whether a policy favoring competition is in the public interest, or in the interest of members of an industry."]

B.   The Ban on Competitive Bidding.

Price is the "central nervous system of the economy," *United States v. Socony-Vacuum Oil Co.*, 310 U.S. 150, 226 n. 59, 60 S.Ct. 811, 845, 84 L.Ed. 1129, and an agreement that "interfere[s] with the setting of price by free market forces" is illegal on its face. *United States v. Container Corp.*, 393 U.S. 333, 337, 89 S.Ct. 510, 512, 21 L.Ed.2d 526. In this case we are presented with an agreement among competitors to refuse to discuss prices with potential customers until after negotiations have resulted in the initial selection of an engineer. While this is not price fixing as such, no elaborate industry analysis is required to demonstrate the anticompetitive character of such an agreement. It operates as an absolute ban on competitive bidding, applying with equal force to both complicated and simple projects and to both inexperienced and sophisticated customers. As the District Court found, the ban "impedes the ordinary give and take of the market place," and substantially deprives the customer of "the ability to utilize and compare prices in selecting engineering services." On its face, this agreement restrains trade within the meaning of § 1 of the Sherman Act.

The Society's affirmative defense confirms rather than refutes the anticompetitive purpose and effect of its agreement. The Society argues that the restraint is justified because bidding on engineering services is inherently imprecise, would lead to deceptively low bids, and would thereby tempt individual engineers to do inferior work with consequent risk to public safety and health.[66] The logic of this argument rests on the assumption that the agreement will tend to maintain the price level; if it had no such effect, it would not serve its intended purpose. The Society nonetheless invokes the Rule of Reason, arguing that its restraint on price competition ultimately inures to the public benefit by preventing the production of inferior work and by insuring ethical behavior. As the preceding discussion of the Rule of Reason reveals, this Court has never accepted such an argument.

It may be, as petitioner argues, that competition tends to force prices down and that an inexpensive item may be inferior to one that is more costly. There is some risk, therefore, that competition will cause some suppliers to market a defective product. Similarly, competitive bidding for engineering projects may be inherently imprecise and incapable of taking into account all the variables which will be involved in the actual performance of the project. Based on these considerations, a purchaser might conclude that his interest in quality—which may embrace the safety of the end product—outweighs

66. [Court's footnote 19.] The Society also points out that competition, in the form of bargaining between the engineer and customer, is allowed under its canon of ethics once an engineer has been initially selected. See n. 6, supra. It then contends that its prohibition of competitive bidding regulates only the *timing* of competition, thus making this case analogous to Chicago Board of Trade, supra, where the Court upheld an exchange rule which forbade exchange members from making purchases after the close of the day's session at any price other than the closing bid price. Indeed, petitioner has reprinted the Government's brief in that case to demonstrate that the Solicitor General regarded the exchange's rule as a form of pricefixing. Reply Brief for Petitioner (addendum). We find this reliance on Chicago Board of Trade misplaced for two reasons. First, petition-er's claim mistakenly treats negotiation between a single seller and a single buyer as the equivalent of competition between two or more potential sellers. Second, even if we were to accept the Society's equation of bargaining with price competition, our concern with Chicago Board of Trade is in its formulation of the proper test to be used in judging the legality of an agreement; that formulation unquestionably stresses impact on competition. Whatever one's view of the application of the Rule of Reason in that case, see L. Sullivan, supra, at 175–182, the Court considered the exchange's regulation of price information as having a positive effect on competition. 246 U.S., at 240–241, 38 S.Ct. at 244–245. The District Court's findings preclude a similar conclusion concerning the effect of the Society's "regulation."

the advantages of achieving cost savings by pitting one competitor against another. Or an individual vendor might independently refrain from price negotiation until he has satisfied himself that he fully understands the scope of his customers' needs. These decisions might be reasonable; indeed, petitioner has provided ample documentation for that thesis. But these are not reasons that satisfy the Rule; nor are such individual decisions subject to antitrust attack.

The Sherman Act does not require competitive bidding; it prohibits unreasonable restraints on competition. Petitioner's ban on competitive bidding prevents all customers from making price comparisons in the initial selection of an engineer, and imposes the Society's views of the costs and benefits of competition on the entire market place. It is this restraint that must be justified under the Rule of Reason, and petitioner's attempt to do so on the basis of the potential threat that competition poses to the public safety and the ethics of its profession is nothing less than a frontal assault on the basic policy of the Sherman Act.

The Sherman Act reflects a legislative judgment that ultimately competition will not only produce lower prices, but also better goods and services. "The heart of our national economic policy long has been faith in the value of competition." *Standard Oil Co. v. Federal Trade Commission,* 340 U.S. 231, 248, 71 S.Ct. 240, 249, 95 L.Ed. 239. The assumption that competition is the best method of allocating resources in a free market recognizes that all elements of a bargain— quality, service, safety, and durability—and not just the immediate cost, are favorably affected by the free opportunity to select among alternative offers. Even assuming occasional exceptions to the presumed consequences of competition, the statutory policy precludes inquiry into the question whether competition is good or bad.

The fact that engineers are often involved in large-scale projects significantly affecting the public safety does not alter our analysis. Exceptions to the Sherman Act for potentially dangerous goods and services would be tantamount to a repeal of the statute. In our complex economy the number of items that may cause serious harm is almost endless—automobiles, drugs, foods, aircraft components, heavy equipment, and countless others, cause serious harm to individuals or to the public at large if defectively made. The judiciary cannot indirectly protect the public against this harm by conferring monopoly privileges on the manufacturers.

By the same token, the cautionary footnote in *Goldfarb,* 421 U.S., at 788–789, n. 17, 95 S.Ct. at 2013, quoted supra, cannot be read as fashioning a broad exemption under the Rule of Reason for learned professions. We adhere to the view expressed in *Goldfarb* that, by their nature, professional services may differ significantly from other business services, and, accordingly, the nature of the competition in such services may vary. Ethical norms may serve to regulate and promote this competition, and thus fall within the Rule of Reason. But the Society's argument in this case is a far cry from such a position. We are faced with a contention that a total ban on competitive bidding is necessary because otherwise engineers will be tempted to submit deceptively low bids. Certainly, the problem of professional deception is a proper subject of an ethical canon. But once again, the equation of competition with deception, like the similar equation with safety hazards, is simply too broad; we may assume that competition is not entirely conducive to ethical behavior, but that is not a reason, cognizable under the Sherman Act, for doing away with competition.

In sum, the Rule of Reason does not support a defense based on the assumption that competition itself is unreasonable. Such a view of the Rule would create the "sea of doubt" on which Judge Taft refused to embark in *Addyston,* and which this Court has firmly avoided ever since.

III

The judgment entered by the District Court, as modified by the Court of Appeals, prohibits the Society from adopting any official opinion, policy statement or guideline stating or implying that competitive bidding is unethical. Petitioner argues that this judgment abridges its First Amendment rights. We find no merit in this contention.

Having found the Society guilty of a violation of the Sherman Act, the District Court was empowered to fashion appropriate restraints on the Society's future activities both to avoid a recurrence of the violation and to eliminate its consequences. While the resulting order may curtail the exercise of liberties that the Society might otherwise enjoy, that is a necessary and, in cases such as this, unavoidable consequence of the violation. Just as an injunction against pricefixing abridges the freedom of businessmen to talk to one another about prices, so too the injunction in this case must restrict the Society's range of expression on the ethics of competitive bidding. The First Amendment does not "make it . . . impossible ever to enforce laws against agreements in restraint of trade . . . ." *Giboney v. Empire Store & Ice Co.,* 336 U.S. 490, 502, 69 S.Ct. 684, 691, 93 L.Ed. 834. In fashioning a remedy, the District Court may, of course, consider the fact that its injunction may impinge upon rights that would otherwise be constitutionally protected, but those protections do not prevent it from remedying the antitrust violations.

. . .

The Society apparently fears that the District Court's injunction, if broadly read, will block legitimate paths of expression on all ethical matters relating to bidding. But the answer to these fears is . . . that the burden is upon the proven transgressor "to bring any proper claims for relief to the court's attention." In this case, the Court of Appeals specifically stated that "[i]f the Society wishes to adopt some other ethical guideline more closely confined to the legitimate objective of preventing deceptively low bids, it may move the district court for modification of the decree." 555 F.2d, at 983. This is, we believe, a proper approach, adequately protecting the Society's interests. We therefore reject petitioner's attack on the District Court's order.

The judgment of the Court of Appeals is *affirmed*.

MR. JUSTICE BRENNAN took no part in the consideration or decision of this case.

MR. JUSTICE BLACKMUN, with whom MR. JUSTICE REHNQUIST joins, concurring in part and concurring in the judgment.

I join Parts I and III of the Court's opinion and concur in the judgment. I do not join Part II because I would not, at least for the moment, reach as far as the Court appears to me to do in intimating that any ethical rule with an overall anticompetitive effect promulgated by a professional society is forbidden under the Sherman Act. In my view, the decision in *Goldfarb v. Virginia State Bar*, 421 U.S. 773, 788–789 n. 17, 95 S.Ct. 2004, 2013, 44 L.Ed.2d 572 (1975), properly left to the Court some flexibility in considering how to apply traditional Sherman Act concepts to professions long consigned to self-regulation. Certainly, this case does not require us to decide whether the "Rule of Reason" as applied to the professions ever could take account of benefits other than increased competition. For even accepting petitioner's assertion that product quality is one such benefit, and that maintenance of the quality of engineering services requires that an engineer not bid before he has made full acquaintance with the scope of a client's desired project, petitioner Society's rule is still grossly overbroad. As petitioner concedes, Rule 11(c) forbids any simultaneous consultation between a client and several engineers, even where the client provides complete information to each about the scope and nature of the desired project before requesting price information. To secure a price estimate on a project, the client must purport to engage a single engineer, and so long as that engagement continues no other member of the Society is permitted to discuss the project with the client in order to provide comparative price information. Though Rule 11(c) does not fix prices directly, and though the customer retains the option of rejecting a particular engineer's offer and beginning negotiations all over again with another engineer, the forced process of sequential search inevitably increases the cost of gathering price information, and hence will dampen price competition, without any calibrated role to play in preventing uninformed bids. Then, too, the Society's rule is overbroad in the aspect noted by Judge Leventhal, when it prevents any dissemination of competitive price information in regard to real property improvements prior to the engagement of a single engineer regardless of "the sophistication of the purchaser, the complexity of the project, or the procedures for evaluating price information." 555 F.2d at 982.

My skepticism about going further in this case by shaping the Rule of Reason to such a narrow last as does the majority, arises from the fact that there may be ethical rules which have a more-than-*de-minimis* anticompetitive effect and yet are important in a progression's proper ordering. A medical association's prescription of standards of minimum competence for licensing or certification may lessen the number of entrants. A bar association's regulation of the permissible forms of price advertising for nonroutine legal services or limitation of in-person solicitation, see *Bates v. State Bar of Arizona,* 433 U.S. 350, 97 S.Ct. 2691, 53 L.Ed.2d 810 (1977), may also have the effect of reducing price competition. In acknowledging that "professional services may differ significantly from other business services" and that the "nature of the competition in such services may vary," but then holding that ethical norms can pass muster under the Rule of Reason only if they promote competition, I am not at all certain that the Court leaves enough elbow room for realistic application of the Sherman Act to professional services.

Mr. Chief Justice Burger, concurring and dissenting.

I concur in the Court's judgment to the extent it sustains the finding of a violation of the Sherman Act but dissent from that portion of the judgment prohibiting petitioner from stating in its published standards of ethics the view that competitive bidding is unethical. The First Amendment guarantees the right to express such a position and that right cannot be impaired under the cloak of remedial judicial action.

NOTES AND QUERIES

1. *The Rule of Reason as a Vehicle for Examining Justifications or Excuses for Otherwise Per Se Unlawful Conduct.* Did the Court explain what "public service" and other "features of the profession" justify a rule of reason analysis in the case of professions? Do not oil companies engage in a "public service" by bringing oil products to the consumer? Should the public service benefits of conserving oil be weighed in cases like *Socony-Vacuum?* Were they weighed in deciding whether the conduct should be labeled price fixing for Sherman Act purposes? Were the traders on the Chicago Board of Trade providing a "public service" by limiting price changes for trading done off the exchange? Which "professions", among the hundreds claiming to be "professions", are entitled to the special considerations of a rule of reason analysis of their joint action restraining trade? Accountants? Beauticians and barbers? Doctors? The oldest profession? Must courts examine every restraint a profession chooses to impose on its members under an extended rule of reason analysis, or just some restraints, like limiting entry into the profession, but not price fixing?[67]

These kinds of issues are likely to spring up as a result of the Court's approach in *National Society of Professional Engineers.* Although the Court rejected the proffered justification for banning competitive bidding, it did not reject the possibility that some restraints imposed by a profession may be justified. Presumably the nature of the activities carried on by a profession, i.e., practicing law or medicine, may justify joint action administering entry examinations to insure the necessary moral or intellectual quali-

---

67. See generally Bauer, Professional Activities and the Antitrust Laws, 50 N.D. Lawyer 570 (1975); Note, The Antitrust Liability of Professional Associa- tions After Goldfarb, 1977 Duke L.J. 1047; Note, The Professions and Non-Commercial Purposes, 11 U.Mich.J.L.Ref. 387 (1978).

ties necessary for the practice.[68] Even after one is admitted to practice in medicine, for example, obtaining hospital staff privileges may require extended review by one's peers, peers who also may be one's competitors in an increasingly competitive profession.[69] What result, if the Bar Association authorized by the state to administer the bar examination decides to raise the standards for passing the bar exam to a level where no more than 50% taking the exam are admitted in any one year? Assume the Bar Association does so because the large numbers of new lawyers competing for business have caused a noticeable increase in unethical practices like "ambulance chasing", unethical "fee splitting", manufactured lawsuits, and the like. Rule of reason or *per se* analysis? Under either line of analysis would the action be lawful or unlawful?[70]

2. *Unique Characteristics of the Business Justifying Rule of Reason Analysis.* The unique circumstances surrounding the licensing of copyrighted music for broadcasting may be read as the basis for triggering an extended rule of reason type of analysis in *Broadcast Music,* supra. Subsequent chapters, e.g., Boycotts, infra Chap. 5, will contain cases where the characteristics of the trade or business require a broader inquiry of the legality of certain restraints than that normally permitted in *per se* analysis. Justice Harlan advocated a similar approach for vertically imposed *maximum* price fixing in his dissent in *Albrecht v. Herald Co.*[71] In that case a monopoly newspaper granting independent carriers exclusive territories prohibited carriers from reselling papers in excess of the newspaper's advertised maximum resale price in their exclusive territories. Justice Harlan argued the economic motivation and consequences of *maximum* price fixing in such a setting differed from those involved in vertically imposed minimum price fixing. Among the other considerations stemming from the vertical nature of the restraint (taken up in Chapter 6 infra), Justice Harlan emphasized the unusual circumstances of a monopoly newspaper needing an efficient and reliable distribution system, yet one which would not result in consumer exploitation by carriers taking advantage of the territorial monopoly granted to them.

3. *Rethinking the Per Se—Rule of Reason Distinction.* As the student reviews this section, consideration should again be given to the way in which the courts are conceptualizing and using *per se*—and rule of reason analysis. Are *per se* and rule of reason analysis two separate categories of substantive rules or a single methodology establishing evidentiary presumptions for identifying conduct impinging antitrust goals and a methodology for ordering sensibly the litigation of the dispute? Consider:

> Conceptualizing *per se* and rule of reason analyses as rules and as separate methods of analysis can be useful in the vast number of cases never litigated and in giving clients advice in most normal circumstances. This perspective tends to break down, however, when something is worth litigating because of unique circumstances or serious factual disputes

---

68. See Levin, "Doctors Sue Hospitals for Staff Privileges as Competition Rises", Wall St. J., Sept. 29, 1981, p. 1, summarizing antitrust and other litigation over denial of hospital privileges and noting a 31% surge in the number of doctors between 1970–1978, while the population grew by only 6.4% and the number of hospital beds declined by 17%.

69. Cf. Feldman v. Gardner, 661 F.2d 1295 (D.C.Cir. 1981) (District of Columbia Court rule limiting sitting for D.C. Bar to those graduating from A.B.A. accredited law school upheld on state action grounds), certiorari denied, ___ U.S. ___, 102 S.Ct. 3483, 73 L.Ed.2d 1365 (1982).

70. See Ronwin v. State Bar of Arizona, 663 F.2d 914 (9th Cir. 1981).

71. 390 U.S. 145, 88 S.Ct. 869, 19 L.Ed.2d 998 (1968), rehearing denied 390 U.S. 1018, 88 S.Ct. 1258, 20 L.Ed.2d 169.

over whether the conduct involved is pursuant to joint-action, falls within a *per se* category or is reasonable if not within a defined category of *per se* illegality.

Difficulties and chaos break out when we conceptualize *per se* and rule of reason doctrine as separate substantive *rules*, rather than a single *method* of analysis generating differing evidentiary presumptions for allocating burdens of proof regarding the degree to which the *quality* of the collaborative activity displaces competition as the rule of trade. . . .

The issue is a *qualitative* one of measuring the impact of the conduct on the ideal of a competitive process in the context of the particular industry or trade and in light of the political, social, and economic purpose for relying on the competitive process as the rule of trade. The issue is not a *quantitative* one of determining how much competition is effected or destroyed by the practice, although power, relevant market, and quantitative effect may aid in determining qualitative impact in some limited circumstances. . . . The spectrum from *per se* to rule of reason analysis is a single methodology presenting varying levels of evidentiary presumptions ordering the analysis of whether there has been an unreasonable displacement of the competition process. Conceptualizing *per se* doctrine as a separate category of rules and rule of reason analysis as necessarily requiring a significant quantitative effect on competition has engendered confusion in the cases. . . . It is not enough to know that a conspiracy to fix prices is *per se* illegal; one must know what facts will give rise to the inference of a conspiracy and what facts will give rise to the inference that the conspiracy is one which will be legally identified as "price fixing". Considerable "rule of reason" type evidence may be required to justify the inference that there is a conspiracy or that it is one to "fix prices". Of even more significance to lawyers than the conclusion reached, is the method by which a court will reach such conclusions, since the analytical framework by which a case is decided provides the intellectual basis from which to extrapolate the implications of the reasoning to other facts and circumstances.

Thinking about *per se* and rule of reason analyses as methods for establishing evidentiary presumptions allocating burdens of proof to structure an analysis of whether or not the competitive process has been displaced pursuant to a contract, combination, or conspiracy clarifies much of the mystery of recent twists and turns in the case law.[72]

Query: Does the above approach clarify the mysteries of the "twists and turns in the case law" you have surveyed in this section?

C. DIVISION OF MARKET

Agreements among competitors dividing customers or territories have long been viewed as even more destructive of the competitive process than horizontal price fixing arrangements. A horizontal market division can eliminate all forms of competition, while horizontal price fixing usually eliminates only price competition. The traditional hostility to horizontal market divisions is evidenced by the dissenting views of Justices Douglas and Black in *United States v. Penn-Olin*

---

72. Flynn, Rethinking Sherman Act Section 1 Analysis: Three Proposals for Reducing the Chaos, 49 Antitrust L.J. 1593 (1982).

Chemical Co.,[73] a joint venture merger case they viewed as a classic horizontal agreement to divide the sodium chlorate market:

> Agreements among competitors to divide markets are per se violations of the Sherman Act. The most detailed, grandiose scheme of that kind is disclosed in Addyston Pipe & Steel Co. v. United States, 175 U.S. 211, 20 S.Ct. 96, 44 L.Ed. 136, where industrialists, acting like commissars in modern communist countries, determined what tonnage should be produced by each company and what territory was 'free' and what was 'bonus.' The Court said: 'Total suppression of the trade in the commodity is not necessary in order to render the combination one in restraint of trade. It is the effect of the combination in limiting and restricting the right of each of the members to transact business in the ordinary way, as well as its effect upon the volume or extent of the dealing in the commodity, that is regarded.' Id., at 244–245, 20 S.Ct. at 108.

While there is general agreement that "naked" horizontal agreements dividing markets are and should be *per se* unlawful, controversy can break out in specific cases over whether the conduct in question is or is not a division of markets, is horizontal or vertical, or is conduct which can be justified or excused in any circumstances.[74]

UNITED STATES v. TOPCO ASSOCIATES, INC.

Supreme Court of the United States, 1972.
405 U.S. 596, 92 S.Ct. 1126, 31 L.Ed.2d 515.

MR. JUSTICE MARSHALL delivered the opinion of the Court.

The United States brought this action for injunctive relief against alleged violation by Topco Associates, Inc. (Topco), of § 1 of the Sherman Act. Following a trial on the merits, the United States District Court for the Northern District of Illinois entered judgment for Topco, 319 F.Supp. 1031, and the United States appealed directly to this Court pursuant to § 2 of the Expediting Act. We noted probable jurisdiction, and we now reverse the judgment of the District Court.

Topco is a cooperative association of approximately 25 small and medium-sized regional supermarket chains that operate stores in some 33 States. Each of the member chains operates independently; there is no pooling of earnings, profits, capital, management, or advertising resources. No grocery business is conducted under the Topco name. Its basic function is to serve as a purchasing agent for its members. In this capacity, it procures and distributes to the

---

73. 378 U.S. 158, 84 S.Ct. 1710, 12 L.Ed.2d 775 (1964). The case is discussed supra, p. 280.

74. See R. Bork, The Antitrust Paradox, pp. 263–64 (1978): "The rule should be restated so that it is illegal per se to fix prices or divide markets (or to eliminate rivalry in any other way) only when the restraint is "naked"—that is, only when the agreement is not ancillary to cooperative productive activity engaged in by the agreeing parties. Only then is the effect of the agreement clearly to restrict output. Many price-fixing and market-division agreements make cooperative productive activity more efficient, and these should be judged, according to the circumstances, by the standards applicable to internal growth of firms or by horizontal merger rules."

members more than 1,000 different food and related nonfood items, most of which are distributed under brand names owned by Topco. The association does not itself own any manufacturing, processing, or warehousing facilities, and the items that it procures for members are usually shipped directly from the packer or manufacturer to the members. Payment is made either to Topco or directly to the manufacturer at a cost that is virtually the same for the members as for Topco itself.

All of the stock in Topco is owned by the members, with the common stock, the only stock having voting rights, being equally distributed. The board of directors, which controls the operation of the association, is drawn from the members and is normally composed of high-ranking executive officers of member chains. It is the board that elects the association's officers and appoints committee members, and it is from the board that the principal executive officers of Topco must be drawn. Restrictions on the alienation of stock and the procedure for selecting all important officials of the association from within the ranks of its members give the members complete and unfettered control over the operations of the association.

Topco was founded in the 1940's by a group of small, local grocery chains, independently owned and operated, that desired to cooperate to obtain high quality merchandise under private labels in order to compete more effectively with larger national and regional chains.[75] With a line of canned, dairy, and other products, the association began. It added frozen foods in 1950, fresh produce in 1958, more general merchandise equipment and supplies in 1960, and a branded bacon and carcass beef selection program in 1966. By 1964, Topco's members had combined retail sales of more than $2 billion; by 1967, their sales totaled more than $2.3 billion, a figure exceeded by only three national grocery chains.

Members of the association vary in the degree of market share that they possess in their respective areas. The range is from 1.5%

75. [Court's footnote 3.] The founding members of Topco were having difficulty competing with larger chains. This difficulty was attributable in some degree to the fact that the larger chains were capable of developing their own private-label programs.

Private-label products differ from other brand-name products in that they are sold at a limited number of easily ascertainable stores. A&P, for example, was a pioneer in developing a series of products that were sold under an A&P label and that were only available in A&P stores. It is obvious that by using private-label products, a chain can achieve significant cost economies in purchasing, transportation, warehousing, promotion, and advertising. These economies may afford the chain opportunities for offering private-label products at lower prices than other brand-name products. This,

in turn, provides many advantages of which some of the more important are: a store can offer national-brand products at the same price as other stores, while simultaneously offering a desirable, lower priced alternative; or, if the profit margin is sufficiently high on private-brand goods, national-brand products may be sold at reduced price. Other advantages include: enabling a chain to bargain more favorably with national-brand manufacturers by creating a broader supply base of manufacturers, thereby decreasing dependence on a few, large national-brand manufacturers; enabling a chain to create a "price-mix" whereby prices on special items can be lowered to attract customers while profits are maintained on other items; and creation of general goodwill by offering lower priced, higher quality goods.

to 16%, with the average being approximately 6%. While it is difficult to compare these figures with the market shares of larger regional and national chains because of the absence in the record of
accurate statistics for these chains, there is much evidence in the
record that Topco members are frequently in as strong a competitive
position in their respective areas as any other chain. The strength of
this competitive position is due, in some measure, to the success of
Topco-brand products. Although only 10% of the total goods sold by
Topco members bear the association's brand names, the profit on
these goods is substantial and their very existence has improved the
competitive potential of Topco members with respect to other large
and powerful chains.

It is apparent that from meager beginnings approximately a quarter of a century ago, Topco has developed into a purchasing association wholly owned and operated by member chains, which possess
much economic muscle, individually as well as cooperatively.

. . .

The United States charged that, beginning at least as early as
1960 and continuing up to the time that the complaint was filed,
Topco had combined and conspired with its members to violate § 1 in
two respects. First, the Government alleged that there existed:

"a continuing agreement, understanding and concert of action
among the co-conspirator member firms acting through Topco, the
substantial terms of which have been and are that each co-conspirator or member firm will sell Topco-controlled brands only within
the marketing territory allocated to it, and will refrain from selling Topco-controlled brands outside such marketing territory."

The division of marketing territories to which the complaint refers
consists of a number of practices by the association.

Article IX, § 2, of the Topco bylaws establishes three categories
of territorial licenses that members may secure from the association:

"(a) *Exclusive*—An exclusive territory is one in which the
member is licensed to sell all products bearing specified trademarks of the Association, to the exclusion of all other persons.

"(b) *Non-exclusive*—A non-exclusive territory is one in which
a member is licensed to sell all products bearing specified trademarks of the Association, but not to the exclusion of others who
may also be licensed to sell products bearing the same trademarks
of the Association in the same territory.

"(c) *Coextensive*—A coextensive territory is one in which two
(2) or more members are licensed to sell all products bearing specified trademarks of the Association to the exclusion of all other
persons. . . ."

When applying for membership, a chain must designate the type of
license that it desires. Membership must first be approved by the
board of directors, and thereafter by an affirmative vote of 75% of
the association's members. If, however, the member whose operations are closest to those of the applicant, or any member whose oper-

ations are located within 100 miles of the applicant, votes against approval, an affirmative vote of 85% of the members is required for approval. Bylaws, Art. I, § 5. Because, as indicated by the record, members cooperate in accommodating each other's wishes, the procedure for approval provides, in essence, that members have a veto of sorts over actual or potential competition in the territorial areas in which they are concerned.

Following approval, each new member signs an agreement with Topco designating the territory in which that member may sell Topco-brand products. No member may sell these products outside the territory in which it is licensed. Most licenses are exclusive, and even those denominated "coextensive" or "non-exclusive" prove to be *de facto* exclusive. Exclusive territorial areas are often allocated to members who do no actual business in those areas on the theory that they may wish to expand at some indefinite future time and that expansion would likely be in the direction of the allocated territory. When combined with each member's veto power over new members, provisions for exclusivity work effectively to insulate members from competition in Topco-brand goods. Should a member violate its license agreement and sell in areas other than those in which it is licensed, its membership can be terminated under the bylaws. Once a territory is classified as exclusive, either formally or *de facto*, it is extremely unlikely that the classification will ever be changed.

The Government maintains that this scheme of dividing markets violates the Sherman Act because it operates to prohibit competition in Topco-brand products among grocery chains engaged in retail operations. The Government also makes a subsidiary challenge to Topco's practices regarding licensing members to sell at wholesale. Under the bylaws, members are not permitted to sell any products supplied by the association at wholesale, whether trademarked or not, without first applying for and receiving special permission from the association to do so. Before permission is granted, other licensees (usually retailers), whose interests may potentially be affected by wholesale operations, are consulted as to their wishes in the matter. If permission is obtained, the member must agree to restrict the sale of Topco products to a specific geographic area and to sell under any conditions imposed by the association. Permission to wholesale has often been sought by members, only to be denied by the association. The Government contends that this amounts not only to a territorial restriction violative of the Sherman Act, but also to a restriction on customers that in itself is violative of the Act.

From the inception of this lawsuit, Topco accepted as true most of the Government's allegations regarding territorial divisions and restrictions on wholesaling, although it differed greatly with the Government on the conclusions, both factual and legal, to be drawn from these facts.

Topco's answer to the complaint is illustrative of its posture in the District Court and before this Court:

> Private label merchandising is a way of economic life in the food retailing industry, and exclusivity is the essence of a private label program; without exclusivity, a private label would not be private. Each national and large regional chain has its own exclusive private label products in addition to the nationally advertised brands which all chains sell. Each such chain relies upon the exclusivity of its own private label line to differentiate its private label products from those of its competitors and to attract and retain the repeat business and loyalty of consumers. Smaller retail grocery stores and chains are unable to compete effectively with the national and large regional chains without also offering their own exclusive private label products.

. . .

> "The only feasible method by which Topco can procure private label products and assure the exclusivity thereof is through trademark licenses specifying the territory in which each member may sell such trademarked products."

Topco essentially maintains that it needs territorial divisions to compete with larger chains; that the association could not exist if the territorial divisions were anything but exclusive; and that by restricting competition in the sale of Topco-brand goods, the association actually increases competition by enabling its members to compete successfully with larger regional and national chains.

The District Court, considering all these things relevant to its decision, agreed with Topco. It recognized that the panoply of restraints that Topco imposed on its members worked to prevent competition in Topco-brand products, but concluded that

> "[w]hatever anti-competitive effect these practices may have on competition in the sale of Topco private label brands is far outweighed by the increased ability of Topco members to compete both with the national chains and other supermarkets operating in their respective territories."

The court held that Topco's practices were procompetitive and, therefore, consistent with the purposes of the antitrust laws. But we conclude that the District Court used an improper analysis in reaching its result.

On its face, § 1 of the Sherman Act appears to bar any combination of entrepreneurs so long as it is "in restraint of trade." Theoretically, all manufacturers, distributors, merchants, sellers, and buyers could be considered as potential competitors of each other. Were § 1 to be read in the narrowest possible way, any commercial contract could be deemed to violate it. The history underlying the formulation of the antitrust laws led this Court to conclude, however, that Congress did not intend to prohibit all contracts, nor even all contracts that might in some insignificant degree or attenuated sense restrain trade or competition. In lieu of the narrowest possible reading of

§ 1, the Court adopted a "rule of reason" analysis for determining whether most business combinations or contracts violate the prohibitions of the Sherman Act. An analysis of the reasonableness of particular restraints includes consideration of the facts peculiar to the business in which the restraint is applied, the nature of the restraint and its effects, and the history of the restraint and the reasons for its adoption.

While the Court has utilized the "rule of reason" in evaluating the legality of most restraints alleged to be violative of the Sherman Act, it has also developed the doctrine that certain business relationships are *per se* violations of the Act without regard to a consideration of their reasonableness. In Northern Pacific R. Co. v. United States, 356 U.S. 1, 5, 78 S.Ct. 514, 518, 2 L.Ed.2d 545 (1958), Mr. Justice Black explained the appropriateness of, and the need for, *per se* rules:

> "[T]here are certain agreements or practices which because of their pernicious effect on competition and lack of any redeeming virtue are conclusively presumed to be unreasonable and therefore illegal without elaborate inquiry as to the precise harm they have caused or the business excuse for their use. This principle of *per se* unreasonableness not only makes the type of restraints which are proscribed by the Sherman Act more certain to the benefit of everyone concerned, but it also avoids the necessity for an incredibly complicated and prolonged economic investigation into the entire history of the industry involved, as well as related industries, in an effort to determine at large whether a particular restraint has been unreasonable—an inquiry so often wholly fruitless when undertaken."

It is only after considerable experience with certain business relationships that courts classify them as *per se* violations of the Sherman Act. See generally Van Cise, The Future of Per Se in Antitrust Law, 50 Va.L.Rev. 1165 (1964). One of the classic examples of a *per se* violation of § 1 is an agreement between competitors at the same level of the market structure to allocate territories in order to minimize competition. Such concerted action is usually termed a "horizontal" restraint, in contradistinction to combinations of persons at different levels of the market structure, e.g. manufacturers and distributors, which are termed "vertical" restraints. This Court has reiterated time and time again that "[h]orizontal territorial limitations . . . are naked restraints of trade with no purpose except stifling of competition." Such limitations are *per se* violations of the Sherman Act.

We think that it is clear that the restraint in this case is a horizontal one, and, therefore, a *per se* violation of § 1. The District Court failed to make any determination as to whether there were *per se* horizontal territorial restraints in this case and simply applied a rule of reason in reaching its conclusions that the restraints were not illegal. . . .

United States v. Sealy, Inc., [388 U.S. 350, 87 S.Ct. 1847, 18 L.Ed. 2d 1238 (1967)], is in fact, on all fours with this case. Sealy licensed manufacturers of mattresses and bedding to make and sell products using the Sealy trademark. Like Topco, Sealy was a corporation owned almost entirely by its licensees, who elected the Board of Directors and controlled the business. Just as in this case, Sealy agreed with the licensees not to license other manufacturers or sellers to sell Sealy-brand products in a designated territory in exchange for the promise of the licensee who sold in that territory not to expand its sales beyond the area demarcated by Sealy. The Court held that this was a horizontal territorial restraint, which was *per se* violative of the Sherman Act.[76]

Whether or not we would decide this case the same way under the rule of reason used by the District Court is irrelevant to the issue before us. The fact is that courts are of limited utility in examining difficult economic problems.[77] Our inability to weigh, in any meaningful sense, destruction of competition in one sector of the economy against promotion of competition in another sector is one important reason we have formulated *per se* rules.

In applying these rigid rules, the Court has consistently rejected the notion that naked restraints of trade are to be tolerated because they are well intended or because they are allegedly developed to increase competition.

Antitrust laws in general, and the Sherman Act in particular, are the Magna Carta of free enterprise. They are as important to the preservation of economic freedom and our free-enterprise system as the Bill of Rights is to the protection of our fundamental personal freedoms. And the freedom guaranteed each and every business, no matter how small, is the freedom to compete—to assert with vigor, imagination, devotion, and ingenuity whatever economic muscle it can muster. Implicit in such freedom is the notion that it cannot be foreclosed with respect to one sector of the economy because certain pri-

---

76. [Court's footnote 9.] It is true that in *Sealy* the Court dealt with price fixing as well as territorial restrictions. To the extent that *Sealy* casts doubt on whether horizontal territorial limitations, unaccompanied by price fixing, are *per se* violations of the Sherman Act, we remove that doubt today.

77. [Court's footnote 10.] There has been much recent commentary on the wisdom of *per se* rules. See, e.g., Comment, Horizontal Territorial Restraints and the Per Se Rule, 28 Wash. & Lee L.Rev. 457 (1971); Averill, Sealy, Schwinn and Sherman One: An Analysis and Prognosis, 15 N.Y.L.F. 39 (1969); Note, Selected Antitrust Problems of the Franchisor: Exclusive Arrangements, Territorial Restrictions, and Franchise Termination, 22 U.Fla.L.Rev. 260, 286

(1969); Sadd, Antitrust Symposium: Territorial and Customer Restrictions After Sealy and Schwinn, 38 U.Cin.L.Rev. 249, 252–253 (1969); Bork, The Rule of Reason and the Per Se Concept, pt. 1, Price Fixing and Market Division, 74 Yale L.J. 775 (1965).

Without the *per se* rules, businessmen would be left with little to aid them in predicting in any particular case what courts will find to be legal and illegal under the Sherman Act. Should Congress ultimately determine that predictability is unimportant in this area of the law, it can, of course, make *per se* rules inapplicable in some or all cases, and leave courts free to ramble through the wilds of economic theory in order to maintain a flexible approach.

vate citizens or groups believe that such foreclosure might promote greater competition in a more important sector of the economy.

The District Court determined that by limiting the freedom of its individual members to compete with each other, Topco was doing a greater good by fostering competition between members and other large supermarket chains. But, the fallacy in this is that Topco has no authority under the Sherman Act to determine the respective values of competition in various sectors of the economy. On the contrary, the Sherman Act gives to each Topco member and to each prospective member the right to ascertain for itself whether or not competition with other supermarket chains is more desirable than competition in the sale of Topco-brand products. Without territorial restrictions, Topco members may indeed "[cut] each other's throats." But we have never found this possibility sufficient to warrant condoning horizontal restraints of trade.

The Court has previously noted with respect to price fixing, another *per se* violation of the Sherman Act, that:

> "The reasonable price fixed today may through economic and business changes become the unreasonable price of to-morrow. Once established, it may be maintained unchanged because of the absence of competition secured by the agreement for a price reasonable when fixed." United States v. Trenton Potteries Co., 273 U.S. 392, 397, 47 S.Ct. 377, 379, 71 L.Ed. 700 (1927).

A similar observation can be made with regard to territorial limitations.

There have been tremendous departures from the notion of a free-enterprise system as it was originally conceived in this country. These departures have been the product of congressional action and the will of the people. If a decision is to be made to sacrifice competition in one portion of the economy for greater competition in another portion this too is a decision that must be made by Congress and not by private forces or by the courts. Private forces are too keenly aware of their own interests in making such decisions and courts are ill-equipped and ill-situated for such decisionmaking. To analyze, interpret, and evaluate the myriad of competing interests and the endless data that would surely be brought to bear on such decisions, and to make the delicate judgment on the relative values to society of competitive areas of the economy, the judgment of the elected representatives of the people is required.

Just as the territorial restrictions on retailing Topco-brand products must fall, so must the territorial restrictions on wholesaling. The considerations are the same, and the Sherman Act requires identical results.

We also strike down Topco's other restrictions on the right of its members to wholesale goods. These restrictions amount to regulation of the customers to whom members of Topco may sell Topco-brand goods. Like territorial restrictions, limitations on customers are intended to limit intra-brand competition and to promote interbrand competition. For the reasons previously discussed, the arena in which Topco members compete must be left to their unfettered choice absent a contrary congressional determination.

We reverse the judgment of the District Court and remand the case for entry of an appropriate decree.

It is so ordered.

Reversed and remanded.

MR. JUSTICE POWELL and MR. JUSTICE REHNQUIST took no part in the consideration or decision of this case.

MR. JUSTICE BLACKMUN, concurring in the result.

The conclusion the Court reaches has its anomalous aspects, for surely, as the District Court's findings make clear, today's decision in the Government's favor will tend to stultify Topco members' competition with the great and larger chains. The bigs, therefore, should find it easier to get bigger and, as a consequence, reality seems at odds with the public interest. The *per se* rule, however, now appears to be so firmly established by the Court that, at this late date, I could not oppose it. Relief, if any is to be forthcoming, apparently must be by way of legislation.

[Mr. Chief Justice Burger in a dissenting opinion argued that the Court was creating a new *per se* rule in circumstances which required the use of the rule of reason.]

NOTES AND QUERIES

(1) *The Analytical Process in Horizontal Division of Market Cases.* As with horizontal price fixing, the *per se* status of market division arrangements is routinely stated but difficult to apply in the cases which are litigated. Conduct labeled a *per se* unlawful market division can include agreements dividing territories as in *Addyston Pipe & Steel* and *Topco*,[78] agreements dividing customers as in *Consolidated Laundries* (supra Chap. II),[79] or agreements dividing the manufacture or sale of certain goods or services.[80] Identification of the conduct can include extensive dispute over the presence of an agreement sufficient for Section 1 purposes (discussed infra Section D) and whether the agreement is horizontal or vertical (see note 2, infra).

The *Gypsum* case requirement for criminal cases—proving that the joint conduct was "undertaken with knowledge of its probable consequences" and

78. See also Gainesville Utilities Department v. Florida Power & Light Co., 573 F.2d 292 (5th Cir. 1978), certiorari denied 439 U.S. 966, 99 S.Ct. 454, 58 L.Ed. 2d 424 (division of markets in regulated utility business violates Sherman Act; not sanctioned by regulatory authorities); Community Builders, Inc. v. City of Phoenix, 652 F.2d 823 (9th Cir. 1981) (division of markets in municipal water supply business exempt state action).

79. See also United States v. Cadillac Overall Supply Co., 568 F.2d 1078 (5th Cir. 1978); United States v. Flom, 558 F.2d 1179 (5th Cir. 1977).

80. See Hartford Empire Co. v. United States, 323 U.S. 386, 65 S.Ct. 373, 89 L.Ed. 322 (1945); Gough v. Rossmoor Corp., 487 F.2d 373 (9th Cir. 1973), complaint dismissed on other grounds 585 F.2d 381 (9th Cir. 1978), certiorari denied 440 U.S. 936, 99 S.Ct. 1280, 59 L.Ed.2d 494 (1979); Sport Shoe of Newark v. Ralph Libonate Co., 1981–2 Trade Cases ¶ 64,230 (D.Del.1981).

had the requisite anticompetitive effects—has also generated difficulties in defining the standard of proof in criminal market division cases.[81]   For example, in *United States v. Koppers Co., Inc.,*[82] defendants charged with dividing the Connecticut road tar business argued *Gypsum* required proof of specific intent and anticompetitive effects before a conviction could be entered.   The Court of Appeals rejected the argument, holding: "Where *per se* conduct is found, a finding of intent to conspire to commit the offense is sufficient; a requirement that intent go further and envision actual anti-competitive results would reopen the very questions of reasonableness which the *per se* rule is designed to avoid."[83]   In *United States v. Brighton Building & Maintenance Co.,*[84] a criminal case charging a horizontal conspiracy to divide customers, the Court of Appeals upheld conviction of the parties, stating: "[I]n order to convict it must be proved that defendants knowingly agreed or formed a combination or conspiracy for the purpose of rigging bids, and intentionally assisted in its furtherance."[85]

   Query: Are these holdings consistent with *Gypsum?*

   The issue of whether there is ever a justification or excuse for imposing horizontal market divisions does not often arise in the context of a defense to a clear cut agreement dividing markets, but as a contest over whether the restraint is horizontal or vertical.   (See note 2, infra.)   Many joint venture and boycott cases frequently have market division features, but are usually litigated as boycott cases (see Chapter 5, infra) or arise as Clayton Act § 7 cases testing the validity of a partial integration under the incipiency standard of that statute.[86]

   Queries: Does *Topco* raise an issue of identification of the conduct as a horizontal market division or an issue of whether there is any justification or excuse for a market division once it is shown?   Does it make any difference whether the Court analyzes the case under one issue or the other?

   (2) *Division of Markets—Horizontal or Vertical?*   Whether a restraint is characterized as horizontal or vertical may affect the decision to have a *per se* rule since the scope of the restraint is presumably broader where the restraint is horizontal than is the case with vertical restraints.   Vertical market restraints will be examined in Chapter 6, infra.   Some cases present a difficult question of identifying the restraint as horizontal or vertical.[87]   In one sense the restraint in *Topco* may be viewed as vertical since the joint activity of the chains which formed Topco created a new entity, an independent business of private brand labelling, and cooperative buying.   Why did the Court characterize the restraint as a horizontal restraint?   When should the Court give effect to the separate legal identity of organizations like Topco and categorize such restraints as vertical restraints?   What central goal of antitrust policy would be defeated by allowing Topco to enforce its territorial restraints?   Its customer restraints?   Is the rationale of *Topco* broader than that of *Socony-Vacuum?*

   81.   See United States v. Cadillac Overall Supply Co., supra n. 79; United States v. Flom, supra n. 79.

   82.   652 F.2d 290 (2d Cir. 1981), certiorari denied 454 U.S. 1083, 102 S.Ct. 639, 70 L.Ed.2d 617.

   83.   Id. at 296, n. 6.

   84.   598 F.2d 1101 (7th Cir. 1979), certiorari denied 444 U.S. 840, 100 S.Ct. 79, 62 L.Ed.2d 52.

   85.   Id. at 1106.

   86.   See Yamaha Motor Co. Ltd. v. Federal Trade Commission, 657 F.2d 971 (8th Cir. 1981) (joint venture dividing world markets for outboard marine motors struck down under Section 7 of the Clayton Act).

   87.   See United States v. Sealy, Inc., 388 U.S. 350, 87 S.Ct. 1847, 18 L.Ed.2d 1238 (1967).   Cf., United States v. Pan American World Airways, Inc., 371 U.S. 296, 83 S.Ct. 476, 9 L.Ed.2d 325 (1963).

In a number of cases, practices which may have started out as vertical or innocuous because of the wide geographic separation of the parties, gradually appear to become horizontal with the growth of the participants or saturation of the market by retailers or franchisees with exclusive territorial rights. Where the arrangement is clearly horizontal and entails an agreement not to invade another's territory or compete in price, the restraint is invariably struck down, despite its innocent origins, on a *per se* basis.[88] Partial integration of functions by formation of a joint venture as in *Topco* or allocation of exclusive territories from the top down, as is done in many franchise relationships, can lend a vertical hue to the arrangement. In such cases, would it make more sense to characterize the conduct as presumptively unlawful subject to justifications of objective and laudatory business reasons for the restraint, pro-competitive consequences, or achievement of efficiencies? Where cases characterize a market division as an "ancillary restraint" to some legitimate economic or business goal, is the result to treat the *per se* rule as an evidentiary presumption rather than a substantive rule? With Topco's sales in excess of $2.4 billion, is there any justification for the continued agreement of its members to refuse to compete in each other's territory in the sale of Topco brand goods?

(3) *Ancillary Restraints and Arrangements to Allocate Particular Markets or Business Among Participating Firms.* The common law doctrine that a contract for the sale of a business may include "reasonable" restraint of the seller's freedom to reengage in the same business in competition with the purchaser survives under the Sherman Act, at least in application to transactions of limited scope involving neither a purpose nor a tendency to impair competition generally in the relevant business or market.[89] But cf. *United States v. General Electric Co.*,[90] in which General Electric was convicted of conspiring with the German Krupp interests to restrain and monopolize trade in hard metal alloys by price-fixing, allocation of markets, and other devices. One detail of the scheme involved the elimination of Thomas Prosser & Sons, American competitors of G. E. formerly supplied by Krupp. G. E.'s subsidiary, Carboloy, purchased the assets and good will of Prosser for $300,000, of which $13,500 was for Prosser's inventory. The balance, payable in annual installments over seven years was contingent on Prosser's not competing with Carboloy. As to this transaction, the Chairman of the Board of Carboloy testified:

"Q. Wasn't that amount paid for the sole purpose of eliminating Thomas Prosser & Sons, Richard Prosser and Roger Prosser from competition with Carboloy in respect to hard metal compositions? A. Well, I don't know what the purpose would be. We settled this affair with Mr. Prosser in a manner satisfactory to him and in a manner satisfactory to us. The assets and good will and so forth that he could turn over to us were not very valuable to us. . . . Q. Isn't it a fact, Dr. Jeffries, that the remaining amount, that is the amount of $300,000, minus $13,500, covered no other consideration than Prosser's undertaking to refrain

88. See United States v. Sealy Inc., 388 U.S. 350, 87 S.Ct. 1847, 18 L.Ed.2d 1238 (1967); American Motor Inns, Inc. v. Holiday Inns, Inc., 521 F.2d 1230 (3d Cir. 1975); Sport Shoe of Newark v. Ralph Libonate, Inc., supra note 9.

89. See for example, Brett v. Ebel, 29 App.Div. 256, 51 N.Y.S. 573 (1898) (enforcing a shipbroker's covenant to re-

frain from engaging in the New York-Haiti shipping trade); John T. Stanley Co. v. Lagomarsino, 53 F.2d 112 (S.D. N.Y.1931); but cf. Norfolk Southern Bus Corp. v. Virginia Dare Transportation Co., 159 F.2d 306 (4th Cir. 1947), certiorari denied 331 U.S. 827, 67 S.Ct. 1349, 91 L.Ed. 1842.

90. 80 F.Supp. 989 (S.D.N.Y.1948).

from competition? A. Well, we got no other value out of the payments so far as I know, than that."

United States v. National Lead Co.,[91] and *Timken Roller Bearing Co. v. United States,*[92] rejected defense arguments that arrangements by which certain national markets were allocated to one or another of the participating firms were lawful because the restraints were merely ancillary to agreements for exchange of patent or trade mark rights. On the other hand, where two firms are engaged in different but related lines of business, and each owns patents useful in the other's field, it may be lawful for each to license the other with limitations that tend to confine each to his own field. See p. 1020, infra. "Agreements among competitors for market division should be and are treated like price control arrangements." Report of the Attorney General's National Committee to Study the Antitrust Laws 26 (1955).

Some academic commentary has picked up on the ancillary and non-ancillary distinction, arguing that only "naked" division of market agreements should be condemned on a *per se* basis.[93] Agreements dividing markets which are "ancillary" to some otherwise justifiable business objective, it is argued, should be measured on a rule of reason basis. Distinguishing the "naked" from the partially clothed and the "ancillary" from the "non-ancillary" is recognized as a difficult analytical task to be guided by the "efficiency" enhancing characteristics of the arrangement.[94] Queries: Is the "ancillary"—"non-ancillary" distinction a workable basis for distinguishing market divisions which ought to be condemned on a *per se* basis from those which should not? What other analytical approach would you suggest?

(4) *Injunctions Against Market Allocating Arrangements.* Where the court finds an illegal contract to pool or allocate markets, its decree may declare the contract unlawful and enjoin the parties from observing its restrictions. In addition, the parties may be directed affirmatively to seek markets which they have previously abjured. Thus an American participant in an international cartel has been ordered to use reasonable efforts to promote the sale of its products in the territories of its foreign co-conspirators, notwithstanding the possibility that the cartel agreement may be legal under the law of the other country so that the American firm might be sued for damages there. *Holophane Co. v. United States.*[95]

(5) *Relief in Topco; a Pyrrhic Victory?* On remand, the district court enjoined territorial exclusivity but explicitly sanctioned practices tending so strongly to restrain extraterritorial selling that the Department of Justice once more appealed to the Supreme Court on the inadequacy of the relief. This time the Supreme Court affirmed by an evenly divided vote.[96] Among practices explicitly permitted were: designation of areas of "prime responsibility", territorial limitation of trademark licenses, and arrangements by which an extraterritorial seller must compensate the prime-responsibility retailer for "goodwill" developed by the latter in its own territory.

91. 332 U.S. 319, 67 S.Ct. 1634, 91 L.Ed. 2077 (1947).

92. 341 U.S. 593, 71 S.Ct. 971, 95 L.Ed. 1199 (1951).

93. See Bork, supra n. 3; Louis, Restraints Ancillary to Joint Ventures and Licensing Agreements: Do *Sealy* and *Topco* Logically Survive *Sylvania* and *Broadcast Music?*, 66 Va.L.Rev. 879 (1980).

94. Id. For a glimpse of the complexities of employing the concept of "efficiency" in legal analysis, see Symposium on Efficiency As A Legal Concern, 8 Hofstra L.Rev. 485–972 (1980).

95. 352 U.S. 903, 77 S.Ct. 144, 1 L.Ed. 2d 114 (1956).

96. 414 U.S. 801, 94 S.Ct. 116, 38 L.Ed.2d 39 (1973) (affirmed by an equally divided Court).

D. "CONTRACT", "COMBINATION", "CONSPIRACY": THE REQUIRED MULTIPLICITY AND CONSENSUS

Section 1 of the Sherman Act, directed against "contract", "combination" or "conspiracy," is explicitly confined to multiparty arrangements. Unilateral action by an entrepreneur may in some cases "restrain" trade; if so, it is reachable only under the monopoly provisions of Section 2 of the Sherman Act or under special statutory provisions such as Sections 2 and 3 of the Clayton Act (discrimination among customers; exclusive dealing), or Section 5 of the Federal Trade Commission Act.[97]

Express agreements or conspiracies between competitors fixing prices, dividing markets or limiting production occur regularly but are seldom litigated fully because there is little room to deny the existence of an agreement or that the agreement is designed to achieve the prohibited result. These kinds of cases are quickly settled by a consent decree, nolo contendere plea or negotiated settlement of damage claims. Another class of cases may occasion an extended evidentiary controversy over the question of whether there was in fact a contract, combination, or conspiracy; or, whether the joint action was in purpose or effect the accomplishment of a category of *per se* illegal conduct. While this class of case may test the discovery and evidentiary rules followed by the courts, they usually do not test the outer boundaries of the legal meaning of "contract," "combination" or "conspiracy" for antitrust purposes.[98]

Those outer limits are tested by cases confronted with the question of who or what may be considered "persons" for purposes of the Sherman Act in the context of parent-subsidiary firms and by cases where it is claimed the displacement of the competitive process as the

97. But see Boise Cascade Corp. v. Federal Trade Commission, 637 F.2d 573 (9th Cir. 1980), refusing to enforce an F.T.C. cease and desist order against delivered pricing in the absence of evidence that the parallel use of a similar delivered pricing system had an anticompetitive effect. The Court's opinion casts doubt upon use of Section 5 to declare parallel business behavior unlawful absent proof of conspiracy or at least some evidence of an anticompetitive effect.

98. "It does not strain credulity that solemnized covenants to conspire are difficult to come by in any price fixing case. Plaintiffs have, nevertheless, unearthed damaging evidence from the mouths, or typewriters, of defendants' own employees.

. . .

"Without belaboring the point by citation of further examples, the record contains documents from which a reasonable jury could find that defendants and other softwood manufacturers were engaged in a conspiracy to fix prices in violation of section 1 of the Sherman Act. . . . The parallel pricing conduct clearly demonstrated in the record plus the numerous items of direct evidence of communication between high level personnel on pricing policy adequately support the jury's verdict."

In re Plywood Antitrust Litigation, 655 F.2d 627, 633–34 (5th Cir. 1981), certiorari granted sub nom. Weyerhaeuser Co. and Willamette Industries, Inc. v. Lyman Lamb Co., 456 U.S. 971, 102 S.Ct. 2232, 72 L.Ed.2d 844 (1982). The Court's opinion should be compared with Boise Cascade Corp. v. Federal Trade Commission, supra note 26, involving the same defendants and facts. The plywood opinion refused to apply collateral estoppel because the suit was under the Sherman Act, the record included specific evidence of joint action in addition to parallel business behavior, and the plaintiffs demonstrated anticompetitive effect through expert testimony.

mechanism for establishing price and allocating resources has occurred without agreement or even direct communication. The latter kind of case arises in oligopoly industries where a mutual awareness, interdependence and course of conduct can result in effects similar to outright agreements displacing the competitive process or lead to the quiet life of the monopolist. "Each firm recognizes that its best choice depends on the choices its rivals make. The firms are interdependent, and they are acutely conscious of it. Their decisions depend then upon the assumptions they make about rival decisions and reactions, and many alternative assumptions might be entertained." [99]

When the alternative assumptions entertained indicate industry behavior is having the effect of tampering with the competitive process, the legal meaning of "contract," "combination" or "conspiracy" can become the central question in determining whether the Sherman Act is applicable. There may be a purpose or effect of fixing or stabilizing prices, but in the absence of joint action amounting to the Sherman Act's concepts of "contract," "combination" or "conspiracy" there can be no violation of Section 1. On the other hand, these concepts take on special meanings in antitrust law, where the concepts are interpreted functionally in light of the goals of the statute—to maintain a competitive process as the rule of trade.

Division (1) of this subchapter deals with the question whether "contract or combination" includes uncoordinated adoption of parallel prices or other commercial policies by multiple entrepreneurs without provable negotiations among them. It will be seen that the courts have drawn the line against inferring agreement from the bare fact of conscious parallel action, but have been astute in finding an extra ingredient of centralized orchestration of policy which will carry parallel action over the line into the forbidden zone of implied contract and combination. The question arises, what changes, if any, should be made in the law to deal with the phenomenon of oligopolistic "parallel action without agreement."

Division (2) of the subchapter deals with the immunity from Section 1 which has been conferred on certain aggregations of entrepreneurs notwithstanding the undeniable existence of trade-restraining contracts among them. If the collaborating entrepreneurs can be conceptualized as being engaged in a "joint enterprise" distinct from the participants, as a corporation is distinct from its shareholders or a partnership is distinct from the partners, the multiparty aspect of the arrangement is sometimes disregarded for purposes of Section 1, especially if the arrangement is seen as having important rule-of-reason justifications. In such cases a question often arises whether the collaboration has employed restraints beyond those necessary for its operation as a joint enterprise, for example by coercing or boycotting non-participants.

99. F.M. Scherer, Industrial Market Structure and Economic Performance, 151 (2d Ed. 1980).

1. PRICE LEADERSHIP; PARALLEL ACTION

PRICE LEADERSHIP

Excerpt from Handler, A Study of the Construction and Enforcement of the
Federal Antitrust Laws, T.N.E.C. Mono. 38 (1941) pp. 40 et seq.[1]

Price leadership has supplanted the price-fixing agreement in many industries as the principal device by which prices are stabilized. Like direct price-fixing, the object and effect of the practice is the establishment of a noncompetitive market price. This end, however, is achieved without any agreement or understanding. The price announcement of one of the companies in the field, typically the dominant concern, or principal producer, is loyally followed by most of its competitors. The price leader sets the market price. It assumes the lead both in advancing and reducing prices. Administrative action of one seller, and not the competition among sellers and the higgling between buyer and seller, determines the market price.

Price leadership occurs primarily in industries in which there are but a limited number of sellers. It is not feasible in the atomistic industries in which there are numerous producers.

An agreement among competitors to sell at the price set by a member of the industry would be in clear contravention of the statute. Price leadership, however, is rarely encompassed by any agreement or understanding, but exists typically as the result of convention. Each producer waits for the announcement of the leader's price before publishing his own price. There need be no meetings, no discussions, no direct interchange of price information, no exchange of assurances, no commitments to adhere to any announced price for the practice to take root in an industry. In other words, all the ingredients of an agreement may be absent, or, if present, they may be so shrewdly concealed that discovery is virtually impossible.

If the leadership is to be followed, the price must be placed at a level which is attractive to the other companies in the field, or the leader must possess sufficient power to compel the observance of its prices by competitors fearful of reprisals.

Complete uniformity does not always exist; in many fields in which price leadership occurs there are occasional variations in the prices of competitors as well as secret "shading" and discrimination of price.

Price uniformity is the necessary consequence of price leadership, except when the leadership is partial or incomplete. If the leader's

1. See also F.M. Scherer, Industrial Market Structure and Economic Performance 151–266 (2d Ed. 1980); Administered Prices: A Compendium on Public Policy, Committee Print, Subcommittee on Antitrust and Monopoly, Senate Judiciary Committee, 88th Cong. 1st Sess. (1963); Hearings on Administered Prices, Subcommittee on Antitrust and Monopoly, Senate Judiciary Committee, 85th Cong. 2d Sess. (1957–8); Auerbach, Administered Prices and Concentration of Economic Power, 47 Minn.L.Rev. 139 (1962); Blair, Administered Prices: A Phenomenon in Search of a Theory, 46 Am.Econ.Rev. 431 (1959).

prices are stationary, the price structure of the industry tends to become rigid. Fluctuations in the leader's price provide only that degree of flexibility which the leader is prepared to vouchsafe the industry. It is not the flexibility which results from the individual responses of buyers and sellers in an unrestrained market and through which supply may be equated with demand. It is a controlled flexibility, which may or may not harmonize with changes in the general price level. Dictation, and not competition, determines price, despite the fact that the followers may be free from the compulsions of an agreement or economic pressure.

Price dictatorships, like other forms of despotism, may be benevolent as well as tyrannical. It is not inconceivable that the controlled price of an enlightened leader may be economically more satisfactory than the haphazard price produced by the blind forces of competition. Such theoretical possibilities, however, did not deter the Supreme Court from forbidding price-fixing agreements, whether reasonable or not. They are entitled to no greater weight in appraising the desirability of price leadership. Private, noncompetitive price-making which is not subject to any effective checks and balances, can in the long run only be detrimental to the public. Price-making is too important a function to be entrusted to the uncontrolled discretion of a single concern or a group acting in concert.

Price leadership and price-fixing are both subject to the same economic and administrative objections. The price set by the leader tends to be sufficiently high to permit the continuance in business of the high-cost, inefficient producers. It exacts a toll from the unorganized purchaser. It lacks the flexibility and resiliency necessary to mitigate cyclical economic disturbances. It destroys the capacity of the business system to adjust itself quickly and effectively to changes in business conditions. It increases the economic pressure on uncontrolled prices and thus unbalances the entire price structure. It unstabilizes production and reduces the opportunities for gainful employment. The sole advantage of leadership is that it may avoid wasteful price wars.

The only difference between direct price-fixing and price leadership is that group control of prices is achieved by agreement in the one case and by convention in the other. If the consequences of a noncompetitive price are evil when established by agreement, they are equally harmful when effected through the tacit acceptance of a leader's price. Unfortunately, the prohibitions of the Sherman Law are limited to the restraints of trade accomplished by contract or combination and do not extend to practices equally reprehensible which do not involve the element of agreement.

Leadership is not limited to price but may relate to production, distribution, and other commercial policies. What is said in the present section about price leadership applies equally to other forms of business leadership. . . .

The prevalence of price leadership reveals the fundamental weakness in the Sherman Act. A law which prohibits merely the means by which evil consequences are engendered rather than the consequences themselves provides an easy avenue of escape. The prohibitions of the Sherman law are directed against the elimination of competition by agreement or understanding. The act is powerless to prevent the elimination of competition by other means. Uniform price and production policies can be pursued without resort to any prohibited agreement. Understandings, if there be any, can be concealed and remain virtually incapable of detection.

Leadership, of course, is not possible in all industries. It is most effective in those industries in which there is concentrated economic power, in which competition is already attenuated. It is thus chiefly used in areas of business life in which the need for competition is most urgent. No believer in a free competitive order will deny the desirability of preventing price leadership from being utilized as a device to eliminate price competition in our concentrated industries. The difficulty is in devising ways and means of doing so.

An outright prohibition of price leadership as such is not feasible. Where leadership is not accomplished by agreement, what would be the precise conduct to be forbidden? Businessmen must be left free to meet the competition of their rivals and this may involve the duplication of another's prices. Where an industry is ordered to abandon price leadership, what in practice must it do to comply with the order? The leader must be permitted to announce its price at some time even though it is no longer the first to publish a price change. Its action may still be followed. The dictates of business judgment may require some adherence by the smaller companies to the price schedule of the dominant concern in the industry. An order directed against an agreement is objective and is capable of enforcement and compliance. Any prohibition of price leadership can only be effective if it is directed against conduct which is similarly objective.

NOTES

(1) *Proof of Contract, Combination, or Conspiracy and Economic Theories of Oligopoly Pricing.* "Economists have developed a multiplicity of oligopoly pricing theories—some simple, some marvels of mathematical complexity. This proliferation of theories is mirrored by an equally rich array of behavioral patterns actually observed under oligopoly. Casual observation suggests that virtually anything can happen. Some oligopolistic industries appear to maintain prices approximating those a pure monopolist would find most profitable. Others gravitate toward price warfare." [2]

For the economist, sorting out when it is appropriate to conclude oligopoly behavior constitutes price fixing is primarily a question of measuring industry performance and the degree it departs from the competitive norm. While economic models may assist the law in identifying the effect of price fixing in oligopoly industries, proof of a Section 1 violation also requires evidence of a contract, combination or conspiracy effectuating price fixing or price stabilization. The latter question is dependent upon the standards giving legal meaning to the concepts of "contract," "combination" or "conspiracy." Identification of the requisite degree of collaborative activity may re-

2. Scherer, supra note 28.

quire considerable evidence of the characteristics of the product and industry involved, the purpose of individual firm behavior, and the overall effect of firm and industry behavior. Cases like *United States v. Container Corp.*[3] appear to make the agreement element of the offense a subsidiary concern where the effect of industry structure and behavior clearly establish anticompetitive effect.

(2) *Other Factors Justifying a Finding of "Contract", "Combination" or "Conspiracy"*. Cases like *Container* and *Gypsum* find the requisite contract justifying application of Section 1 in the exchange of specific price information with the expectation of a reciprocal exchange of price information upon request.[4] Drawing a line between procompetitive and anticompetitive pricing practices in oligopoly industries on this basis has provoked considerable debate. One view suggests that anticompetitive pricing consequences are inherent in oligopoly industries and should be viewed as a structural problem requiring a structural remedy.[5] A second view suggests that not all oligopoly industries behave in an anticompetitive manner; indeed it is rational to assume many are competitive, and in some circumstances knowledge of and matching a competitor's price is an expression of healthy competition, not a subversion of it. Separating the bad from the good oligopoly can be done by inferring that there is an agreement from economic indicia of collusion: *viz.*, fixed relative market share, systematic price discrimination, exchanges of price information, identical bids, regional price variations, abnormal profits and the like.[6] Still another view would infer agreement from a complex set of economic assumptions about efficient industry performance as opposed to observed industry performance.[7] While each proposal recognizes industry structure can lead to parallel behavior having anticompetitive effects, each differs over the degree to which it may be assumed an oligopoly structure justifies a necessary belief of anticompetitive effects, the appropriate way to identify those effects, and the degree to which economic effect measured by a particular abstract model justifies inferring contract, combination or conspiracy.[8] The legal issue of the meaning of "contract", "combination" and "conspiracy" and the character and sufficiency of the evidence to prove it, therefore, derive conflicting signals from academic speculation over the implications of concentrated industries.[9]

3. Supra page 396.

4. For an analysis supporting this approach and urging a wider use of it, see Note, Antitrust Liability For an Exchange of Price Information—What Happened to *Container Corporation?*, 63 Va.L.Rev. 639 (1977). See also Note, The No-Conduct Approach to Monopoly Power and Its Application to Oligopoly, 15 Valparaiso U.L.Rev. 529 (1981) (exploring the use of Section 2 on a "no-conduct" basis for dealing with oligopoly industries); Comment, The Creation of a Separate Rule of Reason: Antitrust Liability For the Exchange of Price Information Among Competitors, 1979 Duke L.J. 1004 (1979) (advocating a rule of reason approach in cases like *Container* and *Gypsum*).

5. Turner, The Definition of Agreement Under the Sherman Act: Conscious Parallelism and Refusals to Deal, 75 Harv.L.Rev. 655 (1962).

6. Posner, Oligopoly and the Antitrust Laws: A Suggested Approach, 21 Stan.L.Rev. 1562 (1969).

7. Markovits, Oligopolistic Pricing Suits, the Sherman Act, and Economic Welfare, 26 Stan.L.Rev. 493 (1974); 26 Stan.L.Rev. 717 (1974); 27 Stan.L.Rev. 307 (1975); 28 Stan.L.Rev. 1 (1975).

8. See Posner, Oligopolistic Pricing Suits, the Sherman Act, and Economic Welfare, 28 Stan.L.Rev. 903 (1976); Spence, Markovits on Imperfect Competition, 28 Stan.L.Rev. 915 (1976); Markovits, A Response to Professor Posner, 28 Stan.L.Rev. 919 (1976).

9. See Brodley, Oligopoly Power Under the Sherman and Clayton Acts—From Economic Theory to Legal Policy, 19 Stan.L.Rev. 285 (1967).

SOLUTIONS TO THE PROBLEM OF OLIGOPOLISTIC PARALLEL ACTION

A wide range of solutions have been suggested to resolve the problems of leadership and parallel market action. Proposals range from government regulation of prices that would otherwise be "administered" oligopolistically to a radical program of deconcentration. Full government regulation would eliminate price leadership but would effectively substitute one administered price for another. Few opt for this solution in view of the high administrative costs of regulation and the poor record of such programs in maintaining rational cost-related prices. Deconcentration of oligopolistic industries might solve the problem of price leadership, since an industry without dominant firms will be unable to maintain parallel market behavior without agreement. The costs of deconcentration may be high, a lively topic of debate among economists, but those who view concentration in industry as responsible for numerous detrimental effects aside from parallel pricing view this solution with favor. Neither regulation nor a radical deconcentration program has been attempted yet, but a number of intermediate solutions have been tried.

1. *"Conscious Parallel Action" Equated With "Agreement."* [10] Proof of conspiracy does not require a showing that an express agreement among the conspirators was concluded. It is sufficient if the existence of a tacit, mutual understanding to restrain trade is proved. The prosecution in such cases often relies upon circumstantial evidence and the inference drawn from the striking similarity of defendants' business policies, a resemblance that exceeds what could be expected absent some element of coordination. Any indication of intentional orchestration of the group's behavior may suffice.

---

10. Cf. Turner, The Definition of Agreement under the Sherman Act, 75 Harv.L.Rev. 655 (1962), arguing that the concept "agreement" should include all interdependent decisions in oligopolistic industries, thus bringing within Section 1 of the Sherman Act the question of reasonableness of all concerted practices. Turner would have excluded price leadership from his proposition because of the difficulty of devising an effective administrable remedy. Cf. Givens, Parallel Business Conditions under the Sherman Act, 5 Antitrust Bull. 273 (1960), arguing for judicial review of the reasonableness of parallel practices, even on prices, without criminal sanctions.

Legal regimes which contemplate affirmative official intervention to control excessive prices or other abuse of concentrated economic power do not hesitate to extend official jurisdiction to non-conspiratorial concert of action. Article 85(1) of the Rome Treaty establishing the European Economic Community applies to "all agreements among enterprises

. . . and all concerted practices". Imperial Chemical Industries Ltd. v. Commission of the European Communities ("Dyestuffs Case"), Court of Justice of the European Communities, July 14, 1972, CCH Common Market Reports, 9/12/72, ¶ 8161, sustained a price-fixing fine on the basis of concerted, but not demonstrably conspiratorial, price increases. The case is also important for sustaining the Commission's jurisdiction against ICI, despite international law objections against "extraterritorial" application of Community law, upon a showing that ICI's continental subsidiary was obeying pricing orders issued by the parent in England.

See also Monopolies and Restrictive Practices Act, 1948, 11 & 12 Geo. 6, c. 66, which covers situations where control is "by two or more persons who, whether voluntarily or not, and whether by agreement or arrangement or not, so conduct their respective affairs as in any way to prevent or restrict competition."

In INTERSTATE CIRCUIT, INC. v. UNITED STATES, [11] the dominant moving picture distributors were held to have conspired with Interstate, a powerful chain of Texas first-run theaters, to compel second-run theaters to charge higher admission and to abandon double-features. Interstate had put its demands in identical letters sent simultaneously to all distributors, each letter naming all the distributors as addressees. After individual negotiations, each distributor yielded substantially to the Interstate demands, although there were some differences in the agreements reached. There was no direct evidence of consultation among the distributors, but the Court adverted to the fact that national officers of the distributors had not been summoned to testify against the possibility of high level conferences. Mr. Justice Stone:

. . . The O'Donnell letter named on its face as addressees the eight local representatives of the distributors, and so from the beginning each of the distributors knew that the proposals were under consideration by the others. Each was aware that all were in active competition and that without substantially unanimous action with respect to the restrictions for any given territory there was risk of a substantial loss of the business and good will of the subsequent-run and independent exhibitors, but that with it there was the prospect of increased profits. There was, therefore, strong motive for concerted action, full advantage of which was taken by Interstate and Consolidated in presenting their demands to all in a single document. . . .

While the District Court's finding of an agreement of the distributors among themselves is supported by the evidence, we think that in the circumstances of this case such agreement for the imposition of the restrictions upon subsequent-run exhibitors was not a prerequisite to an unlawful conspiracy. It was enough that, knowing that concerted action was contemplated and invited, the distributors gave their adherence to the scheme and participated in it. Each distributor was advised that the others were asked to participate; each knew that cooperation was essential to successful operation of the plan. They knew that the plan, if carried out, would result in a restraint of commerce, which, we will presently point out, was unreasonable within the meaning of the Sherman Act, and knowing it, all participated in the plan. The evidence is persuasive that each distributor early became aware that the others had joined. With that knowledge they renewed the arrangement and carried it into effect for the two successive years.

It is elementary that an unlawful conspiracy may be and often is formed without simultaneous action or agreement on the part of the conspirators. Acceptance by competitors, without previous agreement, of an invitation to participate in a plan, the necessary consequence of which, if carried out, is restraint of interstate com-

11.   306 U.S. 208, 59 S.Ct. 467, 83 L.Ed. 610 (1939).

merce, is sufficient to establish an unlawful conspiracy under the Sherman Act.[12]

If distributors, each trying to achieve for their own product a maximum share of exhibition business, know that all of them will have to meet the best terms offered by any one of them, is their common response to Interstate's demands evidence of competition or monopoly? Is this a business where "uniformity" of the product must lead to identical prices and terms in a competitive market? If joint action by the licensors be regarded as monopolistic rather than competitive, can it be justified as necessary to meet the monopolistic power of Interstate?

With the *Interstate* case, compare THEATRE ENTERPRISES v. PARAMOUNT FILM DISTRIBUTING CORP.,[13] affirming a verdict for defendants in a treble damage action, and declaring: "Circumstantial evidence of consciously parallel behavior may have made heavy inroads into the traditional judicial attitude toward conspiracy, but 'conscious parallelism' has not yet read conspiracy out of the Sherman Act entirely."

There are of course limitations on the Government's ability to prove agreement by inference from behavior. As in other situations, the defendant must be permitted to rebut the Government's proof. In CONTINENTAL BAKING CO. v. UNITED STATES,[14] a conviction of price conspiracy was reversed where defendants were not permitted to introduce evidence of common market factors to explain price uniformity. The lower court had considered the evidence immaterial once there was proof that the competitors had met and discussed price policies. Pevely Dairy Co. v. United States,[15] reversed the conviction of two companies for conspiring to fix wholesale and retail prices of milk in the St. Louis area. There was some evidence of actual consultation between the defendants regarding prices, but the conviction rested heavily on the record of uniform and approximately simultaneous price movements. A divided Court of Appeals held this insufficient to prove conspiracy where the companies were required by federal regulation to pay the same prices to farmers for raw milk, labor costs were standardized by union contracts, and the product sold was standardized by local health ordinances.[16]

12. Id. at 222–227, 59 S.Ct., at 472–474, 83 L.Ed., at 618–620. Litigation over the distribution practices of film producers still continues and still raises similar conspiracy issues. See Wilder Enterprises, Inc. v. Allied Pictures Corp., 632 F.2d 1135 (4th Cir. 1980).

13. 346 U.S. 537, 74 S.Ct. 257, 98 L.Ed. 273 (1954).

14. 281 F.2d 137 (6th Cir. 1960).

15. 178 F.2d 363 (8th Cir. 1949), certiorari denied 339 U.S. 942, 70 S.Ct. 794, 94 L.Ed. 1358 (1950).

16. Prosecutions were dismissed in parallel pricing cases in United States v. General Motors Corp., 369 F.Supp. 1306

(E.D.Mich.1974); United States v. Arkansas Fuel Corp., CCH Trade Reg. Rep. ¶ 69,619 (D.Okl.1960) (common reaction of major oil companies to Suez crisis); United States v. Eli Lilly & Co., 24 F.R.D. 285 (D.N.J.1959) (Salk Vaccine case in which defendant drug companies explained price rigidity as resulting from provision in public procurement contracts giving the Government the benefit of any price concession made to any customer).

Several private damage cases have also refused to infer agreement from parallel business behavior standing alone. See Syufy Enterprises v. National General Theatres, Inc., 575 F.2d 233 (9th Cir. 1978), certiorari denied 439 U.S. 954, 99

It is generally held that parallel business behavior, standing alone and subject to various competitive or neutral explanations, is not sufficient to overcome a defendant's denial of conspiracy. In the absence of some additional "plus" indicating a conspiracy to achieve an unlawful end as the reasonably probable explanation for the parallel behavior, the evidence is insufficient to present a question of fact for the jury.[17]

These cases should be contrasted with a line of cases holding that a contract, combination, or conspiracy may be inferred from an *unexplained* parallel course of behavior in circumstances where it is reasonable to require an explanation for the parallel behavior. In *Bogosian v. Gulf Oil Corp.*,[18] the plaintiffs charged several major oil companies with a "course of interdependent consciously parallel action" amounting to an unlawful "combination" with the purpose of tying the sale of gasoline by branded retailers to short term gasoline station leases and franchises. The trial court dismissed the complaint for failure to allege a "combination" or "conspiracy." In reversing dismissal of the complaint, the Court of Appeals held allegations of an unlawful "combination" were sufficient for notice pleading purposes and that the concept of "combination" is interchangeable with the concepts of "contract" or "conspiracy." The Court went on to observe:

> The law is settled that proof of consciously parallel business behavior is circumstantial evidence from which an agreement, tacit or express, can be inferred but that such evidence, without more, is insufficient unless the circumstances under which it occurred make the inference of rational, independent choice less attractive than that of concerted action. We recently articulated those circumstances in *Venzie Corp. v. United States Mineral Products Co.*, 521 F.2d 1309 (3d Cir. 1975):
>
>> "(1) a showing of acts by defendants in contradiction of their own economic interests . . . ; and
>>
>> "(2) satisfactory demonstration of a motivation to enter an agreement . . ."
>
> *Id.* at 1314 . . . .

Plaintiffs argue that, given an opportunity to conduct discovery, they will prove that both of these circumstances are present. They contend that independent self interest would indicate that each oil company seek to market gasoline to their competitors' les-

S.Ct. 352, 58 L.Ed.2d 345; Kreager v. General Electric Co., 497 F.2d 468 (2d Cir. 1974), certiorari denied 419 U.S. 861, 95 S.Ct. 111, 42 L.Ed.2d 95, rehearing denied 419 U.S. 1041, 42 L.Ed.2d 319, 95 S.Ct. 530.

17. See First National Bank of Arizona v. Cities Service Co., 391 U.S. 253, 88 S.Ct. 1575, 20 L.Ed.2d 569 (1968); Weit v. Continental Illinois National Bank & Trust Co., 641 F.2d 457 (7th Cir. 1981),

certiorari denied 455 U.S. 988, 102 S.Ct. 1610, 71 L.Ed.2d 847 (1982). See also Boise Cascade Corp. v. Federal Trade Commission infra p. 517. (Parallel business behavior without proof of anticompetitive effect insufficient to uphold cease and desist order against delivered pricing practice).

18. 561 F.2d 434 (3d Cir. 1977), certiorari denied 434 U.S. 1086, 98 S.Ct. 1280, 55 L.Ed.2d 791 (1978).

sees, and that the failure to so compete can be explained only by a mutual understanding, tacit or expressed, that gasoline be marketed to lessee-dealers on an exclusive basis. The motivation to participate in such an agreement, of course, is the elimination of price competition among oil companies at the wholesale level. We need not, at this time, consider whether this theory would necessarily carry the day, for we are satisfied that, at the least, it does not appear to a certainty that plaintiffs can prove no set of facts which under *Venzie* would entitle them to reach the jury. . . .

The detailed statement of parallel lease provisions contained in plaintiffs' complaint which are alleged to be the product of an unlawful combination clearly meets these requirements. It was not necessary for plaintiffs to plead the basis upon which that combination will be proven. The goals of efficient judicial administration are retarded, not advanced, when the pleadings are used as a battleground for legal skirmishes without the necessary factual development upon which to focus decision. We think it was error to conclude that the complaint failed to state a claim under Section 1.

Plaintiffs also contend that even if their complaints are construed not to allege a combination, that an allegation of interdependent consciously parallel action states a § 1 claim. Neither plaintiffs nor defendants offer a definition of interdependence, however. A situation of interdependence has been said to exist when, in a highly concentrated market, there is an awareness that, because of the limited number of sellers, any variation in price or price-related structures will necessarily have a demonstrable effect on the sales of others such that each firm bases its decisions, at least in part, on the anticipated reactions of the others to its initiative. . . .

If these theories are to be tested, it should be done on a fully developed factual record which probes the conflicting economic facts on which they are premised. The complaint is much too blunt an instrument with which to forge fundamental policies regarding the meaning of competition in concentrated industries. We conclude that the ruling that the specific allegation of interdependent consciously parallel action made here fails to state a claim should be vacated so that the issue can be decided, if necessary, after the relevant facts are fully developed.[19]

The uniform and unexplained granting of a 15% discount to major advertising agencies by several major publishers, while charging advertisers dealing directly with publishers the full rate, for many years after a consent decree enjoining an express agreement to do so, was found sufficient evidence of contract, combination or conspiracy to withstand a summary judgment motion in *Ambrook Enterprises v. Time, Inc.*[20] Relying on the *Bogosian* case, a majority of the Court

19.   561 F.2d at 446–47.

20.   612 F.2d 604 (2d Cir. 1979), certiorari dismissed pursuant to Rule 53, 448

U.S. 914, 101 S.Ct. 35, 65 L.Ed.2d 1179 (1980).

found the failure to explain the conduct in light of the past antitrust case and the benefit the practice conferred on advertising agencies provided a sufficient factual basis for allowing a fact finder to draw the inference of contract, combination or conspiracy.

It has also been argued that conscious parallel market behavior amounts to a "combination" under section 1 because ordinary rules of statutory interpretation require that some content be read into that term which is not encompassed by the terms "contract" and "conspire." [21]

2. *"Facilitating Devices" Triggering Enforcement Discretion.* The public announcement of an intention to initiate government suits or prosecutions under stated circumstances enumerating certain practices which will be viewed with suspicion when used in a concentrated industry can curb anticompetitive oligopoly pricing practices. Like taxpayers forewarned of I.R.S. policy to investigate closely certain categories of deductions, firms potentially subject to government antitrust litigation and the risk of treble damage suits following thereafter can be expected to heed warnings defining circumstances in which enforcement officials will bring suit.

In recognition of these realities, President Carter's antitrust chief made public a memo to enforcement personnel instructing them to give "highest priority" to investigations of the use of certain parallel pricing practices in concentrated industries.[22] Called "facilitating devices"[23] because they are practices thought to facilitate mutual cooperation in maintaining a non-competitive price structure in a concentrated industry,[24] the memo identified the practices as follows: the common adoption of a delivered pricing system or freight equalization practices;[25] common use of price books or other pricing formulas;[26] standardization of products;[27] standardization of credit or oth-

---

21. Note, "Combinations" in Restraint of Trade: A New Approach to Section 1 of the Sherman Act, 1966 Utah L.Rev. 75.

22. See J. Shennefield, Memorandum on Shared Monopolies, reprinted in 874 ATRR pp. F–1 (July 27, 1978).

23. See Kestenbaum, What Is "Price Signalling" and Does It Violate The Law?, 49 Antitrust L.J. 911 (1980).

24. The theory is well set forth and analyzed in F. M. Scherer, Industrial Market Structure and Economic Performance, pp. 151–295 (2d Ed. 1980); L. Sullivan, Antitrust, pp. 331–73 (1977). See also Blechman, Conscious Parallelism, Signalling and Facilitating Devices: The Problem of Tacit Collusion Under The Antitrust Laws, 24 N.Y.L.Sch.L.Rev. 881 (1979); Posner, Oligopoly And The Antitrust Laws: A Suggested Approach, 21 Stan.L.Rev. 1562 (1969); Turner, The Definition of Agreement Under The Sherman Act: Conscious Parallelism and Re-

fusals To Deal, 75 Harv.L.Rev. 655 (1962).

25. These are practices aimed at making transportation costs uniform, so that competitors end up charging a similar end price without regard to plant location vis-a-vis the customer. Individual decisions to absorb freight costs in order to compete in distant markets can be competitive; collusion to charge higher freight costs or absorb freight costs in order to stabilize or make uniform prices is anticompetitive. See Trade Association activities infra p. 500.

26. See United States v. General Electric Co., 1977–2 Trade Cases ¶ 61,659 (E.D.Pa.1977), discussed infra, p. 453.

27. See L. Sullivan, Antitrust, pp. 275–77 (1977); Hearings, Voluntary Industrial Standards—1976, Subcom. on Antitrust & Monop., U.S. Senate Judiciary Comm., 94th Cong., 1st & 2d Sess. (1975–76); Bakke, Joint Efforts In Developing Standards, 44 Antitrust L.J. 337

er terms of sale; [28] most favored nations agreements with customers or other forms of price protection; [29] and, exchanges or publication of price and transaction information.[30] The memo outlined four "evidentiary elements" which may be used in conjunction with proof of the uniform use of a "facilitating device" to prove the presence of an agreement in restraint of trade:

First, a parallel course of conduct by firms in a concentrated industry with respect to the adoption of, or adherence to, a business practice that may be used as a facilitating mechanism;

Second, an awareness by each firm that its rivals are following a parallel course with respect to the suspect practice;

Third, an anticompetitive benefit derived by each firm from this parallel course of conduct; and

Fourth, action contradictory to the independent self-interest of each firm, in that a single firm would not have adopted the practice unless it was also adopted by its major rivals.

It is important to note these elements operate as a whole and that proof of all four elements demonstrates both the existence of an 'agreement' and its operation as a restraint of trade.

Queries: After *Gypsum,* would proof that the prices in a concentrated industry have risen in a uniform manner for the past five years and parallel practices like an agreement to announce current prices to individual customers through an industry trade publication and the uniform adoption of similar credit terms be sufficient to sustain a criminal conviction for price fixing? [31] A finding of unlawful price fixing in a civil case seeking equitable relief? A finding of an unfair trade practice under § 5 of the F.T.C. Act? [32] A finding of violation in a treble damage action?

3. *Counteracting the Consequences of the "Unprovable" Conspiracy.* See Identical Bidding in Public Procurement, Tenth Report of the Attorney General under Exec. Order 19036 (1971). Procurement officers are required to report instances of identical bidding to the Attorney General. Tabulation of identical bids in the public procurement is an important source of civil and criminal actions instituted by the Department of Justice. (p. 20) Identical bidding declined

(1975); Note, Antitrust Problems of Trade Association Product Safety Standardization, 55 Iowa L.Rev. 439 (1969); Note, Promoting Product Quality Information: A Proposed Limited Antitrust Exemption For Producers, 30 Stan.L.Rev. 563 (1978).

28. See Catalano, Inc. v. Target Sales, Inc., supra page 388; cf. United States v. Citizens & Southern National Bank, 422 U.S. 86, 95 S.Ct. 2099, 45 L.Ed.2d 41 (1975).

29. See United States v. General Electric Co., infra p. 453.

30. See United States v. Container Corp., supra p. 396; United States v.

United States Gypsum Corp., supra p. 400.

31. Cf. United States v. Continental Group, Inc., 603 F.2d 444 (3d Cir. 1979), certiorari denied 444 U.S. 1032, 100 S.Ct. 703, 62 L.Ed.2d 668 (1980); United States v. Society of Independent Gasoline Marketers, 624 F.2d 461 (4th Cir. 1980); United States v. Foley, 598 F.2d 1323 (4th Cir. 1979), certiorari denied 444 U.S. 1043, 100 S.Ct. 727, 62 L.Ed.2d 728 (1980).

32. Cf., Boise Cascade Corp. v. Federal Trade Commission, supra note 26.

over the ten years of the reporting program from 2550 to 674. (p. 20) Petroleum and chemicals were top-ranking product categories for the occurrence of identical bids. (p. 12) As to the continuance of identical bidding by General Electric, Westinghouse, Allis-Chalmers, etc. in Federal Procurement Classification 6120 (transformers and power equipment), see p. 85. "Identical bidding" may be avoided by proposing non-identical ranges of prices for subdivisions of the contract, so that the contract is shared by the bidders, one prevailing on one part of the procurement, another bidder prevailing on a different part. See pp. 16, 18. Lottery or other non-price criteria govern the award in 25% of identical bid procurement. (p. 14) Preferential treatment of small business controlled 5% of the awards.

On the Government's supplemental efforts to break up bid matching by General Electric and Westinghouse, see p. 453 infra.

4. *Tax Incentives to Encourage Price Competition in Oligopolistic Industries.* In AMERICAN TOBACCO CO. v. UNITED STATES,[33] evidence of price leadership among the Big Three cigarette producers helped sustain the conviction of monopoly. Nicholls, Price Policies in the Cigarette Industry (1951), found that the major tobacco companies followed essentially the same price policies after the anti-trust case as before and that the Big Three had increased their combined share of the national production from 68 to 76 per cent. (p. 402) Although approving a program of dissolution of the dominant companies, Nicholls favored as remedial action: (1) a tax on advertising, at progressively higher rates for larger firms; and (2) reduction of the general level of excise taxes on cigarettes plus substitution of ad valorem for flat taxes. High flat taxes mean that a large component of the retail price is fixed by law. The relative significance of competitive price cuts is therefore minimized. Ad valorem taxation would offer an incentive to price competition since every cut in price would be matched by a tax reduction. See Ch. 29, Can the Cigarette Industry Be Made More Competitive?

5. *Public Exposure of Oligopoly Pricing Decisions to Discourage Excessive Prices.* Government action to expose oligopoly pricing is sometimes effective in restraining excessive price increases. The price setters respond to a number of factors including the fear of threatened investigation, the pressure of public opinion, and political pressure ranging from appeals to patriotism to explicit concessions in exchange for price restraint.

Professor J. K. Galbraith proposed that dominant firms in concentrated industries be required to give advance notice of intention to raise prices, so that legislative committees might investigate the propriety of the increase and focus public attention on the question, before the increase becomes effective.[34] S. 215, 86th Cong. 1st Sess.

---

33. 328 U.S. 781, 66 S.Ct. 1125, 90 L.Ed. 1575 (1946).

34. Hearings on Administered Prices, Subcommittee on Antitrust and Monopoly, Senate Committee on the Judiciary, 85th Cong. (1957–8). The Subcommit-

tee's Report on Administered Prices in the Steel Industry is S.Rep. 1387, 85th Cong., 2d Sess. (1958). The Subcommittee also issued reports on administered prices in automobiles, bread, and drugs. The report on drugs, S.Rep. 448, 87th

(1959) proposed to require price increase notifications of all corporations having capital, surplus, and undivided profits over $10,000,000, in any line of commerce where 50% or more of annual United States sales are made by eight or fewer corporations. Notice would be given to the Federal Trade Commission, the Attorney General, the Senate and the House. The FTC would hold a public hearing on the "justifiability of the proposed increase and . . . impact of such increase upon competition and the economy."

Public "investigation" of prices can be seen as an attempt at "control by persuasion":

> This new technique of regulation by legislative investigation aims to influence corporate policy by constantly reminding men who wield enormous power that they will somehow be held accountable. Its sanctions are the subpoena, with its personal inconvenience and possibility of embarrassing disclosures, adverse public opinion, the likelihood of stimulating regular law enforcement agencies to more active supervision, the prospect of political disfavor at other points where government impinges on business, e.g., taxation, tariffs, labor relations. It is regulation defined by no law and possibly inconsistent with traditional ideas of separation of powers. Its effectiveness cannot be measured. It exists because we have not found other practicable methods of dealing with aggregations of economic power which have grown beyond our normal controls.[35]

6. *Use of Section 2 Combination and Conspiracy to Monopolize Theories.* The Chapter 2 discussion of combination and conspiracy to monopolize theories presents another way to deal with oligopoly pricing practices. The *American Tobacco* case (supra p. 172) and the F.T.C.'s cereal case (supra p. 176) both alleged that parallel business practices in highly concentrated industries constituted conspiracies to monopolize. The resolution of both cases illustrates that the limitations of a Section 2 combination or conspiracy to monopolize theory for dealing with anticompetitive parallel business behavior in concentrated industries are the same as those encountered by a Section 1 theory: *viz.*, what factors in which circumstances will be found legally sufficient to prove the presence of a contract, combination or conspiracy? This central dilemma of oligopoly pricing cases, as well as the quandry of implementing an appropriate remedy where a violation is found, have been principal factors in generating legislative proposals like the Industrial Reorganization Act, reprinted supra, p. 176.[36]

Cong. 1st Sess. (1961) focuses on patent and promotional practices as instruments of oligopoly.

35. Schwartz, Administered Prices, Oligopoly and the Sherman Act, 12 ABA Antitrust Section Rep. 17, 26 (1958).

36. See also H. Goldschmid, H. M. Mann, & J. F. Weston (Eds.), Industrial Concentration: The New Learning, pp. 339–426 (1974); Note, The No-Conduct Approach to Monopoly Power and Its Application to Oligopoly, 15 Valparaiso U.L. Rev. 529 (1981).

NOTES AND QUERIES

(1) *Implying Agreement From Parallel Business Behavior and the Adequacy of Remedies.* It has been argued that certain forms of parallel business behavior, like price leadership, should not be made the basis for inferring an agreement under Section 1 because of the inadequacy of the usual Section 1 remedies.[37] Simply enjoining the conduct does not eliminate the root causes of the problem; *viz.,* an imperfection of market structure. Remedies short of restructuring the industry may either prove inadequate or require extensive supervision of all types of communication with customers or the world in general.

For example, relief in the *Container Corp.* case prohibited the exchange of current price quotes to specific customers or potential customers and discussions with competitors about prices "for the purpose or with the effect of inviting compatible or harmonious pricing practices or otherwise stabilizing prices. . . ." Over the objections of the Government, a prohibition upon the exchange of pricing manuals, price lists, or any similar pricing material used to compute prices was modified by the clause "unless such has been made generally available to the customers of the defendant to which such pricing material is applicable." [38]

The significance of the Government's objection to an exchange of pricing information, price books, and the like made known through dissemination to customers is illustrated by the further proceedings to modify the consent decrees entered in the famous electrical industry price fixing cases.[39] A government investigation uncovered evidence that G.E. and Westinghouse, one year after entry of the consent decrees in the civil cases arising out of the electrical equipment conspiracies, adopted and rigorously followed identical pricing policies in the pricing and bidding for sales of heavy electrical equipment. The trial court described the pricing policies and the effect of them as follows:

> In 1963 both General Electric and Westinghouse published similar and unusually extensive price books enabling each to predict not only the exact price that the other would bid in a particular situation, but also the precise type and size of the machine. Both companies also adopted a price protection plan which provided that if the price was lowered by a manufacturer for a particular customer, any buyer within the previous six month period would be given an identical discount retroactively. Thus, each manufacturer was assured that the other would not engage in discounting because of the substantial self-imposed penalty involved. Also, both companies published a list of outstanding bids whenever there was a price change so that there would be no confusion as to which customers were being charged the old rate and thus no suspicions of discounting would be aroused. These practices resulted in a pattern of equal pricing in the sale of large turbine generators and the government contends that contemporaneous internal documents indicate that this result was the deliberate intent of the defendants.[40]

37. See Turner, supra note 52.

38. United States v. Container Corp., 1970 Trade Cases ¶ 73,091 (D.N.C.1970).

39. See p. 335, supra.

40. United States v. General Electric Co., 1977–2 Trade Cases ¶ 61,659 (E.D. Pa.1977). The competitive impact statement appears in 42 Fed.Reg. 17004 (1977). The case is discussed in Epstein, Theory of Second-Best in Operation: A Comment on the 1977 Modification of the Electrical Equipment Consent Decrees, 22 Antitrust Bull. 503 (1977).

Under threat of a government price fixing suit, G.E. [41] and Westinghouse [42] agreed to a modification of the earlier consent decrees: *Public* statements of pricing policy and publication of outstanding quotations were restricted. Each manufacturer was prohibited from *examining* price-related documents which the other might legitimately supply to individual customers. The supplementary restraints were designed to cut off information from which either duopolist "might infer the pricing policy or strategy of the other."

Queries: Is this kind of remedy in the public interest? Are customers entitled to know what others in the industry are being charged for similar equipment? Is the root of the difficulty the failure to remedy a non-competitive industry structure and the stretching of Section 1 conspiracy doctrine to achieve some remedy in the absence of a viable means for restructuring the industry? [43] Should (do?) courts refuse to infer contract, combination or conspiracy in circumstances where the remedy is likely to be ineffective or inappropriate?

(2) *Presidents and Prices.* [44] On April 11, 1962, the U. S. Steel Corp. announced a price increase of $6 per ton, a move immediately followed by Bethlehem Steel and most other major producers. On April 12, President Kennedy denounced "a tiny handful of steel executives" for "wholly unjustifiable and irresponsible" action in pursuit of "private power and profit . . . utter contempt for the interests of 185 million Americans." The President was aroused because a wage agreement had just been negotiated between the steel industry and the steel workers in which the parties purported to exercise mutual restraint in compliance with the administration's anti-inflation policy. That policy was directed at keeping American goods competitive in the world market, stemming the adverse flow of international payments, and keeping down the costs of defense and foreign aid. The President's castigation was accompanied by threat of governmental countermeasures, including diversion of government purchase contracts away from the steel companies participating in the increase, unfavorable legislative action in pending tax relief bills, and grand jury and FTC investigation of possible violation of the antitrust laws. Attorney General Robert Kennedy's FBI agents were abroad at 3 A.M. serving subpoenas. Blough, President of U. S. Steel, defended the increase as non-collusive and necessary to finance efficient new plants to make the American industry "more competitive". Inland Steel and Kaiser Steel decided not to raise their prices, and on April 13, U. S. Steel, Bethlehem and the others rescinded the price increase. If Inland's refusal to go along required the others to back down, is this industry competitive? If public interest is to control steel pricing, are available legal mechanisms adequate and fair?

The story was repeated with minor variations in confrontations between President Johnson and the big metal producers in 1965.[45] Prospective increases in aluminum and copper prices believed to be inconsistent with "guidelines" approved by the President and his Council of Economic Advisers were forestalled by intimations that government stockpiles would be liq-

41. United States v. General Electric Co., 1977–2 Trade Cases ¶ 61,660 (E.D. Pa.1977).

42. United States v. Westinghouse Electric Corp., 1977–2 Trade Cases ¶ 61,662 (E.D.Pa.1977).

43. See Epstein, supra note 68.

44. See Sheahan, The Wage-Price Guideposts (1970); Schultz and Aliber, Guidelines, Informal Controls, and the Market Place (1966); Auerbach, Presidential Administration of Prices and Wages, 35 G.Wash.L.Rev. 191 (1966).

45. The account which follows is pieced together largely from the New York Times, Dec. 3, 1965 to Jan. 6, 1966. See also Time Magazine, Jan. 14, 1966, p. 77.

uidated to hold down prices. On December 31, Bethlehem Steel announced a $5 per ton increase on certain types of structural steel, of which Bethlehem was the leading producer (38%), attributing the increase to rising costs. On the same day Gardner Ackley, Chairman of the Council of Economic Advisers, denounced the increase as inflationary and "profiteering from the Vietnam war", pointing out that Bethlehem's profits had increased 83% in the preceding two years. President Johnson, in Texas, declared that the increase was unwarranted, and that it was "time to consider the larger national interest, to weigh the impact of unnecessary price action against the sacrifices of our men in Vietnam." Government sources insisted that labor costs *per ton* had actually fallen, due to increased mechanization, and that steel imports were rising to the detriment of our balance of payments. It was announced that the government, which buys 25% of structural steel, would shift its business to companies which refrained from following Bethlehem.

Time Magazine reported, Jan. 14, 1966, p. 77, that:

> Part of the Administration's pique, it developed, came from the fact that Bethlehem had not informed the White House in advance of its plans— though no law or custom yet dictates such action by U. S. businessmen.

Blough, President of U. S. Steel, was summoned to the White House to confer with the Secretary of the Treasury and the Secretary of Defense, after he had publicly stated that "Price increases cause inflation like wet sidewalks cause rain." It was reported that government spokesmen privately admitted that the specific increase was not significantly inflationary, but they insisted that the psychological effect of increases in bellwether steel prices would be intolerable. A compromise was reached. Blough agreed to hold the increase to $2.75 and at the same time to cut $9 per ton on cold rolled steel from Pittsburgh, California (cf. western basing point controversy referred to at p. 503 infra). Since Bethlehem's original proposal would, according to the accounts, have raised the country's steel bill by $1/4$ of 1%, and Ackley welcomed the settlement as adding only $1/10$ of 1%, the steel industry appeared to have achieved 40% of its target.

(3) *Informal Requirement of Notice of Price Increases.* The Wall Street Journal reported, Feb. 10, 1966, p. 3, that Professor Otto Eckstein, newly retired member of the Council of Economic Advisers, told a symposium of the U. S. Chamber of Commerce, "Businessmen should check out prospective price increases with the Administration to see if they square with its anti-inflationary "guideposts". He

> thus brought into the open what others in the Administration have been suggesting privately. Their aim is to squelch possible inflationary price increases without the strains and mutual embarrassment that accompany open clashes . . . the Commerce Department would be a logical point of contact for businessmen. The Council of Economic Advisers is certainly another possibility . . . Defending the concept, Mr. Eckstein said officials don't want to leave prices only to the market place because this didn't work out very well in the past. Despite the efforts of monetary and fiscal policy to influence the economy in the 1950s, he said, there was both inflation and slack in the economy. The guidepost concept, he said, focuses attention on the largest industries, and he argued that it is far from the Korean-war type system of direct price and wage controls. As the three-man council's chief guidepost specialist for the past few years, he said, he had only the part-time help of a handful of staff people, while in the Korean-war some 16,000 Federal employes sought to apply much more comprehensive control. The current approach, Mr. Eckstein said, is

far better than such alternatives as accepting inflation, choking off economic growth, breaking up large corporations to increase competition or applying controls.

Professor Arthur F. Burns, former economic adviser to President Eisenhower and Chairman of the Federal Reserve Board during the Nixon and Ford Administrations charged that while the guideposts restrain the prices of some large corporations the public is left free to spend the money thus saved "to bid up the prices of the thousand and one items that for one reason or another escape the scrutiny of Government officials . . ." Mr. Burns said the guideposts, while having no basis in law, have lost much of their voluntary character through Government actions that he called coercive, capricious, and discriminatory."

An Associated Press despatch of Feb. 28, 1966: "The President's Council of Economic Advisers said Monday U. S. Steel Corp. *plans* price adjustments that will amount to a two-tenths of one percent increase in the total price of steel." (Italics supplied). Chairman Ackley reviewed for the press the company's advance justification of the increase, particularly compensating decreases in some categories of steel prices.

(4) *Pitfalls of Informality.* Irwin M. Stelzer, The Current Regulatory Scene: Rules, Guideposts and Levers, address to the National Association of Business Economists, New York, May 19, 1967:

The Council [of Economic Advisors] notes, "Only in rare cases has the Council been told that it had no right to question private decisions." I think it is fair to state that this constitutes a form of price regulation very close to that which is characteristic of utility industries. The Council has objected to a price increase (i.e., filed a complaint); the companies have then "explained the reasons why a price increase was considered appropriate"; "the Government representatives [have then] presented any information available to them which appeared relevant to the price decision." This is, in all except the legal safeguards, a classic utility rate case.

There is, I think a real danger in abandoning those traditional legal procedures that are an integral part of true utility regulation. This is nowhere better demonstrated than in the recent asphalt price dispute. The Department of the Interior reportedly was considering relaxing import restrictions because of a 25-per-cent increase in prices for middle-layer seal and tacking asphalt in certain eastern states between 1965 and 1966. At this point an enterprising Wall Street Journal staff reporter decided to substitute for cross-examining counsel. [The Wall Street Journal, April 10, 1967, p. 9]. He checked with Interior, which repeated the 25-per-cent figure and suggested he check with the Office of Emergency Planning, from whence it came. The OEP man, having read press reports of the 25-per-cent figure, was reportedly "in a state of mild shock"; he pointed out that the 25-per-cent increase related to the price of asphalt "laid in place," and hence included labor and machinery cost increases. For further information the reporter was referred to the Bureau of Public Roads which had provided OEP with *its* figure. The Public Roads man was described as "apologetic." He had belatedly discovered that the 1966 laid-in-place price data he had used had been distorted by Vermont's reporting the prices paid for costlier asphalt-aggregate blends. Elimination of this Vermont error reduced the Public Roads' increase figure to 13.7 per cent. Whether elimination of labor cost and other irrelevant items contained in the laid-in-place figure would bring the 1965–66 increase to the one-percent level alleged to be fact by one oil company, I do not know. But we would all have a better chance of finding out if some formal method could be evolved for reviewing these matters.

As I have indicated, a data problem such as this would have been quickly uncovered in a competently-tried utility rate case in which legal safeguards protected the rights of the company. But I am reluctant to suggest that all non-utilities rush to Interior, the CEA and other agencies with demands that decision-making be made in a formal, utility fashion. Having participated in many rate cases, I do not recommend them to you as a forum within which *you* should seek to have your pricing decisions tested.

What then is the alternative? It seems to me that advance articulation of your pricing policy and compilation of the data required to analyze it are crucial. This would provide management with a quasi-regulatory "kit"—the equivalent of an affirmative "case." If it did nothing else, it would at least make available to the relevant government agencies accurate and meaningful price and other data. And such preparation might have the useful ancillary effect of causing management to reappraise some of the policies which may, upon articulation, appear not quite as sensible *from a business viewpoint* as they were thought to be.

(5) *The Decline of "Jawboning" and Advent of "Reaganomics".* Confrontation between the White House and business on pricing decisions began a noticeable decline in the 70's. The Carter Administration, pre-occupied by "stagflation", soaring energy prices and pressing international concerns, emphasized a policy of deregulation of such industries as airlines, surface transportation and oil and natural gas prices. A relatively activist antitrust enforcement program, consideration of proposals like "no conduct monopoly," (supra p. 176) and investigations of concentrated industries pursuant to "facilitating devices" theories of liability under Section 1 appeared to be the order of the day for dealing with oligopoly pricing in the economy.

The advent of the Reagan Administration has brought strict monetary controls, the claimed magic of "supply-side" economics through massive tax cuts and substantial budget cuts in social programs, and a significant reorientation of government responsibilities away from social programs and toward substantial increases in defense expenditures. Along with these significant shifts in macro-economic policy and re-definitions of the appropriate role of government in economic affairs has come a significant shift in antitrust enforcement policy. Instead of a general government concern and suspicion about pricing policies of powerful firms and parallel pricing practices in concentrated industries, *laissez faire* is the order of the day. Enforcement policy appears to be limited to prosecution of horizontal cartel arrangements and deregulation. Concerns about firm size are dismissed with the statement that "bigness is not necessarily bad"; concerns about economic concentration, vertical market restraints, conglomerate mergers and the like are generally dismissed by reference to the predictions of neo-classical economic theory suggesting that firm size and concentration levels are the result of "efficiencies" or economies of scale. In the absence of horizontal collusion, it is claimed, antitrust or other government intervention is counterproductive and destructive of natural market forces determining price, resource allocation, and innovation.

It is unlikely, therefore, that either Presidential confrontation or activist antitrust enforcement will be relied upon to deter parallel business behavior in concentrated industries under "Reaganomics." As with "supply-side" economics, monetarism, and the other significant changes of direction by the Reagan Administration, the wisdom of substantial and significant changes in antitrust enforcement policy must await the test of time and a growing chorus of dissent as to both the propriety and wisdom of the course chosen.

(5) *Queries.* According to the foregoing accounts, what non-profit considerations should enter into a businessman's price determinations? On these issues, what sort of documentation should we expect to find in the executive files of leading corporations as having been presented to their price-makers at the time of decision? How should the question of possibly desirable price *decreases* be handled?

2. JOINT ENTERPRISE AND INTRA–ENTERPRISE CONSPIRACY

Because the prohibitions of Section 1 of the Sherman Act run only against multi-party arrangements, the legality of a given arrangement may turn on whether the participants are to be regarded as constituting a single enterprise or a collaboration of several enterprises. The range of possibilities is wide. On the one hand, it would be possible to regard a league of football teams as a single enterprise engaged in presenting a spectacle consisting of a series of competitive games, culminating in championship matches, and requiring for success central control of scheduling, prices, broadcasts, and player relationships; and this despite the independence of ownership, investment, management, and profits of each team and the fierce competition between them within the framework of the league.[46] Twelve hundred newspapers, members of Associated Press, might be regarded as engaged in a single "joint enterprise" for collecting and disseminating national and international news.[47] On the other hand, the wholly-owned subsidiaries of a single parent corporation, carrying out identical operations in separate states or countries, or closely related operations in the same geographic area, certainly are distinct entities for many legal purposes and may be so for purposes of the antitrust laws. The relationship between independent firms is sometimes cast in the legal form of "agency" in order to achieve antitrust immunity for their collaboration, since all action taken by the agents can be attributed to the single principal.[48]

Judicial classification of a particular arrangement as involving a single or several enterprises will be affected by many factors, including the legal nature of the association, views as to the desirability of the practices under attack, the distinction between creative mutual aid and use of collective power for predatory or coercive purposes,

---

46. But cf. Smith v. Pro Football, Inc., infra p. 543; Radovich v. National Football League, 352 U.S. 445, 77 S.Ct. 390, 1 L.Ed.2d 456 (1957).

47. But cf. Associated Press v. United States, p. 557 infra.

48. United States v. General Electric Co., 272 U.S. 476, 47 S.Ct. 192, 71 L.Ed. 362 (1926), (G. E. fixing retail price of lamps sold by 21,000 retailers); but cf. United States v. Masonite Corp., 316 U.S.

265, 62 S.Ct. 1070, 86 L.Ed. 1461 (1942), (manufacturer designates its principal competitors as agents to sell product at a common price); Federal Trade Commission v. Curtis Publishing Co., 260 U.S. 568, 43 S.Ct. 210, 67 L.Ed. 408 (1923) (substituting "agency" for "dealer" contracts permits magazine publisher to restrict "agents" to dealing exclusively in his publications notwithstanding Section 3 of the Clayton Act).

and feasibility of alternative arrangements to accomplish valid objectives of the collaboration while minimizing its anti-competitive features.[49]

With growing frequency, cataloging joint action as a "joint venture" or "agency," rather than as a contract or conspiracy of independent entities, is relied upon to argue that Section 1 should not be applied, or to claim that the conduct in question not be judged by a *per se* rule. In each of these instances, sorting out the applicability of antitrust policy in particular cases is made to turn on legalistic definitions of who or what are "persons" for antitrust purposes. Avoiding harsh or unwise results caused by using *per se* and rule of reason analyses as rules rather than tools leads to manipulation of the definition of "person" in cases where some countervailing considerations justify or require that joint action be treated as action by a unitary being. Requiring the concept of "person" to carry so much substantive weight has not brought light to the question of whether there is an unlawful displacement of the competitive process in violation of the policies of Section 1 of the Sherman Act. While other areas of law may create unitary artificial legal entities for agency, corporate or other purposes, the definition of person and who it is that may combine or conspire for antitrust purposes must be understood and used in light of the purpose of the statute to prohibit unreasonable displacements of the competitive process by an objectionable form of joint action under the circumstances.

NOTE

(1) *Joint Pricing in Securities Underwriting.* In re *National Association of Securities Dealers, Inc.*, 20 S.E.C. 508 (1945) [known as the "P.S.I. Case," because it related to securities of the Public Service Company of Indiana]. The Securities Exchange Commission held that the Association had no power to impose fines on securities dealers who violated an agreement with investment bankers by reselling P.S.I. bonds at less than the "offering price" set by the bankers. The fines were imposed for violation of an association rule that "A member, in the conduct of his business, shall observe high standards of commercial honor and just and equitable principles of trade." The application of this rule to compel observance of price-fixing agreements was held unlawful because Section 15A(b) (7) of the Securities Exchange Act of 1934 requires that association rules be designed "to remove impediments to . . . a free and open market" and forbids rules which fix minimum profits or schedules of prices. However, the Commission went out of its way to declare the agreements valid and not contrary to the Sherman Act. It was concerned only with the "great danger in permitting the NASD's disciplinary powers to be used in support of the underwriters' judgment of what is a fair minimum price", thus adding to the ordinary legal sanctions for enforcing the agreements.

Among the grounds given by the Commission for believing that agreements to stabilize the price of a security while it is being distributed do not

---

49. On the general subject of joint venture see pp. 555–584 infra. For an excellent article surveying joint venture doctrine in antitrust and proposing an analytical system for separating lawful and unlawful joint ventures, see Brodley, Joint Ventures and Antitrust Policy, 95 Harv.L.Rev. 1523 (1982).

violate the antitrust laws were the following: that any given security issue forms only a minute fraction of the total volume of available securities so that the underwriters are subject to substantial competition in setting the price; that stabilization agreements last only for several months; that stabilization operations by the investment bankers syndicate, including the buying up of offerings made below their price, are necessary to counter the "artificial" price depressant influence of the sudden increase in supply of the security being distributed; that the collaboration of huge syndicates of investment bankers is necessary if the capital requirements of giant industries are to be met promptly and cheaply; that the collaboration involved is really a "joint venture" rather than a "coming together of heretofore independent competitors for the purpose of lessening competition among themselves."[50]

United States v. Morgan,[51] was a suit against the principal investment bankers of the United States seeking to enjoin an alleged combination or conspiracy to restrain and monopolize the business of underwriting and distributing new issues of securities. Among the elements of the scheme charged by the Department of Justice were:

(a) common adherence to the "triple concept" of "traditional banker," "historical position" and "reciprocity."

Under the traditional banker concept, that banker who first manages an underwriting for a particular issuer is deemed entitled to manage in the future all additional security issues offered by such issuer. . . . Under the concept of historical position once a banker participates as a member of a buying group in the purchase of the securities of a particular issuer, such banker is deemed entitled to participate on substantially the same terms as a member of the buying group in all future issues offered by such issuer. Under the concept of reciprocity the defendant banking firms recognize a mutual obligation to exchange participations with one another in the buying groups which they respectively manage.

(b) Concerted opposition to establishment, by government action or otherwise, of competitive bidding by investment bankers for new security issues,[52] and formation of syndicates so large as to preclude or impede competitive bidding.

(c) Collective determination of the price at which each new issue should be sold to the public, arrived at through the defendants' common participation in each new syndicate led by the appropriate traditional banker.

(d) Maintenance of standard profit margins for dealers through syndicate contract provisions like those referred to in the P.S.I. Case, supra.

The court summarized the evidence in a 200-page opinion and found against the government on the issue of conspiracy, holding instead that the practices of the industry were the result of natural evolution to meet the needs of issuers. A review of federal legislation and administration in the

---

50. The Securities Exchange Commission was explicitly authorized to regulate stabilization operations conducted on a national securities exchange, but not on the "over-the-counter" market involved in the NASD case. See 3 Loss, Securities Regulation 1576 et seq. (1961).

51. 118 F.Supp. 621 (S.D.N.Y.1953).

52. Cf. Annual Reports of the Securities and Exchange Commission on the re-duction of underwriting spreads (i.e., bankers' profit margin) attributable to its rules requiring competitive bidding for securities subject to the Public Utility Holding Company Act of 1935, Seventh Annual Report (1941) pp. 98–102; Tenth Annual Report (1944) pp. 105–107; Eighteenth Annual Report (1952) pp. 129–131.

fields of banking and securities regulation satisfied the court that Congress had, at least by acquiescence, approved the syndicate practices. In addition, the court declared that the "rule of reason" applied even to price-fixing agreements under the circumstances of the investment banking business.[53] With respect to defendants' contention that each syndicate should be regarded as a legal unit rather than a combination or conspiracy of independent firms, the court took note of the fact that at one time it was the practice for the entire issue to be purchased by the originating banker, who then resold shares to other banker members of the syndicate, who in turn sold to dealers. After the enactment of the Securities Act of 1933, the strict liability for false statements which that Act imposed on the underwriter, as well as certain tax considerations, led to a change in syndicate practice. Each banker member of the syndicate now purchased his share of the issue direct from the corporation. The court held this change of practice did not preclude a finding that the syndicate was to be treated as a legal unit for purposes of the Sherman Act:

> Against this factual background of substance, such a purely fortuitous and incidental feature as the taking of title by the underwriters in severalty, as they now do, . . . cannot possibly be controlling. To make it so would indeed make the law an ass. Nor does it make sense to separate the underwriting participants from the selected dealers as one might separate the sheep from the goats, simply because of the formal transfer of title from one to the other. It is axiomatic under the Sherman Act that matters of form must always be subordinated to matters of substance. Basically the underwriting participants and the dealers who constitute the selling group are in the same boat together, pulling in unison toward the same mark.

> It matters not whether the members of the team be called "partners," "quasi-partners," "joint adventurers" or what not; the significant fact vis-a-vis the Sherman Act is that they are acting together in a single, integrated, unitary, cooperative enterprise, the purpose of which is not "raising, fixing, pegging, or stabilizing the price" of anything, nor the exercise of any manner of control over general market prices, but solely the distribution of a new security issue in an orderly manner.[54]

---

53. 118 F.Supp. at 687–690.

54. The Morgan Case is debated in Steffen, The Investment Bankers' Case, 64 Yale L.J. 169 (1954); Whitney, The Investment Bankers' Case—Including a Reply to Professor Steffen, 64 Yale L.J. 319 (1955); Steffen, The Investment Bankers' Case: Observations in Rejoinder, 64 Yale L.J. 863 (1955); Whitney, The Investment Bankers' Case: A Surrejoinder, 64 Yale L.J. 873 (1955). See 3 Loss, Securities Regulation 1615 et seq. (1961); United States v. National Association of Securities Dealers, Inc., 422 U.S. 694, 95 S.Ct. 2427, 45 L.Ed.2d 486 (1975) (antitrust immunity in distribution practices of mutual fund shares under the Investment Company Act); Pozen, Competition and Regulation in the Stock Markets, 73 Mich.L. Rev. 317 (1974).

INTRA–ENTERPRISE CONSPIRACY

Excerpt from Report of Attorney General's National Committee to Study the
Antitrust Laws 30–36 (1955).[55]

The situations commonly lumped together under the phrase "intracorporate conspiracy" may more precisely be considered under the following three headings:

(a) Conspiracy solely between a corporation and its officers or between its officers acting on its behalf;

(b) Conspiracy solely between a parent corporation and its subsidiaries or between two or more such subsidiaries;

(c) Conspiracy solely between two or more corporations, the stock in each of which is owned by the same natural person or persons.

. . .

It has long been the law that where a corporation commits a substantive crime, the officers and directors who participated in the illicit venture are guilty of criminal conspiracy. Accordingly, where a corporation monopolizes in violation of Section 2, the officers and directors responsible for such action may be guilty of a conspiracy to monopolize under that section. By a parity of reasoning, if the monopoly scheme is carried out by a parent corporation and its subsidiaries, instead of by a single corporation, the group may be held for a conspiracy to commit the substantive offense of monopolization. But because Section 1 of the Sherman Act does not make restraining trade, as distinguished from a Section 2 charge of monopolizing trade, a substantive offense, it does not follow as a matter of logic that the concerted action of corporate officers acting on the corporation's behalf, or of subsidiaries' action on behalf of their parent, constitutes a conspiracy in violation of Section 1.

The early case of Patterson v. United States[56] concluded that a group of corporate employees could be held guilty of violating Sections 1 and 2 of the Sherman Act, the corporation not being a party to the prosecution, where the employees carried out a predatory policy looking to a monopoly of the cash register business. Despite the holding in Patterson as well as White Bear under Section 1, plaintiffs in both cases charged violations of Section 2, thus making unnecessary to the result the brief discussion of the applicability of Section 1 to these facts. Where there is no charge of violating Section 2, coupled

---

55. See also L. Sullivan, Antitrust, § 148 (1977); Willis & Pitofsky, Antitrust Consequences of Using Corporate Subsidiaries, 43 N.Y.U.L.Rev. 20 (1968); Note, All In The Family: When Will Internal Discussion Be Labeled Intra-Enterprise Conspiracy?, 14 Duq.L.Rev. 63 (1975); Note, Intra-Enterprise Conspiracy Under Section 1 of the Sherman Act: A Suggested Standard, 75 Mich.L.Rev. 717 (1977); Parsons, Developments in The Doctrine of Intra-Enterprise Conspiracy, 39 A.B.A. Antitrust L.J. 968 (1970); Intra-Enterprise Conspiracy Under the Sherman Act, 63 Yale L.J. 372 (1954); Schwartz, Relations With Affiliated Customers, Symposium on Antitrust Law (Commerce Clearing House, 1953) p. 214.

56. 222 F. 599, 618 (6th Cir. 1915), certiorari denied 238 U.S. 635, 35 S.Ct. 939. [This and the following footnotes to the excerpt are those of the Committee.]

with the Section 1 charge, the only reported decisions on the question have found no conspiracy in restraint of trade in joint action solely between a corporation and its officers acting on its behalf.[57]

The Committee believes these decisions are correct.[58] Restraining trade is not illegal, but only contracting, combining and conspiring in restraint of trade. Since a corporation can only act through its officers, and since the normal commercial conduct of a single trader acting alone may restrain trade, many activities of any business could be interdicted were joint action solely by the agents of a single corporation acting on its behalf itself held to constitute a conspiracy in restraint of trade.

A different situation may sometimes be presented by the charge of a trade-restraining conspiracy between a parent and its subsidiary or between two corporations owned by the same corporation or individuals.

. . .

The most recent case to consider the question is United States v. Timken Roller Bearing Co.[59] That Section 1 case charged arrangements between the American Timken and a major foreign competitor for limiting their competition in the American and World markets. British Timken had evolved between 1909 and 1928 as an enterprise jointly controlled by the American Company and a British firm which was American Timken's principal potential competitor. The French company was organized by the British and American interests controlling British Timken. At the time of the trial, the American company owned 30 percent of the stock of the British Company, one Dewar owned 24 percent, and the balance was publicly held. Both Dewar and the defendant owned 50 percent of the stock of the French company. Dewar died while the appeal was pending. Under preexisting contracts, Timken had the right to purchase Dewar's stock from his estate, which option Timken later exercised. The original arrangements were held unjustified by the patents then owned by Timken, and their continuation after the expiration of the patents was held violative of Section 1.

57. Nelson Radio & Supply Co. v. Motorola, Inc., 200 F.2d 911, 914 (5th Cir., 1952), certiorari denied 345 U.S. 925, 73 S.Ct. 783, 97 L.Ed. 1356 (1953); Marion County Co-op. Association v. Carnation Co., 114 F.Supp. 58 (W.D.Ark.1953); see also Union Pacific Coal Co. v. United States, 173 F. 737, 745 (8th Cir. 1909); Arthur v. Kraft-Phenix Cheese Corp., 26 F.Supp. 824, 830 (D.Md.1937).

58. The Antitrust Division charged conspiracy in restraint of trade solely between a corporation and its officers in United States v. Lorain Journal Co., 92 F.Supp. 794 (N.D.Ohio 1950), affirmed 342 U.S. 143, 72 S.Ct. 181, 96 L.Ed. 162 (1951); and in United States v. Times-Picayune Publishing Co., 105 F.Supp. 670 (E.D.La.1952), reversed 345 U.S. 594, 73 S.Ct. 872, 97 L.Ed. 1277 (1953). In the former case, the District Court found for the Government under an alternate charge of attempting to monopolize in violation of Section 2 and refused to decide the Section 1 question. In the Times-Picayune case, the Government dropped the Section 1 conspiracy charge before the final argument in the District Court.

59. 83 F.Supp. 284 (N.D.Ohio 1949), affirmed 341 U.S. 593, 71 S.Ct. 971, 95 L.Ed. 1199 (1951).

The majority opinion stated:

. . . The fact that there is common ownership or control of the contracting corporations does not liberate them from the impact of the antitrust laws. . . . Nor do we find any support in reason or authority for the proposition that agreements between legally separate persons and companies to suppress competition among themselves and others can be justified by labeling the project a "joint venture." Perhaps every agreement and combination to restrain trade could be so labeled.

The language of the Timken majority has caused alarm among some corporations who carry on their business through subsidiaries. They fear that the opinion makes unlawful the action of a parent company in establishing prices for or dividing markets between its subsidiaries—actions that a single corporation not bent on monopoly may generally take with impunity.

The use of subsidiaries is generally induced by normal, prudent business considerations. No social objective would be attained were subsidiaries enjoined from agreeing not to compete with each other or with their parent. To demand internal competition within and between the members of a single business unit is to invite chaos without promotion of the public welfare.

The substance of the Supreme Court decisions is that concerted action between a parent and subsidiary or between subsidiaries which has for its purpose or effect coercion or unreasonable restraint on the trade of strangers to those acting in concert is prohibited by Section 1. Nothing in these opinions should be interpreted as justifying the conclusion that concerted action solely between a parent and subsidiary or subsidiaries, the purpose and effect of which is not coercive restraint of the trade of strangers to the corporate family, violates Section 1.

. . .

It is obviously unrealistic to expect or to command wholly-owned affiliates to compete. Insofar as the decision in Kiefer-Stewart,[60] or the decree in Timken may be considered to rest on such a hypothesis, we recommend that the Supreme Court reconsider it. While the decision on illegality in both cases can be otherwise justified, we believe the remedy provided in the Timken case, requiring competition among companies now fully controlled by American Timken, sacrifices substance to form. Both before and after the litigation, the Timken enterprise represented a permanent combination of the American Company and its chief foreign competitor. Especially since stock ownership constituted the essence of the combination, the obvious remedy should have been dissolution, as indicated in cases like United States v. Southern Pacific Co.[61]

60. 340 U.S. 211, 71 S.Ct. 259, 95 L.Ed. 219 (1951), rehearing denied 340 U.S. 939, 71 S.Ct. 487, 95 L.Ed. 678.

61. 259 U.S. 214, 42 S.Ct. 496, 66 L.Ed. 907 (1922).

NOTES AND QUERIES

(1) *When Is a "Person" Not a "Person" for Purposes of Antitrust Contract, Combination and Conspiracy Analysis?* The definition of "person" for Sherman Act purposes, found in Section 8 of the original Act,[62] simply includes corporations and associations within the meaning of the concept and does not define who or what is excluded from the concept. In several circumstances, courts are confronted with defining who or what is *not* a person for purposes of the contract, combination and conspiracy requirements under Section 1 of the Sherman Act. The issue sometimes arises in the context of a claim that a corporation and its officers or employees have conspired to violate Section 1. Despite the fact that a corporation and its employees are separate "persons" for other purposes and that corporate employees may be considered separate persons for the purposes of other conspiracy laws,[63] the courts have generally refused to hold that a corporation and its employees are separate persons capable of combining and conspiring with respect to corporate activity for Section 1 purposes. In *Nelson Radio & Supply Co., Inc. v. Motorola, Inc.*[64] the Court of Appeals explained the rationale for the rule as follows:

> Surely discussions among those engaged in the management, direction and control of a corporation concerning the price at which the corporation will sell its goods, the quantity it will produce, the type of customers or market to be served, or the quality of goods to be produced do not result in the corporation being engaged in a conspiracy in unlawful restraint of trade under the Sherman Act. . . . The defendant is a corporate person and as such it can act only through its officers and representatives. It has the right as a single manufacturer to select its customers and to refuse to sell its goods to anyone for any or no reason whatsoever. It does not violate the Act when it exercises its rights through its officers and agents, which is the only medium through which it can possibly act.[65]

The *Nelson Radio* rule has been criticized by Judge Wisdom in *Dussouy v. Gulf Coast Investment Corp.*,[66] a diversity suit claiming violations of the Louisiana antitrust laws. Dussouy, an insurance salesman employed by a customer to obtain insurance for a home being financed by the defendant, claimed that the defendant and its employees conspired to coerce borrowers and their insurance agents to place policies with a particular insurance company. The court, in reversing dismissal of the complaint, held that a corporation and its employees can be treated as separate persons for purposes of conspiracy under the Louisiana antitrust law.[67] Judge Wisdom observed:

> The concept of intracorporate conspiracy raises difficult conceptual problems, and the courts have reached varying results on whether such a conspiracy is possible. For purposes of federal antitrust law, a corpora-

62. 15 U.S.C.A. § 7: "That the word "person" or "persons", wherever used in this act shall be deemed to include corporations and associations existing under or authorized by the laws of either the United States, the laws of any of the Territories, the laws of any State, or the laws of any foreign country."

63. See L. Sullivan, Antitrust p. 324 (1977).

64. 200 F.2d 911 (5th Cir. 1952), certiorari denied 345 U.S. 925, 73 S.Ct. 783, 97 L.Ed. 1356 (1953).

65. 200 F.2d at 914. See also Tose v. First Pennsylvania Bank, N.A., 648 F.2d 879, 893–94 (3d Cir. 1981), certiorari denied 454 U.S. 893, 102 S.Ct. 390, 70 L.Ed. 2d 208.

66. 660 F.2d 594 (5th Cir. 1981).

67. The Louisiana antitrust act is virtually identical to the Sherman Act. The relevant conspiracy section provides: "Every contract, combination in the form

tion cannot conspire with its officers or employers. That rule is not unquestioned. See Novotny v. Great American Savings & Loan Association, 3 Cir. 1978, 584 F.2d 1235, 1257 n. 117 (en banc), vacated on other grounds, 442 U.S. 336, 99 S.Ct. 2345, 60 L.Ed.2d 957 (1979); see generally L. Sullivan, Handbook of the Law of Antitrust § 114 (1977). The rationale for that rule is two-fold: first, agency principles attribute the acts of agents of a corporation to the corporation, so that all of their acts are considered to be those of a single legal actor, negating the multiplicity of actors necessary to conspiracy, and, second, applying the prohibition of combinations in restraint of trade contained in section 1 of the Sherman Act to activities by a single firm renders meaningless section 2, which prohibits monopolization and attempt to monopolize.

There are, however, strong arguments against the *Nelson Radio* rule. The original purposes of the rule attributing agents' acts to a corporation were to enable corporations to act, permitting the pooling of resources to achieve social benefits and, in the case of tortious acts, to require a corporation to bear the costs of its business enterprise. But extension of the rule to preclude the possibility of intracorporate conspiracy does not serve either of these goals. See Note, *Intracorporate Conspiracies under 42 U.S.C. § 1985(c): The Impact of Novotny v. Great American Savings & Loan Association*, 13 Ga.L.Rev. 591, 602–03 (1979). Some courts have found this reasoning persuasive when dealing with problems outside the federal antitrust area. For instance, in *Novotny v. Great American Savings & Loan Association*, the Third Circuit, although it did not consider whether the corporation could be a party to the conspiracy, held that the officers and directors of a single corporation could be liable for conspiracy under 42 U.S.C. § 1985(c). Similarly, a corporation can be convicted of criminal charges of conspiracy based solely on conspiracy with its own employees. In these situations, the action by an incorporated collection of individuals creates the 'group danger' at which conspiracy liability is aimed, and the view of the corporation as a single legal actor becomes a fiction without a purpose. Also, courts have fashioned an exception to the rule that a corporation cannot conspire with its employees: when the officers of a corporation act for their own personal purposes, they become independent actors, who can conspire with the corporation. See *Johnston v. Baker*, 3 Cir. 1971, 445 F.2d 424; R. Eickhoff, *Fletcher Cyclopedia of the Law of Private Corporations* §§ 4884, 5032.1 (1978).

Apparently Louisiana has found the arguments against the *Nelson Radio* rule persuasive even in the antitrust area, or, at the very least, it recognizes exceptions to the rule. Thus, in *Tooke & Reynolds v. Bastrop Ice & Storage*, 171 La. 781, 135 So. 239 (1931), the Louisiana Supreme Court held that a corporation 'with its individual members, shareholders, and managers formed a combination' that could violate the prohibition of combinations in restraint of trade. Id., 135 So. at 242. More recently, the Louisiana appellate courts have held it error, although harmless error, to refuse a requested jury instruction that a corporation could conspire with its own employees. *Economy Carpets Manufacturers & Distributors v. Better Business Bureau*, 361 So.2d 234 (La.App.1978), writ denied, 440 U.S. 915, 99 S.Ct. 1231, 59 L.Ed.2d 464 (1979). The *Economy Carpets* court held that the error was harmless because there was no evidence that the employees conspired, indicating that not every action by

of trust or otherwise, or conspiracy in restraint of trade or commerce in this state is illegal." La.Rev.Stat.Ann. § 51:122 (1950).

a corporation will be a conspiracy. Louisiana courts, then, may accept the view that a conspiracy in restraint of trade between a corporation and its employees is possible only when the employees act for personal purposes. Fortunately, we need not decide that point. Although it is unclear whether the court meant that there was no evidence of any agreement (which would suggest that employees are actors independent of the corporation only when they act for their own purposes), or that there was no evidence of the malicious agreement in restraint of trade requisite under Louisiana law, it is clear that the court thought that a corporation could in some circumstances conspire with its employees in violation of La.Rev.Stat.Ann. § 51:121 et seq. We must accept the early holding of the Louisiana Supreme Court in *Tooke & Reynolds* and the more recent statement of the Louisiana appellate court allowed to stand by the Louisiana Supreme Court, as authoritative statements of Louisiana law.[68]

It has also been held that a partnership agreement may be treated as a contract of the individual partners where it restrains the trade of individual partners by unreasonable penalties for withdrawing from the partnership and entry into competition with the partnership.[69]

(2) *Parent-Subsidiary and Subsidiary-Subsidiary Conspiracies.* In *Kiefer-Stewart Co. v. Joseph E. Seagram & Sons, Inc.,*[70] the Supreme Court held that an agreement between two wholly-owned subsidiaries of one parent corporation, that neither would sell to wholesale liquor distributors who resold at prices above the maxima set by the sellers, violated the Sherman Act:

> [S]uch agreements, no less than those to fix minimum prices, cripple the freedom of traders and thereby restrain their ability to sell in accordance with their own judgment. We reaffirm what we said in United States v. Socony-Vacuum Oil Co., 310 U.S. 150, 223, 60 S.Ct. 811, 844, 84 L.Ed. 1129: 'Under the Sherman Act a combination formed for the purpose and with the effect of raising, depressing, fixing, pegging, or stabilizing the price of a commodity in interstate or foreign commerce is illegal *per se.*' . . . Respondents next suggest that their status as 'mere instrumentalities of a single manufacturing-merchandising unit' makes it impossible for them to have conspired in a manner forbidden by the Sherman Act. But this suggestion runs counter to our past decisions that common ownership and control does not liberate corporations from the impact of the antitrust laws. The rule is especially applicable where, as here, respondents hold themselves out as competitors.[71]

After the *Kiefer-Stewart* decision, Seagrams disincorporated the subsidiaries and operated them as "divisions" of a wholly owned subsidiary corporation. One division of the subsidiary sold Frankfort Distillers branded products, another sold "Four Roses" branded products, and a third division sold products under the "Calvert" brand. Despite the continued holding out of the brands as competitors, it was held by the Ninth Circuit in *Joseph E. Seagram & Sons v. Hawaiian Oke & Liquors, Ltd.,*[72] that a conspiracy to terminate a retailer could not be found between the unincorporated divisions of a single

68. 660 F.2d at 603–04.

69. See Wegman v. London, 648 F.2d 1072 (5th Cir. 1981).

70. 340 U.S. 211, 71 S.Ct. 259, 95 L.Ed. 219 (1951).

71. Id. at 213–15, 71 S.Ct., at 260–61, 95 L.Ed., at 223–24.

72. 416 F.2d 71 (9th Cir. 1969), certiorari denied 396 U.S. 1062, 90 S.Ct. 752, 24 L.Ed.2d 755, rehearing denied 397 U.S. 1003, 90 S.Ct. 1113, 25 L.Ed.2d 415 (1970).

corporation. The Supreme Court appears to have held otherwise in *Poller v. Columbia Broadcasting System*, infra p. 781.

The Ninth Circuit, despite Supreme Court precedent holding that corporations availing themselves of incorporated subsidiaries are not saved "from any of the obligations that the antitrust law[s] impose on separate entities,"[73] has also found that parent-subsidiary *corporations* operated as a "single unified structure" or as a single economic entity should not be held capable of conspiring for Sherman Act purposes.[74] In *William Inglis & Sons Baking Co. v. International Telephone & Telegraph Continental Baking Co., Inc.*,[75] the plaintiff charged ITT and its wholly owned subsidiary, Continental Baking Co., with a conspiracy to drive it out of business. The Court of Appeals explained its rationale on intra-enterprise conspiracy:

> The district court granted summary judgment for Continental, in part because it found that Continental and ITT, because of their parent-subsidiary relationship, were legally incapable of conspiring to violate the law. We disagree.

> "An antitrust conspiracy, no less than other proscribed conspiracies, requires a plurality of actors concerting their efforts towards a common goal." *Mutual Fund Investors, Inc. v. Putnam Management Co.*, 553 F.2d 620, 625 (9th Cir. 1977). Continental is the wholly owned subsidiary of ITT. The issue is whether they should be treated as distinct economic entities for purposes of the antitrust conspiracy laws. The Supreme Court repeatedly has held that "common ownership and control does not liberate corporations from the impact of the antitrust laws . . . especially where [they] hold themselves out as competitors." . . . However, just as the fact of common ownership alone should not insulate corporations from the antitrust laws, this court has held that "the mere formality of separate incorporation is not, without more, sufficient to provide the capability for conspiracy." . . .

> Within these perimeters a court must examine the facts of the particular case to determine whether related corporate entities are capable of conspiracy. The purpose of this examination is to determine whether the corporations have "antitrust significance as separate economic units." . . . ITT is not engaged in the production or sale of bread, nor does it perform any related business function other than that of a holding company for a conglomeration of other business. As Continental emphasizes, this is not a situation in which concerted activity by a parent and its subsidiary would restrain trade between the two, or between the subsidiary and another subsidiary in the same family engaged in the same or a related line of business. . . . Nor is this a case of vertically related operating companies, such as a manufacturer and distributor, a wholesaler and retailer, or a supplier and purchaser, in which the power of one is used to restrain trade between the other and its competitors. . . .

73. Perma Life Mufflers, Inc. v. International Parts Corp., 392 U.S. 134, 142, 88 S.Ct. 1981, 1986, 20 L.Ed.2d 982, 992 (1968).

74. See Las Vegas Sun, Inc. v. Summa Corp., 610 F.2d 614, 617 (9th Cir. 1980), certiorari denied 447 U.S. 906, 100 S.Ct. 2988, 64 L.Ed.2d 855; Mutual Fund Investors, Inc. v. Putnam Management Co., 553 F.2d 620, 625 (9th Cir. 1977);

Harvey v. Fearless Farris Wholesale, Inc., 589 F.2d 451, 456 (9th Cir. 1978); Knutson v. Daily Review, Inc., 548 F.2d 795, 802 (9th Cir. 1976), certiorari denied 433 U.S. 910, 97 S.Ct. 2977, 53 L.Ed.2d 1094 (1977).

75. 668 F.2d 1014 (9th Cir. 1981), certiorari denied ___ U.S. ___, 103 S.Ct. 58, ___ L.Ed.2d ___ (1982).

Nevertheless, we do not believe that the doctrine of intra-enterprise conspiracy is limited to such situations. The lack of competition between Continental and ITT in the wholesale bread market and the lack of a vertical operating relationship between the companies are facts that militate against a finding of capacity to conspire, but they are not conclusive. Our reading of cases within our circuit . . . convinces us that two corporations, although part of the same corporate "family," are capable of conspiring unless they function as a single economic unit.

The existing record provides no reliable answer to whether Continental and ITT did or did not so function. Nothing in the record shows conclusively that ITT directed Continental's pricing activity in the northern California market. In fact, the evidence indicates that Continental was given considerable operating autonomy. In any event, the district court apparently did not explore the details of the ITT-Continental relationship because of its conclusion that the two were incapable of conspiring so long as ITT did not compete in the wholesale bread market and did not act as a manufacturer or supplier to Continental. Such an exploration was necessary before the summary judgment motion could be properly considered. The possibility of less than total involvement of a large holding company in the competitive affairs of one of its operating subsidiaries in a way that might strengthen an anticompetitive assault perpetrated by that subsidiary, is of sufficient concern to antitrust policy to require further investigation of an alleged conspiracy.[76]

Queries: Does the Court's analysis confuse "capacity" to conspire with the question of whether two corporations with the capacity to conspire did in fact conspire? Should antitrust liability under Section 1 turn on whether a multi-faceted business is carried on through separately incorporated subsidiaries or affiliates, a holding out of unincorporated subdivisions as competitors, or the operation of the business as a legally and economically single enterprise? How else could a court draw a line defining who or what are separate "persons" for purposes of proving "contract, combination or conspiracy"? Should the Court examine the structure of the allegedly offending enterprise under a "mini-rule-of-reason" analysis to determine whether parts of the enterprise should be considered separate persons for purposes of finding agreement? Is this what the Court was advocating in the *Inglis* case?

Conglomerate corporations may be viewed as an aggregation of disparate enterprises tied together under the auspices of the equivalent of a "central bank," *viz.*, the conglomerate parent company. The parent company provides financing and other services to the subsidiary companies, as well as general management supervision measured by yearly financial performance. Should the parent and subsidiary companies have the benefits of a family relationship for these purposes, but none of the antitrust risks of being treated as separate entities for antitrust purposes? If Continental had conspired with an outside bank to finance a predatory pricing campaign against Inglis & Sons, would a court inquire into whether the outside bank and Continental had the "capacity" to conspire, were "separate economic units" or had "antitrust significance as separate economic units"? Does it make more sense in the case of conglomerates sued for the predatory pricing tactics of a subsidiary to treat parent and subsidiary as separate "persons" for antitrust conspiracy purposes in light of the risks of cross-subsidization of subsidiary

---

76.   668 F.2d at 1054–58.

price wars backed by the parent conglomerate or other subsidiaries in the family?

(3) *Alternative Methods for Analyzing Intra-Enterprise Conspiracy Cases.* Among the many alternative methods for analyzing intra-enterprise conspiracy cases have been proposals that a finding of conspiracy in intra-enterprise conspiracy cases only be made where the arrangement or agreement has the purpose or effect of coercing outsiders or only where parent and/or subsidiary hold themselves out as competitors.[77] Another proposed approach would preclude finding a conspiracy where "a parent firm controls the day-to-day operations of its subsidiaries" on the theory that the multi-corporate enterprise is, in reality, of "one mind."[78]

Each of these approaches may have merit in specific cases, but none appears to provide a workable and predictable framework for all cases. The basic question remains whether joint conduct, carried out by artificial or natural persons or within the context of a relationship the law recognizes as a single entity for some other purpose (i.e., the employer-employee relationship and the doctrine of respondeat superior), unreasonably restrains trade in ways the antitrust laws condemn. Conflict between antitrust policy and business or other legal justification for using subsidiaries can confuse the process of sorting out when personhood should be recognized and when it should be ignored. Recognition of business, tax and other justifications for the use of subsidiary corporations, divisions, conglomerates and so on, can collide with the use of *per se* and rule of reason analysis as rigid rules of illegality and legality once two or more "persons" agree. Would it make more sense to treat *per se* and rule of reason analysis as a single method of analysis establishing evidentiary presumptions of illegality and legality for identified categories of conduct and subject to various defenses? And, in the case of intra-enterprise conspiracy, recognize as a defense subject to examination or rebuttal, the intra-enterprise nature of the alleged conspirators, the circumstances in which the activity takes place, and its impact upon the competitive process?

(4) *Implying Understandings With Outsiders.* A business decision which is superficially unilateral or the apparent product of intra-enterprise decisions by functionally different branches of the enterprise, e.g., a petroleum company's refusal to renew the franchise of a service station dealer who follows an independent price policy, may be found to result from an implied understanding with all the other dealers, who follow the supplier's suggested price policy.[79]

(5) *The Corporation as a Combination Exempted From the Antitrust Laws by State Action; Federal Incorporation?* A business corporation is functionally a "combination"—often on a gigantic scale—of investors, managers, entrepreneurs, and workers. Only legal fiction confers upon the cor-

77. The various proposals are surveyed in Kempf, Bathtub Conspiracies: Has Seagram Distilled a More Potent Brew?, 24 Bus.Law 173 (1968); McQuade, Conspiracy, Multi-Corporate Enterprises and Section 1 of the Sherman Act, 41 Va.L.Rev. 183 (1955); Willis & Pitofsky, Antitrust Consequences of Using Corporate Subsidiaries, 43 N.Y.U.L.Rev. 20 (1968); Note, All in The Family: When Will Internal Discussion be Labeled Intra-Enterprise Conspiracy?, 14 Duq.L.Rev. 63 (1975).

78. Note, Intra-Enterprise Conspiracy Under Section 1 of the Sherman Act: A Suggested Standard, 75 Mich.L.Rev. 717 (1977).

79. Compare Simpson v. Union Oil Co., p. 601 infra and Quinn v. Mobil Oil Co., 375 F.2d 273 (1st Cir. 1967), certiorari dismissed 389 U.S. 801, 88 S.Ct. 8, 19 L.Ed.2d 56 (1967).

poration a conceptual "unity," authorizing it to sue and ~~be~~
name, to hold property, to make contracts, and to incur de~~bts~~
~~ble~~ invention of "corporate personality" and the accomp~~anying~~
limited liability, shielding the shareholder participants fro~~m~~
corporate debts, vastly reduced the risks of entrepreneur~~ial~~
pooling of interests among small capitalists. Despite th~~e artifici-~~
rial character of the corporation, it would be absurd i~~n applying~~
antitrust laws to disregard the legal fiction of corporate unity. The corporation could not function if agreement among the officers as to the prices to be
charged for the company's products or agreement among them not to produce more than X products would be examinable under Section 1. It is notable nevertheless that the nature and scope of this artificial entity, enjoying
partial immunity from the federal antitrust laws, is determined by *state* incorporation laws. The states have engaged in a competitive scramble for
corporate favor by progressively relaxing their incorporation laws, to the
point where lawyers and entrepreneurs have virtually uncontrolled discretion
in organizing megacorporations of unlimited scope, controlling numerous legally distinct subsidiaries, and with voting and other arrangements that assure management virtual independence in fixing their own emoluments and
limiting shareholder control of the corporate destiny. It is not surprising
therefore to find, on the one hand, a demand for a federal corporation law
applicable to large interstate and international business, and, on the other
hand, some tendency under the antitrust laws to treat a gigantic corporation
as a combination under Section 1 of the Sherman Act, especially if the corporation operates in visibly distinct enterprises through separate, though wholly-owned, subsidiaries.[80]

(6) *Query.* Should it be illegal (a) for any firm, or (b) for a dominant
firm, to deal with its subsidiaries or affiliates on terms more favorable than
are accorded to others? Cf. consent decree requiring General Motors Corp.
to refrain from exercising its influence over dealers to get them to finance
their purchases through General Motors Acceptance Corp. General Motors
was required to provide facilities in its plants for other financing firms if it
provided such facilities for GMAC.[81]

E. TRADE ASSOCIATIONS

1. INTRODUCTION

Adam Smith observed in "THE WEALTH OF NATIONS": "People of
the same trade seldom meet together, even for merriment and diversion, but that the conversation ends in a conspiracy against the public
or in some contrivance to raise prices."[82] That trade association
meetings and communications afford excellent opportunities for "contracts, combinations, and conspiracies" in restraint of trade is undeni-

80. See Nader et al., Taming the Giant Corporation (1976); Nader et al., Con-
stitutionalizing the Corporation: The
Case for the Federal Chartering of Giant
Corporations (1976).

81. United States v. General Motors
Corp., CCH Trade Reg. Serv. 1952–53 De-

cisions, ¶ 67,324 (N.D.Ill.1952). See p.
994 infra on discrimination by one segment of a vertically integrated enterprise
in favor of another segment of the same
enterprise.

82. 1 Wealth of Nations 117 (Every-
man's Ed. 1910).

e. On the other hand, there are innocent and even beneficial aspects of association among persons interested in common business and governmental problems; and the First Amendment stands in the way of official constraints of freedom of speech and association.

The principled yet practical resolution of the tensions between the beneficial effects of trade association activities and the antitrust risks created by an association of competitors pursuing common industry goals illustrates well each step of the analytical process in section 1 litigation outlined in the previous sections of this chapter. Indeed, many of the leading cases in this chapter have concerned the analysis of activities having their genesis in trade association activities. In this section we focus on trade association activities affecting prices, for the purposes of bringing together and demonstrating the interaction of the various elements of the analysis of horizontal price fixing restraints arising under section 1 and to illustrate many of the recurring problems lawyers encounter when counseling clients about establishing, supervising or participating in a trade association.

There are several thousand trade associations at the national, regional, and local levels. Lawyers not only play an important role in advising such organizations about antitrust, tax and other legal constraints, but usually belong to associations of lawyers which are at least analogous to, if not corresponding exactly with, industrial or trade groups more readily identified as "trade associations." Whether a particular grouping of persons engaged in the same trade be called a professional association or a trade association, antitrust concerns are a significant constraint upon the structure and operation of the organization. Adam Smith's observation is as realistic today as it was three centuries ago, because many of the most pressing common concerns of people of the same trade concern features of the competitive process in that trade: i.e., pricing practices; methods of distribution; customer relations; product standardization; advertising practices; new technologies affecting the trade; cost and inventory information; dealings with customers, suppliers or shippers; and the "ethics" of the trade. Preventative counseling, by lawyers alert to the antitrust risks peculiar to trade association activities, can assure that the "merriment and diversion" generated in meetings by people of the same trade are not rudely disrupted by a government antitrust investigation or are not later made the basis for a successful treble damage action.

BACKGROUND AND SCOPE OF OPERATIONS

Excerpt from Wilcox, Competition and Monopoly in American Industry, T.N.E.C. Mono. 21 (1940) pp. 225 et seq.

The trade association movement is a product of the past 30 years. The few associations that were formed during the latter half of the nineteenth century were, in the main, impotent, clandestine, or ephemeral. Trade organization, in the twentieth century, took its initial impetus from the enunciation of the rule of reason by the Supreme Court in 1911 and from the publication of a popular book on

"The New Competition" by Arthur J. Eddy in 1912, both statements holding out the hope that competitors might cooperate in common activities and remain within the law. The formation of associations was further stimulated in 1917 and 1918 by the function assigned to them by the War Industries Board in the procurement of supplies, and again in 1933 and 1934 by the opportunity afforded them to adopt and administer codes of fair competition under the National Industrial Recovery Act. In 1940 there were more than 8,000 trade associations— local, regional, and national—in the United States, some 2,000 of them national in scope.

Association Activities [83]

The functions performed by trade associations for the benefit of their members are numerous and diverse. Many of them do not appear to be inconsistent with the preservation of competition; many others may involve the imposition of restraints. Typical association activities include cooperative industrial research, market surveys, the development of new uses for products, the provision of traffic information, the operation of employment bureaus, collective bargaining with organized labor, mutual insurance, commercial arbitration, the publication of trade journals, joint advertising and publicity, and joint representation before legislative and administrative agencies, all of them undertakings that may serve a trade without disservice to its customers. But they also include the establishment of common cost accounting procedures, the collection and dissemination of statistics, the operation of price reporting plans, the standardization of products, terms of contracts, and price lists and differentials, the provision of credit information, the interchange of patent rights, the administration of basing point systems, the joint purchasing of supplies, and the promulgation of codes of business ethics, each of them practices which may operate to restrain competition in quality, service, price, or terms of sale. . . .[84]

Cost Accounting

Conspicuous among association activities is the promotion of cost accounting, or, in association parlance, cost education. As described, by Burns, this educational work is carried on through six grades. In the first, the association provides its members with standard forms for use in cost determination. This is expected to eliminate any price cutting that might arise from ignorance of costs. It may also carry the suggestion that no seller's price should fall below his costs as set forth on the standard forms. In the second grade, the association

---

83. See Lamb & Shields, Trade Association Law and Practice (1971); Symposium, 18 Antitrust Bull. 167 (1973); Symposium, 19 Antitrust Bull. 681 (1974); Rich, The Conduct of Trade Association Meetings, 46 Brooklyn Law Review 205 (1980); Olson, Trade Associations and Other Associations of Competitors, Antitrust Advisor 495 (C.A. Hills rev. ed. 1978).

84. See Herold, How Can an Association Avoid Antitrust Problems—A Private Practitioners Perspective, 22 Antitrust Bull. 299 (1977).

prescribes detailed procedures for computing costs, showing its members the proper way to figure charges for materials, the proper way to compute depreciation, and the proper way to distribute overhead. This is designed to reduce the price disparities that might result from the employment of diverse methods of calculation. In the third grade, the association suggests a uniform mark-up. Each of its members is encouraged to add the same percent of profit to his costs to get his price. But one member may undersell another if he has lower costs. In the fourth grade, however, the association publishes some sort of an average of the costs of all the firms in the trade. Where this figure is adopted by members in place of their individual actual costs, it affords a basis for the establishment of a common price. But prices may still vary if members do not add a uniform mark-up to the uniform cost. In the fifth grade, therefore, says Burns, "Some associations have taken the final step and included an allowance for profit in the so-called average costs. Average costs then become merely a suggested selling price, uniform for all, and provide a means by which to define and detect price cutting and a stimulus to attempts to eliminate it." In the sixth and final grade, the association undertakes to enforce adherence to the average "costs". Through editorials published in trade journals, through resolutions passed at association meetings, and through conferences and correspondence between association officials and members of the trade, it endeavors to persuade all sellers that they should adopt the common estimate of "cost" and therefore charge a common price.

Not every association has carried cost education through all six grades. But every student of the activity has recognized that it is subject to abuse. Whitney, for instance, lists three methods of controlling prices: direct, through price fixing; indirect, through persuasion; and technical, through cost accounting. The Federal Trade Commission quotes a statement made by the secretary of the National Association of Cost Accountants at a meeting of the American Trade Association executives: "I cannot see a great deal in uniform costing unless it does lead to an exchange of information and a comparison of costs with a view to securing a certain amount of cost standardization which is something entirely different from uniformity of method . . . It is perfectly true that the exchange of information is likely to have an influence on price levels in the industry, but why shouldn't it?" According to the Commission, "These words sum up very well the philosophy of cost accounting and cost comparison as a trade association activity." The study of average cost data by the members of an industry "will promote uniformity of practice in computing costs and generally influence them in the direction of uniformity of prices." It is, moreover, "the natural tendency of trade associations to include everything possible in costs and thus to swell the amount". The Commission therefore concludes: "Among the many legitimate kinds of trade association activities which may easily and imperceptibly pass over from the stage of useful service to that of abuse and even illegality, there are probably few more prone to this sort of transition than cost-accounting work." . . .

Statistical Activities

The statistical activities of trade associations may affect prices by influencing the production policies of member firms. Association statistics cover such matters as the volume of production, inventories, unfilled orders, idle capacity, shipments, and sales. Reports on the volume of production may show output as a ratio of capacity and compare it with some ratio designated as "normal". They may compare output with orders or with shipments. They may compare it with the quantity produced during some "normal" period in the past. Such comparisons are likely to carry the suggestion that production is getting out of hand. The consequent curtailment amounts, says Burns, "to adapting production to demand and avoiding the accumulation of unsold stocks. It is implied that when demand declines there is only one proper response, viz., an equal reduction of output." In some cases, association reports have compared changes in the volume of one member's output with changes in the total output of the trade. "These calculations are aimed at deterring the firm whose sales have been falling from attempting to increase its sales by increased sales effort or price cutting at a time when the sales of all firms are falling. Thus a 'demoralized market' is avoided. Such an interpretation of the statistics must tend to fix the distribution of business between firms. Insofar as price cutting is deterred when business falls off, there is also a tendency to maintain unchanged prices." Reports on the volume of inventories likewise "are likely to be used as a guide to production policy, production being diminished when stocks are accumulating and increased when stocks are falling. . . . The existing price of the product tends to be maintained and production adjusted to changes in demand at the unchanging price." So, too, with reports on unfilled orders. If they reveal an increase in the volume of such orders, output may rise; but if they reveal a decline, it is probable that output will be curtailed and the established price maintained. Reports on the volume of idle capacity may have a similar effect. They serve to warn the members of the trade that a price cut may provoke a price war. They may also deter existing firms from adding to their equipment and new firms from entering the field, even though it might be possible to put the added capacity to work at a lower price. Whitney's three methods of price control are paralleled by three methods of controlling production: direct, through quota systems; indirect, through persuasion; and technical, through the collection and dissemination of statistics.

Price Reporting Systems [85]

Trade association statistics cover prices as well as production. Through their price reporting systems, association members make available to one another, and sometimes to outsiders, information concerning the prices at which products have been, are being, or are to

85. For a survey of recent cases, see Bass, Price Fixing and Trade Associations, 46 Brooklyn L.Rev. 213 (1980).

be sold. It is argued that such systems, by increasing the amount of knowledge available to traders, must lessen the imperfection of markets and make for more effective competition. Whether they do so, in fact, depends upon the characteristics of the industries which use them and upon the characteristics of the plans themselves.

For a price reporting system to increase the effectiveness of competition in a trade, many conditions must be fulfilled. As for the characteristics of the trade: Sellers must be numerous, each of them relatively small, and no one of them dominant. Entrance to the field must not be obstructed by legal barriers or by large capital requirements. Otherwise a reporting system may implement a price agreement, or promote price leadership, and facilitate the application of pressure against price cutters. Moreover, the market for the trade must not be a declining one. Supply, demand, and price must not be subject to violent fluctuation. The product must consist of small units turned out in large volume and sales must be frequent. Otherwise sellers will have a stronger incentive than usual to restrict competition and, even though numerous, they may agree upon a common course of action. Under such circumstances, a price reporting plan may serve as a convenient instrument for the administration of a scheme of price control. And finally, the demand for the product of the trade must be elastic, falling as prices rise and rising as prices fall. Otherwise it is not to be expected that the provision of fuller information would force a seller to reduce his price.

So, too, with the characteristics of the reporting plan itself: The price reports must not be falsified. If members do not return their lowest prices, if the association excludes such prices from the figures it reports, competitive reductions to meet the lowest figure actually charged will not occur. The reports must be available to all sellers on equal terms. If they are not, the sellers who fail to see them will not be informed of lower prices that they otherwise might meet. The reports must also be available to buyers. If information is withheld from them, they cannot seek out the seller who has filed the lowest price or compel another seller to meet this price to make a sale. The reports must not identify individual traders. The reporting agency must be neutral, keeping each seller's returns in confidence and transmitting the collective information to all concerned. If price cutters are openly or secretly identified, those who desire to sell at higher prices may employ persuasion or even sterner methods to bring them into line. The prices reported must be limited to past transactions. If current or future prices are exchanged, sellers will hesitate to cut their charges to make a sale, since they will know that lower figures will instantly be met. Each seller must be free to change his price at any time. If a seller cannot cut a price until sometime after he has filed the lower figure, thus affording his rivals an opportunity to meet it instantly, the chances that he will do so are accordingly reduced. The plan must carry no recommendation as to price policy. If the publication of average "costs" suggests the figures to be filed, if uniform charges are voted at trade meetings then the reporting system becomes a method of policing the observance of a common price. The system, finally, must make no provision for the supervision of prices charged or for the imposition of penalties on those who sell below the figures they have filed. If association officials supervise the filing and persuade sellers whose quotations are low to raise them, if penalties are imposed on those who quote figures below those recommended or sell at figures below those quoted, then the reporting plan becomes but an incident in the whole price fixing scheme. When every one of these conditions is fulfilled, a price reporting system may promote effective competition. But where any one of them is unsatisfied, price reporting is likely to implement the non-competitive arrangements within the trade. It follows that competition must more often be dismissed than increased through the operation of price reporting plans.

Standardization [86]

The standardization of products, terms of contracts, and price lists and differentials, though frequently advantageous to buyers and sellers alike, is also subject to abuse. Standardization of products contributes to convenience and lessens waste. But it may limit competition in quality, restrict the consumer's range of choice, and by eliminating the sale of cheaper grades, compel him to buy a better and a more expensive product than the one that he desires.[87] Standardization of the terms of contracts saves time, prevents misunderstanding, and affords a common basis for the comparison of prices. If limited to such matters as allowable variations in the quality of goods delivered, the time when title passes, and the method to be employed in the settlement of disputes, it does not restrain competition. But a trade may go on to establish common credit terms, create uniform customer classifications, eliminate or standardize discounts, forbid free deals, limit guarantees, restrict the return of merchandize, minimize allowances on trade-ins, fix handling charges, forbid freight absorption, discourage long-term contracts, and agree upon a common policy with respect to guarantees against price declines. In the judgment of the Federal Trade Commission, "the standardization of terms of sale, and of elements in the sales contract, appears to be entirely desirable, and at least as beneficial to the buyer as to the seller, and yet it is hard to arrive cooperatively at such standardization without an agreement on some element in the price paid". At best, such an agreement restricts the scope of competition and deprives buyers of options which they are entitled to enjoy. At worst, it serves to supplement other elements in a comprehensive scheme of price control, preventing indirect departures from the established price and facilitating its enforcement through the operation of a price reporting plan. So, also, the standardization of price lists and differentials involving the selection of a single variety or size of product

86. See Wachtel, Products Standards and Certification Programs, 13 Antitrust Bull. 1 (1968); Blecher, Product Standards and Certification Programs, 46 Brooklyn L.Rev. 223 (1980).

87. Cf. National Macaroni Manufacturing Association v. Federal Trade Commission, 345 F.2d 421 (7th Cir. 1965) (condemning standardization of quantity of scarce ingredient).

for use as a base in quoting prices and the adoption of a system of uniform extras and discounts for use in computing the prices of other varieties and sizes, contributes to the convenience with which negotiations may be carried on. But here again, as the Trade Commission has observed, "the simplification of the process of quotation doubtless facilitates agreement on prices between sellers; and the devising of a base price list, or of standard differentials, by an association may be accompanied by elements of agreement that are contrary to the anti-trust laws."

Credit Bureaus

The provision, through a central bureau, of information on credit risks increases the safety with which credit may be granted. If confined to the exchange of ledger data on individual buyers in response to specific requests and accompanied by no recommendation as to policy, it helps the members of a trade without injustice to their customers. But an association may go on to limit the freedom of members to extend credit where they please, to circulate blacklists, to boycott delinquent debtors without affording them a hearing, to set up uniform terms to govern the extension of credit, and to employ the denial of credit as a means of controlling the channels of distribution or enforcing the maintenance of a resale price. . . .

Cooperation or Conspiracy? [88]

. . . It is impossible to measure the extent to which members of trade associations are actually engaged in cooperating to serve the public and in conspiring against it. The line between cooperation and conspiracy is not an easy one to draw. The courts, to be sure, must attempt to draw it. Price reporting, for instance, is held to be legal if reports are confined to past transactions, is of uncertain legality if they cover current or future transactions [89] and if members are required to adhere to the prices they have filed, and is illegal if essential information is withheld from buyers, if sellers are identified, if members agree upon the prices they will file, and if adherence to these prices is enforced by detailed supervision and by the imposition of penalties. But no one can say with confidence how many of the price reporting systems now in operation fail to overstep this line. . . . Nor can there ever be assurance that the merriment, diversion, and conversation, of which Adam Smith once spoke, do not lead to the conspiracies or contrivances to raise prices which he feared, unless an agent of the Federal Government is placed in every trade association office to read all correspondence, memoranda, and reports, attend all meetings, listen to all conversations, participate in all

88. See Section D, this chapter, supra; Dolan, How An Association is Investigated and What Is The Government Looking For – A Federal Trade Commission Perspective, 22 Antitrust Bull. 273 (1977).

89. The decision in United States v. Container Corp., supra p. 396, found agreement in the act of exchanging price information, and found that it was a *per se* unlawful agreement to fix prices because of its stabilizing effect on prices.

the merriment and diversion, and issue periodic reports on what transpires. No such systematic oversight is now authorized by law.

NOTES AND QUERIES

(1) *Other Practices of Trade Associations of Antitrust Significance.*
Although the principal focus of this chapter and subsection is on horizontal restraints affecting price, it is appropriate to mention summarily other categories of trade association activities which may raise antitrust issues.[90]

(a) Membership Restrictions.[91] Requirements for membership in an association may appear reasonable to members of the association, but unreasonable to those excluded thereby. The antitrust concern with membership requirements, often cast in terms of boycott analysis (see Chapter 5, infra), increases with the success of a trade association, the significance of its services to members, and where membership in an association is a virtual prerequisite to engaging in the trade or a profession.[92] Restrictions upon membership, reasonable in light of the trade involved and objectively administered in light of the particular circumstances involved, are generally upheld.[93] Judicial review on antitrust standards of the administration of reasonable membership restrictions might still be available, however, in cases where membership is a prerequisite to practicing a trade or profession. It is generally conceded, for example, that successful passage of a bar examination—even an examination administered by practicing lawyers—is a justifiable limitation on entry into the practice of law.[94] However, in *Ronwin v.*

90. See generally, Lamb & Shields, Trade Association Law & Practice (1971); L. Sullivan, Handbook on the Law of Antitrust, 265–311 (1977).

91. One of the first successful treble damage actions under the Sherman Act involved arbitrary membership requirements in an association of manufacturers of tiles, mantels and grates. See Montague & Co. v. Lowry, 193 U.S. 38, 24 S.Ct. 307, 48 L.Ed. 608 (1904). The validity of membership restrictions remains a frequently litigated issue. For surveys of the recent litigation, see Dallas, Trade Association Membership and the Antitrust Laws, 46 Brooklyn L.Rev. 193 (1980); Haddock, The Right of Trade Associations to Deny Membership and To Expel Members, 13 Antitrust Bull. 555 (1968).

92. A widespread circumstance in Adam Smith's day and singled out by Smith as a principal source of the inequality of wages. See A. Smith, The Wealth of Nations pp. 118–43 (Mod.Lib.Ed. 1937). Membership in an association as a condition of engaging in a trade is most common today in those activities labeled a "profession," although not exclusively so. For a perceptive survey of recent litigation involving membership and related activities restricting entry to a trade or profession, see Ponsoldt, The Application of Sherman Act Antiboycott Law to Industry Self-Regulation: An Analysis Integrating Nonboycott Sherman Act Principles, 55 So.Cal.L.Rev. 1 (1981).

93. See e.g., Deesen v. Professional Golfers' Association, 358 F.2d 165 (9th Cir. 1966), certiorari denied 385 U.S. 846, 87 S.Ct. 72, 17 L.Ed.2d 76 (1967) (qualifications for participating in professional golf tournaments); Neeld v. National Hockey League, 594 F.2d 1297 (9th Cir. 1979) (regulation barring one-eyed hockey player upheld as reasonable safety regulation); Cooney v. American Horse Show Association, Inc., 495 F.Supp. 424 (S.D.N.Y.1980) (suspension of trainer from horse shows for violation of drug rules).

94. Jean Baptise Say, a nineteenth century economist, wrote:

"[A]s society is possessed of a natural right to regulate the exercise of any class of industry, that without regulation might prejudice the rest of the community, physicians, surgeons, and apothecaries are with perfect justice subjected to an examination into their professional ability. The lives of their fellow-citizens are dependent upon their skill, and a test of that skill may fairly be established; but it does not seem advisable to limit the number of practitioners nor the plan of their education. Society has no interest further than to ascertain their qualification."

State Bar of Arizona,[95] the Ninth Circuit reversed dismissal of a claim under the Sherman Act charging that the bar examiners limited the number of those passing the examination to a bar association pre-determined number in order to restrict competition in the practice of law in Arizona. Unreasonable administration of a reasonable membership restriction, as well as adoption of arbitrary or unreasonable membership limitations,[96] may collide with antitrust policy where done with a purpose or effect of restraining trade.

(b) Joint Action Dealing With or Influencing Government.[97] A major area for trade association activities is in collecting and disseminating data on the impact of government upon the trade or business of the members and vice-versa. Collecting and disseminating regulatory, political, judicial, and legislative actions affecting a trade association's membership is a growth industry. The use of trade associations to lobby and influence government and its decision-making process is also a growth industry in an era when governmental decision-making can have a profound impact upon competitive and other conditions of the trade or when the powers of government can be manipulated to alter competitive conditions or government largess to favor the interests of an association's membership. Concerted industry activity to influence government can raise complex antitrust and First Amendment issues,[98] where the joint action exceeds the boundaries of legitimate petitioning of one's government or constitutes a misuse of the functions of a particular branch of government.[99] While discussion of those complexities is reserved for treatment elsewhere,[1] suffice it to note here that one of the more significant activities of many trade associations is in providing members with information about the actions of state and national governments affecting the trade or industry, as well as seeking to influence those actions of government by bringing the membership's views or information about the trade or industry to the attention of government decision makers.

(c) Products Standards and Certification Programs.[2] Trade associations, as well as government agencies like the National Bureau of Standards and independent testing agencies like Underwriter's Laboratory, engage in programs aimed at standardizing products (i.e., the number of scanning lines on

In the administration of bar examinations may candidates be required to have a law degree from an "accredited" law school; i.e., one meeting academic or other standards established by the A.B.A. or the American Association of Law Schools? See Feldman v. Gardner, 661 F.2d 1295 (D.C.Cir.1981) (upholding such a requirement where it was adopted by the courts regulating admission to the bar), certiorari denied ___ U.S. ___, 102 S.Ct. 3483, 73 L.Ed.2d 1366 (1982).

95. 663 F.2d 914 (9th Cir. 1981).

96. See e.g. United States v. Realty Multi-List, Inc., 629 F.2d 1351 (5th Cir. 1981), 5 CCH Trade Reg. Rep. ¶ 50,815 (1982) (proposed consent decree).

97. See generally, 1 P. Areeda & D. Turner, Antitrust Law Ch. 2A (1978); L. Sullivan, Handbook of the Law of Antitrust, 731–43 (1977); Chapter 7, infra.

98. See First, Private Interest and Public Control: Government Action, The First Amendment and the Sherman Act, 1975 Utah L.Rev. 9.

99. See Note, Limiting the Antitrust Immunity for Concerted Attempts to Influence Courts and Adjudicative Agencies: Analogies to Malicious Prosecution and Abuse of Process, 86 Harv.L.Rev. 715 (1973).

1. See Chapter 7, infra.

2. See L. Sullivan, Handbook on the Law of Antitrust, 275-82 (1977); Bakke, Joint Efforts in Developing Standards, 44 Antitrust L.J. 337 (1975); Blecker, Product Standards and Certification Programs, 46 Brooklyn L.Rev. 223 (1980); Ponsoldt, The Application of Sherman Act Antiboycott Law to Industry Self-Regulation: An Analysis Integrating Nonboycott Sherman Act Principles, 55 So.Cal.L.Rev. 1, 50 (1981); Wachtel, Product Standards and Certification Programs, 13 Antitrust Bull. 1 (1968); Note, Promoting Product-Quality Information: A Proposed Limited Antitrust Exemption for Producers, 30 Stan.L.Rev. 563 (1978).

T.V. receivers) or certifying the safety of products (i.e., electrical devices or other products presenting potential health or safety risks).[3] While certification and safety standards may bring many obvious and needed benefits to consumers and industry, they may also be used as devices to fix prices or exclude new innovations or particular competitors by manipulation of the standards or certification. While testing the safety or durability of such products as gas burners for use in a furnace and awarding a seal of approval to devices meeting widely known standards is a beneficial activity, manipulation of the standards or of the testing of the device to exclude a particular manufacturer's products can result in antitrust liability on a boycott theory.[4]

As Wilcox observed, supra p. 477: "The standardization of products, terms of contracts, and price lists and differentials, though frequently advantageous to buyers and sellers alike, is also subject to abuse. Standardization of products contributes to convenience and lessens waste. But it may limit competition in quality, restrict the consumer's range of choice, and by eliminating the sale of cheaper grades, compel him to buy a better and a more expensive product than the one that he desires." Standardization of the terms of contracts saves time, prevents misunderstanding, and affords a common basis for the comparison of prices. If limited to such matters as allowable variations in the quality of goods delivered, the time when title passes, and the method to be employed in the settlement of disputes, it does not restrain competition. But a trade may go on to establish common credit terms, create uniform customer classifications, eliminate or standardize discounts, forbid free deals, limit guarantees, restrict the return of merchandise, minimize allowances on trade-ins, fix handling charges, forbid freight absorption, discourage long-term contracts, and agree upon a common policy with respect to guarantees against price declines.[5]

In light of these risks, the Federal Trade Commission has been particularly active in supervising standards and certifications programs, having issued both an "Advisory Opinion" setting forth a series of factors to be evaluated in assessing the legality of a particular program[6] and a detailed "Proposed Trade Regulation Rule" governing such programs.[7] Considerable controversy was generated by the proposed rule. Congress, in the "F.T.C. Improvements Act of 1980",[8] prohibited the F.T.C. from issuing a trade regulation rule under § 18 of the Act governing certification programs.[9] The Commission was left with authority to evaluate such programs on a case-by-case

3. It has been estimated that approximately 400 groups are engaged in product standards and certification programs. F.T.C., Standards and Certification, Proposed Rule and Staff Report 16–17 (1978).

4. See Radiant Burners, Inc. v. Peoples Gas, Light & Coke Co., 364 U.S. 656, 81 S.Ct. 365, 5 L.Ed.2d 358 (1961); Hydrolevel Corp. v. American Society of Mechanical Engineers, 635 F.2d 118 (1980), affirmed __ U.S. __, 102 S.Ct. 1935, 72 L.Ed.2d 330 (1982). But see Eliason Corp. v. National Sanitation Foundation, 614 F.2d 126 (6th Cir. 1980), certiorari denied 449 U.S. 826, 101 S.Ct. 89, 66 L.Ed.2d 29. These issues are explored further, infra pp. 549–554.

5. See National Macaroni Manufacturer's Association v. Federal Trade Commission, 345 F.2d 421 (7th Cir. 1965);

Milk & Ice Cream Can Institute v. Federal Trade Commission, 152 F.2d 478 (7th Cir. 1946).

6. See American Standards Institute, Inc., 78 F.T.C. 1628 (1971).

7. 43 Fed. Reg. 57269 (Dec. 7, 1978); reprinted in 4 CCH Trade Reg. Rep. ¶ 38,047. Legislation regulating standards and certification programs was also considered by Congress in the mid-70's. See S. 3555, 94th Cong., 2d Sess. (1976). Extensive hearings were held exploring the activities of voluntary testing organizations. See Hearings, Voluntary Standards and Certification Act—1976, Subcommittee on Antitrust and Monopoly of the Senate Judiciary Comm., 94th Cong., 2d Sess. (1976).

8. 94 Stat. 374 (1980).

9. 15 U.S.C. § 57A.

basis under existing antitrust laws or possibly to regulate by rulemaking under § 6(g) of the F.T.C. Act.[10]

(g) Codes of "Ethics".[11] Trade associations often adopt codes of "ethics" to govern the conduct of members of the profession. Ethical constraints, aimed at regulating misleading, dishonest or dangerous practices and objectively administered usually pose no antitrust risk. However, codes of "ethics" are often used to mask anticompetitive activity; either intentionally or because the members' perception of what is "ethical" and what is not ethical does not equate with the law's perception of the public interest.[12] While the assumption of regulatory authority over the ethical conduct of the members of a trade may be tolerated up to a certain point, ethical constraints displacing the competitive process establishing price and other conditions of engaging in the trade or business collide with the national policy mandating competition as the rule of trade and the deeper political question of the degree to which private groups ought or ought not be allowed to assume powers more properly vested in a democratic government.[13]

(2) *The Status of Professional Associations Under the Antitrust Laws.* Review the discussion of *Goldfarb* and *National Society of Professional Engineers*, supra pp. 415–423, regarding a possible "justification" for professionals engaging in otherwise *per se* unlawful practices. Is there any justification for treating professional associations any different than trade associations for purposes of antitrust analysis of their activities? Are there risks to public health, safety and welfare if unbridled competition is allowed to take place in such areas as the practice of law or medicine?[14] Is restricting competition the only way to curb any dangerous or fraudulent practices which might result? To what extent should the traditional professions any longer be assumed to be dedicated to some "higher calling" of pursuing the interests of clients or patients and the public interest rather than the self-interest of the members of the profession? Is the ultimate choice either regulation by some objective and non-interested governmental authority or full and free competition—but no intermediate state of affairs such as self-regulation?[15]

---

10. 15 U.S.C. § 46(g). For a description of the legislative battle over F.T.C. regulation of standards and certification programs, see Riegel, The FTC in the 1980's: An Analysis of the FTC Improvements Act of 1980, 26 Antitrust Bull. 449, 461–67 (1981).

11. See Ponsoldt, supra note 54 at 44–47.

12. See, e.g., National Society of Professional Engineers v. United States, supra p. 415.

13. See Fashion Originators' Guild of America v. F.T.C., infra p. 532.

14. The justification for banning lawyer advertising offered by the 1969 version of the Code of Professional Responsibility stated:

The traditional ban is rooted in the public interest. Competitive advertising would encourage extravagant, artful, self-laudatory, brashness in seeking business and thus hoodwink laymen. Furthermore, it would inevitably produce unrealistic expectations

in particular cases, and bring about distrust in the law and lawyers. Thus, public confidence in the legal system is impaired with such advertising for professional services. The attorney-client relationship is personal and unique and should not be established because of the results of pressures and deception.

Mark Green observed with regard to this rationale that: "It is interesting how an organization of lawyers would assume the worst about their members." Green, "A Consumer Advocates' View", in Regulating the Professions, 271, 275 (1980) (R. Blair & S. Rubin Eds.).

15. "Self-regulation in the professions is indeed self-serving. Its ultimate aim and realized effect is to increase professionals' incomes beyond the levels that would obtain in perfectly competitive professional-service markets. Self-regulation accomplishes this by restricting entry and information and by various market-division schemes, which enhance the individual professional's ability to engage in price discrimination among in-

2. DATA COLLECTION AND DISSEMINATION

AMERICAN COLUMN & LUMBER CO. v. UNITED STATES

Supreme Court of the United States, 1921.
257 U.S. 377, 42 S.Ct. 114, 66 L.Ed. 284.

[Digest: The Government charged that the adoption and operation of an "Open Competition Plan" by the members of the American Hardwood Manufacturers Association unreasonably restrained trade in violation of Section 1 of the Sherman Act. The Association was comprised of 400 members operating hardwood mills in the United States. Although the membership comprised only 5 percent of the total number of hardwood mills, they produced one-third of the total production of the United States. The Association leadership proposed that members engage in a program of collecting and disseminating production and marketing information. Called "The Open Competition Plan", the purpose of the proposal was explained to members of the Association as follows:

> The chief concern of the buyer, as we all know, is to see that the price he pays is no higher than that of his competitors, against whom he must sell his product in the market. The chief concern of the seller is to get as much as anybody else for his lumber; in other words to get what is termed the top of the market for the quality he offers. By making prices known to each other they will gradually tend toward a standard *in harmony with market conditions*, a situation advantageous to both buyer and seller.

> The theoretical proposition at the basis of the Open Competition Plan is that

> *Knowledge regarding prices actually made is all that is necessary to keep prices at reasonably stable and normal levels.*

> The Open Competition Plan is a central clearing house for information on prices, trade statistics and practices. By keeping all members fully and quickly informed of what the others have done, the work of the Plan results in *a certain uniformity of trade practice*. There is no agreement to follow the practice of others, *although members do follow their most intelligent competitors*, if they know what these competitors have been actually doing.

> The monthly meetings held in various sections of the country each month have improved *the human relations* existing between the members before the organization of this Plan.

> Competition, blind, vicious, unreasoning, may stimulate trade to abnormal activity, but such condition is no more sound than

come groups and which enhance the profession's prospects for achieving super-perfect price discrimination within the more narrowly defined submarkets, both service and geographic. Society permits these self-serving practices to persist, in exchange for a guarantee of a certain minimal level of competence on the part of the professionals that serve it. It is a bargain that *our* society, at least, has in the main shown little inclination to repudiate." J. Horowitz, The Economic Foundations of Self-Regulation in the Professions, in Regulating the Professions, 3, 16 (1980) (R. Blair & S. Rubin Eds.).

that medieval spirit some still cling to of taking a club and going out and knocking the other fellow and taking away his bone.

The keynote to modern business success is mutual confidence and co-operation. *Co-operative competition, not cutthroat competition.* Co-operation is a matter of business, because it pays, because it enables you to get the best price for your product, because you come into closer *personal contact with the market.*

Co-operation will only replace *undesirable competition* as you develop a co-operative spirit. For the first time in the history of the industry, the hardwood manufacturers are organized into one compact, comprehensive body, equipped to serve the whole trade in a thorough and efficient manner. . . . More members mean more power to do more good for the industry. With co-operation of this kind we will very soon have enlisted in our efforts practically every producing interest, *and you know what that means.*

To achieve these ends, the Plan required each participant to make the following reports to the secretary for the plan:

1. A *daily* report of all sales actually made, with the name and address of the purchaser, the kind, grade and quality of lumber sold and all special agreements of every kind, verbal or written with respect thereto. "The reports to be exact copies of orders taken."

2. A *daily* shipping report, with exact copies of the invoices, all special agreements as to terms, grade, etc. The classification shall be the same as with sales.

3. A *monthly* production report, showing the production of the member reporting during the previous month, with the grades and thickness classified as prescribed in the Plan.

4. A *monthly* stock report by each member, showing the stock on hand on the first day of the month, sold and unsold, green and dry, with the total of each, kind, grade and thickness.

5. Price-lists. Members must file at the beginning of each month price-lists showing prices f.o.b. shipping point, which shall be stated. New prices must be filed with the association as soon as made.

6. Inspection reports. These reports are to be made to the association by a service of its own, established for the purpose of checking up grades of the various members and the Plan provides for a chief inspector and sufficient assistants to inspect the stocks of all members from time to time.

The Plan provided that these reports would be subject to audit by representatives of the Association and that members failing to report would not receive the Association's summary and analysis of the members' individual reports. The Plan required the Secretary to send to each member:

1. A *monthly* summary showing the production of each member for the previous month, "subdivided as to grade, kind, thickness," etc.

2. A *weekly* report, not later than Saturday, of all sales, to and including the preceding Tuesday, giving each sale and the price, and the name of the purchaser.

3. On Tuesday of each week the secretary must send to each member a report of each shipment by each member, complete up to the evening of the preceding Thursday.

4. He must send a *monthly* report, showing the individual stock on hand of each member and a summary of all stock, green and dry, sold and unsold. This report is very aptly referred to by the managing statistician as a monthly inventory of the stock of each member.

5. Not later than the 10th of each month the secretary shall send a summary of the price-lists furnished by members, showing the prices asked by each, and any changes made therein must be immediately transmitted to all the members.

6. A market report letter shall be sent to each member of the association (whether participating in the plan or not) pointing "out changes in conditions both in the producing and consuming sections, giving a comparison of production and sales and in general an analysis of the market conditions."

The Plan called for regional monthly meetings to discuss the reports and other matters of concern to the members. Regular meetings were held and the association statistician collected and disseminated further information prior to each meeting pursuant to an eleven part questionnaire. Among the eleven questions were the following:

(4) What was your total production of hardwood during the last month? What do you estimate your production will probably be for the next two months?

(10) Do you expect to shut down within the next few months on account of shortage of logs or for any other reason? If so, please state how long you will be idle.

(11) What is your view of market conditions for the next few months and what is the general outlook for business? State the reasons for your conclusion.

The majority opinion noted that while the Plan on paper called only for the collection and dissemination of information on "past transactions," these three questions plainly invited an estimate and discussion of future market conditions and coordination of future prices.

The Plan also called for the association's statistician to distribute a "monthly report letter" to all members. The letter was a statement of the statistician's estimate of current and future market conditions based on information about supply, demand and prices.]

MR. JUSTICE CLARKE delivered the opinion of the Court.

This elaborate plan for the interchange of reports does not simply supply to each member the amount of stock held, the sales made and the prices received, by every other member of the group, thereby furnishing the data for judging the market, on the basis of supply and demand and current prices. It goes much farther. It not only furnishes such information, with respect to stock, sales and prices, but also reports, giving the views of each member as to "market conditions for the next few months"; what the production of each will be for the next "two months"; frequent analyses of the reports by an expert, with, we shall see, significant suggestions as to both future prices and production; and opportunities for future meetings for the interchange of views, which the record shows were very important. It is plain that the only element lacking in this scheme to make it a familiar type of the competition suppressing organization is a definite agreement as to production and prices. But this is supplied: By the disposition of men "to follow their most intelligent competitors," especially when powerful; by the inherent disposition to make all the money possible, joined with the steady cultivation of the value of "harmony" of action; and by the system of reports, which makes the discovery of price reductions inevitable and immediate. The sanctions of the plan obviously are financial interest, intimate personal contact, and business honor, all operating under the restraint of exposure of what would be deemed bad faith and of trade punishment by powerful rivals.

The principles of law by which we must judge of the legality of the scheme of doing business thus provided for, as it was worked out in practice, are clearly settled by the anti-trust statute and the decisions of this court interpreting it. . . .

Obviously the organization of the defendants constitutes a combination and confessedly they are engaged in a large way in the transportation and sale of lumber in interstate commerce so that there remains for decision only the question whether the system of doing business adopted resulted in that direct and undue restraint of interstate commerce which is condemned by this anti-trust statute. . . .

Much more of like purport appears in the minutes of the meetings throughout the year, but this is sufficient to convincingly show that one of the prime purposes of the meetings, held in every part of the lumber district, and of the various reports, was to induce members to co-operate in restricting production, thereby keeping the supply low and the prices high, and that whenever there was any suggestion of running the mills to an extent which would bring up the supply to a point which might affect prices, the advice against operations which might lead to such result was put in the strongest possible terms. The co-operation is palpable and avowed, its purpose is clear, and we shall see that it was completely realized.

Next, the record shows clearly that the members of the combination were not satisfied to secure, each for himself, the price which might be obtainable even as the result of co-operative restriction of production, but that throughout the year they assiduously cultivated, through the letters of Gadd, speaking for them all, and through the discussions at the meetings, the general conviction that higher and higher prices were obtainable and a disposition on the part of all to demand them. The intention to create such a common purpose is too clear to be doubted, evidenced as it is by the following excerpts from much of like character in the testimony . . ..

[The Court quoted extensively from minutes of several meetings where members were urged to limit production and concluded the evidence showed "convincingly" that this was the purpose of the weekly meetings. Further quotations from the minutes were relied upon to demonstrate that the *purpose* of cutting production was to raise prices. Testimonials to the Plan's *effect* of raising prices, in the form of letters from the members, were relied upon to conclude the record demonstrated that not only was the purpose of the plan "to encourage members to unite in pressing for higher and higher prices without regard to cost," but that this purpose "was fully realized." The Court continued:]

These quotations are sufficient to show beyond discussion that the purpose of the organization, and especially of the frequent meetings, was to bring about a concerted effort to raise prices regardless of cost or merit, and so was unlawful, and that the members were soon entirely satisfied that the Plan was "carrying out the purpose for which it was intended."

As to the price conditions during the year: Without going into detail, the record shows that the prices of the grades of hardwood in most general use were increased to an unprecedented extent during the year. Thus, the increases in prices of varieties of oak, range from 33.3 per cent. to 296 per cent. during the year; of gum, 60 per cent. to 343 per cent., and of ash, from 55 per cent. to 181 per cent. While it is true that 1919 was a year of high and increasing prices generally, and that wet weather may have restricted production to some extent, we cannot but agree with the members of the Plan themselves, as we have quoted them, and with the District Court, in the conclusion that the united action of this large and influential membership of dealers contributed greatly to this extraordinary price increase.

Such close co-operation, between many persons, firms, and corporations controlling a large volume of interstate commerce, as is provided for in this Plan, is plainly in theory, as it proved to be in fact, inconsistent with that free and unrestricted trade which the statute contemplates shall be maintained, and that the persons conducting the association fully realized this is apparent from their protesting so often as they did, in many of their confidential communications appearing in this record, that their purposes were not unlawful, that they sought only to supplant cutthroat competition with what in their own judgment would be "fair and reasonable competition," and to obtain, not make, fair prices, and by their repeated insistence that the Sherman Law, "designed to prevent the restraint of trade, is itself one of the greatest restrainers of trade, and should be repealed."

To call the activities of the defendants, as they are proved in this record, an "Open Competition Plan" of action is plainly a misleading misnomer.

Genuine competitors do not make daily, weekly, and monthly reports of the minutest details of their business to their rivals, as the defendants did; they do not contract, as was done here, to submit their books to the discretionary audit, and their stocks to the discretionary inspection, of their rivals, for the purpose of successfully competing with them; and they do not submit the details of their business to the analysis of an expert, jointly employed, and obtain from him a "harmonized" estimate of the market as it is, and as, in his specially and confidentially informed judgment, it promises to be. This is not the conduct of competitors, but is so clearly that of men united in an agreement, express or implied, to act together and pursue a common purpose under a common guide that, if it did not stand confessed a combination to restrict production and increase prices in interstate commerce, and as, therefore, a direct restraint upon that commerce, as we have seen that it is, that conclusion must inevitably have been inferred from the facts which were proved. To pronounce such abnormal conduct on the part of 365 natural competitors, controlling one-third of the trade of the country in an article of prime necessity, a "new form of competition," and not an old form of combination in restraint of trade, as it so plainly is, would be for this court to confess itself blinded by words and forms to realities which men in general very plainly see, and understand and condemn, as an old evil in a new dress and with a new name.

The Plan is, essentially, simply an expansion of the gentleman's agreement of former days, skillfully devised to evade the law. To call it open competition, because the meetings were nominally open to the public, or because some voluminous reports were transmitted to the Department of Justice, or because no specific agreement to restrict trade or fix prices is proved, cannot conceal the fact that the fundamental purpose of the Plan was to procure "harmonious" individual action among a large number of naturally competing dealers with respect to the volume of production and prices, without having any specific agreement with respect to them, and to rely for maintenance of concerted action in both respects, not upon fines and forfeitures as in earlier days, but upon what experience has shown to be the more potent and dependable restraints, of business honor and social penalties—cautiously reinforced by many and elaborate reports, which would promptly expose to his associates any disposition in any member to deviate from the tacit understanding that all were to act together under the subtle direction of a single interpreter of their common purposes, as evidenced in the minute reports of what they had done and in their expressed purposes as to what they intended to do.

In the presence of this record it is futile to argue that the purpose of the Plan was simply to furnish those engaged in this industry, with widely scattered units, the equivalent of such information as is contained in the newspaper and government publications with respect to the market for commodities sold on Boards of Trade or Stock Exchanges. One distinguishing and sufficient difference is that the published reports go to both seller and buyer, but these reports go to

the seller only; and another is that there is no skilled interpreter of
the published reports, such as we have in this case, to insistently recommend harmony of action likely to prove profitable in proportion as
it is unitedly pursued.

Convinced, as we are, that the purpose and effect of the activities
of the Open Competition Plan, here under discussion, were to restrict
competition, and thereby restrain interstate commerce in the manufacture and sale of hardwood lumber, by concerted action in curtailing production and in increasing prices, we agree with the District
Court that it constituted a combination and conspiracy in restraint of
interstate commerce within the meaning of the Anti-Trust Act of 1890
(26 Stat. 209), and the decree of that court must be affirmed.

MR. JUSTICE HOLMES, dissenting.

When there are competing sellers of a class of goods, knowledge
of the total stock on hand, of the probable total demand, and of the
prices paid, of course will tend to equalize the prices asked. But I
should have supposed that the Sherman Act did not set itself against
knowledge—did not aim at a transitory cheapness unprofitable to the
community as a whole because not corresponding to the actual conditions of the country. I should have thought that the ideal of commerce was an intelligent interchange made with full knowledge of the
facts as a basis for a forecast of the future on both sides. A combination to get and distribute such knowledge, notwithstanding its tendency to equalize, not necessarily to raise, prices, is very far from a
combination in unreasonable restraint of trade. It is true that it is a
combination of sellers only, but the knowledge acquired is not secret,
it is public, and the buyers, I think I may assume, are not less active
in their efforts to know the facts. A combination in unreasonable
restraint of trade imports an attempt to override normal market conditions. An attempt to conform to them seems to me the most reasonable thing in the world. I see nothing in the conduct of the appellants that binds the members even by merely social sanctions to
anything that would not be practised, if we could imagine it, by an
all-wise socialistic government acting for the benefit of the community as a whole. The parties to the combination are free to do as they
will.

I must add that the decree as it stands seems to me surprising in
a country of free speech that affects to regard education and knowledge as desirable. It prohibits the distribution of stock, production,
or sales reports, the discussion of prices at association meetings, and
the exchange of predictions of high prices. It is true that these acts
are the main evidence of the supposed conspiracy, but that to my
mind only shows the weakness of the Government's case. I cannot
believe that the fact, if it be assumed, that the acts have been done
with a sinister purpose, justifies excluding mills in the backwoods
from information, in order to enable centralized purchasers to take
advantage of their ignorance of the facts.

I agree with the more elaborate discussion of the case by my
BROTHER BRANDEIS.

MR. JUSTICE BRANDEIS, dissenting, with whom MR. JUSTICE
McKENNA concurs.

. . . In the case before us there was clearly no coercion.
There is no claim that a monopoly was sought or created. There is
no claim that a division of territory was planned or secured. There is
no claim that uniform prices were established or desired. There is no
claim that by agreement, force or fraud, any producer, dealer, or consumer was to be or has in fact been controlled or coerced. The Plan
is a voluntary system for collecting from these independent concerns
detailed information concerning the business operations of each, and
its opinions as to trade conditions, prospects, and policy, and of collat-
ing, interpreting, and distributing the data so received among the
members of the Association and others. No information gathered under the Plan was kept secret from any producer, any buyer, or the
public. Ever since its inception in 1917, a copy of every report made
and of every market letter published has been filed with the Department of Justice, and with the Federal Trade Commission. The district meetings were open to the public. Dealers and consumers were
invited to participate in the discussions, and to some extent have done
so.

It is claimed that the purpose of the Open Competition Plan was
to lessen competition. Competition among members was contemplated and was in vigorous operation. The Sherman Law does not prohibit every lessening of competition; and it certainly does not command that competition shall be pursued blindly, that business rivals
shall remain ignorant of trade facts, or be denied aid in weighing
their significance. It is lawful to regulate competition in some degree. Chicago Board of Trade v. United States, 246 U.S. 231, 38 S.Ct.
242, 62 L.Ed. 683. But it was neither the aim of the Plan, nor the
practice under it, to regulate competition in any way. Its purpose
was to make rational competition possible, by supplying data not otherwise available, and without which most of those engaged in the
trade would be unable to trade intelligently.

The hardwood lumber mills are widely scattered. The principal
area of production is the Southern States. But there are mills in Minnesota, New York, New England, and the Middle States. Most plants
are located near the sources of supply, isolated, remote from the larger cities and from the principal markets. No official, or other public,
means have been established for collecting from these mills and from
dealers data as to current production, stocks on hand, and market
prices. Concerning grain, cotton, coal, and oil, the government collects and publishes regularly, at frequent intervals, current information on production, consumption, and stocks on hand; and Boards of
Trade furnish freely to the public details of current market prices of
those commodities, the volume of sales, and even individual sales, as
recorded in daily transactions. Persons interested in such commodities are enabled through this information to deal with one another on

an equal footing. The absence of such information in the hardwood
lumber trade enables dealers in the large centers more readily to secure advantage over the isolated producer. And the large concerns,
which are able to establish their own bureaus of statistics, secure an
advantage over smaller concerns. Surely it is not against the public
interest to distribute knowledge of trade facts, however detailed.
Nor are the other features of the Plan—the market letters and the
regional conferences—an unreasonable interference with freedom in
trade. Intelligent conduct of business implies, not only knowledge of
trade facts, but an understanding of them. To this understanding
editorial comment and free discussion by those engaged in the business and by others interested are aids. Opinions expressed may be
unsound; predictions may be unfounded; but there is nothing in the
Sherman Law which should limit freedom of discussion, even among
traders.

It is insisted that there was a purpose to curtail production. No
evidence of any such purpose was introduced. There was at no time
uniformity in the percentage of production to capacity. On the contrary, the evidence is uncontradicted that the high prices induced
strenuous efforts to increase production. Weather and labor conditions had made production difficult. Tractors were purchased at
great cost to get the logs out of the forests which excessive rains had
rendered inaccessible to the usual methods of transport. The current
sales of new machinery to hardwood lumber mills were on an unprecedented scale. Where equipment and supply of logs permitted, mills
were run at night to overcome the restrictions upon production which
the bad weather had imposed. There were, it is true, from time to
time, warnings, in the "Market Letters" and otherwise, against overproduction—warnings which seem not to have been heeded. But
surely Congress did not intend by the Sherman Act to prohibit self-
restraint—and it was for self-restraint that the only appeal was
made. The purpose of the warnings was to induce mill owners to
curb their greed—lest both they and others suffer from the crushing
evils of overproduction. Such warning or advice, whether given by
individuals or the representatives of an association, presents no element of illegality.

It is urged that this was a concerted effort to enhance prices.
There was at no time uniformity in prices. So far as appears, every
mill charged for its product as much as it could get. There is evidence that the hardwood mills expected, by adopting the Plan, to earn
more in profits, and to do so, at least in part, by getting higher prices
for their product. It may be that the distribution of the trade data,
the editorial comment, and the conferences enabled the producers to
obtain, on the average, higher prices than would otherwise have been
possible. But there is nothing in the Sherman Law to indicate that
Congress intended to condemn co-operative action in the exchange of
information, merely because prophecy resulting from comment on the
data collected may lead, for a period, to higher market prices. Congress assumed that the desire to acquire and to enjoy property is the
safest and most promising basis for society, and to that end it sought,

among other things, to protect the pursuit of business for private profit. Its purpose, obviously, was not to prevent the making of profits, or to counteract the operation of the law of supply and demand. Its purpose was merely to prevent restraint. The illegality of a combination under the Sherman Law lies, not in its effect upon the price level, but in the coercion thereby affected. It is the limitation of freedom, by agreements which narrow a market, which constitutes the unlawful restraint.

The co-operation which is incident to this plan does not suppress competition. On the contrary, it tends to promote all in competition which is desirable. By substituting knowledge for ignorance, rumor, guess, and suspicion, it tends also to substitute research and reasoning for gambling and piracy, without closing the door to adventure, or lessening the value of prophetic wisdom. In making such knowledge available to the smallest concern, it creates among producers equality of opportunity. In making it available, also, to purchasers and the general public, it does all that can actually be done to protect the community from extortion. If, as is alleged, the Plan tends to substitute stability in prices for violent fluctuations, its influence, in this respect, is not against the public interest. The evidence in this case, far from establishing an illegal restraint of trade, presents, in my opinion, an instance of commendable effort by concerns engaged in a chaotic industry to make possible its intelligent conduct under competitive conditions.

The refusal to permit a multitude of small rivals to co-operate, as they have done here, in order to protect themselves and the public from the chaos and havoc wrought in their trade, by ignorance, may result in suppressing competition in the hardwood industry. These keen business rivals, who sought through co-operative exchange of trade information to create conditions under which alone rational competition is possible, produce in the aggregate about one-third of the hardwood lumber of the country. This court held in United States v. U. S. Steel Corporation, 251 U.S. 417, 40 S.Ct. 293, 64 L.Ed. 343, 8 A.L.R. 1121, that it was not unlawful to vest in a single corporation control of 50 per cent. of the steel industry of the country; and in United States v. United Shoe Machinery Co., 247 U.S. 32, 38 S.Ct. 473, 62 L.Ed. 968, the court held that it was not unlawful to vest in a single corporation control of practically the whole shoe machinery industry. May not these hardwood lumber concerns, frustrated in their efforts to rationalize competition, be led to enter the inviting field of consolidation? And, if they do, may not another huge trust, with highly centralized control over vast resources, natural, manufacturing, and financial, become so powerful as to dominate competitors, wholesalers, retailers, consumers, employees, and, in large measure, the community?

QUERIES

(1) Is there any evidence in these opinions bearing on the question whether the Hardwood Association was a league of small backwoods sawmills or

of "large concerns, which are able to establish their own bureaus of statistics"?

(2) In what respect, if any, would the trade statistics activities of "an allwise socialistic government acting for the benefit of the community as a whole" differ from the "Open Competition Plan"? *Wouldn't*

(3) If you were General Counsel to a trade association of the same scope and character as the Hardwood Association, precisely what changes in activities would you recommend after reading the *American Column and Lumber* case?

(4) Should the fact that there was no "coercion" upon members to raise or maintain prices or to restrict production save the plan? Should producers of one-third of the nation's hardwood be free to have full discussion of prices and come to voluntary understandings as to future prices, so long as they make no enforceable commitments?

(5) Is "discussion" of future prices by competitors protected by the First Amendment to the Federal Constitution? [16]

(6) If a little backwoods sawyer is ignorantly selling lumber at a price satisfactory to himself but $6 below "the market," is there a community interest in eliminating the discrepancy? If so, what agency should the community employ for that purpose?

MAPLE FLOORING MANUFACTURER'S ASSOCIATION v. UNITED STATES

Supreme Court of the United States, 1925.
268 U.S. 563, 45 S.Ct. 578, 69 L.Ed. 1093.

[The following is a digest of the Court's opinion:] The Maple Flooring Association was an organization of twenty-two manufacturers of maple, beech and birch flooring. Its members produced upwards of 70% of this type of flooring, although they had only about a third of the national manufacturing capacity and controlled a small proportion of the total stand of such timber. The Association distributed among its members periodic reports based on weekly and monthly member reports on sales, prices, production, selling commissions, inventory, unfilled orders and new orders booked, for each variety of

---

16. See pp. 340–341, supra.

Compare the problem of the extent to which employers may constitutionally be forbidden to express themselves to their employees on the subject of the selection or rejection of a union to represent them in collective bargaining with the employer. Section 8(1) of the National Labor Relations Act of 1935, 29 U.S.C.A. § 158, made it an unfair labor practice for an employer to "interfere with, restrain, or coerce" employees in the exercise of their right of self-organization. Under this section the employer's freedom to speak on unionization issues was sharply curtailed. But cf. National Labor Relations Board v. Virginia Electric & Power Co., 314 U.S. 469, 479, 62 S.Ct. 344, 349, 86 L.Ed. 348 (1941), reversing the Board where it held utterances by the employer to be unfair labor practices, without finding that the utterances were "raised to the stature of coercion by . . . the surrounding circumstances."

The Labor-Management Relations Act of 1947 ("Taft-Hartley Act") provided that:

"The expressing of any views, argument, or opinion, or the dissemination thereof, whether in written, printed, graphic, or visual form, shall not constitute or be evidence of an unfair labor practice . . . if such expression contains no threat of reprisal or force or promise of benefit." 29 U.S.C.A. § 158(c).

See generally, Gorman, Labor Law 148–56 (1976).

flooring. Prior to 1923 the Association reports identified the mill concerned in each transaction reported. The Association also distributed among its members a quarterly computation of average cost of finished flooring, and a freight rate book showing rail rates from Cadillac, Michigan to numerous consumption points in the United States. At monthly meetings the members discussed the published statistics and manufacturing and marketing conditions, but on advice of counsel there was no discussion of future prices.

The average cost figures were obtained as follows: the cost of rough lumber was computed by averaging the purchase prices in five or ten selected transactions. The percentage of waste in converting the rough lumber into flooring was ascertained by test runs made by selected members of the Association. Manufacturing costs were ascertained by questionnaires in which members were asked to give information as to labor costs, cost of warehousing, insurance and taxes, interest at 6% on the value of the plant, selling expense including commissions and cost of advertising, and depreciation of plant. From the total thus ascertained there was deducted the net profit from wood and other by-products. The aggregate cost, thus ascertained, of all flooring produced by members was divided by total production to give an average cost for flooring. Since this average did not take into account differences in types and grades of flooring, officials of the Association made an adjustment, on a basis not disclosed by the evidence, to arrive at "average cost" of particular types and grades.

It was the Government's theory that the intent and necessary effect of this scheme was to stabilize prices by suggesting that members sell at a standard price, made up of the average cost plus freight from Cadillac (regardless of actual shipping point) plus a standard profit. As evidence of the purpose behind the Association's activities, the Government showed that since 1913 the defendants had maintained a number of successive trade organizations, gradually modifying, under government pressure, more obvious price support plans closely resembling the present arrangements. Thus a previous freight rate book used by defendants in connection with a so-called "minimum price plan" had incorporated a schedule of prices based upon average cost plus 10% profit plus freight from Cadillac. This plan had been abandoned in 1920. Thereafter and until 1923 the Association had included in its computation of average cost 5% for "contingencies".

The defendants justified the cost calculation and dissemination of prices and other information regarding past transactions as mere exchange of information not different in purpose or effect from similar trade information distributed by the government in other trades. Association reports were read by 90 to 95 per cent of the buyers of flooring, were furnished to the Department of Commerce, and were available to anyone. The use of the freight book was defended as a convenience to members in calculating their own selling prices. Buyers in this trade preferred to have price quotations include transportation to their own place of business ("delivered prices"). Most of the members of the Association were located in Michigan and Wisconsin and the Cadillac rates were about equal to the average rates from their mills to principal consuming centers. Delays in obtaining rate figures from local railroad agents in defendants' mill towns had frequently interfered with prompt quotation of prices to customers.

A decree against the defendants was reversed by the Supreme Court, 6 to 3. Mr. Justice Stone, writing the majority opinion, held that the challenged arrangement involved no more tendency to stabilize prices than necessarily followed from the dissemination of trade information:

> "Persons who unite in gathering and disseminating information in trade journals and statistical reports on industry; who gather and publish statistics as to the amount of production of commodities in interstate commerce, and who report market prices, are not engaged in unlawful conspiracies in restraint of trade merely because the ultimate result of their efforts may be to stabilize prices or limit production through a better understanding of economic laws and a more general ability to conform to them, for the simple reason that the Sherman Law neither repeals economic laws nor prohibits the gathering and dissemination of information. Sellers of any commodity who guide the daily conduct of their business on the basis of market reports would hardly be deemed to be conspirators engaged in restraint of interstate commerce. They would not be any the more so merely because they became stockholders in a corporation or joint owners of a trade journal, engaged in the business of compiling and publishing such reports . . .
>
> "We decide only that trade associations or combinations of persons or corporations which openly and fairly gather and disseminate information as to the cost of their product, the volume of production, the actual price which the product has brought in past transactions, stocks of merchandise on hand, approximate cost of transportation from the principal point of shipment to the points of consumption, as did these defendants, and who, as they did, meet and discuss such information and statistics without however reaching or attempting to reach any agreement or any concerted action with respect to prices or production or restraining competition, do not thereby engage in unlawful restraint of commerce." [17]

NOTES AND QUERIES

(1) *Trade Association Data Collection and Dissemination After Container Corp. and Gypsum.* At this juncture, *United States v. Container Corp.* (supra p. 396) and *United States v. United States Gypsum Co.* (supra p. 400) should be reviewed from the perspective of their impact upon

---

17. See also Tag Manufacturers Institute v. Federal Trade Commission, 174 F.2d 452 (1st Cir., 1949), setting aside a cease and desist order against a trade association price reporting plan; In re Vitrified China Ass'n, 49 F.T.C. 1571 (1953). The Maple Flooring and Tag Manufacturers decisions are criticized in Stocking, The Rule of Reason, Workable Competition, and the Legality of Trade Association Activities, 21 U.Chi.L.Rev. 527 (1954).

trade association data collection and dissemination activities. *Container Corp.* remains the leading Supreme Court decision for defining the boundary between a lawful and unlawful exchange of information about industry conditions.[18] Would the conduct in *American Column & Lumber* and *Maple Flooring* be sufficient to sustain a criminal conviction for price fixing after *Gypsum*? How much evidence of an effect on prices is necessary to infer a specific intent to fix prices? Does *Container Corp.* overrule *Maple Flooring*? How much of an effect of "stabilizing prices" as a result of collecting and disseminating past information on production, inventory, pricing, shipping costs and the like is necessary to prove the effect of the joint action is to displace the competitive process establishing price rather than enhance the competitive process by enabling individual firms to maximize their efficiency as a result of knowledge of their competitors' costs?

(2) *Characteristics of the Industry and the Effect of an Exchange of Information.* In comparing cases like *Container Corp., Gypsum, American Column* and *Maple Flooring,* industry structure and the nature of the product, its method of production, and the means for distributing the product—as well as whether the information exchanged is with regard to past or future transactions and conditions—appear to be significant in drawing the line between legality and illegality. In determining the level of antitrust risk in collecting and disseminating specific categories of information it may make a difference whether the industry is concentrated or not, what percentage of industry production is involved in the activity, whether the product is fungible or not, whether transportation costs are a significant or minimal part of total cost, whether manufacturing processes are substantially identical throughout the industry or not and so on. The facts unique to each industry involved in data collection and dissemination and the specific types of information being collected in light of the characteristics of the industry are particularly significant in judging the pro- or anti-competitive effects of the activity.

For example, a closer examination of the industry and categories of information collected in *Maple Flooring* demonstrates the kinds of questions which should be considered in counseling a trade association in this area. Would you expect the cost of rough lumber to vary by as much as 100%, depending on the section of the country, availability to transportation, etc.? Or would you suppose this to be an industry in which raw material costs are substantially uniform throughout the country? Who selects the "five or ten selected transactions" and what might influence the choice of the transactions to be included in the averaging? If raw material costs vary widely how will information as to the national average help any individual manufacturer to set his selling price? Will he increase his selling price if he learns that the national average is higher than his own cost, or will that be impossible because presumably he is already charging as much as his own immediate competition will permit? Will he reduce his selling price if he knows that the national average cost of rough lumber is lower than he pays? Of what order of magnitude would you expect variations in selling expense to be? Is 6% interest on value of the plant a "cost"? In estimating the waste in converting rough lumber into flooring would a trade association officer have any interest in selecting the most efficient converters? If you were a floor-

18. Lower courts, have had a tendency to ignore or limit the implications of *Container Corp.* See Comment, Antitrust Liability for an Exchange of Price Information—What Happened to *Container Corporation,* 63 Va.L.Rev. 639 (1977).

ing manufacturer how would the association's computed average cost of flooring enter into your calculations?

(3) *Decrees Limiting Exchange of Information.* An association of manufacturers of machine-made chain and individual members of the association consented to a judgment containing the following provisions:

IV. The defendant Association is enjoined and restrained from collecting from or circulating, reporting, or recommending to any manufacturer of machine-made chain any costs or averaged costs of manufacture or sale of machine-made chain, any prices or terms used or to be used in connection with the sale of machine-made chain, or any formulae for computing such costs or prices.

V. The consenting defendants are jointly and severally enjoined and restrained from entering into, adhering to, or maintaining, or claiming any rights under any contract, combination, agreement, understanding, plan, or program with any other defendant, with any other manufacturer of machine-made chain, or with any association or central agency of or for manufacturers of machine-made chain:

(A) To fix, determine, establish or maintain prices, pricing methods, discounts or other terms and conditions used or to be used by such defendant or by any other person in connection with the manufacture or sale of machine-made chain;

(B) To circulate or exchange, directly or indirectly, any price lists or price quotations applicable to machine-made chain with any other machine-made chain manufacturers in advance of the publication, circulation or communication of such price lists or price quotations to the customers of such defendant;

(C) To circulate or exchange, directly or indirectly, any statistics representing costs of operation with any other machine-made chain manufacturer, for the purpose or with the effect of fixing prices or, otherwise restraining trade.

. . .

VII. Within sixty (60) days following the date of the entry of this Final Judgment, each of the consenting defendants, other than the defendant Association, is ordered and directed to cease utilizing any cost or pricing formulae or part thereof which has not been independently arrived at by such consenting defendant, and which has been theretofore furnished to such defendant by the defendant Association, or by any other manufacturer of machine-made chain, as a means of determining in whole or in part the price or prices at which such consenting defendant will sell any style, size or design of machine-made chain.

VIII. Within sixty (60) days following the date of the entry of this Final Judgment, each of the defendants, other than the defendant Association, and the consenting defendant M. S. Co., Inc., is ordered and directed:

(A) To withdraw his or its presently effective price lists for machine-made chain (or, where no price list has been issued, withdraw his or its presently prevailing prices); and

(B) To individually review the machine-made chain prices withdrawn in conformity with Section VIII(A) herein, on the basis of his or its individual cost figures and individual judgment as to profits, and issue a new price list (or, where no price list has been issued, issue new prices) on the basis of such independent review.[19]

Query: Should members of the Association be permitted to exchange price lists among themselves once they are in the hands of customers? [20]

(4) *Information Exchange and Game Theory.* It is a truism of economics that perfect competition could occur only in "transparent" markets, i.e., where all buyers and all sellers have complete and immediate knowledge of available alternatives. But see Shubik, Information, Theories of Competition, and the Theory of Games, 60 J.Pol.Econ. 145 (1952): "Possibly one of the first steps for many firms in competition to take is to form a trade association among whose functions the dissemination of information is by no means minor. In this way, in a dynamic situation the amount of information available enables many to become few for the purposes of competition." [21]

(5) *Business Advisory Committees.* Trade association representatives increasingly participate in official policy-making through committees organized to advise the government. The danger in this situation that governmental action will become merely a cover for industry self-determination,[22] or that the desires of dominant units in the trade will be translated into law or regulation, has led to proposals to regulate the functioning of these committees.[23] The Antitrust Division of the Department of Justice has issued opinions, based on its construction of the antitrust laws, requiring, among other things, that "the agenda for such committees and their meetings must be initiated and formulated by the Government . . . and any determinations of action to be taken must be made solely by government representatives." [24] The Defense Production Act required that industry representatives, "including trade association representatives", be consulted in the formulation of regulations and orders under the Act, and directed the President to encourage them to make voluntary agreements, which would be exempt from

19. United States v. Machine Chain Manufacturers Association (D.R.I.1955), CCH 1955 Trade Cases, ¶ 68,009; Cf. Chain Institute, Inc. v. Federal Trade Commission, 246 F.2d 231 (8th Cir. 1957). See also GE and Westinghouse decrees, supra p. 453.

20. Upon remand of the *Container* case, the trial court entered a judgment over the Government's objection permitting an exchange of price lists which had been made generally available to customers. United States v. Container Corp., 1970 Trade Cases ¶ 73,091 (D.N.C.1970).

21. See generally, Shubik, Strategy and Market Structure: Competition, Oligopoly and the Theory of Games (1959).

22. See Federal Trade Commission v. Texaco, Inc., 555 F.2d 862 (D.C.Cir. 1977), seeking to enforce subpoenas against a trade association supplying data on gas reserves used in government rate making.

23. See discussion of, product standards and certification programs, supra pp. 480–481.

24. Letter to the Secretary of Commerce, Oct. 19, 1950, CCH Trade Reg. Par. 61,301. See also Interim Report on

The Business Advisory Council for the Department of Commerce, Antitrust Subcommittee of the House Committee on the Judiciary (1955); H.Rep. 576 on H.R. 7390, 85th Cong. 1st Sess. (1957); Ginsburg, Industry Committees, The Antitrust Laws and Industrial Mobilization, Current Business Studies, Jan. 1951. See Federal Committee Act, 5 U.S.C.A. App. § 1 requiring registration of such committees and imposing rules to assure official control and responsibility.

The Federal Trade Commission utilizes industry advisory committees in connection with its program of trade practice conferences. These conferences result in rules specifying practices likely to be regarded as unfair or deceptive and therefore unlawful under Section 5(a) of the Federal Trade Commission Act. Advisory Committees are expressly forbidden to interpret conference rules, to attempt to correct alleged violations, or to receive or screen complaints of violation. 16 C.F.R. § 16.1 (Supp.1958).

As to the F.T.C. conference program in general, see Note, 62 Yale L.J. 912 (1953). As to FTC rule-making authority under the Federal Trade Commission Improvements Act of 1975, see p. 21 supra.

the antitrust laws, to further the objectives of the Act.[25] Where a statute, the Fair Packaging and Labelling Act, 15 U.S.C. § 1454(d), provides a formal procedure by which the Secretary of Commerce is to consult an industry and affected interests in standardizing package size to facilitate comparison shopping, do the antitrust laws foreclose an "informal" consultation with the industry alone prior to the statutory proceeding? [26]

Health and safety standards established by non-profit professional and scientific associations or societies and given effect by government or industry enforcement, may also be developed or administered by voluntary committees from the profession or industry affected by the standards. For example, the American Society of Mechanical Engineers (ASME), a non-profit technical and scientific society, promulgates over 400 codes and standards related to mechanical engineering. Many of the codes become incorporated into federal, state and local regulations. Committees composed of volunteers from ASME's membership draft, revise and interpret the codes. In American Society of Mechanical Engineers, Inc. v. Hydrolevel Corp.,[27] the Society was held liable in a treble damage suit for injuries to a plaintiff driven out of the business of manufacturing safety valves for boilers. Two volunteers serving on ASME's Boiler and Pressure Vessel Code Committee were employees of the leading manufacturer of such devices. The plaintiff had developed an improved boiler cut-off valve. The volunteers employed by a competing valve manufacturer were found to have used ASME's Code committee process to cause ASME to issue a false opinion letter stating the plaintiff's valve did not meet the Code's standards. The Supreme Court affirmed a judgment holding the volunteers, their employer and ASME liable in treble damages. ASME's liability was premised on the agency notions of apparent authority and ratification. Three dissenters objected to the "expansion" of treble damage liability of a non-profit association on a theory of apparent authority.

Query: Should government agencies or non-profit societies be liable for unauthorized anticompetitive activities carried out under their auspices by voluntary members of advisory committees or code committees?

(6) *Foreign Law Alternatives for Regulating Trade Associations.* The British Restrictive Trade Practices Act provides:

> Where specific recommendations (whether express or implied) are made by or on behalf of a trade association to its members or to any class of its members, as to the action to be taken or not taken by them in relation to any particular class of goods or process of manufacture in respect of any matter described in the said subsection (1), this Part of this Act [requiring restrictive agreements to be registered and declared invalid if contrary to the public interest] shall apply in relation to the agreement for the constitution of the association notwithstanding any provision to the contrary therein, as if it contained a term by which each such member, and any person represented on the association by any such member, agreed to comply with those recommendations and any subsequent recommendations made to them by or on behalf of the association as to the

---

25. 50 U.S.C.A.App. §§ 2151, 2158, 2159.

26. See letter of 11/27/68 from Assistant Attorney General to the Chief, Office of Weights & Measures, National Bureau of Standards. ATRR Rep. No. 387, December 10, 1968, p. X–1.

27. 456 U.S. 556, 102 S.Ct. 1935, 72 L.Ed.2d 330 (1982).

action to be taken by them in relation to the same class of goods or process of manufacture and in respect of the same matter.[28]

Query: Would enactment of a comparable provision by Congress change American trade association law?

3. DELIVERED PRICING

Trade association activities which risk being labeled "price fixing" may also arise when joint activity tampers with one element of the cost of the members' goods or services. Trade association activity designed to standardize credit terms, regulate the blend of different wheats sold as "Durum wheat", limit pricing signs at gasoline stations, eliminate the distribution of trading stamps and limit warranties have all been found to be *per se* unlawful "price fixing" because of the effect of the activity upon the ultimate price to consumers. (See Notes: "Ambiguous Price Fixing—How *Per Se* is the *Per Se* Rule?", supra p. 388 and "Indirect Price Fixing," supra p. 390).

A perennial arena of trade association activity of this sort raising "price fixing" risks concerns association activity involving the method by which transportation charges are established and included in the ultimate sales price of the members' goods. In industries with significant transportation costs for bringing their goods to market, there may be pressures to standardize the method for computing transportation charges into the final price quoted a buyer. Distant mills may be able to compete in markets not otherwise open to them if transportation charges for a given product are made uniform and included in the price all sellers quote buyers in that market. Buyers and sellers could avoid the need for computing actual transportation charges from a variety of points and the cumbersome task of keeping track of complex rate books. Think of how confusing and time-consuming it might be if each time you wished to mail a letter, the actual transportation cost from the point from which you mail the letter to the place you wish to send it had to be computed.

A variety of different delivered pricing systems have evolved to alleviate these problems. In the postal system, for example, charges for first class mail are the same no matter where the delivery is to be made in the country. This is called a single zone pricing system, where the post office will be charging more for transporting some letters (e.g. across the street) than it actually costs—charging "phantom freight"—while it will be charging less than its actual transportation costs for delivering other letters (e.g., across the country) and will thereby be "absorbing" transportation costs in its quoted price for the service. Charges for parcel post delivery may be based on a system of arbitrary geographic zones with different rates for ship-

---

28. 4 & 5 Eliz. II, Ch. 68, Sec. 6(7) (1956). The Japanese antitrust laws contain a specific law regulating the activities of trade associations. The law, The Trade Association Act, is now Section 8 of the Antimonopoly Act and contains a laundry list of specific "dos" and "don'ts" for trade associations and is administered by the Fair Trade Commission. See Japan Ministry of Finance, I Guide to the Economic Laws of Japan 38–42 (1979); H. Iyori, Antimonopoly Legislation In Japan 57–62 (1969).

ping from one zone to each of the others. This is called a multiple zone pricing system. Or, as in the *Cement* case which follows, prices which include a transportation charge may be quoted to buyers using a "basing point"—or a particular geographic location from which transportation charges are computed—regardless of the place from which the goods are shipped and the actual transportation costs.

Uniformity in the use of a particular delivered pricing system can cause substantial price uniformity in the sale of an industry's output. Proof that uniformity results from collaboration rather than competition is often derived from the involvement of trade associations seeking to standardize transportation charges among their members.

FEDERAL TRADE COMMISSION v. CEMENT INSTITUTE

Supreme Court of the United States, 1948.
333 U.S. 683, 68 S.Ct. 793, 92 L.Ed. 1010.

MR. JUSTICE BLACK delivered the opinion of the Court.

We granted certiorari to review the decree of the Circuit Court of Appeals which, with one judge dissenting, vacated and set aside a cease and desist order issued by the Federal Trade Commission against the respondents. 7 Cir., 157 F.2d 533. Those respondents are: The Cement Institute, an unincorporated trade association composed of 74 corporations which manufacture, sell and distribute cement; the 74 corporate members of the Institute; and 21 individuals who are associated with the Institute. It took three years for a trial examiner to hear the evidence which consists of about 49,000 pages of oral testimony and 50,000 pages of exhibits. . . .

The proceedings were begun by a Commission complaint of two counts. The first charged that certain alleged conduct set out at length constituted an unfair method of competition in violation of § 5 of the Federal Trade Commission Act. The core of the charge was that the respondents had restrained and hindered competition in the sale and distribution of cement by means of a combination among themselves made effective through mutual understanding or agreement to employ a multiple basing point system of pricing. It was alleged that this system resulted in the quotation of identical terms of sale and identical prices for cement by the respondents at any given point in the United States. This system had worked so successfully, it was further charged, that for many years prior to the filing of the complaint, all cement buyers throughout the nation, with rare exceptions, had been unable to purchase cement for delivery in any given locality from any one of the respondents at a lower price or on more favorable terms than from any of the other respondents.

The second count of the complaint, resting chiefly on the same allegations of fact set out in Count I, charged that the multiple basing point system of sales resulted in systematic price discriminations between the customers of each respondent. These discriminations were made it was alleged, with the purpose of destroying competition in price between the various respondents in violation of § 2 of the

Clayton Act, 38 Stat. 730, as amended by the Robinson-Patman Act, 49 Stat. 1526. That section, with certain conditions which need not here be set out, makes it "unlawful for any person engaged in commerce, . . . either directly or indirectly, to discriminate in price between different purchasers of commodities of like grade and quality. . . ." 15 U.S.C. § 13, 15 U.S.C.A. § 13.

Resting upon its findings, the Commission ordered that respondents cease and desist from "carrying out any planned common course of action, understanding, agreement, combination, or conspiracy" to do a number of things, all of which things, the Commission argues, had to be restrained in order effectively to restore individual freedom of action among the separate units in the cement industry. Certain contentions with reference to the order will later require a more detailed discussion of its terms. For the present it is sufficient to say that, if the order stands, its terms are broad enough to bar respondents from acting in concert to sell cement on a basing point delivered price plan which so eliminates competition that respondents' prices are always identical at any given point in the United States. . . .

The Multiple Basing Point Delivered Price System.—Since the multiple basing point delivered price system of fixing prices and terms of cement sales is the nub of this controversy, it will be helpful at this preliminary stage to point out in general what it is and how it works. A brief reference to the distinctive characteristics of "factory" or "mill prices" and "delivered prices" is of importance to an understanding of the basing point delivered price system here involved.

Goods may be sold and delivered to customers at the seller's mill or warehouse door or may be sold free on board (f.o.b.) trucks or railroad cars immediately adjacent to the seller's mill or warehouse. In either event the actual cost of the goods to the purchaser is, broadly speaking, the seller's "mill price" plus the purchaser's cost of transportation. However, if the seller fixes a price at which he undertakes to deliver goods to the purchaser where they are to be used, the cost to the purchaser is the "delivered price." A seller who makes the "mill price" identical for all purchasers of like amount and quality simply delivers his goods at the same place (his mill) and for the same price (price at the mill). He thus receives for all f.o.b. mill sales an identical net amount of money for like goods from all customers. But a "delivered price" system creates complications which may result in a seller's receiving different net returns from the sale of like goods. The cost of transporting 500 miles is almost always more than the cost of transporting 100 miles. Consequently if customers 100 and 500 miles away pay the same "delivered price," the seller's net return is less from the more distant customer. This difference in the producer's net return from sales to customers in different localities under a "delivered price" system is an important element in the charge under Count I of the complaint and is the crux of Count II.

The best known early example of a basing point price system was called "Pittsburgh plus." It related to the price of steel. The Pittsburgh price was the base price, Pittsburgh being therefore called a price basing point. In order for the system to work, sales had to be made only at delivered prices. Under this system the delivered price of steel from anywhere in the United States to a point of delivery anywhere in the United States was in general the Pittsburgh price plus the railroad freight rate from Pittsburgh to the point of delivery. Take Chicago, Illinois, as an illustration of the operation and consequences of the system. A Chicago steel producer was not free to sell his steel at cost plus a reasonable profit. He must sell it at the Pittsburgh price plus the railroad freight rate from Pittsburgh to the point of delivery. Chicago steel customers were by this pricing plan thus arbitrarily required to pay for Chicago produced steel the Pittsburgh base price plus what it would have cost to ship the steel by rail from Pittsburgh to Chicago had it been shipped. The theoretical cost of this fictitious shipment became known as "phantom freight." But had it been economically possible under this plan for a Chicago producer to ship his steel to Pittsburgh, his "delivered price" would have been merely the Pittsburgh price, although he actually would have been required to pay the freight from Chicago to Pittsburgh. Thus the "delivered price" under these latter circumstances required a Chicago (non-basing point) producer to "absorb" freight costs. That is, such a seller's net returns became smaller and smaller as his deliveries approached closer and closer to the basing point.

Several results obviously flow from use of a single basing point system such as "Pittsburgh plus" originally was. One is that the "delivered prices" of all producers in every locality where deliveries are made are always the same regardless of the producers' different freight costs. Another is that sales made by a non-base mill for delivery at different localities result in net receipts to the seller which vary in amounts equivalent to the "phantom freight" included in, or the "freight absorption" taken from the "delivered price."

As commonly employed by respondents, the basing point system is not single but multiple. That is, instead of one basing point, like that in "Pittsburgh plus," a number of basing point localities are used. In the multiple basing point system, just as in the single basing point system, freight absorption or phantom freight is an element of the delivered price on all sales not governed by a basing point actually located at the seller's mill.[29] And all sellers quote identical delivered prices in any given locality regardless of their different costs of production and their different freight expenses. Thus the multiple and single systems function in the same general manner and produce the same consequences—identity of prices and diversity of net re-

29. [Footnotes 91 through 95 are from the Court's opinion.] A base mill selling cement for delivery at a point outside the area in which its base price governs, and inside the area where another base mill's lower delivered price governs, adopts the latter's lower delivered price. The first base mill thus absorbs freight and becomes as to such sales a non-base mill.

turns.[30] Such differences as there are in matters here pertinent are therefore differences of degree only. . . .

Alleged Errors in re Introduction of Evidence.—The complaint before the Commission, filed July 2, 1937, alleged that respondents had maintained an illegal combination for "more than eight years last past." In the Circuit Court of Appeals and in this Court the Government treated its case on the basis that the combination began in August, 1929, when the respondent Cement Institute was organized. The Government introduced much evidence over respondents' objections, however, which showed the activities of the cement industry for many years prior to 1929, some of it as far back as 1902. It also introduced evidence as to respondents' activities from 1933 to May 27, 1935, much of which related to the preparation and administration of the NRA Code for the cement industry pursuant to the National Industrial Recovery Act, 48 Stat. 195, held invalid by this Court, in Schechter Poultry Corp. v. United States, 295 U.S. 495, 55 S.Ct. 837, 79 L.Ed. 1570, 97 A.L.R. 947. All of the testimony to which objection was made related to the initiation, development, and carrying on of the basing point practices.

Respondents contend that the pre-1929 evidence, especially that prior to 1919, is patently inadmissible with reference to a 1929 combination, many of whose alleged members were non-existent in 1919. They also urge that evidence of activities during the NRA period was improperly admitted because § 5 of Title I of the NRA provided that any action taken in compliance with the code provisions of an industry should be "exempt from the provisions of the antitrust laws of the United States." And some of the NRA period testimony relating to basing point practices did involve references to code provisions. The Government contends that evidence of both the pre-1929 and the NRA period activities of members of the cement industry tends to show a continuous course of concerted efforts on the part of the industry, or at least most of it, to utilize the basing point system as a

---

30. The Commission in its findings explained how the multiple basing point system affects a seller's net return on sales in different localities and how the delivered price is determined at any particular point. "Substantially all sales of cement by the corporate respondents are made on the basis of a delivered price; that is, at a price determined by the location at which actual delivery of the cement is made to the purchaser. In determining the delivered price which will be charged for cement at any given location, respondents use a multiple basing-point system. The formula used to make this system operative is that the delivered price at any location shall be the lowest combination of base price plus all-rail freight. Thus, if Mill A has a base price of $1.50 per barrel, its delivered price at each location where it sells cement will be $1.50 per barrel plus the all-rail freight from its mill to the point of deliv-

ery, except that when a sale is made for delivery at a location at which the combination of the base price plus all-rail freight from another mill is a lower figure, Mill A uses this lower combination so that its delivered price at such location will be the same as the delivered price of the other mill. At all locations where the base price of Mill A plus freight is the lowest combination, Mill A recovers $1.50 net at the mill, and at locations where the combination of base price plus freight of another mill is lower, Mill A shrinks its mill net sufficiently to equal that price. Under these conditions it is obvious that the highest mill net which can be recovered by Mill A is $1.50 per barrel, and on sales where it has been necessary to shrink its mill net in order to match the delivered price of another mill, its net recovery at the mill is less than $1.50." 37 F.T.C. at 147–148.

means to fix uniform terms and prices at which cement would be sold, and that the Commission had properly so regarded this evidence. The Circuit Court of Appeals agreed with respondents that the Commission had erroneously considered both the NRA period evidence and the pre-1929 evidence in making its findings of the existence of a combination among respondents.

We conclude that both types of evidence were admissible for the purpose of showing the existence of a continuing combination among respondents to utilize the basing point pricing system.

The Commission did not make its findings of post-1929 combination, in whole or in part, on the premise that any of respondents' pre-1929 or NRA code activities were illegal. The consideration given these activities by the Commission was well within the established judicial rule of evidence that testimony of prior or subsequent transactions, which for some reason are barred from forming the basis for a suit, may nevertheless be introduced if it tends reasonably to show the purpose and character of the particular transactions under scrutiny. Here the trade practices of an entire industry were under consideration. Respondents, on the one hand, insisted that the multiple basing point delivered price system represented a natural evolution of business practices adopted by the different cement companies, not in concert, but separately in response to customers' needs and demands. That the separately adopted business practices produced uniform terms and conditions of sale in all localities was, so the respondents contended, nothing but an inevitable result of long-continued competition. On the other hand, the Government contended that, despite shifts in ownership of individual cement companies, what had taken place from 1902 to the date the complaint was filed showed continued concerted action on the part of all cement producers to develop and improve the basing point system so that it would automatically eliminate competition. In the Government's view the Institute when formed in 1929 simply took up the old practices for the old purpose and aided its member companies to carry it straight on through and beyond the NRA period.

Furthermore, administrative agencies like the Federal Trade Commission have never been restricted by the rigid rules of evidence. And of course rules which bar certain types of evidence in criminal or quasi-criminal cases are not controlling in proceedings like this, where the effect of the Commission's order is not to punish or to fasten liability on respondents for past conduct but to ban specific practices for the future in accordance with the general mandate of Congress.

The foregoing likewise largely answers respondents' contention that there was error in the admission of a letter written by one Treanor in 1934 to the chairman of the NRA code authority for the cement industry. Treanor, who died prior to the filing of the complaint, was at the time president of one of the respondent companies and also an active trustee of the Institute. In the letter he stated among other things that the cement industry was one "above all others that cannot stand free competition, that must systematically restrain competition or be ruined." This statement was made as part of his criticism of the cement industry's publicity campaign in defense of the basing point system. The relevance of this statement indicating this Institute official's informed judgment is obvious. That it might be only his conclusion does not render the statement inadmissible in this administrative proceeding.

All contentions in regard to the introduction of testimony have been considered. None of them justify refusal to enforce this order.

The Old Cement Case.—This Court's opinion in Cement Mfrs.' Protective Ass'n v. United States, 268 U.S. 588, 45 S.Ct. 586, 69 L.Ed. 1104, known as the Old Cement case, is relied on by the respondents in almost every contention they present. We think it has little relevance, if any at all, to the issues in this case.

In that case the United States brought an action in the District Court to enjoin an alleged combination to violate § 1 of the Sherman Act. The respondents were the Cement Manufacturers Protective Association, four of its officers, and nineteen cement manufacturers. The District Court held hearings, made findings of fact, and issued an injunction against those respondents. This Court, with three justices dissenting, reversed upon a review of the evidence. It did so because the Government did not charge and the record did not show "any agreement or understanding between the defendants placing limitations on either prices or production," or any agreement to utilize the basing point system as a means of fixing prices. The Court said "But here the government does not rely upon agreement or understanding, and this record wholly fails to establish, either directly or by inference, any concerted action other than that involved in the gathering and dissemination of pertinent information with respect to the sale and distribution of cement to which we have referred, and it fails to show any effect on price and production except such as would naturally flow from the dissemination of that information in the trade and its natural influence on individual action." Id., at page 606, of 268 U.S., at page 592 of 45 S.Ct., 69 L.Ed. 1104. In the Old Cement case and in Maple Flooring Mfrs.' Ass'n v. United States, 268 U.S. 563, 45 S.Ct. 578, 69 L.Ed. 1093, decided the same day, the Court's attention was focused on the rights of a trade association, despite the Sherman Act, openly to gather and disseminate statistics and information as to production costs, output, past prices, merchandise on hand, specific job contracts, freight rates, etc., so long as the Association did these things without attempts to foster agreements or concerted action with reference to prices, production, or terms of sale. Such associations were declared guiltless of violating the Sherman Act, because "in fact, no prohibited concert of action was found." Corn Products Refining Co. v. Federal Trade Commission, 324 U.S. 726, 735, 65 S.Ct. 961, 966, 89 L.Ed. 1320.

The Court's holding in the Old Cement case would not have been inconsistent with a judgment sustaining the Commission's order here, even had the two cases been before this Court the same day. The issues in the present Commission proceedings are quite different from those in the Old Cement case, although many of the trade practices shown here were also shown there. In the first place, unlike the Old Cement case, the Commission does here specifically charge a combination to utilize the basing point system as a means to bring about uniform prices and terms of sale. And here the Commission has focused attention on this issue, having introduced evidence on the issue which covers thousands of pages. Furthermore, unlike the trial court in the Old Cement case, the Commission has specifically found the existence of a combination among respondents to employ the basing point system for the purpose of selling at identical prices.

In the second place, individual conduct, or concerted conduct, which falls short of being a Sherman Act violation may as a matter of law constitute an "unfair method of competition" prohibited by the Trade Commission Act. A major purpose of that Act, as we have frequently said, was to enable the Commission to restrain practices as "unfair" which, although not yet having grown into Sherman Act dimensions would, most likely do so if left unrestrained. The Commission and the courts were to determine what conduct, even though it might then be short of a Sherman Act violation, was an "unfair method of competition." This general language was deliberately left to the "Commission and the courts" for definition because it was thought that "There is no limit to human inventiveness in this field"; that consequently a definition that fitted practices known to lead towards an unlawful restraint of trade today would not fit tomorrow's new inventions in the field; and that for Congress to try to keep its precise definitions abreast of this course of conduct would be an "endless task." See Federal Trade Commission v. R. F. Keppel & Bro., 291 U.S. 304, 310–312, 54 S.Ct. 423, 426, 78 L.Ed. 814, and congressional committee reports there quoted.

These marked differences between what a court must decide in a Sherman Act proceeding and the duty of the Commission in determining whether conduct is to be classified as an unfair method of competition are enough in and of themselves to make the Old Cement decision wholly inapplicable to our problem in reviewing the findings in this case. That basic problem is whether the Commission made findings of concerted action, whether those findings are supported by evidence, and if so whether the findings are adequate as a matter of law to sustain the Commission's conclusion that the multiple basing point system as practiced constitutes an "unfair method of competition," because it either restrains free competition or is an incipient menace to it.

Findings and Evidence.—It is strongly urged that the Commission failed to find, as charged in both counts of the complaint, that the respondents had by combination, agreements, or understandings among themselves utilized the multiple basing point delivered price system as a restraint to accomplish uniform prices and terms of sale. A subsidiary contention is that assuming the Commission did so find, there is no substantial evidence to support such a finding. We think that adequate findings of combination were made and that the findings have support in the evidence.

The Commission's findings of fact set out at great length and with painstaking detail numerous concerted activities carried on in order to make the multiple basing point system work in such way that competition in quality, price and terms of sale of cement would be non-existent, and that uniform prices, job contracts, discounts, and terms of sale would be continuously maintained. The Commission found that many of these activities were carried on by the Cement Institute, the industry's unincorporated trade association, and that in other instances the activities were under the immediate control of groups of respondents. Among the collective methods used to accomplish these purposes, according to the findings, were boycotts; discharge of uncooperative employees; organized opposition to the erection of new cement plants; selling cement in a recalcitrant price cutter's sales territory at a price so low that the recalcitrant was forced to adhere to the established basing point prices; discouraging the shipment of cement by truck or barge; and preparing and distributing freight rate books which provided respondents with similar figures to use as actual or "phantom" freight factors, thus guaranteeing that their delivered prices (base prices plus freight factors) would be identical on all sales whether made to individual purchasers under open bids or to governmental agencies under sealed bids. These are but a few of the many activities of respondents which the Commission found to have been done in combination to reduce or destroy price competition in cement. After having made these detailed findings of concerted action, the Commission followed them by a general finding that "the capacity, tendency, and effect of the combination maintained by the respondents herein in the manner aforesaid is to . . . promote and maintain their multiple basing point delivered-price system and obstruct and defeat any form of competition which threatens or tends to threaten the continued use and maintenance of said system and the uniformity of prices created and maintained by its use." The Commission then concluded that "The aforesaid combination and acts and practices of respondents pursuant thereto and in connection therewith, as hereinabove found, under the conditions and circumstances set forth, constitute unfair methods of competition in commerce within the intent and meaning of the Federal Trade Commission Act." And the Commission's cease and desist order prohibited respondents "from entering into, continuing, cooperating in, or carrying out any planned common course of action, understanding, agreement, combination, or conspiracy between and among any two or more of said respondents . . ." to do certain things there enumerated.

Thus we have a complaint which charged collective action by respondents designed to maintain a sales technique that restrained competition, detailed findings of collective activities by groups of respondents to achieve that end, then a general finding that respondents maintained the combination, and finally an order prohibiting the continuance of the combination. It seems impossible to conceive that anyone reading these findings in their entirety could doubt that the

Commission found that respondents collectively maintained a multiple basing point delivered price system for the purpose of suppressing competition in cement sales. The findings are sufficient. The contention that they were not is without substance.

Disposition of this question brings us to the related contention that there was no substantial evidence to support the findings. We might well dispose of the contention as this Court dismissed a like one with reference to evidence and findings in a civil suit brought under the Sherman Act in Sugar Institute v. United States, 297 U.S. 553, 601, 56 S.Ct. 629, 643, 80 L.Ed. 859: "After a hearing of extraordinary length, in which no pertinent fact was permitted to escape consideration, the trial court subjected the evidence to a thorough and acute analysis which has left but slight room for debate over matters of fact. Our examination of the record discloses no reason for overruling the court's findings in any matter essential to our decision." In this case, which involves the evidence and findings of the Federal Trade Commission, we likewise see no reason for upsetting the essential findings of the Commission. Neither do we find it necessary to refer to all the voluminous testimony in this record which tends to support the Commission's findings.

Although there is much more evidence to which reference could be made, we think that the following facts shown by evidence in the record, some of which are in dispute, are sufficient to warrant the Commission's finding of concerted action.

When the Commission rendered its decision there were about 80 cement manufacturing companies in the United States operating about 150 mills. Ten companies controlled more than half of the mills and there were substantial corporate affiliations among many of the others. This concentration of productive capacity made concerted action far less difficult than it would otherwise have been. The belief is prevalent in the industry that because of the standardized nature of cement, among other reasons, price competition is wholly unsuited to it. That belief is historic. It has resulted in concerted activities to devise means and measures to do away with competition in the industry. Out of those activities came the multiple basing point delivered price system. Evidence shows it to be a handy instrument to bring about elimination of any kind of price competition. The use of the multiple basing point delivered price system by the cement producers has been coincident with a situation whereby for many years, with rare exceptions, cement has been offered for sale in every given locality at identical prices and terms by all producers. Thousands of secret sealed bids have been received by public agencies which corresponded in prices of cement down to a fractional part of a penny.[31]

31. The following is one among many of the Commission's findings as to the identity of sealed bids:

An abstract of the bids for 6,000 barrels of cement to the United States Engineer Office at Tucumcari, New Mexico, opened April 23, 1936, shows the following:

Occasionally foreign cement has been imported, and cement dealers have sold it below the delivered price of the domestic product. Dealers who persisted in selling foreign cement were boycotted by the domestic producers. Officers of the Institute took the lead in securing pledges by producers not to permit sales f.o.b. mill to purchasers who furnished their own trucks, a practice regarded as seriously disruptive of the entire delivered price structure of the industry.

During the depression in the 1930's, slow business prompted some producers to deviate from the prices fixed by the delivered price system. Meetings were held by other producers; an effective plan was devised to punish the recalcitrants and bring them into line. The plan was simple but successful. Other producers made the recalcitrant's plant an involuntary base point. The base price was driven down with relatively insignificant losses to the producers who imposed the punitive basing point, but with heavy losses to the recalcitrant who had to make all its sales on this basis. In one instance, where a producer had made a low public bid, a punitive base point price was put on its plant and cement was reduced 10% per barrel; further reductions quickly followed until the base price at which this recalcitrant had to sell its cement dropped to 75¢ per barrel, scarcely one-half of its former base price of $1.45. Within six weeks after the base price hit 75¢ capitulation occurred and the recalcitrant joined a Portland cement association. Cement in that locality then bounced back to $1.15, later to $1.35, and finally to $1.75.

The foregoing are but illustrations of the practices shown to have been utilized to maintain the basing point price system. Respondents offered testimony that cement is a standardized product, that "cement is cement," that no differences existed in quality or usefulness, and that purchasers demanded delivered price quotations because of the high cost of transportation from mill to dealer. There was evidence, however, that the Institute and its members had, in the interest of eliminating competition, suppressed information as to the variations in quality that sometimes exist in different cements.[32] Respondents introduced the testimony of economists to the effect that competition alone could lead to the evolution of a multiple basing point system of uniform delivered prices and terms of sale for an industry with a standardized product and with relatively high freight

Name of Bidder	Price per Bbl.
Monarch	$3.286854
Ash Grove	3.286854
Lehigh	3.286854
Southwestern	3.286854
U. S. Portland Cement Co.	3.286854
Oklahoma	3.286854
Consolidated	3.286854
Trinity	3.286854
Lone Star	3.286854
Universal	3.286854
Colorado	3.286854

All bids subject to 10¢ per barrel discount for payment in 15 days. (Com.Ex. 175-A.) See 157 F.2d at page 576.

32. See Sugar Institute v. United States, 297 U.S. 553, 600, 56 S.Ct. 629, 643, 80 L.Ed. 859: "The fact that because sugar is a standardized commodity, there is a strong tendency to uniformity of price, makes it the more important that such opportunities as may exist for fair competition should not be impaired."

costs. These economists testified that for the above reasons no inferences of collusion, agreement, or understanding could be drawn from
the admitted fact that cement prices of all United States producers
had for many years almost invariably been the same in every given
locality in the country. There was also considerable testimony by
other economic experts that the multiple basing point system of delivered prices as employed by respondents contravened accepted economic principles and could only have been maintained through collusion.

The Commission did not adopt the views of the economists produced by the respondents. It decided that even though competition
might tend to drive the price of standardized products to a uniform
level, such a tendency alone could not account for the almost perfect
identity in prices, discounts, and cement containers which had prevailed for so long a time in the cement industry. The Commission
held that the uniformity and absence of competition in the industry
were the results of understandings or agreements entered into or carried out by concert of the Institute and the other respondents. It
may possibly be true, as respondents' economists testified, that cement producers will, without agreement express or implied and without understanding explicit or tacit, always and at all times (for such
has been substantially the case here) charge for their cement precisely, to the fractional part of a penny, the price their competitors
charge. Certainly it runs counter to what many people have believed,
namely, that without agreement, prices will vary—that the desire to
sell will sometimes be so strong that a seller will be willing to lower
his prices and take his chances. We therefore hold that the Commission was not compelled to accept the views of respondents' economist-
witnesses that active competition was bound to produce uniform cement prices. The Commission was authorized to find understanding,
express or implied, from evidence that the industry's Institute actively worked, in cooperation with various of its members, to maintain
the multiple basing point delivered price system; that this pricing
system is calculated to produce, and has produced, uniform prices and
terms of sale throughout the country; and that all of the respondents
have sold their cement substantially in accord with the pattern required by the multiple basing point system.

Some of the respondents contend that particularly as to them crucial findings of participation by them in collective action to eliminate
price competition and to bring about uniformity of cement prices are
without testimonial support. . . .

These companies support their separate contentions for particularized consideration by pointing out among other things that there was
record evidence which showed differences between many of their
sales methods and those practiced by other respondents. Each says
that there was no direct evidence to connect it with all of the practices found to have been used by the Institute and other respondents
to achieve delivered price uniformity.

The record does show such differences as those suggested. It is
correct to say, therefore, that the sales practices of these particular

respondents, and perhaps of other respondents as well, were not at all times precisely like the sales practices of all or any of the others. For example, the Commission found that in 1929 all of the central California mills became basing points. There was evidence that the Institute's rate books did not extend to the states in which some of the California companies did business. The Commission found that "In Southern California the basing point system of pricing is modified by an elaborate system of zone prices applicable in certain areas," that the California system does not require separate calculations to determine the delivered price at each destination, but that complete price lists were published by the companies showing delivered prices at substantially all delivery points. Northwestern and Superior assert that among other distinctive practices of theirs, they were willing to and did bid for government contracts on a mill price rather than a delivered price basis. Huron points out that it permitted the use of trucks to deliver cement, which practice, far from being consistent with the plan of others to maintain the basing point delivered price formulas, was frowned on by the Institute and others as endangering the success of the plan. Marquette emphasizes that it did not follow all the practices used to carry out the anti-competition plan, and urges that although the Commission rightly found that it had upon occasion undercut its competitors, it erroneously found that its admitted abandonment of price cutting was due to the combined pressure of other respondents, including the Institute.

What these particular respondents emphasize does serve to underscore certain findings which show that some respondents were more active and influential in the combination than were others, and that some companies probably unwillingly abandoned competitive practices and entered into the combination. But none of the distinctions mentioned, or any other differences relied on by these particular respondents, justifies a holding that there was no substantial evidence to support the Commission's findings that they cooperated with all the others to achieve the ultimate objective of all—the elimination of price competition in the sale of cement. These respondents' special contentions only illustrate that the Commission was called upon to resolve factual issues as to each of them in the light of whatever relevant differences in their practices were shown by the evidence. For aside from the testimony indicating the differences in their individual sales practices, there was abundant evidence as to common practices of these respondents and the others on the basis of which the Commission was justified in finding cooperative conduct among all to achieve delivered price uniformity.

The evidence commonly applicable to these and the other respondents showed that all were members of the Institute and that the officers of some of these particular respondents were or had been officers of the Institute. We have already sustained findings that the Institute was organized to maintain the multiple basing point system as one of the "customs and usages" of the industry and that it participated in numerous activities intended to eliminate price competition through the collective efforts of the respondents. Evidence before the Commission also showed that the delivered prices of these respondents, like those of all the other respondents, were, with rare exceptions, identical with the delivered prices of all their competitors. Furthermore, there was evidence that all of these respondents, including those who sold cement on a zone basis in sections of southern California, employed the multiple basing point delivered price system on a portion of their sales.

Our conclusion is that there was evidence to support the Commission's findings that all of the respondents, including the California companies, Northwestern Portland and Superior Portland, Huron and Marquette, cooperated in carrying out the objectives of the basing point delivered price system.

Unfair Methods of Competition.—We sustain the Commission's holding that concerted maintenance of the basing point delivered price system is an unfair method of competition prohibited by the Federal Trade Commission Act. In so doing we give great weight to the Commission's conclusion, as this Court has done in other cases. In Federal Trade Commission v. R. F. Keppel & Bro., 291 U.S. 304, 314, 54 S.Ct. 423, 427, 78 L.Ed. 814, the Court called attention to the express intention of Congress to create an agency whose membership would at all times be experienced, so that its conclusions would be the result of an expertness coming from experience. We are persuaded that the Commission's long and close examination of the questions it here decided has provided it with precisely the experience that fits it for performance of its statutory duty. The kind of specialized knowledge Congress wanted its agency to have was an expertness that would fit it to stop at the threshold every unfair trade practice—that kind of practice, which if left alone, "destroys competition and establishes monopoly." Federal Trade Commission v. Raladam Co., 283 U.S. 643, 647, 650, 51 S.Ct. 587, 591, 75 L.Ed. 1324, 79 A.L.R. 1191.

We cannot say that the Commission is wrong in concluding that the delivered-price system as here used provides an effective instrument which, if left free for use of the respondents, would result in complete destruction of competition and the establishment of monopoly in the cement industry. That the basing point price system may lend itself to industry-wide anti-competitive practices is illustrated in the following among other cases: United States v. United States Gypsum Co. et al., 333 U.S. 364, 68 S.Ct. 525, Sugar Institute v. United States, 297 U.S. 553, 56 S.Ct. 629, 80 L.Ed. 859. We uphold the Commission's conclusion that the basing point delivered price system employed by respondents is an unfair trade practice which the Trade Commission may suppress. . . .

The Order.— . . . Most of the objections to the order appear to rest on the premise that its terms will bar an individual cement producer from selling cement at delivered prices such that its net return from one customer will be less than from another, even if the particular sale be made in good faith to meet the lower price of a competitor. The Commission disclaims that the order can possibly be so understood. Nor do we so understand it. As we read the order, all of its separate prohibiting paragraphs and sub-paragraphs, which need not here be set out, are modified and limited by a preamble. This preamble directs that all of the respondents "do forthwith cease and desist from entering into, continuing, cooperating in, or carrying out any planned common course of action, understanding, agreement, combination or conspiracy, between and among any two or more of said respondents, or between any one or more of said respondents and others not parties hereto, to do or perform any of the following things. . . ." Then follow the prohibitory sentences. It is thus apparent that the order by its terms is directed solely at concerted, not individual activity on the part of the respondents. . . .

The Commission's order should not have been set aside by the Circuit Court of Appeals. Its judgment is reversed and the cause is remanded to that court with directions to enforce the order. It is so ordered.

Reversed and remanded.[33]

MR. JUSTICE DOUGLAS and MR. JUSTICE JACKSON took no part in the consideration or decision of these cases.

MR. JUSTICE BURTON dissented.

NOTES AND QUERIES

(1) *Queries.* If Pittsburgh is a basing point for steel, the delivered price paid by customers of Pittsburgh will be higher, by the amount of rail freight, as the point of delivery becomes more remote from Pittsburgh. However, if Chicago is also a basing point, the delivered price for steel from Pittsburgh, to customers located beyond the midpoint between Pittsburgh and Chicago, will fall as Chicago is approached, since the Pittsburgh shipper is now in Chicago's freight-advantage territory. In this territory Pittsburgh sellers will quote delivered prices that include freight charges calculated as if the

---

33. Compare Cement Makers Federation Agreement, (British Restrictive Practices Court 1961), p. 31 supra, and the decision denying approval of a "rationalization cartel" for the South German cement industries, [1962], WuW 206.

For a review of the history of the Cement Institute and its predecessor confederacies, regarding them as unofficial but nevertheless "governmental" power aggregations engaged in defending their own "security" against other hostile groups, private and governmental, see Latham, Giantism and Basing Points: A Political Analysis, 58 Yale L.J. 383 (1949); Cf. McAllister and Quigg, The Art of Selecting and Exploiting Half-Truths: A Reply to "Giantism and Basing Points", 58 Yale L.J. 1068 (1949); Latham, Lament for Cement, Being an Answer to a Reply, 58 Yale L.J. 1079 (1949); McAllister and Trigg, Rejoinder, 58 Yale L.J. 1090 (1949).

Wallace and Douglas, Antitrust Policies and the New Attack on the Federal Trade Commission, 19 U.Chi.L.Rev. 684 (1952), describes the legislative struggle to undo the effects of the Cement case, including proposals to abolish the Commission, to define "price" as the delivered price (so that uniformity in delivered price could not be held discriminatory), and to deprive price uniformity and rigidity of evidentiary significance on the issue of conspiracy.

Loescher, Inert Antitrust Administration: Formula Pricing and the Cement Industry, 65 Yale L.J. 1 (1955), criticised the Department of Justice decision in 1953 to abandon its eight year old suit against the cement industry seeking injunctive relief under the Sherman Act. He argued that the FTC order was ineffective because of the limitation to "planned common course of action," and because it did not require sellers to quote *both* delivered and f.o.b. prices, the former affording an opportunity for competitive freight absorption.

shipments were coming from Chicago, although the steel is actually shipped from Pittsburgh. In Chicago itself, Pittsburgh steel will sell for no more than Chicago steel, and at approximately the same price as Pittsburgh customers are paying for steel produced in adjoining plants. Thus a Pittsburgh Steel Co. penetrates into the market of the Chicago Steel Co. Presumably, the Chicago Steel Co. will seek business in Pittsburgh on the same basis.

If the Pittsburgh Co. faces effective competition in its home market, will it be able to earn enough money on nearby sales to make up for the "freight absorption" on distant sales? How is it able to charge rail freight rates if there are Pittsburgh competitors able and willing to ship by barge and charge only barge rates? Must it be assumed that, in the hypothetical case of the Pittsburgh-Chicago multiple basing point system, each company has some kind of protection against local competition? What kind?

Why does Chicago, which seems to have excess capacity available for Pittsburgh customers, permit the Pittsburgh Co. to penetrate the Chicago market, when it could use its capacity in serving the Chicago market where it has a natural advantage over the Pittsburgh Co.?

Will steel costs and prices be reduced because of fuller use of Pittsburgh's plant capacity when it sells to Chicago? Or will the Pittsburgh Co., under the multiple basing point system, lose as much Pittsburgh business to Chicago sellers as it gains customers in Chicago?

If Pittsburgh is shipping steel to Chicago which might have been produced in Chicago, and Chicago is shipping to Pittsburgh ("cross-hauling"), the total transportation cost included in the price steel consumers have to pay must be greater than if each company sold f.o.b. its own plant, i.e., charged full freight to all customers. Will this increase the total price consumers pay for steel, with a corresponding restriction in steel consumption as some buyers are diverted to other materials?

Would railroads be for or against basing point pricing?

Is "interpenetration" of markets a necessary result of competitive striving for each other's customers, and also a necessary condition for the existence of competition between Pittsburgh and Chicago sellers? Or is it possible only by collusion or price leadership establishing a general price level high enough to permit uneconomic cross-hauling? If competition is enhanced by multiple basing point systems, why do businessmen find it desirable to use and defend the system?

In order to obtain the fullest benefits from admitting remote sellers as competitors, would it be desirable to have a price level high enough to permit San Francisco steel to be shipped to New York? Swedish steel to Pittsburgh, and Birmingham steel to Calcutta?[34]

Why should standardization of the product be thought to make competition "unsuitable" to the cement industry? Does the belief of the industry that competition is unsuitable to trade in a standardized product mean (a) that price competition is likely to be too rigorous ("cutthroat") where individual sellers cannot claim a quality superiority, so that measures must be taken to restrain the rivalry, or (b) that trade rivals selling a standard product will have no incentive to cut prices, since they know that their competitors will have to match the price immediately, so that it is useless to rely on competitive controls? In the latter case must prices be "administered" either by the industry or by the government?

34. See Stocking, Basing Point Pricing and Regional Development: A Case   Study of the Iron and Steel Industry (1954).

If a product is standardized, is there more or less reason to maintain competition in plant location and transportation costs?

In a business dealing with a standardized product like cement, where great contracts are let on sealed bids, what prevents a manufacturer who knows that everybody else is bidding 3.286854 from bidding 3.286853 and thus securing all the trade? In such a business would "open competition" plans, requiring each producer to publicize his current offering price promptly, tend to stimulate competition or restrain competition?

(2) *The Controversy Over F.T.C. Regulation of Delivered Pricing.* Three other developments in the regulation of delivered pricing systems generated considerable controversy in the late 40's. In *Corn Products Refining Co. v. Federal Trade Commission*,[35] and *Federal Trade Commission v. A.E. Staley Manufacturing Co.*,[36] the Supreme Court held that the use of a single basing point delivered pricing system constituted unlawful price discrimination in violation of the Robinson-Patman Act. (See Chapter 8 infra). Then in *Triangle Conduit & Cable Co. v. Federal Trade Commission*,[37] the Seventh Circuit upheld an F.T.C. cease and desist order against the use of a delivered pricing system on a theory that the parallel use of the system by several manufacturers (without proof of an overt combination or conspiracy to do so) constituted an unfair method of competition in violation of Section 5 of the F.T.C. Act. *Triangle Conduit* was affirmed by an equally divided Supreme Court.[38] Meanwhile, the F.T.C. had issued a Statement of Policy on delivered pricing practices to its staff [39] stating that widespread industry use of certain forms of delivered pricing systems justified the inference of unlawful collusion, even in the absence of express evidence of collusion. The statement concluded: "The inference of collusion from the character of a geographic price structure becomes more persuasive as the structure itself becomes more complex, more rigid, and more inconsistent with the immediate competitive interests of various enterprises which follow it. Having explored the problem in a number of instances through legal prosecutions and economic investigations, the Commission now holds the view that sustained observance of single or multiple basing point systems which are complex and rigid is in itself substantial even though not necessarily conclusive evidence of collusion. . . ."[40]

These developments suggested that the unilateral use of most delivered pricing systems was potentially unlawful under the Robinson-Patman Act and that the F.T.C. could attack the parallel adoption and use of a delivered pricing system as an unfair method of competition under Section 5.[41] Legislation was passed by Congress and vetoed by President Truman attempting to clarify the status of the unilateral and parallel adoption of delivered pricing systems within an industry.[42] Thereafter, probably as a result of the emergency of the Korean War and changes in F.T.C. personnel, the contro-

---

35. 324 U.S. 726, 65 S.Ct. 961, 89 L.Ed. 1320 (1945).

36. 324 U.S. 746, 65 S.Ct. 971, 89 L.Ed. 1338 (1945).

37. 168 F.2d 175 (7th Cir. 1948).

38. Sub nom., Clayton Mark & Co. v. Federal Trade Commission, 336 U.S. 956, 69 S.Ct. 888, 93 L.Ed. 1110 (1949).

39. Statement of Federal Trade Commission Policy Toward Geographic Pricing Practices (October 12, 1948), quoted in L. Schwartz & J. Flynn, Antitrust and Regulatory Alternatives, 564–65 (5th Ed. 1977).

40. Id.

41. See Kittelle & Lamb, The Implied Conspiracy Doctrine and Delivered Pricing, 15 L. & Contemp. Prob. 277 (1950).

42. See DuBose, The Delivered Price Controversy and the O'Mahoney Bill, 38 Geo.L.J. 200 (1950); Latham, The Politics of Basing Point Legislation, 15 L. & Contemp. Prob. 272 (1950).

versy subsided. Only occasional cases have been brought against the use of delivered pricing systems in particular industries.[43]

In a recent case, *Boise Cascade Corp. v. Federal Trade Commission*,[44] the F.T.C. challenged the adoption and use by Southeastern Plywood producers of a zone pricing system long followed by plywood producers in the Pacific Northwest. Despite an absence of evidence of overt collusion by southeastern producers to adopt a west coast basing point and a system of zone pricing, the Commission found a violation of Section 5 in the industry-wide adoption of an artificial freight factor and issued a cease and desist order. The Ninth Circuit refused to enforce the cease and desist order, stating:

> It is important to stress that the weight of the case law and the Commission's own policy statement make it clear that we are looking for at least tacit agreement to use a formula which has the effect of fixing prices. Indeed, none of the delivered pricing cases support a finding of a section 5 violation for the bare existence of an industry-wide artificial freight factor. In each case, the system had been utilized, tacitly or overtly, to match prices and avoid price competition. We thus hold that in the absence of evidence of overt agreement to utilize a pricing system to avoid price competition, the Commission must demonstrate that the challenged pricing system has actually had the effect of fixing or stabilizing prices. Without such effect, a mere showing of parallel action will not establish a section 5 violation.[45]

After reviewing the evidence and finding "no evidence" that the price of plywood "has been unresponsive to market conditions", the court concluded:

> [T]he law of delivered pricing is well forged, having been developed by the Commission and courts over years of litigation. . . . [T]he weight of the case law, as well as the practices and statements of the Commission, establish the rule that the Commission must find either collusion or actual effect on competition to make out a section 5 violation for use of delivered pricing. In this setting at least, where the parties agree that the practice was a natural and competitive development in the emergence of the southern plywood industry, and where there is a complete absence of evidence implying overt conspiracy, to allow a finding of a section 5 violation on the theory that the mere widespread use of the practice makes it an incipient threat to competition would be to blur the distinction between guilty and innocent commercial behavior. Since we have found that there is not substantial evidence in the record to support the Commission's finding of anti-competitive effect, it follows that the Commission's order may not be enforced.[46]

In parallel treble damage litigation by plaintiffs claiming injury as the result of a conspiracy by the same defendants to adopt a common delivered pricing system by southeastern plywood manufacturers, independent evidence of a conspiracy to use a common delivered pricing system was found sufficient to sustain a jury verdict finding the uniform adoption of the west coast basing point was pursuant to a conspiracy in violation of § 1 of the Sherman Act.[47]

43. See Federal Trade Commission v. National Lead Co., 352 U.S. 419, 77 S.Ct. 502, 1 L.Ed.2d 438 (1957) (upholding finding that unilateral adoption and use of a zone pricing system matching competitor's sales a violation of Section 5); Chain Institute, Inc. v. Federal Trade Commission, 246 F.2d 231 (8th Cir. 1957), certio-

rari denied 355 U.S. 895, 78 S.Ct. 269, 2 L.Ed.2d 192.

44. 637 F.2d 573 (9th Cir. 1980).

45. 637 F.2d at 576–77.

46. Id. at 682.

47. In re Plywood Antitrust Litigation, 655 F.2d 627 (5th Cir. 1981), certio-

Query: Should evidence of the uniform use of a zone pricing system with an effect of stabilizing prices be sufficient to show a violation of Section 5 of the F.T.C. Act?

F. ALTERNATIVE APPROACHES FOR REGULATING HORIZONTAL RESTRAINTS

A policy of prohibiting joint action displacing the competitive process which relies on the adversary system for its enforcement, is only one approach to the larger question of how and for what objectives ought society's economic affairs be organized. The companion course of Regulated Industries explores the approach of affirmatively using government authority to limit, or in some circumstances prohibit, competition by restricting entry into a business and/or affirmatively regulating the price at which particular goods or services may be sold. Intervention regulating entry and price is usually an exception, chosen where it is believed the market process cannot work because of inherent natural monopoly characteristics of the industry or because physical or other limitations severely limit the resource that is being exploited. It is also not unknown for affirmative regulation to be imposed as the result of the political power of the previously regulated seeking to control competing technologies, or for industries to actively seek out regulation to escape the risks of a competitive market regime. The dangerous nature of a product may require regulation of the seller and the circumstances of sale, while the characteristics of providing a service may require education and training before one is permitted to practice the art. A patient undergoing open heart surgery may be entitled to some guarantee of the surgeon's knowledge and skills beyond self-serving declarations on these questions by the seller of the service. Other activities may be placed exclusively in governmental hands because the market will not or cannot provide a necessary service for all at a reasonable price or because the activity is vital to public health and safety. In contrast to the state owned and planned economies based on Marxist theory, however, the basic presumption in most western societies is in favor of relying upon a free market process, where possible and appropriate, to allocate resources, establish price, stimulate innovation and meet the short and long range economic, political and social demands of society. Pragmatism tempers the preferences to varying degrees throughout the economy, making ours a mixed economy: partly free, partly regulated, partly socialized, and various combinations of all three.[48]

rari granted sub nom. Weyerhauser Co. and Willamette Industries, Inc. v. Lyman Lamb Co., 456 U.S. 971, 102 S.Ct. 2232, 72 L.Ed.2d 844 (1982).

48. The contrasts between socialist and market oriented societies are well demonstrated in Schwartz, American Antitrust and Trading With State-Controlled Economies, 25 Antitrust Bull. 513 (1980).

It should be noted that there are those who favor carrying the "free market" ideology and approach to the point of viewing *any* government interference with its operation (antitrust enforcement included) as counterproductive.[49] Libertarian tendencies also occur in the analysis of specific horizontal arrangements of widespread significance. For example, it has been argued that the activities of O.P. E.C., fixing the world price and production of crude oil, has conferred a long-run benefit on society by providing an early signal of inevitable long-term price increases, encouraging conservation and stimulating the search for new supplies of oil and alternative energy sources.[50] If one ignores such factors as the 30 to 1 ratio of price to cost of production, the massive wealth transfer from buyers to suppliers, the heavy human and economic toll paid in the form of recession in many industrial countries and deprivation in much of the third world, increased world tensions, and the other adverse effects of a cartel-fixed price for a basic commodity, one might agree with the analysis. In the main, however, most modern western societies have come to rely upon some degree of a state enforced policy of competition, i.e., fostering programs to enhance competition and using the legal system to prevent or punish private arrangements designed to displace the competitive process in those areas of the economy not otherwise socialized or regulated by affirmative government edict limiting entry, regulating price, controlling supply or otherwise regulating the activity.

The touchstones for federal and state antitrust regulation in the United States have been the legal concepts of "contract", "combination" and "conspiracy" and the legal/economic concepts of "restraint of trade" and "monopolization". Reliance upon these concepts as vehicles of analysis, and as the basis for defining the line of illegality, while employing the common law adversary process as the method for sorting out the prohibited from the permissible, necessarily charts the direction of analysis along well defined legal paths, forecloses consideration of other approaches for dealing with private arrangements affecting the competitive process, and results in a distinctively American approach to the regulation of the "free market" sector of the economy. Other governments relying on market forces as a regulatory tool have followed diverse paths to implement antitrust policy.

A remarkable spread of the American idea of a government enforced antitrust policy took place after the Second World War. In part, the policy was imposed on nations like Japan and Germany by the occupation forces in order to prevent the reincarnation of powerful industrial combinations controlling the state and blamed for contributing to the rise of fascist, totalitarian, or military dictatorships.[51] Since that time, antitrust enforcement of varying levels of intensity

---

49. Neo-classical economic theorizing can come close to this state of affairs by narrowly defining the goals of antitrust policy. See Bork, supra pp. 39–40.

50. P.W. MacAvoy, "To OPEC, With Many Thanks," New York Times, Business Section, P. 1, Col. 1 (Nov. 23, 1980).

51. See J. Montgomery, Forced To Be Free: The Artificial Revolution in Germa-

has become an institutionalized part of the legal/economic regulation of the "free market" economies of most western nations. Integration of European economies into the Common Market has also seen the use of antitrust policy as a way of preventing private arrangements from inhibiting or detracting from the free flow of goods and services among the member states.[52] The United Nations adopted in 1980 a resolution approving "Equitable Principles and Rules for the Control of Restrictive Business Practices" which borrows heavily from antitrust theory in defining restrictive business practices.[53] Although it is not enforceable and is limited to defining the obligations of member states, the resolution reflects a remarkable world-wide consensus embracing antitrust principles as tools for regulating world trade.[54]

These developments provide a basis for comparing different methods for achieving similar antitrust ends. The conceptual analytical touchstones of the legislation which follows and the forums in which it is enforced should be compared and contrasted with the approaches of American law sketched out in previous chapters. Several bases for comparison should be considered:

What types of collaboration are covered? What are the stated and implicit purposes? What safeguards against exploitation are specified? What enforcement methods are relied upon and what remedies are available?

Among types of collaboration are: cooperatives, agricultural and other; joint selling and joint buying arrangements; price and production agreements in "sick industries"; rationalization cartels (agreements assigning particular products or markets to designated members of the cartel presumably to achieve lower costs by specialization and larger scale of operations).

Among safeguards against exploitation may be: requiring that the tolerated restraint of trade be "necessary" to achieve the objective; requiring that the "least restrictive" method of pursuing the objective be chosen; requiring that collective price-setting be with "due regard" to the rest of the economy and the public weal (i.e., not governed solely by the concerns of the cartelized industry); insisting upon the temporary character of the "crisis cartel" by demanding that price constraints be accompanied by a "planned adjustment of capacity to demand" (i.e., a disinvestment program such as might be accomplished by competitive suppression of marginal firms); assuring that cost-savings from specialization will, in part at least, be

ny and Japan (1957); E. Hadley, Antitrust in Japan (1970).

52. A.D. Neale & D. G. Goyder, The Antitrust Laws of the U.S.A. 476 (3d Ed. 1980): "The one area of consensus that lay behind Articles 85 and 86 of the Treaty of Rome was that the formation of the Common Market through the dismantling of tariffs and other trade barriers should not be frustrated by allowing private cartel agreements or dominant firms to

erect new or substitute obstacles to trade between member countries."

53. U.N. Doc. TD/RBP/CONF/10 (1980), reprinted in 19 Int'l Legal Materials 815 (1980).

54. See Benson, The U.N. Code of Restrictive Business Practices: An International Antitrust Code is Born, 30 Am.U.L. Rev. 1031 (1981); Davidow, International Antitrust Codes: The Post Acceptance Phase, 26 Antitrust Bull. 567 (1981).

passed on to consumers; entrusting the price-fixing power not to the cartel but to the supervising governmental authority; allocating the burden of proof of justification to the proponent of the restraint; assuring that the tribunal which must pass on the restraint is structured so as to assure predominance of public over parochial industry concerns.

Analyze the following by the criteria suggested above.

TREATY OF ROME [55]

(1957)

European Economic Community

Article 85

(1) The following shall be deemed to be inconsistent with the Common Market and shall be prohibited namely: all agreements between firms, all decisions by associations of firms and all concerted practices likely to affect trade between Member States and which have the object or effect of preventing, restraining or distorting competition within the Common Market, and in particular those which:

(a) directly or indirectly fix buying or selling prices or other trading terms,

(b) limit or control production, marketing, technical development or investments,

(c) effect the sharing of markets or sources of supply,

(d) apply to trade partners unequal conditions in respect of equivalent transactions, thereby placing them at a competitive disadvantage,

(e) make the conclusion of a contract subject to the acceptance by trade partners of additional goods or services which are not by their nature or by the custom of the trade related to the subject matter of such contract.

(2) Any agreement or decision prohibited by this Article shall be automatically null and void.

(3) The provisions of Clause 1 may nevertheless be declared inapplicable

55. For recent surveys of developments under Articles 85 and 86, see R. Folsom, Corporate Competition Law in the European Communities (1978); Hacker, Article 86—Some Recent Developments, Parts 1 & 2, 128 New L.J. 907, 1005 (1978), 130 New L.J. 40, 163 (1980); Korak, Interpretation and Application of Article 86 of the Treaty of Rome, 53 N.D.Law. 768 (1978); Lang, Compliance With the Common Market's Antitrust Law, 14 Int.Law. 485 (1980); Comment, Antitrust Under the Treaty of Rome, 11 Int.Law. 369 (1977); Comment, A Survey of Antitrust Law in the European Economic Community, 16 Santa Clara L.Rev. 535 (1976). Regular reports of enforcement actions in the common market are published by CCH in Common Market Reports and summaries are published as an annex to the General Report on the Activities of The Communities. Articles on significant developments in foreign antitrust are published in each issue of the Antitrust Bulletin.

— to any agreement or category of agreements, between firms,

— to any decision or category of decisions of associations of firms or

— to any concerted practice or category of concerted practices

which contributes towards improving the production or distribution of goods or promoting technical or economic progress while reserving to users a fair share in the profit which results, without

(a) imposing upon the firms concerned any restriction which is not essential for the attainment of these objects, or

(b) giving such firms the power to eliminate competition in respect of a substantial portion of the products in question.

Article 86

It shall be inconsistent with the Common Market and prohibited so far as the trade between Member States may be thereby affected for one or more firms to abuse a dominant position in the Common Market or any substantial part thereof.

The following practices shall in particular be deemed to be an abuse:

(a) the direct or indirect imposition of buying or selling prices or other unfair trading terms;

(b) the limitation of production, marketing or technical development to the prejudice of consumers;

(c) the application of trade partners of unequal conditions in respect of equivalent transactions, thereby placing them at a competitive disadvantage;

(d) subjecting the conclusion of a contract to the acceptance by trade partners of additional goods or services which are not by their nature or by the custom of the trade related to the subject matter of such contract.

TREATY OF PARIS

(1951)
European Coal & Steel Community

[Article 65 of the Treaty, after forbidding agreements and concerted practices which would tend to impede "the normal operation of competition", provides for "Rationalization Cartels" as follows]:

(2) However, the High Authority will authorize enterprises to agree among themselves to specialize in the production of, or to engage in joint buying or selling of specified products, if the High Authority finds:

(a) that such specialization or such joint buying or selling will contribute to a substantial improvement in the production or marketing of the products in question; and

(b) that the agreement in question is essential to achieve such effects, and does not impose any restriction not necessary for that purpose; and

(c) that it is not susceptible of giving the interested enterprises the power to influence prices, or to control or limit production or marketing of an appreciable part of the products in question within the common market, or of protecting them from effective competition by other enterprises within the common market.[56]

THE UNITED NATIONS RESOLUTION ON EQUITABLE PRINCIPLES AND RULES FOR THE CONTROL OF RESTRICTIVE BUSINESS PRACTICES

(1980)

SECTION A—Objectives

Taking into account the interests of all countries, particularly those of developing countries, the Set of Multilaterally Agreed Equitable Principles and Rules are framed in order to achieve the following objectives:

1. To ensure that restrictive business practices do not impede or negate the realization of benefits that should arise from the liberalization of tariff and non-tariff barriers affecting world trade, particularly those affecting the trade and development of developing countries.

2. To attain greater efficiency in international trade and development, particularly that of developing countries, in accordance with national aims of economic and social development and existing economic structures, such as through:

(a) The creation, encouragement and protection of competition;

(b) Control of the concentration of capital and/or economic power;

(c) Encouragement of innovation.

3. To protect and promote social welfare in general and, in particular, the interests of consumers in both developed and developing countries.

---

56. One of the early acts of the High Authority was to dissolve the German coal sales cartel, which handled the entire output of the Ruhr. Three independent agencies were set up; but they were permitted to maintain a Joint Office for cooperation in "emergency" situations, pooling of transport, estimating production and sales, engaging in joint research and advertising, and supplying all consumers ordering more than 50,000 tons a year. Producers' sales direct to wholesalers were limited to those handling specified large tonnages. The arrangement proved unsuccessful in establishing sales agencies. See Bulletin of The European Community for Coal and Steel, April 1956, p. 4; Bull. of the European Economic Community, March-April 1959, p. 227. See Comptoirs de Vente v. Haute Autorité, VI Receuil de la Jurisprudence de la Cour de Justice des Communautés Européennes 49 (1960). In 1969 substantially all the Ruhr coal producers were merged into a single giant firm "designed to revive the sick industry." Under both German and European Community law, mergers are subject to few controls unless they "abuse" a "dominant" position. The Ruhr combine was carried out with governmental financial support. See Ruhr Companies Form Coal Group, New York Times, July 19, 1969, p. 35.

SECTION B—Definitions and scope of application

For the purpose of this Set of Multilaterally Agreed Equitable Principles and Rules

(i) Definitions:

1. "Restrictive business practices" means acts or behaviour of enterprises which, through an abuse or acquisition and abuse of a dominant position of market power, limit access to markets or otherwise unduly restrain competition, having or being likely to have adverse effects on international trade, particularly that of developing countries, and on the economic development of these countries, or which through formal, informal, written or unwritten agreements or arrangements among enterprises have the same impact.

2. "Dominant position of market power" refers to a situation where an enterprise, either by itself or acting together with a few other enterprises, is in a position to control the relevant market for a particular good or service or group of goods or services.

. . .

SECTION D—Principles and Rules for enterprises, including transnational corporations

1. Enterprises should conform to the restrictive business practices laws, and the provisions concerning restrictive business practices in other laws, of the countries in which they operate, and in the event of proceedings under these laws should be subject to the competence of the courts and relevant administrative bodies therein.

. . .

3. Enterprises, except when dealing with each other in the context of an economic entity wherein they are under common control, including through ownership, or otherwise not able to act independently of each other, engaged on the market in rival or potentially rival activities, should refrain from practices such as the following when, through formal, informal, written or unwritten agreements or arrangements, they limit access to markets or otherwise unduly restrain competition, having or being likely to have adverse effects on international trade, particularly that of developing countries, and on the economic development of these countries:

   (a) agreements fixing prices including as to exports and imports;

   (b) collusive tendering;

   (c) market or customer allocation arrangements;

   (d) allocation by quota as to sales and production;

   (e) collective action to enforce arrangements—e.g., by concerted refusals to deal;

   (f) concerted refusal of supplies to potential importers;

   (g) collective denial of access to an arrangement, or association, which is crucial to competition.

4. Enterprises should refrain from the following acts or behaviour in a relevant market when, through an abuse [57] or acquisition

---

57. [Footnote in the original.] Whether acts or behaviour are abusive or not should be examined in terms of their purpose and effects in the actual situa-

and abuse of a dominant position of market power, they limit access to markets or otherwise unduly restrain competition, having or being likely to have adverse effects on international trade, particularly that of developing countries, and on the economic development of these countries:

(a) predatory behavior towards competitors, such as using below cost pricing to eliminate competitors;

(b) discriminatory (i.e. unjustifiably differentiated) pricing or terms or conditions in the supply or purchase of goods or services, including by means of the use of pricing policies in transactions between affiliated enterprises which overcharge or undercharge for goods or services purchased or supplied as compared with prices for similar or compatible transactions outside the affiliated enterprises;

(c) mergers, takeovers, joint ventures or other acquisitions of control, whether of a horizontal, vertical or a conglomerate nature;

(d) fixing the prices at which goods exported can be resold in importing countries;

(e) restrictions in the importation of goods which have been legitimately marked abroad with a trademark identical or similar to the trademark protected as to identical or similar goods in the importing country where the trademarks in question are of the same origin, i.e., belong to the same owner or are used by enterprises between which there is economic, organizational, managerial or legal interdependence and where the purpose of such restrictions is to maintain artificially high prices;

(f) when not for ensuring the achievement of legitimate business purposes, such as quality, safety, adequate distribution or service:

(i) partial or complete refusals to deal on the enterprise's customary commercial terms;

(ii) making the supply of particular goods or services dependent upon the acceptance of restrictions on the distribution or manufacture of competing or other goods;

(iii) imposing restrictions concerning where, or to whom, or in what form or quantities goods supplied or other goods may be re-sold or exported;

tion, in particular with reference to whether they limit access to markets or otherwise unduly restrain competition, having or being likely to have adverse effects on international trade, particularly that of developing countries, and on the economic development of these countries, and to whether they are:

(a) appropriate in the light of the organizational, managerial and legal relationship among the enterprises concerned, such as in the context of relations within an economic entity and not having restrictive effects outside the related enterprises.

(b) appropriate in light of special conditions or economic circumstances in the relevant market such as exceptional conditions of supply and demand or the size of the market;

(c) of types which are usually treated as acceptable under pertinent national or regional laws and regulations for the control of restrictive business practices;

(d) consistent with the purposes and objectives of these principles and rules.

(iv) **making the supply of particular goods or services dependent upon the purchase of other goods or services from the supplier or his designee.**

NOTES AND QUERIES

(1) *"Crisis Cartels."* The Treaty of 1951 establishing The European Coal and Steel Community as a 6-nation competitive market for specified commodities provided, in Article 61(b), that the High Authority of the Community may fix minimum prices "if it deems that a manifest crisis exists or is imminent and that such a decision is necessary to attain the objectives defined in Article 3." Among the objectives referred to in Article 3 are "lowest prices . . . while at the same time providing normal possibilities of remuneration for capital invested," and expanded production "avoiding inconsiderate exhaustion of . . . resources."

The German Cartel Authority is authorized to approve a cartel agreement "in case of a decline of sales which is the result of a fundamental change in the demand if such agreement or resolution is necessary to effect a planned adjustment of the capacity to the demand and if the regulation is made with due regard to the economy as a whole and the common weal." [58]

(2) *Queries.* How does Article 85 correspond to Section 1 of the Sherman Act? How does it differ? Does the concept "abuse of dominant position" in Article 86 provide a better conceptual basis for analyzing structural problems than the concept of "monopolization" under the Sherman Act? Should a sick industry be assured "normal possibilities of remuneration for capital invested", as under Section 61(b) of the European Coal & Steel Community Treaty? Can a "rationalization cartel" be established without giving the parties "power to influence prices, etc." as provided in Section 65(2)(c) of the European Coal & Steel Community Treaty? Will the economic gains realized by "specialization" under Section 65(2) of the Coal and Steel Treaty be better realized in the long run by competition?

(3) *Adoption of the U.N. Resolution and Its Implications.* The unanimous adoption of the U.N. Resolution on Restrictive Trade Practices in 1980 may be considered surprising in view of the widespread disparity of ideology among nations on how to organize their economic affairs and several decades of failure to negotiate similar statements of international economic policy to govern world trade. One observer attributes the success to the growing worldwide recognition of the need to come to grips with the competitive and investment behavior of multi-national corporations and to the fact that the text of the Resolution is "so lacking in legal form as to nations or enterprises, so gradual in likely application, and so balanced in content and tone, that it presents no imminent threat to the interests of any corporation or government." [59]

---

58. Section 4 of the Law Against Restraint of Competition, Federal Republic of Germany, [1957] 1 BGB 1081. Cf. Section 21(1) of The Restrictive Trade Practices Act, 1956, 4 & 5 Eliz. 2, c. 68 (necessary to avert "serious and persistent adverse effect on the general level of unemployment").

This defense of a minimum pricing scheme failed in Yarn Spinners' Agreement L.R. 1 R.P. 118 (1959), being overbalanced by detriments to the public interest which the Court found in the prospect of higher prices, lower exports, and encouragement to overcapacity.

59. Davidow, International Antitrust Codes: The Post Acceptance Phase, 26 Antitrust Bull. 567, 570 (1981).

Despite the hortatory nature of the Resolution, it is interesting to note parallels between the structure and concepts of the Resolution, the Treaty of Rome, and the Sherman Act. Compare: (i) the definition of "restrictive business practices," found in Section B(1) of the Resolution with Article 85 of the Treaty of Rome and Section 1 of the Sherman Act; (ii) the definition of "dominant position of market power" in Section B(2) of the Resolution with Article 86 of the Treaty of Rome and Section 2 of the Sherman Act; (iii) the treatment of intra-enterprise arrangements in Section D(3) of the Resolution with the treatment of intra-enterprise conspiracy under the Sherman Act discussed supra pp. 458–471; (iv) the concepts "unduly restrain competition", "written or unwritten agreements or arrangements" with the Sherman Act concepts of "rule of reason" and "contract", "combination" and "conspiracy"; (v) the enumerated list of practices set forth in Section D(3) of the Resolution with the practices singled out for *"per se"* treatment under the Sherman Act, and the practices enumerated in Section D(4) of the Resolution with conduct relied upon in Sherman Act § 2 litigation, supra Chapter 2, to prove unlawful monopolization.

(4) *The Antitrust Laws of Nation States.* Most western nations have also incorporated various forms of antitrust policy into their domestic law. While too complex and varied to enumerate or describe here, it should be noted that both the specific legislation and its application vary considerably from country to country in interesting and unexpected ways from the language and application of the U.S. antitrust laws. For example, the Canadian Combines Investigation Act, § 32(1)(c) provides:

> Every one who conspires, combines, agrees or arranges with another person . . . (c) to prevent, or lessen, unduly, competition in the production, manufacture, purchase, barter, sale, storage, rental, transportation or supply of an article, or in the price of insurance upon persons or property, or . . . is guilty of an indictable offense and is liable to imprisonment for two years.[60]

Unlike the Sherman Act's prohibition upon "every" restraint of trade, the Canadian law only condemns those restraints which "unduly" prevent or lessen competition. Recent cases in Canada have imposed a heavy burden to show a violation, requiring "the government to demonstrate that the accused [specifically] intended to lessen competition unduly, that they entered an agreement, and that the agreement entered did, or would have if carried into effect, lessen competition unduly."[61] Unlike the doctrine developed in *Socony-Vacuum*, footnote 59, supra p. 358, proof of an adverse effect upon competition standing alone is not sufficient to find a violation of the Act. "Unduly" has been interpreted to require proof of an intent to achieve a specific anticompetitive effect. Arrangements entered to make rational certain trade practices, therefore, will not be held unlawful even if there is an anticompetitive effect because the intent is not viewed as one aimed specifically at restraining trade for its own sake.

A similar result has been reached under the British Restrictive Trade Practices Act.[62] Under that law, agreements in restraint of trade must be registered with the Registrar of the Restrictive Practices Court. Such agreements are presumptively contrary to the public interest, but may be upheld if the agreement produces one or more specified benefits (i.e., protect

60. Combines Investigation Act, R.S., c. C–23, amended by C. 10 (1st Supp.) c. 10 (2d Supp.) 1974–76, c. 76.

61. Reshenthaler & Stanbury, Recent Conspiracy Decisions In Canada: New Legislation Needed, 26 Antitrust Bull. 839, 850 (1981).

62. 4 & 5 Eliz. II Chap. 68 (1956). The British legislation is discussed supra p. 499.

the public from injury in use of the goods, prevent an increase in unemployment, promote exports, etc.) and is not "unreasonable" on balance to the public or persons not party to the agreement. The statute has been interpreted as permitting a form of rule of reason price fixing in *Black Bolt & Nut Association Agreement.*[63] The analysis in that case has been described as follows: [64]

Forty-four members of a manufacturers' trade association producing ninety per cent of Britain's black bolts and nuts fixed common prices for their products. Their agreement, registered pursuant to the Restrictive Trade Practices Act of 1956, was referred by the Registrar to the Restrictive Practices Court, a tribunal empowered to nullify and enjoin adherence to any trade restrictions it finds contrary to the public interest. Under the act, a restrictive agreement is deemed contrary to the public interest unless the court is satisfied that it meets any of seven enumerated justifications and, further, that it is not "unreasonable," a determination to be made by balancing against its proven justifications any detriment to the public that may result from its operation. In justification of the Black Bolt and Nut Association's agreement the court found that the resulting common price structure eliminated any need for commercial purchasers to "go shopping" for favorable prices. Since shopping adds to a purchaser's cost of doing business, its obviation, concluded the court, produces a saving which is—in the language of one of the statutory justifications—a "specific and substantial benefit" to the public. On balance, because the court believed that the established prices would not be higher than those which free competition would determine, the agreement was held not to be "contrary to the public interest." . . .

The court justified the common price scheme in the present case on the ground that it "saved" purchasers expensive shopping around. This protection of buyers from an assumed indulgence in uneconomic price comparisons fails to reflect several factors which encouraged the court to uphold the agreement. The court was noticeably impressed by technical cooperation and intertrading among members of the industry, which foster what the court thought to be desirable specialization and small firm protection. The court realized, however, that it was confined by an act whose language does not exempt an agreement from condemnation because of industrial efficiency, reasonable prices, small firm survival, or economic specialization. Faced with what it considered a reasonable restriction without specific statutory justification, the court seems to have turned to a supposed benefit—the shopping economy [65]—to qualify the agreement as one yielding a "specific and substantial benefit," thereby avoiding the impact of the statutory presumption. . . .

---

63. L.R. 2 R.P. 50 (1960).

64. Comment, 109 U.Pa.L.Rev. 1034 (1961).

65. The shopping economy is probably imaginary in that it assumes that purchasers will undertake an uneconomic operation. It seems obvious that if it costs more to go shopping than can be realized by savings on lower prices, most purchasers will forego shopping, each relying on one manufacturer who will keep his prices competitive in order not to lose the business. 77 L.Q.Rev. 28, 29 (1961). The court recognized this weakness in its argument, but countered that in times of high demand manufacturers—all of whom must rely on intertrading to fill comprehensive orders—would be unwilling to fill intertrade orders until their own established customers were adequately provided. This would force purchasers to shop around in such times because their usual sole suppliers would be unable to fill all their requirements. This argument, however, overlooks the likelihood of purchasers establishing trade relations with enough manufacturers to cover their entire potential needs. [author's footnote]

The court's reasoning that prices would not be appreciably lower without the price-fixing agreement, especially in an industry displaying a wide range of individual firm profits, implicitly rejects the classical economic theory that the lowest possible price will result from firms of differing efficiencies competing in price. Even more significant, however, was the court's use of the transparent shopping economy rationale to fit into a statutory slot an agreement which it found generally unobjectionable. This manifests a disposition on the part of the court to perpetuate the 1948 act's approach of evaluating the reasonableness of each restriction as the court believes it in fact operates. The 1956 act's presumption is thus disregarded even in instances where the new statute would appear to have foreclosed judicial determination. By expanding the "specific and substantial benefit" justification, the court has effectively determined to enjoy the same discretion in evaluating agreements as did the Monopolies Commission. The exercise of such discretion could significantly alter the impact of the 1956 act upon restrictive practices.

[Ed. The Black Bolt agreement originally excluded large buyers and provided a bidding process for this business. Upon the Court's refusal to countenance this, the agreement was amended to require large users to pay the fixed prices, although the shopping rationale was inapplicable to them. The court sustained this restriction as necessary to prevent erosion of prices on the general list. [1966] 1 W.L.R. 93 (Rest.Pr.Ct.1965). See also Cement Makers Federation Agreement, L.R. 2 R.P. 241 (1961), accepting the argument that concerted price-fixing lowered prices in this field by limiting risks and thus lowering the return which investors required; reliance was also placed on supervision by a highly-regarded gentleman, Sir Malcolm Trustram Eve, as the industry's "independent chairman."]

Chapter 5

COLLECTIVE ACTION: BOYCOTTS AND JOINT VENTURES

A. BOYCOTTS

We owe the term "boycott" to the economic distress of Irish tenant farmers in the late 1870's.[1] Following three years of bad harvests, and the House of Lords' rejection in 1880 of legislation to compensate tenants evicted for nonpayment of rent due to crop failure, landlords in Ireland proceeded to raise rents and increase evictions. The Irish National Land League, formed in 1879, urged tenants to not pay rent and to passively resist eviction. They also devised an additional tactic:[2]

> Captain Boycott was an Englishman, an agent of Lord Earne, and a farmer of Lough Mask, in the wild and beautiful district of Connemara. In his capacity as agent he had served notices upon Lord Earne's tenants, and the tenantry suddenly retaliated in a most unexpected way . . . . The population of the region for miles round resolved not to have anything to do with him, and as far as they could prevent it not to allow any one else to have anything to do with him. His life appeared to be in danger; he had to claim police protection. . . . No one would work for him; no one would supply him with food. He and his wife had to work in their own fields themselves . . . . The Orangemen of the north heard of Captain Boycott and his sufferings, and the way in which he was holding his ground, and they organized assistance and sent him down armed laborers from Ulster. To prevent civil war the authorities had to send a force of soldiers and police to Lough Mask, and Captain Boycott's harvests were brought in, and his potatoes dug by the armed Ulster laborers, guarded always by the little army.

As a result of the events at Lough Mask, "Boycotting" was thereafter freely employed by the League. No League sympathizer was to have any dealings with the boycotted individual; "they were not to be worked for, bought from, sold to." The principle of boycotting "was not aggressive" and "nothing was to be done to the obnoxious person."[3] Nevertheless, in addition to the boycotts urged by the Land League, there were a number of acts of violence and intimidation, which led to the passage of legislation in 1881 increasing the power to arrest persons who incited to crimes of intimidation.

1. The following history is from McCarthy, England Under Gladstone, 1880–1885, published in Harper's Franklin Square Library, No., 505, at 20–25 (1886).

2. Id. at 24.

3. Id.

Boycotts in the United States have been a frequent subject of antitrust litigation. Indeed, antitrust cases involving boycotting behavior date back to the earliest days of the Sherman Act.[4] Nevertheless, it was not until 1978 that the Supreme Court attempted a definition of the term: "The generic concept of boycott refers to a method of pressuring a party with whom one has a dispute by withholding, or enlisting others to withold, patronage or services from the target."[5]

The following cases will show that boycotts (or "joint refusals to deal," as they are sometimes called) can occur in a wide variety of contexts. In reading these cases the student should ask whether the archetypal "Boycott" implicates policy concerns not present in all situations which fit the Supreme Court's definition of a boycott. Are there some reasons for condemning boycotts—or, perhaps, allowing them—which are unrelated to the economic harm they cause? Should all boycotting behavior be covered under the antitrust laws, or should some types of boycotts be exempt? Note, in this connection, that Congress has exempted certain types of labor boycotts from the antitrust laws in Section 6 of the Clayton Act.[6] Finally, if boycotts are to be condemned under the antitrust laws, should they be viewed as *per se* illegal or should they be judged under a rule of reason?

The first case in this section, *Fashion Originators' Guild of America v. Federal Trade Commission*, and the materials following are designed to focus on the question of why boycotts should be viewed as illegal. The *per se*/rule of reason inquiry is explored in *Smith v. Pro-Football, Inc.*, which also indicates how a rule of reason analysis might work in light of the Supreme Court's decision in *National Society of Professional Engineers*, supra p. 352.

4. See Anderson v. United States, 171 U.S. 604, 19 S.Ct. 50, 43 L.Ed. 300 (1898) (members of Traders' Live Stock Exchange, who bought and sold cattle, agreed not to transact business with nonmember traders and not to purchase cattle from any firm that did; held: no restraint of trade). For reviews of past boycott decisions, see, e.g., Barber, Refusals to Deal Under the Federal Antitrust Laws, 103 U.Pa.L.Rev. 847 (1945); Bird, Sherman Act Limitations on Noncommercial Concerted Refusals to Deal, 1970 Duke L.J. 247; First, Competition in the Legal Education Industry (II): An Antitrust Analysis, 54 N.Y.U.L.Rev. 1049 (1979); Kirkpatrick, Commercial Boycotts As Per Se Violations of the Sherman Act, 10 Geo.Wash.L.Rev. 302 (1942).

5. St. Paul Fire & Marine Insurance Co. v. Barry, 438 U.S. 531, 98 S.Ct. 2923, 57 L.Ed.2d 932 (1978) (joint refusal of insurance companies to sell medical malpractice insurance to dissatisfied custom-

ers of one of them; held to be a "boycott" and hence not exempt from the antitrust laws by virtue of McCarran-Ferguson Act).

6. See, e.g., H.A. Artists & Associates, Inc. v. Actors' Equity Association, 451 U.S. 704, 101 S.Ct. 2102, 68 L.Ed.2d 558 (1981) (union's system of regulation of theatrical agents is immune from antitrust liability under statutory labor exemption); cf. Allied International v. International Longshoreman's Association, 640 F.2d 1368 (1st Cir. 1981) (union's refusal to handle cargo from Soviet Union after invasion of Afghanistan, although not exempt under statutory labor exemption, does not give rise to Sherman Act liability; "mere refusal to work," done without anticompetitive purpose or collaboration with nonlabor groups), certiorari denied 456 U.S. 212, 102 S.Ct. 3508, 73 L.Ed. 1382 (1982). The labor exemption is explored further, infra chapter 10.

FASHION ORIGINATORS' GUILD OF AMERICA v. FEDERAL TRADE COMMISSION

Supreme Court of the United States, 1941.
312 U.S. 457, 61 S.Ct. 703, 85 L.Ed. 949.

MR. JUSTICE BLACK delivered the opinion of the Court.

The Circuit Court of Appeals, with modifications not here challenged, affirmed a Federal Trade Commission decree ordering petitioners to cease and desist from certain practices found to have been done in combination and to constitute "unfair methods of competition" tending to monopoly. Determination of the correctness of the decision below requires consideration of the Sherman, Clayton, and Federal Trade Commission Acts.

Some of the members of the combination design, manufacture, sell and distribute women's garments—chiefly dresses. Others are manufacturers, converters or dyers of textiles from which these garments are made. Fashion Originators' Guild of America (FOGA), an organization controlled by these groups, is the instrument through which petitioners work to accomplish the purposes condemned by the Commission. The garment manufacturers claim to be creators of original and distinctive designs of fashionable clothes for women, and the textile manufacturers claim to be creators of similar original fabric designs. After these designs enter the channels of trade, other manufacturers systematically make and sell copies of them, the copies usually selling at prices lower than the garments copied. Petitioners call this practice of copying unethical and immoral, and give it the name of "style piracy." And although they admit that their "original creations" are neither copyrighted nor patented, and indeed assert that existing legislation affords them no protection against copyists, they nevertheless urge that sale of copied designs constitutes an unfair trade practice and a tortious invasion of their rights. Because of these alleged wrongs, petitioners, while continuing to compete with one another in many respects, combined among themselves to combat and, if possible, destroy all competition from the sale of garments which are copies of their "original creations." They admit that to destroy such competition they have in combination purposely boycotted and declined to sell their products to retailers who follow a policy of selling garments copied by other manufacturers from designs put out by Guild members. As a result of their efforts, approximately 12,000 retailers throughout the country have signed agreements to "cooperate" with the Guild's boycott program, but more than half of these signed the agreements only because constrained by threats that Guild members would not sell to retailers who failed to yield to their demands—threats that have been carried out by the Guild practice of placing on red cards the names of non-cooperators (to whom no sales are to be made), placing on white cards the names of cooperators (to whom sales are to be made), and then distributing both sets of cards to the manufacturers.

The one hundred and seventy-six manufacturers of women's garments who are members of the Guild occupy a commanding position in their line of business. In 1936, they sold in the United States more than 38% of all women's garments wholesaling at $6.75 and up, and more than 60% of those at $10.75 and above. The power of the combination is great; competition and the demand of the consuming public make it necessary for most retail dealers to stock some of the products of these manufacturers. And the power of the combination is made even greater by reason of the affiliation of some members of the National Federation of Textiles, Inc.—that being an organization composed of about one hundred textile manufacturers, converters, dyers, and printers of silk and rayon used in making women's garments. Those members of the Federation who are affiliated with the Guild have agreed to sell their products only to those garment manufacturers who have in turn agreed to sell only to cooperating retailers.

The Guild maintains a Design Registration Bureau for garments, and the Textile Federation maintains a similar Bureau for textiles. The Guild employs "shoppers" to visit the stores of both cooperating and non-cooperating retailers, "for the purpose of examining their stocks, to determine and report as to whether they contain . . . copies of registered designs . . . ." An elaborate system of trial and appellate tribunals exists, for the determination of whether a given garment is in fact a copy of a Guild member's design. In order to assure the success of its plan of registration and restraint, and to ascertain whether Guild regulations are being violated, the Guild audits its members books. And if violations of Guild requirements are discovered, as, for example, sales to red-carded retailers, the violators are subject to heavy fines.

In addition to the elements of the agreement set out above, all of which relate more or less closely to competition by so-called style copyists, the Guild has undertaken to do many things apparently independent of and distinct from the fight against copying. Among them are the following: the combination prohibits its members from participating in retail advertising; regulates the discount they may allow; prohibits their selling at retail; cooperates with local guilds in regulating days upon which special sales shall be held; prohibits its members from selling women's garments to persons who conduct businesses in residences, residential quarters, hotels or apartment houses; and denies the benefits of membership to retailers who participate with dress manufacturers in promoting fashion shows unless the merchandise used is actually purchased and delivered.

If the purpose and practice of the combination of garment manufacturers and their affiliates runs counter to the public policy declared in the Sherman and Clayton Acts, the Federal Trade Commission has the power to suppress it as an unfair method of competition. From its findings the Commission concluded that the petitioners, "pursuant to understandings, arrangements, agreements, combinations and conspiracies entered into jointly and severally", had prevented sales in interstate commerce, had "substantially lessened, hindered and suppressed" competition, and had tended "to create in themselves a monopoly." And paragraph 3 of the Clayton Act, 15 U.S.C. § 14, 15 U.S.C.A. § 14, declares "It shall be unlawful for any person engaged in commerce . . . to . . . make a sale or contract for sale of goods . . . on the condition, agreement or understanding that the . . . purchaser thereof shall not use or deal in the goods . . . of a competitor or competitors of the . . . seller, where the effect of such . . . sale, or contract for sale . . . may be to substantially lessen competition or tend to create a monopoly in any line of commerce." The relevance of this section of the Clayton Act to petitioners' scheme is shown by the fact that the scheme is bottomed upon a system of sale under which (1) textiles shall be sold to garment manufacturers only upon the condition and understanding that the buyers will not use or deal in textiles which are copied from the designs of textile manufacturing Guild members; (2) garment manufacturers shall sell to retailers only upon the condition and understanding that the retailers shall not use or deal in such copied designs. And the Federal Trade Commission concluded in the language of the Clayton Act that these understandings substantially lessened competition and tended to create a monopoly. We hold that the Commission, upon adequate and unchallenged findings, correctly concluded that this practice constituted an unfair method of competition.

Not only does the plan in the respects above discussed thus conflict with the principles of the Clayton Act; the findings of the Commission bring petitioners' combination in its entirety well within the inhibition of the policies declared by the Sherman Act itself. Section 1 of that Act makes illegal every contract, combination or conspiracy in restraint of trade or commerce among the several states; Section 2 makes illegal every combination or conspiracy which monopolizes or attempts to monopolize any part of that trade or commerce. Under the Sherman Act "competition, not combination, should be the law of trade." And among the many respects in which the Guild's plan runs contrary to the policy of the Sherman Act are these: it narrows the outlets to which garment and textile manufacturers can sell and the sources from which retailers can buy; subjects all retailers and manufacturers who decline to comply with the Guild's program to an organized boycott; takes away the freedom of action of members by requiring each to reveal to the Guild the intimate details of their individual affairs; and has both as its necessary tendency and as its purpose and effect the direct suppression of competition from the sale of unregistered textiles and copied designs. In addition to all this, the combination is in reality an extra-governmental agency, which prescribes rules for the regulation and restraint of interstate commerce, and provides extra-judicial tribunals for determination and punishment of violations, and thus "trenches upon the power of the national legislature and violates the statute." *

* Compare FOGA's arrangements for protection of original designs with the statutory provisions for "design patents." See p. 948 infra. Would the stan-

. . . . [Petitioners] argue that their boycott and restraint of interstate trade is not within the ban of the policies of the Sherman and Clayton Acts because "the practices of FOGA were reasonable and necessary to protect the manufacturer, laborer, retailer and consumer against the devastating evils growing from the pirating of original designs and had in fact benefited all four." The Commission declined to hear much of the evidence that petitioners desired to offer on this subject. As we have pointed out, however, the aim of petitioners' combination was the intentional destruction of one type of manufacture and sale which competed with Guild members. The purpose and object of this combination, its potential power, its tendency to monopoly, the coercion it could and did practice upon a rival method of competition, all brought it within the policy of the prohibition declared by the Sherman and Clayton Acts. For this reason, the principles announced in Appalachian Coals, Inc. v. United States, 288 U.S. 344, 53 S.Ct. 471, 77 L.Ed. 825, and Sugar Institute v. United States, 297 U.S. 553, 56 S.Ct. 629, 80 L.Ed. 859, have no application here. Under these circumstances it was not error to refuse to hear the evidence offered, for the reasonableness of the methods pursued by the combination to accomplish its unlawful object is no more material than would be the reasonableness of the prices fixed by unlawful combination.

Nor can the unlawful combination be justified upon the argument that systematic copying of dress designs is itself tortious, or should now be declared so by us. In the first place, whether or not given conduct is tortious is a question of state law . . . . In the second place, even if copying were an acknowledged tort under the law of every state, that situation would not justify petitioners in combining together to regulate and restrain interstate commerce in violation of federal law. And for these same reasons, the principles declared in International News Service v. Associated Press, 248 U.S. 215, 39 S.Ct. 68, 63 L.Ed. 211, 2 A.L.R. 293, cannot serve to legalize petitioners' unlawful combination. The decision below is accordingly affirmed.

NOTES AND QUERIES

(1) *What Is Bad About a Boycott?* Review the list of factors Justice Black presents to demonstrate the ways in which the Guild's plan "runs contrary to the policy of the Sherman Act" (p. 534). Well-established precedent supported the proposition that commercial boycotts would violate Section 1 if they narrowed the outlets available to buyers and sellers, the first factor listed.[7] Why did the Court look beyond the anticompetitive effect of such market foreclosure? In a later case Justice Black wrote:[8]

The Sherman Act was designed to be a comprehensive charter of economic liberty aimed at preserving free and unfettered competition as the

dards of novelty and invention administered by FOGA's design registration bureau differ from those of the Patent Office? How would the consequences of "infringement" differ?

7. See, e.g., Montague & Co. v. Lowry, 193 U.S. 38, 24 S.Ct. 307, 48 L.Ed. 608 (1904).

8. Northern Pacific Railway v. United States, 356 U.S. 1, 4, 78 S.Ct. 514, 517, 2 L.Ed.2d 545 (1958).

rule of trade. It rests on the premise that the unrestrained interaction of competitive forces will yield the best allocation of our economic resources, the lowest prices, the highest quality and the greatest material progress, while at the same time providing an environment conducive to the preservation of our democratic political and social institutions.

(2) *Two Cases.* Consider the following cases. Does the conduct involved "run contrary to the policy of the Sherman Act" in the ways suggested in *FOGA?*

(a) The Arab League, composed of sovereign States, is engaged in an effort to combat "Zionism." As part of that effort it commenced (in 1951) a boycott of firms which trade with the State of Israel. The League maintains a central office in Damascus, Syria, to compile and distribute to members a list of target firms. As a condition of doing business in the Arab League countries, the Bechtel Corporation, a large American contractor, has agreed not to hire listed American firms as subcontractors on any of its projects within those countries. Overseas construction contracts amount to $22 billion yearly, of which $7.5 billion are in the involved countries (up from $1 billion last year). Subcontracting costs represent 30%–50% of that amount. Assuming the foreign commerce jurisdictional requirement is met (see p. 178 supra), should Bechtel be sued (criminally?) under Section 1 for the boycott?

(b) The National Organization For Women (NOW), a non-profit organization whose purpose is to bring women "into full participation in the mainstream of American Society," is engaged in an effort to secure ratification of the Equal Rights Amendment. As part of that effort it established an "Economic Sanctions Committee" in its Washington, D.C., office to promote convention boycotts of States which have not yet ratified the ERA. Through this office it distributed "boycott kits" (with information on how to organize a boycott), made extensive mailings and follow-up telephone calls, and maintained a list of unratified states and organizations which have adopted boycott resolutions. NOW claims that more than 120 organizations have joined the boycott, and that unratified States have lost more than $100 million in convention revenues. According to the New York Times, Phyllis Schlafly, an opponent of ERA, "describes the boycott as 'a deliberate malicious campaign against people like waiters and maids in hotels and restaurants and taxicab drivers who don't have anything to do with ratification.' " [9] The Missouri Attorney General, estimating that the boycott has cost Kansas City $8 million and St. Louis $10 million, has accordingly filed a *parens patriae* antitrust suit on behalf of the citizens of Missouri. Should he win?

(3) *Boycotts Adopted for Noncommercial Objectives.* What difference do the motives of the participants make? Should an agreement between a bank credit card company and member banks to refuse card service to "adult book" shops be immune from the Sherman Act if done solely for moral reasons?[10] Would it matter in the *NOW* case if convention site owners in ratified States had made financial contributions to NOW's boycott effort?

9. "Cost of Convention Boycott to States that Have Not Ratified Equal Rights Proposal Put at $100 Million," N.Y. Times, April 4, 1978, p. 17.

10. See Alpha-Sentura Business Services, Inc. v. Interbank Card Association, 1979–2 Trade Cas. ¶ 62,960 (D.Md.1979) (held: not unreasonable; done only for "moral" reasons; plaintiff and defendant were not competitors, and all adult book stores similarly affected).

As to the use of antitrust laws to vindicate civil rights threatened by concerted action, see Marcus, Civil Rights and the Antitrust Laws, 18 U.Chi.L.Rev. 171 (1951). In United States v. The Mortgage Conference of New York, the defendant lenders association was dissolved and members were ordered, inter alia, not to abstain from competing for a mortgage or lease "because such property is owned or occupied or is to be owned

In *Marjorie Webster Junior College v. Middle States Association of Colleges and Secondary Schools, Inc.*, plaintiff, a proprietary educational institution, was denied accreditation by defendant association solely because it was a for-profit school. In reversing an antitrust judgment favorable to plaintiff, Judge Bazelon wrote: [11]

> . . . the proscriptions of the Sherman Act were "tailored . . . for the business world", not for the noncommercial aspects of the liberal arts and the learned professions. In these contexts, an incidental restraint of trade, absent an intent or purpose to affect the commercial aspects of the profession, is not sufficient to warrant application of the antitrust laws
> . . . .

Is an exemption for noncommercially motivated boycotts consistent with the Supreme Court's subsequent decision in *Goldfarb* (pp. 413–414, supra)? [12] Why should any conduct which affects someone's business (or, more broadly, "resource allocation") be totally immune from antitrust scrutiny? Should motive be considered only to the extent that it is helpful in assessing the competitive impact of the restraint, rather than as a ground for a total exemption?

(4) *Boycotts To Fight Inflation.* Consider "President Bars Idea of Boycotts," N.Y. Times, Dec. 13, 1978, p. D1.* Was President Carter acting on advice of antitrust counsel?

> President Carter declared today his opposition to organized consumer boycotts of companies that do not comply with the Administration's wage-price guidelines.

> But while publicly rebuffing his new anti-inflation chief, Alfred E. Kahn, who suggested the boycott only last week, the President offered a qualifier. He observed at his televised news conference today that consumers, as well as state and local governments, "should be conversant with the relative compliance of suppliers" and adopt "the posture of a prudent purchaser."

> The statement by Mr. Kahn, the outspoken chairman of the Council on Wage and Price Stability, that the Government was considering the boycotts as a means of making its voluntary program more effective stirred unusually hostile reaction in the business community, which the President was apparently seeking to defuse. . . .

> The President said flatly: "I don't personally favor any organized boycotts."

> But in suggesting that consumers should still be conversant with the compliance record in making their purchases, the President appeared to be leaving his wage-price monitors considerable authority.

> The Council on Wage and Price Stability said it reserved absolute discretion in determining and disclosing which companies are or are not going along with the guidelines. Its monitoring would be similar to the selective enforcement of the Internal Revenue Service.

or occupied by persons belonging to any particular racial or national group". CCH Trade Cases, 1948–9, ¶ 62,273 (S.D. N.Y.1948) Cf. I. P. C. Distributors v. Chicago Moving Picture Operators Union, 132 F.Supp. 294 (N.D.Ill.1955) (treble damage action for refusal of union employees to handle allegedly communist film).

11.   432 F.2d 650, 654 (D.C.Cir. 1970), certiorari denied 400 U.S. 965, 91 S.Ct. 367, 27 L.Ed. 384.

12 No: Hennessey v. National Collegiate Athletic Association, 564 F.2d 1136, 1148–49 (5th Cir. 1977). See First, Competition in the Legal Education Industry (II): An Antitrust Analysis, 54 N.Y.U.L.Rev. 1049, 1092–99 (1979) (arguing *Marjorie Webster* incorrectly decided).

After the news conference, Mr. Kahn stuck to his guns, issuing a statement saying he was continuing to urge consumers to take compliance into account in deciding where and what to buy. . . .

Private industry has expressed in some cases vehement reaction to the extension of Government influence into the sector of consumer decision-making.

Herbert E. Markley, newly elected chairman of the National Association of Manufacturers, and president of the Timkin Company, told a press luncheon today that the boycott idea was "reprehensible."

"If we were moving into the Hitler government, that's what we'd be trying to do," said the business leader, whose organization represents 12,000 companies accounting for 75 percent of the national industrial output.

"I thought the President was trying to reduce the role of Government today. Those of us who fought in World War II wonder what we fought the war for."

Similarly spirited reaction has come from the United States Chamber of Commerce, whose chief economist, Jack Carlson, characterized consumer boycotts as a "witch hunt against workers and business people" and a "return to McCarthyism."

Mr. Carlson insisted that "consumers should be encouraged to purchase their requirements at the lowest price, as has been the American way for 200 years."

Under the guidelines, wages are to be held to 7 percent increases and prices to a half-percentage point under the average rise in 1976 and 1977.

(5) *Boycotts and the First Amendment.* Reconsider the conduct involved in promoting a boycott, particularly as described in Note (2), along with the frequent association of boycotts with political goals (dating back to Captain Boycott). To what extent might (some) boycotts be protected by the first amendment?

Consider *NAACP v. Claiborne Hardware Co.*,[13] where plaintiffs sought damages arising out of a boycott of white merchants by blacks in Claiborne County, Mississippi, between 1966 and 1972. The boycott was imposed following the rejection by local officials of a list of nineteen demands, seeking, e.g., desegregation of schools and public facilities and the hiring of black police officers. The boycott was effectuated, in part, through the use of "store watchers," who identified blacks who continued to trade with white merchants, and through the publication and public reading of the names of those who violated the boycott. The Mississippi Supreme Court upheld the trial court's finding of liability on a common law tort theory, stressing the acts of violence and coercion which accompanied the boycott; it rejected liability predicated on secondary boycott and state antitrust claims. The United States Supreme Court unanimously reversed, holding that liability in this setting could be imposed only for violent conduct and that the state court's factual findings were inadequate to show that the claimed business losses were proximately caused by violent acts. In the course of his opinion for the Court, Justice Stevens wrote: [14]

The boycott of white merchants at issue in this case took many forms. The boycott was launched at a meeting of a local branch of the NAACP attended by several hundred persons. Its acknowledged purpose was to secure compliance by both civic and business leaders with a lengthy list of demands for equality and racial justice. The boycott was supported by speeches and nonviolent picketing. Participants repeatedly encouraged others to join in its cause.

13. ___ U.S. ___, 102 S.Ct. 3409, 73 L.Ed.2d 1215 (1982).

14. Id. at ___, 102 S.Ct., at 3422–27, 73 L.Ed.2d, at 1232–37.

Each of these elements of the boycott is a form of speech or conduct that is ordinarily entitled to protection under the First and Fourteenth Amendments. The black citizens named as defendants in this action banded together and collectively expressed their dissatisfaction with a social structure that had denied them rights to equal treatment and respect. . . .

Of course, the petitioners in this case did more than assemble peaceably and discuss among themselves their grievances against governmental and business policy. Other elements of the boycott, however, also involved activities ordinarily safeguarded by the First Amendment. In *Thornhill v. Alabama*, 310 U.S. 88, 60 S.Ct. 736, 84 L.Ed. 1093, the Court held that peaceful picketing was entitled to constitutional protection, even though, in that case, the purpose of the picketing "was concededly to advise customers and prospective customers of the relationship existing between the employer and its employees and thereby to induce such customers not to patronize the employer. . . .

Speech itself also was used to further the aims of the boycott. Nonparticipants repeatedly were urged to join the common cause, both through public address and through personal solicitation. These elements of the boycott involve speech in its most direct form. In addition, names of boycott violators were read aloud at meetings at the First Baptist Church and published in a local black newspaper. Petitioners admittedly sought to persuade others to join the boycott through social pressure and the "threat" of social ostracism. Speech does not lose its protected character, however, simply because it may embarrass others or coerce them into action. . . .

In sum, the boycott clearly involved constitutionally protected activity. The established elements of speech, assembly, association and petition, "though not identical, are inseparable." *Thomas v. Collins*, 323 U.S. 516, 530, 65 S.Ct. 315, 322, 89 L.Ed. 430. Through exercise of these First Amendment rights, petitioners sought to bring about political, social, and economic change. Through speech, assembly, and petition—rather than through riot or revolution—petitioners sought to change a social order that had consistently treated them as second-class citizens.

The presence of protected activity, however, does not end the relevant constitutional inquiry. Governmental regulation that has an incidental effect on First Amendment freedoms may be justified in certain narrowly defined instances. A nonviolent and totally voluntary boycott may have a disruptive effect on local economic conditions. This Court has recognized the strong governmental interest in certain forms of economic regulation, even though such regulation may have an incidental effect on rights of speech and association. The right of business entities to "associate" to suppress competition may be curtailed. *National Soc. of Professional Engineers* v. *United States*, 435 U.S. 679, 98 S.Ct. 1355, 55 L.Ed.2d 637. Unfair trade practices may be restricted. Secondary boycotts and picketing by labor unions may be prohibited, as part of "Congress' striking of the delicate balance between union freedom of expression and the ability of neutral employers, employees, and consumers to remain free from coerced participation in industrial strife."

While States have broad power to regulate economic activity, we do not find a comparable right to prohibit peaceful political activity such as that found in the boycott in this case. This Court has recognized that expression on public issues "has always rested on the highest rung of the hierarchy of First Amendment values." . . . There is a "profound national commitment" to the principle that "debate on public issues should be uninhibited, robust, and wide-open." *New York Times v. Sullivan*, 376 U.S. 254, 270, 84 S.Ct. 710, 720, 11 L.Ed.2d 686.

In *Eastern Railroad Presidents Conference v. Noerr Motor Freight*, 365 U.S. 127, 81 S.Ct. 523, 5 L.Ed.2d 464, the Court considered whether the Sherman Act prohibited a publicity campaign waged by railroads against the trucking industry that was designed to foster the adoption of laws destructive of the trucking business, to create an atmosphere of distaste for truckers among the general public, and to impair the relationships existing between truckers and their customers. Noting that the "right of petition is one of the freedoms protected by the Bill of Rights, and we cannot, of course, lightly impute to Congress an intent to invade these freedoms," the Court held that the Sherman Act did not proscribe the publicity campaign. Id., at 137–138, 81 S.Ct., at 529. The Court stated that it could not see how an intent to influence legislation to destroy the truckers as competitors "could transform conduct otherwise lawful into a violation of the Sherman Act." Id., at 138–139, 81 S.Ct., at 530. Noting that the right of the people to petition their representatives in government "cannot properly be made to depend on their intent in doing so," the Court held that "at least insofar as the railroads' campaign was directed toward obtaining governmental action, its legality was not at all affected by any anticompetitive purpose it may have had." Id., at 139–140, 81 S.Ct., at 530. This conclusion was not changed by the fact that the railroads' anticompetitive *purpose* produced an anticompetitive *effect;* the Court rejected the truckers' Sherman Act claim despite the fact that "the truckers sustained some direct injury as an incidental effect of the railroads' campaign to influence governmental action." Id., at 143, 81 S.Ct., at 532.

It is not disputed that a major purpose of the boycott in this case was to influence governmental action. Like the railroads in *Noerr*, the petitioners certainly foresaw—and directly intended—that the merchants would sustain economic injury as a result of their campaign. Unlike the railroads in that case, however, the purpose of petitioners' campaign was not to destroy legitimate competition. Petitioners sought to vindicate rights of equality and of freedom that lie at the heart of the Fourteenth Amendment itself. The right of the States to regulate economic activity could not justify a complete prohibition against a non-violent, politically-motivated boycott designed to force governmental and economic change and to effectuate rights guaranteed by the Constitution itself. We hold that the nonviolent elements of petitioners' activities are entitled to the protection of the First Amendment.[15]

Queries: After *Claiborne Hardware*, could there be a cause of action for damages arising out of an unlawful secondary boycott (violative of Section 8(b)(4) of the National Labor Relations Act) if longshoremen refuse to unload cargoes arriving from or destined for the Soviet Union, in protest against the Soviet Union's invasion of Afghanistan?[16] Would the boycott be worthier of

---

15. [Court's footnote 49.] We need not decide in this case the extent to which a narrowly tailored statute designed to prohibit certain forms of anticompetitive conduct or certain types of secondary pressure may restrict protected First Amendment activity. No such statute is involved in this case. Nor are we presented with a boycott designed to secure aims that are themselves prohibited by a valid state law.

16. See International Longshoremen's Association v. Allied International, 456 U.S. 212, 102 S.Ct. 1656, 72 L.Ed.2d 21 (1982) (boycott violates Section 8(b)(4) and is not constitutionally protected).

Constitutional protection if organizers announced that they sought to pressure the United States into breaking diplomatic relations with the USSR? Does *Claiborne Hardware* have any implications for the constitutionality of using Section 1 of the Sherman Act to restrict the dissemination of trade information?[17]

Per Se or Rule of Reason?

Does *FOGA* adopt a *per se* approach to boycotts? If there were any doubt as to the answer to this question, it was apparently settled in *Klor's, Inc. v. Broadway-Hale Stores, Inc.*[18] George Klor operated a retail appliance store. He complained that appliance manufacturers, in league with a powerful competing appliance distributor, had conspired to refuse to deal with him. The district court granted summary judgment against Klor's on the basis of uncontradicted affidavits that there were hundreds of other dealers in Klor's neighborhood, so that any injury to Klor's would not affect competition, prices, quality, or any other public concern. The Supreme Court (per Justice Black) wrote:[19]

> We think Klor's allegations clearly show one type of trade restraint and public harm the Sherman Act forbids, and that defendants' affidavits provide no defense to the charges. . . . In the landmark case of *Standard Oil Co. v. United States*, this Court read § 1 to prohibit those classes of contracts or acts which the common law had deemed to be undue restraints of trade and those which new times and economic conditions would make unreasonable. . . . The Court recognized that there were some agreements whose validity depended on the surrounding circumstances. It emphasized, however, that there were classes of restraints which from their "nature or character" were unduly restrictive, and hence forbidden by both the common law and the statute. As to these classes of restraints, the Court noted, Congress had determined its own criteria of public harm and it was not for the courts to decide whether in an individual case injury had actually occurred.
>
> Group boycotts, or concerted refusals by traders to deal with other traders, have long been held to be in the forbidden category. They have not been saved by allegations that they were reasonable in the specific circumstances, nor by a failure to show that they "fixed or regulated prices, parcelled out or limited production, or brought about a deterioration in quality." *Fashion Originators' Guild v. Federal Trade Comm'n*, 312 U.S. 457, 466, 467–468. Cf. *United States v. Trenton Potteries Co.*, 273 U.S. 392. Even when they operated to lower prices or temporarily to stimulate competition they were banned. For "such agreements,

17. See decree in National Soc. of Prof. Engineers, pp. 421–422, supra; Note (1), pp. 453–454, supra; California Motor Transport Co. v. Trucking Unlimited, infra pp. 838–842.

18. 359 U.S. 207, 79 S.Ct. 705, 3 L.Ed. 2d 741 (1959).

19. Id. at 210–14, 79 S.Ct. at 708–10, 3 L.Ed.2d at 744–46.

no less than those to fix minimum prices, cripple the freedom of traders and thereby restrain their ability to sell in accordance with their own judgment."

Plainly the allegations of this complaint disclose such a boycott. This is not a case of a single trader refusing to deal with another, nor even of a manufacturer and a dealer agreeing to an exclusive distributorship. Alleged in this complaint is a wide combination consisting of manufacturers, distributors and a retailer. This combination takes from Klor's its freedom to buy appliances in an open competitive market and drives it out of business as a dealer in the defendants' products. It deprives the manufacturers and distributors of their freedom to sell to Klor's at the same prices and conditions made available to Broadway-Hale and in some instances forbids them from selling to it on any terms whatsoever. It interferes with the natural flow of interstate commerce. It clearly has, by its "nature" and "character," a "monopolistic tendency." As such it is not to be tolerated merely because the victim is just one merchant whose business is so small that his destruction makes little difference to the economy. Monopoly can as surely thrive by the elimination of such small businessmen, one at a time, as it can by driving them out in large groups. In recognition of this fact the Sherman Act has consistently been read to forbid all contracts and combinations "which 'tend to create a monopoly,'" whether "the tendency is a creeping one" or "one that proceeds at full gallop."

The Supreme Court has followed the *per se* view of *Klor's* in later cases,[20] but it has also suggested on occasion that it will not hold all boycotts illegal "without more."[21] Compare the analytical approach to the *per se* issue taken in *BMI*, supra p. 385. Using this approach, would the boycott in *FOGA* qualify for *per se* treatment? The boycott in *Klor's?* Are these simply cases in which no good justification was offered—rather than cases standing for the proposition that no good justification *could be* offered?[22] In reading the following cases consider again whether it is better to view the *per se*/rule of reason

20. See United States v. General Motors Corp., 384 U.S. 127, 145–46, 86 S.Ct. 1321, 1330–31, 16 L.Ed.2d 415 (1966); Radiant Burners, Inc. v. Peoples Gas Light & Coke Co., 364 U.S. 656, 659–60, 81 S.Ct. 365, 367, 5 L.Ed.2d 358 (1961).

21. See St. Paul Fire & Marine Insurance Co. v. Barry, 438 U.S. 531, 542–43, 98 S.Ct. 2923, 2930, 57 L.Ed.2d 932 (1978) (noting that question before the Court was whether the conduct in question was a "boycott," not whether it was within the category of boycotts judged per se unreasonable); Silver v. New York Stock Exchange, 373 U.S. 341, 348–49, 83 S.Ct. 1246, 1252, 10 L.Ed.2d 389 (1963) (concerted refusal to deal violated Sherman Act "absent any justification derived from the policy of another statute or otherwise").

22. See Bird, Sherman Act Limitations on Noncommercial Concerted Refusals To Deal, 1970 Duke L.J. 247, 276 ("The problem with *Klor's* is that it is difficult to derive a per se rule from a case in which the defendants offered no justification whatsoever for their conduct."). See generally Bauer, Per Se Illegality of Concerted Refusals to Deal: A Rule Ripe For Reexamination, 79 Colum. L.Rev. 685 (1979).

argument as one dealing with burdens of proof, rather than as one dealing with substantive liability rules.[23]

SMITH v. PRO FOOTBALL, INC.

United States Court of Appeals, District of Columbia Circuit, 1978.
593 F.2d 1173.

WILKEY, CIRCUIT JUDGE:

This private antitrust action challenges the legality of the National Football League (NFL) player selection system, commonly called the "draft." The plaintiff is James McCoy (Yazoo) Smith, a former professional football player who played one season for the Washington Redskins after being drafted by them in 1968. The defendants are Pro-Football, Inc., which operates the Redskins, and the NFL. Smith contends that the draft as it existed in 1968 was an unreasonable restraint of trade in violation of §§ 1 and 3 of the Sherman Act, and that, but for the draft, he would have negotiated a far more lucrative contract when he signed as a player in that year. Smith alleges that he has been injured in his business or property in the amount of the difference between the compensation he actually received and the compensation he would have received had there existed a "free market" for his services.

After a trial to the court, District Judge Bryant held that the NFL draft as it existed in 1968 constituted a "group boycott" and was thus a *per se* violation of the Sherman Act. Alternatively, he held that the draft, tested under the rule of reason, was an unreasonable restraint because it was "significantly more restrictive than necessary" to accomplish whatever legitimate goals the NFL had. Judge Bryant awarded Smith treble damages totaling $276,000. The Redskins and the NFL have appealed the finding of antitrust liability; both sides have appealed the damage award. Relying on the rule of reason, we affirm the finding of antitrust liability and remand for recomputation of damages.

1. BACKGROUND

The NFL draft, which has been in effect since 1935, is a procedure under which negotiating rights to graduating college football players are allocated each year among the NFL clubs in inverse order of the clubs' standing. Under the draft procedures generally followed, the team with the poorest playing-field record during the preceding season has the first opportunity, as among the NFL teams, to select a college player of its choice; the team with the next poorest record has the next choice, and so on until the team with the best record (the winner of the previous year's "Super Bowl") has picked last. At this point, the first "round" of the draft is completed. In 1968 there were 16 succeeding rounds in the yearly draft, the same order of selection being followed in each round. Teams had one choice per round unless they had traded their choice in that round to another team (a

---

23. See pp. 424–425, supra.

fairly common practice). When Smith was selected by the Redskins there were 26 teams choosing in the draft.

The NFL draft, like similar procedures in other professional sports, is designed to promote "competitive balance." By dispersing newly arriving player talent equally among all NFL teams, with preferences to the weaker clubs, the draft aims to produce teams that are as evenly-matched on the playing field as possible. Evenly-matched teams make for closer games, tighter penant races, and better player morale, thus maximizing fan interest, broadcast revenues, and overall health of the sport.

The draft is effectuated through the NFL's "no-tampering" rule. Under this rule as it existed in 1968, no team was permitted to negotiate prior to the draft with any player eligible to be drafted, and no team could negotiate with (or sign) any player selected by another team in the draft. The net result of these restrictions was that the right to negotiate with any given player was exclusively held by one team at any given time. If a college player could not reach a satisfactory agreement with the team holding the rights to his services he could not play in the NFL.

.   .   .

II. ANALYSIS

The legality of the NFL player draft under the antitrust laws is essentially a question of first impression. This case requires us to consider (1) whether the legality of the draft is governed by a *per se* rule or by the rule of reason; (2) whether the draft, if tested by the rule of reason, is a reasonable restraint; and (3) whether, if the draft violates the antitrust laws, the measure of damages adopted by the District Judge was proper. We discuss these issues in turn.

A. *Per Se Illegality*

.   .   .

Plaintiff argues that the NFL draft constitutes a "group boycott" because the NFL clubs concertedly refuse to deal with any player before he has been drafted or after he has been drafted by another team, and that the draft is in consequence a *per se* violation of § 1. The District Court accepted this argument. We reject it. We hold that the NFL player draft is not properly characterized as a "group boycott"—at least not the type of boycott that traditionally has been held illegal *per se*—and that the draft, regardless of how it is characterized, should more appropriately be tested under the rule of reason.

The classic "group boycott" is a concerted attempt by a group of competitors at one level to protect themselves from competition from non-group members who seek to compete at that level. Typically, the boycotting group combines to deprive would-be competitors of a trade relationship which they need in order to enter (or survive in) the level wherein the group operates. The group may accomplish its exclusionary purpose by inducing suppliers not to sell to potential competitors, by inducing customers not to buy from them, or, in some cases, by refusing to deal with would-be competitors themselves. In each instance, however, the hallmark of the "group boycott" is the effort of competitors to "barricade themselves from competition at their own level." It is this purpose to exclude competition that has characterized the Supreme Court's decisions invoking the group boycott *per se* rule.

The NFL player draft differs from the classic group boycott in two significant respects. First, the NFL clubs which have "combined" to implement the draft are not *competitors* in any economic sense. The clubs operate basically as a joint venture in producing an entertainment product—football games and telecasts. No NFL club can produce this product without agreements and joint action with every other team. To this end, the League not only determines franchise locations, playing schedules, and broadcast terms, but also ensures that the clubs receive equal shares of telecast and ticket revenues. These economic joint ventures "compete" on the playing field, to be sure, but here as well cooperation is essential if the entertainment product is to attain a high quality: only if the teams are "competitively balanced" will spectator interest be maintained at a high pitch. No NFL team, in short, is interested in driving another team out of business, whether in the counting-house or on the football field, for if the League fails, no one team can survive.

The draft differs from the classic group boycott, secondly, in that the NFL clubs have not combined *to exclude competitors or potential competitors* from their level of the market. Smith was never seeking to "compete" with the NFL clubs, and their refusal to deal with him has resulted in no decrease in the competition for providing football entertainment to the public. The draft, indeed, is designed not to insulate the NFL from competition, but to improve the entertainment product by enhancing its teams' competitive equality.

In view of these differences, we conclude that the NFL player draft cannot properly be described as a group boycott—at least not the type of group boycott that traditionally has elicited invocation of a *per se* rule. . . .

Our conclusion that the legality of the NFL draft should not be governed by a *per se* rule parallels the conclusion of most courts and commentators that the legality of player restrictions in professional sports should be governed by the rule of reason. . . . While we fully appreciate the administrative convenience of a *per se* rubric, ease of application alone cannot suffice to recommend it. In antitrust law, as elsewhere, we must heed Justice Cardozo's warning to beware "the tyranny of tags and tickets." When anticompetitive effects are shown to result from a particular player selection system "they can be adequately policed under the rule of reason."

B. Rule of Reason

Under the rule of reason, a restraint must be evaluated to determine whether it is significantly anticompetitive in purpose or effect. In making this evaluation, a court generally will be required to analyze "the facts peculiar to the business, the history of the restraint, and the reasons why it was imposed." If, on analysis, the restraint is found to have legitimate business purposes whose realization serves to promote competition, the "anticompetitive evils" of the challenged practice must be carefully balanced against its "procompetitive virtues" to ascertain whether the former outweigh the latter. A restraint is unreasonable if it has the "net effect" of substantially impeding competition.

After undertaking the analysis mandated by the rule of reason, the District Court concluded that the NFL draft as it existed in 1968 had a severely anticompetitive impact on the market for players' services, and that it went beyond the level of restraint reasonably necessary to accomplish whatever legitimate business purposes might be asserted for it. . . .

The draft that has been challenged here is undeniably anticompetitive both in its purpose and in its effect. The defendants have conceded that the draft "restricts competition among the NFL clubs for the services of graduating college players" and, indeed, that the draft "is designed to limit competition" and "to be a 'purposive' restraint" on the player-service market. The fact that the draft assertedly was designed to promote the teams' playing-field equality rather than to inflate their profit margins may prevent the draft's purpose from being described, in subjective terms, as nefarious. But this fact does not prevent its purpose from being described, in objective terms, as anticompetitive, for suppressing competition, is the *telos*, the very essence of the restraint.

The trial judge was likewise correct in finding that the draft was significantly anticompetitive in its *effect*. The draft inescapably forces each seller of football services to deal with one, and only one buyer, robbing the seller, as in any monopsonistic market, of any real bargaining power. The draft, as the District Court found, "leaves no room whatever for competition among the teams for the services of college players, and utterly strips them of any measure of control over the marketing of their talents." The predictable effect of the draft, as the evidence established and as the District Court found, was to lower the salary levels of the best college players. There can be no doubt that the effect of the draft as it existed in 1968 was to "suppress or even destroy competition" in the market for players' services.

The justification asserted for the draft is that it has the legitimate business purpose of promoting "competitive balance" and playing-field equality among the teams, producing better entertainment for the public, higher salaries for the players, and increased financial security for the clubs. The NFL has endeavored to summarize this justification by saying that the draft ultimately has a "procompetitive" effect, yet this shorthand entails no small risk of confusion. The draft is "procompetitive," if at all, in a very different sense from that in which it is anticompetitive. The draft is anticompetitive in its effect on the market for players' services, because it virtually eliminates economic competition among buyers for the services of sellers. The draft is allegedly "procompetitive" in its effect on the playing field; but the NFL teams are not economic competitors on the playing field, and the draft, while it may heighten athletic competition and thus improve the entertainment product offered to the public, does not increase competition in the economic sense of encouraging others to enter the market and to offer the product at lower cost. Because the draft's "anticompetitive" and "procompetitive" effects are not comparable, it is impossible to "net them out" in the usual rule-of-reason balancing. The draft's "anticompetitive evils," in other words, cannot be balanced against its "procompetitive virtues," and the draft be upheld if the latter outweigh the former. In strict economic terms, the draft's demonstrated procompetitive effects are nil.

The defendants' justification for the draft reduces in fine to an assertion that competition in the market for entering players' services would not serve the best interests of the public, the clubs, or the players themselves. This is precisely the type of argument that the Supreme Court only recently has declared to be unavailing. In *National Society of Professional Engineers v. United States*, the Court held that a professional society's ban on competitive bidding violated § 1 of the Sherman Act. In so holding the Court rejected a defense that unbridled competitive bidding would lead to deceptively low bids and inferior work "with consequent risk to public safety and health," terming this justification "nothing less than a frontal assault on the basic policy of the Sherman Act." Ending decades of uncertainty as to the proper scope of inquiry under the rule of reason, the Court stated categorically that the rule, contrary to its name, "does not open the field of antitrust inquiry to any argument in favor of a challenged restraint that may fall within the realm of reason," and that the inquiry instead must be "confined to a consideration of [the restraint's] impact on competitive conditions." . . .

Confining our inquiry, as we must, to the draft's impact on competitive conditions, we conclude that the draft as it existed in 1968 was an unreasonable restraint of trade. The draft was concededly anticompetitive in purpose. It was severely anticompetitive in effect. It was not shown to have any significant offsetting procompetitive impact in the economic sense. Balancing the draft's anticompetitive evils against its procompetitive virtues, the outcome is plain. The NFL's defenses, premised on the assertion that competition for players' services would harm both the football industry and society, are unavailing; there is nothing of procompetitive virtue to balance, because "the Rule of Reason does not support a defense based on the assumption that competition itself is unreasonable."

. . .

Without intimating any view as to the legality of the following procedures, we note that there exist significantly less anticompetitive alternatives to the draft system which has been challenged here. The trial judge found that the evidence supported the viability of a player selection system that would permit "more than one team to draft each player, while restricting the number of players any one team might sign." A less anticompetitive draft might permit a college player to negotiate with the team of his choice if the team that drafted him failed to make him an acceptable offer. The NFL could also conduct a second draft each year for players who were unable to reach agreement with the team that selected them the first time. Most obviously, perhaps, the District Court found that the evidence supported the feasibility of a draft that would run for fewer rounds, applying only to the most talented players and enabling their "average" brethren to negotiate in a "free market". The least restrictive alternative of all, of course, would be for the NFL to eliminate the draft entirely and employ revenue-sharing to equalize the teams' financial resources—a method of preserving "competitive balance" nicely in harmony with the league's self-proclaimed "joint-venture" status.*

We are not required in this case to design a draft that would pass muster under the antitrust laws. We would suggest, however, that under the Supreme Court's decision in *Professional Engineers*, no draft can be justified merely by showing that it is a relatively less anticompetitive means of attaining sundry benefits for the football industry and society. Rather, a player draft can survive scrutiny under the rule of reason only if it is demonstrated to have positive, economically *procompetitive* benefits that offset its anticompetitive effects, or, at the least, if it is demonstrated to accomplish legitimate business purposes and to have a net anticompetitive effect that is *insubstantial*. Because the NFL draft as it existed in 1968 had severe anticompetitive effects and no demonstrated procompetitive virtues, we hold that it unreasonably restrained trade in violation of § 1 of The Sherman Act.

[The remainder of the court's opinion, dealing with the computation of damages, is omitted.]

NOTES AND QUERIES

(1) *Queries.* What is the distinction between the justification offered in *FOGA* (eliminating competition from "style pirates") and the one in *Smith* (eliminating competition for new players to improve the entertainment product)? Why should the latter have led to a rule of reason analysis, but not the former? Are you convinced that the critical factor for applying a *per se* analysis is whether the boycott is directed at horizontal competitors? Would it be *per se* unlawful for all NFL teams to refuse to play sandlot football teams? Should a boycott of all hot-dog vendors not related to the owners by

* Do you see any antitrust problems with the court's solution? Reconsider after reading the material on joint ventures infra, and particularly *Citizen Publishing*.

blood or marriage be subjected to a rule of reason analysis? What is bad about a boycott?

Consider the court's rule of reason analysis. Can you suggest any market in which player draft/team competitive balance might have a procompetitive effect? If so, how would you net the adverse effect in the player labor market against the procompetitive effect? Who has the burden of proof on this issue?

Has the court properly articulated the rule of reason analysis? Consider its suggestions as to less restrictive alternatives (p. 548). What procompetitive benefits would such alternatives offer if team balance is not procompetitive "in the economic sense"? Does the court imply that if the NFL picks the "least restrictive alternative," it has satisfied the Sherman Act?

(2) *Industry Self-Regulation With Unobjectionable Purposes but Anticompetitive Potential Effects. Union Circulation Co. v. Federal Trade Commission*, 241 F.2d 652 (2d Cir. 1957), affirmed an FTC order directing magazine subscription solicitation agencies to drop "no-switching" agreements. Under these agreements an agency would not employ a solicitor who had worked for another agency within one year. According to defendants these agreements were confined in purpose and operation to solicitors who had been guilty of misrepresenting magazines to the customers, false sympathy appeals, and embezzlement of subscription moneys. The industry had tried for 20 years to suppress these practices by jointly sponsored "standards of practice" and a central registry of information on individual solicitors. But enforcement of standards was almost impossible because a solicitor discharged by his agency for fraud could easily find a job with another agency. The court noted that a boycott "whose deleterious effect on competition is not . . . apparent on its face" need not be "illegal *per se*," and that the no-switching agreements were distinguishable from the *per se* decisions like FOGA, above, since:

> These agreements are not designed to coerce retailers, or other independent members of an industry, into abandoning competitive practices of which the concerted parties do not approve. Rather, they are ostensibly directed at "housecleaning" within the ranks of the signatory organizations themselves. . . . Here it appears that the reasonably foreseeable effect of the "no-switching" agreements will be to impair or diminish competition between existing subscription agencies, and to prevent would-be competitors from engaging in similar activity. One probable result of the agreements, because entered into by organizations that represent a very substantial segment of the industry, will be to "freeze" the labor supply, which is the indispensable element of the door-to-door magazine-selling trade. Although only the signatory agencies are bound by the agreements, a crew member working for one of them will hesitate to leave his employer in order to join a newly formed competitor, or an expanding established one, if he knows that he may be out of work for a year in the event that the latter agency does not prove to be successful. The tendency of the "no-switching" agreements is to discourage labor mobility, and thereby the magazine-selling industry may well become static in its composition to the obvious advantage of the large, well-established signatory agencies and to the disadvantage of infant organizations.
> . . . .

One last contention of the petitioners remains to be considered. They claim that the agreements were intended to affect only those crew members who have a record of deceptive selling practices and other fraudulent conduct, and, in practice, that they have been invoked only against such crew members. Whether or not this be true, the agreements considered by the Federal Trade Commission are capable of enforcement against any crew member. The petitioners can not be left to police the magazine-selling industry by a method as ripe for abuse as that offered by such agreements. . . .

The petitioners asked the Commission to modify its original order so as to permit the application of the "no-switching" agreements to solicitors "who in the course of such business have been using unfair methods of competition, or unfair or deceptive acts or practices." The Commission properly refused this request, pointing out that the application and effects of an agreement so restricted had not been explored by it, and thus there was no evidence in the record by which the reasonableness of such a hypothetical agreement could be tested.

For the reasons expressed above, the "no-switching" agreements do not survive the close scrutiny that must be given under Section 5 of the Federal Trade Commission Act to any concerted restraints of trade.

What additional evidence could the respondents be expected to produce to justify narrowing the cease and desist order? Is the implication of the opinion that on some showing the industry would be permitted to blacklist fraudulent solicitors?[24]

(3) *Industry Self-Regulation in the Field of Public Health and Morality.* The major auto manufacturers, in the course of a cooperative program to develop antipollution devices for automobile motors, violated the Sherman Act by agreeing to defer, for a time, installation of the devices.[25]

The Annual Report of the American Civil Liberties Union for 1953 said, at p. 24:

In the spring of 1953, the ACLU Board of Directors adopted a strong statement against the motion picture code, which it considers a serious limitation on freedom of expression in the motion picture field. Whereas in the motion picture industry the major producers have combined to prohibit the use of certain subject matter in motion picture scripts, there is an effective restraint in ideas. The ACLU's interest is that the code, in effect, covers practically the entire industry and makes practically impossible the distribution or exhibition of any U.S.-made motion picture not produced in compliance with code standards.[26]

A New York State Joint Legislative Committee to Study Publication of Comics recommended that "the comic book industry, under the leadership of the largest producers, take immediate steps to organize an effective self-regulatory association with an independent administrator, without industry

---

24. See FTC Advisory Opinion Digest 128, ATRR No. 307, May 30, 1967, p. X–1. By a divided vote, the Commission approved the organization of an industry committee whose "administrator" could fine an agency up to $5,000 for condoning deceptive practices. Rejected was a proposal to authorize the administrator to "recommend" up to one year's suspension of a salesman who willfully violated the ethical code on three separate occasions; but the administrator may maintain a public record of the names of willful violators.

25. See United States v. Automobile Manufacturer's Association, 307 F.Supp. 617 (C.D.Cal.1969) (approving consent decree), affirmed 397 U.S. 248, 90 S.Ct. 1105, 25 L.Ed.2d 280 (1970). For further information about the case, see p. 1032, infra.

26. See Ayer, Bates and Herman, Self Censorship in the Movie Industry, 1970 Wisc.L.Rev. 791.

connections, acting as a review agency." [27] The Magazine Publishers Association resolved that:

> in so far as is legally permissible, the publisher members of Magazine Publishers Association, Inc., through their association and individually, hereby formally offer their cooperation and assistance to the duly constituted legislative and administrative authorities and to interested private groups in carrying out the following program:
>
>> First: The vigilant and vigorous, but fair, enforcement of the legislative bans against such objectionable material through legal prosecutions by appropriate authorities within the framework of existing obscenity statutes;
>>
>> Second: A continuing appraisal by the various legislatures of the existing obscenity statutes with the view of making such revisions or changes as may appear to be required, keeping in mind, however, the necessity of protecting the fundamental constitutional guarantees of freedom of speech and of the press; and
>>
>> Third: The education of the reading public, through a program of publicity on the possible effects of the publication and distribution of salacious, repulsive and otherwise objectionable material upon the people generally, and particularly the youth of our Country.[28]

The New York Herald Tribune, July 28, 1957, reported that "The Distilled Spirits Institute is a mite unhappy with the government of Puerto Rico" for using a girl's picture in an advertisement for rum, contrary to a "voluntary agreement never to use feminine allure in selling high proof products. This is one of several bans the Institute observes as a means of keeping out of Congressional committee rooms, where law-makers are often found attempting to restrict liquor advertising."

The New York Law Journal, September 27, 1979, p. 1 reported:

> A three-member commission with powers to investigate, regulate and fine area nursing homes was appointed yesterday by an association of owners of ninety-five nursing homes in the New York metropolitan area.
>
> The commissioners, appointed by the Greater New York Health Care and Health Facilities Association, have a contract with the owners granting them powers of subpoena and to levy fines. While the $300,000 annual budget for the commission will be provided by the association, the commissioners have been given three-year contracts by the owners and guaranteed independence.
>
> Former Chief Judge Stanley H. Fuld, of the State Court of Appeals, . . . was named chairman of the commission. The other two commissioners are David G. Trager, former U.S. Attorney for the Eastern District of New York . . . and Nicholas Scoppetta, former Deputy Mayor for Criminal Justice. . . .

Investigate Complaints

> The commission, which will hold regular public hearings, is expected to investigate complaints by the public, for which a special telephone "hot line" has been established, initiate investigations on its own, and establish and promulgate a professional code for nursing home operators on standards of professional care, according to the commission's counsel, Robert Goldman. . . .
>
> The commissioners have been given three-year contracts to provide them with independence from the association and its member-owners.
>
> "We're secure in our positions, whatever decisions we make," Mr. Fuld said yesterday.

27. N.Y.Legis.Doc. 37 (1955) p. 9.   28. Id. at pp. 116–117.

In addition, the contract signed by the nursing homes, which make up 60 percent of all homes in the state, provides that a member cannot withdraw from the agreement while an investigation against him is pending.

Fines, which are not limited in amount in the agreement, will be used to purchase equipment for nursing-home residents, improve facilities, subsidize grants for geriatric research or fund scholarships. The commissioners can also recommend withdrawal of a home's license to the state licensing authority.

In what ways would industry self-policing be likely to differ from governmental policing? Would standards be higher or lower? Would enforcement be more or less effective? Would the rights of individual dissenters have more or less protection? Does the Sherman Act bar *any* use of collective pressure in this area? Or only abuse? Under what circumstances would deprivation of membership in a trade association constitute illegal pressure?[29] Note that as direct government controls over business conduct are removed in today's "deregulation" climate, the calls for increased private self-regulation may increase.[30]

(4) *Sherman Act Pressures for Due Process in Industry Self-Regulation. Klor's* was followed in *Radiant Burners, Inc. v. Peoples Gas Light and Coke Co.*, 364 U.S. 656, 81 S.Ct. 365, 5 L.Ed.2d 358 (1961), reversing *per curiam* a decision of the Seventh Circuit dismissing Radiant Burners' complaint. The complaint charged that American Gas Association had refused its "seal of approval" to plaintiff's ceramic gas burner, that its tests for safety and efficiency were arbitrary and influenced by producers and sellers of competing burners, and that public utility members of AGA including Peoples Gas refused to supply gas to burners lacking the seal of approval.

In *Silver v. New York Stock Exchange*, 373 U.S. 341, 83 S.Ct. 1246, 10 L.Ed.2d 389 (1963), Silver was a stockbroker, but not a member of the Exchange. Pursuant to the Exchange's rule, members were permitted to establish private wire connections with him. This permission was withdrawn without notice or hearing. Justice Goldberg's opinion for the Court posed the issue as "whether the Securities Exchange Act has created a duty of exchange self-regulation so pervasive as to constitute an implied repealer of our antitrust laws", and affirmed the principle that "exchange self-regulation is to be regarded as justified in response to antitrust charges only to the extent necessary to protect the achievement of the aims of the Securities Exchange Act." He held that concerted termination of trade relations, which would ordinarily constitute an illegal boycott, might be exempt from the antitrust laws as a result of the duty of self-regulation imposed on the Exchange, but only if fair procedures were followed, including notice and hearing:

. . . The point is not that the antitrust laws impose the requirement of notice and a hearing here, but rather that, in acting without according petitioners these safeguards in response to their request, the Ex-

29. See Levin, The Limits of Self-Regulation, 67 Colum.L.Rev. 603 (1967). Cf. Rosman v. Butchers Local 1, 164 Misc. 378, 298 N.Y.Supp. 343 (1937) (refusing to enjoin a group of kosher butcher shops from picketing a competitor with posters asserting his nonconformity with Orthodox Jewish requirements). See generally Ponsoldt, The Application of Sherman Act Antiboycott Law To Industry Self-Regulation: An Analysis Integrating Nonboycott Sherman Act Principles, 55 S.Cal.L.Rev. 1 (1981).

30. See ATRR No. 1018, June 11, 1981, pp. A–6–A–7 (President Reagan's new F.T.C. Chairman tells executives of Better Business Bureaus that the President " 'wants to encourage volunteerism,' especially with self-regulatory activities," and that there is " 'nothing wrong with voluntary standards and codes of ethics' in industries," provided they do not impede entry).

change has plainly exceeded the scope of its authority under the Securities Exchange Act to engage in self-regulation and therefore has not even reached the threshold of justification under that statute for what would otherwise be an antitrust violation. Since it is perfectly clear that the Exchange can offer no justification under the Securities Exchange Act for its collective action in denying petitioners the private wire connections without notice and an opportunity for hearing, and that the Exchange has therefore violated § 1 of the Sherman Act, there is no occasion for us to pass upon the sufficiency of the reasons which the Exchange later assigned for its action. Thus there is also no need for us to define further whether the interposing of a substantive justification in an antitrust suit brought to challenge a particular enforcement of the rules on its merits is to be governed by a standard of arbitrariness, good faith, reasonableness, or some other measure. It will be time enough to deal with that problem if and when the occasion arises. Experience teaches, however, that the affording of procedural safeguards, which by their nature serve to illuminate the underlying facts, in itself often operates to prevent erroneous decisions on the merits from occurring.

In *Eliason Corp. v. National Sanitation Foundation,*[31] the Sixth Circuit found no unreasonable restraint of trade arising out of NSF's program to test products and issue a seal of approval if the products comply with NSF promulgated standards. The court pointed out that: NSF's standards were developed to promote uniformity in the health requirements that products are required to meet in various jurisdictions; that neither NSF's standards nor the testing fees charged manufacturers were claimed to be unreasonable; that NSF standards are periodically revised; that continued compliance with the standards is strictly enforced; and that NSF is an independent organization, not controlled by manufacturers of any one product and not in competition with the plaintiff.

Where the alleged boycott [of unapproved products] arises from standard-making or even industry self-regulation, the plaintiff must show either that it was barred from obtaining approval of its products on a discriminatory basis from its competitors, or that the conduct as a whole was manifestly anticompetitive or unreasonable. There is no evidence of discrimination or exclusion in this case.[32]

What if the self-regulation, although affording procedural due process, reaches "arbitrary" substantive decisions? Will it be an issue for the antitrust court whether the gas burner standards in the *Radiant Burners* case were "arbitrary" or only whether the association procedures were fair and afforded reasonable opportunity for hearing producers of non-conforming burners? If an industry regulation, backed by "boycott," is legal if the regulation is reasonable, can it be said that boycott is illegal *per se?* Would it make any difference if industry self-regulation were subject to review by an administrative agency?[33] The demand for due process and equal protection

31. 614 F.2d 126 (6th Cir. 1980), certiorari denied 449 U.S. 826, 101 S.Ct. 89, 66 L.Ed.2d 29. For further discussion of trade association efforts regarding standardization, see pp. 477–480, supra.

32. Id. at 129.

33. See United States v. National Association Securities Dealers, Inc., 422 U.S. 694, 95 S.Ct. 2427, 45 L.Ed.2d 486 (1975) (S.E.C. regulatory and supervisory power requires a finding of implied immunity from antitrust liability for a horizontal combination restricting secondary markets for mutual fund shares).

in the conduct of corporate affairs has been advanced on a broader basis than the Sherman Act.[34]

(5) *Proof of Agreement.* As elsewhere in antitrust litigation, where proof of agreement is necessary, inference from parallel behavior may be relied on.[35] Note that a "collective" refusal to deal may be found in the collaboration of affiliated companies, in the collaboration between Supplier and New Distributor who is replacing the aggrieved distributor, or in the collaboration between Supplier and firms, e.g., business brokers, retained by Supplier to carry out his distributorship plans.[36] But where such collaboration goes no further than to replace one distributor with another, leaving competition unimpaired, the mere concert in withdrawing patronage from the original distributor has been held lawful.[37] Can a rule which requires consideration of impact on competition, in some types of concerted refusal to deal, be regarded as a *per se* rule?

(6) *Proposed Approach for Evaluating the Legality of Boycotts.* Consider the following proposal for analyzing boycotts.[38] Is it consistent with the cases you have read? Does it sufficiently narrow the universe of potentially relevant facts? Is it manageable?

> . . . The boycott, and its surrounding setting, must be examined for: (1) market impact, that is, the likely effect on price and output as predicted by microeconomic theory; (2) the impact on trader liberty, based on the extent to which individual entrepreneurs are coerced into acceding to collective demands; (3) the comprehensiveness of the private regulation supported by the boycott sanction; and (4) the extent to which the use of the boycott sanction is outside the bounds of fair rules of behavior. This list helps to resolve the issue of how much evidence must be examined to determine the legality of a boycott. The four factors delimit inquiry; a wide-ranging look at all the reasons for, or against, the boycott is not called for. The question is not whether the boycott is "reasonable," the sort of broad inquiry suggested by an expansive view of the rule of reason. On the other hand, a workable approach should not be limited to a purely economic inquiry.

. . .

34. Cf. "Corporate Regulations as 'Laws' under the Fourteenth Amendment" in Berle, Power 373ff (1970).

35. See Taxi Weekly, Inc. v. Metropolitan Taxicab Board of Trade, Inc., 539 F.2d 907 (2d Cir. 1976); Quality Mercury, Inc. v. Ford Motor Co., 542 F.2d 466 (8th Cir. 1976); Cartrade, Inc. v. Ford Dealers, 446 F.2d 289 (9th Cir. 1971). Delaware Valley Marine Supply Co. v. American Tobacco Co., 297 F.2d 199 (3d Cir. 1961), involved a case of concurrent, but not agreed, refusal to supply plaintiff, a would-be entrant into the business of selling tobacco products to ships. Dismissal of the action for want of proof of conspiracy was sustained. See Turner, The Definition of Agreement Under the Sherman Act: Conscious Parallelism and Refusals to Deal, 75 Harv.L.Rev. 655 (1962). See also text Chapter 4, supra.

36. See Kiefer-Stewart, p. 467 supra; Albrecht v. Herald Co., p. 619 infra; Poll-

er v. Columbia Broadcasting System, p. 781 infra.

37. Joseph E. Seagram & Sons v. Hawaiian Oke & Liquors, Ltd., 416 F.2d 71 (9th Cir. 1969); Ace Beer Distributors, Inc. v. Kohn, 318 F.2d 283 (6th Cir. 1963); Packard Motor Co. v. Webster Motor Co., 100 U.S.App.D.C. 161, 243 F.2d 418 (1957). But cf. Perryton Wholesale, Inc. v. Pioneer Distributing Co., 353 F.2d 618 (10th Cir. 1965), certiorari denied 383 U.S. 945, 86 S.Ct. 1202, 16 L.Ed.2d 208 (wrongful means used to drive out original distributor, e.g., inducing breach of employees' contracts not to work for competitor); Walker Distributing Co. v. Lucky Lager Brewing Co., 323 F.2d 1 (9th Cir. 1963) (alleged attempt to boycott particular brand of beer).

38. First, Competition In The Legal Education Industry (II): An Antitrust Analysis, 54 N.Y.U.L.Rev. 1049, 1111–13 (1979).

The proposed four-factor approach for analyzing boycotts falls between . . . [the new] rule of reason [set out in, e.g., *National Society of Professional Engineers*], which allows recovery only when the plaintiff can show adverse market effects, and the traditional per se test, which requires no proof of predictable anticompetitive effect and allows no "justifications." Although it limits the types of justifications which a defendant can assert, the proposed analysis neither presumes adverse market effect nor bars recovery to a plaintiff (like Klor's) who could satisfy some of the factors even without showing any appreciable adverse market impact. The proposed approach requires a weighing of all four factors.

This compromise approach is preferable, as a matter of history and policy. To ask only whether challenged actions "restrain trade and enhance prices," as the new rule of reason does, is to see "competition" as promoting but one policy—increased efficiency through a market mechanism. This ignores the social and political benefits which arise when economic power is dispersed and fairly used, and when the opportunities for individual decisionmaking are maximized. On the other hand, courts cannot totally ignore economic impact; the Sherman Act is rooted in economic concepts. . . . An approach that recognizes these concerns is thus truer to the common law development of the Sherman Act, and the view of competition policy traditionally articulated.

B. JOINT VENTURES

"Joint ventures" are becoming an increasingly popular way to do business. Established corporations are using them for projects with large capital requirements, as a vehicle for introducing new products, engaging in cooperative research, or developing foreign markets. Joint ventures are attractive because they can be organized for a discrete project or series of projects, the co-venturers need not totally merge all their assets and operations, and each firm has more control than a mere investor while taking less risk than a sole owner.

An important case in the joint venture area is *Timken Roller Bearing Co. v. United States*, decided by the Supreme Court in 1951.[39] The government sued Timken, an American manufacturer of antifriction bearings, under Section 1 of the Sherman Act for conspiring with British Timken, Ltd. (British Timken), and Societe Anonyme Francaise Timken (French Timken) to: (1) allocate trade territories among themselves; (2) fix prices on the products each sold in the other's territory; (3) protect each other's markets and eliminate outside competition; and (4) participate in cartels restricting imports to, and exports from, the United States. Timken owned about 30% of the stock of British Timken; Dewar, an English businessman, owned about 24%. Timken and Dewar were co-owners of French Timken.

Timken claimed its agreements were "reasonable" because ancillary to lawful joint ventures. Justice Black, for the majority, wrote:

We cannot accept the "joint venture" contention. That the trade restraints were merely incidental to an otherwise legitimate

39. 341 U.S. 593, 71 S.Ct. 971, 95 L.Ed. 1199 (1951).

"joint venture" is, to say the least, doubtful. The District Court
found that the dominant purpose of the restrictive agreements into which appellant, British Timken and French Timken entered
was to avoid all competition either among themselves or with
others. Regardless of this, however, appellant's argument must
be rejected. Our prior decisions plainly establish that agreements
providing for an aggregation of trade restraints such as those existing in this case are illegal under the Act. The fact that there is
common ownership or control of the contracting corporations does
not liberate them from the impact of the antitrust laws. Nor do
we find any support in reason or authority for the proposition that
agreements between legally separate persons and companies to
suppress competition among themselves and others can be justified by labeling the project a "joint venture." Perhaps every
agreement and combination to restrain trade could be so labeled
. . . . .

. . .

We also reject the suggestion that the Sherman Act should not
be enforced in this case because what appellant has done is reasonable in view of current foreign trade conditions. The argument in this regard seems to be that tariffs, quota restrictions and
the like are now such that the export and import of antifriction
bearings can no longer be expected as a practical matter; that appellant cannot successfully sell its American-made goods abroad;
and that the only way it can profit from business in England,
France and other countries is through the ownership of stock in
companies organized and manufacturing there. This position ignores the fact that the provisions in the Sherman Act against restraints of foreign trade are based on the assumption, and reflect
the policy, that export and import trade in commodities is both
possible and desirable. Those provisions of the Act are wholly inconsistent with appellant's argument that American business
must be left free to participate in international cartels, that free
foreign commerce in goods must be sacrificed in order to foster
export of American dollars for investment in foreign factories
which sell abroad. Acceptance of appellant's view would make
the Sherman Act a dead letter insofar as it prohibits contracts and
conspiracies in restraint of foreign trade. If such a drastic
change is to be made in the statute, Congress is the one to do it.[40]

Despite the Court's refusal to allow the joint venture label to affect its analysis, the question remains whether the antitrust laws
should allow (some?) joint ventures whose formation or operational
restrictions would otherwise be impermissible. Current law in this
area is unclear, for a number of reasons. For one, the term "joint
venture" lacks precise definition. It is often used to refer to an " 'association of two or more persons to carry on as co-owners an enterprise for one or a series of transactions.' "[41] This covers a wide ar-

---

40. Id. at 597–99, 71 S.Ct. at 974–75,
95 L.Ed. at 1206–07.

41. Brodley, The Legal Status of
Joint Ventures Under the Antitrust

ray of activity. (How many of the cases discussed in Chapter 4 could
be classified as involving joint ventures under this definition?) Another reason for the unclear status of joint ventures is that they oft-
en appear on their face to offer some procompetitive advantages
(e.g., the formation of a new entrant, or the carrying-out of business
no single firm will attempt). This may lead enforcement authorities
to be cautious in bringing suit. Finally, there is no single statute or
theory by which to judge the legality of a joint venture. Joint ventures cut across the Sherman and Clayton Acts and potentially involve a number of separate antitrust claims.

The following materials are organized to focus on the joint venture aspect of the defendants' conduct. The first full case, *Associated Press v. United States*, involves access to the product of the joint
venture; the second, *Citizen Publishing Co. v. United States*, focuses on the problems raised by the relationship between the co-venturers. Students should ask how the joint venture organization affected
the Court's analysis. Were there any particular industry problems
which led the parties to form the joint venture? (Note that both
cases involve the newspaper industry.) Did the Court take account
of them? If you were requested to form a joint venture, could you
structure it to avoid antitrust risks?[42]

ASSOCIATED PRESS v. UNITED STATES

Supreme Court of the United States, 1945.
326 U.S. 1, 65 S.Ct. 1416, 89 L.Ed. 2013.

MR. JUSTICE BLACK delivered the opinion of the Court.

The publishers of more than 1200 newspapers are members of the
Associated Press (AP), a cooperative association incorporated under
the Membership Corporations Law of the State of New York, Consol.
Laws c. 35. Its business is the collection, assembly and distribution
of news. The news it distributes is originally obtained by direct employees of the Association, employees of the member newspapers,
and the employees of foreign independent news agencies with which
AP has contractural relations, such as the Canadian Press. Distribution of the news is made through interstate channels of communication to the various newspaper members of the Association, who pay
for it under an assessment plan which contemplates no profit to AP.

The United States filed a bill in a Federal District Court for an
injunction against AP and other defendants charging that they had
violated the Sherman Anti-Trust Act, in that their acts and conduct
constituted (1) a combination and conspiracy in restraint of trade and
commerce in news among the states, and (2) an attempt to monopolize
a part of that trade.

Laws: A Summary Assessment, 21 Antitrust Bull. 453, 454 (1976).

42. See Brodley, Joint Ventures and
Antitrust Policy, 95 Harv.L.Rev. 1521

(1982), for a comprehensive framework
for analyzing joint ventures, suggesting
standards for presuming antitrust risk
along with incentive-modifying remedies.

The heart of the government's charge was that appellants had by concerted action set up a system of By-Laws which prohibited all AP members from selling news to non-members, and which granted each member powers to block its non-member competitors from membership. These By-Laws, to which all AP members had assented, were, in the context of the admitted facts, charged to be in violation of the Sherman Act. A further charge related to a contract between AP and Canadian Press, (a news agency of Canada, similar to AP) under which the Canadian agency and AP obligated themselves to furnish news exclusively to each other. The District Court, composed of three judges, held that the By-Laws unlawfully restricted admission to AP membership, and violated the Sherman Act insofar as the By-Laws' provisions clothed a member with powers to impose or dispense with conditions upon the admission of his business competitor. Continued observance of these By-Laws was enjoined. The court further held that the Canadian contract was an integral part of the restrictive membership conditions, and enjoined its observance pending abandonment of the membership restrictions. The government's motion for summary judgment, under Rule 56 of the Rules of Civil Procedure, was granted and its prayer for relief was granted in part and denied in part. . . .

These By-Laws, for a violation of which members may be thus fined, suspended, or expelled, require that each newspaper member publish the AP news regularly in whole or in part, and that each shall "promptly furnish to the corporation, through its agents or employees, all the news of such member's district, the area of which shall be determined by the Board of Directors." All members are prohibited from selling or furnishing their spontaneous news to any agency or publisher except to AP. Other By-Laws require each newspaper member to conduct his or its business in such manner that the news furnished by the corporations shall not be made available to any non-member in advance of publication. The joint effect of these By-Laws is to block all newspaper non-members from any opportunity to buy news from AP or any of its publisher members. Admission to membership in AP thereby becomes a prerequisite to obtaining AP news or buying news from any one of its more than twelve hundred publishers. The erection of obstacles to the acquisition of membership consequently can make it difficult, if not impossible for non-members to get any of the news furnished by AP or any of the individual members of this combination of American newspaper publishers.

The By-Laws provide a very simple and non-burdensome road for admission of a non-competing applicant. The Board of Directors in such case can elect the applicant without payment of money or the imposition of any other onerous terms. In striking contrast are the By-Laws which govern admission of new members who do compete. Historically, as well as presently, applicants who would offer competition to old members have a hard road to travel. This appears from the following facts found by the District Court.

AP originally functioned as an Illinois corporation, and at that time an existing member of the Association had an absolute veto power over the applications of a publisher who was or would be in competition with the old member. The Supreme Court of Illinois held that AP, thus operated, was in restraint of trade. Inter-Ocean Publishing Co. v. Associated Press, 184 Ill. 438, 56 N.E. 822. As a result of this decision, the present Association was organized in New York. Under the new By-Laws, the unqualified veto power of the Illinois AP members was changed into a "right of protest" which, when exercised, prevented the AP directors from electing the applicants as in other cases. The old member's protest against his competitor's application could then be overruled only by the affirmative vote of four-fifths of all the members of AP.

In 1931, the By-Laws were amended so as to extend the right of protest to all who had been members for more than 5 years and upon whom no right of protest had been conferred by the 1900 By-Laws. In 1942, after complaints to the Department of Justice had brought about an investigation, the By-Laws were again amended. These By-Laws, presently involved, leave the Board of Directors free to elect new members unless the applicant would compete with old members, and in that event the Board cannot act at all in the absence of consent by the applicant's member competitor. Should the old member object to admission of his competitor, the application must be referred to a regular or special meeting of the Association. As a prerequisite to election, he must (a) pay to the Association 10% of the total amount of the regular assessments received by it from old members in the same competitive field during the entire period from October 1, 1900 to the first day of the month preceding the date of the election of the applicant,[43] (b) relinquish any exclusive rights the applicant may have to any news or news picture services and when requested to do so by his member competitor in that field, must "require the said news or news picture services, or any of them, to be furnished to such member or members, upon the same terms as they are made available to the applicant", and (c) receive a majority vote of the regular members who vote in person or by proxy. These obstacles to membership, and to the purchase of AP news, only existed where there was a competing old member in the same field.

The District Court found that the By-Laws in and of themselves were contracts in restraint of commerce in that they contained provisions designed to stifle competition in the newspaper publishing field. The court also found that AP's restrictive By-Laws had hindered and impeded the growth of competing newspapers. This latter finding, as to the *past* effect of the restrictions, is challenged. We are inclined to think that it is supported by undisputed evidence, but we do not stop to labor the point. For the court below found, and we think correctly, that the By-Laws on their face, and without regard to their

---

43. Under these terms, a new applicant could not have entered the morning field in New York without paying $1,432,142.73, and in Chicago, $416,631.90. For entering the evening field in the same cities it would have cost $1,095,003.21, and $595,772.31, respectively. [Court's footnote.]

past effect, constitute restraints of trade. Combinations are no less unlawful because they have not as yet resulted in restraint. An agreement or combination to follow a course of conduct which will necessarily restrain or monopolize a part of trade or commerce may violate the Sherman Act, whether it be "wholly nascent or abortive on the one hand, or successful on the other." For these reasons the argument, repeated here in various forms, that AP had not yet achieved a complete monopoly is wholly irrelevant. Undisputed evidence did show, however, that its By-Laws had tied the hands of all of its numerous publishers, to the extent that they could not and did not sell any part of their news so that it could reach any of their non-member competitors. In this respect the Court did find, and that finding cannot possibly be challenged, that AP's By-Laws had hindered and restrained the sale of interstate news to non-members who competed with members.

Inability to buy news from the largest news agency, or any one of its multitude of members, can have most serious effects on the publication of competitive newspapers, both those presently published and those which, but for these restrictions, might be published in the future. This is illustrated by the District Court's finding that in 26 cities of the United States, existing newspapers already have contracts for AP news and the same newspapers have contracts with United Press and International News Service under which new newspapers would be required to pay the contract holders large sums to enter the field.[44] The net effect is seriously to limit the opportunity of any new paper to enter these cities. Trade restraints of this character, aimed at the destruction of competition, tend to block the initiative which brings newcomers into a field of business and to frustrate the free enterprise system which it was the purpose of the Sherman Act to protect.

We need not again pass upon the contention that trade in news carried on among the states is not interstate commerce, or that because AP's activities are cooperative, they fall outside the sphere of business. It is significant that when Congress has desired to permit cooperatives to interfere with the competitive system of business, it has done so expressly by legislation.

Nor can we treat this case as though it merely involved a reporter's contract to deliver his news reports exclusively to a single newspaper, or an exclusive agreement as to news between two newspapers in different cities. For such trade restraints might well be "reasonable", and therefore not in violation of the Sherman Act. But however innocent such agreements might be, standing alone, they would assume quite a different aspect if utilized as essential features

44. INS and UP make so-called "asset value" contracts under which if another newspaper wishes to obtain their press services, the newcomer shall pay to the competitor holding the UP or INS contract the stipulated "asset value". [Court's footnote.]

In 1958, INS, being "in failing circumstances," was acquired by UP with the approval of the Department of Justice. 2 Trade Reg.Rep. (CCH) ¶ 4295.15. [Ed. note.]

of a program to hamper or destroy competition. It is in this light that we must view this case.

It has been argued that the restrictive By-Laws should be treated as beyond the prohibitions of the Sherman Act, since the owner of the property can choose his associates and can, as to that which he has produced by his own enterprise and sagacity, efforts or ingenuity, decide for himself whether and to whom to sell or not to sell. While it is true in a very general sense that one can dispose of his property as he pleases, he cannot "go beyond the exercise of this right, and by contracts or combinations, express or implied, unduly hinder or obstruct the free and natural flow of commerce in the channels of interstate trade." United States v. Bausch & Lomb Co., 321 U.S. 707, 722, 64 S.Ct. 805, 813, 88 L.Ed. 1024. The Sherman Act was specifically intended to prohibit independent businesses from becoming "associates" in a common plan which is bound to reduce their competitor's opportunity to buy or sell the things in which the groups compete. Victory of a member of such a combination over its business rivals achieved by such collective means cannot consistently with the Sherman Act or with practical, everyday knowledge be attributed to *individual* "enterprise and sagacity"; such hampering of business rivals can only be attributed to that which really makes it possible—the collective power of an unlawful combination. That the object of sale is the creation or product of a man's ingenuity does not alter this principle. Fashion Originators' Guild, Inc. v. Federal Trade Commission, 312 U.S. 457, 61 S.Ct. 703, 85 L.Ed. 949. It is obviously fallacious to view the By-Laws here in issue as instituting a program to encourage and permit full freedom of sale and disposal of property by its owners. Rather these publishers have, by concerted arrangements, pooled their power to acquire, to purchase, and to dispose of news reports through the channels of commerce. They have also pooled their economic and news control power and, in exerting that power, have entered into agreements which the District Court found to be "plainly designed in the interest of preventing competition."

It is further contended that since there are other news agencies which sell news, it is not a violation of the Act for an overwhelming majority of American publishers to combine to decline to sell their news to the minority. But the fact that an agreement to restrain trade does not inhibit competition in all of the objects of that trade cannot save it from the condemnation of the Sherman Act. It is apparent that the exclusive right to publish news in a given field, furnished by AP and all of its members gives many newspapers a competitive advantage over their rivals. Conversely, a newspaper without AP service is more than likely to be at a competitive disadvantage. The District Court stated that it was to secure this advantage over rivals that the By-Laws existed. It is true that the record shows that some competing papers have gotten along without AP news, but morning newspapers, which control 96% of the total circulation in the United States, have AP news service. And the District Court's unchallenged finding was that "AP is a vast, intricately reticulated organization, the largest of its kind, gathering news from all over the world, the chief single source of news for the American press, universally agreed to be of great consequence."

Nevertheless, we are asked to reverse these judgments on the ground that the evidence failed to show that AP reports, which might be attributable to their own "enterprise and sagacity", are clothed "in the robes of indispensability." The absence of "indispensability" is said to have been established under the following chain of reasoning: AP has made its news generally available to the people by supplying it to a limited and select group of publishers in the various cities; therefore, it is said, AP and its member publishers have not deprived the reading public of AP news; all local readers have an "adequate access" to AP news, since all they need do in any city to get it is to buy, on whatever terms they can in a protected market, the particular newspaper selected for the public by AP and its members. We reject these contentions. The proposed "indispensability" test would fly in the face of the language of the Sherman Act and all of our previous interpretations of it. Moreover, it would make that law a dead letter in all fields of business, a law which Congress has consistently maintained to be an essential safeguard to the kind of private competitive business economy this country has sought to maintain.

The restraints on trade in news here were no less than those held to fall within the ban of the Sherman Act with reference to combinations to restrain trade outlets in the sale of tiles, Montague & Co. v. Lowry, 193 U.S. 38, 24 S.Ct. 307, 48 L.Ed. 608; or enameled iron ware, Standard Sanitary Mfg. Co. v. United States, 226 U.S. 20, 48, 49, 33 S.Ct. 9, 14, 15, 57 L.Ed. 107; or lumber, Eastern States Retail Lumber Dealers' Association v. United States, 234 U.S. 600, 611, 34 S.Ct. 951, 954, 58 L.Ed. 1490, L.R.A.1915A, 788; or women's clothes, Fashion Originators' Guild of America, Inc., et al. v. Federal Trade Commission, supra; or motion pictures, United States v. Crescent Amusement Co., 323 U.S. 173, 65 S.Ct. 254. Here as in the Fashion Originator's Guild case, supra, 312 U.S. 465, 61 S.Ct. 707, 85 L.Ed. 949, "the combination is in reality an extra-governmental agency, which prescribes rules for the regulation and restraint of interstate commerce, and provides extra-judicial tribunals for determination and punishment of violations, and thus 'trenches upon the power of the national legislature and violates the statute.' . . . ". By the restrictive By-Laws each of the publishers in the combination has, in effect, "surrendered himself completely to the control of the association," Anderson v. Shipowners' Ass'n, 272 U.S. 359, 362, 47 S.Ct. 125, 126, 71 L.Ed. 298, in respect to the disposition of news in interstate commerce. Therefore this contractual restraint of interstate trade, "designed in the interest of preventing competition," cannot be one of the "normal and usual agreements in aid of trade and commerce which may be found out to be within the [Sherman] act . . . ." Eastern States Retail Lumber Dealers' Association v. United States, supra, 234 U.S. 612, 613, 34 S.Ct. 954, 955, 58 L.Ed. 1490, L.R.A. 1915A, 788. It is further said that we reach our conclusion by application of the "public utility" concept to the newspaper business.[45] This is not correct. We merely hold that arrangements or combinations designed to stifle competition cannot be immunized by adopting a membership device accomplishing that purpose.

Finally, the argument is made that to apply the Sherman Act to this association of publishers constitutes an abridgment of the freedom of the press guaranteed by the First Amendment. Perhaps it would be a sufficient answer to this contention to refer to the decisions of this Court in Associated Press v. N. L. R. B., supra, and Indiana Farmer's Guide Publishing Co. v. Prairie Farmer Publishing Co., 293 U.S. 268, 55 S.Ct. 182, 79 L.Ed. 356. It would be strange indeed however if the grave concern for freedom of the press which prompted adoption of the First Amendment should be read as a command that the government was without power to protect that freedom. The First Amendment, far from providing an argument against application of the Sherman Act, here provides powerful reasons to the contrary. That Amendment rests on the assumption that the widest possible dissemination of information from diverse and antagonistic sources is essential to the welfare of the public, that a free press is a condition of a free society. Surely a command that the government itself shall not impede the free flow of ideas does not afford nongovernmental combinations a refuge if they impose restraints upon that constitutionally guaranteed freedom. Freedom to publish means freedom for all and not for some. Freedom to publish is guaranteed by the Constitution, but freedom to combine to keep others from publishing is not. Freedom of the press from governmental interference under the First Amendment does not sanction repression of that freedom by private interests. The First Amendment affords not the slightest support for the contention that a combination to restrain trade in news and views has any constitutional immunity.

We now turn to the decree. Having adjudged the By-Laws imposing restrictions on applications for membership to be illegal, the court enjoined the defendants from observing them, or agreeing to observe any new or amended By-Law having a like purpose or effect. It further provided that nothing in the decree should prevent the adoption by the Associated Press of new or amended By-Laws "which will restrict admission, provided that members in the same city and in the same 'field' (morning, evening or Sunday), as an applicant publishing a newspaper in the United States of America or its Territories, shall not have power to impose, or dispense with, any conditions upon his admission and that the By-Laws shall affirmatively declare that the effect of admission upon the ability of such applicant to compete with members in the same city and 'field' shall not be taken into consideration in passing upon his application." . . . Interpreting the decree to mean that AP news is to be furnished to competitors of old mem-

---

45. The "public utility concept" is the idea that certain businesses, like gas, electric, telephone and street-car companies, are under a legal obligation to serve all comers without discrimination. It will be observed that these are businesses in which competition is unlikely and, indeed, generally limited by law, so that the customer has no alternative source of supply. [Ed. note.]

bers without discrimination through By-Laws controlling membership, or otherwise, we approve it.

The court also held that, taken in connection with the restrictive
clauses on admissions to membership, those sections of the By-Laws
violated the Sherman Act which prevented service of AP news to non-
members and prevented AP members from furnishing spontaneous
news to anyone not a member of the Association. It held the agreement between AP and the Canadian Press, under which AP secured
exclusive right to receive the news reports of the Canadian Press and
its members, was also, when taken in connection with the restrictive
membership agreements, in violation of the Sherman Act. It declined
to hold these By-Laws and the agreement with Canadian Press illegal
standing by themselves. It consequently enjoined their observance
temporarily, pending AP's obedience to the decree enjoining the restrictive membership agreements. . . .

The government has appealed from the court's refusal to hold
each of these last-mentioned items a violation of the Sherman Act
standing alone. . . . The fashioning of a decree in an antitrust
case in such way as to prevent future violations and eradicate existing evils, is a matter which rests largely in the discretion of the
court. . . . In the situation thus narrowly presented we are unable to say that the court's decree should have gone further than it
did. Furthermore, the District Court retained the cause for such further proceedings as might become necessary. If, as the government
apprehends, the decree in its present form should not prove adequate
to prevent further discriminatory trade restraints against non-member newspapers, the court's retention of the cause will enable it to
take the necessary measures to cause the decree to be fully and faithfully carried out.

The judgment in all three cases is affirmed.

MR. JUSTICE JACKSON took no part in the consideration or decision
of this case.

MR. JUSTICE DOUGLAS, concurring.

I join in the opinion of the Court. But in view of the broader issues which have been injected into the discussion of the case, I add a
few words to indicate what I deem to be the narrow compass of the
decision.

Every exclusive arrangement in the business or commercial field
may produce a restraint of trade. A manufacturer who has only one
retail outlet for his product may be said to restrain trade in the sense
that other retailers are prevented from dealing in the commodity.
And to a degree, the same kind of restraint may be found wherever a
reporter is gathering news exclusively for one newspaper. But Standard Oil Co. v. United States, 221 U.S. 1, 31 S.Ct. 502, 55 L.Ed. 619,
construed the Sherman Act to include not every restraint but only
those which were unreasonable. Starting from that premise, I assume that it would not be a violation of the Sherman Act if a newspaper in Seattle and one in New York made an agency agreement

whereby each was to furnish exclusively to the other news reports from his locality.

But such an exclusive arrangement, though innocent standing alone, might be part of a scheme which would violate the Sherman Act in one of two respects.

(1) It might be a part of the machinery utilized to effect a restraint of trade in violation of § 1 of the Act. I think the exclusive arrangement employed by the Associated Press had such a necessary effect. As developed in the opinion of the Court, the by-laws of the Associated Press were aimed at the competitors of the Associated Press' members; their necessary effect was to hinder or impede competition with members of the combination. The District Court not only ordered the by-laws to be revised; it enjoined continuance of the exclusive arrangement until the restraint effected by the by-laws had been eliminated. That was plainly within its power. For it is well settled that a feature of an illegal restraint of trade, which is innocent by itself and which may be lawfully used if independently established, may be uprooted along with the other parts of an illegal arrangement. We certainly cannot say that the District Court abused its discretion in adopting that course here as an interim measure pending a revision of the by-laws.

(2) Such an exclusive arrangement as we have here might result in the growth of a monopoly in the furnishing of news, in the access to news, or in the gathering or distribution of news. Those are business activities subject to the Sherman Act as well as other Acts of Congress regulating interstate commerce. The District Court found that in its present stage of development the Associated Press had no monopoly of that character. Those findings are challenged here in the appeal taken by the United States. They are not reached in the present decision for the reason, discussed in the opinion of the Court, that they cannot be tried out on a motion for a summary judgment. The decree which we approve does not direct Associated Press to serve all applicants. It goes no further than to put a ban on Associated Press' practice of discriminating against competitors of its members in the same field or territory. That entails not only a discontinuance of the practice for the future but an undoing of the wrong which has been done. If Associated Press, after the effects of that discrimination have been eliminated, freezes its membership at a given level, quite different problems would be presented. Whether that would result in a monopoly in violation of § 1 of the Act is distinct from the issue in this case.

Only if a monopoly were shown to exist would we be faced with the public utility theory which has been much discussed in connection with this case and adopted by MR. JUSTICE FRANKFURTER. The decrees under the Sherman Act directed at monopolies have customarily been designed to break them up or dissolve them. There have been some exceptions. Thus in United States v. Terminal Railroad Ass'n, 224 U.S. 383, 32 S.Ct. 507, 56 L.Ed. 810, an action was brought under the Sherman Act to dissolve a combination among certain railroads serving St. Louis. The combination had acquired control of all available facilities for connecting railroads on the east bank of the Mississippi with those on the west bank. The Court held that as an alternative to dissolution a plan should be submitted which provided for equality of treatment of all railroads. Whether that procedure would be appropriate in this type of case or should await further legislative action is a considerable question, the discussion of which should not cloud the present decision. What we do today has no bearing whatsoever on it.

MR. JUSTICE FRANKFURTER, concurring.

. . . [W]e have here arrangements whereby members of the Associated Press bind one another from selling local news to non-members and exercise power, which reciprocal self-interest invokes, to help one another in keeping out competitors from membership in the Associated Press, with all the advantages that it brings to a newspaper. . . . [T]hese plainly are agreements in restraint of that commerce. But ever since the Sherman Law was saved from stifling literalness by "the rule of reason," it is not sufficient to find a restraint. The decisive question is whether it is an unreasonable restraint. This depends, in essence, on the significance of the restraint in relation to a particular industry. Compare Chicago Board of Trade v. United States, 246 U.S. 231, 238, 38 S.Ct. 242, 244, 62 L.Ed. 683.

To be sure, the Associated Press is a cooperative organization of members who are "engaged in a commercial business for profit." But in addition to being a commercial enterprise, it has a relation to the public interest unlike that of any other enterprise pursued for profit. A free press is indispensable to the workings of our democratic society. The business of the press, and therefore the business of the Associated Press, is the promotion of truth regarding public matters by furnishing the basis for an understanding of them. Truth and understanding are not wares like peanuts or potatoes. And so, the incidence of restraints upon the promotion of truth through denial of access to the basis for understanding calls into play considerations very different from comparable restraints in a cooperative enterprise having merely a commercial aspect. I find myself entirely in agreement with Judge Learned Hand that "neither exclusively, nor even primarily, are the interests of the newspaper industry conclusive; for that industry serves one of the most vital of all general interests: the dissemination of news from as many different sources, and with as many different facets and colors as is possible. That interest is closely akin to, if indeed it is not the same as, the interest protected by the First Amendment; it presupposes that right conclusions are more likely to be gathered out of a multitude of tongues, than through any kind of authoritative selection. To many this is, and always will be, folly; but we have staked upon it our all." 52 F.Supp. 362, 372.

From this point of view it is wholly irrelevant that the Associated Press itself has rival news agencies. As to ordinary commodities, agreements to curtail the supply and to fix prices are in violation of the area of free enterprise which the Sherman Law was designed to protect. The press in its commercial aspects is also subject to the regulation of the Sherman Law. But the freedom of enterprise protected by the Sherman Law necessarily has different aspects in relation to the press than in the case of ordinary commercial pursuits. The interest of the public is to have the flow of news not trammeled by the combined self-interest of those who enjoy a unique constitutional position precisely because of the public dependence on a free press. A public interest so essential to the vitality of our democratic government may be defeated by private restraints no less than by public censorship.

Equally irrelevant is the objection that it turns the Associated Press into a "public utility" to deny to a combination of newspapers the right to treat access to their pooled resources as though they were regulating membership in a social club. The relation of such restraints upon access to news and the relation of such access to the function of a free press in our democratic society must not be obscured by the specialized notions that have gathered around the legal concept of "public utility".

The short of the matter is that the by-laws which the District Court has struck down clearly restrict the commerce which is conducted by the Associated Press, and the restrictions are unreasonable because they offend the basic functions which a constitutionally guaranteed free press serves in our nation.

MR. JUSTICE ROBERTS, dissenting in part. (CHIEF JUSTICE STONE concurred in this opinion.)

I think the judgment should be reversed. . . .

I assume it cannot be questioned that two or more persons desirous of obtaining news may agree to employ a single reporter, or a staff of reporters, to furnish them news, and agree amongst themselves that, as they share the expense involved, they themselves will use the fruit of the service and will not give it away or sell it. Although the procedure has obvious advantages, and is in itself innocent, I do not know, from the opinion of the court, whether it would be held that the inevitable or necessary operation, or necessary consequence of such an arrangement is to restrain competition in trade or commerce and that it is, consequently, illegal. Many expressions in the opinion seem to recognize that all AP does is to keep for its members that which, at joint expense, its members and employees have produced,—its reports of world events. Thus it is said that nonmembers are denied access to AP news, not, be it observed, to news.

. . . [AP's] purpose is stated by its charter as "The collection and interchange, with greater economy and efficiency, of information and intelligence for publication in the newspaper" of its members. The organization started on a comparatively modest basis, to facilitate exchange of news reports amongst its members. It has grown into a cooperatively maintained news reporting agency having, in addition, its own reporters and agencies for the collection, arrangement, editing, and transmission to its members, of news, gathered by its employees, and those of others with whom it contracts.

The question is whether the Sherman Act precludes such a cooperative arrangement and renders those who participate liable to furnish news copy, on equal terms, to all newspapers which desire it, as the court below has held. If so, it must be because the joint arrangement constitutes a contract, combination or conspiracy in restraint of trade, or a monopolization, or an attempt or combination or conspiracy to monopolize part or all of some branch of interstate or international trade or commerce or is a public utility subject to regulation. . . .

> [JUSTICE ROBERTS then analyzed the record, finding the government's case inadequate under each theory. He emphasized among other things: (1) that comparable worldwide press service was available from United Press, International News Service and others; (2) that many papers had succeeded without AP service, and some who had the choice preferred the competing services; (3) that AP made no effort to prevent its members from using the competing services or to obstruct nonmember access to news, either directly or through other press services.]

The court's opinion, under the guise of enforcing the Sherman Act, in fact renders AP a public utility subject to the duty to serve all on equal terms. This must be so, despite the disavowal of any such ground of decision. The District Court made this public utility theory the sole basis of decision, because it was unable to find support for a conclusion that AP either intended or attempted to, or in fact did, unreasonably restrain trade or monopolize or attempt to monopolize all or any part of any branch of trade within the decisions of this court interpreting and applying the Sherman Act. . . .

Suffice it to say that it is a novel application of the Sherman Act to treat it as legislation converting an organization, which neither restrains trade nor monopolizes it, nor holds itself out to serve the public generally, into a public utility because it furnishes a new sort of illumination—literary as contrasted with physical—by pronouncing a fiat that the interest of consumers—the reading public—not that of competing news agencies or newspaper publishers—requires equal service to all newspapers on the part of AP and that a court of equity, in the guise of an injunction, shall write the requisite regulatory statute. This is government-by-injunction with a vengeance.

Moreover it is to make a new statute by court decision. The Sherman Act does not deal with public utilities as such. They may violate the Act, as may persons engaged in private business. But that Act never was intended and has never before been thought to require a private corporation, not holding itself out to serve the public, whose operations neither were intended to nor tended unreasonably to restrain or monopolize trade, to fulfill the duty incident to a public calling, of serving all applicants on equal terms.

For myself, I prefer to entrust regulatory legislation of commerce to the elected representatives of the people instead of freezing it in the decrees of courts less responsive to the public will.

[JUSTICE MURPHY dissented in a separate opinion, finding no evidence of any program to hamper or destroy competition, but only a successful effort by AP to protect the fruits of its own enterprise from use by competitors. Like JUSTICE ROBERTS, he was particularly concerned over the disposition of the case on motion for summary judgment, i.e., on pleadings and affidavits without testimony, in view of the dangers in "interference by the Government with the private dissemination of information."]

NOTES AND QUERIES

(1) *Queries.* Do any of the opinions finding A.P.'s conduct illegal establish a per se test of illegality? Does Justice Black's approach, in the end, differ much from Justice White's in *BMI*, supra p. 385 (another joint venture)?

Which of the following features of the Associated Press arrangements was most detrimental to competition and the public interest:

(a) discriminatory restriction on admission of competitors?

(b) the provision that members may not supply spot news to anyone except Associated Press? Is this exclusive feature essential to A.P.'s performance of the function of gathering and disseminating nationwide news? How does this affect press services competing with A.P.?

(c) the provision in the contract with Canadian Press preventing it from supplying Canadian news to others than A.P.? If a court sustains the exclusive contract with members, is there any basis on which it might distinguish and enjoin the C.P. exclusive?

(d) the size of A.P., in terms of the number and leading position of its members, bound by exclusive contract?

Draft decree provisions embodying the maximum relief which the government might reasonably have sought against A.P. Would these include:

(a) an obligation to supply Canadian news, at reasonable cost, to nonmembers of A.P. so long as it had exclusive rights to C.P. service?

(b) prohibition of arrangements with members to supply A.P. exclusively?

(c) an obligation upon A.P. to choose within one year either to end the exclusive arrangements or to reduce the number of members to a specified level which would still permit A.P. to have at least one member in every city of consequence, but preclude it from having all papers in any one area tied up in exclusive arrangements?

(2) *Access to Pooled Facilities.* As early as 1912 in *United States v. Terminal Railroad Association*, 224 U.S. 383, 32 S.Ct. 507, 56 L.Ed. 810, the Sherman Act had been used to compel a group of railroads, which jointly controlled St. Louis access and terminal facilities, to reform the terms of their agreements so as to permit nonmember lines to use these facilities.[46]

46. Cf. United States v. Pennsylvania Railroad, 323 U.S. 612, 65 S.Ct. 471, 89 L.Ed. 499 (1945) (railroads, maintaining a nationwide pooling arrangement, under which they use and haul each other's freight cars, may be required by order of the Interstate Commerce Commission to drop a rule imposing special requirement

Gamco, Inc. v. Providence Fruit & Produce Building, 194 F.2d 484 (1st Cir. 1952), held that defendant corporation, together with its directors and certain lessees, combined to violate the Sherman Act by causing the corporation to refuse to renew Gamco's lease and by maintaining a successful ejectment action against Gamco in the state courts, under the following circumstances: Plaintiff was a producer wholesaler in Providence, R. I. Defendant corporation operated the Produce Building, which provided the most favorable storage, selling, and shipping facilities for produce wholesalers along the tracks of the New Haven Railroad in Providence. Stock of defendant was owned by local wholesalers occupying portions of the building. Defendant refused to renew the lease because control of Gamco had passed to a Boston firm, in violation of defendant's policy of leasing only to Rhode Island firms. There was evidence that other premises were available and feasible for produce wholesaling, and that Gamco's ouster would not significantly dampen the sharp competition among the dealers. The District Court judgment for defendant was reversed on appeal. The Court of Appeals declared:

> Defendants contend, however, that a discriminatory policy in regard to the lessees in the Produce Building can never amount to monopoly because other alternative selling sites are available. The short answer to this is that a monopolized resource seldom lacks substitutes; alternatives will not excuse monopolization. . . .

> Admittedly the finite limitations of the building itself thrust monopoly power upon the defendants, and they are not required to do the impossible in accepting indiscriminately all who would apply. Reasonable criteria of selection, therefore, such as lack of available space, financial unsoundness, or possibly low business or ethical standards, would not violate the standards of the Sherman Antitrust Act. But the latent monopolist must justify the exclusion of a competitor from a market which he controls. Where, as here, a business group understandably susceptible to the temptations of exploiting its natural advantage against competitors prohibits one previously acceptable from hawking his wares beside them any longer at the very moment of his affiliation with a potentially lower priced outsider, they may be called upon for a necessary explanation. The conjunction of power and motive to exclude with an exclusion not immediately and patently justified by reasonable business requirements establishes a prima facie case of the purpose to monopolize. Defendants thus had the duty to come forward and justify Gamco's ouster. This they failed to do save by a suggestion of financial unsoundness obviously hollow in view of the fact that the latter's affiliation with Sawyer & Co. put it in a far more secure credit position than it had enjoyed even during its legal tenancy. We therefore hold that, although selection and discrimination among those who would become lessees was necessary, defendants have failed to show that the basis for their action here was innocent of the economic consideration alleged.[47]

to obtain consent of car owner before delivering to ocean-going car ferry, offering coastwise transportation competitive with some of the railroads); Agreement Establishing Air Cargo Incorporated, 9 C.A.B. 468 (1948) (proposal by seventeen certificated air carriers to establish a jointly owned company to consolidate ground facilities for handling air freight approved only on condition that participation should be open to all certificated air carriers); United States v. National

Wrestling Alliance, 1956 Trade Cases ¶ 68,507 (S.D.Iowa 1956) (consent decree requiring association of bookers and promoters of professional wrestling matches to admit any booker or promoter meeting prescribed qualifications, e.g., having engaged in booking or promoting wrestling matches for two years or having promoted at least ten exhibitions in one year).

47. Compare complex litigation over allocation of selling time in state licensed

Municipal Electric Association v. S.E.C., 134 U.S.App.D.C. 145, 413 F.2d 1052 (1969), set aside SEC approval of New England utilities' acquisition of stock in a giant joint venture nuclear power facility because the Commission declined to permit municipal power plants to pursue their claim that they should have been allowed to participate in stock ownership and thus share direct access to inexpensive power and to development opportunities.

(3) *Collective Boycott or Individual Refusal to Deal.*[48] Note that Associated Press was a legal entity, *i.e.*, an incorporated non-profit association, directly engaged in assembling and distributing news. In this respect it was unlike FOGA, which was not itself producing or selling, and therefore could not invoke the right of each producing unit in a competitive economy to select its own customers. Should this distinction have been determinative in favor of A.P.? Would it have been determinative had A.P. been a publicly-held corporation? Can the identity of an enterprise's owners transform it into a "joint venture" whose operations are then subject to Section 1 as being the result of some "contract, combination, or conspiracy"? Consider the court's characterization of the NFL, in *Smith v. Pro-Football*, as a "joint venture."[49] Would this make the NFL's decisions on the sale of television rights (e.g., no broadcasting into the home team's market) subject to Section 1 of the Sherman Act?[50]

tobacco warehouses: Danville Tobacco Association v. Bryant-Buckner Associates, 372 F.2d 634 (4th Cir. 1967), certiorari denied 387 U.S. 907, 87 S.Ct. 1688, 18 L.Ed.2d 624; Bale v. Glasgow Tobacco Board, 339 F.2d 281 (6th Cir. 1964); Rogers v. Douglas Tobacco Board of Trade, 244 F.2d 471 (5th Cir. 1957); Note, Antitrust Problems Raised by Private Regulation of the Auctioning of Leaf Tobacco, 106 U.Pa.L.Rev. 568 (1958).

48. See Fulda, Individual Refusals to Deal: When Does Single-Firm Conduct Become Vertical Restraint?, Law and Cont.Prob. Summer 1965, 590; Mund, The Right to Buy—And Its Denial to Small Business, S.Doc. No. 32, 85th Cong., 1st Sess. (1957) (Senate Comm. on Small Business); Report of Attorney General's National Committee to Study the Antitrust Laws 132–37 (1955); Barber, Refusals to Deal under the Antitrust Laws, 103 U.Pa.L.Rev. 847 (1955).

49. For a review of past cases and discussion of the "joint venture" argument, see North American Soccer League v. National Football League, 505 F.Supp. 659 (S.D.N.Y.1980) (holding NFL Rule, forbidding NFL owners from acquiring interest in another major sports team, not subject to Section 1; NFL a single economic entity in this context), reversed 670 F.2d 1249 (2d Cir.) (NFL not a single economic entity; cross-ownership ban violates Sherman Act under rule of reason analysis), certiorari denied ___ U.S. ___, 103 S.Ct. 499, 74 L.Ed.2d 639 (1982).

50. Yes: United States v. National Football League, 116 F.Supp. 319 (E.D. Pa.1953).

A petition by the National Football League to modify the 1953 decree so as to permit the 14 clubs to convey their television rights as a "package" to Columbia Broadcasting System was denied in United States v. National Football League, 196 F.Supp. 445 (E.D.Pa.1961). Thereupon Congress passed P.L. 87–637, 15 U.S.C.A. §§ 1301–3 (1963), exempting from the antitrust laws joint agreements by members of professional sports leagues conveying their television rights. It is provided that the agreement may not restrict televising except in the home territory of a member club when the club is playing at home, and that it may not permit televising of professional football within 75 miles of intercollegiate games on Friday nights or Saturdays during the football season. Pub.L. 93–107 amended the Communications Act of 1934 to add § 311 which invalidates any agreement to prevent telecasting a game which has been sold out 72 hours before the game starts and requires the holder of the telecasting rights to make them "available . . . on reasonable terms." Cf. United Press dispatch reporting small colleges' warning to the National Collegiate Athletic Association not to permit additional broadcasts of popular big university games, because it would kill attendance at games of smaller schools: "We are satisfied with the controlled television as it was in 1955. But we don't want them to get any ideas about expansion." Philadelphia Evening Bulletin, Jan. 10, 1956, p. 59.

There have been recurrent efforts to amend the antitrust laws to provide explicit exemptions for sports league prac-

Recall from Note (2) that even unilateral refusals to deal may subject the defendant to liability under Section 2 of the Sherman Act. See also *Otter Tail Power Co. v. United States*, supra p. 124 and accompanying Notes. Thus, a joint venture with sufficient market power (AP? Gamco? Terminal R.R.?) might find its refusal to sell its product condemned under Section 2, where done "to foreclose competition, or gain a competitive advantage, or to destroy a competitor." [51] Are the courts therefore applying a *per se* analysis to refusals to deal when the joint venture has monopoly power, but inclining toward a rule of reason when it does not?

(4) *Research Joint Ventures.* In *Berkey Photo, Inc. v. Eastman Kodak Co.*,[52] Berkey claimed that Kodak violated Section 1 of the Sherman Act by conspiring with the General Electric Company and Sylvania Electric Products, Inc., to restrain trade in amateur cameras with flash devices. (Berkey's monopolization claim is explored supra, pp. 140–154.) Berkey proved that in 1963 Sylvania approached Kodak with a prototype of a new battery-powered light device—the flashcube—and a modified Kodak 126 camera to fire it. As a condition for joint development, Kodak required Sylvania not to disclose this invention to any other camera manufacturer. (Why might Sylvania have wanted to disclose the invention to other camera manufacturers?) The result was that, for some time after the flashcube and Kodak flashcube camera were introduced, Kodak was the only manufacturer able to sell cameras using the device. In 1967 Sylvania came to Kodak with the "magicube," a flashcube which did not require batteries for firing. Again, over Sylvania's protests, Kodak insisted that details of the new device be withheld from the public and the trade. This gave Kodak nearly a year and one-half edge over Berkey in bringing a magicube camera to market.

General Electric also approached Kodak (in 1969) with proposals for several new flash devices; one was similar to the magicube, the other used a piezoelectric crystal to ignite the flash. Kodak did not want to introduce two new flash systems simultaneously, so it stalled GE until October 1972, when the two executed a contract to introduce by 1975 GE "piezo" flashlamps and Kodak cameras designed to fire them. Disclosure beforehand to other lamp and camera manufacturers was forbidden. The GE "flipflash" was the result, and again Kodak got the jump on its camera rivals.

The Court of Appeals' opinion on this part of the case follows:

> Berkey contends that Kodak's agreements with the magicube and flip-flash manufacturers violated § 1 of the Sherman Act. In particular, it charges that although Kodak did not make any meaningful technological contribution to either system, the secrecy agreements it extracted from GE and Sylvania prevented other camera makers from competing in the production of cameras that could cooperate with the new flash devices. Evaluating all the evidence presented on these issues, the jury found Kodak's conduct to be unreasonable restraints of trade.

tices. See, for example, S. 950, 89th Cong. 1st Sess. which proposed to exempt arrangements relating to equalization of playing strength, employment and eligibility of players, right to operate within specific geographic areas, and preservation of public confidence in the honesty of sports contests. See also The Superbowl and the Sherman Act: Professional Team Sports and the Antitrust Laws, 81 Harv.L.Rev. 418 (1967), reviewing 1966 legislation authorizing merger of two national football leagues (15 U.S. C.A. §§ 1291–3).

51. Otter Tail Power Co. v. United States, supra p. 125.

52. 603 F.2d 263, 299 (2d Cir. 1979), certiorari denied 444 U.S. 1093, 100 S.Ct. 1061, 62 L.Ed.2d 783 (1980).

Kodak's challenge to these verdicts is relatively simple. It argues that both projects "involved millions of dollars of research and development expense by Kodak," and "led directly to the introduction of innovative new products" that "gained wide success." Accordingly, it urges, Berkey's § 1 claims are nothing more than "a mirror image" of the § 2 predisclosure arguments we rejected in Part II of this opinion [see pp. 147–150 supra].

There is a vast difference, however, between actions legal when taken by a single firm and those permitted for two or more companies acting in concert. To repeat a simple example, a monopolist may, assuming he acquired his power legally, charge any nonpredatory price for his product, but agreements among competitors to raise prices have been recognized as *per se* violations of the Sherman Act since *Socony-Vacuum*. We have stated that we respect innovation, and we have construed § 2 of the Act to avoid an interpretation that would stifle it. But this is *toto caelo* different from an agreement among a few firms to restrict to themselves the rewards of innovation. Such conduct is not immune to examination under § 1. . . . Kodak contends that it is "not a 'restraint of trade,' reasonable or unreasonable, jointly to develop a new product." Where a participant's market share is large, however, we believe joint development projects have sufficient anticompetitive potential to invite inquiry and thus stand on a different footing.

Joint development programs can benefit competition, but they are not without their costs. In analyzing joint research by direct competitors, one commentator has suggested that if several substantial firms in an industry join in research at a scale the remaining firms could not attain, and if the others are not permitted to join the group, the favored competitors might obtain a decisive and unjustified advantage over the rest. L. Sullivan, at 298–303. The benefits and detriments of joint research will vary with the circumstances, Sullivan suggests, and the market power of the participant firms is likely to be the most significant factor. Id.; accord, Turner, Patents, Antitrust and Innovation, 28 U.Pitt.L.Rev. 151, 158–59 (1966).

Kodak and GE, of course, are not direct competitors, and Kodak and Sylvania were at best potential competitors when the magicube was being developed.[53] Nevertheless, because of Kodak's market power over cameras, the exclusionary potential of horizontal research pools was present. In the case of the flipflash, for example, GE indicated early in 1971 that it could be at maximum production in two years. Kodak, however, counselled delay, at one point urging GE project officials to make a show of progress, "even if all you do is 'paint the red base black,'" so that "we'll feel free to work with you." Otherwise, Kodak said, GE could not be assured of being part of Kodak's future flash plans, for "we would then have to ask all [lamp] manufacturers" to submit ideas. A few months later, the two firms executed the formal agreement binding them to joint development of flipflash and nondisclosure to rival lamp and camera manufacturers. From this and other evidence, the jury could have found in

53. [Court's footnote 66.] Until 1962, Argus Camera was operated as a division of Sylvania. In May of that year, Sylvania sold Argus for a small amount of cash and $7.8 million in promissory notes. Over the next seven years, as a result of recapitalizations of Argus, Sylvania was, at various times, a major creditor, common shareholder, and preferred shareholder of its former division, on occasion placing a nominee on Argus's Board of Directors. Berkey contended that Sylvania's relationship with Argus permitted the jury to infer that the lamp manufacturer was a potential camera competitor as well.

the verdict it returned that, without any technological justification, GE kept a desirable innovation off the market for two years solely to suit Kodak's convenience. There is a hollow ring to a claim of justification by appeal to the need to promote innovation, where the result of the conduct was such a clear loss to consumers.

We hasten to add that we do not hold that joint development agreements between a monopolist and a firm in a complementary market are *per se* violations of § 1. It may be, for example, that the market structure is such that only a dominant firm will have the resources necessary to exploit the complementary technology being offered. If such were the case, the alternative to joint development could be no development at all. Accordingly, Judge Frankel appropriately rejected Berkey's request for a *per se* charge. See generally Continental T. V., Inc. v. GTE Sylvania, Inc., 433 U.S. 36, 49–50 & n. 16, 97 S.Ct. 2549, 53 L.Ed.2d 568 (1977). Nevertheless, as Areeda and Turner have noted, joint ventures involving a monopolist have sufficient anticompetitive potential that they must be scrutinized with care lest they be permitted to fortify the already substantial entry barriers inherent in a monopolized market. 3 P. Areeda & D. Turner, supra, at 114. The relevant variables might include: the size of the joint venturers; their share of their respective markets; the contributions of each party to the venture and the benefits derived; the likelihood that, in the absence of the joint effort, one or both parties would undertake a similar project, either alone or with a smaller firm in the other market; the nature of the ancillary restraints imposed and the reasonableness of their relationship to the purposes of the venture. This list is not intended to be exhaustive, nor do we suggest that each element applies to every case. In analyzing joint development agreements, as elsewhere in § 1, "the factfinder [must] weigh all of the circumstances of a case in deciding whether a restrictive practice should be prohibited as imposing an unreasonable restraint on competition," Continental T. V., supra, 433 U.S. at 49, 97 S.Ct. at 2557.

On the record before us, we have little doubt that a properly instructed jury could find that the magicube and flipflash agreements violated § 1.[54] It remains, therefore, to examine Kodak's challenges to the charge to the jury. Kodak asserts that Judge Frankel erred in instructing the jury to consider whether (1) Sylvania's substantial interest in Argus Camera Co. rendered it a potential camera competitor of Kodak, and (2) the "legitimate purposes" of the magicube and flipflash agreements might be accomplished by "less restrictive alternatives" than those actually chosen. We believe, however, that the charge provided accurate guidance for the jury's deliberations.

Kodak claims that there was an absence of evidence that an agreement between it and Sylvania not to compete existed; this assertion, however, misses the point. As we noted above, the possibility of individual entry or expansion into the monopolized market is a highly relevant consideration in assessing a joint venture such as the magicube agreement. We agree with the district judge that Sylvania's large interest in Argus was sufficient to raise for the jury the possibility that absent the joint

---

54. [Court's footnote 67.] In particular, there was in each instance evidence that Kodak used its camera monopoly to extract secrecy agreements from the lamp manufacturers, and that the benefits it derived from the agreements far exceeded the value of its technological contributions. . . .

project with Kodak, Sylvania might have produced magicube cameras with Argus.

. . .

Kodak also challenges a direction that the jury

should consider whether, under all the circumstances, the legitimate objectives of the programs might have been achieved by alternative means with less restrictive effects, including predisclosure or provisions for royalty-free licensing.

Kodak contends that this in effect directed a verdict for Berkey because, in retrospect, lawyers can always "conjure up some method of achieving the business purpose in question that would result in a somewhat lesser restriction of trade," American Motor Inns, Inc. v. Holiday Inns, Inc., 521 F.2d 1230, 1249 (3d Cir. 1975). We agree with the Third Circuit that a better charge would be to require that "the restraints . . . not exceed 'the limits *reasonably necessary* to meet the competitive problems,'" id. (quoting United States v. Arnold, Schwinn & Co., 388 U.S. 365, 380–81, 87 S.Ct. 1856, 18 L.Ed.2d 1249 (1967) (emphasis added by the court)). *American Motor Inns* noted, however, id. at 1248, that the existence of alternatives is obviously of vital concern in evaluating putatively anticompetitive conduct. Judge Frankel's § 1 charge simply presented the availability of less restrictive alternatives to the jury as one among many possibilities to be considered. The quoted paragraph did not in any way diminish the earlier instructions based on the rule of reason, including the specific admonition that no single test determines reasonableness.

Finally, we must address Kodak's contention that even if the less restrictive language passes muster, the reference in this context to predisclosure as a specific alternative does not. As is clear from both the charging conference and Kodak's requests to charge, Kodak views the "fact that these products were developed by two companies, rather than by Kodak alone" as immaterial to the issue of predisclosure. But, given the significantly different posture of single-firm and multi-firm conduct under the Sherman Act and Kodak's arguably minimal technological contributions to the two projects, we believe it was quite appropriate for the jury to consider whether Kodak's refusal to permit Sylvania or GE to disclose their inventions to other camera manufacturers was unreasonable.

Accordingly, we affirm the judgment insofar as it holds Kodak liable for violating § 1 of the Sherman Act by its conduct in the flash programs.

Query. Is this part of *Berkey* consistent with the court's holding that, "as a matter of law," Kodak had no duty under Section 2 of the Sherman Act to predisclose to competing camera manufacturers information about the 110 cartridge and film format (see p. 147, supra)? Does it matter that Sylvania was a reluctant participant in the magicube secrecy agreement?

Research joint ventures frequently face the question whether access to the research produced (or to the joint venture itself) must be open to competitors of the joint venturers. *Berkey* is somewhat unusual factually in that the preservation of lead-time was the critical factor; competitors were apparently able to copy the innovation, but with a time-lag before successful manufacture. Many research joint ventures produce technology protected by patents which cannot be invented around so easily, but can be licensed. Whether a research joint venture must license its patents to outsiders is an issue to be explored more fully infra, Chapter 9.

Both the Department of Justice Antitrust Division and the Environmental Protection Agency have issued Guidelines for research joint ventures. The former attempts to deal comprehensively with potential antitrust problems; the latter is focused exclusively on pollution control.[55]

CITIZEN PUBLISHING CO. v. UNITED STATES

Supreme Court of the United States, 1969.
394 U.S. 131, 89 S.Ct. 927, 22 L.Ed.2d 148.

MR. JUSTICE DOUGLAS delivered the opinion of the Court.

Tucson, Arizona, has only two daily newspapers of general circulation, the Star and the Citizen. The Citizen is the oldest, having been founded before 1900, and is an evening paper published six times a week. The Star, slightly younger than the Citizen, has a Sunday as well as a daily issue. Prior to 1940 the two papers vigorously competed with each other. While their circulation was about equal, the Star sold 50% more advertising space than the Citizen and operated at a profit, while the Citizen sustained losses. Indeed the Star's annual profits averaged about $25,825, while the Citizen's annual losses averaged about $23,550.

In 1936 the stock of the Citizen was purchased by one Small and one Johnson for $100,000 and they invested an additional $25,000 of working capital. They sought to interest others to invest in the Citizen but were not successful. Small increased his investment in the Citizen, moved from Chicago to Tucson, and was prepared to finance the Citizen's losses for at least awhile from his own resources. It does not appear that Small and Johnson sought to sell the Citizen; nor was the Citizen about to go out of business. The owners did, however, negotiate a joint operating agreement between the two papers which was to run for 25 years from March 1940, a term that was extended in 1953 until 1990. By its terms the agreement may be canceled only by mutual consent of the parties.

The agreement provided that each paper should retain its own news and editorial department, as well as its corporate identity. It provided for the formation of Tucson Newspapers, Inc. (TNI), which was to be owned in equal shares by the Star and Citizen and which was to manage all departments of their business except the news and editorial units. The production and distribution equipment of each paper was transferred to TNI. The latter had five directors—two named by the Star, two by the Citizen, and the fifth chosen by the Citizen out of three named by the Star.

The purpose of the agreement was to end any business or commercial competition between the two papers and to that end three types of controls were imposed. First was *price fixing*. The newspapers were sold and distributed by the circulation department of TNI; commercial advertising placed in the papers was sold only by the advertising department of TNI; the subscription and advertising

---

55. The Antitrust Division Guide is reprinted in ATRR No. 992, December 4, 1980, Special Supp.; EPA's is reprinted at 5 CCH Trade Reg.Rep. ¶ 50,423.

rates were set jointly. Second was *profit pooling*. All profits realized were pooled and distributed to the Star and the Citizen by TNI pursuant to an agreed ratio. Third was a *market control*. It was agreed that neither the Star nor the Citizen nor any of their stockholders, officers, and executives would engage in any other business in Pima County, the metropolitan area of Tucson, in conflict with the agreement. Thus competing publishing operations were foreclosed.

All commercial rivalry between the papers ceased. Combined profits before taxes rose from $27,531 in 1940 to $1,727,217 in 1964.

The Government's complaint charged an unreasonable restraint of trade or commerce in violation of § 1 of the Sherman Act, and a monopoly in violation of § 2. The District Court, after finding that the joint operating agreement contained provisions which were unlawful *per se* under § 1, granted the Government's motion for summary judgment.

The case went to trial on the § 2 charge and also on a charge brought under § 7 of the Clayton Act. The latter charge arose out of the acquisition of the stock of the Star by the shareholders of the Citizen pursuant to an option in the joint operating agreement. Arden Publishing Company was formed as the vehicle of acquisition and it now publishes the Star.

At the end of the trial the District Court found that the joint operating agreement in purpose and effect monopolized the only newspaper business in Tucson in violation of § 2 of the Sherman Act.

As respects the Clayton Act charge the District Court found that in Pima County, the appropriate geographic market, the Citizen's acquisition of the Star stock had the effect of continuing in a more permanent form a substantial lessening of competition in daily newspaper publishing that is condemned by § 7.

The decree does not prevent all forms of joint operation. It requires, however, appellants to submit a plan for divestiture and reestablishment of the Star as an independent competitor and for modification of the joint operating ageement so as to eliminate the price-fixing, market control, and profit-pooling provisions. The case is here by way of appeal.

We affirm the judgment. The § 1 violations are plain beyond peradventure. Price-fixing is illegal *per se*. United States v. Masonite Corp., 316 U.S. 265, 276, 62 S.Ct. 1070, 1077, 86 L.Ed. 1461. Pooling of profits pursuant to an inflexible ratio at least reduces incentives to compete for circulation and advertising revenues and runs afoul of the Sherman Act. Northern Securities Co. v. United States, 193 U.S. 197, 328, 24 S.Ct. 436, 453, 48 L.Ed. 679. The agreement not to engage in any other publishing business in Pima County was a division of fields also banned by the Act. Timken Roller Bearing Co. v. United States, 341 U.S. 593, 71 S.Ct. 971, 95 L.Ed. 1199. The joint operating agreement exposed the restraints so clearly and unambiguously as to justify the rather rare use of a summary judgment in the antitrust field. See Northern Pac. R. Co. v. United States, 356 U.S. 1, 5, 78 S.Ct. 514, 518, 2 L.Ed.2d 545.

The only real defense of appellants was the "failing company" defense, a judicially created doctrine. The facts tendered were excluded on the § 1 charge but were admitted on the § 2 charge as well as on the § 7 charge under the Clayton Act. So whether or not the District Court was correct in excluding the evidence under the § 1 charge, it is now before us; and a consideration of it makes plain that the requirements of the failing company doctrine were not met. [The Court's discussion of the failing company defense is reproduced supra, pp. 247–248.]

Neither news gathering nor news dissemination is being regulated by the present decree. It deals only with restraints on certain business or commercial practices. The restraints on competition with which the present decree deals comport neither with the antitrust laws nor with the First Amendment. As we stated in the *Associated Press* case:

> "It would be strange indeed . . . if the grave concern for freedom of the press which prompted adoption of the First Amendment should be read as a command that the government was without power to protect that freedom. . . ."

The other points mentioned are too trivial for discussion. Divestiture of the Star seems to us quite proper. At least there is no showing of that abuse of discretion which authorizes us to recast the decree.

Affirmed.

MR. JUSTICE HARLAN, concurring in the result.

When the owners of the Citizen and the Star embarked upon their joint venture in 1940, they did not believe that they were combining their commercial operations for all time. Rather, their contract provided that the venture would last for 25 years and that the relationship would terminate in 1965 if both parties agreed to go their separate ways. It was only in 1953 that the parties agreed they would not permit their contract to expire in 1965 but would continue their relationship for another quarter century beyond the original termination date.

Nevertheless, both the Department of Justice and my Brethren have decided that the crucial question in this case is whether the original 1940 transaction could be justified on "failing company" grounds. Yet regardless of one's view of the 1940 transaction, the fact remains that if the parties had not renewed their agreement, full competition between the two newspapers would have been restored in 1965 and the Justice Department would never have begun the Sherman Act branch of this lawsuit. It would appear, then, that the decisive issue in this case is not the validity of the original 1940 transaction but the propriety of the decision taken in 1953 in which the term of the joint venture was extended by a quarter century beyond its original termination date.

In defense of the Court's approach, one may argue that if the 1940 agreement had provided that the newspapers' joint venture was to continue indefinitely, we would then have been required to decide this case on the basis of the situation prevailing at the time of the original transaction. In other words, if the agreement had been only slightly different it is arguable that we would have had no choice but to treat the transaction in the same way we would treat a total corporate merger. However this may be, I do not understand why the parties' decision to retain the advantages of flexibility should not be decisive for our purposes. If businessmen believe, after considering all the relevant factors, that future events may deprive their existing arrangements of utility, there is no reason why the antitrust laws should not view the transaction in a similar way.

While the trial court did not analyze the case in the way which I have suggested, it made sufficient factual findings to permit an evaluation of the legality of the 1953 decision extending the joint venture's term. The Court in effect found that in each year between 1940 and 1953, each newspaper operated at a profit. Moreover, in the decade preceding 1953, the joint venture's total profits increased with each succeeding year. Given this pattern of increasing profitability, I would hold that the "failing company" doctrine could not reasonably permit the two newspapers to extend the term of the agreement in 1953 at a time when it was impossible to predict whether full competition could be renewed in 1965.

[Justice Harlan's opinion concludes that, in view of the favorable profit situation which actually existed in 1965, the companies should then have made "a conscientious effort to operate independently" before claiming business necessity for continued joint operation.]

[The dissenting opinion of Justice Stewart is omitted.]

NOTES AND QUERIES

(1) *Queries.* *Citizen Publishing* reminds us that joint ventures can raise Section 7 Clayton Act problems, as well as problems under the Sherman Act. See *United States v. Penn-Olin Chemical Co.*, discussed supra pp. 280–282, the leading case for holding that the establishment of a joint venture and subsequent acquisition of the joint venture's stock is covered by Section 7. What is the difference between assessing a joint venture's legality under the Sherman Act and under the Clayton Act? Will the remedy vary (injunction rather than dissolution)? Is it possible that Sherman Act Section 1 liability is easier to find for joint ventures than Clayton Act Section 7 liability?

(2) *Legislative Response to Citizen Publishing.* Congressional reaction to the Court's decision was swift. The Newspaper Preservation Act was passed in 1970 and provides:[56]

> Sec. 2. In the public interest of maintaining a newspaper press editorially and reportorially independent and competitive in all parts of the United States, it is hereby declared to be the public policy of the United States to preserve the publication of newspapers in any city, community, or metropolitan area where a joint operating arrangement has been here-

---

56. 15 U.S.C.A. § 1801 et seq.

tofore entered into because of economic distress or is hereafter effected in accordance with the provisions of this Act.

Sec. 3. As used in this Act—

(2) The term "joint newspaper operating arrangement" means any contract, agreement, joint venture (whether or not incorporated), or other arrangement entered into by two or more newspaper owners for the publication of two or more newspaper publications, pursuant to which joint or common production facilities are established or operated and joint or unified action is taken or agreed to be taken with respect to any one or more of the following: printing; time, method, and field of publication; allocation of production facilities; distribution; advertising solicitation; circulation solicitation; business department; establishment of advertising rates; establishment of circulation rates and revenue distribution; *Provided:* That there is no merger, combination, or amalgamation of editorial or reportorial staffs, and that editorial policies be independently determined. . . .

(5) The term "failing newspaper" means a newspaper publication which, regardless of its ownership or affiliations, is in probable danger of financial failure.

Sec. 4. (a) It shall not be unlawful under any antitrust law for any person to perform, enforce, renew, or amend any joint newspaper operating arrangement entered into prior to the effective date of this Act, if at the time at which such arrangement was first entered into, regardless of ownership or affiliations, not more than one of the newspaper publications involved in the performance of such arrangement was likely to remain or become a financially sound publication: *Provided:* That the terms of a renewal or amendment of a joint operating arrangement must be filed with the Department of Justice and that the amendment does not add a newspaper publication or newspaper publications to such arrangement.

(b) It shall be unlawful for any person to enter into, perform, or enforce a joint operating arrangement, not already in effect, except with the prior written consent of the Attorney General of the United States. Prior to granting such approval, the Attorney General shall determine that not more than one of the newspaper publications involved in the arrangement is a publication other than a failing newspaper, and that approval of such arrangement would effectuate the policy and purpose of this Act.

(c) Nothing contained in the Act shall be construed to exempt from any antitrust law any predatory pricing, any predatory practice, or any other conduct in the otherwise lawful operations of a joint newspaper operating arrangement which would be unlawful under any antitrust law if engaged in by a single entity. Except as provided in this Act, no joint newspaper operating arrangement or any party thereto shall be exempt from any antitrust law. . . .[57]

What risks may be present in the requirement that the Attorney General, a political appointee serving at the will of the President, must approve new joint ventures? How do the Court's definition of the failing company doctrine and the Act's definition of a "failing newspaper" in Section 3(5) differ? Does the statute adopt the "least restrictive alternative" principle, e.g., by requiring efforts to dispose of the "failing" newspaper to a non-competitor?

57. See Comments, 12 B.C.Ind. & Com.L.Rev. 937 (1971); 46 Ind.L.J. 392 (1971); 32 Univ.Pitt.L.Rev. 347 (1971).

or by requiring joint facilities to be open to other newspapers so far as its capacity permits? [58]

(3) *Other Legislative Joint Ventures.* Congress has mandated or expressly permitted establishment of other joint ventures in order to achieve some national goals or to take account of circumstances regarded as unique to a particular industry. The joint venture to construct and operate an oil pipeline to bring North Slope Alaska oil to the all-weather port of Valdez is an example. Environmental objections and litigation under the National Environmental Policy Act and the Mineral Leasing Act of 1920 had delayed construction of the pipeline by a joint venture formed by four major oil companies.[59] The original joint venture was replaced by Alyeska Pipeline Service Company, a joint venture owned by seven oil companies directly or through subsidiary pipeline companies. In the Trans-Alaskan Pipeline Act,[60] Congress amended the Mineral Leasing Act to permit the granting of permits to Alyeska and declared no further action was required under the National Environmental Policy Act. The Act expressly provides: "The grant of a right-of-way, permit, lease, or other authorization pursuant to this chapter shall grant no immunity from the operation of the federal antitrust laws." [61] Another recent congressional effort in this area is the creation of Comsat, a private corporation jointly owned by communications carriers, the general public and the Government, to promote satellite communications.

(4) *International Joint Ventures.* Recall the Court's summary rejection of the "foreign trade conditions" argument in *Timken,* supra p. 556. Justice Jackson, dissenting in *Timken,* wrote: [62]

[T]he question [is] whether the arrangement is an unreasonable restraint of trade or a method and means of carrying on competition in trade. Timken did not sit down with competitors and divide an existing market between them. It has at all times, in all places, had powerful rivals. It was not effectively meeting their competition in foreign markets, and so it joined others in creating a British subsidiary to go after business best reachable through such a concern and a French one to exploit French markets. Of course, in doing so, it allotted appropriate territory to each and none was to enter into competition with the other or with the parent. Since many foreign governments prohibit or handicap American corporations from owning plants, entering into contracts, or engaging in business directly, this seems the only practical way of waging competition in those areas.

. . . [N]ot all agreements are conspiracies and not all restraints of trade are unlawful. In a world of tariffs, trade barriers, empire or domestic preferences, and various forms of parochialism from which we are by no means free, I think a rule that it is restraint of trade to enter a foreign market through a separate subsidiary of limited scope is virtually to foreclose foreign commerce of many kinds. It is one thing for competitors or a parent and its subsidiaries to divide the United States domestic

58. See Bay Guardian Co. v. Chronicle Publishing Co., 344 F.Supp. 1155 (N.D. Cal.1972) (rejecting several constitutional objections to the Act on a motion to strike the Act as a defense to antitrust claims). The *Bay Guardian* case and the claims of 16 other plaintiffs were settled for $1,350,000 and an agreement to negotiate access to distribution points for competing local papers. See Editor & Publisher, May 31, 1975, p. 7.

59. For a discussion of the formation of the joint venture and the litigation seeking to block construction of the pipeline, see Alyeska Pipeline Service Co. v. Wilderness Society, 421 U.S. 240, 95 S.Ct. 1612, 44 L.Ed.2d 141 (1975).

60. 43 U.S.C.A. § 1651 et seq.

61. 43 U.S.C.A. § 1654.

62. 341 U.S. at 607–08, 71 S.Ct. at 979, 95 L.Ed. at 1211.

market which is an economic and legal unit; it is another for an industry to recognize that foreign markets consist of many legal and economic units and to go after each through separate means. I think this decision will restrain more trade than it will make free.

Query. With which view do you agree? If a joint venture with competitive restrictions on territory (or price?) is necessary to enable United States' corporations to compete in foreign markets, shouldn't a rule of reason apply to weigh pro- and anticompetitive effects? Compare the analysis of the joint venture in *BMI*, supra pp. 380–388. Or is the notion of "necessity" in this context so slippery and subject to manipulation that exceptions from usual *per se* offenses should be granted only under statutory directive. Note, in this connection, the existence of the Webb-Pomerene Act and the Export Trading Company Act of 1982, discussed infra pp. 856–861, granting antitrust exemptions for certain export ventures.[63]

(5) *Spill-Over Effects of Joint Ventures.* Joint ventures may eliminate present or future competition between the co-venturers in a more subtle way than in *Citizen Publishing.* Consider the view of Judge Wyzanski in *United States v. Minnesota Mining & Manufacturing Co.*, 92 F.Supp. 947, 963 (D.Mass.1950), a case involving the legality of a joint venture by the leading American manufacturers of coated abrasives to establish manufacturing plants in foreign countries:

> Up to this point this opinion has considered whether it is a violation of that clause in section 1 of the Sherman Act dealing with "commerce with foreign nations" for the dominant manufacturers in an industry to combine to establish factories in certain foreign countries. . . . But there is another facet of this case as a whole which should not escape mention . . . .. The Government might formalize a charge that this same conduct of defendants constitutes a violation of that clause in section 1 of the Sherman Act governing combinations in restraint of "commerce among the several States". It may very well be that even though there is an economic or political barrier which entirely precludes American exports to a foreign country a combination of dominant American manufacturers to establish joint factories for the sole purpose of serving the internal commerce of that country is a *per se* violation of this other clause of the Sherman Act. The intimate association of the principal American producers in day-to-day manufacturing operations, their exchange of patent licenses and industrial know-how, and their common experience in marketing and fixing prices may inevitably reduce their zeal for competition *inter sese* in the American market. . . . It may, therefore, be subject to condemnation regardless of the reasonableness of the manufacturers' conduct in the foreign countries. In this aspect the reasonableness of the foreign conduct would, like the reasonableness of domestic price-fixing, be irrelevant. Joint foreign factories like joint domestic price-fixing would be invalid *per se* because they eliminate or restrain competition in the American domestic market. That suppression of domestic competition is in each case the fundamental evil, and the good or evil nature of the immediate manifestations of the producers' joint action is a superficial consideration.

(6) *Joint Venturers in Particular Industries—Automobiles.* Volkswagen and Nissan Motor Company (maker of Datsuns) have discussed the

---

63. Specific hypothetical examples of international joint ventures are discussed in the United States Department of Justice, Antitrust Guide For International Operations (1977).

possibility of producing Volkswagens in Japan; Ford and Toyota, and General Motors and Toyota, have attempted to negotiate agreements to build automobiles together in the United States; Chrysler and Peugeot have agreed to produce a subcompact car in the United States by late-1985. How should such ventures be analyzed under the antitrust laws? Consider also "Isuzu Is Set to Sell Its Own Cars in U.S.," N.Y. Times, April 13, 1981, p. D1. Can firms be considered competitors if they are simultaneously acting as independent entities and joint venturers?

For a decade, Isuzu Motors has produced diesel-engine trucks and small commercial vehicles that have been marketed worldwide by the General Motors Corporation, and it will soon begin assembling General Motor's little "J" cars.

But Americans will shortly be introduced to Isuzu under its own name, as the company begins selling its highly regarded diesel-engine passenger cars in the United States. The 65-year-old Japanese company has just kicked off a vigorous advertising campaign in the United States for its diesel-powered models.

Maintaining Links to G. M.

"We are now marketing the Gemini and we will soon introduce a new, very smart coupe, in both diesel and gasoline engines," said Toshio Okamoto, Isuzu's 72-year-old president. "If you see it, you will want to buy it."

Despite Isuzu's growing assertiveness in its own production and marketing plans, Mr. Okamoto denies that his company is becoming more independent of its big United States partner.

"The spirit of our affiliation remains unchanged," he said. "Our relationship can be termed competitive but cooperative. As president, I would like to continue the very fine relationship with G. M. forever."

So close has the link been between the two companies that some people say that Isuzu "should be regarded as a subsidiary of G. M.," as a researcher at the Yamaichi Economic Research Institute put it. In fact, the General Motors Corporation, the world's biggest auto maker, is Isuzu's largest shareholder, with a 34.2 percent share. . . .

However, Mr. Okamoto insisted, "We do not intend to disturb the U. S. market and want to enter it in a very small way." He said the maximum volume envisioned by company planners was 5,000 units a month, mainly diesel passenger cars that "will not compete directly with G. M. products."

Since the 1971 agreement that wedded Isuzu's expertise in diesel-powered commercial vehicles with G. M.'s global marketing, the joint venture has become known as one of the most successful business alliances in Japan.

'Both Companies Benefit'

"Relations are getting better and better, and both companies will benefit from the relationship," said an auto analyst from the Nomura Securities Company. "Isuzu's sales to G. M. will expand very sharply in the next two to three years."

G. M. also says it has high hopes for its future relations with Isuzu. "The next step is very clear," said Loring B. Lyons, vice president of the General Motors Overseas Distribution Corporation in Tokyo, "and that is that Isuzu's future is keyed to a rather full development of the passenger car." Mr. Lyons was referring to Isuzu's role in producing some of the "J" cars. . . .

"Their contributions to G. M.'s downsizing will be very usable," said G. M.'s Mr. Lyons. "Their experts have the ability to take their diesel engines and downsize them like nobody else in the world." Vehicles are downsized when technology used in larger models in adapted for use in smaller ones.

Like other Japanese auto makers, Isuzu is watching closely the outcome of Government talks between the United States and Japan on agreements to limit exports of Japanese cars to the United States.

Isuzu, Toyo Kogyo, which makes Mazdas and is 25 percent owned by the Ford Motor Company, and the Mitsubishi Motors Corporation, 15 percent owned by the Chrysler Corporation, have raised production capacity in order to provide smaller, fuel-efficient models to their American partners.[64]

64. © 1981 by The New York Times Company. Reprinted by permission. Subsequently, the Japanese government imposed "voluntary restraints" on automobile exports to the United States; General Motors made further agreements with Isuzu and Suzuki to have them supply cars to General Motors; and General Motors and Toyota entered into a joint venture, to last twelve years, to produce a subcompact car in the United States. See "G.M. and Toyota to Produce Cars in Joint Venture at Plant on Coast," N.Y.Times, Feb. 15, 1983, p. 1.

Chapter 6

VERTICAL MARKET RESTRAINTS; FRANCHISING

A. INTRODUCTION

Previous chapters have explored horizontal agreements relating to price, allocation of customers and territories, and boycotts. This chapter explores vertical restraints. Theoretical and practical distinctions between horizontal and vertical conduct suggest this separate treatment. The obvious distinction is that vertical restraints often affect only the product or service of a single firm. The effect of the restraint is usually limited to *intra*brand competition, rather than producing the broader *inter*brand effect of a horizontal restraint. In the absence of monopoly, oligopoly or horizontal collusion, consumer injury is not likely to be as manifest as in the case of horizontal restraints.

Those who view antitrust solely in relation to "economic efficiency" are more tolerant of vertical market restraints. When imposed by the rational profit maximizer, it is argued, such restraints often can be presumed to be promoting "efficiency"; when irrationally imposed, they cannot be maintained for long in the face of the discipline of a competitive market. Other schools of thought seek to take account of a wider slice of reality by recognizing that few, if any, markets are perfectly competitive, that competitive behavior is not always rational, and that predatory or vindictive purpose may significantly characterize behavior. Trademarks, brand loyalty, regulatory intervention, information lags, tax advantages at one level of a market but not another, and power derived from distinctive characteristics of the product or market structure may all serve to distort the competitive model.

A further ground of debate relating to the goals of antitrust policy involves the long tradition of protecting the independence of individual entrepreneurs. The individual freedom of retailers, franchisees and others subject to vertically imposed restraints in the operation of their business is clearly affected by vertical market restraints telling them what they can sell, where it may be sold, to whom it may be sold and/or at what price it may be sold. To what extent should antitrust policy be fashioned to protect individual freedom of decision making at each level of a distribution system? To what extent should antitrust policy limit the freedom of suppliers and retailers to mutually impose vertical restraints by contract? Should antitrust policy restrict that right only if there is some risk to "efficiency" or "consumer welfare" as defined by the economic models of some schools of thought? If some level of restraint is to be permitted, how can account be taken of disparities of bargaining power in vertical market relationships and what weight should be given buyer rationality as well as supplier rationality in the calculus? Where does the ultimate interest of consumers reside?

A variety of approaches to vertical restraints, premised on differing underlying assumptions and explanations for why these restraints are imposed in the first place, have been put forth by commentators in recent years. One school of thought argues that suppliers impose vertical market restraints for only one of two reasons:[1] 1) the restraint is a cover for an unlawful horizontal supplier conspiracy or for a "dealer cartel" in which buyers have pressured the supplier to fix the resale price; or 2) the supplier has made a rational business decision, beneficial to consumers, to maximize the efficient distribution, service, and sale of its product in competition with suppliers of similar products. The former, it is argued, can be remedied by the application of traditional horizontal antitrust analysis. As for the latter, absent horizontal collusion, it is claimed such restraints should not be declared *per se* unlawful (and perhaps should be *"per se* lawful") because the restraint is the product of a rational and legitimate business judgment by a supplier and one that is usually beneficial to the consumer by enhancing interbrand competition. For example, a supplier may decide to impose vertical customer and territorial restraints in order to induce retailers to provide suitable sales and service facilities for the product. Retailers will not undertake such investments unless they are protected from "free riders," *viz.,* intrabrand competitors selling in their territory but not making the same investment in sales and servicing facilities and presumably enhancing interbrand competition. Consequently, suppliers in a competitive market ought to be generally free, it is argued, to impose customer and territorial restraints to achieve their goal of enhancing interbrand competition and minimize the risk of "free riders."

On the other hand, it can be argued that implicit in the "free rider" notion are vague and ill-defined assumptions about the scope of a supplier's property rights and the public interest in limiting freedom of contract rights. There is a long tradition in antitrust of limiting a supplier's enforceable property rights to the protection of possessory interests and closely limiting the power to impose conditions upon the buyer's subsequent use of the property once title has been transferred.[2] Restraints upon alienation, in the absence of legislation creating such an enforceable interest, have usually been held to be unlawful by the common law. To the extent that antitrust policy admits

---

1. See Bork, The Rule of Reason and the Per Se Concept: Price Fixing and Market Division (Pt. 2), 75 Yale L.J. 373 (1966); Posner, The Rule of Reason and the Economic Approach: Reflections on the *Sylvania* Decision, 45 U.Chi.L.Rev. 1 (1977); Posner, The Next Step in Antitrust Treatment of Restricted Distribution: Per Se Legality, 48 U.Chi.L.Rev. 6 (1981); Note, A Uniform Rule of Reason for Vertical and Horizontal Nonprice Restraints, 55 So.Cal.L.Rev. 441, 444–49 (1982).

2. See Dr. Miles Medical Co. v. John D. Park & Sons Co., 220 U.S. 373, 31 S.Ct. 376, 55 L.Ed. 502 (1911); United States v. Addyston Pipe & Steel Co., 85 F. 271 (6th Cir. 1898), affirmed 175 U.S. 211, 20 S.Ct. 96, 44 L.Ed. 136 (1899).

of a legitimate need to control "free riders" trading upon a supplier's good will, by permitting enforcement of vertical market restraints, it is implicitly expanding by judicial decree a supplier's property rights in the goods or services sold and colliding with the common law suspicion of restraints upon alienation.[3]

By the same token, recognition of a wider freedom of contract by suppliers and buyers in the name of a need to control "free riders" collides with deeply rooted judicial suspicions of restrictive covenants. Because of a public interest in receiving the benefits of every person's competitive effort, the law has long recognized the community's right to limit the freedom to contract away one's freedom to compete.[4] Indeed, the language of Section 1 of the Sherman Act and the judicial development of the rule of reason are directly traceable to this long standing assertion of governmental power to restrict the freedom of traders to impose or agree upon restrictive covenants limiting one's freedom to compete.[5]

Other commentators see vertical restraints as a way of increasing "transactional" efficiencies by permitting an integration of marketing functions by contractual agreement where it is rational to do so.[6] No presumption of illegality, it is claimed, ought be attached to such arrangements where freely entered into in competitive markets, because the savings arrived at will be passed along to consumers as a result of *inter*brand competition forcing suppliers and retailers agreeing to *inter*brand vertical restraints to meet the competition from substitutes.[7] Still others frame the analysis in terms of balancing power between suppliers and buyers, while juggling industry structure and concentration with the other hand, so as to distinguish the lawful vertical restraint from that which "ought" not be lawful.[8]

This current ferment in the antitrust analysis of vertical market restraints is best understood in terms of its historical evolution and

3. In Dr. Miles Medical Co. v. John D. Park & Sons, supra note 2, Dr. Miles argued that its monopoly over its own goods "carries with it the right to control the entire trade of the produced article, and prevent any competition that otherwise might arise between wholesale and retail dealers." 220 U.S., at 403, 31 S.Ct., at 383, 55 L.Ed., at 517. The court rejected the contention holding: "The fact that the market may not be supplied with the particular article unless he produces it is a practical consequence which does not enlarge his right of property in what he does produce." Id.

4. See Goldschmid, Antitrust's Neglected Stepchild: A Proposal for Dealing with Restrictive Covenants Under Federal Law, 73 Colum.L.Rev. 1193 (1973).

5. See United States v. Addyston Pipe & Steel Co., supra note 2. For arguments favoring a standard of presumptive illegality applied to some or all vertical restraints, see Andersen, The Antitrust Consequences of Manufacturer-Suggested Retail Prices—The Case for Presumptive Illegality, 54 Wash.L.Rev. 763 (1979); Commoner, Vertical Territorial and Customer Restrictions: White Motor and Its Aftermath, 81 Harv.L.Rev. 1419 (1968); Flynn, The Function and Dysfunction of Per Se Rules in Vertical Market Restraints, 58 Wash.U.L.Q. 767 (1980); Jenkenson & Foster, Per Se Rules Against Vertical Restraints: Down But Not Out, 58 Wash.U.L.Q. 795 (1980).

6. See Goldberg, The Law and Economics of Vertical Restrictions: A Relational Perspective, 58 Texas L.Rev. 91 (1979).

7. Id.

8. See Williamson, Assessing Vertical Market Restrictions: Antitrust Ramifications of the Transaction Cost Approach, 127 U.Pa.L.Rev. 953 (1979).

by looking at each type of restraint according to its consequences—
i.e., price fixing, territorial and customer restraints, etc. The initial
section of this chapter examines the development of a *per se* rule for
vertical price fixing and legislative responses seeking to mitigate the
rigor of the rule in certain circumstances under the banner of the
"Fair Trade" movement. Subsequent sections examine other vertical
market restraints—territorial and customer restraints, exclusive dealing, tying, and selection and termination of dealers.

With each of these restraints, it will be important to keep in mind
that a major area for dispute in vertical cases is the problem of defining "contract", "combination" or "conspiracy." As with horizontal
cases, part of the difficulty is how much circumstantial evidence is
required to infer agreement; unlike horizontal cases, however, the issue frequently arises in the context of a threatened and coercive refusal to deal designed to engender conformity without voluntary
agreement. In what circumstances ought a court infer agreement
because of coerced conformity? Should agreement be inferred when
the buyer or supplier refuses to go along with a coercive demand to
agree to a vertical restraint?

Many vertical restraints arise in the context of franchising. Special franchising statutes have been enacted to regulate various aspects of this growing area, a topic on which we conclude the chapter.[9]
The concept of franchising has been used to describe many different
methods of marketing goods or services. In automobile distribution,
for example, franchising refers to a contract with a retailer to market
and service a manufacturer's product under the manufacturer's
brand name.[10] The arrangement may designate a geographic area as
a territory to be served by the dealer and require the dealer to sell
exclusively to retail customers thereby reserving for the manufacturer sales to car rental or police agencies. Another form of franchising, widely used in the soft drink bottling industry, involves the licensing of a distributor to perform part of the manufacturing and
wholesale distribution functions, usually under a contract granting an
exclusive territory to the licensee as well as a license to utilize the
franchisor's trademarks.[11] Franchising in the marketing of petrole-

9. See Brown, Franchising—Realities
and Remedies (2d ed. 1978); Thompson,
Franchise Operations and Antitrust
(1971); Rosenfeld, The Law of Franchising (1970); Business and Legal Problems
of the Franchise (P.L.I.1968); Franchising—Today's Legal and Business Problems (P.L.I.1970); The Economic Effects
of Franchising (Comm. Print), Senate Select Comm. on Small Business, 92d
Cong., 1st Sess. (1971).

10. The automobile industry was one
of the first industries to adopt a franchise method of distribution. It did so, in
part, as a method of raising capital to finance expansion of the industry. For
histories of the industry and its financing
see Seltzer, A Financial History of the

American Automobile Industry (1928);
Hewitt, Automobile Franchise Agreements (1956). Recurring problems in the
automobile franchise relationship led to
the passage of a special statute governing the relationship. See Automobile
Dealers' Day in Court Act, 15 U.S.C.
§§ 1221–25, discussed infra.

11. See Soft Drink Interbrand Competition Act of 1980, 15 U.S.C. §§ 3501–03.
Analysis of the Act and its history may
be found in Abrams, Antitrust Law in
the Soft Drink Industry, 26 Antitrust
Bull. 697 (1981); Stein, The Soft Drink
Interbrand Competition Act of 1980: Antitrust Loses its Fizz, 18 Harv.J. of
Legis. 91 (1981).

um products may involve the exchange of a complex array of interests including the right to the use of a nationally advertised brand name, lease of facilities and real estate owned by the franchisor, authority to make credit card sales, the right to sell nationally advertised tires, batteries and accessories (TBA), and training in the servicing of motor vehicles.[12] Sometimes a contract may require the dealer to take company sponsored TBA (tied product) as a price for lease of the facility or the right to sell gasoline under a nationally advertised trademark (typing product), thereby raising the complex issue of the legality of "tying arrangements" under the antitrust laws.[13] The franchise concept is also employed in pyramid sales schemes whereby participants are induced to recruit others as salesmen of a product, with the expectancy of mounting profits based on the efforts of subsequent recruits in an ever-growing pyramid of "franchised" seller-recruiters.[14]

In recent years, franchising has proliferated to the point where it is estimated that in 1981, $376 billion in retail sales were made through franchise distribution systems—approximately 32 percent of all retail sales.[15] The modern American travelling the roads in an automobile bought from a franchised auto dealer and supplied with franchisee-dispensed gasoline has a wide choice of franchised fast food chains, motels, sports centers or shopping outlets to visit. One may watch a television program disseminated by a broadcaster who holds a government granted franchise and "distributes" network programs under a franchise called a "network affiliation agreement". When a person chooses to move to a new city, he may locate new housing through a nationwide system of franchised realtors and is likely to ship household belongings by an independent trucker franchised by an interstate moving company, or to haul his own belongings in a truck or trailer provided by a franchised rental firm. Marriages and adoptions may be arranged by franchised dating services and adoption agencies; while one's physical well-being may be looked after by franchised health spas and a franchised hospital. One may even spend one's final days in a franchised "nursing home,"

12. Legislative responses to the recurring problems in the gasoline franchising area are explored infra pp. 782–797.

13. Recurring tensions in franchising wholesale and retail distributors of petroleum products have generated numerous legislative investigations. See Hearings, Impact of Gasoline Marketing Practices on the Consumer, Consumer Subcomm. of the Senate Commerce Comm., 93rd Cong., 1st Sess. (1973); Hearings, Marketing Practices in the Gasoline Industry, Subcomm. on Antitrust & Monopoly of the Senate Judiciary Comm., 92nd Cong., 1st & 2nd Sess. (1972).

14. The fraudulent aspects of such schemes vis-a-vis the franchisees, who

are frequently required to pay for joining the scheme, has been recognized. Securities Exchange Commission v. Glenn W. Turner, Enterprises, Inc., 474 F.2d 476 (9th Cir.), certiorari denied 414 U.S. 821, 94 S.Ct. 117, 38 L.Ed.2d 53 (1973); Securities Exchange Commission v. Koscot Interplanetary, Inc., 497 F.2d 473 (5th Cir. 1974); Note, Federal Regulation of Pyramid Sales Schemes, 1974 U.Ill.L.F. 137 (1974); Note, Pyramid Schemes: Dare to be Regulated, 61 Geo.L.J. 1257 (1973).

15. See United States Department of Commerce, Franchising in the Economy, 1979–1981, pp. 1, 12 (1981). The number of franchised establishments is estimated to be 476,000, employing 4.6 million. Id.

be remembered by friends in a franchised funeral establishment, and be buried in a franchised cemetery.

The antitrust and other responses to the growth of franchising, as well as vertical restraints elsewhere, raise again questions previously encountered in the context of horizontal restraints: When is a grouping of "independent" entrepreneurs properly regarded as a "joint enterprise" whose mutual constraints are entitled to a generous "rule of reason" analysis? To what extent should antitrust policy seek to preserve independent economic units at each level of a distribution system, even at some cost to "efficiency"? Should the arbitrary exercise of economic power be subject to legal constraints even where the power is non-conspiratorial and non-monopolistic? To what extent are the antitrust laws a guarantor that each individual's success or failure will be determined by the competitive process viewed in light of the characteristics of the trade involved, as well as a guarantor of competition more generally? Can conflicting goals be synthesized in legal rules that are understandable and predictable, yet take account of the unique characteristics of individual circumstances?

B.   VERTICAL PRICE FIXING

1.   ECONOMIC SIGNIFICANCE AND THE "FAIR TRADE" MOVEMENT

Vertical price fixing accomplished through a seller-buyer agreement and fixing the price at which a buyer or buyers can resell the product was condemned relatively early (1911) in the history of judicial interpretation of the Sherman Act. It was condemned on a basis which did not permit mitigation, excuse or justification:

[A]greements or combinations between dealers, having for their sole purpose the destruction of competition and the fixing of prices, are injurious to the public interest and void. They are not saved by the advantages which the participants expect to derive from the enhanced price to the consumer. . . . [W]here commodities have passed into the channels of trade and are owned by dealers, the validity of agreements to prevent competition and to maintain prices is not to be determined by the circumstance whether they were produced by several manufacturers or by one, or whether they were previously owned by one or by many. The complainant having sold its product at prices satisfactory to itself, the public is entitled to whatever advantage may be derived from competition in the subsequent traffic.[16]

The condemnation of vertical price fixing sparked efforts by small wholesalers and retailers for an exemption from the Sherman Act, so they could continue their traditional practice of fixing retail prices regionally or nationwide. Louis Brandeis, then a Boston lawyer, became a leader in the effort; an effort which has been described as "one of the longest, most relentless, and best organized lobbying ef-

16.   Dr. Miles Medical Co. v. John D. Park & Sons Co., 220 U.S. 373, 408–09, 31 S.Ct. 376, 384–85, 55 L.Ed. 502, 519 (1911).

forts in American history." [17] Brandeis was motivated by an intense dislike of large business firms and a preference for a maximization of the number of small business firms, a position not necessarily in the best interest of the consumer. Brandeis' involvement in the movement to legitimize retail price fixing for the benefit of small business caused one historian to observe: "It shows perhaps better than any other episode precisely for whom Brandeis spoke and why in many ways he was less the 'Peoples Lawyer' than the petty bourgeoisie's lawyer." [18]

The Great Depression of the 1930's and the growth of chains in retail distribution resulted in added pressure from retailers for state legislation permitting some degree of vertical price fixing or "resale price maintenance." [19] Such legislation was passed under the rubric of "Fair Trade" laws. To permit the application of such laws where they might impact on interstate commerce, Congress exempted resale price maintenance agreements pursuant to valid state laws from the prohibitions of Section 1 of the Sherman Act and Section 5 of the Federal Trade Commission Act. The original exemption statute, the Miller-Tydings Act of 1937, was interpreted by the Supreme Court to validate only consensual arrangements between the supplier and the distributor; but the McGuire Act of 1952 made it clear that such an agreement between the supplier and *any distributor* was to bind non-signers, i.e. all distributors.[20] The exemption was limited to vertical price fixing agreements on trademarked goods in "free and open competition" with commodities of the same class produced or distributed by others. The McGuire Act was thus an extreme expression of the view that interbrand competition sufficed to protect the consumer interest, and that supplier-distributor collaboration in the distribution of a trademarked article should be regarded as a legitimate joint enterprise.

At the zenith of the movement, 45 states had Fair Trade laws of varying scope, passionately supported by various classes of small re-

17. T. McCraw, "Rethinking the Trust Question", in Regulation In Perspective, 1, 46 (T. McCraw Ed. 1981).

18. Id. at 47.

19. See generally B. Yamey, The Economics of Resale Price Maintenance (1954); Federal Trade Commission Report on Resale Price Maintenance (1945); Fulda, Resale Price Maintenance, 21 U.Chi.L.Rev. 175 (1954); Bowman, Resale Price Maintenance—A Monopoly Problem, 25 U.Chi.J. of Bus. 141 (1951); Report of the Attorney General's National Committee to Study the Antitrust Laws 149 (1955). Leading articles in the field are reprinted in, "Resale Price Maintenance", 12 J.Rep. Antitrust L. & Econ. 587 *et seq.* (1981). The foregoing are critical of resale price maintenance.

For a vigorous defense of the practice by one who is otherwise an advocate of free competition, see Adams, Resale Price Maintenance: Fact and Fancy, 64 Yale L.J. 967 (1955), to which there was a reply, Herman, A Note on Fair Trade, 65 Yale L.J. 23 (1955), followed by a rebuttal, Adams, Fair Trade and the Art of Prestidigitation, 65 Yale L.J. 196 (1955).

20. Pub.L. No. 542, 66 Stat. 631 (1952); repealed Pub.L. No. 94–145, 89 Stat. 801 (1975), 15 U.S.C.A. §§ 1, 45 (1976 Supp.). As to the narrow interpretation of the Miller-Tydings Act, Pub.L. No. 314, 50 Stat. 693 (1937), see Schwegmann Brothers v. Calvert Distillers Corp., 341 U.S. 384, 71 S.Ct. 745, 95 L.Ed. 1035 (1951), rehearing denied 341 U.S. 956, 71 S.Ct. 1011, 95 L.Ed. 1377.

tailers.[21] By the time Congress enacted the 1975 repeal [22] of the Miller-Tydings and McGuire Acts, only 13 states had Fair Trade laws binding non-signers, while another 23 states had limited or severely restricted Fair Trade laws. Resale price maintenance under Fair Trade laws is now possible only for sales having no effect on interstate commerce. State control of liquor distribution, previously thought to be nearly absolute under the Twenty-first Amendment,[23] has recently been held not to authorize states to delegate price fixing authority to producers and distributors pursuant to a "fair trade" law for alcoholic beverages. In *California Retail Liquor Dealers Association v. Midcal Aluminum Co.*,[24] the Supreme Court narrowly construed the Twenty-first Amendment's grant of exclusive authority to the states over the "transportation and importation" of liquor into the states as not including the power to authorize "fair trade" agreements in the liquor trade in violation of the Sherman Act. The four decades of experience with legally sanctioned vertical price fixing in the liquor trade and elsewhere provide a useful source of information on the economic and other effects of vertical price fixing, many forms of which survived the repeal of the explicit antitrust exemption.

When a supplier, either on his own initiative or under pressure from distributors, undertakes to set the price at which distributors resell his product, the immediate and most obvious consequence is to eliminate price competition among the distributors. It is very much as if the distributors themselves had agreed to avoid price competition. On the average, consumers will have to pay more for the product. Occasionally, the supplier's advertising of a standard retail price may prevent a storekeeper from charging a higher price. Some stud-

21. For example, a trade paper for retailers of photographic equipment analyzed the resale price maintenance problem under the caption "Fair Trade, Karl Marx, and the Superstate:"

"Profit is getting thinner all the time. It is a regrettable fact that many have succumbed to this sly, divisive propaganda against what is claimed to be an outmoded distribution system but which, in reality, is an attack against the 'middle class' which operates the retail stores of America, and is the backbone of our distribution system. . . . WE OF THE 'MIDDLE CLASS' make up about 65% of the total population. In this group, according to the latest Department of Commerce reports, there are 1,783,400 retail stores and 863,900 service establishments, of which 95% are small businesses. Destroy the possibility of making a profit, and the 'middle class' is wiped out and there is nothing left but to become a pawn of an all-powerful State.

"THAT'S A NASTY PICTURE. So far as I know, this is the first time this dangerous drift has been critically examined and attributed to an unthinking acceptance of the 'party line'. Your Bu-

reau sincerely believes that none of us can afford to be lethargic about this situation. Once we're awake and alert we can take positive corrective steps against this creeping form of socialism."

Bulletin No. 3 of the Photo Retailers' Service Bureau, Feb. 8, 1955. On the other hand, Fair Trade laws which require some sellers to abide by prices satisfactory to others have also been denounced as socialistic or "communistic" regimentation of the economy. Concurring opinion, Liquor Store v. Contintental Distilling Corp., 40 So.2d 371, 386 (Fla. 1949).

22. See Consumer Goods Pricing Act, Pub.L. 94–145, 89 Stat. 801 (1975).

23. See Note, Effect of the Twenty-First Amendment On State Authority To Control Intoxicating Liquors, 75 Colum. L.Rev. 1578 (1975). Note, New York State Liquor Market: The Rocky Road To Competition, 54 Cornell L.Rev. 113 (1968); Note, Fair Trade of Liquor In California: Is Bartering For Booze Bad? 6 Cal.West.L.Rev. 282 (1970).

24. 445 U.S. 97, 100 S.Ct. 937, 63 L.Ed.2d 233 (1980), infra p. 813.

ies show that producer-controlled retail prices do not rise as rapidly as free prices in a period of general inflation, perhaps because the larger profit margin makes it possible to absorb cost increases for a time. A producer may wish to avoid the unfavorable long range effect on the market for his product by restraining retailers from making "unreasonable" price increases to exploit a temporary shortage. But the overall effect of resale price maintenance must be to inflate retailer profit margins, as attested not only by economic theory and comparative studies of prices in states which did and those which did not legalize resale price maintenance, but also by the fact that such laws were promoted by retailer organizations and opposed by consumer organizations. Both may be supposed to have known their own interests.

On the other hand, the extent of any increase in price attainable by vertical controls was certainly limited by the availability in fact, and the legal requirement under the Fair Trade laws, of products competitive with the price-fixed product. But oligopoly economics teaches that competition is tempered as the number of price-makers dwindles, even without explicit agreement among them. Thus, the retail price of gasoline will be more stable and uniform among stations if a handful of major refiners are setting resale prices than it would be if each service station operator were setting his own price, since each major supplier can foresee that a price reduction will gain nothing but a matching price reduction by the others, and each knows that the other makes the same calculation. An unorganized multitude of retailers cannot rely on such calculations, since some unpredictable individual may decide rightly or wrongly that his interests will benefit from price-cutting. Moreover, free competition at the retail level often forces competitive price-cutting among suppliers, as retailers seek price concessions to enable them to meet competing retailers' selling prices.[25]

Among the arguments advanced for the proposition that resale price maintenance benefits consumers as well as merchants, despite the higher cash prices paid for the price-fixed articles, are the following. Unrestrained competition among retailers causes some of them to engage in fraudulent practices. For example, a hard-pressed gasoline service station dealer may be driven to pass off inferior gasoline as premium quality gasoline. Unscrupulous merchants use popular

25. This effect is attested by the enactment of state laws to prevent such concessions, e.g., the New Jersey Motor Fuels Practices Act of 1953, 56 N.J.Stat. Ann. §§ 56:6–19 et seq. Significantly, the act made no exception for concessions to meet competition, as does the Robinson-Patman Act. See Philadelphia Evening Bulletin, Dec. 1, 1954, reporting hearing on a complaint under the Act, proposing to revoke the business licenses of 12 leading refiners charged with "fostering gasoline price wars." Cf. Federal Trade Commission v. Sun Oil Co., p. —

supra. See Interim Report on Distribution Practices in the Petroleum Industry, Subcomm. No. 5, Select Comm. on Small Business, H.Rep. No. 1157, 85th Cong., 1st Sess. (1957).

Resale prices of milk are maintained under some regulatory systems as a means of increasing the fund available for paying higher prices to the farmer-producer. See also, "Discount Computer Market Grows as Dealers Unload Excess Supply," Wall St.J., p. 23, Jan. 24, 1983.

brand-name products as "loss leaders," advertising them at less than cost, in order to lure customers to the shop where they will then be overcharged on other articles purchased.

In response to these contentions, it may be argued that fraud is a matter for public policing, and that the temptation to cheat is not substantially reduced by resale price maintenance. There will always be some marginal dealers losing money, and the prospect of increasing profit by chicanery is always open to the unscrupulous. Some "tricks of the trade" appear to be built on resale price maintenance; for example, "when General Electric presented its 1954 model vacuum cleaner to the trade, it announced a list price of $89.95, although the fair trade price was only $79.95. In short, the $89.95 list price was there for the dealer to play with." [26] As for "loss leaders," aside from the want of persuasive evidence that those who would use this form of advertising do in fact charge more for other goods, there is no way of preventing such meretricious "give-aways" unless every article in the store were price-fixed and in addition the store-keeper were prevented from offering his customers free parking, special delivery service, and other valuable attractions.

Resale price maintenance was also defended as providing the necessary margin which enables retailers to provide attractive facilities and services; but opponents took the position that customers should have the choice between low-price-non-service stores and higher-priced elegance. Similarly a merchant should be able to elect one or the other policy as most suited to his resources and market. On the other hand, some argued that price protection was essential to the survival of smaller units, and that the extra cost, if any, which the consumer paid was a kind of insurance premium against extortionate prices he would have had to pay to monopolistic retailers that would have survived unrestrained competition.[27]

The differential effect of resale price maintenance as between large and small merchants was an important aspect of the practice in another respect. Large retailing establishments had open to them the "private brand" escape from the price control mechanism. The producer of a desirable, price-fixed, branded commodity would furnish the same item to his bigger distributors without the brand or with a brand or label specified by the distributor. These distributors then push their "own" brands at lower prices, leaving the smaller merchant to sell decreasing quantities of price-protected items.

As between retailers of the same size, resale price maintenance tended to restrict the more efficient units from expanding their markets. A retailer who was successful in reducing his operating costs might, for example, have been able to sell a product at a lower price while yet maintaining the same profit margin as his higher cost competitor. Fair Trade protected the latter from this threat.

26. Consumer Reports, March 1954, p. 142.

27. But see Fulda, op. cit. supra n. 19, on the prosperity of merchants in non-Fair Trade states.

Another effect of resale price maintenance was the tendency to draw new classes of distributors into the fields where profit margins were fat and secure, thus dividing up the distribution of specific lines of merchandise among more and more units. Professor Fulda reported on this as follows: [28]

> According to The Progressive Grocer, the national magazine of the food trade, 70% of all food and grocery stores sold drug items in 1950, compared with 64% in 1949, 51% in 1946, and 37% in 1941. "[T]he percent of drug sales to total store sales is steadily rising . . .. Customers are becoming more and more accustomed to drug departments in food stores . . .. In all likelihood food stores will become the No. 1 outlet for a number of popular, frequently used drug products . . .. The cause of this development is "the low margin on many food items." Indeed, The Progressive Grocer reported in January 1952 that food stores "depended more and more on the sidelines and supplementary items to balance out their margins and profits. Whether a grocer made a satisfactory profit frequently depended upon how well he merchandised the supplementary lines like drugs and toiletries . . .. Because of their favorable margin an increasing number of grocers added these lines." This year, "nearly 50% of the total U. S. volume in popular health and beauty aids" are being sold in chain and independent retail food stores. More than half of Colgate's dentifrice sales are in food stores, and in Springfield, Massachusetts, three supermarkets sell more Pepsodent than the top fifteen drug stores. All this seems to be due to the fact that the average margin on drug proprietaries is about 33% and on food products 16 or 17%. Thus the success of the druggists in obtaining enactment of fair-trade laws created a new and presumably unexpected competitive peril by inducing an industry, accustomed to get along on much lower margins without a legislative umbrella, to invade their domain. . . .

When repealing the exemption for state fair trade legislation, the Senate Committee Report took note of the failure rate of small retailers in states with and without Fair Trade laws. In states without Fair Trade laws the 1972 firm failure rate per 10,000 firms was 23.3; in states with partially effective Fair Trade laws (laws which did not bind non-assenting wholesalers or retailers to the price fixed by Fair Trade contracts with assenting wholesalers or retailers) the failure rate was 32.2; and in states with fully effective Fair Trade laws (binding non-assenting wholesalers and retailers to the Fair Trade contract price) the failure rate was 35.9.[29] The Committee also reported that the 1956–1972 rate of growth of small retail stores in non-Fair Trade states was 32% higher than the rate of growth in Fair Trade states. The Senate Report relied also on studies which estimated that Fair Trade laws increased prices on fair traded goods 18–27% and that the elimination of fair trade would save consumers

28. Fulda, op. cit. supra n. 19.

29. Consumer Goods Pricing Act of 1975, Sen.Rep.No.94–466, p. 3, 94th Cong. 1st Sess. (1975).

$1.2 billion a year in 1969 dollars.[30] There were few defenders of "Fair Trade" in its final days as antitrust standards governing resale price maintenance were restored to full vigor.

The experience with "Fair Trade" in the United States and repeal of the federal antitrust exemption for state laws authorizing resale price maintenance is also important because of the current debate over whether vertical price fixing agreements ought to remain *per se* unlawful. Followers of a strict neo-classical analysis of antitrust issues argue that the only reasons suppliers would seek to impose or agree to resale price maintenance arrangements are: (1) as a cover for a supplier or dealer cartel fixing prices; or (2) to foster and protect legitimate business interests or goals of the supplier.[31] Where resale price maintenance is used as a cover for supplier or dealer cartel arrangements, it is argued, the traditional *per se* rule against horizontal price fixing is sufficient to remedy the problem. Where there is no horizontal conspiracy, it is claimed, one should assume that a supplier in a competitive market will only impose or agree to resale price maintenance with distributors to obtain a legitimate goal of the supplier in securing an optimal level of dealer presale services. Absent protection from other dealers ("free riders") undercutting a dealer adhering to a supplier imposed resale price agreement, suppliers would be unable to obtain dealers willing to invest in sales facilities, warranty work, and other expensive undertakings a supplier believes necessary to the effective marketing of its product. Thus, it is argued vertical price fixing ought not be subject to a *per se* prohibition.

Several criticisms have been leveled at this line of analysis, a line of analysis reminiscent of the arguments made for "Fair Trade" and sounding like a defense of the desires of the not-so-petty bourgeoise supplier rather than a defense of the consumer's interest. The "free rider" analysis results in displacement of the market process deciding what pre-sale services are efficient and wanted by consumers.[32] Consumers not wishing such services should be free to patronize discounters for the product. Moreover, it is questioned whether such restrictions are objectively beneficial or simply an abstract rationale for justifying the supplier or dealers to take a "free ride" on consumers by charging prices higher than those which would prevail if retailers could compete on price.[33] Further, artificial product differentiation, coupled with resale price maintenance, may be used to encourage dealers to favor and push high-priced goods to the disadvantage of equally or more efficient competitors selling low-priced goods, thereby distorting interbrand competition.[34] In addition, the hypothesis ignores the imbalance of bargaining power found in many

30. Id.

31. Bork, Vertical Restraints: Schwinn Overruled, 1977 Sup.Ct.Rev. 171; Posner, supra note 1. For a survey and criticism of the debate, see Stewart & Roberts, Viability of the Antitrust Per Se Illegality Rule: Schwinn Down, How Many To Go?, 58 Wash.U.L.Q. 727 (1980).

32. See Sullivan, Antitrust, § 145 (1977); Commoner, supra note 5, at 1433; Pitofsky, The Sylvania Case: Antitrust Analysis of Non-Price Vertical Restrictions, 78 Column.L.Rev. 1, 6 (1978).

33. Stewart & Roberts, supra note 31 at 753.

34. Id. at 755–56.

supplier-dealer relationships, assumes perfect competition is the rule rather than a rare exception in reality and gives little or no weight to distributor and consumer rationality as values worthy of consideration.[35] The hypothesis simply assumes supplier rationality subject to a perfectly competitive market to be a sufficient surrogate for these values.

A legalistic objection may also be found in the decision by Congress to repeal the "Fair Trade" exemption. In the Senate Report accompanying the repealer, there is language which might be interpreted as expressing an intent to restore fully a *per se* rule for vertical price fixing. The Report states:

> This proposed legislation repeals the Miller-Tydings Act which enables the States to enact fair trade laws and the McGuire Act which permits States to enact nonsigner provisions. Without these exemptions the agreements they authorize would violate the antitrust laws.
>
> . . .
>
> Opponents were primarily service-oriented manufacturers who claimed retailers would not give adequate service unless they were guaranteed a good margin of profit. [The "free rider" rationale.] However, the manufacturer could solve this problem by placing a clause in the distributorship contract requiring the retailer to maintain adequate service. Moreover, the manufacturer has the right to select distributors who are likely to emphasize service.
>
> . . .
>
> The repeal of fair trade laws does not affect the use of suggested prices by a manufacturer. However, the use of suggested prices in such a way as to coerce adherence to them would be illegal. [36]

Whether the Supreme Court will read the repeal of the Fair Trade exemption as congressional intent to retain the long established *per se* prohibition on vertical price fixing may be decided in *Spray-Rite Service Corp. v. Monsanto Co.*[37] The Court has granted *certiorari* in a case imposing treble damages for vertical price fixing where the Reagan Administration has intervened on the side of the defendant. The Government argued in its *amicus* petition in the case that vertical price fixing should be measured on a rule of reason basis rather than on a standard of *per se* illegality.

35. See Flynn, supra note 5 at 773–74; Goldberg, supra note 6.

36. Consumer Goods Pricing Act of 1975, S.Rep. No. 94–466, 94th Cong., 1st Sess. 1, 3 (1975), reprinted in 1975 U.S. Code Cong. & Ad.News 1569, 1570–1572.

37. 684 F.2d 1226 (7th Cir. 1982), certiorari granted ___ U.S. ___, 103 S.Ct. 1249, ___ L.Ed.2d ___ (1983). The Court, in Continental T. V., Inc. v. G.T.E. Sylvania, Inc., 433 U.S. 36, 51 n. 18, 97 S.Ct. 2549, 2558 n. 18, 53 L.Ed.2d 568, 581 n. 18 (1977), took note of the fact that "Congress . . . has expressed its approval of a *per se* analysis of vertical price restrictions by repealing . . . fair trade pricing at the option of the individual states."

NOTES

(1) *RPM and Political Corruption.* Elimination of resale price competition by law can have the practical political significance illustrated in the following Associated Press dispatch from the Philadelphia Inquirer of Aug. 22, 1953:

> Harrisburg, Aug. 21, (AP).—Gov. John S. Fine said today he supposed that State milk contracts were awarded to dealers "friendly to the Administration." The Governor made the statement when asked to comment on a remark by Alan Reynolds, Secretary of Property and Supplies, that tie bids on some million dollars a year in milk contracts at State institutions were channeled to the Governor's office. . . . Reynolds earlier told a newsman that he had the sole right to break ties in milk contracts under the law but that he sent some of them to Fine's office because "I don't want to give them to someone outside the (Republican) party." Tie bids often occur in milk contracts because of the State's minimum price law. No milk dealer can bid to sell milk at a price under the floor set by the State Milk Control Commission.

(2) *RPM and National Defense.* The terms in which sharp competition is reported in mass publications, as well as trade journals, are revealing. The common phrase for it is "price war", thus lending to competition some of the unfavorable overtones of international blood-letting, and inviting a receptive attitude towards legislation which might bring "peace" to the embattled merchants. The dealer who sells below the standard price will be known to his fellow dealers as a "chiseler" or, in the more elegant phrase of Mr. Justice Holmes, a "knave".[38] Support for the right of the dealer to make a "normal" profit is so powerful that there was a sharp contest in Congress over whether national defense emergency price controls should be paramount over state resale price maintenance laws.[39]

(3) *RPM and Religion.* The Sunday Closing or Blue Laws, held valid by the Supreme Court of the United States as secular regulation despite religious background and language of the statutes, have been tailored by amendment and by discriminatory enforcement to protect some dealers against competition by "discount" stores.[40] The Philadelphia Inquirer, Dec. 31, 1959, pp. 1 and 22, quoted Mayor Dilworth of Philadelphia announcing the following enforcement policy: "big department stores and discount houses should be hit by police action rather than the little neighborhood stores."

2. RESALE PRICE MAINTENANCE UNDER THE ANTITRUST LAWS

In 1911 the Supreme Court held, in *Dr. Miles Medical Co. v. John D. Park & Sons*,[41] that an agreement between a supplier and its distributors to maintain resale prices was an unlawful restraint of trade. The suit was brought against a wholesaler, Park, who was not one of Dr. Miles' authorized distributors, but was acquiring Dr. Miles patent medicines from an authorized distributor at cut-rate prices. Park

---

38. See dissent in Dr. Miles Medical Co. v. John D. Park & Sons, 220 U.S. 373, 412, 31 S.Ct. 376, 386, 55 L.Ed. 502, 520 (1911).

39. See Farragher and Heinemann, Price Controls and Anti-trust Laws, 19 Law and Cont.Prob. 648, 677 (1954).

40. McGowan v. Maryland, 366 U.S. 420, 81 S.Ct. 1101, 6 L.Ed.2d 393 (1961); Two Guys from Harrison-Allentown, Inc. v. McGinley, 366 U.S. 582, 81 S.Ct. 1135, 6 L.Ed.2d 551 (1961).

41. 220 U.S. 373, 31 S.Ct. 376, 55 L.Ed. 502 (1911).

was reselling below the prices stipulated in Dr. Miles' distributor contracts, and was supplying price-cutting retailers. The Court refused to enjoin Park from "maliciously interfering" with, or inducing breach of, the distributor's contract with Dr. Miles.

Argument addressed to the reasonableness of Dr. Miles' effort to control resale prices was unavailing. It was urged in vain that Dr. Miles' product, manufactured under a secret formula, might lawfully have been withheld from the market altogether, so that the public was benefited rather than prejudiced by his making the product available under whatever conditions he chose. It was held to be no justification for the restraint that there were other competing medicines, or that Dr. Miles purpose was to protect its goodwill and the reputation of its product.

The Court's rationale for finding Dr. Miles' conduct unlawful stressed both the common law property prohibition upon restraints on alienation and the common law contractual doctrine prohibiting restrictive covenants. The Court noted that "restraints upon alienation have been generally regarded as obnoxious to public policy" because they interfere with the "great freedom of traffic in such things" and " 'are against trade and traffic and bargaining and contracting between man and man.' " [42] The Court further noted:

> If there be an advantage to the manufacturer in the maintenance of fixed retail prices, the question remains whether it is one which he is entitled to secure by agreements restricting the freedom of trade on the part of dealers who own what they sell. As to this, the complainant can fare no better with its plan of identical contracts than could the dealers themselves if they formed a combination and endeavored to establish the same restrictions, and thus to achieve the same result, by agreement with each other. If the immediate advantage they would thus obtain would not be sufficient to sustain such a direct agreement, the asserted ulterior benefit to the complainant cannot be regarded as sufficient to support the system.[43]

Since *Dr. Miles*, the Supreme Court has gradually evolved and consistently applied a rule of *per se* illegality to resale price maintenance agreements or vertical price fixing.[44] The rule has been applied without regard to whether the price fixed is a maximum or a minimum, and it has been applied to the sale of all products—including those which are trademarked,[45] patented [46] or copyrighted.[47]

---

42. 220 U.S. at 404–405, 31 S.Ct., at 383, 55 L.Ed., at 517.

43. 220 U.S. at 407, 31 S.Ct. at 384, 55 L.Ed. at 518.

44. See Straus v. Victor Talking Machine Co., 243 U.S. 490, 37 S.Ct. 412, 61 L.Ed. 866 (1917); Schwegmann Brothers v. Calvert Distillers Corp., 341 U.S. 384, 71 S.Ct. 745, 95 L.Ed. 1035 (1951); Albrecht v. Herald Co., 390 U.S. 145, 88 S.Ct. 869, 19 L.Ed.2d 998 (1968); Continental T.V., Inc. v. GTE Sylvania, Inc.,

433 U.S. 36, 97 S.Ct. 2549, 2558, 53 L.Ed. 2d 568, 581 (1977).

45. United States v. Bausch & Lomb Optical Co., 321 U.S. 707, 64 S.Ct. 805, 88 L.Ed. 1024 (1944); United States v. Sealy, Inc., 388 U.S. 350, 87 S.Ct. 1847, 18 L.Ed. 2d 1238 (1967).

46. United States v. Univis Lens Co., 316 U.S. 241, 62 S.Ct. 1088, 86 L.Ed. 1408 (1942); Boston Store of Chicago v. Amer-

---

47. See note 47 on page 600.

Whether the courts should continue to apply the rule is one of the questions raised by the materials in this section.

A further issue raised in *Dr. Miles*, and in a number of subsequent vertical price fixing cases, is the question whether the distributor is actually an "agent" of the manufacturer. The vertical price fixing might be lawful in such circumstances, either because "agreement" might be lacking between a principal and agent or because there could be no restraint on alienation (the agent does not own the goods). The lawyers who drafted Dr. Miles' distributor contract set up the relationship between Dr. Miles and the distributor as an agency rather than a sale. Goods were "consigned" to the distributor under an express stipulation that Dr. Miles retained title until sale by the distributor. On the other hand, the contract contained some provisions more consistent with sale than with agency, e.g., looking toward payment by the consignee in advance of his sale of the goods. In any event, the Court was satisfied that, whether or not title passed from Dr. Miles to his authorized distributor, Park had acquired title, either by purchase from an authorized distributor or through an intermediate vendee. If so, any attempt by Dr. Miles to control Park's resale prices would violate the Sherman Act, and the Court refused to apply the law protecting contracts from malicious interference, in aid of such an attempt.

Argument over whether the agency is "genuine" or "sham" has continued to dominate the rhetoric of the resale price maintenance controversy since *Dr. Miles*. In UNITED STATES v. GENERAL ELECTRIC Co.,[48] GE was able to persuade the Supreme Court that its lamp agency contracts with 21,000 retail hardware dealers were "genuine", by the scrupulosity with which its contract reserved title in GE to the retailer's inventory, provided for GE inventory control and inspection, created a "trust" in the proceeds of retail lamps sales until the dealer paid GE, denominated the retailer's margin as a "commission", etc. The result was to sustain a gigantic legal fiction that every householder buying lamps in a shop was dealing directly with the manufacturer, a fiction whose central significance was that GE could fix the price of "its own" lamps in all stores. This result was reached notwithstanding that the store provided all the capital for the retail distribution facility, acquired its stock of lamps through ordinary wholesalers (who held another kind of "agency" contract from GE enabling them to designate retailer subagents), "guaranteed" customer payment for the lamps (i.e., assumed the credit risks), and paid all expenses of storage, delivery, handling and sale. In short, from a practical business point-of-view, the commerce was indistinguishable from any other system of distribution by sale to wholesalers and resale to retailers.

ican Graphophone Co., 246 U.S. 8, 38 S.Ct. 257, 62 L.Ed. 551 (1918).

47. See Straus v. American Publishers Association, 231 U.S. 222, 34 S.Ct. 84, 58 L.Ed. 192 (1913); Bobbs-Merrill Co. v.

Straus, 210 U.S. 339, 28 S.Ct. 722, 52 L.Ed. 1086 (1908).

48. 272 U.S. 476, 47 S.Ct. 192, 71 L.Ed. 362 (1926).

Subsequent cases, however, appear to condemn "agency" or "consignment" as a device for maintaining retail prices. In UNITED STATES v. MASONITE CORP.,[49] conflicting patent claims of two leading producers of building materials were settled with an arrangement under which one became the selling agent for the other. The Court declared its willingness to assume that the agency was conventional and valid apart from the Sherman Act:

> . . . A patentee who employs such an agent to distribute his product certainly is not enlarging the scope of his patent privilege if it may fairly be said that that distribution is part of the patentee's own business and operates only to secure to him the reward for his invention which Congress has provided. But where he utilizes the sales organization of another business—a business with which he has no intimate relationship—quite different problems are posed since such a regimentation of a marketing system is peculiarly susceptible to the restraints of trade which the Sherman Act condemns. And when it is clear, as it is in this case, that the marketing systems utilized by means of the del credere agency agreements are those of competitors of the patentee and that the purpose is to fix prices at which the competitors may market the product, the device is without more an enlargement of the limited patent privilege and a violation of the Sherman Act. . . .[50]

In SIMPSON v. UNION OIL CO.,[51] a retail gasoline service station operator recovered treble damages from a supplier who dropped him when he persisted in cutting the price below that specified pursuant to his "consignment" contract. The Court stated:

> By reason of the lease [Union was lessor of the station premises as well as supplier of gasoline, and the lease was readily cancelable] and "consignment" agreement dealers are coercively laced into an arrangement under which their supplier is able to impose noncompetitive prices on thousands of persons whose prices otherwise might be competitive. The evil of this resale price maintenance program . . . is its inexorable potentiality for and even certainty in destroying competition in retail sales of gasoline by these nominal "consignees" who are in reality small struggling competitors seeking retail gas customers.

> As we have said, an owner of an article may send it to a dealer who may undertake to sell it only at a price determined by the owner. There is nothing illegal about that arrangement. When, however, a "consignment" device is used to cover a vast gasoline distribution system, fixing prices through many retail outlets, the antitrust laws prevent calling the "consignment" an agency, for then the end result of United States v. Socony-Vacuum Oil Co. would be avoided merely by clever manipulation of words, not by differences in substance.[52]

49. 316 U.S. 265, 62 S.Ct. 1070, 86 L.Ed. 1461 (1942).

50. 316 U.S., at 279, 62 S.Ct., at 1078, 86 L.Ed., at 1476.

51. 377 U.S. 13, 84 S.Ct. 1051, 12 L.Ed.2d 98 (1964).

52. 377 U.S., at 21–22, 84 S.Ct., at 1057, 12 L.Ed.2d, at 104–105.

Simpson's right to recover was vindicated despite contentions that the rule here announced was "new", that Union Oil should not be prejudiced by its reliance on the old General Electric rule, and that Simpson had no "equities" since Union Oil had merely declined to renew Simpson's lease and was under no contractual duty to renew.[53]

Subsequent to the decision in *Simpson*, the government renewed its attack upon the G.E. consignment selling program for light bulbs contending that the *Simpson* case had the effect of over-ruling the 1926 *General Electric* case. The district court concluded:

> The law applicable now is that laid down in *Simpson*—that a vast consignment agency system of distribution through independent businessmen, such as we have here, under which there is price fixing by the supplier, is a per se violation of the Sherman Act.[54]

Although the language of *Simpson* and subsequent lower court actions challenging consignment or agency selling can be viewed as foreclosing these devices for avoiding the *per se* prohibition on vertical price fixing,[55] the emphasis in *Simpson* and other cases upon the scope of the consignment selling program, the power of the firm imposing it, and the intent which motivates the adoption of the program all suggest that the courts are engaged in a "mini-rule of reason" analysis to identify the conduct as price fixing when weighing the legitimacy of consignment or agency selling.[56] Consignment selling, at least for purposes other than vertical price fixing by dominant suppliers, remains a viable marketing technique.[57]

But while agreement with one's "agent" as to the price at which he will sell the principal's goods may escape the bite of the Sherman Act, a "contract," "combination" or "conspiracy" with independent entities remains subject to the Act. If a seller announces a policy of refusing to deal with buyers who resell the product or service below the seller's suggested resale price, is there a "contract," "combination" or "conspiracy" for purposes of the antitrust laws either between buyer and seller, if the buyer purchases knowing the terms on which the seller does business, or among buyers, if the seller enter-

---

53. Noted, 78 Harv.L.Rev. 279 (1964). The question whether Simpson was entitled to damages in view of a new interpretation of the validity of consignment selling was further litigated in Simpson v. Union Oil Co., 396 U.S. 13, 90 S.Ct. 30, 24 L.Ed.2d 13 (1969), (damages not properly denied in this case).

54. United States v. General Electric Co., 358 F.Supp. 731, 738 (S.D.N.Y.1973).

55. See Sun Oil Co. v. Federal Trade Commission, 350 F.2d 624, 636 (7th Cir. 1965), certiorari denied 382 U.S. 982, 86 S.Ct. 559, 15 L.Ed.2d 473 (1966). Cf. United States v. Standard Oil Co. (Ohio), 1973–1 Trade Cases ¶ 74,692 (N.D.Ohio 1973) (consent decree requiring SOHIO to sell either through company owned stations or independent stations but not on consignment).

56. See Continental T.V., Inc. v. G.T.E. Sylvania, Inc. p. 639 infra; Rahl, Control of an Agent's Prices: The Simpson Case—A Study in Antitrust Analysis, 61 Nw.U.L.Rev. 1 (1966); Comment, 1966 Utah L.Rev. 75.

57. See Continental T.V., Inc. v. G.T.E. Sylvania, Inc. p. 639 infra; American Oil Co. v. McMullin, 508 F.2d 1345 (10th Cir. 1975); Lehrman v. Gulf Oil Corp., 464 F.2d 26 (5th Cir.), certiorari denied 409 U.S. 1077, 93 S.Ct. 689, 34 L.Ed. 2d 665 (1972), appeal after remand 500 F.2d 659 (5th Cir. 1974), rehearing denied 503 F.2d 1403 (5th Cir.), certiorari denied 420 U.S. 929, 95 S.Ct. 1128, 43 L.Ed.2d 400.

tains protests from them as to price cutting by a rival reseller or if the seller gives them assurances that he will enforce his "Do-Not-Sell-to-Price-Cutters" policy?

UNITED STATES v. PARKE, DAVIS & CO.

Supreme Court of the United States, 1960.
362 U.S. 29, 80 S.Ct. 503, 4 L.Ed.2d 505.

MR. JUSTICE BRENNAN delivered the opinion of the Court.

The Government sought an injunction under § 4 of the Sherman Act against the appellee, Parke, Davis & Company, on a complaint alleging that Parke Davis conspired and combined, in violation of §§ 1 and 3 of the Act, with retail and wholesale druggists in Washington, D. C., and Richmond, Virginia, to maintain the wholesale and retail prices of Parke Davis pharmaceutical products. The violation was alleged to have occurred during the summer of 1956 when there was no Fair Trade Law in the District of Columbia or the State of Virginia. After the Government completed the presentation of its evidence at the trial, and without hearing Parke Davis in defense, the District Court for the District of Columbia dismissed the complaint on the ground that upon the facts and the law the Government had not shown a right to relief. We noted probable jurisdiction of the Government's direct appeal under § 2 of the Expediting Act.

Parke Davis makes some 600 pharmaceutical products which it markets nationally through drug wholesalers and drug retailers. The retailers buy these products from the drug wholesalers or make large quantity purchases directly from Parke Davis. Sometime before 1956 Parke Davis announced a resale price maintenance policy in its wholesalers' and retailers' catalogues. The wholesalers' catalogue contained a Net Price Selling Schedule listing suggested minimum resale prices on Parke Davis products sold by wholesalers to retailers. The catalogue stated that it was Parke Davis' continuing policy to deal only with drug wholesalers who observed that schedule and who sold only to drug retailers authorized by law to fill prescriptions. Parke Davis, when selling directly to retailers, quoted the same prices listed in the wholesalers' Net Price Selling Schedule but granted retailers discounts for volume purchases. Wholesalers were not authorized to grant similar discounts. The retailers' catalogue contained a schedule of minimum retail prices applicable in States with Fair Trade Laws and stated that this schedule was suggested for use also in States not having such laws. These suggested minimum retail prices usually provided a 50% mark up over cost on Parke Davis products purchased by retailers from wholesalers but, because of the volume discount, often in excess of 100% mark up over cost on products purchased in large quantities directly from Parke Davis.

There are some 260 drugstores in Washington, D. C., and some 100 in Richmond, Virginia. Many of the stores are units of Peoples Drug Stores, a large retail drug chain. There are five drug wholesalers handling Parke Davis products in the locality who do business with the drug retailers. The wholesalers observed the resale prices suggested by Parke Davis. However, during the spring and early summer of 1956 drug retailers in the two cities advertised and sold several Parke Davis vitamin products at prices substantially below the suggested minimum retail prices; in some instances the prices apparently reflected the volume discounts on direct purchases from Parke Davis since the products were sold below the prices listed in the wholesalers' Net Price Selling Schedule. The Baltimore office manager of Parke Davis in charge of the sales district which included the two cities sought advice from his head office on how to handle this situation. The Parke Davis attorney advised that the company could legally "enforce an adopted policy arrived at unilaterally" to sell only to customers who observed the suggested minimum resale prices. He further advised that this meant that "we can lawfully say 'we will sell you only so long as you observe such minimum retail prices' but cannot say 'we will sell to you only if you agree to observe such minimum retail prices,' since except as permitted by Fair Trade legislations [sic] agreements as to resale price maintenance are invalid." Thereafter in July the branch manager put into effect a program for promoting observance of the suggested minimum retail prices by the retailers involved. The program contemplated the participation of the five drug wholesalers. In order to insure that retailers who did not comply would be cut off from sources of supply, representatives of Parke Davis visited the wholesalers and told them, in effect, that not only would Parke Davis refuse to sell to wholesalers who did not adhere to the policy announced in its catalogue, but also that it would refuse to sell to wholesalers who sold Parke Davis products to retailers who did not observe the suggested minimum retail prices. Each wholesaler was interviewed individually but each was informed that his competitors were also being apprised of this. The wholesalers without exception indicated a willingness to go along.

Representatives called contemporaneously upon the retailers involved, individually, and told each that if he did not observe the suggested minimum retail prices, Parke Davis would refuse to deal with him, and that furthermore he would be unable to purchase any Parke Davis products from the wholesalers. Each of the retailers was also told that his competitors were being similarly informed.

Several retailers refused to give any assurances of compliance and continued after these July interviews to advertise and sell Parke Davis products at prices below the suggested minimum retail prices. Their names were furnished by Parke Davis to the wholesalers. Thereafter Parke Davis refused to fill direct orders from such retailers and the wholesalers likewise refused to fill their orders. This ban was not limited to the Parke Davis products being sold below the suggested minimum prices but included all the company's products, even those necessary to fill prescriptions.

The president of Dart Drug Company, one of the retailers cut off, protested to the assistant branch manager of Parke Davis that Parke Davis was discriminating against him because a drugstore across the street, one of the Peoples Drug chain, had a sign in its window advertising Parke Davis products at cut prices. The retailer was told that if this were so the branch manager "would see Peoples and try to get them in line." The branch manager testified at the trial that thereafter he talked to a vice-president of Peoples and that the following occurred:

"Q. Well, now, you told Mr. Downey [the vice-president of Peoples] at this meeting, did you not, Mr. Powers, [the assistant branch manager of Parke Davis] that you noticed that Peoples were cutting prices? A. Yes.

"Q. And you told him, did you not, that it had been the Parke, Davis policy for many years to do business only with individuals that maintained the scheduled prices? A. I told Mr. Downey that we had a policy in our catalog, and that anyone that did not go along with our policy, we were not interested in doing business with them.

. . .

"Q. . . . Now, Mr. Downey told you on the occasion of this visit, did he not, that Peoples would stop cutting prices and would abide by the Parke, Davis policy, is that right? A. That is correct.

. . .

"Q. When you went to call on Mr. Downey, you solicited his support of Parke, Davis policies, is not that right? A. That is right.

"Q. And he said, I will abide by your policy? A. That is right."

The District Court found, apparently on the basis of this testimony, that "The Peoples' representative stated that Peoples would stop cutting prices on Parke, Davis' products and Parke, Davis continued to sell to Peoples." [164 F.Supp. 833.]

But five retailers continued selling Parke Davis products at less than the suggested minimum prices from stocks on hand. Within a few weeks Parke Davis modified its program. Its officials believed that the selling at discount prices would be deterred, and the effects minimized of any isolated instances of discount selling which might continue, if all advertising of such prices were discontinued. In August the Parke Davis representatives again called on the retailers individually. When interviewed, the president of Dart Drug Company indicated that he might be willing to stop advertising, although continuing to sell at discount prices, if shipments to him were resumed. Each of the other retailers was then told individually by Parke Davis representatives that Dart was ready to discontinue advertising. Each thereupon said that if Dart stopped advertising he would also. On August 28 Parke Davis reported this reaction to Dart. Thereafter all of the retailers discontinued advertising of Parke Davis vitamins at less than suggested minimum retail prices and Parke Davis and the wholesalers resumed sales of Parke Davis products to them. However, the suspension of advertising lasted only a month. One of the retailers again started newspaper advertising in September and, despite efforts of Parke Davis to prevent it, the others quickly followed suit. Parke Davis then stopped trying to promote the retailers' adherence to its suggested resale prices, and neither it nor the wholesalers have since declined further dealings with them. A reason for this was that the Department of Justice, on complaint of Dart Drug Company, had begun an investigation of possible violation of the antitrust laws.

The District Court held that the Government's proofs did not establish a violation of the Sherman Act because "the actions of [Parke Davis] were properly unilateral and sanctioned by law under the doctrine laid down in the case of United States v. Colgate & Co., 250 U.S. 300, 39 S.Ct. 465, 63 L.Ed. 992. . . ." 164 F.Supp. at page 829.

The Colgate case came to this Court on writ of error under the Criminal Appeals Act, 34 Stat. 1246, from a District Court judgment dismissing an indictment for violation of the Sherman Act. The indictment proceeded solely upon the theory of an unlawful combination between Colgate and its wholesale and retail dealers for the purpose and with the effect of procuring adherence on the part of the dealers to resale prices fixed by the company. However, the District Court construed the indictment as not charging a combination by agreement between Colgate and its customers to maintain prices. This Court held that it must disregard the allegations of the indictment since the District Court's interpretation of the indictment was binding and that without an allegation of unlawful *agreement* there was no Sherman Act violation charged. The Court said:

"The purpose of the Sherman Act is to prohibit monopolies, contracts and combinations which probably would unduly interfere with the free exercise of their rights by those engaged, or who wish to engage, in trade and commerce—in a word to preserve the right of freedom to trade. In the absence of any purpose to create or maintain a monopoly, the act does not restrict the long recognized right of trader or manufacturer engaged in an entirely private business, freely to exercise his own independent discretion as to parties with whom he will deal; and, of course, he may announce in advance the circumstances under which he will refuse to sell." 250 U.S. at page 307, 39 S.Ct. at page 468.

The Government concedes for the purposes of this case that under the Colgate doctrine a manufacturer, having announced a price maintenance policy, may bring about adherence to it by refusing to deal with customers who do not observe that policy. The Government contends, however, that subsequent decisions of this Court compel the holding that what Parke Davis did here by entwining the wholesalers and retailers in a program to promote general compliance with its price maintenance policy went beyond mere customer selection and created combinations or conspiracies to enforce resale price maintenance in violation of §§ 1 and 3 of the Sherman Act.

The history of the Colgate doctrine is best understood by reference to a case which preceded the Colgate decision, Dr. Miles Medical

Co. v. John D. Park & Sons Co., 220 U.S. 373, 31 S.Ct. 376, 55 L.Ed. 502. Dr. Miles entered into written contracts with its customers obligating them to sell its medicine at prices fixed by it. The Court held that the contracts were void because they violated both the common law and the Sherman Act. The Colgate decision distinguished Dr. Miles on the ground that the Colgate indictment did not charge that company with selling its products to dealers *under agreements* which obligated the latter not to resell except at prices fixed by the seller. The Colgate decision created some confusion and doubt as to the continuing vitality of the principles announced in Dr. Miles. This brought United States v. Schrader's Son, Inc., 252 U.S. 85, 40 S.Ct. 251, 64 L.Ed. 471, to the Court. The case involved the prosecution of a components manufacturer for entering into price-fixing agreements with retailers, jobbers and manufacturers who used his products. The District Court dismissed, saying:

> "Granting the fundamental proposition stated in the Colgate case, that the manufacturer has an undoubted right to specify resale prices and refuse to deal with any one who fails to maintain the same, or, as further stated, the act does not restrict the long-recognized right of a trader or manufacturer engaged in an entirely private business freely to exercise his own independent discretion as to parties with whom he will deal, and that he of course may announce in advance the circumstances under which he will refuse to sell, it seems to me that it is a distinction without a difference to say that he may do so by the subterfuges and devices set forth in the [Colgate] opinion and not violate the Sherman Anti-Trust Act, yet if he had done the same thing in the form of a written agreement, adequate only to effectuate the same purpose, he would be guilty of a violation of the law. . . ." D.C., 264 F. 175, 184.

This Court reversed, and said:

> "The court below misapprehended the meaning and effect of the opinion and judgment in [Colgate]. We had no intention to overrule or modify the doctrine of Dr. Miles Medical Co. v. John D. Park & Sons Co., where the effort was to destroy the dealers' independent discretion through restrictive agreements." 252 U.S. at page 99, 40 S.Ct. at page 253.

The Court went on to explain that the statement from Colgate quoted earlier in this opinion meant no more than that a manufacturer is not guilty of a combination or conspiracy if he merely "indicates his wishes concerning prices and declines further dealings with all who fail to observe them . . ."; however there is unlawful combination where a manufacturer "enters into agreements—whether express or implied from a course of dealing or other circumstances—with all customers . . . which undertake to bind them to observe fixed resale prices." Ibid.

The next decision was Frey & Son, Inc., v. Cudahy Packing Co., 256 U.S. 208, 41 S.Ct. 451, 65 L.Ed. 892. That was a treble damage suit alleging a conspiracy in violation of the Sherman Act between the manufacturer and jobbers to maintain resale prices. The plaintiff recovered a judgment. The Court of Appeals for the Fourth Circuit reversed on the authority of Colgate. The Court of Appeals concluded [261 F. 65, 67]: "There was no formal written or oral agreement with jobbers for the maintenance of prices" and in that circumstance held that under Colgate the trial court should have directed a verdict for the defendant. In holding that the Court of Appeals erred, this Court referred to the decision in Schrader as holding that the "essential agreement, combination or conspiracy might be implied from a course of dealing or other circumstances," so that in Cudahy, "Having regard to the course of dealing and all the pertinent facts disclosed by the present record, we think whether there existed an unlawful combination of agreement between the manufacturer and jobbers was a question for the jury to decide, and that the Circuit Court of Appeals erred when it held otherwise." 256 U.S. at page 210, 41 S.Ct. at page 451.

But the Court also held improper an instruction which was given to the jury that a violation of the Sherman Act might be found if the jury should find as facts that the defendant "indicated a sales plan to the wholesalers and jobbers, which plan fixed the price below which the wholesalers and jobbers were not to sell to retailers, and . . . [that] defendant called this particular feature of this plan to their attention on very many different occasions, and . . . [that] the great majority of them not only [expressed] no dissent from such plan, but actually [cooperated] in carrying it out by themselves selling at the prices named . . . ." 256 U.S. 210–211, 41 S.Ct. 452, 65 L.Ed. 892. However, the authority of this holding condemning the instruction has been seriously undermined by subsequent decisions which we are about to discuss. Therefore, Cudahy does not support the District Court's action in this case, and we cannot follow it here. Less than a year after Cudahy was handed down, the Court decided Federal Trade Commission v. Beech-Nut Packing Co., 257 U.S. 441, 42 S.Ct. 150, 66 L.Ed. 307, which presented a situation bearing a marked resemblance to the Parke Davis program.

In Beech-Nut the company had adopted a policy of refusing to sell its products to wholesalers or retailers who did not adhere to a schedule of resale prices. Beech-Nut later implemented this policy by refusing to sell to wholesalers who sold to retailers who would not adhere to the policy. To detect violations the company utilized code numbers on its products and instituted a system of reporting. When an offender was cut off, he would be reinstated upon the giving of assurances that he would maintain prices in the future. The Court construed the Federal Trade Commission Act, 15 U.S.C.A. § 41 et seq. to authorize the Commission to forbid practices which had a "dangerous tendency unduly to hinder competition or create monopoly." [257 U.S. at page 454, 42 S.Ct. at page 154.] The Sherman Act was held to be a guide to what constituted an unfair method of competition. The company had urged that its conduct was entirely legal under the Sherman Act as interpreted by Colgate. The Court rejected this contention, saying that "the Beech-Nut system goes far beyond the simple refusal to sell goods to persons who will not sell at stated prices, which in the Colgate Case was held to be within the legal right of the producer." Ibid. The Court held further that the nonexistence of contracts covering the practices was irrelevant since "[t]he specific facts found show suppression of the freedom of competition by methods in which the company secures the co-operation of its distributors and customers, which are quite as effectual as agreements express or implied intended to accomplish the same purpose." Id., 257 U.S. at page 455, 42 S.Ct. at page 155. That the Court considered that the Sherman Act violation thus established was dispositive of the issue before it is shown by the ground taken by Mr. Justice McReynolds in dissent. The parties had stipulated that there were no contracts covering the policy. Relying on his view of Colgate, he asked : "How can there be methods of co-operation . . . when the existence of the essential contracts is definitely excluded?" Id., 257 U.S. at page 459, 42 S.Ct. at page 156. The majority did not read Colgate as requiring such contracts; rather, the Court dispelled the confusion over whether a combination effected by contractual arrangements, express or implied was necessary to a finding of Sherman Act violation by limiting Colgate to a holding that when the only act specified in the indictment amounted to saying that the trader had exercised his right to determine those with whom he would deal, and to announce the circumstances under which he would refuse to sell, no Sherman Act violation was made out. However, because Beech-Nut's methods were as effective as agreements in producing the result that "all who would deal in the company's products are constrained to sell at the suggested prices," 257 U.S. at page 455, 42 S.Ct. at page 155, the Court held that the securing of the customers' adherence by such methods constituted the creation of an unlawful combination to suppress price competition among the retailers.

That Beech-Nut narrowly limited Colgate and announced principles which subject to Sherman Act liability the producer who secures his customers' adherence to his resale prices by methods which go beyond the simple refusal to sell to customers who will not resell at stated prices, was made clear in United States v. Bausch & Lomb Optical Co., 321 U.S. 707, 722, 64 S.Ct. 805, 813, 88 L.Ed. 1024:

> "The Beech-Nut case recognizes that a simple refusal to sell to others who do not maintain the first seller's fixed resale price is lawful but adds as to the Sherman Act, 'He [the seller] may not, consistently with the act, go beyond the exercise of this right, and by contracts or combinations, express or implied, unduly hinder or obstruct the free and natural flow of commerce in the channels of interstate trade.' 257 U.S. at page 453, 42 S.Ct. at page 154. The Beech-Nut Company, without agreements, was found to suppress the freedom of competition by coercion of its customers through special agents of the company, by reports of competitors about customers who violated resale prices, and by boycotts of price cutters. . . ."

Bausch & Lomb, like the instant case, was an action by the United States to restrain alleged violations of §§ 1 and 3 of the Sherman Act. The Court, relying on Beech-Nut, held that a distributor, Soft-Lite Lens Company, Inc., violated the Sherman Act when, as was the case with Parke Davis, the refusal to sell to wholesalers was not used simply to induce acquiescence of the wholesalers in the distributor's published resale price list; the wholesalers "accepted Soft-Lite's proffer of a plan of distribution by cooperating in prices, limitation of sales to and approval of retail licensees. That is sufficient. . . . Whether this conspiracy and combination was achieved by agreement or by acquiescence of the wholesalers coupled with assistance in effectuating its purpose is immaterial." 321 U.S. at page 723, 64 S.Ct. at page 813. Thus, whatever uncertainty previously existed as to the scope of the Colgate doctrine, Bausch & Lomb and Beech-Nut plainly fashioned its dimensions as meaning no more than that a simple refusal to sell to customers who will not resell at prices suggested by the seller is permissible under the Sherman Act. In other words, an unlawful combination is not just such as arises from a price maintenance *agreement*, express or implied; such a combination is also organized if the producer secures adherence to his suggested prices by means which go beyond his mere declination to sell to a customer who will not observe his announced policy.

In the cases decided before Beech-Nut the Court's inquiry was directed to whether the manufacturer had entered into illicit contracts, express or implied. The District Court in this case apparently assumed that the Government could prevail only by establishing a contractual arrangement, albeit implied, between Parke Davis and its customers. Proceeding from the same premise Parke Davis strenuously urges that Rule 52 of the Rules of Civil Procedure compels an affirmance of the District Court since under that Rule the finding that there were no contractual arrangements should "not be set aside unless clearly erroneous." But Rule 52 has no application here. The District Court premised its ultimate finding that Parke Davis did not violate the Sherman Act on an erroneous interpretation of the standard to be applied. The Bausch & Lomb and Beech-Nut decisions cannot be read as merely limited to particular fact complexes justifying the inference of an agreement in violation of the Sherman Act. Both cases teach that judicial inquiry is not to stop with a search of the record for evidence of purely contractual arrangements. The Sherman Act forbids combinations of traders to suppress competition. True, there results the same economic effect as is accomplished by a prohibited combination to suppress price competition if each customer, although induced to do so solely by a manufacturer's announced policy, independently decides to observe specified resale prices. So long as Colgate is not overruled, this result is tolerated but only when it is the consequence of a mere refusal to sell in the exercise of the manufacturer's right "freely to exercise his own independent discretion as to parties with whom he will deal." [250 U.S. 300, 39 S.Ct. 468.] When the manufacturer's actions, as here, go beyond mere announcement of his policy and the simple refusal to deal, and he employs other means which effect adherence to his resale prices, this countervailing consideration is not present and therefore he has put together a combination in violation of the Sherman Act. Thus, whether an unlawful combination or conspiracy is proved is to be judged by what the parties actually did rather than by the words they used. Because of the nature of the District Court's error we are reviewing a question of law, namely, whether the District Court applied the proper standard to essentially undisputed facts.

The program upon which Parke Davis embarked to promote general compliance with its suggested resale prices plainly exceeded the limitations of the Colgate doctrine and under Beech-Nut and Bausch & Lomb effected arrangements which violated the Sherman Act. Parke Davis did not content itself with announcing its policy regarding retail prices and following this with a simple refusal to have business relations with any retailers who disregarded that policy. Instead Parke Davis used the refusal to deal with the wholesalers in order to elicit their willingness to deny Parke Davis products to retailers and thereby help gain the retailers' adherence to its suggested minimum retail prices. The retailers who disregarded the price policy were promptly cut off when Parke Davis supplied the wholesalers with their names. The large retailer who said he would "abide" by the price policy, the multi-unit Peoples Drug chain, was not cut off. In thus involving the wholesalers to stop the flow of Parke Davis products to the retailers, thereby inducing retailers' adherence to its suggested retail prices, Parke Davis created a combination with the retailers and the wholesalers to maintain retail prices and violated the Sherman Act. Although Parke Davis' originally announced wholesalers' policy would not under Colgate have violated the Sherman Act if its action thereunder was the simple refusal without more to deal with wholesalers who did not observe the wholesalers' Net Price Selling Schedule, that entire policy was tainted with the "vice of . . . illegality," cf. United States v. Bausch & Lomb Optical Co., 321 U.S. 707, 724, 64 S.Ct. 805, 814, 88 L.Ed. 1024, when Parke Davis used it as the vehicle to gain the wholesalers' participation in the program to effectuate the retailers' adherence to the suggested retail prices.

Moreover, Parke Davis also exceeded the "limited dispensation which [Colgate] confers," Times-Picayune Pub. Co. v. United States, 345 U.S. 594, 626, 73 S.Ct. 872, 890, 97 L.Ed. 1277, in another way, which demonstrates how far Parke Davis went beyond the limits of the Colgate doctrine. With regard to the retailers' suspension of advertising, Parke Davis did not rest with the simple announcement to the trade of its policy in that regard followed by a refusal to sell to the retailers who would not observe it. First it discussed the subject with Dart Drug. When Dart indicated willingness to go along the other retailers were approached and Dart's apparent willingness to cooperate was used as the lever to gain their acquiescence in the program. Having secured those acquiescences Parke Davis returned to Dart Drug with the report of that accomplishment. Not until all this was done was the advertising suspended and sales to all the retailers resumed. In this manner Parke Davis sought assurances of compliance and got them, as well as the compliance itself. It was only by actively bringing about substantial unanimity among the competitors that Parke Davis was able to gain adherence to its policy. It must be admitted that a seller's announcement that he will not deal with customers who do not observe his policy may tend to engender confidence in each customer that if he complies his competitors will also. But if a manufacturer is unwilling to rely on individual self-interest to bring about general voluntary acquiescence which has the collateral effect of eliminating price competition, and takes affirmative action to achieve uniform adherence by inducing each customer to adhere to avoid such price competition, the customers' acquiescence is not then a matter of individual free choice prompted alone by the desirability of the product. The product then comes packaged in a competition-free wrapping—a valuable feature in itself—by virtue of concerted action induced by the manufacturer. The manufacturer is thus the organizer of a price maintenance combination or conspiracy in violation of the Sherman Act. . . .

The District Court also alternatively rested its judgment of dismissal on the holding that ". . . even if the unlawful conditions alleged in the Complaint had actually been proved, since 1956 they no longer existed, and . . . [there is] no reason to believe, or even surmise, the unlawful acts alleged can possibly be repeated . . . ." 164 F.Supp. 827, 829, 830. We are of the view that the evidence does not justify any such finding. The District Court stated that "the compelling reason for defendant's so doing [ceasing its efforts] was forced upon it by business and economic conditions in its field." There is no evidence in the record that this was the reason and any such conclusion must rest on speculation. It does not appear even that Parke Davis has announced to the trade that it will abandon the practices we have condemned. So far as the record indicates any reason, it is that Parke Davis stopped its efforts because the Department of Justice had instituted an investigation. . . .

On the record before us the Government is entitled to the relief it seeks. The courts have an obligation, once a violation of the antitrust laws has been established, to protect the public from a continuation of the harmful and unlawful activities. A trial court's wide discretion in fashioning remedies is not to be exercised to deny relief altogether by lightly inferring an abandonment of the unlawful activities from a cessation which seems timed to anticipate suit.

The judgment is reversed and the case remanded to the District Court with directions to enter an appropriate judgment enjoining Parke Davis from further violations of the Sherman Act unless the company elects to submit evidence in defense and refutes the Government's right to injunctive relief established by the present record.

It is so ordered.

Judgment reversed and case remanded with directions.

MR. JUSTICE STEWART, concurring.

I concur in the judgment. The Court's opinion amply demonstrates that the present record shows an illegal combination to maintain retail prices. I therefore find no occasion to question, even by innuendo, the continuing validity of the Colgate decision, 250 U.S. 300, 39 S.Ct. 465, 63 L.Ed. 992, or of the Court's ruling as to the jury instruction in Cudahy, 256 U.S. 210–211, 41 S.Ct. 451, 452, 65 L.Ed. 892.

MR. JUSTICE HARLAN, whom MR. JUSTICE FRANKFURTER and MR. JUSTICE WHITTAKER join, dissenting.

The Court's opinion reaches much further than at once may meet the eye, and justifies fuller discussion than otherwise might appear warranted. Scrutiny of the opinion will reveal that the Court has done no less than send to its demise the Colgate doctrine which has been a basic part of antitrust law concepts since it was first announced in 1919 in United States v. Colgate & Co., 250 U.S. 300, 39 S.Ct. 465, 63 L.Ed. 992.

. . .

Bearing down heavily on the statement in Beech-Nut that the conduct there involved showed more than "the simple refusal to sell," 257 U.S. at page 454, 42 S.Ct. at page 154, 66 L.Ed. 307 (see also Bausch & Lomb, supra, 321 U.S. at page 722, 64 S.Ct. at page 813, 88 L.Ed. 1024), the Court finds that Parke Davis' conduct exceeded the permissible limits of Colgate in two respects. The first is that Parke Davis announced that it would, and did, cut off wholesalers who continued to sell to price-cutting retailers. The second is that the Company in at least one instance reported its talks with one or more retailers to other retailers; that in "this manner Parke Davis sought assurances of compliance and got them"; and that it "was only by actively bringing about substantial unanimity among the competitors that Parke Davis was able to gain adherence to its policy."

There are two difficulties with the Court's analysis on these scores. The first is the findings of the District Court. As to refusals to sell to wholesalers, the lower court found that such conduct did not involve any concert of action, but was wholly unilateral on Parke Davis' part. And I cannot see how such unilateral action, permissible in itself, becomes any less unilateral because it is taken simultaneously with similar unilateral action at the retail level. As to the other respect in which the Court holds Parke Davis' conduct was illegal, the District Court found that the Company did not make "the enforcement of its policies, as to any one wholesaler or retailer dependent upon the action of any other wholesaler or retailer." And it further stated that the "evidence is clear that both wholesalers and retailers valued defendant's business so highly that they acceded to its policy," and that such acquiescence was not brought about by "coercion" or "agreement." Even if this were not true, so that concerted action among the retailers at the "horizontal" level might be inferred, as the Court indicates, under the principles of Interstate Circuit, Inc., v. United States, 306 U.S. 208, 59 S.Ct. 467, 83 L.Ed. 610, I do not see how that itself would justify an inference that concerted action at the "vertical" level existed between Parke Davis and the retailers or wholesalers.

The second difficulty with the Court's analysis is that even reviewing the District Court's findings only as a matter of law, as the Court purports to do, the cases do not justify overturning the lower court's resulting conclusions. Beech-Nut did not say that refusals to sell to wholesalers who persisted in selling to cut-price retailers—conduct which was present in that case (257 U.S. at page 448, 42 S.Ct. at page 152, 66 L.Ed. 307)—was a *per se* infraction of the Colgate rule, but only that it was offensive if it was the result of cooperative group action. While the Court in Beech-Nut and Bausch & Lomb inferred from the aggresive, widespread, highly organized, and successful merchandising programs involved there that such concerted action existed in those cases, the defensive, limited, unorganized, and unsuccessful effort of Parke Davis to maintain its resale price policy [58] does not justify our disregarding the District Court's finding to the contrary in this case.

In light of the whole history of the Colgate doctrine, it is surely this Court, and not the District Court, that has proceeded on erroneous premises in deciding this case. Unless there is to be attributed to the Court a purpose to overturn the findings of fact of the District Court—something which its opinion not only expressly disclaims doing, but which would also be in plain definance of the Federal Rules of Civil Procedure, Rule 52(a), and principles announced in past cases. I think that what the Court has really done here is to throw the Colgate doctrine into discard.

To be sure, the Government has explicitly stated that it does not ask us to overrule Colgate, and the Court professes not to do so. But contrary to the long understanding of bench and bar, the Court treats Colgate as turning not on the absence of the concerted action explicitly required by §§ 1 and 3 of the Sherman Act, but upon the Court's notion of "countervailing" social policies. I can regard the Court's profession as no more than a bow to the fact that Colgate, decided more than 40 years ago, has become part of the economic regime of the country upon which the commercial community and the lawyers who advise it have justifiably relied.

If the principle for which Colgate stands is to be reversed, it is, as the Government's position plainly indicates, something that should be

---

58. [Footnote 4 from the opinion.] The District Court found, among other things, that the efforts of Parke, Davis in the District of Columbia and Virginia came about only after some of its competitors had engaged in damaging local "deep price cutting" on Parke, Davis products (Fdg. 12); that Parke, Davis' sales in those areas constituted less than 5% of the total pharmaceutical sales therein (Fdg. 3); that these efforts followed the legal advice previously given by the Company's counsel (Fdg. 12); that Parke, Davis did not have "any regular-

ized or systematic machinery for maintaining its suggested minimum prices as to either retailers or wholesalers" (Fdg. 10); that the entire episode lasted only from July to the fall of 1956, when the Company "in good faith" abandoned all further such efforts (Fdgs. 12, 27); and that since that time retailers in these areas "have continuously sold and advertised Parke, Davis products at cut prices, and have been able to obtain those products from both the wholesalers and/or Parke, Davis itself." (Fdg. 27).

left to the Congress. It is surely the emptiest of formalisms to profess respect for Colgate and eviscerate it in application.

I would affirm.[59]

NOTES AND QUERIES

(1) *Justice Holmes, Vertical Price Fixing, The Public Interest and Price Cutting "Knaves."* Beginning with the *Dr. Miles* case, Justice Holmes dissented from decisions holding vertical price fixing illegal. In the *Dr. Miles* case Holmes observed:

> I think that at least it is safe to say that the most enlightened judicial policy is to let people manage their own business in their own way, unless the ground for interference is very clear. . . . The Dr. Miles Medical Company knows better than we do what will enable it to do the best business. We must assume its retail price to be reasonable, . . . so I see nothing to warrant my assuming that the public will not be served best by the company being allowed to carry out its plan. I cannot believe that in the long run the public will profit by this court permitting knaves to cut reasonable prices for some ulterior purpose of their own, and thus to impair, if not to destroy, the production and sale of articles which it is assumed to be desirable that the public should be able to get.[60]

Holmes, again in dissent, reasserted his views about vertical price fixing in *Federal Trade Commission v. Beech-Nut Packing Co.,*[61] where a majority upheld an F.T.C. finding that an elaborate plan for enforcing resale price maintenance was an "unfair method of competition" in violation of § 5 of the F.T.C. Act. Holmes stated:

> There are obvious limits of propriety to the persistent expression of opinions that do not command the agreement of the Court. But as this case presents a somewhat new field—the determination of what is unfair competition within the meaning of the Federal Trade Commission Act—I venture a few words to explain my dissent. I will not recur to fundamental questions. The ground on which the respondent is held guilty is that its conduct has a dangerous tendency, unduly to hinder competition or to create monopoly. It is enough to say that this I cannot understand. So far as the Sherman Act is concerned I had supposed that its policy was aimed against attempts to create a monopoly in the doers of the condemned act or to hinder competition with them. Of course there can be nothing of that sort here. The respondent already has the monopoly of its own goods with the full assent of the law and no one can compete with it with regard to those goods, which are the only ones concerned. It seems obvious that the respondent is not creating a monopoly in them for anyone else, although I see nothing to hinder its doing so by conveying them all to one single vendee. The worst that can be said, so far as I see, is that it hinders competition among those who purchase from it. But it

59. See Dam & Pitofsky, Is The Colgate Doctrine Dead? 37 Antitrust L.J. 503 (1970); Turner, The Definition of Agreement under the Sherman Act, 75 Harv.L.Rev. 655 (1962); Levi, The Parke, Davis-Colgate Doctrine: The Ban on Resale Price Maintenance, 1960 Sup.Ct.Rev. 257; Mund, The Right to Buy, Staff Report for the Select Committee on Small Business, U. S. Senate, 86th Cong. 1st Sess. (1959).

On difficulties in proving that collaboration between supplier and competing distributors was the cause of plaintiff's dismissal as a distributor, see Klein v. American Luggage Works, Inc., 323 F.2d 787 (3d Cir. 1963).

60. 220 U.S., at 411–12, 31 S.Ct., at 386, 55 L.Ed., at 520.

61. 257 U.S. 441, 42 S.Ct. 150, 66 L.Ed. 307 (1922).

seems to me that the very foundation of the policy of the law to keep competition open is that the subject-matter of the competition would be open to all but for the hindrance complained of. I cannot see what that policy has to do with a subject-matter that comes from a single hand that is admitted to be free to shut as closely as it will. And, to come back to the words of the statute, I cannot see how it is unfair competition to say to those to whom the respondent sells, and to the world, you can have my goods only on the terms that I propose, when the existence of any competition in dealing with them depends upon the respondent's will. I see no wrong in so doing, and if I did I should not think it a wrong within the possible scope of the word unfair. Many unfair devices have been exposed in suits under the Sherman Act, but to whom the respondent's conduct is unfair I do not understand.

[Justices McKenna and Brandeis joined in this opinion. Justice McReynolds dissented in a separate opinion.]

(2) *Queries.* To whom was Beech-Nut's conduct unfair? Consumers? Grocers who, because of greater efficiency, can sell Beech-Nut products at a lower profit margin than their retail competitors? Are such grocers "knaves"?

One grocer prefers to attract customers by providing services, like charge accounts and delivery; another grocer chooses to advertise extensively; a third cuts prices. Is competition between them "fair" if the third man is told by his supplier (or by the government) that he may not cut prices? Would it be "fair competition" if the first were told to eliminate credit and deliveries? Would there still be "fair competition" if all three were told to sell at the same prices, without advertising or services?

Was Beech-Nut's price-fixing effort directed solely to "its own goods"? Were the grocers its agents?

If X owns the only tin mine, with the usual owner's right to produce or not to produce, ought he therefore be allowed to set the price at which his vendees resell tin, or tin products, or foods sold in tin cans?

Can Dealer compel Supplier to continue relations with him while the Dealer is litigating the validity of Supplier's resale price policy? Is refusal to deal with somebody who is suing you a violation of the antitrust laws? [62] Is there any other basis for compelling Supplier to continue to supply, assuming that any contractual relationship between the parties has expired, e.g., by failure to renew an annually renewable franchise? [63]

---

62. Compare Bergen Drug Co. v. Parke, Davis & Co., 307 F.2d 725 (3d Cir. 1962) with House of Materials, Inc. v. Simplicity Pattern Co., 298 F.2d 867 (2d Cir. 1962).

63. See generally, Goldberg, The Law and Economics of Vertical Restrictions: A Relational Perspective, 58 Texas L.Rev. 91 (1979). Legislation aimed at franchise abuses in particular industries has been adopted which severely limits the right of franchisors to terminate or fail to renew the franchise relationship. See, e.g., Petroleum Marketing Practices Act, 15 U.S.C. § 2801, *et seq.*, discussed infra p. 788; Comment, Retail Gasoline Franchise Terminations and Nonrenewals Under Title I Of The Petroleum Market-

ing Practices Act, 1980 Duke L.J. 522. Simpson v. Union Oil Co., p. 601 supra; Quinn v. Mobil Oil Co., 375 F.2d 273 (1st Cir. 1967), certiorari dismissed 389 U.S. 801, 88 S.Ct. 8, 19 L.Ed.2d 56. There may be remedies available under state common law or statute, see Shell Oil Co. v. Marinello, 63 N.J. 402, 307 A.2d 598 (1973), certiorari denied 415 U.S. 920, 94 S.Ct. 1421, 39 L.Ed.2d 475 (1974). It has been argued that such remedies have not been adequate. See Bohling, Franchise Termination Under the Sherman Act: Populism and Relational Power, 53 Texas L.Rev. 1180, 1182 (1975); Note, Constitutional Obstacles to State "Good Cause" Restrictions on Franchise Terminations, 74 Colum.L.Rev. 1487 (1974).

(3) *Inadequately Enforced "Suggested" Resale Price as a Deceptive Trade Practice.* While a supplier who goes too far in enforcing dealer adherence to suggested resale prices may run the risk of violating Section 1 of the Sherman Act, a supplier who is too cavalier about dealers manipulating discounts from suggested resale prices may run the risk of violating Section 5 of the F.T.C. Act.[64]

In *Baltimore Luggage Co. v. Federal Trade Commission,*[65] the Fourth Circuit sustained the Commission's decision that "pre-ticketing" (labeling the item with a suggested retail price) at a level of prices higher than that charged by 387 out of the supplier's 1276 distributors was deceptive. But in *Rayex Corp. v. Federal Trade Commission,*[66] the Second Circuit set aside a similar Commission order for want of substantial evidence, notwithstanding testimony that sunglasses preticketed at $4.95 were sold by Rayex for $9 a dozen to wholesalers, who charged retailers $14.40, that Rayex preticketed at "what the customer requests", and that in midtown Manhattan, according to a wholesaler witness, only 25% of retail sales were at $4.95. The Court wanted proof of "actual recurrent and frequent sales within a given trade area" with variations shown not to be due to seasonal variations. The Commission's policy on "preticketing" as a violation of § 5 has been summarized as follows: [67]

> The Federal Trade Commission warns manufacturers who affix preticketed prices on nationally distributed goods that they may well find themselves impaled on the horns of a dilemma. If their distributors habitually sell below the ticketed price, the preticketing constitutes a deceptive practice; on the other hand, rigid adherence to the marked price may indicate illegal restraint of trade.

> The occasion for issuing this broad warning was presented by a sunglass manufacturer that put different price tags on different pairs of the same quality sunglasses in order to accommodate retailers who sold the glasses at widely varying prices. In the Commission's view, this clearly constituted a deceptive practice since it provided "high-priced dealers with a deceptive crutch upon which to carry their goods to market."

> The Commission goes much further, however, in its denunciation of preticketing generally. It notes that preticketed prices are not false or misleading in an industry characterized by price rigidity or uniformity, that is, one in which all dealers are content to sell at the price suggested. Nevertheless, it warns that such rigidity and uniformity of price "may make preticketing even more suspect as a manifestation of some form of illegal restraint of trade."

ALBRECHT v. HERALD CO.

Supreme Court of the United States, 1968.
390 U.S. 145, 88 S.Ct. 869, 19 L.Ed.2d 998.

MR. JUSTICE WHITE delivered the opinion of the Court.

A jury returned a verdict for respondent in petitioner's suit for treble damages for violation of § 1 of the Sherman Act. . . . The

64. Federal Trade Commission Advisory Opinion, National Outerwear & Sportswear Association, Inc., [1976–79 Transfer Binder, Federal Trade Commission Complaints & Orders] (CCH) ¶ 21,183 (1976).

65. 296 F.2d 608 (4th Cir.), certiorari denied 369 U.S. 860, 82 S.Ct. 949, 8 L.Ed. 2d 17 (1962).

66. 317 F.2d 290 (2d Cir. 1963).

67. 30 U.S. Law Week 1161 (April 17, 1962).

question is whether the denial of petitioner's motion for judgment notwithstanding the verdict was correctly affirmed by the Court of Appeals. . . . Respondent publishes the Globe-Democrat, a morning newspaper distributed in the St. Louis metropolitan area by independent carriers who buy papers at wholesale and sell them at retail. There are 172 home delivery routes. Respondent advertises a suggested retail price in its newspaper. Carriers have exclusive territories which are subject to termination if prices exceed the suggested maximum. Petitioner, who had Route 99, adhered to the advertised price for some time but in 1961 raised the price to customers. After more than once objecting to this practice, respondent wrote petitioner on May 20, 1964, that because he was overcharging and because respondent had reserved the right to compete should that happen, subscribers on Route 99 were being informed by letter that respondent would itself deliver the paper to those who wanted it at the lower price. In addition to sending these letters to petitioner's customers, respondent hired Milne Circulation Sales, Inc., which solicited readers for newspapers, to engage in telephone and house-to-house solicitation of all residents on Route 99. As a result, about 300 of petitioner's 1,200 customers switched to direct delivery by respondent. Meanwhile respondent continued to sell papers to petitioner but warned him that should he continue to overcharge, respondent would not have to do business with him. Since respondent did not itself want to engage in home delivery, it advertised a new route of 314 customers as available without cost. Another carrier, George Kroner, took over the route knowing that respondent would not tolerate overcharging and understanding that he might have to return the route if petitioner discontinued his pricing practice. On July 27 respondent told petitioner that it was not interested in being in the carrier business and that petitioner could have his customers back as long as he charged the suggested price. Petitioner brought this lawsuit on August 12. In response, petitioner's appointment as a carrier was terminated and petitioner was given 60 days to arrange the sale of his route to a satisfactory replacement. Petitioner sold his route for $12,000, $1,000 more than he had paid for it but less than he could have gotten had he been able to turn over 1,200 customers instead of 900.

Petitioner's complaint charged a combination or conspiracy in restraint of trade under § 1 of the Sherman Act. At the close of the evidence the complaint was amended to charge only a combination between respondent and "plaintiff's customers and/or Milne Circulation Sales, Inc. and/or George Kroner." The case went to the jury on this theory, the jury found for respondent, and judgment in its favor was entered on the verdict. The court denied petitioner's motion for judgment notwithstanding the verdict, which asserted that under United States v. Parke, Davis & Co., 362 U.S. 29, 80 S.Ct. 503, 4 L.Ed. 2d 505 (1960), and like cases, the undisputed facts showed as a matter of law a combination to fix resale prices of newspapers which was *per se* illegal under the Sherman Act. The Court of Appeals affirmed. In its view "the undisputed evidence fail[ed] to show a Sherman Act violation," because respondent's conduct was wholly unilateral and there was no restraint of trade. The previous decisions of this Court were deemed inapposite to a situation in which a seller establishes maximum prices to be charged by a retailer enjoying an exclusive territory and in which the seller, who would be entitled to refuse to deal simply engages in competition with the offending retailer. We disagree with the Court of Appeals and reverse its judgment.

On the undisputed facts recited by the Court of Appeals respondent's conduct cannot be deemed wholly unilateral and beyond the reach of § 1 of the Sherman Act. That section covers combinations in addition to contracts and conspiracies, express or implied. The Court made this quite clear in United States v. Parke, Davis & Co., 362 U.S. 29, 80 S.Ct. 503, 4 L.Ed.2d 505 (1960), where it held that an illegal combination to fix prices results if a seller suggests resale prices and secures compliance by means in addition to the "mere announcement of this policy and the simple refusal to deal . . . ." Id., at 44, 80 S.Ct. at 512. Parke, Davis had specified resale prices for both wholesalers and retailers and had required wholesalers to refuse to deal with noncomplying retailers. It was found to have created a combination "with the retailers, and the wholesalers to maintain retail prices . . . ." Id., at 45, 80 S.Ct. at 512. The combination with retailers arose because their acquiescence in the suggested prices was secured by threats of termination; the combination with wholesalers arose because they cooperated in terminating price-cutting retailers.

If a combination arose when Parke, Davis threatened its wholesalers with termination unless they put pressure on their retail customers, then there can be no doubt that a combination arose between respondent, Milne, and Kroner to force petitioner to conform to the advertised retail price. When respondent learned that petitioner was overcharging, it hired Milne to solicit customers away from petitioner in order to get petitioner to reduce his price. It was through the efforts of Milne, as well as because of respondent's letter to petitioner's customers, that about 300 customers were obtained for Kroner. Milne's purpose was undoubtedly to earn its fee, but it was aware that the aim of the solicitation campaign was to force petitioner to lower his price. Kroner knew that respondent was giving him the customer list as part of a program to get petitioner to conform to the advertised price, and he knew that he might have to return the customers if petitioner ultimately complied with respondent's demands. He undertook to deliver papers at the suggested price and materially aided in the accomplishment of respondent's plan. Given the uncontradicted facts recited by the Court of Appeals, there was a combination within the meaning of § 1 between respondent, Milne, and Kroner, and the Court of Appeals erred in holding to the contrary.[68]

68. [Court's footnote 6]. Petitioner's original complaint broadly asserted an illegal combination under § 1 of the Sherman Act. Under *Parke, Davis* petitioner could have claimed a combination between respondent and himself, at least as of the day he unwillingly complied with respondent's advertised price. Likewise,

The Court of Appeals also held there was no restraint of trade, despite the long-accepted rule in § 1 cases that resale price fixing is a *per se* violation of the law whether done by agreement or combination.[69]

In *Kiefer-Stewart*, liquor distributors combined to set maximum resale prices. The Court of Appeals held the combination legal under the Sherman Act because in its view setting maximum prices ". . . constituted no restraint on trade and no interference with plaintiff's right to engage in all the competition it desired." 182 F.2d 228, 235 (C.A. 7th Cir. 1950). This Court rejected that view and reversed the Court of Appeals, holding that agreements to fix maximum prices "no less than those to fix minimum prices, cripple the freedom of traders and thereby restrain their ability to sell in accordance with their own judgment."[70] 340 U.S. 211, 213, 71 S.Ct. 259, 260.

We think *Kiefer-Stewart* was correctly decided and we adhere to it. Maximum and minimum price fixing may have different conse-

he might successfully have claimed that respondent had combined with other carriers because the firmly enforced price policy applied to all carriers, most of whom acquiesced in it. See United States v. Arnold, Schwinn & Co., 388 U.S. 365, 372, 87 S.Ct. 1856, 1862, 18 L.Ed.2d 1249 (1967). These additional claims, however, appear to have been abandoned by petitioner when he amended his complaint in the trial court.

Petitioner's amended complaint did allege a combination between respondent and petitioner's customers. Because of our disposition of this case it is unnecessary to pass on this claim. It was not, however, a frivolous contention. [Citations omitted.]

69. [Court's footnote 7, edited]. Our Brother Harlan seems to state that suppliers have no interest in programs of minimum resale price maintenance, and hence that such programs are "essentially" horizontal agreements between dealers even when they appear to be imposed unilaterally and individually by a supplier on each of his dealers. Although the empirical basis for determining whether or not manufacturers benefit from minimum resale price programs appears to be inconclusive, it seems beyond dispute that a substantial number of manufacturers formulate and enforce complicated plans to maintain resale prices because they deem them advantageous. . . . As a theoretical matter, it is not difficult to conceive of situations in which manufacturers would rightly regard minimum resale price maintenance to be in their interest. Maintaining minimum resale prices would benefit manufacturers when the total demand for their product would not be increased as much by the lower prices brought about by dealer competition as by some other nonprice, demand-creating activity. In particular, when total consumer demand (at least within that price range marked at the bottom by the minimum cost of manufacture and distribution and at the top by the highest price at which a price-maintenance scheme can operate effectively) is affected less by price than by the number of retail outlets for the product, the availability of dealer services, or the impact of advertising and promotion, it will be in the interest of manufacturers to squelch price competition through a scheme of resale price maintenance in order to concentrate on nonprice competition. Finally, if the retail price of each of a group of competing products is stabilized through manufacturer-imposed price maintenance schemes, the danger to all the manufacturers of severe interbrand price competition is apt to be alleviated.

70. [Court's footnote 8]. Our Brother Harlan appears to read *Kiefer-Stewart* as prohibiting only combinations of suppliers to squeeze retailers from the top. Under this view, scarcely derivable from the opinion in that case, signed contracts between a single supplier and his many dealers to fix maximum resale prices would not violate the Sherman Act. With all deference, we reject this view, which seems to stem from the notion that there can be no agreement violative of § 1 unless that agreement accrues to the benefit of both parties, as determined in accordance with some *a priori* economic model. Cf. Comment, The Per Se Illegality of Price-Fixing—Sans Power, Purpose, or Effect, 19 U.Chi.L.Rev. 837 (1952).

quences in many situations. But schemes to fix maximum prices, by substituting the perhaps erroneous judgment of a seller for the forces of the competitive market, may severely intrude upon the ability of buyers to compete and survive in that market. Competition, even in a single product, is not cast in a single mold. Maximum prices may be fixed too low for the dealer to furnish services essential to the value which goods have for the consumer or to furnish services and conveniences which consumers desire and for which they are willing to pay. Maximum price fixing may channel distribution through a few large or specifically advantaged dealers who otherwise would be subject to significant nonprice competition. Moreover, if the actual price charged under a maximum price scheme is nearly always the fixed maximum price, which is increasingly likely as the maximum price approaches the actual cost of the dealer, the scheme tends to acquire all the attributes of an arrangement fixing minimum prices. It is our view, therefore, that the combination formed by the respondent in this case to force petitioner to maintain a specified price for the resale of the newspapers which he had purchased from respondent constituted, without more, an illegal restraint of trade under § 1 of the Sherman Act.

We also reject the suggestion of the Court of Appeals that *Kiefer-Stewart* is inapposite and that maximum price fixing is permissible in this case. The Court of Appeals reasoned that since respondent granted exclusive territories, a price ceiling was necessary to protect the public from price gouging by dealers who had monopoly power in their own territories. . . . The assertion that illegal price fixing is justified because it blunts the pernicious consequences of another distribution practice is unpersuasive. If, as the Court of Appeals said, the economic impact of territorial exclusivity was such that the public could be protected only by otherwise illegal price fixing itself injurious to the public, the entire scheme must fall under § 1 of the Sherman Act.

In sum, the evidence cited by the Court of Appeals makes it clear that a combination in restraint of trade existed. Accordingly, it was error to affirm the judgment of the District Court which denied petitioner's motion for judgment notwithstanding the verdict. The judgment of the Court of Appeals is reversed and the case is remanded to that court for further proceedings consistent with this opinion.

Reversed and remanded.

[Justice Douglas concurred but indicated that remand should also take account of the legality of the exclusive territorial division of markets utilized in the distribution of newspapers.]

MR. JUSTICE HARLAN, dissenting.

While I entirely agree with the views expressed by my Brother Stewart and have joined his dissenting opinion, the Court's disregard of certain economic considerations underlying the Sherman Act warrants additional comment.

I.

The practice of setting genuine price "ceilings," that is maximum prices, differs from the practice of fixing minimum prices, and no accumulation of pronouncements from the opinions of this Court can render the two economically equivalent.

The allegation of a combination of persons to fix maximum prices undoubtedly states a Sherman Act cause of action. In order for a plaintiff to win such a § 1 case, however, he must be able to prove the existence of the alleged combination, and the defendant must be unable, either by virtue of a *per se* rule or by failure of proof at trial, to show an adequate justification. It is on these two points that price ceilings differ from price floors: to hold that a combination may be inferred from the vertical dictation of a maximum price simply because it may be permissible to infer a combination from the vertical dictation of a minimum price ignores economic reality; to conclude that no acceptable justification for fixing maximum prices can be found simply because there is no acceptable justification for fixing minimum prices is to substitute blindness for analysis.

Resale price maintenance, a practice not involved here, lessens horizontal intrabrand competition. The effects, higher prices, less efficient use of resources, and an easier life for the resellers, are the same whether the price maintenance policy takes the form of a horizontal conspiracy among resellers or of vertical dictation by a manufacturer plus reseller acquiescence. This means two things. First, it is frequently possible to infer a combination of resellers behind what is presented to the world as a vertical and unilateral price policy, because it is the resellers and not the manufacturer who reap the direct benefits of the policy. Second, price floors are properly considered *per se* restraints, in the sense that once a combination to create them has been demonstrated, no proffered justification is an acceptable defense. Following the rule of reason, combinations to fix price floors are invariably unreasonable: to the extent that they achieve their objective, they act to the direct detriment of the public interest as viewed in the Sherman Act. In the absence of countervailing fair trade laws, all asserted justifications are, upon examination, found wanting, either because they are too trivial or elusive to warrant the expense of a trial (as is the case, for example, with a defense that price floors maintain the prestige of a product) or because they run counter to Sherman Act premises (as is the case with the defense that price maintenance enables inefficient sellers to stay in business).

Vertically imposed price ceilings are, as a matter of economic fact that this Court's words cannot change, an altogether different matter. Other things being equal, a manufacturer would like to restrict those distributing his product to the lowest feasible profit margin, for in this way he achieves the lowest overall price to the public and the largest volume. When a manufacturer dictates a minimum resale price he is responding to the interest of his customers, who may treat his product better if they have a secure high margin of profits.

When the same manufacturer dictates a price ceiling, however, he is acting directly in his own interest, and there is no room for the inference that he is merely a mechanism for accomplishing anticompetitive purposes of his customers.

Furthermore, the restraint imposed by price ceilings is of a different order from that imposed by price floors. In the present case the Court uses again the fallacious argument that price ceilings and price floors must be equally unreasonable because both "cripple the freedom of traders and thereby restrain their ability to sell in accordance with their own judgment." The fact of the matter is that this statement does not in itself justify a *per se* rule in either the maximum or minimum price case, and that the real justification for a *per se* rule in the case of minimums has not been shown to exist in the case of maximums.

It has long been recognized that one of the objectives of the Sherman Act was to preserve, for social rather than economic reasons, a high degree of independence, multiplicity, and variety in the economic system. Recognition of this objective does not, however, require this Court to hold that every commercial act that fetters the freedom of some trader is a proper subject for a *per se* rule in the sense that it has no adequate provable justification. The *per se* treatment of price maintenance is justified because analysis alone, without the burden of a trial in each individual case, demonstrates that price floors are invariably harmful on balance. Price ceilings are a different matter: they do not lessen horizontal competition; they drive prices toward the level that would be set by intense competition, and they cannot go below this level unless the manufacturer who dictates them and the customer who accepts them have both miscalculated. Since price ceilings reflect the manufacturer's view that there is insufficient competition to drive prices down to a competitive level, they have the arguable justification that they prevent retailers or wholesalers from reaping monopoly or supercompetitive profits.

When price floors and price ceilings are placed side by side, then, and the question is asked of each, "Does analysis justify a no-trial rule?" the answers must be quite different. Both practices share the negative attribute that they restrict individual discretion in the pricing area, but only the former imposes upon the public the much more significant evil of lessened competition, and, as just seen, the latter has an important arguable justification that the former does not possess. As the Court's opinion partially but inexplicitly recognizes, in a maximum price case the asserted justification must be met on its merits, and not by incantation of a *per se* rule developed for an altogether different situation.

II.

The Court's discovery in this case of (a) a combination and (b) a restraint that is *per se* unreasonable is beset with pitfalls. The Court relies directly on combinations with Milne and Kroner, two third parties who were simply hired and paid to do telephoning and distributing jobs that respondent could as effectively have done itself. Neither had any special interest in respondent's objective of setting a price ceiling. If the critical question is whether a company pays one of its own employees to perform a routine task, or hires an outsider to do the same thing, the requirement of a "combination" in restraint of trade has lost all significant meaning. The point is more than that the words in a statute ought to be taken to mean something of substance. The premise of § 1 adjudication has always been that it is quite proper for a firm to set its own prices and determine its own territories, but that it may not do so in conjunction with another firm with which, in combination, it can generate market power that neither would otherwise have. A firm is not "combining" to fix its own prices or territory simply because it hires outside accountants, market analysts, advertisers by telephone or otherwise, or delivery boys. Once it is recognized that Kroner had no interest whatever in forcing his competitor to *lower* his price, and was merely being paid to perform a delivery job that respondent could have done itself, it is clear respondent's activity was in its essence unilateral.

The Court's difficulties on all of its theories stem from its unwillingness to face the ultimate conclusion at which it has actually arrived: it is unlawful for one person to dictate price floors or price ceilings to another; any pressure brought to bear in support of such dictation renders the dictator liable to any dictatee who is damaged. The reason for the Court's reluctance to state this conclusion bluntly is transparent: this statement of the matter takes no account of the absence of a combination or conspiracy.

This does not mean, however, that no combination or conspiracy could ever be inferred in such an ostensibly unilateral situation. It would often be proper to infer, in situations in which a manufacturer dictates a minimum price to a retailer, that the manufacturer is the mechanism for enforcing a very real combinatorial restraint among retailers who should be competing horizontally. Instead of undertaking to analyze when this inference would be proper, the Court has in the past followed the rough approximation adopted in *Parke, Davis:* there is no "combination" when a manufacturer simply states a resale price and announces that he will not deal with those who depart from it; there is a combination when the manufacturer goes one inch further. The magical quality in this transformation is more apparent than real, for the underlying horizontal combination may frequently be there and the Court has simply failed to state what it is.

. . .

For the reasons stated in my Brother Stewart's opinion and those stated here, I would affirm the judgment below.

[Justice Stewart, joined by Justice Harlan, dissented on the ground that the grant of exclusive territories was lawful and respondent's act of soliciting customers was pro-competitive, not anti-competitive.]

NOTES AND QUERIES

(1) *Implying "Agreement" Because of Coercion.* *Albrecht* is a controversial case because it may be viewed as an opinion expanding the concept of "combination" or as a case where any joint action coercing a distributor to follow a supplier's pricing dictates will be defined as a "contract", "combination" or "conspiracy" for Sherman Act purposes.[71] Similarly, the Court has held that distributors who go along unwillingly with the coercive dictates of a supplier may make that joint action the "contract", "combination" or "conspiracy" allegation necessary for Section 1 analysis.[72] The connection between the joint action and the unlawful end may be attenuated where coercion is present.[73] The more direct the consequences of the coercion are in purpose and effect in pressuring the distributor to obey the supplier's resale pricing policies, the more willing courts appear to infer, imply, or discover the necessary agreement for Section 1 purposes.[74]

These realities have the consequences of narrowing the *Colgate* doctrine[75] and expanding the intra-enterprise conspiracy doctrine.[76] Coercion aimed at obtaining adherence with resale pricing policies by threatening a refusal to deal must be done with "Doric simplicity" to avoid the implication of agreement.[77]

Consider, for example, the FTC's proceeding against Russell Stover Candies, Inc., for engaging in unlawful vertical price fixing by "designating" resale prices and announcing it would refuse to deal with retailers reselling below the designated prices.[78] The stipulated facts showed Stover sold through 18,000 retail outlets, refused to deal with known price cutters, secured compliance with its resale price policies on 94.4% of its products sold at retail, and that a substantial number of retailers desired to sell at less than the Stover designated prices but did not do so because of Stover's announced policy of cutting off price-cutting retailers. FTC complaint counsel set forth two theories for finding the requisite agreement: (1) *"[U]nwilling* compliance by dealers to avoid termination by a manufacturer . . . is bilateral

---

71. "[B]ecause of its analytical shortcomings, *Albrecht* has contributed more to confusing the law than clarifying it." Comment, Maximum Price Fixing: A Per Se Violation of the Sherman Act, 1969 Law & Soc. Order 476, 488.

72. Perma Life Mufflers, Inc. v. International Parts Corp., 392 U.S. 134, 88 S.Ct. 1981, 20 L.Ed.2d 982 (1968).

73. "[S]ince *Albrecht v. Herald Co.*, antitrust lawyers have become accustomed to the idea that co-conspirators need not be friends; they can be enemies or even innocent bystanders." Anderson, The Antitrust Consequences of Manufacturer-Suggested Retail Prices—The Case for Presumptive Illegality, 54 Wash.L.Rev. 763, 774 (1979).

74. See, e.g., Spray-Rite Service Corp. v. Monsanto Co., supra n. 37; Sahm v. V–1 Oil Co., 402 F.2d 69 (10th Cir. 1968); Yentsch v. Texaco, Inc., 630 F.2d 46 (2d Cir. 1980); Malcolm v. Marathon Oil Co., 642 F.2d 845 (5th Cir., Unit B), certiorari denied 454 U.S. 1125, 102 S.Ct. 975, 71 L.Ed.2d 113 (1981).

75. For an argument suggesting the *Colgate* doctrine should be substantially abolished, see Anderson, *supra* note 73.

76. See Handler & Smart, The Present Status of the Intracorporate Conspiracy Doctrine, 3 Cardozo L.Rev. 23 (1981); Note, Intra-Enterprise Conspiracy Under Section 1 of the Sherman Act: A Suggested Standard, 75 Mich.L.Rev. 717 (1977).

77. The phrase "Doric simplicity" is from a case where the Second Circuit upheld an allegation of conspiracy based on a pattern of dealer coercion. George W. Warner & Co. v. Black & Decker Manufacturing Co., 277 F.2d 787, 790 (2d Cir. 1960): "The Supreme Court has left a narrow channel through which a manufacturer may pass even though the facts would have to be of such Doric simplicity as to be somewhat rare in this day of complex business enterprises."

78. In the Matter of Russell Stover Candies, Inc., 3 Trade Reg.Rep. (CCH) ¶ 21,933 (F.T.C. 1, 1982).

conduct and, thus an agreement for purposes of the Sherman Act"; and (2) *"willing* compliance with a manufacturer's pricing policies by the great majority of dealers, knowing that competitor dealers are being 'invited' by the manufacturer to charge the same prices, and knowing that the manufacturer is making continued dealing contingent upon compliance, amounts to a series of vertical agreements between the manufacturer and the dealers."

After an extensive survey of the post-*Colgate* cases, three out of four Commissioners found Stover was engaged in an unlawful combination to fix resale prices in violation of § 1 of the Sherman Act and § 5 of the F.T.C. Act. In an opinion by Commissioner Pertschuk, the majority held:

> Our review of Supreme Court and lower court cases convinces us that, despite the Court's original pronouncement concerning the right of a manufacturer to threaten termination for failing to comply with pricing policies, that right has been circumscribed by a prohibition on the securing of unwilling compliance through the coercion inherent in threatened termination. We recognize that our interpretation is not free from doubt. Despite the strong language in a number of opinions, e.g., *Albrecht, Schwinn, Hanson* and *Yentsch*,[79] that coercion from threatened termination which leads to unwilling compliance is sufficient for finding an agreement, there are other factors which could be relied upon as distinguishing it from the case presented here. For example, in *Albrecht*, the supplier hired a substitute distributor. In *Schwinn* the manufacturer could be said to have exercised substantial economic leverage over the distributors. In *Yentsch*, the manufacturer apparently threatened termination a number of times rather than just once and, as in *Hanson*, the supplier had the right to terminate the dealer's lease.

> However, we do not believe that these cases should be read to compel the conclusion that they should be limited to their precise facts. Such an interpretation, we believe, elevates form over substance by focusing on factors which are actually tangential to the real ongoing relationship between suppliers and distributors. No doubt, there has been a tendency for some "extra" factor, beyond threatened termination, though not necessarily significant in itself, to be present in the evidentiary record when courts have analyzed a claim that a dealer has been coerced into compliance with the manufacturer's pricing policies. The presence of this "extra" factor seems to have provided at least an arguable rationale, though doing some theoretical damage in the process, for maintaining the Court's original statement of the *Colgate* doctrine. *Parke, Davis*, in fact, appeared to sanction this very type of analysis. However, the logic of the Court's statements in *Albrecht, Perma Life*, and other post-*Parke, Davis* opinions convinces us that the *Parke, Davis* "plus factor" requirement for an agreement to be found was not intended to be essential where unwilling compliance resulting from threatened termination is present. While it is true that there is no Supreme Court holding to this effect, we must interpret *Colgate* in light of a history of an evolving standard and a series of clarifying cases. In effect, the "plus factor" requirement has evolved to serve as a device for the courts to infer the presence of coercion, a concept that the Court has utilized to connote bilateral behavior. Here, coercion is clearly present and provides direct evidence that bilateral behavior, and hence agreements, existed. Consequently, we believe

79. [The references are to Albrecht v. Herald Co., discussed supra; United States v. Arnold, Schwinn & Co., discussed infra pp. 631–637; Hanson v. Shell Oil Co., 541 F.2d 1352 (9th Cir.), certiorari denied 429 U.S. 1074, 97 S.Ct. 813, 50 L.Ed.2d 792 (1976); Yentsch v. Texaco, discussed infra p. 781.—Ed.]

that, were the Court faced with the factual record presented here, an agreement would be found.

We conclude, therefore, that there is no sound legal distinction between coercion resulting from the threat of cancelling a lease or terminating a franchise and coercion resulting from a communicated policy of terminating supply of products for resale to dealers who fail to comply with the manufacturer's pricing policies. In both sets of situations the distributor is induced to act contrary to its preferences in order to avoid termination or other sanctions. It is important to note that we are not dealing here with mere parallel behavior, that is, where dealers decide independently to charge the same prices suggested by manufacturers. Rather, we are faced with an unambiguous factual record establishing that a number of dealers comply with Stover's pricing policy in order to avoid termination. Absent the threat of termination, they would charge lower prices. This conduct—a threatened action of refusal to continue dealing, followed by unwilling compliance in order to avoid the threatened sanction, followed by continued dealing—is the antithesis of unilateral behavior.[80]

The majority went on to reject complaint counsel's second theory for inferring a combination; that Stover "invited" dealers to fix resale prices and the dealers acquiesced. The majority reasoned that drawing the inference of combination or conspiracy from widespread dealer compliance, without more, was a rule not supported by precedent and a rule which would unduly interfere with a supplier's initial selection of dealers.

The majority then defined the scope of the Colgate doctrine as follows:

We conclude that the *Colgate* doctrine, as it stands today, does not preclude, as a matter of law, a finding of agreement when a buyer unwillingly complied with a supplier's pricing policies in order to avoid termination. There is no sound basis, either in legal precedent or theory, for reaching the illogical result that this conduct is only unilateral. . . . We see no logical basis for concluding that a dealer who restricts his pricing policies in return for some assurance of continued dealing has not entered into an agreement with the supplier. An announced policy of terminating non-complying dealers is the practical equivalent of providing some assurances of future dealing in return for the dealer's restricting his pricing policies.

We emphasize that our view of the *Colgate* doctrine does not restrict the discretion of a seller in deciding with whom he will deal initially. An initial decision to distribute only through non-discounters, for example, would not give rise to a finding of bilateral conduct. Initial customer selection, standing alone, does not raise an inference of unwilling compliance on the part of the distributor because there is no conduct required of the distributor for future dealing. Conditioning *continued* dealing on any particular conduct, e.g., charging particular prices, on the other hand, is the equivalent of a communicated threat of termination.

We believe this right of *initial* customer selection is the meaning of *Colgate* as it stands today. Thus, we agree with respondent that there continues to be a *Colgate* doctrine and that it can be stated in terms of the "long recognized right of trader or manufacturer, engaged in an entirely private business freely to exercise his own independent discretion as to parties with whom he will deal." . . . However, this phrase, as we have seen, has been much qualified as the Court has continually re-

80. 3 Trade Reg.Rep. at p. 22,363-64.

fined its meaning. It does not mean that compliance with a pricing policy in order to avoid termination, as is presented in this case, does not give rise to an agreement.

We also emphasize that our interpretation of *Colgate* does not effect the right of a seller to suggest resale prices. The very term "suggested" prices implies that the dealer is free to follow them if he wishes. Compliance with suggested prices, entirely based on the dealer's own preferences and without influence of a threat of termination or other sanctions, does not lead to a finding of combination between the dealer and the manufacturer.[81]

Commission Chairman Miller dissented principally on the grounds that resale price maintenance should not be *per se* unlawful and that the majority's "coercion doctrine" goes beyond the "more appropriate economic concept of a response to true market power" and "displaces the more principled analysis of 'combination' that has developed in horizontal restraint cases under the Sherman and F.T.C. Acts." [82]

Query: If the FTC's view in *Russell Stover* becomes the general rule, will there be anything left of *Colgate?*

(2) *The Per Se Illegality of Vertical Maximum Price Fixing. Albrecht* is also a controversial case because it applies a *per se* rule to vertical *maximum* price fixing agreements. Critics of the rule argue that firms imposing maximum resale prices on distributors promote "consumer welfare" because the supplier's only interest in doing so is to maximize unit sales at the lowest efficient cost.[83] The counter-arguments again assert that the antitrust laws are designed to promote the freedom of traders, long term consumer welfare is benefited by so doing,[84] and sellers seeking the advantages of vertical integration by contract should not be allowed to do so with regard to pricing unless they are willing to bear the risks of vertical integration as well.[85] Cases like *Albrecht* also point out that today's maximum price may become tomorrow's minimum price and that courts are ill-suited to supervise continually private pricing arrangements displacing the competitive process.

The question of the antitrust treatment of maximum price fixing arrangements was before the Supreme Court once again in *Arizona v. Maricopa County Medical Society*, supra p. 367, a horizontal arrangement of physicians operating under the aegis of non-profit foundations for medical care and setting maximum fees for medical care reimbursed by approved insurance plans. In reaffirming the *per se* rule against *horizontal* maximum price fixing, the Court cited with approval the *Albrecht* case and its ban on *vertical* maximum price fixing. See p. 371, supra.

(3) *Queries.* Does the majority opinion in *Albrecht* develop a meaning for the concept "combination" that differs from the meaning of "contract"

81. Id. at 22, 369–70.

82. Id. at 22, 372–73.

83. Easterbrook, Maximum Price Fixing, 48 U.Chi.L.Rev. 886 (1981); Blair & Kaserman, The *Albrecht* Rule and Consumer Welfare: An Economic Analysis, 33 U.Fla.L.Rev. 461 (1981).

84. See Anderson, supra note 73; Redlich, The Burger Court and the Per Se Rule, 44 Albany L.Rev. 1 (1979).

85. Flynn, The Function and Dysfunction of Per Se Rules in Vertical Market

Restraints, 58 Wash.U.L.Q. 767, 792 (1980) ("[A] test of presumptive illegality is probably justified in view of the impact of the conduct on the independence of traders, intrabrand price competition, and the tradition of narrowly circumscribing the exercise of monopoly power by those seeking the advantage of vertical integration without its attendant risks and burdens.")

or "conspiracy"? Could this case have been brought under Section 2 as an attempt to monopolize? How would you state the "Colgate doctrine" after *Parke, Davis* and *Albrecht?* Can you think of any justifications, other than preservation of independents, mentioned by Justice Harlan, for a *per se* rule against vertical *maximum* price fixing? Do the reasons set forth for banning horizontal maximum price fixing in *Arizona v. Maricopa County Medical Society* apply equally to vertical conspiracies to fix maximum prices?

C. VERTICAL RESTRAINTS ON TERRITORIES, CLASSES OF CUSTOMERS AND LOCATION

An agreement between supplier and dealer may provide that the latter shall have the exclusive right to handle supplier's goods in a defined territory. If dealers holding such exclusive franchises are located far enough apart, each will have a more or less effective monopoly in selling the particular brand of automobile or television set which he handles. Thus the problem of maintaining resale prices satisfactory to the dealer can be solved without reliance on Fair Trade legislation or consignment selling. Indeed this system may be more effective than fair-trading in a business like automobile retailing, where most of the price-cutting takes the form of higher allowances on the used car which the customer turns in when buying a new car. The Fair Trade acts did not necessarily permit vertical control of the price of the new car sold by the dealer, but clearly did not authorize control of prices paid by the retailer for trade-in cars of the same or other makes. But if a franchisee were the exclusive Ford dealer in his market, his margin between new and used car prices would have to face competition only from dealers in other automobiles.

Despite the ease with which exclusive franchising lends itself to restraint of competition among dealers, its legality is fairly well established.[86] It rests primarily upon the axiom that sellers in a competitive unregulated economy are free to limit the number of, and to select, their customers. It is true that a contract between producer and dealer, binding the producer to refrain from appointing additional dealers in the territory, goes somewhat beyond the mere unfettered exercise of producer's choice to deal or not to deal.[87] The producer's freedom is restrained. This kind of restraint can be defended on grounds that do not, at least directly, compromise the competitive ide-

---

86. United States v. Bausch & Lomb Optical Co., 321 U.S. 707, 64 S.Ct. 805, 88 L.Ed. 1024 (1944); Brosius v. Pepsi-Cola Co., 155 F.2d 99 (3d Cir. 1946); Great Atlantic & Pacific Tea Co. v. Cream of Wheat Co., 227 F. 46 (2d Cir. 1915); Report of Attorney General's National Committee to Study the Antitrust Laws 27–29 (1955).

Compare Ebb, The Grundig-Consten Case Revisited, 115 U.Pa.L.Rev. 855 (1967), reviewing the law of the European Economic Community. The case involved an exclusive distributorship granted by a German manufacturer to a French firm. The German firm also transferred its French trademark thus precluding itself and others from competing with the French firm. The arrangement was held incompatible with the principle of transnational competition embodied in the Rome Treaty.

87. See Quality Mercury, Inc. v. Ford Motor Co., 542 F.2d 466 (8th Cir. 1976); Eastex Aviation, Inc. v. Sperry & Hutchison Co., 522 F.2d 1299 (5th Cir. 1975); Packard Motor Car Co. v. Webster Motor Car Co., 243 F.2d 418, 421 (D.C.Cir.) (Bazelon, J., dissenting), certiorari denied 355 U.S. 822, 78 S.Ct. 29, 2 L.Ed.2d 38 (1957).

al. A producer may decide as a matter of commercial policy to set high standards for his dealers, to demand that they be of good credit, financial and otherwise, that they be well located, that they maintain elegant and expensive show-rooms, and that they furnish reliable service facilities to the ultimate consumer. Such a policy might be difficult to carry out unless the producer can concentrate his distribution through a few favored distributors, who are encouraged to invest the necessary funds and effort because they are assured of reaping the full benefit thereof. The restraint might be defended as ancillary to the sale of a share of the manufacturer's good will.[88]

On the other hand vertical restraints imposed on independent businesses as to customers, territories or location might be viewed as a form of vertical integration by contract without the necessity of capital investment required by acquisition. In addition, the supplier may be able to achieve many of the advantages of vertical integration while shifting most of the risks to the distributor bound by customer, territory or location restrictions. In some industries where marketing is chaotic, exposure to tort and other forms of liability is substantial, compliance with state or local regulation is complex and expensive, or unionization of marketing employees is feared, restrictive licensing of independent outlets may maximize the supplier's return on ultimate sales while retaining control of the channels of distribution with a minimum exposure to the risks and costs associated with marketing the product. Gasoline retailing through branded stations and jobbers has many of these characteristics and has provoked much antitrust litigation.[89]

From the point of view of dealers interested in protection from competition by other dealers in the same product, the mobility of customers may seriously weaken the advantages gained by restricted distribution. A customer dissatisfied with the "official" automobile dealer in the territory in which he happens to live, may shop around in other territories to purchase the same model. Dealers begin to press the manufacturer for franchise provisions which prevent or discourage both dealers and customers from crossing the territorial boundaries. In the vernacular of the auto dealers, "cross-selling" or "bootlegging" of automobiles must be halted.[90] The situation of the dealer, caught between supplier's pressure to maintain sales under the implicit threat of cancellation of the franchise and dwindling sales due to price-cutting by competing dealers, has been extensively re-

---

88. The courts have sustained on such reasoning a covenant, in the lease of a motion picture film to a "first-run" theater, that the same film would not be reshown in the same area until after a reasonable "clearance" period. See cases reviewed in Orbo Theatre Corp. v. Loew's, Inc., 156 F.Supp. 770, 778 (D.D.C.1957).

89. Gasoline marketing practices and litigation are reviewed in Hearings, Marketing Practices in the Gasoline Industry,

Subcomm. on Antitrust & Monopoly of the Senate Comm. on the Judiciary, 3 Vols. (1970–1972).

Franchise terminations and non-renewals in the gasoline industry are now regulated by the Petroleum Marketing Practices Act, 15 U.S.C. §§ 2801, *et seq.*

90. Cf. United States v. General Motors Corp., 384 U.S. 127, 86 S.Ct. 1321, 16 L.Ed.2d 415 (1966).

viewed in Congressional hearings, Federal Trade Commission reports, and economic treatises.[91]

Judicial analysis of customer and territory restraints has reflected these cross-currents. In WHITE MOTOR CO. v. UNITED STATES, 372 U.S. 253, 83 S.Ct. 696, 9 L.Ed.2d 738 (1963), the Court reversed a district court holding that customer and territory restrictions were *per se* unlawful. The Court remanded for further proceedings, citing a need to know more about the "economic and business stuff out of which these arrangements emerge" to determine whether they should be measured by a rule of reason test or whether a *per se* test should be adopted. Settlement of the case by consent decree deprived the Court of the opportunity to examine the "economic and business stuff" of vertical market restraints in the context of marketing trucks.[92] Four years later however, enough "stuff" was apparently furnished in a case testing the legitimacy of vertical customer and territory restraints in the marketing of bicycles.

The case, *United States v. Arnold, Schwinn & Co.*,[93] was a civil case challenging Schwinn's practices of allocating exclusive territories to jobbers and wholesalers and confining retail sales to sales by franchised Schwinn retailers. While franchised retailers were free to sell other brands of bicycles, the Schwinn franchise required that they obtain Schwinn bicycles from the wholesaler authorized to sell in their territory and that franchisees refrain from selling Schwinn bicycles to unauthorized retailers. Wholesalers were assigned specific exclusive territories and were required to sell only to franchised Schwinn accounts and only to accounts within the wholesaler's exclusive territory.

After a 70-day trial, the district court held the territorial restrictions on the resale of products sold by Schwinn to distributors were *per se* unlawful, while the territorial restrictions on wholesaler transactions where they acted as agents or consignees for direct shipments by Schwinn to franchised retailers were not unlawful. The district court also upheld Schwinn's customer limitations on franchised retailers, prohibiting retailers from selling to discount houses and unfranchised retailers for resale to the public.

---

91. An excellent summary and analysis is provided by Kessler and Brenner, Automobile Dealer Franchises: Vertical Integration by Contract, 66 Yale L.J. 1135 (1957). See also Note, Restricted Channels of Distribution, 75 Harv.L.Rev. 795 (1962); Scherer, Industrial Market Structure and Economic Performance 586–90 (2d Ed. 1980). Hearings, Exclusive, Territorial Allocation Legislation, Subcomm. on Antitrust & Monopoly of the Senate Comm. on the Judiciary, 92d Cong., 1st Sess. (1972); Hearings, Franchise Legislation, Subcomm. on Antitrust & Monopoly of the Senate Comm. on the Judiciary, 90th Cong., 1st Sess. (1967); Hearings, Distribution Problems Affecting Small Business, Subcomm. on Anti-

trust & Monopoly of the Senate Comm. on the Judiciary, 89th Cong. 1st & 2nd Sess. (1965–66).

Automobile franchising is regulated by the Automobile Dealers' Day in Court Act, 15 U.S.C. §§ 1221–1225.

92. The consent decree enjoined the division of customers and territories. White Motor Co. v. United States, 1964 Trade Cases, ¶ 79,762 (N.D.Ohio 1964). Lower federal courts however, generally applied a rule of reason analysis. See Sandura Co. v. Federal Trade Commission, 339 F.2d 847 (6th Cir. 1964).

93. 388 U.S. 365, 87 S.Ct. 1856, 18 L.Ed.2d 1249 (1967).

On appeal, the Supreme Court viewed the case as a challenge to Schwinn's vertical territory and customer restraints and one free of a horizontal or vertical price fixing conspiracy. Justice Fortas, writing for the majority analyzed the legality of the restraints as follows: [94]

We first observe that the facts of this case do not come within the specific illustrations which the Court in *White Motor* articulated as possible factors relevant to a showing that the challenged vertical restraint is sheltered by the rule of reason because it is not anticompetitive. Schwinn was not a newcomer, seeking to break into or stay in the bicycle business. It was not a "failing company." On the contrary, at the initiation of these practices, it was the leading bicycle producer in the Nation. Schwinn contends, however, and the trial court found, that the reasons which induced it to adopt the challenged distribution program were to enable it and the small, independent merchants that made up its chain of distribution to compete more effectively in the marketplace. Schwinn sought a better way of distributing its product: a method which would promote sales, increase stability of its distributor and dealer outlets, and augment profits. But this argument, appealing as it is, is not enough to avoid the Sherman Act proscription; because, in a sense, every restrictive practice is designed to augment the profit and competitive position of its participants. Price fixing does so, for example, and so may a well-calculated division of territories. The anti-trust outcome does not turn merely on the presence of sound business reason or motive. Here, for example, if the test of reasonableness were merely whether Schwinn's restrictive distribution program and practices were adopted "for good business reasons" and not merely to injure competitors, or if the answer turned upon whether it was indeed "good business practice," we should not quarrel with Schwinn's eloquent submission or the finding of the trial court. But our inquiry cannot stop at that point. Our inquiry is whether, assuming nonpredatory motives and business purposes and the incentive of profit and volume considerations, the effect upon competition in the marketplace is substantially adverse. The promotion of self-interest alone does not invoke the rule of reason to immunize otherwise illegal conduct. It is only if the conduct is not unlawful in its impact in the marketplace or if the self-interest coincides with the statutory concern with the preservation and promotion of competition that protection is achieved. Chicago Board of Trade, 246 U.S., at 238, 38 S.Ct., at 243.

On this basis, restraints as to territory or customers, vertical or horizontal, are unlawful if they are "ancillary to the price-fixing" (White Motor Co. v. United States, supra, 372 U.S., at 260, 83 S.Ct. at 700) or if the price fixing is "an integral part of the whole distribution system." (Bausch & Lomb, supra, 321 U.S., at 720, 64 S.Ct., at 812). In those situations, it is needless to inquire further

---

94. Id. at 374–382, 87 S.Ct., at 1863–1867, 18 L.Ed.2d, at 1257–1262.

into competitive effect because it is established doctrine that, unless permitted by statute, the fixing of prices at which others may sell is anticompetitive, and the unlawfulness of the price fixing infects the distribution restrictions. At the other extreme, a manufacturer of a product other and equivalent brands of which are readily available in the market may select his customers, and for this purpose he may "franchise" certain dealers to whom, alone, he will sell his goods. Cf. United States v. Colgate & Co., 250 U.S. 300, 39 S.Ct. 465, 63 L.Ed. 992 (1919). If the restraint stops at that point—if nothing more is involved than vertical "confinement" of the manufacturer's own sales of the merchandise to selected dealers, and if competitive products are readily available to others, the restriction, on these facts alone, would not violate the Sherman Act. It is within these boundary lines that we must analyze the present case.

. . .

. . . [T]he Government argues that it is illogical and inconsistent to forbid territorial limitations on resales by distributors where the distributor owns the goods, having bought them from Schwinn, and, at the same time, to exonerate arrangements which require distributors to confine resales of the goods they have bought to "franchised" retailers. It argues that requiring distributors, once they have purchased the product, to confine sales to franchised retailers is indistinguishable in law and principle from the division of territory which the decree condemns. Both, the Government argues, are in the nature of restraints upon alienation which are beyond the power of the manufacturer to impose upon its vendees and which, since the nature of the transaction includes an agreement, combination or understanding, are violations of § 1 of the Sherman Act. . . . We agree, and upon remand, the decree should be revised to enjoin any limitation upon the freedom of distributors to dispose of the Schwinn products, which they have bought from Schwinn, where and to whomever they choose. The principle is of course, equally applicable to sales to retailers, and the decree should similarly enjoin the making of any sales to retailers upon any condition, agreement or understanding limiting the retailer's freedom as to where and to whom it will resell the products.

The appellant vigorously argues that, since this remedy is confined to situations where the distributor and retailer acquire title to the bicycles, it will provide only partial relief; that to prevent the allocation of territories and confinement to franchised retail dealers, the decree can and should be enlarged to forbid these practices, however effected—whether by sale and resale or by agency, consignment, or the Schwinn Plan. [Direct shipments to retailers upon orders of wholesalers acting as agents]. But we are dealing here with a vertical restraint embodying the unilateral program of a single manufacturer. We are not dealing with a combination of manufacturers, as in *Klor's* or of distributors, as in *General Motors.* We are not dealing with a "division" of territory in the sense of an allocation by and among the distributors, see *Sealy,* supra, or an agreement among distributors to restrict their competition, see *General Motors,* supra. We are here concerned with a truly vertical arrangement, raising the fundamental question of the degree to which a manufacturer may not only select the customers to whom he will sell, but also allocate territories for resale and confine access to his product to selected, or franchised, retailers. We conclude that the proper application of § 1 of the Sherman Act to this problem requires differentiation between the situation where the manufacturer parts with title, dominion, or risk with respect to the article, and where he completely retains ownership and risk of loss.

As the District Court held, where a manufacturer *sells* products to his distributor subject to territorial restrictions upon resale, a *per se* violation of the Sherman Act results. And, as we have held, the same principle applies to restrictions of outlets with which the distributors may deal and to restraints upon retailers to whom the goods are sold. Under the Sherman Act, it is unreasonable without more for a manufacturer to seek to restrict and confine areas or persons with whom an article may be traded after the manufacturer has parted with dominion over it. *White Motor,* supra; *Dr. Miles,* supra. Such restraints are so obviously destructive of competition that their mere existence is enough. If the manufacturer parts with dominion over his product or transfers risk of loss to another, he may not reserve control over its destiny or the conditions of its resale.[95]   To permit this would sanction franchising and confinement of distribution as the ordinary instead of the unusual method which may be permissible in an appropriate and impelling competitive setting, since most merchandise is distributed by means of purchase and sale. On the other hand, as indicated in *White Motor,* we are not prepared to introduce the inflexibility which a *per se* rule might bring if it were applied to prohibit all vertical restrictions of territory and all franchising, in the sense of designating specified distributors and retailers as the chosen instruments through which the manufacturer, retaining ownership of the goods, will distribute them to the public. Such a rule might severely hamper smaller enterprises resorting to reasonable methods of meeting the competition of giants and of merchandising through independent dealers, and it might sharply accelerate the trend towards vertical integration of the distribution process. But to allow this freedom where the manufacturer has parted with dominion over the goods—the usual marketing situation—would violate the ancient rule against re-

95. [Footnote 6 in original] We have no occasion here to consider whether a patentee has any greater rights in this respect. Compare United States v. General Electric Co., 272 U.S. 476, 47 S.Ct. 192, 71 L.Ed. 362 (1926), with United States v. New Wrinkle, Inc., 342 U.S. 371, 72 S.Ct. 350, 96 L.Ed. 417 (1952); United States v. Line Material Co., 333 U.S. 287, 68 S.Ct. 550, 92 L.Ed. 701 (1948); and United States v. Masonite Corp., 316 U.S. 265, 62 S.Ct. 1070, 86 L.Ed. 1461 (1942).

straints on alienation and open the door to exclusivity of outlets and limitation of territory further than prudence permits.

The Government does not here contend for a *per se* rule as to agency, consignment, or Schwinn-Plan transactions even though these may be used—as they are here—to implement a scheme of confining distribution outlets as in this case. Where the manufacturer retains title, dominion, and risk with respect to the product and the position and function of the dealer in question are, in fact, indistinguishable from those of an agent or salesman of the manufacturer, it is only if the impact of the confinement is "unreasonably" restrictive of competition that a violation of § 1 results from such confinement, unencumbered by culpable price fixing. Simpson v. Union Oil Co., 377 U.S. 13, 84 S.Ct. 1051, 12 L.Ed.2d 98 (1964). As the District Court found, Schwinn adopted the challenged distribution programs in a competitive situation dominated by mass merchandisers which command access to large-scale advertising and promotion, choice of retail outlets, both owned and franchised, and adequate sources of supply. It is not claimed that Schwinn's practices or other circumstances resulted in an inadequate competitive situation with respect to the bicycle market; and there is nothing in this record—after elimination of the price-fixing issue—to lead us to conclude that Schwinn's program exceeded limits reasonably necessary to meet the competitive problems posed by its more powerful competitors. In these circumstances, the rule of reason is satisfied.

We do not suggest that the unilateral adoption by a single manufacturer of an agency or consignment pattern and the Schwinn type of restrictive distribution system would be justified in any and all circumstances by the presence of the competition of mass merchandisers and by the demonstrated need of the franchise system to meet that competition. But certainly, in such circumstances, the vertically imposed distribution restraints—*absent* price fixing and in the presence of adequate sources of alternative products to meet the needs of the unfranchised—may not be held to be *per se* violations of the Sherman Act. The Government, in this Court, so concedes in this case.

. . .

. . . Once the manufacturer has parted with title and risk, he has parted with dominion over the product, and his effort thereafter to restrict territory or persons to whom the product may be transferred—whether by explicit agreement or by silent combination or understanding with his vendee—is a *per se* violation of § 1 of the Sherman Act.

Justices Stewart and Harlan dissented from the majority's application of a *per se* rule to vertical territory and customer restraints where title to the goods had passed to a Schwinn franchised distributor. Stressing the significance of franchising to the preservation of small business and the adverse impact of the majority's adoption of *per se* rules upon the operation of a strong distribution system, the dissent characterized the majority opinion as one premised on a "wooden and irrelevant formula" [96] likely to compel vertical integration. Professing to see no reason for distinguishing between sale and agency transactions and no evidence of the competitive effects of Schwinn's distribution system, the dissent observed: [97]

> Centuries ago, it could perhaps be assumed that a manufacturer had no legitimate interest in what happened to his products once he had sold them to a middleman and they had started their way down the channel of distribution. But this assumption no longer holds true in a day of sophisticated marketing policies, mass advertising, and vertically integrated manufacturer-distributors. Restrictions like those involved in a franchising program should accordingly be able to claim justification under the ancillary restraints doctrine.

> In any event, the state of the common law 400 or even 100 years ago is irrelevant to the issue before us: the effect of the antitrust laws upon vertical distributional restraints in the American economy today. The problems involved are difficult and complex, and our response should be more reasoned and sensitive than the simple acceptance of a hoary formula. "It does seem possible that the nineteenth and twentieth centuries have contributed legal conceptions growing out of new types of business which make it inappropriate" for the Court to base its "overthrow of contemporary commercial policies on judicial views of the reign of Queen Elizabeth." [98] Moreover, the Court's answer makes everything turn on whether the arrangement between a manufacturer and his distributor is denominated a "sale" or "agency." Such a rule ignores and conceals the "economic and business stuff out of which" a sound answer should be fashioned. White Motor Co. v. United States, supra, 372 U.S., at 263, 83 S.Ct., at 702. The Court has emphasized in the past that these differences in form often do not represent "differences in substance." Simpson v. Union Oil Co., 377 U.S. 13, 22, 84 S.Ct. 1051, 1057. Draftsmen may cast business arrangements in different legal molds for purposes of commercial law, but these arrangements may operate identically in terms of economic function and competitive effect. It is the latter factors which are the concern of the antitrust laws. The record does not show that the purposes of Schwinn's franchising program and the competitive consequences of its implementation differed, depending on whether Schwinn sold its products to wholesalers or resorted to the agency, consignment, or Schwinn Plan methods of distribution. And there is no reason generally to suppose that variations in the formal legal packaging of franchising programs produce differences in their actual impact in the marketplace. Our experience is to the contrary. As stated in

96. Id. at 394, 87 S.Ct., at 1873, 18 L.Ed.2d, at 1269.

97. Id. at 392–394, 87 S.Ct., at 1872–1873, 18 L.Ed.2d, at 1267-1269.

98. [Footnote 17 in original] Chafee, Equitable Servitudes on Chattels, 41 Harv.L.Rev. 945, 983.

United States v. Masonite Corp., 316 U.S. 265, 278, 280, 62 S.Ct. 1070, 1077:

> "[T]his Court has quite consistently refused to allow the form into which the parties chose to cast the transaction to govern.
>
> · · ·
>
> "So far as the Sherman Act is concerned the result must turn not on the skill with which counsel has manipulated the concepts of 'sale' and 'agency' but on the significance of the business practices in terms of restraint of trade."

The impact of today's decision on Schwinn may be slight, because over 75% of its distribution is done through the Schwinn Plan, which the Court upholds. Perhaps Schwinn can rearrange the legal terminology of its other distributional arrangements to avoid "the ancient rule against restraints on alienation" which the Court adopts. Perhaps other manufacturers who use sales as a means of distribution in a franchise or analogous marketing system can do likewise. If they can, the Court has created considerable business for legal draftsmen. If they cannot, vertical integration and the elimination of small independent competitors are likely to follow. Meanwhile, the Court has, *sua sponte*, created a bluntly indiscriminate and destructive weapon which can be used to dismantle a vast variety of distributional systems—competitive and anticompetitive, reasonable and unreasonable.

In view of the commendably careful and realistic approach the Court has taken in analyzing the basic structure of Schwinn's marketing program, it is particularly disappointing to see the Court balk at the label "sale," and turn from reasoned response to a wooden and irrelevant formula.

The *Schwinn* decision provoked considerable controversy, both in the courts and in the academy.[99] It was apparent that careful planning and draftsmanship could avoid the application of the *per se* rule by relying upon the unilateral selection of sole outlets in widely sepa-

99. See generally Comegys, Moderator, Restraints in Distribution: *General Motors, Sealy and Schwinn,* a Symposium on Ancillary Restrictions, 36 ABA Antitrust L.J. 84 (1967); Handler, Twenty-Fifth Annual Antitrust Review, 73 Colum.L.Rev. 415, 458–59 (1973); Handler, The Twentieth Annual Antitrust Review—1967, 53 Va.L.Rev. 1667, 1680–86 (1967); Keck, The Schwinn Case, 23 Bus. Lawyer 669 (1968); McLaren, Marketing Limitations on Independent Distributors and Dealers—Prices, Territories, Customers, and Handling of Competitive Products, 13 Antitrust Bull. 161, 168 (1968); Orrick, Marketing Restrictions Imposed to Protect the Integrity of 'Franchise' Distribution Systems, 36 ABA Antitrust L.J. 63, 69–72 (1967); Pollock, Antitrust Problems in Franchising, 15 N.Y.L.F. 106, 110–13 (1969); Pollock, Alternative Distribution Methods After Schwinn, 63 Nw.L.Rev. 595 (1968); Sadd, Territorial and Customer Restrictions After Sealy and Schwinn, 38 U.Cin.L.Rev. 249 (1969); Williams, Distribution and the Sherman Act—The Effects of General Motors, Schwinn and Sealy, 1967 Duke L.J. 732, 740 (1967); Note, Restrictive Distribution Arrangements after the Schwinn Case, 53 Cornell L.Rev. 515 (1967); The Supreme Court, 1966 Term, 81 Harv.L.Rev. 69, 235–38 (1967); Note, Territorial Restrictions and Per Se Rules—A Re-evaluation of the Schwinn and Sealy Doctrines, 70 Mich.L.Rev. 616 (1972); Comment, Vertical Territorial Restraints and the Per Se Concept, 18 Buffalo L.Rev. 153, 161 (1969); Comment, The Impact of the Schwinn Case on Territorial Restrictions, 46 Texas L.Rev. 497, 511 (1968).

rate geographic areas, unilateral refusals to deal with distributors selling in territories or to customers not of the supplier's liking, assignment of areas of "primary responsibility" to franchisees, or the orchestration of distribution on an agency or consignment basis rather than a sales basis. The competitive consequences of such devices appeared to differ little from outright vertical agreements restricting a franchisee's resale to specific territories or customers, thereby lending weight to the observation that the *Schwinn* rationale was "an exercise in barren formalism." [1]

Courts quickly encountered cases where the public interest either legitimately required or arguably justified express customer or territorial restraints. For example, in *Tripoli Co. v. Wella Corp.,*[2] the Third Circuit upheld a vertical customer restraint restricting the resale of dangerous hair-care products to professional beauticians. The court found the products posed a risk of serious physical injury if not administered by trained professionals and the restraints were necessary to protect the public and to protect the manufacturer from liability should the products fall into untrained hands.

Other courts, most noticeably the Tenth Circuit, limited the implications of *Schwinn* by emphasizing the court's reliance upon Schwinn's "firm and resolute enforcement" of its vertical restrictions. These courts held that there must be proof of both "firm and resolute enforcement" of the restrictions, beyond the formal contractual agreement to the restrictions, before the restraint would be considered *per se* unlawful.[3]

Territorial limitations were found justifiable but *per se* unlawful because of *Schwinn* in the case of a producer of pasteurized beer claiming the restrictions were necessary to maintain the quality of its pasteurized beer while in transit. In *Adolph Coors Co. v. Federal Trade Commission,*[4] the Tenth Circuit expressed misgivings about applying a *per se* rule while upholding an F.T.C. cease and desist order against Coors' territorial restrictions upon distributors:

> Although we are compelled to follow the *Schwinn per se* rule rendering Coors' territorial restrictions on resale illegal *per se*, we believe that the *per se* rule should yield to situations where a

1. Baker, Vertical Restraints in Times of Change: From *White* to *Schwinn* to *Where?*, 44 Antitrust L.J. 537 (1975).

2. 425 F.2d 932 (3d Cir.), certiorari denied 400 U.S. 831, 91 S.Ct. 62, 27 L.Ed.2d 62 (1970). See also Clairol, Inc. v. Boston Discount Center of Berkley, Inc., 608 F.2d 1114 (6th Cir. 1979). For cases in which a *Tripoli* type justification was found wanting, see Pitchford v. Pepi, Inc., 531 F.2d 92 (3d Cir. 1975), certiorari denied 426 U.S. 935, 96 S.Ct. 2649, 49 L.Ed.2d 387 (1976); Carter-Wallace, Inc. v. United States, 196 Ct.Cl. 35, 449 F.2d 1374 (1971).

3. See Colorado Pump & Supply Co. v. Febco, Inc., 472 F.2d 637 (10th Cir.),

certiorari denied 411 U.S. 987, 93 S.Ct. 2274, 36 L.Ed.2d 965 (1973); World of Sleep, Inc. v. Stearns & Foster Co., 525 F.2d 40 (10th Cir. 1975). See also Janel Sales Corp. v. Lanvin Parfums, Inc., 396 F.2d 398 (2d Cir.), certiorari denied 393 U.S. 938, 89 S.Ct. 303, 21 L.Ed.2d 275 (1968). Contra, Copper Liquor, Inc. v. Adolph Coors Co., 506 F.2d 934, rehearing en banc denied 509 F.2d 758 (5th Cir. 1975). See Annot., 30 A.L.R. Fed. 19 (1976).

4. 497 F.2d 1178 (10th Cir. 1974), certiorari denied 419 U.S. 1105, 95 S.Ct. 775, 42 L.Ed.2d 801 (1975).

unique product requires territorial restrictions to remain in business. For example, speed of delivery, quality control of the product, refrigerated delivery, and condition of the Coors product at the time of delivery may justify restraints on trade that would be unreasonable when applied to marketing standardized products. . . . Perhaps the Supreme Court may see the wisdom of grafting an exception to the *per se* rule when a product is unique and where the manufacturer can justify its territorial restraints under the rule of reason.[5]

Territorial divisions pursuant to trademark, patent and other forms of licensing continued to be analyzed on a rule of reason basis on the rationale that licensing was not the equivalent of a sale and therefore the *Schwinn* premise did not apply.[6]

Academic criticism of *Schwinn* echoed these justifications for vertical customer and territory restraints, while also suggesting others.[7] Proponents of an exclusively neo-classical analysis of antitrust issues were more harshly critical of *Schwinn* and similar cases, arguing that the only time firms in a competitive market would seek to impose territory or customer restraints, in the absence of horizontal collusion, is when economic efficiency and consumer welfare warranted such action.[8] Amidst the growing controversy and ten years after the decision in *Schwinn*, the Supreme Court once again granted *certiorari* in a case raising the issue of the appropriate antitrust analysis of vertical non-price restraints.

CONTINENTAL T.V., INC. v. GTE SYLVANIA, INC.

Supreme Court of the United States, 1977.
433 U.S. 36, 97 S.Ct. 2549, 53 L.Ed.2d 568.

MR. JUSTICE POWELL delivered the opinion of the Court.

Franchise agreements between manufacturers and retailers frequently include provisions barring the retailers from selling franchised products from locations other than those specified in the agreements. This case presents important questions concerning the

5. 497 F.2d at 1187. The Fifth Circuit, in a private treble damage action attacking the same restrictions placed by Coors on distributors in Texas, suggested that the exceptions the Tenth Circuit would like to see engrafted on the *Schwinn* rule "might engulf the rule itself" and if any such exceptions were to be allowed, the manufacturer should be required to demonstrate "the absence of means less restrictive of competition to achieve the same end." Copper Liquor, Inc. v. Adolph Coors Co., supra note 3 at 947. See also, Anderson v. American Automobile Association, 454 F.2d 1240 (9th Cir. 1972).

6. See ABA Antitrust Section, Monograph No. 2, Vertical Restrictions Limiting Intrabrand Competition 17–19 (1977);

Sullivan, Antitrust § 144 (1977); McLaren, Marketing Limitations on Independent Distributors and Dealers, 13 Antitrust Bull. 161 (1968).

7. The most comprehensive analysis of the consequences of *Schwinn* was the ABA Antitrust Section Monograph No. 2, Vertical Restrictions Limiting Intrabrand Competition (1977).

8. Bork, The Rule of Reason and The Per Se Concept: Price Fixing and Market Division II, 75 Yale L.J. 373 (1966); Posner, Antitrust Policy and The Supreme Court: An Analysis of the Restricted Distribution, Horizontal Merger and Potential Competition Decisions, 75 Colum. L.Rev. 243 (1975).

appropriate antitrust analysis of these restrictions under § 1 of the
Sherman Act, 15 U.S.C. § 1, and the Court's decision in United States
v. Arnold, Schwinn & Co., 388 U.S. 365, 87 S.Ct. 1856, 18 L.Ed.2d
1249 (1967).

I

Respondent GTE Sylvania, Inc. (Sylvania) manufactures and sells
television sets through its Home Entertainment Products Division.
Prior to 1962, like most other television manufacturers, Sylvania sold
its televisions to independent or company-owned distributors who in
turn resold to a large and diverse group of retailers. Prompted by a
decline in its market share to a relatively insignificant 1 to 2% of national television sales, Sylvania conducted an intensive reassessment
of its marketing strategy, and in 1962 adopted the franchise plan
challenged here. Sylvania phased out its wholesale distributors and
began to sell its televisions directly to a smaller and more select
group of franchised retailers. An acknowledged purpose of the
change was to decrease the number of competing Sylvania retailers
in the hope of attracting the more aggressive and competent retailers
thought necessary to the improvement of the company's market position. To this end, Sylvania limited the number of franchises granted
for any given area and required each franchisee to sell his Sylvania
products only from the location or locations at which he was
franchised. A franchise did not constitute an exclusive territory, and
Sylvania retained sole discretion to increase the number of retailers
in an area in light of the success or failure of existing retailers in
developing their market. The revised marketing strategy appears to
have been successful during the period at issue here, for by 1965 Sylvania's share of national television sales had increased to approximately 5 percent, and the company ranked as the Nation's eighth
largest manufacturer of color television sets.

This suit is the result of the rupture of a franchisor-franchisee
relationship that had previously prospered under the revised Sylvania
plan. Dissatisfied with its sales in the city of San Francisco, Sylvania
decided in the spring of 1965 to franchise Young Brothers, an established San Francisco retailer of televisions, as an additional San Francisco retailer. The proposed location of the new franchise was approximately a mile from a retail outlet operated by petitioner
Continental T.V., Inc. (Continental), one of the most successful Sylvania franchisees. Continental protested that the location of the new
franchise violated Sylvania's marketing policy, but Sylvania persisted
in its plans. Continental then cancelled a large Sylvania order and
placed a large order with Phillips, one of Sylvania's competitors.

During this same period, Continental expressed a desire to open a
store in Sacramento, Cal., a desire Sylvania attributed at least in part
to Continental's displeasure over the Young Brothers decision. Sylvania believed that the Sacramento market was adequately served by
the existing Sylvania retailers and denied the request. In the face of
this denial, Continental advised Sylvania in early September 1965,

that it was in the process of moving Sylvania merchandise from its San Jose, Cal., warehouse to a new retail location that it had leased in Sacramento. Two weeks later, allegedly for unrelated reasons, Sylvania's credit department reduced Continental's credit line from $300,000 to $50,000. In response to the reduction in credit and the generally deteriorating relations with Sylvania, Continental withheld all payments owed to John P. Maguire & Co., Inc. (Maguire), the finance company that handled the credit arrangements between Sylvania and its retailers. Shortly thereafter, Sylvania terminated Continental's franchises, and Maguire filed this diversity action in the United States District Court for the Northern District of California seeking recovery of money owed and of secured merchandise held by Continental.

The antitrust issues before us originated in cross-claims brought by Continental against Sylvania and Maguire. Most important for our purposes was the claim that Sylvania had violated § 1 of the Sherman Act by entering into and enforcing franchise agreements that prohibited the sale of Sylvania products other than from specified locations. At the close of evidence in the jury trial of Continental's claims, Sylvania requested the District Court to instruct the jury that its location restriction was illegal only if it unreasonably restrained or suppressed competition. Relying on this Court's decision in United States v. Arnold, Schwinn & Co., supra, the District Court rejected the proffered instruction in favor of the following one:

"Therefore, if you find by a preponderance of the evidence that Sylvania entered into a contract, combination or conspiracy with one or more of its dealers pursuant to which Sylvania exercised dominion or control over the products sold to the dealer, after having parted with title and risk to the products, you must find any effort thereafter to restrict outlets or store locations from which its dealers resold the merchandise which they had purchased from Sylvania to be a violation of Section 1 of the Sherman Act, regardless of the reasonableness of the location restrictions."

In answers to special interrogatories, the jury found that Sylvania had engaged "in a contract, combination or conspiracy in restraint of trade in violation of the antitrust laws with respect to location restrictions alone," and assessed Continental's damages at $591,505, which was trebled pursuant to 15 U.S.C. § 15 to produce an award of $1,774,515.

On appeal, the Court of Appeals for the Ninth Circuit, sitting en banc, reversed by a divided vote. 537 F.2d 980 (1976). The court acknowledged that there is language in *Schwinn* that could be read to support the District Court's instruction but concluded that *Schwinn* was distinguishable on several grounds. Contrasting the nature of the restrictions, their competitive impact, and the market shares of the franchisors in the two cases, the court concluded that Sylvania's location restriction had less potential for competitive harm than the restrictions invalidated in *Schwinn* and thus should be judged under the "rule of reason" rather than the *per se* rule stated in

Schwinn. The court found support for its position in the policies of the Sherman Act and in the decisions of other federal courts involving nonprice vertical restrictions.

We granted Continental's petition for certiorari to resolve this important question of antitrust law. 429 U.S. 893, 97 S.Ct. 252, 50 L.Ed.2d 176 (1976).

II

We turn first to Continental's contention that Sylvania's restriction on retail locations is a *per se* violation of § 1 of the Sherman Act as interpreted in *Schwinn.* The restrictions at issue in *Schwinn* were part of a three-tier distribution system comprising, in addition to Arnold, Schwinn & Co. (Schwinn), 22 intermediate distributors and a network of franchised retailers. Each distributor had a defined geographic area in which it had the exclusive right to supply franchised retailers. Sales to the public were made only through franchised retailers, who were authorized to sell Schwinn bicycles only from specified locations. In support of this limitation, Schwinn prohibited both distributors and retailers from selling Schwinn bicycles to non-franchised retailers. At the retail level, therefore, Schwinn was able to control the number of retailers of its bicycles in any given area according to its view of the needs of that market.

As of 1967 approximately 75% of Schwinn's total sales were made under the "Schwinn Plan." Acting essentially as a manufacturer's representative or sales agent, a distributor participating in this plan forwarded orders from retailers to the factory. Schwinn then shipped the ordered bicycles directly to the retailer, billed the retailer, bore the credit risk, and paid the distributor a commission on the sale. Under the Schwinn Plan, the distributor never had title to or possession of the bicycles. The remainder of the bicycles moved to the retailers through the hands of the distributors. For the most part, the distributors functioned as traditional wholesalers with respect to these sales, stocking an inventory of bicycles owned by them to supply retailers with emergency "fill-in" requirements. A smaller part of the bicycles that were physically distributed by the distributors were covered by consignment and agency arrangements that had been developed to deal with particular problems of certain distributors. Distributors acquired title only to those bicycles that they purchased as wholesalers; retailers, of course, acquired title to all of the bicycles sold by them.

In the District Court, the United States charged a continuing conspiracy by *Schwinn* and other alleged coconspirators to fix prices, allocate exclusive territories to distributors, and confine Schwinn bicycles to franchised retailers. Relying on United States v. Bausch & Lomb Co., 321 U.S. 707, 64 S.Ct. 805, 88 L.Ed. 1024 (1944), the Government argued that the nonprice restrictions were *per se* illegal as part of a scheme for fixing the retail prices of Schwinn bicycles. The District Court rejected the price-fixing allegation because of a failure of proof and held that Schwinn's limitation of retail bicycle sales to

franchised retailers was permissible under § 1. The court found a
§ 1 violation, however, in "conspiracy to divide certain borderline or
overlapping counties in the territories served by four Midwestern cycle distributors." The court described the violation as a "division of
territory by agreement between the distributors . . . horizontal
in nature," and held that Schwinn's participation did not change that
basic characteristic. The District Court limited its injunction to apply
only to the territorial restrictions on the resale of bicycles purchased
by the distributors in their roles as wholesalers.

Schwinn came to this Court on appeal by the United States from
the District Court's decision. Abandoning its *per se* theories, the
Government argued that Schwinn's prohibition against distributors
and retailers selling Schwinn bicycles to nonfranchised retailers was
unreasonable under § 1 and that the District Court's injunction
against exclusive distributor territories should extend to all such restrictions regardless of the form of the transaction. The Government
did not challenge the District Court's decision on price-fixing, and
Schwinn did not challenge the decision on exclusive distributor territories.

The Court acknowledged the Government's abandonment of its
per se theories and stated that the resolution of the case would require an examination of "the specifics of the challenged practices and
their impact upon the marketplace in order to make a judgment as to
whether the restraint is or is not 'reasonable' in the special sense in
which § 1 of the Sherman Act must be read for purposes of this type
of inquiry." Despite this description of its task, the Court proceeded
to articulate the following "bright line" *per se* rule of illegality for
vertical restrictions: "Under the Sherman Act, it is unreasonable
without more for a manufacturer to seek to restrict and confine areas
or persons with whom an article may be traded after the manufacturer has parted with dominion over it." But the Court expressly stated
that the rule of reason governs when "the manufacturer retains title,
dominion, and risk with respect to the product and the position and
function of the dealer in question are, in fact, indistinguishable from
those of an agent or salesman of the manufacturer."

Application of these principles to the facts of *Schwinn* produced
sharply contrasting results depending upon the role played by the distributor in the distribution system. With respect to that portion of
Schwinn's sales for which the distributors acted as ordinary wholesalers, buying and reselling Schwinn bicycles, the Court held that the
territorial and customer restrictions challenged by the Government
were *per se* illegal. But, with respect to that larger portion of
Schwinn's sales in which the distributors functioned under the
Schwinn Plan and under the less common consignment and agency
arrangements, the Court held that the same restrictions should be
judged under the rule of reason. The only retail restriction challenged by the Government prevented franchised retailers from supplying nonfranchised retailers. The Court apparently perceived no

material distinction between the restrictions on distributors and retailers, for it held that:

> "The principle is, of course, equally applicable to sales to retailers, and the decree should similarly enjoin the making of any sales to retailers upon any condition, agreement or understanding limiting the retailer's freedom as to where and to whom it will resell the products."

Applying the rule of reason to the restrictions that were not imposed in conjunction with the sale of bicycles, the Court had little difficulty finding them all reasonable in light of the competitive situation in "the product market as a whole."

In the present case, it is undisputed that title to the televisions passed from Sylvania to Continental. Thus, the *Schwinn per se* rule applies unless Sylvania's restriction on locations falls outside *Schwinn's* prohibition against a manufacturer attempting to restrict a "retailer's freedom as to where and to whom it will resell the products." As the Court of Appeals conceded, the language of *Schwinn* is clearly broad enough to apply to the present case. Unlike the Court of Appeals, however, we are unable to find a principled basis for distinguishing *Schwinn* from the case now before us.

Both Schwinn and Sylvania sought to reduce but not to eliminate competition among their respective retailers through the adoption of a franchise system. Although it was not one of the issues addressed by the District Court or presented on appeal by the Government, the Schwinn franchise plan included a location restriction similar to the one challenged here. These restrictions allowed Schwinn and Sylvania to regulate the amount of competition among their retailers by preventing a franchisee from selling franchised products from outlets other than the one covered by the franchise agreement. To exactly the same end, the Schwinn franchise plan included a companion restriction, apparently not found in the Sylvania plan, that prohibited franchised retailers from selling Schwinn products to nonfranchised retailers. In *Schwinn* the Court expressly held that this restriction was impermissible under the broad principle stated there. In intent and competitive impact, the retail customer restriction in *Schwinn* is indistinguishable from the location restriction in the present case. In both cases the restrictions limited the freedom of the retailer to dispose of the purchased products as he desired. The fact that one restriction was addressed to territory and the other to customers is irrelevant to functional anti-trust analysis, and indeed, to the language and broad thrust of the opinion in *Schwinn*.[9] As Chief Justice

9. [Footnote 12 in original] The distinctions drawn by the Court of Appeals and endorsed in Mr. Justice White's separate opinion have no basis in *Schwinn*. The intrabrand competitive impact of the restrictions at issue in *Schwinn* ranged from complete elimination to mere reduction; yet, the Court did not even hint at any distinction on this ground. Similarly, there is no suggestion that the *per se* rule was applied because of Schwinn's prominent position in its industry. That position was the same whether the bicycles were sold or consigned, but the Court's analysis was quite different. In light of Mr. Justice White's emphasis on the "superior consumer acceptance" enjoyed by the Schwinn brand name, we note that the Court rejected precisely that premise in *Schwinn*. Applying the

Hughes stated in Appalachian Coals, Inc. v. United States, 288 U.S. 344, 360, 377, 53 S.Ct. 471, 474, 480, 77 L.Ed. 825 (1933), "Realities must dominate the judgment. . . . The Anti-Trust Act aims at substance."

III

Sylvania argues that if *Schwinn* cannot be distinguished, it should be reconsidered. Although *Schwinn* is supported by the principle of *stare decisis*, we are convinced that the need for clarification of the law in this area justifies reconsideration. *Schwinn* itself was an abrupt and largely unexplained departure from White Motor Co. v. United States, 372 U.S. 253, 83 S.Ct. 696, 9 L.Ed.2d 738 (1963), where only four years earlier the Court had refused to endorse a *per se* rule for vertical restrictions. Since its announcement, *Schwinn* has been the subject of continuing controversy and confusion, both in the scholarly journals and in the federal courts. The great weight of scholarly opinion has been critical of the decision,[10] and a number of the federal courts confronted with analogous vertical restrictions have sought to limit its reach.[11] In our view, the experience of the past 10 years should be brought to bear on this subject of considerable commercial importance.

rule of reason to the restrictions imposed in nonsale transactions, the Court stressed that there was "no showing that [competitive bicycles were] not in all respects reasonably interchangeable as articles of competitive commerce with the Schwinn product" and that it did "not regard Schwinn's claim of product excellence as establishing the contrary." Although *Schwinn* did hint at preferential treatment for new entrants and failing firms, the District Court below did not even submit Sylvania's claim that it was failing to the jury. Accordingly, Mr. Justice White's position appears to reflect an extension of *Schwinn* in this regard. Having crossed the "failing firm" line, Mr. Justice White neither attempts to draw a new one nor to explain why one should be drawn at all.

10. [Footnote 13 in original] A former Assistant Attorney General for Antitrust has described *Schwinn* as "an exercise in barren formalism" that is "artificial and unresponsive to the competitive needs of the real world." Baker, Vertical Restraints in Times of Change: From *White* to *Schwinn* to Where?, 44 Antitrust L.J. 537 (1975). See e.g., Handler, The Twentieth Annual Antitrust Review—1967, 53 Va.L.Rev. 1667 (1967); McLaren, Territorial and Customer Restrictions, Consignments, Suggested Retail Prices and Refusals to Deal, 37 Antitrust L.J. 137 (1968); Pollock, Alternative Distribution Methods After *Schwinn*, 63

Nw.U.L.Rev. 595 (1968); Posner, Antitrust Policy and the Supreme Court: An Analysis of the Restricted Distribution, Horizontal Merger and Potential Competition Decisions, 75 Colum.L.J. 282 (1975). But see Louis, Vertical Distributional Restraints Under *Schwinn* and *Sylvania:* An Argument for the Continuing Use of a Partial *Per Se* Approach, 75 Mich.L. Rev. 275 (1976); Zimmerman, Distribution Restrictions After *Sealy* and *Schwinn*, 12 Antitrust Bull. 1181 (1967). For a more inclusive list of articles and comments, see 537 F.2d, at 988 n. 13.

11. [Footnote 14 in original] . . . Thus, the statement in *Schwinn* that post-sale vertical restrictions as to customers or territories are "unreasonable without more," 388 U.S., at 379, 87 S.Ct., at 1865, has been interpreted to allow an exception to the *per se* rule where the manufacturer proves "more" by showing that the restraints will protect consumers against injury and the manufacturer against product liability claims. See, e.g., Tripoli Co. v. Wella Corp., 425 F.2d 932, 936–938 (CA3 1970) (en banc). Similarly, the statement that Schwinn's enforcement of its restrictions had been "firm and resolute," 388 U.S., at 372, 87 S.Ct., at 1862, has been relied upon to distinguish cases lacking that element. See, e.g., Janel Sales Corp. v. Lanvin Parfums Inc., 396 F.2d 398, 406 (CA2 1968). . . .

The traditional framework of analysis under § 1 of the Sherman Act is familiar and does not require extended discussion. Section 1 prohibits "[e]very contract, combination . . . or conspiracy, in restraint of trade or commerce." Since the early years of this century a judicial gloss on this statutory language has established the "rule of reason" as the prevailing standard of analysis. Standard Oil Co. v. United States, 221 U.S. 1, 31 S.Ct. 502, 55 L.Ed. 619 (1911). Under this rule, the fact-finder weighs all of the circumstances of a case in deciding whether a restrictive practice should be prohibited as imposing an unreasonable restraint on competition. *Per se* rules of illegality are appropriate only when they relate to conduct that is manifestly anti-competitive. As the Court explained in Northern Pac. R. Co. v. United States, 356 U.S. 1, 5, 78 S.Ct. 514, 518, 2 L.Ed.2d 545 (1958), "there are certain agreements or practices which because of their pernicious effect on competition and lack of any redeeming virtue are conclusively presumed to be unreasonable and therefore illegal without elaborate inquiry as to the precise harm they have caused or the business excuse for their use." [12]

In essence, the issue before us is whether *Schwinn's per se* rule can be justified under the demanding standards of *Northern Pac. R. Co.* The Court's refusal to endorse a *per se* rule in *White Motor Co.* was based on its uncertainty as to whether vertical restrictions satisfied those standards. Addressing this question for the first time, the Court stated:

> "We need to know more than we do about the actual impact of these arrangements on competition to decide whether they have such a 'pernicious effect on competition and lack . . . any redeeming virtue' (Northern Pac. R. Co. v. United States, supra, 356 U.S. p. 5, 78 S.Ct. 514) and therefore should be classified as *per se* violations of the Sherman Act." 372 U.S., at 263, 83 S.Ct., at 702.

Only four years later the Court in *Schwinn* announced its sweeping *per se* rule without even a reference to *Northern Pac. R. Co.* and with no explanation of its sudden change in position. We turn now to consider *Schwinn* in light of *Northern Pac. R. Co.*

The market impact of vertical restrictions [13] is complex because of their potential for a simultaneous reduction of intrabrand competition

---

12. [Footnote 16 in original] *Per se* rules thus require the Court to make broad generalizations about the social utility of particular commercial practices. The probability that anticompetitive consequences will result from a practice and the severity of those consequences must be balanced against its pro-competitive consequences. Cases that do not fit the generalization may arise, but a *per se* rule reflects the judgment that such cases are not sufficiently common or important to justify the time and expense necessary to identify them. Once established, *per se* rules tend to provide guidance to the business community and to minimize the burdens on litigants and the judicial system of the more complex rule of reason trials, but those advantages are not sufficient in themselves to justify the creation of *per se* rules. If it were otherwise, all of antitrust law would be reduced to *per se* rules, thus introducing an unintended and undesirable rigidity in the law.

13. [Footnote 18 in original] As in *Schwinn*, we are concerned here only with nonprice vertical restrictions. The *per se* illegality of price restrictions has

and stimulation of interbrand competition.[14] Significantly, the Court in *Schwinn* did not distinguish among the challenged restrictions on the basis of their individual potential for intrabrand harm or interbrand benefit. Restrictions that completely eliminated intrabrand competition among Schwinn distributors were analyzed no differently than those that merely moderated intrabrand competition among retailers. The pivotal factor was the passage of title: All restrictions were held to be *per se* illegal where title had passed, and all were evaluated and sustained under the rule of reason where it had not. The location restriction at issue here would be subject to the same pattern of analysis under *Schwinn*.

It appears that this distinction between sale and nonsale transactions resulted from the Court's effort to accommodate the perceived intrabrand harm and interbrand benefit of vertical restrictions. The *per se* rule for sale transactions reflected the view that vertical restrictions are "so obviously destructive" of intrabrand competition that their use would "open the door to exclusivity of outlets and limitation of territory further than prudence permits." [15] Conversely, the

been established firmly for many years and involves significantly different questions of analysis and policy. As Mr. Justice White notes, some commentators have argued that the manufacturer's motivation for imposing vertical price restrictions may be the same as for nonprice restrictions. There are, however, significant differences that could easily justify different treatment. In his concurring opinion in *White Motor Co.*, Mr. Justice Brennan noted that, unlike nonprice restrictions, "[r]esale price maintenance is not designed to, but almost invariably does in fact, reduce price competition not only *among* sellers of the affected product, but quite as much *between* that product and competing brands." 372 U.S. at 268, 83 S.Ct., at 704. Professor Posner also recognized that "industry-wide resale price maintenance might facilitate cartelizing." . . . Furthermore, Congress recently has expressed its approval of a *per se* analysis of vertical price restrictions by repealing those provisions of the Miller-Tydings and McGuire Acts allowing fair trade pricing at the option of the individual States. Consumer Goods Pricing Act of 1975, Pub.L. 94–145 (1975), amending 15 U.S.C. § 45(a). No similar expression of congressional intent exists for nonprice restrictions.

14. [Footnote 19 in the original.] Interbrand competition is the competition among the manufacturers of the same generic product—television sets in this case—and is the primary concern of antitrust law. The extreme example of a deficiency of interbrand competition is monopoly, where there is only one manu-facturer. In contrast, intrabrand competition is the competition between the distributors—wholesale or retail—of the product of a particular manufacturer.

The degree of intrabrand competition is wholly independent of the level of interbrand competition confronting the manufacturer. Thus, there may be fierce intrabrand competition among the distributors of a product produced by a monopolist and no intrabrand competition among the distributors of a product produced by a firm in a highly competitive industry. But when interbrand competition exists, as it does among television manufacturers, it provides a significant check on the exploitation of intrabrand market power because of the ability of consumers to substitute a different brand of the same product.

15. [Footnote 21 in original] The Court also stated that to impose vertical restrictions in sale transactions would "violate the ancient rule against restraints on alienation." 388 U.S., at 380, 87 S.Ct., at 1866. The isolated reference has provoked sharp criticism from virtually all of the commentators on the decision, most of whom have regarded the Court's apparent reliance on the "ancient rule" as both a misreading of legal history and a perversion of antitrust analysis. . . . We quite agree with Mr. Justice Stewart's dissenting comment in *Schwinn* that "the state of the common law 400 or even 100 years ago is irrelevant to the issue before us: the effect of the antitrust laws upon vertical distributional restraints in the American econo-

continued adherence to the traditional rule of reason for nonsale transactions reflected the view that the restrictions have too great a potential for the promotion of interbrand competition to justify complete prohibition.[16] . . .

Vertical restrictions reduce intrabrand competition by limiting the number of sellers of a particular product competing for the business of a given group of buyers. Location restrictions have this effect because of practical constraints on the effective marketing area of retail outlets. Although intrabrand competition may be reduced, the ability of retailers to exploit the resulting market may be limited both by the ability of consumers to travel to other franchised locations and, perhaps more importantly, to purchase the competing products of other manufacturers. None of these key variables, however, is affected by the form of the transaction by which a manufacturer conveys his products to the retailers.

Vertical restrictions promote interbrand competition by allowing the manufacturer to achieve certain efficiencies in the distribution of his products. These "redeeming virtues" are implicit in every decision sustaining vertical restrictions under the rule of reason. Economists have identified a number of ways in which manufacturers can use such restrictions to compete more effectively against other manufacturers. See, e.g., Preston, Restrictive Distribution Arrangements: Economic Analysis and Public Policy Standards, 30 Law & Contemp. Prob. 506, 511 (1965).[17] For example, new manufacturers and manu-

my today." 388 U.S., at 392, 87 S.Ct., at 1872.

We are similarly unable to accept Judge Browning's interpretation of *Schwinn*. In his dissent below he argued that the decision reflects the view that the Sherman Act was intended to prohibit restrictions on the autonomy of independent businessmen even though they have no impact on "price, quality, and quantity of goods and services," 537 F.2d, at 1019. This view is certainly not explicit in *Schwinn*, which purports to be based on an examination of the "impact [of the restrictions] upon the marketplace." 388 U.S., at 374, 87 S.Ct., at 1863. Competitive economies have social and political as well as economic advantages, see e.g., Northern Pac. R. Co. v. United States, 356 U.S., at 4, 78 S.Ct., at 517, but an antitrust policy divorced from market considerations would lack any objective benchmarks. As Justice Brandeis reminded us, "Every agreement concerning trade, every regulation of trade, restrains. To bind, to restrain is of their very essence." Chicago Board of Trade v. United States, 246 U.S., at 238, 38 S.Ct., at 244. Although Mr. Justice White's opinion endorses Judge Browning's interpretation, *post*, at 2567, it purports to distinguish *Schwinn* on grounds

inconsistent with that interpretation, post at 2568.

16. [Footnote 22 in original] In that regard, the Court specifically stated that a more complete prohibition "might severely hamper smaller enterprises resorting to reasonable methods of meeting the competition of giants and of merchandising through independent dealers." 388 U.S., at 380, 87 S.Ct., at 1866. The Court also broadly hinted that it would recognize additional exceptions to the *per se* rule for new entrants in an industry and for failing firms, both of which were mentioned in *White Motor* as candidates for such exceptions. Id., at 374, 87 S.Ct., at 1863. The Court might have limited the exceptions to the *per se* rule to these situations, which present the strongest arguments for the sacrifice of intrabrand competition for interbrand competition. Significantly, it chose instead to create the more extensive exception for nonsale transactions which is available to all businesses, regardless of their size, financial health, or market share. This broader exception demonstrates even more clearly the Court's awareness of the "redeeming virtues" of vertical restrictions.

17. [Footnote 23 in original] Marketing efficiency is not the only legitimate reason for a manufacturer's desire to ex-

facturers entering new markets can use the restrictions in order to induce competent and aggressive retailers to make the kind of investment of capital and labor that is often required in the distribution of products unknown to the consumer. Established manufacturers can use them to induce retailers to engage in promotional activities or to provide service and repair facilities necessary to the efficient marketing of their products. Service and repair are vital for many products, such as automobiles and major household appliances. The availability and quality of such services affect a manufacturer's good will and the competitiveness of his product. Because of market imperfections such as the so-called "free rider" effect, these services might not be provided by retailers in a purely competitive situation, despite the fact that each retailer's benefit would be greater if all provided the services than if none did. Posner, supra, n. 13, at 285; cf. P. Samuelson, Economics 506–507 (10th ed. 1976).

Economists also have argued that manufacturers have an economic interest in maintaining as much intrabrand competition as is consistent with the efficient distribution of their products. Although the view that the manufacturer's interest necessarily corresponds with that of the public is not universally shared, even the leading critic of vertical restrictions concedes that *Schwinn's* distinction between sale and nonsale transactions is essentially unrelated to any relevant economic impact. Comanor, Vertical Territorial and Customer Restrictions: White Motor and Its Aftermath, 81 Harv.L.Rev. 1419, 1422 (1968).[18] Indeed, to the extent that the form of the transaction is related to interbrand benefits, the Court's distinction is inconsistent with its articulated concern for the ability of smaller firms to compete effectively with larger ones. Capital requirements and administrative expenses may prevent smaller firms from using the exception for nonsale transactions.[19]

We conclude that the distinction drawn in *Schwinn* between sale and nonsale transactions is not sufficient to justify the application of

ert control over the manner in which his products are sold and serviced. As a result of statutory and common law developments, society increasingly demands that manufacturers assume direct responsibility for the safety and quality of their products. For example, at the federal level, apart from more specialized requirements, manufacturers of consumer products have safety responsibilities under the Consumer Product Safety Act, 15 U.S.C. § 2051 et seq., and obligations for warranties under the Consumer Product Warranties Act, 15 U.S.C. § 2301 et seq. . . .

18. [Footnote 25 in original] Professor Comanor argues that the promotional activities encouraged by vertical restrictions result in product differentiation and, therefore, a decrease in interbrand competition. This argument is flawed by its necessary assumption that a large

part of the promotional efforts resulting from vertical restrictions will not convey socially desirable information about product availability, price, quality and services. Nor is it clear that a *per se* rule would result in anything more than a shift to less efficient methods of obtaining the same promotional effects.

19. [Footnote 26 in original] We also note that *per se* rules in this area may work to the ultimate detriment of the small businessmen who operate as franchisees. To the extent that a *per se* rule prevents a firm from using the franchise system to achieve efficiencies that it perceives as important to its successful operation, the rule creates an incentive for vertical integration into the distribution system, thereby eliminating to that extent the role of independent businessmen.

a *per se* rule in one situation and a rule of reason in the other. The question remains whether the *per se* rule stated in *Schwinn* should be expanded to include non-sale transactions or abandoned in favor of a return to the rule of reason. We have found no persuasive support for expanding the rule. As noted above, the *Schwinn* Court recognized the undesirability of "prohibit[ing] all vertical restrictions of territory and all franchising . . .." 388 U.S., at 379–380, 87 S.Ct., at 1866.[20] And even Continental does not urge us to hold that all such restrictions are *per se* illegal.

We revert to the standard articulated in *Northern Pac. R. Co.*, and reiterated in *White Motor,* for determining whether vertical restrictions must be "conclusively presumed to be unreasonable and therefore illegal without elaborate inquiry as to the precise harm they have caused or the business excuse for their use." Such restrictions, in varying forms, are widely used in our free market economy. As indicated above, there is substantial scholarly and judicial authority supporting their economic utility. There is relatively little authority to the contrary. Certainly, there has been no showing in this case, either generally or with respect to Sylvania's agreements, that vertical restrictions have or are likely to have a "pernicious effect on competition" or that they "lack . . . any redeeming virtue." [21] Accordingly, we conclude that the *per se* rule stated in *Schwinn* must be overruled. In so holding we do not foreclose the possibility that particular applications of vertical restrictions might justify *per se* prohibition under *Northern Pac. R. Co.* But we do make clear that departure from the rule of reason standard must be based upon demonstrable economic effect rather than—as in *Schwinn*—upon formalistic line drawing.

In sum, we conclude that the appropriate decision is to return to the rule of reason that governed vertical restrictions prior to *Schwinn.* When competitive effects are shown to result from particular vertical restrictions they can be adequately policed under the rule of reason, the standard traditionally applied for the majority of anticompetitive practices challenged under § 1 of the Act. Accordingly, the decision of the Court of Appeals is affirmed.

20. [Footnote 27 in original] Continental's contention that balancing intrabrand and interbrand competitive effects of vertical restrictions is not a "proper part of the judicial function," Petitioner Brief, at 52, is refuted by *Schwinn* itself. United States v. Topco Associates, Inc., 405 U.S. 596, 92 S.Ct. 1126, 31 L.Ed.2d 515 (1972), is not to the contrary, for it involved a horizontal restriction among ostensible competitors. 405 U.S., at 608, 92 S.Ct., at 1133.

21. [Footnote 29 in original] The location restriction used by Sylvania was neither the least nor the most restrictive provision that it could have used. But we agree with the implicit judgment in *Schwinn* that a *per se* rule based on the nature of the restriction is, in general, undesirable. Although distinctions can be drawn among the frequently used restrictions, we are inclined to view them as differences of degree and form. We are unable to perceive significant social gain from channeling transactions into one form or another. Finally, we agree with the Court in *Schwinn* that the advantages of vertical restrictions should not be limited to the categories of new entrants and failing firms. Sylvania was faltering, if not failing, and we think it would be unduly artificial to deny it the use of valuable competitive tools.

Mr. Justice Rehnquist took no part in the consideration or decision of this case.

Mr. Justice White, concurring in the judgment.

Although I agree with the majority that the location clause at issue in this case is not a *per se* violation of the Sherman Act and should be judged under the rule of reason, I cannot agree that this result requires the overruling of United States v. Arnold, Schwinn & Co., 388 U.S. 365, 87 S.Ct. 1856, 18 L.Ed.2d 1249 (1967). In my view this case is distinguishable from *Schwinn* because there is less potential for restraint of intrabrand competition and more potential for stimulating interbrand competition. As to intrabrand competition, Sylvania, unlike Schwinn, did not restrict the customers to whom or the territories where its purchasers could sell. As to interbrand competition, Sylvania, unlike Schwinn, had an insignificant market share at the time it adopted its challenged distribution practice and enjoyed no consumer preference that would allow its retailers to charge a premium over other brands. In two short paragraphs, the majority disposes of the view, adopted after careful analysis by the Ninth Circuit en banc below, that these differences provide a "principled basis for distinguishing *Schwinn*," despite holdings by three Courts of Appeals and the District Court on remand in *Schwinn* that the *per se* rule established in that case does not apply to location clauses such as Sylvania's. To reach out to overrule one of this Court's recent interpretations of the Sherman Act, after such a cursory examination of the necessity for doing so, is surely an affront to the principle that considerations of *stare decisis* are to be given particularly strong weight in the area of statutory construction.

One element of the system of interrelated vertical restraints invalidated in *Schwinn* was a retail customer restriction prohibiting franchised retailers from selling Schwinn products to nonfranchised retailers. The Court rests its inability to distinguish *Schwinn* entirely on this retail customer restriction, finding it "[i]n intent and competitive impact . . . indistinguishable from the location restriction in the present case," because "[i]n both cases the restrictions limited the freedom of the retailer to dispose of the purchased products as he desired." The customer restriction may well have, however, a very different "intent and competitive impact" than the location restriction: it prevents discount stores from getting the manufacturer's product and thus prevents intrabrand price competition. Suppose, for example, that interbrand competition is sufficiently weak that the franchised retailers are able to charge a price substantially above wholesale. Under a location restriction, these franchisees are free to sell to discount stores seeking to exploit the potential for sales at prices below the prevailing retail level. One of the franchised retailers may be tempted to lower its price and act in effect as a wholesaler for the discount house in order to share in the profits to be had from lowering prices and expanding volume.

Under a retail customer restriction, on the other hand, the franchised dealers cannot sell to discounters, who are cut off altogether from the manufacturer's product and the opportunity for intrabrand price competition. This was precisely the theory on which the Government successfully challenged Schwinn's customer restrictions in this Court. The District Court in that case found that "[e]ach one of [Schwinn's franchised retailers] knows also that he is not a wholesaler and that he cannot sell as a wholesaler or act as an agent for some other unfranchised dealer, such as a discount house retailer who has not been franchised as a dealer by Schwinn." The Government argued on appeal, with extensive citations to the record, that the effect of this restriction was "to keep Schwinn products out of the hands of discount houses and other price cutters so as to discourage price competition in retailing. . . .

It is true that, as the majority states, Sylvania's location restriction inhibited to some degree "the freedom of the retailer to dispose of the purchased products" by requiring the retailer to sell from one particular place of business. But the retailer is still free to sell to any type of customer—including discounters and other unfranchised dealers—from any area. I think this freedom implies a significant difference for the effect of a location clause on intrabrand competition.

. . .

In my view there are at least two considerations, both relied upon by the majority to justify overruling *Schwinn*, that would provide a "principled basis" for instead refusing to extend *Schwinn* to a vertical restraint that is imposed by a "faltering" manufacturer with a "precarious" position in a generic product market dominated by another firm. The first is that, as the majority puts it, "when interbrand competition exists, as it does among television manufacturers, it provides a significant check on the exploitation of intrabrand market power because of the ability of consumers to substitute a different brand of the same product." Second is the view, argued forcefully in the economic literature cited by the majority, that the potential benefits of vertical restraints in promoting interbrand competition are particularly strong where the manufacturer imposing the restraints is seeking to enter a new market or to expand a small market share. The majority even recognizes that *Schwinn* "hinted" at an exception for new entrants and failing firms from its *per se* rule.

In other areas of the antitrust law, this Court has not hesitated to base its rules of *per se* illegality in part on the defendant's market power. Indeed, in the very case from which the majority draws its standard for *per se* rules, Northern Pac. R. Co. v. United States, 356 U.S. 1, 5, 78 S.Ct. 514, 518, 2 L.Ed.2d 545 (1958), the Court stated the reach of the *per se* rule against tie-ins under § 1 of the Sherman Act as extending to all defendants with "sufficient economic power with respect to the tying product to appreciably restrain free competition in the market for the tied product. . . ." And the Court subsequently approved an exception to this *per se* rule for "infant industries" marketing a new product. United States v. Jerrold Electronics Corp., 187 F.Supp. 545 (ED Pa.1960), aff'd per curiam, 365 U.S. 567,

81 S.Ct. 755, 5 L.Ed.2d 806 (1961). . . . I see no doctrinal obstacle to excluding firms with such minimal market power as Sylvania's from the reach of the *Schwinn* rule.[22]

I have, moreover, substantial misgivings about the approach the majority takes to overruling *Schwinn*. The reason for the distinction in *Schwinn* between sale and nonsale transactions was not, as the majority would have it, "the Court's effort to accommodate the perceived intrabrand harm and interbrand benefit of vertical restrictions," the reason was rather, as Judge Browning argued in dissent below, the notion in many of our cases involving vertical restraints that independent businessmen should have the freedom to dispose of the goods they own as they see fit.

. . .

After summarily rejecting this concern, reflected in our interpretations of the Sherman Act, for "the autonomy of independent businessmen," the majority not surprisingly finds "no justification" for Schwinn's distinction between sale and nonsale transactions because the distinction is "essentially unrelated to any relevant economic impact." But while according some weight to the businessman's interest in controlling the terms on which he trades in his own goods may be anathema to those who view the Sherman Act as directed solely to economic efficiency,[23] this principle is without question more deeply embedded in our cases than the notions of "free rider" effects and distributional efficiencies borrowed by the majority from the "new economics of vertical relationships." Perhaps the Court is right in partially abandoning this principle and in judging the instant nonprice vertical restraints solely by their "relevant economic impact"; but the precedents which reflect this principle should not be so lightly rejected by the Court. The rationale of *Schwinn* is no doubt difficult to discern from the opinion, and it may be wrong; it is not, however, the aberration the majority makes it out to be here.

I have a further reservation about the majority's reliance on "relevant economic impact" as the test for retaining *per se* rules regarding vertical restraints. It is common ground among the leading advocates of a purely economic approach to the question of distribution restraints that the economic arguments in favor of allowing vertical nonprice restraints generally apply to vertical price restraints as well. Although the majority asserts that "the *per se* illegality of price restrictions . . . involves significantly different questions of analysis and policy," I suspect this purported distinction may be as difficult to justify as that of *Schwinn* under the terms of the majority's analysis. Thus Professor Posner, in an article cited five times by the majority, concludes, "I believe the law should treat price and nonprice

---

22. [Footnote 8 in original] Cf. Sandura Co. v. FTC, 339 F.2d 847, 850 (CA6 1964) (territorial restrictions on distributors imposed by small manufacturer "competing with and losing ground to the 'giants' of the floorcovering industry" is not *per se* illegal). . . .

23. [Footnote 9 in original] E.g., Bork, Legislative Intent and the Policy of the Sherman Act, 9 J.Law & Econ. 7 (1966); Bork, The Rule of Reason and the *Per Se* Concept: Price Fixing and Market Division I, 74 Yale L.J. 775 (1965).

restrictions the same and that it should make no distinction between the imposition of restrictions in a sale contract and their imposition in an agency contract." Antitrust Policy and the Supreme Court: An Analysis of the Restricted Distribution, Horizontal Merger and Potential Competition Decisions, 75 Colum.L.Rev. 282, 298 (1975). Indeed, the Court has already recognized that resale price maintenance may increase output by inducing "demand-creating activity" by dealers (such as additional retail outlets, advertising and promotion, and product servicing) that outweighs the additional sales that would result from lower prices brought about by dealer price competition. Albrecht v. Herald Co., 390 U.S. 145, 151 n. 7, 88 S.Ct. 869, 872, 19 L.Ed.2d 998 (1968). These same output-enhancing possibilities of nonprice vertical restraints are relied upon by the majority as evidence of their "social utility and economic soundness," and as a justification for judging them under the rule of reason. The effect, if not the intention, of the Court's opinion is necessarily to call into question the firmly established *per se* rule against price restraints.

Although the case law in the area of distributional restraints has perhaps been less than satisfactory, the Court would do well to proceed more deliberately in attempting to improve it. In view of the ample reasons for distinguishing *Schwinn* from this case and in the absence of contrary congressional action, I would adhere to the principle that

> ". . . each case arising under the Sherman Act must be determined upon the particular facts disclosed by the record, and . . . the opinions in those cases must be read in the light of their facts and of a clear recognition of the essential differences in the facts of those cases, and in the facts of any new case to which the rule of earlier decisions is to be applied." Maple Flooring Manufacturers Association v. United States, 268 U.S. 563, 579, 45 S.Ct. 578, 583, 69 L.Ed. 1093 (1925).

In order to decide this case, the Court need only hold that a location clause imposed by a manufacturer with negligible economic power in the product market has a competitive impact sufficiently less restrictive than the *Schwinn* restraints to justify a rule of reason standard, even if the same weight is given here as in *Schwinn* to dealer autonomy. I therefore concur in the judgment.

MR. JUSTICE BRENNAN with whom MR. JUSTICE MARSHALL joins, dissenting.

I would not overrule the *per se* rule stated in United States v. Arnold, Schwinn & Co., 388 U.S. 365, 87 S.Ct. 1856, 18 L.Ed.2d 1249 (1967), and would therefore reverse the decision of the Court of Appeals for the Ninth Circuit.

NOTES AND QUERIES

(1) *The Court's Assumptions and Methodology of Analysis in Sylvania.* An avalanche of litigation and commentary has followed *Sylvania*.[24] The Court's extensive citation and discussion of theoretical economic analysis of vertical restraints was seen as a significant shift in the predicate for antitrust analysis generally—from one emphasizing a multiplicity of social, political and economic goals to one principally emphasizing neo-classical economic goals of "efficiency" and "consumer welfare." [25] Moreover, the Court's reliance upon the deductive analytical methodology of some schools of economic thought, rather than the more complex inductive method of legal analysis, was seen by some observers as opening a gap between the theory and the reality of vertical restraints in particular cases.[26]

The Court set forth a paradigm which presumes vertical non-price restraints to be consistent with a competitive process. The paradigm is premised upon the assumptions that the market is competitive, that suppliers are motivated to maximize profit but constrained in their choice of means for doing so by interbrand competitors, and that if the means chosen include vertical market divisions and resale restraints, they must necessarily be designed to improve distributional efficiencies. Improved distributional "efficiencies," including point of sales services, advertising, and other promotions will result in higher sales or transactional efficiencies producing savings for the consumer and a stimulation of interbrand competition offsetting the anticompetitive effects resulting from foreclosure of intrabrand competition.[27]

24. The post-*Sylvania* litigation is surveyed in the leading articles and commentaries commenting on the case and its implications. See Altschuler, *Sylvania*, Vertical Restraints, and Dual Distribution, 25 Antitrust Bull. 1 (1980); Bohling, A Simplified Rule of Reason for Vertical Restraints: Integrating Social Goals, Economic Analysis and *Sylvania*, 64 Iowa L.Rev. 465 (1979); Baker, Interconnected Problems of Doctrine and Economics in the Section One Labyrinth: Is *Sylvania* a Way Out? 67 Va.L.Rev. 1457 (1981); Brett & Wallace, *Sylvania* and the Dual Distribution Dilemma, 26 N.Y.L.S.L.Rev. 971 (1981); Flynn, The Function and Dysfunction of *Per Se* Rules in Vertical Market Restraints, 58 Wash.U.L.Q. 767 (1980); Goldberg, The Law and Economics of Vertical Restrictions: A Relational Perspective, 58 Tex. L.Rev. 1 (1979); Jinkinson & Foster, Per Se Rules Against Vertical Restraints: Down But Not Out, 58 Wash.U.L.Q. 795 (1980); Pitofsky, The *Sylvania* Case: Antitrust Analysis of Vertical Non-Price Restraints, 78 Colum.L.Rev. 1 (1978); Posner, The Rule of Reason and The Economic Approach: Reflections on the *Sylvania* Decision, 45 U.Chi.L.Rev. 1 (1977); Posner, The Next Step in the Antitrust Treatment of Restricted Distribution: Per Se Legality, 48 U.Chi.L.Rev. 6 (1981); Stewart & Roberts, Viability of the Antitrust Per Se Illegality Rule: *Schwinn* Down, How Many to Go, 58 Wash.U.L.Q.

727 (1980); Williamson, Assessing Vertical Market Restrictions: Antitrust Ramifications of the Transaction Cost Approach, 127 U.Pa.L.Rev. 953 (1979); Zeleck, Stern & Dunfee, The Rule of Reason Decision Model After *Sylvania*, 68 Cal.L.Rev. 13 (1980).

25. "A great deal of doctrinal baggage about the social purposes of these laws . . . was silently jettisoned." Bork, Vertical Restraints: Schwinn Overruled, 1977 Sup.Ct.Rev. 171, 172. See also Bohling, supra note 24 at 495; Comment, Franchising and Vertical Customer-Territorial Restrictions: *GTE Sylvania* and the Demise of the Social Goals of the Sherman Act, 9 Tex.Tech.L. Rev. 267, 287–92 (1978).

26. "The *Sylvania* opinion substituted axiomatic theological propositions for a reflective analysis of the reality of the dispute before the Court in light of the goals of the law. A mechanical deductive process of reasoning from fixed rules has been substituted for what ought to be a complex inductive and deductive process of legal analysis in light of the facts of the case and the goals of the law." Flynn, supra note 24 at 776.

27. See Posner, The Rule of Reason and the Economic Approach: Reflections on the *Sylvania* Decision, 45 U.Chi.L. Rev. 1 (1977), for a more elaborate explication of this form of analysis. See also Bork, supra note 25.

Critics of this approach include those who attack the narrow assumptions of the Court's paradigm,[28] the Court's method for balancing the pro-competitive and anticompetitive potential of the restraints in particular cases,[29] and some who attack the basic assumption that competitive markets do in fact exist and that it should be assumed that vertical restraints are an expression of their existence.[30] In the last named category are those who claim the economy is not one governed by consumer sovereignty, but it is an economy managed by powerful firms operating in concentrated industries, with the power and motivation to manipulate demand. In such a world, it is argued, it should not be presumed that manufacturers institute vertical restrictions to increase efficiency, lower marginal costs, increase profits and promote consumer welfare. Rather, such restraints should be presumed to be means for promoting artificial product differentiation based on advertising and promotional gimmickry and an exercise in market power causing consumer prices to rise, and thereby stimulating interbrand non-price competition insulating manufacturers from interbrand price competition.[31]

Placed in the context of a "planned economy," one where powerful firms dictate consumer wants rather than vice-versa, it is argued that vertical restraints should be assumed to be devices for promoting the interests of the manufacturer rather than the consumer. Those interests have been described as follows:

> The mature corporation seeks to emancipate itself from the unpredictability of the market by exercising control over all phases of production. It would be absurd to seek this control over production and then leave purchases to the random fate of individual entrepreneurial skill or consumer taste. Effective planning requires control over consumer behavior and control over product distribution. Through the use of vertical restrictions the mature corporation gains an amount of control over the action of the independent trader tantamount to vertical integration. Further, vertical restrictions provide sufficient protection from the eroding effects of intrabrand market competition to enable the firm to maintain price levels adequate to wage a successful campaign to mold and control consumer demand.

> Thus, in the most concentrated and powerful sector of the economy, the assumptions of the classical paradigm, that producers seek to maximize profits and consumers control the allocation of society's resources, is replaced with the following: that producers seek to gain security and stability through effective planning and a maximum rate of growth, and that consumer demand is effectively molded and controlled to insure that

28. See, e.g., Redlich, The Burger Court and the Per Se Rule, 44 Albany L.Rev. 1, 50–56 (1979); Flynn, supra note 24; Lewis, Vertical Distribution Restraints After *Sylvania:* A Postscript and Comment, 76 Mich.L.Rev. 265 (1977). For a more comprehensive analysis and criticism of the reliance upon narrow economic models in resolving antitrust policy issues, see Fox, The Modernization of Antitrust: A New Equilibrium, 66 Cornell L.Rev. 1140 (1981).

29. See, e.g., Bohling, supra note 24; Pitofsky, supra note 24; Zeleck, Stern & Dunfee, supra note 24.

30. See Comanor, Vertical Territorial and Customer Restrictions: *White Motor* and Its Aftermath, 81 Harv.L.Rev. 1419 (1968); Note, Vertical Nonprice Restrictions and Antitrust Policy: Assumptions Re-examined, 1977 Utah L.Rev. 719. See generally Leff, Economic Analysis of Law: Some Realism About Nominalism, 60 Va.L.Rev. 451 (1974); Polinsky, Economic Analysis as a Potentially Defective Product: A Buyer's Guide to Posner's Economic Analysis of the Law, 87 Harv. L.Rev. 1655 (1974); Sullivan, Economics and More Humanistic Disciplines: What are the Sources of Wisdom for Antitrust?, 125 U.Pa.L.Rev. 1214 (1977).

31. For a more elaborate explanation, see W.D. Slawson, The New Inflation, Chaps. 1–2 (1981).

stability and growth. With increased economic development, power passes from the consumer to the producer in determining where and how society's resources should be allocated and the use of vertical restrictions helps preserve this shift of power.

Vertical restrictions are thus crucial to the effective planning of the mature corporation and unless the goals of planning are in concert with the present and future needs of the public, vertical restrictions which promote and preserve such goals must not be wholeheartedly endorsed as redounding to the consumers' benefit.[32]

Queries: What evidence did the Court rely upon to presume vertical non-price restraints are an expression of the workings of a competitive market? Does the Court's methodology establish workable standards for sorting out whether the restraints in a particular case are pro- or anti-competitive? What are the consequences of assuming vertical restraints are an expression of planning for the benefit of the "mature corporation," rather than the expression of efficient interbrand competition for the benefit of the consumer?

(2) *Ninth Circuit Opinions in Continental T.V.* Among interesting features of the opinions in the lower court were:

(a) Judge Ely's argument against per se prohibition of location clauses that they were less restrictive than the exclusive dealership, a practice generally upheld.[33]

(b) Judge Kilkenny's argument in dissent that the trial judge had not submitted the case to the jury on the theory of *per se* illegality of the location clause standing alone, but on the theory that it was part of a conspiracy to restrict territories in which dealers could resell.

(c) Judge Chambers' protest against the influence of law review comments.

(d) Judge Browning's demonstration that the Sherman Act was intended to further social and political goals other than economic efficiency, including freedom of commercial policy for independent businessmen,[34] and his argu-

---

32. Note, supra note 30 at 732–33.

33. 537 F.2d at 997.

34. [Consolidating two of Judge Browning's footnotes] . . . 'There is little evidence that Sherman and the others had any idea of imposing an economist's model of competition on American industry. They did not consult economists of the time; and if they had done so, they would have found little support for any such course.' A. Neale, The Antitrust Laws of the United States of America 13 (2d ed. 1970). In striking contrast to the views of the Congress, economists of the late 1800's considered 'trusts' and other combinations to be a natural evolutionary advance, and monopolies to be both inevitable and potentially beneficial. Letwin, Congress and the Sherman Antitrust Law: 1887–1890, 23 U.Chi.L.Rev. 221, 237–38 (1956). Considering the level of economic thought prevailing in 1890, it is inconceivable that Congress passed the Sherman Act 'out of an exclusive preoccupation with the idea that prices should always equal marginal

costs.' Blake & Jones, In Defense of Antitrust, 65 Colum.L.Rev. 377, 384 (1965).

'In the congressional debates, the Sherman Act was urged as a means of dealing with great trusts that had accumulated tremendous power threatening small businessmen, the consuming public, and the social order. Its purpose was variously conceived to be to preserve free and full competition, to protect the public against high prices, and to protect small business and individual freedom against corporate wealth and power. In the broad, general terms of the debates, the Senators appeared to regard these social, political, and economic purposes as consistent, collateral thrusts of the Act.' Bohling, Franchise Terminations Under the Sherman Act: Populism and Relational Power, 53 Texas L.Rev. 1180, 1189 (1975). 'The legislators were well aware of the common law on restraints of trade, and of the powers of monopolists to hurt the public by raising price, deteriorating product, and restricting production. At the same time, there was at least equal

ment that the Supreme Court has recognized the inappropriateness for the judiciary of issues such as net economic gain in balancing restraint of intrabrand competition against enhanced interbrand competition.[35]

(e) Judge Duniway's refusal to enter into the economic debate.[36]

(3) *Sylvania, The "Rule of Reason" and Post-Sylvania Litigation.* The *Sylvania* opinion has also been criticized for its failure to spell out the factors to be considered in a rule of reason analysis and how those factors are to be weighed and blended in a particular case.[37] Left unclear were such questions as the role—if any—of relevant market analysis, how one balances the intrabrand and interbrand effects of the restraint, the role of an imbalance in bargaining power in the equation, the significance of purpose or intent, the implications of vertical price fixing in the analysis of non-price restraints, the weight to be given the availability of "less restrictive alternatives," and which side has the burden of proving what. One scholar has described the situation as follows:

> There is no existing analytical framework for applying a rule of reason generally, and certainly none for applying it to vertical non-price restraints. The technique of the *Sylvania* majority—quoting a long list of factors without any indication of priority or weight to be accorded each factor—unfortunately is standard operating procedure.[38]

On remand of the *Sylvania* case, for example, the trial court alluded to the ambiguities posed by requiring a rule of reason analysis without spelling out what should be considered and how it should be weighed.[39] In granting Sylvania's motion for summary judgment on the location restriction, the trial court concluded: "[I]t is interbrand competition, rather than intrabrand, which is the primary concern of antitrust law" [40] and that "Sylvania's location practice has an overall pro-competitive effect." [41] In support of the pro-competitive effect of the restraint, the Court cited evidence that Sylvania had

concern with the fate of small producers, driven out of business, or deprived of the opportunity to enter it, by all powerful aggregations of capital.' C. Kaysen & D. Turner, Antitrust Policy 19 (1959). . . . "

35. [T]he Court said in United States v. Topco Associates, Inc., supra, 405 U.S. at 609–10, 92 S.Ct. at 1134, 31 L.Ed.2d at 526:

The fact is that courts are of limited utility in examining difficult economic problems. Our inability to weigh, in any meaningful sense, destruction of competition in one sector of the economy against promotion of competition in another is one important reason we have formulated per se rules.

If the courts were required to review such issues under a "rule of reason," unpredictable ad hoc determinations as to what is or is not illegal under the Sherman Act would result. The Supreme Court suggested that a rule of reason should be applied in this area only if Congress were to decide that predictability is unimportant and that the courts should be "free to ramble through the wilds of

economic theory in order to maintain a flexible approach." . . .

36. . . . I express no views as to the conflicting policy arguments that appear in the respective opinions of Judges Browning, Ely and Kilkenny. I cannot, however, refrain from making one small observation. I am puzzled by the notion that because the courts are not very well equipped to decide between conflicting notions of economic policy, they should pick one side of such an argument and erect it into a rule of per se illegality."

37. See, e.g., Bohling, supra note 24 at 503; Flynn, supra note 24 at 783; Posner, The Next Step in the Antitrust Treatment of Restricted Distribution: Per Se Legality, 48 U.Chi.L.Rev. 6, 14–18 (1981); Zeleck, Stern & Dunfee, supra note 24 at 14.

38. Pitofsky, supra note 24 at 34.

39. Continental T.V., Inc. v. GTE Sylvania, Inc., 461 F.Supp. 1046, 1052 n. 10 (N.D.Cal.1978), affirmed 694 F.2d 1132 (9th Cir. 1982).

40. 461 F.Supp. at 1052.

41. Id.

increased its market share from 1 or 2% to 5%, "thereby becoming an effective interbrand competitor." [42] No examination of the impact of the restraint on intrabrand competition was apparently offered or requested; nor was it explained how a plaintiff could demonstrate a vertical restraint to be unreasonable.

Various proposed models for a rule of reason analysis of vertical restraints have been put forth in the literature.[43] Among the proposals are the following:

(1) "[f]ocus on the single question whether the restriction is intended to cartelize distribution or, on the contrary, to promote the manufacturer's own interests." [44]

(2) Declare all purely vertical restrictions on distribution, including price restrictions, *per se* lawful.[45]

(3) A "presumptive illegality" test whereby a plaintiff would be required to show the restraint caused some harm to competition or an individual competitor which could be rebutted by a defendant proving the restraint was imposed for a legitimate business purpose and was the least restrictive means for achieving the purpose.[46]

(4) Presumptive illegality for vertical non-price restraints imposed by a core member of a "tightly knit oligopoly" possessing market power, which restriction "significantly inhibits" a distributor in its efforts to win customers from competing intrabrand distributors. Where the presumption is triggered, several defenses would be available; i.e., the failing company defense, new entrant, protection of public health and safety, and the like.[47]

(5) "First, the plaintiff would be required to prove that the effect of the challenged restriction is to substantially eliminate intrabrand competition. If the plaintiff were successful in proving this, the burden would shift to the defendant to establish that the restriction was both reasonable and that it was adopted for a proper business purpose. The defendant could meet the necessary burden by demonstrating that the restraint was instituted to enhance distributional efficiency, to increase product safety, or to eliminate free riders. The traditional newcomer or failing-product defenses also would be available.

Once the defendant established a proper business purpose, the restriction would be presumed permissible subject to rebuttal by the plaintiff. Rebuttal by the plaintiff could be accomplished without resort to broad economic proof concerning the effect of the relevant market. Thus, the plaintiff could attempt to establish that the restraint was an unreasonable infringement on plaintiff's business discretion because of the improper

42. Id. The court of appeals affirmed the district court's judgment. See 43 ATRR 715 (9th Cir. 1982).

43. A survey of several of the proposals may be found in Meehan & Larner, A Proposed Rule of Reason for Vertical Restraints on Competition, 26 Antitrust Bull. 195 (1981).

44. Posner, The Rule of Reason and the Economic Approach: Reflections on the *Sylvania* Decision, 45 U.Chi.L.Rev. 1, 17 (1977). Professor Posner, appointed to the Seventh Circuit after publication of this article, has had the opportunity to

apply his test in Valley Liquors, Inc. v. Renfield Importers, Ltd., 678 F.2d 742 (7th Cir. 1982).

45. Posner, The Next Step in the Antitrust Treatment of Restricted Distribution: Per Se Legality, 48 U.Chi.L.Rev. 6 (1981).

46. Note, A Uniform Rule of Reason for Vertical and Horizontal Nonprice Restraints, 55 So.Cal.L.Rev. 465–66 (1982).

47. Zeleck, Stern & Dunfee, supra note 24 at 13.

ends to be achieved by the restriction or the existence of a number of alternatives that would have significantly less restrictive effects on the plaintiff's business discretion.

Finally, plaintiff would have the opportunity to open the case to an economic analysis of the effect of the practice on interbrand competition in the relevant market. Thus, the plaintiff could, if it so elected, attempt to establish the unreasonableness of the restraint through a demonstration of its harmful effect on interbrand competition. The defendant's market power and product differentiation would, of course, be highly relevant to the resolution of this issue." [48]

(6)(i) All airtight vertical territorial restrictions imposed by a supplier that dominates over fifty percent of the market should be declared *per se illegal.*

(ii) All less restrictive vertical restraints imposed by a dominant firm should be *carefully scrutinized* under a *presumption* of *illegality.*

(iii) All airtight vertical territorial restrictions imposed by a manufacturer without market power should be *carefully scrutinized* under a *rule of reason* analysis, with special emphasis on whether a *less restrictive alternative* would suffice and *emphasis* on *market structure.*

(iv) All less restrictive vertical territorial restraints imposed by nondominant companies are to be judged according to a rule of reason analysis which includes consideration of market structure with a presumption of legality for any firm with less than ten percent of the market.

(v) All vertically imposed nonprice restraints employed by a new entrant or failing company should be rebuttably presumed to be legal.[49]

(7) "Because of the conduct's impact on trader and consumer freedom and the lessening of intrabrand competition, a presumption of illegality, without regard to market power or structure, is warranted as a beginning guidepost to analysis when the conduct is a product of a vertical contract, combination, or conspiracy explicitly imposing resale price maintenance or territorial or customer divisions. The test is a beginning guidepost because it is uncertain whether the facts will raise the inference that the conduct results from a contract or conspiracy or is within the per se category. It is not certain whether a justification or excuse for the conduct is factually present in the case or warranted as a matter of policy under all the circumstances unique to the dispute. Moreover, the test is a qualitative one because the legal essence of the offense under section 1 is contractual or conspiratorial conduct that unreasonably displaces the competitive process. The inquiry is a qualitative one not dependent on the amount of commerce displaced or even that any commerce is displaced. The Authors' [of Proposal #6] attempt to make the primary focus of a section 1 analysis of vertical market tests a measure of quantitative market displacement not only greatly complicates the trial of such cases and converts the analysis into a section 2 inquiry, but also would require the reversal of substantial and significant long standing legal precedent to the contrary.

Before that additional chaos is brought on to comply with the implications of *Sylvania,* other means for sensibly moderating the overly broad implications of both *Schwinn* and *Sylvania* should be explored. The con-

48. Bohling, supra note 24 at 513–16.   **49.** Stewart & Roberts, supra note 24 at 758–59.

ceptualization of the per se and rule of reason methodology as a series of evidentiary presumptions of varying levels of rebuttability is a more convincing path to follow. The moderately presumptive illegal classification of contractual air-tight vertical restraints as to price, customers, and territories makes good sense. It provides a method for sorting out the conduct in question in light of the goals of the law, i.e., proof of an objective need to provide significant point of sales services, efficiently market a product, gain entry into a market, or protect public health or safety in light of peculiar risks associated with the product. The restraint, however, should be ancillary to these otherwise lawful objectives and no more restrictive than objectively necessary to overcome the presumption of illegality—questions of fact that must be resolved in the circumstances of the restraint and peculiarities of the business." [50]

Query: With which proposed test, if any, do you agree? Why?

(4) *"Horizontal" or "Vertical"? Sylvania's Implications for Dual Distribution.* Considerable controversy has arisen about *Sylvania's* meaning in the case of restraints imposed by dual distributors—sellers who both supply and compete with distributors they impose restraints upon.[51] For example, an oil company may decide to operate wholly-owned wholesale or retail outlets, or to reserve large commercial accounts for direct sales by itself rather than permitting franchised wholesalers or retailers to service the account. Franchised wholesalers or retailers operating in competition with company-owned outlets frequently complain about the pricing practices of the company-owned outlet which can be used to discipline retailers at variance with company pricing policies.

Franchisors operating at the wholesale or retail level through independently incorporated subsidiaries or even separate divisions and who seek to restrict customers or territories of their independent franchisees by agreement or unilateral refusal to deal increase their antitrust risks. What may have begun as a vertical restraint phrased in terms of a location clause or primary responsibility clause may later develop into or be seen as a horizontal division of markets between the retailing branch of the vertically integrated firm and its independent retail competitors. The boycott concept may come into play when wholesale or retail subsidiaries, other franchisees or franchisor services are utilized by a supplier to deter a franchisee from exercising independent judgment about prices, services, territories or customers.

The courts are split over whether to characterize such conduct as horizontal and subject to a rule of *per se* illegality, or whether to view the restraint as vertical and subject to the ill-defined and more generous test of the rule of reason.[52]

50. Flynn, supra note 24, at 789–90. See also Pitofsky, supra note 24, at 28, for a similar proposal.

51. See, Copy-Data Systems, Inc. v. Toshiba America, Inc., 663 F.2d 405 (2d Cir. 1981); Abadir & Co. v. First Mississippi Corp., 651 F.2d 422 (5th Cir. Unit A 1981); Rubbermaid, Inc. v. Federal Trade Commission, 575 F.2d 1169 (6th Cir. 1978); Sargent-Welch Scientific Co. v. Ventron Corp., 567 F.2d 701 (7th Cir. 1977), certiorari denied 439 U.S. 822, 99 S.Ct. 87, 58 L.Ed.2d 113 (1978); Roesch,

Inc. v. Star Cooler Corp., 671 F.2d 1168 (8th Cir. 1982); Cowley v. Braden Industries, Inc., 613 F.2d 751 (9th Cir.), certiorari denied 446 U.S. 965, 100 S.Ct. 2942, 64 L.Ed.2d 824 (1980).

52. The cases are analyzed in Altschuler, Sylvania, Vertical Restraints and Dual Distribution, 25 Antitrust Bull. 1 (1980). See also Note, Dual Distribution and the Horizontal-Vertical Dichotomy of Nonprice Restrictions, 17 Tulsa L.J. 306 (1981).

Among the proposals for resolving this ambiguity traceable to *Sylvania* [53] have been the following:

(1) "Where a supplier retains an area or class of customers exclusively for itself, it is in effect agreeing horizontally with distributors in adjacent territories that they will not compete. Since the manufacturer as dealer is no longer interested exclusively in a high volume, low markup sales policy, the reasons for displacing the traditional per se rules against horizontal market division disappear; any justification could equally be asserted (and would be rejected under current law) on behalf of horizontal territorial allocations. Of course, where the manufacturer appoints many dealers (itself along with others) in every area, or imposes reasonable primary responsibility burdens on the dealers, reduction in intra-brand competition may be insignificant. It would not be sensible in those circumstances to characterize such an arrangement as horizontal market division and therefore illegal per se." [54]

(2) "In determining whether to apply the per se or rule of reason standard, courts should undertake a two-step analysis. Essentially, the greater the supplier's share of the intrabrand market (at the retail level) and the greater its share of the interbrand market (at the manufacturing level), the more willing courts should be to apply the per se standard of illegality. Whenever the dual distributor possesses substantial market power (enjoys the ability to raise prices in excess of costs and normal profits for a sustained period of time) in both the intrabrand and interbrand markets, the per se rule of illegality should apply.

The first step in this analysis entails measurement of the dual distributor's share of the retail market in which it deals. . . . The purpose of this test of intrabrand competition is readily apparent. As the dual distributor's share of retail sales increases, *ceteris paribus*, his incentive to sacrifice some profits as a manufacturer in order to reap monopoly profits as a retailer increases. . . .

The second step in this proposed analysis focuses on the competitiveness of the interbrand market. . . . If the dual distributor's interbrand market share is small or consumers can easily substitute other brands for the dual distributor's brand and these substitutes are accessible, then vertical restrictions can serve a useful purpose in promoting interbrand competition and, even if they did not, the power of individual dealers to raise markups as a result of the restrictions will be tightly constrained. Therefore, if the intrabrand and interbrand market shares are small, the rule of reason analysis should be employed to place upon the plaintiff the burden of showing that these restraints are in fact anticompetitive. When the dual distributor has a very large market share, and is in fact a monopolist or oligopolist in the manufacture of the product, courts should apply the per se rule of illegality." [55]

(3) "[T]he plaintiff should be required to indicate early on whether or not the restraint is alleged to be unlawful because it is imposed by a manufacturer-distributor (or a manufacturer-retailer) seeking to protect itself from intrabrand competition from other distributors to whom it sells.

53. "Dual distribution . . . introduces problems of categorization that *Sylvania* left unexplained. . . . [T]he applicability of the rule of reason in a particular case depends entirely on how the challenged restraints are characterized." Altschuler, supra note 52 at 2.

54. Pitofsky, The *Sylvania* Case: Antitrust Analysis of Vertical Non-Price Restraints, 78 Colum.L.Rev. 1, 32 (1978).

55. Note, Antitrust Treatment of Intrabrand Territorial Restraints Within a Dual Distribution System, 56 Tex.L.Rev. 1486, 1504–05 (1978).

The plaintiff's ability to provide *prima facie* support for such a contention is subject to review on summary judgment and the case should be dismissed in the absence of strong proof that the defendant realizes a substantial part of its income as a distributor, and enjoys sufficient profitability and freedom from interbrand competition to establish that such a horizontally operating restraint can rationally be found to be anti-competitive in purpose and effect. Thus, the manufacturer whose distribution activity is minimal or highly competitive is presumed (almost conclusively) to be operating in a vertical mode. However, if the plaintiff can ultimately establish the requirements of a horizontal impact, the restraint should be found to be unlawful unless the defendant can come forward with sufficient evidence to persuade the finder of fact that the benefits for interbrand competition are sufficient to justify the imposition of the restraint. This is, of course, likely to be a difficult burden, since a horizontally imposed restraint will rarely be defensible. If, however, the plaintiff is unable or unwilling to take on the burden of establishing that the manufacturer-distributor has imposed the restraint to protect itself as a distributor, the case should proceed as would any other rule of reason case under *Sylvania* analyzing a vertically imposed restraint. The governing rules on burdens of proof for such cases would prevail and the dual distribution status of the defendant could be evidentiary of the purpose and effect of the restraint, but would not create any rules of *per se* unlawfulness (or lawfulness) or any presumptions." [56]

Query: With which proposed test do you agree? Do any of the proposals require unduly complex trials? Should the complexity of litigation be a factor in determining whether to adopt a particular test?

(5) *Sylvania's Implications for Vertical Price Fixing.* Justice White's concurring opinion in *Sylvania* points out that the majority's logic justifying a rule of reason approach to vertical non-price restraints warrants similar treatment for vertical price fixing. Some lower courts have agreed with Justice White's analysis and have refused to apply a *per se* rule to vertical price fixing.

For example, in *Eastern Scientific Co. v. Wild Heerbrugg Instruments, Inc.,* [57] the plaintiff was a Rhode Island distributor of scientific instruments manufactured by Wild Heerbrugg. The distribution arrangement imposed no limitations on Eastern's sales within Rhode Island but Wild demanded that Eastern not sell below list outside of Rhode Island. Eastern was terminated upon its refusal to comply with Wild's demands, a practice the Court described as a policy of territorial restriction enforced by price maintenance restraints. In remanding the case for a new trial in light of the intervening *Sylvania* decision, the Court observed:

[W]e are unable to conceive of how the resale price restrictions used to enforce the assigned territories in the present case can possibly have a greater anti-competitive effect than a pure policy of territorial restrictions. [58]

Queries. Do you agree? What if Wild had not imposed territorial restraints but required all dealers to resell at list prices? Should the latter restraint be treated any differently than a pure territorial restriction or a

56. Brett & Wallace, *Sylvania* and the Dual Distribution Dilemma, 26 N.Y. L.S.L.Rev. 971, 1004–05 (1981).

57. 572 F.2d 883 (1st Cir.), certiorari denied 439 U.S. 833, 99 S.Ct. 112, 58 L.Ed.2d 128 (1978). Cf. In re Nissan Antitrust Litigation, 577 F.2d 910 (5th Cir. 1978), certiorari denied 439 U.S. 1072, 99 S.Ct. 843, 59 L.Ed.2d 38 (1979).

58. 572 F.2d at 885.

territorial restriction enforced by resale price restraints on sales outside the assigned territory? Consider the following:

> [Intrabrand restraints] may be imposed to enable the manufacturer to capture the profit arising from an advantage that his product has over a rival's product, and to do so by eliminating the possibility that his dealers will compete such profits away through intrabrand competition. This is called the competitive-advantages rationale. Restrictions imposed under the competitive-advantages rationale are unjustifiable because they remove market forces that would otherwise lower prices to consumers, without inducing greater dealer services. Moreover, such restrictions are unnecessary to spur the manufacturer to improve his product's quality or his efficiency; that incentive comes from interbrand, not intrabrand, competition. Most important, the competitive-advantages rationale for intrabrand restraints explains the Supreme Court's distinction between price and nonprice restraints.
>
> . . .
>
> [P]rice restraints are almost always likely to be explained by the competitive-advantages rationale and never by the dealer-services rationale. [Dealer services rationale is defined as restricting intrabrand competition to induce dealers to undertake greater non-price competition like advertising, showrooms, repair service, etc.]
>
> . . .
>
> Economic analysis usually assumes that intrabrand restraints directly increase manufacturers' profits only when imposed by a manufacturers' cartel and assumes that otherwise they increase dealer margins, either in response to a dealer cartel or in an attempt to increase dealer services. Although each of these explanations is valid under some circumstances, they each miss an important alternative explanation: the competitive-advantages theory. That theory states that a manufacturer profits directly from intrabrand restrictions when they enable him to keep his price to dealers higher than would otherwise be possible. With active intrabrand competition, the dealers' profitability on a particular brand decreases and the manufacturer can be forced to lower his wholesale price to compensate for his brand's lower profitability in the retail market. Without active intrabrand competition, the manufacturer can maintain higher wholesale prices. Restraints imposed under the competitive-advantages rationale decrease consumer welfare and are unjustifiable.[59]

(6) *Sylvania and Boycott Principles in Enforcement of Vertical Market Restraints.* As will be developed more fully infra, pp. 762–782, boycott principles are relied upon in an increasing number of vertical restraint cases. The boycott alleged is a "vertical" boycott, claiming that the plaintiff distributor was terminated or otherwise disciplined by his supplier at the behest of competing distributors complaining about the distributor's pricing or other marketing practices. A supplier agreeing to act upon the complaints and to terminate or discipline the distributor for violating vertical market restraints runs the antitrust risk that the conduct will be identified as an "agreement" and one to "boycott" the terminated or disciplined distributor.

In the *Schwinn* era, such conduct was labled as *per se* unlawful.[60] In the post-*Sylvania* era, courts have accorded diverse treatment to these claims.

59. Gerhart, The "Competitive Advantage" Explanation for Intrabrand Restraints: An Antitrust Analysis, 1981 Duke L.J. 417, 429–30, 447.

60. See, e.g., Eastex Aviation, Inc. v. Sperry & Hutchinson Co., 522 F.2d 1299 (5th Cir. 1975).

The courts are divided over whether the conduct should be *per se* unlawful when the underlying objective of the termination is to fix resale prices, although the majority of courts have applied a *per se* rule. Vertical enforcement of customer and territorial limitations at the instance of competing distributors has received a more mixed reception, depending upon whether the facts support the view that enforcement of the restrictions is motivated by the unilaterally determined self-interest of the supplier or whether the conduct is motivated by the self-interest of competing distributors seeking to minimize intrabrand competition. In the latter instance, one under Supreme Court review in *Spray-Rite Service Corp. v. Monsanto Co.*, the case takes on the overtones of a horizontal group boycott and is treated as *per se* illegal.[61] The horizontal-vertical dichotomy is made the dividing line between *per se* and rule of reason analysis.

Queries. Should a *per se* rule be applied when a supplier terminates a distributor at the behest of a competing distributor for violating territorial or customer limitations imposed by the supplier? Should there be proof that the supplier has significant market power in a relevant market before the conduct is declared unlawful? Would you require proof that the primary motive for cutting off the distributor was the self-interest of the competing distributor and not the supplier's self-interest?[62] What light, if any, does *Sylvania* shed on these questions?

D.   EXCLUSIVE DEALING

Freedom of dealers to make independent decisions in the conduct of their business may be restricted not only in respect of their resale prices and trading territory, but also in respect of their sources of supply. It often makes good business sense for a manufacturer to obtain from his distributors contractual commitments to handle his line and no other. In this way the manufacturer can be assured that the distributor will work hard and faithfully to sell his goods. It will be worth while to provide special training to the distributor, where the complex character of the wares calls for special skill. A distributor who confines himself to a single manufacturer's line can more easily stock various sizes or models in adequate supply. An attempt to carry full stock on several lines may require an excessive inventory and thus over-extend the dealer's financial commitments, increas-

---

61.   684 F.2d 1226 (7th Cir. 1982), certiorari granted 457 U.S. 1106, 103 S.Ct. 1249, ___ L.Ed.2d ___ (1983). See also Com-Tel, Inc. v. DuKane Corp., 669 F.2d 404 (6th Cir. 1982); Hobart Brothers Co. v. Malcolm T. Gilliland, Inc., 471 F.2d 894 (5th Cir.), certiorari denied 412 U.S. 923, 93 S.Ct. 2736, 37 L.Ed.2d 150 (1973); Valley Liquors, Inc. v. Renfield Importers, Ltd., 678 F.2d 742 (7th Cir. 1982).

62.   In Valley Liquors, Inc. v. Renfield Importers, Ltd., supra note 61, on appeal from the denial of a motion for preliminary injunction to prevent termination, Judge Posner found that the "possibility" that a termination was motivated by supplier self-interest was sufficient to rebut an inference of collusion between the supplier and distributors competing with the plaintiff. Judge Posner went on in dicta: (1) To invoke a *per se* analysis there must be proof that the motive of the supplier *and* competing distributors was to restrain price competition, but making motive the touchstone for legality involves "a certain unreality." (2) The test for "unreasonableness" in dealer termination cases requires proof that the restraint made consumers "worse off" after weighing the effects on both intrabrand and interbrand competition; a "short-cut" way to measure such an effect is to show the defendant has "significant market power" by examining market share in a "carefully defined" relevant product and geographic market.

ing the credit risk which the supplier must take into account in setting his price. To the extent that the dealer is obliged to take all his requirements from the one producer, the producer can plan his own manufacturing operations more confidently, schedule more efficiently, and save on sales expense. Lower costs achieved in this way might make the producer a more effective competitor against other producers, and lead to lower prices. Although this kind of integration does not provide permanent assurance of a "firm market," as does acquisition of a customer (see *Columbia Steel* case, p. 209 supra), it has compensating advantages. The producer need not invest his own capital in the controlled outlets. He avoids tort and other liabilities of an employer at the distributing level, e.g., under state law, minimum wage and social security legislation. It may permit one to achieve many of the advantages of vertical integration while escaping the burdens of doing so.

On the other hand, it is apparent that if one producer enters into exclusive arrangements with all leading distributors, other producers are severely handicapped in reaching consumers, even with a better or cheaper product. Also, if several leading producers enter into exclusive dealing arrangements, each with his own "family" of distributors, so that all distributors are tied to one or another supplier, it will be difficult for a new producer to break into the field, or for an existing producer to increase his share of the business. The effects are similar to those analyzed in vertical merger cases like *Brown Shoe*, supra p. 251.

Obviously we are dealing with a legal device which lends itself to restraint of trade or monopoly, but which can hardly be classified as unreasonable *per se* except, perhaps, where it is employed by dominant firms.

Several closely related terms are used to describe the variations in business relationships having the legal and economic characteristics of "exclusive dealing." Professor Sullivan defines them as follows: "An exclusive dealing contract involves a commitment by a buyer to deal only with a particular seller. The related device, a requirements contract, may entail a commitment by a buyer to take all he needs of a given product for a specified period from the seller, or may entail a commitment by a seller to supply all of the buyer's needs, or both. These arrangements tend to foreclose a portion of the market from competitors and to reduce free choice, as do tying arrangements." [63]

"Tying", which is considered in the next section, may be regarded as a variant of exclusive dealing. The seller of some highly regarded or scarce or patented article A refuses to sell it unless the buyer also purchases a less desirable commodity B. Sale of B is "tied" to the sale of A. It is evident that the seller can do this only when for some reason he is not subject to effective competition from other suppliers

---

63. L. Sullivan, Antitrust, 471 (1977). See also, Hyde v. Jefferson Parish Hospital District No. 2, 686 F.2d 286 (5th Cir. 1982), certiorari granted ___ U.S. ___, 103 S.Ct. 1271, ___ L.Ed.2d ___ (1983) (case raising distinction between tying and exclusive dealing).

of commodity A; i.e., he has some kind of partial or complete "monopoly" in the tying product, perhaps entirely lawful as under a patent. It is also evident that he must want more money for B, or a larger volume of sales, than he could get in normal competition with other suppliers of B, else he could sell his B without resort to tying. By tying, therefore, the seller "protects" his market for B. He maintains his ability to sell B at a non-competitive price by using his A power to exclude competitors who can furnish B but not A.[64]

The Sherman Act accorded the usual respect to the "good business reasons" which could be advanced to show that these restrictive practices were reasonable and not prejudicial to public interests.[65] A tougher regime was inaugurated in Section 3 of the Clayton Act.

Although the problem of exclusive dealing is considered in this chapter primarily with reference to restraints which suppliers impose on dealers and customers, it should not be forgotten that similar restrictions may be imposed by a powerful customer upon a weak supplier.[66] Or a supplier and customer may find it to their advantage to enter into mutually exclusive obligations.

Akin to exclusive dealing and tying is the practice known as "reciprocity": arrangements by which large firms prefer each other commercially or by which a powerful firm exploits its buying power as a lever for promoting sales to firms from which it is buying.

SECTION 3 OF THE CLAYTON ACT OF 1914

15 U.S.C.A. § 14.

It shall be unlawful for any person engaged in [federally regulated] commerce, in the course of such commerce, to lease or make a sale or contract for sale of goods, wares, merchandise, machinery, supplies, or other commodities, whether patented or unpatented, for use, consumption, or resale within the United States or any Territory thereof or the District of Columbia or any insular possession or other place under the jurisdiction of the United States,* or fix a price charged therefor, or discount from, or rebate upon, such price, on the condition, agreement, or understanding that the lessee or purchaser thereof shall not use or deal in the goods, wares, merchandise, machinery, supplies, or other commodities

---

64. See generally L. Sullivan, Antitrust, 431–471 (1977); Markovits, Tie-Ins and Reciprocity: A Functional, Legal, and Policy Analysis, 58 Texas L.Rev. 1363 (1980); Marvel, Exclusive Dealing, 25 J.L. & Econ. 1 (1982); Markovits, Tie-ins, Reciprocity and the Leverage Theory, 76 Yale L.J. 1397 (1967); Kessler and Stern, Competition, Contract and Vertical Integration, 69 Yale L.J. 1 (1959); Turner, The Validity of Tying Arrangements Under the Antitrust Laws, 72 Harv.L. Rev. 50 (1958); Bowman, Tying Arrangements and the Leverage Problem, 67 Yale L.J. 19 (1957).

65. United States v. United Shoe Machine Co. of New Jersey, 247 U.S. 32, 38 S.Ct. 473, 62 L.Ed. 968 (1918); cf. United Shoe Machine Corp. v. United States, 258 U.S. 451, 42 S.Ct. 363, 66 L.Ed. 708 (1922).

66. See Twin City Sportservice, Inc. v. Charles O. Finley & Co., 676 F.2d 1291 (9th Cir. 1982).

* What policy is expressed in this exemption of restraints abroad? Nationalist unconcern for exploitation of the foreign consumer? Cf. Webb-Pomerene Export Act, p. 856, infra. Would it be lawful for one American exporter to tie up in an exclusive dealing contract the dominant London distributor, thus cutting out of the London market a competing American exporter?

of a competitor or competitors of the lessor or seller, where the effect of such lease, sale, or contract for sale or such condition, agreement, or understanding may be to substantially lessen competition or tend to create a monopoly in any line of commerce.

NOTES

(1) *Lease or Sale; Agency.* Section 3 is explicitly limited to imposition of exclusive dealing restraints upon customers by suppliers; corresponding exploitation of buying power to constrain suppliers is reachable under the Sherman Act or under Section 5 of the Federal Trade Commission Act.[67] Even supplier imposed restraints may escape Section 3 to the extent that transactions can be cast as "agency" or "consignment" rather than sale or lease.[68] Moreover, the mere refusal to sell to distributors who handle competing lines cannot readily be brought within the proscriptions of a statute framed in terms of "sell or lease". Cf. the following argument from the Government's unsuccessful *amicus* petition for certiorari to review *Amplex v. Outboard Marine Corp.:* [69]

> The government's right to antitrust relief, and the cancelled dealer's right to recover, is well established in cases of concerted refusals to deal, as where suppliers act together or at the behest of rival dealers. The Court has also sustained the government's right to relief under the Sherman Act against a supplier who uses an announced policy of refusal to deal as a means of putting together a combination to maintain resale prices. But this Court has not yet expressly passed upon the question, presented here, of the cancelled dealer's right to relief against such a supplier—i.e., one who uses refusal to deal as a means to secure compliance with an anticompetitive program embodied in tacit agreements with acquiescent dealers.

> A substantial number of lower courts, however, have held that the cancelled dealer cannot recover. The leading case is Nelson Radio & Supply Co. v. Motorola, Inc., 200 F.2d 911 (C.A.5), cert. denied 345 U.S. 925, 73 S.Ct. 783, 97 L.Ed. 1356 [additional citations] contra, Lessig v. Tidewater Oil Co., 327 F.2d 459 (C.A.9), cert. denied 377 U.S. 993, 84 S.Ct. 1920, 12 L.Ed.2d 1046. Under this line of authority, which the court below followed, the dealer disciplined by cancellation or non-renewal of his franchise when he refuses to agree to an arrangement in violation of the antitrust laws has no remedy, because Section 3 of the Clayton Act and Section 1 of the Sherman Act prohibit only executed sales or agreements on restrictive conditions—and not refusals to deal.

> To be sure, these decisions recognize that the defendant supplier has made sales to and agreements with dealers other than the plaintiff. But those sales and agreements, even though they may violate the antitrust laws, are deemed immaterial on the ground that "it is the absence of a contract with the plaintiff, not the presence of the agreements with distributors in other parts of the country, of which the plaintiff must complain" . . . The result is to deny redress to the dealer who has suffered injury for his unwillingness to fall in line by acceding to an unlawful program. Such an anomalous result is not justified by the

67. Cf. Lawlor v. National Screen Service Corp., 238 F.2d 59 (3d Cir. 1957).

68. Federal Trade Commission v. Curtis Publishing Co., 260 U.S. 568, 43 S.Ct. 210, 67 L.Ed. 408 (1923).

69. 380 F.2d 112 (4th Cir. 1967), certiorari denied 389 U.S. 1036, 88 S.Ct. 768, 19 L.Ed.2d 823 (1968).

broad language of Section 4 of the Clayton Act and would defeat the objectives of Congress in creating the private antitrust remedy.

We urge, therefore, that a refusal to deal is actionable under Section 4 of the Clayton Act, which simply requires that the injury be "by reason of anything forbidden in the antitrust laws," when it is used to secure, or in an attempt to secure, agreement to a proposal which, if acceded to, would (1) comprise one of a set of contracts in unreasonable restraint of trade, or (2) constitute one of a number of sales agreements made on condition or understanding of unlawful exclusive dealing. To the extent, if any, that such a ruling may further curtail "the limited dispensation" conferred on refusals to deal under the doctrine of United States v. Colgate & Co., 250 U.S. 300, 39 S.Ct. 465, 63 L.Ed. 992, as already qualified in United States v. Parke, Davis & Co., 362 U.S. 29, 80 S.Ct. 503, 4 L.Ed.2d 505, we would urge that such curtailment is required for the proper enforcement of the antitrust laws.

It has been held that an ongoing and continuous course of dealing "may ripen into an implied or informal agreement or understanding" [70] for exclusive dealing within the limitations of § 3 of the Clayton Act.

(2) *Goods or Other Commodities.* Section 3 is applicable only where the restraint is associated with the supply of tangible goods and only where the restraint is directed against another's supply of tangible goods. Thus, exclusive dealing arrangements with respect to transportation, communications, or other services would not be covered by the section.[71] Nor would extensions of credit.[72] In such circumstances, the validity of an exclusive dealing arrangement would be tested under the less rigorous standards of the Sherman Act [73] or § 5 of the F.T.C. Act.[74] Should banks be free, subject only to the Sherman Act, to make loans on preferential terms to persons who buy computer services, travel agency services, or tangible goods from the bank or its affiliates? Is the potential for unfair competition or risky credit practices such that banks should be confined to the "banking business"?

(3) *Condition, Agreement or Understanding Not to Use or Deal; "Practical Effect."* If the "practical effect" of an explicit provision is to preclude the purchaser's dealing with a competitor of the supplier, Section 3 applies notwithstanding that the provision does not literally foreclose all

70. McElhenney Co. v. Western Auto Supply Co., 269 F.2d 332, 337 (4th Cir. 1959); Dillon Materials Handling, Inc. v. Albion Industries, 567 F.2d 1299, 1302 (5th Cir.), certiorari denied 439 U.S. 832, 99 S.Ct. 111, 58 L.Ed.2d 127 (1978).

71. Cf. Associated Press v. Taft-Ingalls Corp., 340 F.2d 753 (6th Cir. 1965) (regional news services); Times-PiCayune Publishing Co. v. United States, 345 U.S. 594, 73 S.Ct. 872, 97 L.Ed. 1277 (1953) (advertising); Battle v. Liberty National Life Insurance Co., 493 F.2d 39, rehearing denied 503 F.2d 567 (5th Cir. 1974), certiorari denied 419 U.S. 1110, 95 S.Ct. 784, 42 L.Ed.2d 807 (1975) (service contract).

72. But cf. Fortner Enterprises, Inc. v. U.S. Steel Corp., p. 707 infra, and judgments under the Sherman Act against the Big Three motor car manufacturers based on alleged coercion of their auto-mobile dealers to finance their automobile purchases through finance companies affiliated with the respective manufacturers. United States v. General Motors Corp., 121 F.2d 376 (7th Cir.), certiorari denied 314 U.S. 618, 62 S.Ct. 105, 86 L.Ed. 497, rehearing denied 314 U.S. 710, 62 S.Ct. 178, 86 L.Ed. 566 (1941); Chrysler Corp. v. United States, 314 U.S. 583, 62 S.Ct. 356, 86 L.Ed. 471 (1941); same case 316 U.S. 556, 62 S.Ct. 1146, 86 L.Ed. 1668 (1942); Ford Motor Co. v. United States, 335 U.S. 303, 69 S.Ct. 93, 93 L.Ed. 24 (1948).

73. See Twin City Sportservice, Inc. v. Charles O. Finley & Co., 512 F.2d 1264 (9th Cir. 1975) (Finley I); Twin City Sportservice, Inc. v. Charles O. Finley & Co., Inc., 676 F.2d 1291 (9th Cir. 1982) (Finley II).

74. See Federal Trade Commission v. Brown Shoe Co., Inc., infra p. 755.

dealing with such competitor. Thus, an agreement by a department store to handle only one line of dress patterns at its premises designated in the franchise agreement falls within Section 3, although handling another line of patterns would have been permissible at other premises. *Standard Fashion Co. v. Magrane-Houston Co.*[75] But cf., *Federal Trade Commission v. Sinclair Refining Co.*,[76] overruling the administrative finding of practical effect where gasoline pumps and storage tanks were supplied to service station dealers on condition that they be used solely with Sinclair's gasoline. The court substituted its own conclusion that a service station dealer could readily handle other brands of gasoline by installing pumps and tanks of other refiners, or by buying his own equipment.[77] It is not illegal, in connection with the appointment of an exclusive distributor for a designated territory, to provide that he shall be "responsible" for the effective exploitation of that market, an obligation which may of course discourage him from dispersing his sales effort over more than one supplier's line. Cf. *Atlantic Refining Co. v. Federal Trade Commission*, p. 757 infra and *Continental T.V., Inc. v. GTE Sylvania, Inc.* p. 639 supra.

STANDARD OIL CO. OF CALIFORNIA v. UNITED STATES

Supreme Court of the United States, 1949.
337 U.S. 293, 69 S.Ct. 1051, 93 L.Ed. 1371.

MR. JUSTICE FRANKFURTER delivered the opinion of the Court.

This is an appeal to review a decree enjoining the Standard Oil Company of California and its wholly-owned subsidiary, Standard Stations, Inc., from enforcing or entering into exclusive supply contracts with any independent dealer in petroleum products and automobile accessories. The use of such contracts was successfully assailed by the United States as violative of § 1 of the Sherman Act and § 3 of the Clayton Act.

The Standard Oil Company of California, a Delaware corporation, owns petroleum-producing resources and refining plants in California and sells petroleum products in what has been termed in these proceedings the "Western area"—Arizona, California, Idaho, Nevada, Oregon, Utah and Washington. It sells through its own service stations, to the operators of independent service stations and to industrial users. It is the largest seller of gasoline in the area. In 1946 its combined sales amounted to 23% of the total taxable gallonage sold there in that year: sales by company-owned service stations constituted 6.8% of the total, sales under exclusive dealing contracts with independent service stations, 6.7% of the total; the remainder were sales to industrial users. Retail service-station sales by Standard's six leading competitors absorbed 42.5% of the total taxable gallonage; the remaining retail sales were divided between more than seventy small companies. It is undisputed that Standard's major competitors employ similar exclusive dealing arrangements. In 1948 only 1.6% of

75. 258 U.S. 346, 42 S.Ct. 360, 66 L.Ed. 653 (1922).

76. 261 U.S. 463, 43 S.Ct. 450, 67 L.Ed. 746 (1923).

77. Cf., Magnus Petroleum Co. v. Skelly Oil Co., 599 F.2d 196 (7th Cir.), cer-

tiorari denied 444 U.S. 916, 100 S.Ct. 231, 62 L.Ed.2d 171 (1979) (partial requirements contract upheld because fuel oil distributor free to purchase product elsewhere).

retail outlets were what is known as "split-pump" stations, that is, sold the gasoline of more than one supplier.

Exclusive supply contracts with Standard had been entered into as of March 12, 1947, by the operators of 5,937 independent stations, or 16% of the retail gasoline outlets in the Western area, which purchased from Standard in 1947, $57,646,233 worth of gasoline and $8,200,089.21 worth of other products. Some outlets are covered by more than one contract so that in all about 8,000 exclusive supply contracts are here in issue. These are of several types, but a feature common to each is the dealer's undertaking to purchase from Standard all his requirements of one or more products. Two types, covering 2,777 outlets, bind the dealer to purchase of Standard all his requirements of gasoline and other petroleum products as well as tires, tubes, and batteries. The remaining written agreements, 4,368 in number, bind the dealer to purchase of Standard all his requirements of petroleum products only. It was also found that independent dealers had entered 742 oral contracts by which they agreed to sell only Standard's gasoline. In some instances dealers who contracted to purchase from Standard all their requirements of tires, tubes, and batteries, had also orally agreed to purchase of Standard their requirements of other automobile accessories. Of the written agreements, 2,712 were for varying specified terms; the rest were effective from year to year but terminable "at the end of the first 6 months of any contract year, or at the end of any such year, by giving to the other at least 30 days prior thereto written notice. . . ." Before 1934 Standard's sales of petroleum products through independent service stations were made pursuant to agency agreements, but in that year Standard adopted the first of its several requirements-purchase contract forms, and by 1938 requirements contracts had wholly superseded the agency method of distribution.

Between 1936 and 1946 Standard's sales of gasoline through independent dealers remained at a practically constant proportion of the area's total sales; its sales of lubricating oil declined slightly during that period from 6.2% to 5% of the total. Its proportionate sales of tires and batteries for 1946 were slightly higher than they were in 1936, though somewhat lower than for some intervening years; they have never, as to either of these products, exceeded 2% of the total sales in the Western area.

Since § 3 of the Clayton Act was directed to prohibiting specific practices even though not covered by the broad terms of the Sherman Act, it is appropriate to consider first whether the enjoined contracts fall within the prohibition of the narrower Act. . . .

Obviously the contracts here at issue would be proscribed if § 3 stopped short of the qualifying clause beginning, "where the effect of such lease, sale, or contract for sale . . . ." If effect is to be given that clause, however, it is by no means obvious, in view of Standard's minority share of the "line of commerce" involved, of the fact that that share has not recently increased, and of the claims of these contracts to economic utility, that the effect of the contracts may be to lessen competition or tend to create a monopoly. It is the qualifying clause, therefore, which must be construed.

The District Court held that the requirement of showing an actual or potential lessening of competition or a tendency to establish monopoly was adequately met by proof that the contracts covered "a substantial number of outlets and a substantial amount of products, whether considered comparatively or not." Given such quantitative substantiality, the substantial lessening of competition—so the court reasoned—is an automatic result, for the very existence of such contracts denies dealers opportunity to deal in the products of competing suppliers and excludes suppliers from access to the outlets controlled by those dealers. Having adopted this standard of proof, the court excluded as immaterial testimony bearing on "the economic merits or demerits of the present system as contrasted with a system which prevailed prior to its establishment and which would prevail if the court declared the present arrangement [invalid]." The court likewise deemed it unnecessary to make findings, on the basis of evidence that was admitted, whether the number of Standard's competitors had increased or decreased since the inauguration of the requirements-contract system, whether the number of their dealers had increased or decreased, and as to other matters which would have shed light on the comparative status of Standard and its competitors before and after the adoption of that system. The court concluded:

"Grant that, on a comparative basis, and in relation to the entire trade in these products in the area, the restraint is not integral. Admit also that control of distribution results in lessening of costs and that its abandonment might increase costs. . . . Concede further, that the arrangement was entered into in good faith, with the honest belief that control of distribution and consequent concentration of representation were economically beneficial to the industry and to the public, that they have continued for over fifteen years openly, notoriously and unmolested by the Government, and have been practised by other major oil companies competing with Standard, that the number of Standard outlets so controlled may have decreased, and the quantity of products supplied to them may have declined, on a comparative basis. Nevertheless, as I read the latest cases of the Supreme Court, I am compelled to find the practices here involved to be violative of both statutes. For they affect injuriously a sizeable part of interstate commerce, or,—to use the current phrase—'an appreciable segment' of interstate commerce."

The issue before us, therefore, is whether the requirement of showing that the effect of the agreements "may be to substantially lessen competition" may be met simply by proof that a substantial portion of commerce is affected or whether it must also be demonstrated that competitive activity has actually diminished or probably will diminish.

[The opinion here reviews a number of decisions construing Section 3 of the Clayton Act, showing that, prior to International

Salt Co. v. United States, 332 U.S. 392, 68 S.Ct. 12, 92 L.Ed. 20 (1947), a "dominant" position in the market had been one of the circumstances leading to the conclusion that the restrictive clause would probably lessen competition substantially.]

It is thus apparent that none of these cases controls the disposition of the present appeal, for Standard's share of the retail market for gasoline, even including sales through company-owned stations, is hardly large enough to conclude as a matter of law that it occupies a dominant position, nor did the trial court so find. The cases do indicate, however, that some sort of showing as to the actual or probable economic consequences of the agreements, if only the inferences to be drawn from the fact of dominant power, is important, and to that extent they tend to support appellant's position. . . .

But then came International Salt Co. v. United States, 332 U.S. 392, 68 S.Ct. 12, 92 L.Ed. 20. That decision, at least as to contracts tying the sale of a nonpatented to a patented product, rejected the necessity of demonstrating economic consequences once it has been established that "the volume of business affected" is not "insignificant or insubstantial" and that the effect of the contracts is to "foreclose competitors from [a] substantial market." Id. at page 396, 68 S.Ct. at page 15, 92 L.Ed. 20. Upon that basis we affirmed a summary judgment granting an injunction against the leasing of machines for the utilization of salt products on the condition that the lessee use in them only salt supplied by defendant. It was established by pleadings or admissions that defendant was the country's largest producer of salt for industrial purposes, that it owned patents on the leased machines, that about 900 leases were outstanding, and that in 1944 defendant sold about $500,000 worth of salt for use in these machines. It was not established that equivalent machines were unobtainable, it was not indicated what proportion of the business of supplying such machines was controlled by defendant, and it was deemed irrelevant that there was no evidence as to the actual effect of the tying clauses upon competition. It is clear, therefore, that unless a distinction is to be drawn for purposes of the applicability of § 3 between requirements contracts and contracts tying the sale of a nonpatented to a patented product, the showing that Standard's requirements contracts affected a gross business of $58,000,000 comprising 6.7% of the total in the area goes far toward supporting the inference that competition has been or probably will be substantially lessened.

In favor of confining the standard laid down by the International Salt case to tying agreements, important economic differences may be noted. Tying agreements serve hardly any purpose beyond the suppression of competition. The justification most often advanced in their defense—the protection of the good will of the manufacturer of the tying device—fails in the usual situation because specification of the type and quality of the product to be used in connection with the tying device is protection enough. If the manufacturer's brand of the tied product is in fact superior to that of competitors, the buyer will presumably choose it anyway. The only situation, indeed, in which the protection of good will may necessitate the use of tying clauses is where specifications for a substitute would be so detailed that they could not practicably be supplied. In the usual case only the prospect of reducing competition would persuade a seller to adopt such a contract and only his control of the supply of the tying device, whether conferred by patent monopoly or otherwise obtained, could induce a buyer to enter one. The existence of market control of the tying device, therefore, affords a strong foundation for the presumption that it has been or probably will be used to limit competition in the tied product also.

Requirements contracts, on the other hand, may well be of economic advantage to buyers as well as to sellers, and thus indirectly of advantage to the consuming public. In the case of the buyer, they may assure supply, afford protection against rises in price, enable long-term planning on the basis of known costs, and obviate the expense and risk of storage in the quantity necessary for a commodity having a fluctuating demand.* From the seller's point of view, requirements contracts may make possible the substantial reduction of selling expenses, give protection against price fluctuations, and—of particular advantage to a newcomer to the field to whom it is important to know what capital expenditures are justified—offer the possibility of a predictable market. They may be useful, moreover, to a seller trying to establish a foothold against the counterattacks of entrenched competitors. Since these advantages of requirements contracts may often be sufficient to account for their use, the coverage by such contracts of a substantial amount of business affords a weaker basis for the inference that competition may be lessened than would similar coverage by tying clauses, especially where use of the latter is combined with market control of the tying device A patent, moreover, although in fact there may be many competing substitutes for the patented article, is at least prima facie evidence of such control. And so we could not dispose of this case merely by citing International Salt Co. v. United States, 332 U.S. 392, 68 S.Ct. 12, 92 L.Ed. 20.

Thus, even though the qualifying clause of § 3 is appended without distinction of terms equally to the prohibition of tying clauses and of requirements contracts, pertinent considerations support, certainly as a matter of economic reasoning, varying standards as to each for the proof necessary to fulfill the conditions of that clause. If this distinction were accepted, various tests of the economic usefulness or restrictive effect of requirements contracts would become relevant. Among them would be evidence that competition has flourished despite use of the contracts, and under this test much of the evidence tendered by appellant in this case would be important. Likewise bearing on whether or not the contracts were being used to suppress competition, would be the conformity of the length of their term to

---

* Is this case concerned with a *requirements* contract (i.e., one in which the seller assumes an obligation to provide all that the buyer needs) or with an *exclusive supply* contract (i.e., one in which the buyer cuts himself off from all other sources of supply? How can the latter ever benefit the buyer?

the reasonable requirements of the field of commerce in which they were used. Still another test would be the status of the defendant as a struggling newcomer or an established competitor. Perhaps most important, however, would be the defendant's degree of market control, for the greater the dominance of his position, the stronger the inference that an important factor in attaining and maintaining that position has been the use of requirements contracts to stifle competition rather than to serve legitimate economic needs.

Yet serious difficulties would attend the attempt to apply these tests. We may assume, as did the court below, that no improvement of Standard's competitive position has coincided with the period during which the requirements-contract system of distribution has been in effect. We may assume further that the duration of the contracts is not excessive and that Standard does not by itself dominate the market. But Standard was a major competitor when the present system was adopted, and it is possible that its position would have deteriorated but for the adoption of that system. When it is remembered that all the other major suppliers have also been using requirements contracts, and when it is noted that the relative share of the business which fell to each has remained about the same during the period of their use, it would not be farfetched to infer that their effect has been to enable the established suppliers individually to maintain in their own standing and at the same time collectively, even though not collusively, to prevent a late arrival from wresting away more than an insignificant portion of the market. If, indeed, this were a result of the system, it would seem unimportant that a short-run by-product of stability may have been greater efficiency and lower costs, for it is the theory of the antitrust laws that the long-run advantage of the community depends upon the removal of restraints upon competition.

Moreover, to demand that bare inference be supported by evidence as to what would have happened but for the adoption of the practice that was in fact adopted or to require firm prediction of an increase of competition as a probable result of ordering the abandonment of the practice, would be a standard of proof if not virtually impossible to meet, at least most ill-suited for ascertainment by courts.[78] Before the system of requirements contracts was instituted, Standard sold gasoline through independent service-station operators as its agents, and it might revert to this system if the judgment below were sustained. Or it might, as opportunity presented itself, add service stations now operated independently to the number managed by its subsidiary, Standard Stations, Inc. From the point of view of maintaining or extending competitive advantage, either of these alternatives would be just as effective as the use of require-

---

78. [This and the following two footnotes are from the opinion, renumbered.] The dual system of enforcement provided for by the Clayton Act must have contemplated standards of proof capable of administration by the courts as well as by the Federal Trade Commission and other designated agencies. Our interpretation of the Act, therefore, should recognize that an appraisal of economic data which might be practicable if only the latter were faced with the task may be quite otherwise for judges unequipped for it either by experience or by the availability of skilled assistance.

ments contracts, although of course insofar as they resulted in a tendency to monopoly they might encounter the anti-monopoly provisions of the Sherman Act. As appellant points out, dealers might order petroleum products in quantities sufficient to meet their estimated needs for the period during which requirements contracts are now effective, and even that would foreclose competition to some degree. So long as these diverse ways of restricting competition remain open, therefore, there can be no conclusive proof that the use of requirements contracts has actually reduced competition below the level which it would otherwise have reached or maintained.

We are dealing here with a particular form of agreement specified by § 3 and not with different arrangements, by way of integration or otherwise, that may tend to lessen competition. To interpret that section as requiring proof that competition has actually diminished would make its very explicitness a means of conferring immunity upon the practices which it singles out. Congress has authoritatively determined that those practices are detrimental where their effect may be to lessen competition. It has not left at large for determination in each case the ultimate demands of the "public interest," as the English lawmakers, considering and finding inapplicable to their own situation our experience with the specific prohibition of trade practices legislatively determined to be undesirable, have recently chosen to do.[79] Though it may be that such an alternative to the present system as buying out independent dealers and making them dependent employees of Standard Stations, Inc., would be a greater detriment to the public interest than perpetuation of the system, this is an issue like the choice between greater efficiency and freer competition, that has not been submitted to our decision. We are faced, not with a broadly phrased expression of general policy, but merely a broadly phrased qualification of an otherwise narrowly directed statutory provision.

In this connection it is significant that the qualifying language was not added until after the House and Senate Bills reached Conference. The conferees responsible for adding that language were at pains, in answering protestations that the qualifying clause seriously weakened the Section, to disclaim any intention seriously to augment the burden of proof to be sustained in establishing violation of it.[80] It seems hardly likely that, having with one hand set up an express prohibition against a practice thought to be beyond the reach of the Sherman Act, Congress meant, with the other hand, to reestablish the necessity of meeting the same tests of detriment to the public interest as that Act had been interpreted as requiring. Yet the economic investigation which appellant would have us require is of the same broad scope as was adumbrated with reference to unreasonable re-

79. The Monopolies and Restrictive Practices (Inquiry and Control) Act, 1948, adopted July 30, 1948. . . .

80. . . . Senator Chilton, one of the managers on the part of the Senate, denying that the clause weakened the bill, stated that the words "where the ef-

fect may be" mean "where it is possible for the effect to be." Id. at 16002. Senator Overman, also a Senate conferee, argued that even the elimination of competition in a single town would substantially lessen competition. Id. at 15935.

straints of trade in Chicago Board of Trade v. United States, 246 U.S. 231, 38 S.Ct. 242, 62 L.Ed. 683. To insist upon such an investigation would be to stultify the force of Congress' declaration that requirements contracts are to be prohibited wherever their effect "may be" to substantially lessen competition. If in fact it is economically desirable for service stations to confine themselves to the sale of the petroleum products of a single supplier, they will continue to do so though not bound by contract, and if in fact it is important to retail dealers to assure the supply of their requirements by obtaining the commitment of a single supplier to fulfill them, competition for their patronage should enable them to insist upon such an arrangement without binding them to refrain from looking elsewhere.

We conclude, therefore, that the qualifying clause of § 3 is satisfied by proof that competition has been foreclosed in a substantial share of the line of commerce affected. It cannot be gainsaid that observance by a dealer of his requirements contract with Standard does effectively foreclose whatever opportunity there might be for competing suppliers to attract his patronage, and it is clear that the affected proportion of retail sales of petroleum products is substantial. In view of the widespread adoption of such contracts by Standard's competitors and the availability of alternative ways of obtaining an assured market, evidence that competitive activity has not actually declined is inconclusive. Standard's use of the contracts creates just such a potential clog on competition as it was the purpose of § 3 to remove wherever, were it to become actual, it would impede a substantial amount of competitive activity.

Since the decree below is sustained by our interpretation of § 3 of the Clayton Act, we need not go on to consider whether it might also be sustained by § 1 of the Sherman Act. . . .

The judgment below is affirmed.

MR. JUSTICE JACKSON, with whom THE CHIEF JUSTICE and MR. JUSTICE BURTON join, dissenting.

I am unable to join the judgment or opinion of the Court for reasons I will state, but shortly.

Section 3 of the Clayton Act does not make any lease, sale, or contract unlawful unless "the effect of such lease, sale, or contract for sale or such condition, agreement, or understanding may be to substantially lessen competition or tend to create a monopoly in any line of commerce." It is indispensable to the Government's case to establish that either the actual or the probable effect of the accused arrangement is to substantially lessen competition or tend to create a monopoly.

I am unable to agree that this requirement was met. To be sure, the contracts cover "a substantial number of outlets and a substantial amount of products, whether considered comparatively or not." But that fact does not automatically bring the accused arrangement within the prohibitions of the statute. The number of dealers and the volume of sales covered by the arrangement of course was sufficient to be substantial. That is to say, this arrangement operated on enough commerce to violate the Act, provided its effects were substantially to lessen competition or create a monopoly. But proof of their quantity does not prove that they had this forbidden quality and the assumption that they did, without proof, seems to me unwarranted.

Moreover, the trial court not only made the assumption but it did not allow the defendant affirmatively to show that such effects do not flow from this arrangement. Such evidence on the subject as was admitted was not considered in reaching the decision that these contracts are illegal.

I regard it as unfortunate that the Clayton Act submits such economic issues to judicial determination. It not only leaves the law vague as a warning or guide, and determined only after the event, but the judicial process is not well adapted to exploration of such industry-wide, and even nation-wide questions.

But if they must decide, the only possible way for the courts to arrive at a fair determination is to hear all relevant evidence from both parties and weigh not only its inherent probabilities of verity but also compare the experience, disinterestedness and credibility of opposing witnesses. This is a tedious process and not too enlightening, but without it a judicial decree is but a guess in the dark. That is all we have here and I do not think it is an adequate basis on which to upset long-standing and widely practiced business arrangements.

I should therefore vacate this decree and direct the court below to complete the case by hearing and weighing the Government's evidence and that of defendant as to the effects of this device.

However, if the Court refuses to do that, I cannot agree that the requirements contract is *per se* an illegal one under the antitrust law, and that is the substance of what the Court seems to hold. I am not convinced that the requirements contract as here used is a device for suppressing competition instead of a device for waging competition. If we look only at its effect in relation to particular retailers who become parties to it, it does restrain their freedom to purchase their requirements elsewhere and prevents other companies from selling to them. Many contracts have the effect of taking a purchaser out of the market for goods he already has bought or contracted to take. But the retailer in this industry is only a conduit from the oil fields to the driver's tank, a means by which the oil companies compete to get the business of the ultimate consumer—the man in whose automobile the gas is used. It means to me, if I must decide without evidence, that these contracts are an almost necessary means to maintain this all-important competition for consumer business, in which it is admitted competition is keen. The retail stations, whether independent or company-owned, are the instrumentalities through which competition for this ultimate market is waged.

It does not seem to me inherently to lessen this real competition when an oil company tries to establish superior service by providing the consumer with a responsible dealer from which the public can

purchase adequate and timely supplies of oil, gasoline and car accessories of some known and reliable standard of quality. No retailer,
whether agent or independent, can long remain in business if he does
not always, and not just intermittently, have gas to sell.* Retailers'
storage capacity usually is limited and they are in no position to accumulate large stocks. They can take gas only when and as they can
sell it. The Government can hardly force someone to contract to
stand by, ever ready to fill fluctuating demands of dealers who will
not in turn undertake to buy from that supplier all their requirements. And it is important to the driving public to be able to rely on
retailers to have gas to retail. It is equally important that the wholesaler have some incentive to carry the stocks and have the transport
facilities to make the irregular deliveries caused by varied consumer
demands.

It may be that the Government, if required to do so, could prove
that this is a bad system and an illegal one. It may be that the defendant, if permitted to do so, can prove that it is, in its overall aspects, a good system and within the law. But on the present record
the Government has not made a case.

If the Courts are to apply the lash of the antitrust laws to the
backs of businessmen to make them compete, we cannot in fairness
also apply the lash whenever they hit upon a successful method of
competing. That insofar as I am permitted by the record to learn the
facts, appears to be the case before us. I would reverse.

MR. JUSTICE DOUGLAS. . . . It is plain that a filling station
owner who is tied to an oil company for his supply of products is not
an available customer for the products of other suppliers. The same
is true of a filling station owner who purchases his inventory a year
in advance. His demand is withdrawn from the market for the duration of the contract in the one case and for a year in the other. The
result in each case is to lessen competition if the standard is day-to-
day purchases. Whether it is a substantial lessening of competition
within the meaning of the Antitrust Laws is a question of degree and
may vary from industry to industry.

The Court answers the question for the oil industry by a formula
which under our decisions promises to wipe out large segments of
independent filling station operators. The method of doing business
under requirements contracts at least keeps the independents alive.
They survive as small business units. The situation is not ideal from
either their point of view or that of the nation. But the alternative
which the Court offers is far worse from the point of view of both.

The elimination of these requirements contracts sets the stage for
Standard and the other oil companies to build service-station empires
of their own. The opinion of the Court does more than set the stage
for that development. It is an advisory opinion as well, stating to the

---

* In most retail trades the retailer is
not required by contract to take all his
needs from one supplier. This has not
led to "intermittent" supply. Why? Are
there peculiar conditions in the petroleum
business? Has the Standard Oil decision
resulted in "intermittent" supply of gasoline to service stations?

oil companies how they can with impunity build their empires. The formula suggested by the Court is either the use of the "agency" device, which in practical effect means control of filling stations by the oil companies, cf. Federal Trade Commission v. Curtis Co., 260 U.S. 568, 43 S.Ct. 210, 67 L.Ed. 408, or the outright acquisition of them by subsidiary corporations or otherwise. See United States v. Columbia Steel Co., supra. Under the approved judicial doctrine either of those devices means increasing the monopoly of the oil companies over the retail field.

When the choice is thus given, I dissent from the outlawry of the requirements contract on the present facts. The effect which it has on competition in this field is minor as compared to the damage which will flow from the judicially approved formula for the growth of bigness tendered by the Court as an alternative. Our choice must be made on the basis not of abstractions but of the realities of modern industrial life.

Today there is vigorous competition between the oil companies for the market. That competition has left some room for the survival of the independents. But when this inducement for their survival is taken away, we can expect that the oil companies will move in to supplant them with their own stations. There will still be competition between the oil companies. But there will be a tragic loss to the nation. The small, independent business man will be supplanted by clerks. Competition between suppliers of accessories (which is involved in this case) will diminish or cease altogether. The oil companies will command an increasingly larger share of both the wholesale and the retail markets.

That is the likely result of today's decision. The requirements contract which is displaced is relatively innocuous as compared with the virulent growth of monopoly power which the Court encourages. The Court does not act unwittingly. It consciously pushes the oil industry in that direction. The Court approves what the Antitrust Laws were designed to prevent. It helps remake America in the image of the cartels.

NOTES AND QUERIES

(1) *Effect on Competition; Rule of Reason or Per Se.* The decision in *Standard Oil of California* evoked a flood of criticism of the majority's refusal to give weight to economic analysis of the consequences of requirements contracts, when "competition has been foreclosed in a substantial share of the line of commerce affected." The majority opinion was attacked as creating a *per se* illegality rule in the face of the congressional mandate, under the final clause of Section 3, to inquire into "effect." The Federal Trade Commission, with the approval of the Attorney General's National Committee to Study the Antitrust Laws, proceeded to inquire into economic effect of challenged requirements contracts notwithstanding *Standard Oil.*[81]

81. See Kintner, The Revitalized Federal Trade Commission, 30 N.Y.U.L.Rev. 1143, 1177 et seq. (1955) ("the resurgence of critical market analysis," p. 1183); Report of the Attorney General's National Committee to Study the Antitrust Laws 141 et seq. (1955); Lockhart and Sachs, The Relevance of Economic Factors in

But cf. *Dictograph Products, Inc. v. Federal Trade Commission,*[82] reading the legislative history of section 3, as "in no way [supporting] the view that it was designed to reinstate the same Sherman Act tests which had, at that very time, been determined to be inadequate."

The enforcement agencies, victorious in attacks on long-term (5 year) requirements or exclusive dealing contracts, have, by appropriate limitations in injunctive relief, permitted continuance of one-year contracts in special circumstances. *Federal Trade Commission v. Motion Picture Advertising Service Co.,*[83] (to enable respondent to offer prospective advertisers assurance of continuity and coverage in the showing of their filmed advertisements, moving picture theaters may properly be bound to take all their advertising films from respondent for one year); *United States v. American Can Co.,*[84] (canning companies may be obliged to take their annual canning season requirements of cans from supplier). Can these be regarded as market-determined customary units of trade?

In *Twin City Sportservice, Inc. v. Charles O. Finley & Co., Inc.,*[85] the Ninth Circuit upheld a finding that a 15 year exclusive dealing contract for concession services for a major league baseball team was an unreasonable restraint of trade under § 1 of the Sherman Act. The Court held exclusive dealing contracts must be tested under the "rule of reason" and that the contract in question was unreasonable because its length exceeded the time needed to recapture the concessionaire's investment and contained a "follow the franchise" clause. The latter clause bound the team even if the franchise was moved to another city and had resulted in Finley's team (Oakland A's) being bound by an exclusive dealing contract signed by Connie Mack in 1950 when the team was known as the Philadelphia Athletics. Stating that its decision was not based solely on the length of the contract term, the Court cited such additional factors as the effect of the contract and its "follow the franchise" clause on competing concessionaires, Sportservice market share (24%) and "vast financial resources", and the absence of any justification for the length and other restrictive characteristics of the contract involved.

(2) *Tampa Electric and a Structuralist Approach to Exclusive Dealing.* In *Tampa Electric Co. v. Nashville Coal Co.,*[86] a Clayton Act § 3 challenge was raised by Nashville Coal to a 20-year exclusive dealing contract for $128 million in coal for Tampa Electric's newly constructed coal fired generating plants. Nashville was obligated to deliver the coal subject to a base price of $6.40/ton with an escalator clause for rising labor and other costs up to $8.80/ton. Although the coal in question constituted less than 1% of the coal produced in the relevant market, the lower courts

Determining Whether Exclusive Arrangements Violate Section 3 of the Clayton Act, 65 Harv.L.Rev. 913 (1952); but cf. Schwartz, Potential Impairment of Competition—the Impact of Standard Oil Company of California v. United States on the Standard of Legality under the Clayton Act, 98 U.Pa.L.Rev. 10 (1949).

82. 217 F.2d 821 (2d Cir. 1954).

83. 344 U.S. 392, 73 S.Ct. 361, 97 L.Ed. 426 (1953).

84. 87 F.Supp. 18 (N.D.Cal.1949).

85. 676 F.2d 1291 (9th Cir. 1982).

86. 365 U.S. 320, 81 S.Ct. 623, 5 L.Ed. 2d 580 (1961). See Bork, The *Tampa Electric* Case and the Problem of Exclusive Arrangements Under the Clayton Act, 1961 Sup.Ct.Rev. 267; Miller, Some Observations on the Lawfulness of Long Term Contracts for the Purchase of Energy Supplies by Public Utilities in Interstate Commerce, 49 Geo.L.J. 673 (1961); Weston, Antitrust Highlights: *Tampa Electric* and the Clayton Act, 19 Antitrust Sec.Rep. 211 (1961).

held $128,000,000 of coal was "not insubstantial" and the contract was illegal under § 3 of the Clayton Act. In reversing, the Supreme Court held:

"In practical application, even though a contract is found to be an exclusive-dealing arrangement, it does not violate the section unless the court believes it probable that performance of the contract will foreclose competition in a substantial share of the line of commerce affected. Following the guidelines of earlier decisions, certain considerations must be taken. *First*, the line of commerce, i.e., the type of goods, wares, or merchandise, etc., involved must be determined, where it is in controversy, on the basis of the facts peculiar to the case. *Second*, the area of effective competition in the known line of commerce must be charted by careful selection of the market area in which the seller operates, and to which the purchaser can practicably turn for supplies. In short, the threatened foreclosure of competition must be in relation to the market affected. . . .

Third, and last, the competition foreclosed by the contract must be found to constitute a substantial share of the relevant market. That is to say, the opportunities for other traders to enter into or remain in that market must be significantly limited. . . . .

To determine substantiality in a given case, it is necessary to weigh the probable effect of the contract on the relevant area of effective competition, taking into account the relative strength of the parties, the proportionate volume of commerce involved in relation to the total volume of commerce in the relevant market area, and the probable immediate and future effects which pre-emption of that share of the market might have on effective competition therein. It follows that a mere showing that the contract itself involves a substantial number of dollars is ordinarily of little consequence.[87]

The Court found that the contract foreclosed less than 1% of the market for coal in the area and there was no coercion to enter the contract. Its effect was therefore *de minimus* and posed no threat to competition or tendency to restrain trade.

Query: Is this analysis consistent with the opinions in *Standard Stations?*[88] Does the Court's opinion require a sophisticated structural analysis?[89]

87. 365 U.S. at 327–29, 81 S.Ct. at 628–29, 5 L.Ed.2d at 386–87.

88. In American Motor Inns, Inc. v. Holiday Inns, Inc., 521 F.2d 1230 (3d Cir. 1975) the court described the difference between the two cases as follows:

"In *Standard Oil* Justice Frankfurter, speaking for the Court, eschewed any economic investigation by the judiciary in determining whether the effect of a given exclusive dealing agreement " 'may be' to substantially lessen competition". Rather, under his quantitative substantiality test, a case would be made out under section 3 merely upon a showing that the exclusive dealing arrangement involved a significant share of the relevant market, or possibly even upon a showing that the arrangement involved a substantial volume of commerce. 337 U.S., at 299,

310–14, 69 S.Ct., 1051, 1062. *See* Von Kalinowski, Antitrust Laws and Trade Regulations, §§ 13.04, 13.05 (1971). The *Standard Oil* test was heavily criticized as being too mechanical and as depriving the public of the economic advantages of exclusive dealing contracts over alternative arrangements. *See, e.g.,* Kessler & Stern, "Competition Contracts, and Vertical Integration," 69 Yale L.J. 1 (1959); Schwartz, Potential Impairment of Competition— The Impact of *Standard Oil of California v. United States* on the Standard of Legality Under the Clayton Act, 98 U.Pa.L.Rev. 10 (1949); Lockhart & Sacks, "The Relevance of Economic Factors in Determining Whether Exclusive Arrangements Violate Sec-

89. See note 89 on page 683.

(3) *"Quantitative Substantiality" v. "Qualitative Substantiality".*
The effects clause of section 3 is phrased in terms of proof of an effect
which "may be to *substantially* lessen competition or tend to create a monopoly in any line of commerce". (Emphasis added). Did the Court adopt a
"quantitative" test (the amount of commerce involved) or a "qualitative" test
(the impact of the restraint upon the competitive ideal) for the "substantiality" requirement of section 3 in *Standard Oil of California?* In *Tampa
Electric?*

(4) *Exclusive Dealing Under the Sherman Act.* Exclusive dealing contracts may also be challenged as an unreasonable restraint of trade or unlawful monopolization under the Sherman Act. The Sherman Act is usually
invoked where a jurisdictional element of the more relaxed standards of § 3
of the Clayton Act is not present; i.e., the contract is for services rather than
for "goods or commodities."

The relatively few opinions testing exclusive dealing contracts under the
Sherman Act usually rely upon the vague standards of the *Tampa Electric*
case and require proof of a qualitatively substantial lessening of competition
in a defined relevant product and geographic market.[90] If the particular exclusive dealing arrangement is found not to be a violation of § 3 of the Clayton Act it is held to be *a fortiori* not a violation of the Sherman Act.[91]

(5) *Exclusive Dealing in Regulated Industries; Administrative Review.*
In *Marine Space Enclosures v. Federal Maritime Commission,*[92] the FMC
had approved without hearing (on the ground that a full hearing had been
held before the New York City Council) arrangements under which the Port
Authority would build and operate a maritime passenger terminal to be made

tion 3 of the Clayton Act," 65 Harv.
L.Rev. 913 (1952).

In *Tampa Electric* the Court adopted a
somewhat different standard for measuring the legality of exclusive dealing contracts under section 3. . . . [T]he new
test, commonly denominated the qualitative substantiality test, introduced
greater flexibility and requires the courts
actually to evaluate the restrictiveness
and the economic usefulness of the challenged practice in relation to the business
factors extant in the market. *See* Von
Kalinowski, *supra,* §§ 13.04, 13.05, 14.04;
Bok, The Tampa Electric Case and the
Problem of Exclusive Arrangements Under the Clayton Act, 1961 Sup.Ct.Rev.
267; Note, 75 Harv.L.Rev. 202 (1961);
Susser v. Carvel Corp., 332 F.2d 505,
516–17 (2d Cir. 1964). Although the Supreme Court has modified the rigid rule
articulated in *Standard Oil,* it has not indicated that the result in *Standard Oil*
would differ from *Tampa Electric.* Indeed, the *Tampa Electric* opinion impliedly endorses the result reached in
Standard Oil. See 365 U.S., at 328–29,
81 S.Ct., at 628–29. . . . "

89. See Sullivan, Antitrust 479 (1977).

90. See American Motor Inns, Inc. v.
Holiday Inns, Inc., 521 F.2d 1230 (3d Cir.
1975): Northwest Power Products, Inc.
v. Omark Industries, Inc., 576 F.2d 83
(5th Cir. 1978), rehearing denied 579 F.2d

643, certiorari denied 439 U.S. 1116, 99
S.Ct. 1021, 59 L.Ed.2d 75 (1979); Dillon
Materials Handling, Inc. v. Albion Indus-
tries, 567 F.2d 1299 (5th Cir. 1978), certio-
rari denied 439 U.S. 832, 99 S.Ct. 111, 58
L.Ed.2d 127; Magnus Petroleum Co., Inc.
v. Skelly Oil Co., 599 F.2d 196 (7th Cir.
1979), certiorari denied 444 U.S. 916, 100
S.Ct. 231, 62 L.Ed.2d 171; First Bever-
ages, Inc. v. Royal Crown Cola Co., 612
F.2d 1164 (9th Cir. 1980), certiorari de-
nied 447 U.S. 924, 100 S.Ct. 3016, 65
L.Ed.2d 1116; Twin City Sportservice,
Inc. v. Charles O. Finley & Co., Inc., 676
F.2d 1291 (9th Cir. 1982); Murray v.
Toyota Motor Distributors, Inc., 664 F.2d
1377, (9th Cir. 1982), certiorari denied __
U.S. __, 102 S.Ct. 2905, 73 L.Ed.2d 1314.

91. For exclusive dealing under Section 5 of the Federal Trade Commission
Act, see Federal Trade Commission v.
Brown Shoe Co., Inc., 384 U.S. 316, 86
S.Ct. 1501, 16 L.Ed.2d 587 (1966); In The
Matter of General Motors Corp., 3 Trade
Reg. Rep. ¶ 21,931 (FTC 1982) (upholding
distribution of G.M. crash parts to G.M.
franchisees); In the Matter of Beltone
Electronics Corp., 3 Trade Reg. Rep. ¶
21,934 (FTC 1982) (upholding exclusive
dealing by leading manufacturer of hearing aids).

92. 137 U.S.App.D.C. 9, 420 F.2d 577
(1969).

available only to shiplines which agreed to use the new terminal exclusively. The Port Authority was not to allow non-signatory carriers to use the terminal, and also agreed that it would not build or authorize any other passenger terminal. These mutually exclusive provisions were designed to assure the revenues of the new terminal and thus cover the interest charges on the bonds. The restraints were, however, to endure for 70 years, while the bonds matured in 20. Marine Space Enclosures, interested in operating a different terminal, challenged the Commission's order. In setting the order aside and remanding for a hearing, the Court took note of the fact that, "at the prodding of the Justice Department", FMC had modified its order so as to retain jurisdiction to consider applications filed after 20 years to build additional facilities, but held this inadequate. The court articulated standards to guide the FMC in the new hearing. The burden of proof was put on the proponent of the restraint. The feasibility of less restrictive alternatives must be explored. A restraint is to be authorized only if necessary to achieve the public objective:

> This is responsive to the dominant consideration that anticompetitive restraints, the kind that would be illegal or of doubtful legality if used in an unregulated industry, are in some ways contrary to the public interest that shapes rules governing persons in directly regulated industry.

A natural gas pipeline company may be permitted to charge higher rates for gas delivered to customers who take some of their requirements from competing suppliers, if the pipeline company makes a sufficient demonstration to the Federal Power Commission of "need" for such partial requirements rates. Such need might be found in the prospect of diversion of sales to the competitor resulting in less than full utilization of pipeline company's facilities, and unfairly saddling the full-requirements customers with a disproportionate share of the capital costs of the system. The company might consequently lose sales to full-requirements customers, or forfeit the possibility of expanding its market to such customers, unless alternative rate adjustments can be devised to keep and attract such sales.[93]

To what extent is the rationale for tolerating some "requirements" selling under a regulatory regime applicable to businesses in the "free" sector?

(6) *Broadcast Station Affiliations With Networks; Option Time.* [94] Federal Communications Commission Rules provide:

> (a) *Exclusive affiliation of station.* No license shall be granted to a television broadcast station having any contract, arrangement, or understanding, express or implied, with a network organization under which the station is prevented or hindered from, or penalized for, broadcasting the programs of any other network organization.
>
> . . .
>
> (d) *Station commitment of broadcast time.* No license shall be granted to a television broadcast station having any contract, arrangement, or understanding, express or implied, with any network organization, which provides for optioning of the station's time to the network

---

93. Cf. Atlantic Seaboard Corp. v. Federal Power Commission, 131 U.S.App. D.C. 291, 404 F.2d 1268 (1968) (need held insufficiently shown, and alternatives available).

94. 47 C.F.R. § 73.658 (1981).

For a comprehensive discussion of the significance of "option time" and other features of affiliation contracts in televi-

sion, see Report on Network Broadcasting (Roscoe L. Barrow, Director), H.Rep. No.1297. House Committee on Interstate and Foreign Commerce, 85th Cong., 2d Sess. (1958). See also Report on The Television Industry, Antitrust Subcommittee, House Committee on the Judiciary, 85th Cong., 1st Sess. (1957).

organization, or which has the same restraining effect as time optioning. As used in this section, time optioning is any contract, arrangement, or understanding, express or implied, between a station and a network organization which prevents or hinders the station from scheduling programs before the network agrees to utilize the time during which such programs are scheduled, or which requires the station to clear time already scheduled when the network organization seeks to utilize the time.

(e) *Right to reject programs.* No license shall be granted to a television broadcast station having any contract, arrangement, or understanding, express or implied, with a network organization which, with respect to programs offered or already contracted for pursuant to an affiliation contract, prevents or hinders the station from: (1) Rejecting or refusing network programs which the station reasonably believes to be unsatisfactory or unsuitable or contrary to the public interest, or (2) substituting a program which, in the station's opinion, is of greater local or national importance.

The validity of this type of regulation as an exercise of the Commission's statutory power "to encourage the larger and more effective use of radio in the public interest" and "to make special regulations applicable to radio stations engaged in chain broadcasting" was sustained in *National Broadcasting Co. v. United States.* [95] "The effect of this [exclusive affiliation] provision was to hinder the growth of new networks, to deprive the listening public in many areas of service to which they were entitled, and to prevent station licensees from exercising their statutory duty of determining which programs would best serve the needs of their community." The broadcasting chains defended exclusive affiliation as essential to chain broadcasting, which had played an important part in the development of radio and had provided a strong incentive for advertisers to finance expensive programs. The FCC regulation prohibiting networks from acting as agents for their affiliated stations in the sale of non-network time has also been upheld.[96]

(7) *Option Time in Television Broadcasting,* excerpt from *Barrow, Antitrust and Regulated Industry: Promoting Competition in Broadcasting,* 1964 Duke L.J. 282, 289–292:

Time optioning received extensive study by the Commission's Broadcast Network Study staff, established in 1955.[97] This group concluded that time optioning restrained competition contrary to the public interest, that the practice was not necessary to the operation of healthy networks, and that the practice should be prohibited under the public interest standard. It concluded further that the practice contravened the antitrust laws.

Following issuance of the staff report, the Commission held hearings thereon and concluded by a four to three vote that time optioning was reasonably necessary to the successful conduct of network operations and, thus, was in the public interest.[98]

95. 319 U.S. 190, 63 S.Ct. 997, 87 L.Ed. 1344 (1943). Access rules for cable television requiring cable systems to maintain a specified number of channels and provide for local access were struck down as beyond the Commission's statutory authority in Federal Communications Commission v. Midwest Video Corp., 440 U.S. 689, 99 S.Ct. 1435, 59 L.Ed.2d 692 (1979).

96. Metropolitan Television Co. v. Federal Communications Commission, 289 F.2d 874 (D.C.Cir.1961).

97. [This and the following eight footnotes are from the original text. They have been renumbered.] The option time practice is discussed and analyzed in Network Broadcasting 279–401.

98. FCC 58–37 (1958), FCC Docket No. 12285.

In accordance with an understanding between the Commission and the Department, the Commission submitted its ultimate findings on time optioning to the Antitrust Division and requested a formal opinion on the antitrust aspects of the practice.[99] By letter of February 27, 1959, the Assistant Attorney General in charge of the Antitrust Division rendered a formal opinion to the FCC Chairman in which it was concluded that "viewed either as an 'exclusive dealing' or 'tying' device, the Commission's own findings require the conclusion that option time runs afoul of the Sherman Act." The exclusive dealing analysis, in brief, was that time optioning predisposed or obliged affiliates to take network programs, thereby unduly restricting competition by independent program sources, nonnetwork advertisers, and independent stations and unduly restricting new network entry. The tying device analysis was that desired programs were tied to undesired programs, contrary to the principles established in United States v. Paramount Pictures, Inc.[1] and Northern Pac. Ry. Co. v. United States.[2] While finding that time optioning ran afoul of the Sherman Act, the Department did not file an antitrust suit to prohibit the practice. On inquiry by the press, the Department explained that it would await disposition of the time optioning proceeding before the Commission.

The case law relating to antitrust aspects of broadcasting handed down since this formal opinion was rendered does not derogate from the position that the option time practice "runs afoul" of the Sherman Act.[3]

---

99. FCC 59–33 (1959), FCC Docket No. 12285. The understanding had been that findings on both the "time optioning" and "must buy" practices would be submitted for opinion on the antitrust aspect. However, thereafter the "must buy" practice was voluntarily discontinued. Accordingly, the findings on "must buy" were not transmitted. Prior to 1957, CBS and NBC engaged in the so-called "must buy" practice, under which the advertiser, as a condition to using the network service, was required to purchase time from a "basic" group of stations designated by call letter. It was found that some advertisers were required under this practice to take some stations not desired and that, in exchange for the economic advantage of being placed on the "must buy" list, some stations accepted network programs which they would not otherwise have been disposed to carry. Network Broadcasting, 523. Also, the practice was of doubtful legality under § 1 of the Sherman Act, since it was similar to the "tie-in" and "block booking" practices condemned in Times-Picayune Publishing Co. v. United States, 345 U.S. 594, 73 S.Ct. 872, 97 L.Ed. 1277 (1953), and United States v. Paramount Pictures, Inc., 334 U.S. 131, 68 S.Ct. 915, 92 L.Ed. 1260 (1948). Network Broadcasting 502–22. Following these findings and the recommendation that the practice be prohibited, CBS and NBC voluntarily discontinued the practice.

1. 334 U.S. 131, 68 S.Ct. 915, 92 L.Ed. 1260 (1948).

2. 356 U.S. 1, 78 S.Ct. 514, 2 L.Ed.2d 545 (1958).

3. In United States v. Loew's, Inc., 371 U.S. 38, 83 S.Ct. 97, 9 L.Ed.2d 11 (1962), the Supreme Court held that block booking of copyrighted motion pictures for television exhibition was a tying arrangement in violation of § 1 of the Sherman Act. The Court emphasized that the fact that the block booking arose in the context of television, rather than motion pictures, was not a basis for distinction. Id. at 48. In CBS v. Amana Refrigeration, Inc., 295 F.2d 375 (7th Cir. 1961), it was held that the television "service" is not a "commodity" within the Clayton Act. However, the decision does not preclude a finding that option time is an unreasonable restraint, or even a per se violation, contrary to § 1 of the Sherman Act. United States v. CBS, 215 F.Supp. 694 (S.D.N.Y.1963), involved a CBS compensation plan which had a strong clearance incentive in the nature of a substitute for option time. A motion for final judgment without trial was denied on the ground that a *per se* violation of the antitrust laws had not been established and that determination of the legality of the restraint should be reached on the basis of a trial. American Mutual Insurance Co. v. American Broadcasting-Paramount Theatres, Inc., 221 F.Supp. 848 (S.D.N.Y. 1963), involved a network requirement that the advertiser accept, as a condition

Although the Commission has stated that its regulation of broadcasting must be compatible with the antitrust laws, it did not choose to follow the formal opinion that time optioning violated the Sherman Act. Rather, it issued a notice of rule making, looking toward a further limitation of time optioning. Thereafter, it modified the option time rule so as to reduce the period subject to option from three to two and one-half hours in each of the four segments of the broadcast day, and it provided greater flexibility to the broadcaster in rejecting programs offered by the network during option time.[4] An appeal was taken from the Commission's decision, one basis being that time optioning violated the antitrust laws.[5] Thereafter, the Commission moved to remand the case for a review of its report and order in the option time matter, and the motion was granted. After further notice of rule making, the Commission, by a six to one vote, determined that time optioning was not essential to the operation of networks and prohibited time optioning on the ground that the practice restrained competition contrary to the public interest. The decision was not based, in whole or in part, on the antitrust laws.[6]

In putting to one side industry contentions that it was inappropriate for the FCC to reconsider the time optioning matter, the Commission stated that it must be free at any point in time to weigh the restraining effect of a practice against its essentiality. Insofar as the public interest standard is concerned, this is a sound doctrine. Broadcasting is a dynamic industry and, as circumstances in the industry change, the FCC has a duty to evaluate the changed circumstances in the light of the public interest standard. However, any such evaluation must be compatible with the antitrust laws. It may be noted that since the Commission's report and order on time optioning rely upon the public interest standard in prohibiting the practice rather than upon the antitrust laws, the door is left open to reinstate the practice in the event that changing circumstances warrant such action.

Three related developments have further weakened network control of programming on affiliated television stations. The "Prime Time" rule (47 C.F.R. § 73.658(k)) restricts network programming to three of the four hours considered prime evening viewing hours. A suit by the Antitrust Division sought to restrict the amount of network programming which is network produced in order to open network programming to independent producers.[7] The "Family Hour" rule adopted by the National Association of Broad-

to advertising over the network, a total of 130 stations or the financial equivalent thereof (the so-called "minimum buy" practice), whereas the advertiser desired only ninety-five stations. The network's motion for summary judgment was denied since the complaint alleged a possible tying arrangement under § 1 of the Sherman Act.

4. FCC 60–1089 (1960), FCC Docket No. 12859.

5. Times-Mirror Broadcasting Co. v. United States, Case No. 16068 (D.C.Cir. 1961).

6. 28 Fed.Reg. 5501 (1963); FCC 63–497 (1963), FCC Docket No. 12859. The FCC denied three petitions for reconsideration of this report and order. FCC 63–802 (1963), FCC Docket No. 12859.

7. The three suits have had a complicated and curious history, summarized in Kubin, The Antitrust Implications of Network Television Programming, 27 Hastings L.J. 1207 (1976); Note, Regulatory Approaches to Television Network Control of the Program Procurement Process: An Historical Perspective, 8 Ford. Urb.L.J. 563, 578 (1980). The suits have been settled by consent decree. See United States v. National Broadcasting Co., 1978–1 Trade Cases ¶ 61,855, ¶ 61,842 (C.D.Cal.1978); United States v. American Broadcasting Co., Inc., 1981–1 Trade Cases ¶ 64,150 (C.D.Cal.1980); United States v. CBS, Inc., 1980–81 Trade Cases ¶ 63,594 (C.D.Cal.1980).

casters, reserving the first hour of prime time for programming suitable for family viewing, was struck down by a district court in a suit by writers of television scripts, but that ruling was vacated by the Ninth Circuit on jurisdictional grounds.[8]

There is reason to believe that the greater freedom of choice by individual broadcasters, achieved by restricting network programming control, has not raised the level of programming. Broadcasters substitute movie reruns and other inexpensive material in place of more expensive network alternatives.[9] Is this "market response," in a regulated industry, vindicated by Sherman Act principles? The FCC has made exceptions for specified types of favored network programs, e.g., news, education.

With the growing presence of cable television, direct satellite-to-home television, "low power" television, and home video recorders, considerable debate and discussion about the structure and regulation of the broadcasting industry has been taking place.[10] It is possible that a major re-writing of the regulatory scheme for broadcasting will take place, with increased reliance upon competition to regulate the quality of programming content as well as the economic relationships between broadcasters and the suppliers of programming material.

KINTNER, THE ANATOMY OF RECIPROCITY

56 American Bar Association Journal 232 (1970).
(reprinted by permission of the author and copyright owner)

"Reciprocity", like "conglomerate", is fast becoming one of the major taboo words of antitrust law. Like most taboos, it is steeped in a considerable amount of mystery and confusion. There is a great deal of misunderstanding on the part of businessmen as to what aspects of their conduct constitute reciprocal relationship, and there is an equal amount of misunderstanding on the part of Government enforcement agencies as to the exact nature and functions of those business officials most frequently accused of engaging in reciprocal dealings. It is my hope to shed some light on both these shadowy areas.

Reciprocity as a generic term means nothing more than a mutual exchange of benefits or privileges. In the context of a business rela-

8. Writers Guild of America v. Federal Communications Commission, 423 F.Supp. 1064 (C.D.Cal.1976), vacated sub nom., Writers Guild of America, West, Inc. v. American Broadcasting Co., Inc., 609 F.2d 355 (9th Cir. 1979). The refusal of the F.C.C. to adopt a series of proposed rules aimed at improving children's television programming was upheld in Action for Children's Television v. Federal Communications Commission, 564 F.2d 458 (D.C.Cir.1977).

9. Schwartz, The Cultural Deficit in Broadcasting, 26 J.Com. 58 (1976).

10. These issues are explored more fully in Schwartz, Flynn & First, Free Enterprise and Economic Organization: Government Regulation, Chs. 2 & 3 (6th Ed. 1983). See also Owen, Structural Approaches to the Problem of Network Economic Dominance, 1979 Duke L.J. 191; Schuessler, Structural Barriers to the Entry of Additional Television Networks: The Federal Communications Commission's Spectrum Management Policies, 54 So.Cal.L.Rev. 875 (1981); Kreiss, Deregulation of Cable Television and the Problem of Access Under the First Amendment, 54 So.Cal.L.Rev. 1001 (1981); Note, A Regulatory Approach to Diversifying Commercial Television Entertainment, 89 Yale L.J. 694 (1980). Direct satellite television broadcasting has recently been authorized by the F.C.C. See "Direct Satellite-to-Home TV is Given Nod; FCC May End Certain Curbs on Networks", Wall St. J., June 24, 1982, p. 15.

tionship, reciprocity could be described broadly as any form of mutual exchange of purchases. Not every situation in which two companies exchange purchases is tantamount to a violation of the antitrust laws. Reciprocity, as a legal concept, comprehends a far narrower scope of business conduct than the dictionary definition of the word. There must be some additional dimensions to reciprocal activity before it can be circumscribed as unlawful.

These additional dimensions may be found whenever the reciprocal relationship has the effect of introducing an alien or irrelevant element into the selection process normally followed by businessmen in choosing the suppliers with whom they place their orders. Thus, illegal reciprocity encompasses either (1) voluntary agreements which contradict the normal and usual bases for product selection (quality, price and service) in favor of the overriding influence of continued mutual dealings or (2) coerced purchases that have the effect of nullifying the buyer's freedom of choice through the application of purchasing leverage. In both instances, the normal competitive process is subverted by the guarantee of return patronage, a consideration totally unrelated to the products offered for sale.

It should be noted that quality, price and service are not the only considerations open to a businessman in making a purchase. Human nature being what it is, various personal likes and dislikes frequently play an influential role in purchasing, and there is nothing in the antitrust laws that requires a businessman to purchase from an individual he does not like or to avoid doing business with a friend. It is only when his conduct abuses the competitive process and systematically forecloses other competitors that his personal idiosyncrasies are required to take a back seat to the public policy favoring free and open competition.

Before examining what activity does constitute illegal reciprocity, we should examine one form of conduct that does not amount to an illegal reciprocal arrangement. Much of the current legal commentary concerning reciprocity focuses on a category of conduct variously described as unilateral, psychological or "golden rule" reciprocity.[11] Essentially, it involves those situations wherein one company makes purchases in the hope or expectation that its purchasing volume will stimulate the vendor to reciprocate. The fact that this type of conduct is described as reciprocity only serves to highlight the confusion and lack of standardized definitions in this field. Unilateral action may well be an attempt at reciprocity, but it can never logically constitute actual reciprocity because there is no accomplished mutual arrangement. Much of the speculation in this area is a carry-over from the application of concepts of reciprocity in the context of merger law, where the potential for reciprocity is a proper consideration un-

11. [This and the following eleven footnotes are from the original.] See, e.g., Flinn, Reciprocity and Related Products Under the Sherman Act, 37 Antitrust L.J. 156 (1968); Kaapcke, Reciprocity Under the Antitrust Laws, 22 Bus. Law, 557 (1967); Krash, Legality of Reciprocity Under Section 7 of the Clayton Act, 9 Antitrust Bull. 93 (1964).

der an incipiency statute.[12]   However, even when reciprocity is examined in the perspective of a proposed merger, there must be the potential for actual reciprocity rather than unilateral action by an individual purchaser.

Beyond the contradictions inherent in the phrase "unilateral reciprocity", there is the further fact that the purchasing practices in question must be capable of stimulating reciprocity.   This can be achieved only if there is an expectation of additional future purchases of significant volume to create some potential for leverage.   This leverage rarely, if ever, can be achieved through a single purchase and will ordinarily result only from a continuous course of dealings. When the purchasing pattern is of sufficient size to have a coercive effect, any purchasing arrangements that do not reflect decisions based on price, quality or service will fall into one of the more traditional categories of illegal reciprocity, and there is no need to examine them on a unilateral basis.   When the purchase lacks such coercive potential, then no alien factor has been injected into product selection, and the competitive process has not been subverted.   It would seem, therefore, that any description of unilateral action as a form of reciprocity serves only to perpetuate an obvious misnomer.

Under the present state of the law, there are only two forms of reciprocal conduct that have been declared to violate the antitrust laws.   While the potential for reciprocity has had an extremely broad application in the merger context, only voluntary reciprocal agreements and coerced reciprocal arrangements have been condemned as being independent violations of the Sherman Act or of Section 5 of the Federal Trade Commission Act.

The first category, mutual or negotiated reciprocity, occurs when both parties voluntarily enter into a reciprocal arrangement whereby each conditions his purchases on continued patronage by the other. This is the traditional situation of back-scratching that usually comes to mind when one speaks of reciprocity.   Since it has the effect of making the mutual arrangement the overriding consideration in supplier selection, it constitutes that "alien factor" our antitrust laws prohibit from influencing the competitive forces of the marketplace. For the most part, these arrangements are now a rarity.   Businessmen have come to recognize not only their illegality, but also the damaging effect they can have on the corporate flexibility so necessary to corporate expansion and growth.   Since neither party is at the economic mercy of the other, it is usually just bad business for a corporation to involve itself in an arrangement that would restrict its ability to solicit lower prices from competing sellers.

12.   This article will not attempt to examine the vast area of "reciprocity effect", which concerns the allegation of potential reciprocity as an anticompetitive prospect of a proposed or completed merger.   Suffice it to mention the recent Justice Department suit against the Ling-Tempco-Vought acquisition of Jones & Laughlin Steel Company, Civil No. 69–438 (W.D.Pa., April 14, 1969), and the FTC proceeding against White Consolidated Industries for its acquisition of Allis-Chalmers, FTC Press Release, March 6, 1969, both of which are premised solely on reciprocity effect.

A far more predatory reciprocal activity is coerced reciprocity. This form of mutual dealing is ordinarily the result of a purchasing superiority or leverage on the part of one of the corporations involved that is used as a weapon to exact reciprocating purchases from a disadvantaged seller. It is this area of reciprocity that has been the subject of recent investigation and litigation by both the Justice Department[13] and the Federal Trade Commission.[14] While the exact state of the law is far from clear,* it is possible to identify certain fundamental elements of coercive reciprocity. As its name would imply, there must always be some element of coercion capable of eliciting the desired response. But coercion, like beauty, is a relative consideration, and it is largely determined by the party at whom it is directed. Thus, in every instance, it must be demonstrated that the party charged with coercive reciprocity had the purchasing power capable of forcing others to comply with its wishes.

This "power" is more frequently referred to as "leverage". Leverage most certainly can be an actual, present purchasing volume of sufficient size that another corporation would be willing to reciprocate merely to maintain the *status quo*. Leverage also might be buying power still in a potential stage, that is, an unplaced order for a large quantity of goods that might be used to induce reciprocation as a condition to its placement with a particular seller.

The crucial question is "How much leverage is enough?" Since this pressure is usually applied with some degree of subtlety, the necessary purchasing leverage must be determined by examination of external factors such as the relative size and purchasing volume of the parties concerned. This does not mean absolute size but rather comparative size of the reciprocal purchases in question. If a multimillion dollar corporation sells to a local manufacturer and in turn purchases from that manufacturer, the question of purchasing leverage would be determined with reference to the sales volume between those two companies rather than the comparative corporate size of the two entities.

Once a purchasing disparity is established and it can be demonstrated that there is the power to exert leverage, it then becomes necessary to demonstrate facts and circumstances to support an inference that leverage actually was applied. One way of doing this has been to show the existence of purchases or purchasing patterns that do not reflect considerations based solely on cost, quality and service. The weakness of this approach, as was noted earlier, is the fact that a

13. E.g., United States v. General Tire & Rubber Company, Civil No. C-67-155 (N.D.Ohio, filed March 2, 1967); United States v. United States Steel Corporation, Civil No. 69-728 (W.D.Pa., filed June 13, 1969).

14. E.g., Chase Bag Company, Trade Reg.Rep. ¶ 18,758 (May 2, 1969); GAF Corporation, Trade Reg.Rep. ¶ 18,694 (March 18, 1969); Union Camp Corporation, Trade Reg.Rep. ¶ 18,669 (February 12, 1969); American Standard, Inc., Trade Reg.Rep. ¶ 18,167 (January 24, 1968).

* [Editors' note.] Since publication of this article, two circuits have held coerced reciprocity to be *per se* unlawful. See Betaseed, Inc. v. U. & I., Inc., 681 F.2d 1203 (9th Cir. 1982); Spartan Grain & Mill Co. v. Ayers, 581 F.2d 419 (5th Cir. 1978), certiorari denied 444 U.S. 381, 100 S.Ct. 59, 62 L.Ed.2d 39 (1979).

businessman is not obliged to make his purchases solely on the bases of cost, quality and service. He is free to respond to a certain degree of personal prejudice or preference and cannot be called to task under the antitrust laws because his decision to buy did not reflect the soundest possible business judgment.[15] Consequently, another method has been employed to demonstrate the likelihood that purchasing leverage was applied, namely, that there was the opportunity, and even the predisposition, to apply the purchasing leverage. This is done typically by reference to the existence of a corporate department invested with the responsibility of maintaining market relations with other corporations.

The present tripartite rationale for demonstrating coercive reciprocity appears to be (1) that the corporation has the necessary purchasing leverage, (2) that it has the facilities and the predisposition for applying that leverage and (3) that it has purchase agreements reflecting the application of that leverage because they are not based solely on considerations of cost, quality and service. Like a three-legged bench, this argument will not stand if any leg is missing. The issues of leverage and leverage-produced agreements are usually subject to economic and statistical proof, while the middle element of "means" or "opportunity" can only be established from an examination of corporate conduct.

It is with respect to the element of corporate conduct that trade relations departments or similarly named parts of corporate structures have received controversial attention. While Government representatives have avowed repeatedly that the existence of these departments creates no presumptions of reciprocity, they nonetheless have sought to use the existence of trade relations departments as an inferential basis for showing the application of purchasing leverage. In two of the most recent pieces of litigation, an attempt has been made to equate the existence of a trade relations department with the performance of illegal reciprocal functions.[16] This attitude not only makes these departments a particularly sensitive area of the corporate anatomy, but also reflects a disturbing lack of knowledge on the part of the Government concerning the legitimate and essential functions performed by market relations departments in the day-to-day operation of a corporation.

Trade relations, like public relations, advertising and other aspects of corporate promotion and image, constitute an essential ingredient in the operation of a corporation in today's sophisticated market

15. Obviously, personal prejudice must be clearly distinguished from both predatory business practices and those prejudices created or induced by others in the industry. A businessman may not arbitrarily engage in a systematic program of discrimination against certain individuals, even though personally motivated, if his conduct has monopolistic effects or inflicts anticompetitive injury. Similarly, the prejudice cannot be that created by favorable business dealings with other competitors if it is tantamount to a combination.

16. See, United States v. United States Steel Corporation, Civil No. 69–728 (W.D.Pa., filed June 13, 1969); United States v. General Tire & Rubber Company, Civil No. C–67–155 (N.D.Ohio, filed March 2, 1967).

place. As an essential, its functions must be performed, either by a specialist trained in trade relations or by other personnel involved in the marketing operations of the corporation. The absence of a trade relations division in a corporate structure simply means that those duties are being performed by someone with another title, perhaps less well equipped for the job and less acquainted with the legitimate bounds.

Nor is it realistic to equate the trade relations function with reciprocal dealing alone. Numerous and diverse duties are performed by this department pursuant to its role as a corporate ambassador, and these encompass a far wider range of subject matter than the mere collection of purchase and sales data.[17] To draw the inferences the Government has sought to extract from the mere existence of independent trade relations departments carries, as a necessary prerequisite, the equally erroneous inference that reciprocal dealings are the only reason for the existence of the departments. Purchase and sales contracts with other corporations constitute only a very small portion of the over-all responsibilities of a trade relations representative, and even these responsibilities generally do not involve any ultimate decision to purchase.

A far more realistic approach would acknowledge the diverse roles performed by a trade relations representative as an integral part of the marketing of a corporation's product and would focus only on instances in which the corporation has abused the proper functions of the trade relations department. This would avoid the obvious shortcomings in any Government attempt to impute misconduct through mere status. The existence of the department would remain a proper reflection of legitimate corporate activities, and inferences of reciprocal conduct would be confined to those situations in which the Government could demonstrate an abuse or misuse of the legitimate ends of the trade relations function.

Despite the infirmities in any attempt to establish reciprocal conduct from the mere existence of a trade relations department, recent litigation has indicated that the Antitrust Division of the Justice Department will continue to press courts to accept this argument. It has been the consistent position of Justice in its recent public statements on reciprocity[18] that, whenever it suspects that a company is engaging in reciprocal dealings, it will attempt to establish the actual application of purchasing leverage from the mere existence of a corporate department with trade relations responsibilities. In the light of this, it is valuable to examine the recent litigation on reciprocal dealings with a view toward cataloguing the various types of corpo-

17. Garrison & Hooker, Trade Relations: Some Misconceptions and Realities, 22 Bus.Law. 1137 (1967).

18. See, e.g., Address by Roland W. Donnem, Director of Antitrust Policy Planning, Department of Justice, to American Bar Association Annual Meeting, in Dallas, Texas, August 12, 1969; Address by Baddia J. Rashid, Director of Antitrust Operations, Department of Justice, to Federal Bar Association Annual Meeting, in Miami Beach, Florida, September 4, 1969.

rate conduct the Antitrust Division considers particularly relevant to the question of reciprocity.

The starting point for any examination of the case law on reciprocal dealings would have to be the decision of the United States District Court for the Southern District of New York in United States v. General Dynamics Corporation, 258 F.Supp. 36 (D.C.N.Y.1966). In that case, General Dynamics attempted to use its purchasing leverage with its suppliers to increase the sales of its subsidiary, Liquid Carbonic. The court acknowledged the use of leverage but refused to find a violation based exclusively on reciprocal dealings because there was an insufficient effect on interstate commerce. Despite the outcome of the case, the court identified certain aspects of corporate activity as clear indications of reciprocal dealings. Special attention was given to the fact that sales prospects for Liquid Carbonic were categorized on the basis of their sales to General Dynamics, and those companies having more than $10,000 in sales to General Dynamics were "targeted" for special sales pressure. The court also noted that sales representatives for Liquid Carbonic frequently contacted their counterparts in the "targeted" companies rather than negotiating with the purchasing agent. Finally, the court dwelt on the existence of an extensive sales program, replete with all pertinent supplier information and "designed to exploit the sales generating capacity latent in defendant's purchasing power".

The *General Dynamics* decision represents the only recent judicial decision involving an independent cause of action based solely on coercive reciprocity. While the discussion of reciprocity is unavoidably intermingled with consideration of potential reciprocity in a merger context, it is clear that the court felt that the facts were adequate to sustain proof that General Dynamics had pursued a systematic course of applying purchasing leverage to achieve coerced reciprocity.

After *General Dynamics*, the Department of Justice instituted two other suits alleging a violation of the Sherman Act based on illegal reciprocity. In each of these cases, the Government cited the existence of a trade relations department to support the inference that reciprocal dealings were, in fact, being engaged in by the defendants. This was a far cry from the special sales program of General Dynamics and represented a major extension of Justice's position on inferring reciprocal relationships. The department is apparently willing to attribute certain presumptive conduct to a corporate department merely by virtue of its existence.

In the first of these suits, involving the General Tire & Rubber Company,[19] the Government is attempting to prove an illegal concert of action among affiliates in the form of a deliberate and sustained campaign to make sales by reciprocal dealings. A primary ingredient in the Government's allegation of a systematic course of conduct is

19. United States v. General Tire & Rubber Company, Civil No. C–67–155 (N.D.Ohio, filed March 2, 1967).

its reference to the existence of trade relations departments in the corporate entities involved. While this case is in pretrial stages, a ruling on a Government subpoena for documents sheds some light on the type of conduct the Justice Department considers to be related to the existence of reciprocal dealings. The Government requested all purchase and sales data in the possession of the trade relations department as well as all information pertaining to suppliers and customers of the corporation. A request was also made for all file cards and telephone numbers in the possession of the trade relations department, from which the Government apparently hopes to identify particular individuals in other companies with whom trade relations personnel had regular and personal contact. Among the relief sought by the Government against General Tire & Rubber Company is the dissolution of the trade relations department within the corporation.

The third and most recent suit involves the United States Steel Corporation.[20] Once again, the Government asserted the existence of a trade relations department to support its contention of reciprocity. The suit was settled by a consent decree in August, 1969, wherein U. S. Steel is prohibited from maintaining any statistical compilations that compare sales to and purchases from suppliers. The company is also forbidden to issue any customer lists that identify or recommend purchases to any corporate representative involved in purchasing. Finally, U. S. Steel agreed to dissolve its commercial relations section and not to create any successor department directed toward conducting trade relations that involve reciprocal arrangements.

The original form of this consent decree directed U. S. Steel to withdraw from the Trade Relations Association. As a result of the objections of that association,[21] the language was changed, not only to delete any reference to the Trade Relations Association but also to clarify the fact that U. S. Steel was prohibited only from joining associations whose trade relations activities contribute to the creation of reciprocal dealings. This is perhaps the only instance wherein the Justice Department tacitly has agreed that the functions of a trade relations representative are far more comprehensive than the single area of dealings with customers and suppliers that might afford a potential for reciprocal arrangement if abused.

One very able Justice Department representative has referred to the U. S. Steel consent decree as demonstrating "how a direct challenge to a systematic reciprocity program may provide a basis for relief aimed at the system itself, and not just the resulting agreements".[22] The unfortunate and perhaps unjustifiable conclusion to be drawn from this statement is that the Government still does not

20. United States v. United States Steel Corporation, Civil No. 69–728 (W.D. Pa., filed June 13, 1969), final judgment consented to August 4, 1969, 424 A.T. R.R. at A–11 (August 26, 1969).

21. The Trade Relations Association sought to intervene in the action to protect its interests and also contemplated an action for trade libel. The Justice Department responded by rewording the proposed consent judgment. 424 A.T. R.R. at A–11 (August 26, 1969).

22. Address by Baddia Rashid, supra note 61 [8 in orig.]

distinguish between valid trade relations functions and abuses of those functions resulting in reciprocity. It can be expected, therefore, that future suits will continue the present policy of equating status with conduct and misinterpreting the trade relations role. Until the broader aspects of the trade relations function receive recognition, it is important to understand the kinds of conduct Government enforcement agencies consider to be indicative of reciprocal dealings. It is clear from the litigation to date that responsible counsel should advise corporate executives charged with the trade relations functions to observe the following guidelines:

1. Do not maintain statistics on purchases from and sales to suppliers for the purpose of isolating "target" companies.

2. Do not catalogue customers on the basis of your purchases from them.

3. Do not supply your sales departments with purchasing statistics.

4. Do not supply your purchasing department with sales statistics.

5. Do not deal with sales representatives when selling or with buyers when making purchases. Always deal through the proper channel on the other side of the transaction.

6. Do not combine the trade relations function with either the line-purchasing or the line-selling functions, and do not invest the trade relations representative with authority to consummate directly either purchases or sales.

7. Do not suddenly eliminate a trade relations department or intentionally disguise it under some other title or department. Nothing creates a stronger inference of guilt than an attempt to conceal otherwise acceptable conduct.

In addition to these few simple precautions, there are some affirmative steps a corporation can take to insure its full and complete adherence to the law. There is no better safeguard against violation of the antitrust laws than a knowledgeable understanding of how those laws affect the corporation. It is essential to obtain a maximum degree of participation by top-level corporate personnel in associations designed to instruct the businessman in his obligations under the antitrust laws. Corporate executives should take the time to participate in educational programs so that they can better direct the activities of their corporations in a manner that will avoid any unnecessary confrontation with the antitrust laws.

The most significant single step that any corporation can take is to adopt a well-defined policy concerning reciprocal dealings. This policy should reflect a complete "open-door" approach to the solicitation of sales and the placement of orders. The existence of a firm corporate policy on this matter provides the best possible defense against any attempted application of purchasing leverage by another corporation. If corporate representatives are well informed on company policies on reciprocal dealings, they are better equipped to dismiss overtures for reciprocal arrangements. Finally, every corporation with an established trade relations department should clearly define and make public the powers and responsibilities of that department.

It is only by these efforts that corporations will succeed in educating both the public and the Government about the true role of the trade relations representative. These educational measures will highlight the diverse responsibilities of that position and properly minimize the potential for illegal reciprocal dealings.[23]

E. TYING ARRANGEMENTS

1. INTRODUCTION [24]

Section 3 of the Clayton Act was intended to encompass "tying arrangements," i.e., the conditioning of the sale of one product (tying product) upon the purchase of a second product (tied product). The idea is that the transaction is on the condition that the purchaser will not buy the tied product from a competitor of the seller. As indicated in the discussion of International Salt Co. v. United States in the *Standard Oil* opinion, supra p. 673, the Supreme Court has concluded that tying arrangements "serve hardly any purpose beyond the suppression of competition," and therefore are presumptively unlawful where there is "sufficient economic power" in the tying product (and the other jurisdictional requisites of Section 3 are present). Among the competitive dangers said to be generated by tying are forcing the buyer into taking an unwanted product,[25] the foreclosure of competitors of the seller from the tied product market,[26] the extension of market power from the tying product market to the tied product mar-

23. For further analysis of reciprocity see generally, V, P. Areeda & D. Turner, Antitrust Law, ch. 11C–1 (1980); L. Sullivan, Antitrust 490–95 (1977); Markovits, Tie-Ins and Reciprocity: A Functional, Legal and Policy Analysis, 58 Texas L.Rev. 1363 (1980); Flinn, Reciprocity and Related Topics Under The Sherman Act, 37 Antitrust L.J. 156 (1968).

24. See generally L. Sullivan, Antitrust, pp. 431–471 (1977); Baker, The Supreme Court and The Per Se Tying Rule: Cutting the Gordian Knot, 66 Va. L.Rev. 1183 (1980); Bauer, A Simplified Approach to Tying Arrangements: A Legal and Economic Analysis, 33 Vand.L. Rev. 283 (1980); Bowman, Tying Arrangements and the Leverage Problem, 67 Yale L.J. 19 (1957); Ferguson, Tying Arrangements and Reciprocity: An Economic Analysis, 30 Law & Contemp.Probs. 552 (1965); Markovits, Tie-Ins and Reciprocity: A

Functional, Legal and Policy Analysis, 58 Texas L.Rev. 1363 (1980); Markovits, Tie-Ins, Leverage, and The American Antitrust Laws, 80 Yale L.J. 195 (1970); Pearson, Tying Arrangements and Antitrust Policy, 60 Nw.U.L.Rev. 626 (1965); Slawson, A Stronger Simpler Tie-In Doctrine, 25 Antitrust Bull. 671 (1980); Turner, The Validity of Tying Arrangements Under the Antitrust Laws, 72 Harv.L.Rev. 50 (1958); Wheeler, Some Observations on Tie-Ins, the Single Product Defense, Exclusive Dealing and Regulated Industries, 60 Calif.L.Rev. 1557 (1972).

25. See, Fortner Enterprise, Inc. v. United States Steel Corp., (Fortner I), infra p. 702.

26. See United States v. Loew's, Inc., 371 U.S. 38, 83 S.Ct. 97, 9 L.Ed.2d 11 (1962).

ket (particularly where the tying product is patented or copyright-ed),[27] the reduction of consumer alternatives for purchasing particular goods,[28] the increase of barriers to entry into both the tied and tying product markets[29] and the use of hidden price discrimination in pricing the tied or the tying product.[30] In view of these potential hazards of tying arrangements, they have been singled out by Congress in Section 3 of the Clayton Act for special treatment and they have traditionally been treated harshly when brought before the courts.

Because of the jurisdictional limitations upon Section 3 of the Clayton Act (see pp. 668–670 supra), some tying arrangements can be attacked only under the Sherman Act or Section 5 of the Federal Trade Commission Act. In *Northern Pacific Railway Co. v. United States*,[31] the Court designated tying as a *per se* violation of Section 1 of the Sherman Act, and held illegal Northern Pacific's practice of requiring grantees or lessees of Northern Pacific land adjoining the railroad right-of-way to ship their products over the Northern Pacific, provided its rates were equal to those of competing carriers:

> Where such conditions are successfully exacted competition on the merits with respect to the tied product is inevitably curbed. . . . They deny competitors free access to the market for the tied product, not because the party imposing the tying requirements has a better product or a lower price but because of his power or leverage in another market. At the same time buyers are forced to forego their free choice between competing products. For these reasons "tying agreements fare harshly under the laws forbidding restraints of trade." They are unreasonable in and of themselves whenever a party has sufficient economic power with respect to the tying product to appreciably restrain free competition in the market for the tied product and a "not insubstantial" amount of interstate commerce is affected. . . . Of course where the seller has no control or dominance over the tying product so that it does not represent an effectual weapon to pressure buyers into taking the tied item any restraint of trade attributable to such tying arrangements would obviously be insignificant at most. As a simple example, if one of a dozen food stores in a community were to refuse to sell flour unless the buyer also took sugar it would hardly tend to restrain competition in sugar if its competitors were ready and able to sell flour by itself.

A careful reading of the Court's language indicates that the "per se" test adopted for tying is unlike the per se tests adopted else-

27. See, International Salt Co. v. United States, 332 U.S. 392, 68 S.Ct. 12, 92 L.Ed. 20 (1947). See also discussion of tying in Chap. 9, infra pp. 998–1020. See also Lavey, Patents, Copyrights, and Trademarks as Sources of Market Power in Antitrust Cases, 27 Antitrust Bull. 433 (1982).

28. See Slawson, supra note 24 at 676–77.

29. Id. at 681. See also United Shoe Machinery Corp. v. United States, 258 U.S. 451, 42 S.Ct. 363, 66 L.Ed. 708 (1922).

30. See Bauer, supra note 24 at 291–97.

31. 356 U.S. 1, 78 S.Ct. 514, 2 L.Ed.2d 545 (1958).

where.[32] The Court's test left considerable room for litigation over
whether a particular arrangement does in fact constitute a tying arrangement: viz., when are two physically distinct things to be regarded, for antitrust purposes, as a commercial unit rather than a tying
product and a tied product? As a moment's reflection about the oft-
mentioned plight of the one-legged customer in a shoe store may indicate, what might be a rational package for merchandizing goods to
some or most persons might be an unwanted "tying arrangement" to
another person. When is there "sufficient economic power with respect to the tying product to appreciably restrain free competition in
the market for the tied product"? How much is a "not insubstantial"
amount of interstate commerce affected by the tie? Litigation since
Northern Pacific has repeatedly encountered each of these questions
and has regularly failed to resolve finally most of them. Extensive
controversy also exists concerning the motivation for employing a tying arrangement and the economic consequences of doing so.

F. M. SCHERER, INDUSTRIAL MARKET STRUCTURE AND ECONOMIC PERFORMANCE

(2d Ed. 1980) [33]

Tying contracts: Businesses have diverse reasons for attempting to tie the sale of one product to that of another. First, a firm
may have monopoly power over one product by virtue of patent
protection, strong product differentiation, or scale economies; and
it may try to exploit this leverage in a second market where, without the tie, it could earn no more than a normal return. Thus, it
adds to its monopoly profits in the tying good market the profits it
can realize by exercising power over price in at least part of the
tied good market. The economics of such ties are similar to those
of downstream integration by a firm to obtain control over the
purchase of inputs complementary in production to the input on
which the firm enjoys monopoly power. Second and closely related, the profits attainable from coordinated monopoly pricing of
two goods which, for example, are complements in use, will generally be higher than those realized by setting a monopoly price for
each commodity separately. This is so because, by ignoring interdependence between the demand functions of complementary
products, a producer in effect fails to adjust for all the variables
affecting its profit maximum, just as oligopolists producing the
same product maximize joint profits only when they take into account fully the interdependence of their demand functions. Third,
tying is sometimes a convenient way of discriminating in price according to intensity of demand. Suppose, for instance, that one

copying machine user makes 3,000 copies per month, while another makes 10,000 copies per month. It would be difficult for a company selling only copying machines to price its machines in such a way as to extract more revenue from the more intensive user. But if the machine maker can tie the purchase of special copying paper to the purchase of its machine, and if it can wield sufficient leverage in the paper market to realize a supranormal profit margin there, it will be able to secure additional profits from the high-volume user. An analogous but more complex variant occurs when firms sell related but separable products only at a single package or "bundled" price. Fourth, the producer of a technically complex machine may engage in tying to control the quality of materials and supplies used with its machine, so that the reputation of its product is not sullied by breakdowns caused through the use of faulty supplies. Fifth, certain economies may be realized by producing or distributing the tied and tying goods together. For example, supplies of special copying machine paper or ink may be delivered by maintenance personnel in the course of routine service visits, saving separate delivery costs. It is doubtful, however, whether the savings realized in this way could be very substantial. Finally, tying contracts may be employed to evade governmental price controls—e.g., when a firm supplying some commodity such as gas or telephone service whose price is regulated requires customers to buy from it fixtures and attachments whose prices are not effectively controlled.

Sorting out which of these uses of tying arrangements should be permitted and which should be condemned and in what circumstances one or the other result should follow has provoked considerable controversy. On the one hand are those who view tying arrangements as a displacement of consumer freedom of choice and seldom productive of any worthwhile efficiencies or pro-competitive benefits that may not be achieved by less restrictive alternatives.[34] The opposing view, usually relying upon neo-classical "economic analysis", emphasizes seller rationality, rather than buyer freedom of choice, as the touchstone for analysis and suggests tying arrangements should be assumed to be pro-competitive in the absence of structural market conditions giving rise to a threat to competition generally.[35] Rather than being condemned on a *per se* or presumptively illegal basis, it is argued, tying should be analyzed on a rule of reason basis, because it should be presumed rational sellers operating in competitive markets would only employ the device where it is efficient to do so. As is the case with other vertical market restraints, the substantive debate is one over the goals of antitrust policy as well as the methodology by which those goals are implemented efficiently within the context of

34. See Bauer, supra note 24; Slawson, supra note 24.

35. See Baker, supra note 24; Bowman, supra note 24; Markovits, supra note 24. See also, Hyde v. Jefferson Parish Hospital District No. 2, 686 F.2d 286 (5th Cir. 1982), certiorari granted ___ U.S. ___, 103 S.Ct. 1271, ___ L.Ed.2d ___ (1983). (Anesthesiologist exclusive dealing contract with hospital *per se* unlawful; government brief argues tying should not be *per se*).

the adversary process.[36] Unlike the debate elsewhere however, the controversy over tying arrangements is considerably complicated by the vagaries of the concepts used to identify the conduct, the shifting emphasis given the elements of the offense from case to case, and the ambiguity over the *"per seness"* of the offense. These factors in turn have generated inconsistencies in the methodology followed from one court to the next in analyzing a tying arrangement in the circumstances of a particular case. All these features of tying arrangements are well illustrated by the two decisions in the *Fortner* case, the most recent pronouncements on tying arrangements by the Supreme Court.*

36. The practical problems with an extensive economic analysis of tying arrangements and the goals of antitrust policy impinged by such practices were summed up by the court in Moore v. Jas. H. Matthews & Co., 550 F.2d 1207, 1212–13 (9th Cir. 1977):

The rationale for proscribing the practice of tie-ins rests on the leverage theory. . . . .

Competitors in the tied product market are injured if they cannot offer their products on an equal basis with the distributor of the tying product. Buyers are injured because they forego choices among products and services and the public is harmed by the adverse effect on the market for the tied product.

These reasons for the presumptive illegality of tie-ins have been questioned persuasively by commentators and economists. See, e.g., Posner, Exclusionary Practices and the Antitrust Laws, 41 U.Chi.L.Rev. 506 (1974); Bowman, Tying Arrangements and the Leverage Problem, 67 Yale L.J. 19 (1957). Underlying their criticism is the belief that enforcement and interpretation of the antitrust laws should be governed by economic principles for maximizing consumer welfare. The effect of this premise would be to shift our focus from the traditional interests in avoiding "coerced sacrifice[s] of alternatives" to an analysis of the tie-in's effect on economic efficiency.

. . .

The clear implication from a purely economic standpoint is that tie-ins should be considered on a case-by-case basis because they are not inherently detrimental. They can in fact be beneficial.

The difficulty with adopting such an approach is well-recognized and it derives from the nature of courts and the costs of judicial enforcement. The problem stems from the unwillingness, if not the inability, of courts to undertake complex economic decision making in the face of economic indeterminacy and over-crowded court calendars.

As courts, we engage in our own balancing of notions about efficiency and have concluded that rules of presumptive illegality serve two vital functions. First, the *per se* rule:

avoids the necessity for an incredibly complicated and prolonged economic investigation . . . in an effort to determine at large whether a particular restraint has been unreasonable—an inquiry so often wholly fruitless . . . .

Northern Pacific Ry. Co., supra, 356 U.S. at 5, 78 S.Ct. at 518.

Second, the Court's steadfast refusal to heed arguments premised solely on the theory of consumer welfare recognizes the fact that enforcement of the antitrust laws requires rules which are both predictable and workable. The test of presumptive illegality is such a mechanism. It protects competition "on the merits," *Northern Pacific Ry. Co.,* supra, 356 U.S. at 6, 78 S.Ct. 514, by identifying situations which diminish equality of opportunity in competitive markets and proscribing them.

* The *Hyde,* case supra n. 35, pending argument before the Court, may become a leading tying case.

2.   IDENTIFYING A TYING ARRANGEMENT AND THE
DEGREE OF *Per Se* ILLEGALITY

FORTNER ENTERPRISES, INC. v. UNITED STATES STEEL CORP. (FORTNER I)

Supreme Court of the United States, 1969.
394 U.S. 495, 89 S.Ct. 1252, 22 L.Ed.2d 495.

MR. JUSTICE BLACK delivered the opinion of the Court.

This case raises a variety of questions concerning the proper standards to be applied by a United States district court in passing on a
motion for summary judgment in a civil antitrust action. Petitioner,
Fortner Enterprises, Inc., filed this suit seeking treble damages and
an injunction against alleged violations of §§ 1 and 2 of the Sherman
Act. . . . The complaint charged that respondents, United States
Steel Corp. and its wholly owned subsidiary, the United States Steel
Homes Credit Corp., had engaged in a contract, combination, and conspiracy to restrain trade and to monopolize trade in the sale of prefabricated houses. It alleged that there was a continuing agreement
between respondents "to force corporations and individuals, including
the plaintiff, as a condition to availing themselves of the services of
United States Steel Homes Credit Corporation, to purchase at artificially high prices only United States Steel Homes . . . ." Specifically, petitioner claimed that in order to obtain loans totaling over
$2,000,000 from the Credit Corp. for the purchase and development of
certain land in the Louisville, Kentucky, area, it had been required to
agree, as a condition of the loans, to erect a prefabricated house manufactured by U. S. Steel on each of the lots purchased with the loan
proceeds. Petitioner claimed that the prefabricated materials were
then supplied by U. S. Steel at unreasonably high prices and proved
to be defective and unusable, thus requiring the expenditure of additional sums and delaying the completion date for the development.
Petitioner sought treble damages for the profits thus lost, along with
a decree enjoining respondents from enforcing the requirement of the
loan agreement that petitioner use only houses manufactured by U.
S. Steel.

. . . [T]he District Court entered summary judgment for respondents, holding that petitioner's allegations had failed to raise any
question of fact as to a possible violation of the antitrust laws, 293
F.Supp. 762. Noting that the agreement involved here was essentially a tying arrangement, under which the purchaser was required to
take a tied product—here prefabricated homes—as a condition of being allowed to purchase the tying product—here credit, the District
Judge held that petitioner had failed to establish the prerequisites of
illegality under our tying cases, namely sufficient market power over
the tying product and foreclosure of a substantial volume of commerce in the tied product. The Court of Appeals affirmed without
opinion 6 Cir., 404 F.2d 936, and we granted certiorari, 393 U.S. 820,
89 S.Ct. 126, 21 L.Ed.2d 92 (1968). Since we find no basis for sus-

taining this summary judgment, we reverse and order that the case proceed to trial.

We agree with the District Court that the conduct challenged here primarily involves a tying arrangement of the traditional kind. The Credit Corp. sold its credit only on the condition that petitioner purchase a certain number of prefabricated houses from the Homes Division of U. S. Steel. Our cases have made clear that, at least when certain prerequisites are met, arrangements of this kind are illegal in and of themselves, and no specific showing of unreasonable competitive effect is required. The discussion in Northern Pacific R. Co. v. United States, 356 U.S. 1, 5–6, 78 S.Ct. 514, 518, 2 L.Ed.2d 545 (1958), is dispositive of this question:

[The opinion quotes the language from *Northern Pacific* quoted supra p. 698.]

. . .

Despite its recognition of this strict standard, the District Court held that petitioner had not even made out a case for the jury. The court held that respondents did not have "sufficient economic power" over credit, the tying product here, because although the Credit Corp.'s terms evidently made the loans uniquely attractive to petitioner, petitioner had not proved that the Credit Corp. enjoyed the same unique attractiveness or economic control with respect to buyers generally. The court also held that the amount of interstate commerce affected was "insubstantial" because only a very small percentage of the land available for development in the area was foreclosed to competing sellers of prefabricated houses by the contract with petitioner. We think it plain that the District Court misunderstood the two controlling standards and misconceived the extent of its authority to evaluate the evidence in ruling on this motion for summary judgment.

A preliminary error that should not pass unnoticed is the District Court's assumption that the two prerequisites mentioned in *Northern Pacific* are standards that petitioner must meet in order to prevail on the merits. On the contrary, these standards are necessary only to bring into play the doctrine of *per se* illegality. Where the standards were found satisfied in *Northern Pacific*, and in International Salt Co. v. United States, 332 U.S. 392, 68 S.Ct. 12, 92 L.Ed. 20 (1947), this Court approved summary judgment *against* the defendants but by no means implied that inability to satisfy these standards would be fatal to a plaintiff's case. A plaintiff can still prevail on the merits whenever he can prove, on the basis of a more thorough examination of the purposes and effects of the practices involved, that the general standards of the Sherman Act have been violated. Accordingly, even if we could agree with the District Court that the *Northern Pacific* standards were not satisfied here, the summary judgment against petitioner still could not be entered without further examination of petitioner's general allegations that respondents conspired together for the purpose of restraining competition and acquiring a monopoly in the market for prefabricated houses.

. . .

We need not consider, however, whether petitioner is entitled to a trial on this more general theory, for it is clear that petitioner raised questions of fact which, if proved at trial, would bring this tying arrangement within the scope of the *per se* doctrine. The requirement that a "not insubstantial" amount of commerce be involved makes no reference to the scope of any particular market or to the share of that market foreclosed by the tie, and hence we could not approve of the trial judge's conclusions on this issue even if we agreed that his definition of the relevant market was the proper one.[37] An analysis of market shares might become relevant if it were alleged that an apparently small dollar-volume of business actually represented a substantial part of the sales for which competitors were bidding. But normally the controlling consideration is simply whether a total amount of business, substantial enough in terms of dollar-volume so as not to be merely *de minimis*, is foreclosed to competitors by the tie, for as we said in *International Salt*, it is "unreasonable, *per se*, to foreclose competitors from any substantial market" by a tying arrangement, 332 U.S. at 396, 68 S.Ct. at 15.

The complaint and affidavits filed here leave no room for doubt that the volume of commerce allegedly foreclosed was substantial. It may be true, as respondents claim, that petitioner's annual purchases of houses from U. S. Steel under the tying arrangement never exceeded $190,000, while more than $500,000 in annual sales was involved in the tying arrangement held illegal in *International Salt*, but we cannot agree with respondents that a sum of almost $200,000 is paltry or "insubstantial." In any event, a narrow focus on the volume of commerce foreclosed by the particular contract or contracts in suit would not be appropriate in this context. As the special provision awarding treble damages to successful plaintiffs illustrates, Congress has encouraged private antitrust litigation not merely to compensate those who have been directly injured but also to vindicate the important public interest in free competition. For purposes of determining whether the amount of commerce foreclosed is too insubstantial to warrant prohibition of the practice, therefore, the relevant figure is the total volume of sales tied by the sales policy under challenge, not the portion of this total accounted for by the particular plaintiff who brings suit. In *International Salt* the $500,000 total represented the volume of tied sales to all purchasers, and although this amount was directly involved because the case was brought by the Government against the practice generally, the case would have been no less worthy of judicial scrutiny if it had been

---

37. [Court's footnote 1.] Since the loan agreements obligated petitioner to erect houses manufactured by U. S. Steel on the land acquired, the trial judge thought the relevant foreclosure was the percentage of the undeveloped land in the county that was no longer open for sites on which homes made by competing producers could be built. This apparently was an insignificant .00032%. But of course the availability of numerous vacant lots on which houses might legally be erected would be small consolation to competing producers once the economic demand for houses had been pre-empted by respondents. It seems plain that the most significant percentage figure with reference to the tied product is the percentage of annual sales of houses, or prefabricated houses, in the area that was foreclosed to other competitors by the tying arrangement.

brought by one individual purchaser who accounted for only a fraction of the $500,000 in tied sales. In the present case, the annual sales allegedly foreclosed by respondents' tying arrangements throughout the country totaled almost $4,000,000 in 1960, more than $2,800,000 in 1961, and almost $2,300,000 in 1962. These amounts could scarcely be regarded as insubstantial.

The standard of "sufficient economic power" does not, as the District Court held, require that the defendant have a monopoly or even a dominant position throughout the market for the tying product. Our tie-in cases have made unmistakably clear that the economic power over the tying product can be sufficient even though the power falls far short of dominance and even though the power exists only with respect to some of the buyers in the market. . . . As we said in the *Loew's* case, 371 U.S. at 45, 83 S.Ct. at 102: "Even absent a showing of market dominance, the crucial economic power may be inferred from the tying product's desirability to consumers or from uniqueness in its attributes."

These decisions rejecting the need for proof of truly dominant power over the tying product have all been based on a recognition that because tying arrangements generally served no legitimate business purpose that cannot be achieved in some less restrictive way, the presence of any appreciable restraint on competition provides a sufficient reason for invalidating the tie. Such appreciable restraint results whenever the seller can exert some power over some of the buyers in the market, even if his power is not complete over them and over all other buyers in the market. In fact, complete dominance throughout the market, the concept that the District Court apparently had in mind, would never exist even under a pure monopoly. Market power is usually stated to be the ability of a single seller to raise price and restrict output, for reduced output is the almost inevitable result of higher prices. Even a complete monopolist can seldom raise his price without losing some sales; many buyers will cease to buy the product, or buy less, as the price rises. Market power is therefore a source of serious concern for essentially the same reason, regardless of whether the seller has the greatest economic power possible or merely some lesser degree of appreciable economic power. In both instances, despite the freedom of some or many buyers from the seller's power, other buyers—whether few or many, whether scattered throughout the market or part of some group within the market—can be forced to accept the higher price because of their stronger preferences for the product, and the seller could therefore choose instead to force them to accept a tying arrangement that would prevent free competition for their patronage in the market for the tied product. Accordingly, the proper focus of concern is whether the seller has the power to raise prices, or impose other burdensome terms such as a tie-in, with respect to any appreciable number of buyers within the market.

The affidavits put forward by petitioner clearly entitle it to its day in court under the standard. The construction company president stated that competitors of U. S. Steel sold prefabricated houses and built conventional homes for at least $400 less than U. S. Steel's price for comparable models. Since in a freely competitive situation buyers would not accept a tying arrangement obligating them to buy a tied product at a price higher than the going market rate, this substantial price differential with respect to the tied product (prefabricated houses) in itself may suggest that respondents had some special economic power in the credit market. In addition, petitioner's president, A. B. Fortner, stated that he accepted the tying condition on respondents' loan solely because the offer to provide 100% financing, lending an amount equal to the full purchase price of the land to be acquired, was unusually and uniquely advantageous to him. He found that no such financing was available to his corporation on any such cheap terms from any other source during the 1959–1962 period. His views on this were supported by the president of a finance company in the Louisville area, who stated in an affidavit that the type of advantageous financing plan offered by U. S. Steel "was not available to Fortner Enterprises or any other potential borrower from or through Louisville Mortgage Service Company or from or through any other lending institution or mortgage company to this affiant's knowledge during this period."

We do not mean to accept petitioner's apparent argument that market power can be inferred simply because the kind of financing terms offered by a lending company are "unique and unusual." We do mean, however, that uniquely and unusually advantageous terms can reflect a creditor's unique economic advantages over his competitors.[38] Since summary judgment in antitrust cases is disfavored, the claims of uniqueness in this case should be read in the light most favorable to petitioner. They could well mean that U. S. Steel's subsidiary Credit Corp. had a unique economic ability to provide 100% financing at cheap rates. The affidavits show that for a three-to-four-year period no other financial institution in the Louisville area was willing to match the special credit terms and rates of interest available from U. S. Steel. Since the possibility of a decline in property values, along with the difficulty of recovering full market value in a foreclosure sale, makes it desirable for a creditor to obtain collateral greater in value than the loan it secures, the unwillingness of competing financial institutions in the area to offer 100% financing probably reflects their feeling that they could not profitably lend money on the risks involved. U. S. Steel's subsidiary Credit Corp., on the other hand, may well have had a substantial competitive advantage in providing this type of financing because of economies resulting from the

38. [Court's footnote 2.] Uniqueness confers economic power only when other competitors are in some way prevented from offering the distinctive product themselves. Such barriers may be legal, as in the case of patented and copyrighted products, e.g., *International Salt; Loew's*, or physical, as when the product is land, e.g., *Northern Pacific.* It is true that the barriers may also be economic, as when competitors are simply unable to produce the distinctive product profitably, but the uniqueness test in such situations is somewhat confusing since the real source of economic power is not the product itself but rather the seller's cost advantage in producing it.

nationwide character of its operations. In addition, potential competitors such as banks and savings and loan associations may have been prohibited from offering 100% financing by state or federal law. Under these circumstances the pleadings and affidavits sufficiently disclose the possibility of market power over borrowers in the credit market to entitle petitioner to go to trial on this issue.

It may also be, of course, that these allegations will not be sustained when the case goes to trial. It may turn out that the arrangement involved here serves legitimate business purposes and that U. S. Steel's subsidiary does not have a competitive advantage in the credit market. But on the record before us it would be impossible to reach such conclusions as a matter of law, and it is not our function to speculate as to the ultimate findings of fact. We therefore conclude that the showing made by petitioner was sufficient on the market power issue.

Brief consideration should also be given to respondents' additional argument that even if their unique kind of financing reflected economic power in the credit market, and even if a substantial volume of commerce was affected, the arrangement involving credit should not be held illegal under normal tie-in principles. In support of this, respondents suggest that every sale on credit in effect involves a tie. They argue that the offering of favorable credit terms is simply a form of price competition equivalent to the offering of a comparable reduction in the cash price of the tied product. Consumers should not, they say, be deprived of such advantageous services, and they suffer no harm because they can buy the tangible product with credit obtained elsewhere if the combined price of the seller's credit-product package is less favorable than the cost of purchasing the components separately.

All of respondents' arguments amount essentially to the same claim—namely, that this opinion will somehow prevent those who manufacture goods from ever selling them on credit. But our holding in this case will have no such effect. There is, at the outset of every tie-in case, including the familiar cases involving physical goods, the problem of determining whether two separate products are in fact involved. In the usual sale on credit the seller, a single individual or corporation, simply makes an agreement determining when and how much he will be paid for his product. In such a sale the credit may constitute such an inseparable part of the purchase price for the item that the entire transaction could be considered to involve only a single product. It will be time enough to pass on the issue of credit sales when a case involving it actually arises. Sales such as that are a far cry from the arrangement involved here, where the credit is provided by one corporation on condition that a product be purchased from a separate corporation, and where the borrower contracts to obtain a large sum of money over and above that needed to pay the seller for the physical products purchased. Whatever the standards for determining exactly when a transaction involves only a "single product," we cannot see how an arrangement such as that present in this case could ever be said to involve only a single product.

Nor does anything in respondents' arguments serve to distinguish credit from other kinds of goods and services, all of which may, when used as tying products, extend the seller's economic power to new markets and foreclose competition in the tied product. The asserted business justifications for a tie of credit are not essentially different from the justifications that can be advanced when the tying product is some other service or commodity. Although advantageous credit terms may be viewed as a form of price competition in the tied product, so is the offer of any other tying product on advantageous terms. In both instances, the seller can achieve his alleged purpose, without extending his economic power, by simply reducing the price of the tied product itself.

The potential harm is also essentially the same when the tying product is credit. The buyer may have the choice of buying the tangible commodity separately, but as in other cases the seller can use his power over the tying product to win customers that would otherwise have constituted a market available to competing producers of the tied product. "[C]ompetition on the merits with respect to the tied product is inevitably curbed." *Northern Pacific*, 356 U.S. at 6, 78 S.Ct. at 518, 2 L.Ed.2d 545. Nor can it be assumed that because the product involved is money needed to finance a purchase, the buyer would not have been able to purchase from anyone else without the seller's attractive credit. A buyer might have a strong preference for a seller's credit because it would eliminate the need for him to lay out personal funds, borrow from relatives, put up additional collateral, or obtain guarantors, but any of these expedients might have been chosen to finance a purchase from a competing producer if the seller had not captured the sale by means of his tying arrangement.

In addition, barriers to entry in the market for the tied product are raised since, in order to sell to certain buyers, a new company not only must be able to manufacture the tied product but also must have sufficient financial strength to offer credit comparable to that provided by larger competitors under tying arrangements. If the larger companies have achieved economies of scale in their credit operations, they can of course exploit these economies legitimately by lowering their credit charges to consumers who purchase credit only, but economies in financing should not, any more than economies in other lines of business, be used to exert economic power over other products that the company produces no more efficiently than its competitors.

For all these reasons we can find no basis for treating credit differently in principle from other goods and services. Although money is a fungible commodity—like wheat or, for that matter, unfinished steel—credit markets, like other markets, are often imperfect, and it is easy to see how a big company with vast sums of money in its treasury could wield very substantial power in a credit market. Where this is true, tie-ins involving credit can cause all the evils that the antitrust laws have always been intended to prevent, crippling other companies that are equally, if not more, efficient in producing their own products. Therefore, the same inquiries must be made as to economic power over the tying product and substantial effect in the tied market, but where these factors are present no special treatment can be justified solely because credit, rather than some other product, is the source of the tying leverage used to restrain competition.

The judgment of the Court of Appeals is reversed, and the case is remanded with directions to let this suit proceed to trial.

Reversed and remanded.

MR. JUSTICE WHITE, with whom MR. JUSTICE HARLAN joins, dissenting.

The judicially developed proscription of certain kinds of tying arrangements has been commonly understood to be this: an antitrust defendant who ties the availability of one product to the purchase of another violates § 1 of the Sherman Act if he both has sufficient market power in the tying product and affects a substantial quantity of commerce in the tied product. This case further defines the degree of market power which is sufficient to invoke the tying rule. . . .

The Court does not purport to abandon the general rule that some market power in the tying product is essential to a § 1 violation. But it applies the rule to permit proscription of a seller's extension of favorable credit terms conditioned on the purchase of an agreed quantity of the seller's product without any offer of proof that the seller has any market power in the credit market itself. Although the credit extended was for the purchase and development of land on which the purchased houses were to be built, the Court's logic dictates the same result if unusually attractive credit terms had been offered simply for the purchase of the houses themselves. Proscription of the sale of goods on easy credit terms as an illegal tie without proof of market power in credit not only departs from established doctrine but also in my view should not be outlawed as *per se* illegal under the Sherman Act. Provision of favorable credit terms may be nothing more or less than vigorous competition in the tied product, on a basis very nearly approaching the price competition which it has always been the policy of the Sherman Act to encourage. Moreover, it is far from clear that, absent power in the credit market, credit financing of purchases should be regarded as a tie of two distinct products any more than a commodity should be viewed as tied to its own price. Since provision of credit by sellers may facilitate competition, since it may provide essential risk or working capital to entrepreneurs or businessmen, and since the logic of the majority's opinion does away in practice with the requirement of showing market power in the tying product while retaining that requirement in form, the majority's *per se* rule is inappropriate. I dissent.

. . . .

There is general agreement in the cases and among commentators that the fundamental restraint against which the tying proscription is meant to guard is the use of power over one product to attain power over another, or otherwise to distort freedom of trade and competition in the second product. This distortion injures the buyers of the second product, who because of their preference for the seller's brand of the first are artificially forced to make a less than optimal choice in the second. And even if the customer is indifferent among brands of the second product and therefore loses nothing by agreeing to use the seller's brand of the second in order to get his brand of the first,[39] such tying agreements may work significant restraints on competition in the tied product. The tying seller may be working toward a monopoly position in the tied product[40] and, even if he is not, the practice of tying forecloses other sellers of the tied product and makes it more difficult for new firms to enter that market. They must be prepared not only to match existing sellers of the tied product in price and quality, but to offset the attraction of the tying product itself. Even if this is possible through simultaneous entry into production of the tying product, entry into both markets is significantly more expensive than simple entry into the tied market, and shifting buying habits in the tied product is considerably more cumbersome and less responsive to variations in competitive offers.[41] In addition to these anticompetitive effects in the tied product, tying arrangements may be used to evade price control in the tying product through clandestine transfer of the profit to the tied product;[42] they may be used as a counting device to effect price discrimination;[43] and they may be used to force a full line of products on the customer [44] so

39. [This and the next 6 footnotes are from the dissenting opinion.] Theoretically, the tie may do the tier little good unless the buyer is in that position. Even if the seller has a complete monopoly in the tying product, this is the case. The monopolist can exact the maximum price which people are willing to pay for his product. By definition, if his price went up he would lose customers. If he then refuses to sell the tying product without the tied product, and raises the price of the tied product above market, he will also lose customers. The tying link works no magic. However, difficulty in extracting the full monopoly profit without the tie, Burstein, A Theory of Full-Line Forcing, 55 Nw.U.L.Rev. 62 (1960), or the marginal advantage of a guaranteed first refusal from otherwise indifferent customers of the tied product, or other advantages mentioned in the text, may make the tie beneficial to its originator.

40. If the monopolist uses his monopoly profits in the first market to underwrite sales below market price in the second, his monopoly business becomes less profitable. There remains an incentive to do so nonetheless when he thinks he can obtain a monopoly in the tied product as well, permitting him later to raise prices without fear of entry to recoup the monopoly profit he has foregone. But just as the firm whose deep pocket stems from monopoly profits in the tying product may make this takeover, so may anyone else with a deep pocket from whatever source.

41. Even when the terms of the tie allow a competitor to obtain the business in the tied product simply by offering a price lower than, rather than equal to, the tier's the Court has found sufficient restriction in the tied product, as in the *Northern Pacific* case.

42. Bowman, Tying Arrangements and the Leverage Problem, 67 Yale L.J. 19, 21–23 (1957).

43. Id., at 23–24.

44. Burstein, A Theory of Full-Line Forcing, 55 Nw.U.L.Rev. 62 (1960).

as to extract more easily from him a monopoly return on one unique product in the line.[45]

All of these distortions depend upon the existence of some market power in the tying product quite apart from any relationship which it might bear to the tied product. In this case, what proof of any market power in the tying product has been alleged? Only that the tying product—money—was not available elsewhere on equally good terms, and perhaps not at all. . . .

· · ·

I cannot join such a complete evisceration of the requirement that market power in the tying product be shown before a tie-in becomes illegal under § 1. Certainly it is unnecessary to erect a § 1 *per se* ban on promotional tie-ins in order to protect the tied product market. If the resulting exclusion of competitors is of sufficient significance to threaten competition in that market, the transaction may be reached as a requirements contract under § 3 of the Clayton Act. If the promotional tie is in effect price discrimination, that too can be examined under statutes designed for that purpose. Moreover, the transaction could be dealt with as an unfair method of competition under § 5 of the Federal Trade Commission Act. . . .

The principal evil at which the proscription of tying aims is the use of power in one market to acquire power in, or otherwise distort, a second market. This evil simply does not exist if there is no power in the first market. The first market here is money, a completely fungible item. I would not apply a *per se* rule here without independent proof of market power. Cutting prices in the credit market is more likely to reflect a competitive attempt to offset the market power of others in the tied product than it is to reflect existing market power

---

45. Tie-ins may also at times be beneficial to the economy. Apart from the justifications discussed in the text are the following. They may facilitate new entry into fields where established sellers have wedded their customers to them by ties of habit and custom. Brown Shoe Co. v. United States, 370 U.S. 294, 330, 82 S.Ct. 1502, 1526, 8 L.Ed.2d 510 (1962); Note, Newcomer Defenses: Reasonable Use of Tie-ins, Franchises, Territorials, and Exclusives, 18 Stan.L.Rev. 457 (1966). They may permit clandestine price cutting in products which otherwise would have no price competition at all because of fear of retaliation from the few other producers dealing in the market. They may protect the reputation of the tying product if failure to use the tied product in conjunction with it may cause it to misfunction. Compare International Business Machines Corp. v. United States, 298 U.S. 131, 138–140, 56 S.Ct. 701, 705, 80 L.Ed. 1085 (1936), and Standard Oil Co. v. United States, 337 U.S. 293, 306, 69 S.Ct. 1051, 1058, 93 L.Ed. 1371 (1949), with Pick Mfg. Co. v. General Motors Corp., 80 F.2d 641 (C.A.7th Cir. 1935), aff'd, 299 U.S. 3, 57 S.Ct. 1, 81 L.Ed. 4 (1936). And, if the tied and tying products are functionally related, they may reduce costs through economies of joint production and distribution. These benefits which may flow from tie-ins, though perhaps in some cases a potential basis for an affirmative defense, were not sufficient to avoid the imposition of a *per se* proscription, once market power has been demonstrated. But in determining whether even the market-power requirement should be eliminated, as the logic of the majority opinion would do, extending the *per se* rule to absolute dimensions, the fact that tie-ins are not entirely unmitigated evils should be borne in mind.

in the credit market. Those with real power do not offer uniquely advantageous deals to their customers; they raise prices.

. . .

[Justices Fortas and Stewart concurred in Justice White's dissent, but added an opinion stressing the view that the provision of credit was ancillary to the business of selling the houses and should not be considered a tying arrangement.]

UNITED STATES STEEL CORP. v. FORTNER ENTERPRISES, INC. (FORTNER II)

Supreme Court of the United States, 1977.
429 U.S. 610, 97 S.Ct. 861, 51 L.Ed.2d 80.

MR. JUSTICE STEVENS delivered the opinion of the Court.

In exchange for respondent's promise to purchase prefabricated houses to be erected on land near Louisville, Ky., petitioners agreed to finance the cost of acquiring and developing the land. Difficulties arose while the development was in progress, and respondent ("Fortner") commenced this treble damage action, claiming that the transaction was a tying arrangement forbidden by the Sherman Act. Fortner alleged that competition for prefabricated houses (the tied product) was restrained by petitioners' abuse of power over credit (the tying product). A summary judgment in favor of petitioners was reversed by this Court. Fortner Enterprises v. U. S. Steel, 394 U.S. 495 (Fortner I). We held that the agreement affected a "not insubstantial" amount of commerce in the tied product and that Fortner was entitled to an opportunity to prove that petitioners possessed "appreciable economic power" in the market for the tying product. The question now presented is whether the record supports the conclusion that petitioners had such power in the credit market.[46]

---

46. [This and the following 6 footnotes are from the Court's opinion renumbered]. As explained at the outset of the opinion, *Fortner I* involved "a variety of questions concerning the proper standards to be applied by a United States district court in passing on a motion for summary judgment in a civil antitrust action." 394 U.S., at 496. Petitioners do not ask us to reexamine *Fortner I*, which left only the economic power question open on the issue of whether a *per se* violation could be proved. On the other hand, Fortner has not pursued the suggestion in *Fortner I* that it might be able to prove a § 1 violation under the rule of reason standard. 394 U.S., at 500. Thus, with respect to § 1, only the economic power issue is before us.

In *Fortner I*, the Court noted that Fortner also alleged a § 2 violation, namely, that petitioners "conspired together for the purpose of . . . acquiring a monopoly in the market for pre-

fabricated houses." 394 U.S., at 500. The District Court held that a § 2 violation had been proved. Although the Court of Appeals did not reach this issue, a remand is unnecessary. It is clear that neither the District Court's findings of fact nor the record supports the conclusion that § 2 was violated. The District Court found only that "the defendants did combine or conspire to *increase sales* of prefabricated house packages by United States Steel Corporation by the making of loans to numerous builders containing the tie-in provision" and that "the sole purpose of the loan programs of the Credit Corporation was specifically and deliberately to *increase the share of the market* of United States Steel Corporation in prefabricated house packages. . . ." App., at 1603 (emphasis added) But "increasing sales" and "increasing market share" are normal business goals, not forbidden by § 2 without other evidence of an intent to monopolize. The evidence in this case does not bridge the

The conclusion that a violation of § 1 of the Sherman Act had been proved was reached only after two trials. At the first trial following our remand, the District Court directed a verdict in favor of Fortner on the issue of liability, and submitted only the issue of damages to the jury. The jury assessed damages, before trebling, of $93,200. The Court of Appeals reversed the directed verdict and remanded for a new trial on liability. The parties then waived the jury; the trial judge heard additional evidence, and entered extensive findings of fact which were affirmed on appeal. Both courts held that the findings justified the conclusion that petitioners had sufficient economic power in the credit market to make the tying arrangement unlawful.

Before explaining why we disagree with the ultimate conclusion of the courts below, we first describe the tying arrangement and then summarize the findings on the economic power issue.

I

Only the essential features of the arrangement between the parties need be described. Fortner is a corporation which was activated by an experienced real estate developer for the purpose of buying and improving residential lots. One petitioner, United States Steel Corporation, operates a "Home Division" which manufactures and assembles components of prefabricated houses; the second petitioner, the "Credit Corporation," is a wholly owned subsidiary, which provides financing to customers of the Home Division in order to promote sales. Although their common ownership and control make it appropriate to regard the two as a single seller, they sell two separate products—credit and prefabricated houses. The credit extended to Fortner was not merely for the price of the homes. Petitioners agreed to lend Fortner over $2,000,000 in exchange for Fortner's promise to purchase the components of 210 homes for about $689,000. The additional borrowed funds were intended to cover Fortner's cost of acquiring and developing the vacant real estate, and the cost of erecting the houses.

The impact of the agreement on the market for the tied product (prefabricated houses) is not in dispute. On the one hand, there is no claim—nor could there be—that the Home Division had any dominance in the prefabricated housing business. The record indicates that it was only moderately successful, and that its sales represented a small fraction of the industry total.[47] On the other hand, we have

gap between the District Court's findings of intent to increase sales and its legal conclusion of conspiracy to monopolize. Moreover, petitioners did not have a large market share or dominant market position. . . . No inference of intent to monopolize can be drawn from the fact that a firm with a small market share has engaged in nonpredatory competitive conduct in the hope of increasing sales.

Yet as we conclude, . . . that is all the record in this case shows.

47. In 1960, for example, the Home Division sold a total of 1,793 houses for $6,747,353. There were at least four larger prefabricated home manufacturers, the largest of which sold 16,804 homes in that year. In the following year the Home Division's sales declined while the sales of each of its four princi-

already held that the dollar value of the sales to respondent was sufficient to meet the "not insubstantial" test described in earlier cases. See 394 U.S., at 501–502. We therefore confine our attention to the source of the tying arrangement—petitioners' "economic power" in the credit market.

II

The evidence supporting the conclusion that the Credit Corporation had appreciable economic power in the credit market relates to four propositions: (1) petitioners were owned by one of the Nation's largest corporations; (2) petitioners entered into tying arrangements with a significant number of customers in addition to Fortner; (3) the Home Division charged respondent a noncompetitive price for its prefabricated homes; and (4) the financing provided to Fortner was "unique," primarily because it covered 100% of Fortner's acquisition and development costs.

The Credit Corporation was established in 1954 to provide financing for customers of the Home Division. The United States Steel Corporation not only provided the equity capital, but also allowed the Credit Corporation to use its credit in order to borrow money from banks at the prime rate. Thus, although the Credit Corporation itself was not a particularly large company, it was supported by a corporate parent with great financial strength.

The Credit Corporation's loan policies were primarily intended to help the Home Division sell its products.[48] It extended credit only to customers of the Home Division, and over two-thirds of the Home Division customers obtained such financing. With few exceptions, all the loan agreements contained a tying clause comparable to the one challenged in this case. Petitioner's home sales in 1960 amounted to $6,747,353. Since over $4,600,000 of these sales were tied to financing provided by the Credit Corporation,[49] it is apparent that the tying arrangement was used with a number of customers in addition to Fortner.

The least expensive house package that Fortner purchased from the Home Division cost about $3,150. One witness testified that petitioner's price was $455 higher than the price of comparable components in a conventional home; another witness, to whom the District Court made no reference in its findings, testified that petitioners' price was $443 higher than a comparable prefabricated product. Whether the price differential was as great as 15% is not entirely

pal competitors remained steady or increased.

48. After reviewing extensive evidence taken from the files of the Credit Corporation, including a memorandum stating that "our only purpose in making the loan . . . is shipping houses," the District Court expressly found "that the Credit Corporation was not so much concerned with the risks involved in loans but whether they would help sell houses."

49. This figure is not stated in the District Court's findings; it is derived from the finding of total sales and the finding that 68% of the sales in 1960 were made to dealers receiving financial assistance from the Credit Corporation. See App., at 1589–1590.

clear, but the record does support the conclusion that the contract required Fortner to pay a noncompetitive price for petitioners' houses.

The finding that the credit extended to Fortner was unique was based on factors emphasized in the testimony of Fortner's expert witness, Dr. Masten, a professor with special knowledge of lending practices in the Kentucky area. Dr. Masten testified that mortgage loans equal to 100% of the acquisition and development cost of real estate were not otherwise available in the Kentucky area; that even though Fortner had a deficit of $16,000, its loan was not guaranteed by a shareholder, officer, or other person interested in its business; and that the interest rate of 6% represented a low rate under prevailing economic conditions. Moreover, he explained that the stable price levels at the time made the risk to the lender somewhat higher than would have been the case in a period of rising prices. Dr. Masten concluded that the terms granted to respondent by the Credit Corporation were so distinctly unique that it was almost inconceivable that the funds could have been acquired from any other source. It is a fair summary of his testimony, and of the District Court's findings, to say that the loan was unique because the lender accepted such a high risk and the borrower assumed such a low cost.

The District Court also found that banks and federally insured savings and loan associations generally were prohibited by law from making 100% land acquisition and development loans, and "that other conventional lenders would not have made such loans at the time in question since they were not prudent loans due to the risk involved." App., at 1596.

Accordingly, the District Court concluded "that all of the required elements of an illegal tie-in agreement did exist since the tie-in itself was present, a not insubstantial amount of interstate commerce in the tied product was restrained and the Credit Corporation did possess sufficient economic power or leverage to effect such restraint."

III

Without the finding that the financing provided to Fortner was "unique," it is clear that the District Court's findings would be insufficient to support the conclusion that the Credit Corporation possessed any significant economic power in the credit market.

Although the Credit Corporation is owned by one of the Nation's largest manufacturing corporations, there is nothing in the record to indicate that this enabled it to borrow funds on terms more favorable than those available to competing lenders, or that it was able to operate more efficiently than other lending institutions. In short, the affiliation between the petitioners does not appear to have given the Credit Corporation any cost advantage over its competitors in the credit market. Instead, the affiliation was significant only because the Credit Corporation provided a source of funds to customers of the

Home Division. That fact tells us nothing about the extent of petitioners' economic power in the credit market.

The same may be said about the fact that loans from the Credit Corporation were used to obtain house sales from Fortner and others. In some tying situations a disproportionately large volume of sales of the tied product resulting from only a few strategic sales of the tying product may reflect a form of economic "leverage" that is probative of power in the market for the tying product. If, as some economists have suggested, the purpose of a tie-in is often to facilitate price discrimination, such evidence would imply the existence of power that a free market would not tolerate. But in this case Fortner was only required to purchase houses for the number of lots for which it received financing. The tying product produced no commitment from Fortner to purchase varying quantities of the tied product over an extended period of time. This record, therefore, does not describe the kind of "leverage" found in some of the Court's prior decisions condemning tying arrangements.

The fact that Fortner—and presumably other Home Division customers as well—paid a noncompetitive price for houses also lends insufficient support to the judgment of the lower court. Proof that Fortner paid a higher price for the tied product is consistent with the possibility that the financing was unusually inexpensive and that the price for the entire package was equal to, or below, a competitive price. And this possibility is equally strong even though a number of Home Division customers made a package purchase of homes and financing.[50]

The most significant finding made by the District Court related to the unique character of the credit extended to Fortner. This finding is particularly important because the unique character of the tying product has provided critical support for the finding of illegality in prior cases. Thus, the statutory grant of a patent monopoly in International Salt Co. v. United States, 332 U.S. 392, the copyright monopolies in United States v. Paramount Pictures, Inc., 334 U.S. 131, and

---

50. Relying on Advance Business Systems and Supply Co. v. SCM Corp., 415 F.2d 55 (CA4 1969), cert. denied, 397 U.S. 920, Fortner contends that acceptance of the package by a significant number of customers is itself sufficient to prove the seller's economic power. But this approach depends on the absence of other explanations for the willingness of buyers to purchase the package. See id., at 68. In the *Northern Pacific* case, for instance, the Court explained that:

"The very existence of this host of tying arrangements is itself compelling evidence of the defendant's great power, at least where, as here, no other explanation has been offered for the existence of these restraints. The 'preferential routing' clauses conferred no benefit on the purchasers or lessees. While they got the land they wanted by yielding their freedom to deal with competing carriers, the defendant makes no claim that it came any cheaper than if the restrictive clauses had been omitted. In fact any such price reduction in return for rail shipments would have quite plainly constituted an unlawful rebate to the shipper. So far as the Railroad was concerned its purpose obviously was to fence out competitors, to stifle competition."

As this passage demonstrates, this case differs from *Northern Pacific* because use of the tie-in in this case can be explained as a form of price competition in the tied product, whereas that explanation was unavailable to the Northern Pacific Railroad.

United States v. Loew's Inc., 371 U.S. 38, and the extensive land hold-ings in Northern Pacific R. Co. v. United States, 356 U.S. 1, repre-sented tying products that the Court regarded as sufficiently unique to give rise to a presumption of economic power.

As the Court plainly stated in its prior opinion in this case, these decisions do not require that the defendant have a monopoly or even a dominant position throughout the market for a tying product. They do, however, focus attention on the question whether the seller has the power within the market for the tying product, to raise prices or to require purchasers to accept burdensome terms that could not be exacted in a completely competitive market. In short, the ques-tion is whether the seller has some advantage not shared by his com-petitors in the market for the tying product.

Without any such advantage differentiating his product from that of his competitors, the seller's product does not have the kind of uniqueness considered relevant in prior tying clause cases.[51] The Court made this point explicitly when it remanded this case for trial:

> "We do not mean to accept petitioner's apparent argument that market power can be inferred simply because the kind of fi-nancing terms offered by a lending company are 'unique and un-usual.' We do mean, however, that uniquely and unusually ad-vantageous terms can reflect a creditor's unique economic advantages over his competitors. 394 U.S., at 505.

An accompanying footnote explained that:

> "Uniqueness confers economic power only when other competi-tors are in some way prevented from offering the distinctive prod-uct themselves. Such barriers may be legal, as in the case of pat-ented and copyrighted products, e. g., *International Salt, Loew's,* or physical, as when the product is land, e.g., *Northern Pacific.* It is true that the barriers may also be economic, as when competi-tors are simply unable to produce the distinctive product profita-bly, but the uniqueness test in such situations is somewhat con-fusing since the real source of economic power is not the product itself but rather the seller's cost advantage in producing it." Id., at n. 2.

Quite clearly, if the evidence merely shows that credit terms are unique because the seller is willing to accept a lesser profit—or to incur greater risks—than its competitors, that kind of uniqueness will not give rise to any inference of economic power in the credit market. Yet this is, in substance, all that the record in this case indicates.

The unusual credit bargain offered to Fortner proves nothing more than a willingness to provide cheap financing in order to sell

51. One commentator on *Fortner I* noted:

"The Court's uniqueness test is ade-quate to identify a number of situa-tions in which this type of foreclosure is likely to occur. Whenever there are some buyers who find a seller's prod-uct uniquely attractive, and are there-fore willing to pay a premium above the price of its nearest substitute, the seller has the opportunity to impose a tie to some other good." The Logic of Foreclosure, 79 Yale L.J. 86, 93–94 (1969).

expensive houses.[52]   Without any evidence that the Credit Corporation had some cost advantage over its competitors—or could offer a
form of financing that was significantly differentiated from that
which other lenders could offer if they so elected—the unique character of its financing does not support the conclusion that petitioners
had the kind of economic power which Fortner had the burden of
proving in order to prevail in this litigation.

The judgment of the Court of Appeals is reversed.

MR. CHIEF JUSTICE BURGER, with whom MR. JUSTICE REHNQUIST
joins, concurring.

I concur in the Court's opinion and write only to emphasize what
the case before us does *not* involve; I join on the basis of my understanding of the scope of our holding.   Today's decision does not impli-
cate ordinary credit sales of only a single product and which therefore cannot constitute a tying arrangement subject to *per se* scrutiny
under § 1 of the Sherman Act.   In contrast to such transactions, we
are dealing here with a peculiar arrangement expressly found by the
Court in *Fortner I* to involve two separate products sold by two separate corporations.   394 U.S. 495, 507.   Consequently, I read the
Court's assumption that a tie-in existed in this case, required as it is
by the law of the case, to cast no doubt on the legality of credit financing by manufacturers or distributors.

NOTES AND QUERIES

(1) *The Goals of Antitrust Policy Impinged by Tying Arrangements.*
Commentators on tying arrangements reach different results on the legality
or illegality of particular tying arrangements depending upon whether they
emphasize the effect of the arrangement on buyer freedom of choice [53] or the
effect of a seller's use of tying upon competition generally in the tying and
tied product markets.[54]   Proponents of the former view end up advocating a
strict rule of *per se* illegality for tying, while advocates of the latter view
end up urging a "rule of reason" be applied in tying cases.

Queries.   What goals of antitrust policy did the majority in *Fortner I*
seek to implement in their analysis?   The dissent in *Fortner I*?   The Court
in *Fortner II*?   Should the antritrust laws protect the right of a single buyer
to be free from being required to buy a tied product in order to obtain a
tying product, in the absence of a necessary or legitimate business reason
for selling the two products together? [55]   Should any of the opinions in both

---

52.   The opinion of the Court in *Fortner I* notes that smaller companies might
not have the "financial strength to offer
credit comparable to that provided by
larger competitors under tying arrangements." 394 U.S., at 509.   Fortner's expert witness was unaware of the financing practices of competing sellers of
prefabricated homes, App., at 1691–1692,
but there is nothing to suggest that they
were unable to offer comparable financing if they chose to do so.

53.   See Bauer, supra note 24; Slawson, supra note 24.

54.   See Baker, supra note 24; Markovits, Tie-Ins and Reciprocity: A Functional, Legal and Policy Analysis, 58 Texas
L.Rev. 1363 (1980).

55.   See Ware v. Trailer Mart, Inc.,
623 F.2d 1150 (6th Cir. 1980) (upholding
right of consumer to challenge trailer
park requirement that lessees purchase
trailer they use in park from the park
owner); Bogus v. American Speech &
Hearing Association, 582 F.2d 277 (3d
Cir. 1978) (membership restriction invalid
tying restriction).

Fortners be labeled as a test of "qualitative substantiality" or a test of "quantitative substantiality"? [56]

(2)(A) *Involuntary Ties and Two Separate Products.* In *Times-Picayune Publishing Co. v. United States,* [57] the Times-Picayune was the leading newspaper of New Orleans, and the only morning paper. Its publisher also owned the States, one of the two evening papers. The publisher instituted a "unit plan" in the sale of advertising, under which advertisers could not buy space in one of its papers without inserting the same copy in the other. As a result, advertisers who might have preferred to use the independent evening paper, the Item, were compelled to use the States if they wished to have access to the Times-Picayne. The government sued to enjoin the unit plan as a violation of Sections 1 and 2 of the Sherman Act, Section 3 of the Clayton Act being unavailable because advertising is not a "commodity". The district court found that the Times-Picayune was "dominant" in view of the fact that it had almost half of the total newspaper circulation and 40% of the advertising. The court also found that this dominance had been used to effect illegal "tie-in" sales of advertising in the States. Held (5–4): (1) A 40% position in advertising does not establish "dominance" in view of the fact that equality among the three papers would reduce this only to 33%; dominance in readership is irrelevant, since the relevant market here is not sale of news but of advertising space. (2) The decisions on tying are inapplicable, since they involve the forced purchase of "a second distinct commodity", whereas here "the readership 'bought' by advertisers in the Times-Picayune was the self-same 'product' sold by the States and, for that matter, the Item." (3) Applying the rule of reason, the unit plan was lawful here, since there was no showing of specific intent to monopolize or to injure the Item otherwise than by normal competition.[58] The unit plan is commonly employed in selling advertising in papers that have morning and evening editions, to achieve operating and administrative economies.[59]

Times-Picayune, as well as *Fortner I,* have been criticized for their failure to articulate standards for determining whether there are two separate

56. As to the "qualitative"—"quantitative" distinction, see p. 683 supra.

57. 345 U.S. 594, 73 S.Ct. 872, 97 L.Ed. 1277 (1953).

58. But see Death of the New Orleans Item, Time Magazine, Aug. 4, 1958, p. 47:

   . . . Rising costs and lagging ad sales . . . forced Publisher David Stern III to sell the afternoon New Orleans *Item* (circ. 101,604) to the Times-Picayune Publishing Co., which owns both the morning *Times-Picayune* (circ. 189,758) and the afternoon *States* (circ. 101,916). Contributing to the 81-year-old *Item's* failure: the "unit" ad rate of the *Times-Picayune* and *States,* which forced national and classified advertisers to take space in both papers, or neither. The *Times-Picayune* announced that, just to keep competition alive, it would resell the *Item* to any bidder willing to match the $3,400,000 price within 60 days. But the *Item* was clearly marked for merger with the *States,* and New Orleans

was fated to join the ranks of the monopoly-ownership newspaper cities.

Tying is also common in the condominium business. Condominium purchasers are usually required to purchase long-term service or recreational contracts as part of the condominium package. For litigation of such a practice, see Chatham Condominium Associations v. Century Village, Inc., 597 F.2d 1002 (5th Cir. 1979).

59. For the subsequent history of events in the New Orleans newspaper market, see Barber Newspaper Monopoly in New Orleans: The Lessons for Antitrust Policy, 26 La.L.Rev. 503 (1964). Barber argued that the economics of the newspaper industry push almost inexorably to single paper dominance in a market and argued that the solution would be to permit newspapers to share printing plants. The Newspaper Preservation Act, supra p. 579 permits such arrangements for newspapers qualifying under the Act.

products for purposes of tying analyses.[60] Subsequent cases can find little objective guidance from these cases for identifying the existence of a tying arrangement.[61] Even worse, it has been argued, the Courts have permitted the question of one or two products to be used as a vehicle for analyzing something else: namely, defenses to a tie under the smokescreen of a metaphysical and confusing discussion of whether a particular sales arrangement should be considered the sale of a single product or the sale of a tied and tying product.[62]

Hirsh v. Martindale-Hubbell, Inc.[63] is an illustration of a confusing *ad hoc* factual judgment approach to the single product versus two product issue. Hirsh, an attorney, claimed that the defendant publisher of the leading directory of attorneys was imposing two different tying arrangements on attorneys seeking to advertise in the defendant's directory. The first alleged tie was a requirement that attorneys purchasing advertising (tying product) in the directory purchase a copy of the directory itself (tied product). The second alleged tie involved the two different types of attorney advertising accepted by Martindale-Hubbell. In addition to the regular listing of an attorney's name in the directory, one could purchase advertising called "information cards" listing the attorney's phone number, zip code, associates, areas of specialization, references and representative clients. In the biographical sections of the directory, listing only attorneys meeting certain minimal ethical and competency standards, advertising called "professional cards" could be purchased which is more expansive than that included in "informative card" advertising. Martindale-Hubbell required attorneys purchasing "professional card" advertising (tying product) to also purchase "informative card" advertising (tied product), as well as a copy of the directory. Both forms of advertising in the directory are considered essential to attorneys seeking the referral of legal business.

In finding neither of the two alleged tying arrangements constituted the sale of two separate products, a panel of the Ninth Circuit reasoned as follows:

> "There is, at the outset of every tie-in-case, . . . the problem of determining whether two separate products are in fact involved." . . . In determining whether an aggregation of items constitutes one or more products for antitrust purposes, we must look to the function of the aggregation. . . . This necessarily requires an inquiry into the nature of the relationship between the alleged tying product (the advertising) and the alleged tied product (the Directory). . . . In evaluating this relationship, we must consider whether the aggregation serves to facilitate competition by promoting product quality or whether it, in fact, amounts

---

60. See Bauer, supra note 24 at 306. Several scholars have proposed tests for determining whether the arrangement should be considered one or two products. See Austin, The Tying Arrangement: A Critique and Some New Thoughts, 1967 Wis.L.Rev. 88, 116–18; Ross, The Single Product Issue in Antitrust Tying: A Functional Approach, 23 Emory L.J. 963 (1974); Wheeler, Some Observations on Tie-Ins, The Single Product Defense, Exclusive Dealing and Regulated Industries, 60 Calif.L.Rev. 1557 (1972); Note, 31 Ohio St.L.J. 861 (1970); Note, 46 S.Cal.L.Rev. 160 (1972); Note, 85 Harv.L.Rev. 670 (1979).

61. Bauer suggests, as a "useful beginning" to the analysis, that: "Courts should look at the prevailing practices by which the product(s) is sold industry-wide; whether the products are sold in fixed or variable quantities; whether there is some cost savings or other efficiency in selling the product(s) together; the practical functions served by selling the items in a package; and the motive of the seller in choosing this method of distribution." Bauer, supra note 24 at 307.

62. Bauer, supra note 24 at 307.

63. 674 F.2d 1343 (9th Cir. 1982).

to no more than a naked effort to impede competition on the merits. Our examination of the relationship between the items at issue here leads us to conclude that the Directory and the advertising it contains constitute but a single product.

Martindale offers advertising attorneys a system of legal advertising. The effective operation of that system requires both the printing of information regarding advertising attorneys and the circulation of that information. Through its subscription requirement, Martindale, is able to supply both. To characterize the printing of the information and the circulation of that information as mere separable components of that system is to ignore the practical realities of advertising.

Generally, an attorney advertising in the Directory is seeking to obtain the referral of legal business through the dissemination of information regarding his legal qualifications. In order for this effort to succeed, the attorney's advertisement must reach those persons with legal work available for referral. Because other attorneys are frequently the most productive source of referrals, circulation of the Directory among them is particularly important. Through its subscription requirement, Martindale is able to offer prospective advertisers a guaranteed circulation among other advertising attorneys. Because circulation is one of the principal determinants of the value of specific advertising space, this guaranteed circulation greatly increases the desirability of advertising in the Directory and tends to spur sales of additional professional and informative card advertising. As more attorneys place advertisements in the Directory, the volume of information contained therein tends to expand. This increased information content renders the Directory itself a more effective tool for persons seeking to refer legal work to others and thereby tends to expand circulation of the Directory. This expanded circulation, in turn, renders advertising in the Directory more desirable by ensuring prospective advertisers a wider readership. From the foregoing, it is apparent that the aggregate sale of the Directory and the advertising it contains renders each more effective than if only sold separately. We believe this synergistic interrelationship between the Directory and the advertising precludes a finding that they are separate products. Here, the whole is truly greater than the sum of its parts; it is . . . a different product. *Broadcast Music, Inc. v. CBS*, 441 U.S. 1, 21–22, 99 S.Ct. 1551, 1563, 60 L.Ed.2d 1 (1978)." [64]

Queries. Do you agree? Is the buyer of advertising in the directory being required to purchase something he or she does not want? What effect on competing sellers of directories and/or lawyer advertising would you expect these arrangements have? Should the Court have evaluated the benefits and detriments of the alleged tying arrangements to buyers and competitors?

Courts confronted with a seemingly justifiable tying arrangement but a *per se* rule of illegality, sometimes take refuge in the ambiguities of the two product issue to avoid a harsh or unjustified result. For example, in *Dehy-*

64. 674 F.2d at 1347–48. For similar cases, see Foster v. Maryland State Savings & Loan Association, 590 F.2d 928 (D.C.Cir. 1978), certiorari denied 439 U.S. 1071, 99 S.Ct. 842, 59 L.Ed.2d 37 (1979) (lender required borrowers to use bank's lawyer for services associated with a loan; not a tie); Krehl v. Baskin-Robbins Ice Cream Co., 664 F.2d 1348 (9th Cir. 1982) (trademark license and ice cream sold to the franchisee by the franchisor under the license not two separate products).

drating Process Co. v. A. O. Smith Corp.,[65] defendant was exonerated of violating Section 3 by selling a storage silo and unloading device only in combination. Plaintiff was compelled to buy both although it needed only the unloader. There was uncontradicted evidence that defendant had adopted the "tying" policy only after seven years of experience selling the component separately, during which period they had a record of 50 percent complaints of malfunction where other producers' silos were employed. Aldrich J.:

> We may agree with the plaintiff that the compulsory joining of two "separate" articles is a per se violation of the act. This statement, however, solves nothing. Articles, though physically distinct, may be related through circumstances. The sound business interests of the seller or, phrasing it another way, a substantial hardship apart from the loss of the tie-in sale may be such a circumstance. It would not be thought, for example, that a one-legged man could insist on purchasing only a left shoe. Whatever may be meant by per se, we must first consider what may be fairly treated by a seller as inseparable.[66]

Query: Should the courts mitigate the rigor of a *per se* test for tying arrangments in cases like *Martindale-Hubbell* and *Dehydrating Process* by recognizing limited grounds for justification of the tying arrangement, rather than develop metaphysical tests for two separate products or for power in the tying product?

(B) *Voluntary Ties and Two Separate Products.* The sale of two articles together does not establish that one was used as a "tie" to push the sale of the other; the joint sales may have been for the mutual convenience of both seller and buyer. In *American Manufacturers Mutual Insurance Co. v. American Broadcasting-Paramount Pictures, Inc.,*[67] a television broadcasting network offered an advertiser a "package" of stations which would carry the advertiser's sponsored program. The advertiser expressed a desire for a less expensive package including only certain of the stations, but agreed to the original proposal after the network procrastinated in responding. Held: absent a showing that the advertiser seriously bargained for an untied contract, the evidence was insufficient to establish an illegal extension of economic power to new markets or a foreclosure of competitors: a "mere statement of bargaining terms" which the seller might not insist on or be able to insist on does not violate the antitrust laws. On the other hand, acceptance by a franchisee of a standard franchise contract with tying provisions that the franchisee could not reasonably expect to bargain away will not bar a subsequent antritrust suit for damages by the franchisee. *Perma Life Mufflers, Inc. v. International Parts Corp.*[68]

Coercion is seen as significant because if the buyer was free to purchase the tied product elsewhere but voluntarily purchased it from the seller, none of the evils of a tying arrangement would be present.[69] There are a large and growing number of cases seeking to draw the line between a voluntary and involuntary tie, a question of fact subject to the widely fluctuating opinions as to what factors demonstrate sufficient coercion to cross the line be-

65. 292 F.2d 653 (1st. Cir.), certiorari denied 368 U.S. 931, 82 S.Ct. 368, 7 L.Ed. 2d 194 (1961).

66. 292 F.2d at 655.

67. 446 F.2d 1131 (2d Cir. 1971), certiorari denied 404 U.S. 1063, 92 S.Ct. 737, 30 L.Ed.2d 752 (1972).

68. 392 U.S. 134, 88 S.Ct. 1981, 20 L.Ed.2d 982 (1968).

69. The cases are surveyed in Bauer, supra note 24, at 309–14; Austin, The Individual Coercion Doctrine in Tie-In Analysis: Confusing and Irrelevant, 65 Calif. L.Rev. 1143 (1977); Varner, Voluntary Ties and the Sherman Act, 50 So.Cal.L. Rev. 271 (1977).

tween a transaction of mutual convenience and one imposing a tying arrangement.[70]

The issue whether the joint sale was a "mutual convenience" transaction or a "tying arrangement" may also be critical in determining whether franchisees may collectively maintain a "class action." In such an action the "common" issues of law and fact must predominate. In *Ungar v. Dunkin' Donuts, Inc.*,[71] the Third Circuit held that the necessity of proving coercion as to each franchisee precluded the use of the class action procedure. The same Court reached the opposite result one year later in *Bogosian v. Gulf Oil Corp.*,[72] a significant class action case challenging the widespread practice of oil companies tying the purchase of gasoline from the lessor to the lease of a gasoline station to a franchisee dealer.[73]

(3) *Proving Sufficient Economic Power.*

(A) *Power in The Tying Product.* The requirement of proof of "sufficient economic power" over the tying product has been the source of additinal ambiguity and confusion. There is debate about what it means, how it can be shown, when it must be shown, and even whether it should be a requirement at all.[74] The general standards which have been employed by the courts in the past have been summarized by the Eighth Circuit in *Rosebrough Monument Co. v. Memorial Park Cemetery Association.*[75] In that case a manufacturer of burial markers and monuments successfully challenged a policy adopted by a trade association of St. Louis cemeteries requiring the preparation of the foundation for monuments or grave markers to be done exclusively by the cemetery that owns the lot.[76] In finding the practice a tying arrangement where there was "sufficient economic power" in the tying product to be *per se* unlawful, the court reasoned:

> Among the factors cited by the Supreme Court that are relevant to our inquiry whether appellees hold sufficient economic power are (1) the unique characteristics of the tying product or its desirability to consumers, (2) the noncompetitive nature of the price sought for the tied product, (3) the volume of sales of the tied product or service (foundation preparation), and (4) the size of the companies owning and operating the tying product (cemetery lots). As to these four elements, the record reflects that appellees possessed sufficient economic power to impose an appreciable restraint on free competition.

70. In Photovest Corp. v. Fotomat Corp., 606 F.2d 704 (7th Cir. 1979), certiorari denied 445 U.S. 917, 100 S.Ct. 1278, 63 L.Ed.2d 601 (1980), discussed supra p. 158, the defendant franchisor of kiosks providing film services was charged with fraudulently inducing franchisees to accept a tying arrangement. The Court held an "untruthful representation may constitute breach of contract or fraud" but it cannot supply the "missing link" of power in the tying product inducing the tie to create an illegal tying arrangement. 606 F.2d at 723.

71. 531 F.2d 1211 (3d Cir. 1976), certiorari denied 429 U.S. 823, 97 S.Ct. 74, 50 L.Ed.2d 84.

72. 561 F.2d 434 (3d Cir. 1977), certiorari denied 434 U.S. 1086, 98 S.Ct. 1280, 55 L.Ed.2d 791 (1978).

73. See generally Matheson, Class Action Tying Cases: A Framework for Certification Decisions, 76 Nw.U.L.Rev. 855 (1982).

74. See Slawson, supra note 24, Hyde v. Jefferson on Parish Hosp. Dist. No. 2, supra n. 35.

75. 666 F.2d 1130 (8th Cir. 1981), certiorari denied ___ U.S. ___, 102 S.Ct. 2915, 73 L.Ed.2d 1321 (1982).

76. For a similar case where cemetery lot buyers were required to purchase grave markers and monuments from the cemetery see, Moore v. Jas. H. Matthews & Co., 550 F.2d 1207 (9th Cir. 1977), remanded for recomputation of damages, 682 F.2d 830 (1982).

Monopoly power or dominance in the tying market need not be shown. Sufficient economic power exists if the supplier of the tying product has sufficient leverage in the market to increase prices or to force a significant number of buyers to accept burdensome terms.

It is unnecessary for appellant to prove by voluminous economic data that appellees have a strangle hold on the tying market. Where the sellers are of sufficient size to exert some power, control or dominance over the tying product, the threshold standard of economic power has been met.

Summarizing the case law in the area, we find that in order to answer the question of economic power we look to whether the characteristics of the tying product are unique. For example, the statutory grant of a patent monopoly in *International Salt Co.*, supra, 332 U.S. at 395–96, 68 S.Ct. at 14–15, the copyright monopolies in *United States v. Loew's, Inc.*, 371 U.S. 38, 49, 83 S.Ct. 97, 104, 9 L.Ed.2d 11 (1962), and the extensive land holding in *Northern Pacific*, supra, 356 U.S. at 8–12, 78 S.Ct. at 519–21, represented tying products that the Court regarded as sufficiently unique to give rise to a presumption of economic power.

Uniqueness alone, however, is not always sufficient to infer economic power. In *Fortner II*, while the evidence showed that the credit terms offered by Fortner were unique because of Fortner's willingness to accept a lesser profit, the Supreme Court held that the unique element did not give rise to an inference of economic power in the tied market.

Fortner II, however, is distinguishable from the case at bar. Appellants have shown the cemetery owners have an unique economic advantage which enables them to offer a package arrangement for the burial and supply and installation of the monuments that is significantly differentiated from that which the manufacturer of grave memorials can offer.

It can hardly be denied that cemeteries are distinct enterprises and have a unique public function. A cemetery lot, like any piece of real estate, is unique. Further, only a limited number of people have the enormous resources required to start their own cemetery. The capital cost of starting a cemetery is far greater than the cost of manufacturing monuments or markers. Also, zoning restrictions in St. Louis and its neighboring counties make the construction of a new cemetery almost prohibitive. The costs and regulations associated with opening a cemetery prevent appellant from offering the tying product in the unique manner that appellees offer it.

The Supreme Court in several cases has considered the volume of sales in determining whether a particular tying arrangement shows sufficient economic power to establish a violation of § 1 of the Sherman Act.

In *Standard Oil Co. v. United States*, 337 U.S. 293, 69 S.Ct. 1051, 93 L.Ed. 1371 (1949) (*Standard Oil of California*), the Supreme Court held that control of 6.7 percent of the retail gasoline market permitted an inference of substantial economic power. More recently, a 10 percent share of the market has been seen to be sufficient economic power to establish a *prima facie* case. *Cornwell Quality Tools Co. v. C.T.S. Co.*, 446 F.2d 825, 831 (9th Cir. 1971) (*Cornwell Tools*) (exclusive dealing contract with territorial restrictions), cert. denied, 404 U.S. 1049, 92 S.Ct. 715, 30 L.Ed.2d 740 (1972); . . .

The case before us falls within the quantitative analysis used in *Standard Oil of California,* . . . and *Cornwell Tools*. The tying products in the case at bar are the cemetery lots supplied by appellees. Appellees accounted for 22 percent of the burials performed in the market area in 1978, and the exclusive foundation preparation policy, upon which appellant bases its claim, is uniformly followed by nearly all of the cemeteries in St. Louis.

The minimum percentage of market dominance required to establish economic power has never been specified; nevertheless, in deciding this case we need not define in detail the line of demarcation between sufficient and insufficient economic power. It suffices to hold that appellees' level of economic power is sufficient to fall within the broad authority of the Sherman Act.[77]

Queries. What precisely is meant by "sufficient economic power"? Does the concept shift and change depending on whether the adverse impact on the competitive process is seen as foreclosure of the tied product market or coercion of buyers of the tying product to take a product they do not want? Did the Court in *Fortner II* limit the range of considerations to market foreclosure and ignore the impact of the arrangement upon buyers of the tying product?[78]

(B) *Proving Market Foreclosure—The Relevance of Relevant Market Analysis.* At least one court has read *Fortner II* as necessarily requiring "definition of the relevant market and identification of the competitors therein to determine whether there are exclusionary effects in the market for the tied product, and whether the seller has some advantage not shared by his competitors in the market for the tying product." [79]

Queries. Does *Fortner II* require proof of a relevant market for the tied and tying markets in order to prove the requisite anticompetitive effects? How *"per se"* is the rule if relevant market analysis is required?[80] If relevant market analysis is required, how does one measure power in the tying market and exclusionary effect in the tied market? How much power and

77. 666 F.2d at 1142–43.

78. For an argument tying *Fortner II* with *Sylvania* and claiming the Court has limited the range of considerations to market foreclosure, see Baker, The Supreme Court and the Per Se Tying Rule: Cutting the Gordian Knot, 66 Va.L.Rev. 1235 (1980).

79. In re Data General Corp. Antitrust Litigation, 529 F.Supp. 801, 809 (N.D.Cal.1981). In an earlier opinion the court held Data General tied the licensing of its computer software (tying product) to the purchase of its central processing units (tied product) and the only issue for trial was the sufficiency of Data General's power over the tying product and the effect of the tying in the tied and tying markets. In re Data General Corp. Antitrust Litigation, 490 F.Supp. 1089 (N.D.Cal.1980). In overturning the jury verdict in favor of the plaintiffs, the trial judge held there was insufficient evidence to support a finding that defendant had sufficient economic power in the system software market to injure competition in the markets for general purpose minicomputers or microprocessors or in the "submarket" for software compatible with defendant's central processing units. The Court did not analyze the effect on buyers forced to buy a product (defendant's computer) they did not want.

80. Cf. Flynn, Rethinking Sherman Act Section 1 Analysis: Three Proposals for Reducing the Chaos, 49 Antitrust L. J. 1593, 1617–18 (1982): "[O]nce the court saw the case was not within a rule of *per se* illegality, it concluded it was necessary to apply the rule of reason and no restraint is unreasonable unless it adversely effects or destroys competition in the entire market. For some reason, the court concluded that market analysis was an indispensable element of all rule of reason cases, rather than whether the restraint is justified by legitimate business purposes, and is no more restrictive than necessary—the traditional way of conceptualizing Section 1 rule of reason cases. The inquiry is the same as it is in *per se* cases; *viz.*, whether the competitive process has been unreasonably displaced by a contract, combination or conspiracy and not whether competition has been destroyed in the line of commerce involved."

exclusionary effect are necessary before the practice will be declared illegal? Does *Fortner II* provide any guidance?

(C) *The Relevance of Power and Exclusionary Effect to the Antitrust Goals Impinged by Tying Arrangements.* Some commentators have criticized the requirement of proof of "sufficient economic power" as a separate element in tying analysis. They see its origins as questionable and its emphasis in *Fortner II* as a means for the Court to circumvent the law of the case in *Fortner I*, finding the arrangement the sale of two separate products in the first instance.[81] Instead of sufficient economic power and adverse effects being separate elements of analysis, it is argued they should either be dropped from the analysis or, in some cases, be made part of the analysis of the question of whether there are two separate products.[82] Rather than ameliorate the *per se* standard by requiring proof of a relevant market and an adverse effect in that market, Professor Bauer argues: [83]

> [T]he *per se* rule respecting tying arrangements should be restated and even expanded.
>
> An analogy may be drawn to the rule of price fixing. Price fixing is unreasonable *per se*, even though this form of conduct may not always injure competition. That rule is justified because price fixing often injures competition; it never benefits competition; and it is simply not a worthwhile expenditure of judicial resources to separate out the injurious from the benign. Similarly, having shown that tie-ins often injure competition, why must one go further to show that they always injure competition, if the defenders of this conduct can come forward with only slight justifications for allowing the conduct to continue, other than the specific benefits which the rule argued for in this Article would recognize as defenses? On the other hand, if the rule argued for by the economists— requiring individual examination of the effects of each tie-in—were accepted, the sellers' hope of persuading the trier of fact of their benign intentions would lead to expansion of tying arrangements. . . .
>
> Once there is a finding that the conduct constitutes a tying arrangement, the next step is to determine whether it violates the antitrust laws. It has not been made sufficiently clear why this inquiry should be necessary at all. In part the inquiry arises from the assumption that unless the seller has some significant market power in the tying product market, it will be unable to enforce the tie and hence unable either to coerce the buyer or to foreclose its competitors in the tied product market. This Article suggests that coercion is inherent in any true tie-in; that the inquiry regarding the defendant's market power should therefore become part of the determination of the existence of the tie, rather than a part of the liability issue; and that any overestimate of this market power will be relatively unimportant, since condemning even noninjurious ties will have little if any adverse societal effects. . . .
>
> There has been a great deal of analysis, both in the cases and in the literature, devoted to different factual patterns and different approaches for demonstrating this market power. This Article argues that *Fortner*

---

81. See Bauer, supra note 24; Slawson, supra note 24. But see Baker, supra note 24, arguing that tying arrangements be assessed on a rule of reason basis.

82. A position adopted in Bell v. Cherokee Aviation Corp., 660 F.2d 1123, 1131 (6th Cir. 1981) and Bogosian v. Gulf Oil Corp., 561 F.2d 434, 449 (3d Cir. 1977), certiorari denied 434 U.S. 1086, 98 S.Ct. 1280, 55 L.Ed.2d 791 (1978).

83. Bauer, A Simplified Approach to Tying Arrangements: A Legal & Economic Analysis, 33 Vand.L.Rev. 283 (1980), quoting from 305, 317–18, 320–21 (footnotes omitted). Used by permission.

II and the trend it fostered represent an unhealthy and inappropriate deviation from prior treatment of tying arrangements. Until *Fortner II*, in each case in which the Court found a tying arrangement present, it also concluded that the conduct violated the antitrust laws. In *Fortner II*, however, the Court found that notwithstanding the existence of the tie-in, there was no injury to competition and therefore no violation. Although the Court had previously stated on several occasions that tying arrangements rarely have any procompetitive value, here it allowed U.S. Steel's practice to stand undisturbed. *Fortner II* is part of the Court's new "economic realism," under which conduct will not be condemned unless adverse economic effects are clear. Since one of the evils described in earlier cases—foreclosure of competitors—was not present here, the Court found the arrangement lawful. It reached this conclusion by finding that U.S. Steel did not have sufficient economic power in the credit (tying product) market.

This evaluation of the seller's market power is relevant to determine whether it has the ability to impose the tie. It is unclear, however, why it is critical that the seller's competitors might have offered the tying product but chose not to. There should be two key inquiries in the tying analysis: Were competitors (and competition) injured? Was the buyer coerced? Even if competitors were not foreclosed, the Court in *Fortner II* ignored another significant evil of tie-ins—that the buyer was forced to take products that it did not want, at least not from that seller. Clearly, U.S. Steel had enough power in the credit market to force Fortner to take its prefabricated homes. Given an admittedly express tie, and given that the buyer was forced to take goods it did not want, it should be unnecessary to evaluate the impact of this conduct on U. S. Steel's competitors.

Query: Do you agree with this line of analysis?

(D) *Further Queries*. Would *Fortner II* have been decided otherwise if the record had contained evidence that U.S. Steel, alone among sellers of prefabricated houses, could borrow money at the prime rate? What if three other "major" steel companies selling prefabs had the same advantage, but the rest of the industry, comprising dozens of smaller companies doing, in the aggregate, 60 percent of the business, had to pay higher rates of interest or simply could not refinance such deals with the banks? If a showing of unique advantage in the tying credit is necessary to condemn a tie, why are banks themselves flatly forbidden to tie sales to loans?[84] Why should a lending subsidiary of a giant conglomerate be treated differently, when the issue is not extension of credit on goods sold, but financing general operations in the context of which goods will be sold?[85]

(4) *A Not Insubstantial Amount of Commerce*. In *Fortner I*, the requirement was said to be satisfied by showing that "a total amount of business, substantial enough in terms of dollar volume so as not to be merely *de minimus*, is foreclosed to competition by the tie." There is general agreement that this requirement is a relatively non-controversial and straightforward application of the "quantitative substantiality" test.[86] Moreover, it was held in *Fortner I* that a treble damage plaintiff could rely upon the amount involved for all purchases subject to the tie and not just those

---

84. See Bank Holding Company Act, 12 U.S.C.A. § 1972.

85. See Costner v. Blount National Bank, 578 F.2d 1192 (6th Cir. 1978) (tying bank loan agreement for an auto dealership to a requirement that the dealership sell its commercial installment paper to the bank *per se* violation of Bank Holding Company Act; no need to prove economic power in the tying product market).

86. See Bauer, supra note 24 at 323.

purchases made by the plaintiff in order to establish a violation of the law. This suggests that the amount of commerce necessary to impugn a tie-in can be less than must be shown to invalidate an exclusive dealing arrangement. Can it ever be "de minimus" if it is enough to be worth suing about? Are we here concerned with merely a different way of expressing the *"per se"* character of the tying prohibition? See p. 683 supra, defining the difference between "quantitative" and "qualitative" substantiality.

(5) *Defenses or Justifications for a Tying Arrangement.* While it may appear anomalous to permit defenses or justifications for conduct which has been labeled *per se* unlawful, it is apparent that courts have been doing so implicitly and explicitly. Implicit recognition of a defense occurs when courts manipulate the issue of whether there is a tie or "power" in the tying product to avoid a result of illegality where the court believes there is a justification or defense for imposing a tying arrangement.[87] Several courts have avoided this confusing line of analyses by explicitly recognizing possible defenses to what would otherwise be an unlawful tying arrangement.[88]

At least four defenses or justifications have been acknowledged or recognized: (1) Goodwill Defense; (2) Business Justification Defense; (3) The New Entrant Justification; and (4) The Efficiencies Defense. Because of "the fact that any tie-in presumably promotes the business interest of the party imposing the restraint, the justifications deemed 'legitimate' are few and narrowly construed. . . . Even with respect to the few exceptions which have been accepted, an asserted justification will prevail only in the absence of less restrictive alternatives." [89]

The "goodwill defense", often arising in franchising arrangements, is a recognition of the necessity for insuring uniformity of quality in goods or services sold under a common brand or trademark.[90] Requiring the purchase of goods or services sold by the franchisee to be bought from the franchisor or designated sellers is a frequent practice in franchising. "Both the franchisor and the franchisee are concerned that all other franchisees offer goods or services of uniform quality; dissatisfaction by a customer with one franchisee may dissuade her from patronizing all other franchisees." [91] As suggested by the materials in subsection 3, infra p. 732, this defense is frequently limited by the availability of the less restrictive alternative of establishing quality specifications for goods or services sold by the

87. *Times Picayune, Fortner (I)* and *Fortner (II)* have been criticized on this basis. See Bauer, supra note 24 at 306. Several lower court opinions have followed a similar course. See E.g., Krehl v. Baskin-Robbins Ice Cream Co., 664 F.2d 1348 (9th Cir. 1982) (discussed infra p. 739; Principe v. McDonald's Corp., 631 F.2d 303 (4th Cir. 1980), certiorari denied 451 U.S. 970, 101 S.Ct. 2047, 68 L.Ed.2d 349 (1981) (see p. 744 infra); Hirsh v. Martindale-Hubbell, Inc., 674 F.2d 1343 (9th Cir. 1982) (discussed supra p. 720).

88. See, e.g., Siegel v. Chicken Delight, Inc., 448 F.2d 43 (9th Cir. 1971), certiorari denied 405 U.S. 955, 92 S.Ct. 1172, 31 L.Ed.2d 232 (1972) (reprinted p. 732 infra); United States v. Jerrold Electronics Corp., 187 F.Supp. 545 (E.D.Pa. 1960), affirmed per curiam, 365 U.S. 567, 81 S.Ct. 755, 5 L.Ed.2d 806 (1961). The cases are surveyed in Bauer, supra note 24 at 324–327.

89. In re Data General Corp. Antitrust Litigation, 490 F.Supp. 1089, 1120 (N.D.Cal.1980).

90. See Bauer, supra note 24, at 324; Hensley, Franchise Tying: Gauging the Economic Power of a Trademark, 15 U.C. Davis L.Rev. 405, 414–23 (1981). Early cases recognized the defense. See Federal Trade Commission v. Sinclair Refining Co., 261 U.S. 463, 43 S.Ct. 450, 67 L.Ed. 746 (1923); Pick Manufacturing Co. v. General Motors Corp., 80 F.2d 641 (7th Cir. 1935), affirmed per curiam, 299 U.S. 3, 57 S.Ct. 1, 81 L.Ed. 5 (1936). In view of the expanded use of a "less restrictive alternative" analysis, such cases are of doubtful validity today. See Bogosian v. Gulf Oil Corp., 561 F.2d 434 (3d Cir. 1977), certiorari denied 434 U.S. 1086, 98 S.Ct. 1280, 55 L.Ed.2d 791 (1978).

91. Bauer, supra note 24, at 314.

franchisee without forcing the purchase of them from or through the franchisor. It has, on occasion, prevailed, where the trademarks and goods sold under the mark are so closely related that there are no sources for the goods other than the franchisor.[92]

The "business justification" defense asserts that the proper functioning of the tying product requires the use of the tied product.[93] The defense was asserted in the *International Salt* case,[94] where it was claimed that use of inferior salt would cause the patented salt injection machine to malfunction—a problem users would blame on the machine. While the court rejected the defense on a less restrictive alternative basis (no claim or proof of the machine "is allergic" to salt produced by others), the defense has been recognized in a limited number of cases. The leading case remains *Dehydrating Process Co. v. A. O. Smith Corp.*, the case of the defective silo discussed supra p. 722, where the court observed in upholding the tying arrangement in light of malfunctions in the loading equipment: "The antitrust laws do not require a business to cut its own throat." [95]

The "new entrant defense" has been suggested as a possible justification for tying in circumstances where the arrangement appears necessary for a firm to enter and stake out a share of a new market.[96] The leading case suggesting the defense and the significant limitations upon it is *United States v. Jerrold Electronics Corp.* [97] Jerrold pioneered in CATV systems, using a merchandising plan that offered all components and a servicing contract as a single unit. The court found this arrangement reasonable in its inception in view of the fact that a "wave of system failures at the start would have greatly retarded, if not destroyed, this new industry", but also found that the need for tying in the service contract with sale of components disappeared eventually, at different times in different sections of the country:

> . . . Jerrold has the burden on this point. Since it is not necessary for purposes of granting the relief requested to find more than that at sometime during its use, Jerrold's tie-in of services to equipment became unreasonable, this court makes no finding as to when this occurred. It is content to say that, while Jerrold has satisfied this court that its policy was reasonable at its inception, it has failed to satisfy us that it remained reasonable throughout the period of its use, even allowing it a reasonable time to recognize and adjust its policies to changing conditions. Accordingly, the court concludes that the defendants' refusal to sell Jerold equipment except in conjunction with a service contract violated § 1 of the Sherman Act during part of the time this policy was in effect.[98]

While this defense is often mentioned, it is rarely asserted or recognized.

92. See Krehl v. Baskin-Robbins Ice Cream Co., supra note 31. Other justifications for imposing tying arrangements in the context of franchising, premised primarily on neo-classical economic theorizing, are elaborately discussed in Note, A New Approach to the Legality of Franchising Tie-Ins, 129 U.Pa.L.Rev. 1267 (1981).

93. See Bauer, supra note 67 at 325–26; Notes: 49 Calif.L.Rev. 746 (1961); 62 Mich.L.Rev. 1413 (1964); 17 West Res.L.Rev. 257 (1965).

94. International Salt v. United States, 332 U.S. 392, 68 S.Ct. 12, 92 L.Ed. 20 (1947). A similar defense was assert-

ed and rejected in International Business Machines Corp. v. United States, 298 U.S. 131, 56 S.Ct. 701, 80 L.Ed. 1085 (1936).

95. 292 F.2d at 657.

96. Bauer, supra note 24, at 326; Notes: 18 Stan.L.Rev. 457 (1960); 70 Yale L.J. 804 (1961).

97. 187 F.Supp. 545 (E.D.Pa.1960), affirmed per curiam, 365 U.S. 567, 81 S.Ct. 755, 5 L.Ed.2d 806 (1961).

98. 187 F.Supp. at 558. Cf. United States v. Eastman Kodak Co., 1954 Trade Cases ¶ 67,920 (W.D.N.Y.1954) (consent decree requiring separation of charge for color film and processing). See an-

The "efficiencies" or "economies" defense proceeds from the notion that it is cheaper or more efficient for some reason to produce and sell two separate products as a package rather than sell them separately.[99] For example, a new automobile may be sold to a customer as a package with independently produced tailpipe, tires and windshield wipers attached to the automobile. At some point, the adding on of additional items may stray beyond the boundaries of a legitimate packaging of components because it is efficient to do so and become a tying arrangement forcing the buyer to take unwanted items like air conditioning or an expensive car stereo system.[1] Drawing that line depends very much upon the facts of a particular case, and the line remains both obscure and poorly defined. Implicit recognition of the defense however may be found in *Times-Picayune Publishing Co. v. United States*, discussed supra p. 719, where the Court upheld the newspaper's requirement that buyers of general display and classified advertising could only purchase insertions appearing in both morning and evening editions of the newspaper. The Court upheld the practice, in part, because "uncontradicted testimony suggests that unit insertions of classified ads substantially reduce the publisher's overhead costs."[2] The opinion has been criticized because the practice contributed to the demise of *Times-Picayune's* only competition in New Orleans[3] and, it has been suggested, a savings to the seller not passed along to buyers should not be allowed to justify an otherwise unnecessary tying arrangement.[4]

Other defenses or justifications for tying arrangements, particularly in the rapidly evolving area of franchising discussed *infra*,[5] might be expected to be asserted or recognized in future litigation.[6] Both the justification and scope of any such defenses will depend directly upon what assumptions are made about the evils tying poses to the public interest. Is the prohibition designed to protect competition in the tying and tied markets only, or is it also designed to protect or maximize the freedom of buyers to purchase one product or service without being required to purchase a product or service they do not want?

(6) *Constructing a Rational Framework for Analyzing Tying Arrangements.* The general analytical confusion and conceptual ambiguity associated with the antitrust analysis of tying arrangements have caused several scholars to propose reform of the standards adopted heretofore.[7] Part

nouncement by International Business Machines Corp. on June 23, 1969, of the "unbundling" of charges for computer hardware and for "software" service. Wall St.J., June 24, 1969, p. 38.

99. Bauer, supra note 24.

1. Cf. Calnetics Corp. v. Volkswagen of America, Inc., 532 F.2d 674 (9th Cir.), certiorari denied 429 U.S. 940, 97 S.Ct. 355, 50 L.Ed.2d 309 (1976); Automatic Radio Manufacturing Co. v. Ford Motor Co., 242 F.Supp. 852 (D.Mass.1965).

2. 345 U.S. at 623, 73 S.Ct. at 888, 97 L.Ed., at 1298.

3. See Barber, Newspaper Monopoly in New Orleans: The Lessons for Antitrust Policy, 24 La.L.Rev. 503 (1964).

4. Bauer, supra note 24 at 327.

5. See Markovits, Tie-Ins and Reciprocity: A Functional, Legal and Policy

Analysis, 58 Texas L.Rev. 1363 (1980); Note, A New Approach to the Legality of Franchising Tie-Ins, 129 U.Pa.L.Rev. 1267 (1981).

6. See, e.g., Rosebrough Monument Co. v. Memorial Park Cemetery Association, supra note 75 (statutory obligation to provide perpetual care justifies tie; rejected); Hirsch v. Martindale-Hubbell, Inc., supra note 63 ("synergistic" effect of tying advertising to purchase of lawyer directory is a case of the whole being greater than the sum of its parts); Siegel v. Chicken Delight, Inc., infra p. 732 (tie used to measure and collect revenue, rejected; tie necessary to prevent disclosure of trade secrets, rejected).

7. See Baker, supra note 24; Bauer, supra note 24; Markovits, supra note 24; Slawson, supra note 24.

of the confusion over tying arrangements is traceable to shifting and changing views about the values and goals of antitrust policy said to be impinged by such practices. A further source of the confusion and ambiguity may be attributable to the *per se* character of the offense, where the *per se* concept is misunderstood and treated as an inflexible rule not admitting of mitigation, justification or excuse once conduct is identified as within the category of *per se* illegality.[8] Courts seeking to avoid the otherwise inflexible rule of *per se* illegality can only do so by artificially manipulating one or more elements defining the offense so that the conduct no longer fits the category of "tying arrangement".

One proposed reform [9] suggests that tying arrangements be deemed presumptively unlawful and that the issue of whether there is a tying arrangement is the crucial question to the creation of the presumption of illegality. In determining the question of whether there is a tying arrangement, express tying arrangements should be presumed unlawful subject only to the defenses outlined in Note 5, supra. Implied tying should also be presumptively unlawful, subject to the same defenses. In determining whether to infer a pattern of conduct should be designated a tying arrangement, the power of the seller and the use made of that power can be a relevant consideration to distinguish a transaction of mutual convenience from tying. Otherwise, "power" in the tying product should not be considered in light of the presumption that tying arrangements serve hardly any purpose beyond the suppression of competition and the salutary effects of having clear-cut and predictable rules for the benefit of those subject to the law and those administering it.

Query: Do you agree with this proposal? Does it take adequate account of all the possible reasons for employing tying arrangements outlined by Professor Scherer, supra p. 699. Does the proposal elevate the value of protecting buyer freedom of choice above the value of potential benefits to competition generally?

(7) *Problem.* The Buffalo Bills, a professional football team with a monopoly of live professional football contests in Buffalo, New York, began requiring season ticket holders to purchase tickets for three pre-season exhibition games as a condition of obtaining season's tickets. Holders of season's tickets obtain advantages over purchasers of individual game tickets in seat selection, first call on post-season playoff tickets, and preferential seat selection for the following season's games. Your clients, Mr. and Mrs. Smith, season ticket holders, object to this practice, claiming it is a tying arrangement forcing them "to buy three tickets at $10 each for lousy preseason games" in order to buy season tickets for regular games. Twenty thousand other season ticket holders are subject to the same requirements. The Smiths wish to know whether they can sue the Buffalo Bills for this practice. What advice would you give them?[10]

8. For an analysis of the *per se* concept as a tool of analysis establishing evidentiary presumptions of varying levels of rebutability see Flynn, Rethinking Sherman Act Section 1 Analysis: Three Proposals for Reducing the Chaos, 49 Antitrust L.J. 1593 (1982).

9. Bauer, supra note 24, at 328.

10. See, Coniglio v. Highwood Services, Inc., 495 F.2d 1286 (2d Cir.), certiorari denied 419 U.S. 1022, 95 S.Ct. 498, 42 L.Ed.2d 296 (1974) (upholding dismissal of complaint on grounds of no injury to competitor because monopolist has no competition; injury to buyers dismissed as a "causal determinant of the proscribed restraint on competition in the tied market"). *Accord*, Driskill v. Dallas Cowboys Football Club, Inc., 498 F.2d 321 (5th Cir. 1974). See generally Austin, The Legality of Ticket Tie-ins In Intercollegiate Athletics, 15 U.Rich.L.Rev. 1 (1980).

3. TYING, TRADEMARKS, AND FRANCHISING

SIEGEL v. CHICKEN DELIGHT, INC.

United States Court of Appeals for the Ninth Circuit, 1971.
448 F.2d 43, certiorari denied 405 U.S. 955, 92 S.Ct. 1172, 1173,
31 L.Ed.2d 232 (1972).

MERRILL, CIRCUIT JUDGE: This antitrust suit is a class action in which certain franchisees of Chicken Delight seek treble damages for injuries allegedly resulting from illegal restraints imposed by Chicken Delight's standard form franchise agreements. The restraints in question are Chicken Delight's contractual requirements that franchisees purchase certain essential cooking equipment, dry-mix food items, and trade-mark bearing packaging exclusively from Chicken Delight as a condition of obtaining a Chicken Delight trade-mark license. These requirements are asserted to constitute a tying arrangement, unlawful per se under § 1 of the Sherman Act.

After five weeks of trial to a jury in the District Court, plaintiffs moved for a directed verdict, requesting the court to rule upon four propositions of law: (1) That the contractual requirements constituted a tying arrangement as a matter of law; (2) that the alleged tying products—the Chicken Delight name, symbols, and system of operation—possessed sufficient economic power to condemn the tying arrangement as a matter of law; (3) that the tying arrangement had not, as a matter of law, been justified; and (4) that, as a matter of law, plaintiffs as a class had been injured by the arrangement.

The court ruled in favor of plaintiffs on all issues except part of the justification defense, which it submitted to the jury. On the questions submitted to it, the jury rendered special verdicts in favor of plaintiffs. Chicken Delight has taken this interlocutory appeal from the trial court rulings and verdicts.

I. FACTUAL BACKGROUND

Over its eighteen years existence, Chicken Delight has licensed several hundred franchisees to operate home delivery and pick-up food stores. It charged its franchisees no franchise fees or royalties. Instead, in exchange for the license granting the franchisees the right to assume its identity and adopt its business methods and to prepare and market certain food products under its trademark, Chicken Delight required its franchisees to purchase a specified number of cookers and fryers and to purchase certain packaging supplies and mixes exclusively from Chicken Delight.[11] The prices fixed for these

---

11. [This and the following 5 footnotes are from the Court's opinion, renumbered]. From the organization's beginning in 1952 until 1959, the franchisees were required to purchase, in addition to the cookers and fryers, the batter mix and two types of packaging. Additional packaging items were added in 1959 and in 1961; and in 1963, the beginning of the period in question in this suit, barbecue rib seasoning mix which had previously been specified to and made by the franchisees became a required item. More packaging items were added in 1963 and 1964.

purchases were higher than, and included a percentage markup which exceeded that of, comparable products sold by competing suppliers.

II. THE EXISTENCE OF AN UNLAWFUL TYING ARRANGEMENT

In order to establish that there exists an unlawful tying arrangement plaintiffs must demonstrate *First*, that the scheme in question involves two distinct items and provides that one (the tying product) may not be obtained unless the other (the tied product) is also purchased. *Second*, that the tying product possesses sufficient economic power appreciably to restrain competition in the tied product market. *Third*, that a "not insubstantial" amount of commerce is affected by the arrangement. Chicken Delight concedes that the third requirement has been satisfied. It disputes the existence of the first two. Further it asserts that, even if plaintiffs should prevail with respect to the first two requirements, there is a *fourth* issue: whether there exists a special justification for the particular tying arrangement in question. United States v. Jerrold Electronics Corp., 187 F.Supp. 545 (E.D.Pa.1960), aff'd per curiam, 365 U.S. 567, 81 S.Ct. 755, 5 L.Ed.2d 806 (1961).

A. Two Products

The District Court ruled that the license to use the Chicken Delight name, trade-mark, and method of operations was "a tying item in the traditional sense," the tied items being the cookers and fryers, packaging products, and mixes.

The court's decision to regard the trade-mark or franchise license as a distinct tying item is not without precedent. In Susser v. Carvel Corp., 332 F.2d 505 (2d Cir. 1964), all three judges regarded as a tying product the trade-mark license to ice cream outlet franchisees, who were required to purchase ice cream, toppings and other supplies from the franchisor. Nevertheless, Chicken Delight argues that the District Court's conclusion conflicts with the purposes behind the strict rules governing the use of tying arrangements.

The hallmark of a tie-in is that it denies competitors free access to the tied product market, not because the party imposing the arrangement has a superior product in that market, but because of the power or leverage exerted by the tying product. Rules governing tying arrangements are designed to strike, not at the mere coupling of physically separable objects, but rather at the use of a dominant desired product to compel the purchase of a second, distinct commodity. In effect, the forced purchase of the second, tied product is a price exacted for the purchase of the dominant, tying product. By shutting competitors out of the tied product market, tying arrangements serve hardly any purpose other than the suppression of competition.

Chicken Delight urges us to hold that its trade-mark and franchise licenses are not items separate and distinct from the packaging, mixes, and equipment, which it says are essential components of the franchise system.[12] To treat the combined sale of all these items as a tie-in for antitrust purposes, Chicken Delight maintains, would be like applying the antitrust rules to the sale of a car with its tires or a left shoe with the right. Therefore, concludes Chicken Delight, the lawfulness of the arrangement should not be measured by the rules governing tie-ins. We disagree.

In determining whether an aggregation of separable items should be regarded as one or more items for tie-in purposes in the normal cases of sales of products the courts must look to the function of the aggregation. Consideration is given to such questions as whether the amalgamation of products resulted in cost savings apart from those reductions in sales expenses and the like normally attendant upon any tie-in, and whether the items are normally sold or used as a unit with fixed proportions.[13]

Where one of the products sold as part of an aggregation is a trade-mark or franchise license, new questions are injected. In determining whether the license and the remaining ("tied") items in the aggregation are to be regarded as distinct items which can be traded in distinct markets, consideration must be given to the function of trade-marks.

The historical conception of a trade-mark as a strict emblem of source of the product to which it attaches has largely been abandoned. The burgeoning business of franchising has made trade-mark licensing a widespread commercial practice and has resulted in the development of a new rationale for trade-marks as representations of product quality. This is particularly true in the case of a franchise system set up not to distribute the trade-marked goods of the franchisor, but, as here, to conduct a certain business under a common trade-mark or trade name. Under such a type of franchise, the

12. Appellant, in urging us not to distinguish between the trade-mark and the product it represents, relies in part upon Supreme Court language to the effect that there is no property in a trade-mark except as a right appurtenant to an established business in connection with which the mark is employed. United Drug Co. v. Theodore Rectanus Co., 248 U.S. 90, 97, 39 S.Ct. 48, 63 L.Ed. 141 (1918). But the Court did not mean that a mark and the product or business which it identifies are one and the same; it meant simply that, unlike a copyright or a patent, a trade-mark does not confer upon its owner the right to prohibit a competitor's use of the mark unless the owner himself uses the mark in connection with an existing business.

13. It should be readily apparent that, measured against these tests, the package sales here in question are quite different from the sale of an automobile and its tires or a left shoe and the right. In particular, there are several factors in this case which other courts have deemed sufficient to find a tie-in. Undisputed testimony at trial established that other franchisors in fast food businesses similar to that of Chicken Delight sold their licenses separate from the essential supplies. The various supplies sold here were sold individually and in differing amounts, rather than in a preassembled package, and the franchisees were billed accordingly. At no time were the franchisees required to purchase all their various supplies from Chicken Delight. Chicken Delight did not itself manufacture the tied items. See Associated Press v. Taft-Ingalls Corp., 340 F.2d 753, 764 (6th Cir. 1965); United States v. Jerrold Electronics Corp., supra, 187 F.Supp. at 559.

trade-mark simply reflects the goodwill and quality standards of the enterprise which it identifies. As long as the system of operation of the franchisees lives up to those quality standards and remains as represented by the mark so that the public is not misled, neither the protection afforded the trade-mark by law nor the value of the trade-mark to the licensee depends upon the source of the components.

This being so, it is apparent that the goodwill of the Chicken Delight trade-mark does not attach to the multitude of separate articles used in the operation of the licensed system or in the production of its end product. It is not what is used, but how it is used and what results that have given the system and its end product their entitlement to trade-mark protection. It is to the system and the end product that the public looks with the confidence that established goodwill has created.

Thus, sale of a franchise license, with the attendant rights to operate a business in the prescribed manner and to benefit from the goodwill of the trade name, in no way requires the forced sale by the franchisor of some or all of the component articles. Just as the quality of a copyrighted creation cannot by a tie-in be appropriated by a creation to which the copyright does not relate, United States v. Paramount Pictures, Inc., 334 U.S. 131, 158, 68 S.Ct. 915, 92 L.Ed. 1260 (1948), so here attempts by tie-in to extend the trade-mark protection to common articles (which the public does not and has no reason to connect with the trade-mark) simply because they are said to be essential to production of that which is the subject of the trademark, cannot escape antitrust scrutiny.

Chicken Delight's assertions that only a few essential items were involved in the arrangement does not give us cause to reach a different conclusion. The relevant question is not whether the items are essential to the franchise, but whether it is essential to the franchise that the items be purchased from Chicken Delight. This raises not the issue of whether there is a tie-in but rather the issue of whether the tie-in is justifiable, a subject to be discussed below.

We conclude that the District Court was not in error in ruling as matter of law that the arrangement involved distinct tying and tied products.

B. *Economic Power*

Under the per se theory of illegality, plaintiffs are required to establish not only the existence of a tying arrangement but also that the tying product possesses sufficient economic power to appreciably restrain free competition in the tied product markets.

Chicken Delight points out that while it was an early pioneer in the fast food franchising field, the record establishes that there has recently been a dramatic expansion in this area, with the advent of numerous firms, including many chicken franchising systems, all competing vigorously with each other. Under the circumstances, it contends that the existence of the requisite market dominance remained a jury question.

The District Court ruled, however, that Chicken Delight's unique registered trade-mark, in combination with its demonstrated power to impose a tie-in, established as matter of law the existence of sufficient market power to bring the case within the Sherman Act.

We agree. In Fortner Enterprises, Inc. v. United States Steel Corp., [Fortner I] 394 U.S. 495, 502–503, 89 S.Ct. 1252, 1258, 22 L.Ed.2d 495 (1969), it is stated:

> "The standard of 'sufficient economic power' does not, as the District Court held, require that the defendant have a monopoly or even a dominant position throughout the market for the tying product. Our tie-in cases have made unmistakably clear that the economic power over the tying product can be sufficient even though the power falls far short of dominance and even though the power exists only with respect to some of the buyers in the market."

Later, at page 504, 89 S.Ct. at page 1259, it is stated:

> "Accordingly, the proper focus of concern is whether the seller has the power to raise prices, or impose other burdensome terms such as a tie-in, with respect to any appreciable number of buyers within the market."

In United States v. Loew's, Inc., 371 U.S. 38, 45, 83 S.Ct. 97, 102, 9 L.Ed.2d 11 (1962), it is stated:

> "Even absent a showing of market dominance, the crucial economic power may be inferred from the tying product's desirability to consumers or from uniqueness in its attributes."

It can hardly be denied that the Chicken Delight trade-mark is distinctive; that it possesses goodwill and public acceptance unique to it and not enjoyed by other fast food chains.

It is now clear that sufficient economic power is to be presumed where the tying product is patented or copyrighted. . . .

Just as the patent or copyright forecloses competitors from offering the distinctive product on the market, so the registered trade-mark presents a legal barrier against competition. It is not the nature of the public interest that has caused the legal barrier to be erected that is the basis for the presumption, but the fact that such a barrier does exist. Accordingly we see no reason why the presumption that exists in the case of the patent and copyright does not equally apply to the trade-mark.[14]

---

14. Our conclusion conflicts with that of the majority of the *Susser* case, supra, 332 F.2d at 518–521, which, after a careful review of the facts in that case, held that sufficient economic power had not been demonstrated. But the *Susser* court understood the economic power test to require a showing of "market dominance." We think that interpretation has since been rejected by the Supreme Court in Fortner Enterprises, Inc. v. United States Steel Corp., supra. [Fortner I]

Thus we conclude that the District Court did not err in ruling as matter of law that the tying product—the license to use the Chicken Delight trade-mark—possessed sufficient market power to bring the case within the Sherman Act.

C. *Justification*

Chicken Delight maintains that, even if its contractual arrangements are held to constitute a tying arrangement, it was not an unreasonable restraint under the Sherman Act. Three different bases for justification are urged.

First, Chicken Delight contends that the arrangement was a reasonable device for measuring and collecting revenue. There is no authority for justifying a tying arrangement on this ground. Unquestionably, there exist feasible alternative methods of compensation for the franchise licenses, including royalties based on sales volume or fees computed per unit of time, which would neither involve tie-ins nor have undesirable anticompetitive consequences.[15]

Second, Chicken Delight advances as justification the fact that when it first entered the fast food field in 1952 it was a new business and was then entitled to the protection afforded by United States v. Jerrold Electronics Corp., supra, 187 F.Supp. 545. As to the period here involved—1963 to 1970—it contends that transition to a different arrangement would be difficult if not economically impossible.

We find no merit in this contention. Whatever claim Chicken Delight might have had to a new business defense in 1952—a question we need not decide—the defense cannot apply to the 1963–70 period. To accept Chicken Delight's argument would convert the new business justification into a perpetual license to operate in restraint of trade.

The third justification Chicken Delight offers is the "marketing identity" purpose, the franchisor's preservation of the distinctiveness, uniformity and quality of its product.

In the case of a trade-mark this purpose cannot be lightly dismissed. Not only protection of the franchisor's goodwill is involved. The licensor owes an affirmative duty to the public to assure that in the hands of his licensee the trade-mark continues to represent that which it purports to represent. For a licensor, through relaxation of quality control, to permit inferior products to be presented to the public under his licensed mark might well constitute a misuse of the mark. 15 U.S.C. §§ 1055, 1127; See Note, "Quality Control and the Antitrust Laws in Trade-mark Licensing," [72 Yale L.J. 1171 (1963)].

However, to recognize that such a duty exists is not to say that every means of meeting it is justified. Restraint of trade can be justified only in the absence of less restrictive alternatives. In cases

---

15. It bears noting that Chicken Delight's competitors in the fast food franchising business did not find it necessary to use tie-ins.

such as this, where the alternative of specification is available,[16] the language used in Standard Oil Co. v. United States, supra, 337 U.S. at 306, 69 S.Ct. at 1058, 93 L.Ed. 1371, in our view states the proper test, applicable in the case of trade-marks as well as in other cases:

> ". . . the protection of the good will of the manufacturer of the tying device—fails in the usual situation because specification of the type and quality of the product to be used in connection with the tying device is protection enough. . . . The only situation, indeed, in which the protection of good will may necessitate the use of tying clauses is where specifications for a substitute would be so detailed that they could not practicably be supplied."

The District Court found factual issues to exist as to whether effective quality control could be achieved by specification in the case of the cooking machinery and the dip and spice mixes. These questions were given to the jury under instructions; and the jury, in response to special interrogatories, found against Chicken Delight.

As to the paper packaging, the court ruled as matter of law that no justification existed. It stated, 311 F.Supp. at page 851:

> "Defendants' showing on paper packaging is nothing more than a recitation of the need for distinctive packaging to be used uniformly by all franchisees in identifying the hot foods. This was not contested. However, the admissions in evidence clearly demonstrate that the tied packaging was easily specifiable. In fact the only specifications required were printing and color. Moreover, defendants have admitted that any competent manufacturer of like products could consistently and satisfactorily manufacture the packaging products if defendants furnished specifications. Those suppliers could have sold to the franchisees through normal channels of distribution."

We agree. One cannot immunize a tie-in from the antitrust laws by simply stamping a trade-mark symbol on the tied product—at least where the tied product is not itself the product represented by the mark.

We conclude that the District Court was not in error in holding as matter of law (and upon the limited jury verdict) that Chicken Delight's contractual requirements constituted a tying arrangement in violation of § 1 of the Sherman Act. Upon this aspect of the case, judgment is affirmed.

· · ·

Upon the issue of damages, judgment is reversed and the case remanded for limited new trial.

NOTES AND QUERIES

(1) *Trademark as the Tying Product.* Until recently, the *Chicken Delight* treatment of trademarks as a separate tying product in franchise li-

---

16. There may, of course, be cases where some extraordinary condition forecloses specification, e.g., where it would divulge a trade secret.

censing situations was widely followed.[17] The wisdom of treating a trade-
mark as a separate product in franchising generally and the analytical
methodology followed in *Chicken Delight* were called into question, however, in *Krehl v. Baskin-Robbins Ice Cream Co.*[18] The plaintiff franchisees of
Baskin-Robbins claimed the defendant's policy of conditioning the grant of a
Baskin-Robbins franchise upon the purchase of ice cream exclusively from
Baskin-Robbins constituted an unlawful tying arrangement. The Court of
Appeals defined the issue as "whether the Baskin-Robbins trademark may
be properly treated as an item separate from the ice cream it purportedly
represents." [19] In finding the trademark and Baskin-Robbins ice cream one
product, the Court reasoned:

> Where, as in *Chicken Delight*, the tied products are commonplace arti-
> cles, the franchisor can easily maintain its quality standards through oth-
> er means less intrusive upon competition.[20] Accordingly, the coerced pur-
> chase of these items amounts to little more than an effort to impede
> competition on the merits in the market for the tied products.[21] *See
> Northern Pacific Railway Co. v. United States*, 356 U.S. 1, 6, 78 S.Ct.
> 514, 518, 2 L.Ed.2d 545 (1958).

> Where a distribution type system, such as that employed by Baskin-
> Robbins, is involved, significantly different considerations are presented.
> See McCarthy, Trademark Franchising and Antitrust: The Trouble with
> Tie-ins, 58 Cal.L.Rev. 1085, 1108 (1970). Under the distribution type sys-
> tem, the franchised outlets serve merely as conduits through which the
> trademarked goods of the franchisor flow to the ultimate consumer.
> These goods are generally manufactured by the franchisor or, as in the
> present case, by its licensees according to detailed specifications.[22] In
> this context, the trademark serves a different function. Instead of identi-
> fying a business format, the trademark in a distribution franchise system
> serves merely as a representation of the end product marketed by the
> system. "It is to the system and the *end product* that the public looks
> with the confidence that the established goodwill has created." *Chicken
> Delight*, 448 F.2d at 49 (emphasis added). Consequently, sale of substan-
> dard products under the mark would dissipate this goodwill and reduce
> the value of the trademark. The desirability of the trademark is there-
> fore utterly dependent upon the perceived quality of the product it repre-
> sents. Because the prohibition of tying arrangements is designed to

---

17. See Carpa, Inc. v. Ward Foods,
536 F.2d 39 (5th Cir. 1976); Northern v.
McGraw-Edison Co., 542 F.2d 1336
(8th Cir. 1976); McCarthy, Trademark
Franchising and Antitrust: The Trouble
with Tie-Ins, 58 Calif.L.Rev. 1085 (1970).

18. 664 F.2d 1348 (9th Cir. 1982).

19. Id. at 1352.

20. [This and the following three footnotes are from the Court's opinion, renumbered.] Provision of specifications
for the manufacture of these products is
one means often available to insure that
franchisees maintain quality standards.
See *Chicken Delight*, 448 F.2d at 51.
Where, as here, the alleged tied product
is manufactured pursuant to secret formulae, the specification alternative is not
available. See id. at n.9. [Note 5 supra,
p. 728].

21. In some cases, however, this co-
erced purchase may be justified as neces-
sary to prevent the sale of inferior goods
under the franchisor's trademark. See
Chicken Delight, 448 F.2d at 51; Note,
*Quality Control and the Antitrust
Laws in Trade-Mark Licensing*, 72 Yale
L.J. 1171 (1963).

22. Franchisees argue that, because
some Baskin-Robbins ice cream is manufactured by licensees instead of BRICO
[Baskin-Robbins] the trademark must be
a separate product. We reject this contention. Regardless of whether the ice
cream is manufactured by BRICO or its
licensees, the trademark still serves only
to identify that distinctive ice cream
made in accordance with secret formulae
and processes developed by BRICO.

strike solely at the use of a dominant *desired* product to compel the purchase of a second *undesired* commodity, id. at 47, the tie-in doctrine can have no application where the trademark serves only to identify the alleged tied product.[23] The desirability of the trademark and the quality of the product it represents are so inextricably interrelated in the mind of the consumer as to preclude any finding that the trademark is a separate item for tie-in purposes.

Queries. Do you agree with the court's result and the way it got there? How does one distinguish between a "business format" franchise pursuant to trademark licensing and a "distribution type" franchise pursuant to trademark licensing? Should a major oil company be free to require its branded franchise retailers to purchase all their gasoline from the oil company?[24] What if the oil company obtains significant portions of its gasoline from other oil companies pursuant to "exchange agreements"?[25] Would the court's opinion make more sense if the court followed *Chicken Delight's* methodology and found two products and a tie but one that is subject to the "goodwill defense" discussed supra p. 728? Is the question of whether there are two products or a defense like the "goodwill defense" a question of law for the judge or one of fact for the jury?[26]

(2) *Presumption of Power in Tying to a Patent, Copyright or Trademark.* In *United States v. Loew's, Inc.,*[27] the Court declared that "when the tying product is patented or copyrighted . . . sufficiency of economic power is presumed." The courts are not unanimous on the question of whether power should be presumed where the tying product is a trademark. *Chicken Delight* relied upon the "uniqueness" test of *Fortner I* to erect a legal presumption of power where the tying product is a trademark. In a leading pre-*Fortner I* decision, *Susser v. Carvel Corp.*[28] franchisees operating ice cream stores under Carvel trademarks claimed Carvel was engaging in a *per se* violation of the antitrust laws by requiring franchisees to buy all or part of their supplies from Carvel. The majority refused to presume the existence of power where the tying product is a trademark, requiring proof

23. In this situation, it is simply impossible for the trademark to be desirable if the product it represents is perceived as undesirable. Of course, franchisees may find the purchase of Baskin-Robbins ice cream undesirable because it prevents them from selling a less expensive brand of ice cream under the Baskin-Robbins trademark. The antitrust laws, however, are not designed to facilitate such a fraud upon the consumer.

24. See Bogosian v. Gulf Oil Corp., 561 F.2d 434 (3d Cir. 1977), certiorari denied 434 U.S. 1086, 98 S.Ct. 1280, 55 L.Ed.2d 791 (1978); Redd v. Shell Oil Co., 524 F.2d 1054 (10th Cir. 1975), certiorari denied 425 U.S. 912, 96 S.Ct. 1508, 47 L.Ed.2d 762 (1976); Hamro v. Shell Oil Co., 674 F.2d 784 (9th Cir. 1982).

25. An "exchange agreement" is where one oil company supplies a second with product for distribution in territory where the second has no or limited refining capacity. The second returns the favor in areas where the first has no or

limited refining capacity. The exchange is usually made on specifications. The practice has been widespread in the petroleum industry. See Hearings, Marketing Practices in the Gasoline Industry, Antitrust Subc., Sen. Judiciary Committee, 91st Cong., 1st Sess. (1970 and 1971). In the *Redd* case, supra note 24, Shell was engaged in supplying Redd pursuant to an "exchange agreement." The facts are summarized in detail in the trial court opinion. Redd v. Shell Oil Co., 1974–2 Trade Cases ¶ 75,390 (D.Utah).

26. See Hawkins v. Holiday Inns, Inc., 1976–1 Trade Cas. ¶ 60,847 (D.Tenn. 1976) (whether the "Great Sign" is one product or two is a jury question; summary judgment inappropriate).

27. 371 U.S. 38, 45, 83 S.Ct. 97, 9 L.Ed.2d 11 (1962).

28. 332 F.2d 505 (2d Cir. 1964), certiorari dismissed as improvidently granted 381 U.S. 125, 85 S.Ct. 1364, 14 L.Ed.2d 284 (1965).

of such power by an examination of the soft ice cream franchising market. Judge Lumbard, in dissent on this point, stated:

> . . . in the light of the Supreme Court's decision in United States v. Loew's, Inc., supra, I believe that such power may be presumed from the use of the Carvel trademark as the principal feature of the Carvel franchise system. In Loew's, the Court declared that "when the tying product is patented or copyrighted . . . sufficiency of economic power is presumed." 371 U.S. at 45, 83 S.Ct. at 2102, n. 4. I can find little reason to distinguish, in determining the legality of an allegedly unlawful tying arrangement, between the economic power generated by a patent or copyright on the one hand and that generated by a trademark on the other. In all three cases, the Congress has granted a statutory monopoly which places in the hands of the owner the right, within the limitations of federal law, to do as he will with the protected product. The value of the patent, copyright or trademark is, of course, directly proportionate to the consumer desirability of the protected product.

> I can find no reason not to extend this presumption of economic power to trademarks.[29] In any event, the claims which Carvel itself proffers lend added weight to the presumption, for Carvel's claim of economic justification is founded upon the substantial value of its trademark and the necessity for contractual restraints upon its dealers to protect that value.[30]

Do you agree? In both *Chicken Delight* and *Carvel* there was widespread competition in the fast food and ice cream business. By presuming power because the tying product is a trademark, are *Chicken Delight* and Judge Lumbard suggesting that trademark tie-ins are banned because of their impact on the freedom of individual franchisees even though the impact of the tying arrangement upon competition in general may not be economically significant?[31] Is this analysis still valid after *Fortner II* and *Sylvania*?

Turning the question about, can you think of any "economic benefits" to society, beyond those recognized by the defenses outlined supra p. 728, from

---

29. [Footnote 6 in original] The protection given to trademarks is in some respects even more extensive than that given either patents or copyrights. The duration of a trademark, for example, may, during continued use, be extended beyond 20 years without limit of time, 15 U.S.C. §§ 1058–59, whereas a patent expires after 17 years, 35 U.S.C. § 154, and a copyright after 28 years, subject to a renewal period of 28 years, 17 U.S.C. § 24.

30. 332 F.2d at 1512–13.

31. For critical analysis of *Chicken Delight*, see Hensley, infra note 37; Note Franchise Tie-Ins and Antitrust: A Critical Analysis, 60 Iowa L.Rev. 122 (1974). In *Carvel Corp.*, FTC Docket 8574, July 19, 1965, as reported in Antitrust and Trade Reg.Rep. No. 212, Aug. 3, 1965, A–14, the FTC, going further than the Court of Appeals for the Second Circuit when it upheld the same franchise provisions in a treble-damage suit, ruled that supplies-purchasing restrictions in franchises granted by the same soft-ice-cream freezing-equipment manufacturer were not illegal tie-in arrangements. Because the trademark license that attracted prospective dealers "conceptually cannot constitute a 'tying' product," the Commission set aside an examiner's decision that the franchise agreements are illegal tying arrangements violative of the unfair-methods-of-competition ban in Section 5 of the FTC Act.

The Commission held that, even if the trademark license could be treated as a tying product, there would be no illegal tie-in. First of all the trademark license "could never be regarded as a separable 'product' apart from" the ice cream mix and other supplies. Second, there is a lack of evidence that the manufacturer possesses sufficient economic power or dominance in the soft ice cream market through its control of the trademark as the "tying" product to appreciably restrain trade in the "tied" products—soft ice cream mix and commissary items. . . .

allowing franchisors to impose tying arrangements on franchisees?[32] Would franchisor image advertising and other efforts to build product differentiation likely increase if franchisors were allowed wide freedom to impose tying arrangements on franchisees? Will such non-price competition benefit society?[33] Should a disparity in bargaining power between franchisor and franchisee be considered?[34]

(3) *The Lanham Act and Trademarks.*[35] In most forms of franchising, a trademark license is central to the franchising agreement. A trademark or brand is a symbol by which a producer or distributor identifies his goods or service and distinguishes them from those of other sellers.[36] Consumer preference for goods of a particular brand may be built up if goods so marked are regularly found to be of excellent or standard quality, and by advertising. Such goods may command a premium price over other articles of equal intrinsic merit. To the extent that the seller succeeds in so differentiating his product, he has accomplished something which can be described, depending on one's point of view, either as insulating the product from competition of other products which the consumer does not recognize as equivalents, or as engaging in effective competitive merchandising, using means which are lawful and open to all sellers.

The right of a seller to the exclusive use of a particular symbol receives legal protection. At a minimum, the law prohibits a seller from deceiving the public by palming off his goods as those of another, benefit to the brand owner being only an incidental effect of public police measures against fraudulent or deceptive practices. But proponents of strong trademark protection emphasize that the purpose of trademark legislation goes beyond pro-

---

32. Compare the views of Bauer, supra note 24, with Hensley, infra note 37. For an analysis of the hypothetical benefits of franchise tying derived from economic theorizing, see Markovits, supra note 24; Note, A New Approach to the Legality of Franchising Tie-Ins, 129 U.Pa.L.Rev. 1267 (1981).

33. See W. D. Slawson, The New Inflation: The Collapse of Free Markets (1981) (attributing, the phenomenon of chronic inflation, in part, to the proliferation of non-price competition).

34. Federal and state franchise legislation surveyed in section F, infra p. 782, is often premised in part on a widespread recognition of a need to redress the imbalance of bargaining power between franchisors and franchisees. The latter often have all their resources invested in the business of the franchise and are vulnerable to demands and pressures by the franchisor—particularly by threat of franchise termination. Franchisees, particularly retail gasoline dealers, frequently complain about being forced to pump gasoline at a loss and to work long hours for below minimum wages. See Hearings, Divorcement of Motor Fuel Service Stations, Sen.Jud. Comm., 97th Cong., 1st Sess. (1981). See generally Bohling, Franchise Terminations Under the Sher-

man Act: Populism and Relational Power, 53 Texas L.Rev. 1180 (1975).

35. On trademarks generally, see ALI–ABA Course of Study: Unfair Competition, Trademarks and Copyrights, 1977; McCarthy, Trademarks and Unfair Competition (2 vols. 1973); Seidel, Dubroff, Gonda, Trademark Law and Practice (1963); Callmann, Unfair Competition, Trademarks and Monopolies (4th Ed., 1981); Nims, Unfair Competition and Trademarks (4th ed. 1947). Annual surveys of trademark developments appear each year in the Trademark Reporter. See, e.g., 71 Trademark Rep. 285 (1981); 70 Trademark Rep. 493 (1980). See also McCarthy, Important Trends In Trademark and Unfair Competition Law During the Decades of the 1970's, 71 Trademark Rep. 93 (1981).

36. The law recognizes not only marks of individual producers but also "collective" and "certification" marks. Collective marks are those used "by the members of a cooperative, an association or other collective group . . ." Certification marks are those used by persons other than the owner to certify regional or other origin, material, quality or other characteristics, including the fact that work was performed by members of a union. 15 U.S.C.A. §§ 1054, 1127.

tection of the public to include, as an independent goal, protection of the trademark owner's "investment." [37]

Although trademarks enjoy legal protection under the common law of unfair competition, federal legislation now plays a crucial role. The Lanham Trademark Act of 1946, 15 U.S.C.A. §§ 1051 et seq., provides for federal registry of trademarks by application to the U.S. Patent and Trademark Office. Registration may be denied on various grounds, e.g., that the mark is deceptive, immoral,[38] "merely descriptive," or that it so resembles a mark already in use "as to be likely, when applied to the goods of the applicant, to cause confusion or mistake or to deceive purchasers." [39] Registration is denied to marks which are merely descriptive, in order to prevent a merchant from appropriating to his exclusive use parts of the common language. Similar considerations, as well as the doctrine of "abandonment", lead to forfeiture of the right to exclusive use of a mark to the extent that the owner has permitted it to lose its distinctive character and to become a generic term commonly applied to articles of that sort regardless of source.[40] Functional features of an article may not be registered or protected as trademarks, even though they are specially designed to serve also as identifying devices.[41]

The Patent and Trademark Office, after satisfying itself that applicant is entitled to the mark he claims, will issue a certificate of registration, which constitutes prima facie evidence of validity, ownership, and registrant's exclusive right to use the mark in all commerce subject to federal regulation. Five years use of a registered mark makes the registrant's right "incontestable" except on a few specified grounds, including fraud in procuring registration, or proof that the mark is the common descriptive name of any article.[42]

A mark is assignable "with that part of the goodwill of the business connected with the use of and symbolized by the mark. . . . Provided, that any assigned registration may be cancelled at any time if the registered mark is being used by, or with the permission of, the assignee so as to misrepresent the source of the goods or services. . . ." [43] Thus if Mr. Upright sells his business to Mr. Scoundrel, Mr. Scoundrel may continue to use the trademarks assigned to him with the business. Also, within limits, the ingredients or quality of a trademarked product may be changed without notice to the public.[44] A trademark may also be licensed for use by someone

37. See Hensley, Franchise Tying: Gauging the Economic Power of a Trademark, 15 U.C. Davis L.Rev. 405 (1981); S.Rep.No.1333, 79th Cong., 2d Sess. (1946) p. 6, relating to the Lanham Trade-Mark Act of 1946; Morse-Starrett Products Co. v. Steccone, 86 F.Supp. 796, 803 (N.D.Calif.1949).

38. See In re McGinley, 206 USPQ 753 (TTAB 1979), reviewing several cases involving "immoral" or "scandalous" applications for registration.

39. 15 U.S.C.A. § 1052.

40. 15 U.S.C.A. § 1127; Du Pont Cellophane Co. v. Waxed Products Co., 85 F.2d 75 (2d Cir. 1936), certiorari denied 299 U.S. 601, 57 S.Ct. 194, 81 L.Ed. 443.

41. See, for example, Sylvania Electric Product Co. v. Dura Electric Lamp Co., 247 F.2d 730 (3d Cir. 1957) (spot of colored chemical inside electric lamps used to check vacuum in bulb during manufacture). But see Dallas Cowboys Cheerleaders, Inc. v. Pussycat Cinema, Ltd., 604 F.2d 200 (2d Cir. 1979) (cheerleader uniform a trademark; protected from infringement by use in a film, "Debbie Does Dallas," described by the Court as "a gross and revolting sex film." Id. at 202.)

42. 15 U.S.C.A. § 1065. The leading case on the incontestability of a mark is Union Carbide Corp. v. Ever-Ready Inc., 531 F.2d 366 (7th Cir. 1976), certiorari denied 429 U.S. 830, 97 S.Ct. 91, 50 L.Ed.2d 94.

43. 15 U.S.C.A. § 1060.

44. Cf. Independent Baking Powder Co. v. Boorman, 175 F. 448 (D.N.J.1910). Plaintiff's predecessor sold alum baking powder under a number of different trademarks, including "Solar". "Solar"

other than the owner, if the owner maintains some control over the quality of the goods sold under the mark by the licensee.[45] Trademark licensors may face strict liability in torts for injuries caused by the trademarked product or service being marketed by licensees under a franchise.[46]

The interface of antitrust and trademark law in the area of franchising is pronounced because the trademark license is at the heart of most modern franchising.[47] Franchisors licensing the use of their trademark have an obligation under section 5 of the Lanham Act to maintain quality control of the use of the mark so that the public is not deceived.[48] However, section 33(b) (7) of the Act makes the use of the mark "to violate the antitrust laws of the United States" a defense to an action enforcing the exclusive use of the mark.[49] Although it has long been held that a trademark may not be used to violate the antitrust laws,[50] the scope of a trademark licensor's responsibility to maintain quality control under the Lanham Act and the extent to which the methods adopted to do so constitute antitrust violations remain a fruitful source of litigation. The availability of less restrictive alternatives than exclusive dealing or tying requirements (i.e., specifications of quality) frequently causes courts to find that the licensor has exceeded legitimate tactics in the pursuit of quality control, thereby overstepping the bounds of legitimate trademark protection.

PRINCIPE v. McDONALD'S CORP.

United States Court of Appeals for the Fourth Circuit, 1980.
631 F.2d 303, certiorari denied 451 U.S. 970, 101 S.Ct. 2047, 68 L.Ed.2d 349 (1981).

PHILLIPS, SENIOR CIRCUIT JUDGE delivered the opinion of the Court.

· · ·

The appellants, Frank A. Principe, Ann Principe and Frankie, Inc., a family owned corporation, are franchisees of McDonald's System,

was assigned to plaintiff, the assignor continuing in business under the other marks. Plaintiff substituted phosphate for alum in "Solar" baking powder. Held: Plaintiff's trademark rights were forfeited when it substituted an important ingredient, regarded by the trade and the public as distinguishing the product, even if the change was an improvement.

45. Du Pont Co. v. Celanese Corp., 167 F.2d 484 (C.C.P.A.1948); Broeg v. Duchaine, 319 Mass. 711, 67 N.E.2d 466 (1946).

46. See Behringer & Otte, Liability and the Trademark Licensor: Advice For the Franchisor of Goods Or Services, 19 Am.Bus. 109 (1981).

47. See Brown, Franchising: Trap for the Trusting (1969); Brown, Franchising—Realities and Remedies (rev.ed. 1981); Rosenfeld, The Law of Franchising (1970); Thompson, Franchising and Antitrust (1971); Treece, Trademark Licensing and Vertical Restraints in Franchising Agreements, 116 U.Pa.L.Rev. 435 (1968).

48. 15 U.S.C.A. § 1055. See also, 15 U.S.C.A. §§ 1115(b)(2), 1127.

49. See 15 U.S.C.A. § 1115(b)(7). This section was inserted in the final version of the bill which became the Lanham Act at the insistence of Senator O'Mahoney to make clear that trademarks can not be used to violate the antitrust laws. See 92 Cong.Rec. pp. 7872–73, 7523 (79th Cong. 2d Sess. 1946); Puritan Sportswear Corp. v. Shure, 307 F.Supp. 377 (W.D.Pa.1969); Phi Delta Theta Fraternity v. J. A. Buchroeder & Co., 251 F.Supp. 968 (W.D.Mo.1966). See generally Hill, Antitrust Violations as a Defense to Trademark Infringement, 71 Trademark Rep. 148 (1981); Smith, Trademarks and Antitrust: The Misuse Defense Under Section 33(b)(7) of the Lanham Act, 4 Harv.J.L. & Pub.Pol. 161 (1981).

50. See Timken Roller Bearing Co. v. United States, 341 U.S. 593, 71 S.Ct. 971, 95 L.Ed. 1199 (1951); United States v. Bausch & Lomb Optical Co., 321 U.S. 707, 64 S.Ct. 805, 88 L.Ed. 1024 (1944).

Inc. The Principes acquired their first franchise, a McDonald's hamburger restaurant in Hopewell, Virginia, in 1970. At that time, they executed a twenty year franchise license agreement and a store lease of like duration. In consideration for their rights under these agreements, the Principes paid a $10,000 license fee and a $15,000 security deposit, and agreed to remit 2.2 per cent of their gross receipts as royalties under the franchise agreement and 8.0 per cent as rent under the lease.[51] In 1974, Frank Principe and his son, Raymond, acquired a second franchise in Colonial Heights, Virginia, on similar terms. The Colonial Heights franchise subsequently was transferred to Frankie, Inc., a corporation owned jointly by Frank and Raymond Principe.

The Principes sought to purchase a third franchise in 1976 in Petersburg, Virginia. Robert Beavers, McDonald's regional manager, concluded the plaintiffs lacked sufficient management depth and capabilities to take on a third store without impairing the quality of their existing operations. During the next twenty months, the Principes obtained corporate review and reconsideration of the decision to deny them the franchise. They were notified in May 1978 that the Petersburg franchise was being offered to a new franchisee.

They filed this action a few days later alleging violations of federal and state antitrust and securities laws and state franchising laws. Counts I and II alleged McDonald's violated federal antitrust laws by tying store leases and $15,000 security deposit notes to the franchise rights at the Hopewell and Colonial Heights stores. Count XII alleged McDonald's denied the Principes a third franchise in retaliation for their refusal to follow McDonald's pricing guidelines. The remaining counts, alleging violations of state and federal antitrust and securities laws, as well as Virginia franchising laws, were dismissed prior to trial and are not before us on this appeal.

Following discovery the district court granted summary judgment for McDonald's on the security deposit note tie in claims. District Judge D. Dortch Warriner found the notes represented deposits against loss and do not constitute a product separate from the store leases to which they pertain.

The court directed a verdict for McDonald's on the store lease tie in counts at the close of all the evidence. Relying on the decision of this court in *Phillips v. Crown Central Petroleum Corp.*, 602 F.2d 616 (4th Cir.), cert. denied, 444 U.S. 1074, 100 S.Ct. 1021, 62 L.Ed.2d 756 (1980), Judge Warriner held the Principes had failed to introduce any evidence of McDonald's power in the tying product market, which he held is the food retailing market. The court held, however, McDonald's sells only one product: the license contract and store lease are component parts of the overall package McDonald's offers its prospective franchisees. Accordingly, Judge Warriner held as a matter of law there was no illegal tie in.

51. (This and the following 4 footnotes are from the Court's opinion, renumbered.) Since 1970 McDonald's has increased the franchise fee to $12,500, the franchise royalty to three per cent and the rent payment to 8.5 per cent.

The remaining issue, whether McDonald's denied the Principes a third franchise in retaliation for their pricing independence, went to the jury which held for the defendants.   The jury returned an unsolicited note stating they felt the Principes had been wronged, although price fixing was not the reason, and should be awarded the Petersburg franchise.   The court disregarded the jury's note and entered judgment on the verdict for McDonald's.

. . .

II

At the time this suit was filed, McDonald's consisted of at least four separate corporate entities.   McDonald's Systems, Inc. controlled franchise rights and licensed franchisees to sell hamburgers under the McDonald's name.   Franchise Realty Interstate Corporation (Franchise Realty) acquires real estate, either by purchase or long term lease, builds McDonald's hamburger restaurants, and leases them [52] either to franchisees or to a third corporation, McOpCo. McOpCo, which is not a party to this suit, operates about one-fourth of the McDonald's restaurants in the United States as company stores.   Straddling this triad is McDonald's Corporation, the parent, who owns all the stock of the other defendants. . . .

McDonald's is not primarily a fast food retailer.   While it does operate over a thousand stores itself, the vast majority of the stores in its system are operated by franchisees.   Nor does McDonald's sell equipment or supplies to its licensees.   Instead its primary business is developing and collecting royalties from limited menu fast food restaurants operated by independent business people.

McDonald's develops new restaurants according to master plans that originate at the regional level and must be approved by upper management.   Regional administrative staff meet at least annually to consider new areas into which McDonald's can expand.   Once the decision is made to expand into a particular geographic area, specialists begin to search for appropriate restaurant sites.

McDonald's uses demographic data generated by the most recent census and its own research in evaluating potential sites.   McDonald's attempts to analyze and predict demographic trends in the geographic area.   This process serves a two fold purpose: (1) by analyzing the demographic profile of a given market area, McDonald's hopes to determine whether the residents are likely to buy fast food in sufficient quantities to justify locating a restaurant there; (2) by anticipating future growth, McDonald's seeks to plan its expansion to maximize the number of viable McDonald's restaurants within a given geographic area.   Based on a comparison of data for various available sites, the regional staffs select what they believe is the best site

---

52. The McDonald's system of restaurants included some 4465 stores in 1978, 99 per cent of which were owned by Franchise Realty. See Martino v. McDonald's System, Inc., 81 F.R.D. 81, 84 (N.D.Ill.1979).

in each geographic area. Occasionally no available site suits McDonald's requirements and expansion must be postponed.

The regional staffs compile master plans for expansion once particular sites are selected. These generally extend three years into the future and are broken down by site and month. Each proposed new restaurant is assigned projected dates for acquisition of the land, ground breaking and opening. These dates vary from location to location because of differences in restaurant size, zoning and special permit requirements and various other factors. The completed master plans must be approved first by regional management and later by corporate management.

. . .

After the specifics of each proposed new restaurant are approved, McDonald's decides whether the store will be company operated or franchised. If the decision is to franchise the store McDonald's begins the process of locating a franchisee. This involves offering the store either to an existing franchisee or to an applicant on the franchise waiting list. Applicants need not live near the store in order to be offered the franchise, and they need not accept the first franchise they are offered. The Principes lived in Kenosha, Wisconsin, and rejected eleven separate McDonald's restaurants before accepting their first franchise in Hopewell, Virginia. McDonald's often does not know who will operate a franchised store until it is nearly completed because a new restaurant may be offered to and rejected by several different applicants.

Meanwhile, Franchise Realty acquires the land, either by purchase or long term lease and constructs the store. Acquisition and development costs averaged over $450,000 per store in 1978. All McDonald's restaurants bear the same distinctive features with a few exceptions due to architectural restrictions: the golden arches motif, the brick and glass construction and the distinctive roofline. According to the defendants, these features identify the stores as a McDonald's even where zoning restrictions preclude other advertising or signs.

As constructed, McDonald's restaurants are finished shells; they contain no kitchen or dining room equipment. Furnishing store equipment is the responsibility of the operator, whether a franchisee or McOpCo. McDonald's does provide specifications such equipment must meet, but does not sell the equipment itself.

Having acquired the land, begun construction of the store and selected an operator, McDonald's enters into two contracts with the franchisee. Under the first, the franchise agreement, McDonald's grants the franchisee the rights to use McDonald's food preparation system and to sell food products under the McDonald's name. The franchise pays a $12,500 franchise fee and agrees to remit three per cent of his gross sales as a royalty in return. Under the second contract, the lease, McDonald's grants the franchisee the right to use the particular store premises to which his franchise pertains. In return, the franchisee pays a $15,000 refundable security deposit (as evidence of which he receives a twenty year non-negotiable non-interest bear-

ing note) and agrees to pay eight and one half per cent of his gross
sales as rent. These payments under the franchise and lease agreements are McDonald's only sources of income from its franchised restaurants. The franchisee also assumes responsibility under the lease
for building maintenance, improvements, property taxes and other
costs associated with the premises. Both the franchise agreement
and the lease generally have twenty year durations, both provide that
termination of one terminates the other, and neither is available separately.

III

The Principes argue McDonald's is selling not one but three distinct products, the franchise, the lease and the security deposit note.
The alleged antitrust violation stems from the fact that a prospective
franchisee must buy all three in order to obtain the franchise.

As evidence that this is an illegal tying arrangement, the
Principes point to the unfavorable terms on which franchisees are required to lease their stores. Not only are franchisees denied the opportunity to build equity and depreciate their property, but they must
maintain the building, pay for improvements and taxes, and remit 8.5
per cent of their gross sales as rents. In 1978 the gross sales of the
Hopewell store generated about $52,000 in rent. That figure nearly
equalled Franchise Realty's original cost for the site and corresponds
to more than a fourth of the original cost of the entire Hopewell restaurant complex. At that rate of return, the Principes argue, Franchise Realty will have recouped its entire investment in four years
and the remainder of the lease payments will be pure profit. The
Principes contend that the fact the store rents are so high proves that
McDonald's cannot sell the leaseholds on their own merits.

Nor has McDonald's shown any need to forbid its licensees to own
their own stores, the Principes say. Appellants contend that McDonald's is the only fast food franchisor that requires its licensees not
only to pay royalties but to lease their stores from the franchisor.
. . . Before 1959 McDonald's itself permitted franchisees to own
their own stores. McDonald's could maintain its desired level of uniformity by requiring franchisees to locate and construct stores according to company specifications. The Company could even provide
planning and design assistance as it apparently does in connection
with food purchasing and restaurant management. The Principes argue McDonald's has not shown that the success of its business or the
integrity of its trademarks depends on company ownership of all
store premises.

A separate tied product is the note that evidences the lessee's
$15,000 security deposit, according to the appellants. The Principes
argue the security deposit really is a mandatory contribution to Mc-
Donald's working capital, not security against damage to the store or
breach of the lease contract. By tying the purchase of these $15,000
twenty year non-negotiable non-interest bearing notes to that of the
franchise, McDonald's allegedly has generated a capital fund that to-

talled over $45 million in 1978. It is argued that no one would purchase such notes on their own merits. The Principes assert that only by requiring franchisees to purchase the notes as a condition of obtaining a franchise has McDonald's been able to sell them at all.

McDonald's responds that it is not in the business of licensing use of its name, improving real estate for lease or selling long term notes. Its only business is developing a system of hamburger restaurants and collecting royalties from their sales. The allegedly tied products are but parts of the overall bundle of franchise benefits and obligations. According to McDonald's, the appellants are asking the court to invalidate the way McDonald's does business and to require it to adopt the licensing procedures of its less successful competitors. Federal antitrust laws do not compel such a result, McDonald's contends.

IV

. . . Because we agree with McDonald's that the lease, note and license are not separate products but component parts of the overall franchise package, we hold on the facts of this case there was no illegal tie in. Accordingly, we affirm the summary judgment and directed verdict for McDonald's on the tying claims.

As support for their position, the Principes rely primarily on the decision of the Ninth Circuit in *Siegel v. Chicken Delight, Inc.*, 448 F.2d 43 (9th Cir. 1971), cert. denied, 405 U.S. 955, 92 S.Ct. 1172, 31 L.Ed.2d 232 (1972), one of the first cases to address the problem of franchise tie-ins. Chicken Delight was what McDonald's characterizes as a "rent a name" franchisor: It licensed franchisees to sell chicken under the Chicken Delight name but did not own store premises or fixtures. The company did not even charge franchise fees or royalties. Instead, it required its franchisees to purchase a specified number of cookers and fryers and to purchase certain packaging supplies and mixes exclusively from Chicken Delight. These supplies were priced higher than comparable goods of competing sellers. . . .

In addressing Chicken Delight's argument that the allegedly tied products all were essential components of the franchise system, the Ninth Circuit looked to the "function of the aggregation." 448 F.2d at 48. Viewing the essence of a Chicken Delight franchise as the franchisor's trademark, the court sought to determine whether requiring franchisees to purchase common supplies from Chicken Delight was necessary to ensure that their operations lived up to the quality standards the trademark represented. Judged by this standard, the aggregation was found to consist of separate products . . .. In the court's view, Chicken Delight had attempted "to extend trade-mark protection to common articles (which the public does not and has no reason to connect with the trade-mark)", id., a classic kind of illegal tying arrangement.

The Principes urge this court to apply the *Chicken Delight* reasoning to invalidate the McDonald's franchise lease note aggregation.

They urge that McDonald's can protect the integrity of its trademarks by specifying how its franchisees shall operate, where they may locate their restaurants and what types of buildings they may erect. Customers do not and have no reason to connect the building's owner with the McDonald's operation conducted therein. Since company ownership of store premises is not an essential element of the trademark's goodwill, the Principes argue, the franchise, lease and note are separable products tied together in violation of the antitrust laws.[53]

In *Phillips v. Crown Central Petroleum Corporation*, supra, 602 F.2d at 627, this court spoke of the "emerging law of tie ins in franchise settings". We noted that "the very essence of a franchise is the purchase of several related products in a single competitively attractive package." Id. at 628, see also *Ungar v. Dunkin' Donuts of America, Inc.*, 531 F.2d 1211, 1224 (3d Cir.), cert. denied, 429 U.S. 823, 97 S.Ct. 74, 50 L.Ed.2d 84 (1976). Franchising has come a long way since the decision in *Chicken Delight*.

Without disagreeing with the result in *Chicken Delight*, we conclude that the court's emphasis in that case upon the trademark as the essence of a franchise is too restrictive. Far from merely licensing franchisees to sell products under its trade name, a modern franchisor such as McDonald's offers its franchisees a complete method of doing business. It takes people from all walks of life, sends them to its management school, and teaches them a variety of skills ranging from hamburger grilling to financial planning. It installs them in stores whose market has been researched and whose location has been selected by experts to maximize sales potential. It inspects every facet of every store several times a year and consults with each franchisee about his operation's strengths and weaknesses. Its regime pervades all facets of the business, from the design of the

---

53. Such a result would not be entirely unprecedented. In Photovest Corporation v. Fotomat Corporation, 606 F.2d 704, 724–725 (9th Cir. 1979), cert. denied, 445 U.S. 917, 100 S.Ct. 1278, 63 L.Ed.2d 601 (1980), the Seventh Circuit held Fotomat's practice of requiring its franchisees to lease kiosks from the franchisor is an illegal tying arrangement. In Northern v. McGraw-Edison Company, 542 F.2d 1336 (8th Cir. 1976), cert. denied, 429 U.S. 1097, 97 S.Ct. 1115, 51 L.Ed.2d 544 (1977), the Eighth Circuit found a tying violation where a franchisor licensed its trademarks to dealer agents who, in turn, assembled complete dry cleaning operations and leased them as "going businesses" to franchisees. Similarly, in Carpa, Inc. v. Ward Foods, Inc., 536 F.2d 39 (5th Cir. 1976), the court found an illegal tie in where a seafood restaurant franchisee was required to lease a completed restaurant from his franchisor.

However, none of these decisions dealt in any detail with the issue before this court: whether a franchise package granting the right to conduct a business in a specific company owned store can be separated into tying and tied products. Both *Northern* and *Capra, Inc.* were concerned primarily with equipment and supplies tie ins; store leases were only the vehicles by which the illegally tied packages were conveyed. While *Photovest* is closer to the present case, it is distinguished by the fact that Fotomat merely leased space in shopping center parking lots, installed prefabricated kiosks, and subleased to franchisees. There was no argument that Fotomat had greater expertise than its franchisees, conducted elaborate market research, or invested substantial sums of money. The Seventh Circuit did not elaborate its reasons for finding the franchise and lease separable. Because none of these cases dealt with the two product question in depth, we do not find them controlling as precedents.

menu board to the amount of catsup on the hamburgers, nothing is left to chance. This pervasive franchisor supervision and control benefits the franchisee in turn. His business is identified with a network of stores whose very uniformity and predictability attracts customers. In short, the modern franchisee pays not only for the right to use a trademark but for the right to become a part of a system whose business methods virtually guarantee his success. It is often unrealistic to view a franchise agreement as little more than a trademark license.

Given the realities of modern franchising, we think the proper inquiry is not whether the allegedly tied products are associated in the public mind with the franchisor's trademark, but whether they are integral components of the business method being franchised. Where the challenged aggregation is an essential ingredient of the franchised system's formula for success, there is but a single product and no tie in exists as a matter of law.

Applying this standard to the present case, we hold the lease is not separable from the McDonald's franchise to which it pertains. McDonald's practice of developing a system of company owned restaurants operated by franchisees has substantial advantages, both for the company and for franchisees. It is part of what makes a McDonald's franchise uniquely attractive to franchisees.

First, because it approaches the problem of restaurant site selection systematically, McDonald's is able to obtain better sites than franchisees could select. Armed with its demographic information, guided by its staff of experts and unencumbered by preferences of individual franchisees, McDonald's can wield its economic might to acquire sites where new restaurants will prosper without undercutting existing franchisees' business or limiting future expansion. Individual franchisees are unlikely to possess analytical expertise, undertake elaborate market research or approach the problem of site selection from an area wide point of view.[54] Individual franchisees benefit from the McDonald's approach because their stores are located in areas McDonald's has determined will produce substantial fast food business and on sites where that business is most likely to be diverted to their stores. Because McDonald's purposefully locates new stores where they will not undercut existing franchisees' business, McDonald's franchisees do not have to compete with each other, a substantial advantage in the highly competitive fast food industry.

Second, McDonald's policy of owning all of its own restaurants assures that the stores remain part of the McDonald's system. McDonald's franchise arrangements are not static: franchisees retire or die; occasionally they do not live up to their franchise obligations and must be replaced; even if no such contingency intervenes, the agreements normally expire by their own terms after twenty years. If

54. Nor would requiring corporate approval of franchisees' site selection decisions be a satisfactory alternative. McDonald's regional manager testified that the Company's planning and acquisition experts are unlikely to stay with McDonald's if their roles become purely advisory.

franchisees owned their own stores, any of these events could disrupt McDonald's business and have a negative effect on the system's goodwill. Buildings whose architecture identified them as former McDonald's stores would sit idle or be used for other purposes. Replacement franchisees would have to acquire new and perhaps less desirable sites, a much more difficult and expensive process after the surrounding business area has matured. By owning its own stores, McDonald's assures its continued presence on the site, maintains the store's patronage even during management changes and avoids the negative publicity of having former McDonald's stores used for other purposes. By preserving the goodwill of the system in established markets, company store ownership produces attendant benefits for franchisees.

Third, because McDonald's acquires the sites and builds the stores itself, it can select franchisees based on their management potential rather than their real estate expertise or wealth. Ability to emphasize management skills is important to McDonald's because it has built its reputation largely on the consistent quality of its operations rather than on the merits of its hamburgers. A store's quality is largely a function of its management. McDonald's policy of owning its own stores reduces a franchisee's initial investment, thereby broadening the applicant base and opening the door to persons who otherwise could not afford a McDonald's franchise.[55] Accordingly, McDonald's is able to select franchisees primarily on the basis of their willingness to work for the success of their operations. Their ability to begin operating a McDonald's restaurant without having to search for a site, negotiate for the land, borrow hundreds of thousands of dollars and construct a store building is of substantial value to franchisees.

Finally, because both McDonald's and the franchisee have a substantial financial stake in the success of the restaurant, their relationship becomes a sort of partnership that might be impossible under other circumstances. McDonald's spends close to half a million dollars on each new store it establishes. Each franchisee invests over $100,000 to make the store operational. Neither can afford to ignore the other's problems, complaints or ideas. Because its investment is on the line, the Company cannot allow its franchisees to lose money. This being so, McDonald's works with its franchisees to build their business, occasionally financing improvements at favorable rates or even accepting reduced royalty payments in order to provide franchisees more working capital.

All of these factors contribute significantly to the overall success of the McDonald's system. The formula that produced systemwide success, the formula that promises to make each new McDonald's store successful, that formula is what McDonald's sells its franchisees. To characterize the franchise as an unnecessary aggregation of separate products tied to the McDonald's name is to miss the point

---

55. The record establishes that the Principes could not have obtained financing to construct their first restaurant themselves.

entirely. Among would be franchisees, the McDonald's name has come to stand for the formula, including all that it entails. We decline to find that it is an illegal tie in. Cf. *Kugler v. Aamco Automatic Transmissions, Inc.*, 460 F.2d 1214, 1215–16 (8th Cir. 1972) (franchise and mandatory advertising constitute a single product); *In re 7-Eleven Franchise Litigation*, 1974–2 Trade Cases ¶ 75,429 (N.D. Cal.) (convenience store franchise package is not separable into tied and tying products).

We have examined the Principes' other contentions and do not believe they warrant extended discussion. The security deposit note was just that: evidence of a security deposit on a lease which we have held was a legitimate part of the franchise package. . . . The jury's unsolicited comment that the Principes had been wronged was expressly qualified by their statement that price fixing was not the reason. The district court correctly determined that the note did not affect the integrity of the jury verdict.

Affirmed.[*]

NOTES AND QUERIES

(1) *Queries.* What was McDonald's selling and what was Principe buying? Is McDonald's in the trademark licensing business? The restaurant construction business? The real estate business? The fast food business? The restaurant site selection business? The restaurant management training business? Should the Court have investigated the effects of McDonald's practices in any of these markets? What result would this Court have reached if McDonald's had required franchisees to purchase all their food requirements (i.e. hamburger, pickles, sesame seed buns, etc.), paper goods, and cooking equipment from McDonald's as part of the franchise licensing package? Did the court articulate standards for determining the circumstances in which the individual elements of a franchise agreement will be defined as one product or several products?[56] If there are separate products being sold as a package in *Principe*, is the tie voluntary?[57] A tie subject to the defenses outlined supra Note 5, p. 728?

(2) *Tying and Franchise Packaging.* In many franchise marketing systems, franchisors are often engaged in activities consumers do not ordinarily associate with the products or services being marketed. For example, major oil companies are among the largest owners of real estate in every communi-

[*] [McDonald's was subsequently awarded the bulk of its requested $36,000 in costs for prevailing in the litigation; the trial court stressed the importance and riskiness of the litigation as a reason for McDonald's having incurred high litigation costs. See 42 ATRR 834 (1982).—Ed.]

56. Commentary on the *Principe* case has been critical of the Court's single product analysis. See Note, Antitrust Franchising—*Principe v. McDonald's Corp.*—Big Mac Attacks The Chicken Delight Rule, 7 J.Corp.L. 137 (1981); Note, The McDonald's Antitrust Litigation: Real Estate Tying Agreements in Trademark Franchising, 13 J.Marsh.L. Rev. 607 (1980); Note, *Principe v. McDonald's Corporation*: The Separability Issue in Franchise Tying Arrangements, 12 Loyola U.L.Rev. 839 (1981); Note, Product Separability in Franchise Tying Arrangements: The Fourth Circuit's New Rule, 38 Wash. & Lee L.Rev. 1195 (1981).

57. Cf. Kypta v. McDonald's Corp., 671 F.2d 1282 (11th Cir.) (upholding grant of a defendant's summary judgment motion in a case similar to *Principe*, on the ground that plaintiff had not shown actual injury), certiorari denied __ U.S. __, 103 S.Ct. 127, 74 L.Ed.2d 109 (1982).

ty in the country. Land is purchased for the construction of service stations which are then leased to franchisees for the marketing of petroleum products under trademarks owned by the franchisor. As in the *Principe* case, the arrangement is to the benefit of small business because it enables an individual to be in business without a large capital investment; provides instant consumer recognition of a widely advertised trademark; can be the source of management training and business advice; and provides the individual with product supply and access to such additional marketing benefits as a national credit card and advertising promotions. The franchisor is benefited by having an outlet for its products, the entreprenurial effort of an independent businessman, extensive control over retailer activity, and a shifting of business risk for tort and other liabilities to the franchisee. Many of the advantages of vertical integration may be obtained by contract, while some of the investment risks and regulatory burdens of doing so may be avoided.

There usually is an imbalance in bargaining power in the relationship when the franchisor is the franchisee's landlord, banker for credit sales, trademark licensor, and supplier.[58] When trouble breaks out and the dispute is cast in antitrust terms, allegations of unlawful tying, exclusive dealing, and other vertical restraints are frequently made.[59] Several courts have recognized the trademark license, building lease, credit card rights, and supply agreements as separate products for purposes of the analysis. For example, in *Bogosian v. Gulf Oil Corp.*,[60] on a motion for certification of a class action, the Court held a gas station lease and a trademark license could both be tying products for purposes of determining whether the major oil companies were unlawfully requiring gasoline retailers to purchase petroleum products from their landlord and/or trademark licensor.

In *Photovest Corp. v. Fotomat Corp.*,[61] see p. 158 supra, the Court found Fotomat's practice of tying film processing to the franchise license to operate under the Fotomat trademarks and the practice of requiring franchisees to lease drive-thru kiosks and the land upon which they sat from the franchisor also constituted unlawful tying.

At least four different approaches to franchising tying allegations can be discerned from the cases. The *Chicken Delight* approach defines physically or legally distinct items in the franchise package as separate products for tying purposes subject to narrowly drawn defenses limited by "least restrictive alternative" analysis. *Krehl v. Baskin-Robbins* and *Principe* base the analysis of whether there is unlawful tying on the one product-two product element, with little analysis beyond the facts peculiar to each case of when two or more items will be considered a single product for tying purposes.[62] A third approach, suggested by both *Krehl* and *Principe*, is to distinguish

58. See Bohling, Franchise Terminations Under the Sherman Act: Populism and Relational Power, 53 Tex.L.Rev. 1180 (1975).

59. See Harkins, Tying and the Franchisee, 47 Antitrust L.J. 903 (1978).

60. 561 F.2d 434 (3d Cir. 1977), certiorari denied 434 U.S. 1086, 98 S.Ct. 1280, 55 L.Ed.2d 791 (1978).

61. 606 F.2d 704 (7th Cir. 1979).

62. See Dore, The "Total Product" Approach to Analysis of Alleged Tying Arrangements, 34 Wash. & Lee L.Rev.

409 (1977). For a survey of two product analysis, see Zeidman, The Two Product Test in Franchising: If You Want to Get X, You Gotta Buy Y, 1980 Ariz.St.L.J., 433 (1980); Note, Trademark Franchising and Antitrust Law: The Two-Product Rule for Tying Arrangements, 27 Syracuse L.Rev. 953 (1976). A similar analytical problem exists where complementary products are sold as a unit, i.e., a camera and the flash attachment or a computer and memory units. See Note, An Economic and Legal Analysis of Physical Tie-Ins, 89 Yale L.J. 769 (1980).

between different forms of franchising in defining whether there is a single product or a tying arrangement. The F. T. C., in Trade Practice Rules regulating franchisor disclosure of the terms and conditions of a franchise,[63] discussed infra p. 761, has distinguished at least three kinds of franchising: (1) The "business format" or "rent-a-name" franchise, where the franchisor licenses the franchisee to sell goods or services meeting the franchisor's quality standards under the franchisor's trademark; (2) The "product franchisee" where the franchisor licenses the franchisee to sell the franchisor's trademarked products at retail; and (3) The "business opportunity" franchise where the franchisor puts the franchisee into the business of distributing goods or services produced under a third party trademark. While there are considerable variations on the theme, *Chicken Delight* is an example of (1), *Krehl* is an example of (2), and *Principe* has many of the earmarks of (3). When analyzed under the tying rubric, there is a tendency to treat the "business format" franchise as a product separate from the products sold under the franchise, while in "product" franchises like *Krehl* courts tend to lump the franchise and the product sold under it together as a single product. The "business opportunity" franchise system has received a mixed result with cases like *Photovest* treating the individual elements of the franchise as separate products and *Principe* viewing them as a single package.

A fourth approach, one advocated by some commentators, is to apply a "rule of reason" approach to franchise tying.[64] As elsewhere in antitrust, the factors to be considered in the analysis and their relative weight are left undefined and vague, other than the suggestion that primary emphasis be given the effect of the practice in the tying and tied product markets. The goal of this line of analysis is to measure injury to competitors of the franchisor or its suppliers, rather than injury to franchisees. The franchisee response, in part, has been to seek special legislation (discussed infra p. 782) addressing franchisor abuse in the selection, termination and ongoing franchisor-franchisee relationship rather than trust their fortunes to the meandering vagaries of antitrust policy as it grapples with franchise tying arrangements.

(3) *Tie-Ins Under Section 5 of the F.T.C. Act.* In *Federal Trade Commission v. Gratz,*[65] the Commission found that a dominant distributor of U. S. Steel Corporation's steel ties for cotton bales was refusing to sell scarce steel ties to any customer who would not buy a corresponding amount of jute bagging, in which the cotton bale is wrapped. The Supreme Court set aside the Commission's cease and desist order, saying:

> Nothing is alleged which would justify the conclusion that the public suffered injury or that competitors had reasonable ground for complaint. All question of monopoly or combination being out of the way, a private merchant, acting with entire good faith, may properly refuse to sell except in conjunction, such closely associated articles as ties and bagging.

Gratz was expressly overruled in *Federal Trade Commission v. Brown Shoe Co.,*[66] sustaining the Commission's order under Section 5 against a provision in the Brown franchise agreement requiring dealers to "concentrate" on sale of Brown shoes and to "have no lines conflicting" therewith, as a condition to obtaining certain special services from the Brown organization.

---

63. See 16 CFR §§ 436.1 et seq. (1981).

64. See Hensley, Franchise Tying: Gauging the Economic Power of a Trademark, 15 U.C. Davis L.Rev. 405 (1981).

65. 253 U.S. 421, 40 S.Ct. 572, 64 L.Ed. 993 (1920).

66. 384 U.S. 316, 86 S.Ct. 1501, 16 L.Ed.2d 587 (1966).

The Supreme Court declined to require proof of effect on competition such as would be required in a proceeding under Section 3 of the Clayton Act.

In *Sperry and Hutchinson Co. v. Federal Trade Commission* [67] it appeared that S & H, the dominant firm in the field, sold redeemable "green stamps" to grocers and other retailers. They are willing to pay for the stamps and absorb the cost as advertising (or increase the consumer price) because customers are motivated to return to the S & H franchisees to fill up their stamp books in sufficient numbers to trade in for the gadgets in which they are redeemable. Among the objections to such an arrangement are that: (i) it tends to tie the sale of groceries to the sale of gadgets; (ii) it tends, like a requirements contract, to constrain the housewife's choice of grocery suppliers; (iii) it impairs competition in groceries by making price comparisons more difficult; (iv) it inflates the price of groceries not only by the amounts paid to S & H by the grocers but by the labor and administrative costs involved in handling and issuing the stamps; (v) it imposes inconvenience on the housewife to the extent that she must spend time and energy going to the redemption centers; (vi) since many stamps never are redeemed, the value attributed to the stamps in advertising by the issuer and the stores never materializes for a substantial number of housewives.

The market response to some of the foregoing was the appearance of "trading stamp exchanges", that is, firms that would exchange "green stamps" for "gold stamps", or pay cash for stamps, thus giving the customer greater freedom to shop at stores issuing different varieties of stamps. In a number of suits brought in state courts throughout the country, S & H invoked trademark and contractual rights, and secured injunctions against the handling of its stamps by trading stamp exchanges. The FTC issued a cease and desist order against interference by lawsuit or otherwise with the conduct of the exchanges. The court set this order aside, by a vote of 2–1 saying:

> To be the type of practice that the Commission has power to declare "unfair" the act complained of must fall within one of the following types of violations: (1) a per se violation of antitrust policy, (2) a violation of the letter of either the Sherman, Clayton or Robinson-Patman Act, or (3) a violation of the spirit of these acts as recognized by the Supreme Court of the United States.

The Supreme Court held that the Court of Appeals "erred" in its construction of Section 5 of the F.T.C. Act, and stated:

> [L]egislative and judicial authorities alike convince us that the Federal Trade Commission does not arrogate excessive power to itself if, in measuring a practice against the elusive, but congressionally mandated standard of fairness, it, like a court of equity, considers public values beyond simply those enshrined in the letter or encompassed in the spirit of the antitrust laws.[68]

Although the Court found error in the legal standard applied by the Fifth Circuit, the Court affirmed the setting aside of the order and the case was remanded on the grounds that the facts in the record did not accord with the legal theory the F.T.C. adopted for entry of its order.

Query: May the F.T.C. condemn conduct having some but not all the elements of a tie-in under the antitrust laws as an unfair method of competi-

67. 432 F.2d 146 (5th Cir. 1970).

68. Federal Trade Commission v. Sperry & Hutchinson Co., 405 U.S. 233, 244, 92 S.Ct. 898, 905, 31 L.Ed.2d 170 (1972).

tion? On F.T.C. discretion under Section 5 to supplement the anti-discrimination controls specified in the Clayton and Robinson-Patman Acts, see p. 905.

The issue of trading stamps redeemable in merchandise, or "profit-sharing" coupons, may be subjected to special taxation or prohibited, on the theory that such schemes partake of the evils of lotteries or gaming and so are within the police power of the States.[69]

(4) *"Full-Line Forcing"; Excessive Sales Pressure on Franchisee by Multi-Line Firms as Tie-In Under Section 5: Atlantic Refining Co. v. Federal Trade Commission;*[70] *Federal Trade Commission v. Texaco, Inc.* [71]. A giant Petroleum Company markets gasoline and auto accessories, including tires, through "independent" service stations under contracts and leases readily terminable by the supplier, e.g., for failure effectively to market supplier's wares. Following a period during which Petroleum Company has been purchasing tires and other accessories for resale through its dealer system, it shifts to a new plan under which a giant tire company sells directly to the service station. Tire Company pays Petroleum Company an overriding commission on sales to the service stations, and representatives of the two companies call jointly on the dealers to urge "vigorously" the promotion of Tire Company products. There was no requirement that dealers refrain from handling products of competing suppliers. The F.T.C. found that the effect of the plan was as though Petroleum Company had agreed with Tire Company to require its dealers to buy Tire Company products. Refusing to hear evidence concerning the improved efficiency of the overriding commission as against the purchase-resale distribution system, the Commission not only ordered the parties to cease overt coercion of dealers, but also banned any arrangements under which Petroleum Company receives a commission on sales by Tire Company through Petroleum Company's distribution system.

The Supreme Court sustained the Commission's orders, emphasizing the "broad delegation" of authority to define unfair practices which Congress intended to confer on the FTC, the Commission's responsibility to halt anti-competitive practices in their "incipiency", the unequal bargaining power of the big petroleum companies and their dealers, and the "vice" of:

> " 'utilization of economic power in one market to curtail competition in another . . .' Here the TBA [tires, batteries, and accessories] manufacturer has purchased the oil company's economic power and used it as a partial substitute for competitive merit in gaining a major share of the TBA market. The nonsponsored brands do not compete on the even terms of price and quality competition; they must overcome, in addition, the influence of the dominant oil company that has been paid to induce its dealers to buy the recommended brand."[72]

Must the F.T.C. prove "coercion"?[73] Is the purchase-resale plan also illegal? Is Petroleum company less likely to use its inherent economic power to force dealers to push tires which it has bought from Tire company and there-

69. Rast v. Van Deman & Lewis, 240 U.S. 342, 36 S.Ct. 370, 60 L.Ed. 679 (1916); but cf. Sperry & Hutchinson Co. v. Hoegh, 246 Iowa 9, 65 N.W.2d 410 (1954).

70. 381 U.S. 357, 85 S.Ct. 1498, 14 L.Ed.2d 443 (1965).

71. 393 U.S. 223, 89 S.Ct. 429, 21 L.Ed.2d 394 (1968).

72. Id. at 230, 89 S.Ct. at 433, 21 L.Ed., at 400.

73. Cf. Tire Sales Corp. v. Cities Service Oil Co., 637 F.2d 467 (7th Cir. 1980), certiorari denied 451 U.S. 920, 101 S.Ct. 1999, 68 L.Ed.2d 312 (1981) (similar facts; proof of dealer coercion required in private suit by tire wholesaler cut off by oil company from supplying company dealers).

fore owns, rather than tires which it is selling on commission? If the Commission opinion fails to articulate any respect in which sales-commission is more restrictive than purchase-resale, which it replaced, should the order be set aside? Is it unlawful for Petroleum company to require its dealers to handle its tires, batteries, and accessories, as well as its gasoline?[74] Is the "double-teaming" sales effort the crucial circumstance in the cases? Are the cases to be viewed as partial "mergers"?

"Full line forcing" often occurs in hard goods products, where a retailer is required to take an entire line of products in order to purchase a portion of the line. For example, a hardware store may agree to become a dealer for "X" Company's entire line of power tools in order to sell "X's" popular power drill. So long as the dealer is free in fact, as in *Schwinn* and *Sylvania*, to carry competing power tools, such transactions are seldom challenged,[75] absent coercion like that condemned in the tying cases or injury to competitors in the TBA cases.

(5) *Who Is "Injured" by the Restraint; Standing of the Franchisor to Sue.* Billy Baxter, Inc. v. Coca Cola Co.,[76] denied standing in the following circumstances. Billy Baxter marketed flavoring extracts for soft-drinks to franchised bottlers who in turn, supplied retail soft-drink dealers. Defendants, giant producers and distributors of extracts used in bottling soft drinks, allegedly combined with their franchised bottlers to bring pressure to bear on soft drink retailers so as to limit access to the retail market by plaintiff and his franchisees. The court held that the "target" of the violations, if any, was retailers' purchases from bottlers, and that any damage done to franchisor was "incidental". Billy Baxter neither sold bottled drinks, nor so dominated the activities of his franchisees as to be identified with them, even though the royalties he received from them in exchange for use of his trademark and processes would be adversely affected by defendants' restraints on retailers.

But cf. *Karseal Corp. v. Richfield Oil Corp.*,[77] (franchisor selling the identical product which his franchisees resold to retailers is sufficiently identified with the product to be within the "target area" of defendant's exclusionary practices directed to retail outlets); *Perkins v. Standard Oil of California* [78] and *Malamud v. Sinclair Oil Co.*[79] (real estate investment companies financing retail gas stations have standing to challenge oil company franchising practices denying expansion of retail franchises).[80]

"Standing" in antitrust cases is a question of considerable controversy, generally.[81] Varying tests of "target area", "remoteness" etc., have been employed by the courts to define who may sue. In *Blue Shield of Virginia v. McCready* [82] the Supreme Court upheld the antitrust "standing" of a con-

---

74. See Burstein, A Theory of Full-Line Forcing, 55 Nw.L.Rev. 62 (1960).

75. See Sullivan, Antitrust 456.

76. 431 F.2d 183 (2d Cir. 1970).

77. 221 F.2d 358 (9th Cir. 1955).

78. 395 U.S. 642, 89 S.Ct. 1871, 23 L.Ed.2d 599 (1969).

79. 521 F.2d 1142 (6th Cir. 1975).

80. Berger & Bernstein, An Analytical Framework for Antitrust Standing, 86 Yale L.J. 809 (1977); Flynn, Rethinking Sherman Act Section 1 Analysis: Three Proposals for Reducing the Chaos, 49 Antitrust L.J. 1593 (1982); see Sher-

man, Antitrust Standing: From *Loeb* to *Malamud*, 51 N.Y.U.L.Rev. 374 (1976); Tyler, Private Antitrust Litigation: The Problem of Standing, 49 U.Colo.L.Rev. 269 (1978). Cf. Long Island Lighting Co. v. Standard Oil Co. (Cal.), 521 F.2d 1269 (2d Cir. 1975), certiorari denied 423 U.S. 1073, 96 S.Ct. 855, 47 L.Ed.2d 83 (1976).

81. See articles cited supra note 80.

82. ___ U.S. ___, 102 S.Ct. 2540, 73 L.Ed.2d 149 (1982). See also, Associated General Contractors of California, Inc. v. California State Council of Carpenters, ___ U.S. ___, 103 S.Ct. 897, 74 L.Ed.2d 723 (1983) (Dismissing antitrust claim;

sumer denied reimbursement by Blue Shield for psychotherapy services provided by a clinical psychologist. Claiming Blue Shield was engaged in a conspiracy with the Neuropsychiatric Society of Virginia to deny consumer reimbursement unless the service was billed through a physician, McCready sought treble damages. The trial court denied McCready standing on the ground that the object of the alleged conspiracy was to exclude clinical psychologists from the psychotherapy market and that McCready was not in the area of the economy threatened by a breakdown of competitive conditions. In upholding the Fourth Circuit's reversal of the district court and finding McCready had "standing" to sue, the Court held McCready's injury was "clearly foreseeable; indeed it was a necessary step in effecting the ends of the illegal conspiracy."

Query. What are the implications of the *McCready* case in franchise tying cases? Do franchisees subject to a tie have standing to attack tying aimed at suppliers competing with the franchisor? Do suppliers seeking to supply franchisees subject to an unlawful tying arrangement have standing to attack a tying arrangement aimed at franchisees?

(6) *Tying in Regulated Industries.* Tying and other anticompetive practices by regulated industries, where not sanctioned by the regulatory legislation or the agency administering the law, are subject to the antitrust laws.[83] But cf. *Washington Gas Light Co. v. Virginia Electric & Power Co.*,[84] and *Gas Light Co. v. Georgia Power Co.*,[85] involving steep rate discounts offered by electric companies to home builders installing all-electric appliances, thus taking business from the gas companies. Application of the Sherman Act was held precluded because the antitrust laws are inapplicable to "state action". Approval of the rates by the state utility commission, or even failure to intervene against the rates when there was jurisdiction to do so, was regarded as state action. But cf. *Cantor v. Detroit Edison Co.*,[86] substantially narrowing the state action doctrine as applied to voluntary rate filings having an anticompetitive effect. *Columbia Gas of New York, Inc. v. New York State Electric & Gas Corp.*,[87] held that similar rates could be challenged under state antitrust legislation. Could the scope of federal antitrust jurisdiction be cut back, without amendment of federal law, by states' undertaking to regulate and cartelize businesses within their territory?

(7) *Tying to the Bell System's Telephone Monopoly; Scope of the Lawful Monopoly.* Telephone companies provide subscribers with a telephone and access to the telephone system through a cable linked to the subscriber's home or office. State approved rates are charged for the lease of the telephone and the cable. Additional charges may be imposed for choosing a telephone in a color other than black, touchtone dialing, or longer wiring. May the telephone company refuse to deal with customers who insist upon buying their own telephone or who install their own accessories?[88] May the telephone company charge higher rates for system access to those who use their

injury "indirect" and not "antitrust injury".

83. See Northern Pacific Railway Co. v. United States, 356 U.S. 1, 78 S.Ct. 514, 2 L.Ed.2d 545 (1958); Otter Tail Power Co. v. United States, supra p. 124; United States v. Philadelphia National Bank, supra p. 220; California Motor Transport Co. v. Trucking Unlimited, infra p. 838.

84. 438 F.2d 248 (4th Cir. 1971).

85. 440 F.2d 1135 (5th Cir. 1971).

86. 428 U.S. 579, 96 S.Ct. 3110, 49 L.Ed.2d 1141 (1976).

87. 28 N.Y.2d 117, 320 N.Y.S.2d 57, 268 N.E.2d 790 (1971).

88. See In the Matter of Carterphone, 13 F.C.C.2d 420 (1968); Litton Systems, Inc. v. Southwestern Bell Telephone Co., 539 F.2d 418 (5th Cir. 1976); Benjamin & Read, Ma Bell Fights for Her Monopoly, N.Y. Times Sunday Magazine (Nov. 28, 1976) p. 32; Symposium, Antitrust and Monopoly Policy in the Communications

own equipment in order to make up for revenues lost by their refusal to take company supplied equipment?[89] *North Carolina Utilities Commission v. Federal Communications Commission* (North Carolina II),[90] sustained the Commission's regulations establishing a system for registering terminal devices which may be attached to the AT&T network without carrier-supplied connecting devices. This followed *North Carolina Utilities Commission v. Federal Communications Commission* (North Carolina I),[91] which sustained FCC jurisdiction over terminal devices used for both interstate and intrastate traffic. The Federal Communications Act explicitly reserves state jurisdiction over intrastate communication and rates, but the court held that the Commission's power is paramount where a communications device is used for both interstate and intrastate calls, even though the usage is overwhelmingly intrastate. The dissenting judge believed that the Commission had failed to address itself to the issue of the economic consequence of opening up the terminal business to independent competition through the registration system. His perception of the evidence was that competition in terminal devices would require increase in intrastate communications rates, and that the underlying issue was how should the regulated monopoly be defined.

The controversy over tying arrangements, the scope of state regulation, and the future structure and operation of the Bell System and the telecommunications industry generally promises to remain with us. Continued judicial and Congressional involvement in the controversy can be expected well into the 80's with settlement of the Governments' monopolization case against AT&T, and the rapid evolution of new technologies, disrupting existing markets and forging new ones.[92]

F. SELECTION AND TERMINATION OF DEALERS

1. INTRODUCTION

Many of the cases set forth or discussed in the previous sections of this chapter have arisen in the context of franchising. As noted in the Introduction, supra p. 588, franchising has been a rapidly evolving and growing form of marketing in recent decades; approximately

Industry, 13 Antitrust Bull. 871 (1968); Note, F.C.C. Computer Inquiry: Interfaces of Competitive and Regulated Markets, 71 Mich.L.Rev. 172 (1972); Text note on Consent Decree Reorganizing A.T. & T., supra p. 192.

Federal Communications Commission regulation prevails over efforts by state regulatory commissions to restrict the attachment of "foreign" devices to phones interconnected with the AT&T system. North Carolina Utilities Commission v. Federal Communications Commission, 537 F.2d 787 (4th Cir. 1976).

89. See "Divestiture in Regulated Industries", supra p. 191, describing the controversy over dissolution of the Bell System by consent decree. Considerable controversy exists over the terms and conditions upon which competing carriers will be allowed access in and out of the divested local companies.

90. 552 F.2d 1036 (4th Cir. 1977).

91. 537 F.2d 787 (4th Cir. 1976).

92. See generally Symposium, Communications Regulation, 69 Calif.L. 497 (1981); Symposium, Law and the Emerging Video Technologies, 25 N.Y.L.Sch.L. Rev. 863 (1980).

$332.7 billion or 32% of all retail sales in 1981 took place through franchised outlets of one sort or another.[93]

While franchising has been a relatively long-standing marketing system in areas like automobile sales and retail gasoline distribution,[94] there has been little economic analysis of the phenomena or settled public policy as to how franchising should or should not be regulated.[95] The varying forms of franchising, described supra p. 755, have some of the characteristics of vertical integration by contract, a joint venture, a fiduciary relationship, a common enterprise or mutual investment scheme for profit, a trademark or other licensing of "property" rights, or a status relationship similar to those found in the law of agency.

Not surprisingly, the complexity of defining what franchising is and the uncertainty about its economic, social, and other consequences have provoked varying legal responses to the phenomena. The legal process has become involved in regulating the initiation of the relationship, the ongoing relationship and the termination of franchisees or dealers in several different ways. For example, the F.T.C. by Trade Practice Rule [96] and several states by statute or state securities regulation [97] have imposed disclosure requirements upon franchisors soliciting new franchisees in response to widespread fraud and misrepresentations in the recruitment of dealers or franchisees.[98] In addition to the disclosure of audited financial information, the F.T.C. rule requires the disclosure of such information as the franchisor's business experience, litigation and bankruptcy history and policy on termination, cancellation and renewal.[99] Several states

93. U.S. Dept. of Commerce, Franchising in the Economy: 1979–81 p. 12 (1981).

94. The history of franchising in the United States is set forth in E. Lewis & R. Hancock, The Franchise System of Distribution (1963).

95. For general surveys of franchising, see H. Brown, Franchising: Trap for the Trusting (1970); J. Curry, Partners for Profit: A Study of Franchising (1966); D. Thompson, Franchise Operations and Antitrust (1971). The history and evolution of the McDonald's franchise system is traced by one of its founders in R. Kroc, Grinding It Out, The Making of McDonald's (1977).

96. 16 C.F.R. § 436.1, et seq. (1981). The Commission has also issued Guides to Compliance with F.T.C. Franchising Rule, Trade Reg. Rep. (CCH) No. 396, Part II (Aug. 1, 1979). The Rule is analyzed in Tifford, The Federal Trade Commission Trade Regulation Rule on Franchises and Business Opportunity Ventures, 36 Bus.L. 1051 (1981); Note, The Federal Trade Commission Franchise Disclosure Rule, 13 J.Marsh.L.Rev. 637 (1980).

97. State and federal laws regulating franchising are collected in a looseleaf service published by Commerce Clearing House titled "Business Franchise Guide." State and federal securities law regulation may also apply. See Comment, What Is a Security? Howey, Turner Enterprises and Franchise Agreements, 22 Kan.L.Rev. 55 (1973); Securities Act Release No. 5211, Securities Exchange Act Release No. 9387, Applicability of Securities Laws to Multilevel Distributorship and Pyramid Sales Plans (Nov. 30, 1971). State franchise disclosure statutes are collected in Business Franchise Guide (CCH) ¶ 3010 et seq. For a comprehensive survey of state laws regulating franchising, see Note, State Regulation of Franchising, 59 Minn.L.Rev. 1027 (1975). On state termination and non-renewal legislation, see Eaton, State Regulation of Franchise and Dealership Terminations: An Overview, 49 Antitrust L.J. 1331 (1981); Caffey, Franchise Termination and Nonrenewal Legislation: Recent Developments and Trends in State Legislation, 49 Antitrust L.J. 1343 (1981).

98. See H. Brown, supra note 95; Note, supra note 96 at 638.

99. 16 C.F.R. § 436.1.

require similar disclosures for franchise solicitations made within their borders. Many states and the F.T.C. are developing uniform disclosure standards based on the Uniform Franchise Offering Circular developed by the Midwest Securities Commissioners Association.[1]

Other responses to the franchising phenomena include the use of federal and state antitrust laws to counter particular abuses occurring in the relationship and the enactment of special franchise legislation either to govern the selection, ongoing relationship or termination of franchisees generally or to regulate the relationship in particular industries like auto retailing or gasoline marketing. The next subsection is designed to survey briefly the use of antitrust policy to regulate franchising. While an exhaustive treatment of the rapidly growing area of special franchise statutory developments is beyond the scope of these materials, part 3 of this section briefly summarizes and reviews the significant federal and state statutory developments regulating dealer non-renewal or termination. The attorney representing a supplier, dealer, or regulatory agency concerned with franchising must be alert to the potential relevance of a wide and rapidly evolving array of legal tools bearing upon the selection, ongoing relationship, and termination of supplier-dealer and franchisor-franchisee. In both the planning of the business relationship and the resolution of disputes arising during or at the end of the relationship, the resourceful and imaginative counselor will find there is a wide and growing variety of legal paths relevant to a particular problem he or she confronts. While antitrust doctrine may often be a relevant consideration, one should not ignore the often more direct approach of special franchise legislation or other legal approaches which may be available.[2]

2. ANTITRUST LIMITATIONS UPON DEALER SELECTION AND TERMINATION

AMERICAN MOTOR INNS, INC. v. HOLIDAY INNS, INC.

United States Court of Appeals, Third Circuit, 1975.
521 F.2d 1230.

[Digest. Holiday Inns, Inc. (HI) operates the nation's largest chain of motels, three times the size of its nearest competitor. HI owns and operates 281 "inns" itself and licenses 1099 other inns built and operated by franchisees under the HI trademark. American Motor Inns, Inc. (AMI) is HI's largest franchisee, operating 48

1. The Circular and Comments on it are reproduced in Business Franchise Guide (CCH) ¶ 5700, et seq. For an extensive analysis of the Maryland franchise disclosure law, see Shapiro & Carolan, Franchise Law Compliance: Before the Logo Hits the Streets, 10 U.Balt.L. Rev. 1 (1980).

2. Reference should also be made to the common law and statutory developments peculiar to each state. See H. Brown, Code Impact on Existing Franchises, 87 Com.L.J. 83 (1982); Chisum, State Regulation of Franchising: The Washington Experience, 48 Wash.L. Rev. 293 (1973); Symposium, Recent Developments in the Law Affecting Franchise Organization, 1980 Ariz.St.L.J. 433; Note, Franchises: Statutory and Common Law Causes of Action in Missouri, 45 Mo.L.Rev. 42 (1980); Note, Business Opportunity Purchasers Act: The Unfulfilled Promise to Ohio Franchisees, 41 Ohio St. L.J. 477 (1980).

franchised HI Hitt motels. AMI applied to HI for a franchise to operate an HI franchised motel at Newark Airport. AMI had submitted the winning bid to the City of Elizabeth, New Jersey, for a parcel
of land adjacent to the site of a new terminal at the Newark Airport
conditioned on a requirement that $1 million of construction of a new
hotel-motel complex be completed within 18 months. HI followed its
normal procedure of sending written notices of AMI's application to
the three HI franchised inns nearest the proposed location (the notices were called "radius letters") and referred the application and
responses to the "radius letters" to its "Franchise Committee." If
the "radius letters" produced an objection, the Franchise Committee
could only deny the application and refer the application to the Board
of Directors of HI for review of the application and objections.
AMI's application was objected to by the owners of a franchised Holiday Inn near the existing Newark Airport; the objector had unsuccessfully bid on the Elizabeth property as the site for a new HI
franchised hotel-motel. HI rejected AMI's application. AMI then requested HI's permission to build on the Elizabeth site an inn to be
franchised by the Sheraton hotel chain. HI's permission was required because the standard HI franchise agreement barred HI franchisees from operating non-Holiday Inns. HI refused to waive the
non-Holiday Inn clause. HI claimed that this clause was necessary in
order to encourage franchisees to make maximum use of HI's
"Holidex" advanced reservation system, a centralized computer reservation system with terminals in all Holiday Inns. Past experience
with franchisees owning non-HI inns indicated they would not use the
system to refer customers to HI inns in cities where the franchisee
owned a non-HI inn. By barring ownership of non-HI inns and requiring franchisees to refer customers seeking advanced reservations
to other HI inns, HI found it could make maximum use of its Holidex
system and franchisees could mutually benefit each other. The District Court found 38% of the total occupancy of all Holiday Inns
originated through "Holidex", and reservations made by one inn for
another inn accounted for 21.4% of total occupancy.

HI also followed a policy of reserving certain cities (152 cities with
281 inns) for itself by operating wholly owned inns in those cities and
refusing to license franchisee-owned inns in those cities or permitting
franchisees to build non-HI inns in those cities. AMI claimed and the
trial court found that this policy together with the "radius letter"
practice and the non-Holiday Inn clause in the franchise agreements
constituted a horizontal allocation of markets. The district court also
found a conspiracy to deny AMI its Newark application and a national conspiracy to divide markets through the "radius letters" practice.
It held that the non-HI inn clause was an unreasonable restraint of
trade, and that HI's practice of reserving certain cities to itself, coupled with restrictive provisions of the franchise agreement and other
HI policies, constituted an unreasonable restraint of trade. After trial on the liability issues, treble damages of $4 million were stipulated
to by the parties and the court awards injunctive relief to AMI. HI
appealed.]

ADAMS, CIRCUIT JUDGE.

In the present case the district court found that HI treated "as a veto" the objections by its existing franchisees to AMI's application for a license at the Elizabeth location. After carefully reviewing the entire record, we cannot say that the trial judge's findings of fact in this regard are clearly erroneous.

By thus permitting its existing franchisees to determine whether a potential competitor would be allowed to enter the Elizabeth-Newark market, HI enabled its franchisees already in the Elizabeth-Newark area to divide that market between themselves, thus precluding further intrabrand competition. Such conduct constitutes a horizontal market allocation that is a violation of the Sherman Act.

HI's treatment of the responses to the radius letters regarding AMI's Newark application is similar to the practice which the Supreme Court determined to be *per se* unlawful in United States v. Topco Associates. . . .

Concededly, HI, in the case at hand, was not created, nor is it in general controlled, by its licensees, as Topco was. Further, there are no rigidly defined territories—as in Topco—within which HI's Newark-area franchisees have the exclusive right to operate. However, according to the finder of fact here, HI treated the franchisees' objections to AMI's application as dispositive and thus allowed its licensees, like the existing Topco members, to determine whether the applicant would be allowed to compete with them. Although there are no explicit limits on the area over which the [Newark] franchisees exercise veto power, the radius letters from HI, together with the significance accorded to the franchisees' objections, function like the combination of the exclusivity provisions and the veto power over new members in *Topco* "effectively to insulate members from competition" under the Holiday Inn Trademark.

HI's action in denying AMI's application, according to the trial court, was not taken unilaterally, but rather in concert with one or more of its licensees. If HI had acted independently in refusing AMI's request, such conduct might have been akin to the vertical restraints in *Schwinn*. But where, as here, the action in question is ascertained by the finder of fact to be joint or collaborative, it is sufficient to constitute a "combination or conspiracy" within the meaning of the Sherman Act.

· · ·

The district court concluded that HI's practice of sending radius letters to the three inns nearest the proposed sites effected a general or national conspiracy among HI's franchisees, as well as a local one, to divide the market among themselves. Each Holiday Inn, the court found, was able to impede the granting of a franchise which the existing licensee believed would compete with his own motor hotel. "Holiday Inns franchisees," the court held, "have utilized the parent HI . . . to allocate territories horizontally so as to restrict intrabrand competition."

We agree with HI, however, that the issue of a general or national conspiracy was not fairly litigated in the trial court because AMI and the trial judge on a number of occasions indicated to counsel for HI that, apart from the non-Holiday Inn clause and the company town policy, there remained in the case no issue as to a national conspiracy. [The Court proceeded to quote extensively from the record demonstrating that HI had been precluded from litigating the purpose and effect of the use of "radius letters" on a national basis and concluded the issue should be remanded for further proceedings.]

AMI contends, and the district court determined that the restriction on Holiday Inn franchisees' ownership of motor hotels other than Holiday Inns constituted an unreasonable restraint of trade which violated the Sherman Act.

. . .

The district court's analysis of the non-Holiday Inn clause refers to three considerations in support of its conclusion that the clause is condemned under section 1 of the Sherman Act: (1) "The Holidex system can be protected adequately without a 'device' as restrictive of competition as the non-Holiday Inn clause;" (2) the non-Holiday Inn clause results in "the foreclosure of all hostelers competing with HI from doing business with all HI franchisees;" and (3) "the effect of the . . . clause 'is the intended one of reducing and preventing competition among Holiday Inns franchisees and between franchised inns and company-owned inns.' "

The trial judge's explanation of the grounds for his conclusion that the non-Holiday Inn clause is unlawful, however, does not reflect any exploration into one of the major determinants under the rule-of-reason test—the impact of the restraint on competition within the relevant market. In *Schwinn* the Supreme Court said, "Our inquiry is whether . . . the effect upon competition in the market place is substantially adverse." It is only if the *impact* of the restriction is to unreasonably restrain competition that it is illegal. . . .

Here the district court's opinion terminates its Sherman Act analysis of the clause after finding that the clause was intended to and did reduce competition among HI and its franchisees, and that the Holiday Inn referral system could be protected by other means. The analysis does not take into account whether the competition eliminated by the clause is significant within the context of the total competition extant in the industry, nor does the analysis attempt in any way to measure the effect of the challenged restriction on the market structure.

In addition, the district court does not point to any testimony to the effect that the challenged clause makes it any more onerous for other motel operators to compete effectively with HI or its franchisees. Although the court made some findings relevant to the anticompetitive effect of the clause, the portion of the opinion reflecting the legal analysis of the non-Holiday Inn clause under the Sherman Act does not demonstrate that considerations like the number or size of the firms in the industry or HI's market share played any part in the court's decision on this question. Indeed, the court does not, in deciding the Sherman Act issue, even discuss what the relevant market is, although the cases make it clear that such a market definition is fundamental to evaluating the reasonableness of the restraint.

Because the district court opinion does not demonstrate that in making his rule of reason analysis the trial judge took into account many of the relevant conditions in the industry, that portion of the judgment regarding the reasonableness of the non-Holiday Inn clause must be vacated. Since the parties may have adduced at trial relevant information which is not manifested in the district court's opinion, the case will be remanded for a re-evaluation of this question by the district court on the basis of the existing record. . . .

If the restraint on competition caused by the non-Holiday Inn clause is otherwise reasonable, HI's purpose in adopting the clause, as found by the trial judge here, does not by itself render the clause a violation of the Sherman Act. Concededly, an agreement is inimical to section 1 if it results in an otherwise *reasonable* restraint of trade but was *designed* to achieve a forbidden restraint. Thus a contract, regardless of its actual effect, contravenes the Act if it was intended as part of a scheme to monopolize or to fix prices or to drive a competitor out of the market. In the present case, however, the trial judge found that the intended effect was the one which was in fact achieved. The issue remains, therefore, whether that resultant restriction on competition is, under the circumstances of this case, unreasonable.

Although relevant to ascertaining the reasonableness of the non-Holiday Inn clause, it is not determinative that the Holidex system could, as the district court found, be "protected adequately" by less restrictive alternatives. In a rule of reason case, the test is not whether the defendant deployed the least restrictive alternative. Rather the issue is whether the restriction actually implemented is "fairly necessary" in the circumstances of the particular case, or whether the restriction "exceed[s] the outer limits of restraint reasonably necessary to protect the defendant."

The Ninth Circuit has stated in Siegel v. Chicken Delight, Inc. that "Restraint of trade can be justified only in the absence of less restrictive alternatives." The restraint involved here, however, unlike the tie-in at issue in *Siegel*, is not *per se* unlawful. Like the Ninth Circuit, the Fifth Circuit has also, in Copper Liquor, Inc. v. Adolph Coors Co., utilized the "least restrictive alternative" test. There again, however, as in *Siegel* the restraint which the defendant sought to justify was one which the Fifth Circuit considered to be so detrimental in its effect on competition as to be *per se* unlawful.

In its descriptions of the rule of reason inquiry, the Supreme Court has never indicated that, regardless of the other circumstances present, the availability of an alternative means of achieving the asserted business purpose renders the existing arrangement unlawful if that alternative would be less restrictive of competition no matter to how small a degree. . . .

Application of the rigid "no less restrictive alternative" test in cases such as this one would place an undue burden on the ordinary conduct of business. Entrepreneurs such as HI would then be made guarantors that the imaginations of lawyers could not conjure up some method of achieving the business purpose in question that would result in a somewhat lesser restriction of trade. And courts would be placed in the position of second-guessing business judgments as to what arrangements would or would not provide "adequate" protection for legitimate commercial interests.

. . .

HI offers an additional argument which, if accepted, would enable the Court to conclude that the non-Holiday Inn clause is lawful under the Sherman Act without going through the full rule of reason analysis. HI contends that the non-Holiday Inn clause is, in effect, an exclusive dealing agreement. Although section 3 of the Clayton Act is admittedly not applicable to the non-Holiday Inn clause because no goods are involved, HI asserts that the clause cannot violate the Sherman Act because the clause satisfies the standards of section 3 of the Clayton Act, and that such standards impose tighter restraints on exclusive dealing arrangements than does the Sherman Act.

HI would seem to be correct in stating that an exclusive dealing arrangement which satisfies the test of legality set out in the Clayton Act would a fortiori be lawful under the less stringent Sherman Act. It would also appear true that the non-Holiday Inn clause is analogous, for antitrust purposes, to an exclusive dealing contract. We cannot say, however, on the basis of the record before us, that the clause would necessarily satisfy the standards encompassed within section 3 of the Clayton Act.

In *Tampa Electric*[3] the Supreme Court set forth a three-step analysis for evaluating the legitimacy of an exclusive-dealing arrangement under the Clayton Act:

> *First*, the line of commerce . . . involved must be determined, where it is in controversy, on the basis of the facts peculiar to the case. *Second*, the [geographic] area of effective competition in the known line of commerce must be charted . . . .. *Third*, and last, the competition foreclosed by the contract must be found to constitute a substantial share of the relevant market.[4]

To ascertain whether the exclusive dealing contract in issue forecloses competition in a substantial share of the relevant market,

> it is necessary to weigh the probable effect of the contract on the relevant area of effective competition, taking into account the relative strength of the parties, the proportionate volume of commerce involved in relation to the total volume of commerce in the relevant market area, and the probable immediate and future ef-

3. Tampa Electric Co. v. Nashville Coal Co., 365 U.S. 320, 81 S.Ct. 623, 5 L.Ed.2d 580 (1961).

4. 365 U.S., at 327–28, 81 S.Ct. at 628, 5 L.Ed.2d at 587.

fects which pre-emption of that share of the market might have on effective competition therein.[5]

Here the trial judge stated, "I would hold that the relevant 'product' market is national hotel-motel chains or referral groups." The court's rationale for adopting that product market—or line of commerce—was simply that "[t]he only justification for the non-Holiday Inn clause seriously pressed by HI . . . has been the clause's role in protecting the Holidex System of computerized national referrals." Applying the last two prongs of the tripartite test set out in *Tampa Electric*, he determined that, since Holiday Inns operate nationwide, the relevant geographic area was the United States, and that the non-Holiday Inn clause foreclosed hotel-motel groups which competed with HI from doing business with 14.7% of the relevant market. That degree of market foreclosure, the trial judge concluded, constituted a "substantial share" of the market and would render the non-Holiday Inn clause unlawful under the Clayton Act.

Here, the opinion of the district court does not demonstrate a consideration of sufficient factors to constitute the type of economic analysis explicated by the Supreme Court in *Tampa Electric*. In the portion of his opinion which concludes that the non-Holiday Inn clause would violate the Clayton Act standards, the trial judge in effect relied exclusively on statistics relating to the percentage of the market foreclosed. The district court did not indicate that it had considered "the probable immediate and future effects which preemption of that share of the market might have" within the competitive context of that industry, nor did it in any way advert to the "relative strength of the parties."

Tampa Electric makes clear that in deciding whether an exclusive dealing contract violates section 3, the judiciary must take into account the economic justification for the arrangement. HI argues that the non-Holiday Inn clause protects the Holidex referral system, enables the International Association of Holiday Inns to assess the member inns for joint improvements like the Holiday Inn University, and promotes competition in the hotel-motel industry by fostering a sense of loyalty among HI's franchisees which stimulates a free exchange among the innkeepers of ideas and suggested improvements. Although AMI disputes the significance of some of these business justifications for the clause, the district court, under *Tampa Electric*, should have assessed the clause's restraint on competition in light of these asserted justifications.

Holiday Inns constitute the largest hotel-motel group in the country; the Holiday Inn chain is three times the size of its largest competitor. In view of these factors if the non-Holiday Inn clause does, as the district court determined, foreclose competitors of HI from 14.7% of the market, the clause may well offend the limitations which the Clayton Act places on exclusive contracts. The trial judge, how-

---

5.   365 U.S. at 329, 81 S.Ct. at 629, 5 L.Ed.2d at 588.

ever, has not made clear that he conducted the broad inquiry required by *Tampa Electric*.

. . . It would seem that the proper demarcation of the market in this case would depend on (1) whether Holiday Inns are reasonably interchangeable with other hotels or motor inns, insofar as the traveling public is concerned, or (2) whether HI's franchisees are reasonably fungible with other persons as potential franchisees for other hotel-motel chains. Since the factual issues relevant to interchangeability have not been resolved, this Court is unable to define the limits of the market or markets involved here, and thus we are unable to assess the degree to which the non-Holiday Inn clause forecloses competition in such markets.

We cannot, therefore, decide whether HI is correct in asserting that the non-Holiday Inn clause is an exclusive dealing agreement which satisfies the even more exacting requirements of the Clayton Act. . . .

The district court concluded that the combined effect of the radius letter procedure, the company-town policy and the non-Holiday Inn clause was a horizontal allocation of territories which is *per se* unlawful. . . .

We have already decided that the question of what significance HI generally or nationally affords to objections in response to radius letters regarding applications for new franchises was, in effect, withdrawn from consideration during the course of the trial. Therefore, we are not in a position to judge whether the radius letter procedure in combination with the non-Holiday Inn clause results in an unreasonable restraint of trade on a national basis.

The combination of the company-town policy and the non-Holiday Inn clause, however, does create a basis for finding a horizontal conspiracy between HI, operating on the retail level as a motel-operator, and HI's franchisees. For example, the district court found that the "company-town policy standing alone prevents AMI from building a Holiday Inn in competition with the company-owned inns in Fort Worth. The non-Holiday Inn clause also prevents AMI from building a Sheraton Inn in Fort Worth." The net result of the two practices is that HI and its franchisees have agreed to a division of territories.

The district court concluded that the company-town policy, standing alone, would be satisfactory because, although it resulted in an allocation of territories, it was imposed unilaterally by HI. When the company-town policy is joined with the non-Holiday Inn clause, however, the element of "contract, combination or conspiracy" is fulfilled by the presence of the non-Holiday Inn clause in the franchise agreement, whether or not the non-Holiday Inn clause alone is valid.

Acts by a franchisor, such as HI, that create otherwise unreasonable restraints of trade are not insulated from the antitrust laws by the fact that such company functions as a franchisor as well as a motel operator. The circumstances of this case are similar to those

in Hobart Brothers v. Malcolm T. Gilliand, Inc.[6] Hobart, a manufacturer of welding equipment and supplies, sold its products through
distributors and also competed with those distributors by selling directly to ultimate users. Gilliand was a distributor of Hobart's products and manufactured a line which competed with Hobart's products. The Fifth Circuit held that the distribution agreement between
Hobart and Gilliand that restricted Gilliand's sales of Hobart products to a specified territory constituted a horizontal allocation of territories which was a *per se* violation of the Sherman Act since, as
rival distributors, the two firms operated on the same market level.[7]

In the present case, since HI, in one of its capacities, was dealing
on the same market level as its franchisees, its contracts that, in effect, foreclosed such franchisees from operating either Holiday Inns
or non-Holiday Inns in cities where HI operated an inn, except with
HI's permission, constitute market allocation agreements among competitors. The district court therefore did not err in ruling that the
combination of the non-Holiday Inn clause and the company-town policy constituted an unlawful restraint of trade. . . .

I. CONCLUSION.

The judgment of the district court will be affirmed in part, reversed in part, and vacated in part, as set forth in detail below:

A. The judgment is affirmed insofar as it found a combination or conspiracy with respect to the application for a franchise at
the Newark airport.

B. The finding of a national conspiracy to allocate markets
through the use of radius letters is reversed.

C. The judgment regarding the question whether the non-Holiday Inn clause alone constitutes an unreasonable restraint of
trade is vacated and the cause is remanded for a re-evaluation of
the reasonableness of the clause on the basis of the evidence already adduced.

6. [Court's footnote 84.] 471 F.2d 894
(5th Cir. 1973).

7. [Court's footnote 85.] See Interphoto Corp. v. Minolta Corp., 295
F.Supp. 711 (S.D.N.Y.), aff'd per curiam,
417 F.2d 621 (2d Cir. 1969) (Territorial
customer restrictions in distributorship
agreement between Minolta, which sold
its cameras both through its own distribution system and through independent
distributors and Interphoto, an independent distributor of Minolta's cameras,
constitutes a horizontal market allocation). Cf. United States v. McKesson and
Robbins, Inc., 351 U.S. 305, 76 S.Ct. 937,
100 L.Ed. 1209 (1956) (Agreements between McKesson, a drug manufacturer
which also operated as a distributor, and
its independent distributors, relating to
the resale price of McKesson products,

are not insulated from the Sherman Act
by the McGuire and Miller-Tydings Acts
because the agreements are between
competing distributors rather than between a manufacturer and a distributor).

HI cites Capital Temporaries, Inc. v.
Olsten Corp., 506 F.2d 658 (2d Cir. 1974),
to support its argument that a noncompe-
tition agreement between a franchisee
and its franchisor, who also competes
with the franchisee, is not a horizontal
conspiracy. That case, however, is not
on point in this respect because the non-
competition agreement there related only
to the franchisee's competing with his
own franchised operations, and an ancillary limitation on the franchisee's competing with the franchisor within a limited time after termination of his franchise
and within a limited geographic area.

D. The judgment will be reversed insofar as it determined that the combined effect of the radius-letter procedure, the company-town policy and the non-Holiday Inn clause constituted an unreasonable restraint of trade.

E. The judgment will be affirmed to the extent that it determined that the combination of the company-town policy and the non-Holiday Inn clause constituted an unreasonable restraint of trade.

F. The amount of damages will be reconsidered in light of this opinion and any subsequent determination regarding liability made by the district court on remand.

The cause will be remanded to the district court for further proceedings consistent with this opinion.

NOTES AND QUERIES

(1) *Queries*: What advice would you have given Holiday Inns, Inc. upon receiving the application from American Motor Inns, Inc. for a franchise to operate a Holiday Inn at the Newark Airport? In light of the Court's conclusions A–E, how would you advise Holiday Inns, Inc. to change its practices or its standard franchise agreement to avoid future antitrust difficulties? Would you advise American Motor Inns, Inc. that it is free to construct non-Holiday Inns wherever it wishes without much risk that Holiday Inns, Inc. can lawfully cancel its existing franchises or refuse to grant its future applications for new Holiday Inn franchises?

(2) *Regulating Dealer Selection by Antitrust Policy.* The refusal to select one as a dealer or authorize an existing dealer to open at a new location as in *Holiday Inns, Principe,* and *Sylvania* can trigger an antitrust dispute. Where the decision is a unilateral one of the franchisor, the necessary contract, combination or conspiracy element for a § 1 violation is not present. Where, however, there is franchisor consultation with existing franchisees or evidence of existing franchisees urging the franchisor not to appoint the dealer, the requisite duality may be present.[8] Active dealer opposition and coercion of their supplier not to deal may convert the restraint into one labeled a vertical restraint to boycott the potential dealer. See Note, infra p. 779.

Existing dealers or franchisees jointly pressuring their common supplier or franchisor not to deal with a potential dealer or franchisee may also be liable on a horizontal boycott theory. In *Com-Tel, Inc. v. DuKane Corp.,*[9] franchisees of a sound equipment manufacturer were held to have committed a horizontal group boycott when they conspired to deny the plaintiff, a successful bidder on a public contract specifying the franchisor's sound equipment, access to the equipment. The court held:

Although the primary concern of the antitrust laws is with interbrand competition, intrabrand competition is still a concern, especially in cases such as this where no benefits from increased interbrand competition may or did result from the vertical restrictions. This arrangement must be viewed as a horizontal attempt to exclude a competitor on the horizon-

8. See Com-Tel, Inc. v. DuKane Corp., 669 F.2d 404 (6th Cir. 1982); Contractor Utility Sales Co., Inc. v. Certain-Teed Products Corp., 638 F.2d 1061 (7th Cir. 1981); Borger v. Yamaha International Corp., 625 F.2d 390 (2d Cir. 1980).

9. 669 F.2d 404 (6th Cir. 1982).

tal level and to restrict interbrand competition without an offsetting benefit to interbrand competition.[10]

The court rejected the further argument that "proof of a general exclusion
from competition must be offered, and that exclusion from one job is insufficient to make out an antitrust violation" with the observation:

> [T]he intent of the per se categories is to root out without further inquiry
> those behaviors which have a 'pernicious' effect on competition in the
> marketplace. . . . [E]xclusionary conduct has a pernicious effect on
> competition when one project is affected. It is the market behavior, not
> the impact of the behavior itself, that warrants condemnation of the per
> se rule.[11]

Query: Do you agree that the exclusion of a single potential dealer on a
single job should be an actionable federal antitrust claim on a *per se* basis?[12]
Recall the Supreme Court's decision in *Klor's,* supra p. 541.

BATTLE v. LUBRIZOL CORP.

United States Court of Appeals, Eighth Circuit, 1982.
673 F.2d 984, rehearing *en banc* granted, 43 ATRR 774 (Oct. 21, 1982).*

McMILLIAN, CIRCUIT JUDGE.

[Digest: Plaintiffs distributed defendant's product Lubrizol
2085A, a rustproofing compound. They obtained the product from
Jenkin-Guerin, Inc., a wholesale distributor of chemical compounds,
operating as a franchised Lubrizol distributor. Jenkin-Guerin packaged and sold Lubrizol 2085A under the trademark "Anchor Tuflex."
Unable to compete for a share of the automobile rustproofing market
because of the price they paid Jenkin-Guerin, plaintiffs approached
Lubrizol with a proposal to distribute Lubrizol 2085A in the marine
vessel and industrial rust-proofing markets. Because of competitive
pricing in the marine vessel market, plaintiffs requested and received
a direct supply of Lubrizol 2085A at a lower price than they could
receive from Jenkin-Guerin.

Upon receiving their distributorship, plaintiffs began marketing
the product in the automotive market under the tradename "Armor
Shield" at a cheaper price than Jenkin-Guerin's "Anchor Tuflex".
The President of Jenkin-Guerin, Jack Krause, made a series of calls
to Lubrizol complaining about plaintiffs' sale and pricing of 2085A in
the automotive market. Thereafter, Lubrizol cut off plaintiffs direct
supply of 2085A. Plaintiffs have only been able to obtain the product
from another Lubrizol distributor at higher prices than they paid as a

---

10. 669 F.2d at 412.

11. Id. at 414.

12. "[The] requirement that a plaintiff prove a relevant market in a Section
1 case and a quantitative impact in that
market is unnecessary if one views the
purpose of Section 1 as protecting the
plaintiff from a contract or conspiracy
unreasonably displacing the competitive
process as the mechanism for determining plaintiff's success or failure in trade
or commerce. Whether the rest of the

market is impacted or not is usually not
relevant in Section 1 cases to a determination of whether a plaintiff's rights under the antitrust laws have been violated." Flynn, Rethinking Sherman Act
Section 1 Analysis: Three Proposals for
Reducing the Chaos, 49 Antitrust L.J.
1593, 1625 (1982).

* The *en banc* decision remains
pending as of the manuscript deadline for
these materials.

direct distributor. Plaintiffs filed suit under § 1 of the Sherman Act claiming defendants Lubrizol, Jenkin-Guerin and Krause conspired to terminate plaintiffs' distributorship for the purpose of restraining price competition.]

. . . Appellants do not offer evidence to prove an anticompetitive effect on the market and rely solely on the principle enunciated in *Cernuto, Inc. v. United Cabinet Corp.*, 595 F.2d 164 (3d Cir. 1979) (*Cernuto*), that the concerted action alleged here, aimed at limiting price competition, has a *per se* anticompetitive impact on the market. The district court followed the *per se* analysis in *Cernuto*, but found the evidence insufficient to support a reasonable inference that appellants' termination by Lubrizol was motivated by a desire to protect Jenkin-Guerin from price competition and granted summary judgment against appellants.

For reversal appellants argue that the evidence was sufficient to support an inference that Lubrizol stopped selling directly to appellants in order to protect appellants' competitor, Jenkin-Guerin, from price competition. For the reasons discussed below, we reverse and remand for further proceedings.

. . .

"Vertical" Horizontal Restraint or "Horizontal" Vertical Agreement?

This case presented the following question of law: after *Continental T.V., Inc. v. GTE Sylvania, Inc.*, 433 U.S. 36, 97 S.Ct. 2549, 53 L.Ed.2d 568 (1977) (*GTE Sylvania*), is the *per se* rule or the rule of reason appropriate in determining whether a technically vertical restraint of trade, which smacks of horizontal pricing interference, unduly restrains trade under § 1 of the Sherman Act. . . .

The Supreme Court . . . declared in *GTE Sylvania* that because vertical trade restraints, i.e., those imposed by a supplier or manufacturer on a distributor, may have redeeming procompetitive aspects, a rule of reason analysis should be used to determine the net effect on the market. In *GTE Sylvania*, a manufacturer terminated the plaintiff's distributorship when the plaintiff began to sell the product at an outlet outside its allotted territory. The Court upheld this action, reasoning that while the manufacturer's exclusive franchise marketing plan might stifle *intrabrand* competition or competition among dealers of the same product in a given area, it could also serve to stimulate *interbrand* competition or competition among different manufacturers of comparable products.

Appellees argue that *GTE Sylvania* precludes use of the *per se* rule for any vertically imposed restraint except those expressly retained by the *GTE Sylvania* decision, i.e., price fixing and resale price maintenance, id. at 51 n. 18, 97 S.Ct. at 2558, n. 18. See *Oreck Corp. v. Whirlpool Corp.*, 579 F.2d 126 (2d Cir.) (en banc), cert. denied, 439 U.S. 946, 99 S.Ct. 340, 58 L.Ed.2d 338 (1978) (applying rule of reason analysis); accord, *Gough v. Rossmoor Corp.*, 585 F.2d 381

(9th Cir. 1978), cert. denied, 440 U.S. 936, 99 S.Ct. 1280, 59 L.Ed.2d 494 (1979); *H & B Equipment Co. v. International Harvester Co.*, 577 F.2d 239 (5th Cir. 1978); see generally Comment, *Vertical Agreements to Terminate Competing Distributors: Oreck Corp. v. Whirlpool Corp.*, 92 Harv.L.Rev. 1160 (1979) (supporting *Oreck*); Comment, *Vertical Agreement as Horizontal Restraint: Cernuto, Inc. v. United Cabinet Corp.*, 128 U.Pa.L.Rev. 622 (1980) (supporting *Cernuto*). We agree, however, with the Third Circuit that such an expansive interpretation of *GTE Sylvania* is unwarranted absent a clear expression of such intent by the Supreme Court. *Cernuto*, supra, 595 F.2d at 167 n.15, citing *GTE Sylvania*, supra, 433 U.S. at 51 n.18, 97 S.Ct. at 2558 n.18. See also *Contractor Utility Sales Co. v. Certain-Teed Products Corp.*, 638 F.2d 1061, 1072 n.9 (7th Cir. 1981) (*Contractor Utility*). Like the *Cernuto* court, "we are not persuaded that the law's tolerance of reasonable restraints designed to improve the manufacturer's competitive position may be converted into a blanket allowance of *any* marketing decision made by a manufacturer." 595 F.2d at 167–68 (emphasis in original). As noted by Professor Sullivan,

> It does not follow from the fact that a manufacturer may, when franchising a dealer, commit itself not to franchise another in a territory defined by the manufacturer, that it may, having earlier franchised two or more dealers, agree at the request of one to terminate the others. It is not merely that the latter promise liquidates palpable interests of existing traders, while the former does not (a difference which is real enough, and which is charged with meaning for the procedural and damage aspects of the law); it is also that the competitive effect of the first promise is less severe than that of the second. The first commitment forecloses potential intrabrand competition only; the second stamps out existing competition at the behest of a firm which is suffering under it.
>
>   •   •   •
>
>   . . . When the manufacturer sets up a dealership structure and binds itself not to add dealers in any existing territory, we truly have a vertical structure. But when an existing dealer enlists the manufacturer to choke off one of the dealer's competitors, although the "agreement" which enables Section 1 to be invoked is vertical [(manufacturer-dealer)], the restraint thereby achieved is horizontal in its impact [(dealer-dealer)]; it is an attack by one dealer against another.

L. Sullivan, Antitrust § 148, at 427–29 (1977). "The supplier [or manufacturer] participates merely as the 'enforcement agent' in furthering the distributors' [or dealers'] anticompetitive and horizontal purposes." Comment, *Vertical Agreement as Horizontal Restraint*, supra, 128 U.Pa.L.Rev. at 635, citing Posner, *The Rule of Reason and the Economic Approach: Reflections on the Sylvania Decision*, 45 U.Chi.L.Rev. 1, 17 (1977) (Professor Posner recently advanced a *per se* legality theory of restricted distribution; see Posner,

*The Next Step in the Antitrust Treatment of Restricted Distribu-
tion: Per Se Legality*, 48 U.Chi.L.Rev. 6 (1981)).

Moreover, there are significant differences between the alleged
conspirators' intent and the competitive impact found in *GTE Sylvania* and in the present case. First, as noted in *Cernuto*,

> [w]hen a manufacturer acts on its own, in pursuing its own mar-
> ket strategy, it is seeking to compete with other manufacturers by
> imposing what may be defended as reasonable vertical restraints.
> This would appear to be the rationale of the *GTE Sylvania* deci-
> sion. However, if the action of a manufacturer or other supplier
> is taken at the direction of its customer, the restraint becomes pri-
> marily horizontal in nature in that one customer is seeking to sup-
> press its competition by utilizing the power of a common supplier.
> Therefore, although the termination in such a situation is, itself, a
> vertical restraint, the desired impact is horizontal and on the deal-
> er, not the manufacturer, level.

595 F.2d at 168. Thus, the alleged purpose and effect of the dealer
termination in the present case was to eliminate or reduce intrabrand
competition at the dealer or distributor level and not to increase interbrand competition at the manufacturer or supplier level as in *GTE
Sylvania*. Second, *GTE Sylvania* involved a nonprice vertical restraint, a restriction on the location from which the dealer could sell
the manufacturer's products. 433 U.S. at 37, 97 S.Ct. at 2551. In
contrast, price and price competition was allegedly the key factor in
the present case and in *Cernuto*, supra, 595 F.2d at 168–69; in each
case the dealer complained to the manufacturer that the competing
dealer was selling the manufacturer's products in its territory and at
lower prices.

In *United States v. General Motors Corp.*, 384 U.S. 127, 86 S.Ct.
1321, 16 L.Ed.2d 415 (1966) (a decision prior to, but expressly affirmed by *GTE Sylvania*, supra, 433 U.S. at 58 n.28, 97 S.Ct. at 2561
n.28), the Court found a *per se* violation where the manufacturer
bowed to retailers' complaints by pressuring other retailers not to
deal with discounters. Although *General Motors* involved dual conspiracies, retailer-retailer and retailer-manufacturer, the Court's application of the *per se* rule points to the importance of the underlying
horizontal nature of the arrangement. 384 U.S. at 144–45, 86 S.Ct. at
1330–1331. Substance should be more important than form.

We do not think the horizontal impact is diminished because the
alleged combination or conspiracy consists of only one member of the
plaintiff's distribution level and a common supplier. Compare *Alloy
International Co. v. Hoover-NSK Bearing Co.*, 635 F.2d 1222, 1224
(7th Cir. 1980) (single dealer), *and Cernuto*, supra, 595 F.2d at 165
(single dealer), with *Gough v. Rossmoor Corp.*, supra, 585 F.2d at
387 ("In all cases so far holding such restraints to be *per se* unreasonable, there has been some horizontal concert of action taken
against the victims of the restraint."); *Oreck Corp. v. Whirlpool Co.*,
supra, 579 F.2d at 131–33; *H & B Equipment Co. v. International
Harvester Co.*, supra, 577 F.2d at 245 ("Conspiracies between a man-

ufacturer and its distributors are only treated as horizontal, however, when the source of the conspiracy is a combination of the distributors."). As noted in Comment, *Vertical Agreement as Horizontal Restraint*, supra, 128 U.Pa.L.Rev. at 641–42 (emphasis in original, footnotes omitted):

> [H]orizontal plurality is not the real determinant of per se unreasonableness. The essence of a violation of section 1 of the Sherman Act is agreement to pursue illegal conduct. A combination to cut a retailer off from a source of supply is not any less an illegal agreement because only one, rather than a plurality, of the parties is on the affected level. Nor is the effect of the combination any less harmful. A dealer's success in using the refusal-to-deal weapon to strike at a competitor depends on enlisting the cooperation of their mutual supplier, not the other competing dealers.

If a distributor can establish that a manufacturer or common supplier terminated its existing supply relationship at the request of a competing distributor and the termination was motivated by a desire on the part of the manufacturer to reduce or eliminate price competition for the other distributor, then a *per se* violation of § 1 of the Sherman Act has been established. *Contractor Utility*, supra, 638 F.2d at 1072 & n.9; *Alloy International Co. v. Hoover-NSK Bearing Co.*, supra, 635 F.2d at 1224; *Cernuto*, supra, 595 F.2d at 170. Here, the district court found that the evidence, when viewed in the light most favorable to appellants, was sufficient to support the reasonable inference that Lubrizol and Jenkin-Guerin acted in concert, but insufficient to support the reasonable inference that Lubrizol acted with a desire to protect Jenkin-Guerin from price competition, and therefore granted summary judgment against appellants. 513 F.Supp. at 998–99. We will address these requirements individually.

Concerted Action

In finding an inference of concerted action, the district court considered: (1) Krause's telephone calls to Lubrizol complaining of appellants' competition and the subsequent termination by Lubrizol of appellants and (2) evidence that Krause boasted to his office staff that, first, he could pressure Lubrizol into cutting off appellants' supply and, later, that he had in fact been successful. The district court concluded that the evidence of Krause's complaints and Lubrizol's subsequent termination of appellants' direct supply, standing alone, was insufficient to raise an inference of concerted action, id. at 997, but that this evidence, when considered with Krause's statements to his office staff, was sufficient to raise an inference of concerted action. Id. at 998.

· · ·

In *Edward J. Sweeney & Sons v. Texaco, Inc.*, 637 F.2d 105 (3d Cir. 1980), cert. denied, 451 U.S. 911, 101 S.Ct. 1981, 68 L.Ed.2d 300 (1981), the Third Circuit considered a similar question. Sweeney, a discount gasoline wholesaler and distributor, had a favorable hauling agreement changed and later his distributorship terminated after other Texaco retailers complained of his price cutting practices. In affirming a summary judgment against Sweeney, the majority held as a matter of law that the mere temporal relation between complaints by competitors and termination by a common supplier does not necessarily raise an inference of concerted action . . .. To hold otherwise would disrupt normal and reasonable business communications between a supplier and its customers. . . .

In *Sweeney*, the majority reviewed Sweeney's evidence and concluded that the evidence failed to show that Texaco's actions had contradicted the refiner's economic self-interest, proof of acts against economic interest and motivation to enter an agreement being the " 'two elements generally considered critical in establishing conspiracy from evidence of parallel business behavior.' " Id. at 114, citing *Venzie Corp. v. United States Mineral Products Co.*, 521 F.2d 1309, 1314 (3d Cir. 1975). By lowering the hauling allowance, Texaco saved $58,000 per year in sales to Sweeney, an action not in contradiction to its economic interests and which thus negated one element necessary to establishing concerted action circumstantially. Moreover, the majority also found that the facts "militate[d] strongly against a causal relation between the complaints and Texaco's actions." Texaco had realized its unfavorable position in its hauling agreement with Sweeney some five years prior to taking action. It had also learned of Sweeney's practice of representing non-Texaco fuel as Texaco fuel and had received many consumer complaints about service and credit card irregularities at Sweeney's stations.

We agree with the majority in *Sweeney* that the mere receipt by a manufacturer of dealer complaints about another dealer's market behavior would not be sufficient evidence to raise an inference of concerted action. . . . However, we do not agree that "even if appellants had demonstrated that Texaco's actions were in response to these complaints, such evidence alone would not show the necessary concerted action." Id. at 110, 116. To the contrary, we conclude that proof of a dealer's complaints to the manufacturer about a competitor dealer's price cutting and the manufacturer's action *in response* to such complaints would be sufficient to raise an inference of concerted action. See id. at 124–25 (Sloviter, J., dissenting). A showing of *responsive action* on the part of the manufacturer is necessary; there must be evidence of a causal relationship between the competitor dealer's price-related complaints and the manufacturer's action. "[T]he mere fact that the manufacturer/supplier took some action will not suffice to establish the requisite combination unless such action was taken in response to such complaints." Id. at 125 (Sloviter, J., dissenting).

We hold only that evidence of receipt by the manufacturer of a competitor dealer's price-related complaints and responsive action by the manufacturer against the offending dealer raises a reasonable inference of concerted action in violation of section 1 of the Sherman Act. Such evidence does not conclusively establish liability. As noted in Comment, *Vertical Agreement as Horizontal Restraint*, supra, 128 U.Pa.L.Rev. at 647–48 (footnotes omitted):

> A manufacturer may have numerous legitimate reasons for terminating a dealer that coincide with the illegitimate reasons of the distributor demanding termination of its competitor. For instance, a violation of a distribution contract may come to the manufacturer's attention only through the complaint of another dealer that maintains a close and jealous watch upon its rivals' activities.* . . .
>
> . . .
>
> . . . This evidence might include explanations such as the dealer's violation of a marketing agreement, protection of product integrity, unsatisfactory dealer performance, instability of the dealer's business, the dealer's dishonesty, shortage of supply, or reorganization of the marketing system.

Here, we think there was sufficient evidence to raise an inference of concerted action. Appellants presented evidence that Krause complained to Lubrizol about appellants' price cutting and sales to Jenkin-Guerin customers in January 1980, that Lubrizol actually received these complaints, that the Lubrizol officials who made supply decisions knew about these complaints and the substance of the complaints, and that Lubrizol terminated appellants' direct supply of Lubrizol 2085A in February 1980, thus eliminating appellants as competitors on the same level of distribution as Jenkin-Guerin and reducing the difference between appellants' prices and Jenkin-Guerin's prices. This evidence is circumstantial. However, we think that it is most unlikely that antitrust plaintiffs, like any other plaintiffs alleging conspiracy, will have direct evidence.

Lubrizol argues that it terminated appellants' direct supply because appellants violated their marketing agreement to develop principally marine applications for Lubrizol 2085A and because appellants were dishonest in their pre-distribution negotiations. Lubrizol also argues that its actions were unilateral and wholly independent of Krause's complaints. We think that these arguments are properly directed to the jury. The jury could have reasonably found that, as appellants contend, Lubrizol terminated appellants' direct supply pursuant to an understanding or agreement with Jenkin-Guerin for the purpose of reducing price competition between Jenkin-Guerin and appellants or that, as Lubrizol and Jenkin-Guerin contend, Lubrizol independently decided to terminate appellants' direct supply and did so for reasons that were not price-related.

Price-related Complaints

. . .

* Indeed, one of the manufacturer's most valuable sources of information about the operation of its distribution channel is communications from its dealers. See Comment, *Vertical Agreements to Terminate Competing Distributors: Oreck Corp. v. Whirlpool Co.*, 92 Harv.L.Rev. 1160, 1169 (1979).

We agree that there is no direct evidence that Lubrizol was motivated by a desire to protect Jenkin-Guerin from price competition. We would be somewhat surprised to find any direct evidence of this nature. However, there was sufficient circumstantial evidence, when viewed most favorably to appellants, to suggest that Lubrizol terminated appellants' direct supply of Lubrizol 2085A in order to protect Jenkin-Guerin from price competition. Krause's complaints clearly referred to appellants' lower prices; Krause wanted to know whether Lubrizol would continue to sell Lubrizol 2085A to appellants. The record indicates that Jenkin-Guerin was Lubrizol's third largest purchaser of Lubrizol 2085A during 1979 and most of 1980. Under the circumstances, we think that this evidence reasonably supports an inference that Lubrizol was motivated by a desire to protect Jenkin-Guerin from price competition.

Accordingly, we reverse the order of summary judgment and remand the case for further proceedings. The only issue before us on appeal was the propriety of summary judgment. We of course express no opinion whatsoever with respect to the merits of the position of any party to this action.

[Benson, Senior District Judge, dissented on the ground that the District Court's opinion was supported by sufficient evidence.]

NOTES AND QUERIES

(1) *Dealer Terminations and "Vertical Boycotts"*. Cases alleging supplier acquiescence or compliance with the demands of a dealer to terminate a competing price-cutting dealer have generated a split in the circuits over the substantive standard to be applied to such conduct. *Lubrizol* and *Cernuto* held such conduct *per se* unlawful. *Oreck v. Whirlpool Corp.* did not view the conduct as "price fixing," holding it subject to a rule of reason analysis which requires the plaintiff to demonstrate an injury to competition in a relevant market. The Supreme Court may resolve the question in the pending case of *Spray-Rite Service Corp. v. Monsanto Co.*, where proof of injury to a relevant market was held not esential in a dealer termination case alleging *per se* unlawful vertical price fixing.[13]

The degree to which antitrust policy may be used to control dealer terminations and to redress the usual imbalance of bargaining power favoring franchisors over franchisees depends upon which line of cases is followed. Several cases, particularly in the retail gasoline industry,[14] have followed the

13. 684 F.2d 1226 (7th Cir. 1982), certiorari granted ___ U.S. ___, 103 S.Ct. 1249, ___ L.Ed.2d ___ (1983). The holding that one must prove injury to competition in a relevant market in a rule of reason case is a questionable one. In National Society of Profession Engineers v. United States, 435 U.S. 679, 690, 98 S.Ct. 1355, 1364–65, 55 L.Ed.2d 637, 649 (1978), the Court described the analysis under a rule of reason as follows: "The test prescribed . . . is whether the challenged contracts or acts 'were unreasonably restrictive of competitive conditions.' Unreasonableness under that test could be based either (1) on the nature or character of the contracts, or (2) on surrounding circumstances giving rise to the inference or presumption that they were intended to restrain trade and enhance prices. Under either branch of the test, the inquiry is confined to a consideration of impact on competitive conditions." See also Flynn, Rethinking Sherman Act Section 1 Analysis: Three Proposals for Reducing the Chaos, 49 Antitrust L.J. 1593 (1982).

14. See Yentsch v. Texaco, Inc., 630 F.2d 46 (2d Cir. 1980); Arnott v. Ameri-

Cernuto-Lubrizol line of reasoning, either by labeling the restraint "horizontal" or by adopting the view that displacement of the competitive process by conduct labeled *per se* unlawful is illegal without regard to the amount of commerce displaced. See Note, "Protecting Competition Versus Protection of a Competitive Process", supra Chap. 4, p. 361; *Albrecht v. Herald Co.*, supra p. 617.

(2) *Sufficiency of the Evidence to Prove Dealer Termination Unlawful.* The decision in *Lubrizol* also raises the evidentiary and procedural issue of the sufficiency of the evidence to get to a jury in a dealer termination case claiming the cut-off was for an illegal purpose. This issue also effects significantly the degree to which antitrust policy may be relied upon to regulate franchisor-franchisee relationships. When a case pits a powerful franchisor against a small franchisee or dealer whose livelihood is destroyed by a termination of the franchise, being able to get to a jury can often spell the difference between success or failure for the dealer.

For example, in a case pending argument before the Supreme Court, *Spray-Rite Service Corp. v. Monsanto Co.*,[15] the Seventh Circuit affirmed a $10.5 million jury verdict for a terminated distributor of Monsanto's herbicides. Citing *Lubrizol* and rejecting *Edward J. Sweeney & Sons, Inc. v. Texaco, Inc.*[16] (discussed in *Lubrizol*) the Court held:

> We believe . . . that proof of termination following competitor complaints is sufficient to support an inference of concerted action. . . . Proof of distributorship termination in response to competing distributorship complaints about the terminated distributor's pricing policies is sufficient to raise an issue of concerted action.

In a less generous opinion, *Contractor Utility Sales Co. v. Certain-Teed Products Corp.*,[17] the Seventh Circuit upheld a directed verdict for a franchisor which explained its dealings with competing dealers of its pipe as unilateral business activity. The Court observed:

> Although Section 1 does not require production of a smoking gun in order to establish an unlawful conspiracy, we certainly cannot fault the district court for granting a directed verdict where the plaintiff fails to produce even a puff of smoke indicating that such a gun existed and was used. Cusco's [plaintiff] evidence established only that Certain-Teed unilaterally performed a number of activities and that those activities may have had anti-competitive effects.[18]

It is risky to draw any generalizations from these and other cases attempting to define the line between legitimate questions for a jury and insufficient evidence to warrant sending the case to a jury. Each case must necessarily be measured on its own facts until a definitive ruling occurs in the *Spray-Rite* or some similar case.

can Oil Co., 609 F.2d 873 (8th Cir. 1979), certiorari denied, 446 U.S. 918, 100 S.Ct. 1852, 64 L.Ed.2d 272 (1980); Umphres v. Shell Oil Co., 512 F.2d 420 (5th Cir. 1975), certiorari denied 423 U.S. 929, 96 S.Ct. 278, 46 L.Ed.2d 257; Lehrman v. Gulf Oil Corp., 464 F.2d 26 (5th Cir. 1972), certiorari denied 409 U.S. 1077, 93 S.Ct. 687, 34 L.Ed.2d 665; Quinn v. Mobil Oil Co., 375 F.2d 273 (1st Cir. 1967), certiorari dismissed, 389 U.S. 801, 88 S.Ct. 8, 19 L.Ed. 2d 56; Broussard v. Socony Mobil Oil

Co., 350 F.2d 346 (5th Cir. 1965); Lessig v. Tidewater Oil Co., 327 F.2d 459 (9th Cir. 1964), certiorari denied 377 U.S. 993, 84 S.Ct. 1920, 12 L.Ed.2d 1046.

15. Supra note 13.

16. 637 F.2d 105 (3d Cir. 1980), certiorari denied 451 U.S. 911, 101 S.Ct. 1981, 68 L.Ed.2d 300 (1981).

17. 638 F.2d 1061 (7th Cir. 1981).

18. Id. at 1075.

(3) *Dealer Terminations Without Complaints From Competitors.* Can it ever be unlawful under Section 1 to terminate (or refuse to renew) a dealer where there have been no complaints from competing dealers? Would the supplier's conduct necessarily be unilateral? Reconsider, e.g., *Albrecht v. Herald Co.* and accompanying Notes, supra p. 617. Consider also *Yentsch v. Texaco, Inc.,*[19] where plaintiff dealer claimed Texaco terminated his franchise because of his refusal to comply with Texaco's maximum resale pricing policies (the dealer charged higher prices). The Court of Appeals held the "required combination" could be proved by "(1) an express or implied agreement, or (2) the securing of actual adherence to prices by means beyond mere refusal to deal."[20] The Court found the facts supported a theory of "combination" by coercion:

> We think there was sufficient evidence here, although just barely, to find an illegal combination to maintain resale prices between Texaco and other Connecticut service station dealers, and between Texaco and Yentsch. Texaco went beyond *Colgate's* safe harbor of announcement plus mere refusal to deal by creating a coercive business climate in which its dealers knew of the low price policy, understood the consequences of failure to comply and thus generally complied.[21]

The Court cited as factors "creating a coercive business climate" Texaco's repeated threats to Yentsch and other Texaco dealers in Connecticut that their franchise and station lease would be cancelled if they did not lower prices and increase volume; interoffice memos by Texaco marketing personnel stressing a policy of securing dealer compliance by franchise terminations or threats thereof; extensive price monitoring of dealers by Texaco representatives; and Texaco's repeated coercion of Yentsch to follow Texaco's pricing policy by threats to not renew his franchise and cancellation of his franchise for refusing to comply with Texaco's policy. In addition to finding such activity satisfied the "Parke Davis-Albrecht" standards for finding a Sherman Act combination, the Court also found the evidence sufficient to support a finding of plaintiff's "actual adherence" to Texaco's price dictates, stating that this "coerced 'agreement' with Texaco alone was sufficient to violate § 1 of the Sherman Act."[22]

(4) *Intra-Enterprise Conspiracy and Dealer Termination.* In *Poller v. Columbia Broadcasting System, Inc.,*[23] frequently cited for its holding that summary judgments are disfavored in antitrust litigation,[24] a UHF T.V. station which had an affiliation agreement with CBS claimed CBS terminated the affiliation as part of a conspiracy to exclude plaintiff's station from the Milwaukee market, to obtain its equipment below cost when the station failed to succeed without network affiliation, and to destroy UHF broadcasting in favor of VHF broadcasting nationally. Named as alleged co-conspirators were an individual employed by CBS to obtain a competing UHF station in his own name, the seller of the competing UHF station, certain CBS officers and a CBS division (CBS T.V.). In reversing the lower court grant of

19. 630 F.2d 46 (2d Cir. 1980).

20. Id. at 52.

21. Id. at 53–4.

22. Id. at 54.

23. 368 U.S. 464, 82 S.Ct. 486, 7 L.Ed. 2d 458 (1962).

24. "We believe that summary procedures should be used sparingly in complex antitrust litigation where motive and intent play leading roles, the proof is largely in the hands of the alleged conspirators, and hostile witnesses thicken the plot. It is only when the witnesses are present and subject to cross-examination that their credibility and the weight to be given their testimony can be appraised. Trial by affidavit is no substitute for trial by jury which so long has been the hallmark of 'even handed justice.' " 368 U.S., at 473, 82 S.Ct., at 491, 7 L.Ed.2d, at 464.

summary judgment for the defendants the Court stated: "It may be that CBS by independent action could have exercised its granted right to cancel . . . [the] affiliation upon six months notice and independently purchased its own outlet in Milwaukee. However, if such a cancellation and purchase were part and parcel of unlawful conduct or agreement with others or were conceived in a purpose to unreasonably restrain trade, control a market, or monopolize, then such conduct might well run afoul of the Sherman Law." [25] Left unclear was who could be "others" for purposes of a conspiracy.

As in the case of horizontal restraints, see Chapter 4 supra p. 458, there is ambiguity over when it is appropriate to consider subsidiaries, divisions, corporate parents or corporate employees as separate "persons" capable of conspiring for Sherman Act purposes.[26] The issue can be an important one in dealer termination cases, because many franchisors are subsidiaries of conglomerate corporations or operate through several subsidiaries or unincorporated divisions.

Queries. Should the court in *Principe*, supra p. 744 have found McDonald's separately incorporated divisions for licensing the trademark and constructing the restaurants were separate persons capable of conspiring? [27] Should the Court in *Yentsch* have found a conspiracy between the employees of Texaco's marketing division to terminate Yentsch for his refusal to abide by Texaco's resale price policies? [28] Should an agreement between officials of a conglomerate and officers of its wholly-owned subsidiary franchisor to cut off franchisees engaged in price-cutting be considered a conspiracy for antitrust purposes?[29]

3. STATUTORY AND OTHER REGULATION OF DEALER TERMINATIONS AND NONRENEWALS

a. Federal Legislation

Franchise agreements usually specify a limited period for which the relationship shall continue, provide for cancellation by the franchisor or franchisee during the term of the agreement, and permit renewal of the agreement at the option of the parties. Short terms, threats of cancellation on short notice, and the risk of nonrenewal have all been recognized as sources of leverage in the hands of a franchisor to coerce franchisees in the operation of the franchise.[30] Franchisors may need such authority to protect the reputation of their businesses, eliminate poorly-performing franchisees, or achieve other legitimate business objectives. Frequently, however, the franchisor terminates because the franchisee refused to engage in an-

25. 368 U.S., at 468–9, 82 S.Ct., at 488–9, 7 L.Ed.2d, at 462.

26. For a critical review of the cases see Handler & Smart, The Present Status of The Intracorporate Conspiracy Doctrine, 3 Cardozo L.Rev. 23 (1982).

27. See Kiefer-Stewart Co. v. Joseph Seagram & Sons, 340 U.S. 211, 71 S.Ct. 259, 95 L.Ed. 219 (1951) (discussed supra p. 467).

28. Cf., Dussouy v. Gulf Coast Investment Corp., 660 F.2d 594 (5th Cir. 1981) (discussed supra p. 465).

29. See William Inglis & Sons Baking Co. v. ITT Continental Baking Co., Inc., 668 F.2d 1014 (9th Cir. 1981), certiorari denied __ U.S. __, 103 S.Ct. 58, 74 L.Ed.2d 61 (1982) (discussed supra p. __).

30. See Hearings, Franchise Legislation, Subcommm. on Antitrust & Monopoly of the Senate Judiciary Comm., 90th Cong., 1st Sess. (1967); Hearings, Distribution Problems Affecting Small Business, Subcom. on Antitrust & Monopoly of the Senate Judiciary Comm., 89th Cong., 2nd Sess. (1966).

ticompetitive activity or to follow other unreasonable demands.[31] Termination may also take place because the franchisor wishes to take over the franchisee's business or establish a business which might compete with the franchisee.[32] The mere threat of termination is likely to cause a franchisee to follow the dictates of the franchisor—whether legitimate or not—since the franchisee faces destruction of his business and loss of prospective income if termination takes place. Litigation against threatened termination, or for treble damages resulting from termination, may not be worthwhile even with the lure of generous attorneys' fees contingent on victory. The costs and risks of litigation are too high, or the client is not disposed to sacrifice an on-going relationship with the franchisor even for the possibility of a treble damage award. While antitrust litigation may be an effective remedy in some cases and clearly limits the exercise of termination authority to achieve anti-competitive goals, it cannot completely redress the imbalance of power in most modern franchising relationships. Franchisees have been particularly active and successful in obtaining state legislation dealing specifically with franchisor termination and nonrenewal practices.[33]

Legislative response to imbalance in the franchisor-franchisee relationship has not been limited to action at the state level. The disparity of bargaining power in the relationship of automobile dealers and automobile manufacturers and widespread abuse of that relationship led to federal legislative intervention in automobile franchising. Twenty years later, even more widespread abuses by oil companies in their dealings with retail service station franchisees led to the adoption of federal legislation regulating terminations and nonrenewals in that business. The difficulties of franchised auto dealers had not gone unnoticed by the auto manufacturers. But the efforts to resolve franchisee complaints by intracorporate measures failed to meet the demands of franchised auto dealers.[34] There is some paradox in the extension of special franchise security to auto dealers, surely the most powerful class of franchisees, and more than a little doubt whether the interests of automobile buyers are best served by loosening the disciplinary authority of the company to push sales (promoting intrabrand competition), to compel faithful performance of warranty obligations, and to refrain from deceptive practices. What may be posed here is a variant of the ancient political issue: whether the monarch or the barons will deal more kindly with the plebs.

31. See Bohling, Franchise Terminations Under the Sherman Act: Populism and Relational Power, 53 Texas L.Rev. 1180 (1975); Gellhorn, Limitations on Contract Termination Rights—Franchise Cancellations, 1967 Duke L.J. 465.

32. See Eastman Kodak Co. v. Southern Photo Materials Co., 273 U.S. 359, 47 S.Ct. 400, 71 L.Ed. 684 (1927); Poller v. Columbia Broadcasting System, Inc., 368 U.S. 464, 82 S.Ct. 486, 7 L.Ed.2d 458 (1962), p. 781 supra.

33. See Eaton, State Regulation of Franchise and Dealership Terminations, 49 Antitrust L.J. 1331 (1981); Fern & Klein, Restrictions On Terminations and Nonrenewal of Franchises: A Policy Analysis, 36 Bus.L. 1041 (1981).

34. See P. Drucker, Concept of the Corporation, pp. 101–10 (1946) (describing the functioning of the G. M. franchising system). See also Macauley, infra note 36.

AUTOMOBILE DEALERS' DAY IN COURT ACT

15 U.S.C.A. § 1221 et seq.

An Act

To supplement the antitrust laws of the United States, in order to balance the power now heavily weighted in favor of automobile manufacturers, by enabling franchise automobile dealers to bring suit in the district courts of the United States to recover damages sustained by reason of the failure of automobile manufacturers to act in good faith in complying with the terms of franchises or in terminating or not renewing franchises with their dealers.

Sec. 1. . . . (e) The term "good faith" shall mean the duty of each party to any franchise, and all officers, employees, or agents thereof to act in a fair and equitable manner toward each other so as to guarantee the one party freedom from coercion, intimidation, or threats of coercion or intimidation from the other party: *Provided*, That recommendation, endorsement, exposition, persuasion, urging or argument shall not be deemed to constitute a lack of good faith.

Sec. 2. An automobile dealer may bring suit against any automobile manufacturer engaged in commerce, in any district court of the United States in the district in which said manufacturer resides, or is found, or has an agent, without respect to the amount in controversy, and shall recover the damages [35] by him sustained and the cost of suit by reason of the failure of said automobile manufacturer from and after the passage of this Act to act in good faith in performing or complying with any of the terms or provisions of the franchise, or in terminating, canceling, or not renewing the franchise with said dealer: *Provided*, That in any such suit the manufacturer shall not be barred from asserting in defense of any such action the failure of the dealer to act in good faith. . . .

NOTES AND QUERIES

(1) *Background.* The foregoing legislation was enacted as a result of complaints by franchised automobile dealers, especially those of General Motors and Ford, that they had been put under tremendous pressure by the manufacturers to sell excessive quotas of new cars in the course of a production and sales race among the leading companies. Some dealers, unable to meet their quotas, had their franchises cancelled. The threat of cancellation led other dealers to engage in "bootlegging," i.e., sale of cars at cut prices in the territory of other dealers, whose ability to meet their own quotas was thus undermined. In Congress and before the state legislatures dealers pressed their demand that the companies take steps to prevent bootlegging and that their freedom to cancel or refuse to renew franchises be restricted. While seeking to firm up their own franchises against company pressure to sell more cars, dealers looked to the companies to use the cancellation threat to stop other dealers from bootlegging.[36]

35. Bateman v. Ford Motor Co., 302 F.2d 63 (3d Cir. 1962), held that injunctive relief was available in addition to the remedy of damages expressly provided by the Act.

36. See S. Macauley, Law And The Balance of Power—The Automobile Manufacturers and Their Dealers (1966); Macauley, Changing a Continuing Relationship Between a Large Corporation and

(2) *Constitutionality.* The constitutionality of the Automobile Dealer Day in Court Act has not been authoritatively settled.[37]   Cf. *General Motors Corp. v. Blevins,*[38] invalidating a state law of Colorado upon the ground, among others, that it was unconstitutionally vague to prohibit cancellation "unfairly, without due regard to the equities of the dealer, and without just provocation." General Motors argued that a law which would require it "in the operation of its private business to continue business relations with dealers without its consent is beyond the scope of the police power." But cf. *Willys Motors, Inc. v. Northwest Kaiser-Willys, Inc.,*[39] sustaining Minnesota statute forbidding cancellation "without just cause."

(3) *Good Faith.* Good faith was found lacking where the manufacturer carried out his threat to terminate relations on the ground that the dealer was cutting prices, even though the manufacturer was exercising his conceded right unilaterally to refuse to deal with price-cutters. *Autowest, Inc. v. Peugeot, Inc.*[40] It was recognized in the *Autowest* case that a dealer must prove something more than threat to terminate on a lawful ground, "for otherwise the manufacturer would be precluded from insisting upon reasonable and valid contractual provisions." Here, the insistence on maintaining resale prices provided the extra ingredient because this violated "the spirit of the antitrust laws, which the Franchise Act was designed to supplement." It was also observed that a distinction would be drawn between a manufacturer's insistence on mutually beneficial conditions, e.g., adequate inventory and service facilities, and conditions benefiting the manufacturer primarily. Resale price maintenance fell into the latter category as an obstacle to the dealer's expansion of his sales and gross profit.

"Good faith" was found lacking where Chrysler dropped a dealer for failure to fulfill his "minimum sales responsibility" (average performance of Chrysler dealers in the region) after he had made substantial investment in expanded facilities at Chrysler's urging at the same time that plans were being made to terminate his franchise and turn his facilities over to a new Chrysler-sponsored dealer.[41] Although it has been suggested that "good faith" is narrowly limited to acts of "coercion and intimidation",[42] it has been held that a manufacturer's "wrongful demand" of a dealer under "all the facts and circumstances" may be made the basis of a jury finding an absence

Those Who Deal With It: Auto Manufacturers, Their Dealers, and the Legal System, 1965 Wis.L.Rev. 740 (1965). It should be noted that the Act does not preclude the application of antitrust policy to disputes involving dealers and manufacturers. See United States v. General Motors Corp., 384 U.S. 127, 86 S.Ct. 1321, 16 L.Ed.2d 415 (1966); Martin B. Glauser Dodge Co. v. Chrysler Corp., 570 F.2d 72 (3d Cir. 1977). See generally Symposium, Franchisor-Franchisee Relationships—Antitrust Considerations, 47 Antitrust L.J. 869 (1978).

37. Since the adoption of the Act, there have been over 100 court opinions interpreting it. The Supreme Court, however, has yet to review a case arising under the statute. See Donovan, Federal Laws Affecting the Right Of A Franchisor To Terminate or Not Renew A Franchise: Automobile Dealers Day In Court Act, 49 Antitrust L.J. 1353 (1981);

cf. Woodward Motor Co. v. General Motors Corp., 298 F.2d 121 (5th Cir. 1962) (issue raised but passed over in view of judgment for defendant on the merits).

See generally Kessler and Brenner, Automobile Dealer Franchises: Vertical Integration by Contract, 66 Yale L.J. 1135 (1957); Comment, The Automobile Dealer Franchise Act: A "New Departure" in Federal Legislation? 52 Nw. U.L.Rev. 253 (1957).

38. 144 F.Supp. 381 (D.Colo.1956).

39. 142 F.Supp. 469 (D.Minn.1956).

40. 434 F.2d 556 (2d Cir. 1970).

41. Madsen v. Chrysler Corp., 261 F.Supp. 488 (N.D.Ill.1966), vacated 375 F.2d 773 (7th Cir. 1967) (complaint dismissed without prejudice on grounds of mootness.)

42. See Donovan, supra note 37 at 1357.

of "good faith". In *Marquis v. Chrysler Corp.*,[43] it was held that unfair minimum sales requirements plus Chrysler's acquisition of a site for a new location in the dealer's area and cancellation of the dealer's franchise "was precisely the kind of intimidating and overbearing manufacturer conduct that the Act was designed to proscribe."[44] In *Colonial Ford, Inc. v. Ford Motor Co.*,[45] the Act was applied to Ford's financing subsidiary where leverage from financing a dealer's operations and the threat of franchise termination were used to force a dealer to accept a third party stockholder in the dealership.

On the other hand, manufacturers have been found to be in "good faith" when terminating dealers for dealer breach of a location clause,[46] refusing to renew a dealer with which it had legitimate disputes over warranty claims,[47] terminating a dealer who objected to carrying the manufacturer's full line including unwanted large cars,[48] and terminating a dealer who refused to build adequate repair facilities.[49] In *Autohaus Brugger, Inc. v. Saab Motors, Inc.*[50] the Court spelled out its perception of the "good faith" requirement:

> There is no question that the failure to exercise good faith within the meaning of the Act has a limited and restricted meaning. It is not to be construed liberally. It does not mean "good faith" in a hazy or general way, nor does it mean unfairness. The existence or nonexistence of "good faith" must be determined in the context of actual or threatened coercion or intimidation.

> In order to prove lack of good faith the manufacturer's actions must be unfair and inequitable in addition to being for the purpose of coercion and intimidation.

> Coercion or intimidation must include a wrongful demand which will result in sanctions if not complied with, and it is necessary to consider not only whether the manufacturer brought pressure to bear on the dealer, but also his reason for doing so.

> When a termination or nonrenewal of a franchise is involved, there must be a "causal connection" between the dealer's resistance to the coercive conduct and the termination or nonrenewal for there to be a lack of good faith under the Act.

> The existence of coercion or intimidation depends upon the circumstances arising from each particular case. However, unless the transactions between the parties involve coercion or intimidation, or threats or coercion or intimidation, the duty of good faith imposed by the Act does not prohibit a manufacturer's "recommendation, endorsement, exposition, persuasion, urging or argument normal in competitive commercial rela-

43. 577 F.2d 624 (9th Cir. 1978).

44. Id. at 635.

45. 577 F.2d 106 (10th Cir. 1978), affirmed on rehearing 592 F.2d 1126 (10th Cir.), certiorari denied 444 U.S. 837, 100 S.Ct. 73, 62 L.Ed.2d 48 (1979).

46. Golden Gate Acceptance Corp. v. General Motors Corp., 597 F.2d 676 (9th Cir. 1979).

47. Autohaus Brugger, Inc. v. Saab Motors, Inc., 567 F.2d 901 (9th Cir. 1978),

certiorari denied 436 U.S. 946, 98 S.Ct. 2848, 56 L.Ed.2d 787.

48. Bob Maxfield, Inc. v. American Motors Corp., 637 F.2d 1033 (5th Cir. Unit A 1981) certiorari denied 454 U.S. 860, 102 S.Ct. 315, 70 L.Ed.2d 158.

49. Ed Houser Enterprises, Inc. v. General Motors Corp., 595 F.2d 366 (7th Cir. 1979).

50. Supra note 47.

tionships." House Report 2850 (1956 U.S.Code Cong. & Admin.News at p. 4596).[51]

(4) *Generalized Dealer Security.* Puerto Rico enacted the following provisions in 1964–6:

> Notwithstanding the existence in a dealer's contract of a clause reserving to the parties the unilateral right to terminate the existing relationship, no principal or grantor may terminate said relationship or refuse to renew said contract on its normal expiration, except for just cause.

> Just cause [is defined as] nonperformance of any of the essential obligations of the dealer's contract, on the part of the dealer, or any action or omission on his part that adversely and substantially affects the interests of the principal or grantor in promoting the marketing or distribution of the merchandise or service.[52]

The legislative committee report on this act declared:

> The Commonwealth of Puerto Rico can not remain indifferent to the growing number of cases in which domestic and foreign enterprises, without just cause, eliminate their dealers, concessionaires, or agents, as soon as these have created a favorable market and without taking into account their legitimate interests.

> The Legislative Assembly of Puerto Rico declares that reasonable stability in the dealer's relationship in Puerto Rico is vital to the general economy of the country, to the public interest and to the general welfare, and in the exercise of its police power it deems it necessary to regulate, insofar as pertinent, the field of said relationship, so as to avoid the abuse caused by certain practices.

In *Fornaris v. Ridge Tool Co.,*[53] the retrospective application of this law to preexisting dealerships was held unconstitutional as a drastic alteration of contractual rights, converting a "relationship terminable by either party without cause into one which, short of breach by the other party, can be terminated only by making substantial payments and without protection for its economic interests." This decision was reversed by the United States Supreme Court with directions to remand to the Supreme Court of Puerto Rico for an authoritative interpretation of "just cause" in the "Spanish tradition".[54]

---

51. 567 F.2d at 911. The Court also enumerated several instances "where courts have found that manufacturer's actions do lack good faith and violate the Act, see *McGeorge Car Co., Inc. v. Leyland Motor Sales, Inc.,* 504 F.2d 52 (4th Cir. 1974) (where the manufacturer tried to compel the dealer to accept an undesirable line of cars by withholding delivery to the dealer of a highly successful line of cars); *Rea v. Ford Motor Co.,* 497 F.2d 577 (3d Cir. 1974) (where the manufacturer threatened to cease shipping Ford cars, unless a separate corporation, in which dealer was a principal stockholder, resigned its franchise as an Oldsmobile dealer in a neighboring town); *Autowest, Inc. v. Peugeot, Inc.,* 434 F.2d 556 (2d Cir. 1970) (where the manufacturer terminated the dealer because the dealer resisted the manufacturer's coercion to follow the suggested resale price);

Randy's Studebaker Sales, Inc. v. Nissan Motor Corp., supra (where the manufacturer used the nonrenewal weapon, as well as curtailment of car deliveries in order to coerce the dealer into a program of retail price fixing); and *Shor-Line Rambler, Inc. v. American Motor Sales,* 543 F.2d 601 (7th Cir. 1976) (where the manufacturer put unreasonable and unrealistic demands on the dealer to build new facilities, increase credit, and make extensive personnel changes, then terminated the dealership when it could not comply.)"

52. 10 L.P.R.A. § 278(a). Cf. S. 2321 and S. 2507, 90th Cong., 1st Sess., and hearings thereon, reported in ATRR No. 327, October 17, 1967, p. A–12.

53. 423 F.2d 563 (1st Cir. 1970).

54. 400 U.S. 41, 91 S.Ct. 156, 27 L.Ed. 2d 174 (1970).

(5) *Queries.*[55]   In organizing a Round Table discussion of the Automobile Dealers Day in Court Act for the December 1956 meeting of the Association of American Law Schools, Professor James A. Rahl posed the following questions:

(1) whether the Act is a good method of solving the problems involved;

(2) whether the Act is well-adapted for use in other industries involving franchised dealers;

(3) whether this kind of legislation is reconcilable with old or new antitrust policy assumptions and with ideas about free contract, competition and bargaining;

(4) whether what we have here is a new phase of something begun with NRA, Robinson-Patman, Fair Trade, or whether it is a Galbraithian approach toward countervailing power;

(5) whether our preoccupation with the problems of small business means more of this kind of legislation and less emphasis upon traditional antitrust enforcement.

Under the Act, could the mere failure to renew a franchise upon grounds of the dealer's unsatisfactory performance give rise to liability, absent previous threats not to renew?   Would proof of previous warning that his franchise would be terminated if he didn't sell more cars be sufficient proof of "coercion"?   Would the issue of "good faith" turn on whether the company-fixed quota of sales was "reasonable"?

PETROLEUM MARKETING PRACTICES ACT OF 1978

15 U.S.C.A. § 2801 et seq.

Sec. 102.   **(a) Except as provided in subsection (b) and section 103, no franchisor engaged in the sale, consignment, or distribution of motor fuel in commerce may—**

(1) terminate any franchise (entered into or renewed on or after the date of enactment of this Act) prior to the conclusion of the term, or the expiration date, stated in the franchise; or

(2) fail to renew any franchise relationship (without regard to the date on which the relevant franchise was entered into or renewed).

(b)(1) Any franchisor may terminate any franchise (entered into or renewed on or after the date of enactment of this Act) or may fail to renew any franchise relationship, if—

(A) the notification requirements of section 104 are met;   and

(B) such termination is based upon a ground described in paragraph (2) or such nonrenewal is based upon a ground described in paragraph (2) or (3).

---

55. Some answers are offered in Macaulay, supra note 36, Notes on Automobile Dealers Franchise Act: a New Departure in Federal Legislation, 52 Nw. U.L.Rev. 253 (1957);   Automobile Dealers Franchise Act: Another Experiment in Federal Class Legislation, 25 G.W.L.Rev. 667 (1957).

(2) For purposes of this subsection, the following are grounds for termination of a franchise or nonrenewal of a franchise relationship:

(A) A failure by the franchisee to comply with any provision of the franchise, which provision is both reasonable and of material significance to the franchise relationship, if the franchisor first acquired actual or constructive knowledge of such failure—

(i) not more than 120 days prior to the date on which notification of termination or nonrenewal is given, if notification is given pursuant to section 104(a); or

(ii) not more than 60 days prior to the date on which notification of termination or nonrenewal is given, if less than 90 days notification is given pursuant to section 104(b)(1).

(B) A failure by the franchisee to exert good faith efforts to carry out the provisions of the franchise, if—

(i) the franchisee was apprised by the franchisor in writing of such failure and was afforded a reasonable opportunity to exert good fatih efforts to carry out such provisions; and

(ii) such failure thereafter continued within the period which began not more than 180 days before the date notification of termination or nonrenewal was given pursuant to section 104.

(C) The occurrence of an event which is relevant to the franchise relationship and as a result of which termination of the franchise or nonrenewal of the franchise relationship is reasonable, if such event occurs during the period the franchise is in effect and the franchisor first acquired actual or constructive knowledge of such occurrence—

(i) not more than 120 days prior to the date on which notification of termination or nonrenewal is given, if notification is given pursuant to section 104(a); or

(ii) not more than 60 days prior to the date on which notification of termination or nonrenewal is given, if less than 90 days notification is given pursuant to section 104(b)(1).

(D) An agreement, in writing, between the franchisor and the franchisee to terminate the franchise or not to renew the franchise relationship, if—

(i) such agreement is entered into not more than 180 days prior to the date of such termination or, in the case of nonrenewal, not more than 180 days prior to the conclusion of the term, or the expiration date, stated in the franchise;

(ii) the franchisee is promptly provided with a copy of such agreement, together with the summary statement described in section 104(d); and

(iii) within 7 days after the date on which the franchise is provided a copy of such agreement, the franchisee has not posted by certified mail a written notice to the franchisor repudiating such agreement.

(E) In the case of any franchise entered into prior to the date of the enactment of this Act and in the case of any franchise entered into or renewed on or after such date (the term of which is 3 years or longer, or with respect to which the franchisee was offered a term of 3 years or longer), a determination made by the franchisor in good faith and in the normal course of business to withdraw from the marketing of motor fuel through retail outlets in the relevant geographic market area in which the marketing premises are located, if—

(i) such determination—

(I) was made after the date such franchise was entered into or renewed, and

(II) was based upon the occurrence of changes in relevant facts and circumstances after such date;

(ii) the termination or nonrenewal is not for the purpose of converting the premises, which are the subject of the franchise, to operation by employees or agents of the franchisor for such franchisor's own account; and

(iii) in the case of leased marketing premises—

(I) the franchisor, during the 180-day period after notification was given pursuant to section 104, either made a bona fide offer to sell, transfer, or assign to the franchisee such franchisor's interests in such premises, or, if applicable, offered the franchisee a right of first refusal of at least 45 days duration of an offer, made by another, to purchase such franchisor's interest in such premises; or

(II) in the case of the sale, transfer, or assignment to another person of the franchisor's interest in such premises in connection with the sale, transfer, or assignment to such other person of the franchisor's interest in one or more other marketing premises, if such other person offers, in good faith, a franchise to the franchisee on terms and conditions which are not discriminatory to the franchisee as compared to franchises then currently being offered by such other person or franchises then in effect and with respect to which such other person is the franchisor.

(3) For purposes of this subsection, the following are grounds for nonrenewal of a franchise relationship:

(A) The failure of the franchisor and the franchisee to agree to changes or additions to the provisions of the franchise, if—

(i) such changes or additions are the result of determinations made by the franchisor in good faith and in the normal course of business; and

(ii) such failure is not the result of the franchisor's insistence upon such changes or additions for the purpose of preventing the renewal of the franchise relationship.

(B) The receipt of numerous bona fide customer complaints by the franchisor concerning the franchisee's operation of the marketing premises, if—

(i) the franchisee was promptly apprised of the existence and nature of such complaints following receipt of such complaints by the franchisor; and

(ii) if such complaints related to the condition of such premises or to the conduct of any employee of such franchisee, the franchisee did not promptly take action to cure or correct the basis of such complaints.

(C) A failure by the franchisee to operate the marketing premises in a clean, safe, and healthful manner, if the franchisee failed to do so on two or more previous occasions and the franchisor notified the franchisee of such failures.

(D) In the case of any franchise entered into prior to the date of the enactment of this Act (the unexpired term of which, on such date of enactment, is 3 years or longer) and, in the case of any franchise entered into or renewed on or after such date (the term of which was 3 years or longer, or with respect to which the franchisee was offered a term of 3 years or longer), a determination made by the franchisor in good faith and in the normal course of business, if—

(i) such determination is—

(I) to convert the leased marketing premises to a use other than the sale or distribution of motor fuel,

(II) to materially alter, add to, or replace such premises,

(III) to sell such premises, or

(IV) that renewal of the franchise relationship is likely to be uneconomical to the franchisor despite any reasonable changes or reasonable additions to the provisions of the franchise which may be acceptable to the franchisee;

(ii) with respect to a determination referred to in subclause (II) or (IV), such determination is not made for the purpose of converting the leased marketing premises to operation by employees or agents of the franchisor for such franchisor's own account; and

(iii) in the case of leased marketing premises such franchisor, during the 90–day period after notification was given pursuant to section 104, either—

(I) made a bona fide offer to sell, transfer, or assign to the franchisee such franchisor's interests in such premises; or

(II) if applicable, offered the franchisee a right of first refusal of at least 45–days duration of an offer, made by another, to purchase such franchisor's interest in such premises.

(c) As used in subsection (b)(2)(C), the term "an event which is relevant to the franchise relationship and as a result of which termination of the franchise or nonrenewal of the franchise relationship is reasonable" includes events such as—

. . .

[The Act enumerates 12 categories of "events" precluding the continued operation of the franchise, including such factors as fraud or criminal misconduct by the franchisee, bankruptcy, expiration of the underlying lease, willful adulteration or misbranding of products, etc.]

Sec. 104. [This section spells out in detail specific time limits within which notice of termination or nonrenewal must be given, as well as the content of the notice.]

Sec. 105. [**This section establishes jurisdiction in U.S. district courts to entertain actions for failure to comply with the Act. Relief may include damages and preliminary and permanent injunctive relief.**]

Sec. 106. **(a) To the extent that any provision of this title applies to the termination (or the furnishing of notification with respect thereto) of any franchise, or to the nonrenewal (or the furnishing of notification with respect thereto) of any franchise relationship, no State or any political subdivision thereof may adopt, enforce, or continue in effect any provision of any law or regulation (including any remedy or penalty applicable to any violation thereof) with respect to termination (or the furnishing of notification with respect thereto) of any such franchise or to the nonrenewal (or the furnishing of notification with respect thereto) of any such franchise relationship unless such provision of such law or regulation is the same as the applicable provision of this title.**

(b) Nothing in this title authorizes any transfer or assignment of any franchise or prohibits any transfer or assignment of any franchise as authorized by the provisions of such franchise or by any applicable provision of State law which permits such transfer or assignment without regard to any provision of the franchise.

NOTES AND QUERIES

(1) *Comparison With Auto Dealer Act.* The Petroleum Marketing Practices Act's (P.M.P.A.) standards for determining the legality of a termination or non-renewal are far more specific and complex than the Auto Dealers' Act. In part, the draftsmen sought to avoid the vagueness of a general "good faith" standard found in many state statutes and in the Auto Dealers' Act.[56] The Act also establishes in Section 104 rigorous notice standards before termination or nonrenewal may take place. Spelling out the permissible conditions, time frame, and content of the notice of termination or non-renewal was thought necessary to redress the great imbalance of bargaining power between oil company franchisors and dealer franchisees, as well as remedy what one commentator has described as "a prime example of the worst abuses in franchising."[57] Failure to comply with these requirements of the Act may result in injunctive relief requiring the continuation of the relationship or damages.[58]

Query: With which approach do you agree—the general standards of the Auto Dealers' Act or the specific standards of the Petroleum Marketing Act? Which statute imposes the more significant limitations upon franchisor rights? Which affords franchisees the most protection?

(2) *Distinguishing Between Terminations and Nonrenewals.* Notice that the Act draws a distinction between termination during the franchise term and nonrenewals at the end of the term. Why distinguish between the two?

56. Comment, Retail Gasoline Franchise Terminations and Nonrenewals Under Title I of the Petroleum Marketing Practices Act, 1980 Duke L.J. 522, 531.

57. Brown, Franchising—A Fiduciary Relationship, 49 Tex.L.Rev. 650, 657 (1971). See also Jordan, Unconscionabil-ity at the Gas Station, 62 Minn.L.Rev. 813 (1978).

58. See Davy v. Murphy Oil Co., 488 F.Supp. 1013 (W.D.Mich.1980); Noe v. Mobil Oil Corp., 503 F.Supp. 213 (E.D.Mo. 1980); Blankenship v. Atlantic-Richfield Co., 478 F.Supp. 1016 (D.Or.1979).

(3) *Litigation Under the Petroleum Marketing Act.* A substantial number of cases have been litigated under the Act, many of them unreported. While it is still too early to conclude whether the Act will be liberally construed in favor of franchisees, several courts have rigorously enforced the notice requirements of the Act [59] and other courts have recognized the remedial purposes of the Act and the desire of Congress [60] to redress the imbalance of balancing power between franchisor and franchisee by closely regulating terminations and non-renewals. For example, in *Brach v. Amoco Oil Co.,* [61] the Court stated:

> The statutory scheme of the PMPA seeks to strike a balance between the interests of the participants in a petroleum marketing franchise relationship. Congress recognized the disparity of bargaining power between franchisor and franchisee and the harsh consequences of suddenly terminating a business for which the franchisee has worked long and hard to develop goodwill. Echoing those concerns, the PMPA commits gasoline franchisors to a franchise marriage of sorts, the dissolution of which is available only on specific grounds. While most of the grounds relate to serious franchisee misconduct, others reflect an intent to permit the franchisor to exercise reasonable business judgment. The franchisor, for example, may act upon a determination made in good faith and in the normal course of business to withdraw from the geographic market, that renewal is likely to be uneconomical, or to convert the premises to another use. Although one prerequisite to invoking any of those grounds is the existence of a three-year lease, compromises were nonetheless made which would allow a franchisor to "buy out" a franchisee under a short-term lease based on any of the enumerated business decisions, or to make the marriage more comfortable by imposing good faith changes to the franchise. But the one thing the Act is clearly intended to prevent is the appropriation of hard-earned goodwill which occurs when a franchisor arbitrarily takes over a business that the franchisee has turned into a successful going concern.

> As the statutory scheme shows, "the grounds specified as justification for termination or nonrenewal of a franchise are intentionally broad enough to provide to franchisors the flexibility which may be needed to respond to changing market conditions or consumer preferences," yet are not "so broad as to deny franchisees meaningful protections from arbitrary or discriminatory terminations and nonrenewals or to prevent fulfillment of the reasonable renewal expectations of franchisees." [62]

A challenge to the Act's constitutionality, because the non-renewal provisions were made applicable to franchise relationships established prior to enactment, was rejected in *Brach* with the comment: "We do not sit in judgment on the wisdom of Congress' chosen scheme. . . . It is enough that the Act rationally furthers legitimate congressional concerns and does not unreasonably burden existing property rights." [63]

b. State Legislation and Regulation

Franchisee complaints about the imbalance of bargaining power in the relationship and arbitrary terminations and non-renewals have

---

59. See cases cited supra note 57.

60. For the legislative history of the Act see House Rep. No. 95–161, 95th Cong., 1st Sess. (1977); S.Rep. No. 95–731, 95th Cong., 2d Sess. (1978). Excerpts from the Senate Report are set forth in 3 U.S.Code Cong. & Admin. News 873 (1978).

61. 677 F.2d 1213 (7th Cir. 1982).

62. 677 F.2d at 1220.

63. Id. at 1225.

provoked a variety of responses at the state level—not all of them legislative. In the leading case of SHELL OIL CO. v. MARINELLO,[64] the New Jersey courts—on common law contract and equity principles— held that a franchise contract clause giving the franchisor an absolute right to terminate a franchisee on ten days' notice was void and unenforceable. The New Jersey Supreme Court further held that "public policy requires that there be read into the existing lease and dealer agreements, and all future lease and dealer agreements . . . the restriction that Shell not have the unilateral right to terminate, cancel or fail to renew the franchise . . . in [the] absence of a showing that Marinello has failed to substantially perform his obligations under the lease and dealer agreement, i.e., for good cause. . . . " The Court acknowledged that the consequence of its decision was to give "Marinello's franchise . . . legal existence for an indefinite period, subject to his substantially performing his obligations thereunder." The Court suggested that Marinello's franchise might even pass to his heirs, but declined to decide in the case before it whether the "relationship is so personal it would not survive." [65]

The jurisprudential implications of cases like *Marinello* and state statutes curbing the authority of franchisors to terminate in accordance with express contractual provisions are interesting and profound. They may reflect a modern tendency to discriminate sharply between contract as a regulator of discrete *transactions* and contracts which establish *"status relationships."* The older notion of being bound by a bargain gives way to societal standards of what a bargain should be, especially in "contracts of adhesion," standardized agreements drawn by the more powerful participant in the "bargaining." Public intervention, whether by positive regulation or under the rubric of "unconscionability," [66] equitable reformation, or antitrust law, will refer to the realities of such relationships, with little deference to traditional contract law.[67] (or antitrust standards?). The relationship of retail service station operators to major oil companies was described by Judge Wisdom in an F.T.C. tying case against Shell Oil Company [68] as follows:

> The relationship of a major oil company to its service station dealer goes beyond the bigness-littleness antithesis that exists in innumerable contract negotiations and in the operations of a modern, large business. The inherent leverage a major oil company has over its dealers results from the market structure of the industry and the special dependence on the company of the service station

64. 120 N.J.Super. 357, 294 A.2d 253 (Ch.Div.1972), modified & affirmed 63 N.J. 402, 307 A.2d 598 (1973), certiorari denied 415 U.S. 920, 94 S.Ct. 1421, 39 L.Ed.2d 475 (1974).

65. 63 N.J. at 411, 307 A.2d at 603.

66. See Uniform Commercial Code § 2–302 (1970); Leff, Unconscionability and the Code—The Emperor's New Clause, 115 U.Pa.L.Rev. 485 (1967); Murray, Unconscionability: Unconscionability, 31 U.Pitt.L.Rev. 1 (1969); White & Summers, Uniform Commercial Code, Chap. 4 (1972).

67. Cf. Gilmore, The Death of Contract (1974); Friedman, Contract Law In America (1965).

68. Shell Oil Co. v. Federal Trade Commission, 360 F.2d 470 (5th Cir. 1966), certiorari denied 385 U.S. 1002, 87 S.Ct. 703, 17 L.Ed.2d 541 (1967), and 385 U.S. 1002, 87 S.Ct. 705, 17 L.Ed.2d 541.

dealer (who is usually also a lessee). The classic market factors of price, quality, attractiveness, and whatever enables a retailer to resell goods at a profit are pre-empted by the TBA distribution system superimposed from on high by *deus ex machina.* A man operating a gas station is bound to be over-awed by the great corporation that is his supplier, his banker, and his landlord. When he hears that Shell will benefit from his patronage of sponsored TBA outlets, the velvet glove of request has within it the mailed fist of command. His interest in catering to Shell's sponsorship of certain TBA will be especially strong when the time for lease renewal approaches (once a year) or when a change in rental or commission appears in sight. The run of the mill service station dealer is a man of limited means who has, for him, a sizable investment in his station. Much of the value of that investment is in goodwill attached to the gasoline he sells, the TBA he stocks, and the location of the station where he sells these products. While it is true that it is expensive for Shell to switch dealers, it is far more expensive, in relative terms, for a dealer to lose his station.[69]

New Jersey [70] and several other states have enacted statutes regulating termination of franchises in specified industries or generally.[71] In some states cancellation is permitted only for "good cause." [72] Other states require only that the franchisor compensate a terminated franchisee for inventory, supplies, and equipment purchased by the franchisee.[73] The constitutionality of state franchise termination legislation has been attacked on varying grounds, including preemption by the Lanham Act,[74] impairment of contract rights,[75] and undue burden on interstate commerce.[76]

69. Id. at 487. Cf. Atlantic Refining Co. v. Federal Trade Commission, supra p. 757.

70. N.J.Stat.Ann. §§ 56–10–1 et seq. (Supp.1976).

71. States with general franchise termination laws are: Arkansas, California, Connecticut, Delaware, Hawaii, Indiana, Mississippi, Missouri, Nebraska, New Jersey, Virginia, Washington, and Wisconsin. The statutes are collected in Business Franchise Guide (CCH). ¶ 4000 et seq. For surveys of state termination law, see Caffey, Franchise Termination and Nonrenewal Legislation: Recent Developments and Trends In State Legislation, 49 Antitrust L.J. 1343 (1981); Note, Regulation of Franchising, 59 Minn.L. Rev. 1027 (1975).

72. See N.J.Stat.Ann. § 56–10–5 (Supp. 1975).

73. See Conn.Gen.Stat.Ann. § 42–133f (b) (Supp.1976).

74. See Marinello v. Shell Oil Co., 511 F.2d 853 (3d Cir. 1975), reversing a district court holding that the New Jersey Franchise Act was preempted by the Lanham Act; See Note, Constitutional Obstacles to State "Good Cause" Restrictions on Franchise Terminations, 74 Colum.L.Rev. 1487 (1974); Note, Franchise Terminations and Refusals to Renew: The Lanham Act and Preemption of State Regulation, 60 Iowa L.Rev. 122 (1974).

75. See Globe Liquor Co. v. Four Roses Distillers Co., 281 A.2d 19 (Del. Sup.Ct.), certiorari denied 404 U.S. 873, 92 S.Ct. 103, 30 L.Ed.2d 117 (1971), holding the Delaware Franchise Act, 6 Del. Code Ann. § 2551 et seq. (Supp.1976), an unconstitutional impairment of contracts and taking of property.

76. See Note, Constitutional Obstacles to State "Good Cause" Restrictions on Franchise Terminations, supra note 74. See also American Motors Sales Corp. v. Division of Motor Vehicles, 592 F.2d 219 (4th Cir. 1979) (upholding the Virginia Auto Dealers Act). State franchise laws may also raise conflict of laws questions. See C.A. May Marine Supply Co. v. Brunswick Corp., 557 F.2d 1163 (5th Cir. 1977) (Upholding application of

The Supreme Court has turned aside attacks on state franchise regulation on two occasions in recent years. In EXXON CORP. v. GOVERNOR OF MARYLAND,[77] the Court upheld a Maryland statute prohibiting producers or refiners of petroleum products from operating retail service stations in the State.[78] The Court rejected oil company claims that the statute violated the Due Process Clause, the Commerce Clause, or was preempted by federal legislation. In NEW MOTOR VEHICLE BOARD v. ORRIN W. FOX CO.,[79] the Court upheld a California statute [80] which required auto manufacturers proposing to open or relocate a retail dealership within the area of a protesting dealer of the manufacturer, to obtain the approval of a state agency before opening the dealership. The Court upheld the statute over claims that the statute violated due process and was in conflict with the Sherman Act. On the due process argument, the majority held (Brennan, J.):

> Even if the right to franchise had constituted a protected interest when California enacted the Automobile Franchise Act, California's Legislature was still constitutionally empowered to enact a general scheme of business regulation that imposed reasonable restrictions upon the exercise of the right. . . . At least since the demise of the concept of "substantive due process" in the area of economic regulation, this Court has recognized that, "[l]egislative bodies have broad scope to experiment with economic problems . . ." *Ferguson v. Skrupa*, 372 U.S. 726, 730, 83 S.Ct. 1028, 1031, 10 L.Ed.2d 93 (1963). States may, through general ordinance, restrict the commercial use of property, and the geographical location of commercial enterprises, ... Moreover, "[c]ertain kinds of business may be prohibited; and the right to conduct a business, or to pursue a calling, may be conditioned. . . . [S]tatutes prescribing the terms upon which those conducting certain businesses may contract, or imposing terms if they do enter into agreements, are within the state's competency."

> In particular, the California Legislature was empowered to subordinate the franchise rights of automobile manufacturers to the conflicting rights of their franchisees where necessary to prevent unfair or oppressive trade practices. "[S]tates have power to legislate against what are found to be injurious practices in their internal commercial and business affairs, so long as their laws do not run afoul of some specific federal constitutional prohibition, or of some valid federal law. . . . [T]he due process clause is [not] to be so broadly construed that the Congress and state legislatures are put in a straight jacket when they attempt to suppress business and industrial conditions which they regard as offensive to the public welfare."

Wisconsin franchise law to termination of a Georgia franchisee).

77. 437 U.S. 117, 98 S.Ct. 2207, 57 L.Ed.2d 91 (1978).

78. Md.Annot.Code, Art. 56, § 157E (1972 Repl.Vol., 1976 Cum.Supp.).

79. 439 U.S. 96, 99 S.Ct. 403, 58 L.Ed.2d 361 (1978).

80. Calif.Veh.Code Annot. §§ 3062–63 (West Supp. 1978).

Further, the California Legislature had the authority to protect the conflicting rights of the motor vehicle franchisees through customary and reasonable procedural safeguards; i.e., by providing existing dealers with notice and an opportunity to be heard by an impartial tribunal—the New Motor Vehicle Board—before their franchisor is permitted to inflict upon them grievous loss. Such procedural safeguards cannot be said to deprive the franchisor of due process. States may, as California has done here, require businesses to secure regulatory approval *before* engaging in specified practices.[81]

In response to the claim that the law conflicted with the Sherman Act because it gave existing dealers power to delay the establishment of competing dealerships, the majority held:

The dispositive answer is that the Act's regulatory scheme is a system of regulation, clearly articulated and affirmatively expressed, designed to displace unfettered business freedom in the matter of the establishment and relocation of automobile dealerships. The regulation is therefore outside the reach of the antitrust laws under the "state action" exemption.[82]

81. 439 U.S., at 106–8, 99 S.Ct., at 410–11, 58 L.Ed.2d, at 374–5.

82. Id. at 109, 99 S.Ct., at 412, 58 L.Ed.2d, at 376.

Chapter 7

JUDICIALLY CREATED DEFENSES AND EXEMPTIONS

A. INTRODUCTION

The broad brush Congress used in drafting the antitrust laws, their status as "a charter of freedom" with a "generality and adaptability" comparable to that found in constitutional provisions",[1] and the across-the-board application of antitrust policy to all sectors of interstate and foreign commerce are factors which have contributed to the necessity for legislative and judge-made defenses and exemptions. Over the years, Congress has enacted a hodge-podge of statutory schemes inconsistent with the antitrust laws,[2] completely regulating some industries, partially regulating others, or exempting some or all of the activity of a particular business from the general policies of the antitrust laws.[3] In some cases, regulation or exemption has been deemed necessary because of the "natural monopoly" characteristics of the business. In others, risks to consumers or the commonweal have been seen as justifications for affirmative government intervention to protect public health and safety in, for example, the marketing of drugs; to prevent fraud or unwise investments in the sale and distribution of securities; to protect peoples' savings in banking operations; or to prevent risks to the environment by the release of toxic wastes or pollutants and risks to our very survival by the manufacture or distribution of nuclear materials. Other exemptions can only be explained in terms of the felt necessities of the times in which they were enacted, or the presence of existing regulation requiring the further regulation of new technologies competing with the old. Airline regulation was originally adopted to help promote an infant industry, while sheltering it from the risks of new entry and cutthroat competition thought likely to preclude the establishment of strong national and international carriers.[4] Trucking regulation is an example of regulation of an emerging technology which

1. Appalachian Coals, Inc. v. United States, 288 U.S. 344, 359–60, 53 S.Ct. 471, 474, 77 L.Ed. 825, 830 (1933).

2. The major statutes exempting particular industries or singling them out for special treatment are collected in 4 Trade Reg. Rep. (CCH) ¶ 25,000 et seq.

3. See 1 P. Areeda & D. Turner, Antitrust Law, 134 et seq. (1978); Symposi-

um, Antitrust Exemptions and Immunities, 48 Antitrust L.J. 909 (1980).

4. See generally R. Caves, Air Transport and Its Regulators: An Industry Study (1962). For an analysis of the impact of deregulation, see T. Keeler, The Revolution in Airline Regulation, in Case Studies in Regulation 53 (L. Weiss & M. Klass, Eds. 1981).

could compete with a powerful and entrenched regulated one, the railroads.[5]

Other statutory exemptions from antitrust policy find their primary *raison d'etre* in the political clout of the exempted industry. Newspaper publishers were able to "persuade" Congress to exempt joint operating arrangements by the "Newspaper Preservation Act"; [6] small retailers enjoyed a forty-year exemption for vertical price fixing under the "Fair Trade" exemption; [7] soft drink bottlers [8] and professional sports teams receive specialized treatment under laws tailored to meet what they perceive to be unique circumstances affecting their business; and the insurance industry obtained a wideranging exemption for the "business of insurance" [9] within a few months of the Supreme Court's decision applying the antitrust laws to their business.[10] Proposed exemptions of this type tend to appear more regularly before Congress in this era of Political Action Committees (PAC's), sometimes with only a thin veneer of justification for what is otherwise an exercise of political power for displacing the competitive process as the basic rule of trade.[11]

Many of these exemptions and schemes of affirmative regulation are studied in the related courses of Regulated Industries, Securities Regulation, Insurance Law, Environmental Law, Health Care Regulation, and so on. We do not take them up here in any extended detail. This chapter focuses, rather, on those judicially created doctrines, which attempt to accommodate the conflict between the antitrust laws and government regulation. The materials are organized on the following plan. Section B examines federal statutory exemptions from antitrust, whether express or implied, and the doctrine of primary jurisdiction. Section C looks at state and local schemes of regulation, and the judicially created "state action" doctrine which is designed to reconcile such legislation with the federal antitrust laws. Section D explores the constitutional defenses which can be asserted when the allegedly anticompetitive scheme involves approaches to governmental units—executive, legislative, judicial, or administrative—seeking government action which restrains trade. The chapter concludes with an examination of the interplay of foreign economic

5. "[The Motor Carrier] Act was passed and has been enforced with the explicit purpose and effect of protecting railroads against the intensified competition of motor carriers and protecting motor carriers from one another." 2 A. Kahn, The Economics of Regulation: Principles and Institutions 14 (1970).

6. See supra p. 579.

7. See supra p. 590.

8. See supra p. 588.

9. McCarran-Ferguson Act, 15 U.S. C.A. §§ 1012–13.

10. United States v. South-Eastern Underwriters Association, 322 U.S. 533, 64 S.Ct. 1162, 88 L.Ed. 1440 (1942).

11. See "Cash Politics: Special Interest Money Increasingly Influences What Congress Enacts", W.St.J., July 26, 1982, p. 1 (discussing bill to exempt medical professionals from F.T.C. jurisdiction; of the 192 House Sponsors, 186 of them are recipients of campaign contributions from the A.M.A.'s Political Action Committee); "House Vote On Broad Antitrust Immunity For Ship Lines To Test Effect of Lobbying", W.St.J., Sept. 15, 1982, p. 12 ($1 million in campaign "gifts" given congressional candidates by proponents of bill to allow shipping lines to jointly set rates and divide territories).

regulation and the federal antitrust laws, focusing specifically on the "act of state" and "sovereign compulsion" defenses.

In considering these defenses and exemptions it is well to remember that the antitrust laws can at times act as a defense for conduct which might give rise to liability under other laws. A familiar example is the doctrine of patent "abuse" (explored infra pp. 978–1039), whereby an infringer of a patent can avoid a suit for damages by showing that the patentee abused its statutory privilege by using the patent to commit an antitrust violation. Another example is the doctrine of "antitrust illegality"—a party sued for breach of a contract asserts that the contract is unenforceable because enforcement would command a violation of the antitrust laws. The Supreme Court's 1982 decision in *Kaiser Steel Corp. v. Mullins* [12] breathed new life into this doctrine, allowing an employer to assert antitrust illegality in defense to a suit enforcing a term in a collective bargaining agreement.

B. PRIMARY JURISDICTION AND IMPLIED EXEMPTION [13]

Regulatory statutes seldom contain specific language detailing the interrelationship between antitrust policy and the regulatory scheme adopted. An inability to foresee all the factual circumstances and controversies which might arise in the activity regulated, as well as evolutions in the business regulated and its technologies long after regulation is imposed, may justify a reluctance by Congress to be overly specific in spelling out the relationship. Courts confronted with an antitrust dispute related in some degree with a regulatory scheme have found it necessary to develop analytical concepts and methods for reconciling antitrust policy and a particular regulatory scheme within the factual confines of a particular case. Three interrelated and frequently confused doctrines have been developed by the courts to analyze such cases sensibly: (1) express exemption; (2) implied exemption; and (3) primary jurisdiction.

In a limited number of circumstances, Congress has expressly and unambiguously exempted certain activities from the antitrust laws.[14] Even in these circumstances, controversy over the scope of the express exemption can break out around the periphery of the exemption. For example, the Congressional exemption from federal anti-

---

12. 455 U.S. 72, 102 S.Ct. 851, 70 L.Ed.2d 833 (1982).

13. For general surveys, see 1 P. Areeda & D. Turner, Antitrust Law, 134–237 (1978); K. Davis, Administrative Law Text § 19.01 (1972); E. Giellhorn & R. Pierce, Regulated Industries, 366–75 (1982); L. Sullivan, Antitrust, 743–51 (1977); Botein, Primary Jurisdiction: The Need For Better Court/Agency Interaction, 29 Rutgers L.Rev. 867 (1976); Shulman, Application of the Antitrust Laws to Regulated Industries, 44 Tenn.L.Rev. 1 (1976); Travis, Primary Jurisdiction: A

General Theory and Its Application to the Securities Exchange Act, 63 Calif.L.Rev. 926 (1975); Symposium, Antitrust and Deregulation: Government Policy at the Crossroads, 50 Antitrust L.J. 359 (1982); Symposium, Current Antitrust Exemptions and Immunities, 48 Antitrust L.J. 909 (1979).

14. See, e.g., Reed-Bulwinkle Act, 49 U.S.C.A. § 10706 (rate agreements by carriers and approved by ICC); Shipping Act of 1916, 46 U.S.C.A. §§ 813a, 814 (exempting FMB approved rate agreements between carriers).

trust regulation for the insurance industry under the McCarran-Ferguson Act [15] is expressly limited to "the business of insurance" is only available to the extent the conduct in question is regulated by state law, and is further limited by a proviso excepting from the exemption conduct amounting to a "boycott", "coercion" or "intimidation". Controversy has occurred about the meaning of each of these limitations upon the scope of the express exemption.[16]

The more common and far more analytically complex case is one of "implied" exemption—the claim that Congress "intended" to exempt regulated conduct from antitrust even though it did not do so by express statutory language spelling out the exemption.[17] Divining Congressional intent can be a complex task, and it has been persuasively argued:

> [T]wo grounds—and only two grounds—will support an implied repeal: the first is irreconcilability and the second is an affirmative showing of legislative intent to repeal by implication. The latter criterion has only been satisfied in cases in which the repealing act contains a directive to the regulatory agency to police the interplay of competitive forces. The irreconcilability criterion requires, at a minimum, that the statutes [antitrust and regulatory] produce differing results. This finding alone is not sufficient however. Rather, to find 'irreconcilability' there must be a determination that repeal of the antitrust laws is necessary to make the regulatory act work. This requires an appreciation of the nature of the various regulatory acts.[18]

Although a survey of the "various regulatory acts" and the multitude of court opinions interpreting them in the context of a claim of implied antitrust immunity is beyond the scope of these materials, it is important to emphasize that the courts have repeatedly rejected claims of an implied blanket immunity for all activity of a regulated industry and have only recognized implied immunity "for particular and discrete transactions and occurrences." [19] The analytical methodology employed is well illustrated by Judge Greene's opinion in an early phase of the Antitrust Division's suit against AT&T seeking dissolution of the company on the ground of unlawful monopolization.[20]

15. 15 U.S.C.A. §§ 1011–15. See generally, Carlson, The Insurance Exemption From The Antitrust Laws, 57 Tex.L.Rev. 1127 (1979); Sullivan & Wiley, Recent Antitrust Developments: Defining the Scope of Exemptions, Expanding Coverage, and Refining the Rule of Reason, 27 U.C.L.A.L.Rev. 266, 268–291 (1979).

16. See Union Labor Life Insurance Co. v. Pireno, ___ U.S. ___, 102 S.Ct. 3002, 73 L.Ed.2d 647 (1982) (peer review not "business of insurance"); Group Life & Health Insurance Co. v. Royal Drug Co., 440 U.S. 205, 99 S.Ct. 1067, 59 L.Ed. 2d 261 (1979) (insurance company contracts with pharmacies fixing fees paid pharmacies for filling prescriptions not business of insurance); St. Paul Fire & Marine Insurance Co. v. Barry, 438 U.S. 531, 98 S.Ct. 2923, 57 L.Ed.2d 932 (1978) (definition of boycott; conduct not exempt).

17. See Balter & Day, Implied Antitrust Repeals: Principles for Analysis, 86 Dickinson L.Rev. 447 (1982); Comment, Antitrust and Regulated Industries: A Critique and Proposal for Reform of the Implied Immunity Doctrine, 57 Tex.L. Rev. 751 (1979).

18. Balter & Day, supra note 17 at 465–66.

19. Id. at 472.

20. United States v. American Telephone & Telegraph Co., 461 F.Supp. 1314, 1320–30 (D.D.C.1978).

(Discussed supra. p. 192). In response to a motion to dismiss the suit on a claim that Congress had committed regulation of the activity in question to the F.C.C. under the Communications Act of 1934,[21] Judge Greene wrote:

> Telecommunications carriers clearly do not enjoy an express statutory immunity from antitrust enforcement with respect to the activities here involved. While Congress has not hesitated in so many words to exempt the practices of other industries from the antitrust laws, and while it has statutorily exempted some activities of telephone companies from those laws, it has not done so with respect to the conduct which is the subject matter of this complaint. Likewise, defendants have cited nothing in the legislative history of the statutes regulating the telecommunications industry which would lead to the conclusion that an antitrust immunity was contemplated when those statutes were enacted. Thus, if the Court lacks jurisdiction, it could only be because defendants enjoy an immunity by implication, resulting from an incompatibility between the antitrust laws and the statutes which regulate the telecommunications industry.

> The problem created by the tension between the antitrust laws and economic regulation has been long recognized. Broadly speaking the antitrust laws are rooted in the proposition that the public interest is best protected by competition, free from artificial restraints such as price-fixing and monopoly. The theory of regulation, on the other hand, presupposes that with respect to certain areas of economic activity the judgment of expert agencies may produce results superior to those of the marketplace, and that for this reason competition in a particular industry will not necessarily serve the public interest. Because of these divergent objectives, it could be, and has been, argued that whenever the Congress has established a scheme of regulation through an independent commission, it must be deemed to have determined that the antitrust laws should not apply to the industry thus being regulated. That, however, is not the law.

> The Supreme Court has repeatedly noted that 'repeals of the antitrust laws by implication from a regulatory statute are strongly disfavored, and have only been found in cases of plain repugnancy between the antitrust and regulatory provisions.'

Regulated industries are not per se exempt from the Sherman Act,[22] and they are not necessarily exempt even if the conduct

---

21. 47 U.S.C.A. §§ 151 et seq.

22. [Court's footnote 23.] The antitrust laws apply notwithstanding regulation in such industries as the production of natural gas (California v. Federal Power Commission, 369 U.S. 482, 82 S.Ct. 901, 8 L.Ed.2d 54 (1962)); generation and transmission of electric power (Otter Tail Power Co. v. United States, supra); national banking (United States v. Philadelphia National Bank, supra); securities and commodities exchanges (Silver v. New York Stock Exchange, supra; Ricci v. Chicago Mercantile Exchange, 409 U.S. 289, 93 S.Ct. 573, 34 L.Ed.2d 525 (1973)); and broadcasting (United States v. Radio Corporation of America, 358 U.S. 334, 79 S.Ct. 457, 3 L.Ed.2d 354 (1959)).

complained of in an antitrust context has been expressly approved by the agency charged with regulating the particular industry.

. . .

Regulated conduct is, however, deemed to be immune by implication from the antitrust laws in two relatively narrow instances: (1) when a regulatory agency has, with congressional approval, exercised explicit authority over the challenged practice itself (as distinguished from the general subject matter) in such a way that antitrust enforcement would interfere with regulation, and (2) when regulation by an agency over an industry or some of its components or practices is so pervasive that Congress is assumed to have determined competition to be an inadequate means of vindicating the public interest.

. . .

The FCC—unlike, for example, the SEC in the stock exchange cases—has consistently taken the position that antitrust enforcement through court action is not precluded in this area.

. . .

Among the considerations it cited in support of its position, the Commission stressed, *inter alia*, that, while under section 214 of the Communications Act, 47 U.S.C. § 214, it has exclusive market entry authority, antitrust actions not only do not necessarily conflict with that authority, but might even complement it in appropriate circumstances; the courts and the Commission have concurrent responsibilities, but when there is a conflict, the doctrine of primary jurisdiction is adequate to resolve the matter; the Commission has never considered its authority over equipment interconnection to displace the antitrust laws; and even with respect to tariffs, since . . . they often become effective without Commission scrutiny or approval, the courts appropriately exercise antitrust jurisdiction.

An examination of the complaint in this proceeding against the implied immunity doctrine and its philosophic underpinnings verifies the Commission's conclusion. The allegations of the complaint describe conduct that quite obviously was not stimulated by regulatory supervision or coercion; it is of a character that reflects defendants' business judgment that its profits might be maximized if potential competitors were discouraged from entering the various markets AT&T controls.

. . .

In such a posture, the abstract philosophical differences between regulation and competition will hardly serve to oust the antitrust laws from their normal function and effect. The purpose of the implied immunity rule is to eliminate adherence to antitrust standards when there are irreconcilable differences between the antitrust laws and federal regulatory statutes.[23] But the antitrust

23. [Court's footnote 42.] Immunity will be implied only if necessary to make the regulatory statutes work, "and even then only to the minimum extent necessa-

laws cannot be held hostage to a supposed irreconcilability between antitrust and regulatory enforcement when no such irreconcilability exists in fact, nor can the alleged unlawful actions of defendants be deemed protected from the Sherman Act by the cloak
of generalized regulation of AT&T by the Commission.

．　．　．

For these reasons, the Court rejects defendants' contention
that the Court lacks antitrust jurisdiction over the matters alleged
in the complaint.   However, in the event that it should subsequently appear after the issues have been crystallized—e.g., after
discovery has been completed—that with respect to some of defendants' conduct the Commission has special expertise or there
may be a conflict between antitrust enforcement and regulation,
the issues relating to such conduct will be referred to the Commission under the doctrine of primary jurisdiction.[24]

The doctrine of "primary jurisdiction" referred to by Judge
Greene is sometimes confused with the doctrine of implied immunity.
"Primary jurisdiction" is not concerned with whether Congress intended to preclude the application of antitrust policy to a particular
dispute, but only with the question of whether the antitrust court
should suspend the resolution of some questions of fact or law over
which it does have antitrust jurisdiction, until passed upon by the regulatory authority whose jurisdiction encompasses the activity involved.   Such initial deference is the usual practice in three situations: (1) when resolution of the case involves complex factual
inquiries particularly within the province of the regulatory body's expertise; (2) when interpretation of administrative rules is required;
and (3) when interpretation of the regulatory statute involves broad
policy determination within the special ken of the regulatory agency.
This deference to statutory interpretation extends even to questions

ry."   Gordon v. New York Stock Exchange, 422 U.S., at 685, 95 S.Ct., at
2613.

24. [Court's footnote 45.] While the
term "primary jurisdiction" has been
widely used, including by the U. S. Supreme Court, it deserves some clarification. A referral under that doctrine does
not oust a court of jurisdiction; it merely
serves as a means for requesting a regulatory agency to make preliminary factual and legal determinations while reserving to the court the authority to decide
the ultimate questions. Judge Waddy's
opinion of November 24, 1976, concluded
that some of the issues herein might be
referred to the FCC under that doctrine.
It is clear from Ricci v. Chicago Mercantile Exchange, supra, that such a referral
is appropriate particularly where there is
a need to resolve possible conflicts between the objectives of the antitrust laws
and the regulatory standards, and where
an adjudication of such issues by the regulatory body will be of material aid in the
ultimate decision of the antitrust issues.
It is my intention, as it was Judge Waddy's, to make such appropriate references to the FCC. According to the
Commission (Memorandum as *amicus
curiae*, p. 29) issues which substantially
affect the following matters should be referred to it under the principle of primary jurisdiction: (1) entry into or exit from
a communications carrier market; (2)
FCC orders requiring interconnection;
and (3) tariff provisions which the Commission has approved or precluded. It
would be premature at this point to conclude the extent to which these conditions exist with respect to particular issues in this case, or whether there may
be other matters appropriate for referral
to the Commission.

of jurisdiction.　As stated by the court of appeals in *Southern Railway Co. v. Combs:* [25]

The doctrine of primary jurisdiction does not determine whether a court or an administrative body ultimately shall be responsible for resolving an issue.　Rather it is used to determine which tribunal shall make the initial determination.　The doctrine permits courts to suspend the resolution of issues, which are originally cognizable in the courts, until such time as an administrative body, with special competence in the field, has an opportunity to present its views.　This concept was recently summarized in Port of Boston Marine Terminal Ass'n v. Rederiaktiebolaget Transatlantic, 400 U.S. 62, 91 S.Ct. 203, 27 L.Ed.2d 203 (1970), wherein the Court stated:

'When there is a basis for judicial action, independent of agency proceedings, courts may route the threshold decision as to certain issues to the agency charged with primary responsibility for governmental supervision or control of the particular industry or activity involved.'　400 U.S. at 68, 91 S.Ct. at 208.

Here we are calling upon the agency to interpret the statute upon which its jurisdiction rests.　This differs from the traditional primary jurisdiction case wherein complex issues of fact or the interpretation of administrative rules are involved.　Far East Conference v. United States, 342 U.S. 570, 72 S.Ct. 492, 96 L.Ed. 576 (1952).　However, where the interpretation of specific statutory provisions involve [s] [sic] consideration of broad national policies, courts have not hesitated to defer questions of jurisdiction to insure the most thoughtful resolution.　In J.M. Huber Corp. v. Denman, 367 F.2d 104 (5th Cir. 1966), Judge Brown wrote:

'At the outset we recognize that this is a new application of the doctrine of primary jurisdiction.　But considering the broad aim of this device and the consequent flexibility of it there is really nothing startling about submitting to an agency for initial decision the question of its own jurisdiction.

'That that question of law happens to be one of jurisdiction does not force a different result.　To the contrary, justification for judicial deferral of the jurisdictional question for initial resolution by an agency is even stronger than for a non-jurisdictional question.　This is demonstrated by the many cases upholding the jurisdiction of administrative agencies to determine the coverage of their respective statutes and barring all attempts through judicial proceedings to avoid such determination.'　(Footnotes omitted.)　367 F.2d at 111–112.

We believe deference to the N.M.B. is appropriate in this case because far reaching considerations of national policy underlie the legal issues.　By availing ourselves of the Board's experience, we believe the groundwork will be laid for '.　.　.　a more informed and precise determination by the Court of the scope and meaning

25.　484 F.2d 145 (6th Cir. 1973).

of the statute. . . . ' Federal Maritime Board v. Isbrandtsen Co., Inc., 356 U.S. 481, 498–499, 78 S.Ct. 851, 862, 2 L.Ed.2d 926 (1958).[26]

The effect of judicial reference of a question to an administrative agency should be agency action on the question referred and then further court action in the antitrust case,[27] although in some cases agency action might be dispositive where the agency has the power to approve the challenged activities.[28] Unlike a finding of express or implied exemption, however, where the primary jurisdiction doctrine is applied review is had of the trial court's action and that review is on antitrust standards. Where the doctrines of express or implied exemption are applied, on the other hand, review is of the agency's action on the standards set forth in the regulatory statute, and usually with the judicial deference due the expertise of administrative agency fact finding. As a practical matter, the initial sorting out of the question of which doctrine applies in a particular case is of great significance in deciding what law applies, the degree to which antitrust considerations may or may not be accorded weight, and whether the antitrust remedies of criminal sanctions or treble damages are available in a particular case. An express or implied exemption finding precludes the application of antitrust standards and remedies; while an application of the primary jurisdiction doctrine does not necessarily preclude the use of antitrust standards and remedies to adjudicate the dispute but may only defer the adjudication pending an initial decision by the agency. It is, of course, not infrequent that a court may find none of these doctrines applicable in a case involving activity by a regulated industry—even where the agency has some jurisdiction over the activity in question. As Judge Greene pointed out in the *AT&T* case, supra, in such cases antitrust policy and regulatory policy are seen as compatible and not antagonistic.

NOTES AND QUERIES

(1) *Deregulation and Narrowing the Doctrines of Implied Immunity and Primary Jurisdiction.* At one time the doctrines of implied immunity and primary jurisdiction were generously applied in antitrust cases posing challenges to activity by industries regulated in whole or part at the federal and state level. Substantial scholarly criticism of the casual application of the doctrines, and the resulting widespread immunity from antitrust,[29] led to

---

26. 484 F.2d at 149–50.

27. "Under true primary jurisdiction, the court retains jurisdiction to render the ultimate decision as well as relief, refers one or more issues to the agency, and then takes the agency's action for what it deems it is worth. Although true primary jurisdiction has existed for decades, a vital feature is still unclear—namely, the extent of a court's freedom to ignore an agency's decision." Botein, supra note 13 at 889.

28. "[T]he practical effect of applying the doctrine of primary jurisdiction has

sometimes been to preclude such enforcement entirely if the agency has the power to approve the challenged activities. . . ." United States v. Philadelphia National Bank, 374 U.S. 321, 353–54, 83 S.Ct. 1715, 1736–37, 10 L.Ed.2d 915, 939–40 (1963).

29. See Schwartz, Legal Restrictions of Competition in the Regulated Industries: An Abdication of Judicial Responsibility, 67 Harv.L.Rev. 436, 464 et seq. (1954); Baxter, NYSE Fixed Commission Rates: A Private Cartel Goes Public, 22 Stan.L.Rev. 675, 683ff (1970); Jaffe, Pri-

a gradual narrowing of doctrines in recent years by way of a more rigorous judicial analysis of the regulatory scheme involved and the specific activity being questioned, with an on-going presumption against finding an intent to preempt antitrust policy or stay the court's hand pending agency action.[30] The tendency to narrow the application of these doctrines has further accelerated in recent years, with the "deregulation movement" questioning regulatory regimes adopted many decades ago during the distress of the Depression to regulate industries which have now changed significantly.[31] The reasons for this widespread concern have been succinctly summarized by President Carter's National Commission For The Review of Antitrust Laws and Procedures:

> The roots of the current reexamination of antitrust immunities and economic regulation are several. They include the following diverse factors:
>
> (1) A realization that the problems of the Great Depression were not problems involving specific industries, but were economy-wide;
>
> (2) A new recognition that the limitations on our national resources require a far greater emphasis on efficiency in their use;
>
> (3) A growing awareness that the persistence of inflation is not entirely a macroeconomic problem, but is associated with specific performance problems in particular industries arising in part from economic regulation; and
>
> (4) An increasing resistance to governmental interference with entrepreneurial and consumer freedom of choice.

Contributing to the reexamination of regulatory policy has been a rapidly expanding body of academic literature, empirical studies, and legislative reports critical of much economic regulation. It has been widely observed in such studies that economic regulation tends almost invariably to take on a protectionist cloak. The regulator too often mistakes industry-wide prosperity with success. Paradoxically, this type of regulation may not produce high profits because protectionist regulation tends to discourage input cost control and in many cases to decrease efficiency. In other

mary Jurisdiction Reconsidered, 102 U.Pa.L.Rev. 577 (1954); Judicial Doctrine of Primary Jurisdiction as Applied in Antitrust Suits, Staff Report to the Antitrust Subcommittee of the House Committee on the Judiciary, 84th Cong., 2d Sess. (1956).

30. Among decisions refusing to find implied repeal or exemption of the antitrust laws in the face of a regulatory statute are Nader v. Allegheny Airlines, Inc., 426 U.S. 290, 96 S.Ct. 1978, 48 L.Ed. 2d 643 (1976); Otter Tail Power Co. v. United States, supra p. 124; Hughes Tool Co. v. Trans World Airlines, Inc., 409 U.S. 363, 93 S.Ct. 647, 34 L.Ed.2d 577 (1973); Carnation Co. v. Pacific Conference, 383 U.S. 213, 86 S.Ct. 781, 15 L.Ed. 2d 709 (1966); United States v. Philadelphia National Bank, supra p. 220; California v. Federal Power Commission, 369 U.S. 482, 82 S.Ct. 901, 8 L.Ed.2d 54 (1962); United States v. Radio Corp. of

America, 358 U.S. 334, 79 S.Ct. 457, 3 L.Ed.2d 354 (1959) (despite approval of transaction by Federal Communications Commission); United States Alkali Association v. United States, 325 U.S. 196, 65 S.Ct. 1120, 89 L.Ed. 1554 (1945) (export association subject to Federal Trade Commission); Georgia v. Pennsylvania Railroad, 324 U.S. 439, 65 S.Ct. 716, 89 L.Ed. 1051 (1945) (railroad rate conference); United States v. Borden Co., 308 U.S. 188, 60 S.Ct. 182, 84 L.Ed. 181 (1939) (jurisdiction of the Department of Agriculture).

31. See Krutter, Judicial Enforcement of Competition in the Regulated Industries, 12 Creighton L.Rev. 1041 (1979); Symposium, Antitrust and Deregulation: Government Policy at the Crossroads, 50 Antitrust L.J. 359 (1982); Note, Vanishing Immunity: The Antitrust Assault on Regulated Industries, 27 Loyola L.Rev. 187 (1981).

instances, profits may be dissipated by wasteful types of service competition.

Observers have also cited increasing examples of regulatory mismatches between asserted legislative purposes and actual industry conditions. Particular attention has been directed to the widespread tendency to apply entry and pricing regulation that is suitable for the problems of natural monopoly to industries that are structurally conducive to competition.

Another fundamental issue concerns the use of economic regulation as an indirect method of subsidizing certain consumers at the expense of others. Most observers have noted that this method of providing cross-subsidies is highly inefficient and often causes unintended, costly dislocations. Similarly, health and safety regulation is generally thought to be more efficiently accomplished through directly targeted regulatory schemes rather than by price, entry, or output controls.

It is clear that existing antitrust immunity and regulatory schemes result in significant economic costs. A sampling of some of the more authoritative studies demonstrates the costs of anticompetitive regulation. A General Accounting Office study pegged the cost of air transport regulation at almost $2 billion a year. Various students of the trucking industry have found that regulation costs nearly a billion 1969 dollars annually, with trucking rates being inflated by 5 to 10 percent. Estimates of the impact of the Federal Maritime Commission's regulation of ocean shipping have shown rates may be as much as 45 percent higher than they would be under competitive conditions. The federal milk marketing order system, just one component of total farm regulation, was estimated by various methods to cause a dead weight social loss of at least $100 million annually, as well as inducing an income transfer of another $200 million per year.

During the last two decades, there also has emerged a new judicial awareness of the need to scrutinize antitrust immunities and to consider the role of competition in regulated industries. The Supreme Court in the *Philadelphia National Bank* case [32] stated that '[t]he fact that banking is a highly regulated industry critical to the Nation's welfare makes the play of competition not less important but more so.' This appreciation of the role of competition in regulated industries was also evident in a series of decisions that declared the applicability of antitrust principles to a number of substantially regulated activities, and that approved or mandated greater agency attentiveness to competitive principles in carrying out 'public interest' decisionmaking.[33]

The more restrictive court interpretations of the implied immunity and primary jurisdiction doctrines are apparent in cases like *Otter Tail Power Co. v. United States,* supra p. 124. The Supreme Court rejected claims by Otter Tail that regulation of interstate transmission of electricity by the Federal Power Act ousted antitrust jurisdiction over claims Otter Tail used its monopoly power over transmission of power to monopolize the local distribution of power. Although the Federal Power Act authorized the F.P.C. (now

---

32. Supra pp. 220–236.

33. 1 Report To The President And The Attorney General of the National Commission For The Review of Antitrust Laws and Procedures, 180–82 (1979)

(hereinafter cited as NCRALP Report). The Report advocates substantial deregulation of surface transportation, insurance, agriculture, ocean shipping, and export associations.

F.E.R.C.) to order involuntary connections,[34] the Court held antitrust jurisdiction to enjoin refusals to deal or order wheeling of power was not displaced by regulatory authority. The F.P.C. authority to order interconnection was held not to preempt antitrust jurisdiction over an unlawful refusal to deal [35] and the absence of F.P.C. authority to order wheeling of power was held no bar to an antitrust court doing so.[36] The majority left open the question of the future interplay between F.P.C. and antitrust jurisdiction with the comment that future disputes would be subject to F.P.C. perusal and "[i]t will be time enough to consider whether the antitrust remedy may override the power of the Commission . . . if and when the Commission denies the interconnection and the District Court nevertheless undertakes to direct it." [37]

(2) *Query:* A bill introduced in the 94th Congress, The Competition Improvements Act of 1976, and reintroduced in the 95th Congress [38] provides:

> Sec. 3(a). Notwithstanding any other provision of law, no federal agency shall take any action, the effect of which may be substantially to

34. Section 202(b), 16 U.S.C.A. § 824a(b), provided: "Whenever the Commission, upon application of any State commission or of any person engaged in the transmission or sale of electric energy, and after notice to each State commission and public utility affected and after opportunity for hearing, finds such action necessary or appropriate in the public interest it may by order direct a public utility (if the Commission finds that no undue burden will be placed upon such public utility thereby) to establish physical connection of its transmission facilities with the facilities of one or more other persons engaged in the transmission or sale of electric energy, to sell energy to or exchange energy with such persons: *Provided,* That the Commission shall have no authority to compel the enlargement of generating facilities for such purposes, nor to compel such public utility to sell or exchange energy when to do so would impair its ability to render adequate service to its customers. The Commission may prescribe the terms and conditions of the arrangement to be made between the persons affected by any such order, including the apportionment of cost between them and the compensation or reimbursement reasonably due to any of them."

35. "It is clear, then, that Congress rejected a pervasive regulatory scheme for controlling the interstate distribution of power in favor of voluntary commercial relationships. When these relationships are governed in the first instance by business judgment and not regulatory coercion, courts must be hesitant to conclude that Congress intended to override the fundamental national policies embodied in the antitrust laws. This is particularly true in this instance because Congress, in passing the Public Utility Holding Company act, which included

Part II of the Federal Power Act, was concerned with "restraint of free and independent competition" among public utility holding companies. See 15 U.S.C. § 79a(b)(2).

"Thus, there is no basis for concluding that the limited authority of the Federal Power Commission to order interconnections was intended to be a substitute for, or to immunize Otter Tail from, antitrust regulation for refusing to deal with municipal corporations." 410 U.S., at 374–75, 93 S.Ct., at 1028, 35 L.Ed.2d, at 366.

36. "So far as wheeling is concerned, there is no authority granted the Commission under Part II of the Federal Power Act to order it, for the bills originally introduced contained common carrier provisions which were deleted. The Act as passed contained only the interconnection provision set forth in § 202(b). The common carrier provision in the original bill and the power to direct wheeling were left to the 'voluntary coordination of electric facilities.' Insofar as the District Court ordered wheeling to correct anticompetitive and monopolistic practices of Otter Tail, there is no conflict with the authority of the Federal Power Commission." 410 U.S., at 376, 93 S.Ct. at 1028–29, 35 L.Ed.2d, at 367.

37. 410 U.S., at 377, 93 S.Ct., at 1029, 35 L.Ed.2d, at 367. Under the Public Utility Regulatory Policies Act of 1978, enacted after *Otter Tail*, the Commission has been given increased power to require interconnection and wheeling. See 16 U.S.C.A. §§ 824a–1, 824i–824k.

38. S. 2028, 94th Cong., 1st Sess. (1976); S. 2625, 95th Cong., 2d Sess. (1978). See Hearings The Competitive Improvements Act of 1975, Subcommittee on Antitrust and Monopoly, Comm.

lessen competition, or tend to create a monopoly, or to create or maintain a situation involving a significant burden on competition, unless it finds that—

(1) Such action is necessary to accomplish an overriding statutory purpose of the agency;

(2) The anticompetitive effects of such action are clearly outweighed by significant and demonstrable benefits to the general public; and,

(3) The objectives of the action and the overriding statutory purpose cannot be accomplished in substantial part by alternative means having lesser anticompetitive effects.

If this proposal becomes law, would it provide a workable standard for reconciling a policy favoring competition with regulatory statutes governing particular industries? [39]

C. THE STATE ACTION OR *"PARKER V. BROWN"* DOCTRINE [40]

1. ANTICOMPETITIVE STATE REGULATION

The state action (or "Parker v. Brown") doctrine was judicially developed to accommodate the federal antitrust laws to a system in which economic regulation is shared with the states.[41] State economic regulation is not uncommon, and consequently the issue has frequently arisen as to when and under what circumstances a state should be permitted to control certain industries or activities by imposing a regulatory scheme that supplants a federal policy favoring competition. In resolving the clash between a state or local government's regulatory plan and federal antitrust policy, the courts have moved from a broad judicially created exemption in favor of state regulation to a significantly narrower exemption for anticompetitive conduct authorized or mandated by state or local laws and regulation. The evolution of the Court's thinking in this area is a fascinating

on the Judiciary, 94th Cong., 1st Sess. (1975–76).

39. For arguments in support of the Bill, see 1 NCRALP Report 307–16 (1979).

40. See generally 1 P. Areeda & D. Turner, Antitrust Law, pp. 67–114 (1978); L. Sullivan, Antitrust, 731–40 (1977); First, Private Interest and Public Control: Government Action, The First Amendment and The Sherman Act, 1975 Utah L.Rev. 9; Flynn, Trends in Federal Antitrust Doctrine Suggesting Future Directions for State Antitrust Enforcement, 4 J.Crop.L. 479 (1979); Fox, The Supreme Court and the Confusion Surrounding the State Action Doctrine, 48 Antitrust L.J. 1571 (1980); Areeda, Antitrust Immunity for "State Action" After *Lafayette*, 95 Harv.L.Rev. 435 (1981); Kennedy, Of Lawyers, Lightbulbs, and Raisins: An Analysis of the State Action Doctrine Under the Antitrust Laws, 74 Nw.U.L.Rev. 31 (1979); Rogers, State Action Antitrust Immunity, 49 U.Colo.L.Rev. 147 (1978); Rose, Municipal Activities and the Antitrust Laws After *City of Lafayette*, 5 U.Det. Urb.L.J. 438 (1980); Sullivan & Wiley, Recent Antitrust Developments: Defining the Scope of Exemptions, Expanding Coverage, and Defining the Rule of Reason, 27 U.C.L.A.L.Rev. 265 (1979); Symposium, Municipal Antitrust Liability, 1980 Ariz.St.L.J. 245.

41. See First, supra note 40; Morgan, Sherman Act Violations and State Action, 33 Ark.L.Pro.L.Rev. 273 (1981).

chapter in American federalism, initially paralleling the Court's new-found concern about its authority to strike down state economic regulation on substantive due process grounds but gradually recognizing that undue deference to state regulation might create a major loophole from federal antitrust regulation. Shifting pluralities of Supreme Court Justices are now trying to hit upon a consistent formula and sensible analytical methodology to resolve the state-federal clash over economic regulation.[42]

In the seminal case of *Parker v. Brown* [43] the Supreme Court addressed the question whether a price maintenance program for raisins, directed by officials of a state commission, should be enjoined as violative of the Sherman Act. The Court held that the program did not violate the Sherman Act—the state, "as sovereign, imposed the restraint as an act of government which the Sherman Act did not undertake to prohibit": [44]

> [T]he prorate program here was never intended to operate by force of individual agreement or combination. It derived its authority and its efficacy from the legislative command of the state and was not intended to operate or become effective without the command. . . .

> There is no suggestion of a purpose to restrain state action in the Act's legislative history. The sponsor of the bill which was ultimately enacted as the . . . Sherman Act declared that it prevented only "business combinations."

> True, a state does not give immunity to those who violate the Sherman Act by authorizing them to violate it or by declaring that their action is lawful. . . . Although the organization of a prorate zone is proposed by the producers, and a prorate program, approved by the Commission, must also be approved by referendum of the producers, it is the state, acting through the Commission, which adopts the program and which enforces it with penal sanctions, in the execution of a governmental policy.[45]

Implicit in the Court's analysis were several limitations upon a broad grant of immunity for state sanctioned restraints, factors which have come to predominate current development of the doctrine: (1) The possible application of a preemption analysis where state law authorizes a violation of federal law; (2) Inquiry into whether the conduct is authorized or mandated by state law as opposed to being the product of private action; (3) An examination into whether the policy is intended by the state to regulate the conduct in question as the sovereign act of a government; (4) An inquiry into the extent of

42. For an historical survey of the evolution of the doctrine, see First, supra note 40.

43. 317 U.S. 341, 63 S.Ct. 307, 87 L.Ed. 315 (1943).

44. "[S]ince Congress' authority under the commerce clause was extremely limited at the time it passed the Sherman Act, it is doubtful whether the members of Congress ever considered the possibility of applying the Act to state action." Slater, Antitrust and Government Action, A Formula for Narrowing Parker v. Brown, 69 Nw.U.L.Rev. 71, 84 (1974).

45. 317 U.S., at 350–52, 63 S.Ct., at 314, 87 L.Ed., at 326.

private participation in the conduct claimed to be illegal, and the degree to which the action is "actively supervised" by state officials.

Several recent decisions of the Supreme Court, applying various combinations of the above factors, have significantly narrowed the scope of the "state action" defense. *Goldfarb v. Virginia State Bar*,[46] for example, was a private suit under Section 1 of the Sherman Act against state and county bar associations for publishing and enforcing minimum fee schedules. The Court held:

> Here we need not inquire further into the state action question because it cannot fairly be said that the State of Virginia through its Supreme Court Rules required the anticompetitive activities of either respondent. . . . Respondents' arguments, at most, constitute the contention that their activities complemented the objective of the ethical codes. In our view that is not state action for Sherman Act purposes. It is not enough that, as the County Bar puts it, anticompetitive conduct is 'prompted' by state action; rather, anticompetitive activities must be compelled by direction of the State acting as sovereign. . . . The fact that the State Bar is a state agency for some limited purposes does not create an antitrust shield that allows it to foster anticompetitive practices for the benefit of its members.[47]

Another important case was *Cantor v. Detroit Edison Co.*,[48] which involved a light bulb retailer's allegations that Detroit Edison's practice of providing its customers with "free" light bulbs, as set out in tariffs filed with the Michigan Public Service Commission, violated Sections 1 and 2 of the Sherman Act and Section 3 of the Clayton Act. The Supreme Court rejected Detroit Edison's assertion that the state action defense applied by virtue of the fact that the light bulb program was controlled by the state's Public Service Commission. A plurality of four (Justices Stevens, Brennan, White and Marshall) held the *Parker* defense not available at all to a private defendant, purporting to distinguish *Parker* on the ground that it applied only to defendants who were state officials. Other parts of the majority's opinion, however, appeared to establish a test for resolving the conflict between the Sherman Act and inconsistent state regulation which would examine 1) whether the state's participation in the restraint was "so dominant that it would be unfair to hold a private party responsible for his conduct in implementing it"; or 2) whether there should be an "implied exemption" from the Sherman Act where necessary "to make the [state] regulatory Act work." [49]   This analyti-

46. 421 U.S. 773, 95 S.Ct. 2004, 44 L.Ed.2d 572 (1975).

47. 421 U.S., at 790–91, 95 S.Ct., at 2015, 44 L.Ed.2d, at 587.

48. 428 U.S. 579, 96 S.Ct. 3110, 49 L.Ed.2d 1141 (1976).

49. See 428 U.S., at 592–97, 96 S.Ct., at 3118–21, 49 L.Ed.2d, at 1150–53. On petition by Detroit Edison to terminate the free light bulb tariff, the Michigan Public Service Commission refused to allow Detroit Edison to discontinue it, terming it a "cost containment program," and ordered general hearings on the question whether the program should be imposed "statewide." See Re Detroit Edison Co., 25 PUR 4th 314 (Mich.P.S.C. 1978).

cal approach, however, was eventually replaced by the test put forward in the following case.

CALIFORNIA RETAIL LIQUOR DEALERS ASSOCIATION v. MIDCAL ALUMINUM, INC.

Supreme Court of the United States, 1980.
445 U.S. 97, 100 S.Ct. 937, 63 L.Ed.2d 233.

MR. JUSTICE POWELL delivered the opinion of the Court.

I

Under § 24866(b) of the California Business and Professions Code, all wine producers, wholesalers, and rectifiers must file with the State fair trade contracts or price schedules. If a wine producer has not set prices through a fair trade contract, wholesalers must post a resale price schedule for that producer's brands. No state-licensed wine merchant may sell wine to a retailer at other than the price set "either in an effective price schedule or in an effective fair trade contract . . . ." Id., § 24862 (West Supp.1979).

The State is divided into three trading areas for administration of the wine pricing program. A single fair trade contract or schedule for each brand sets the terms for all wholesale transactions in that brand within a given trading area. Similarly, state regulations provide that the wine prices posted by a single wholesaler within a trading area bind all wholesalers in that area. A licensee selling below the established prices faces fines, license suspension, or outright license revocation. The State has no direct control over wine prices, and it does not review the reasonableness of the prices set by wine dealers.

Midcal Aluminum, Inc. is a wholesale distributor of wine in Southern California. In July 1978, the Department of Alcoholic Beverage Control charged Midcal with selling 27 cases of wine for less than the prices set by the effective price schedule of the E & J Gallo Winery. The Department also alleged that Midcal sold wines for which no fair trade contract or schedule had been filed. Midcal stipulated that the allegations were true and that the State could fine it or suspend its license for those transgressions. Midcal then filed a writ of mandate in the California Court of Appeal for the Third Appellate District asking for an injunction against the State's wine pricing system.

The Court of Appeals ruled that the wine pricing scheme restrains trade in violation of the Sherman Act, 15 U.S.C. § 1 *et seq.* The court relied entirely on the reasoning in *Rice v. Alcoholic Beverage Control Appeals Bd.*, 21 Cal.3d 431, 146 Cal.Rptr. 585, 579 P.2d 476 (1978), where the California Supreme Court struck down parallel restrictions on the sale of distilled liquors. In that case, the court held that because the State played only a passive part in liquor pricing, there was no *Parker v. Brown* immunity for the program.

"In the price maintenance program before us, the state plays no role whatever in setting the retail prices. The prices are established by the producers according to their own economic interests, without regard to any actual or potential anticompetitive effect; the state's role is restricted to enforcing the prices specified by the producers. There is no control or 'pointed re-examination,' by the state to insure that the policies of the Sherman Act are not 'unnecessarily subordinated' to state policy." 21 Cal.3d, at 445, 146 Cal.Rptr., at 595, 579 P.2d, at 486.

Rice also rejected the claim that California's liquor pricing policies were protected by § 2 of the Twenty-first Amendment, which insulates state regulation of intoxicating liquors from many federal restrictions. The court determined that the national policy in favor of competition should prevail over the state interests in liquor price maintenance—the promotion of temperance and the preservation of small retail establishments. The court emphasized that the California system not only permitted vertical control of prices by producers, but also frequently resulted in horizontal price fixing. Under the program, many comparable brands of liquor were marketed at identical prices.[50] Referring to congressional and state legislative studies, the court observed that resale price maintenance has little positive impact on either temperance or small retail stores. See p. 947, infra.

In the instant case, the State Court of Appeal found the analysis in *Rice* squarely controlling. . . .

II

The threshold question is whether California's plan for wine pricing violates the Sherman Act. This Court has ruled consistently that resale price maintenance illegally restrains trade. In *Dr. Miles Medical Co. v. Park & Sons Co.*, 220 U.S. 373, 407, 31 S.Ct. 376, 384, 55 L.Ed. 502 (1911), the Court observed that such arrangements are "designed to maintain prices . . ., and to prevent competition among those who trade in [competing goods]." See *Albrecht v. Herald Co.*, 390 U.S. 145, 88 S.Ct. 869, 19 L.Ed.2d 998 (1968); *United States v. Parke, Davis & Co.*, 362 U.S. 29, 80 S.Ct. 503, 4 L.Ed.2d 505 (1960); *United States v. Schrader's Son, Inc.*, 252 U.S. 85, 40 S.Ct. 251, 64 L.Ed. 471 (1920).

. . .

California's system for wine pricing plainly constitutes resale price maintenance in violation of the Sherman Act. The wine producer holds the power to prevent price competition by dictating the

---

50. [Court's footnote 3.] The court cited record evidence that in July 1976, five leading brands of gin each sold in California for $4.89 for a fifth of a gallon, and that five leading brands of scotch whiskey sold for either $8.39 or $8.40 a fifth. Rice v. Alcoholic Beverage Control Appeals Bd., 21 Cal.3d 431, 454, and nn. 14, 16, 146 Cal.Rptr. 585, 600, and nn. 14, 16, 579 P.2d 476, 491–492, and nn. 14, 16 (1978).

prices charged by wholesalers.　As Mr. Justice Hughes pointed out in *Dr. Miles,* such vertical control destroys horizontal competition as effectively as if wholesalers "formed a combination and endeavored to establish the same restrictions . . . by agreement with each other."　220 U.S., at 408, 31 S.Ct., at 384.　Moreover, there can be no claim that the California program is simply intrastate regulation beyond the reach of the Sherman Act.

Thus, we must consider whether the State's involvement in the price-setting program is sufficient to establish antitrust immunity under *Parker v. Brown,* 317 U.S. 341, 63 S.Ct. 307, 87 L.Ed. 315 (1943). That immunity for state regulatory programs is grounded in our federal structure.　"In a dual system of government in which, under the Constitution, the states are sovereign, save only as Congress may constitutionally subtract from their authority, an unexpressed purpose to nullify a state's control over its officers and agents is not lightly to be attributed to Congress."　In *Parker v. Brown,* this Court found in the Sherman Act no purpose to nullify state powers. Because the Act is directed against "individual and not state action," the Court concluded that state regulatory programs could not violate it.

Under the program challenged in *Parker,* the state Agricultural Prorate Advisory Commission authorized the organization of local cooperatives to develop marketing policies for the raisin crop.　The Court emphasized that the Advisory Commission, which was appointed by the governor, had to approve cooperative policies following public hearings: "It is the state which has created the machinery for establishing the prorate program. . . . [I]t is the state, acting through the Commission, which adopts the program and enforces it . . . ."　In view of this extensive official oversight, the Court wrote, the Sherman Act did not apply.　Without such oversight, the result could have been different.　The Court expressly noted, "a state does not give immunity to those who violate the Sherman Act by authorizing them to violate it, or by declaring that their action is lawful . . . ."　Id., at 351, 63 S.Ct., at 314.

Several recent decisions have applied *Parker's* analysis.　In *Goldfarb v. Virginia State Bar,* 421 U.S. 773, 95 S.Ct. 2004, 44 L.Ed.2d 572 (1975), the Court concluded that fee schedules enforced by a state bar association were not mandated by ethical standards established by the State Supreme Court.　The fee schedules therefore were not immune from antitrust attack.　"It is not enough that . . . anticompetitive conduct is 'prompted' by state action; rather, anticompetitive conduct must be compelled by direction of the State acting as a sovereign."　Id., at 791, 95 S.Ct., at 2015.　Similarly, in *Cantor v. Detroit Edison Co.,* 428 U.S. 579, 96 S.Ct. 3110, 49 L.Ed.2d 1141 (1976), a majority of the Court found that no antitrust immunity was conferred when a state agency passively accepted a public utility's tariff.　In contrast, Arizona rules against lawyer advertising where held immune from Sherman Act challenge because they "reflect[ed] a clear articulation of the State's policy with regard to professional behavior" and were "subject to pointed reexamination by the policymaker—the Arizona Supreme Court—in enforcement proceedings." *Bates v. State Bar of Arizona*, 433 U.S. 350, 362, 97 S.Ct. 2691, 2698, 53 L.Ed.2d 810 (1977).

Only last Term, this Court found antitrust immunity for a California program requiring state approval of the location of new automobile dealerships. *New Motor Vehicle Bd. of Calif. v. Orrin W. Fox Co.*, 439 U.S. 96, 99 S.Ct. 403, 58 L.Ed.2d 361 (1978). That program provided that the State would hold a hearing if an automobile franchisee protested the establishment or relocation of a competing dealership. In view of the State's active role, the Court held, the program was not subject to the Sherman Act. The "clearly articulated and affirmatively expressed" goal of the state policy was to "displace unfettered business freedom in the matter of the establishment and relocation of automobile dealerships."

These decisions establish two standards for antitrust immunity under *Parker v. Brown*. First, the challenged restraint must be "one clearly articulated and affirmatively expressed as state policy"; second, the policy must be "actively supervised" by the State itself. *City of Lafayette v. Louisiana Power & Light Co.*, 435 U.S. 389, 410, 98 S.Ct. 1123, 1135, 55 L.Ed.2d 364 (1978) (opinion of Brennan, J.). The California system for wine pricing satisfies the first standard. The legislative policy is forthrightly stated and clear in its purpose to permit resale price maintenance. The program, however, does not meet the second requirement for *Parker* immunity. The State simply authorizes price-setting and enforces the prices established by private parties. The State neither establishes prices nor reviews the reasonableness of the price schedules; nor does it regulate the terms of fair trade contracts. The State does not monitor market conditions or engage in any "pointed reexamination" of the program. The national policy in favor of competition cannot be thwarted by casting such a gauzy cloak of state involvement over what is essentially a private price fixing arrangement. As *Parker* teaches, "a state does not give immunity to those who violate the Sherman Act by authorizing them to violate it, or by declaring that their action is lawful . . . ." 317 U.S., at 351, 63 S.Ct., at 314.

III

[Part III of the Court's opinion rejected the claim that the 21st Amendment's reservation of power to the States to regulate liquor importation and distribution precluded application of the Sherman Act to the wine trade. The Court held the 21st Amendment did not oust all federal jurisdiction to regulate liquor distribution under the commerce clause, the state's 21st Amendment interest must be balanced against the Federal Government's commerce clause interest, and the federal interest in enforcing the national policy in favor of competition was more substantial than the questionable interest of California in mandating resale price maintenance for wine.]

MR. JUSTICE BRENNAN did not take part in the consideration or decision in this case.

NOTES AND QUERIES

(1) *State Supervision.* How could California comply with the *Midcal* test? Would the state be required to fix the price retailers could charge, as well as authorizing resale price maintenance, to satisfy the requirement of "supervision"? [51] What result if the state had closely monitored the pricing system or retained a veto authority over the prices fixed, but did nothing to preclude the maintenance of an unreasonably high price floor? [52] Does this standard impose an unmanageable task on courts in deciding if a particular supervisory mechanism is sufficiently active? Is the supervision requirement satisfied in a situation in which a statute in restraint of trade is self-executing and judicial enforcement provides an adequate check against abuse? [53] Why should state legislatures be restrained under the Sherman Act from choosing less intrusive "passive regulation" which relies in large measure on assistance from private groups? Why can't a state choose a "gauzy cloak" in preference to elaborate regulation? [54]

(2) *"Clear" Articulation and "Affirmative" Expression of State Policy.* In *Bates v. State Bar of Arizona* [55] the Supreme Court reviewed Arizona's rules prohibiting advertising by lawyers, rules which had been adopted by the Arizona Supreme Court at the behest of the bar association. The Court's opinion distinguished the bar association's private activity from the private activity of distributing light bulbs in *Cantor*: [56]

> . . . [A]ppellants argue by analogy to *Cantor* that no immunity should result from the bar's success in having the code adopted by the State. They also assert that the interest embodied in the Sherman Act must prevail over the state interest in regulating the bar. Particularly is this the case, they claim, because the advertising ban is not tailored so as to intrude upon the federal interest to the minimum extent necessary.
>
> . . . *Cantor* would have been an entirely different case if the claim had been directed against a public official or public agency, rather than against a private party. Here, the appellant's claims are against the State. The Arizona Supreme Court is the real party in interest; it adopted the rules, and it is the ultimate trier of fact and law in the enforcement process. . . . Second, the Court emphasized in *Cantor* that the State had no independent regulatory interest in the market for light bulbs.

51. On the concerns raised by private regulation, cf. Boycott Chapter, pp. 535–541. See generally, W. Page, Antitrust, Federalism, and the Regulatory Process: A Reconstruction and Critique of State Action Exemption After *Midcal Aluminum*, 61 B.U.L.Rev. 1099 (1981).

52. M. Handler, Reforming the Antitrust Laws 65 (1982).

53. Cf. Morgan v. Division of Liquor Control, 664 F.2d 353 (2d Cir. 1981) (upholding Connecticut statute requiring liquor manufacturers and wholesalers to file their price list with state and requiring prices not to be less than "cost" as defined by the statute).

54. See Allied Artists Picture Corp. v. Rhodes, 679 F.2d 656, 662 (6th Cir. 1982)

(Ohio statute prohibiting "blind bidding" and requiring motion picture distributors to screen films for all interested theatre operators prior to bidding, held a self-executing statute; active state supervision by judicial review of statute's application to particular cases sufficient "supervision" to satisfy *Midcal*); Ronwin v. State Bar of Arizona, 686 F.2d 692 (9th Cir. 1982) (state supervision of the grading of bar exam not sufficiently "articulated" for immunity).

55. 317 U.S., at 351, 63 S.Ct., at 314, 87 L.Ed., at 326.

56. 433 U.S. 350, 97 S.Ct. 2691, 53 L.Ed.2d 810 (1977).

There was no suggestion that the bulb program was justified by flaws in the competitive market or was a response to health or safety concerns. And an exemption for the program was not essential to the State's regulation of electric utilities. In contrast, the regulation of the activities of the bar is at the core of the State's power to protect the public.[57]

The *Bates* notion of requiring an important independent state interest incident to the application of the state action defense was incorporated in the two-prong test adopted in *Midcal*.

Queries. Is the distinction between interests that lie at the "core" of state interests (e.g., regulation of the bar) and insubstantial interests (e.g., light bulb marketing) really a subjective judgment on what is an adequate state interest?[58] Isn't this type of inquiry a question of substantive due process which the courts have, since the late 1930's, refused to undertake?[59] While it may be argued that the state action defense should arise only in the context of a challenge to the exercise of an essential governmental function, rather than to shelter "proprietary" functions undertaken by the state, the same distinction has been repeatedly assailed as untenable in cases involving substantive due process.

(3) *F.T.C. Rulemaking and State Action.* The Federal Trade Commission has authority to issue rules defining "unfair or deceptive acts or practices."[60] Pursuant to this authority, the F.T.C. issued a rule defining as an unfair and deceptive act and practice the restricting of advertising of ophthalmic goods and services.[61] Forty-five states and the ethical rules of national associations of optometrists and ophthalmologists prohibited or restricted advertising of eye examinations and opthalmic goods and services. One part of the rule made it an unfair or deceptive act or practice for a state or local entity to enforce a prohibition on the dissemination of information concerning ophthalmic goods or services or the dissemination of information concerning eye examinations by any refractionist.

In *American Optometric Association v. Federal Trade Commission*,[62] the court of appeals remanded that part of the F.T.C.'s rulemaking purporting to preempt enforcement of state and local laws restricting advertising of opthalmic services for reconsideration in light of *Bates*. Noting the rule was adopted prior to the *Bates* decision and that *Bates* left room for some state regulation of advertising by professionals while striking down a general prohibition of lawyer advertising on First Amendment grounds, the court questioned whether the rule was any longer necessary. The court also remanded the rule because "the diminished need for the rule intensifies questions which go "to the very heart of the case" in at least two areas:[63]

---

57. 433 U.S., at 361, 97 S.Ct., at 2697, 53 L.Ed.2d, at 822.

58. See Note, State Action and The Sherman Antitrust Act: Should the Antitrust Laws Be Given a Preemptive Effect?, 14 Conn.L.Rev. 135, 160 (1980). See also New Motor Vehicle Board v. Orrin W. Fox Co., 439 U.S. 96, 99 S.Ct. 403, 58 L.Ed.2d 361 (1978) (upholding state regulation of new auto dealerships as a valid exercise of state power of economic regulation).

59. For examples of the type of inquiry the Court's test requires, see Mobilfone of Northeastern Pennsylvania, Inc. v. Commonwealth Telephone Co., 571 F.2d 141 (3d Cir. 1978) (state's interest in regulating mobile telephone paging service held sufficient); Euster v. Eagle Downs Racing Association, 677 F.2d 992 (3d Cir. 1982) (upholding state regulation of fees to be paid jockeys at race tracks within the state).

60. 15 U.S.C.A. § 57a.

61. 16 CFR § 456, 43 Fed.Reg. 23,992, 25,995 (1978).

62. 626 F.2d 896 (D.C.Cir.1980).

63. Id. at 910.

The first such area results from the fact that the Commission's proposed pre-emption of state law is almost as thorough as human ingenuity could make it. Consequently, the Commission has at least approached the outer boundaries of its authority and may have infringed on that deference to the states' exercise of their police powers dictated by the principles of federalism. The rule therefore raises several interrelated issues: Did Congress authorize the Commission to pre-empt state laws? If so, did the scope of the Commission's delegated power permit it to pre-empt state laws to the extent of pre-empting the whole field of ophthalmic advertising? Does the "state action" doctrine of *Parker v. Brown*, 317 U.S. 341, 63 S.Ct. 307, 87 L.Ed. 315 (1943), forbid the agency to issue this rule? Has the Commission exceeded its jurisdiction in treating the states as persons under the Magnuson-Moss Act? The relevance of the changes which followed *Bates* is that answers to these questions may well depend in some measure on the extent to which a federal regulation gratuitously intrudes on the exercise of the police powers of the states.[64]

Queries: After *Midcal*, does the F.T.C. by rulemaking have the authority to preempt anticompetitive state regulation not clearly articulating a valid state interest for the regulation? Authority to preempt state regulation not sufficiently active in its supervision of the anticompetitive activity?

(4) *Harmonizing Federal Antitrust and Valid State Regulation.* Federal antitrust law may still be applicable to conduct affirmatively regulated pursuant to a valid exercise of state regulatory authority if there is in fact no true conflict between state regulatory policy and antitrust liability. Much like the analytical process followed in the implied immunity doctrine cases at the federal level, discussed supra p. 800, a court may engage in a detailed examination of the state regulatory scheme to determine whether there is an intent to oust reliance upon competition or an irreconcilable conflict between the specific regulation imposed and application of the antitrust laws to the conduct in question. For example, in *Sound, Inc. v. American Telephone & Telegraph Co.*,[65] the court upheld application of the antitrust laws to an alleged scheme by A.T.&T. to manipulate rates filed with the Iowa State Commerce Commission for Bell terminal equipment so as to exclude the plaintiff

64. [Court's footnote 6]. We note that in Katherine Gibbs School (Inc.) v. Federal Trade Commission, 612 F.2d 658 (2d Cir. 1979), the Second Circuit recently expressed its dissatisfaction with the preemption provision of a Commission rule promulgated under the Magnuson-Moss Act and entitled "Proprietary Vocational and Home Study Schools," 16 C.F.R. § 438 (1979). That provision read:

This trade regulation rule preempts any provision of any state law, rule, or regulation which is inconsistent with or otherwise frustrates the purpose of the provisions of this trade regulation rule, except where the Commission has exempted such a state or local law, rule or regulation. If, upon, [sic] application of any appropriate state or local governmental agency, the Commission determines that the state statutory or

regulatory provision affords greater protection to students than the comparable provision of the Commission's rule then the state requirement will be applicable to the extent specified in the Commission's determination on the exemption application.

16 C.F.R. § 438.9 (1979). The court found that, in light of its conclusion that the Commission had failed to identify with sufficient specificity the acts or practices it deemed deceptive, "the breadth of the preemption provision is such that it places in issue an indefinite variety of state laws and regulations governing the contractual relations between vocational schools and their students." 612 F.2d at 667. But see Judge Newman's dissent in that case.

65. 631 F.2d 1324 (8th Cir. 1980).

from the terminal telephone equipment market. In rejecting A.T.&T.'s claim that its conduct was exempt by virtue of state action, the court stated:

[T]he determination of whether state regulation of private action is 'state action' and therefore exempt from the antitrust laws is not an easy task. 'Like many other phantasmagoria of the law, we know it is there, but it is hard to define precisely what it is, and, unlike obscenity, we do not always know it even when we see it.' We are convinced, however, that the following factors are relevant to our determination: the existence and nature of any relevant statutorily expressed policy; the nature of the regulatory agency's interpretation and application of its enabling statute, including the accommodation of competition by the regulator; the fairness of subjecting a regulated private defendant to the mandates of antitrust law; and the nature and extent of the state's interest in the specific subject matter of the challenged activity.

Nothing in the Iowa statutes establishing the Iowa State Commerce Commission or its system of regulating public utilities even remotely suggests an intention to require anticompetitive conduct on the part of a public utility. Nothing in the statutes resembles the direct establishment of a program of resale price maintenance as in *Midcal* or the proscription of advertising as in *Bates*, nor is there any other explicit requirement of action prohibited by the Sherman Act. On the contrary, the statute prohibits rates 'in violation of any provision of law,' which presumably includes the Sherman Act. By requiring just and reasonable rates and charges, the statute provides a means of preventing the abuse of monopoly power by public utilities; it does not purport to aid an industry by giving it a competitive advantage as did the State of California in *Parker v. Brown*. . . . We thus are unable to find in the state statutes any clearly articulated or affirmatively expressed policy of replacing competition with regulation in the telephone terminal equipment market.[66]

It has also been held, in a similar case by a seller of terminal equipment suing A.T.&T. under the antitrust laws, that although conduct regulated by the state may not be immune "state action," the presence of state regulation must be considered in determining whether the conduct does in fact violate the antitrust laws.[67]

2. ANTI–COMPETITIVE MUNICIPAL REGULATION AND ACTIVITY

COMMUNITY COMMUNICATIONS CO., INC. v. CITY OF BOULDER

Supreme Court of the United States, 1982.
455 U.S. 40, 102 S.Ct. 835, 70 L.Ed.2d 810.

JUSTICE BRENNAN delivered the opinion of the Court.

The question presented in this case, in which the District Court for the District of Colorado granted preliminary injunctive relief, is whether a "home rule" municipality, granted by the state constitution extensive powers of self-government in local and municipal matters, enjoys the "state action" exemption from Sherman Act liability announced in *Parker v. Brown*, 317 U.S. 341, 63 S.Ct. 307, 87 L.Ed.2d 315 (1943).

---

66. 631 F.2d at 1334–35.

67. Phonetelle, Inc. v. American Telephone & Telegraph Co., 664 F.2d 716, 737 (9th Cir. 1981).

I

Respondent City of Boulder is organized as a "home rule" municipality under the Constitution of the State of Colorado.[68] The City is thus entitled to exercise "the full right of self-government in both local and municipal matters," and with respect to such matters the City Charter and ordinances supersede the laws of the State. Under that Charter, all municipal legislative powers are exercised by an elected City Council. In 1964 the City Council enacted an ordinance granting to Colorado Televents, Inc., a 20-year, revocable, non-exclusive permit to conduct a cable television business within the City limits. This permit was assigned to petitioner in 1966, and since that time petitioner has provided cable television service to the University Hill area of Boulder, an area where some 20% of the City's population lives, and where, for geographical reasons, broadcast television signals cannot be received.

From 1966 until February 1980, due to the limited service that could be provided with the technology then available, petitioner's service consisted essentially of re-transmissions of programming broadcast from Denver and Cheyenne, Wyo. Petitioner's market was therefore confined to the University Hill area. However, markedly improved technology became available in the late 1970s, enabling petitioner to offer many more channels of entertainment than could be provided by local broadcast television. Thus presented with an opportunity to expand its business into other areas of the City, petitioner in May 1979 informed the City Council that it planned such an expansion. But the new technology offered opportunities to potential competitors, as well, and in July 1979 one of them, the newly formed Boulder Communications Company (BCC), also wrote to the City Council, expressing its interest in obtaining a permit to provide competing cable television service throughout the City.

The City Council's response, after reviewing its cable television policy, was the enactment of an "emergency" ordinance prohibiting petitioner from expanding its business into other areas of the City for a period of three months. The City Council announced that during

68. [This and the following 4 footnotes are from the majority opinion, renumbered.] The Colorado Home Rule Amendment, Colo.Const., Art. XX, § 6, provides in pertinent part:

"The people of each city or town of this state, having a population of two thousand inhabitants . . ., are hereby vested with, and they shall always have, power to make, amend, add to or replace the charter of said city or town, which shall be its organic law and extend to all its local and municipal matters.

"Such charter and the ordinances made pursuant thereto in such matters shall supersede within the territorial limits and other jurisdiction of said city or town any law of the state in conflict therewith.

. . .

"It is the intention of this article to grant and confirm to the people of all municipalities coming within its provisions the full right of self-government in both local and municipal matters.

. . .

"The statutes of the state of Colorado, so far as applicable, shall continue to apply to such cities and towns, except insofar as superseded by the charters of such cities and towns or by ordinance passed pursuant to such charters."

this moratorium it planned to draft a model cable television ordinance and to invite new businesses to enter the Boulder market under its terms, but that the moratorium was necessary because petitioner's continued expansion during the drafting of the model ordinance would discourage potential competitors from entering the market.

Petitioner filed this suit in the United States District Court for the District of Colorado, and sought, *inter alia*, a preliminary injunction to prevent the City from restricting petitioner's proposed business expansion, alleging that such a restriction would violate § 1 of the Sherman Act. The City responded that its moratorium ordinance could not be violative of the antitrust laws, either because that ordinance constituted an exercise of the City's police powers, or because Boulder enjoyed antitrust immunity under the *Parker* doctrine. The District Court considered the City's status as a home rule municipality, but determined that that status gave autonomy to the City only in matters of local concern, and that the operations of cable television embrace "wider concerns, including interstate commerce . . . [and] the First Amendment rights of communicators." 485 F.Supp. 1035, 1038–1039 (1980). Then, assuming *arguendo* that the ordinance was within the City's authority as a home rule municipality, the District Court considered *City of Lafayette v. Louisiana Power & Light Co.*, 435 U.S. 389, 98 S.Ct. 1123, 55 L.Ed.2d 364 (1978), and concluded that the *Parker* exemption was "wholly inapplicable," and that the City was therefore subject to antitrust liability. Petitioner's motion for a preliminary injunction was accordingly granted.

On appeal, a divided panel of the United States Court of Appeals for the Tenth Circuit reversed. 630 F.2d 704 (1980). The majority, after examining Colorado law, rejected the District Court's conclusion that regulation of the cable television business was beyond the home rule authority of the City. The majority then addressed the question of the City's claimed *Parker* exemption. It distinguished the present case from *City of Lafayette* on the ground that, in contrast to the municipally operated revenue-producing utility companies at issue there, "no proprietary interest of the City is here involved." After noting that the City's regulation "was the only control or active supervision exercised by state or local government, and . . . represented the only expression of policy as to the subject matter," the majority held that the City's actions therefore satisfied the criteria for a *Parker* exemption, *id.*, at 708.[69] We reverse.

---

69. The majority cited California Retail Liquor Dealers Assn. v. Midcal Aluminum, Inc., 445 U.S. 97, 100 S.Ct. 937, 63 L.Ed.2d 233 (1980), as support for its reading of *City of Lafayette*, and concluded "that *City of Lafayette* is not applicable to a situation wherein the governmental entity is asserting a governmental rather than a proprietary interest, and that instead the *Parker-Midcal* doctrine is applicable to exempt the City from antitrust liability."

The dissent urged affirmance, agreeing with the District Court's analysis of the antitrust exemption issue. The dissent also considered the City's actions to violate "[c]ommon principles of contract law and equity," as well as the First Amendment rights of petitioner and its customers, both actual and potential. The petition for certiorari did not present the First Amendment question, and we do not address it in this opinion.

II

A

Parker v. Brown, supra, addressed the question whether the federal antitrust laws prohibited a State, in the exercise of its sovereign powers, from imposing certain anticompetitive restraints. . . . *Parker* noted that California's program "derived its authority . . . from the legislative command of the state," and went on to hold that the program was therefore exempt, by virtue of the Sherman Act's own limitations, from antitrust attack. . . .

The availability of this exemption to a State's municipalities was the question presented in *City of Lafayette*, supra. In that case, petitioners were Louisiana cities empowered to own and operate electric utility systems both within and beyond their municipal limits. Respondent brought suit against petitioners under the Sherman Act, alleging that they had committed various antitrust offenses in the conduct of their utility systems, to the injury of respondent. Petitioners invoked the *Parker* doctrine as entitling them to dismissal of the suit. The District Court accepted this argument and dismissed. But the Court of Appeals for the Fifth Circuit reversed, holding that a "subordinate state governmental body is not *ipso facto* exempt from the operation of the antitrust laws," 532 F.2d 431, 434 (1976) (footnote omitted), and directing the District Court on remand to examine "whether the state legislature contemplated a certain type of anticompetitive restraint," ibid.

This Court affirmed. In doing so, a majority rejected at the outset petitioners' claim that, quite apart from *Parker*, "Congress never intended to subject local governments to the antitrust laws." A plurality opinion for four Justices then addressed petitioners' argument that *Parker*, properly construed, extended to "all governmental entities, whether state agencies or subdivisions of a State, . . . simply by reason of their status as such." The plurality opinion rejected this argument, after a discussion of *Parker*, *Goldfarb v. Virginia State Bar*, 421 U.S. 773, 95 S.Ct. 2004, 44 L.Ed.2d 572 (1975), and *Bates v. State Bar of Arizona*, 433 U.S. 350, 97 S.Ct. 2697, 53 L.Ed. 2d 810 (1977).[70] These precedents were construed as holding that the *Parker* exemption reflects the federalism principle that we are a nation of *States*, a principle that makes no accommodation for sovereign subdivisions of States. The plurality opinion said that:

> "Cities are not themselves sovereign; they do not receive all the federal deference of the States that create them. *Parker's* limitation of the exemption to 'official action directed by a state,' is consistent with the fact that the States' subdivisions generally have

---

70. The Chief Justice, in a concurring opinion, focused on the nature of the challenged activity rather than the identity of the parties to the suit. 435 U.S., at 420, 98 S.Ct., at 1140. He distinguished between "the proprietary enterprises of municipalities," id., at 422, 98 S.Ct., at 1141 (footnote omitted), and their "traditional government functions," id., at 424, 98 S.Ct., at 1142, and viewed the *Parker* exemption as extending to municipalities only when they engaged in the latter.

not been treated as equivalents of the States themselves. In light of the serious economic dislocation which could result if cities were free to place their own parochial interests above the Nation's economic goals reflected in the antitrust laws, we are especially unwilling to presume that Congress intended to exclude anticompetitive municipal action from their reach." 435 U.S., at 412–413, 98 S.Ct., at 1136–37.

The opinion emphasized, however, that the state as sovereign might sanction anticompetitive municipal activities and thereby immunize municipalities from antitrust liability. Under the plurality's standard, the *Parker* doctrine would shield from antitrust liability municipal conduct engaged in "pursuant to state policy to displace competition with regulation or monopoly public service." This was simply a recognition that a State may frequently choose to effect its policies through the instrumentality of its cities and towns. It was stressed, however, that the "state policy" relied upon would have to be "clearly articulated and affirmatively expressed." This standard has since been adopted by a majority of the Court. *New Motor Vehicle Board of California v. Orrin W. Fox Co.*, 439 U.S. 96, 109, 99 S.Ct. 403, 411–12, 58 L.Ed.2d 361 (1978); *California Retail Liquor Dealers Assn. v. Midcal Aluminum, Inc.*, 445 U.S. 97, 105, 100 S.Ct. 937, 943, 63 L.Ed.2d 233 (1980).[71]

B

Our precedents thus reveal that Boulder's moratorium ordinance cannot be exempt from antitrust scrutiny unless it constitutes the action of the State of Colorado itself in its sovereign capacity, see *Parker*, or unless it constitutes municipal action in furtherance or implementation of clearly articulated and affirmatively expressed state policy, see *City of Lafayette, Orrin W. Fox Co.*, and *Midcal*. Boulder argues that these criteria are met by the direct delegation of powers to municipalities through the Home Rule Amendment to the Colorado Constitution. It contends that this delegation satisfies both the *Parker* and the *City of Lafayette* standards. We take up these arguments in turn.

---

71. In *Midcal* we held that a California resale price maintenance system, affecting all wine producers and wholesalers within the State, was not entitled to exemption from the antitrust laws. In so holding, we explicitly adopted the principle, expressed in the plurality opinion in *City of Lafayette*, that anticompetitive restraints engaged in by state municipalities or subdivisions must be "clearly articulated and affirmatively expressed as state policy" in order to gain an antitrust exemption. *Midcal*, 445 U.S., at 105, 100 S.Ct., at 943. The price maintenance system at issue in *Midcal* was denied such an exemption because it failed to satisfy the "active state supervision" criterion described in *City of Lafayette*, 435 U.S., at 410, 98 S.Ct., at 1135, as underlying our decision in Bates v. State Bar of Arizona, 433 U.S. 350, 97 S.Ct. 2697, 53 L.Ed.2d 810 (1977). Because we conclude in the present case that Boulder's moratorium ordinance does not satisfy the "clear articulation and affirmative expression" criterion, we do not reach the question whether that ordinance must or could satisfy the "active state supervision" test focused upon in *Midcal*.

(1)

Respondent's *Parker* argument emphasizes that through the Home Rule Amendment the people of the State of Colorado have vested in the City of Boulder *"every power* theretofore possessed by the legislature . . . in local and municipal affairs." The power thus possessed by Boulder's City Council assertedly embraces the regulation of cable television, which is claimed to pose essentially local problems. Thus, it is suggested, the City's cable television moratorium ordinance is an "act of government" performed by the City *acting as the state* in local matters, which meets the "state action" criterion of *Parker.*

We reject this argument: it both misstates the letter of the law and misunderstands its spirit. The *Parker* state action exemption reflects Congress' intention to embody in the Sherman Act the federalism principle that the States possess a significant measure of sovereignty under our Constitution. But this principle contains its own limitation: Ours is a *"dual* system of government," which has no place for sovereign cities. As this Court stated long ago, all sovereign authority "within the geographical limits of the United States" resides either with

> "the Government of the United States, or [with] the States of the Union. *There exist within the broad domain of sovereignty but these two.* There may be cities, counties, and other organized bodies with limited legislative functions, but they are all derived from, or exist in, subordination to one or the other of these." *United States v. Kagama,* 118 U.S. 375, 379, 6 S.Ct. 1109, 1111, 30 L.Ed. 228 (1886) (emphasis added).

The dissent in the Court of Appeals correctly discerned this limitation upon the federalism principle: "We are a nation not of 'city-states' but of States." *Parker* itself took this view. When *Parker* examined Congress' intentions in enacting the antitrust laws, the opinion noted that "nothing in the language of the Sherman Act or in its history . . . suggests that its purpose was to restrain a state or its officers or agents from activities *directed by its legislature.* . . . [And] an unexpressed purpose to nullify a *state's control over its officers and agents* is not lightly to be attributed to Congress." Thus *Parker* recognized Congress' intention to limit the state action exemption based upon the federalism principle of limited state sovereignty. *City of Lafayette, Orrin W. Fox Co.,* and *Midcal* reaffirmed both the vitality and the intrinsic limits of the *Parker* state action doctrine. It was expressly recognized by the plurality opinion in *City of Lafayette* that municipalities "are not themselves sovereign," and that accordingly they could partake of the *Parker* exemption only to the extent that they acted pursuant to a clearly articulated and affirmatively expressed state policy. The Court adopted this view in *Orrin W. Fox Co.,* and *Midcal.* We turn then to Boulder's contention that its actions were undertaken pursuant to a clearly articulated and affirmatively expressed state policy.

(2)

Boulder first argues that the requirement of "clear articulation and affirmative expression" is fulfilled by the Colorado Home Rule Amendment's "guarantee of local autonomy." It contends, quoting from *City of Lafayette*, that by this means Colorado has "comprehended within the powers granted" to Boulder the power to enact the challenged ordinance, and that Colorado has thereby "contemplated" Boulder's enactment of an anticompetitive regulatory program. Further, Boulder contends that it may be inferred, "from the authority given" to Boulder "to operate in a particular area"—here, the asserted home rule authority to regulate cable televison—"that the *legislature* contemplated the kind of action complained of." Boulder therefore concludes that the "adequate state mandate" required by *City of Lafayette*, is present here.

But plainly the requirement of "clear articulation and affirmative expression" is not satisfied when the State's position is one of mere *neutrality* respecting the municipal actions challenged as anticompetitive. A State that allows its municipalities to do as they please can hardly be said to have "contemplated" the specific anticompetitive actions for which municipal liability is sought. Nor can those actions be truly described as "comprehended within the powers *granted,*" since the term, "granted," necessarily implies an affirmative addressing of the subject by the State. The State did not do so here: The relationship of the State of Colorado to Boulder's moratorium ordinance is one of precise neutrality. As the majority in the Court of Appeals below acknowledged, "we are here concerned with City action in the absence of any regulation whatever by the State of Colorado. Under these circumstances there is no interaction of state and local regulation. We have only the action or exercise of authority by the City." Indeed, respondent argues that as to local matters regulated by a home rule city, the Colorado General Assembly is without power to act. Thus on respondent's view, Boulder can pursue its course of regulating cable television competition, while another home rule city can choose to prescribe monopoly service, while still another can elect free-market competition: and all of these policies are equally "contemplated," and "comprehended within the powers granted." Acceptance of such a proposition—that the general grant of power to enact ordinances necessarily implies state authorization to enact specific anticompetitive ordinances—would wholly eviscerate the concepts of "clear articulation and affirmative expression" that our precedents require.

III

Respondent argues that denial of the *Parker* exemption in the present case will have serious adverse consequences for cities, and will unduly burden the federal courts. But this argument is simply an attack upon the wisdom of the longstanding congressional commitment to the policy of free markets and open competition embodied in the antitrust laws. Those laws, like other federal laws imposing civil or criminal sanctions upon "persons," of course apply to municipalities as well as to other corporate entities.[72] Moreover, judicial enforcement of Congress' will regarding the state action exemption renders a State "no less able to allocate governmental power between itself and its political subdivisions. It means only that when the State itself has not directed or authorized an anticompetitive practice, the State's subdivisions in exercising their delegated power must obey the antitrust laws." *City of Lafayette*, 435 U.S., at 416, 98 S.Ct., at 1138. As was observed in that case,

> Today's decision does not threaten the legitimate exercise of governmental power, nor does it preclude municipal government from providing services on a monopoly basis. *Parker* and its progeny make clear that a State properly may . . . direct or authorize its instrumentalities to act in a way which, if it did not reflect state policy, would be inconsistent with the antitrust laws. . . . [A]ssuming that the municipality is authorized to provide service on a monopoly basis, these limitations on municipal action will not hobble the execution of legitimate governmental programs. Id., at 416–417, 98 S.Ct., at 1138–39 (footnote omitted).

The judgment of the Court of Appeals is reversed, and the action remanded for further proceedings consistent with this opinion.

It is so ordered.

JUSTICE WHITE took no part in the consideration or decision of this case.

JUSTICE STEVENS, concurring.

The Court's opinion, which I have joined, explains why the City of Boulder is not entitled to an exemption from the antitrust laws. The dissenting opinion seems to assume that the Court's analysis of the exemption issue is tantamount to a holding that the antitrust laws have been violated. The assumption is not valid. The dissent's dire predictions about the consequences of the Court's holding should therefore be viewed with skepticism.

· · ·

72. See City of Lafayette, supra, 435 U.S., at 394–397, 98 S.Ct., at 1127–28.

We hold today only that the Parker v. Brown exemption was no bar to the District Court's grant of injunctive relief. This case's preliminary posture makes it unnecessary for us to consider other issues regarding the applicability of the antitrust laws in the context of suits by private litigants against government defendants. As we said in City of Lafayette, "[i]t may be that certain activities, which might appear anticompetitive when engaged in by private parties, take on a different complexion when adopted by a local government." 435 U.S., at 417 n. 48, 98 S.Ct., at 1139 n. 48. Compare e.g., National Society of Professional Engineers v. United States, 435 U.S. 679, 687–692, 98 S.Ct. 1155, 1163–65, 55 L.Ed. 2d 637 (1978) (considering the validity of anticompetitive restraint imposed by private agreement) with Exxon Corp. v. Governor of Maryland, 437 U.S. 117, 133, 98 S.Ct. 2207, 2217–18, 57 L.Ed.2d 91 (1978) (holding that anticompetitive effect is an insufficient basis for invalidating a state law). Moreover, as in City of Lafayette, 435 U.S., at 401–402, 98 S.Ct., at 1130–31, we do not confront the issue of remedies appropriate against municipal officials.

JUSTICE REHNQUIST, with whom THE CHIEF JUSTICE and JUSTICE O'CONNOR join, dissenting.

The Court's decision in this case is flawed in two serious respects, and will thereby impede, if not paralyze, local governments' efforts to enact ordinances and regulations aimed at protecting public health, safety, and welfare, for fear of subjecting the local government to liability under the Sherman Act, 15 U.S.C. § 1 *et seq.* First, the Court treats the issue in this case as whether a municipality is "exempt" from the Sherman Act under our decision in *Parker v. Brown,* 317 U.S. 341, 63 S.Ct. 307, 87 L.Ed. 315 (1943). The question addressed in *Parker* and in this case is not whether State and local governments are *exempt* from the Sherman Act, but whether statutes, ordinances, and regulations enacted as an act of government are *preempted* by the Sherman Act under the operation of the Supremacy Clause. Second, in holding that a municipality's ordinances can be "exempt" from antitrust scrutiny only if the enactment furthers or implements a "clearly articulated and affirmatively expressed state policy," the Court treats a political subdivision of a State as an entity indistinguishable from any privately owned business. As I read the Court's opinion, a municipality may be said to *violate* the antitrust laws by enacting legislation in conflict with the Sherman Act, unless the legislation is enacted pursuant to an affirmative state policy to supplant competitive market forces in the area of the economy to be regulated.

I

Preemption and exemption are fundamentally distinct concepts. Preemption, because it involves the Supremacy Clause, implicates our basic notions of federalism. Preemption analysis is invoked whenever the Court is called upon to examine "the interplay between the enactments of two *different* sovereigns—one federal and the other state." Handler, Antitrust—1978, 78 Colum.L.Rev. 1363, 1379 (1978). We are confronted with questions under the Supremacy Clause when we are called upon to resolve a purported conflict between the enactments of the federal government and those of a State or local government, or where it is claimed that the federal government has occupied a particular field exclusively, so as to foreclose any state regulation. Where preemption is found, the state enactment must fall without any effort to accommodate the State's purposes or interests. Because preemption treads on the very sensitive area of Federal-State relations, this Court is "reluctant to infer preemption," and the presumption is that preemption is not to be found absent the clear and manifest intention of Congress that the federal act should supersede the police powers of the States.

In contrast, exemption involves the interplay between the enactments of a single sovereign—whether one enactment was intended by Congress to relieve a party from the necessity of complying with a prior enactment. Since the enactments of only one sovereign are involved, no problems of federalism are present. The court interpreting the statute must simply attempt to ascertain congressional intent, whether the exemption is claimed to be express or implied. The presumptions utilized in exemption analysis are quite distinct from those applied in the preemption context. In examining exemption questions, "the proper approach . . . is an analysis which reconciles the operation of both statutory schemes with one another rather than holding one completely ousted."

With this distinction in mind, I think it quite clear that questions involving the so-called "state action" doctrine are more properly framed as being ones of preemption rather than exemption. Issues under the doctrine inevitably involve state and local regulation which, it is contended, are in conflict with the Sherman Act.

· · ·

Unlike the instant case, *Parker, Midcal,* and *New Motor Vehicle Bd.* involved challenges to a state statute. There was no suggestion that a State *violates* the Sherman Act when it enacts legislation not saved by the *Parker* doctrine from invalidation under the Sherman Act. Instead, the statute is simply unenforceable because it has been preempted by the Sherman Act. By contrast, the gist of the Court's opinion is that a municipality may actually violate the antitrust laws when it merely enacts an ordinance invalid under the Sherman Act, unless the ordinance implements an affirmatively expressed state policy. According to the majority, a municipality may be liable under the Sherman Act for enacting anticompetitive legislation, unless it can show that it is acting simply as the "instrumentality" of the State.

Viewing the *Parker* doctrine in this manner will have troubling consequences for this Court and the lower courts who must now adapt antitrust principles to adjudicate Sherman Act challenges to local regulation of the economy. . . . Among the many problems to be encountered will be whether the *"per se"* rules of illegality apply to municipal defendants in the same manner as they are applied to private defendants. Another is the question of remedies. The Court understandably leaves open the question whether municipalities may be liable for treble damages for enacting anticompetitive ordinances which are not protected by the *Parker* doctrine.[73]

· · ·

Before this Court leaps into the abyss and holds that municipalities may *violate* the Sherman Act by enacting economic and social legislation, it ought to think about the consequences of such a decision in terms of its effect both upon the very antitrust principles the Court desires to apply to local governments and on the role of the

---

73. [Footnote 2 of Justice Rehnquist's opinion.] It will take a considerable feat of judicial gymnastics to conclude that municipalities are not subject to treble damages to compensate any person "injured in his busines or property." Section 4 of the Clayton Act, 15 U.S.C. § 15, is mandatory: "any person who shall be injured in his business or property by reason of anything forbidden in the antitrust laws . . . shall recover threefold the damages by him sustained." See Lafayette v. Louisiana Power & Light Co., 435 U.S. 389, 442-443, 98 S.Ct. 1123, 1151–52, 55 L.Ed.2d 364 (1978) (Blackmun, J., dissenting).

federal courts in examining the validity of local regulation of the economy.

Analyzing this problem as one of federal preemption rather than exemption will avoid these problems. We will not be confronted with the anomaly of holding a municipality liable for enacting anticompetitive ordinances. The federal courts will not be required to engage in a standardless review of the reasonableness of local legislation. Rather, the question simply will be whether the ordinance enacted is preempted by the Sherman Act. I see no reason why a different rule of preemption should be applied to testing the validity of municipal ordinances than the standard we presently apply in assessing state statutes. I see no reason why a municipal ordinance should not be upheld if it satisfies the *Midcal* criteria: the ordinance survives if it is enacted pursuant to an affirmative policy on the part of the city to restrain competition and if the city actively supervises and implements this policy. As with the case of the State, I agree that a city may not simply authorize private parties to engage in activity that would violate the Sherman Act. As in the case of a State, a municipality may not become "a participant in a private agreement or combination by others for restraint of trade."

. . .

II

By treating the municipal defendant as no different from the private litigant attempting to invoke the *Parker* doctrine, the Court's decision today will radically alter the relationship between the States and their political subdivisions. Municipalities will no longer be able to regulate the local economy without the imprimatur of a clearly expressed state policy to displace competition. The decision today effectively destroys the "home rule" movement in this country, through which local governments have obtained, not without persistent state opposition, a limited autonomy over matters of local concern. The municipalities that stand most to lose by the decision today are those with the most autonomy. Where the State is totally disabled from enacting legislation dealing with matters of local concern, the municipality will be defenseless from challenges to its regulation of the local economy. In such a case, the State is disabled from articulating a policy to displace competition with regulation. Nothing short of altering the relationship between the municipality and the State will enable the local government to legislate on matters important to its inhabitants. In order to defend itself from Sherman Act attacks, the home rule municipality will have to cede its authority back to the State. It is unfortunate enough that the Court today holds that our Federalism is not implicated when municipal legislation is invalidated by a federal statute. It is nothing less than a novel and egregious error when this Court uses the Sherman Act to regulate the relationship between the States and their political subdivisions.[74]

74. See also Hybud Equipment Corp. v. City of Akron, 455 U.S. 931, 102 S.Ct. 1416, 71 L.Ed.2d 640 (1982) (reversing 6th Circuit opinion, 654 F.2d 1187, up-

NOTES AND QUERIES

(1) *Dual Federalism: A Limitation on Municipal Regulation.* Should cities be free to adopt anticompetitive regulation independent of a compelling and uniform state policy once the city has been delegated the relevant powers of the State? The majority labor the point that "[o]urs is a 'dual system of government,' . . . which has no place for sovereign cities."[75] In *Lafayette* the Court elaborated that:

. . . the fact that governmental bodies sued are cities, with substantially less than statewide jurisdiction, has significance. When cities, each of the same status under state law, are equally free to approach a policy decision in their own way, the anticompetitive restraints adopted as policy by any one of them, may express its own preference, rather than that of the state.[76]

The underlying concern of the Court is that in 1972 there were 62,437 different units of local government[77] with broad potential to make economic choices without regard to their anticompetitive effects. Providing cities an equal footing with sovereign states in regulatory matters arguably opens a "serious chink in the armor of antitrust protection"[78] and leaves the potential for controlling abuses of public power at the local level wanting.

Queries: Does Justice Rehnquist's dissent in *City of Boulder* take account of this type of concern? Is the need for this concern diminished in the principal case because the scope of the decision is limited to home rule municipalities and, presumably, non-home-rule municipalities can only act pursuant to express state authority anyway? Does Justice Rehnquist quarrel with the importance the majority attached to the fact that the state had expressed no clearly articulated and affirmatively expressed state policy but instead was merely neutral regarding the municipalities regulatory scheme? On the other hand, does the majority take account of the fact that the state may be precluded from acting in the area by the home rule provision of the state constitution?

(2) *Preemption v. Implied Exemption: Shifting the Presumption of Validity or Violation.* Justice Rehnquist, in dissent, asserts that the "state action" doctrine is not an "exemption" at all, but instead a matter of federal preemption.[79] It is a position advocated by several commentators on the state action doctrine.[80] The "exemption" analysis seems to have gained a

---

holding city ordinance establishing city owned waste disposal unit and eliminating competition in waste disposal; remanded for reconsideration in light of *City of Boulder*).

75. See also Kurek v. Pleasure Driveway and Park District of Peoria, 557 F.2d 580, 590 (7th Cir. 1977) ("We simply see little sense in automatically treating as mandates the activities of local governmental units when these activities may vary substantially from unit to unit and may be wholly lacking in any express or implied state authorization or command."; cf. Pueblo Aircraft Service, Inc. v. City of Pueblo, 679 F.2d 805 (10th Cir. 1982).

76. 435 U.S., at 414, 98 S.Ct., at 1137, 55 L.Ed.2d, at 383. The Municipal Yearbook, 1982 p. xiii shows a 1977 total of 79,862 "Local governmental units" bro-

ken down as follows: counties, 3,042; municipalities, 18,862; townships, 16,822; school districts, 15,174; and, special districts, 25,962.

77. Id. at 407, 98 S.Ct., at 1134, 55 L.Ed.2d, at 379.

78. Id. at 408, 98 S.Ct., at 1134, 55 L.Ed.2d, at 380.

79. 455 U.S., at 63, 102 S.Ct., at 847, 70 L.Ed.2d, at 826.

80. See M. Handler, Reforming the Antitrust Laws 59–68 (1982); Note, State Action and the Sherman Antitrust Act: Should the Antitrust Laws Be Given a Preemptive Effect?, 14 Conn.L.Rev. 135 (1981); Note, Applicability of Federal Antitrust Laws to State and Municipal Action: A Case Against the Current Approach, 16 Houston L.Rev. 903 (1979). Compare First, Private Interest and Pub-

foothold in *Parker,* and was reiterated in *Cantor, Lafayette,* and *Midcal.* In *Cantor,* the Court relied on three points to refute the argument that "federal antitrust laws should not be applied in areas of the economy pervasively regulated by state agencies":

> First, merely because certain conduct may be subject both to state regulation and to the federal antitrust laws does not necessarily mean that it must satisfy inconsistent standards; second, even assuming inconsistency, we could not accept the view that the federal interest must inevitably be subordinated to the State's; and finally, even if we were to assume that Congress did not intend the antitrust laws to apply to areas of the economy primarily regulated by a State, that assumption would not foreclose the enforcement of the antitrust laws in an essentially unregulated area such as the market for electric light bulbs.[81]

The process of reconciling these considerations with state law, the Court suggested, could be fashioned by creating an implied exemption to federal antitrust standards where the conflict proves to be irreconcilable.

The Court's explanation of its method for analyzing such cases was fashioned along the lines followed in resolving conflicts between federal regulation and federal antitrust law.[82] The analysis begins with a presumption against implied exemption from the antitrust laws.[83] This presumption has been carried over to state action cases where the reconciliation methodology entails harmonizing enactments by *different* sovereigns in cases like *Cantor.* Despite telling objections by a powerful dissent in *Cantor* that the analogy limped,[84] if it did not fall flat on its face,[85] the majority suggested that a court must follow primary jurisdiction standards "at least as severe as those applied to federal regulatory legislation."[86]

Preemption analysis, on the other hand, specifically delineates areas in which state law impermissively conflicts with the federal law.[87] Unlike the implied exemption analysis, the presumption in preemption analysis appears to cut in favor of the state enactment. Justice Rehnquist argued in his dissent in *The City of Boulder* case: "[b]ecause preemption treads on the very sensitive area of Federal-State relations, this Court is 'reluctant to infer preemption' . . . and the presumption is that preemption is not to be found absent the clear and manifest intentions of Congress that the federal act

lic Control: Government Action, The First Amendment, and The Sherman Act, 1975 Utah L.Rev. 9, 45, arguing for a test which would hold anticompetitive state action "preempted" only where it conflicts with the Sherman Act's political goal of "public control" of the economy.

81. 428 U.S., at 595, 96 S.Ct., at 3119, 49 L.Ed.2d, at 1152.

82. See discussion, Primary Jurisdiction and Implied Exemption, supra pp. 800–810.

83. 428 U.S., at 595–97, 96 S.Ct., at 3119–21, 49 L.Ed.2d, at 1152–54.

84. 428 U.S., at 614, 96 S.Ct., at 3128, 49 L.Ed.2d, at 1164. (Justices Stewart, Powell, & Rehnquist).

85. "The Court's analysis rests on a mistaken premise. The 'implied immuni-

ty' doctrine employed by this Court to reconcile federal antitrust laws and federal regulatory statutes cannot, rationally, be put to the use for which the Court would employ it. That doctrine, a species of the basic rule that repeals by implication are disfavored, comes into play only when arguably inconsistent *federal* statutes are involved. 'Implied repeal' of federal antitrust laws by inconsistent state regulatory statutes is not only 'not favored', . . . it is impossible." 428 U.S., at 629, 96 S.Ct., at 3136, 49 L.Ed.2d, at 1172.

86. 428 U.S., at 597, 96 S.Ct., at 3121, 49 L.Ed.2d, at 1153.

87. See Morgan, Sherman Act Violations and State Action, 33 Ark.L.Rev. 273, 283 (1981).

should supersede the power of the states."[88] Consequently, preemption arguments may begin with a presumption in favor of the state law and turn on the nature or degree of the interference with federal policy free of a bias favoring competition.[89]

It has been argued that there are numerous advantages to applying preemption anaylsis, as opposed to exemption analysis. First, it is conceptually more accurate to employ preemption analysis when determining when a law of one jurisdiction overrides the law of a different jurisdiction. The implied exemption analysis is based on the assumption that the laws should and can be reconciled as if they were espoused from a single consistent sovereign.

Second, the implied exemption analysis creates problems in the sense that an enactment may amount to a Sherman Act violation and thus result in treble damage liability for a state or municipality. The preemption analysis avoids construing the enactment of a law itself as a violation because the preempted enactment is void and unenforceable. No treble damages may necessarily arise, but instead a municipality's improper attempts to enforce the preempted law may be enjoined on grounds independent of the antitrust laws.

Third, the standards applied in the state action cases of "clear articulation", "active supervision", and a legitimate "state interest" appear to have little objective meaning or identifiable parentage. Predicting how they will be applied in a particular case may be considerably more difficult than reliance on the more generally understood and better developed standards relied upon in preemption analysis. Cf. *Affiliated Capital Corp. v. City of Houston*, 700 F.2d 226 (5th Cir. 1983).

(3) *The Reincarnation of Substantive Due Process?* The narrowing of the state action doctrine, and the resulting standards by which the antitrust validity of state and local regulation are judged, appear to place the courts in the position of assessing the wisdom of state and local legislation on the subjective standards of the validity of the state's interest, the articulation of that interest, and the degree of state supervision. Parallel developments in expanding judicial review of state and local advertising regulation by recognizing "commercial speech" as within the ambit of First Amendment protections [90] and the use of § 1983 of the Civil Rights Act of 1871 to limit state economic regulation unfairly restricting individual economic freedom,[91] have given rise to the warning that the Court is reincarnating the doctrine of substantive due process abandoned in the late '30's under threat of President Roosevelt's court packing plan.[92] Under that doctrine, the Court reviewed the substantive merit of federal, state and local economic regulation, striking

88. 455 U.S., at 61, 102 S.Ct., at 846, 70 L.Ed.2d, at 825. See also, J. Norwack, R. Rotunda, and J. Young, Constitutional Law (1978) (preemption analysis will favor federal antitrust law only upon a showing that the state law will " 'impair federal superintendence of the field' and impermissibly interfere with the effectuation of Congressional objectives").

89. See Handler, supra note 81; Morgan, supra note 88. But see First, supra note 40, arguing that the primacy of federal competition policy requires antitrust enforcement, absent a clear showing that Sherman Act liability would conflict with state regulatory goals; and that even in cases of conflict, certain types of state regulatory schemes should be preempted

if they conflict with the Sherman Act's political goals.

90. See Virginia State Board of Pharmacy v. Virginia Citizens Consumer Council, Inc., 425 U.S. 748, 96 S.Ct. 1817, 48 L.Ed.2d 346 (1976); Bates v. State Bar of Arizona, 433 U.S. 350, 97 S.Ct. 2691, 53 L.Ed.2d 810 (1977). See generally Jackson & Jeffries, Commercial Speech: Economic Due Process and The First Amendment, 65 Va.L.Rev. 1 (1979).

91. Gibson v. Berryhill, 411 U.S. 564, 93 S.Ct. 1689, 36 L.Ed.2d 488 (1973).

92. Flynn, Trends In Federal Antitrust Doctrine Suggesting Future Directions For State Antitrust Enforcement, 4 J.Corp.L. 479, 499 (1979).

down that regulation not equating with the Court's vision of appropriate or wise economic regulation.[93] The drift of Supreme Court opinions in the state action, commercial speech, and Civil Rights Act economic cases has drawn the following observation:

> The Court's pursuit of an economic vision of the appropriate balance between competition and regulation, through a narrowing of state action immunity, expansion of free speech and use of the Civil Rights Act to curb arbitrary state economic regulation with an emphasis upon competition over regulation, has been proceeding apace at the federal level. Increased activity by the federal antitrust enforcement agencies in industries regulated and before the agencies engaged in that regulation have sensitized federal courts to the economic values of competition wherever possible and the necessity for careful examination of the legislative scheme of regulation whenever an exemption is claimed for conduct otherwise contrary to the competitive ideal. Some federal regulatory agencies have even become sensitized to the values of competition and the potential for viewing competition as a regulatory tool or at least as a basis from which to reexamine the assumptions of a regulatory scheme laid down many years before in different times and circumstances.

> However, when federal court jurisdiction and federal antitrust policy are brought to bear on state and local regulation the issues become considerably more complex by concerns for federalism, fears of federal judicial revival of substantive due process and the bewildering array of fragmented state and local regulations frequently enacted with less than a coherent social or economic goal in mind and no legislative or administrative record of the reasons for regulation. Indeed, these would appear to be the primary reasons for the Court's failure to articulate a coherent, consistent and acceptable standard for defining a state action exemption from the federal antitrust laws and a willingness to expand first amendment free speech concepts to commercial speech despite the serious political and social implications of doing so.[94]

Queries. Do you agree with this observation? How can such cases be resolved sensibly without the Court substituting its economic philosophy for that of state and local legislative bodies? Most of the states have enacted their own antitrust statutes.[95] Would it make more sense for the federal courts to remand state action cases to state courts for an implied exemption or primary jurisdiction analysis of the state regulatory law in question vis-a-vis the state's antitrust law, before proceeding with the federal antitrust case?

D.   FIRST AMENDMENT DEFENSES AND THE "NOERR–PENNINGTON" DOCTRINE [96]

A public relations and lobbying campaign by a railroad trade association aimed at discrediting truckers and influencing the adoption

---

93. The leading articles on substantive due process are Hetherington, State Economic Regulation and Substantive Due Process, 53 Nw.L.Rev. 13 (1958); Paulsen, The Persistence of Substantive Due Process In The States, 34 Minn.L. Rev. 91 (1950). The issue is explored further in Schwartz, Flynn & First, Free Enterprise and Economic Organization: Government Regulation, ch. 1 (6th Ed. 1983).

94. Flynn, supra note 93 at 501.

95. The state antitrust laws are collected in 4 Trade Reg.Rep. (CCH) ¶ 30,000.

96. See generally 1 P. Areeda & D. Turner, Antitrust Law pp. 36–56 (1978);

and retention of state laws "destructive of the trucking business" gave rise to the *Noerr-Pennington* doctrine. The truckers filed a treble damage suit claiming the railroads' campaign was "vicious, corrupt and fraudulent" and motivated solely to destroy the truckers as competitors of the railroads. The trial court found the railroads violated the Sherman Act. The court awarded treble damages and issued an injunction. The Supreme Court reversed in *Eastern Railroad Presidents Conference v. Noerr Motor Freight, Inc.*,[97] and launched what has now become known as the *Noerr-Pennington* doctrine:

> We accept, as the starting point for our consideration of the case, the same basic construction of the Sherman Act adopted by the courts below—that no violation of the Act can be predicated upon mere attempts to influence the passage or enforcement of laws. It has been recognized, at least since the landmark decision of this Court in *Standard Oil Co. of New Jersey v. United States*, that the Sherman Act forbids only those trade restraints and monopolizations that are created, or attempted, by the acts of "individuals or combinations of individuals or corporations." Accordingly, it has been held that where a restraint upon trade or monopolization is the result of valid governmental action, as opposed to private action, no violation of the Act can be made out. These decisions rest upon the fact that under our form of government the question whether a law of that kind should pass, or if passed be enforced, is the responsibility of the appropriate legislative or executive branch of government so long as the law itself does not violate some provision of the Constitution.
>
> We think it equally clear that the Sherman Act does not prohibit two or more persons from associating together in an attempt to persuade the legislature or the executive to take particular action with respect to a law that would produce a restraint or a monopoly. Although such associations could perhaps, through a process of expansive construction, be brought within the general proscription of "combinations[s] . . . in restraint of trade", they bear very little if any resemblance to the combinations normally held violative of the Sherman Act, combinations ordinarily

L. Sullivan, Antitrust Law 731–43 (1977); Balmer, Sham Litigation and The Antitrust Laws, 29 Buffalo L.Rev. 39 (1980); Bern, The Noerr-Pennington Immunity For Petitioning in Light of *City of Lafayette's* Restriction on The State Action Immunity, 1980 Ariz.St.L.J. 279; Bien, Litigation as an Antitrust Violation: Conflict Between The First Amendment and The Sherman Act, 16 U.San Fran.L.Rev. 41 (1981); Fischel, Antitrust Liability for Attempts to Influence Government Action: The Bases and Limits of the Noerr-Pennington Doctrine, 45 U.Chi.L.Rev. 80 (1977); E. Sullivan, The First Amendment Defenses to Antitrust Litigation, 46 Mo.L.Rev. 517 (1981); Symposium, Antitrust and The Constitution—Collision Course?, 48 Antitrust L.J. 1331 (1979); Note, Noerr-Pennington Antitrust Immunity and Proprietary Governmental Activity, 1981 Ariz.St.L.J. 749; Note, Limiting The Antitrust Immunity for Concerted Attempts to Influence Courts and Adjudicative Agencies: Analogies to Malicious Prosecution and Abuse of Process, 86 Harv.L.Rev. 715 (1973); Note, Protest Boycotts Under the Sherman Act, 128 U.Pa.L.Rev. 1131 (1980).

97.   365 U.S. 127, 81 S.Ct. 523, 5 L.Ed. 2d 464 (1961).

characterized by an express or implied agreement or understanding that the participants will jointly give up their trade freedom, or help one another to take away the trade freedom of others through the use of such devices as price-fixing agreements, boycotts, market-division agreements, and other similar arrangements. This essential dissimilarity between an agreement jointly to seek legislation or law enforcement and the agreements traditionally condemned by § 1 of the Act, even if not itself conclusive on the question of the applicability of the Act, does constitute a warning against treating the defendants' conduct as though it amounted to a common-law trade restraint. And we do think that the question is conclusively settled, against the application of the Act, when this factor of essential dissimilarity is considered along with the other difficulties that would be presented by a holding that the Sherman Act forbids associations for the purpose of influencing the passage or enforcement of laws.

In the first place, such a holding would substantially impair the power of government to take actions through its legislature and executive that operate to restrain trade. In a representative democracy such as this, these branches of government act on behalf of the people and, to a very large extent, the whole concept of representation depends upon the ability of the people to make their wishes known to their representatives. To hold that the government retains the power to act in this representative capacity and yet hold, at the same time, that the people cannot freely inform the government of their wishes would impute to the Sherman Act a purpose to regulate, not business activity, but political activity, a purpose which would have no basis whatever in the legislative history of that Act. Secondly, and of at least equal significance, such a construction of the Sherman Act would raise important constitutional questions. The right of petition is one of the freedoms protected by the Bill of Rights, and we cannot, of course, lightly impute to Congress an intent to invade these freedoms. Indeed, such an imputation would be particularly unjustified in this case in view of all the countervailing considerations enumerated above. For these reasons, we think it clear that the Sherman Act does not apply to the activities of the railroads at least insofar as those activities comprised mere solicitation of governmental action with respect to the passage and enforcement of laws. . . .

. . . The proscriptions of the Act, tailored as they are for the business world, are not at all appropriate for application in the political arena. Congress has traditionally exercised extreme caution in legislating with respect to problems relating to the conduct of political activities, a caution which has been reflected in the decisions of this Court interpreting such legislation. All of this caution would go for naught if we permitted an extension of the Sherman Act to regulate activities of that nature simply because those activities have a commercial impact and involve conduct that can be termed unethical.

There may be situations in which a publicity campaign, ostensibly directed toward influencing governmental action, is a mere sham to cover what is actually nothing more than an attempt to interfere directly with the business relationships of a competitor and the application of the Sherman Act would be justified. But this certainly is not the case here. No one denies that the railroads were making a genuine effort to influence legislation and law enforcement practices. . . . Under these circumstances, we conclude that no attempt to interfere with business relationships in a manner proscribed by the Sherman Act is involved in this case.[98]

The *Noerr* limitation upon the use of the Sherman Act to attack efforts to influence government action for the purpose of restraining trade was elaborated upon in *United Mine Workers v. Pennington.*[99] In that case, small coal mine operators charged that the union and large coal companies had conspired to persuade the Secretary of Labor to impose, under the Walsh-Healey Act, a high minimum wage structure on small operators selling coal to the TVA and to persuade the TVA to limit spot purchases of coal, a substantial portion of which were exempt from Walsh-Healey.[1] In reversing a lower court treble damage award against the union for failure to include in jury instructions a proper defense instruction based on *Noerr*, the Court stated:

In *Eastern R.R. Presidents Conf. v. Noerr Motor Freight, Inc.*, the Court rejected an attempt to base a Sherman Act conspiracy on evidence consisting entirely of activities of competitors seeking to influence public officials. The Sherman Act, it was held, was not intended to bar concerted action of this kind even though the resulting official action damaged other competitors at whom the campaign was aimed. Furthermore, the legality of the conduct "was not at all affected by any anticompetitive purpose it may have had," even though the "sole purpose in seeking to influence the passage and enforcement of laws was to destroy the truckers as competitors for the long-distance freight business." Nothing could be clearer from the Court's opinion than that anticompetitive purpose did not illegalize the conduct there involved.

We agree with the UMW that both the Court of Appeals and the trial court failed to take proper account of the Noerr case. In approving the instructions of the trial court with regard to the approaches of the union and the operators to the Secretary of Labor and to the TVA officials, the Court of Appeals considered Noerr as applying only to conduct "unaccompanied by a purpose or intent to further a conspiracy to violate a statute. It is the illegal purpose or intent inherent in the conduct which vitiates the con-

98. 365 U.S., at 135–44, 81 S.Ct., at 528–33, 5 L.Ed.2d, at 469–75.

99. 381 U.S. 657, 85 S.Ct. 1585, 14 L.Ed.2d 626 (1965).

1. The Walsh-Healey Act, 41 U.S.C.A. § 35, *et seq.*, authorizes the Secretary of Labor to set a minimum wage for employees of firms selling goods in excess of $10,000 to any U.S. Government agency, department or instrumentality.

duct which would otherwise be legal." Noerr shields from the Sherman Act a concerted effort to influence public officials regardless of intent or purpose. . . . Joint efforts to influence public officials do not violate the antitrust laws even though intended to eliminate competition. Such conduct is not illegal, either standing alone or as part of a broader scheme itself violative of the Sherman Act. . . .[2]

Noerr and *Pennington* appeared to create a generous shelter from potential antitrust liability for joint action seeking to influence government to adopt or implement policies injuring competitors in the name of protecting the higher values expressed by the First Amendment. The breadth of the exemption, however, was soon questioned by the following case.

CALIFORNIA MOTOR TRANSPORT CO. v. TRUCKING UNLIMITED

Supreme Court of the United States, 1972.
404 U.S. 508, 92 S.Ct. 609, 30 L.Ed.2d 642.

Opinion of the Court by MR. JUSTICE DOUGLAS, Announced by MR. CHIEF JUSTICE BURGER.

This is a civil suit under § 4 of the Clayton Act, 38 Stat. 731, 15 U.S.C. § 15, for injunctive relief and damages instituted by respondents, who are highway carriers operating in California, against petitioners, who are also highway carriers operating within, into, and from California. Respondents and petitioners are, in other words, competitors. The charge is that the petitioners conspired to monopolize trade and commerce in the transportation of goods in violation of the antitrust laws. The conspiracy alleged is a concerted action by petitioners to institute state and federal proceedings to resist and defeat applications by respondents to acquire operating rights or to transfer or register those rights. These activities, it is alleged, extend to rehearings and to reviews or appeals from agency or court decisions on these matters.

The District Court dismissed the complaint for failure to state a cause of action. The Court of Appeals reversed, 432 F.2d 755.

The present case is akin to Eastern Railroad Presidents Conference v. Noerr Motor Freight Inc., where a group of trucking companies sued a group of railroads to restrain them from an alleged conspiracy to monopolize the long-distance freight business in violation of the antitrust laws and to obtain damages. We held that no cause of action was alleged insofar as it was predicated upon mere attempts to influence the Legislative Branch for the passage of laws or the Executive Branch for their enforcement. . . .

We followed that view in United Mine Workers v. Pennington.

The same philosophy governs the approach of citizens or groups of them to administrative agencies (which are both creatures of the

---

2. 381 U.S., at 669, 85 S.Ct., at 1593, 14 L.Ed.2d, at 636.

legislature, and arms of the executive) and to courts, the third branch of Government. Certainly the right to petition extends to all departments of the Government. The right of access to the courts is indeed but one aspect of the right of petition.

We conclude that it would be destructive of rights of association and of petition to hold that groups with common interests may not, without violating the antitrust laws, use the channels and procedures of state and federal agencies and courts to advocate their causes and points of view respecting resolution of their business and economic interests *vis-à-vis* their competitors.

We said, however, in *Noerr* that there may be instances where the alleged conspiracy "is a mere sham to cover what is actually nothing more than an attempt to interfere directly with the business relationships of a competitor and the application of the Sherman Act would be justified."

In that connection the complaint in the present case alleged that the aim and purpose of the conspiracy was "putting their competitors, including plaintiff, out of business, of weakening such competitors, of destroying, eliminating and weakening existing and potential competition, and of monopolizing the highway common carriage business in California and elsewhere."

More critical are other allegations, which are too lengthy to quote, and which elaborate on the "sham" theory by stating that the power, strategy, and resources of the petitioners were used to harass and deter respondents in their use of administrative and judicial proceedings so as to deny them "free and unlimited access" to those tribunals. The result, it is alleged, was that the machinery of the agencies and the courts was effectively closed to respondents, and petitioners indeed became "the regulators of the grants of rights, transfers and registrations" to respondents—thereby depleting and diminishing the value of the businesses of respondents and aggrandizing petitioners' economic and monopoly power. See Note, 57 Calif.L.Rev. 518 (1969).

Petitioners rely on our statement in *Pennington* that "*Noerr* shields from the Sherman Act a concerted effort to influence public officials regardless of intent or purpose." In the present case, however, the allegations are not that the conspirators sought "to influence public officials," but that they sought to bar their competitors from meaningful access to adjudicatory tribunals and so to usurp that decisionmaking process. It is alleged that petitioners "instituted the proceedings and actions . . . with or without probable cause, and regardless of the merits of the cases." The nature of the views pressed does not, of course, determine whether First Amendment rights may be invoked; but they may bear upon a purpose to deprive the competitors of meaningful access to the agencies and courts. As stated in the opinion concurring in the judgment, such a purpose or intent, if shown, would be "to discourage and ultimately to prevent the respondents from invoking" the processes of the administrative agencies and courts and thus fall within the exception to *Noerr*.

The political campaign operated by the railroads in *Noerr* to obtain legislation crippling truckers employed deception and misrepresentation and unethical tactics. . . .

Yet unethical conduct in the setting of the adjudicatory process often results in sanctions. Perjury of witnesses is one example. Use of a patent obtained by fraud to exclude a competitor from the market may involve a violation of the antitrust laws, as we held in Walker Process Equipment, Inc. v. Food Machinery & Chemical Corp., 382 U.S. 172, 175–177, 86 S.Ct. 347, 349–350, 15 L.Ed.2d 247. Conspiracy with a licensing authority to eliminate a competitor may also result in an antitrust transgression. Continental Ore Co. v. Union Carbide & Carbon Corp., 370 U.S. 690, 707, 82 S.Ct. 1404, 1414, 8 L.Ed.2d 777; Harman v. Valley National Bank, 339 F.2d 564 (CA9 1964). Similarly, bribery of a public purchasing agent may constitute a violation of § 2(c) of the Clayton Act, as amended by the Robinson-Patman Act. Rangen, Inc. v. Sterling Nelson & Sons, 351 F.2d 851 (CA9 1965).

There are many other forms of illegal and reprehensible practice which may corrupt the administrative or judicial processes and which may result in antitrust violations. Misrepresentations, condoned in the political arena, are not immunized when used in the adjudicatory process. Opponents before agencies or courts often think poorly of the other's tactics, motions, or defenses and may readily call them baseless. One claim, which a court or agency may think baseless, may go unnoticed; but a pattern of baseless, repetitive claims may emerge which leads the factfinder to conclude that the administrative and judicial processes have been abused. That may be a difficult line to discern and draw. But once it is drawn, the case is established that abuse of those processes produced an illegal result, *viz.*, effectively barring respondents from access to the agencies and courts. Insofar as the administrative or judicial processes are involved, actions of that kind cannot acquire immunity by seeking refuge under the umbrella of "political expression."

Petitioners, of course, have the right of access to the agencies and courts to be heard on applications sought by competitive highway carriers. That right, as indicated, is part of the right of petition protected by the First Amendment. Yet that does not necessarily give them immunity from the antitrust laws.

It is well settled that First Amendment rights are not immunized from regulation when they are used as an integral part of conduct which violates a valid statute. Giboney v. Empire Storage & Ice Co., 336 U.S. 490, 69 S.Ct. 684, 93 L.Ed. 834. In that case Missouri enacted a statute banning secondary boycotts and we sustained an injunction against picketing to enforce the boycott, saying:

"It is true that the agreements and course of conduct here were as in most instances brought about through speaking or writing. But it has never been deemed an abridgment of freedom of speech or press to make a course of conduct illegal merely because the conduct was in part initiated, evidenced, or carried out by means of language, either spoken, written, or printed. . . . Such an expansive interpretation of the constitutional guaranties of speech and press would make it practically impossible ever to enforce laws against agreements in restraint of trade as well as many other agreements and conspiracies deemed injurious to society." 336 U.S., at 502, 69 S.Ct., at 691.

In Associated Press v. United States, 326 U.S. 1, 65 S.Ct. 1416, 89 L.Ed. 2013, we held that the Associated Press was not immune from the antitrust laws by reason of the fact that the press is under the shelter of the First Amendment. . . .

The rationale of those cases, when applied to the instant controversy, makes the following conclusions clear: (1) that any carrier has the right of access to agencies and courts, within the limits, of course, of their prescribed procedures, in order to defeat applications of its competitors for certificates as highway carriers; and (2) that its purpose to eliminate an applicant as a competitor by denying him free and meaningful access to the agencies and courts may be implicit in that opposition.

First Amendment rights may not be used as the means or the pretext for achieving "substantive evils" which the legislature has the power to control. Certainly the constitutionality of the antitrust laws is not open to debate. A combination of entrepreneurs to harass and deter their competitors from having "free and unlimited access" to the agencies and courts, to defeat that right by massive, concerted, and purposeful activities of the group are ways of building up one empire and destroying another. As stated in the opinion concurring in the judgment, that is the essence of those parts of the complaint to which we refer. If these facts are proved, a violation of the antitrust laws has been established. If the end result is unlawful, it matters not that the means used in violation may be lawful.

What the proof will show is not known, for the District Court granted the motion to dismiss the complaint. . . . On their face the above-quoted allegations come within the "sham" exception in the *Noerr* case, as adapted to the adjudicatory process.

Accordingly we affirm the Court of Appeals and remand the case for trial.

So ordered.

Judgment affirmed and case remanded.*

MR. JUSTICE POWELL and MR. JUSTICE REHNQUIST took no part in the consideration or decision of this case.

MR. JUSTICE STEWART, with whom MR. JUSTICE BRENNAN joins, concurring in the judgment.

In the *Noerr* case this Court held, in a unanimous opinion written by Mr. Justice Black, that a conspiracy by railroads to influence legislative and executive action in order to destroy the competition of

---

* [Compare the Court's subsequent decision in National Association for Advancement of Colored People v. Claiborne Hardware Co., discussed supra pp. 538–540. Are the decisions consistent?— Ed.]

truckers in the long-haul freight business was wholly immune from the antitrust laws. . . . Today the Court retreats from *Noerr*, and in the process tramples upon important First Amendment values. For that reason I cannot join the Court's opinion.

. . .

The Court concedes that the petitioners' "right of access to the agencies and courts to be heard on applications sought by competitive highway carriers . . . is part of the right of petition protected by the First Amendment." Yet, says the Court, their joint agreement to exercise that right "does not necessarily give them immunity from the antitrust laws." *Ante*, at 613. It is difficult to imagine a statement more totally at odds with *Noerr*. For what that case explicitly held is that the joint exercise of the constitutional right of petition *is* given immunity from the antitrust laws.

While disagreeing with the Court's opinion, I would nonetheless remand this case to the District Court for trial. The complaint contains allegations that the petitioners have:

1. *Agreed* jointly to finance and to carry out and publicize a consistent, systematic and uninterrupted program of opposing 'with or without probable cause and regardless of the merits' every application, with insignificant exceptions, for additional operating rights or for the registration or transfer of operating rights, before the California PUC, the ICC, and the courts on appeal.

2. *Carried out* such agreement (a) by appearing as protestants in all proceedings instituted by plaintiffs and others in like position or by instituting complaints in opposition to applications or transfers or registrations; (b) by establishing a trust fund to finance the foregoing, consisting of contributions monthly in amounts proportionate to each defendant's annual gross income; (c) by publicizing and making known to plaintiffs and others in like position the foregoing program.

Under these allegations, liberally construed, the respondents are entitled to prove that the real *intent* of the conspirators was not to invoke the processes of the administrative agencies and courts, but to discourage and ultimately to prevent the respondents from invoking those processes. Such an intent would make the conspiracy "an attempt to interfere directly with the business relationships of a competitor and the application of the Sherman Act would be justified."

It is only on this basis that I concur in the judgment of the Court.

NOTES AND QUERIES

(1) *"Sham" vs. "Non-Sham" Activity Influencing Government.* In *Otter Tail Power Co. v. United States*, supra p. 124, a part of the conduct claimed exclusionary was the filing of lawsuits against municipal bond issues to be used for financing municipal power systems taking over Otter Tail franchises. The Court remanded that part of the case for reconsideration in light of its intervening decision in *Trucking Unlimited*, and described its

opinion in *Trucking Unlimited* as one "where we held that the principle of *Noerr* may also apply to the use of administrative or judicial processes where the purpose is to suppress competition as evidenced by repetitive lawsuits carrying the hallmark of insubstantial claims and thus within the 'mere sham' exception announced in *Noerr.*"[3] This language has spawned a split of opinion as to whether a single baseless lawsuit can be within the concept of "sham" and constitute a ground for Sherman Act liability.[4]

Disputes have also arisen with regard to how "baseless" the litigation must be and what standards a court must apply to determine that question. Suggestions have ranged from requiring proof that the conduct amounts to the tort of malicious prosecution or abuse of process[5] to the creation of a presumption of validity in invoking governmental processes which can only be overcome by "clear and convincing evidence."[6] Other opinions have based a finding of "sham" on unethical conduct like withholding vital information in securing a patent, or committing fraud, bribery, misrepresentation or perjury in the litigation process.[7] The multiplicity of opinions and proposed tests has led the Ninth Circuit to observe: "There is no precise definition to the sham exception. . . . The easiest way to explain it is by saying the *Noerr-Pennington* doctrine does not exempt attempts to influence the government which are a sham."[8]

(2) *Commercial Governmental Activity—An Exception to Noerr-Pennington?* Although not expressly mentioned by Supreme Court opinions, several lower court opinions have been carving out an exception from the *Noerr-Pennington* doctrine for "commercial" or "proprietary" activity by government.[9] When government acts in a commercial or proprietary capacity—selling franchises or buying goods or services, for example—some courts have imposed antitrust liability for conspiracies to restrain trade in the carrying out of the activity. It has been argued that the fact of government involvement should have no bearing on immunity: "The fact that the government is the victim of an otherwise improper act by a private party cannot immunize the action. . . . It would be perverse to hold that the identity of the victim saves the seller."[10]

---

3. 410 U.S. 366, 380, 93 S.Ct. 1022, 1031, 35 L.Ed.2d 359, 369 (1973).

4. See Vendo Co. v. Lektro-Vend Corp., 433 U.S. 623, 97 S.Ct. 2881, 53 L.Ed.2d 1009 (1977) (Justices Stevens, Brennan, Marshall & White arguing a single baseless suit can be a "sham"); Technicron Medical Information Systems Corp. v. Green Bay Packaging, Inc., 480 F.Supp. 124 (E.D.Wis.1979). But see MCI Communications Corp. v. American Telephone & Telegraph Co., 1983 Trade Cases ¶ 65,137 (7th Cir. 1983) (there must be a pattern of baseless suits).

5. See Clipper Express v. Rocky Mountain Motor Tariff Bureau, 690 F.2d 1240 (9th Cir. 1982); Note, Limiting the Antitrust Immunity for Concerted Attempts to Influence Courts and Adjudicative Agencies: Analogies to Malicious Prosecution and Abuse of Process, 86 Harv.L.Rev. 715 (1973).

6. See Subscription Television v. Southern California Theatre Owners Association, 576 F.2d 230 (9th Cir. 1978).

7. The opinions are surveyed in Balmer, Sham Litigation and The Antitrust Laws, 29 Buff.L.Rev. 39 (1980); Bien, Litigation as an Antitrust Violation: Conflict Between The First Amendment and The Sherman Act, 16 U.S.F.L.Rev. 41 (1981); Crawford & Tschaepe, The Erosion of the Noerr-Pennington Immunity, 13 St. Mary's L.J. 291 (1981); Litton Systems, Inc. v. American Telephone & Telegraph Co., 700 F.2d 785 (2d Cir. 1983).

8. Ernest W. Hahn, Inc. v. Codding, 615 F.2d 830, 837 n. 8 (9th Cir. 1980).

9. See generally Robinson, Reconciling Antitrust and The First Amendment, 48 Antitrust L.J. 1335, 1342–49 (1980); Note, Noerr-Pennington Antitrust Immunity and Proprietary Government Activity, 1981 Ariz.St.L.J. 749.

10. 1 P. Areeda & D. Turner, Antitrust Law ¶ 206(c) (1978). See First, supra note 40, suggesting that there is no need for First Amendment protection in those commercial contexts where the government has already determined that

Queries. Do you agree? Should bribery of or bid rigging by government purchasing agents conspiring with sellers be immune from antitrust liability? Should a distinction be drawn between suits brought by injured competitors and suits brought by the government victimized? Between suits seeking to hold the government liable and suits seeking to hold private parties or government employees liable? After the *City of Lafayette* state action case, should appeals to a governmental proprietary entity like a city owned power company to engage in anticompetitive conduct be protected by the First Amendment?

(3) *The Interrelation of the State Action Doctrine and the Noerr-Pennington Doctrine.* In cases where a municipality can claim no state action immunity under the standards of *City of Lafayette* and *City of Boulder*, the question arises whether the municipality and those who have petitioned the municipality to engage in anticompetitive conduct not clearly articulated and authorized by state law can claim *Noerr-Pennington* immunity. "Put more directly, does it follow that if the government can't do it, the people can't petition for it"? [11]

Different results have been reached on the question, even in the same case—*In re Airport Car Rental Antitrust Litigation.*[12] Small car rental agencies charged that Hertz, Avis and National conspired with airport authorities to adopt and enforce standards for airport car rental concessions designed to exclude plaintiffs. On an initial summary judgment motion, the trial court upheld the complaint on the ground that the *Noerr-Pennington* exemption was not available for attempts to influence government "commercial activity". The Court also linked its decision to the *Parker* doctrine: "[T]he rationale of *Noerr-Pennington* would not extend to attempts to influence government officials acting in a manner that was not protected 'state action' under *Parker. . . . Noerr-Pennington* presupposes *Parker v. Brown* immunity: if the governmental or agency action is valid as under state authority (despite anticompetitive effects), then seeking to influence the action and a successful outcome are also exempt." [13]

Motions for summary judgment were renewed by the defendants after the case was assigned to a different judge. The second judge rejected the claim of a broad "commercial activity" exception to *Noerr-Pennington* and held the defendant's joint activity seeking a competitive edge over their rivals by influencing governmental commercial activity was protected communication with government, a holding subsequently affirmed by the Ninth Circuit. The Court refused to link *Noerr-Pennington* immunity to *Parker* immunity by requiring the subject matter petitioned about be a subject matter the governmental agency could validly execute under the rationale of *Parker* and *City of Lafayette.* The court observed: "Persons contemplating joint activities to influence public officials cannot predict with any degree of certainty whether the officials or their agencies could in some future lawsuits be held liable under the antitrust laws for engaging in the activities sought to be influenced." [14]

its policy is to seek economic efficiency within a market framework.

11. Bern, The Noerr-Pennington Immunity for Petitioning In Light of *City of Lafayette's* Restriction on the State Action Immunity, 1980 Ariz.St.L.J. 279, 282.

12. 474 F.Supp. 1072 (N.D.Cal.1979); 521 F.Supp. 568 (N.D.Cal.1981).

13. 474 F.Supp. at 1990–91 and quoting Huron Valley Hospital Inc. v. City of Pontiac, 466 F.Supp. 1301, 1315 (E.D. Mich.1979).

14. 521 F.Supp. at 584–85, affirmed 693 F.2d 84 (9th Cir. 1982).

Queries. After *City of Boulder,* should the *Noerr-Pennington* doctrine be applied to joint activity soliciting anticompetitive municipal activity not clearly articulated and affirmatively expressed by state law as within the municipality's authority? Would such a rule constitute too great a "chilling" of First Amendment rights in light of *Noerr?* Could such conduct be considered a "sham" under *Trucking Unlimited?*

E.   INTERNATIONAL TRADE [15]

1.   AN OVERVIEW

The application of American antitrust policy to international trade is a rapidly expanding and complex area. Only a summary overview of the major issues affecting the exercise of court jurisdiction over "commerce . . . with foreign nations" granted by §§ 1 and 2 of the Sherman Act and some of the specialized statutes dealing with foreign trade are presented here. (See also, Chapter 4, § F, supra p. 518). The growing interrelationship of world trade, operation of U.S. corporations and subsidiaries abroad and foreign ones here, attempts to regulate international trade by the United Nations, and direct involvement of nation states in commercial activity, have all served to create an expanding area of antitrust speciality—international antitrust law and practice.

American courts have not been immune from these developments. Antitrust jurisdiction is often invoked to adjudicate disputes having their origins outside the United States and aimed at our international or domestic trade, or disputes originating in the United States and aimed at international trade. Jurisdictional and "comity" questions abound, as do issues of the proper relationship of American law to those of other nation states, the scope of the judicial power vis-a-vis that of the other branches of government in foreign affairs, and the propriety of using American law to call into question the actions of foreign government-owned commercial enterprises or sovereign acts commanding anticompetitive conduct affecting the interstate or foreign commerce of the United States.

---

15. See generally 1 P. Areeda & D. Turner, Antitrust Law 254–78 (1978); J. Atwood & K. Brewster, Antitrust and American Business Abroad (2d Ed. 1981); W. Fugate, Foreign Commerce and The Antitrust Laws (2d Ed. 1973); B. Hawk, United States, Common Market and International Antitrust (1979); A. D. Neale & D. G. Goyder, The Antitrust Laws of the U.S.A., Chap. XI (3d Ed. 1980); Dept. of Justice, Antitrust Guide for International Operations (1977); Symposium, Antitrust and International Trade, 49 Antitrust L.J. 1185 (1981); Symposium, Transnational Issues in American Antitrust Law, 2 Nw.J.Int.L. & Bus. 334 (1980); Symposium, American Antitrust Laws and Foreign Governments, 13 J.Int. L. & Econ. 137 (1978); Symposium, Application of U.S. Antitrust Laws to International Trade and Investment, 5 N.C.J.Int. L. & Comm.Reg. 91 (1980).

J. ATWOOD, INTERNATIONAL ANTITRUST ISSUES IN THE COURTS AND CONGRESS

50 Antitrust L.J. 257 (1982).[16]

For some decades, the United States has been uniquely aggressive in applying its antitrust law to international trade. Uniquely aggressive, but not unique. Other nations, particularly Germany, have been known to scrutinize international transactions under their local competition laws, and for some time the Commission of the European Communities has warned that the Treaty of Rome's antitrust articles would be applied to all conduct, local or not, that adversely affected competition within the Community.[17] But the United States, more than any other nation, has applied its antitrust laws with at least some degree of consistency and vigor in international trade. Beginning with the early international shipping cases [18] and running through the exhilarating days of *Alcoa*,[19] *Timken*,[20] and *Minnesota Mining*,[21] the United States put the world business community on notice that the Sherman Act had to be reckoned with in U.S. foreign commerce.

This isn't to say that United States law was wholly uninhibited, or that United States policies pressed single-mindedly for more and more competition in freer and freer markets. There were hesitancies [22] and cross-currents,[23] and some of the practical and political problems that can arise from too expansive an application of American law began to emerge. But still the tradition of a vigorous role for American antitrust in international trade seemed basically unchallenged. In 1978, for example, it was not preposterous to learn that a private suit had been filed in U.S. federal court challenging OPEC's pricing-setting arrangements as an antitrust violation.[24] In any other legal system, such a suit would have been unthinkable, but in the United States it had to be taken very seriously.

16. Copyright, American Bar Association, 1982. Reprinted by permission of the American Bar Association and Mr. Atwood. (Footnotes have been renumbered.)

17. For a recent statement, see Commission of the European Communities, Tenth Report on Competition Policy 20 (1980): "Articles 85 and 86 apply to all agreements and practices that have economic consequences within the Community by affecting competition and trade, whatever the nationality or location of some or all of the parties."

18. United States v. Pacific & Arctic Ry., 228 U.S. 87 (1913); Thomsen v. Cayser, 243 U.S. 66 (1917).

19. United States v. Aluminum Co. of America, 148 F.2d 416 (2d Cir. 1945).

20. Timken Roller Bearing Co. v. United States, 341 U.S. 593 (1951).

21. United States v. Minnesota Mining & Mfg. Co., 92 F.Supp. 947 (D.Mass. 1950).

22. A notable example was the cutting back of the Justice Department's investigation, spanning the 1940s and 1950s, of the international petroleum companies. For description of the case, see 1 J. Atwood & K. Brewster, Antitrust and American Business Abroad 44–47 (2d ed. 1981).

23. See 1 J. Atwood & K. Brewster, supra . . . , ch. 3.

24. International Ass'n of Machinists v. Organization of Petroleum Exporting Countries, No. 78–5012–AAH (C.D.Cal. 1979). The suit ultimately failed on act-of-state grounds. International Ass'n of Machinists v. Organization of Petroleum Exporting Countries, 649 F.2d 1354 (9th Cir. 1981), certiorari denied 454 U.S. 1163, 102 S.Ct. 1036, 71 L.Ed.2d 319 (1982).

In the recent few years, though, there has begun a process of serious rethinking. The realization has come that freely applying American law in the international sphere may be more difficult than was once thought, and carries both risks and costs for American interests. Objections to the "rough rider" tradition of American antitrust have come principally from two sources: American business, which argues that its competitiveness and profitability in export and foreign markets have suffered, and foreign governments, which object to the "legal imperialism" which occurs when American law is applied to conduct which another sovereign regards as within its sole jurisdiction. Added to this criticism has been the growing belief, both at home and abroad, that the United States was no longer entitled—as arguably it was in the immediate post-war period—to pursue its own policies and preferences without careful regard to what our allies and trading partners might think.

Not deaf to these criticisms and concerns, the American courts, Congress, and even enforcement officials are now reevaluating just how and when U.S. antitrust should apply internationally. Some significant changes in the law seem to be emerging and in this paper, I will try to give a capsule report on the areas of recent activity and importance.

I. JURISDICTION AND ABSTENTION

First is the ever-popular topic of jurisdiction and its close cousin: abstention.

American antitrust jurisdiction reached its doctrinal zenith in *Alcoa*,[25] which as interpreted over the years came to mean that American law would apply, even as against foreign conduct and foreign actors, where the conduct had a substantial and foreseeable effect on United States domestic or foreign commerce. This effects theory of jurisdiction raised eyebrows abroad, but United States courts and prosecutors became convinced that alternative approaches which focused on the nationality of the actors or on the locus of the conduct were too inflexible and too often missed conduct which significantly impinged on American interests and which should therefore be subject to American law.

Despite *Alcoa's* age—it was decided in 1945—remarkably little elaboration emerged on its basic test of substantial and foreseeable effects. Gloss of some importance, though, was recently provided by the Second Circuit's . . . decision in *National Bank of Canada*.[26] The decision is potentially significant on a number of issues, including the application of *Alcoa's* jurisdictional test.

The plaintiff was a Canadian bank, and it sued one of its Canadian competitors and Interbank, the U.S. Master Charge organization, challenging a decision by those two defendants to enforce a nonas-

25. United States v. Aluminum Co. of America, 148 F.2d 416 (2d Cir. 1945).

26. National Bank of Canada v. Interbank Card Ass'n, 1980–81 Trade Cas. ¶ 63,836 (2d Cir. 1981).

signment clause in the Master Charge Canadian license agreements, thereby preventing the plaintiff from obtaining a Master Charge license. Given that the plaintiff was a Canadian bank and complaining about a restraint on its Canadian operations, the obvious question arose whether its claims fell within the Sherman Act's jurisdictional scope. The court of appeals concluded that they did not. Two things about the court's opinion are noteworthy. First, it stated in unusually clear terms what would seem to be an indisputable point: that anticompetitive effects within a foreign market do not trigger Sherman Act jurisdiction; U.S. law is not applicable simply because conduct by an American firm is at issue and claimed to have had adverse effects abroad. A showing of an impact on U.S. commerce—either U.S. domestic commerce, or U.S. exports or imports—is necessary.[27]

More novel, though, was the court's statement on the *type* of effects which must be shown. Drawing from the principles in the Supreme Court's *Brunswick* decision,[28] the court stated that U.S. jurisdiction "is not supported by every conceivable repercussion of the action . . . on United States commerce."[29] Simply demonstrating an effect on U.S. commerce is not sufficient; a plaintiff must show an "*anticompetitive* effect either of the violation or of anticompetitive acts made possible by the violation."[30] Only such anticompetitive effects "constitute effects sufficient to confer jurisdiction."[31]

. . .

. . . The Second Circuit seems to be saying that Sherman Act jurisdiction may not be based solely on a showing that the export trade of an American defendant was restricted by the challenged conduct; there must be a showing of a restrictive effect on the U.S. trade of someone *other than the defendant*, because self-denial by an American defendant will be presumed to be in that party's interest. I will return to this point in a moment, in my discussion of substantive law as it bears on exports.

B. COMITY AS A LIMITATION ON JURISDICTION

In addition to this clarification, or perhaps narrowing, of the effects test by *National Bank of Canada*, another significant development has occurred on the jurisdictional front. Whatever refinements are possible on the effects standard, the *Alcoa* approach to jurisdiction has been increasingly criticized as basically flawed because of its completeness. Specifically, the effects doctrine does not take account of the interests of *other* governments which might counsel against the application of United States law to particular transactions. That is, however significant and foreseeable the effects of a transaction on American commerce, there might be equally compelling grounds for the conclusion that an American antitrust court ought not intervene.

27. 1980–1 Trade Cas. at 78,471–72.

28. Brunswick Corp. v. Pueblo Bowl-O-Mat, Inc., 429 U.S. 477 (1977).

29. 1980–81 Trade Cas. at 78,472.

30. Id. (emphasis added).

31. Id.

Almost by definition, an international transaction is likely to affect the policies and interests of other governments, and a jurisdictional standard which looks only at United States policies and interests and not those of other affected governments can be challenged as unacceptably narrow-minded in today's world of interdependent national economies and interests.

The judicial response, although somewhat hesitant, has been to accept the principle, at least, that comity among nations requires a balancing of the respective interests of affected states to see whether a United States court should assert antitrust jurisdiction over an international transaction, even where the effects standard of jurisdiction is satisfied. In the words of Kingman Brewster, comity provides a "jurisdictional rule of reason," [32] allowing an antitrust court to consider a range of relevant factors bearing on the appropriateness of adjudication under American law. The two leading antitrust cases embracing the comity principle, *Timberlane* [33] and *Mannington Mills*,[34] have been generally praised by both commentators and government officials for showing a new and needed sensitivity to the international ramifications of extraterritorial antitrust enforcement.

These two decisions, though, were on pretrial motions, and serious questions still remain on the practicality of comity as a jurisdictional rule in complex litigation and, more worrisome still, in day-to-day counseling and decision-making by businesses. The courts have concluded that a long list of factors are relevant to the comity analysis, including complex factual and policy questions that are not susceptible of easy evaluation or quantification. Also, some courts have expressed concern about their competence to weigh the foreign policy issues which may be presented in sensitive antitrust litigation,[35] and it is not entirely clear what amici role should be played by foreign governments or the Justice Department in private suits.[36] And while foreign governments generally welcome this new willingness by the U.S. legal system to take their interests into account, they are not exactly thrilled by the fact that the weighing process is to be conducted in an American courtroom rather than at a negotiating table in the ministry of foreign affairs.

In sum, most are agreed that comity analysis is a long-needed addition to the American approach to antitrust jurisdiction. But many questions and concerns remain as to its usefulness to antitrust counselors and its workability in the combative framework of litigation.

32. K. Brewster, Antitrust and American Business Abroad (1958). See also 1 J. Atwood & K. Brewster, supra . . . ., 156–80.

33. Timberlane Lumber Co. v. Bank of America, 549 F.2d 597 (9th Cir. 1976).

34. Mannington Mills, Inc. v. Congoleum Corp., 595 F.2d 1287 (3d Cir. 1979).

35. See In re Uranium Antitrust Litigation, 480 F.Supp. 1138, 1148 (N.D.Ill. 1979).

36. Compare In re Uranium Antitrust Litigation, 617 F.2d 1248, 1256 (7th Cir. 1980), with Letter of Robert B. Owen, Legal Adviser of the Department of State, to John H. Shenefield, Associate Attorney General (Mar. 17, 1980), reprinted in 74 Am.J.Int'l L. 665 (1980), and Letter of John H. Shenefield, Associate Attorney General, to Hon. Prentice H. Marshall (May 6, 1980), reprinted in 5 Trade Reg. Rep. (CCH) ¶ 50,416.

C. ABSTENTION

[Discussion of the Act of State Doctrine omitted, see subsection 2, infra p. 863.]

D. ENFORCEMENT AND/OR ADJUDICATIVE JURISDICTION

Still on the threshold question of jurisdiction, let me say a few words about another facet of the problem. Even if a court satisfies itself that it has jurisdiction over the dispute and that the act of state doctrine does not compel abstention, there may still be other obstacles of a jurisdictional nature that could affect the conduct of the litigation. I am referring to what is frequently labeled enforcement jurisdiction, although the current draft of the *Revised Restatement of Foreign Relations* divides the subject by dealing separately with "jurisdiction to enforce" and "jurisdiction to adjudicate." [37] Jurisdiction to enforce refers to the power of a court to compel compliance with its judgments, while jurisdiction to adjudicate deals with the power to compel compliance with legal process such as subpoenas and discovery orders.

Questions of enforcement or adjudicative jurisdiction are subject to somewhat different considerations and rules than is the case for subject-matter jurisdiction, which I have discussed up to this point. For one, there is probably somewhat greater international consensus on proper rules for enforcement and adjudicative jurisdiction than there is for subject-matter jurisdiction. The FTC recently found this out in the *Saint-Gobain* litigation, where the court invoked general principles of international law to quash an investigative subpoena served upon a French company in a manner that the French government found offensive. [38] Generally speaking, the principle of territoriality will have far greater sway on questions of enforcement and adjudicative jurisdiction than it will on questions of subject-matter jurisdiction.

Further, unlike the case in disputes over subject matter jurisdiction, U.S. courts may encounter foreign statutory law that directly conflicts with their exercise of enforcement or adjudicative jurisdiction. For some decades, U.S. antitrust courts have encountered foreign blocking statutes, designed to frustrate the ability of American authorities to order discovery of documents or other evidence located within a foreign jurisdiction. [39] A more recent development has been the passage of foreign legislation that prohibits the enforcement of U.S. antitrust judgments by foreign courts. [40] And as of last year, we

37. Revised Restatement of the Foreign Relations Law of the United States § 401 (Tent. draft No. 2, 1981).

38. FTC v. Compagnie de Saint-Gobain-Pont-a-Mousson, 636 F.2d 1300 (D.C.Cir.1980).

39. E.g., Business Records Protection Act, Ont.Rev.Stat. ch. 54 (1970). A re-

cent example is the new French statute, Law No. 80–538, [1980] J.O. 1799.

40. E.g., Australia's Foreign Antitrust Judgments (Restriction of Enforcement) Act of 1979, No. 13 (1979).

now have the famous claw-back provision of the British Protection of Trading Interests Act.[41] It creates an automatic statutory cause of action under which a British firm that feels abused by a treble-damage judgment of an American court can "claw-back" two-thirds of any portion it is forced to pay in the United States. Statutes of this sort are becoming quite popular among foreign parliaments, reflecting alarmingly widespread hostility to extraterritorial orders of American courts.

So far the principal area of dispute with foreign governments has been over discovery orders, rather than over the enforcement of final judgments. Particularly in the recent flurry of suits over uranium supply contracts and the international uranium cartel,[42] questions of foreign discovery and blocking orders have dominated the attention of the courts and parties. From an outsider's perspective, I would guess that those who found themselves defending antitrust charges were substantially hurt by the foreign blocking orders, rather than benefited by them, given the sanctions which courts have shown a willingness to impose where their discovery orders went unheeded. But leaving that aside, the prolonged, sometimes bitter, and surely expensive uranium litigation is clear evidence that substantial problems remain to be solved on the vexing subject of international antitrust discovery.

II. EXPORTS

Let me now turn—finally—to matters of substance. Again, time requires that I omit detail, but a few important substantive points on both exports and imports are worth some attention.

On exports, I have already mentioned the complaints of the American business community that U.S. exports are handicapped in international trade because of the heavy burden of American antitrust. Some of these complaints seem to be exaggerated, some are not. It is interesting to note, for example, that a standard British legal text on international trade goes out of its way to warn British businessmen that, if they deal with American firms, they can expect antitrust complications even on sales to third-market countries.[43] Obviously, then, a Britisher might be inclined—for example—towards choosing a German as a joint venture partner rather than an American. This may simply be a special case of the "perception" problem—American exports are deterred not because antitrust is unduly burdensome, but because it is *perceived* to be burdensome. The result, nevertheless, is unfortunate.

41. 1980, c. 11, § 6.

42. See, e.g., In re Uranium Antitrust Litigation, 617 F.2d 1248 (7th Cir. 1980); Westinghouse Elec. Corp. Uranium Contracts Litigation, 563 F.2d 992 (10th Cir. 1977); General Atomic Co. v. Exxon Nuclear Co., Civ. No. 78-0223-E (S.D.Cal. Apr. 23, 1981) (Magistrate's Findings and Ruling on Exxon's Motion for an Order Imposing Sanctions); United Nuclear Corp. v. General Atomic Co., 629 P.2d 231 (N.M.1980), appeal dismissed, 101 S.Ct. 1966 (1981).

43. C. Schmitthoff, Export Trade 228–29 (7th ed. 1980).

Most of the concerns of American business are traceable to one fundamental uncertainty in the law. It comes down to the question whether U.S. antitrust is intended to protect foreign consumers and foreign business operating in their own home markets. I have mentioned the jurisdictional ruling in *National Bank of Canada* that anticompetitive effects within a foreign market are not, alone, sufficient to trigger Sherman Act jurisdiction.[44] But what is less clear is whether, as a matter of substantive law, the Sherman Act prohibits restraints in U.S. export trade which, let us assume, *do* limit U.S. export trade in an anticompetitive manner, but where the consequences of the restraint are felt principally in a foreign market. An example might be an agreement by two American computer companies not to export from the United States at lower than an agreed price. Let us assume that there are no "spillover" effects on the domestic market, so that the thrust of the anticompetitive agreement is felt only by foreign customers. Does the Sherman Act apply to such an export restraint?

Surprisingly, there is no clear answer to this question. Some authority would suggest that, yes, the Sherman Act does prohibit the restraint and that a foreign consumer can sue in U.S. courts for treble damages. In addition to some district court opinions along these lines,[45] the Supreme Court's decision in *Pfizer Inc. v. Government of India*[46] is some support for this proposition. The Court's ruling was a narrow one: that foreign governments are "persons" as that term is used in Section 4 of the Clayton Act treble-damage provision, but the *Pfizer* opinion contains broad language suggesting as well that foreign buyers have both standing and a legitimate antitrust grievance, under American law, when they purchase American price-fixed goods abroad. On the other side of this question, the Justice Department has maintained that the interests of foreign buyers and competitors in foreign markets should be protected principally by foreign law, and that the Sherman Act should not be extended to encompass export restraints insofar as foreign interests are at issue.[47] This view gains support from the legislative history of the Sherman Act,[48] from some very substantial policy arguments, and from judicial comments—as in *National Bank of Canada*—to the effect that voluntary restraints among American exporters are not a subject of American legal concern where the complainant is a foreign buyer or competitor.[49]

. . .

44. National Bank of Canada v. Interbank Card Ass'n, 1980–81 Trade Cas. ¶ 63,836 (2d Cir. 1981).

45. See e.g., Waldbaum v. Worldivision Enterprises, Inc., 1978–2 Trade Cas. ¶ 62,378 (S.D.N.Y.1978); Industria Siciliana Asfalti, Bitumi, S.p.A. v. Exxon Research & Engr. Co., 1977–1 Trade Cas. ¶ 61,256, 1977–2 Trade Cas. ¶ 61,636 (S.D. N.Y.1977).

46. 434 U.S. 308 (1978).

47. See, e.g., U.S. Dep't of Justice, Antitrust Division, Antitrust Guide for International Operations 4–7 (1977).

48. See 1 J. Atwood & K. Brewster, supra . . . at 22–25.

49. 1980–81 Trade Cas. at 78,472. But cf. United States v. Minnesota Mining & Mfg. Co., 92 F.Supp. 947 (D.Mass. 1950).

III. IMPORTS

On imports, some modest movement toward retrenchment can be seen in the recent cases. In what must be one of the longest judicial decisions ever written—more than 200 pages in the *Federal Supplement*—Judge Becker in March rejected a comprehensive antitrust attack by Zenith against the Japanese color television manufacturers.[50] Zenith's most predictable claim—that its Japanese competitors conspired to import televisions into the United States at predatory prices—failed for lack of proof of an agreement. A number of its other claims, such as an alleged customer allocation agreement among the Japanese producers, were rejected for lack of standing; normally, Judge Becker observed, a U.S. competitor is benefited rather than hurt if its foreign competitors agree to limit their competition in the American market.

The *Zenith* litigation, with the massive effort it represented on the plaintiff side, attests to the difficulty of using American antitrust as a means of reducing competition from importers. By contrast, the American automobile producers were successful in getting import relief through the political process, when earlier this year the Reagan Administration announced an agreement with the Japanese government that the latter would direct its producers to reduce their U.S. imports. Antitrust has not, so far at least, been an obstacle to this form of import restraint, and indeed the arrangement was the occasion for a rather unorthodox letter from the U.S. attorney general to the Japanese ambassador,[51] assuring him that Japanese companies complying with MITI [52] export directives to implement the accord would "likely" enjoy a governmental-compulsion defense if sued by an American antitrust plaintiff.

A quite different import-related arrangement [has] survived an antitrust challenge . . .   In *United States v. Westinghouse* [53] the government challenged a pattern of patent licensing agreements between Westinghouse on the one hand and two of the Japanese Mitsubishi companies on the other. It appears that Westinghouse was principally the licensor and the Japanese firms the licensees. Justice's objections were somewhat more complex than suggested in the court opinions, but as interpreted by the courts they amounted to this: the license agreements ran along national, territorial lines, such that Westinghouse licensed its rights under its Japanese patents but retained its rights under U.S. and Canadian patents to exclude competition. Since Westinghouse was regarded as dominant in the U.S. market and the Japanese firms were among the few potential entrants, and since the territorial licensing pattern served to keep the

---

50. Zenith Radio Corp. v. Matsushita Elec. Indus. Co., 513 F.Supp. 1100 (E.D. Pa.1981).

51. Letter of May 7, 1981, from Attorney General William French Smith to Ambassador Yoshio Okawara, reprinted in 1981–1 Trade Cas. ¶ 63,998.

52. Ministry of International Trade and Industry.

53. United States v. Westinghouse Elec. Corp., 648 F.2d 642 (9th Cir. 1981).

Japanese firms out of the United States, Justice claimed that the agreements unreasonably restrained U.S. imports and should be modified to requiring licensing of the U.S. patent rights.

Both the district court and . . . the Ninth Circuit found this theory unconvincing. Patent rights are national and territorial by their nature, the courts reasoned, and a patent holder's decision to license some rights but not others is unobjectionable. It would have been one thing if Westinghouse had obtained an affirmative commitment from its foreign licensees not to import into the United States, but all it had done was to license its foreign patents but not its American ones. Under these circumstances, there was no agreement preventing the imports; instead, it was the U.S. patent laws which kept Mitsubishi products at home. "[A] holder of United States patents has a right to refuse to license them," and—the court of appeals observed—"[t]he antitrust laws do not grant to the government a roving commission to reform the economy at will." [54]

CONCLUSION

While the *Westinghouse* opinion deals with a relatively narrow point—it does not, surely, legitimate territorial allocation agreements in the absence of underlying patents—it represents another instance where some of the more extravagant notions of U.S. antitrust reach and grasp have been put to rest. I return to my basic theme: We live in a complex and interdependent world, where different national laws, policies, and economic systems have to interact in a constructive and, one hopes, civil way. This in turn requires moderation by governments in applying their national laws to international transactions. As part of this process—and there are other parts I haven't even eluded to—U.S. antitrust seems to be taking a slightly lower profile in international trade. For the most part, this should be welcomed. The United States should not lose sight of the importance of competitive and open international markets, but trying to achieve that through the device of antitrust litigation can often be both futile and divisive.

NOTES AND QUERIES

(1) *Factors Influencing the Exercise of Court Authority Under the Antitrust Laws to Regulate Restraints in Foreign Commerce.* In the leading case of *Mannington Mills, Inc. v. Congoleum Corp.,*[55] a suit charging the defendant conspired with foreign firms to exclude the plaintiff from foreign markets by fraudulently obtaining patents in 26 nations, the court listed the factors to be balanced in determining whether to exercise jurisdiction over a restraint affecting foreign commerce as follows:

1. Degree of conflict with foreign law or policy;

2. Nationality of the parties;

---

54. Id. at 648. [The case is discussed further, infra p. 867.]

55. 595 F.2d 1287 (3d Cir. 1979).

3. Relative importance of the alleged violation of conduct here compared to that abroad;

4. Availability of a remedy abroad and the pendency of litigation there;

5. Existence of intent to harm or affect American commerce and its foreseeability;

6. Possible effect upon foreign relations if the court exercises jurisdiction and grants relief;

7. If relief is granted, whether a party will be placed in the position of being forced to perform an act illegal in either country or be under conflicting requirements by both countries;

8. Whether the court can make its order effective;

9. Whether an order for relief would be acceptable in this country if made by the foreign nation under similar circumstances;

10. Whether a treaty with the affected nations had addressed the issue.[56]

Commenting on *Mannington* and the other leading case on the question, *Timberlane Lumber Co. v. Bank of America*,[57] Professor Louis B. Schwartz[58] summarized the analytical methodology required as follows:

> There emerges from *Timberlane* and *Mannington* the so-called tripartite analysis of the problem of applying antitrust law to multinational trade:
>
>   i.   determining whether the challenged activity had sufficient impact on American interests to support, as a matter of international law, American legislative intervention.
>
>   ii.   balancing legitimate foreign national concerns and shared comity interests against the U.S. commitment to preserve competition, in deciding whether to exercise jurisdiction. This is the so-called "jurisdictional rule of reason."
>
>   iii.   determining, with regard to the peculiar circumstances of international trade, what constitutes an "unreasonable" restraint of trade or other violation of the antitrust laws. This, in contrast with (i) and (ii), looks toward modification of the *substantive* antitrust rules rather than limitation of jurisdiction.
>
> To the foregoing I would be inclined to add as a separate item for consideration, . . . :
>
>   iv.   determining whether legitimate foreign concerns can be adequately accommodated through modulating relief rather than "abstention" under (ii) above or ad hoc modification of well-settled rules under (iii).
>
> As a practical matter there will be a few cases that reach litigation where the substantial impact on American foreign commerce required by (i) is in doubt. I regard with suspicion abstention and judicial ventures into diplomacy implied under (ii), at least absent any intervention by our Department of State to demonstrate that our foreign relations would be jeopardized by normal judicial operations. Accordingly, I regard (iii) and

---

56. Id. at 1297-98.

57. 549 F.2d 597 (9th Cir. 1976).

58. Schwartz, American Antitrust and Trading With State Controlled Economies, 25 Antitrust Bull. 513 (1980).

(iv) as the main vehicles for judicial recognition of the special problems of international trade.[59]

(2) *The Webb Pomerene Act—U.S. Law Sanctioning Export Cartels.* To help American firms compete in foreign markets with more powerful rivals as well as bargain on equal footing with European buying cartels, the Webb-Pomerene Act of 1918[60] exempts from antitrust all "association[s] entered into for the sole purpose of engaging in export trade and actually engaged solely in such export trade" or "agreement[s] made . . . in the course of export trade by such association." To be eligible, however, the association or agreement must not be "in restraint of trade within the United States" or restrain "the export trade of any domestic competitor." The Act further provides that no such association may "artificially or intentionally" enhance or depress "prices within the United States". When an association falls short of these standards the Federal Trade Commission may "make to such association recommendations for the readjustment of its business in order that it may thereafter maintain its organization and management and conduct its business in accordance with law."

President Carter's Commission to Review the Antitrust Laws[61] made the following recommendations and analysis with regard to the Act:

Recommendations

The Webb-Pomerene exemption should be reexamined by the Congress. If it is retained, it should be amended in at least two ways:

(a) The antitrust immunity for export associations should be made contingent on a showing of particularized need.

(b) Services should be included within the Act's coverage.

Historical Background

. . .

Although the Webb-Pomerene Act has been in existence for 60 years, it has been subjected to FTC or judicial interpretation infrequently. The most significant interpretation of the Act by the FTC is contained in an advisory opinion issued in 1924, known as the "Silver Letter."[62] In that letter, the FTC declared that the membership of Webb associations could exist for the sole purpose of fixing prices and allocating sales for export markets. Most associations formed after the "Silver Letter" have limited their commercial activities to fixing prices rather than performing selling and exporting functions which are now usually handled by the individual members.[63] Thus, the common feature of export associations today is not

59. Id. at 536-7.

60. 15 U.S.C.A. §§ 61-65. See generally, Report of the Attorney General's National Committee to Study the Antitrust Laws, 109 et seq. (1955); Note, A Reexamination of Export Cartels in World Trade, 19 Va.L.Int.L. 151 (1978).

61. 1 Report to The President and The Attorney General of The National Commission For The Review of Antitrust Laws and Procedures, 295-306 (1979). See generally McDermid, The Antitrust Commission and The Webb-Pomerene Act, 37 Wash. & Lee L.Rev. 105 (1980);

Ainacher, Sweeney & Tollison, A Note on The Webb-Pomerene Law and The Webb Cartels, 23 Antitrust Bull. 371 (1978).

62. [Footnotes are from the Report and are renumbered.] See Staff Report to the Federal Trade Commission, Webb-Pomerene Associations: A 50-Year Review 102–06 (1967) [hereinafter cited as FTC Webb-Pomerene Report] (Appendix D), where the Silver Letter is reprinted in full.

63. Allison, Antitrust and Foreign Trade: Exemption for Export Associations, 11 Houston L.Rev. 1124, 1130 & n.

their performance or efficiency or cost-reducing functions, but rather the pursuit of traditional cartel-related activities.

During the 60 years of the statute's existence, only two major judicial decisions on the subject have been rendered. In *United States v. United States Alkali Export Association*,[64] the court held that the Webb Act did not immunize from antitrust prosecution cartel agreements between export associations and foreign competitors; therefore, such associations could not lawfully agree with any individual or group of foreign producers or sellers to fix prices, set quotas, or allocate customers abroad.[65]

In *United States v. Minnesota Mining and Manufacturing Co.*,[66] the court held that the Webb exemption is not available to members of an export association who jointly establish and operate manufacturing companies abroad. The greater significance of this case, however, is its identification of conduct that is permissible under the Act. In denying the Government's plea for dissolution of the defendant association, the court found that a Webb association could: (1) agree to export only through that association, (2) agree that the association would purchase goods only from member producers, (3) refuse to deal with nonmembers, (4) fix prices for goods bought for export, (5) fix prices at which foreign distributors could sell the product, (6) agree not to withdraw from the association at will, (7) require its foreign distributors to refrain from handling the relevant product of competitors, and (8) charge higher prices to American exporters than to foreign distributors.[67]

The Exemption in Practice

Despite the high expectations at the time of its enactment, it is generally agreed today that the Act has failed to promote U.S. exports materially during its 60 years of existence.[68] The hope that the antitrust exemption would result in the formation of hundreds of associations serving as joint selling agencies for small firms has not been realized.

The 1967 FTC study shows that from 1918 to 1965, there were only a total of 130 active associations registered with the FTC.[69] As of November 1978, there were only 29 active Webb associations.[70] Membership in these currently active associations consists of approximately 300 firms, although this figure includes duplications resulting from multiple association membership by some firms. More than one-third of Webb associations have four or less members, while two-thirds have nine or less members.

50 (1974); Larson, An Economic Analysis of the Webb-Pomerene Act, 13 J. Law & Econ. 461 (1970). The FTC has on several occasions studied the functions of Webb associations. In 1929, one of its studies concluded that most of the associations formed since the Silver Letter had price-setting as their primary function. This was also the finding by the FTC in studies made in 1945, 1953, and 1963. See FTC Webb-Pomerene Report, supra . . ., at 28–30, 48–49.

64. 86 F.Supp. 59 (S.D.N.Y.1949).

65. Id. at 70.

66. 92 F.Supp. 947, 963 (D.Mass. 1950).

67. Id. at 964–65.

68. See, e.g., Antitrust Commission Hearings 103 (July 27, 1978, afternoon session) (testimony of Emil Finley, President, International Commodities Export Corp.); FTC Webb-Pomerene Report, supra . . . at 23.

69. FTC Webb-Pomerene Report, supra . . . at 23.

70. Federal Trade Commission, Summary and Analysis of Survey of Webb-Pomerene Associations 6 n. 13 (Nov. 9, 1978) (staff memorandum) [hereinafter cited as 1978 FTC Survey].

The 1967 FTC study revealed that successful export associations are usually characterized by a membership consisting of the leaders of an oligopolistic industry involving a homogeneous product. The results also indicated that large firms were the most common beneficiaries of the Webb-Pomerene Act.[71] Of the 465 companies that were members of export associations during the 1958–1962 period, only 79 members (17%) had assets of one million dollars or less, and only 101 members (22%) had assets of one to five million dollars. In contrast, larger firms accounted for nearly 80 percent of all exports assisted by the Webb exemption.[72]

"One of the most striking findings" of its 1967 survey, the FTC stated, was the "comparative insignificance" of the contribution of Webb associations to total U.S. exports over the years.[73] During the 1958–1962 period, Webb-assisted exports accounted for only 2.4% of total U.S. merchandise exports.[74] In 1967 the FTC concluded that "[i]n no major area of the world is the total amount of U.S. exports increased to a significant degree by Webb-Pomerene association activity."[75] It further stated that the Webb Act provided notable assistance to only a few "[a]mong the myriad products in foreign trade channels."[76]

The latest FTC studies confirm these conclusions. Assisted exports in 1976, the latest year for which the FTC has data, were only 1.5% of the total U.S. exports, relatively one-third less than in 1962.[77]

The FTC empirical review in 1967 established that, in the majority of cases, firms seeking the antitrust exemption have been those "least in need of it, being capable of supporting export programs on their own accounts and, in fact, typically doing so."[78] Moreover, associations that have been formed basically represent only a few products of a standardized nature.

A principal criticism directed against the Webb-Pomerene Act is that Webb association activities adversely affect domestic markets.[79] Opponents of the Act argue that, by encouraging anticompetitive combinations in export trade, it invites the opportunity for similar restraints in domestic trade.[80] While there have been instances of an export agreement being overtly extended to the domestic market,[81] the more likely "spillover" effect of export associations relates to the exchange, among domestic

71. FTC Webb-Pomerene Report, supra . . . at 32–34, 44–45; see also Antitrust Commission Hearings 95 (July 27, 1978, afternoon session) (testimony of Robert P. Beshar, New York, N.Y., and former Dir., Bureau of Int'l Commerce, Dep't of Commerce); id at 105 (testimony of Emil Finley).

72. FTC Webb-Pomerene Report, supra . . . at 44.

73. Id. at 35, 42.

74. Id. at 36.

75. Id. at 42.

76. Id.

77. 1978 FTC Survey, supra . . . at 15.

78. FTC Webb-Pomerene Report, supra . . . at 59.

79. See, e.g., Larson, supra note 6, at 497–98; Diamond, The Webb-Pomerene Act and Export Trade Association, 44 Colum.L.Rev. 805, 826–32 (1944); Note, Webb-Pomerene vs. Foreign Economic Policy, 99 U.Pa.L.Rev. 1195, 1212–15 (1951).

80. See, e.g., Antitrust Commission Hearings 100 (July 27, 1978, afternoon session) (testimony of Emil Finley); Allison, supra note 6, at 1138–39; International Aspects of Antitrust, 1967: Hearings Before the Subcomm. on Antitrust and Monopoly of the Senate Comm. on the Judiciary, 90th Cong., 1st Sess. 124 (1967) (statement of Donald F. Turner, Ass't Att'y Gen., Antitrust Div., Dep't of Justice) [hereinafter cited as International Antitrust Hearings].

81. See United States v. United States Alkali Export Ass'n, 86 F.Supp. 59 (S.D. N.Y.1949).

producers in oligopolistic markets, of export information on future prices, costs, and production. The exchange of such information regarding foreign markets, all of which the Webb Act permits, can facilitate parallel pricing in the domestic market, or enable large oligopolists to coexist both at home and abroad.

Another objection is that the exemption is too broad to accomplish the stated objectives of the Act. The Sherman and Clayton Acts might not prevent the type of procompetitive joint export ventures that are set up by sellers to derive economies of scale or to create countervailing market power.[82] Furthermore, other means are available to achieve the desired results without compromising this country's basic attitudes toward competition. For example, export agents or brokers could be used to provide most, if not all, of the same services export associations were originally designed to provide.

A further criticism of the exemption is the questionable theoretical basis for allowing American firms to cartelize United States export trade.[83] A major premise of the Act was that the existence of foreign selling cartels placed domestic firms at a competitive disadvantage. It is not clear, however, why U.S. companies should be considered disadvantaged and in need of protection under such circumstances. Traditional cartel theory shows that firms operating outside of cartels often benefit from the high prices set by the cartel. A nonmember American exporter would be free to charge a lower price and take business away from the cartel. This theoretical argument is further strengthened by the fact that seldom has a Webb association member cited protection from a foreign cartel as its reason for joining the association.[84]

Finally, opponents also object that the exemption undermines United States Government credibility in advocating strong international antitrust rules.[85] As Robert Beshar, a witness appearing before the Commission, described it, "Webb-Pomerene is a bloody embarrassment" to the United States.[86] In foreign markets, U.S. Webb associations are rightly regarded as cartels. As a result, some nations have authorized the formation of national import or buying cartels to offset the market power of Webb associations.[87] Such a consequence can have an adverse effect on American competitors of the Webb association, who must then deal as individuals with the foreign import cartel.

Arguments in Favor of Retention of the Act

Supporters of the Webb exemption argue today, as they did in 1918, that there is nothing inherently anticompetitive about Webb associations and that real benefits can accrue to small manufacturers who operate in a highly concentrated market if they join together for purposes of export. The argument is advanced that many American firms continue to need today, as they did in the past, a means by which they can attempt to eliminate the economic disparity that exists between themselves individu-

82. See, e.g., International Antitrust Hearings, supra note . . . at 123 (statement of Donald F. Turner); K. Brewster, Antitrust and American Business Abroad 455 (1958).

83. Larson, supra . . . at 485.

84. Id. at 486.

85. International Antitrust Hearings, supra . . . at 124 (statement of Donald F. Turner).

86. See Antitrust Commission Hearings 97 (July 27, 1978, afternoon session) (testimony of Robert P. Beshar).

87. FTC Webb-Pomerene Report, supra . . . at 58.

ally and monopsonistic foreign buyers. The joint negotiating posture permitted by the Act might also be useful in dealing with foreign governments concerning trade or tax matters. The argument also is made that, in order for firms to compete effectively in foreign markets, they need to obtain the economies of scale achieved by their larger rivals, both domestic and foreign, and that such advantages can be provided through the use of Webb associations.

Supporters of the exemption thus maintain that the Act remains useful. It removes uncertainty concerning the legality of joint exporting arrangements and, at least for some companies, actually encourages export activity. Supporters believe the Act would be even more useful in increasing the volume of U.S. export trade, if the antitrust immunity applied to services as well as goods. It is argued that one of the main reasons the Webb Act has been underutilized is that the export of services has been excluded from the Act's exemption. Adding services to its coverage would be useful, especially to small and medium-sized companies interested in bidding on larger foreign contracts.

· · ·

Conclusions

The Commission, because of time constraints and competing priorities, was not able to examine these issues at length. While all the answers are not clear, the questions raised concerning the exemption as presently drafted are substantial. The Act as drafted creates opportunities for significant anticompetitive spillover effects in domestic commerce. It creates an adverse environment for pro-competitive diplomatic initiatives. It would seem, moreover, that the pro-competitive purposes of Webb associations could be accomplished without antitrust immunity. In short, the methodological approach utilized by the Commission, when applied to the Webb-Pomerene Act immunity, would on the current record counsel its elimination. As a result, a number of Commissioners favor outright repeal of the Act.

· · ·

If the Congress concludes that some exemption in this area is desirable, any reformulated immunity statute should be limited to situations where the public benefits outweigh the potential harms.

· · ·

To guard against the costs of any particular association outweighing any public benefits, any immunity grant should require a demonstration that the proposed association would not adversely affect either the domestic or international trade of the United States. In addition, any exemption granted should permit the President or his representative to prohibit or modify an export agreement if he finds that it may be in violation of treaties or other international obligations. The exemption could then become a bargaining tool in bilateral negotiations with other countries.

In response to the National Commission's Report, bills were introduced in the 97th Congress to expand—not abolish—export cartel antitrust immunity. The result was the "Export Trading Company Act of 1982." [88] Title III of the Act allows the Secretary of Commerce, with the concurrence of the At-

88. Pub.L.No. 97–290, 96 Stat. 1233,
15 U.S.C.A. §§ 4001–03.

torney General, to issue export trade certificates of review ("ETC's") to any applicant engaged in exporting goods or services whose operations, inter alia, will not result in a "substantial lessening of competition" within the United States or "unreasonably" affect prices within the United States. Antitrust immunity is granted for suits "based on conduct which is specified in, and complies with the terms of, a certificate." [89] Title IV of the Act establishes a more general antitrust immunity for conduct involving export trade. It provides that the Sherman Act does not apply to trade or commerce with foreign nations unless the conduct has a "direct, substantial, and reasonably foreseeable effect" on import trade or on interstate commerce. This immunity applies without regard to whether an ETC has been obtained.[90] Whether these provisions substantially clarify the application of the antitrust laws to export activities—particularly for competitors who form export cartels— will depend initially on the content of regulations drafted by the Department of Commerce. It may be that, in the absence of a total antitrust immunity, it is simply not possible to write a bill which provides the unambiguous direction that business firms desire.[91]

Queries. Would you have voted for this new legislation? Could current antitrust precedent adequately take account of whatever procompetitive effects export cartels might have? Do you see any danger, in terms of the United States' position internationally, in enacting legislation which in essence proclaims our indifference to American firms restraining competition and raising prices abroad? [92]

(3) *Antidumping Legislation—Applying Anti-price Discrimination Legislation to Imports.* The Revenue Act of 1916 [93] and the Wilson Tariff Act of 1930 [94] prohibit the systematic import of articles into the United States for sale "at a price substantially less than the actual market value or wholesale price of such articles at the time of exportation." Criminal fines and treble damage suits by injured parties are provided by the Revenue Act of 1916, while the Tariff Commission (now the International Trade Commission) is given jurisdiction by the Wilson Tariff Act to determine whether "unfair methods of competition and unfair acts in the importation of articles into the United States" are being committed. Upon finding a violation, the Commission is authorized to issue a cease and desist order and order exclusion of articles imported in violation of the Act. Other sanctions, adopted by amendments in 1976 and 1979, include the imposition of duties on articles being dumped into the United States.[95]

Worldwide recession and claims that foreign producers are dumping products at substantially lower prices on U.S. markets have generated pressures for enforcement of these otherwise neglected statutes. The cumbersome

89. See Sections 303, 306.

90. See Section 402.

91. Compare "Industry, Government Officials Question Usefulness of Export Trading Legislation," 43 ATRR 694 (1982) (critic terms bill " 'an abomination' "); "Late Addition May Prove To Be Key To Export Act," Legal Times of Wash., Oct. 11, 1982, p. 1 (asserting that firms will rely on general antitrust immunity provided by Act and not bother with certification provisions).

92. See Daishowa International v. North Coast Export Co., 1982–2 Trade Cas. ¶ 64,774 (N.D.Cal.1982) (rejecting "implied exemption" for conduct by foreign "buyers' cartel" allegedly formed to counteract efforts of plaintiff Webb-Pomerene association; no "reciprocal immunity" under Webb-Pomerene Act).

93. 15 U.S.C.A. §§ 71–74.

94. 19 U.S.C.A. §§ 1304, 1337 & 1351.

95. See Note, U.S. Legislation Import Relief Options: A Comparison of Procedures, 13 N.Y.U.J.Int'l L. & Pol. 1049 (1981).

procedures for enforcing these laws and the complexities of proving a violation have undoubtedly limited their effectiveness.

Query. Should the Sherman Act be used in cases of foreign producers dumping imports at below "cost" on U.S. markets? [96] Would such cases encounter the same difficulties uncovered in defining predatory pricing in Sherman Act § 2 cases? (See Note, *supra* p. 130).[97]

(4) *The Application of U.S. Antitrust Laws to Extraterritorial Restraints and the Doctrine of Forum Non Conveniens.* Where an extraterritorial restraint directly affects imports into the United States, a court may apply the antitrust laws to the restraint even though the situs of the conduct is wholly outside the United States. The doctrine of *forum non conveniens* is not applicable in suits under the Sherman Act.

For example, in *Industrial Investment Development Corp. v. Mitsui & Co.,*[98] an American corporation and its two Hong Kong subsidiaries sued a Japanese corporation, its American subsidiary, and an Indonesian corporation for a conspiracy to exclude the plaintiffs from harvesting trees in Borneo, Indonesia. Plaintiffs alleged the conspiracy to deprive them of a timber concession in Borneo prevented them from exporting logs from Borneo to the United States and other countries.

In reversing a district court dismissal of the complaint on a motion for summary judgment, the Court of Appeals held:

A restraint that directly or substantially affects the flow of commerce into or out of the United States is within the scope of the Sherman Act.

. . .

The competition between two American importers to obtain a source of supply on foreign territory affects the foreign commerce of the United States.

. . .

The district court agreed with defendants' contention that Indonesia was a more convenient forum for this Sherman Act suit. This conclusion was error. The common law doctrine of *forum non conveniens* is inapplicable to suits brought under the United States antitrust laws. *United States v. National City Lines, Inc.,* 334 U.S. 573, 68 S.Ct. 1169, 92 L.Ed. 1584 (1948).

In *National City Lines,* the district court dismissed a case brought under §§ 1 and 2 of the Sherman Act on the ground that another United States district court was a more convenient forum. The Supreme Court reversed, holding that the venue provisions of 15 U.S.C. § 22 leave no room for judicial discretion to apply the common law doctrine of *forum non conveniens.* Defendants argue that *National City Lines* is distinguishable because it dealt with *forum non conveniens* "in a purely venue-related context." This argument is wrong for several reasons. First, it misstates the facts of *National City Lines,* which involved a dismissal, not a change-of-venue order. Second, it misconceives the holding of *National City Lines,* which was that 15 U.S.C. § 22 was a statutory elimination of judicial discretion concerning where the case should be tried. Third, it ignores the reasons behind that holding, which apply with even

---

96. See Zenith Radio Corp. v. Matsushita Electric Industrial Co., Ltd., supra note 51.

97. Cf. Schwartz, American Antitrust and Trading With State Controlled Economies, 25 Antitrust Bull. 513, 553 (1980): "The antitrust laws are ill-adapted to policing the fairness of cheap imports."

98. 671 F.2d 876 (5th Cir. 1982).

greater force to this case. Those reasons were (1) that Congress had enacted the broad venue provisions of 15 U.S.C. § 22 to leave the choice of forum, within certain bounds, to plaintiffs' convenience, (2) that permitting the application of *forum non conveniens* "inevitably would lengthen litigation already overextended," a prophecy that has come to pass in this case; and (3) that the application of the doctrine would be difficult in antitrust cases, "in which the violations charged are nationwide or nearly so in scope and effect, and the defendants are numerous companies widely scattered in the location of their places of incorporation, principal offices, and places of carrying on business and participating in the scheme." Id. at 591, 68 S.Ct., at 1179. The holding and rationale of *National City Lines* apply fully to this case.

Even without the authority of *National City Lines*, we would reach the conclusion that antitrust cases cannot be dismissed on the ground that a foreign country is a more convenient forum. Sections 1 and 2 of the Sherman Act do not by their terms purport to define civil obligations owed by one party to another; they make it felonious to restrain unreasonably or to monopolize the commerce of the United States. The treble damages action created for "private attorneys general" by § 4 of the Clayton Act, while "designed primarily as a remedy," is designed at least in part to "penaliz[e] wrongdoers and deter [ ] wrongdoing." Since it is a well-established principle of international law that "[t]he Courts of no country execute the penal laws of another," we have little doubt that the Indonesian courts would quite properly refuse to entertain plaintiffs' Sherman Act claim. A dismissal for *forum non conveniens*, then, would be the functional equivalent of a decision that defendants' acts are beyond the reach of the Sherman Act. Defendants cannot use the rules of *forum non conveniens* as a substitute for the rules concerning the extraterritorial application of the Act.

Queries. What are the consequences of this decision? Does it make any sense to litigate the merits of a controversy taking place wholly within Indonesia in a U.S. court because of allegations that it has some effects on U.S. imports? Should there be a requirement that the effect on U.S. imports be substantial and a preliminary inquiry on the effect question be held before the Court permits the case to continue? [99]

2. THE ACT OF STATE DOCTRINE [1]

Unlike the state action defense which is utilized to resolve conflicts between two domestic sovereigns, the act of state doctrine aids

---

99. See National Bank of Canada v. Inter-Bank Card Association, supra note 27.

1. See generally 1 P. Areeda & D. Turner, Antitrust Law, 272–78 (1978); J. Atwood & K. Brewster, Antitrust and American Business Abroad (2d Ed. 1981); W. Fugate, Foreign Commerce and The Antitrust Laws (2d Ed. 1973); Department of Justice, Antitrust Guide for International Operations (1977); Crocker, Sovereign Immunity and the Suit Against OPEC, 12 Case West.L.J. 215 (1980); Hawk, Act of State Doctrine, Noerr-Pennington Abroad and Foreign Government Compulsion Defense, 47 Antitrust L.J.

987 (1978); Meal, Governmental Compulsion and European Community Antitrust Law, 20 Colum.J.Trans.L. 51 (1981); Rahl, Antitrust and International Transactions—Recent Developments, 46 Antitrust L.J. 965 (1978); Schwartz, Arab Boycott and The American Responses: Antitrust Law or Executive Discretion, 54 Tex.L.Rev. 1260 (1976); Schwartz, Antitrust and Trading with State Controlled Economies, 25 Antitrust Bull. 513 (1980); Timburg, Sovereign Immunity and The Act of State Defenses: Transnational Boycotts and Economic Coercion, 55 Tex. L.Rev. 1 (1976); Note, The Act of State Doctrine: The Need for a Commercial

in the delineation of the scope of international and extraterritorial applications of the U.S. antitrust laws vis-a-vis the law of some other nation-state. Although the legal grey areas arising in this field are prolific, the original "black letter" act of state doctrine suggests that courts will decline to adjudicate issues that would require them to scrutinize the public acts of a foreign sovereign within its own territory.[2] The doctrine, however, is not generally applied to acts not performed exclusively within the foreign sovereign's territory [3] and to acts taking place wholly within a foreign state but not mandated by the foreign sovereign.[4]

The act of state doctrine has been characterized as an aspect of international "comity" and of the constitutional allocation of foreign relations responsibility to the Executive. "Comity," in a legal sense, is neither a matter of absolute obligation on the one hand nor mere courtesy and good will on the other.[5] It is a doctrine of self-imposed courtesy and deference, not a binding rule of law. To the extent the act of state doctrine is founded upon the exclusive power of the Executive over foreign affairs, however, it takes on the characteristics of a rule of law and is not merely a matter of judicial self restraint and deference.

The act of state doctrine was spelled out by the Ninth Circuit in *International Association of Machinists & Aerospace Workers v. The Organization of Petroleum Exporting Countries (OPEC)*,[6] where the Court of Appeals upheld dismissal of the union's antitrust suit charging that OPEC violated section 1 of the Sherman Act by fixing the price of imported oil. The Court of Appeals refused to consider the case on the basis of a claim of sovereign immunity,[7] but dismissed on the basis of the act of state doctrine, stating:

Exception in Antitrust Litigation, 18 San Diego L.Rev. 813 (1981); Note, Sherman Act Litigation: A Generic Approach to Objective Territorial Jurisdiction and the Act of State Doctrine, 84 Dick.L.Rev. 645 (1980); Note, The Applicability of the Antitrust Laws to International Cartels Involving Foreign Governments, 91 Yale L.J. 765 (1982).

2. Section 41 of The Restatement (Second) of Foreign Relations Law of the United States provides:

§ 41. Act of Foreign State: General Rule. Except as otherwise provided by statute or the rules stated in §§ 42 and 43, a court in the United States, having jurisdiction under the rule stated in § 19 to determine a claim asserted against a person in the United States or with respect to a thing located there, or other interest localized there, will refrain from examining the validity of an act of a foreign state by which that state has exercised its jurisdiction to give effect to its public interests.

See also Hovenkamp, Can A Foreign Sovereign Be An Antitrust Defendant?, 32 Syr.L.Rev. 879 (1980).

3. See United Nuclear Corp. v. General Atomic Co., 1980–81 Trade Cases ¶ 63,639 (N.M.S.Ct.1980), certiorari denied 444 U.S. 911, 100 S.Ct. 222, 62 L.Ed. 2d 145 (1979); Hunt v. Mobil Oil Corp., 550 F.2d 68 (2d Cir. 1977).

4. See Industrial Investment Development Corp. v. Mitsui & Co., Ltd., 594 F.2d 48 (5th Cir. 1979), certiorari denied 445 U.S. 903, 100 S.Ct. 1078, 63 L.Ed.2d 318 (1980).

5. See Lowenfeld, Book Review, Antitrust, Interest Analysis and The New Conflict of Laws, 95 Harv.L.Rev. 1976 (1982).

6. 649 F.2d 1354 (9th Cir. 1981), certiorari denied 454 U.S. 1163, 102 S.Ct. 1036, 71 L.Ed.2d 319 (1982).

7. Id. at 1355–58. The trial court dismissed on this basis, but the Court of Appeals refused to be drawn into the problem of characterizing the acts in question (fixing oil prices) as within or without the

The act of state doctrine declares that a United States court will not adjudicate a politically sensitive dispute which would require the court to judge the legality of the sovereign act of a foreign state. This doctrine was expressed by the Supreme Court in *Underhill v. Hernandez*, 168 U.S. 250, 252, 18 S.Ct. 83, 84, 42 L.Ed. 456 (1897):

> Every sovereign State is bound to respect the independence of every other sovereign State, and the courts of one country will not sit in judgment on the acts of the government of another done within its own territory.

The doctrine recognizes the institutional limitations of the courts and the peculiar requirements of successful foreign relations. To participate adeptly in the global community, the United States must speak with one voice and pursue a careful and deliberate foreign policy. The political branches of our government are able to consider the competing economic and political considerations and respond to the public will in order to carry on foreign relations in accordance with the best interests of the country as a whole. . . .

While the act of state doctrine has no explicit source in our Constitution or statutes, it does have "constitutional underpinnings." *Banco Nacional de Cuba v. Sabbatino*, 376 U.S. 398, 423, 84 S.Ct. 923, 937, 11 L.Ed.2d 804 (1964). The Supreme Court has stated that the act of state doctrine

> arises out of the basic relationships between branches of government in a system of separation of powers . . . .. The doctrine as formulated in past decisions expresses the strong sense of the Judicial Branch that its engagement in the task of passing on the validity of foreign acts of state may hinder rather than further this country's pursuit of goals both for itself and for the community of nations as a whole in the international sphere. Id.

. . .

The doctrine of sovereign immunity is similar to the act of state doctrine in that it also represents the need to respect the sovereignty of foreign states. The two doctrines differ, however, in significant respects. The law of sovereign immunity goes to the jurisdiction of the court. The act of state doctrine is not jurisdictional. *Ricaud v. American Metal Co.*, 246 U.S. 304, 309, 38 S.Ct. 312, 313, 62 L.Ed. 733 (1918). Rather, it is a prudential doctrine designed to avoid judicial action in sensitive areas. Sovereign immunity is a principle of international law, recognized in the United States by statute. It is the states themselves, as defendants, who may claim sovereign immunity. The act of state doctrine is a domestic legal principle, arising from the peculiar role of American courts. It recognizes not only the sovereignty of for-

"commercial activity" exception to the Foreign Sovereign Immunities Act, 28 U.S.C.A. § 1603(d). See discussion of the Act, infra p. 869.

eign states, but also the spheres of power of the co-equal branches of our government. Thus a private litigant may raise the act of state doctrine, even when no sovereign state is a party to the action. See, e.g., *Timberlane Lumber Co. v. Bank of America*, 549 F.2d 597, 606 (9th Cir. 1976). The act of state doctrine is not diluted by the commercial activity exception which limits the doctrine of sovereign immunity. While purely commercial [8] activity may not rise to the level of an act of state, certain seemingly commercial activity will trigger act of state considerations. As the district court noted, OPEC's "price-fixing" activity has a significant sovereign component. . . . This court has stated that the motivations of the sovereign must be examined for a public interest basis. *Timberlane*, 549 F.2d at 607. When the state *qua state* acts in the public interest, its sovereignty is asserted. The courts must proceed cautiously to avoid an affront to that sovereignty. Because the act of state doctrine and the doctrine of sovereign immunity address different concerns and apply in different circumstances, we find that the act of state doctrine remains available when such caution is appropriate, regardless of any commercial component of the activity involved.

In addition to the public interest factor, a federal court must heed other indications which call for act of state deference. The doctrine does not suggest a rigid rule of application. In the *Sabbatino* case, the Supreme Court suggested a balancing approach:

> some aspects of international law touch more sharply on national nerves than do others; the less important the implications of an issue are for our foreign relations, the weaker the justification for exclusivity in the political branches. 376 U.S., at 428, 84 S.Ct., at 940.

· · ·

A further consideration is the availability of internationally-accepted legal principles which would render the issues appropriate for judicial disposition. As the Supreme Court stated in *Sabbatino*,

> It should be apparent that the greater the degree of codification or consensus concerning a particular area of international law, the more appropriate it is for the judiciary to render decisions regarding it, since the courts can then focus on the application of an agreed principle to circumstances of fact rather than on the sensitive task of establishing a principle not inconsistent with the national interest or with international justice. 376 U.S., at 428, 84 S.Ct., at 940.

---

8. [Court's footnote 8]. In Alfred Dunhill of London, Inc. v. Cuba, 425 U.S. 682, 698, 96 S.Ct. 1854, 1863, 48 L.Ed.2d 301 (1976), the court held that purely commercial activity does not require judicial deference under the act of state doctrine. The Dunhill case suggested but did not decide the question of whether the act of state doctrine is subsumed by the doctrine of sovereign immunity. Compare opinion of Justice White, 425 U.S. 682, 705 at n. 18, 96 S.Ct. 1854, 1866 at n. 18, 48 L.Ed.2d 301, with Justice Marshall's dissent, 425 U.S., at 725–728, 96 S.Ct., at 1875.

While conspiracies in restraint of trade are clearly illegal under domestic law, the record reveals no international consensus condemning cartels, royalties, and production agreements. The United States and other nations have supported the principle of supreme state sovereignty over natural resources. The OPEC nations themselves obviously will not agree that their actions are illegal. We are reluctant to allow judicial interference in an area so void of international consensus. An injunction against OPEC's alleged price-fixing activity would require condemnation of a cartel system which the community of nations has thus far been unwilling to denounce. The admonition in *Sabbatino* that the courts should consider the degree of codification and consensus in the area of law is another indication that judicial action is inappropriate here.[9]

NOTES AND QUERIES

(1) *The Rationale of the Act of State Doctrine.* The theoretical foundation that buttresses the act of state doctrine is multifaceted and has been shifting. There has been a shift in focus from the notions of sovereignty and the dignity of independent nations,[10] to concerns for preserving the "basic relationships between branches of government in a system of separation of powers" and not hindering the executive's conduct of foreign policy by judicial review of foreign acts.[11] More recently, the doctrine has garnered new support from various theories of comity, conflicts of law and interest analysis.[12]

The conflict of laws approach "meshes the jurisdictional question with the issue of justiciability, i.e., whether jurisdiction should be exercised."[13] Does this task make the analysis of the case more difficult? Cf. *Mannington Mills, Inc. v. Congoleum Corp.,*[14] (discussed supra p. 854) in which the court clearly asks the questions (jurisdiction and justiciability) separately but finds unavoidable overlapping of analysis in reaching a decision. Judge Adams, in his concurring opinion in *Mannington* takes exception to the view that "a court may conclude that it is invested with subject matter jurisdiction under the Sherman Act but may nonetheless abstain from exercising such jurisdiction in deference to considerations of international comity."[15] He continues "rather, it seems that those considerations are properly to be weighed at the outset when the court determines whether jurisdiction *vel non* exists . . .

9. 649 F.2d at 1358–62. See generally Crocker, Sovereign Immunity and The Suit Against OPEC, 12 Case West.L.J. 215 (1980); Hovenkamp, Can A Foreign Sovereign Be An Antitrust Defendant?, 32 Syracuse L.Rev. 879 (1981); Note, Act of State Doctrine Applied As a Bar to Antitrust Suit Against Foreign Sovereigns, 17 Tex.Int.L.J. 82 (1982); Note, The Applicability of The Antitrust Laws to International Cartels Involving Foreign Governments, 91 Yale L.J. 765 (1982).

10. See American Banana Co. v. United Fruit Co., 213 U.S. 347, 29 S.Ct. 511, 53 L.Ed. 826 (1909).

11. See Banco Nacional de Cuba v. Sabbatino, 376 U.S. 398, 84 S.Ct. 923, 11 L.Ed.2d 804 (1964).

12. See Mannington Mills, Inc. v. Congoleum Corp., 595 F.2d 1287, 1292 (3d Cir. 1979).

13. See J. O. von Kalinowski, 1 Antitrust Laws & Trade Reg. § 5.02 (1982).

14. 595 F.2d 1287 (3d Cir. 1979).

15. Id. at 1299.

and that possible repercussions abroad should be examined by the court when and if it formulates a remedy." [16]

Query. Do you agree?

(2) *Identifying "Acts" as Acts of State.* "Several types of public acts warrant act of state status. Nationalization and expropriation decrees traditionally have been regarded as acts of state. In general courts also have considered legislative enactments, regulatory decrees and the executive use of police power to be acts of state." [17] Nevertheless, ambiguity can arise in activities involving or related to the actions of a government.

In *Timberlane Lumber Co. v. Bank of America,*[18] plaintiff's milling operations were completely shut down subject to a Honduran court-ordered attachment, and the Ninth Circuit determined such a court order arising from the dispute between private parties was not sufficient evidence of an act of state.[19] In *Mannington,* the Third Circuit decided that an issuance of a foreign patent was also not an act of state but only a "ministerial" act.[20] The scope of the doctrine can contract or expand depending on what a court will consider an "act" for act of state purposes, just as the scope of the state action doctrine depends on the factors a court will consider in characterizing activity *state* action activity.[21] Some have construed *Mannington* as potentially restricting the act of state doctrine dramatically by applying semantic distinctions to state regulatory acts.[22]

(3) *Applicability of Doctrine When the Act of a State Violates International Law.* A further issue on the scope of the doctrine arose in *Banco Nacional de Cuba v. Sabbatino,*[23] as to whether the act of state doctrine is applicable where the act of the foreign sovereign is allegedly in violation of a rule of international law.[24] The Supreme Court held that the act of state doctrine prohibited a challenge to the validity of a Cuban expropriation decree by which the Cuban plaintiff acquired certain sugar belonging to a Cuban corporation whose stock was principally owned by United States residents. In affirming the applicability of act of state doctrine, notwithstanding the alleged violation of international law, the Court weighed "the following factors: (1) the degree of international consensus on the applicable international law . . . , (2) the ability of the courts to aid the executive in providing a fair and adequate remedy for the aggrieved United States citizen; (3) the likelihood of disagreement between the executive and the judiciary over the disposition of the case; and (4) the danger that adjudication would have severe foreign relation repercussions." [25] Following the Court's decision, however, "Congress legislated an important exception to the doctrine in cases involving acts of state in violation of international law." [26]

---

16. Id.

17. Note, The Act of State Doctrine and U.S. Antitrust Law, 12 Law and Policy Int.Bus. 503, 510 (1980).

18. 549 F.2d 597 (9th Cir. 1976).

19. Id. at 608.

20. 595 F.2d at 1294.

21. See discussion of state action, supra p. 810.

22. Note, The Act of State Doctrine and the U.S. Antitrust Law, 12 Law and Policy in Int.Bus. 503, 508, 515 (1980).

23. 376 U.S. 398, 84 S.Ct. 923, 11 L.Ed.2d 804 (1964).

24. See Note, Act of State Doctrine Applied as a Bar to Antitrust Suit Against Foreign Sovereigns, 17 Texas Int.Law J. 82, 86 n. 21 (1982).

25. Note, The Applicability of Antitrust Laws to International Cartels Involving Foreign Governments, 91 Yale L.J. 765, 783 (1982).

26. "The Hickenlooper Amendment to the Foreign Assistance Act of 1965, 22 U.S.C. § 2370(e)(2) (1976), attempted to reverse *Sabbatino's* holding that the act of state doctrine applies even though the act is allegedly in violation of international law. The amendment provides that, subject to certain exceptions, the act of

(4) *The Sovereign Compulsion Defense.* The sovereign compulsion defense is a corrollary to the act of state defense, in the sense that it provides a private party, not an instrumentality of a foreign state, a means for defending its conduct on the ground that its challenged activity was compelled by a foreign sovereign. This defense was successfully invoked in *Interamerican Refining Corp. v. Texaco Maracaibo, Inc.*,[27] in which the defendant was coerced to participate in a boycott imposed by the Venezuelan government that prohibited the sale of Venezuelan crude oil to the plaintiffs. The court stated that "when a nation compels a trade practice, firms there have no choice to obey. Acts of business become effectively acts of the sovereign." [28]

Query. Should sovereign compulsion of a private party to engage in conduct violating U.S. law be a defense?

(5) *Sovereign Immunities Defense and the Foreign Sovereign Immunities Act.* While the act of state doctrine is a limitation on the subject matter available for scrutiny under the antitrust laws, the doctrine of foreign sovereign immunity has been described as a limitation on the jurisdiction of the court,[29] and has been likened to an issue of personal jurisdiction. The concepts are closely related but not altogether congruent. Sovereign immunity is defined by statute, the Foreign Sovereign Immunity Act of 1976,[30] which contains an affirmative declaration of the substantive law permitting as well as limiting jurisdiction, namely, that a foreign state is liable for commercial activities "in the same manner and to the same extent as a private individual under like circumstances."

That limitation on the sovereign immunities defense was further spelled out by § 1605(a) of the Act as follows:

A foreign state shall not be immune from the jurisdiction of the courts of the United States or of the States in any case . . . (2) in which the action is based upon commercial activity carried on in the United States by the foreign state; or upon an act performed in the United States in connection with the commercial activity of the foreign state elsewhere; or upon an act outside the territory of the United States in connection with the commercial activity of the foreign state elsewhere and that act causes a direct effect in the United States." [31]

Section 1606 of the act provides:

As to any claim for relief with respect to which a foreign state is not entitled to immunity . . . the foreign state shall be liable in the same manner and to the same extent as a private individual under like circumstances; but a foreign state except for an agency or instrumentality thereof shall not be liable for punitive damages. . . .[32]

state doctrine is not to be used to prevent federal courts from examining a confiscation or other taking in violation of international law. Id. See Restatement (Second) of Foreign Relations Law of the United States § 41, comment b (1965)." The Act of State Doctrine and U.S. Antitrust Law, 12 Law and Policy in Int.Bus. 503, 511 n. 49 (1980).

27. 307 F.Supp. 1291 (D.Del.1970).

28. Id. at 1298.

29. See Schwartz, Antitrust and Trading with State Controlled Economies, 25 Antitrust Bull. 513, 539 (1980).

30. 28 U.S.C.A. §§ 1330, 1332, 1391, 1441, 1602–1611. The legislative history of the Act is reported in 1976 U.S.Code Cong. & Ad.News 6604, 6617. See generally Kahole & Vega, Immunity and Jurisdiction: Toward a Uniform Body of Law In Actions Against Foreign States, 18 Colum.J.Transnat'l L. 211 (1979); Kane, Suing Foreign Sovereigns: A Procedural Compass, 34 Stan.L.Rev. 385 (1982).

31. 28 U.S.C.A. § 1605.

32. 28 U.S.C.A. § 1606.

Section 1603(d) of the Act defines commercial activity as "either a regular course of commercial conduct or a particular commercial transaction or act. The commercial character of an activity shall be determined by reference to the nature of the course of conduct or particular transaction or act, rather than by reference to its purpose." [33]

In *Outboard Marine Corp. v. Pezetel* [34] an American golfcart producer brought suit against a Polish golfcart exporter and U.S. distributors under Sections 1 and 2 of the Sherman Act.[35] The Polish exporter claimed immunity on the ground that the activity was that of the sovereign because Poland has a state controlled economy and subsidized the industry. The judge by-passed the question of distinguishing Pezetel from Poland. Proceeding on the assumption of the identity of Pezetel with Poland, the court held that even a sovereign was subject to the antitrust laws when engaged in commercial activity, and that under the literal terms of the FSIA, the commercial character of Pezetel's activities must be determined by reference to the transaction itself "rather than by reference to its purpose." [36] Cf. *International Association of Machinists v. Organization of Petroleum Exporting Countries*,[37] (discussed supra p. 864), in which District Judge Hauk's opinion indicated that the association of foreign sovereigns represented by OPEC were immune from antitrust scrutiny notwithstanding the commercial underpinning of their challenged activities.[38]

It should be noted that the "use of the word 'person' in the antitrust law did not create a 'hard and fast rule of exclusion' of governmental bodies." [39] Nor did the Foreign Sovereign Immunities Act, which clearly expressed that Congress intended that "foreign sovereigns can sometimes be defendants in litigation in American courts with respect to their commercial activities," contemplate exclusion of a foreign sovereign's commercial activity from judicial scrutiny under the antitrust laws.[40] Nevertheless it has been argued that the antitrust laws are "ill-adapted" to coping with even the commercial activities of sovereign nation.[41]

Queries. Do you agree? What alternatives are available? [42]

33. 28 U.S.C.A. § 1603(d).

34. 461 F.Supp. 384 (D.Del.1978). The case is discussed in Schwartz, supra note 31.

35. The action was also based on the Wilson Tariff Act and the Antidumping Act of 1916, discussed supra p. 861.

36. 461 F.Supp. at 395. See also National American Corp. v. Federal Republic of Nigeria, 448 F.Supp. 622, 641 (S.D. N.Y.1978).

37. 477 F.Supp. 553, 572 (C.D.Cal. 1979), affirmed on other grounds 649 F.2d 1354 (9th Cir. 1981), certiorari denied 454 U.S. 1163, 102 S.Ct. 1036, 71 L.Ed.2d 319 (1982).

38. See Hovenkamp, Can A Foreign Sovereign be an Antitrust Defendant?, 32 Syracuse L.Rev. 879, 889 (1981).

39. Pfizer v. Government of India, 434 U.S. 308, 98 S.Ct. 584, 54 L.Ed.2d 563 (concluding the foreign sovereign could be a "person" for purposes of Section 4 of the Clayton Act.)

40. Hovenkamp, supra note 40 at 894–897.

41. Schwartz, supra note 31 at 553.

42. See Wilson Tariff Act discussion supra p. 861.

Chapter 8

PRICE DISCRIMINATION

A. INTRODUCTION; LEGISLATIVE TEXTS

Statutory provisions forbidding price discrimination have been part of our national economic policy since 1887, when Congress established the Interstate Commerce Commission and banned "unjust discrimination" in railroad rates—i.e., charging different rates to different persons for "a like and contemporaneous service in the transportation of a like kind of traffic under substantially similar circumstances and conditions."[1] Subsequent legislation, enacted in 1903 and 1906, strengthened this prohibition.[2] This legislation reflected widespread concern that railroad rates were "unfair," in part because large shippers (such as Standard Oil) were able to obtain lower rates than their competitors. Not only was this condemned as inequitable; lower rates were also seen as the foundation of monopoly power for the recipient.[3]

Congress enacted the first general prohibitions on price discrimination in 1914, in Section 2 of the Clayton Act. This part of the Clayton Act, like others previously studied,[4] was intended to strengthen the Sherman Act to make clear that certain practices would be considered unlawful. The debate over price discrimination here emphasized its use as a method for a discriminating seller to strategically build monopoly by engaging in localized price cutting designed to eliminate competition (termed "primary-line" discrimination, because the effects on competition are felt at the seller's level). As one commentator of the time wrote, "[l]ocal price-cutting has been a frequent and familiar weapon of the trusts," citing particularly the record before the Supreme Court in the monopolization case against Standard Oil in

1. "An Act to Regulate Commerce," ch. 104, § 2, 24 Stat. 379 (1887). Section 3 made unlawful any "undue or unreasonable preference" to any person, locality, or "particular description of traffic"; section 4 forbade charging more for a shorter haul than a longer haul. The problem of price discrimination in regulated industries is explored further in Schwartz, Flynn & First, Free Enterprise and Economic Organization: Government Regulation (6th Ed. 1983).

2. See Elkins Act, ch. 708, 32 Stat. 847 (1903); Hepburn Act, ch. 3591, 34 Stat. 584 (1906).

3. See, e.g., Report of the Attorney General of the United States 10–11 (1906) (railroad discriminations "have been one efficient cause in building up the combinations called trusts"; discussing increased criminal prosecutions for rebating under 1903 Act); Scofield v. Lake Shore & Michigan Southern Railway Co., 43 Ohio St. 571, 609, 3 N.E. 907, 923 (1885) (suit by competing shippers protesting discriminatory rates given Standard Oil).

4. See Chs. 3 (mergers) and 6 (exclusive dealing and tying), supra.

which Standard's willingness to engage in local price cutting was detailed.[5]

Congress has continued to legislate against discriminatory rates in industries whose prices it regulates.[6] In 1936 Congress strengthened Section 2 of the Clayton Act by passing the Robinson-Patman Act amendments, which were intended to deal more fully with "secondary-line" discrimination (i.e., price discrimination whose competitive effects are felt at the buyer's level).[7] Despite this long record of legislative condemnation, however, doubts persist as to the wisdom of outlawing price discrimination. A seller cutting prices to consumers in selected markets is likely doing so in response to localized competition from other sellers. Why forbid this responsive pricing, unless, perhaps, Section 2 of the Sherman Act is violated? Similarly, a seller cutting prices to only some ("large") buyer/distributors is likely responding to the buyer's competitive threat to take its business elsewhere. Why forbid giving a lower price, particularly if the effect of the prohibition may be to keep the price up at the level of the "inefficient" smaller distributors? Indeed, discriminatory price concessions (sometimes secret) can constitute an important dynamic force for disrupting oligopoly price structures. A buyer offered a price or service concession by one seller is in a position to secure the same or better from other sellers. Other buyers learn about it and insist on comparable reductions; and so the price reduction may become general. A law against price discrimination may thus tend to produce that rigidity in prices against which the antitrust laws were, in part, directed. (Note that the early legislation strengthening prohibitions on price discrimination by railroads was supported by the railroads themselves, to enable them to better resist shipper pressures for lower rates.[8])

To state the criticisms of a law prohibiting discriminatory prices does not settle the debate over the wisdom of such legislation. Can legislators (and judges interpreting the statute) ignore the apparent historical evidence that firms have strategically used discriminatory prices to thwart local competition?[9] Is it possible that discriminatory

5. Stevens, Unfair Competition, 29 Pol.Sci.Quar. 282, 284 (1914). Stevens' article was widely quoted in the debate over the Federal Trade Commission and Clayton Acts.

6. See, e.g., Shipping Act of 1916, 46 U.S.C.A. § 812 First; Motor Carrier Act of 1935, 49 U.S.C.A. § 317(b); Federal Aviation Act of 1958, 49 U.S.C.A. § 1374(b). States generally prohibit regulated utilities from engaging in unreasonable price discrimination.

7. Although the original language of Section 2 of the Clayton Act was not apparently limited to primary-line discrimination (see n. 11, p. 873 infra), it was not until 1929 that the Supreme Court made clear that secondary-line discrimination was covered. See George Van Camp &

Sons v. American Can Co., 278 U.S. 245, 49 S.Ct. 112, 73 L.Ed. 311 (1929).

8. See G. Kolko, Railroads and Regulation 94–101 (1965).

9. For recent evidence of this practice, see Borden, Inc. v. Federal Trade Commission, 674 F.2d 498 (6th Cir. 1982) (affirming FTC's finding that Borden violated Section 2 of the Sherman Act by engaging in localized predatory pricing targeted at a growing competitor), petition for certiorari filed 51 U.S.L.W. 3150 (Aug. 25, 1982); 44 ATRR 521 (1983) (proposed settlement, weakening order upheld by court of appeals; forbids pricing that would yield "net revenue during any fiscal quarter for any sales district below Respondent's variable cost").

price concessions to large buyers disadvantage otherwise more efficient smaller firms?   What of the Congressionally expressed policy to preserve "equality of opportunity" by allowing all distributors at the same functional level to "start on equal competitive footing"? [10]

This chapter is designed to explore the basic policy issues raised by a statutory ban on price discrimination.   The materials are organized as follows: First is the text of the relevant provisions of Section 2 of the Clayton Act, as amended by the Robinson-Patman Act, followed by Notes exploring several elements of a violation of the statute.   Section B of the chapter focuses in greater depth on the question of competitive injury, and buyer liability.   Section C explores the defenses of cost justification and meeting competition.

SECTION 2 OF THE CLAYTON ACT AS AMENDED BY THE ROBINSON–PATMAN ACT OF 1936 [11]

15 U.S.C.A. § 13.

Sec. 2(a).   (*Price*) **It shall be unlawful for any person engaged in commerce, in the course of such commerce, either directly or indirectly, to discriminate in price between different purchasers of commodities of like grade and quality, where either or any of the purchases involved in such discrimination are in commerce, where such commodities are sold for use, consumption, or resale within the United States or any territory thereof or the District of Columbia or any insular possession or other place under the jurisdiction of the United States, and where the effect of such discrimination may be substantially to lessen competition or tend to create a monopoly in any line of commerce, or to injure, destroy, or prevent competition with any person who either grants or knowingly receives the benefit of such discrimination, or with customers of either of them:** *Provided,* **That nothing herein contained shall prevent differentials which make only due allowance for differences in the cost of manufacture, sale, or delivery resulting from the differing methods or quantities in which such commodities are to such purchasers sold or delivered. . . .**

---

10. Federal Trade Commission v. Sun Oil Co., 371 U.S. 505, 520, 83 S.Ct. 358, 9 L.Ed.2d 466 (1963) (citing House Committee Report relating "guiding ideal" of the Robinson-Patman Act amendments to the Clayton Act).

11. Prior to the Robinson-Patman Act amendments, Section 2 of the Clayton Act provided:

Sec. 2.   That it shall be unlawful for any person engaged in commerce, in the course of such commerce, either directly or indirectly to discriminate in price between different purchasers of commodities, which commodities are sold for use, consumption, or resale within the United States or any Territory thereof or the District of Columbia or any insular possession or other place under the jurisdiction of the United States, where the effect of such discrimination may be to substantially lesssen competition or tend to create a monopoly in any line of commerce: Provided, That nothing herein contained shall prevent discrimination in price between purchasers of commodities on account of differences in the grade, quality, or quantity of the commodity sold, or that makes only due allowance for difference in the cost of selling or transportation, or discrimination in price in the same or different communities made in good faith to meet competition: And provided further, That nothing herein contained shall prevent persons engaged in selling goods, wares, or merchandise in commerce from selecting their own customers in bona fide transactions and not in restraint of trade.

Sec. 2(b). **Upon proof being made, at any hearing on a complaint under this section, that there has been discrimination in price or services or facilities furnished, the burden of rebutting the prima-facie case thus made by showing justification shall be upon the person charged with a violation of this section, and unless justification shall be affirmatively shown, the Commission is authorized to issue an order terminating the discrimination:** *Provided, however,* **That nothing herein contained shall prevent a seller rebutting the prima-facie case thus made by showing that his lower price or the furnishing of services or facilities to any purchaser or purchasers was made in good faith to meet an equally low price of a competitor, or the services or facilities furnished by a competitor.**

Sec. 2(c). *(Paying or accepting commission brokerage or other compensation)* **It shall be unlawful for any person engaged in commerce, in the course of such commerce, to pay or grant, or to receive or accept, anything of value as a commission, brokerage, or other compensation, or any allowance or discount in lieu thereof, except for services rendered in connection with the sale or purchase of goods, wares, or merchandise, either to the other party to such transaction or to an agent, representative, or other intermediary therein where such intermediary is acting in fact for or in behalf, or is subject to the direct or indirect control, of any party to such transaction other than the person by whom such compensation is so granted or paid.**

Sec. 2(d). *(Paying Selected Buyers for Services and Facilities)* **It shall be unlawful for any person engaged in commerce to pay or contract for the payment of anything of value to or for the benefit of a customer of such person in the course of such commerce as compensation or in consideration for any services or facilities furnished by or through such customer in connection with the processing, handling, sale, or offering for sale of any products or commodities manufactured, sold, or offered for sale by such person, unless such payment or consideration is available on proportionally equal terms to all other customers competing in the distribution of such products or commodities.**

Sec. 2(e). *(Providing Services and Facilities to Selected Buyers)* **It shall be unlawful for any person to discriminate in favor of one purchaser against another purchaser or purchasers of a commodity bought for resale, with, or without processing, by contracting to furnish or furnishing, or by contributing to the furnishing of, any services or facilities connected with the processing, handling, sale, or offering for sale of such commodity so purchased upon terms not accorded to all purchasers on proportionally equal terms.**

Sec. 2(f). **It shall be unlawful for any person engaged in commerce, in the course of such commerce, knowingly to induce or receive a discrimination in price which is prohibited by this section.**

NOTES AND QUERIES

(1) *Bibliography.* On discrimination under the antitrust laws, see ABA Antitrust Section, the Robinson-Patman Act (vol. I 1980) (a useful monograph reviewing the policy arguments and case law, plus bibliography); Dirlam & Kahn, Fair Competition (1954); Oppenheim and Weston, The Lawyer's Robinson-Patman Act Sourcebook (1971); Kintner, A Robinson-Patman

Primer (1970); Baxter, A Parable, 23 Stan.L.Rev. 973 (1961) (wittily exploring some amazing paradoxes of prohibiting price discrimination in the Land of Oz); Cooper, Price Discrimination Law and Economic Efficiency, 75 Mich. L.Rev. 972 (1978).   The Department of Justice, in 1977, released a 320 page report setting out then-current views on the Robinson-Patman Act, its legislative history, and a critical evaluation of the economic assumptions underlying the statute.   For foreign developments, see Grant, Recent Developments in the Control of Price Discrimination in Countries Outside North America, 26 Antitrust Bull. 593 (1981).

(2) *Jurisdictional Scope.*   The commerce referred to in the Robinson-Patman Act is interstate, foreign and other commerce subject to federal control, as defined by section 1 of the Clayton Act.   *Moore v. Mead's Fine Bread Co.*[12] held that a discrimination was "in the course of such commerce" where a company doing business in several states cut its bread price in Santa Rosa, New Mexico, to the prejudice of a local competitor.   The Court, per Douglas, J., stated:

> The victim, to be sure, is only a local merchant; and no interstate transactions are used to destroy him.   But the beneficiary is an interstate business; the treasury used to finance the warfare is drawn from interstate, as well as local, sources which include not only respondent but also a group of interlocked companies engaged in the same line of business; and the prices on the interstate sales, both by respondent and by the other Mead companies, are kept high while the local prices are lowered.   If this method of competition were approved, the pattern for growth of monopoly would be simple.   As long as the price warfare was strictly intrastate, interstate business could grow and expand with impunity at the expense of local merchants.   The competitive advantage would then be with the interstate combines, not by reason of their skills or efficiency but because of their strength and ability to wage price wars.   The profits made in interstate activities would underwrite the losses of local price-cutting campaigns.   No instrumentality of interstate commerce would be used to destroy the local merchant and expand the domain of the combine.   But the opportunities afforded by interstate commerce would be employed to injure local trade.   Congress, as guardian of the Commerce Clause, certainly has power to say that those advantages shall not attach to the privilege of doing an interstate business.

The Supreme Court later held, however, that the jurisdictional reach of the Robinson-Patman Act ("in commerce") was not as broad as the reach of the Sherman Act.[13]   Although Congress subsequently expanded Section 7 of the Clayton Act to reach activities "affecting commerce," [14] it has not likewise broadened the Robinson-Patman Act.

(3) *Discrimination in Price; Sale Requirement.*   Section 2(a) covers only discriminations in price, a price "discrimination" being synonymous with a price differential.[15]   Discrimination in the terms of sale (e.g., credit terms) are not, in themselves, illegal unless they are found to be indirect price dis-

---

12.   348 U.S. 115, 75 S.Ct. 148, 99 L.Ed. 145 (1954).

13.   See Gulf Oil Corp. v. Copp Paving Co., 419 U.S. 186, 95 S.Ct. 392, 42 L.Ed. 2d 378 (1974) (purely intrastate sales of asphaltic concrete not "in commerce," rejecting argument that application of product to interstate highways afforded sufficient "nexus to commerce" to meet

requirement; at least one of the discriminatory transactions must cross a state line).

14.   see p. 213, supra.

15.   Federal Trade Commission v. Anheuser-Busch, Inc., 363 U.S. 536, 549, 80 S.Ct. 1267, 4 L.Ed.2d 1385 (1960).

criminations.[16] It is not illegal to offer differently situated customers the same price (e.g., a large retailer and a wholesaler), even though this "equality" could adversely affect competition between the two (e.g., the large retailer could have a competitive advantage over a smaller retailer who must buy from the wholesaler).[17] Nor is it illegal under the Act to simply make an offer to sell at a different price, or to simply refuse to sell at any price.[18] Finally, intra-enterprise transfers are normally not characterized as "sales," so that it is possible for an integrated manufacturer-retailer to favor its own outlets over independents without violating the Act.[19]

To what extent would you want to vary these rules? Are there times when apparent equality is actually "discriminatory"?[20] Should sellers be allowed to affirmatively favor less well-situated buyers? Would it be desirable to more closely scrutinize intra-enterprise transfers? Or would such scrutiny result in the loss of the efficiencies of vertical integration?

(4) *Commodities.* Section 2(a) of the Robinson-Patman Act is limited to price discrimination in the distribution of "commodities." Certain service discriminations are reached by §§ 2(d) and (e) [see infra], but only "in connection with" commodity transactions. It follows that discriminatory prices in the sale of advertising time on broadcasting networks or discrimination in the terms of loans made by a bank would be reachable only under the Sherman Act, or, in some cases, the Federal Trade Commission Act.[21] Would you favor extending the statute to "non-commodities," such as services (doctors? lawyers?) or real estate? Note that discrimination in the pricing of transportation services (e.g., rail, motor carrier, airline) is covered by current regulatory statutes; similarly, states generally forbid unreasonable discrimination in public utility rates (e.g., electric power). With rate controls on airline fares removed at the end of 1982,[22] should the Robinson-Patman Act be amended to cover them?

16. See Viviano Macaroni Co. v. Federal Trade Commission, 411 F.2d 255 (3d Cir. 1969) (violation of 2(a) to offer only one customer a 2% discount if payment is made in 20 days, while all others get the discount only if payment made in 10 days). The Senate bill amending Section 2, and the bill originally introduced in the House, would have forbidden discrimination in price *or* terms of sale, but the final House bill forbade only a price discrimination. See Patman, Complete Guide to the Robinson-Patman Act 291, 306, 316 (1963).

17. The legality of selling at the same price to a wholesaler and retailer could be affected by the application of the "indirect purchaser" doctrine; if the wholesaler's selling policies are effectively controlled by the manufacturer, then the purchaser from the wholesaler may be considered to have purchased directly from the manufacturer. See Purolator Products, Inc. v. Federal Trade Commission, 352 F.2d 874 (7th Cir. 1965), certiorari denied 389 U.S. 1045, 88 S.Ct. 758, 19 L.Ed.2d 837 (1968).

18. See ABA Antitrust Section, The Robinson-Patman Act: Policy and Law 50 (Vol. I 1980) (citing cases). Note that Section 2(a) provides that "nothing herein

contained shall prevent persons . . . from selecting their own customers in bona fide transactions and not in restraint of trade."

19. See, e.g., Island Tobacco Co., Ltd. v. R.J. Reynolds Industries, Inc., 513 F.Supp. 726 (D. Hawaii 1981) (reviewing cases).

20. "[T]he majestic equality of the laws . . . forbids the rich as well as the poor to sleep under bridges, to beg in the streets, and to steal bread." Anatole France, Le Lys Rouge 117–118 (Calman & Levy, eds., 1925).

21. See Blake and Blum, Network TV Rate Practices: a Case Study in Failure of Social Control of Price Discrimination, 74 Yale L.J. 1339 (1965); Note, Antitrust Implications of Network TV Quantity Advertising Discounts, 65 Colum.L.Rev. 1213 (1965). But cf. Times-Mirror Co. v. Federal Trade Commission, 1979–2 Trade Cas. ¶ 62,756 (C.D.Cal.1979) (refusing to enjoin FTC proceeding charging § 2(a) violation for granting volume discounts to large purchasers of newspaper advertising linage). The F.T.C. later dismissed its complaint. See n. 33, infra.

22. See 49 U.S.C.A. § 1551(a)(2)(B) (Supp.1982).

(5) *Comparable Units—"Like Grade and Quality."* If goods are not "of like grade and quality," the constraints of section 2(a) of the Robinson-Patman Act are inapplicable; the supplier need not cost-justify different prices for substantially different commodities. Commodities may be of like grade and quality even though they are not physically identical, if they are functional and commercial equivalents.[23] A group of related but physically quite distinct products, customarily offered by suppliers as an identifiable "line" of goods, may be treated as the unit of comparison.[24] Query: Is the sale of identical goods at different prices to different customers, who compete with each other, lawful if the lower price is governed by a long-term supply contract made much earlier? [25]

As to the situation where the commodities are physically identical but commercially distinct, see *Federal Trade Commission v. Borden Co.*[26] which held that canned milk packed under Borden's nationally advertised brand was "of like grade and quality" with chemically identical milk packed under private brands for some of Borden's customers, despite substantial consumer preference for Borden's brand reflected in a higher market price.

Queries: (i) Should the difference in market value between branded and private label goods not be accepted as removing the ban of the Robinson-Patman Act?

(ii) Should the answer to question (i) be affected by (a) any value judgment as to the social utility of advertising; (b) the fact that some suppliers have sold the same goods under different brands, using one as a "fighting brand" on which prices are cut to meet competition or to discourage price cutting; (c) the fact that it is easier for chain and department stores and mail order houses to have their own brands affixed by the supplier and to push these private brands while smaller distributors are left only with higher-priced nationally advertised brands?

(iii) Would it be lawful for a supplier to allocate all his advertising expense to the cost of his branded line, and so cost-justify a lower price to purchasers of non-branded goods?

(iv) What can be said for and against dealing with the brand problem as a question of whether the price discrimination adversely affects competition in the manner specified in Section 2(a)?

On remand, the FTC order in Borden was set aside for want of a sufficient showing of competitive injury, in view of the fact that Borden was willing to sell unlabelled milk to all customers and that no competitive advantage is conferred on the buyer of the cheaper, unlabelled milk where the difference in price does not exceed the difference in market value.[27] What if

23. American Can Co. v. Bruce's Juices, Inc., 187 F.2d 919, 190 F.2d 73 (5th Cir. 1951) (cans sold to competing canners differed by .02 inches in height; seller refused to supply shorter and cheaper cans to one canner; recovery for discrimination allowed); Atalanta Trading Corp. v. Federal Trade Commission, 258 F.2d 365 (2d Cir. 1958) (promotional allowances granted to grocery chain in connection with sale of some pork products need not be made available to other customers who purchase other pork products, even though the products have sufficient "cross-elasticity of demand" that consumers shift from one to another in response to small changes in price relationships). See Kimball, "Like Grade and Quality", 1967 Utah L.Rev. 251, 257.

24. See, e.g., Callaway Mills Co. v. Federal Trade Commission, 362 F.2d 435 (5th Cir. 1966).

25. See Texas Gulf Sulphur Co. v. J.R. Simplot Co., 418 F.2d 793 (9th Cir. 1969).

26. 383 U.S. 637, 86 S.Ct. 1092, 16 L.Ed.2d 153 (1966).

27. 381 F.2d 175 (5th Cir. 1967).

Borden had refused to sell unlabelled milk to anyone but the big chain groceries? [28]

(6) *Brokerage Allowances.* Section 2(c) of the Robinson-Patman Act attempts to deal with a potential route for avoiding 2(a)—disguising discriminatory price cuts to favored buyers as "brokerage commissions" which are then paid to firms which do not really perform any brokerage functions. Under 2(c) sellers are forbidden from paying commissions to an intermediary who acts for or on behalf of the buyer, or under the buyer's control; there is no qualification for assessing competitive impact. A seller's outright reductions in price to a buyer who deals directly with the seller, eliminating the seller's need for a broker, is forbidden if the reduction is considered to be "in lieu" of brokerage payments; the cost-savings involved in by-passing the middleman is not a defense under 2(c).

On the difficulties of distinguishing between discounts "in lieu" of brokerage and discounts related to cost savings, see *Central Retailer-Owned Grocers, Inc. v. Federal Trade Commission,* where the court of appeals reversed a Commission finding of a violation of 2(c) despite the fact that the cost savings asserted were approximately equal to the brokerage commissions that the sellers paid on sales to other buyers.[29] See also *Federal Trade Commission v. Henry Broch & Co.,*[30] where the Supreme Court upheld an F.T.C. finding that a seller's broker violated 2(c) when it cut its usual brokerage commission so as to make a sale to one particular buyer who was unwilling to pay the price the seller charged to all other customers. Over a dissent that this would lead to static brokerage rates and keep sellers from passing cost savings through to buyers, the Court wrote:

Congress enacted the Robinson-Patman Act to prevent sellers and seller's brokers from yielding to the economic pressures of a large buying organization by granting unfair preferences in connection with the sale of goods. The form in which the buyer pressure is exerted is immaterial and proof of its existence is not required. It is rare that the motive in yielding to a buyer's demands is not the "necessity" for making the sale. . . . If respondent merely paid over part of his commission to the buyer, he clearly would have violated the Act. We see no distinction of substance between the two transactions. . . .

It is suggested that reversal of this case would establish an irrevocable floor under commission rates. We think that view has no foundation in fact or in law. Both before and after the sales to Smucker, respondent continued to charge the usual 5% on sales to other buyers. There is nothing in the Act, nor is there anything in this case, to require him to continue to charge 5% on sales to all customers. A price reduction based upon alleged savings in brokerage expenses is an "allowance in lieu of brokerage" when given only to favored customers. Had respondent, for example, agreed to accept a 3% commission on all sales to all buyers there plainly would be no room for finding that the price reductions were violations of § 2(c). Neither the legislative history nor the purposes of the Act would require such an absurd result, and neither the Commission nor the courts have ever suggested it. Here, however, the reduction in brokerage was made to obtain this particular order and this order only and therefore was clearly discriminatory. . . .

28. See Jordan, Robinson-Patman Aspects of Dual Distribution by Brand of Consumer Goods, 50 Cornell L.Q. 394 (1965).

29. 319 F.2d 410 (7th Cir. 1963).

30. 363 U.S. 166, 80 S.Ct. 1158, 4 L.Ed.2d 1124 (1960).

(7) *Seller's Discriminatory Payments and Services to Buyers.* The Robinson-Patman Act also covers the granting of payments (Section 2(d)) or services (Section 2(e)) to buyers on other than "proportionally equal terms." In *Federal Trade Commission v. Simplicity Pattern Co., Inc.*,[31] the Supreme Court refused to read into sections 2(d) and 2(e) the justifications and defenses found in sections 2(a) and 2(b). Thus these payments and services cannot be defended by showing that there was no adverse effect on competition or that cost savings in dealing with the favored customer were at least equal to the special concessions made to him. The thrust of sections 2(d) and 2(e) is the affirmative requirement of "proportional equality":

> . . . We cannot supply what Congress has studiously omitted. Simplicity's arguments to the contrary are based essentially on the ground that it would be "bad law and bad economics" to make discriminations unlawful even where they may be accounted for by cost differentials or where there is no competitive injury. Entirely aside from the fact that this Court is not in a position to review the economic wisdom of Congress, we cannot say that the legislative decision to treat price and other discriminations differently is without a rational basis. In allowing a "cost justification" for price discriminations and not for others, Congress could very well have felt that sellers would be forced to confine their discriminatory practices to price differentials, where they could be more readily detected and where it would be much easier to make accurate comparisons with any alleged cost savings. And, with respect to the absence of competitive injury requirements, it suffices to say that the antitrust laws are not strangers to the policy of nipping potentially destructive practices before they reach full bloom.

When a manufacturer deals directly with large retailers and also with wholesalers who resell to small retailers competing with the direct-buying retailers, must he equalize his promotional aids (i) as between his wholesaler customers and his direct-buying retail customers, or (ii) as between the competing retailers, some of whom are not his "customers"? *Federal Trade Commission v. Fred Meyer, Inc.*, 390 U.S. 341, 88 S.Ct. 904, 19 L.Ed.2d 1222 (1968), held that the manufacturer must equalize among the retailers, notwithstanding that section 2(d) speaks of equalizing among "customers". This construction in the face of the statutory language was deemed necessary to effectuate the overall intent of Congress to eliminate all devices by which large buyers gained discriminatory preferences over smaller ones by virtue of their greater purchasing power.

(8) *Enforcement.* The Robinson-Patman Act amendments to Section 2 of the Clayton Act, like other provisions of the Clayton Act, may be enforced by private suits for treble damages and by government civil suits brought either by the Justice Department or the Federal Trade Commission. Historically, government enforcement has fallen almost exclusively to the FTC; the Antitrust Division has never had much sympathy for the statute.[32] FTC enforce-

---

31. 360 U.S. 55, 79 S.Ct. 1005, 3 L.Ed. 2d 1079 (1959).

32. See Calvani, Effect of Current Developments on the Future of the Robinson-Patman Act, 48 Antitrust L.J. 1692, 1698 (1979–80) (FTC enforcement data, 1965–1978). Section 3 of the Robinson-Patman Act makes it a crime to be a knowing party to certain discriminatory sales transactions; to engage in geographic price discrimination to eliminate a competitor; or to sell goods at unreasonably low prices to eliminate a competitor. This statute is not part of the Clayton Act, and there is accordingly no private treble-damage remedy for its breach. See Nashville Milk Co. v. Carnation Co., 355 U.S. 373, 78 S.Ct. 352, 2 L.Ed.2d 340 (1958). The statute has virtually never been enforced criminally. For a rare example, see United States v. National Dairy Products Corp., 372 U.S.

ment has declined markedly over the past decade, although the Commission still files some cases.[33] It is the threat of private litigation which keeps the statute alive, although several recent judicial opinions have made successful recovery more difficult.[34]

B. COMPETITIVE INJURY; BUYER LIABILITY

1. PRIMARY–LINE INJURY

UTAH PIE CO. v. CONTINENTAL BAKING CO.

Supreme Court of the United States, 1967.
386 U.S. 685, 87 S.Ct. 1326, 18 L.Ed.2d 406.

MR. JUSTICE WHITE delivered the opinion of the Court.

This suit for treble damages and injunction under §§ 4 and 16 of the Clayton Act, 38 Stat. 731, 737, 15 U.S.C. §§ 15 and 26 was brought by petitioner, Utah Pie Company, against respondents, Continental Baking Company, Carnation Company and Pet Milk Company. The complaint charged a conspiracy under §§ 1 and 2 of the Sherman Act, and violations by each respondent of § 2(a) of the Clayton Act as amended by the Robinson-Patman Act. The jury found for respondents on the conspiracy charge and for petitioner on the price discrimination charge. Judgment was entered for petitioner for damages and attorneys' fees and respondents appealed on several grounds. The Court of Appeals reversed, addressing itself to the single issue of whether the evidence against each of the respondents was sufficient to support a finding of probable injury to competition within the meaning of § 2(a) and holding that it was not. We granted certiorari. We reverse.

The product involved is frozen dessert pies—apple, cherry, boysenberry, peach, pumpkin, and mince. The period covered by the suit comprised the years 1958, 1959, and 1960 and the first eight months of 1961. Petitioner is a Utah corporation which for 30 years had been baking pies in its plant in Salt Lake City and selling them in Utah and surrounding States. It entered the frozen pie business in late 1957. It was immediately successful with its new line and built a new plant

29, 83 S.Ct. 594, 9 L.Ed.2d 561 (1963) (holding statute constitutional insofar as indictment charged selling below cost for the purpose of destroying competition).

33. For recent examples, see YKK (USA), Inc., 3 Trade Reg.Rep. ¶ 21,819 (FTC 1981); Miles Laboratories, Inc., 3 Trade Reg.Rep. ¶ 21,813 (FTC 1981). But cf. "Times Mirror, in Reversal, Plans to Fight Settlement of Antitrust Case on Ad Rates," Wall St. Journal, Sept. 28, 1981, p. 16: After agreeing to settlement with FTC of Robinson-Patman Act charge, newspaper wants case thrown

out; agreement negotiated in 1980 " 'when distinctly different regulatory and marketplace conditions existed' "— i.e. before Reagan administration took office. The F.T.C. ultimately dismissed its complaint, citing public comments on the proposed settlement that "overwhelming urged rejection." See 43 ATRR 55, 198 (1982).

34. See, e.g., J. Truett Payne Co. v. Chrysler Motors Corp., infra p. 902; Wm. Inglis & Sons Baking Co. v. ITT Continental Baking Co., Inc., infra p. 887.

in Salt Lake City in 1958. The frozen pie market was a rapidly expanding one: 57,060 dozen frozen pies were sold in the Salt Lake City
market in 1958, 111,729 dozen in 1959, 184,569 dozen in 1960, and
266,908 dozen in 1961. Utah Pie's share of this market in those years
was 66.5%, 34.3%, 45.5%, and 45.3% respectively, its sales volume
steadily increasing over the four years. Its financial position also improved. Petitioner is not, however, a large company. At the time of
the trial, petitioner operated with only 18 employees, nine of whom
were members of the Rigby family, which controlled the business.
Its net worth increased from $31,651.98 on October 31, 1957 to
$68,802.13 on October 31, 1961. Total sales were $238,000 in the year
ended October 31, 1957, $353,000 in 1958, $430,000 in 1959, $504,000
in 1960 and $589,000 in 1961. Its net income or loss for these same
years was a loss of $6,461 in 1957, and net income in the remaining
years of $7,090, $11,897, $7,636, and $9,216.

Each of the respondents is a large company and each of them is a
major factor in the frozen pie market in one or more regions of the
country. Each entered the Salt Lake City frozen pie market before
petitioner began freezing dessert pies. None of them had a plant in
Utah. By the end of the period involved in this suit Pet had plants in
Michigan, Pennsylvania, and California; Continental in Virginia, Iowa, and California; and Carnation in California. The Salt Lake City
market was supplied by respondents chiefly from their California operations. They sold primarily on a delivered price basis.

The "Utah" label was petitioner's proprietary brand. Beginning
in 1960, it also sold pies of like grade and quality under the controlled
label "Frost 'N' Flame" to Associated Grocers and in 1961 it began
selling to American Food Stores under the "Mayfresh" label. It also,
on a seasonal basis, sold pumpkin and mince frozen pies to Safeway
under Safeway's own "Bel-air" label.

The major competitive weapon in the Utah market was price. The
location of petitioner's plant gave it natural advantages in the Salt
Lake City marketing area and it entered the market at a price below
the then going prices for respondents' comparable pies. For most of
the period involved here its prices were the lowest in the Salt Lake
City market. It was, however, challenged by each of the respondents
at one time or another and for varying periods. There was ample
evidence to show that each of the respondents contributed to what
proved to be a deteriorating price structure over the period covered
by this suit, and each of the respondents in the course of the ongoing
price competition sold frozen pies in the Salt Lake market at prices
lower than it sold pies of like grade and quality in other markets considerably closer to its plants. . . .

I.

We deal first with petitioner's case against the Pet Milk Company.
Pet entered the frozen pie business in 1955, acquired plants in Pennsylvania and California and undertook a large advertising campaign
to market its "Pet-Ritz" brand of frozen pies. Pet's initial emphasis

was on quality, but in the face of competition from regional and local companies and in an expanding market where price proved to be a crucial factor, Pet was forced to take steps to reduce the price of its pies to the ultimate consumer. These developments had consequences in the Salt Lake City market which are the substance of petitioner's case against Pet.

First, Pet successfully concluded an arrangement with Safeway, which is one of the three largest customers for frozen pies in the Salt Lake market, whereby it would sell frozen pies to Safeway under the latter's own "Bel-air" label at a price significantly lower than it was selling its comparable "Pet-Ritz" brand in the same Salt Lake market and elsewhere. The initial price on "Bel-air" pies was slightly lower than Utah's price for its "Utah" brand of pies at the time, and near the end of the period the "Bel-air" price was comparable to the "Utah" price but higher than Utah's "Frost 'N' Flame" brand. Pet's Safeway business amounted to 22.8%, 12.3%, and 6.3% of the entire Salt Lake City market for the years 1959, 1960, and 1961, respectively, and to 64%, 44%, and 22% of Pet's own Salt Lake City sales for those same years.

Second, it introduced a 20-ounce economy pie under the "Swiss Miss" label and began selling the new pie in the Salt Lake market in August 1960 at prices ranging from $3.25 to $3.30 for the remainder of the period. This pie was at times sold at a lower price in the Salt Lake City market than it was sold in other markets.

Third, Pet became more competitive with respect to the prices for its "Pet-Ritz" proprietary label. For 18 of the relevant 44 months its offering price for Pet-Ritz pies was $4 per dozen or lower, and $3.70 or lower for six of these months. According to the Court of Appeals, in seven of the 44 months Pet's prices in Salt Lake were lower than prices charged in the California markets. This was true although selling in Salt Lake involved a 30- to 35-cent freight cost.

The Court of Appeals first concluded that Pet's price differential on sales to Safeway must be put aside in considering injury to competition because in its view of the evidence the differential had been completely cost justified and because Utah would not in any event have been able to enjoy the Safeway custom. Second, it concluded that the remaining discriminations on "Pet-Ritz" and "Swiss Miss" pies were an insufficient predicate on which the jury could have found a reasonably possible injury either to Utah Pie as a competitive force or to competition generally.

We disagree with the Court of Appeals in several respects. First, there was evidence from which the jury could have found considerably more price discrimination by Pet with respect to "Pet-Ritz" and "Swiss Miss" pies than was considered by the Court of Appeals. In addition to the seven months during which Pet's prices in Salt Lake were lower than prices in the California markets, there was evidence from which the jury could reasonably have found that in 10 additional months the Salt Lake City prices for "Pet-Ritz" pies were discriminatory as compared with sales in western markets other than California. Likewise, with respect to "Swiss Miss" pies, there was evidence in the record from which the jury could have found that in five of the 13 months during which the "Swiss Miss" pies were sold prior to the filing of this suit, prices in Salt Lake City were lower than those charged by Pet in either California or some other western market.

Second, with respect to Pet's Safeway business, the burden of proving cost justification was on Pet and, in our view, reasonable men could have found that Pet's lower priced, "Bel-air" sales to Safeway were not cost justified in their entirety. Pet introduced cost data for 1961 indicating a cost saving on the Safeway business greater than the price advantage extended to that customer. These statistics were not particularized for the Salt Lake market, but assuming that they were adequate to justify the 1961 sales, they related to only 24% of the Safeway sales over the relevant period. The evidence concerning the remaining 76% was at best incomplete and inferential. It was insufficient to take the defense of cost justification from the jury, which reasonably could have found a greater incidence of unjustified price discrimination than that allowed by the Court of Appeals' view of the evidence.

With respect to whether Utah would have enjoyed Safeway's business absent the Pet contract with Safeway, it seems clear that whatever the fact is in this regard, it is not determinative of the impact of that contract on competitors other than Utah and on competition generally. There were other companies seeking the Safeway business, including Continental and Carnation, whose pies may have been excluded from the Safeway shelves by what the jury could have found to be discriminatory sales to Safeway. What is more, Pet's evidence that Utah's unwillingness to install quality control equipment prevented Utah from enjoying Safeway's private label business is not the only evidence in the record relevant to that question. There was other evidence to the contrary. The jury would not have been compelled to find that Utah Pie could not have gained more of the Safeway business.

Third, the Court of Appeals almost entirely ignored other evidence which provides material support for the jury's conclusion that Pet's behavior satisfied the statutory test regarding competitive injury. This evidence bore on the issue of Pet's predatory intent to injure Utah Pie.[35] As an initial matter, the jury could have concluded that Pet's discriminatory pricing was aimed at Utah Pie; Pet's own man-

---

35. [This and the following 2 footnotes are from the original; renumbered.] The dangers of predatory price discrimination were recognized in Moore v. Mead's Fine Bread Co., 348 U.S. 115, 75 S.Ct. 148, 99 L.Ed. 145, where such pricing was held violative of § 2(a). Subsequently, the Court noted that "the decisions of the federal courts in primary-line-competition cases . . . consistently emphasize the unreasonably low prices and the predatory intent of the defendants." F.T.C. v. Anheuser-Busch, Inc., 363 U.S. 536, 548, 80 S.Ct. 1267, 1274, 4 L.Ed.2d 1385. . . .

Chief Justice Hughes noted in a related antitrust context that "knowledge of actual intent is an aid in the interpretation of facts and prediction of consequences." Appalachian Coals, Inc. v. United States, 288 U.S. 344, 372, 53 S.Ct. 471, 478, 77 L.Ed. 825, and we do not think it unreasonable for courts to follow that lead. Although the evidence in this regard against Pet seems obvious, a jury would be free to ascertain a seller's intent from

agement, as early as 1959, identified Utah Pie as an "unfavorable factor," one which "d[u]g holes in our operation" and posed a constant "check" on Pet's performance in the Salt Lake City market. Moreover, Pet candidly admitted that during the period when it was establishing its relationship with Safeway, it sent into Utah Pie's plant an industrial spy to seek information that would be of use to Pet in convincing Safeway that Utah Pie was not worthy of its custom. Pet denied that it ever in fact used what it had learned against Utah Pie in competing for Safeway's business. The parties, however, are not the ultimate judges of credibility. But even giving Pet's view of the incident a measure of weight does not mean the jury was foreclosed from considering the predatory intent underlying Pet's mode of competition. Finally, Pet does not deny that the evidence showed it suffered substantial losses on its frozen pie sales during the greater part of the time involved in this suit, and there was evidence from which the jury could have concluded that the losses Pet sustained in Salt Lake City were greater than those incurred elsewhere. It would not have been an irrational step if the jury concluded that there was a relationship between price and the losses.

It seems clear to us that the jury heard adequate evidence from which it could have concluded that Pet had engaged in predatory tactics in waging competitive warfare in the Salt Lake City market. Coupled with the incidence of price discrimination attributable to Pet, the evidence as a whole established, rather than negated, the reasonable possibility that Pet's behavior produced a lessening of competition proscribed by the Act.

II.

Petitioner's case against Continental is not complicated. . . . [I]n June 1961, it took the steps which are the heart of petitioner's complaint against it. Effective for the last two weeks of June it offered its 22-ounce frozen apple pies in the Utah area at $2.85 per dozen. It was then selling the same pies at substantially higher prices in other markets. The Salt Lake City price was less than its direct cost plus an allocation for overhead. Utah's going price at the time for its 24-ounce "Frost 'N' Flame" apple pie sold to Associated Grocers was $3.10 per dozen, and for its "Utah" brand $3.40 per dozen. At its new prices, Continental sold pies to American Grocers in Pocatello, Idaho, and to American Food Stores in Ogden, Utah. Safeway, one of the major buyers in Salt Lake City, also purchased 6,250 dozen, its requirements for about five weeks. Another purchaser ordered 1,000 dozen. Utah's response was immediate. It reduced its price on all of its apple pies to $2.75 per dozen. Continental refused Safeway's request to match Utah's price, but renewed its offer at the same prices effective July 31 for another two-week period. Utah filed suit on September 8, 1961. Continental's total sales of frozen pies increased from 3,350 dozen in 1960 to 18,800 dozen in 1961. Its market share increased from 1.8% in 1960 to 8.3% in 1961. . . .

surrounding economic circumstances, which would include persistent unprofita- ble sales below cost and drastic price cuts themselves discriminatory. . . .

. . . The jury could rationally have concluded that had Utah not lowered its price, Continental, which repeated its offer once, would have continued it, that Safeway would have continued to buy from Continental and that other buyers, large as well as small, would have followed suit. It could also have reasonably concluded that a competitor who is forced to reduce his price to a new all-time low in a market of declining prices will in time feel the financial pinch and will be a less effective competitive force.

. . .

IV.

Section 2(a) does not forbid price competition which will probably injure or lessen competition by eliminating competitors, discouraging entry into the market or enhancing the market shares of the dominant sellers. But Congress has established some ground rules for the game. Sellers may not sell like goods to different purchasers at different prices if the result may be to injure competition in either the sellers' or the buyers' market unless such discriminations are justified as permitted by the Act. This case concerns the sellers' market. In this context, the Court of Appeals placed heavy emphasis on the fact that Utah Pie constantly increased its sales volume and continued to make a profit. But we disagree with its apparent view that there is no reasonably possible injury to competition as long as the volume of sales in a particular market is expanding and at least some of the competitors in the market continue to operate at a profit. Nor do we think that the Act only comes into play to regulate the conduct of price discriminators when their discriminatory prices consistently undercut other competitors. It is true that many of the primary line cases that have reached the courts have involved blatant predatory price discriminations employed with the hope of immediate destruction of a particular competitor. On the question of injury to competition such cases present courts with no difficulty, for such pricing is clearly within the heart of the proscription of the Act. Courts and commentators alike have noted that the existence of predatory intent might bear on the likelihood of injury to competition. In this case there was some evidence of predatory intent with respect to each of these respondents.[36] There was also other evidence upon which the jury could rationally find the requisite injury to competition. The frozen pie market in Salt Lake City was highly competitive. At times Utah Pie was a leader in moving the general level of prices down, and at other times each of the respondents also bore responsibility for the

---

36. It might be argued that the respondents' conduct displayed only fierce competitive instincts. Actual intent to injure another competitor does not, however, fall into that category, and neither, when viewed in the context of the Robinson-Patman Act, do persistent sales below cost and radical price cuts themselves discriminatory. Nor does the fact that a local competitor has a major share of the market make him fair game for discriminatory price cutting free of Robinson-Patman Act proscriptions. "The Clayton Act proscription as to discrimination in price is not nullified merely because of a showing that the existing competition in a particular market had a major share of the sales of the product involved." . . .

downward pressure on the price structure. We believe that the Act reaches price discrimination that erodes competition as much as it does price discrimination that is intended to have immediate destructive impact. In this case, the evidence shows a drastically declining price structure which the jury could rationally attribute to continued or sporadic price discrimination. The jury was entitled to conclude that "the effect of such discrimination," by each of these respondents, "may be substantially to lessen competition . . . or to injure, destroy, or prevent competition with any person who either grants or knowingly receives the benefit of such discrimination . . . ." The statutory test is one that necessarily looks forward on the basis of proven conduct in the past. Proper application of that standard here requires reversal of the judgment of the Court of Appeals.[37]

. . .

MR. JUSTICE STEWART, with whom MR. JUSTICE HARLAN joins, dissenting.

I would affirm the judgment, agreeing substantially with the reasoning of the Court of Appeals as expressed in the thorough and conscientious opinion of Judge Phillips.

There is only one issue in this case in its present posture: Whether the respondents engaged in price discrimination "where the effect of such discrimination may be substantially to lessen competition or tend to create a monopoly in any line of commerce, or to injure, destroy, or prevent competition with any person who either grants or knowingly receives the benefit of such discrimination . . . ." Phrased more simply, did the respondents' actions have the anticompetitive effect required by the statute as an element of a cause of action?

The Court's own description of the Salt Lake City frozen pie market from 1958 through 1961, shows that the answer to that question must be no. In 1958 Utah Pie had a quasi-monopolistic 66.5% of the market. In 1961—after the alleged predations of the respondents—Utah Pie still had a commanding 45.3%, Pet had 29.4%, and the remainder of the market was divided almost equally between Continental, Carnation, and other, small local bakers. Unless we disregard the lessons so laboriously learned in scores of Sherman and Clayton Act cases, the 1961 situation has to be considered more competitive than that of 1958. Thus, if we assume that the price discrimination proven against the respondents had any effect on competition, that effect must have been beneficent.

37. Each respondent argues here that prior price discrimination cases in the courts and before the Federal Trade Commission, in which no primary line injury to competition was found, establish a standard which compels affirmance of the Court of Appeals' holding. But the cases upon which the respondents rely are readily distinguishable. In Anheuser-Busch, Inc. v. F.T.C., 289 F.2d 835, 839, there was no general decline in price structure attributable to the defendant's price discriminations, nor was there any evidence that the price discriminations were "a single lethal weapon aimed at a victim for a predatory purpose." . . .

That the Court has fallen into the error of reading the Robinson-Patman Act as protecting competitors, instead of competition, can be seen from its unsuccessful attempt to distinguish cases relied upon by the respondents. Those cases are said to be inapposite because they involved "no general decline in price structure," and no "lasting impact upon prices." But lower prices are the hallmark of intensified competition.

The Court of Appeals squarely identified the fallacy which the Court today embraces:

". . . a contention that Utah Pie was entitled to hold the extraordinary market share percentage of 66.5, attained in 1958, falls of its own dead weight. To approve such a contention would be to hold that Utah Pie was entitled to maintain a position which approached, if it did not in fact amount to a monopoly, and could not exist in the face of proper and healthy competition." 349 F.2d 122, 155.

I cannot hold that Utah Pie's monopolistic position was protected by the federal antitrust laws from effective price competition, and I therefore respectfully dissent.

NOTES AND QUERIES

(1) *Interplay With the Sherman Act.* Review the materials discussing "predatory" pricing as a violation of Section 2 of the Sherman Act, supra pp. 130–135. How does the Supreme Court's approach to the sellers' pricing policies in *Utah Pie* differ from the approaches taken recently by the courts of appeals in Section 2 cases? Was the Supreme Court as concerned with the relation of price to cost (average variable cost? marginal cost?)? Was other evidence of "predation" more relevant to the Supreme Court?

Should the standard for judging the competitive effect of a discriminatory price cut in Robinson-Patman Act cases be the same as the standard for judging the legality of price cuts in Section 2 cases? In *William Inglis & Sons Baking Co. v. ITT Continental Baking Co., Inc.,* the Ninth Circuit addressed this issue: [38]

Appellant's Robinson-Patman Act claim was based substantially on the same facts underlying the attempt to monopolize claim. Inglis contended that price differentials between Continental's private label and advertised bread constituted price discrimination in violation of section 2(a) of the Clayton Act, as amended by the Robinson-Patman Act. Inglis also

---

38. 668 F.2d 1014, 1039–42 (9th Cir. 1981), certiorari denied ___ U.S. ___, 103 S.Ct. 58, 74 L.Ed.2d 61 (1982). See also International Air Industries, Inc. v. American Excelsior Co., 517 F.2d 714 (5th Cir. 1975) (affirming judgment for defendant in suit alleging violations of section 2 of the Sherman Act and section 2(a) of the Robinson-Patman Act; applies same standard, holding defendant's pricing was competitive rather than anticompetitive, since its prices were at all times above both its marginal and average costs, despite defendant's memorandum stating: "If we are committed to a pro-gram of stunting the possible growth of Vebco (the plaintiff) and keeping our foot in this quite sizeable . . . market, then the real question we have here is just what price do we need to determine as our lowest price level."); Areeda and Turner, Predatory Pricing and Related Practices Under § 2 of the Sherman Act, 88 Harv.L.Rev. 697 (1975) (rule of presumptive legality under the Sherman Act for monopolist pricing at or above marginal cost should be applied for firms with a lesser degree of market power in Robinson-Patman Act cases).

identified (1) discrimination in the price of private label bread between California and Nevada and (2) discrimination in the price of advertised bread between California and Nevada. The district court entered JNOV and, in the alternative, a new trial, in favor of Continental because it found that Inglis had failed to prove (1) the requisite effect on competition, and (2) causation.

. . .

2. *Proof of Predatory Intent in Primary-Line Cases*

In this case we confront the issue whether the principles . . . [governing] proof of predatory intent in an attempt to monopolize claim pursuant to section 2 of the Sherman Act are equally applicable to proof of predatory intent in a primary-line Robinson-Patman Act suit. We hold that they are. We have previously recognized that where "a price differential threatens a primary line injury, . . . section 2 of the Sherman Act . . . and section 2(a) of the Clayton Act . . . are directed at the same economic evil and have the same substantive content." There exists no reason to establish principles for primary-line price discrimination cases different from those we recognized in attempt to monopolize cases.

It follows, therefore, that we disagree with the district court's holding that in its primary-line Robinson-Patman Act claim Inglis was required to prove that Continental's prices were below its marginal cost of production. A plaintiff may establish the required effects on competition in a primary-line case even though the defendant's prices were shown to be above marginal cost. However, unless the plaintiff proves that the prices were below the defendant's average variable cost, the plaintiff bears the burden of establishing that the anticipated benefits of the prices depended on their anticipated destructive effect on competition. If the plaintiff does prove pricing below average variable cost, the burden shifts to the defendant to establish a legitimate business justification for its conduct. Accordingly, we must reverse the district court's entry of JNOV.

However, no abuse of its discretion occurred when the trial court ordered a new trial on the Robinson-Patman Act claim. Although Inglis did establish that Continental's prices were in many instances below average total cost, it failed to establish by sufficient evidence either that Continental's prices were below average variable cost or that the benefits of Continental's prices depended on their anticipated tendency to eliminate competition. Finally, . . . these deficiencies are not remedied by the direct evidence of intent offered by Inglis at trial.

3. *Sherman and Robinson-Patman Compared*

An injury to competition proscribed by section 2(a) of the Robinson-Patman Act perhaps may be established without proof of predatory intent or predatory pricing, however. Therefore, we do not hold that there exists a complete substantive synchronization of the Sherman and Robinson-Patman Acts. However, no basis for establishing the requisite competitive injury, other than by proof of predatory intent and predatory pricing, is evident in the record before us, nor has Inglis argued one. Certainly, the mere fact that Inglis suffered losses and eventually ceased operations is not sufficient to establish a section 2(a) Robinson-Patman

Act violation. In primary-line Robinson-Patman Act cases, such as is this one, the distinction between vigorous, but honest, price competition and predatory assaults on the competitive process is just as important as it is to Sherman Act cases brought under its section 2. Under these circumstances the analytical standards should be no different.

Two other differences between the substantive requirements of the Sherman and Robinson-Patman Acts should be mentioned, although neither alters the result of the case. First, the offense of attempted monopolization requires proof of a dangerous probability of success while section 2(a) of the Robinson-Patman Act requires only a showing that the price discrimination "may" substantially lessen competition. In this case, however, the distinction is of little significance. . . .

The second difference lies in the scope of the competitive injury envisioned by the two statutes. While section 2 of the Sherman Act requires attempted monopolization of a "part" of commerce, and thus is concerned with competitive conditions generally in the line of commerce affected, section 2(a) of Robinson-Patman requires only an impermissible effect on competition by others with the seller employing discriminatory prices. Once again, this difference does not alter our result here. Under either statute Inglis has failed to present sufficient evidence to sustain the jury's verdict.

(2) *Phillips, Price Discrimination and the Large Firm: Hobson's Choice in the Pectin Industry*, 43 Va.L.Rev. 685 (1957), pointed out that the impact of a firm's price changes on the share of the market enjoyed by its rivals is correlated with the proportion of the market originally controlled by the firm:

Suppose, for example, a firm has demand elasticity such that the quantity demanded increases by 2 per cent for each 1 per cent decrease in price. If the firm has 50 per cent of the total market demand volume, a reduction of its price by, say, 10 per cent increases its volume by 20 per cent. The other firms find, on the average, a 20 per cent reduction in the quantity demanded from them so long as their prices remain unchanged. If the initial firm had 80 per cent of the market to start with, the 10 per cent drop in price would have raised its volume to 96 per cent of the market; the remaining firms' share would have been cut from 20 per cent to but 4 per cent, or a drop of 80 per cent. . . .

The same logic shows that a firm with but 10 per cent of the market has little influence on its rivals. If it lowers price by 10 per cent and the quantity demanded from it rises by 20 per cent, its percentage share of the market increases to 12 per cent. The other firms, which had 90 per cent to start with, would be left with 88 per cent, an averge drop in demand of only about 2.2 per cent. The small firm, even with considerable demand elasticity, is impotent before a large competitor since large percentage increases in the quantity demanded from the small firm are but small percentage decreases for the large one. . . . The large firm can hurt the small, but the small cannot hurt the larger.

Professor Phillips noted, however, that a dominant firm could inhibit the expansion of a local competitor as well by a uniform national decrease of price as by a discriminatory local decrease.

(3) *Queries.* Is a national supplier's local competitor injured only by the low price locally or by the discrimination? Must the local competitor prove that the low price was "subsidized" out of profits realized on the higher

prices supplier gets elsewhere? [39] What is the appropriate relief in cases of geographic price discrimination injurious to local competition at the primary level? Should the Federal Trade Commission order the respondent to refrain from local price cutting where it is in competition with any other seller having "a substantially smaller volume of sales"? or where the "lower price undercuts the lowest price offered to that purchaser by any other seller having a substantially smaller volume of sales"? [40]

2. SECONDARY–LINE INJURY

FEDERAL TRADE COMMISSION v. MORTON SALT CO.

Supreme Court of the United States, 1948.
334 U.S. 37, 68 S.Ct. 822, 92 L.Ed. 1196.

MR. JUSTICE BLACK delivered the opinion of the Court.

The Federal Trade Commission, after a hearing, found that the respondent, which manufactures and sells table salt in interstate commerce, had discriminated in price between different purchasers of like grades and qualities, and concluded that such discriminations were in violation of § 2 of the Clayton Act, 38 Stat. 730, as amended by the Robinson-Patman Act, 49 Stat. 1526, 15 U.S.C. § 13, 15 U.S.C.A. § 13.

. . .

Respondent manufactures several different brands of table salt and sells them directly to (1) wholesalers or jobbers, who in turn resell to the retail trade, and (2) large retailers, including chain store retailers. Respondent sells its finest brand of table salt, known as Blue Label, on what it terms a standard quantity discount system available to all customers. Under this system the purchasers pay a delivered price and the cost to both wholesale and retail purchasers of this brand differs according to the quantities bought. These prices are as follows, after making allowance for rebates and discounts:

	Per case
Less-than-carload purchases	$1.60
Carload purchases	1.50
5,000-case purchases in any consecutive 12 months	1.40
50,000-case purchases in any consecutive 12 months	1.35

Only five companies have ever bought sufficient quantities of respondent's salt to obtain the $1.35 per case price. These companies could buy in such quantities because they operate large chains of retail stores in various parts of the country. [41] As a result of this low price these five companies have been able to sell Blue Label salt at retail

---

39. Yes: Shore Gas & Oil Co. v. Humble Oil & Refining Co., 224 F.Supp. 922 (D.N.J.1963). Not deciding: Wm. Inglis v. ITT Continental, supra (even if causal connection between price discrimination and damages must be shown by proving cross-subsidization, district court erred in holding that cross-subsidization can be inferred only when discriminating low price was below marginal cost).

40. Cf. Forster Manufacturing Co. v. Federal Trade Commission, 335 F.2d 47

(1st Cir. 1964), certiorari denied 380 U.S. 906, 85 S.Ct. 887, 13 L.Ed.2d 794 (1965), order amended on remand, F.T.C. Docket 7207, July 23, 1965.

41. [Footnotes 41 to 46 are from the Court's opinion, renumbered.] These chain stores are American Stores Company, National Tea Company, Kroger Grocery Co., Safeway Stores, Inc., and Great Atlantic & Pacific Tea Company.

cheaper than wholesale purchasers from respondent could reasonably sell the same brand of salt to independently operated retail stores, many of whom competed with the local outlets of the five chain stores.

Respondent's table salts, other than Blue Label, are also sold under a quantity discount system differing slightly from that used in selling Blue Label. Sales of these other brands in less-than-carload lots are made at list price plus freight from plant to destination. Carload purchasers are granted approximately a 5 per cent discount; approximately a 10 per cent discount is granted to purchasers who buy as much as $50,000 worth of all brands of salt in any consecutive twelve-month period. Respondent's quantity discounts on Blue Label and on other table salts were enjoyed by certain wholesalers and retailers who competed with other wholesalers and retailers to whom these discounts were refused.

In addition to these standard quantity discounts, special allowances were granted certain favored customers who competed with other customers to whom they were denied.

First. Respondent's basic contention, which it argues this case hinges upon, is that its "standard quantity discounts, available to all on equal terms, as contrasted for example, to hidden or special rebates, allowances, prices or discounts, are not discriminatory, within the meaning of the Robinson-Patman Act." Theoretically, these discounts are equally available to all, but functionally they are not. For as the record indicates (if reference to it on this point were necessary) no single independent retail grocery store, and probably no single wholesaler, bought as many as 50,000 cases or as much as $50,000 worth of table salt in one year. Furthermore, the record shows that, while certain purchasers were enjoying one or more of respondent's standard quantity discounts, some of their competitors made purchases in such small quantities that they could not qualify for any of respondent's discounts, even those based on carload shipments. The legislative history of the Robinson-Patman Act makes it abundantly clear that Congress considered it to be an evil that a large buyer could secure a competitive advantage over a small buyer solely because of the large buyer's quantity purchasing ability. The Robinson-Patman Act was passed to deprive a large buyer of such advantages except to the extent that a lower price could be justified by reason of a seller's diminished costs due to quantity manufacture, delivery or sale, or by reason of the seller's good faith effort to meet a competitor's equally low price.

Section 2 of the original Clayton Act had included a proviso that nothing contained in it should prevent "discrimination in price . . . on account of differences in the grade, quality, or quantity of the commodity sold, or that makes only due allowance for difference in the cost of selling or transportation . . . ." That section has been construed as permitting quantity discounts, such as those here, with-

out regard to the amount of the seller's actual savings in cost attributable to quantity sales or quantity deliveries. The House Committee
Report on the Robinson-Patman Act considered that the Clayton
Act's proviso allowing quantity discounts so weakened § 2 "as to render it inadequate, if not almost a nullity." [42] The Committee considered the present Robinson-Patman amendment to § 2 "of great importance." Its purpose was to limit "the use of quantity price
differentials to the sphere of actual cost differences. Otherwise,"
the report continued, "such differentials would become instruments
of favor and privilege and weapons of competitive oppression." The
Senate Committee reporting the bill emphasized the same purpose,[43]
as did the Congressman in charge of the Conference Report when
explaining it to the House just before final passage. And it was in
furtherance of this avowed purpose—to protect competition from all
price differentials except those based in full on cost savings—that
§ 2(a) of the amendment provided "That nothing herein contained
shall prevent differentials which make only due allowance for differences in the cost of manufacture, sale, or delivery resulting from the
differing methods or quantities in which such commodities are to
such purchasers sold or delivered."

The foregoing references, without regard to others which could be
mentioned, establish that respondent's standard quantity discounts
are discriminatory within the meaning of the Act, and are prohibited
by it whenever they have the defined effect on competition.

Second. The Government interprets the opinion of the Circuit
Court of Appeals as having held that in order to establish "discrimination in price" under the Act the burden rested on the Commission
to prove that respondent's quantity discount differentials were not
justified by its cost savings. Respondent does not so understand the
Court of Appeals decision, and furthermore admits that no such burden rests on the Commission. We agree that it does not. First, the
general rule of statutory construction that the burden of proving justification or exemption under a special exception to the prohibitions of
a statute generally rests on one who claims its benefits, requires that
respondent undertake this proof under the proviso of § 2(a). Secondly, § 2(b) of the Act specifically imposes the burden of showing justification upon one who is shown to have discriminated in prices. And
the Senate committee report on the bill explained that the provisos of
§ 2(a) throw "upon any who claims the benefit of those exceptions
the burden of showing that their case falls within them." [44] We think
that the language of the Act, and the legislative history just cited,
show that Congress meant by using the words "discrimination in
price" in § 2 that in a case involving competitive injury between a
seller's customers the Commission need only prove that a seller had
charged one purchaser a higher price for like goods than he had

42. H. Rep. No. 2287, 74th Cong., 2d
Sess. 7.

43. Sen. Rep. No. 1502, 74th Cong., 2d
Sess. 4–6.

44. Sen.Rep. No. 1502, 74th Cong., 2d
Sess. 3. See also 80 Cong.Rec. 3599,
8241, 9418.

charged one or more of the purchaser's competitors.[45] This construction is consistent with the first sentence of § 2(a) in which it is made unlawful "to discriminate in price between different purchasers of commodities of like grade and quality, where either or any of the purchases involved in such discrimination are in commerce . . . and where the effect of such discrimination may be . . . to injure, destroy, or prevent competition with any person who either grants or knowingly receives the benefit of such discrimination, or with customers of either of them . . . .."

Third. It is argued that the findings fail to show that respondent's discriminatory discounts had in fact caused injury to competition. There are specific findings that such injuries had resulted from respondent's discounts although the statute does not require the Commission to find that injury has actually resulted. The statute requires no more than that the effect of the prohibited price discriminations "may be substantially to lessen competition . . . or to injure, destroy, or prevent competition." After careful consideration of this provision of the Robinson-Patman Act, we have said that "the statute does not require that the discriminations must in fact have harmed competition, but only that there is a reasonable possibility that they 'may' have such an effect." Corn Products Co. v. Federal Trade Comm., 324 U.S. 726, 742, 65 S.Ct. 961, 969, 89 L.Ed. 1320. Here the Commission found what would appear to be obvious, that the competitive opportunities of certain merchants were injured when they had to pay respondent substantially more for their goods than their competitors had to pay. The findings are adequate.

Fourth. It is urged that the evidence is inadequate to support the Commission's findings of injury to competition. As we have pointed out, however, the Commission is authorized by the Act to bar discriminatory prices upon the "reasonable possibility" that different prices for like goods to competing purchasers may have the defined effect on competition. That respondent's quantity discounts did result in price differentials between competing purchasers sufficient in amount to influence their resale price of salt was shown by evidence. This showing in itself is adequate to support the Commission's appropriate findings that the effect of such price discriminations "may be substantially to lessen competition . . . and to injure, destroy and prevent competition."

The adequacy of the evidence to support the Commission's findings of reasonably possible injury to competition from respondent's price differentials between competing carload and less-than-carload purchasers is singled out for special attacks here. It is suggested that in considering the adequacy of the evidence to show injury to competition respondent's carload discounts and its other quantity discounts should not be treated alike. The argument is that there is an obvious saving to a seller who delivers goods in carload lots. Assum-

45. See Moss v. Federal Trade Comm., 2 Cir., 148 F.2d 378, 379, holding that proof of a price differential in itself constituted "discrimination in price," where the competitive injury in question was between sellers. See also Federal Trade Comm. v. Cement Institute et al., 333 U.S. 683, 68 S.Ct. 793, 92 L.Ed. 1010.

ing this to be true, that fact would not tend to disprove injury to the merchant compelled to pay the less-than-carload price. For a ten-cent carload price differential against a merchant would injure him competitively just as much as a ten-cent differential under any other name. However relevant the separate carload argument might be to the question of justifying a differential by cost savings, it has no relevancy in determining whether the differential works an injury to a competitor. Since Congress has not seen fit to give carload discounts any favored classification we cannot do so. Such discounts, like all others, can be justified by a seller who proves that the full amount of the discount is based on his actual savings in cost. The trouble with this phase of respondent's case is that it has thus far failed to make such proof.

It is also argued that respondent's less-than-carload sales are very small in comparison with the total volume of its business and for that reason we should reject the Commission's finding that the effect of the carload discrimination may substantially lessen competition and may injure competition between purchasers who are granted and those who are denied this discriminatory discount. To support this argument, reference is made to the fact that salt is a small item in most wholesale and retail businesses and in consumers' budgets. For several reasons we cannot accept this contention.

There are many articles in a grocery store that, considered separately, are comparatively small parts of a merchant's stock. Congress intended to protect a merchant from competitive injury attributable to discriminatory prices on any or all goods sold in interstate commerce, whether the particular goods constituted a major or minor portion of his stock. Since a grocery store consists of many comparatively small articles, there is no possible way effectively to protect a grocer from discriminatory prices except by applying the prohibitions of the Act to each individual article in the store.

Furthermore, in enacting the Robinson-Patman Act Congress was especially concerned with protecting small businesses which were unable to buy in quantities, such as the merchants here who purchased in less-than-carload lots. To this end it undertook to strengthen this very phase of the old Clayton Act. The committee reports on the Robinson-Patman Act emphasized a belief that § 2 of the Clayton Act had "been too restrictive in requiring a showing of general injury to competitive conditions . . .." The new provision, here controlling, was intended to justify a finding of injury to competition by a showing of "injury to the competitor victimized by the discrimination." [46]

46. In explaining this clause of the proposed Robinson-Patman Act, the Senate Judiciary Committee said:

"This clause represents a recommended addition to the bill as referred to your committee. It tends to exclude from the bill otherwise harmless violations of its letter, but accomplishes a substantial broadening of a similar clause now contained in section 2 of the Clayton Act. The latter has in practice been too restrictive, in requiring a showing of general injury to competitive conditions in the line of commerce concerned; whereas the more immediately important concern is in injury to the competitor victimized by the discrimination. Only through such injuries, in fact, can the larger general injury result, and to catch the weed in

Since there was evidence sufficient to show that the less-than-carload purchasers might have been handicapped in competing with the more favored carload purchasers by the differential in price established by respondent, the Commission was justified in finding that competition might have thereby been substantially lessened or have been injured within the meaning of the Act.

Apprehension is expressed in this Court that enforcement of the Commission's order against respondent's continued violations of the Robinson-Patman Act might lead respondent to raise table salt prices to its carload purchasers. Such a conceivable, though, we think, highly improbable contingency, could afford us no reason for upsetting the Commission's findings and declining to direct compliance with a statute passed by Congress.

The Commission here went much further in receiving evidence than the statute requires. It heard testimony from many witnesses in various parts of the country to show that they had suffered actual financial losses on account of respondent's discriminatory prices. Experts were offered to prove the tendency of injury from such prices. The evidence covers about two thousand pages, largely devoted to this single issue—injury to competition. It would greatly handicap effective enforcement of the Act to require testimony to show that which we believe to be self-evident, namely, that there is a "reasonable possibility" that competition may be adversely affected by a practice under which manufacturers and producers sell their goods to some customers substantially cheaper than they sell like goods to the competitors of these customers. This showing in itself is sufficient to justify our conclusion that the Commission's findings of injury to competition were adequately supported by evidence.

Fifth. The Circuit Court of Appeals held, and respondent here contends, that the order was too sweeping, that it required the respondent to "conduct its business generally at its peril," and that the Commission had exceeded its jurisdiction in entering such an order. Reliance for this contention chiefly rests on National Labor Relations Board v. Express Publishing Co., 312 U.S. 426, 61 S.Ct. 693, 85 L.Ed. 930. That case held that the Labor Board could not broadly enjoin violations of all the provisions of the statute merely because a single violation of one of the Act's many provisions had been found. But it also pointed out that the Labor Board, "Having found the acts which constitute the unfair labor practice . . . is free to restrain the practice and other like or related unlawful acts." It there pointed out that this Court had applied a similar rule to a Federal Trade Commission order in Federal Trade Comm. v. Beech Nut Co., 257 U.S. 441, 455, 42 S.Ct. 150, 155, 66 L.Ed. 307, 19 A.L.R. 882. In the latter case the Court not only approved restraint of the unlawful price-fixing practices found, but "any other equivalent co-operative means of accomplishing the maintenance of prices fixed by the company." We

the seed will keep it from coming to flower." S. Rep. No. 1502, 74th Cong., 2d Sess. 4. See also H. Rep. No. 2287, 74th Cong., 2d Sess. 8; 80 Cong.Rec. 9417.

think the Commission's order here, save for the provisos in (a) and (b) later considered, is specifically aimed at the pricing practices found unlawful, and therefore does not run counter to the holding in the Express Publishing Co. case. Certainly the order in its relation to the circumstances of this case is only designed "to prevent violations, the threat of which in the future is indicated because of their similarity or relation to those unlawful acts which the Board [Commission] has found to have been committed by the . . . [respondent] in the past." National Labor Relations Board v. Express Publishing Co., supra, 312 U.S. at pages 436, 437, 61 S.Ct. at page 700.

The specific restraints of paragraphs (a) and (b) of the order are identical, except that one applies to prices respondent charges wholesalers and the other to prices charged retailers. It is seen that the first part of these paragraphs, preceding the provisos, would absolutely bar respondent from selling its table salt, regardless of quantities, to some wholesalers and retailers at prices different from that which it charged competing wholesalers and retailers for the same grade of salt. The Commission had found that respondents had been continuously engaged in such discriminations through the use of discounts, rebates and allowances. It had further found that respondent had failed to show justification for these differences by reason of a corresponding difference in its costs. Thus the restraints imposed by the Commission upon respondent are concerned with the precise unlawful practices in which it was found to have engaged for a number of years. True, the Commission did not merely prohibit future discounts, rebates, and allowances in the exact mathematical percentages previously utilized by respondent. Had the order done no more than that, respondent could have continued substantially the same unlawful practices despite the order, by simply altering the discount percentages and the quantities of salt to which the percentages applied. Paragraphs (a) and (b) up to the language of the provisos are approved.

The provisos in (a) and (b) present a more difficult problem. They read: "Provided, however, that this shall not prevent price differences of less than five cents per case which do not tend to lessen, injure or destroy competition among such wholesalers [retailers]." The first clause of the provisos, but for the second qualifying clause, would unequivocally permit respondent to maintain price differentials of less than five cents as between competing wholesalers and as between competing retailers. This clause would appear to benefit respondent, and no challenge to it, standing alone, is here raised. But respondent seriously objects to the second clause of the proviso which qualifies the permissive less-than-five-cent differentials provided in the first clause. That qualification permits such differentials only if they do "not tend to lessen, injure, or destroy competition." Respondent points out that where a differential tends in no way to injure competition, the Act permits it. "The Commission," so respondent urges, "must either find and rule that a given differential injures competition, and then prohibit it, or it must leave that differential entirely alone." Whether, and under what circumstances, if any, the

Commission might prohibit differentials which do not of themselves tend to injure competition, we need not decide, for the Commission has not in either (a) or (b) taken action which forbids such noninjurious differentials. But other objections raised to the qualifying clauses require consideration.

One of the reasons for entrusting enforcement of this Act primarily to the Commission, a body of experts, was to authorize it to hear evidence as to given differential practices and to make findings concerning possible injury to competition. Such findings are to form the basis for cease and desist orders definitely restraining the particular discriminatory practices which may tend to injure competition without justification. The effective administration of the Act, insofar as the Act entrusts administration to the Commission, would be greatly impaired, if, without compelling reasons not here present, the Commission's cease and desist orders did no more than shift to the courts in subsequent contempt proceedings for their violation the very fact questions of injury to competition, etc., which the Act requires the Commission to determine as the basis for its order. The enforcement responsibility of the courts, once a Commission order has become final either by lapse of time or by court approval, is to adjudicate questions concerning the order's violation, not questions of fact which support that valid order.

Whether on this record the Commission was compelled to exempt certain differentials of less than five cents we do not decide. But once the Commission exempted the differentials in question from its order, we are constrained to hold that as to those differentials, it could not then shift to the courts a responsibility in enforcement proceedings of trying issues of possible injury to competition, issues which Congress has primarily entrusted to the Commission.

This leaves for consideration the objection to paragraph (c) of the order which reads: "By selling such products to any retailer at prices lower than prices charged wholesalers whose customers compete with such retailer." The only criticism here urged to (c) is that it bars respondent from selling to a retailer at a price lower than that charged a wholesaler whose customers compete with the retailer. Section 2(a) of the Act specifically authorizes the Commission to bar discriminatory prices which tend to lessen or injure competition with "any person who either grants or knowingly receives the benefit of such discrimination, or with customers of either of them." This provision plainly supports paragraph (c) of the order.*

We sustain the Commission's order with the exception of the provisos in paragraphs (a) and (b) previously set out. Since the qualifying clauses constitute an important limitation to the provisos, we think the Commission should have an opportunity to reconsider the entire provisos in light of our rejection of the qualifying clauses, and to refashion these provisos as may be deemed necessary. This the

* Does this mean that a wholesaler is entitled to a lower price than a retailer whose volume or method of purchase results in cost savings to the manufacturer? Compare "functional discounts", p. 904 infra.

Commission may do upon the present evidence and findings or it may hear other evidence and make other findings on this phase of the case, should it conclude to do so.

The judgment of the Circuit Court of Appeals is reversed and the proceedings are remanded to that court to be disposed of in conformity with this opinion.

Reversed.

MR. JUSTICE JACKSON, with whom MR. JUSTICE FRANKFURTER joins, dissenting in part.

While I agree with much of the Court's opinion, I cannot accept its most significant feature, which is a new interpretation of the Robinson-Patman Act that will sanction prohibition of any discounts "if there is a reasonable *possibility* that they 'may' have the effect" to wit: to lessen, injure, destroy or prevent competition. [Emphasis supplied.] I think the law as written by the Congress and as always interpreted by this Court requires that the record show a reasonable *probability* of that effect. The difference, as every lawyer knows, is not unimportant and in many cases would be decisive.

The law rarely authorizes judgments on proof of mere possibilities. After careful consideration this Court has, at least three times and as late as 1945, refused to interpret these laws as doing so. . . .

With these interpretations on our books the Robinson-Patman Act was passed.

When the latter Act came before this Court in 1945, this same question was carefully considered and Chief Justice Stone, with the concurrence of all but two members of the Court and with no disagreement noted on this point, wrote: "It is to be observed that § 2(a) does not require a finding that the discriminations in price have in fact had an adverse effect on competition. The statute is designed to reach such discriminations 'in their incipiency,' before the harm to competition is effected. It is enough that they 'may' have the prescribed effect. Cf. Standard Fashion Co. v. Magrane-Houston Co., 258 U.S. 346, 356–357, 42 S.Ct. 360, 362, 66 L.Ed. 653. But as was held in the Standard Fashion case, supra, with respect to the like provisions of § 3 of the Clayton Act, . . . prohibiting tying clause agreements, the effect of which 'may be substantially to lessen competition,' the use of the word 'may' was not to prohibit discriminations having 'the mere possibility' of those consequences, but to reach those which would probably have the defined effect on competition." Corn Products Refining Company v. Federal Trade Commission, 324 U.S. 726, 738, 65 S.Ct. 961, 967, 89 L.Ed. 1320.

It is true that later the opinion uses the language as to possibility of injury now quoted in part by the Court as the holding of that case. But the phrase appears in such form and context and is so irreconcilable with the earlier careful and complete statement, set out above, that the inconsistency must appear to a fair reader as one of those inadvertencies into which the most careful judges sometimes fall. It is the only authority for making a thrice-rejected rule of interpretation a prevailing one. I know of no other instance in which this Court has ever held that administrative orders applying drastic regulation of business practices may hang on so slender a thread of inference.

The Court uses overtones of hostility to all quantity discounts, which I do not find in the Act, but they are translated into a rule which is fatal to any discount the Commission sees fit to attack. To say it is the law that the Commission may strike down any discount "upon the reasonable possibility that different prices for like goods to competing purchasers may substantially injure competition," coupled with the almost absolute subservience of judicial judgment to administrative experience, cf. Securities and Exchange Commission v. Chenery Corp., 332 U.S. 194, 67 S.Ct. 1575, means that judicial review is a word of promise to the ear to be broken to the hope. The law of this case, in a nutshell, is that no quantity discount is valid if the Commission chooses to say it is not. That is not the law which Congress enacted and which this Court has uniformly stated until today.

The Robinson-Patman Act itself, insofar as it relates to quantity discounts, seems to me, on its face and in light of its history, to strive for two results, both of which should be kept in mind when interpreting it.

On the one hand, it recognizes that the quantity discount may be utilized arbitrarily and without justification in savings effected by quantity sales, to give a discriminatory advantage to large buyers over small ones. This evil it would prohibit. On the other hand, it recognizes that a business practice so old and general is not without some basis in reason, that much that we call our standard of living is due to the wide availability of low-priced goods made possible by mass production and quantity distribution, and hence that whatever economies result from quantity transactions may, and indeed should, be passed down the line to the consumer. I think the Court's disposition of this case pretty much sanctions an obliteration of the difference between discounts which the Act would foster and those it would condemn.

It will illustrate my point to discuss only two of the discounts involved—two which the Commission and the Court lump together and treat exactly alike, but which to me require under the facts of this case quite different inferences as to their effect on competition.

In addition to a general ten-cent per case carload lot discount, there is what we may call a quota discount, by which customers who purchase 5,000 or more cases in a twelve-month period get a further rebate of 10 cents per case, while those who purchase 50,000 or more cases in such periods get an additional 5 cents per case. The application of this schedule to distribution of the table salt involved is substantially illustrated by one of the Company's exhibits, from which we find:

Cases purchased	Number customers	Discount per case
1–500	3,643	0
501–4,999	343	0
5,000–10,000	35	.10
10,000–49,999	14	.10
50,000 and over	5	.15

It thus appears that out of approximately 4,000 customers only 54 receive either of these two quota discounts in practice, and the larger one is available to only four or five major chain store organizations. The quota discounts allowed a customer are not related to any apparent difference in handling costs but are based solely on the volume of his purchases, which in turn depends largely on the volume of his sales, and these in turn are surely influenced by his lowered costs which he can reflect in his retail prices.

I agree that these facts warrant a *prima facie* inference of discrimination and sustain a finding of discrimination unless the Company, which best knows why and how these discounts are arrived at and which possesses all the data as to costs, comes forward with a justification. I agree, too, that the results of this system on respondent's customer list is enough to warrant the inference that the effects "may be substantially to lessen competition or tend to create a monopoly."

Even applying the stricter test of probability, I think the inference of adverse effect on competition is warranted by the facts as to the quota discounts. It is not merely probable but I think it is almost inevitable that the further ten-cent or fifteen-cent per case differential in net price of salt between the large number of small merchants and the small number of very large merchants, accelerates the trend of the former towards extinction and of the latter towards monopoly.

However, a very different problem is presented by the differential of 10 cents per case when delivered in carload lots. This carload price applies to various small purchasers who pool their orders to make a carload shipment and to all who pick up their orders, no matter how small, at the company warehouses which are maintained in ten cities. The evidence is that less than $^1/_{10}$ of 1% of the respondent's total salt business fail to get the benefit of this carload-lot discount.

It does not seem to me that one can fairly draw the inference that competition *probably* is affected by the carload-lot discount. Indeed, the discount is so small in proportion to price, salt is so small an item in wholesale or retail business and in the consumer's budget that I should think it far-fetched even to find it reasonably *possible* that competition would be *substantially* affected. Hence, the discount, whether more or less than the exact savings in handling, would not fall under condemnation of the statute. The incidents of this discount on customers is not arbitrarily determined by the volume of their business but depends upon an obvious difference in handling and delivery costs.

The Commission has forbidden respondent to continue this car-load-lot differential. The Commission has no power to prescribe prices, so that it can order only that the differential be eliminated. Unless competitive conditions make it impossible, the respondent's self-interest would dictate that it abolish the discount and maintain the higher base price, rather than make the discount universally applicable.* The result would be to raise the price of salt 10 cents per case to 99.9% of respondent's customers because ¹/₁₀ of 1% were not in a position to accept carload shipments. This is a quite different effect than the elimination of the quota discount.

It seems to me that a discount which gives a lowered cost to so large a proportion of respondent's customers and is withheld only from those whose conditions of delivery obviously impose greater handling costs, does not permit the same inferences of effect on competition as the quota discounts which reduce costs to the few only and that on a basis which ultimately is their size.

The two types of discount involved here seem to me to fall under different purposes of the Act and to require different conclusions of fact as to effect on competition. Accordingly, I should sustain the court below insofar as it sets aside the cease and desist order as to carload-lot discounts.

NOTES AND QUERIES

(1) *Discounts Based on Aggregate Annual Purchases.* Such discounts are difficult to defend even when substantial numbers of buyers have access to the larger discounts. In most situations the difference in prices would be sufficient to divert trade, and it will be hard to show significant savings in dealing with large buyers if the discount is related to aggregate purchases rather than to efficient deliveries in single large shipments.[47]

(2) *Secondary-Line Injury to Competition.* Proof of a difference in price charged to purchasers who compete on resale may suffice to establish a prima facie case under section 2(a),[48] but discriminators have succeeded with a variety of defenses either negativing anticompetitive effect or attributing it to something other than the discrimination. For example, in *Minneapolis-Honeywell Regulator Co. v. Federal Trade Commission,*[49] the Seventh Circuit Court of Appeals set aside an order by the FTC which had found a quantity discount schedule in violation of the Robinson-Patman Act. M-H

---

* Does the company have power to raise the price? Or is it prevented from doing so by competition? Is it not charging all it can get?

47. Mid-South Distributors v. Federal Trade Commission, 287 F.2d 512 (5th Cir. 1961); Standard Motor Products v. Federal Trade Commission, 265 F.2d 674 (2d Cir. 1959); Moog Industries v. Federal Trade Commission, 238 F.2d 43 (8th Cir. 1956), aff'd per curiam 355 U.S. 411, 78 S.Ct. 377, 2 L.Ed.2d 370 (1958); American Can Co. v. Bruce's Juices, Inc., 187 F.2d

919, 190 F.2d 73 (5th Cir. 1951); but cf. American Can Co. v. Russellville Canning Co., 191 F.2d 38 (8th Cir. 1951).

48. John B. Hull, Inc. v. Waterbury Petroleum Products, Inc., 588 F.2d 24, 28 (2d Cir. 1978), certiorari denied 440 U.S. 960, 99 S.Ct. 1502, 59 L.Ed.2d 773 (1979). See generally Brooks, Injury to Competition under the Robinson-Patman Act, 109 U.Pa.L.Rev. 777 (1961).

49. 191 F.2d 786 (7th Cir. 1951).

prices on temperature controls for oil burners ranged from $13.75 to $17.35 depending on the quantity purchased. The wholesale price of oil burners, into which temperature controls were incorporated by oil burner manufacturers, ranged from $45 to $114.50. On evidence that manufacturers paying the higher price for controls did not necessarily charge higher prices for their oil burners, the court concluded, contrary to the Commission, that variations in the price of controls did not affect competition among oil burner manufacturers. "Even though we assume that the burden of proving absence of injury to competition falls on the accused, we think M–H has met that burden with respect to its competitor competition."

Another example is *American Oil Co. v. Federal Trade Commission.*[50] In that case a retail gasoline "price war" had broken out in Smyrna, Georgia. Refiners, American among others, made price concessions to their harried dealers to enable them to meet competition. As a result American's price to its Smyrna dealers was at times as much as 11.5 cents a gallon lower than to American dealers in nearby Marietta. There was evidence that some customers switched from Marietta to Smyrna stations. Prices returned to normal after 18 days. The court held that there was no substantial evidence "to support a conclusion that this temporary and transient limited economic impact was the result of American's discriminatory price reduction"; and that, because American's concessions were the result rather than the cause of the "price war," injury sustained by Marietta dealers followed from the fierce competition rather than American's discrimination. Diversion of trade alone would establish only harm to competitors, not harm to competition, unless the impact was such as to impair "ability to compete." [51]

Query. Should *Morton Salt's* "presumption" of secondary line injury be applied only in cases of systematic price discrimination favoring large buyers over small ones? [52]

(3) *Private Damages for Secondary-Line Injury.* In *J. Truett Payne Co. v. Chrysler Motors Corp.*[53] the plaintiff claimed injury arising out of a "sales incentive" program under which it paid more money to purchase automobiles for resale than did its competitors. Justice Rehnquist wrote for the Court:

> Petitioner first contends that once it has proved a price discrimination in violation of § 2(a) it is entitled at a minimum to so-called "automatic damages" in the amount of the price discrimination. Petitioner concedes that in order to recover damages it must establish cognizable injury attributable to an antitrust violation and some approximation of damage. It insists, however, that the jury should be permitted to infer the requi-

50. 325 F.2d 101 (7th Cir. 1963).

51. See also Borden Co. v. Federal Trade Commission, 381 F.2d 175 (5th Cir. 1969) (remand of Borden, discussed supra p. 877, holds no secondary-line injury to competition; Borden never denied private label brand to any customer who requested it; where price differential merely reflects consumer preference for premium brand, price difference "creates no competitive advantage to the recipient of the cheaper private brand product"); Tri-Valley Packing Association v. Federal Trade Commission, 329 F.2d 694 (9th Cir. 1964) (remanding to the Commission for inquiry whether the discrimination could have had anticompetitive impact where the customer had access to markets where he could have bought at the lower price).

52. See Falls City Industries, Inc. v. Vanco Beverage, Inc., ___ U.S. ___, 103 S.Ct. 1282, ___ L.Ed.2d ___ (1983) (*Morton Salt*'s prima facie rule requires "proof of a substantial price discrimination between competing purchasers over time"; Court rejects, as an argument properly for Congress, contention that *Morton Salt* be applied only in cases of large buyer preference or seller predation).

53. 451 U.S. 557, 101 S.Ct. 1923, 68 L.Ed.2d 442 (1981).

site injury and damage from a showing of a substantial price discrimination. Petitioner notes that this Court has consistently permitted such injury to be inferred in injunctive actions brought to enforce § 2(a), e.g., Federal Trade Commission v. Morton Salt Co., 334 U.S. 37, 68 S.Ct. 822, 92 L.Ed. 1196 (1948), and argues that private suits for damages under § 4 should be treated no differently. We disagree.[54]

By its terms § 2(a) is a prophylactic statute which is violated merely upon a showing that "the effect of such discrimination *may be* substantially to lessen competition." (Emphasis supplied.) As our cases have recognized, the statute does not "require that the discriminations must in fact have harmed competition." Section 4 of the Clayton Act, in contrast, is essentially a remedial statute. It provides treble damages to "any person who *shall be injured* in his business or property by reason of anything forbidden in the antitrust laws. . . ." (Emphasis supplied.) To recover treble damages, then, a plaintiff must make some showing of actual injury attributable to something the antitrust laws were designed to prevent. It must prove more than a violation of § 2(a), since such proof establishes only that injury *may* result.

Our decision here is virtually governed by our reasoning in Brunswick Corp. v. Pueblo Bowl-O-Mat, Inc., 429 U.S. 477, 97 S.Ct. 690, 50 L.Ed.2d 701 (1977). There we rejected the contention that the mere violation of § 7 of the Clayton Act, which prohibits mergers which *may* substantially lessen competition, gives rise to a damage claim under § 4. . . . Likewise in this cases, proof of a violation does not mean that a disfavored purchaser has been actually "injured" within the meaning of § 4.

Query. How could Payne have demonstrated injury? Would it have been adequate to show that his market share declined 4% in one year (but then rose 2% the following)? That he had gone out of business even though he had approximately 25% of the market? That his customers told him he was being undersold? Should it matter that Payne did not show that the favored retailers actually lowered retail prices on the cars?

The Supreme Court did not decide whether these facts evidenced injury, remanding the case for a clearer determination whether defendant had even violated Section 2(a), an issue not addressed by the court of appeals, before deciding whether proof of injury was sufficient. As for the need to show lower retail prices by favored purchasers, the Court noted:[55]

> Respondent suggests that petitioner's inability to show that his favored competitors lowered their retail sales price should defeat recovery. That argument assumes that evidence of a lower retail price is the *sine qua non* of antitrust injury, that the disfavored purchaser is simply not "injured" unless the favored purchaser has lowered his price. If the favored purchaser has lowered his retail price, for example, the disfavored purchaser will lose sales to the extent it does not match that lower price. Similarly, if the disfavored purchaser matches the lower price, it will lose profits. Because petitioner has not shown that the favored purchasers have lowered their retail price, petitioner is arguably foreclosed from showing that it lost either sales or profits. Justice Cardozo seemingly

---

54. [Court's footnote 2.] The automatic damage theory has split the lower courts. [Citations omitted.]

55. 451 U.S. at 564 n. 4, 101 S.Ct. at 1928 n. 4, 68 L.Ed.2d at 449 n. 4. For the opinion on remand, see 670 F.2d 575 (5th Cir. 1982) (holding proof insufficient to show lessening of competition, antitrust injury, or amount of damages), certiorari denied ___ U.S. ___, 103 S.Ct. 212, 74 L.Ed.2d 169.

adopted this position in ICC v. United States, 289 U.S. 385, 390–391, 53 S.Ct. 607, 609, 77 L.Ed. 1273 (1933), a case involving rate discrimination under the Interstate Commerce Act:

> "If by reason of the discrimination, the preferred producers have been able to divert business that would otherwise have gone to the disfavored shipper, damage has resulted to the extent of the diverted profits. If the effect of the discrimination has been to force the shipper to sell at a lowered price . . . damage has resulted to the extent of the reduction. But none of these consequences is a necessary inference from discrimination without more."

Petitioner argues that is an overly narrow view of antitrust injury. To the extent a disfavored purchaser must pay more for its goods than its competitors, it is less able to compete. It has fewer funds available with which to advertise, make capital expenditures and the like. Although the inability of petitioner to show that the favored retailers lowered their retail price makes petitioner's argument particularly weak, we find it unnecessary to decide in this case whether such failure as a matter of law demonstrates no competitive injury.

(4) *Functional Discounts.* Manufacturers frequently distribute products through a variety of channels—to wholesalers, or to different varieties of jobbers, or directly to retailers. Although it is common practice to sell to these customers at different prices (i.e., to wholesalers at lower prices than retailers), legality under Section 2(a) is not assured by the mere fact that the available discounts depend on the purchaser's function. Indeed, despite Congressional concern in 1936 over the legality of such pricing,[56] the Robinson-Patman Act includes no special provisions for functional discounts. Such discounts are treated like any other type of differential pricing of commodities "of like grade and quality," to be examined for injury to competition and possible statutory defenses (e.g., cost justification).[57] Thus, even if the discrimination does not impair competition between immediate buyers, because the buyers fall into different functional classes, it may be illegal if it impairs competition "with customers" of the favored (wholesale) buyer. Further, the cost justification defense, although legally available, may not save many functional discounts because the discount often exceeds the cost differential to the seller in supplying wholesalers and (large) retailers.

Would you favor legislation exempting functional discounts from the Act? If so, how would you distinguish "wholesalers" from "retailers"? Should all such discriminatory prices be exempt, or only those which make "due allowance" for the wholesaler's costs in performing its stocking and distribution function? Would you *require* that buyers grant functional discounts to wholesalers, on the theory that unless wholesalers are given lower prices than direct buying retailers, smaller retailers who buy from the wholesalers will be unable to compete? [58]

(5) *Cooperative Purchasing.* Section 4 of the Robinson-Patman Act declares that nothing in the act shall prevent a cooperative association from returning to its members any part of the association's earnings. Neverthe-

56. See Attorney General's National Comm. to Study the Antitrust Laws 203–204 (1955).

57. See generally Van Cise, How to Quote Functional Prices, in How to Comply With the Robinson-Patman Act (Commerce Clearing House, 1957); Note, Functional Discounts under the Robin-

son-Patman Act: The Standard Oil Litigation, 67 Harv.L.Rev. 294 (1953). The cases are reviewed in ABA Antitrust Section, The Robinson-Patman Act: Policy and Law 58–64 (vol. I 1980).

58. See H.R. 12562, 94th Cong., 2d Sess. (1976); H.R. 12688, 94th Cong., 2d Sess. (1976).

less, this section does not save discriminatory discounts to buyer cooperatives organized to take advantage of volume discount systems set up by suppliers in favor of big buyers. Despite a purpose to achieve competitive parity, the cooperatives were told that the discounts were unlawful in view of the prejudicial effect on nonmember buyers. "When David slays Goliath no one else may be hurt." [59]

(6) *Breadth of Cease and Desist Orders. Federal Trade Commission v. Ruberoid Co.*, 343 U.S. 470, 72 S.Ct. 800, 96 L.Ed. 1081 (1952):

> . . . the Commission is not limited to prohibiting the illegal practice in the precise form in which it is found to have existed in the past. If the Commission is to attain the objectives Congress envisioned, it cannot be required to confine its road block to the narrow lane the transgressor has travelled . . . it is argued that the order went too far in prohibiting all price differentials between competing purchasers, although only differentials of 5% or more were found. But the Commission found that very small differences in price were material factors in competition among Ruberoid's customers, and Ruberoid offered no evidence to the contrary. In this state of the record the Commission was not required to limit its prohibition to the specific differential shown to have been adopted in the past violations of the statute.

The Court also held that the cease and desist order was valid without express provisos excepting cost-justified and competitively justified price differences, "because we think the provisos are necessarily implicit in every order issued under the authority of the Act . . . [but] the seller, in contesting enforcement or contempt proceedings, may plead only those facts constituting statutory justification which it has not had a previous opportunity to present."

The courts will not stay a cease and desist order merely on the ground that respondent is a small factor in the industry, and competing suppliers, not proceeded against by the Commission, are alleged to be offering even greater discriminatory discounts confronting respondent with drastic competitive consequences. [60]

Kauper, Cease and Desist: The History, Effect, and Scope of Clayton Act Orders of the Federal Trade Commission, 66 Mich.L.Rev. 1095 (1968), makes the following points among others: (i) Orders under the Clayton Act should be more circumspect (closer to the proscriptions of the statute and to the actual violation found) than orders under section 5 of the Federal Trade Commission Act; Congress delegated authority more broadly under Section 5. (ii) Orders should be more circumscribed where, as under the Clayton Act since the Finality Act of 1959, violations become subject to sanctions without preliminary judicial scrutiny. (iii) Although orders approaching the comprehensiveness of the statute are undesirable because they transfer to the courts questions of legality of subsequent behavior which the statutory scheme contemplates shall initially be determined by the administrative agency, orders must be broad enough to reach likely evasions, especially in the case of respondents who have engaged in a variety of practices within the spectrum of illegality. (iv) The courts in reviewing FTC orders should insist on "least restrictions" in view of the desirability of maintaining competitive pricing flexibility.

---

59. See Mid-South Distributors v. Federal Trade Commission, 287 F.2d 512, 520 (5th Cir. 1961), certiorari denied 368 U.S. 838, 82 S.Ct. 36, 7 L.Ed.2d 39.

60. Federal Trade Commission v. Universal-Rundle Corp., 387 U.S. 244, 87 S.Ct. 1622, 18 L.Ed.2d 749 (1967).

3. Buyer Liability

GREAT ATLANTIC & PACIFIC TEA CO., INC. v. FEDERAL TRADE COMMISSION

Supreme Court of the United States, 1979.
440 U.S. 69, 99 S.Ct. 925, 59 L.Ed.2d 153.

MR. JUSTICE STEWART delivered the opinion of the Court.

The question presented in this case is whether the petitioner, the Great Atlantic and Pacific Tea Company (A & P), violated § 2(f) of the Robinson-Patman Act, as amended, 15 U.S.C. § 13(f), by knowingly inducing or receiving illegal price discriminations from the Borden Company (Borden).

The alleged violation was reflected in a 1965 agreement between A & P and Borden under which Borden undertook to supply "private label" milk to more than 200 A & P stores in a Chicago area that included portions of Illinois and Indiana. This agreement resulted from an effort by A & P to achieve cost savings by switching from the sale of "brand label" milk (milk sold under the brand name of the supplying dairy) to the sale of "private label" milk (milk sold under the A & P label).

To implement this plan, A & P asked Borden, its longtime supplier, to submit an offer to supply under private label certain of A & P's milk and other dairy product requirements. After prolonged negotiations, Borden offered to grant A & P a discount for switching to private label milk provided A & P would accept limited delivery service. Borden claimed that this offer would save A & P $410,000 a year compared to what it had been paying for its dairy products. A & P, however, was not satisfied with this offer and solicited offers from other dairies. A competitor of Borden, Bowman Dairy, then submitted an offer which was lower than Borden's.[61]

At this point, A & P's Chicago buyer contacted Borden's chain store sales manager and stated, "I have a bid in my pocket. You [Borden] people are so far out of line it is not even funny. You are not even in the ball park." When the Borden representative asked for more details, he was told nothing except that a $50,000 improvement in Borden's bid "would not be a drop in the bucket."

Borden was thus faced with the problem of deciding whether to rebid. A & P at the time was one of Borden's largest customers in the Chicago area. Moreover, Borden had just invested more than five million dollars in a new dairy facility in Illinois. The loss of the A & P account would result in underutilization of this new plant. Under these circumstances, Borden decided to submit a new bid which doubled the estimated annual savings to A & P, from $410,000 to $820,000. In presenting its offer, Borden emphasized to A & P that

61. [Court's footnote 2.] The Bowman bid would have produced estimated annual savings of approximately $737,000 for A & P as compared with the first Borden bid, which would have produced estimated annual savings of $410,000.

it needed to keep A & P's business and was making the new offer in order to meet Bowman's bid. A & P then accepted Borden's bid after concluding that it was substantially better than Bowman's.

I

Based on these facts, the Federal Trade Commission filed a three-count complaint against A & P. Count I charged that A & P had violated § 5 of the Federal Trade Commission Act by misleading Borden in the course of negotiations for the private label contract, in that A & P had failed to inform Borden that its second offer was better than the Bowman bid. Count II, involving the same conduct, charged that A & P had violated § 2(f) of the Robinson-Patman Act by knowingly inducing or receiving price discriminations from Borden. Count III charged that Borden and A & P had violated § 5 of the Federal Trade Commission Act by combining to stabilize and maintain the retail and wholesale prices of milk and other dairy products.

An Administrative Law Judge found, after extended discovery and a hearing that lasted over 110 days, that A & P had acted unfairly and deceptively in accepting the second offer from Borden and had therefore violated § 5 of the Federal Trade Commission Act as charged in Count I. The Administrative Law Judge similarly found that this same conduct had violated § 2(f) of the Robinson-Patman Act. Finally, he dismissed Count III on the ground that the Commission had not satisfied its burden of proof.

On review, the Commission reversed the Administrative Law Judge's finding as to Count I. Pointing out that the question at issue was what amount of disclosure is required of the buyer during contract negotiations, the Commission held that the imposition of a duty of affirmative disclosure would be "contrary to normal business practice and we think, contrary to the public interest." Despite this ruling, however, the Commission held as to Count II that the identical conduct on the part of A & P had violated § 2(f) of the Robinson-Patman Act, finding that Borden had discriminated in price between A & P and its competitors, that the discrimination had been injurious to competition, and that A & P had known or should have known that it was the beneficiary of unlawful price discrimination.

. . .

A & P filed a petition for review of the Commission's order in the Court of Appeals for the Second Circuit. The court held that substantial evidence supported the findings of the Commission, and that as a matter of law A & P could not successfully assert a meeting competition defense because it, unlike Borden, had known that Borden's offer was better than Bowman's. . . . Because the judgment of the Court of Appeals raises important issues of federal law, we granted certiorari.

II

The Robinson-Patman Act was passed in response to the problem perceived in the increased market power and coercive practices of chain stores and other big buyers that threatened the existence of small independent retailers. Notwithstanding this concern with buyers, however, the emphasis of the Act is in § 2(a), which prohibits price discriminations by sellers. Indeed, the original Patman Bill as reported by Committees of both Houses prohibited only seller activity, with no mention of buyer liability. Section 2(f) of the Act, making buyers liable for inducing or receiving price discriminations by sellers, was the product of a belated floor amendment near the conclusion of the Senate debates.

As finally enacted, § 2(f) provides:

"That it shall be unlawful for any person engaged in commerce, in the course of such commerce, knowingly to induce or receive a discrimination in price *which is prohibited by this section*." (Emphasis added.)

Liability under § 2(f) thus is limited to situations where the price discrimination is one "which is prohibited by this section." While the phrase "this section" refers to the entire § 2 of the Act, only subsections (a) and (b) dealing with seller liability involve discriminations in price. Under the plain meaning of § 2(f), therefore, a buyer cannot be liable if a prima facie case could not be established against a seller or if the seller has an affirmative defense. In either situation, there is no price discrimination "prohibited by this section." The legislative history of § 2(f) fully confirms the conclusion that buyer liability under § 2(f) is dependent on seller liability under § 2(a).

. . .

III

The petitioner, relying on this plain meaning of § 2(f) . . . , argues that it cannot be liable under § 2(f) if Borden had a valid meeting competition defense. The respondent, on the other hand, argues that the petitioner may be liable even assuming that Borden had such a defense. The meeting competition defense, the respondent contends, must in these circumstances be judged from the point of view of the buyer. Since A & P knew for a fact that the final Borden bid beat the Bowman bid, it was not entitled to assert the meeting competition defense even though Borden may have honestly believed that it was simply meeting competition. Recognition of a meeting competition defense for the buyer in this situation, the respondent argues, would be contrary to the basic purpose of the Robinson-Patman Act to curtail abuses by large buyers.

A

The short answer to these contentions of the respondent is that Congress did not provide in § 2(f) that a buyer can be liable even if the seller has a valid defense. The clear language of § 2(f) states that a buyer can be liable only if he receives a price discrimination "prohibited by this section." If a seller has a valid meeting competition defense, there is simply no prohibited price discrimination.

. . .

B

[This] Court [has] warned against interpretations of the Robinson-Patman Act which "extend beyond the prohibitions of the Act and, in so doing, help give rise to a price uniformity and rigidity in open conflict with the purposes of other antitrust legislation." Imposition of § 2(f) liability on the petitioner in this case would lead to just such price uniformity and rigidity.

In a competitive market, uncertainty among sellers will cause them to compete for business by offering buyers lower prices. Because of the evils of collusive action, the Court has held that the exchange of price information by competitors violates the Sherman Act. United States v. Container Corp., 393 U.S. 333, 89 S.Ct. 510, 21 L.Ed. 2d 526. Under the view advanced by the respondent, however, a buyer, to avoid liability, must either refuse a seller's bid or at least inform him that his bid has beaten competition. Such a duty of affirmative disclosure would almost inevitably frustrate competitive bidding and, by reducing uncertainty, lead to price matching and anticompetitive cooperation among sellers.

Ironically, the Commission itself, in dismissing the charge under § 5 of the Federal Trade Commission Act in this case, recognized the dangers inherent in a duty of affirmative disclosure:

"The imposition of a duty of affirmative disclosure, applicable to a buyer whenever a seller states that his offer is intended to meet competition, is contrary to normal business practice and, we think, contrary to the public interest."

. . .

"We fear a scenario where the seller automatically attaches a meeting competition caveat to every bid. The buyer would then state whether such bid meets, beats, or loses to another bid. The seller would then submit a second, a third, and perhaps a fourth bid until finally he is able to ascertain his competitor's bid."

The effect of the finding that the same conduct of the petitioner violated § 2(f), however, is to impose the same duty of affirmative disclosure which the Commission condemned as anticompetitive, "contrary to the public interest," and "contrary to normal business practice," in dismissing the charge under § 5 of the Federal Trade Commission Act. Neither the Commission nor the Court of Appeals offered any explanation for this apparent anomaly.

[W]e decline to adopt a construction of § 2(f) that is contrary to its plain meaning and would lead to anticompetitive results. Accordingly, we hold that a buyer who has done no more than accept the lower of two prices competitively offered does not violate § 2(f) provided the seller has a meeting competition defense.

. . .

Accordingly, the judgment is reversed.

It is so ordered.

[Justice Stevens did not participate in the decision; Justice White concurred in Parts I, II, and III of the Court's opinion. The dissenting opinion of Justice Marshall is omitted.]

NOTES AND QUERIES

(1) *Prior Cases.* Section 2(f) has not been extensively used. The major Supreme Court case in the area prior to *A & P* is *Automatic Canteen Co. v. Federal Trade Commission.*[62] There the Court established that only *knowing* receipt of an *illegal* concession violated the section; the buyer must be aware not only that he is receiving a lower price but also that it is illegal. The Court allowed knowledge of illegality to be inferred from certain fact situations, e.g.: "a buyer who knows that he buys in the same quantities as his competitor and is served by the seller in the same manner or with the same amount of exertion as the other buyer can fairly be charged with notice that a substantial price differential cannot be justified." If the methods of service or quantities of purchase differ, a *prima facie* case could be established by a showing that "such differences could not give rise to sufficient savings in the cost of manufacture, sale or delivery to justify the price differential, and that the buyer, knowing these were the only differences, should have known that they could not give rise to sufficient cost savings." Knowledge would be inferred from a substantial disparity between the cost differential and the price differential.

The Court rejected the Government's contention that a large price differential and nothing more was sufficient to show a *prima facie* case, shifting to the recipient the burden of coming forward with evidence of seller's justification for discrimination. The Court was concerned that indiscriminate attacks on price concessions secured by buyers might "help give rise to a price uniformity and rigidity in open conflict with the purposes of other antitrust legislation." They wished to preserve "that sturdy bargaining between buyer and seller for which scope was presumably left in the areas of our economy not otherwise regulated."

(2) *Queries.* What result under *A & P* if: (a) Borden had accidentally learned about Bowman's offer and then came back to A & P with an intentionally lower price, but without telling A & P that it knew it was beating Bowman's price. The lower price would invalidate Borden's meeting competition defense (see p. 908, supra). Would A & P's liability therefore be affected? If so, how could A & P guard against liability? (b) A & P told Borden that its offer was not low enough, although it already was below Bowman's, and Borden then rebid in response to this intentional misrepresentation? Should the "lying buyer" be treated any differently than the silent one? Could it under *A & P?*[63]

62. 346 U.S. 61, 73 S.Ct. 1017, 97 L.Ed. 1454 (1953).

63. The Court in A & P noted that because A & P was not a lying buyer, "we need not decide whether such a buyer could be liable under § 2(f) even if the seller has a meeting-competition defense." 440 U.S. at 82 n. 15, 99 S.Ct. at 934, 59 L.Ed.2d at 164. See Kroger Co. v. Federal Trade Commission, 438 F.2d

(3) *Use of Section 5 of the Federal Trade Commission Act. Grand Union Co. v. Federal Trade Commission* [64] sustained an FTC order under section 5 against a big buyer's inducing or receiving discriminatory advertising allowances. Section 2(d) of the Robinson-Patman Act, which deals with such allowances, is explicitly applicable to the seller who pays the allowance; section 2(f), which does explicitly reach buyers' receiving illicit payments, is limited to discriminations in *price*, and thus was inapplicable to receipt of advertising allowances. The court held that the Commission had not overextended the substantive coverage of the Robinson-Patman Act, because Congress could not have intended to permit buyers to receive what sellers were prohibited from giving. The omission of explicit provision for buyer responsibility under section 2(d) must be regarded as inadvertent. See Rahl, Does Section 5 of the Federal Trade Commission Act Extend the Clayton Act?, 5 Antitrust Bull. 533 (1960), arguing against the use of section 5 to avoid specific limitations formulated by Congress in defining Clayton Act offenses. Rahl conceded, however, that the section can be used to reach cases where the Clayton Act is inapplicable because of a "merely technical deficiency," e.g. that the transaction involves agency rather than sales, or services rather than goods. He would not permit it to be used "to create lower qualitative standards" than those prescribed in the Clayton Act.

C. DEFENSES

-----

1. MEETING COMPETITION

STANDARD OIL CO. v. FEDERAL TRADE COMMISSION

Supreme Court of the United States, 1951.
340 U.S. 231, 71 S.Ct. 240, 95 L.Ed. 239.

MR. JUSTICE BURTON delivered the opinion of the Court.

In this case the Federal Trade Commission challenged the right of the Standard Oil Company, under the Robinson-Patman Act, to sell gasoline to four comparatively large "jobber" customers in Detroit at a less price per gallon than it sold like gasoline to many comparatively small service station customers in the same area. The company's defenses were that (1) the sales involved were not in interstate commerce and (2) its lower price to the jobbers was justified because made to retain them as customers and in good faith to meet an equally low price of a competitor. The Commission, with one member dissenting, ordered the company to cease and desist from making such a price differential. The Court of Appeals slightly modified the order and required its enforcement as modified. We granted certiorari on petition of the company because the case presents an important issue under the Robinson-Patman Act which has not been settled by this Court. The case was argued at our October Term, 1949, and reargued at this term.

1372 (6th Cir. 1971), certiorari denied 404 U.S. 871, 92 S.Ct. 59, 30 L.Ed.2d 115 (finding lying buyer liable under Section 2(f)).

64. 300 F.2d 92 (2d Cir. 1962).

For the reasons hereinafter stated, we agree with the court below that the sales were made in interstate commerce but we agree with petitioner that, under the Act, the lower price to the jobbers was justified if it was made to retain each of them as a customer and in good faith to meet an equally low price of a competitor.

I. Facts.

Reserving for separate consideration the facts determining the issue of interstate commerce, the other material facts are summarized here on the basis of the Commission's findings. The sales described are those of Red Crown gasoline because those sales raise all of the material issues and constitute about 90% of petitioner's sales in the Detroit area.

Since the effective date of the Robinson-Patman Act, June 19, 1936, petitioner has sold its Red Crown gasoline to its "jobber" customers at its tank-car prices. Those prices have been $1\frac{1}{2}$ cents per gallon less than its tank-wagon prices to service station customers for identical gasoline in the same area. In practice, the service stations have resold the gasoline at the prevailing retail service station prices.[65] Each of petitioner's so-called "jobber" customers has been free to resell its gasoline at retail or wholesale. Each, at some time, has resold some of it at retail. One now resells it only at retail. The others now resell it largely at wholesale. As to resale prices, two of the "jobbers" have resold their gasoline only at the prevailing wholesale or retail rates. The other two, however, have reflected, in varying degrees, petitioner's reductions in the cost of the gasoline to them by reducing their resale prices of that gasoline below the prevailing rates. The effect of these reductions has thus reached competing retail service stations in part through retail stations operated by the "jobbers" and in part through retail stations which purchased gasoline from the "jobbers" at less than the prevailing tank-wagon prices. The Commission found that such reduced resale prices "have resulted in injuring, destroying, and preventing competition between said favored dealers and retail dealers in respondent's [petitioner's] gasoline and other major brands of gasoline . . .." 41 F.T.C. 263, 283. The distinctive characteristics of these "jobbers" are that each (1) maintains sufficient bulk storage to take delivery of gasoline in tank-car quantities (of 8,000 to 12,000 gallons) rather than in tank-wagon quantities (of 700 to 800 gallons) as is customary for service stations; (2) owns and operates tank wagons and other facilities for delivery of gasoline to service stations; (3) has an established business sufficient to insure purchases of from one to two million gallons a year; and (4) has adequate credit responsibility.[66] While the cost of petitioner's

65. [Footnotes 65 to 68 are from the original opinions. They have been renumbered.] About 150 of these stations are owned or leased by the customer independently of petitioner. Their operators buy all of their gasoline from petitioner under short-term agreements. Its other 208 stations are leased or subleased from petitioner for short terms.

66. Not denying the established industry practice of recognizing such dealers as a distinctive group for operational convenience, the Commission held that petitioner's classification of these four

sales and deliveries of gasoline to each of these four "jobbers" is no doubt less, per gallon, than the cost of its sales and deliveries of like gasoline to its service station customers in the same area, there is no finding that such difference accounts for the entire reduction in price made by petitioner to these "jobbers," and we proceed on the assumption that it does not entirely account for that difference.

Petitioner placed its reliance upon evidence offered to show that its lower price to each jobber was made in order to retain that jobber as a customer and in good faith to meet an equally low price offered by one or more competitors. The Commission, however, treated such evidence as not relevant. . . .

III.   There Should Be a Finding as to Whether or Not Petitioner's Price Reduction Was Made in Good Faith to Meet a Lawful Equally Low Price of a Competitor

Petitioner presented evidence tending to prove that its tank-car price was made to each "jobber" in order to retain that "jobber" as a customer and in good faith to meet a lawful and equally low price of a competitor. Petitioner sought to show that it succeeded in retaining these customers, although the tank-car price which it offered them merely approached or matched, and did not undercut, the lower prices offered them by several competitors of petitioner. The trial examiner made findings on the point but the Commission declined to do so, saying: "Based on the record in this case the Commission concludes as a matter of law that it is not material whether the discriminations in price granted by the respondent to the said four dealers were made to meet equally low prices of competitors. The Commission further concludes as a matter of law that it is unnecessary for the Commission to determine whether the alleged competitive prices were in fact available or involved gasoline of like grade or quality or of equal public acceptance. Accordingly the Commission does not attempt to find the facts regarding those matters because, even though the lower prices in question may have been made by respondent in good faith to meet the lower prices of competitors, this does not constitute a defense in the face of affirmative proof that the effect of the discrimination was to injure, destroy and prevent competition with the retail stations operated by the said named dealers and with stations operated by their retailer-customers."   41 F.T.C. 263, 281–282.

The court below affirmed the Commission's position.

There is no doubt that under the Clayton Act, before its amendment by the Robinson-Patman Act, this evidence would have been material and, if accepted, would have established a complete defense to the charge of unlawful discrimination. At that time the material provisions of § 2 were as follows: "Sec. 2. That it shall be unlawful

dealers as "jobbers" was arbitrary because it made "no requirement that said jobbers should sell only at wholesale." 41 F.T.C. at 273. We use the term "job- ber" in this opinion merely as one of convenience and identification, because the result here is the same whether these four dealers are wholesalers or retailers.

for any person engaged in commerce, in the course of such commerce, either directly or indirectly to discriminate in price between different purchasers of commodities . . . where the effect of such discrimination may be to substantially lessen competition or tend to create a monopoly in any line of commerce: *Provided, That nothing herein contained shall prevent* discrimination in price between purchasers of commodities on account of differences in the grade, quality, or quantity of the commodity sold, or that makes only due allowance for difference in the cost of selling or transportation, or *discrimination in price in the same or different communities made in good faith to meet competition: And provided further,* That nothing herein contained shall prevent persons engaged in selling goods, wares, or merchandise in commerce from selecting their own customers in bona fide transactions and not in restraint of trade." (Emphasis added within the first proviso.)

The question before us, therefore, is whether the amendments made by the Robinson-Patman Act deprived those facts of their previously recognized effectiveness as a defense. The material provisions of § 2, as amended, are quoted below, showing in italics those clauses which bear upon the proviso before us. The modified provisions are distributed between the newly created subsections (a) and (b). These must be read together and in relation to the provisions they supersede. The original phrase "That nothing herein contained shall prevent" is still used to introduce each of the defenses. The defense relating to the meeting of the price of a competitor appears only in subsection (b). There it is applied to discriminations in services or facilities as well as to discriminations in price, which alone are expressly condemned in subsection (a). In its opinion in the instant case, the Commission recognizes that it is an absolute defense to a charge of price discrimination for a seller to prove, under § 2(a), that its price differential makes only due allowances for differences in cost or for price changes made in response to changing market conditions. Each of these three defenses is introduced by the same phrase "nothing . . . shall prevent", and all are embraced in the same word "justification" in the first sentence of § 2(b). It is natural, therefore, to conclude that each of these defenses is entitled to the same effect, without regard to whether there also appears an affirmative showing of actual or potential injury to competition at the same or a lower level traceable to the price differential made by the seller. The Commission says, however, that the proviso in § 2(b) as to a seller meeting in good faith a lower competitive price is not an absolute defense if an injury to competition may result from such price reduction. We find no basis for such a distinction between the defenses in § 2(a) and (b).

The defense in subsection (b), now before us, is limited to a price reduction made to meet in good faith an equally low price of a competitor. It thus eliminates certain difficulties which arose under the original Clayton Act. For example, it omits reference to discriminations in price "in the same or different communities . . ." and it thus restricts the proviso to price differentials occurring in actual competition. It also excludes reductions which undercut the "lower price" of a competitor. None of these changes, however, cut into the actual core of the defense. That still consists of the provision that wherever a lawful lower price of a competitor threatens to deprive a seller of a customer, the seller, to retain that customer, may in good faith meet that lower price. Actual competition, at least in this elemental form, is thus preserved.

Subsections 2(a) and (b), as amended, are as follows:

"Sec. 2. (a) That it shall be unlawful for any person engaged in commerce, in the course of such commerce, either directly or indirectly, to discriminate in price between different purchasers of commodities of like grade and quality . . . where the effect of such discrimination may be substantially to lessen competition or tend to create a monopoly in any line of commerce, or to injure, destroy, or prevent competition with any person who either grants or knowingly receives the benefit of such discrimination, or with customers of either of them: *Provided, That nothing herein contained shall prevent* differentials which make only due allowance for differences in the cost of manufacture, sale, or delivery resulting from the differing methods or quantities in which such commodities are to such purchasers sold or delivered: . . . *And provided further, That nothing herein contained shall prevent* price changes from time to time . . . in response to changing conditions affecting the market for or the marketability of the goods concerned . . . .

"(b) Upon proof being made, at any hearing on a complaint under this section, that there has been discrimination in price or services or facilities furnished, *the burden of rebutting the prima-facie case thus made by showing justification* shall be upon the person charged with a violation of this section, and *unless justification shall be affirmatively shown,* the Commission is authorized to issue an order terminating the discrimination: *Provided, however, That nothing herein contained shall prevent* a seller rebutting the prima-facie case thus made by *showing that his lower price or the furnishing of services or facilities to any purchaser or purchasers was made in good faith to meet an equally low price of a competitor, or the services or facilities furnished by a competitor.*" (Emphasis added in part.) 49 Stat. 1526, 15 U.S.C. § 13(a) and (b), 15 U.S.C.A. § 13(a, b).

This right of a seller, under § 2(b), to meet in good faith an equally low price of a competitor has been considered here before. Both in Corn Products Refining Co. v. Federal Trade Comm., 324 U.S. 726, 65 S.Ct. 961, 89 L.Ed. 1320, and in Federal Trade Comm. v. A.E. Staley Mfg. Co., 324 U.S. 746, 65 S.Ct. 971, 89 L.Ed. 1338, evidence in support of this defense was reviewed at length. There would have been no occasion thus to review it, under the theory now contended for by the Commission. While this Court did not sustain the seller's defense in either case, it did unquestionably recognize the relevance of the evidence in support of that defense. The decision in each case was based upon the insufficiency of the seller's evidence to establish its defense, not upon the inadequacy of its defense as a matter of law. . . .

All that petitioner asks in the instant case is that its evidence be considered and that findings be made by the Commission as to the sufficiency of that evidence to support petitioner's defense under § 2(b).

In addition, there has been widespread understanding that, under the Robinson-Patman Act, it is a complete defense to a charge of price discrimination for the seller to show that its price differential has been made in good faith to meet a lawful and equally low price of a competitor. This understanding is reflected in actions and statements of members and counsel of the Federal Trade Commission. Representatives of the Department of Justice have testified to the effectiveness and value of the defense under the Robinson-Patman Act. We see no reason to depart now from that interpretation.[67]

The heart of our national economic policy long has been faith in the value of competition. In the Sherman and Clayton Acts, as well as in the Robinson-Patman Act, "Congress was dealing with competition, which it sought to protect, and monopoly, which it sought to prevent." A.E. Staley Mfg. Co. v. Federal Trade Comm., 7 Cir., 135 F.2d 453, 455. We need not now reconcile, in its entirety, the economic theory which underlies the Robinson-Patman Act with that of the Sherman and Clayton Acts.[68]

67. Attention has been directed again to the legislative history of the proviso. This was considered in the Corn Products and Staley cases. See especially, 324 U.S. at pages 752–753, 65 S.Ct. at page 974. We find that the legislative history, at best, is inconclusive. It indicates that it was the purpose of Congress to limit, but not to abolish, the essence of the defense recognized as absolute in § 2 of the original Clayton Act, 38 Stat. 730, where a seller's reduction in price had been made "in good faith to meet competition . . . ." For example, the legislative history recognizes that the Robinson-Patman Act limits that defense to price differentials that do not undercut the competitor's price, and the amendments fail to protect differentials between prices in different communities where those prices are not actually competitive. There is also a suggestion in the debates, as well as in the remarks of this Court in the Staley case, supra, that a competitor's lower price, which may be met by a seller under the protection of § 2(b), must be a lawful price. . . . there was a statement made by the managers on the part of the House of Representatives, accompanying the conference report, which said that the new clause was a "provision relating to the question of meeting competition, intended to operate only as a rule of evidence in a proceeding before the Federal Trade Commission . . . ." H.R. Rep. No. 2951, 74th Cong., 2d Sess. 7. The Chairman of the House Conferees also received permission to print in the Record an explanation of the proviso. 80 Cong. Rec. 9418. This explanation emphasizes the same interpretation as that put on the proviso in the Staley case to the effect that the lower price which lawfully may be met by a seller must be a lawful price. That statement, however, neither justifies disregarding the proviso nor failing to make findings of fact where evidence is offered that the prices met by the seller are lawful prices and that the meeting of them is in good faith.

68. It has been suggested that, in theory, the Robinson-Patman Act, 15 U.S. C.A. §§ 13, 13a, 13b, 21a, as a whole is inconsistent with the Sherman and Clayton Acts, 15 U.S.C.A. §§ 1–7, 15 note, 12 et seq. See Adelman, Effective Competition and the Antitrust Laws, 61 Harv.L. Rev. 1289, 1327–1350; Burns, The Anti-Trust Laws and the Regulation of Price Competition, 4 Law & Contemp.Prob. 301; Learned & Isaacs, The Robinson-

It is enough to say that Congress did not seek by the Robinson-Patman Act either to abolish competition or so radically to curtail it that a seller would have no substantial right of self-defense against a price raid by a competitor. For example, if a large customer requests his seller to meet a temptingly lower price offered to him by one of his seller's competitors, the seller may well find it essential, as a matter of business survival, to meet that price rather than to lose the customer. It might be that this customer is the seller's only available market for the major portion of the seller's product, and that the loss of this customer would result in forcing a much higher unit cost and higher sales price upon the seller's other customers. There is nothing to show a congressional purpose, in such a situation, to compel the seller to choose only between ruinously cutting its prices to all its customers to match the price offered to one, or refusing to meet the competition and then ruinously raising its prices to its remaining customers to cover increased unit costs. There is, on the other hand, plain language and established practice which permits a seller, through § 2(b), to retain a customer by realistically meeting in good faith the price offered to that customer, without necessarily changing the seller's price to its other customers.

In a case where a seller sustains the burden of proof placed upon it to establish its defense under § 2(b), we find no reason to destroy that defense indirectly, merely because it also appears that the beneficiaries of the seller's price reductions may derive a competitive advantage from them or may, in a natural course of events, reduce their own resale prices to their customers. It must have been obvious to Congress that any price reduction to any dealer may always affect competition at that dealer's level as well as at the dealer's resale level, whether or not the reduction to the dealer is discriminatory. Likewise, it must have been obvious to Congress that any price reductions initiated by a seller's competitor would, if not met by the seller, affect competition at the beneficiary's level or among the beneficiary's customers just as much as if those reductions had been met by the seller. The proviso in § 2(b), as interpreted by the Commission, would not be available when there was or might be an injury to competition at a resale level. So interpreted, the proviso would have such little, if any, applicability as to be practically meaningless. We may, therefore, conclude that Congress meant to permit the natural consequences to follow the seller's action in meeting in good faith a lawful and equally low price of its competitor.

In its argument here, the Commission suggests that there may be some situations in which it might recognize the proviso in § 2(b) as a complete defense, even though the seller's differential in price did injure competition. In support of this, the Commission indicates that in each case it must weigh the potentially injurious effect of a seller's price reduction upon competition at all lower levels against its benefi-

Patman Law: Some Assumptions and Expectations, 15 Harv.Bus.Rev. 137; McAllister, Price Control by Law in the United States: A Survey, 4 Law & Contemp.Prob. 273.

cial effect in permitting the seller to meet competition at its own level. In the absence of more explicit requirements and more specific standards of comparison than we have here, it is difficult to see how an injury to competition at a level below that of the seller can thus be balanced fairly against a justification for meeting the competition at the seller's level. We hesitate to accept § 2(b) as establishing such a dubious defense. On the other hand, the proviso is readily understandable as simply continuing in effect a defense which is equally absolute, but more limited in scope than that which existed under § 2 of the original Clayton Act.

The judgment of the Court of Appeals, accordingly, is reversed and the case is remanded to that court with instructions to remand it to the Federal Trade Commission to make findings in conformity with this opinion. It is so ordered.

Reversed and remanded.

MR. JUSTICE REED, dissenting.

[The dissenting opinion relied heavily on a review of the legislative history of the Robinson-Patman Act, particularly a statement by Representative Utterback, Chairman of the House Managers, in connection with the adoption of the Conference Report by the House, that the proviso "does not set up the meeting of competition as an absolute bar to the charge of discrimination under the bill. It merely permits it to be shown in evidence . . ." The opinion continues:]

The statutory development and the information before Congress concerning the need for strengthening the competitive price provision of the Clayton Act made clear that the evil dealt with by the proviso of § 2(b) was the easy avoidance of the prohibition against price-discrimination. The control of that evil was an important objective of the Robinson-Patman Act. The debates, the Commission's report and recommendation and statutory changes show this. The Conference Report and the explanation by one of the managers, Mr. Utterback, are quite definitive upon the point. Because of experience under the Clayton Act, Congress refused to continue its competitive price proviso. Yet adoption of petitioner's position would permit a seller of nationally distributed goods to discriminate in favor of large chain retailers, for the seller could give to the large retailer a price lower than that charged to small retailers, and could then completely justify its discrimination by showing that the large retailer had first obtained the same low price from a local low-cost producer of competitive goods. This is the very type of competition that Congress sought to remedy. To permit this would not seem consonant with the other provisions of the Robinson-Patman Act, strengthening regulatory powers of the Commission in "quantity" sales, special allowances and changing economic conditions.

The structure and wording of the Robinson-Patman Amendment to the Clayton Act also conduce to our conclusion. In the original Clayton Act, § 2 was not divided into subsections. In that statute, § 2 stated the body of the substantive offense, and then listed, in a series of provisos, various circumstances under which discriminations in price were permissible. Thus the statute provided that discriminations were not illegal if made on account of differences in the grade of the commodity sold, or differences in selling or transportation costs. Listed among these absolute justifications of the Clayton Act appeared the provision that "nothing herein contained shall prevent discrimination in price . . . made in good faith to meet competition". The Robinson-Patman Act, however, made two changes in respect of the "meeting competition" provision, one as to its location, the other in the phrasing. Unlike the original statute, § 2 of the Robinson-Patman Act is divided into two subsections. The first, § 2(a), retained the statement of substantive offense and the series of provisos treated by the Commission as affording full justifications for price discriminations; § 2(b) was created to deal with procedural problems in Federal Trade Commission proceedings, specifically to treat the question of burden of proof. In the process of this division, the "meeting competition" provision was separated from the other provisos, set off from the substantive provisions of § 2(a), and relegated to the position of a proviso to the procedural subsection, § 2(b). Unless it is believed that this change of position was fortuitous, it can be inferred that Congress meant to curtail the defense of meeting competition when it banished this proviso from the substantive division to the procedural. In the same way, the language changes made by § 2(b) of the Robinson-Patman Act reflect an intent to diminish the effectiveness of the sweeping defense offered by the Clayton Act's "meeting of competition" proviso. The original provisos in the Clayton Act, and the provisos now appearing in § 2(a), are worded to make it clear that nothing shall prevent certain price practices, such as "price . . . differentials . . . [making] . . . due allowance for differences in the cost of manufacture . . .," or "price changes . . . in response to changing conditions affecting the market for . . . the goods concerned . . . ." But in contrast to these provisions, the proviso to § 2(b) does not provide that nothing "shall prevent" a certain price practice; it provides only that "nothing . . . shall prevent a seller rebutting . . . [a] . . . prima facie case . . . by showing" a certain price practice—meeting a competitive price. The language thus shifts the focus of the proviso from a matter of substantive defense to a matter of proof. Consistent with each other, these modifications made by the Robinson-Patman Act are also consistent with the intent of Congress expressed in the legislative history.

THE CHIEF JUSTICE and MR. JUSTICE BLACK join in this dissent.

MR. JUSTICE MINTON took no part in the consideration or decision of this case.

NOTES AND QUERIES

(1) *Verification of Competing Offer.* In *United States v. United States Gypsum Co.*[69] (discussed supra pp. 400–408) the defendants claimed that they had engaged in interseller price verification (telephoning competitors to determine the price currently being offered to a specific customer) for the purpose of complying with the meeting competition defense, and that they consequently should not be liable under Section 1 of the Sherman Act even if the result were to stabilize prices. The Supreme Court held that interseller price verification was not a requirement for the Section 2(b) defense:

> A good-faith belief, rather than absolute certainty, that a price concession is being offered to meet an equally low price offered by a competitor is sufficient to satisfy the Robinson-Patman's § 2(b) defense. While casual reliance on uncorroborated reports of buyers or sales representatives without further investigation may not, as we noted earlier, be sufficient to make the requisite showing of good faith, nothing in the language of § 2(b) . . . indicates that direct discussions of price between competitors are required. Nor has any court, so far as we are aware, ever imposed such a requirement.

> The so-called problem of the untruthful buyer which concerned the Court of Appeals does not in our view call for a different approach to the § 2(b) defense. The good-faith standard remains the benchmark against which the seller's conduct is to be evaluated, and we agree with the government and the FTC that this standard can be satisfied by efforts falling short of interseller verification in most circumstances where the seller has only vague, generalized doubts about the reliability of its commercial adversary—the buyer.[70] Given the fact specific nature of the inquiry, it is difficult to predict all the factors the FTC or a court would consider in appraising a seller's good faith in matching a competing offer in these circumstances. Certainly, evidence that a seller had received reports of similar discounts from other customers, or was threatened with a termination of purchases if the discount were not met, would be relevant in this regard. Efforts to corroborate the reported discount by seeking documentary evidence or by appraising its reasonableness in terms of available market data would also be probative as would the seller's past experience with the particular buyer in question.

> There remains the possibility that in a limited number of situations a seller may have substantial reasons to doubt the accuracy of reports of a competing offer and may be unable to corroborate such reports in any of the generally accepted ways. Thus the defense may be rendered unavailable since unanswered questions about the reliability of a buyer's representations may well be inconsistent with a good-faith belief that a com-

---

69. 438 U.S. 422, 98 S.Ct. 2864, 57 L.Ed.2d 854 (1978).

70. [Court's footnote 29.] "Although a seller may take advantage of the meeting competition defense only if it has a commercially reasonable belief that its price concession is necessary to meet an equally low price of a competitor, a seller may acquire this belief, and hence perfect its defense, by doing everything reasonably feasible—short of violating some other statute, such as the Sherman Act—

to determine the veracity of a customer's statement that he has been offered a lower price. If, after making reasonable, lawful, inquiries, the seller cannot ascertain that the buyer is lying, the seller is entitled to make the sale. There is no need for a seller to discuss price with his competitors to take advantage of the meeting competition defense." (Citations omitted.) Brief of Petitioner, 86–87, and n. 78.

peting offer had in fact been made.[71] As an abstract proposition, resort to interseller verification as a means of checking the buyer's reliability seems a possible solution to the seller's plight, but careful examination reveals serious problems with the practice.

Both economic theory and common human experience suggest that interseller verification—if undertaken on an isolated and infrequent basis with no provision for reciprocity or cooperation—will not serve its putative function of corroborating the representations of unreliable buyers regarding the existence of competing offers. Price concessions by oligopolists generally yield competitive advantages only if secrecy can be maintained; when the terms of the concession are made publicly known, other competitors are likely to follow and any advantage to the initiator is lost in the process. See generally F. Scherer, Industrial Market Structure and Economic Performance 208–209, 449 (1970); P. Areeda, Antitrust Analysis 230–231 (1974); Note, Meeting Competition Under the Robinson-Patman Act, 90 Harv.L.Rev. 1476, 1480–1481 (1977). See also United States v. Container Corp., 393 U.S., at 337, 89 S.Ct., at 512. Thus, if one seller offers a price concession for the purpose of winning over one of his competitor's customers, it is unlikely that the same seller will freely inform its competitor of the details of the concession so that it can be promptly matched and diffused. Instead, such a seller would appear to have at least as great an incentive to misrepresent the existence or size of the discount as would the buyer who received it. Thus verification, if undertaken on a one shot basis for the sole purpose of complying with the § 2(b) defense, does not hold out much promise as a means of shoring up buyers' representations.

The other variety of interseller verification is, like the conduct charged in the instant case, undertaken pursuant to an agreement, either tacit or express, providing for reciprocity among competitors in the exchange of price information. Such an agreement would make little economic sense, in our view, if its sole purpose were to guarantee all participants the opportunity to match the secret price concessions of other participants under § 2(b) of the Robinson-Patman Act. For in such circumstances, each seller would know that his price concession could not be kept from his competitors and no seller participating in the information exchange arrangement would, therefore, have any incentive for deviating from the prevailing price level in the industry. See United States v. Container Corp., 393 U.S., at 336–337, 89 S.Ct., at 512. Regardless of its putative purpose, the most likely consequence of any such agreement to exchange price information would be the stabilization of industry prices. Instead of facilitating use of the § 2(b) defense, such an agreement would have the effect of eliminating the very price concessions which provide the main element of competition in oligopolistic industries and the primary occasion for resort to the meeting competition defense.

Especially in oligopolistic industries such as the gypsum board industry, the exchange of price information among competitors carries with it the added potential for the development of concerted price-fixing arrangements which lie at the core of the Sherman Act's prohibitions. The Department of Justice's 1977 Report on the Robinson-Patman Act focused on the growing use of the Act as a cover for price fixing. . . .

---

71. [Court's footnote 31.] We need not and do not decide that in all such circumstances the defense would be unavailable. The case by case interpretation and elaboration of the § 2(b) defense is properly left to the other federal courts and the FTC in the context of concrete fact situations. . . .

We are left, therefore, on the one hand, with doubts about both the need for and the efficacy of interseller verification as a means of facilitating compliance with § 2(b) of the Robinson-Patman Act, and, on the other, with recognition of the tendency for price discussions between competitors to contribute to the stability of oligopolistic prices and open the way for the growth of prohibited anticompetitive activity. To recognize even a limited "controlling circumstance" exception for interseller verification in such circumstances would be to remove from scrutiny under the Sherman Act conduct falling near its core with no assurance, and indeed with serious doubts, that competing antitrust policies would be served thereby. In Automatic Canteen v. FTC, 346 U.S. 61, 74, 73 S.Ct. 1017, 1024, 97 L.Ed. 1454 (1953), the Court suggested that as a general rule the Robinson-Patman Act should be construed so as to insure its coherence with "the broader antitrust policies that have been laid down by Congress;" that observation buttresses our conclusion that exchanges of price information—even when putatively for purposes of Robinson-Patman Act compliance—must remain subject to close scrutiny under the Sherman Act.[72]

(2) *"Good Faith" Meeting an Illegal Price or System.* It is not good faith meeting of competition to match a price offer which seller knows or should have known was itself illegally discriminatory.[73] Although the burden of proving bad faith in such circumstances is on the party asserting it, the rule against meeting illegal prices confronts the business firm with the hard choices of either granting the discriminatory price and facing litigation, or seeking uncertain administrative or judicial relief while the competitor illegally obtains the business.

As to whether adopting competitor's pricing "system" can be justified as good faith meeting of competition, see the Supreme Court's decision in *Federal Trade Commission v. A. E. Staley Manufacturing Co.* involving adoption of a basing point system: Section 2(b) "does not concern itself with pricing systems or even with all the seller's discriminatory prices to buyers. It speaks only of the seller's 'lower' price and of that only to the extent that it is made 'in good faith to meet an equally low price of a competitor.' The Act thus places emphasis on individual competitive situations, rather than upon a general system of competition."[74] Compare *Callaway Mills Co. v. Federal Trade Commission,*[75] where the court of appeals rather remarkably overruled an exercise of administrative discretion with a judicial determination that, under the peculiar circumstances of the carpet trade, the volume discount schedules prevalent in the industry were an appropriate way of doing business:

> We have found no authority which holds that in all circumstances the allowance of volume discounts according to a plan or "system" as distinguished from "individual competitive" responses is condemned per se . . . It is only when no reasonable and prudent person would conclude that the adopted system is a reasonable method of meeting the lower price of a competitor that it is condemned. (p. 442)

72. See also Great Atlantic & Pacific Tea Co. v. Federal Trade Commission, discussed supra pp. 906–910, upholding meeting competition defense where seller was told by long-time customer that seller's offer was "not even in the ball park," although customer was unwilling to give seller specific price necessary to make the sale; Court notes that under *Gypsum* the seller could not attempt to verify competitor's bid without risking Sherman Act liability.

73. Standard Oil Co. v. Brown, 238 F.2d 54 (5th Cir. 1956).

74. 324 U.S. 746, 753, 65 S.Ct. 971, 975, 89 L.Ed. 1338, 1344 (1945). For further discussion of the use of basing point systems, see pp. 500–504, supra.

75. 362 F.2d 435 (5th Cir. 1966).

In a more recent case, *Falls City Industries, Inc. v. Vanco Beverage, Inc.*,[76] the Supreme Court held that pricing on a state-wide basis, which produced lower beer prices in one state than in a neighboring state, might qualify for the meeting competition defense. Sellers choosing to price on a territorial basis, rather than on a customer-by-customer basis, must show that the decision was a "genuine, reasonable response to prevailing competitive circumstances," was "tailored to the competitive situation," and was limited "to that group of customers reasonably believed to have the lower price available to it from competitors." *Staley* was distinguished as a case in which the pricing system was preconceived and not truly responsive to competitors' prices. The Court also held in *Falls City* that the meeting competition defense was not lost even though the price difference between the two states was the result of the seller *raising* prices in one state to "follow the leader" there.

(3) *"Like Grade and Quality" in Meeting Competitive Price.* See *Callaway Mills Co. v. Federal Trade Commission*, 362 F.2d 435 (5th Cir. 1966), where the F.T.C.'s position is quoted as follows:

"Both the courts and the Commission have consistently denied the shelter of the defense to sellers whose products, because of intrinsic superior quality or intense public demand, normally commands a price higher than that usually received by sellers of competitive goods. For example, the defense will not lie when the price of Lucky Strikes is dropped to the level of a 'poorer grade of cigarettes,' Porto Rican American Tobacco Co. v. American Tobacco Co., 30 F.2d 234, 237 (2d Cir. 1929), cert. denied, 279 U.S. 858 (1929); when the price of Budweiser beer is dropped to match the price of 'nonpremium' local beers, Anheuser-Busch, Inc., 54 F.T.C. 277, set aside for other reasons, 265 F.2d 677 (7th Cir. 1959), rev'd. 363 U.S. 536 (1960), again set aside for other reasons 289 F.2d 835 (7th Cir. 1961); and, when the price of a 'premium' automatic control is set above the price of less acceptable controls, Minneapolis-Honeywell Regulator Co., 44 F.T.C. 351, rev'd. on other grounds, 191 F.2d 786 (7th Cir. 1951), cert. dismissed, 344 U.S. 206 (1952)."

The court denied the applicability of these precedents on the ground that they involved products for which the public was shown to be willing to pay more:

The Commission committed error on this point by equating "grade and quality" with "salability." The two are not synonymous. It is obvious that the consuming public, being far less aware of such factors as "craftsmanship and materials" than professional carpetmakers, cannot easily discern differences in quality between comparable carpeting. Furthermore, the public is greatly influenced by such intangibles as color, design, display, advertising, and similar factors. So long as petitioners conclusively show that their products at various price levels generate public demand (or "salability") substantially equivalent to that of competitors' carpeting at the same price levels, considerations of "grade and quality" become unnecessary and indeed superfluous, for the most "grade and quality" can do is tend to show "salability."

(4) *"Aggressive" Meeting of Competition. Sunshine Biscuits, Inc. v. Federal Trade Commission*, 306 F.2d 48 (7th Cir. 1962), held that the meeting competition defense extended to quoting a discriminatorily low price to

76. ___ U.S. ___, 103, S.Ct. 1282, ___
L.Ed.2d ___ (1983).

take a customer away from a supplier's competitor, as well as to retain an existing customer:

. . . The plain meaning of the term "purchaser" is one who buys, and no connotation of the term is justified that would limit its meaning to those purchasers who had been customers of the seller before his lowering of prices to meet those of a competitor.

There are other reasons, however, for us to conclude that the Commission is not justified in making the distinction that a seller's good faith competitive price reduction to old customers is permissible under Section 2(b) while the same reduction to a new customer is not. These reasons, which are discussed by Commissioner Elman in his dissenting opinion, are first, that the distinction made by the Commission is unworkable as a practicality, and, second, that it is economically unsound.

Commissioner Elman makes the point that the Commission's distinction is unworkable because of the practical difficulty in distinguishing between an old and a new customer. As he says:

"Does an 'old' customer retain that status forever, regardless of the infrequency or irregularity of his purchases? Suppose an 'old' customer transfers his business to another seller offering a lower price; how long a period of grace does the first seller have in which to meet the lower competitive price? If he waits too long, will the 'old' customer be regarded as a 'new' one, and hence unapproachable because Section 2(b) no longer applies? If so, how long is too long? And if not, does it suffice that the buyer has at any time in the past, no matter how remote, been a customer of the respondent."

If a seller may seek customers by offering discriminatory low prices, what would be left of Robinson-Patman? Must a defensive discriminatory price cut be extended to all customers to whom the competing offer has been made, or may the Supplier "discriminate" among customers who have similar competing offers, giving defensive discounts to some but not others? Does the requirement of "good faith" meeting of competition bar the latter alternative? If a powerful customer backs his demand for a discriminatory low price with a threat that otherwise he will establish his own manufacturing enterprise to supply his requirements at a cost equal to the discounted price he wants, will Seller's compliance be a good faith meeting of [potential] competition? Would compliance constitute an agreement to restrain potential competition, violating the Sherman Act?

(5) *Supplier's Discriminatory Concessions to Some Dealers to Enable Them to Meet Their Competition. Federal Trade Commission v. Sun Oil Co.,* 371 U.S. 505, 83 S.Ct. 358, 9 L.Ed.2d 466 (1963). In the course of a gasoline "price war" in Jacksonville, Florida, McLean, who owned and operated a Sun Oil station, found himself losing out to Super Test, a 65-station chain of cut-rate gas stations which had opened a branch across the street from McLean. Naturally, Sun's sales to McLean also declined. To encourage McLean to cut his retail price and maintain the volume of his sales, Sun made a discriminatory price cut in his favor. Some regular Sun customers then switched from their usual Sun stations to McLean's. The FTC filed a complaint against Sun, charging illegal price discrimination in McLean's favor and also a violation of FTCA § 5 based on the alleged price-fixing agreement between Sun and McLean, viz., that he would reduce his price if granted a price concession. The Supreme Court held the meeting competition defense unavailable to Sun. "Equally low price of a competitor" in § 2(b) means "of a competitor of the seller".

The conclusion was based largely on analysis of the language and legislative history of the Robinson-Patman Act. Justice Goldberg's opinion for the Court rejected Sun's policy argument that it was coming to the aid of a small independent businessman, because this aid was at the expense of other small businessmen, including other Sun dealers:

To allow a supplier to intervene and grant discriminatory price concessions designed to enable its customer to meet the lower price of a retail competitor who is unaided by his supplier would discourage rather than promote competition. So long as the price cutter does not receive a price "break" from his own supplier, his lawful reductions in price are presumably a function of his own superior merit and efficiency. To permit a competitor's supplier to bring his often superior economic power to bear narrowly and discriminatorily to deprive the otherwise resourceful retailer of the very fruits of his efficiency and convert the normal competitive struggle between retailers into an unequal contest between one retailer and the combination of another retailer and his supplier is hardly an element of reasonable and fair competition. We see no justification for such a result in § 2(b). Restriction of the defense to those situations in which a supplier responds to the price concessions of its own competitor—another supplier—maintains general competitive equities. Fairness demands neither more nor less. We discern in § 2 neither a purpose to insulate retailers from lawful and normal competitive pressures generated by other retailers, nor an intent to authorize suppliers, in response to such pressures created solely at the retail level, to protect, discriminatorily, sales to one customer at the expense of other customers.

It is argued, however, that to deny Sun the right to reduce its prices as it did here is to impair price flexibility and promote price rigidity, the very antithesis of competition. We think that the contrary is the case. While allowance of the discriminatory price cut here may produce localized and temporary flexibility, it inevitably encourages maintenance of the long-range and generalized price rigidity which the discrimination in fact protects. So long as the wholesaler can meet challenges to his pricing structure by wholly local and individualized responses, it has no incentive to alter its overall pricing policy. Moreover, as indicated, the large supplier's ability to "spot price" will discourage the enterprising and resourceful retailer from seeking to initiate price reductions on his own. Such reasoning may be particularly applicable in the oligopolistic environment of the oil industry.

We see no reason to permit Sun discriminatorily to pit its greater strength at the supplier level against Super Test, which, so far as appears from the record, is able to sell its gasoline at a lower price simply because it is a more efficient merchandiser, particularly when Super Test's challenge as an "independent" may be the only meaningful source of price competition offered the "major" oil companies, of which Sun is one.

Respondent Sun makes several other arguments in support of its position. First, it asserts that the interpretation of § 2(b) urged here by the Commission completely ignores the competitive realities of the gasoline vending business. In essence, Sun argues that, practically viewed, Super Test was not merely a competitor of McLean, but also a competitor of Sun. Oil companies, whether major or minor, integrated or nonintegrated, it is asserted, compete not at the wholesaler or jobber level, but almost exclusively at the retail level. All competition, Sun says, is directed to sales of the final product—gasoline—to the motoring consumer, and anything that threatens to reduce the sales of a branded gasoline at the retailer's pump is a threat to the supplier whose business is a direct function of its stations' marketing success or failure. It is contended that the individual station is but a "conduit" for the supplier and that Sun is thus in competition with Super Test, considered even only as a retailer.

In a very real sense, however, every retailer is but a "conduit" for the goods which it sells and every supplier could, in the same sense, be considered a competitor of retailers selling competing goods. We are sure Congress had no such broad conception of competition in mind when it established the § 2(b) defense and, certainly, it intended no special exception for the petroleum industry. It is difficult to perceive convincing reasons rationally confining the thrust of respondent's argument to an area narrow enough to preclude effective emasculation of the prohibitions on discrimination contained in § 2(a). Only differences of degree distinguish the situation of the gasoline station operator from that of many other retail outlets, and in numerous instances the distinction, if any, is slight. The "conduit" theory contains no inherent limitations and its acceptance would so expand the § 2(b) defense as to effect a return to the broader "meeting competition" provision of the Clayton Act, which the Robinson-Patman Act amendments superseded.

Sun also argues that the effect of a decision holding the § 2(b) defense unavailable to it in these circumstances will be to prolong and aggravate the destructive price wars which periodically reoccur in the marketing of gasoline. Whether relevant or not, this contention is best put wholly to one side. Such price warfare appears to be caused by a number of basic factors, not the least of which are industry overcapacity and the propensity of some major refiners to engage in so-called "dual marketing" under which, in order to increase their overall sales and utilize idle facilities, they not only sell branded gasoline to their own dealers but also sell unbranded gasoline to independent retailers or jobbers, often at a lower price. See S.Rep.No.2810, 84th Cong., 2d Sess. 16–19. Whatever we do here can neither eliminate nor mitigate the major economic forces which are productive of these price wars. Moreover, it is wholly unclear whether allowance of the price discrimination prolongs or shortens the war's duration.

The Court expressly disclaimed intimating what the result might be if (i) there were evidence that Super Test was an integrated wholesaler-retailer [which might, in its wholesaler aspect, be regarded as a competitor of Sun], or (ii) there were evidence that Super Test's supplier was making price concessions to help Super Test keep up its volume during the price war. Should the meeting competition defense be applicable in either of these situations, or does the fact that in neither of these cases would any other supplier be offering McLean a low price to justify a defensive discount by Sun to him preclude the defense?

In considering alternative courses open to Sun, the Court referred, in footnote 17, 371 U.S. at 527–28, to the possibility of "feathered" discounts:

Since Sun made no attempt here to utilize a so-called "feathered" discount to its dealers, under which the amount of the price allowance diminishes as it reaches stations further away from the center of the price war, we need not expressly pass upon such practice. However, it may be noted that a properly designed and limited price reduction system fashioned in such a manner might, under appropriate circumstances, be found to have obviated substantial competitive harm to the other Sun dealers and thereby negated a violation of § 2(a) such as is here charged. Of course, improperly designed or too sharply drawn "feathering" gradations may produce precisely the same effect as no gradation at all, and consequently fall within the same ban as an outright illegal discrimination.

(6) *Aftermath of Sun Oil.* Would you advise the FTC to adopt the following policy statement? [77]

Meeting Competition Defense: The Supreme Court has held in *Sun Oil* that a supplier of gasoline may not avail itself of the Section 2(b) meeting competition defense to justify price reductions made to enable a dealer-customer to meet the competition of another dealer but left open the question of whether a supplier is permitted by Section 2(b) to reduce its price to selected dealers to meet the price of either an integrated supplier-retailer or another supplier who has granted a reduction to its own customer.

The nature of the distribution system in the petroleum industry is such that suppliers of gasoline normally do not compete with one another on sales to the same dealer. That they are in competition with one another, however, is an undeniable fact. In the actualities of competition in the marketing of gasoline, it is only by reducing its wholesale price that the supplier can respond defensively to another supplier's price cut which is reflected in the retail price at which that supplier's gasoline is sold. This is true whether the supplier who initiates the price cut is selling to lessee dealers or through retail outlets which it owns and operates. In either case the competing supplier who reduces its price to its customers which may enable them to post a competitive retail price is in fact acting in response to a price cut by its own competitor, a supplier, rather than by a competitor of its customer. Consequently, we are of the opinion that a price reduction by one supplier to its customer which is reflected in the latter's retail price may be lawfully met by a comparable reduction by another supplier to its customer.

While it is of course unlikely that a supplier would always know precisely the wholesale price at which its competitor is selling, or changes in that price, Section 2(b) does not require that price discriminations be justified by a showing that in fact they met a competitive price. The supplier need show only the existence of facts which would lead a reasonable and prudent person to believe that the granting of a lower price would in fact meet the equally low price of a competitor. If the competitor who initiated the price reduction is an integrated supplier-retailer, the supplier claiming the defense need only show that it was aware of this fact and that its concession to its dealer did not exceed the amount of its competitor's retail price reduction. If the competing supplier sells to independent dealers, the supplier claiming the protection of 2(b) must establish that it had reason to believe that it was meeting only a reduction in its competitor's wholesale price and not a reduction in the retail price initiated by a dealer without the assistance of a supplier.

77. See 3 CCH Trade Reg.Rep. ¶ 10,373 (FTC Policy adopted June 10, 1967).

2. Cost Justification

UNITED STATES v. BORDEN CO.

Supreme Court of the United States, 1962.
350 U.S. 460, 82 S.Ct. 1309, 8 L.Ed.2d 627.

Mr. Justice Clark delivered the opinion of the Court.

This is a direct appeal from a judgment dismissing the Government's Section 2(a) Clayton Act suit in which it sought an injunction against the selling of fluid milk products by the appellees, the Borden Company and Bowman Dairy Company, at prices which discriminate between independently owned grocery stores and grocery store chains. The District Court in an unreported decision found the pricing plan of each dairy to be a prima facie violation of § 2(a) but concluded that these discriminatory prices were legalized by the cost justification proviso of § 2(a), which permits price differentials as long as they "make only due allowance for differences in the cost of manufacture, sale, or delivery resulting from the differing methods or quantities in which such commodities are to such purchasers sold or delivered." To review the Government's contention that the District Court had improperly permitted cost justifications based on the *average* cost of dealing with broad groups of customers unrelated in cost-saving factors, we noted probable jurisdiction, 368 U.S. 924, and directed the parties to brief and argue the case separately as to each appellee, 368 U.S. 963. However, finding the same problem at the root of the cost justifications of each appellee, we have dealt with both in this single opinion. We have concluded that the class cost justifications submitted to the District Court by the appellees did not satisfy their burden of showing that their respective discriminatory pricing plans reflected only a "due allowance" for cost differences.

By way of background, we first point out that the present appeal is merely a glimpse of protracted litigation between the parties which began in 1951 and which has not yet seen its end. The original complaint charged violations of §§ 1 and 2 of the Sherman Act and § 2(a) of the Clayton Act. The District Court dismissed the suit, holding that there was no proof of the alleged Sherman Act violations and that no equitable relief was necessary under the Clayton Act charge because appellees were already restrained by a consent decree entered in a private antitrust case. On direct appeal we affirmed the dismissal of the Sherman Act charges but held erroneous the refusal to grant an injunction on the Clayton Act claim solely because of the existence of the private decree. 347 U.S. 514. On remand the case was reopened and on its prima facie case the Government introduced recent general price schedules and illustrated their effect on sample stores to show that each appellee was still engaged in illegal price discriminations notwithstanding the consent decree. In defense the appellees each introduced voluminous cost studies in justification of their pricing systems. The entire case was submitted via stipulations, depositions, and briefs. There was no dispute as to the existence of price discrimination; the sole question was whether the differences in price reflected permissible allowances for variances in cost.

In view of our disposition, we need not relate the facts in detail. Both appellees are major distributors of fluid milk products in metropolitan Chicago. The sales of both dairies to retail stores during the period in question were handled under plans which gave most of their customers—the independently owned stores—percentage discounts off list price which increased with the volume of their purchases to a specified maximum while granting a few customers—the grocery store chains—a flat discount without reference to volume and substantially greater than the maximum discount available under the volume plan offered independent stores. These discounts were made effective through schedules which appeared to cover all stores; however, the schedules were modified by private letters to the grocery chains confirming their higher discounts. Although the two sets of discounts were never officially labeled "independent" and "chain" prices, they were treated, called, and regarded as such throughout the record.

To support their defense that the disparities in price between independents and chains were attributable to differences in the cost of dealing with the two types of customers, the appellees introduced cost studies which will be described separately because of their differing content and analytical approach.

The Borden pricing system produced two classes of customers. The two chains, A & P and Jewel, with their combined total of 254 stores constituted one class. The 1,322 independent stores, grouped in four brackets based on the volume of their purchases, made up the other. Borden's cost justification was built on comparisons of its average cost per $100 of sales to the chains in relation to the average cost of similar sales to each of the four groups of independents. The costs considered were personnel (including routemen, clerical and sales employees), truck expenses, and losses on bad debts and returned milk. Various methods of cost allocation were utilized: Drivers' time spent at each store was charged directly to that store; certain clerical expenses were allocated between the two general classes; costs not susceptible of either of the foregoing were charged to the various stores on a per stop, per store, or volume basis.

Bowman's cost justification was based on differences in volume and methods of delivery. It relied heavily upon a study of the cost per minute of its routemen's time. It determined that substantial portions of this time were devoted to three operations, none of which were ever performed for the 163 stores operated by its two major chain customers. These added work steps arose from the method of collection, i.e., cash on delivery and the delayed collections connected therewith, and the performance of "optional customer services." The customer services, performed with varying frequency depending upon the circumstances, included "services that the driver may be requested to do, such as deliver the order inside, place the containers in a refrigerator, rearrange containers so that any product remaining unsold from yesterday will be sold first today, leave cases of products at different spots in the store, etc." The experts conducting the study calculated as to these elements a "standard" cost per unit of product delivered: the aggregate time required to perform the services, as determined by sample time studies, was divided by the total number of units of product delivered. In essence, the Bowman justification was merely a comparison of the cost of these services in relation to the disparity between the chain and independent prices. Although it was shown that the five sample independents in the Government's prima facie case received the added services it was not shown or found that all 2,500 independents supplied by Bowman partook of them. On the basis of its studies Bowman estimated that about two-thirds of the independent stores received the "optional customer services" on a daily basis and that "most store customers pay the driver in cash daily."

On these facts, stated here in rather summary fashion, the trial court held that appellees had met the requirements of the proviso of § 2(a) on the theory that the general cost differences between chain stores as a class and independents as a class justified the disparities in price reflected in appellees' schedules. In so doing the trial court itself found "the studies . . . imperfect in some respects . . . ." It noted the "seemingly arbitrary" nature of a classification resulting "in percentage discounts which do not bear a direct ratio to differences in volume of sales." But it found "this mode of classification is *not* wholly arbitrary—after all, most chain stores do purchase larger volumes of milk than do most independent stores." We believe it was erroneous for the trial court to permit cost justifications based upon such classifications.

The burden, of course, was upon the appellees to prove that the illegal price discrimination, which the Government claimed and the trial court found present, was immunized by the cost justification proviso of § 2(a). Such is the mandate of § 2(b) as interpreted by this Court in Federal Trade Comm'n v. Morton Salt Co., 334 U.S. 37, 44–45, 68 S.Ct. 822, 92 L.Ed. 1196, 1 A.L.R.2d 260 (1948). There can be no doubt that the § 2(a) proviso as amended by the Robinson-Patman Act contemplates, both in express wording and legislative history, a showing of actual cost differences resulting from the differing methods or quantities in which the commodities in question are sold or delivered. The only question before us is how accurate this showing must be in relation to each particular purchaser.

Although the language of the proviso, with some support in the legislative history, is literally susceptible of a construction which would require any discrepancy in price between any two purchasers to be individually justified, the proviso has not been so construed by those charged with its enforcement. The Government candidly recognizes in its briefs filed in the instant case that "[a]s a matter of practical necessity . . . when a seller deals with a very large number of customers, he cannot be required to establish different cost-reflecting prices to each customer." In this same vein, the practice of grouping customers for pricing purposes has long had the approval of the Federal Trade Commission. We ourselves have noted the "elusiveness of cost data" in a Robinson-Patman Act proceeding. Automatic Canteen Co. v. Federal Trade Comm'n, 346 U.S. 61, 68, 73 S.Ct. 1017, 97 L.Ed. 1454 (1953). In short, to completely renounce class pricing as justified by class accounting would be to eliminate in practical effect the cost justification proviso as to sellers having a large number of purchasers, thereby preventing such sellers from passing on economies to their customers. It seems hardly necessary to say that such a result is at war with Congress' language and purpose.

But this is not to say that price differentials can be justified on the basis of arbitrary classifications or even classifications which are representative of a numerical majority of the individual members. At some point practical considerations shade into a circumvention of the proviso. A balance is struck by the use of classes for cost justification which are composed of members of such selfsameness as to make the averaging of the cost of dealing with the group a valid and reasonable indicium of the cost of dealing with any specific group member. High on the list of "musts" in the use of the average cost of customer groupings under the proviso of § 2(a) is a close resemblance of the individual members of each group on the essential point or points which determine the costs considered.

In this regard we do not find the classifications submitted by the appellees to have been shown to be of sufficient homogeneity. Certainly, the cost factors considered were not necessarily encompassed within the manner in which a customer is owned. Turning first to Borden's justification, we note that it not only failed to show that the economies relied upon were isolated within the favored class but affirmatively revealed that members of the classes utilized were substantially unlike in the cost saving aspects considered. For instance, the favorable cost comparisons between the chains and the larger independents were for the greater part controlled by the higher average volume of the chain stores in comparison to the average volume of the 80-member class to which these independents were relegated. The District Court allowed this manner of justification because "most chain stores do purchase larger volumes of milk than do most independent stores." However, such a grouping for cost justification purposes, composed as it is of some independents having volumes comparable to, and in some cases larger than, that of the chain stores, created artificial disparities between the larger independents and the chain stores. It is like averaging one horse and one rabbit. As the Federal Trade Commission said in In the Matter of Champion Spark Plug Co., 50 F.T.C. 30, 43 (1953): "A cost justification based on the difference between an estimated average cost of selling to one or two large customers and an average cost of selling to all other customers cannot be accepted as a defense to a charge of price discrimination." This volume gap between the larger independents and the chain stores was further widened by grouping together the two chains, thereby raising the average volume of the stores of the smaller of the two chains in relation to the larger independents. Nor is the vice in the Borden class justification solely in the paper volumes relied upon, for it attributed to many independents cost factors which were not true indicia of the cost of dealing with those particular consumers. To illustrate, each independent was assigned a portion of the total expenses involved in daily cash collections, although it was not shown that all independents paid cash and in fact Borden admitted that only a "large majority" did so.

Likewise the details of Bowman's cost study show a failure in classification. Only one additional point need be made. Its justification emphasized its costs for "optional customer service" and daily cash collection with the resulting "delay to collect." As shown by its study these elements were crucial to Bowman's cost justification. In the study the experts charged all independents and no chain store with these costs. Yet, it was not shown that all independents received these services daily or even on some lesser basis. Bowman's studies indicated only that a large majority of independents took these services on a daily basis. Under such circumstances the use of these cost factors across the board in calculating independent store costs is not a permissible justification for it possibly allocates costs to some independents whose mode of purchasing does not give rise to them. The burden was upon the profferer of the classification to negate this possibility and this burden has not been met here. If these factors control the cost of dealing, then their presence or absence might with more justification be the password for admission into the various price categories.[78]

The appellees argue in the alternative that their cost justifications can be sufficiently unscrambled to remove any taint the Court may find in them and still show a cost gap sufficient to justify the price disparity between the chains and any independent. This mass of underlying statistical data not considered by the trial court and now tied together by untried theories can best be evaluated on remand, and we therefore do not consider its sufficiency here.

In sum, the record here shows that price discriminations have been permitted on the basis of cost differences between broad customer groupings, apparently based on the nature of ownership but in any event not shown to be so homogeneous as to permit the joining together of these purchasers for cost allocations purposes. If this is the only justification for appellees' pricing schemes, they are illegal. We do not believe that an appropriate decree would require the trial court continuously to "pass judgment on the pricing practices of these defendants." As to the issuance of an injunction, however, the case is now 11 years old and we have no way of knowing whether equitable relief is in order. Certainly a relevant factor in such consideration would be whether the practices described above are still being

---

78. [Court's footnote 13.] Another suspect feature is that classifications based on services received by independents were apparently frozen—making it impossible for them to obtain larger discounts by electing not to receive the cost-determinative services—with no justifiable business reason offered in support of the practice.

followed in any form. This the record here does not show. Such matters can only be ascertained upon the presently existing facts and the careful application of the principles we have enunciated. For that purpose the case is reversed and remanded.

[JUSTICE FRANKFURTER did not participate in the decision. JUSTICE DOUGLAS concurred on the ground that, in a case such as this where buying is not centralized and the cost justification factors relate to services supplied or not supplied at individual stores, store-by-store costs are the only relevant criteria. JUSTICE HARLAN dissented.]

NOTES

(1) *Averaging Cost Savings for Multi-Product "Line".* The respondent need not cost-justify on a product-by-product basis, if in its business the customary unit of dealing is a multi-product "line", e.g., automobile replacement parts, carpeting in a variety of colors, grades, materials.[79] The rationale, and therefore the limits of application, of this doctrine has been stated as follows:

> While the use of the weighted average price for the whole line seems reasonable in this case, it might, of course, be quite different where demand was primarily for individual items and the volume of sales depended on price differences and other similar competitive factors. In the tube industry, however, this was clearly not the case. Demand for tubes was inelastic. It was determined not by competitive factors but by the structure of the radio set sought to be kept running. For such a market only the weighted average price would appear to have competitive significance. . . . Section 2(a) of the Act requires cost justification only where price differentials may result in adverse competitive effects. It would seem appropriate, therefore, to offer a cost defense that deals with the particular price differential which may have caused the injury. Here it seems clear that any injury would have to stem from the average price difference on the entire line, and not from the differentials which prevailed on individual tube types.[80]

(2) *Quantity Limits Proviso.* One provision of the Robinson-Patman Act clearly expressed a Congressional intent to preclude cost justification in some situations. The following sentence appears in section 2(a) immediately after the proviso as to cost justification:

> **The Federal Trade Commission may, after due investigation and hearing to all interested parties, fix and establish quantity limits, and revise the same as it finds necessary as to particular commodities or classes of commodities, where it finds that available purchasers in greater quantities are so few as to render differentials on account thereof unjustly discriminatory or promotive of monopoly in any line of commerce; and the foregoing shall then not be con-**

79. Federal Trade Commission v. Standard Motor Products, Inc., 371 F.2d 613 (2d Cir. 1967); Callaway Mills Co. v. Federal Trade Commission, 362 F.2d 435 (5th Cir. 1966).

80. Chairman Howrey, concurring in dismissal of complaint in Sylvania Electric Products, Inc., 51 F.T.C. 282 (1954).

strued to permit differentials based on differences in quantities greater than those so fixed and established.

The quantity limits proviso has become virtually a dead letter.[81]

81. See Federal Trade Commission v. B.F. Goodrich Co., 242 F.2d 31 (D.C.Cir. 1957) (setting aside, because of defective findings, an order forbidding discounts on tires for purchases in excess of a carload).

THE LEGAL MONOPOLIES

Chapter 9

PATENT AND COPYRIGHT

A. INTRODUCTION; LEGISLATIVE TEXTS

Patent and copyright law explicitly confer or recognize the right
of an inventor or author to prevent others from engaging in defined
areas of economic activity. In one sense, therefore, these laws may
be said to authorize monopoly or restraint of trade; and it is customary to speak of the "monopoly" granted by these laws. One who
seeks to appraise the legislation from this point of view would study
the circumstances that limit the scope of the monopoly, and would
ask to what extent the restraint may be found "reasonable" because
of public benefits. One would note, for example, that the author of a
novel may enjoy a legal monopoly of that book; yet he must sell it in
"free and open" competition with all other books, copyrighted or not,
and with all other forms of instruction or diversion. The same is true
to a lesser extent of patents for invention; but there will often be
few or no substitutes for a patented article or process embodying basic advances in technology. As for public ends to be served, the Constitution itself declares, in Article I, Section 8, clause 8, that:

> **The Congress shall have Power . . . To Promote the Pro-
> gress of Science and useful Arts, by securing for limited Times To
> Authors and Inventors the exclusive Right to their respective Writ-
> ings and Discoveries.**[1]

There is, however, another conception of patent and copyright
law, which emphasizes the "property" aspect of the rights. It seems
natural that one should "own" what he creates, and ownership implies a right to exclude. The "letters patent," on this view, constitute
a mere official acknowledgment or record of what belongs to the author or inventor, comparable to a recorded deed to real estate. Although patent and copyright law must reflect this point of view, as
all law must reflect widely held conceptions, the positive law by no
means accords an unqualified natural right to all one's creations.
For example, as will be seen below, the most fundamental discoveries
of science, denominated "laws of nature," are excluded from patent
protection for reasons of expediency. Moreover, it will be recalled
that even the most traditional property rights, in land, may be limited

---

1. See Irons and Sears, The Constitutional Standard of Invention—The Touchstone for Patent Reform, in Patent Symposium, 1973 Utah L.Rev. 653.

in the interest of preserving competition, as may other traditional rights such as freedom of contract and association.

In Patents and Free Enterprise,[2] Professor Walton Hamilton pointed out that patents came into being in England not as an incentive to invention but as a grant of special privilege at the pleasure of an absolute monarch. Such grants were sometimes made with public interests in mind, as when foreigners were given trading privileges (not necessarily exclusive) in England in order to encourage their immigration and the establishment of new industries. In the course of time the public advantage in such transactions became little more than a pretense, and exclusive privileges were sold by the crown as a source of revenue or awarded as a gift to favorite courtiers. The oppressive character of these privileges was aggravated by the practice of giving the patentee authority to engage in private policing of his rights, e.g., by carrying out forcible searches for contraband goods manufactured in violation of his exclusive rights. Star Chamber and Court of Exchequer, tribunals which came to be identified with absolutist monarchy, asserted jurisdiction over controversies arising out of the royal grants. In the time of Elizabeth and James I, the patent issue became part of a broader struggle between "royal prerogative" and the growing conception of a monarchy limited by constitutional principles.

The Statute of Monopolies (set out pp. 1–2, supra) is the genesis of modern patent-for-invention legislation.[3] Passed in 1623, it declared generally that grants of exclusive trading privileges were void, but made exception for patents issued to the "true and first inventor" of "new manufactures." A number of the Colonies enacted patent laws following the English example (e.g., Massachusetts in 1641), and Congress passed the first federal patent law in 1790. Many European countries also enacted patent legislation around the turn of the eighteenth century, but by the middle of the nineteenth century an anti-patent movement arose, resulting, for example, in Switzerland's rejection of five proposed patent bills between 1849 and 1863. The anti-patent movement collapsed in the last quarter of the nineteenth century, however, as the proponents of free competition and free trade lost support in an era of economic depression and rising nationalism. Patent abolitionists have not re-emerged.[4]

The Statute of Monopolies provided for letters patent to the "true and first inventor" so long as the patent "be not contrary to the law, nor mischievous to the state, by raising prices of commodities at home, or hurt of trade, or generally inconvenient." Thus the Statute recognized the tension between patents as reward for invention and patents as restriction on the competitive process.

2. Monograph 31, Temporary National Economic Committee, Chapt. II (1941). Patent System (1925) is a useful sourcebook.

3. On the history of patents see Fox, Monopolies and Patents (1947); Price, English Patents of Monopoly (1906); Wood, Patents and Antitrust Law (1942) Chap. I. Vaughn, The Economics of Our

4. See Machlup, An Economic Review of the Patent System, Study No. 15 of the Subcomm. on Patents, Trademarks, and Copyright, of the Sen.Jud.Comm. 85th Cong., 2d Sess. 3–6 (1958).

The materials in this chapter are intended to focus on this tension. Although there is a similar tension in the copyright system, patent materials will receive greater emphasis because of the critical importance of patent protection in our industrial economy.   The materials are organized on the following plan: First is a textual presentation of the statutory outlines of the patent system, including the procedures for obtaining a patent; accompanying Notes provide further detail and contrast the patent and copyright protections.   The first full case, *Diamond v. Chakrabarty*, and the accompanying Notes are designed to focus on the question of why we have a patent system, with particular emphasis on the relation between patent protection and innovation.   Subsequent sections deal with the conflict between patent protection and the antitrust laws (patent licensing, restrictions on pricing and distribution of patented products, tying, and the interchange of patent rights) and the conflict between federal policy (patent and antitrust) and potentially inconsistent state law.

STATUTORY FRAMEWORK OF THE PATENT SYSTEM

A patent grants the patentee the right, for seventeen years, "to exclude others from making, using or selling" the patented invention in the United States (35 U.S.C.A. § 154).   Patents can be issued for the invention or discovery of a "process, machine, manufacture, or composition of matter," or any improvement thereof (§ 101).   There are three related, but conceptually distinct, conditions for patentability: novelty, utility, and non-obviousness.   The Patent Code requires that the invention be "new and useful" (§ 101) and not anticipated in the prior art (§ 102), that the patentee be the first to invent (§ 102), and that the invention cannot have been "obvious" to a person having "ordinary skill in the art" to which the subject matter pertains (§ 103).

To obtain a patent the inventor files an application with the Patent and Trademark Office (PTO).   The application contains a "specification" of the claims, describing the invention and the process for making and using it in "such full, clear, concise, and exact terms" that a person "skilled in the art to which it pertains" could make and use it (§ 112).   The specification performs the function of disclosing the invention to the public once it is patented—an important function of the patent system [5]—as well as clearly indicating the scope of the patentee's claims so that others will not be unduly discouraged from inventing in the same area or "inventing around" the patent.   An examiner then determines whether the applicant has met the statutory standards for patentability, searching the technical literature and the PTO's own files of pending applications and patents.   If the examiner finds another pending application or an unexpired patent which might show priority, an "interference" will be declared and a proceeding held at which the involved parties can contest the issue of priority (§ 135).[6]

5. See Kewanee Oil Co. v. Bicron Corp., infra p. 1050.

6. Protests may also be filed against pending patent applications.   See 37

If the PTO rejects an application, the examiner must state the reasons for rejection; the applicant is then entitled to a reexamination (§ 132). If the agency again rejects the application, the applicant can appeal to the Patent and Trademark Office Board of Appeals. An adverse Board of Appeals decision can then be reviewed either by appeal to United States Court of Appeals for the Federal Circuit or by suit in the district court for the District of Columbia (§§ 134, 141, 145).[7]

Once issued, patents can be enforced through infringement suits seeking damages and injunctive relief (§§ 281, 283, 284). Damages are awarded for not less than "a reasonable royalty for the use made of the invention by the infringer," and may be trebled at the discretion of the court (§ 284).[8] The alleged infringer can defend on the basis of invalidity; by statute, the patent is "presumed valid" and the infringer bears the burden of proving invalidity (§ 282).[9] Courts have strongly tended to exercise independent judgment on patent validity when the issue is raised in judicial proceedings to enforce the patent, perhaps because the PTO appears willing to issue many patents for trivial contributions to technology.[10] Patent infringement litigation can be long and costly,[11] a factor behind legislation enacted in

C.F.R. § 1.291(a). Proposed rules to allow protesters to participate in the proceedings, see 46 Fed.Reg. 3162 (1981), were not adopted. See generally Garrett, "Patent Law Amendments Bring Significant Changes," Legal Times of Washington, March 9, 1981, pp. 18–19.

7. The U.S. Court of Appeals for the Federal Circuit was established in 1982. See "Federal Courts Improvement Act of 1982," Pub.L. 97–164, 96 Stat. 25 (1982). This court hears all cases formerly heard by the Court of Customs and Patent Appeals, and has jurisdiction over appeals in all cases in which jurisdiction is based on a patent question; appeals of the latter variety were formerly heard in all the circuits. *Query:* Will a single appellate court, whose jurisdiction depends on subject matter rather than geography, lead to a more uniform development of patent law and bring greater certainty to patent investments? Or will such a court likely become captured by the "patent industry," much as independent regulatory agencies are often captured by the industries over which they have jurisdiction?

8. See generally Stroup, Patentee's Monetary Recovery From An Infringer, 59 J. POS 362 (1977). It is not a crime to infringe a patent; willful infringement of a copyright "for commercial advantage or private financial gain" is criminal (see 17 U.S.C.A. § 506a). Why should there be a difference? Aren't both "theft"? The criminal provisions of the copyright laws, although rarely invoked in the past, have recently been aimed at tape "pirates" who make unauthorized copies of popular sound recordings. See "Sam

Goody's Faces the Music—In Court," Nat'l Law J., March 23, 1981, p. 10 (detailing trial on twelve count indictment for infringement).

9. The government can seek cancellation of a patent on the basis of fraudulent procurement. See United States v. American Bell Telephone Co., 128 U.S. 315, 9 S.Ct. 90, 32 L.Ed. 450 (1888); 2 Deller's Walker on Patents § 218 (2d ed. 1965). Although the government may not generally sue to set aside a patent on the ground of invalidity, see United States v. American Bell Telephone Co., 167 U.S. 224, 17 S.Ct. 809, 42 L.Ed. 144 (1897), it can challenge validity in an antitrust suit where the question of the patent's validity is relevant to effective relief. See United States v. Glaxo Group, Ltd., 410 U.S. 52, 93 S.Ct. 861, 35 L.Ed.2d 104 (1973).

10. See Oppenheim, Patents and Antitrust: Peaceful Coexistence, 54 Mich.L. Rev. 199, 207–208 (1955): "While this presumption [of validity] had, of course, been recognized in many early cases as an application of the general rule according presumptive validity to decisions of administrative officers, it had been diluted and even ignored, in cases in recent years. This evoked Justice Jackson's famous dissenting remark that 'the only patent that is valid is one which this Court has not been able to get its hands on.' Jungersen v. Ostby & Barton Co., 335 U.S. 560, 572, 69 S.Ct. 269, 274 (1949)."

11. Some relief from excessive patent litigation has come from the Supreme

1980 to allow for reexamination of doubtful patents in the PTO. Congress hoped that this administrative reexamination will clarify validity and increase investor confidence in the certainty of patent rights.[12]

NOTES AND QUERIES

(1) *Bibliography.* On patent law, see Deller's Walker on Patents (2d ed. 1965); Chisum, Patents: A Treatise of the Law of Patentability, Validity and Infringement (1978); Rosenberg, Patent Law Fundamentals (2d ed. 1980); Stedman, Patents and Antitrust—The Impact of Various Legal Doctrines, 1973 Utah L.Rev. 588 (a Patent Symposium); Symposium on Patents, Know-How and Antitrust, 28 U.Pitt.L.Rev. 147 ff (1966). On proposed reform of the Patent Code, see "To Promote The Progress of . . . Useful Arts," Report of the President's Commission on the Patent System (1966); H.R. 5924, 90th Cong., 1st Sess. (1967).

Primarily economic appraisals of the patent system include Bowman, Patent and Antitrust Law (1973), interestingly reviewed by Williamson, 83 Yale L.J. 647 (1974); Mansfield, The Economics of Technical Change (1968); Jewkes, Sawers, and Stillerman, The Sources of Invention (2d ed. rev. 1969); Baxter, Legal Restriction on Exploitation of the Patent Monopoly: An Economic Analysis, 76 Yale L.J. 267 (1966); Kitch, The Nature and Function of the Patent System, 20 J.L. & Econ. 265 (1977).

On copyright law, see Nimmer on Copyright (1982); Copyright Law Revision, H.Rep. 94–1476, Report of the House Committee on the Judiciary on S. 22, 94th Cong., 2d Sess. (1976); Breyer, The Uneasy Case for Copyright, 84 Harv.L.Rev. 281 (1970); Gorman, An Overview of the Copyright Act of 1976, 126 U.Pa.L.Rev. 856 (1978); Latman, The Copyright Law: Howell's Copyright Law Revised and the 1976 Act (5th ed. 1979) (one-volume treatise); Tyerman, The Economic Rationale for Copyright Protection for Published Books: A Reply to Prof. Breyer, 18 U.C.L.A.L.Rev. 1100 (1971); Symposium on Copyright Law Revision, 24 U.C.L.A.L.Rev. 951 (1977).

(2) *Novelty and Priority.* Section 101 authorizes patents only for "new" inventions; section 102(a) precludes issuance of a patent where an invention was known or used by others, even though a later inventor-applicant was unaware of his predecessors' work.[13] Does this requirement that an inven-

---

Court's holding that once a court has declared a patent invalid, the patentee is estopped from asserting the patent's validity in subsequent infringement suits against different parties; mutuality of collateral estoppel does not apply. Blonder-Tongue Laboratories, Inc. v. University of Illinois Foundation, 402 U.S. 313, 91 S.Ct. 1434, 28 L.Ed.2d 788 (1971).

12. See 35 U.S.C.A. §§ 301–307; H.R. Rep.No.96–1307, 96th Cong., 2nd Sess., reprinted in 5 U.S.Code Cong. & Ad. News 6460 (1980).

13. § 101. *Inventions Patentable.* Whoever invents or discovers any new and useful process, machine, manufacture, or composition of matter, or any new and useful improvement thereof, may obtain a patent therefor, subject to the conditions and requirements of this title.

§ 102. *Conditions for Patentability.* A person shall be entitled to a patent unless—

(a) the invention was known or used by others in this country, or patented or described in a printed publication in this or a foreign country, before the invention thereof by the applicant for patent, or

(b) the invention was patented or described in a printed publication in this or a foreign country or in public use or on sale in this country, more than one year prior to the date of the application for patent in the United States, or

(c) he has abandoned the invention, or

(d) the invention was first patented or caused to be patented by the applicant or his legal representatives or assigns in a foreign country prior to the date of the application for patent in this country on an application filed

tor be "a mythically omniscient worker in his chosen field" [14] act as a disincentive to innovation? On the other hand, the knowledge must be public knowledge. Is science promoted by giving Y a 17 year monopoly of a process which X had conceived first and was about to dedicate to the public through scientific journals? Would it be administratively feasible to inquire as to the state of unpublished "knowledge" before issuing a patent? What would patents be worth if unpublished prior knowledge was a valid defense to a suit to enforce the patent? Note that an invention in use in another country can still qualify for a later patent in the United States. Is the patent incentive needed to encourage disclosure and exploitation, in this country, of inventions used abroad and known here?

Not only must the invention be new; the inventor who is awarded the patent must be the first to invent. Is it fair that those who finish later in the race get nothing? Would more resources be invested in research if the rights to an invention could be shared by the first three (ten?) inventors? Is a single jackpot necessary to encourage invention?

(3) *Utility.* An invention must be "useful." Utility includes at least operability, i.e., the invention must accomplish, even if imperfectly, what it purports to accomplish. It is on this ground that the PTO rejects applications covering "perpetual motion machines" and other crank submissions. However, it has been suggested and occasionally held that larger questions of social or ethical values enter into this judgment, e.g., whether the process, though workable, is too dangerous to the life of the operator; [15] whether the only use of the invention is to deceive.[16] Is the PTO the proper forum for deciding the "usefulness" of betting machines, revolvers, prophylactics, or television, in any sense other than the workability of the devices? In view of other legal controls to protect the public against abuse of such devices, would it needlessly complicate the business of securing and enforcing patents to introduce questions of social and ethical value into patent office proceedings? But: Suppose a Du Pont chemist invents a pigment useful for paint and also for textile dyes. Its introduction into the textile dye field would "disturb the price structure" there. Another chemical engineer invents a "contaminant" which renders the pigment unsuitable for textile use. Is the latter invention patentable? [17]

more than twelve months before the filing of the application in the United States, or

(e) the invention was described in a patent granted on an application for patent by another filed in the United States before the invention thereof by the applicant for patent, or

(f) he did not himself invent the subject matter sought to be patented, or

(g) before the applicant's invention thereof the invention was made in this country by another who had not abandoned, suppressed, or concealed it. In determining priority of invention there shall be considered not only the respective dates of conception and reduction to practice of the invention, but also the reasonable diligence of one who was first to conceive and last to reduce to practice, from a time prior to conception by the other.

14. Merit Manufacturing Co. v. Hero Manufacturing Co., 185 F.2d 350, 352 (2d Cir. 1950) (L. Hand, J.).

15. Mitchell v. Tilghman, 86 U.S. (19 Wall.) 287, 397, 22 L.Ed. 125 (1874).

16. Rickard v. Du Bon, 103 F. 868 (2d Cir. 1900) (holding invalid a patented process for artificially spotting the leaves of growing tobacco to imitate commercially valuable natural spotted leaves). Cf. issue of obscenity raised in proceedings to enforce copyright in, e.g., Mitchell Brothers Film Group v. Cinema Adult Theater, 604 F.2d 852 (5th Cir. 1979) (reversing refusal to enforce copyright on "Behind the Green Door," a movie that the district court thought obscene) (reviewing cases), certiorari denied 445 U.S. 917, 100 S.Ct. 1277, 63 L.Ed.2d 601 (1980); Khan v. Leo Feist, Inc., 165 F.2d 188, 193 (2d Cir. 1947) (copyright on song, "Rum and Coca-Cola," enforced despite lines like "Both mother and daughter worken' for the Yankee dollar").

17. Cf. Testimony of Wendell Berge, Assistant Attorney General in charge of the Antitrust Division, in hearings on Scientific and Technical Mobilization before

In *Brenner v. Manson*,[18] the Supreme Court held that a new process for producing certain chemicals which were themselves of unknown utility, except perhaps as objects for scientific study, lacked the utility necessary for patentability. The Court expressed skepticism as to the likelihood that patents would encourage disclosure in this field, since the inventor of a process yielding products of no known utility would have no incentive to withhold the information. But the decision was rested mainly on the surprising proposition that until one knows the uses of the products, the scope of the monopoly conferred on the process cannot be precisely delineated. Justices Harlan and Douglas dissented, on the ground among others that the decision discriminates against "basic" research, discoveries on the basis of which others may take the "perhaps less difficult step leading to a commercially useful item." The opinions disclose a Patent Office practice of issuing patents on chemical *products* without inquiry as to use or upon the sketchiest suggestion of utility.[19]

(4) *Non-obviousness.* In 1952 Congress added a statutory requirement of "non-obviousness" (§ 103) to the requirements of novelty and utility which had been the statutory test since the Patent Act of 1793. The Supreme Court first interpreted this new section in *Graham v. John Deere Co.*,[20] holding that Congress had not intended "to change the general level of patentable invention." Rather, Congress enacted § 103 merely to codify a line of judicial decisions, going back to *Hotchkiss v. Greenwood*,[21] which required for patentability "more ingenuity and skill [than] were possessed by an ordinary mechanic acquainted with the business." Justice Clark observed that Congress apparently intended "to abolish the test it believed this Court announced in the controversial phrase 'flash of creative genius,' used in *Cuno Engineering Corp. v. Automatic Devices Corp.*, 314 U.S. 84 (1941)."

Justice Clark continued: [22]

While the ultimate question of patent validity is one of law, the § 103 condition, which is but one of three conditions, each of which must be satisfied, lends itself to several basic factual inquiries. Under § 103, the scope and content of the prior art to be determined; differences between the prior art and the claims at issue are to be ascertained; and the level of ordinary skill in the pertinent art resolved. Against this background, the obviousness or nonobviousness of the subject matter is determined. Such secondary considerations as commercial success, long felt but unsolved needs, failure of others, etc., might be utilized to give light to the circumstances surrounding the origin of the subject matter sought to be patented. As indicia of obviousness or nonobviousness, these inquiries may have relevancy. See Note, Subtests of "Nonobviousness," 112 U.Pa. L.Rev. 1169 (1964).

. . .

While we have focused attention on the appropriate standard to be applied by the courts, it must be remembered that the primary responsibility for sifting out unpatentable material lies in the Patent Office. . . . We have observed a notorious difference between the standards

the Senate Committee on Military Affairs, Oct. 15 and 21, 1943.

18. 383 U.S. 519, 86 S.Ct. 1033, 16 L.Ed.2d 69 (1966).

19. Cf. Carter-Wallace, Inc. v. Riverton Laboratories, Inc., 433 F.2d 1034 (2d Cir. 1970) (utility of chemical compound can be demonstrated through tests on laboratory animals, rather than humans);

Application of Nelson, 280 F.2d 172 (C.C. P.A.1960).

20. 383 U.S. 1, 86 S.Ct. 684, 15 L.Ed. 2d 545 (1966).

21. 52 U.S. (11 How.) 248, 13 L.Ed. 683 (1850).

22. 383 U.S. at 17–19, 86 S.Ct. at 694–95, 15 L.Ed.2d, at 556–57.

applied by the Patent Office and by the courts. While many reasons can be adduced to explain the discrepancy, one may well be the free rein often exercised by Examiners in their use of the concept of "invention." In this connection we note that the Patent Office is confronted with a most difficult task. Almost 100,000 applications for patents are filed each year. Of these, about 50,000 are granted and the backlog now runs well over 200,000. This is itself a compelling reason for the Commissioner to strictly adhere to the 1952 Act as interpreted here. This would, we believe, not only expedite disposition but bring about a closer concurrence between administrative and judicial precedent.

Although we conclude here that the inquiry which the Patent Office and the courts must make as to patentability must be beamed with greater intensity on the requirements of § 103, it bears repeating that we find no change in the general strictness with which the overall test is to be applied. We have been urged to find in § 103 a relaxed standard, supposedly a congressional reaction to the "increased standard" applied by this Court in its decisions over the last 20 or 30 years. The standard has remained invariable in this Court. . . . He who seeks to build a better mousetrap today has a long path to tread before reaching the Patent Office.

The Supreme Court subsequently applied *Graham* in *Dann v. Johnston* [23] and *Sakraida v. Ag Pro, Inc.* [24] The former involved a patent for a computer program for automatic record keeping of bank checks and deposits; the latter a patent for the "Dairy Establishment," a water flush system to remove cow manure from the floor of a dairy barn. In both cases the Court unanimously reversed lower court findings of patent validity. The Court in *Johnston* emphasized the existence of another patented data processing system for keeping transaction and balance files. Although the two systems were not equivalent, "[t]he gaps between the prior art and respondent's system is simply not so great as to render the system nonobvious to one reasonably skilled in the art." In *Sakraida* the Court wrote: [25]

The scope of the prior art was shown by prior patents, prior art publications, affidavits of people having knowledge of prior flush systems analogous to respondent's, and the testimony of a dairy operator with 22 years experience who described flush systems he had seen on visits to dairy farms throughout the country. . . . [The Court of Appeals] concluded, however, that the element lacking in the prior art was any evidence of an arrangement of the old elements to effect the abrupt release of a flow of water to wash animal wastes from the floor of a dairy barn. Therefore, "although the [respondent's] flush system does not embrace a complicated technical improvement, it does achieve a synergistic result through a novel combination."

We cannot agree . . . .. [T]his assembly of old elements that delivers water directly rather than through pipes or hoses to the barn floor falls under the head of "the work of the skillful mechanic, not that of the inventor." . . .

Though doubtless a matter of great convenience, producing a desired result in a cheaper and faster way, and enjoying commercial success, Dairy Establishment "did not produce a 'new or different function' . . . within the test of validity of combination patents." These desirable benefits "without invention will not make patentability."

23. 425 U.S. 219, 96 S.Ct. 1393, 47 L.Ed.2d 692 (1976).

24. 425 U.S. 273, 96 S.Ct. 1532, 47 L.Ed.2d 784 (1976).

25. Id. at 280–83, 96 S.Ct. at 1536–38, 47 L.Ed.2d at 790–91.

Compare, with these holdings, the following patent (No. 4,022,227) issued in 1977: [26]

METHOD OF CONCEALING PARTIAL BALDNESS

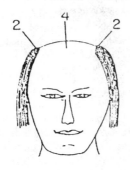

FIG. 1

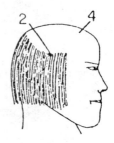

FIG. 2

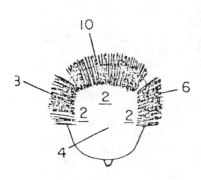

FIG. 3

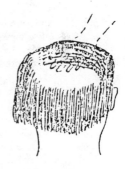

FIG. 5

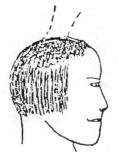

FIG. 4

FIG. 6

26. Compare, also, with the patent in *Sakraida v. Ag Pro, Inc.*, Patent No. 4,286,816, "Device For Collection and Disposal of Pet Waste," issued in 1981. See Gazette of the U.S. Patent & Trademark Office, Sept. 1, 1981, p. 173.

BACKGROUND OF THIS INVENTION

For those people who are partially bald and wish to cover the bald area hair transplants, hair weaving and hairpieces are the most commonly used solutions. The cost of covering bald areas by one of these methods can range from a few hundred dollars to thousands of dollars depending on a person's choice and financial means. Some of these commonly used bald area coverings require periodic care, which generally cost money.

Obviously a partially bald person without the financial means can not afford the luxury of such hair coverings. This person, therefore, has few options; he can attempt to use his own hair to cover the bald area, but generally most people do not have the ability to properly plan a hair style that will look good, and most attempts result in brushing the hair in one direction over the bald area, or he can allow his baldness to show.

. . .

DETAILED DESCRIPTION

In the simplest form of the invention my method is directed to a person who is partially bald as the person illustrated in FIGS. 1, 2 and 3 where there is sufficient hair to cover the bald area and by styling give an appearance of having a full head of hair. To begin with the subject's hair must be allowed to grow long enough to cover the bald area, generally about 3 to 4 inches. Of course, the length of the hair will depend on the size of the bald area, for example, a person who is front to back bald, as in the illustrations of FIGS. 1, 2 and 3, will require more length than a person with a bald spot either in front or in back of the head. In addition, the particular hair style to be performed will dictate the required hair length.

The person's hair line 2, shown in FIGS. 1–3, and bald area 4 suggest that the hair should be divided into three equal sections, sides 6 and 8, and back 10, in starting the method of this invention. A person who has a bald spot in the back of the head could use four equal sections for best results, using my hair styling method. The second step is to take the extra length hair from back area 10 and brushing it forward as in FIG. 4, making sure to cover all of the bald area with hair.

By placing a hand over the hair now covering the bald area and brushing the extra length hair from either of the sides 6 or 8 the hair styling begins to cover the entire bald area. Care should be taken to brush the hair only as it lies over the hand to avoid messing up the hair under the hand. The hair should be arranged and styled at this step since it will soon be covered. To hold the hair in place, hair spray is now applied.

To complete the hair styling the hair from the side of the head either 6 or 8, whichever has not been used, is brushed over the bald area, making sure to cover the hair now covering the bald area with a hand. This top layer of hair is also styled and coated with hair spray. By lightly sweeping the hair into the desired style as the hair spray dries, an appearance of a full head of hair is given, as in FIG. 6.

To cover a bald spot the same procedure is followed, except that hair from in front of the bald spot can be used, if desired to brush toward the back of the head giving an appearance of a full head of hair.

While the above describes the preferred form of this invention, it is apparent that modifications thereof may occur to those skilled in the art, that will fall within the scope of the following claims.

I claim:

1. A method for styling hair to cover bald areas using only the individual's own hair, comprising separating the hair on the head into several substantially equal sections, taking the hair on one section and placing it over the bald area,

then taking the hair on another section and placing it over the first section, and finally taking the hair on the remaining sections and placing it over the other sections whereby the bald area will be completely covered.

2. A method as in claim 1 wherein the hair on a person's head is folded over the bald area beginning with the hair from the back of the head, and then from first one side and then the other.

3. A method as in claim 2 wherein after the hair from the back of the head is folded over the bald area, an object is placed over the hair and hair from a first of the sides is brushed over the object, and after the hair from said first side is folded into place the object is placed over the hair and the hair from the second side is folded over the object.

4. A method as in claim 3, wherein said object is a person's hand the hair spray is applied after the hair from said first side is folded into place and again after said second side being folded into place.

5. A method as in claim 3 wherein the hair from said first side and said second side is given a final styling.

. . .

(5) *Duration of Patent Protection.* Stedman, Invention and Public Policy, 12 Law & Contemp. Probs. 649, 672 (1947):

A given patent, standing alone, is limited to the seventeen-year exclusive right. In practical effect, however, under present methods of operation, a patentee sometimes obtains substantial advantages at the expense of the public which go beyond the scope of his contribution and last much longer than the seventeen years contemplated by the statute. . . .

The first category, and probably the least important in actual effect, is illustrated by delay in the issuance of patents. It is unlikely that many inventors deliberately delay the issuance of patents, and in fact most patents issue within three years after application. Nevertheless, a sufficient number of applications remain pending for five years or more, and extreme cases of flagrant delay involving important patents occur with enough frequency, to make the problem a fairly important one. In one respect the applicant might be deemed to suffer rather than benefit from this lag, since prior to issuance of the patent others may use the invention with impunity, although it is true that the inventor benefits correspondingly at the other end. On the other hand, the applicant may derive a great benefit through delay in issuance of the patent since others, especially if an extensive investment is involved, will be unlikely to use the invention during the application period, knowing they may be compelled to discontinue use when the patent issues. . . .

Improvement patents also become a device for extending one's patent monopoly. True, the original patent expires at the end of seventeen years and is available to anyone who desires to use it. But this is not always sufficient to assure effective competition. Competition, in many fields, is a delicately balanced matter with the advantage going to the one who offers the best product even though its advantage over competitive products may be slight. If a holder of a dominant patent can obtain improvement patents which enable him to continue to put out a better product, after expiration of the basic patent, than his competitors, he may continue to enjoy a substantial competitive advantage, an advantage which is aggravated by his exclusive possession of the field for seventeen years, during which he has established himself on the inside track from the standpoint of goodwill, sales organization, proficiency and know-how, outlets, etc.

Competitors can, of course, prevent this from happening by conducting vigorous research in the field themselves, looking to the acquisition of improvement patents. But as a practical matter the improvement patents are more likely to be found in the hands of the basic patent owner. This for three reasons. First, the dominant patentee constitutes the most likely market for improvement patents independently developed. Second, as indicated above, he may compel licensees, if he does license, to funnel their improvements into his hands. Third, since he alone is in a position to use improvements immediately, he has a greater interest in conducting research in the field than have his competitors, who must perforce await the expiration of his basic patent before they can use any improvements they develop.

Trade-marks also provide a means for retaining a competitive advantage after patent protection has been lost. A trade-mark attached to a patented article, because it is the only name which the public associates with the article, easily becomes identified with the article itself rather than with its producer. As a result, it may be virtually impossible for others to compete effectively, after the patent expires, unless they can use the same mark. In extreme cases the courts have helped to remedy the situation by declaring such marks to be generic in nature and available for use by all producers of the product. It has not been suggested, however, that if the patentee takes appropriate measures to maintain his mark as an indication of origin rather than a description of the article he will lose his exclusive right to it.

Yet, even though the mark is preserved as an indication of origin, the tremendous advantages arising out of public familiarity with the mark—advantages which are greatly augmented by the effective and extensive advertising methods of today—may give the patentee great advantages difficult indeed to overcome.

Trade-mark protection is only one example of the many indirect but highly important competitive advantages that may develop during the seventeen-year period of monopoly. General reputation, development of sales outlets, creation of customer goodwill, the general "know-how" which comes from long operation, all add up to give the patentee an advantage which new competitors in the field may find it difficult, perhaps impossible, to overcome.

See proposal of the President's Commission on the Patent System (1966), that the term of a patent expire 20 years after the earliest filing date to discourage deliberate delays in prosecuting applications. Compare the more recent proposed "Patent Term Restoration Act," discussed infra p. 961, which would extend a patent for up to seven years to account for *post-issuance* regulatory reviews of the product.

(6) *Specification; Doctrine of Equivalents.* The specification, which is a detailed description and/or diagram of the patented invention or process, performs three functions: (1) describing the invention so that persons skilled in the art can reproduce it following the expiration of the patent period, or can study it to work on improvements; (2) establishing validity of the patent by distinguishing the invention from prior art; (3) circumscribing what is foreclosed as infringement during the patent period. Under Section 112, the specification must incorporate a "claims" section in which the applicant fully

delineates the outer boundary of the invention, and which is controlling for the purposes of subsequent infringement litigation.[27]

The specification requirement thus presents a dilemma for the patent applicant. If the applicant claims too broadly, it may be difficult to secure a valid patent. On the other hand, if the applicant claims too narrowly, a subsequent invention may perform " 'substantially the same function, substantially the same way, to obtain the same result' "[28] but elude in some particular a literal reading of the claims. To accommodate the potential unfairness of denying recovery in the latter case, and alleviate this dilemma, the courts have developed the "doctrine of equivalents."[29] Through this doctrine the court may venture beyond a literal reading of claims to capture a patentee's real contribution where it exceeds his stated contribution.[30] Indeed, protection under the doctrine of equivalents tends to be broader when the patent is of a pioneering nature than when it is merely an improvement or perfection of a prior invention.[31]

Is the doctrine of equivalents an unnecessary (and anticompetitive) expansion of the scope of the statutory monopoly granted the patentee?[32] The Justice Department has taken this position, urging the doctrine's abolition in an *amicus* brief in a 1970 Supreme Court case.[33] The Court split four to four on the case, however, thus preserving the doctrine, which lower courts continue to apply.

(7) *Comparison to Copyrights.* Although Congressional power to establish the copyright and patent systems comes from the same Constitutional provision (see p. 935, supra), the two systems differ in several important respects. Fundamentally, patents and copyrights protect different things—patents protect invention, while copyrights protect authorship. Unlike an inventor, an author need not create something novel or useful or unobvious; the work must simply be original:[34]

> "Original" in reference to a copyrighted work means that the particular work "owes its origin" to the "author." No large measure of novelty is necessary . . .. All that is needed to satisfy both the Constitution

27. In many foreign systems the patent application is more open-ended and need include only an articulation of the inventive concept of the applicant's contribution, a determination of the precise outer boundary being left to subsequent litigation. See P. Rosenberg, Patent Law Fundamentals § 14.01 (2d Ed., 1980).

28. Sanitary Refrigerator Co. v. Winters, 280 U.S. 30, 42, 50 S.Ct. 9, 74 L.Ed. 147 (1929).

29. In *Winters*, for example, the Court concluded that infringement might be found although the unauthorized invention did not literally correspond to a single patent claim. See also Winans v. Denmead, 56 U.S. (15 How.) 330, 14 L.Ed. 717 (1853).

30. See, e.g., Graver Tank & Manufacturing Co. v. Linde Air Products Co., 339 U.S. 605, 70 S.Ct. 854, 94 L.Ed. 1097 (1950); Ziegler v. Phillips Petroleum Co., 483 F.2d 858 (5th Cir. 1973), certiorari denied 414 U.S. 1079, 94 S.Ct. 597, 38 L.Ed. 2d 485.

31. See Corning Glass Works v. Anchor Hocking Glass Corp., 374 F.2d 473 (3d Cir. 1967), certiorari denied 389 U.S. 826, 88 S.Ct. 65, 19 L.Ed.2d 80.

32. The potential anticompetitive effects of patents construed too broadly under the doctrine of equivalents are somewhat reduced by the doctrine of "file wrapper estoppel," under which patentees who have reduced claims in response to PTO objections are estopped from later broadening the claims, in court, under the doctrine of equivalents. The "file wrapper" is the folder containing the official record of the case within the PTO. For an illustrative application of the doctrine, see Nationwide Chemical Corp. v. Wright, 584 F.2d 714 (5th Cir. 1978).

33. Tigrett Industries, Inc. v. Standard Industries, Inc., 397 U.S. 586, 90 S.Ct. 1310, 25 L.Ed.2d 590 (1970).

34. Alfred Bell & Co. v. Catalda Fine Arts, 191 F.2d 99, 102–03 (2d Cir. 1951) (Frank, C.J.)

and the statute is that the "author" contributed something more than a "merely trivial" variation, something recognizably "his own." Originality in this context "means little more than a prohibition of actual copying." No matter how poor artistically the "author's" addition, it is enough if it be his own . . . . The "author" is entitled to a copyright if he independently contrived a work completely identical with what went before . . . .

The difference between protecting invention and authorship is related to the type of legal protection afforded by the two systems and the methods for securing that protection. A valid copyright protects only against copying the protected work; a valid patent gives the patentee the right to keep others from making or using the invention even if the infringer engages in no copying. A copyright (since 1978 [35]) "subsists from its creation,"[36] and the copyrighted work need not even be registered at the Copyright Office to obtain copyright protection (although certain infringement remedies and other advantages are available only after registration).[37] This is in obvious contrast to the elaborate examination system, described above, for determining the validity of a patent prior to issuance.

The Copyright Act defines the subject matter of copyright protection in Section 102(a):

Copyright protection subsists, in accordance with this title, in original works of authorship fixed in any tangible medium of expression, now known or later developed, from which they can be perceived, reproduced, or otherwise communicated, either directly or with the aid of a machine or device. Works of authorship include the following categories:

(1) literary works;

(2) musical works, including any accompanying words;

(3) dramatic works, including any accompanying music;

(4) pantomines and choreographic works;

(5) pictorial, graphic, and sculptural works;

(6) motion pictures and other audiovisual works; and

(7) sound recordings.

Copyright protection for works created after January 1, 1978, generally last for the life of the author plus fifty years.[38] Prior law had provided for a twenty-eight year term, with one twenty-eight year renewal.[39] Contrast this to the seventeen year term for patents. Is there any justification for different treatment?

(8) *Design Patents.* Sections 171–173 of 35 U.S.C.A. afford patent protection to the inventor of "any new, original, and ornamental design for an article of manufacture, not known or used by others, etc." Design patents may be had for $3\frac{1}{2}$ years (fee $10), 7 years ($15), or 14 years ($30) at the election of the applicant. The purpose of this monopoly is said to be the encouragement of the beautification of manufactured articles to promote

---

35. The Copyright Act of 1976 (effective for most purposes on January 1, 1978) altered the prior system which had provided statutory protection only upon "publication" with the requisite notice. See Copyright Act of 1909, § 10, 35 Stat. 1078 (1909). For a brief history of copyright laws, see Latman, The Copyright Law: Howell's Copyright Law Revised and the 1976 Act, at 2–11 (5th Ed. 1979).

36. 17 U.S.C.A. § 302(a). Under the current Act a work is created when it is fixed in a tangible medium of expression. 17 U.S.C.A. § 101.

37. See id., §§ 408–412.

38. See 17 U.S.C.A. § 302.

39. See Copyright Act of 1909, §§ 23–24, 35 Stat. 1080 (1909).

their salability. Mechanical utility features are not protected by the design patent.[40]

Is it necessary to confer a monopoly for design in order to stimulate attractive designing, or would competition among sellers give us all the progress we can expect or desire in this field? Patenting of new processes, machines, etc., is said to promote progress in science by getting researchers to disclose their inventions in exchange for the monopoly grant; to what extent does this argument support design patents? Is the Design Patent Act valid under the patent clause of the Constitution?

Note that the 1976 Copyright Act protects "pictorial, graphic, and sculptural works," defined to include "works of artistic craftsmanship insofar as their form but not their mechanical or utilitarian aspects are concerned." [41] Why would one seek a design patent on an article rather than a copyright, in view of the difficulty in satisfying the Patent and Trademark Office that a design is novel and inventive, the time required for Patent and Trademark Office proceedings, and the relatively brief monopoly afforded by design patent? What countervailing advantage is there in patent protection? Should the claimant under several statutes affording design protection be compelled to elect—is more than one statutory monopoly required to fuel the creative fires? [42]

The President's Commission on the Patent System (1966) recommended repeal of the design patent provisions: "Despite the statutory requirement of unobviousness, patents on designs are now granted, in effect, solely on the basis of novelty. Courts often find these patents invalid on the ground that the design is obvious." [43]

40. See generally 2 Deller's Walker on Patents (2d ed. 1964) Ch. VIII.

41. 17 U.S.C.A. § 101.

42. See In re Yardley, 493 F.2d 1389 (C.C.P.A.1974) (issuance of design patent on a watch face adorned with a copyrighted caricature of former Vice President Spiro Agnew; held: areas of protection afforded by the different statutes overlapped, Congress had not required election of protection, and dual protection constitutional). But see 37 C.F.R. § 202.10(b) (copyright office will not register a work of art for which a design patent has previously been issued). The issue of election was not passed on in the landmark case of Mazer v. Stein, 347 U.S. 201, 74 S.Ct. 460, 98 L.Ed. 630 (1953), which allowed copyright protection for a statuette designed for mass production as a lamp base. The Court held that the legislative history and administrative practice showed that "work of art" was not intended to be limited to fine art and that *potential* patentability does not preclude copyright. See id. n.37 (citing cases regarding election as precluding double coverage). On the issue of copyright protection for design, see also Esquire, Inc. v. Ringer, 591 F.2d 796 (D.C. Cir.1978), certiorari denied 440 U.S. 908, 99 S.Ct. 1217, 59 L.Ed.2d 456 (1979) (upholding Register's refusal under 1909 Act to register copyright on outdoor floodlight "of contemporary design"; overall design or configuration of a utilitarian object is not copyrightable; court of appeals acknowledges potential anticompetitive effects of granting protection for product designs).

43. The President's Commission added that "some means *outside* the patent system should be developed for the protection of new and ornamental designs." As to novelty and invention in design patents, see Fields v. Schuyler, 153 U.S.App. D.C. 229, 472 F.2d 1304 (1972), certiorari denied 411 U.S. 987, 93 S.Ct. 2270, 36 L.Ed.2d 965 (1973), rejecting the view that originality should be judged by consumer response, since this would make commercial success determinative of patentability, rather than merely a secondary indicator of patentability. Cf. Thabet Manufacturing Co. v. Koolvent Metal Awning Corp., 226 F.2d 207, 212 (6th Cir. 1955) ("its over-all aesthetic effect must represent a step which has required inventive genius"); Forestek Plating Co. v. Knapp-Monarch Co., 106 F.2d 554, 559 (6th Cir. 1939) ("Every new design of an article manufactured is not patentable. . . . The inventive designer need not possess the skill of a great artist or sculptor, but he must possess more skill than the professional designer, mechanical engineer or metallurgist").

DIAMOND v. CHAKRABARTY

Supreme Court of the United States, 1980.
447 U.S. 303, 100 S.Ct. 2204, 65 L.Ed.2d 144.

MR. CHIEF JUSTICE BURGER delivered the opinion of the Court.

We granted certiorari to determine whether a live, human-made micro-organism is patentable subject matter under 35 U.S.C. § 101.

I

In 1972, respondent Chakrabarty, a microbiologist, filed a patent application, assigned to the General Electric Company. The application asserted 36 claims related to Chakrabarty's invention of "a bacterium from the genus *Pseudomonas* containing therein at least two stable energy-generating plasmids, each of said plasmids providing a separate hydrocarbon degradative pathway." [44] This human-made, genetically engineered bacterium is capable of breaking down multiple components of crude oil. Because of this property, which is possessed by no naturally occurring bacteria, Chakrabarty's invention is believed to have significant value for the treatment of oil spills.

Chakrabarty's patent claims were of three types: first, process claims for the method of producing the bacteria; second, claims for an inoculum comprised of a carrier material floating on water, such as straw, and the new bacteria; and third, claims to the bacteria themselves. The patent examiner allowed the claims falling into the first two categories, but rejected claims for the bacteria. His decision rested on two grounds: (1) that micro-organisms are "products of nature," and (2) that as living things they are not patentable subject matter under 35 U.S.C. § 101.

Chakrabarty appealed the rejection of these claims to the Patent Office Board of Appeals, and the Board affirmed the Examiner on the second ground. . . . The Court of Customs and Patent Appeals, by a divided vote, reversed . . . .. The Government . . . sought certiorari, and we granted the writ . . . .

II

The Constitution grants Congress broad power to legislate to "promote the Progress of Science and the useful Arts, by securing for limited times to authors and inventors the exclusive right to their respective writings and discoveries." Art. I, § 8. The patent laws promote this progress by offering inventors exclusive rights for a

---

44. [Court's footnote 1.] Plasmids are hereditary units physically separate from the chromosomes of the cell. In prior research, Chakrabarty and an associate discovered that plasmids control the oil degradation abilities of certain bacteria. In particular, the two researchers discovered plasmids capable of degrading camphor and octane, two components of crude oil. In the work represented by the patent application at issue here, Chakrabarty discovered a process by which four different plasmids, capable of degrading four different oil components, could be transferred to and maintained stably in a single *Pseudomonas* bacteria, which itself has no capacity for degrading oil.

limited period as an incentive for their inventiveness and research efforts. The authority of Congress is exercised in the hope that "[t]he productive effort thereby fostered will have a positive effect on society through the introduction of new products and processes of manufacture into the economy, and the emanations by way of increased employment and better lives for our citizens." Kewanee [Oil Co. v. Bicron Corp., infra p. 1050].

The question before us in this case is a narrow one of statutory interpretation requiring us to construe 35 U.S.C. § 101, which provides:

> "Whoever invents or discovers any new and useful process, machine, manufacture, or composition of matter, or any new and useful improvement thereof, may obtain a patent therefor, subject to the conditions and requirements of this title."

Specifically, we must determine whether respondent's micro-organism constitutes a "manufacture" or "composition of matter" within the meaning of the statute.

III

In cases of statutory construction we begin, of course, with the language of the statute. And "unless otherwise defined, words will be interpreted as taking their ordinary, contemporary common meaning." We have also cautioned that courts "should not read into the patent laws limitations and conditions which the Legislature has not expressed."

Guided by these canons of construction, this Court has read the term "manufacture" in § 101 in accordance with its dictionary definition to mean "the production of articles for use from raw materials prepared by giving to these materials new forms, qualities, properties, or combinations, whether by hand labor or by machinery." Similarly, "composition of matter" has been construed consistent with its common usage to include "all compositions of two or more substances and . . . all composite articles, whether they be the results of chemical union, or of mechanical mixture, or whether they be gases, fluids, powders, or solids." In choosing such expansive terms as "manufacture" and "composition of matter," modified by the comprehensive "any," Congress plainly contemplated that the patent laws would be given wide scope.

The relevant legislative history also supports a broad construction. The Patent Act of 1793, authored by Thomas Jefferson, defined statutory subject matter as "any new and useful art, machine, manufacture, or composition of matter, or any new or useful improvement [thereof]." Act of Feb. 21, 1793, ch. 11, § 1, 1 Stat. 318. The Act embodied Jefferson's philosophy that "ingenuity should receive a liberal encouragement." V Writings of Thomas Jefferson, at 75–76. Subsequent patent statutes in 1836, 1870, and 1874 employed this same broad language. In 1952, when the patent laws were recodified, Congress replaced the word "art" with "process," but otherwise left Jefferson's language intact. The Committee Reports accompanying the 1952 act inform us that Congress intended statutory subject matter to "include anything under the sun that is made by man."

This is not to suggest that § 101 has no limits or that it embraces every discovery. The laws of nature, physical phenomena, and abstract ideas have been held not patentable. Thus, a new mineral discovered in the earth or a new plant found in the wild is not patentable subject matter. Likewise, Einstein could not patent his celebrated law that $E = mc^2$; nor could Newton have patented the law of gravity. Such discoveries are "manifestations of . . . nature, free to all men and reserved exclusively to none."

Judged in this light, respondent's micro-organism plainly qualifies as patentable subject matter. His claim is not to a hitherto unknown natural phenomenon, but to a nonnaturally occurring manufacture or composition of matter—a product of human ingenuity "having a distinctive name, character [and] use." . . . [T]he patentee has produced a new bacterium with markedly different characteristics from any found in nature and one having the potential for significant utility. His discovery is not nature's handiwork, but his own; accordingly it is patentable subject matter under § 101.

IV

Two contrary arguments are advanced, neither of which we find persuasive.

(A)

The Government's first argument rests on the enactment of the 1930 Plant Patent Act, which afforded patent protection to certain asexually reproduced plants, and the 1970 Plant Variety Protection Act, which authorized patents for certain sexually reproduced plants but excluded bacteria from its protection.[45] In the Government's view, the passage of these Acts evidences congressional understanding that the terms "manufacture" or "composition of matter" do not include living things; if they did, the Government argues, neither Act would have been necessary.

We reject this argument. Prior to 1930, two factors were thought to remove plants from patent protection. The first was the belief that plants, even those artificially bred, were products of nature for purposes of the patent law. . . . The second obstacle to patent

---

45. [Court's footnote 7.] The Plant Patent Act of 1930, 35 U.S.C. § 161, provides in relevant part:

"Whoever invents or discovers and asexually reproduces any distinct and new variety of plant, including cultivated sports, mutants, hybrids, and newly found seedlings, other than a tuberpropogated plant or a plant found in an uncultivated state, may obtain a patent therefor . . . ."

The Plant Variety Protection Act of 1970, provides in relevant part:

"The breeder of any novel variety of sexually reproduced plant (other than fungi, bacteria, or first generation hybrids) who has so reproduced the variety, or his successor in interest, shall be entitled to plant variety protection therefor . . . ." 7 U.S.C. § 2402(a).

protection for plants was the fact that plants were thought not ame-
nable to the "written description" requirement of the patent law.
. . .

In enacting the Plant Patent Act, Congress addressed both of
these concerns. It explained at length its belief that the work of the
plant breeder "in aid of nature" was patentable invention. And it
relaxed the written description requirement in favor of "a description
. . . as complete as is reasonably possible." 35 U.S.C. § 162. No
Committee or Member of Congress, however, expressed the broader
view, now urged by the Government, that the terms "manufacture"
or "composition of matter" exclude living things. . . . Moreover,
. . . the House and Senate Committee reports . . . observe:

> "There is a clear and logical distinction *between the discovery of a*
> *new variety of plant and of certain inanimate things*, such, for
> example, as a new and useful natural mineral. The mineral is cre-
> ated wholly by nature unassisted by man. . . . On the other
> hand, a plant discovery resulting from cultivation is unique, isolat-
> ed, and is not repeated by nature, nor can it be reproduced by
> nature unaided by man. . . ."

Congress thus recognized that the relevant distinction was not between living and inanimate things, but between products of nature,
whether living or not, and human-made inventions. Here, respondent's micro-organism is the result of human ingenuity and research.
Hence, the passage of the Plant Patent Act affords the Government
no support.

Nor does the passage of the 1970 Plant Variety Protection Act
support the Government's position. As the Government acknowledges, sexually reproduced plants were not included under the 1930
Act because new varieties could not be reproduced true-to-type
through seedlings. By 1970, however, it was generally recognized
that true-to-type reproduction was possible and that plant patent protection was therefore appropriate. The 1970 Act extended that protection. There is nothing in its language or history to suggest that it
was enacted because § 101 did not include living things.

In particular, we find nothing in the exclusion of bacteria from
plant variety protection to support the Government's position. The
legislative history gives no reason for this exclusion. . . .
[A]bsent some clear indication that Congress "focused on [the] issues
. . . directly related to the one presently before the Court," there
is no basis for reading into its actions an intent to modify the plain
meaning of the words found in § 101.

(B)

The Government's second argument is that micro-organisms cannot qualify as patentable subject matter until Congress expressly authorizes such protection. Its position rests on the fact that genetic
technology was unforeseen when Congress enacted § 101. From this
it is argued that resolution of the patentability of inventions such as

respondent's should be left to Congress. The legislative process, the Government argues, is best equipped to weigh the competing economic, social, and scientific considerations involved, and to determine whether living organisms produced by genetic engineering should receive patent protection. In support of this position, the Government relies on our recent holding in Parker v. Flook, 437 U.S. 584, 98 S.Ct. 2522, 57 L.Ed.2d 451 (1978), and the statement that the judiciary "must proceed cautiously when . . . asked to extend patent rights into areas wholly unforeseen by Congress."

It is, of course, correct that Congress, not the courts, must define the limits of patentability; but it is equally true that once Congress has spoken it is "the province and duty of the judicial department to say what the law is." Marbury v. Madison, 1 Cranch 137, 177, 2 L.Ed. 60 (1803). Congress has performed its constitutional role in defining patentable subject matter in § 101; we perform ours in construing the language Congress has employed. In so doing, our obligation is to take statutes as we find them, guided, if ambiguity appears, by the legislative history and statutory purpose. Here, we perceive no ambiguity. The subject matter provisions of the patent law have been cast in broad terms to fulfill the constitutional and statutory goal of promoting "the Progress of Science and the useful Arts" with all that means for the social and economic benefits envisioned by Jefferson. Broad general language is not necessarily ambiguous when congressional objectives require broad terms.

Nothing in *Flook* is to the contrary. That case applied our prior precedents to determine that a "claim for an improved method of calculation, even when tied to a specific end use, is unpatentable subject matter under § 101." The Court carefully scrutinized the claim at issue to determine whether it was precluded from patent protection under "the principles underlying the prohibition against patents for 'ideas' or phenomena of nature." We have done that here. *Flook* did not announce a new principle that inventions in areas not contemplated by Congress when the patent laws were enacted are unpatentable *per se*.

To read that concept into *Flook* would frustrate the purposes of the patent law. . . . A rule that unanticipated inventions are without protection would conflict with the core concept of the patent law that anticipation undermines patentability.

Mr. Justice Douglas reminded that the inventions most benefiting mankind are those that "push back the frontiers of chemistry, physics, and the like." A. & P. Tea Co. v. Supermarket Corp., 340 U.S. 147, 154, 71 S.Ct. 127, 131, 95 L.Ed. 162 (1950) (concurring opinion). Congress employed broad general language in drafting § 101 precisely because such inventions are often unforeseeable.

To buttress its argument, the Government, with the support of *amicus,* points to grave risks that may be generated by research endeavors such as respondent's. The briefs present a gruesome parade of horribles. Scientists, among them Nobel laureates, are quoted suggesting that genetic research may pose a serious threat to the human race, or, at the very least, that the dangers are far too substantial to permit such research to proceed apace at this time. We are told that genetic research and related technological developments may spread pollution and disease, that it may result in a loss of genetic diversity, and that its practice may tend to depreciate the value of human life. These arguments are forcefully, even passionately presented; they remind us that, at times, human ingenuity seems unable to control fully the forces it creates—that with Hamlet, it is sometimes better "to bear those ills we have than fly to others that we know not of."

It is argued that this Court should weigh these potential hazards in considering whether respondent's invention is patentable subject matter under § 101. We disagree. The grant or denial of patents on micro-organisms is not likely to put an end to genetic research or to its attendant risks. The large amount of research that has already occurred when no researcher had sure knowledge that patent protection would be available suggests that legislative or judicial fiat as to patentability will not deter the scientific mind from probing into the unknown any more than Canute could command the tides. Whether respondent's claims are patentable may determine whether research efforts are accelerated by the hope of reward or slowed by want of incentives, but that is all.

What is more important is that we are without competence to entertain these arguments—either to brush them aside as fantasies generated by fear of the unknown, or to act on them. The choice we are urged to make is a matter of high policy for resolution within the legislative process after the kind of investigation, examination, and study that legislative bodies can provide and courts cannot. That process involves the balancing of competing values and interests, which in our democratic system is the business of elected representatives. Whatever their validity, the contentions now pressed on us should be addressed to the political branches of the government, the Congress and the Executive, and not to the courts.

. . . Congress is free to amend § 101 so as to exclude from patent protection organisms produced by genetic engineering. Compare 42 U.S.C. § 2181, exempting from patent protection inventions "useful solely in the utilization of special nuclear material or atomic energy in an atomic weapon." Or it may choose to craft a statute specifically designed for such living things. But, until Congress takes such action, this Court must construe the language of § 101 as it is. The language of that section fairly embraces respondent's invention.

Accordingly, the judgment of the Court of Customs and Patent Appeals is affirmed.

Affirmed.

MR. JUSTICE BRENNAN, with whom MR. JUSTICE WHITE, MR. JUS-
TICE MARSHALL, and MR. JUSTICE POWELL join, dissenting.

I agree with the Court that the question before us is a narrow
one. Neither the future of scientific research, nor even, the ability of
respondent Chakrabarty to reap some monopoly profits from his pioneering work, is at stake. Patents on the processes by which he has
produced and employed the new living organism are not contested.
The only question we need decide is whether Congress, exercising its
authority under Art. I, § 8, of the Constitution, intended that he be
able to secure a monopoly on the living organism itself, no matter
how produced or how used. Because I believe the Court has misread
the applicable legislation, I dissent.

The patent laws attempt to reconcile this Nation's deep seated antipathy to monopolies with the need to encourage progress. Given
the complexity and legislative nature of this delicate task, we must be
careful to extend patent protection no further than Congress has provided. In particular, were there an absence of legislative direction,
the courts should leave to Congress the decisions whether and how
far to extend the patent privilege into areas where the common understanding has been that patents are not available.

In this case, however, we do not confront a complete legislative
vacuum. . . . In 1930 Congress enacted the Plant Patent Act
. . . . In 1970 Congress enacted the Plant Variety Protection Act
. . . . Because Congress thought it had to legislate in order to
make agricultural "human-made inventions" patentable and because
the legislation Congress enacted is limited, it follows that Congress
never meant to make patentable items outside the scope of the legislation.

. . .

. . . It is the role of Congress, not this Court, to broaden or
narrow the reach of the patent laws. This is especially true where,
as here, the composition sought to be patented uniquely implicates
matters of public concern.

NOTES AND QUERIES

(1) *Queries.* Will the decision in *Chakrabarty* to grant patent protection: stimulate the genetic engineering industry by attracting investment?
diminish output in the industry by conferring monopolies on patentees?
prove beneficial to society by giving us more (less?) genetic engineering than
an unhindered marketplace would? prove costly to society by creating complex legal battles and discouraging the free publication of research? be irrelevant because exact coverage is today so unclear that firms cannot make
investment decisions based on possible patent protection in the distant future? [46]

46. See "Gene Engineering Industry
Hails Court Ruling as Spur to Growth,"
N.Y. Times, June 17, 1980, p. D16 (discussing efforts of firms attempting to
commercialize genetic engineering);
"Profits in Gene Splicing Bring the Tan-
gled Issue of Ownership to Fore," Wall
St. Journal, Dec. 3, 1980, p. 1 (detailing
disputes over ownership of interferon cell
line and possible effect on willingness of
scientists to publish their research;
" 'The only thing certain is that the pat-

If patents do provide an incentive, should we then reconsider the well-established view that abstract ideas are not patentable? Don't we want to encourage basic research that comes up with new ideas? Note that there has been increasing concern in recent years over a perceived decline in innovation and research and development in the United States.[47] To what extent might (should?) that influence a court to find that a claimed invention is patentable subject matter?

(2) *Patenting New Technology—Computer Programs.* For a number of years the Supreme Court has been struggling with the question whether computer programs—a set of instructions to a computer written in machine or symbolic language making use of one or more formulae ("algorithms")—are patentable subject matter under § 101. In *Gottschalk v. Benson,*[48] the applicant sought a patent for a digital computer program which converted numerical information from one form to another (binary-coded decimal numerals to pure binary numerals); the program was not limited to particular applications or machines and used an algorithm which had "no substantial practical application except in connection with a digital computer." Concluding that a patent on the program "in practical effect would be a patent on the algorithm itself," the Court rejected the claim.

The Court in *Benson* did not foreclose patentability for computer programs. After avoiding the issue in 1976,[49] the Court faced it again in 1978 in *Parker v. Flook.*[50] Flook involved a method for updating "alarm limits" used to signal abnormal conditions during catalytic conversion processes. Again, an algorithm was critical to the claimed invention and the calculations using the algorithm would be performed by computer. The Court rejected the patent, relying on *Benson*, even though there were uses for the algorithm outside the claimed process and the process included steps after applying the algorithm.

In its third decision in the area, *Diamond v. Diehr*[51] (decided after *Chakrabarty*), the Court finally upheld the validity of a patent involving a computer program. Involved was a process for curing synthetic rubber, which used a well known mathematical formula and a computer to perform the calculations. Emphasizing that the applicant did not seek to patent the formula, but only the specific process, the Court held (5–4) that the process was patentable subject matter under Section 101. The majority in *Diehr* stressed that the patent was sought for an industrial process, not a mathematical equation; whether the process was novel and nonobvious was a different question from subject matter patentability. The dissent believed that

ent attorneys are going to get rich,' " says President of Pfizer's research division). On patenting life forms, see generally Note, Implications of the Plant Patent Act for the Patentability of Microorganisms, 39 Md.L.Rev. 376 (1979); Note, Building a Better Bacterium: Genetic Engineering and the Patent Law after Diamond v. Chakrabarty, 81 Colum.L. Rev. 159 (1981); Pros and Cons on the Patentability of Microorganisms Per Se, 7 Am.Pat.L.Ass'n Q.J. 147 (1979).

47. See, e.g., Report of Sen.Comm. on Commerce, Science and Transportation, Subcomm. on Science, Technology and Space, 95th Cong., 2nd Sess. (1978); "Research Lag is Laid to Management," N.Y. Times, Dec. 16, 1978, p. 30 (results

of National Science Foundation study); "Carter Asks Action to Spur Technology," N.Y. Times, Nov. 1, 1979, p. A1.

48. 409 U.S. 63, 93 S.Ct. 253, 34 L.Ed. 2d 273 (1972).

49. See Dann v. Johnston, 425 U.S. 219, 96 S.Ct. 1393, 47 L.Ed.2d 692 (1976), discussed supra p. 942.

50. 437 U.S. 584, 98 S.Ct. 2522, 57 L.Ed.2d 451 (1978).

51. 450 U.S. 175, 101 S.Ct. 1048, 67 L.Ed.2d 155 (1981). See also Diamond v. Bradley, 600 F.2d 807 (C.C.P.A.1979), affirmed by equally divided Court, 450 U.S. 381, 101 S.Ct. 1495, 67 L.Ed.2d 311 (1981) (decided one week after Diamond v. Diehr).

Diehr had simply developed a new method of programming a digital computer to calculate the correct timing in a familiar process, and that under *Benson* and *Flook* there was no patentable invention.

Given the difficulties in distinguishing between a computer program that
is simply a (faster) method of calculation and one that is part of a new process, should the Court have continued to deny patentability to all computer
programs? Consider the views of Justice Stevens, expressed in his dissent
in *Diehr:* [52]

> The broad question whether computer programs should be given pat-
> ent protection involves policy considerations that this Court is not author-
> ized to address. As the numerous briefs *amicus curiae* filed in Gott-
> schalk v. Benson, supra, Dann v. Johnston, supra, Parker v. Flook, supra,
> and this case demonstrate, that question is not only difficult and impor-
> tant, but apparently also one that may be affected by institutional bias.
> In each of those cases, the spokesmen for the organized patent bar have
> uniformly favored patentability and industry representatives have taken
> positions properly motivated by their economic self-interest. Notwith-
> standing fervent argument that patent protection is essential for the
> growth of the software industry, [53] commentators have noted that "this
> industry is growing by leaps and bounds without it." [54] In addition, even
> some commentators who believe that legal protection for computer pro-
> grams is desirable have expressed doubts that the present patent system
> can provide the needed protection.
>
> · · ·
>
> [F]ederal judges have a duty to respond [to the criticism that] the
> cases considering the patentability of program-related inventions do not
> establish rules that enable a conscientious patent lawyer to determine
> with a fair degree of accuracy which, if any, program-related inventions

52. 450 U.S. at 216–18, 101 S.Ct. at
1071–72, 67 L.Ed.2d at 183–84.

53. [Footnote from Justice Stevens'
opinion.] For example, the Association
of Data Processing Service Organizations, appearing as *amicus curiae* in
Flook, made the following policy argument:

"The need of the incentive of patents
for software is at least as great as that
of the incentive available for hardware
because: 'Today, providing computer
software involves greater . . . risk
than providing computer . . . hardware . . . .'

"To a financial giant, the economic
value of a patent may not loom large;
to the small software products companies upon which the future of the development of quality software depends,
the value of the patent in financing a
small company may spell the difference between life and death. To banks
and financial institutions the existence
of a patent or even the potentiality of
obtaining one may well be a decisive
factor in determining whether a loan
should be granted. To prospective investors a patent or the possibility of

obtaining one may be the principal element in the decision whether to invest.

"Making clear that patents may be
available for inventions in software
would unleash important innovative
talent. It would have the direct opposite effect forecast by the . . .
hardware manufacturers; it would enable competition with those companies
and provide the needed incentive to
stimulate innovation." Brief *Amicus
Curiae* for ADAPSO in Parker v.
Flook, 437 U.S. 584, [98 S.Ct. 2522, 57
L.Ed.2d 451] p. 44 (footnote omitted).

54. [Footnote from Justice Stevens'
opinion.] Gemignani, supra, 7 Rut.J.
Comp., Tech. & L., at 309. In a footnote
to that comment, Professor Gemignani
added that the rate of growth of the
software industry "has been even faster
lately than that of the hardware industry
which does enjoy patent protections."
Id., at 309, n. 259. Other commentators
are in accord. See Nycum, Legal Protection for Computer Programs, 1 Comp.L.J.
1, 55–58 (1978); Note, Protection of Computer Programs; Resurrection of the
Standard, 50 N.D.Law 333, 344 (1974).

will be patentable. . . . [I favor] an unequivocal holding that *no* program-related invention is a patentable process under § 101 unless it makes a contribution to the art that is not dependent entirely on the utilization of a computer . . . .

How about granting copyright protection for computer programs (assuming there should be any protection at all)? [55] Recall the different rights granted to patent and copyright holders. Would it be incentive enough to allow the program owner the right to stop others from copying, as opposed to the right to stop others from independently "inventing" the same program? The copyrightability of computer programs was not clear under the Copyright Act of 1909, although the Copyright Office has registered copyrights on computer programs since 1964.[56] In 1974 Congress established a National Commission on New Technological Uses of Copyright Works ("CONTU") to study the copyright issues raised by computer programs. Over the strong dissent of two of its members, the Commission's 1978 Report endorsed the copyrightability of computer programs.[57] Although the legislative history of the 1976 Act indicates that the broad language of Section 102 (see p. 948, supra) was intended to allow copyright protection for computer programs,[58] nevertheless there were no court decisions testing the issue.[59] In 1980 Congress further amended the Copyright Act to reconfirm copyright protection for computer programs.[60]

(3) *Deferring to Congress—Copyright and Cable Television.* By granting patent protection, the Court in *Chakrabarty* (and later in *Diamond v. Diehr*) altered the status quo and placed important new industries within the confines of the general Patent Code. In light of the potential economic and social impact of these changes, should the Court have withheld protection and thereby forced a more tailored legislative solution? Such was the result of Supreme Court decisions in the cable television industry. In *Fortnightly Corp. v. United Artists Television, Inc.,*[61] decided in 1968, the Court held that a cable television operator who merely receives and relays unedited over-the-air television programs is more like a listener than a broadcaster, and hence had not "performed" the copyrighted work within the meaning of

55. See, e.g., Breyer, The Uneasy Case for Copyright, 84 Harv.L.Rev. 281 (1970) (arguing that independent producers of software had little to gain and much to lose with copyright protection; general purpose programs appeared to be salable without protection because usually accompanied by important continuing service supplied by the software firm); Bender, Computer Programs: Should They be Patentable, 68 Colum.L. Rev. 241 (1968). For another way to protect computer programs, see Bender, Trade Secret Software Protection, 5 Am. Patent L. Ass'n Q.J. 49 (1977).

56. See Note, Copyright Protection For Computer Programs, 64 Colum.L. Rev. 1274 (1964).

57. The Report and the opinions of Commissioners Nimmer (concurring) and Hersey (dissenting) are usefully excerpted in Latman & Gorman, Copyright for the Eighties 112–130 (1981).

58. See Latman, supra, at 49–50.

59. See Latman, supra, at 49.

60. See P.L. 96–517, 94 Stat. 3028–29. The provision, part of a bill amending the patent and trademark laws, defines a "computer program" and regulates certain rights of the owner of a copy of a computer program to use the program. Curiously, the bill did not specifically add "computer programs" to the list of examples of "works of authorship" in Section 102; protection still resides in the statute's broad language. See also "Bill Safeguards Data Programs," N.Y. Times, Dec. 4, 1980, p. D1 (reporting "favorable reactions" to legislation from IBM and other major industry organizations with a stake in protection of software, although these groups believe additional legislation still necessary).

61. 392 U.S. 390, 88 S.Ct. 2084, 20 L.Ed.2d 1176 (1968).

the Copyright Act and could not be sued for copyright infringement. Justice Stewart's opinion concluded: [62]

> We have been invited by the Solicitor General in an *amicus curiae* brief to render a compromise decision in this case that would, it is said, accommodate various competing considerations of copyright, communications, and antitrust policy. We decline the invitation. That job is for Congress. We take the Copyright Act of 1909 as we find it. With due regard to changing technology, we hold that the petitioner did not under that law "perform" the respondent's copyrighted works.

Fortnightly was followed by a number of years of political wrangling among the cable television, entertainment, and over-the-air television industries over a legislative solution to determine the proper scope of copyright liability. A needed revision of the Copyright Act of 1909 was stalled until a compromise could be worked out; the jam was broken in 1976 with the new Copyright Act which, in essence, imposes copyright liability on cable television along with a compulsory license and a statutorily imposed fee structure. Noted one commentator: "The cable-television provisions are by far the most lengthy and complex provisions of the new Copyright Act. They must be perused to be believed, if not understood." [63]

(4) *Patent Provisions of the Atomic Energy Act of 1954.* Section 151 of the Atomic Energy Act, 42 U.S.C.A. § 2181, provides that no patent shall be granted "for any invention or discovery which is useful solely in the utilization of special nuclear material or atomic energy in an atomic weapon." [64] Under section 157, the Secretary of Energy can make a monetary award for such inventions disclosed to it. The statute also provides for nonexclusive "reasonable royalty" licensing of patents "affected with the public interest," defined as those covering inventions "of primary importance in the production or utilization of special nuclear material or atomic energy" and whose licensing is of "primary importance" in effectuating the purposes of the Act.[65]

62. Id. at 401–02. In Teleprompter Corp. v. Columbia Broadcasting System, 415 U.S. 394, 94 S.Ct. 1129, 39 L.Ed.2d 415 (1974), the Court reaffirmed *Fortnightly*'s application to cable television, even though such systems relayed "distant" signals and had begun to more closely resemble over-the-air broadcasters.

63. Gorman, An Overview of the Copyright Act of 1976, 126 U.Pa.L.Rev. 856, 878 (1978). Subsequent FCC deregulation of cable television may have upset the compromise reflected in the 1976 Act, and require further amendments. See H.R. 5949, 97th Cong., 2d Sess., described in 24 Pat. Trademark & Copyright J. (BNA) 536 (1982).

64. See Piper v. Atomic Energy Commission, 502 F.2d 1393 (3d Cir. 1974) (focusing on meaning of "useful in the production or utilization of special nuclear material or atomic energy" in section 152 of the A.E.C. Act to deny A.E.C. preemption of patent on certain antiradiation agents). See also Marks and Trowbridge, Framework for Atomic Industry, pp. 25–33 (1955); Boske, Patents Under

the New Atomic Energy Act, 36 J.P.O.S. 867 (1954); Beckett and Merriman, Will the Patent Provisions of the Atomic Energy Act of 1954 Promote Progress or Stifle Invention?, 23 G.Wash.L.Rev. 195 (1954). On patent as well as other problems under the Atomic Energy Act of 1954, see Workshops on legal Problems of Atomic Energy (U. of Mich.Law School 1956); Symposium, 21 Law and Contemp. Prob., Winter Issue 1956; Report of the [McKinney] Panel on the Impact of the Peaceful Uses of Atomic Energy to the Joint Committee on Atomic Energy, 84th Cong., 2d Sess. (1956).

65. 42 U.S.C.A. § 2183. See also The Invention Secrecy Act of 1951, 35 U.S.C.A. § 181 *et seq.*, authorizing the Commissioner of Patents and Trademarks to order patent applications kept secret and patent grants withheld where the publication or disclosure of the invention "would be detrimental to the national security" (§ 181). Under § 183 of the Act an applicant whose patent is so withheld has the right to apply for compensation from the government for the damage caused by the order of secrecy and/or for

Why is this an appropriate area for special treatment? Are such provisions likely to encourage or discourage research in the nuclear energy industry? How should the existence of such a statute have affected the decision in *Chakrabarty*? (See p. 955, supra.)

(5) *Patentability of Medicines.* Should drugs and therapeutic devices be patentable? In a number of countries they are not. The Swiss Patent Act of 1907, art. 2, provides: "A patent may not be obtained . . . for inventions of medicines, food, and beverages, for men and animals [nor for] manufacturing processes used in obtaining such products." [66]

The Principles of Medical Ethics (American Medicine Association, 1949) Chap. 1—General Principles, Sec. 6:

> An ethical physician will not receive remuneration from patents on or the sale of surgical instruments, appliances and medicines, nor profit from a copyright on methods or procedures. The receipt of remuneration from patents or copyrights tempts the owners thereof to retard or inhibit research or to restrict the benefits derivable therefrom to patients, the public or the medical profession. . . .

Efforts to impose compulsory licensing of drug patents, on payment of reasonable royalties, have been unsuccessful.[67] Indeed, more recent efforts have sought to extend the patent term for certain products whose introduction is delayed by federal regulatory review occurring after the patent has been issued; the maximum extension permissible would be seven years.[68] A

the government's use of his invention. This right to compensation is forfeited by violation of a secrecy order (§ 182). If the claimant is not satisfied with the government's award, he has the right to sue for "just compensation" in federal district court or the United States Claims Court (§ 183).

66. See Report of the Canadian Restrictive Trade Practices Comm. on Manufacture, Distribution and Sale of Drugs (1963), recommending elimination of drug patents; Administered Prices—Drugs, S.Rep. 448, 87th Cong., 1st Sess. (1961), especially at 105, 254, marshalling data to show that advances in pharmacology occur as frequently in countries which do not permit patenting of drugs as in countries where drugs may be patented. The Kefauver-Celler Bill, S.1552, H.R.6245, would have required licensing of drug patents after three years at a royalty not in excess of 8%. See testimony against this bill in hearings before the subcommittee, December 7–8, 1961, by Messrs. Rostow, Frost, Markham and others, challenging the statistics and the logic of the report. Frost's views on the significance of patents also appear in a Staff Report prepared by him for the Subcommittee on Patents, Trademarks and Copyrights of the Senate Committee on the Judiciary: The Patent System and the Modern Economy, S.Doc. 22, 85th Cong., 1st Sess. (1958).

The French abandoned their century-old position on pharmaceuticals by De-

cree No. 60–507 of May 30, 1960. Spencer and Chereau, France Decides to Grant Patents for Pharmaceutical Products, 42 J.P.O.S. 640 (1960); cf. Spencer, Recent Changes in French Patent Laws, 36 J.P.O.S. 378 (1954) (difficulties under old law which permitted patents on processes and apparatus but not on drugs).

67. Senator Gaylord Nelson introduced an amendment to S.2812 (1972) to authorize the Federal Trade Commission and the Surgeon General to designate drugs for such licensing if the price to the consumer was more than five times the cost of the producer or higher than the average price to consumers in other countries and if annual sales exceeded $1 million. The Senator referred to testimony in hearings that differentials between prices for the same drugs varied by as much as 20 to 1 depending on whether the drug was patented. 583 ATRR A–12 (Oct. 10, 1972). Representative Rosenthal (D.N.Y.) introduced a bill in three successive Congresses providing for compulsory licensing of prescription drugs; they were not reported out of committee. See H.R.2192, 95th Cong., 1st Sess. (1977); H.R.46, 96th Cong., 1st Sess. (1979); H.R.915, 97th Cong., 1st Sess. (1981).

68. See "Patent Term Restoration Act," S.255, 97th Cong., 1st Sess. (1981), passed by the Senate, 127 Cong.Rec. S7354 (July 9, 1981). The House version of the Act (H.R.6444) failed to pass. See

particular target of the legislation is drugs, which are subject to premarket clearance procedures by the Food and Drug Administration. The Senate Judiciary Committee reported: "There is no valid reason for a better mousetrap to receive 17 years of patent protection and a life-saving drug less than 10 years." [69] Can you think of one?

(6) *Patents and University Research.* Are patents needed to give university researchers an incentive to invent? Or are patents for University research an indirect way to fund higher education, providing a salary supplement to professors and additional income to universities which can be used to hold down tuition rates? See "Patent Policy Announced," in the University of Pennsylvania Almanac, May 22, 1980, p. 12: [70]

> The Trustees have declared it to be the policy of the University of Pennsylvania that any invention or discovery which may result from work carried out on University time or at University expense by special grants or otherwise is the property of the University. Patents on such inventions or discoveries may be applied for in any country by the University in which case the inventor shall assign his interest in the patent application to the University. The University will exercise its ownership of such patent, with or without profit, with due regard for the public interest as well as the interest of all persons concerned.

> · · ·

> The University's share of the returns from patents will . . . be used in such ways as to further research and scholarship, research facilities and equipment, research-related graduate education and involvement, when appropriate, of undergraduates in faculty research programs. On occasions, and they should be of the rarest kind, the President, the Provost and the Trustees may find it justifiable to use the resources from the research foundation for other academic purposes than those noted above. . . .

> Royalties or other income received by the University from patent revenues will be distributed as follows:

> (a) 50% of the first $200,000 net patent revenue will be distributed to the inventor(s);

> (b) 25% of the next $800,000 net patent revenue will be distributed to the inventor(s);

> (c) 15% of the net patent revenue of the next $4,000,000 will be distributed to the inventor(s);

> (d) 10% of the net patent revenue of all subsequent returns will be distributed to the inventor(s).

24 Pat.Trademark & Copyright J. 477 (Sept. 16, 1982).

69. S.Rep.No.97–138, 97th Cong., 1st Sess. 2 (1981).

70. See also "Harvard's Plan for Gene-Splicing Company Meets With Scorn From Other Institutions," Wall St. J., Nov. 12, 1980, p. 37 (Harvard, complaining about high tuition and financial aid rates, considers forming company to exploit gene-splicing process developed at the university); "Seven Concerns Sign Pacts With Stanford For Gene Techniques," Wall St.J., Nov. 18, 1981, p. 4 (license fee of $10,000 annually plus royalties of .5% to 1%, to be split between Stanford and University of California, with price reductions for those who sign before December 15, 1981); Note (8), infra, discussing University and Small Business Patent Act of 1980.

WHY HAVE PATENTS?

Machlup, An Economic Review of the Patent System, Study No. 15 of the
Subcommittee on Patents, Trademarks, and Copyrights, of the
Senate Judiciary Committee, 85th Cong., 2d Sess. (1958).

THE CHIEF ARGUMENTS FOR PATENT PROTECTION

. . .

The four best-known positions on which advocates of patent protection for inventors have rested their case may be characterized as the "natural-law" thesis, the "reward-by-monopoly" thesis, the "monopoly-profit-incentive" thesis, and the "exchange-for-secrets" thesis.

The "natural-law" thesis assumes that man has a natural property right in his own ideas. Appropriation of his ideas by others, that is, their unauthorized use, must be condemned as stealing. Society is morally obligated to recognize and protect this property right.

The "reward-by-monopoly" thesis assumes that justice requires that a man receive reward for his services in proportion to their usefulness to society, and that, where needed, society must intervene to secure him such reward. Inventors render useful services, and the most appropriate way to secure them commensurate rewards is by means of temporary monopolies in the form of exclusive patent rights in their inventions.

The "monopoly-profit-incentive" thesis assumes that industrial progress is desirable, that inventions and their industrial exploitation are necessary for such progress, but that inventions and/or their exploitation will not be obtained in sufficient measure if inventors and capitalists can hope only for such profits as the competitive exploitation of all technical knowledge will permit.

The "exchange-for-secrets" thesis presumes a bargain between inventor and society, the former surrendering the possession of secret knowledge in exchange for the protection of a temporary exclusivity in its industrial use. The presupposition again is that industrial progress at a sustained rate is desirable but cannot be obtained if inventors and innovating entrepeneurs keep inventions secret; in this case, the new technology may only much later become available for general use; indeed, technological secrets may die with their inventors and forever be lost to society. . . .

All four arguments for patent protection have been severely criticized, partly by opponents of any sort of patent protection, partly by advocates who supported one argument but rejected the others. . . . Indeed, if one always cites only the "first and true inventor" of an argument concerning the patent system, one will rarely be able to cite an author of the 20th century.

. . .

SOME BASIC ECONOMIC QUESTIONS

Patents, by giving their owners exclusive rights to the commercial exploitation of inventions, secure to these owners profits (so-called "quasi-rents") which are ultimately collected from consumers as part of the price paid for goods and services. The consumers pay; the patent owners receive. Are the consumers—the non-patent-owning people—worse off for it?

"No; they are not," says one group of economists. Patents are granted on inventions which would not have been made in the absence of a patent system; the inventions make it possible to produce more or better products than could have been produced without them; hence, whatever the consumers pay to the patent owners is only a part of the increase in real income that is engendered by the patent-induced inventions.

"Wrong," says another group of economists. Many of the inventions for which patents are granted would also be made and put to use without any patent system. The consumers could have the fruits of this technical progress without paying any toll charges. Even if *some* inventions are made and used thanks only to the incentives afforded by the patent system, consumers must pay for *all* patented inventions and, hence, lose by the bargain. Moreover, if patents result in monopolistic restrictions which hold down production and hinder the most efficient utilization of resources, it is possible that total real income is less than what it would be without the patent system. Of course, there is impressive technical progress and a substantial growth of national income under the patent system, yet perhaps less so than there would be without patents.

This is but one of the fundamental conflicts in the economics of the patent system. There is another, which is quite independent of any profits collected by the patent owners and of any monopolistic restrictions imposed on production. This second basic problem relates to the overall allocation of productive resources in a developing economy, and to the question whether at any one time the allocation to industrial research and development is deficient, excessive or just right.

It is easy to conceive of the possibility that such allocation is too meager. But can there ever be too much? Is not more research and development always better than less? Is it possible that too much is devoted to the inventive effort of the Nation? This depends on what it is that is curtailed when inventive activity is expanded. More of one thing must mean less of another, and the question is, what it is of which there will be less. . . .

Increased research and development in order to increase the stock of knowledge is a splendid thing for society; so is increased production of productive equipment; and both are valued so highly because they eventually allow increased consumption. Yet, these three— more research, more equipment, more consumption—are alternatives in the sense that, even though all three can increase when productivity increases, a greater increase of one means smaller increases of the others. At any one moment, an increase in the production of knowledge means less equipment and/or less consumption than might otherwise be available. A choice by society to increase research and teaching implies a choice, though usually unconscious, to have in the next years less productive equipment or less consumption, or less of both, than they might have had. . . .

If resources were not transferable at all, neither in the short run nor in the long, then of course research could not encroach on alternative uses of resources. But in this case all incentives to research would be futile, for research could not be increased beyond the limits set by the number of research talents in existence. . . . While the supply of inventive talent and research brains may, in the short run and over a certain range, be relatively inelastic, it need not be so over all ranges and over longer periods. Research and inventive activities *can* be expanded—at the expense of other economic activities.

COMPETITIVE RESEARCH, WASTE, AND SERENDIPITY

Not only is research in general competitive with other economic activities, but research on particular problems and in particular fields is competitive with research on other problems and in other fields. This needs to be mentioned chiefly because in recent years another concept of "competitive research" has received increased attention: different firms and different research teams competing with one another in finding solutions to the same research problem in the same field.

Competition among rival firms which takes the form of a race between their research teams—a race, ultimately, to the patent office—may have various objectives: (*a*) To be the first to find a patentable solution to a problem posed by the needs and preferences of the customers—a better product—or by the technological needs and hopes of the producers—better machines, tools, processes; (*b*) after a competitor has found such a solution and has obtained exclusive patent rights in its exploitation, to find an alternative solution to the same problem in order to be able to compete with him in the same market—in other words, to "invent around" the competitor's patent; and (*c*) after having found and patented the first solution, to find and patent all possible alternative solutions, even inferior ones, in order to "block" competitor's efforts to "invent around" the first patent.

These forms of "competitive research" were described and discussed by antipatent economists during the patent controversy of the 19th century. Concerning the first form, there was much complaint that other inventors who discovered practically simultaneously "the same utility," but were not the first in the race to the patent office, had to forego their "natural privilege of labor" and were barred from using their own inventions. The fact that there was competition in making new inventions was found to be healthy. But that he who lost the race to the patent office should be barred from using his own invention, and should have to search for a substitute invention, was found to be absurd.

What may appear absurd to a disinterested observer, or unjust and unfair to one who lost the right to use the fruit of his own labor and investment, must to an economist appear as sheer economic waste. Of course, one may regard this as an incidental expense of an otherwise beneficial institution, an unfortunate byproduct, an item of social cost, which, perhaps, is unavoidable and must be tolerated in view of the social advantages of the system as a whole. However, from merely defending the need of "inventing around a patent" as a minor item of waste, the discussion has recently proceeded to eulogize it as one of the advantages of the system, indeed as one of its "justifications."

The advantage is seen in the additional "encouragement" to research. If the competitors were given licenses under the patent of the firm that won the race, they would have to pay royalties but would not be compelled to "invent around" it. Exclusivity, however, forces some of them to search for a "substitute invention." But why should this be regarded as an advantage? The idea is probably that, if industrial research is desirable, more research is more desirable, and that it does not matter what kind of knowledge the research effort is supposed to yield. From an economic point of view, research is costly since it absorbs particularly scarce resources which could produce other valuable things. The production of the knowledge of how to do in a somewhat different way what what we have already learned to do in a satisfactory way would hardly be given highest priority in a rational allocation of resources.

This same, or a still lower, evaluation must be accorded to the third form of "competitive research"—inventive effort for the purpose of obtaining patents on all possible alternatives of an existing patented invention just in order to "block" a rival from "inventing around" that patent. In this case inventive talent is wasted on a project which, even (or especially) if it succeeds exactly in achieving its objective, cannot possibly be as valuable as would be other tasks to which the talent might be assigned. When thousands of potential inventions are waiting to be made—inventions which might be of great benefit to society—how can one seriously justify the assignment of a research force to search for inventions that are not intended for use at all—but merely for satisfying a dog-in-a-manger ambition?

There is, however, another "justification" for this kind of "competitive research": it can be summarized in the colorful word "serendipity." This means "the faculty of making happy and unexpected discoveries by accident."[71] The idea is that the research teams en-

---

71. [Footnotes 71 to 74 are from the original, renumbered.] The word was "coined by Horace Walpole upon the title of the fairy tale The Three Princes of Serendip [the former name of Ceylon], the heroes of which 'were always making discoveries, by accidents and sagacity, of things they were not in quest of.' " Oxford Universal English Dictionary (Oxford: 1937) p. 1847. In a recent article entitled "Serendipity: the art of being lucky in a laboratory," it was stated: "Of course, significant chance discoveries are the blue diamonds of laboratory search-

gaged in "inventing around patents," or in inventing to obtain patents to "block" other people's efforts to "invent around patents," might by sheer accident hit upon something really useful. In other words, the work of these research forces is justified by the possibility or probability that they might find something which they did not set out to find.

There is no doubt that these happy accidents occur again and again. But can one reasonably let an effort to produce something without social value take the credit for accidental byproducts that happen to be useful? Can one reasonably assert that research not oriented toward important objectives is more likely to yield useful results than are research efforts that are so oriented? Is it easier to find the important by seeking the unimportant?

. . .

SOME CONFUSIONS, INCONSISTENCIES, AND FALLACIES

. . .

An old fallacy relates to the "adequacy" of the "reward" to the inventor. The assertion has been made, and is still being repeated, that the "rewards" which inventors or their assignees earn through profits from exclusive use of the patented inventions are in proportion to the "social usefulness" of these inventions. There is no reason why this should be so, and in fact no such proportionality, or approximate proportionality, can possibly be shown. It is well known that several inventions which have later proved to be of immense usefulness to society were somewhat "ahead of their time" when they were made and patented, and have earned nothing for their creators. It is firmly established that patents on some trivial gadgets have earned millions for their owners while patents on technically highly significant processes have been financially unrewarding. In general, the profits made from the commercial exploitation of a patent depend in part on the degree of restriction on the output produced under the patent. It is more than probable that the socially most important inventions, say, of drugs or vaccines for the cure or prevention of cancer, would not be allowed to be exploited with the same monopolistic restrictions that are freely tolerated in the exploitation of patents on hair curlers, bottle caps, or television screens.

. . .

The idea that social benefits may be derived from the operation of the patent system misleads many into assuming, without further argument, that social benefits can be derived from existing patents. If one accepts the theory that patent protection has the social function of serving as an incentive for inventive activity, one accepts, by implication, that the beneficial effects of this incentive system must flow,

ing. They are as rare as they are unpredictable. Well-organized research along clearly defined lines is most often the method by which modern science achieves its goal." The Lamp (Standard Oil Co., New Jersey), vol. 35, No. 3 (September 1953), p. 20.

not from existing patents, but from the hope for future profits from future patents; this hope may induce people to undertake certain risky investments and useful activities—to wit, financing and arranging industrial research—which they might not undertake otherwise. Existing patents, on the other hand, restrict the use of inventions already known, and thus they reduce temporarily the full contribution these inventions could make to national output. These restrictions are neither "odious" nor unlawful, nor contrary to public policy; they are "necessary" if any profit is to be derived from the patents. But they are still restrictions, keeping output smaller than it might be otherwise. Consequently, existing patents impose a burden on society, a burden which it has decided to carry in order to hold out to people the chance of obtaining future profits from future patents on future inventions. That existing patents are a social cost, not a social benefit, is most readily appreciated when the patented invention is of such extraordinary importance that society would not tolerate even a temporary restriction in its use. The great inventor of the polio vaccine, Dr. Salk, generously contributed his idea to society without applying for a patent. If he had taken a patent on his process and sold it to a company which exploited it restrictively enough to make high profits, would the American public have stood for it?

· · ·

EVALUATION OF THE PATENT SYSTEM AS A WHOLE

A comparison, even though speculative, of the incremental benefits and costs associated with a little more or a little less patent protection, is more feasible than is an attempt to assess the "total effects" of the system. An economic evaluation of the patent system as a whole implies an analysis of the differences between its existence and nonexistence—perhaps a hopeless task. Nevertheless several different effects, some beneficial, some harmful, have been attributed to the operation of the patent system, and must be reviewed in an attempt at evaluation.

That the patent system succeeds in eliciting the disclosure of technological secrets is a claim widely asserted, though often denied. The chief question is whether, by and large, the period over which inventions could be kept secret, or in which the first invention would not be duplicated by other inventors, is longer than the period for which patents are granted. A negative answer is strongly suggested by the simple reflection that inventions probably are patented only when the inventor or user fears that others would soon find out his secret or independently come upon the same idea. It would follow that the patent system can elicit only those technological secrets which without a patent system would be likely to be dispersed even sooner than they become free for public use under patent protection.

This conclusion disregards the possibility that all the competitors who eventually find out about the novel technology or find it independently will try to keep it secret. However, this would be a "secret" shared by all whose knowledge really matters. For if there is

enough competition among those who are "in the know," the interests of the community are safeguarded.   But there is another advantage in prompt and full disclosure under the patent system, which is
not secured through the process of individual detection or multiple
invention.   Disclosure of an invention through the patent grant may
give "ideas" to technicians in other industries who would not, as a
rule, go out of their ways to "find" the technical information in question but may be glad to take a hint when it is "thrown" at them
through publication in the official gazette.   In other words, dissemination of technical ideas to outsiders should be considered separately
from the availability of the invention to those who would like to use it
in competition with the first inventor.

The claim that the patent system serves to disseminate technological information, and that this accelerates the growth of productivity
in the economy, is not questioned.   In some countries, though not in
all, the patent offices have collected and made publicly available the
vast amount of technical information contained in the hundreds of
thousands of patents, current and past.   But, while this store of
knowledge in public print is a very desirable byproduct of the patent
system, it is not necessarily dependent on it; conceivably, similar collections of technical knowledge could be compiled, perhaps no less efficiently, by special agencies in the absence of patents.

Apart from any effects upon the size of the national income, the
patent system affects the distribution of income.   Indeed this is its
purpose from the point of view of the "just reward" theory: to transfer some of the income increase produced by newly invented technology to the people responsible for it.   The recipients of this income
transfer are often pictured to be those ingenious, independent fellows
called "garret inventors" or "basement inventors"; it was said that
they would be helped by the patent system in their endeavors to go
into business for themselves or to sell their rights to one of the several businessmen competing to acquire these rights for practical application of the inventions.   Yet this is not how things work today.   The
majority of "inventors" are employees of corporations, many working
on the staff of research departments of very big firms.   The income
transferred from the consumers is received by the corporations to
cover their research and development cost (if written off immediately), or as part of their profit either to be reinvested (perhaps in research equipment and innovations) or to be distributed to stockholders.   Is what the consumers pay on this score (as part of the price of
the goods and services they buy) more, or is it less, than the increase
in real income which results—has resulted?   will result?—from the
corporate research and development work?   If it is true that the total
outlay for such work is increased under the patent incentive, this increase means more demand for research personnel and thus will raise
the salaries of the entire staff, old and new, although it is only the
additions to the staff that will increase the rate at which new technology is created.   If the supply of research workers should be completely inelastic, there will be only increased salaries but not more
inventing; and if the corporations should know this, or for any other

reasons fail to increase their outlays for inventive and innovating activities, there will be only increased corporate profits resulting from the patent system. But one never can tell, perhaps the income redistribution accomplished by the system is only a modest portion of the increase in national product which the system induces and which would not occur without it.

The incentive effects of the patent system, which are supposed to yield the new inventions and innovations which in turn produce an increase in national output, are the result of profit expectations based on restrictions of the output produced with the aid of the patented inventions. These output restrictions are the very essence of the patent system because only by restricting output below the competitive level can the patent secure an income to its owner. There need not be any contradiction between the output restrictions and output expansions effected by the patent system. While each existing patent may restrict the utilization of a recently developed piece of technology and thus reduce the output of particular products in particular industries, the system as a whole may promote the development and application of ever new technologies and thus permit an accelerated increase in national product. One is reminded of the famous analogy of the automobile brakes which permit motorists to drive with greater speed.[72] The patents are here likened to the brakes which the "drivers" (entrepreneurs) in the economy can apply and which are to give them the courage to accelerate its progress.[73] The "braking" is the direct and absolutely certain effect, the encouragement is only an indirect effect and not quite so certain, though rather plausible. The output restrictions based on patents are primary effects and testable; the incentive effects are secondary and more conjectural.

These incentives are supposed to generate technological inventions plus innovations—innovation being the first commercial application of a new idea. Invention without application is useless; practical application may depend on patent protection even where invention does not. Thus, even if the patent system were proved to be unnecessary for the promotion of invention—that is, if an adequate flow of inventions were forthcoming without patent incentive—patents might still be needed as encouragement for investment and enterprise to introduce untried techniques and products.[74]

To be eager to do something is not enough if the necessary funds are lacking. Some observers have placed less emphasis on the need for patents as an *incentive* for investment in industrial research, development, and practical innovation than on the need for them as sources of *finance* for such investment. They have argued that only

72. Joseph A. Schumpeter, Capitalism, Socialism, and Democracy (1942), p. 88.

73. The analogy has proved remarkably persuasive although it does not fit the patent story in two essential points: the motorist applies the brakes to his own car when it runs too fast, the patentee applies brakes in order to slow down or stop others, regardless of how fast or cautiously they proceed.

74. Cf. the remark by Judge Frank in Picard v. United Aircraft Corp., 128 F.2d 632, 643 (2d Cir. 1942) [quoted infra, p. 977].

the monopoly profits derived from existing market positions based on past patents can provide the funds for new incentive work and innovating ventures. This argument was perhaps suggested by the observation that the largest research laboratories are in fact maintained by corporations with the strongest patent positions and with high and stable earnings. This, however, does not mean that other firms, not drawing on patent-monopoly profits, could not afford to invest in research. What it probably does mean is that the patent system, because of certain scientific and technological developments of the time, favors certain types of industry, such as chemical and electronic, and that this occasions both the accumulation of masses of patents and the intensive search for new patentable inventions in these industries. But even this explanation probably exaggerates the role of patent monopolies in industrial research. It seems very likely that even without any patents, past, present, or future, firms in these industries would carry on research, development, and innovation because the opportunities for the search for new processes and new products are so excellent in these fields that no firm could hope to maintain its position in the industry if it did not constantly strive to keep ahead of its competitors by developing and using new technologies.

We find ourselves confronted with conflicting theories. On the basis of the theory of the "competitive compulsion to keep ahead" one might think that firms would invent and innovate even without patent protection. But on the basis of the theory of the "competitive elimination of profits" one might think that without patent protection it would not pay to invent and to innovate, and that firms could not afford to invest in research and development. On the strength of the theory of the "sufficiency of the innovator's headstart" one might think that many innovators would have enough time to recover their costs of innovation. But on the strength of the theory of the "nearly perfect competition from imitators" one might think that few innovators would get away without losses.

No conclusive empirical evidence is available to decide this conflict of theories. That the automobile industry developed partly despite patents (when it still had to overcome the barrier of the basic Selden patent) and partly independently of patents (since it refrained from enforcing the exclusive rights obtained) is some presumptive evidence against the theory of the need for patent protection. That in Switzerland and the Netherlands industrial development proceeded rapidly when these countries had no patent laws is not conclusive because, one might say, they shared the fruits of the patent systems elsewhere and profited from the free imitation of technologies developed abroad—an instance of sharing the benefits without sharing the cost. That experts in the chemical, electronic, and other industries testify that their firms could not maintain their research laboratories without patent protection may persuade some, but probably should be discounted as self-serving testimony. That countries with patent laws have made rapid technical progress does not compel the inference that their progress would have been slower without patent laws. None of the empirical evidence at our disposal and none of the theoretical arguments presented either confirms or confutes the belief that the patent system has promoted the progress of the technical arts and the productivity of the economy.

CONCLUDING REMARKS

. . .

If one does not know whether a system "as a whole" (in contrast to certain features of it) is good or bad, the safest "policy conclusion" is to "muddle through"—either with it, if one has long lived with it, or without it, if one has lived without it. If we did not have a patent system, it would be irresponsible, on the basis of our present knowledge of its economic consequences, to recommend instituting one. But since we have had a patent system for a long time, it would be irresponsible, on the basis of our present knowledge, to recommend abolishing it.

NOTES AND QUERIES

(1) *The Innovation Process.* Although the Patent Code allows patents only for "invention," it is now commonplace to consider invention to be only one part of a broader process which includes "innovation" and "diffusion":[75]

An invention, when applied for the first time, is called an innovation. Traditionally, economists have stressed the distinction between an invention and an innovation on the ground that an invention has little or no economic significance until it is applied. This distinction becomes somewhat blurred in cases like Du Pont's nylon, where the inventor and the innovator are the same firm. In these circumstances, which are quite common, the final stages of development may entail at least a partial commitment to a market test. However, in another important class of cases, the inventor is not in a position to—and does not want to—apply his invention, because his business is invention, not production, or because he is a supplier, not a user, of the equipment embodying the innovation, or for some other reason. In these cases, the distinction remains relatively clear-cut.

Regardless of whether the break between invention and innovation is clean, innovation is a key stage in the process leading to the full evaluation and utilization of an invention. The innovator—the firm that is first to apply the invention—must be willing to take the risks involved in introducing a new and untried process, good, or service. In many cases, these risks are high. Although R and D can provide a great deal of information concerning the technical characteristics and the cost of production of the invention—and market research can provide considerable information regarding the demand for it—many areas of uncertainty can be resolved only by actual production and marketing of the invention. By obtaining

75. Mansfield, Rapoport, Schnee, Wagner and Hamburger, Research and Innovation In The Modern Corporation 11–12 (1971). The authors suggest a further breakdown of the innovation process into: applied research; preparation of project requirements; prototype design construction, and testing; planning and construction of manufacturing facilities; manufacturing start-up; marketing start-up. Id. at 112. See also Rogers, Diffusion of Inventions (1962) (reviewing diffusion research studies and theories).

needed information regarding the actual performance of the invention, the innovator plays a vital social role.

Once the invention is introduced for the first time, the diffusion process begins. How rapidly an innovation spreads is obviously of great importance; for example, in the case of a process innovation, it determines how rapidly productivity increases in response to the new process. In a free-enterprise economy, firms and consumers are free to use new technology as slowly or as rapidly as they please, subject, of course, to all the constraints imposed by the marketplace. Diffusion, like the earlier stages in the creation and assimilation of new methods and products, is essentially a learning process. However, instead of being confined to a research laboratory or to a few firms, the learning takes place among a considerable number of users and producers.

When the innovation first appears, potential users are uncertain of its nature and effectiveness, and they tend to view its purchase as an experiment. Sometimes considerable additional research and development is required before the innovation is successful; sometimes, despite attempts at redesign and improvement, the innovation never is a success. Information regarding the existence, characteristics, and availability of the innovation is disseminated by the producers through advertisements and salesmen; information regarding the reaction of users to the innovation tends to be disseminated informally and through the trade press. Learning takes place among the producers of the innovation, as well as the users. Early versions of an innovation often have serious technological problems, and it takes time to work out these bugs. During the early stages of the diffusion process, the improvements in a new process or product may be almost as important as the new idea itself. Moreover, when a new product's design is stabilized, costs of production generally fall in accord with the so-called "learning curve." That is, unit costs of production decrease as the producers gain experience and learn by doing.

. . . .

Mansfield *et al.*, in an empirical study of innovation by chemicals, machinery, and electronics firms, found that traditional "research and development" accounted for less than half the total innovation costs. Almost 40% of the total costs of innovation were consumed by tooling and the design and construction of manufacturing facilities; marketing start-up accounted for almost 15% of total costs. In addition, the authors found that the average probability for technical success was better than 50–50, primarily because the bulk of R & D products studied were aimed at relatively modest technical advances; they also found that the probability of commercial failure was much greater than the probability of technical failure (only about 20 percent of technically successful projects will earn an economic profit). The authors concluded that the amount of resources devoted to innovation is therefore considerably greater than the statistics on it indicate; that when a firm wants to innovate it must be willing to risk more than it has budgeted merely for R & D; and that better coordination of R & D and marketing lies at the heart of successful innovation.[76]

What are the implications for patent policy of this description of the innovation process? Does your response depend on which of the four justifications for patents (see p. 963, supra) you accept? If patents are viewed as incentives for innovation, should they be awarded later in the process than

76. Mansfield *et al.*, supra note 75, at 206–211, 217–18.

the invention stage? Do we give patents to the wrong people (i.e., those who do well at inventing, rather than those who do well at innovating or diffusing)? Even if we make no change in patent law, should we interpret the antitrust laws in a way which would reward innovators with monopoly profits at some stage in the innovation process? You might want to reconsider this question in light of the material discussed infra, pp. 995–996.

(2) *Ford and the Automobile Patent Pool*, condensed from Hamilton, Patents and Free Enterprise.[77] The automobile, covered in whole or part by tens of thousands of patents, achieved its most rapid development during an era of patent truce. In 1879 G. B. Selden, a patent lawyer, applied for a patent on a self-propelled vehicle comprising steering wheel, a liquid hydrocarbon engine of the compression type with the engine running at a speed greater than the driven wheels, a disconnecting means between the two, and a body adapted to either persons or goods. As a result of the breadth of the claims and a series of amendments, his patent was not granted until 1895. Selden licensees formed the Association of Licensed Automobile Manufacturers, contributing $1^{1}/_{4}\%$ of their sales to a fund for enforcing the Selden patent against infringers. A committee of the association determined which new manufacturers should be licensed. In 1905, 19 unlicensed car producers organized the American Motor Car Manufacturers Association for concerted defense against the "legitimate" industry. In 1909 the Selden patent was upheld by a lower federal court, and the independents' organization collapsed. Henry Ford, however, appealed the decision, and in *Columbia Motor Car Co. v. Duerr*, 184 F. 893 (2d Cir. 1911), the scope of the Selden patent was construed very narrowly with the result that Ford was held not to have infringed it.

Ford's experience with patents led him to adopt an extraordinary patent policy. Ford applied for patents on inventions, but only to secure itself against assertions by others of exclusive rights to the technology. The firm licensed all responsible applicants royalty-free. Nor would Ford pay royalties. It enjoyed royalty-free licenses under hundreds of patents and frequently used others without license. In 350 controversies in which Ford was an alleged infringer, including 60 litigated cases, it lost only one suit in a court of last resort.

With the Ford example, the trade association now known as the Automobile Manufacturers' Association set up a patent pool in 1915. The Association took over the licensing of almost all patents of the members in the motor vehicle and accessories field. Any member could use the pooled patents without paying any royalty, on the theory that since many contributed, each was sure to get more than he put in. The agreement lasted until 1925 and covered new inventions developed during that decade. The five-year extension agreed on in 1925, however, applied only to patents held at the beginning of the period. A second renewal in 1930 applied to patents then held by the members, with the result that the patents they had secured between 1925 and 1930 endured as exclusive rights for a maximum of 5 years, but once more subsequently acquired patents were not included. The 1935 renewal did little more than continue the agreement with respect to patents covered by the 1930 contract.

Hamilton attributed the creation of the practically patent-free technology to realization by the early auto manufacturers that reduced costs and a mass

---

77. TNEC Mono. No. 31 (1941) pp. 115–122. See also Welsh, Patents and Competition in the Automobile Industry, 13 Law and Contemp.Prob. 260 (1948); Wood, Patents and Antitrust Law (1942) 145.

market could not be achieved otherwise. He linked the change in attitude to the gradual concentration of the auto business into the hands of the Big Three, each of which can be technologically self-sufficient and has little reason to trade its inventions on an equal basis with the smaller companies in the field.

(3) *The "Lone Inventor."* Machlup, supra, p. 969, dismisses the romantic image of the "garret inventor," pointing out that the majority of inventors today are corporate employees. Jewkes, Sawers and Stillerman, in The Sources of Invention 73–78 (2d ed. rev. 1969), found that, notwithstanding the high concentration of researchers in corporate laboratories, more than half of the important twentieth century inventions investigated by them were produced by individuals outside corporate laboratories. Individual inventions [78] included:

> Air Conditioning; Automatic Transmissions; Bakelite; Ball-point Pen; Catalytic Cracking of Petroleum; Cellophane; Chromium Plating; Cinerama; Cotton Picker; Cyclotron; Domestic Gas Refrigeration; Electric Precipitation; Electron Microscope; Gyro-Compass; Hardening of Liquid Fats; Helicopter; Insulin; Jet Engine; Kodachrome; Magnetic Recording; Penicillin; "Polaroid" Land Camera; Power Steering; Quick Freezing; Radio; Safety Razor; Self-winding Wrist-watch; Streptomycin; Sulzer Loom; Synthetic Light Polarizer; Titanium; Xerography; Zip Fastener.

Corporate contributions were:

> Acrylic Fibres; Cellophane Tape; Continuous Hot-Strip Rolling; Crease Resisting; DDT; Diesel-Electric Locomotive; Duco Lacquers; Fluorescent Lighting; Freon Refrigerants; Krilium; Methyl Methacrylate Polymers; Modern Artificial Lighting; Neoprene; Nylon; Polyethylene; Silicones; Synthetic Detergents; Television; Terylene; Tetraethyl Lead; Transistor.[79]

Is it possible that individuals more often achieve radical breakthroughs because large firms stick to projects entailing small technical risk and near-term results, leaving the pioneering work to others?[80]

(4) *Corporate Invention.* American law treats invention as an intellectual function of human individuals. Several individuals may be joint inventors; a corporation is not recognized as an "inventor" but may acquire rights from inventors by, e.g., purchase, license, or assignment of a patent application pursuant to a contract under which the researcher-inventor has been employed.[81]

Patent practices in American corporate laboratories are exemplified in the following account:[82]

---

78. The author includes in the class of individual inventions those by inventors who were employed in institutions which were, "as in the case of universities, of such a kind that the individuals were autonomous, free to follow their own ideas without hindrance," p. 73.

79. For a critical analysis of Jewkes' thesis, see a review by Gilfillan, 4 Engineering Economist 44 (1958); Dirlam and Thorkelson, Implications of the Individualist Theory of Invention, 6 Antitrust Bull. 173 (1961).

See also Hale and Hale, Monopoly in Motion, 41 Va.L.Rev. 431 (1955), reviewing the extensive contributions of individual inventors and small firms, in the context of a discussion of "dynamic"

competition, which stresses the importance of the development of new products as the principal check on exploitation by producers; Stelzer, Technological Progress and Market Structure, 23 So. Econ.J. 63 (1956), attributing the backward technology in cotton textiles to underconcentration of the industry.

80. See Mansfield, The Economics of Technological Change 92–93 (1968).

81. See Sears, The Corporate Patent—Reform or Retrogression, 22 Vill.L. Rev. 1085 (1977) (criticizing proposals allowing corporate assignees to file for patents).

82. Stavely, A Research Viewpoint of Patents, 37 J.Pat.Off.Soc'y 79 (1955).

How do we go about obtaining the advantages which patents afford us? First, we have been led to believe by our patent attorneys that the keeping of records of research programs and experimental work is a necessary evil to obtaining adequate patent coverage.

Our means of establishing a patent position is based primarily on the initial research assignment, the original data sheet, progress reports and final library reports. Each research project has an identifying number and a written assignment stating the general objectives of the work, as well as some specific objectives. When work is done on the problem, the investigator describes the nature of the work and lists the data he has obtained in that specific series of experiments. The data sheet is signed by the investigator and is witnessed by another member of his laboratory. It is understood that the person witnessing the data sheet should have been present in the laboratory and observed the carrying out of the work recorded. We try to have bench mates witness each other's record experiments except where they are joined in a project which may result in an invention. . . .

Of equal importance, and the first direct step toward recognizing that a patentable invention or discovery may have been made, is the preparation of an invention disclosure. This is stressed with our entire staff at all times, even though today's applicability seems remote, or the product or material appears priced out of today's market. We do this because we feel that if the investigator debates whether or not the disclosure is worthwhile, he may overlook its value in some field or, by procrastination, do nothing. Thus, we urge the preparation of the invention disclosure, and whether or not a patent application is filed later is at the discretion of the Patent Division and research supervisors. We record well over 100 invention disclosures each year from our research staff.

Another advantage of our disclosure practice is that the inventor is early identified with the invention, thus avoiding later complications should the disclosure prove to be an important one. As a result, we have never, in our laboratory, experienced a conflict in priority or identification of the inventors. We do, on occasion, have more than one inventor on a disclosure, which is to be expected when research is coordinated not only between groups in the research department but also in an occasional joint investigation with another department. Another benefit from such practice is that the research supervisors do not tend to "tag along" on the disclosure, thus giving the investigator full credit. . . .

The more promising invention disclosures are selected for patent applications. When specific cases are carefully studied, it may develop that we have not completely explored the field in question, and in such cases we go back into the laboratory and do more work. This is usually of the nature of determining the scope of the invention. In such investigations very interesting additional results often turn up and new avenues of investigation become apparent.

From this point on, the matters are in the hands of the Patent Division unless some experimental demonstrations or expert testimony become necessary to clear up certain points with the Patent Examiners. On this basis of operation we obtain about two dozen patents a year. Some of

The author was Director of the Chemical and Physical Research Laboratories of Firestone Tire & Rubber Co.

these are quite valuable and others, though not of immediate value, may strengthen our position on other patents or activities.

A much debated question is how should the investigator be rewarded. We have no specified reward or bonus system beyond the nominal $1.00 which the investigator receives for each patent application filed. It is our viewpoint that there should be no definite program of rewards or bonuses on patents. The research worker is employed for the specific purpose of making discoveries and obtaining facts. In the modern co-ordinated research laboratory where skills are pooled in the interest of getting prompt answers, a reward system of any kind would create secretiveness and inequalities and thus delay progress. There would be insistent demands by the investigators to work in those fields which offered the quickest and most remunerative returns.

Query. Should an invention produced in a corporate laboratory be judged in light of the state of the art within that laboratory, rather than outside the laboratory, to determine whether it is "nonobvious," particularly where the corporation involved dominates the field technically?[83]

(5) *Patents as Incentive for Investments.* Machlup, supra p. 970, recognizes that more than invention is necessary to produce a useful innovation, and that patents might be needed to encourage investment in developing new products. This theme was elaborated upon by Judge Frank, concurring in *Picard v. United Aircraft Corp.*:[84]

But if we never needed, or do not now need, patents as bait for inventors, we may still need them, in some instances, as a lure to investors. It is sometimes said that there is no need thus to coax investors, because our giant corporations, with their research laboratories, will, without such bait, do the needful. The answer perhaps is that industrial history discloses that those corporations, at times and to some extent, have been prodded into undertaking such research and into developing improvements because of the threat of competition from occasional "outsiders," armed with patent monopolies, and supplied with funds by a few private enterprisers. Thus, paradoxically, monopoly may evoke competition: The threat from patent monopolies in the hands of such "outsiders" may create a sort of competition—a David versus Goliath competition—which reduces the inertia of some huge industrial aggregations that might otherwise be sluggish. . . .

To denounce patents merely because they create monopolies is to indulge in superficial thinking. We may still want our society to be fundamentally competitive. But there has seldom been a society in which there have not been some monopolies, i.e., special privileges. The legal and medical professions have their respective guild monopolies. The owner of real estate, strategically located, has a monopoly; so has the owner of a valuable mine; and so have railroad and electric power companies. The problem is not whether there should be monopolies, but, rather, what monopolies there should be, and whether and how much they should be regulated.

And so patent monopolies may still be socially useful; they may, indeed, as I have said, foster competition. The David Co. v. Goliath, Inc.,

83. See Potts v. Coe, 79 U.S.App.D.C. 223, 145 F.2d 27 (1944) (Arnold, J.) (held: yes) (inventor employed by Teletype Corporation, a wholly-owned subsidiary of AT&T).

84. 128 F.2d 632, 642–43 (2d Cir. 1942), certiorari denied 317 U.S. 651, 63 S.Ct. 46, 87 L.Ed. 524.

kind of competition is dependent on investment in David Co.—the small new competitor. And few men will invest in such a competitor unless they think it has a potential patent monopoly as a slingshot. . . .

Could patents for the purpose of promoting investment be sustained under the patent clause of the Constitution, supra, p. 935? Does the argument for monopoly profits to promote investment in development assume that the market would not allocate adequate capital to such investments if only normal returns were obtainable. Why overrule the market's judgment? Professor Kitch argues that Judge Frank fails to realize "that there is no *a priori* principle dictating that the development of the new is the best use of capital resources. If capital can earn a higher return elsewhere absent the prospect of monopoly for the new product, it may well be because that capital is better applied to the alternative use."[85] Does this assume that there is adequate information about the new product to enable the market to make an accurate assessment?

B.   THE CONFLICT BETWEEN PATENT AND ANTITRUST POLICIES

The right conferred by patent might have been confined to two basic elements: (i) the inventor could himself exploit his creation under the protection of the state granted monopoly, or (ii) he could charge others a non-competitive price for the use of his creation. All efforts beyond that to control the behavior of others would be examined under the antitrust laws. But powerful pragmatic and conceptual justifications supported a different synthesis of patent and antitrust laws. The Industrial Revolution, the increasing capital requirements for engaging in manufacture and distribution, and the growing specialization of functions among individuals and firms led in time to recognition of transferability and subdivision of rights under patent. Among the economic justifications might be listed:

(a) encouragement of qualified people to specialize in invention, by relieving the inventor of the need to engage personally in the exploitation of his discoveries.

(b) more rapid exploitation of the invention by permitting territorial subdivisions of the monopoly through multiple licenses or assignments, thus enlisting locally qualified firms in the commercial development.

(c) more efficient exploitation of the various applications of the discovery by licensing established manufacturers in their respective fields.

The conceptual basis for transferability and subdivision was readily available in the law of property and contract. A patent was surely "property"—hardly distinguishable from the right to exclusive possession of a territorially defined plot of land. Accordingly, one might transfer it, subdivide, lease upon conditions, etc. The strongest and broadest expression of the hold which property notions have in this

85. Kitch, Graham v. John Deere Co.: New Standards For Patents, 1966 S.Ct. Rev. 293, 300 (Kurland ed. 1966).

field appears in the phrase "intellectual property", which serves, in international conventions and elsewhere, to vindicate the most comprehensive protections of invention, authorship, trademarks and trade secrets. Once the "property" notion is firmly embedded, it becomes easy to overlook the fact that this peculiar kind of property is the creation of positive law working through administrative agencies, that its incidents are carefully defined with a view to accomplishing stated public purposes, and that from the beginning patent grants were conditional on their being:

> "not contrary to the law, nor mischievous to the state, by raising prices of commodities at home, or hurt of trade, or generally inconvenient." (Statute of Monopolies, § 6, p. 2 above)

Contract law, too, afforded the widest range to consensual arrangements among entrepreneurs. The contract "licensing" someone under the patent appeared to be subject to state law rather than the federal patent act.[86] Insofar as the federal antitrust laws might become applicable, where interstate or foreign commerce was implicated, the "rule of reason" might be expected to govern the exploitation of an explicitly lawful monopoly, even perhaps as respects such "per se" practices as price fixing, division of markets, boycott, and tying.

Despite the potentials of property and contract law for maximizing returns on patent (and copyright), an accommodation had to be made between these lawful monopolies and the overarching policies of the antitrust laws, as will be seen in the following materials. Not only were the antitrust laws found to be violated by some exercises of patent power, but—more remarkably—some exercises of patent power came to be regarded as "abuse" or unlawful "extension" of patent power even where the same practice might not have reached the level of an antitrust violation if engaged in by one not armed with a legally sanctioned monopoly. Such abuse or extension would lead the courts to deny enforcement of the monopoly against one who was admittedly an infringer. See *Morton Salt Co.* v. *G. S. Suppiger Co.*, p. 998 infra.

1. THE DECISION TO LICENSE[87]

Section 154 of the Patent Code gives the patentee "the right to exclude others from making, using, or selling the invention through-

---

86. See, e.g., Farmland Irrigation Co. Inc. v. Dopplmaier, 48 Cal.2d 208, 308 P.2d 732 (1957), applying California law in holding that a patent license is assignable unless the agreement provides to the contrary. Accord, Unarco Industries, Inc. v. Kelley Co. Inc., 465 F.2d 1303 (7th Cir. 1972). Since a suit for royalties due under a license is a state contract action, a federal declaratory judgment suit brought by the licensee to have the patent declared invalid will be dismissed for want of federal jurisdiction: a case does not "arise under" the patent law merely because invalidity under the patent law

might be a defense in the state action. Thiokol Chemical Corp. v. Burlington Industries, Inc., 448 F.2d 1328 (3d Cir. 1971), certiorari denied 404 U.S. 1019, 92 S.Ct. 684, 30 L.Ed.2d 668.

87. On licensing, see generally Marquis, Limitations on Patent License Restrictions, 58 Iowa L.Rev. 41 (1972); Baxter, Legal Restriction on Exploitation of the Patent Monopoly: An Economic Analysis, 76 Yale L.J. 267 (1966); Buxbaum, Restrictions Inherent in the Patent Monopoly, 113 U.Pa.L.Rev. 633 (1965).

out the United States." Does this right to exclude others from use imply that the patentee has unrestricted freedom to decide not to use the patent at all, or unrestricted freedom to refuse to license others to use the patent?

With respect to the question of non-use, the Supreme Court has on several occasions rejected contentions that would have conditioned patent protection on actual use of the patent technology. A patent may therefore be enforced against another even though the patentee is not producing under it; and the Patent and Trademark Office may be compelled to issue a patent regardless of a disclosed purpose never to use or license the use of the invention. In *Special Equipment Co. v. Coe*,[88] for example, the inventor sought to patent a machine for paring and coring fruit in preparation for canning. The machine comprised two turntables on which some of the operations were carried out, together with a splitting knife which halved the fruit as it passed between the turntables. Perceiving that the operations on the turntables were themselves appropriate for coverage, providing substantial cost savings over hand-paring, the applicant sought patent coverage for the turntable arrangements minus the splitting knife, as well as for the whole machine. The Court of Appeals held that regardless of the possibility that two distinct inventions were disclosed, patent of the subcombination should be denied because applicant had no intention of exploiting the subcombination, but only desired the patent to "protect" his real invention, the entire machine, and to "block" others from developing inventive new machines based on the turntable device. The Supreme Court reversed by a vote of 5–4. Justice Stone, for the majority:

> Congress has frequently been asked to change the policy of the statutes as interpreted by this Court by imposing a forfeiture or providing for compulsory licensing if the patent is not used within a specified time, but has not done so.

> We have no occasion to consider here whether a better rule governing the grant of patents could be devised than that prescribed by Congress, as this Court has interpreted it; or whether the courts on equitable principles should decline to enjoin patent infringements or decline to compel the issue of a patent if and when it appears that the patentee or inventor intends to make no use of the invention. The record neither calls upon nor permits us to decide any of these questions, for it fails to establish that petitioner has any such intention. Petitioner's intended use of the patent to prevent others from appropriating it and by that means from appropriating an essential part of his complete machine is in no way inconsistent with petitioner's making other permissible uses of the subcombination patent. In fact, he does use the subcombination as a part of his completed machine and proposes to

88.   324 U.S. 370, 65 S.Ct. 741, 89 L.Ed. 1006 (1945). See also Continental Paper Bag Co. v. Eastern Paper Bag Co., 210 U.S. 405, 28 S.Ct. 748, 52 L.Ed. 1122 (1908).

ise it. Execution of his declared purpose to prevent
of either of his inventions, whether used separately
vould not prevent his licensing others to make, use
subcombination, on terms which would adequately
ue of the monopoly of both his inventions to which
y the patent laws. And we cannot say that others,
ecure a license to use the complete machine, would
table to secure, or that petitioner would not find it
int, licenses to use the subcombination which the
found to be a useful device which has advanced

for three dissenters, stated:

ppression of a patent came into the law over a
first patent act was passed. In 1886 Judge
that a patentee "is bound either to use the pat-
v others to use it on reasonable or equitable
ip, C.C., 27 F. 204, 212. In 1896 that rule was
rcuit Court of Appeals for the Sixth Circuit in
utton-Fastener Co. v. Eureka Specialty Co., 6
35 L.R.A. 728, where the court stated that a
xclusive, and so clearly within the constitu-
spect of private property that he is neither
very himself, nor permit others to use it."
ed by this Court in Continental Paper Bag
.per Bag Co., 210 U.S. 405, 28 S.Ct. 748, 52 L.Ed.
..., decided in 1908. . . .

I think it is time to be rid of that rule. It is inconsistent with
the Constitution and the patent legislation which Congress has enacted.

· · ·

[S]uppression of patents has become commonplace. Patents
are multiplied to protect an economic barony or empire, not to put
new discoveries to use for the common good. "It is common practice to make an invention and to secure a patent to block off a
competitor's progress. By studying his ware and developing an
improvement upon it, a concern may 'fence in' its rival; by a series of such moves, it may pin the trade enemy within a technology which rapidly becomes obsolete. As often as not such maneuvers retard, rather than promote, the progress of the useful arts.
Invariably their effect is to enlarge and to prolong personal privilege within the public domain." Hamilton, [Patents and Free En-
terprise], p. 161. One patent is used merely to protect another.
The use of a new patent is suppressed so as to preclude experi-
mentation which might result in further invention by competitors.
A whole technology is blocked off. The result is a clog to our
economic machine and a barrier to an economy of abundance.

It is difficult to see how that use of patents can be reconciled with the purpose of the Constitution "to promote the Progress of Science and the Arts." Can the suppression of patents which arrests the progress of technology be said to promote that progress? . . . Take the case of an invention or discovery which unlocks the doors of science and reveals the secrets of a dread disease. Is it possible that a patentee could be permitted to suppress that invention for seventeen years (the term of the letters patent) and withhold from humanity the benefits of the cure? But there is no differencce in principle between that case and any case where a patent is suppressed because of some immediate advantage to the patentee.

I think it is time to return to the earlier, and I think the true, philosophy of the patent system. We should not pass on to Congress the duty to remove the private perquisites which we have engrafted on the patent laws. This Court was responsible for their creation.

With respect to the patentee's freedom to unilaterally refuse to license others, consider *SCM Corp. v. Xerox Corp.*,[89] where the plaintiff claimed, inter alia, that Xerox's refusal to license its plain paper copier patents violated Section 2 of the Sherman Act. Judge Newman, then on the district court, wrote:[90]

No case has been found where a potential competitor has received lost profits as damages because of a patent owner's unilateral refusal to license a valid patent. . . . [T]he need to accommodate the patent laws with the antitrust laws precludes the imposition of damage liability under § 2 for a unilateral refusal to license valid patents. . . .

[T]he prospect of paying potential competitors three times the profits they would have earned if they had been granted patent licenses would pose a grave threat to achieving the objectives of the patent laws. The company facing such a prospect might well decide either to forego basic research and invest in other profit opportunities, or pursue research and forego patent protection, relying instead, especially in a high technology field, on the lead-time it could achieve before reverse engineering enabled competitors to market competitive products. There would be either fewer inventions or, at least, less public disclosure of inventions, or both.

The threat of retrospective treble damage awards for refusing to license is even more serious than the concerns that have been expressed about the wisdom of legislation for compulsory licensing. At least compulsory licensing, if required by statute, puts companies on notice that if their investment produces patentable

89. 463 F.Supp. 983 (D.Conn.1978), affirmed 645 F.2d 1195 (2d Cir. 1981), certiorari denied 455 U.S. 1016, 102 S.Ct. 1708, 72 L.Ed.2d 132 (1982).

90. 463 F.Supp. at 1012–14.

inventions, their investment return is limited to their license royalties plus their profits from marketing products in competition with licensees. That will normally reduce the profits available from exclusive marketing of products, but even if the reduction were substantial, its economic impact would be less inhibiting to research investment than multiple treble damage awards for the profits not earned by potential competitors.

Even if in some industries the aggregate size of damage awards for a refusal to license would not exceed the reduction in profits caused by compulsory licensing, a statutory requirement of licensing would be a known factor to be considered when companies decide the amount of investment appropriate for research. Perhaps the profit reduction would be difficult to estimate, but at least the certainty of the licensing requirement would assist planning not only as to the level of research investment, but also as to the subsequent determination of product prices and license royalty rates.

On the other hand, treble damage awards for a refusal to license would inject major uncertainty into research investment decisions. When those decisions are made, no one can be sure that any one research effort will yield success. But some estimates can be made as to the likely return on capital from a given level of research investment. Those estimates could not possibly take into account the likelihood of antitrust damage awards at some future time. If products are developed and achieve success in the market-place, a decision to grant or refuse licenses would still have to weigh, on pain of treble damage awards, the chances that a fact-finder may one day agree with a potential competitor's definition of the relevant market, claim of monopoly power, and allegation of willful acquisition or maintenance of monopoly power. The inhibiting effect of both the size of damages awards and the uncertainty of their imposition would seriously frustrate achieving the objectives of the patent laws.

Some may contend that these considerations prove too much, that they point toward the elimination of any treble damage awards for antitrust violations, or at least toward their elimination in any case not fully anticipated by a prior adjudication. Whatever one may think of the legitimacy of treble damage awards . . . , the case for imposing damage liability under § 2 is far less substantial when the claimed violation is a unilateral refusal to license a patent. The exercise of that prerogative is a corollary of the explicit statutory grant of the right to exclude others from making, using, or selling the patented invention. 35 U.S.C. § 154. To deny treble damage liability for a monopolist's unilateral refusal to license patents places no limitation on the utility of the private damage action to deter any exclusionary conduct that is not grounded in the very structure of the patent laws. To impose such liability poses a threat to the progress of science and the useful arts not warranted by a reasonable accommodation of the patent and antitrust laws.[91]

NOTES AND QUERIES

(1) *Suppression of Inventions.* Scherer writes:[92]

A further charge against the patent system is that it permits the suppression of inventions from which the public might otherwise benefit. Nearly everyone has heard the recurrent rumor that some shadowy power in the automobile or petroleum industry has obtained and suppressed patents on a carburetor that would let full-sized autos travel 50 miles per gallon of gasoline. Most such rumors, including the present example, prove on investigation to have little or no substance.

Nevertheless, there are occasions (in addition to the "blocking" examples noted by Justice Douglas, supra) when firms have suppressed inventions so as not to interfere with their own currently successful products. For example, in *McDonald v. Johnson & Johnson* a jury found the defendant liable for an attempt to monopolize by virtue of its suppression of a product acquired from the plaintiff which competed with one of the defendant's current products.[93] Does such antitrust liability conflict with the purpose of the patent law by discouraging invention generally? Or might the threat of treble-damage liability for anticompetitive suppression of patented inventions (the jury awarded $56.8 million in *Johnson & Johnson* before trebling) have the positive effect of deterring investment in inventions which will not be exploited?

(2) *Queries.* Recall the established principle that a unilateral refusal to deal by a monopolist can violate Section 2. In *Otter Tail Power Co.* (supra p. 124), for example, the Supreme Court held that Otter Tail's refusal to sell wholesale power to a competing retailer, or to wheel power over its transmission lines, violated Section 2. Is it likely that the threat of treble-damage liability will now deter firms from future investments in long distance transmission lines? Why should the threat of treble damage liability for a refusal to license use of a patent—another capital asset—deter investment in those assets (Judge Newman's concern in *SCM*)? Do we need greater incentives to obtain the necessary level of invention? Wouldn't it be enough to allow non-monopolists the absolute right to refuse to license their patents?

91. The court of appeals affirmed, holding that where a patent was lawfully acquired a patent holder can exercise the patent's "exclusionary power" by refusing to license it. 645 F.2d at 1206. The court added: "We leave for an appropriate case the resolution of the question whether damage liability can accrue to a holder for refusing to license patents that he subsequently abuses through pooling or otherwise." Id., n. 10. See also United States v. Westinghouse Electric Corp., 648 F.2d 642 (9th Cir. 1981) (rejecting Government theory that Westinghouse violated Section 1 by its agreement to license only its foreign patents to Mitsubishi, and its subsequent unwillingness to license its American patents when Mitsubishi was capable of entering the heavily concentrated United States market; even if Mitsubishi, having initially committed itself to Westinghouse technology, could not enter the market because it could not design around Westinghouse absent a license, "no court" has held a patentee must grant further licenses to a competitor because it has already granted some).

92. Scherer, Industrial Market Structure and Economic Performance 452 (2d ed. 1980).

93. 537 F.Supp. 1282 (D.Minn.1982). See also Berkey Photo, Inc. v. Eastman Kodak, supra pp. 572–575 (detailing Kodak's practice of timing new product introductions, done to avoid interference with current products; liability found under Section 1 for agreement not to disclose invention prior to marketing).

(3) *Compulsory Licensing.* "In order to eliminate the use of patents in ways inimical to the public policy inherent in the patent laws, as well as that of the antitrust laws, we recommend that the Congress enact legislation which will require that any future patent is to be available for use by anyone who may desire its use and who is willing to pay a fair price for the privilege. Machinery, either judicial or administrative, should be set up to determine whether the royalty demanded by the patentee may fairly be said to represent reasonable compensation or is intended to set a prohibitive price for such use." Excerpt from Final Report and Recommendations of the Temporary National Economic Committee, S.Doc. 35, 77th Cong., 1st Sess., p. 36 (1941).[94]

Recovery in an infringement suit should be limited to "reasonable compensation without prohibiting the use of the patented invention whenever the court finds that the particular use of the invention in controversy is necessary to the national defense or required by the public health or public safety". First Report of the National Patent Planning Commission (1943), p. 10 (H.Doc. 239, 78th Cong., 1st Sess.).

Provisions for compulsory licensing of patents deemed especially important to the national interest have been included in some statutes, e.g., Atomic Energy Act, see p. 960, supra; 1970 Clean Air Act Amendments. Cf. Patent Commissioner Schuyler, speaking regarding the latter: "effectively removed the incentives of the patent system." Pat., Trademark & Copyright J. (BNA), Feb. 11, 1971, p. A–4. Compulsory licensing has also been ordered as relief in some antitrust decrees. See pp. 1036–1038, infra.

In the United Kingdom, the *Patents Act*, 1977, c. 37, § 48, provides that the comptroller may compel licensing under a patent after three years, on the following grounds:

(a) where the patented invention is capable of being commercially worked in the United Kingdom, that it is not being so worked or is not being so worked to the fullest extent that is reasonably practicable;

(b) where the patented intention is a product, that a demand for the product in the United Kingdom—

(i) is not being met on reasonable terms, or

(ii) is being met to a substantial extent by importation;

(c) where the patented invention is capable of being commercially worked in the United Kingdom, that it is being prevented or hindered from being so worked—

(i) where the invention is a product, by the importation of the product.

(ii) where the invention is a process, by the importation of a product obtained directly by means of the process or to which the process has been applied;

94. This recommendation is criticized on the basis of the evidence before the Committee in Folk, Patents and Industrial Progress (1942) especially at p. 257 et seq.

(d) that by reason of the refusal of the proprietor of the patent to grant a license or licenses on reasonable terms—

(i) a market for the export of any patented product made in the United Kingdom is not being supplied, or

(ii) the working or efficient working in the United Kingdom of any other patented invention which makes a substantial contribution to the art is prevented or hindered, or

(iii) the establishment or development of commercial or industrial activities in the United Kingdom is unfairly prejudiced;

(e) that by reason of conditions imposed by the proprietor of the patent on the grant of licences under the patent, or on the disposal or use of the patented product or on the use of the patented process, the manufacture, use or disposal of materials not protected by the patent, or the establishment or development of commercial or industrial activities in the United Kingdom, is unfairly prejudiced.

2. PRICE CONTROL AND DIVISION OF MARKETS

The strongest affirmation of the "rule of reason" in application to restrictive patent licensing appeared in UNITED STATES v. GENERAL ELECTRIC CO., 272 U.S. 476, 47 S.Ct. 192, 71 L.Ed. 362 (1926), which sustained the right of GE to require in a patent license agreement that Westinghouse, its giant competitor in the electronics field, follow GE's resale practices and prices in distributing electric lamps manufactured by Westinghouse under the license:

[T]he patentee may grant a license to make, use and vend articles under the specifications of his patent for any royalty or upon any condition the performance of which is reasonably within the reward which the patentee by the grant of the patent is entitled to secure. It is well settled . . . that where a patentee makes the patented article and sells it, he can exercise no future control over what the purchaser may wish to do with the article after his purchase. It has passed beyond the scope of the patentee's rights. But the question is a different one which arises when we consider what a patentee who grants a license to one to make and vend the patented article may do in limiting the licensee in the exercise of the right to sell. The patentee may make and grant a license to another to make and use the patented articles but withhold his right to sell them. The licensee in such a case acquires an interest in the articles made. He owns the material of them and may use them. But if he sells them he infringes the right of the patentee, and may be held for damages and enjoined. If the patentee goes further and licenses the selling of the articles, may he limit the selling by limiting the method of sale and the price? We think he may do so provided the conditions of sale are normally and reasonably adapted to secure pecuniary reward for the patentee's monopoly. One of the valuable elements of the exclusive right of a patentee is to acquire profit by the price at which the article is sold. The higher the price, the greater the profit, unless it is prohibitory. When the patentee licenses another to make and vend and retains the right to continue to make and vend on his own account, the price at which his licensee will sell will necessarily affect the price at which he can sell his own patented goods. It would seem entirely reasonable that he should say to the licensee, "Yes, you may make and sell articles under my patent but not so as to destroy the profit that I wish to obtain by making them and selling them myself." He does not thereby sell outright to the licensee the articles the latter may make and sell or vest absolute ownership in them. He restricts the property and interest the licensee has in the goods he makes and proposes to sell.

Qualifications of this extreme statement of the power to fix a licensee's prices appeared in UNITED STATES v. LINE MATERIAL CO., 333 U.S. 287, 68 S.Ct. 550, 92 L.Ed. 701 (1948), where holders of complementary patents covering drop-out fuses pooled their rights and granted licenses to General Electric, Westinghouse, and all other producers of the fuses, so that the entire industry operated under centrally determined prices. The district court dismissed the government's Sherman Act complaint in reliance on *General Electric.* The Supreme Court reversed. Four Justices concurred on the basis of overruling *General Electric.* A fifth Justice rested on narrower grounds, viz. that the combination of patents as the basis for price-fixing on this scale went beyond *General Electric.*[95] The Supreme Court has still not overruled *General Electric.*[96]

NOTES AND QUERIES

(1) *Ancillary Price Control.* In a context of other violations of the Sherman Act by dominant companies, the Supreme Court has several times adverted unfavorably to license provisions which attempt to reinforce price control over the patented product with control over connected transactions. See, for example, license in *United States v. Line Material Co.,* 333 U.S. 287, 294 n. 8, 68 S.Ct. 550, 554 n. 8, 92 L.Ed. 701, 710 n. 8 (1948) ("there shall not be directly, or indirectly, any modification of the prices set . . . as for instance by including in the transaction other material or parts, or labor, or services, at less than the regular prices at which the party making the same is at the time selling such other material or parts or furnishing such labor or services."); cf. *United States v. United States Gypsum Co.,* 333 U.S. 364, 399, 68 S.Ct. 525, 92 L.Ed. 746 (1948) ("the defendants attempted to stabilize plaster prices, and the fact that plaster prices were stabilized only

95. See also United States v. United States Gypsum Co., 333 U.S. 364, 68 S.Ct. 525, 92 L.Ed. 746 (1948); United States v. New Wrinkle, Inc., 342 U.S. 371, 72 S.Ct. 350, 96 L.Ed. 417 (1952) (rejecting a suggested distinction based on the licensor's being a patent holding company solely and not a manufacturing competitor of the licensees); Newburgh Moire Co. v. Superior Moire Co., 237 F.2d 283 (3d Cir. 1956) (power to set prices of manufacturing licenses denied to a relatively small company whose "plurality of licenses" extended to three-fifths of the industry).

96. See United States v. Huck Manufacturing Co., 382 U.S. 197, 86 S.Ct. 385, 15 L.Ed.2d 268 (1965) (affirmed by an equally divided Court).

when plaster was sold in conjunction with [patented] board appears to us to be immaterial").

Cummer-Graham Co. v. Straight Side Basket Corp., 142 F.2d 646 (5th Cir. 1944), involved an action against the Basket Corporation for breach of oral promises to maintain uniform prices for all baskets made by licensees under defendant's patent. The patent covered an attachment on basket making machines, not the basket itself. Plaintiff, one of many licensees, conformed to the agreed prices, with the result that it lost business to price-cutting licensees. There was some evidence of joint action on price policy among licensees, but the court disregarded that. Judgment for defendant was affirmed on the ground that a patent on a machine for making an unpatented product could not confer the right to price-fix the latter: "The licensees use their own materials and capital, and own absolutely the baskets they make," the court observed, analogizing to the freedom of a patented product from price control after the first sale.

(2) *Queries.* When GE required, in its lamp license, that Westinghouse sell lamps at GE's prices, did GE thereby undertake to control the price at which Westinghouse sold unpatented materials and labor put into the lamps by Westinghouse? Is it necessary to confer the privilege of fixing other people's prices in order to maintain the incentive to invent? or is the right to charge royalties, or to practice the invention exclusively, sufficient? The owner of a trademark has the legal power to prevent others from using it in the trademark owner's market. Should he have also the power to license the use of the mark on condition that the licensee follow the licensor's prices? May an "excessive" royalty be condemned as a violation of the antitrust laws on the ground that most of the industry is licensed and the royalty rate in effect sets minimum prices for the equipment in which the patent is incorporated?[97]

(3) *Distinction Between Assignment and License.* Assignments and licenses must be distinguished for some purposes. Section 261 of the Patent Code of 1952 explicitly authorizes assignment of a patent or "any interest therein" and the grant of "an exclusive right under [the] patent to the whole or any specified part of the United States," by writing recorded in the Patent Office. Assignments and licenses are said to be distinguished as proprietary and non-proprietary interests, respectively. A license is said to be any right in the invention other than one which is the subject of assignment under the Act. Thus, an exclusive right to make, use and sell in the city of Philadelphia is an assignment, even though designated a license and even though the agreement calls for the payment of royalties to the "licensor." On the other hand "assignment" of the exclusive right to manufacture and sell fountain pens throughout the United States would be no more than a "license" because it does not embrace the right to "use." This conceptual classification has important substantive and procedural consequences. An assignment is "void" against subsequent purchasers and mortgagees without notice, in the absence of recording. There is no provision for registry of licenses, which may be oral and even implied.[98] Suits for infringement must ordinarily be brought in the name of a person who has a "proprietary" interest in the patent.

97. American Photocopy Equipment Co. v. Rovico, Inc., 359 F.2d 745 (7th Cir. 1966); but cf. same case, 257 F.Supp. 192 (N.D.Ill.1966).

98. Cf. recommendation (1)(c) of the Temporary National Economic Committee in favor of recording licenses. S.Doc. 35, 77 Cong., 1st Sess. (1941) p. 37.

ADAMS v. BURKE

Supreme Court of the United States, 1873.

84 U.S. 453, 21 L.Ed. 700.

[The patentee assigned to Lockhart and Seelye all his right, title and interest in a patent on coffin lids within a ten-mile radius of Boston. He assigned the balance of his interest to Adams, the plaintiff in this infringement suit. Defendant, an undertaker, bought coffins with the patented lids from Lockhart and Seelye, who made and sold them in Boston. Defendant used these coffins in burials 17 miles from Boston.]

MR. JUSTICE MILLER delivered the opinion of the court.

The question presented by the plea in this case is a very interesting one in patent law, and the precise point in it has never been decided by this court, though cases involving some of the considerations which apply to it have been decided, and others of analogous character are frequently recurring. The vast pecuniary results involved in such cases, as well as the public interest, admonish us to proceed with care, and to decide in each case no more than what is directly in issue.

We have repeatedly held that where a person had purchased a patented machine of the patentee or his assignee, this purchase carried with it the right to the use of that machine so long as it was capable of use, and that the expiration and renewal of the patent, whether in favor of the original patentee or of his assignee, did not affect this right. The true ground on which these decisions rest is that the sale by a person who has the full right to make, sell and use such a machine carries with it the right to the use of that machine to the full extent to which it can be used in point of time.

The right to manufacture, the right to sell, and the right to use are each substantive rights, and may be granted or conferred separately by the patentee.

But, in the essential nature of things, when the patentee, or the person having his rights, sells a machine or instrument whose sole value is in its use, he receives the consideration for its use and he parts with the right to restrict that use. The article, in the language of the court passes without the limit of the monopoly. That is to say, the patentee or his assignee having in the act of sale received all the royalty or consideration which he claims for the use of his invention in that particular machine or instrument, it is open to the use of the purchaser without further restriction on account of the monopoly of the patentees.

If this principle be sound as to a machine or instrument whose use may be continued for a number of years, and may extend beyond the

existence of the patent, as limited at the time of the sale, and into the
period of a renewal or extension, it must be much more applicable to
an instrument or product of patented manufacture which perishes in
the first use of it, or which, by that first use, becomes incapable of
further use, and of no further value. Such is the case with the coffin-lids of appellant's patent.

It seems to us that, although the right of Lockhart & Seelye to
manufacture, to sell, and use these coffin-lids was limited to the circle
of ten miles around Boston, that a purchaser from them of a single
coffin acquired the right to use that coffin for the purpose for which
all coffins are used. That so far as the use of it was concerned, the
patentee had received his consideration, and it was no longer within
the monopoly of the patent. It would be to engraft a limitation upon
the right of use not contemplated by the statute nor within the reason of the contract to say that it could only be used within the ten-
mile circle. Whatever, therefore, may be the rule when patentees
subdivide territorially their patents, as to the exclusive right *to make*
or *to sell* within a limited territory, we hold that in the class of machines or implements we have described, when they are once lawfully
made and sold, there is no restriction on their *use* to be implied for
the benefit of the patentee or his assignees or licensees.

A careful examination of the plea satisfies us that the defendant,
who, as an undertaker, purchased each of these coffins and used it in
burying the body which he was employed to bury, acquired the right
to this use of it freed from any claim of the patentee, though purchased within the ten-mile circle and used without it.

The decree of the Circuit Court dismissing the plaintiff's bill is,
therefore, affirmed.

MR. JUSTICE BRADLEY (with whom concurred JUSTICES SWAYNE
and STRONG), dissenting:

The question raised in this case is whether an assignment of a
patented invention for a limited district, such as a city, a county, or a
State, confers upon the assignee the right to sell the patented article
to be used outside of such limited district. The defendant justifies
under such a claim. He uses a patented article outside of the territory within which the patent was assigned to the persons from whom
he purchased it. The plaintiff, who claims under the original patentee, complains that this is a transgression of the limits of the assignment.

If it were a question of legislative policy, whether a patentee
should be allowed to divide up his monopoly into territorial parcels, it
might admit of grave doubt whether a vendee of the patented article
purchasing it rightfully, ought to be restrained or limited as to the
place of its use. But the patent act gives to the patentee a monopoly
of use, as well as of manufacture, throughout the whole United

States; and the eleventh section of the act (of 1836) expressly authorizes not only an assignment of the whole patent, or any undivided part thereof, but a "grant and conveyance of the exclusive right under any patent, to make and *use*, and to grant to others to make and use the thing patented within and throughout any specified part or portion of the United States."

If an assignment under this clause does not confer the same rights within the limited district which the patentee himself previously had in the whole United States, and no more, it is difficult to know what meaning to attach to language however plain. . . .

If it be contended that the right of vending the lids to others enables them to confer upon their vendees the right to use the lids thus sold outside of the limited district, the question at once arises, how can they confer upon their vendees a right which they cannot exercise themselves? The only consistent construction to be given to such an assignment is, to limit all the privileges conferred by it to the district marked out. It is an assignment of the manufacture and use of the patented article within that district, and within that district only.

Difficulties may, undoubtedly, be suggested in special cases. If the patented thing be an article of wearing apparel, sold by the assignee within his district, it is confidently asked, cannot the purchaser wear the article outside of the district? The answer to acute suggestions of this sort would probably be found (in the absence of all bad faith in the parties) in the maxim *de minimis non curat lex.*

On the other hand, the difficulties and the injustice which would follow from a contrary construction to that which I contend for, are very obvious. Take the electric telegraph, for example. Suppose Professor Morse had assigned his patent within and for the New England States. Would such an assignment authorize the vendees of his assignees to use the apparatus in the whole United States? Take the planing machine: would an assignment from Woodworth of his patent within and for the State of Vermont authorize the assignees to manufacture machines *ad libitum*, and sell them to parties to be used in other States? So of Hoe's printing press, and a thousand other machines and inventions of like sort.

Such a doctrine would most seriously affect not only the assignor (as to his residuary right in his patent), but the assignee also. For if it be correct, there would be nothing to prevent the patentee himself, after assigning his patent within a valuable city or other locality, from selling the patent machine or article to be used within the assigned district. By this means, the assignment could be, and in numberless instances would be, rendered worthless. Millions of dollars have been invested by manufacturers and mechanics in these limited assignments of patents in our manufacturing districts and towns, giving them, as they have supposed, the monopoly of the patented machine or article within the district purchased. The decision of the court in this case will, in my view, utterly destroy the value of a great portion of this property. . . .

GENERAL TALKING PICTURES v. WESTERN ELECTRIC CO.

Supreme Court of the United States, 1938.

305 U.S. 124, 59 S.Ct. 116, 83 L.Ed. 81.

MR. JUSTICE BRANDEIS delivered the opinion of the Court.

In this case, we affirmed on May 2, 1938, the judgment of the Circuit Court of Appeals, which held that petitioner had infringed certain patents relating to vacuum tube amplifiers. On May 31st, we granted a rehearing, upon the following questions which had been presented by the petition for certiorari.

1. Can the owner of a patent, by means thereof, restrict the use made of a device manufactured under the patent, after the device has passed into the hands of a purchaser in the ordinary channels of trade, and full consideration paid therefor?

. . .

Upon further hearing we are of opinion that neither question should be answered. For we find that, while the devices embody the inventions of the patents in suit, they were not manufactured or sold "under the patent[s]" and did not "pass into the hands of a purchaser in the ordinary channels of trade."

These are the relevant facts. Amplifiers embodying the invention here involved are useful in several distinct fields. Among these is (a) the commercial field of sound recording and reproducing, which embraces talking picture equipment for theatres, and (b) the private or home field, which embraces radio broadcast reception, radio amateur reception and radio experimental reception. For the commercial field exclusive licenses had been granted by the patent pool [99] to Western

---

99. The patent pool referred to was a system of cross-licenses among the dominant organizations engaged in the manufacture, use, and sale of radio and electronic devices, especially the multi-purpose vacuum tube. Each participant opened its patents to the others on terms which limited each participant to a defined "field" and secured him against competition from the others in that field. Thus the American Telephone and Telegraph Co., top holding company of the Bell System, and its manufacturing subsidiary, Western Electric Co., were assured a virtual monopoly of the technology in its relationship to telephone communication. General Electric Co. and Westinghouse Electric Co. were assigned the field of industrial applications (trans- formers, switches, other power uses). A. T. & T. shared with Radio Corporation of America a monopoly of talking picture apparatus. R.C.A. for the pool licensed manufacturers of radio receivers on standard terms. In 1932 the United States secured a decree under the Sherman Act detaching R.C.A., originally a wholly owned subsidiary of G.E., from domination by that company and Westinghouse. The exclusive features of the cross licenses were terminated so that each participant should be free (without obligation) to license outsiders under its own patents. The restrictive use provisions of the existing cross licenses were not disturbed. See Wood, Patents and the Antitrust Law (1941) pp. 128–145.

Electric Company and Electrical Research Products, Inc. For the private or home field the patent pool granted non-exclusive licenses to about fifty manufacturers. Among these was American Transformer Company. It was licensed "solely and only to the extent and for the uses hereinafter specified and defined . . . to manufacture . . . , and to sell . . . only for radio amateur reception, radio experimental reception and radio broadcast reception . . . licensed apparatus so manufactured by the Licensee. . . ."

The license provided further: "Nothing herein contained shall be regarded as conferring upon the Licensee either expressly or by estoppel, implication or otherwise, a license to manufacture or sell, any apparatus except such as may be manufactured by the Licensee in accordance with the express provision of this Agreement.

Transformer Company, knowing that it had not been licensed to manufacture or to sell amplifiers for use in theatres as part of talking picture equipment, made for that commercial use the amplifiers in controversy and sold them to Pictures Corporation for that commercial use. Pictures Corporation ordered the amplifiers and purchased them knowing that Transformer Company had not been licensed to make or sell them for such use in theatres. Any use beyond the valid terms of a license is, of course, an infringement of a patent. Robinson on Patents, § 916. If where a patented invention is applicable to different uses, the owner of the patent may legally restrict a licensee to a particular field and exclude him from others, Transformer Company was guilty of an infringement when it made the amplifiers for, and sold them to, Pictures Corporation. And as Pictures Corporation ordered, purchased and leased them knowing the facts, it also was an infringer.

The question of law requiring decision is whether the restriction in the license is to be given effect. That a restrictive license is legal seems clear. As was said in United States v. General Electric Co., 272 U.S. 476, 489, 47 S.Ct. 192, 196, 71 L.Ed. 362, the patentee may grant a license "upon any condition the performance of which is reasonably within the reward which the patentee by the grant of the patent is entitled to secure." The restriction here imposed is of that character. The practice of granting licenses for a restricted use is an old one. So far as appears, its legality has never been questioned. The parties stipulated that "it is common practice where a patented invention is applicable to different uses, to grant written licenses to manufacture under United States Letters Patents restricted to one or more of the several fields of use permitting the exclusive or non-exclusive use of the invention by the licensee in one field and excluding it in another field."

As the restriction was legal and the amplifiers were made and sold outside the scope of the license, the effect is precisely the same as if no license whatsoever had been granted to Transformer Company. And as Pictures Corporation knew the facts, it is in no better position than if it had manufactured the amplifiers itself without a license. It is liable because it has used the invention without license to do so.

We have consequently no occasion to consider what the rights of the parties would have been if the amplifier had been manufactured "under the patent" and "had passed into the hands of a purchaser in the ordinary channels of trade." Nor have we occasion to consider the effect of a "licensee's notice" which purports to restrict the use of articles lawfully sold.

Affirmed.

MR. JUSTICE BLACK, dissenting.

Almost a century ago, this Court asserted, and time after time thereafter it has reasserted, that when an article described in a patent is sold and "passes to the hands of a purchaser, it is no longer within the limits of the monopoly. It passes outside of it, and is no longer under the protection of the act of Congress. . . . Contracts in relation to it are regulated by the laws of the State, and are subject to State jurisdiction."

A single departure from his judicial interpretation of the patent statute was expressly overruled within five years, and this Court again reasserted that commodities—once sold—were not thereafter "subject to conditions as to use" imposed by patent owners. In result, the judgment here is a second departure from the traditional judicial interpretation of the patent laws.

As a consequence of the return to the interpretation of the patent statutes previously repudiated and expressly overruled, petitioner is enjoined from making full use of, and must account in triple damages for using, tubes and amplifiers which he owns. He became the owner of the tubes by purchase from various retailers authorized by respondents to sell in the open market. He became the owner of the amplifiers by purchase from a manufacturer who—having the complete right to make them—had contracted to sell only for limited uses. The departure here permits the patentee—by virtue of his contract with the manufacturer—to restrict the uses to which this purchaser and owner may put his tubes and amplifiers.

Notice to the purchaser in any form could not—under the patent law—limit or restrict the use of the amplifiers after they were sold and knowledge by both vendor and purchaser that the articles were purchased for use outside the "field" for which the vendor had been given the right to sell, made the transaction between them no less a sale. Had petitioner—after making the purchase—decided *not* to use these amplifiers in the forbidden fields, or had they been destroyed prior to such use, certainly the mere state of mind of the parties at the time of sale would not have made them both infringers.

Indeed, petitioner could use the amplifiers at all only in combination with tubes which it purchased on the open market from retailers authorized by respondents to sell.   Therefore, even if the state of mind of vendor and purchaser were material, Transformer Company could be considered an infringer only because it sold a commodity which might—depending on possible events after the sale—be used in infringing combination with another lawfully purchased commodity. The patent law was not intended to accomplish such result.   .   .   .

MR. JUSTICE REED joins in this dissent.

MR. JUSTICE ROBERTS took no part in the consideration or decision of the case.

NOTES AND QUERIES

(1) *Queries.*   Can *General Talking Pictures* be distinguished from *Adams v. Burke*? Would the result in *General Talking Pictures* have been different if Transformer Company had sold the amplifiers to Pictures Corporation in an amateur radio and Pictures Corporation had then taken them out and used them in its theaters?

Justice Brandeis, quoting *General Electric* (supra p. 986), states that the patentee may impose license restrictions " 'reasonably within the reward' " of the patent.   Why are restrictions on a licensee's territories or fields of use "reasonably within the reward" before the "first sale"?   Does such a rule properly resolve the conflict between patents and competition policy?   Are such restrictions "inherent" in the patent, if a patentee is to obtain its lawful monopoly reward?[1]

(2) *Post-Sale Distribution Restrictions.   General Talking Pictures* and *Adams v. Burke* were infringement suits by the patentee to enforce patent rights against defendants not party to the licensing agreement.   As *General Electric* indicates, enforcement of restrictions in licensing agreements are not only affected by the patent laws, but also by the antitrust laws.   Thus, post-sale distribution restrictions on the licensee's field of use, or the geographic areas in which the licensee sells the product, are subject to Section 1 of the Sherman Act, like any other distribution restriction.   Recall *GTE-Sylvania* (pp. 646–649, supra) and the material describing the innovation process as broader than simply invention (pp. 972–974, supra).   Should the need to provide monopoly profits for the "diffusion" of new products by a purchaser-distributor be an additional (dispositive?) factor in a rule of reason analysis

---

1. See United States v. Studiengesellschaft Kohle, m.b.H., 670 F.2d 1122 (D.C. Cir. 1981) (upholding, against antitrust challenge, licenses of process patent which restricted some licensees from selling on the open market the product manufactured under the process patent; court rejects distinction between "field-of-use" restrictions which can be imposed under a product patent and a process patent; defendant "sought nothing beyond what the patent itself gave it"); Gibbons, Field Restrictions in Patent Transactions: Economic Discrimination And Restraint of Competition, 66 Colum.L.Rev. 423 (1966); Buxbaum, Restrictions Inherent in the Patent Monopoly: A Comparative Critique, 113 U.Pa.L.Rev. 633 (1965); Selinger, Patent Licensing in the Afterglow of Sylvania: Practicalities of Life Under the Rule of Reason, 63 JPOS 353 (1981).

of territorial or customer restraints?[2] Suppose such agreements have a "horizontal" aspect (e.g., granting or terminating exclusive territorial licenses in agreement with competing licensees)? *Per se* unlawful? Or should all such patent license restrictions be evaluated under a rule of reason?[3]

(3) *Comparisons to Copyright.* Does a copyright holder have the same rights as a patentee to place license restrictions on the user prior to a "first sale"?[4] Consider *Interstate Circuit, Inc. v. United States*,[5] where two powerful theater chains insisted that movie distributors license "A" films on "subsequent runs" subject to two restrictions: the films not appear on a double-feature and not be exhibited at less than a 25 cent (!) admission fee. Justice Stone wrote for the Court:

> Under § 1 of the Copyright Act, the owners of the copyright of a motion picture film acquire the right to exhibit the picture and to grant an exclusive or restrictive license to others to exhibit it. Appellants argue that the distributors were free to license the films for exhibition subject to the restrictions, just as a patentee in a license to manufacture and sell the patented article may fix the price at which the licensee may sell it. That the parallel is not complete is obvious. Because a patentee has power to control the price at which his licensee may sell the patented article, it does not follow that the owner of a copyright can dictate that other pictures may not be shown with the licensed film or the admission price which shall be paid for an entertainment which includes features other than the particular picture licensed.

> We have no occasion now to pass upon these or related questions. Granted that each distributor, in the protection of his own copyright monopoly, was free to impose the present restrictions upon his licensees, we are nevertheless of the opinion that they were not free to use their copyrights as implements for restraining commerce in order to protect Interstate's motion picture theatre monopoly by suppressing competition with it. The restrictions imposed upon Interstate's competitors did not have their origin in the voluntary act of the distributors or any of them. They gave effect to the will and were subject to the control of Interstate, not by virtue of any copyright of Interstate, for it had none, but through its contract with each distributor. Interstate was able to acquire the control

2. Cf. Munters Corp. v. Burgess Industries, Inc., 450 F.Supp. 1195 (S.D.N.Y. 1978) (patentee violated Section 1 by granting purchaser of patented product an exclusive license for the "whole field of evaporative cooling for industrial use"; restriction unreasonable under Sylvania because it was purchaser-induced and not clearly necessary to obtain distribution of product; court factually rejects argument that arrangement was necessary "to open up a new product area").

3. See Mannington Mills, Inc. v. Congoleum Industries, Inc., 610 F.2d 1059 (3d Cir. 1979) (no antitrust "exemption" for termination of licensee after complaints from competing licensees; court expresses "no view" on whether case should be judged under *per se* rule); Mo-

raine Products v. ICI America, Inc., 538 F.2d 134 (7th Cir. 1976) (licensor and licensee, who were competitors, agreed that further licensing will occur only with consent of both parties; *per se* rule held inappropriate), certiorari denied 429 U.S. 941, 97 S.Ct. 357, 50 L.Ed.2d 310.

4. See 17 U.S.C.A. § 109 (copyright holder has no right to restrict disposition after first sale of a copy or phonorecord "lawfully made"). For cases construing this provision, see Latman, supra p. 939, at 176–80.

5. 306 U.S. 208, 59 S.Ct. 467, 83 L.Ed. 610 (1939).

and impose its will by force of its monopoly of first-run theatres in the principal cities of Texas and the threat to use its monopoly position against copyright owners who did not yield to its demands. The purpose and ultimate effect of each of its contracts with the distributors was to restrain its competitors in the theatre business by forcing an increase in their admission price and compelling them through the double feature restriction to make their entertainment less attractive, and to preclude the distributors for the specified time from relaxing the pressure of the restrictions upon them.

. . . Moreover, the provision in Interstate's contracts for the restriction against double billing stipulated for restraint upon competition with Interstate in the exhibition of films in the double bill in which neither Interstate nor the licensor had any interest by way of copyright or otherwise. The patent effect of the contract was to impose an undue restraint both as to admission price and the character of the exhibition upon competing theatre businesses habitually exhibiting the competitive pictures of different copyright owners. Through acceptance of its terms by the principal distributors the contract became the ready instrument by which Interstate succeeded in dominating the business of its competitors in the Texas cities. The fact that the restrictions may have been of a kind which a distributor could voluntarily have imposed, but did not, does not alter the character of the contract as a calculated restraint upon the distribution and use of copyrighted films moving in interstate commerce. Even if it be assumed that the benefit to the distributor from the restrictions is one which it might have secured through its monopoly control of the copyright alone, that would not extend the protection of the copyright to the contract with Interstate and to the resulting restraint upon the competition of its business rivals.

Query. Is it a workable rule for the guidance of bargaining between a movie distributor and a movie exhibitor that any restrictions which the exhibitor wants included in the licensing of other exhibitors be "voluntarily" imposed by the distributor?

(4) *Licensee Dominance of Licensing.* In connection with the observations in the *Interstate* opinion that "restrictions . . . of a kind which a distributor could voluntarily have imposed" [as copyright owner] may become unlawful when used as the instrument by which one licensee dominates the business of its competitors, consider *United States v. L. D. Caulk Co.,* 126 F.Supp. 693 (D.Del.1954). Caulk had an exclusive license from a British company to manufacture and sell in the United States and certain South American countries dental impression material covered by the "Wilding" patent. It was also authorized to grant sub-licenses. Coe and Dental Perfection were sub-licensees. The three companies together sold about 85% of this class of dental impression material. Finding that there were a number of non-licensed, non-royalty-paying competitors moving into the market, Coe and Dental Perfection called upon Caulk and the British patentee to vindicate the patent. Successful infringement suits were brought. Held, on motion for summary judgment: no evidence of conspiracy or combination to restrain trade or monopolize the field, since Caulk never yielded its right to license additional manufacturers though it did not in fact license any, and the licensees did not control the enforcement program. The course of conduct proved was consistent with the proper concern of royalty-paying licensees to prevent infringement.

May licensees of a patent or copyright, in preparation for negotiations with the licensor, agree upon a maximum royalty which any of them will pay? Does this depend on whether they collectively "dominate" the trade? Is collective action by them desirable in order to build countervailing power against the monopoly? Or is it subversion of the constitutional and legislative scheme of rewarding inventors and authors?

3. TYING AND OTHER "EXTENSIONS" OF THE LEGAL MONOPOLY

MORTON SALT CO. v. G. S. SUPPIGER CO.

Supreme Court of the United States, 1942.
314 U.S. 488, 62 S.Ct. 402, 86 L.Ed. 363.

MR. CHIEF JUSTICE STONE delivered the opinion of the Court.

Respondent [Suppiger] brought this suit in the district court for an injunction and an accounting for infringement of its Patent No. 2,060,645, of November 10, 1936, on a machine for depositing salt tablets, a device said to be useful in the canning industry for adding predetermined amounts of salt in tablet form to the contents of the cans.

Upon petitioner's [Morton's] motion, pursuant to Rule 56 of the Rules of Civil Procedure, 28 U.S.C.A. following section 723c, the trial court, without passing on the issues of validity and infringement, granted summary judgment dismissing the complaint. It took the ground that respondent was making use of the patent to restrain the sale of salt tablets in competition with its own sale of unpatented tablets, by requiring licensees to use with the patented machines only tablets sold by respondent. The Court of Appeals for the Seventh Circuit reversed, 117 F.2d 968, because it thought that respondent's use of the patent was not shown to violate § 3 of the Clayton Act, 15 U.S.C. § 14, 15 U.S.C.A. § 14, as it did not appear that the use of its patent substantially lessened competition or tended to create a monopoly in salt tablets. We granted certiorari . . .

The Clayton Act authorizes those injured by violations to maintain suit for treble damages and for an injunction in appropriate cases. But the present suit is for infringement of a patent. The question we must decide it not necessarily whether respondent has violated the Clayton Act, but whether a court of equity will lend its aid to protect the patent monopoly when respondent is using it as the effective means of restraining competition with its sale of an unpatented article.

Both respondent's wholly owned subsidiary and the petitioner manufacture and sell salt tablets used and useful in the canning trade. The tablets have a particular configuration rendering them capable of convenient use in respondent's patented machines. Petitioner makes and leases to canners unpatented salt depositing machines, charged to infringe respondent's patent. For reasons we indicate later, nothing turns on the fact that petitioner also competes with respondent in the sale of the tablets, and we may assume for purposes of this case that petitioner is doing no more than making

and leasing the alleged infringing machines. The principal business
of respondent's subsidiary, from which its profits are derived, is the
sale of salt tablets. In connection with this business, and as an adjunct to it, respondent leases its patented machines to commercial
canners, some two hundred in all, under licenses to use the machines
upon condition and with the agreement of the licensees that only the
subsidiary's salt tablets be used with the leased machines.

It thus appears that respondent is making use of its patent monopoly to restrain competition in the marketing of unpatented articles, salt tablets, for use with the patented machines, and is aiding in
the creation of a limited monopoly in the tablets not within that
granted by the patent. A patent operates to create and grant to the
patentee an exclusive right to make, use and vend the particular device described and claimed in the patent. But a patent affords no
immunity for a monopoly not within the grant, and the use of it to
suppress competition in the sale of an unpatented article may deprive
the patentee of the aid of a court of equity to restrain an alleged
infringement by one who is a competitor. It is the established rule
that a patentee who has granted a license on condition that the patented invention to be used by the licensee only with unpatented
materials furnished by the licensor, may not restrain as a contributory infringer one who sells to the licensee like materials for like use.

The grant to the inventor of the special privilege of a patent monopoly carries out a public policy adopted by the Constitution and
laws of the United States, "to promote the Progress of Science and
useful Arts, by securing for limited Times to . . . Inventors the
exclusive Right . . . ." to their "new and useful" inventions.
United States Constitution, Art. I, § 8, cl. 8; 35 U.S.C. § 31, 35 U.S.
C.A. § 31. But the public policy which includes inventions within the
granted monopoly excludes from it all that is not embraced in the
invention. It equally forbids the use of the patent to secure an exclusive right or limited monopoly not granted by the Patent Office and
which it is contrary to public policy to grant.

It is a principle of general application that courts, and especially
courts of equity, may appropriately withhold their aid where the
plaintiff is using the right asserted contrary to the public interest.
. . . Respondent argues that this doctrine is limited in its application to those cases where the patentee seeks to restrain contributory
infringement by the sale to licensees of competing unpatented article,
while here respondent seeks to restrain petitioner from a direct infringement, the manufacture and sale of the salt tablet depositor. It
is said that the equitable maxim that a party seeking the aid of a
court of equity must come into court with clean hands applies only to
the plaintiff's wrongful conduct in the particular act or transaction
which raises the equity, enforcement of which is sought; that where,
as here, the patentee seeks to restrain the manufacture or use of the
patented device, his conduct in using the patent to restrict competition in the sale of salt tablets does not foreclose him from seeking

relief limited to an injunction against the manufacture and sale of the infringing machine alone.

Undoubtedly "equity does not demand that its suitors shall have led blameless lives", Loughran v. Loughran, 292 U.S. 216, 229, 54 S.Ct. 684, 689, 78 L.Ed. 1219, but additional considerations must be taken into account where maintenance of the suit concerns the public interest as well as the private interests of suitors. Where the patent is used as a means of restraining competition with the patentee's sale of an unpatented product, the successful prosecution of an infringement suit even against one who is not a competitor in such sale is a powerful aid to the maintenance of the attempted monopoly of the unpatented article, and is thus a contributing factor in thwarting the public policy underlying the grant of the patent. Maintenance and enlargement of the attempted monopoly of the unpatented article are dependent to some extent upon persuading the public of the validity of the patent, which the infringement suit is intended to establish. Equity may rightly withhold its assistance from such a use of the patent by declining to entertain a suit for infringement, and should do so at least until it is made to appear that the improper practice has been abandoned and that the consequences of the misuse of the patent have been dissipated.[6]

The reasons for barring the prosecution of such a suit against one who is not a competitor with the patentee in the sale of the unpatented product are fundamentally the same as those which preclude an infringement suit against a licensee who has violated a condition of the license by using with the licensed machine a competing unpatented article, or against a vendee of a patented or copyrighted article for violation of a condition for the maintenance of resale prices [citations]. It is the adverse effect upon the public interest of a successful infringement suit in conjunction with the patentee's course of conduct which disqualifies him to maintain the suit, regardless of whether the particular defendant has suffered from the misuse of the patent. Similarly equity will deny relief for infringement of a trademark where the plaintiff is misrepresenting to the public the nature of his product either by the trademark itself or by his label. . . . The patentee, like these other holders of an exclusive privilege granted in the furtherance of a public policy, may not claim protection of his grant by the courts where it is being used to subvert that policy.

It is unnecessary to decide whether respondent has violated the Clayton Act, for we conclude that in any event the maintenance of the present suit to restrain petitioner's manufacture or sale of the alleged infringing machines is contrary to public policy and that the district court rightly dismissed the complaint for want of equity.

Reversed.

MR. JUSTICE ROBERTS took no part in the decision of this case.

---

6. For examples of the enforcement of patents following abandonment of illegal licensing practices, see Automatic Radio Mfg. Co. v. Hazeltine Research, Inc., 339 U.S. 827, 70 S.Ct. 894, 94 L.Ed. 1312 (1950); Westinghouse Electric Corp. v. Bulldog Electric Prod. Co., 179 F.2d 139 (4th Cir. 1950).

DAWSON CHEMICAL CO. v. ROHM & HAAS CO.

Supreme Court of the United States, 1980.
448 U.S. 176, 100 S.Ct. 2601, 65 L.Ed.2d 696.

[Digest: Propanil is a chemical herbicide used for killing weeds in rice crops. The Monsanto Company had originally obtained a patent on the chemical, but the patent was invalidated in litigation, after which Monsanto dedicated it to the public. Rohm & Haas then obtained a patent on a method for applying propanil so as to inhibit the growth of undesirable plants without killing established crops. Rohm & Haas manufactures and sells propanil, conveying to purchasers of its propanil an "implied license" to practice the patented method.

The Dawson Chemical Company began manufacturing and selling propanil for application to rice crops even before Rohm & Haas received its patent. Dawson markets the chemical in containers on which are printed directions for application in accordance with the method claimed in Rohm & Haas' patent. Rohm & Haas sued Dawson for contributory infringement arising out of the sale of the unpatented propanil along with directions for use. Dawson responded by requesting a license to practice the patented method. When Rohm & Haas refused, Dawson raised a defense of patent misuse and filed an antitrust counterclaim. The district court granted summary judgment to Dawson, holding that Rohm & Haas had misused its patent. The Court of Appeals reversed and the Supreme Court granted certiorari.

The Supreme Court's opinion began by reviewing prior decisions which attempted to deal with the tension between the doctrines of contributory infringement and patent misuse. The Court pointed out that the doctrine of contributory infringement was developed "to protect patent rights from subversion by those who, without directly infringing the patent themselves, engage in acts designed to facilitate infringement by others." The doctrine of patent misuse, on the other hand, was developed to prevent patentees from extending their lawful patent monopoly to unpatented products used in connection with a patented machine (e.g., unpatented movie film with a patented projector; unpatented dry ice with a patented design for a refrigeration package; unpatented salt tablets with a patented dispenser, see *Morton Salt*, supra). The two doctrines came into conflict because suits for contributory infringement often sought to enjoin the intentional sale of unpatented commodities to purchasers who would use them to practice the patent without paying royalties to the patentee; indeed, where the patent involved a process which would be performed by numerous consumers, the only effective way for a patentee to enforce its patent rights would be to stop the contributory infringer.

The leading case dealing with these two doctrines was Mercoid Corp. v. Mid-Continent Investment Co., 320 U.S. 661, 64 S.Ct. 268, 88 L.Ed. 376 (1944). That case involved a combination patent for a domestic heating system comprising a furnace stoker, a stoker switch, and a room thermostat, arranged so that the stoker switch would keep the fire from going out even when the room temperature was above the thermostat setting. Each element of the combination was unpatented. Minneapolis-Honeywell manufactured and sold unpatented stoker switches, and was licensed by the patentee to grant purchasers the right to use the combination patent. Mercoid, a competing manufacturer of switches, was sued for contributory infringement after it knowingly sold stoker switches specially adapted for use in the patented system to persons not licensed under the patent. The Supreme Court held that to allow a contributory infringement suit in such a case would be to extend the aid of a court of equity in expanding the patent beyond the legitimate scope of its monopoly. The Court held it to be irrelevant that the unpatented material or device "is itself an integral part of the structure embodying the patent" or could be characterized as "the heart of the invention." The Court rejected an argument that the necessities of the patentee justified suit for contributory infringement: "If a limited monopoly over the combustion stoker switch were allowed, it would not be a monopoly accorded inventive genius by the patent laws but a monopoly born of a commercial desire to avoid the rigors of competition fostered by the anti-trust laws." The Court concluded by stating that the result of its decision was to limit "substantially" the doctrine of contributory infringement: "What residuum may be left we need not stop to consider."

Following *Mercoid* "corrective legislation" was proposed in three successive Congresses. In 1952 Congress enacted 35 U.S. § 271 which provides:

"(c) Whoever sells a component of a patented machine, manufacture, combination or composition, or a material or apparatus for use in practicing a patented process, constituting a material part of the invention, knowing the same to be especially made or especially adapted for use in an infringement of such patent, and not a staple article or commodity of commerce suitable for substantial noninfringing use, shall be liable as a contributory infringer.

"(d) No patent owner otherwise entitled to relief for infringement or contributory infringement of a patent shall be denied relief or deemed guilty of misuse or illegal extension of the patent right by reason of his having done one or more of the following: (1) derived revenue from acts which if performed by another without his consent would constitute contributory infringement of the patent; (2) licensed or authorized another to perform acts which if performed without his consent would constitute contributory infringement of the patent; (3) sought to enforce his patent rights against infringement or contributory infringement."

Thus, the question presented was whether by virtue of § 271 Rohm & Haas could sue Dawson Chemical for contributory infringement without being barred by the patent misuse doctrine.]

MR. JUSTICE BLACKMUN delivered the opinion of the Court.

. . .

Section 271(c) identifies the basic dividing line between contributory infringement and patent misuse. It adopts a restrictive definition of contributory infringement that distinguishes between staple and nonstaple articles of commerce. It also defines the class of nonstaple items narrowly. In essence, this provision places materials like the dry ice of the *Carbice* case outside the scope of the contributory infringement doctrine. As a result, it is no longer necessary to resort to the doctrine of patent misuse in order to deny patentees control over staple goods used in their inventions.

The limitations on contributory infringement written into § 271(c) are counterbalanced by limitations on patent misuse in § 271(d). Three species of conduct by patentees are expressly excluded from characterization as misuse. First, the patentee may "deriv[e] revenue" from acts that "would constitute contributory infringement" if "performed by another without his consent." This provision clearly signifies that a patentee may make and sell nonstaple goods used in connection with his invention. Second, the patentee may "licens[e] or authoriz[e] another to perform acts" which without such authorization would constitute contributory infringement. This provision's use in the disjunctive of the term "authoriz[e]" suggests that more than explicit licensing agreements is contemplated. Finally, the patentee may "enforce his patent rights against . . . contributory infringement." This provision plainly means that the patentee may bring suit without fear that his doing so will be regarded as an unlawful attempt to suppress competition. The statute explicitly states that a patentee may do "one or more" of these permitted acts, and it does not state that he must do any of them.

In our view, the provisions of § 271(d) effectively confer upon the patentee, as a lawful adjunct of his patent rights, a limited power to exclude others from competition in nonstaple goods. A patentee may sell a nonstaple article himself while enjoining others from marketing that same good without his authorization. By doing so, he is able to eliminate competitors and thereby to control the market for that product. Moreover, his power to demand royalties from others for the privilege of selling the nonstaple item itself implies that the patentee may control the market for the nonstaple good; otherwise, his "right" to sell licenses for the marketing of the nonstaple good would be meaningless, since no one would be willing to pay him for a superfluous authorization.

Rohm & Haas' conduct is not dissimilar in either nature or effect from the conduct that is thus clearly embraced within § 271(d). It sells propanil; it authorizes others to use propanil; and it sues contributory infringers. These are all protected activities. Rohm & Haas does *not* license others to sell propanil, but nothing on the face of the statute requires it to do so. To be sure, the sum effect of Rohm & Haas' actions is to suppress competition in the market for an unpatented commodity. But as we have observed, in this its conduct is no different from that which the statute expressly protects.

The one aspect of Rohm & Haas' behavior that is not expressly covered by § 271(d) is its linkage of two protected activities—sale of propanil and authorization to practice the patented process—together in a single transaction. Petitioners vigorously argue that this linkage, which they characterize pejoratively as "tying," supplies the otherwise missing element of misuse. They fail, however, to identify any way in which this "tying" of two expressly protected activities results in any extension of control over unpatented materials beyond what § 271(d) already allows. Nevertheless, the language of § 271(d) does not explicitly resolve the question when linkage of this variety becomes patent misuse. In order to judge whether this method of exploiting the patent lies within or without the protection afforded by § 271(d), we must turn to the legislative history.

[After noting that § 271 was a part of a general recodification of the patent laws in 1952, that the 1952 Act was approved with "virtually no floor debate," and that the committee reports accompanying the Act also gave "relatively cursory attention to its features," the Court then went on to examine three sets of hearings on legislative proposals that led up to the final enactment. The Court concluded:] It is the consistent theme of the legislative history that the statute was designed to accomplish a good deal more than mere clarification. It significantly changed existing law, and the change moved in the direction of expanding the statutory protection enjoyed by patentees. The responsible congressional committees were told again and again that contributory infringement would wither away if the misuse rationale of the *Mercoid* decisions remained as a barrier to enforcement of the patentee's rights. They were told that this was an undesirable result that would deprive many patent holders of effective protection for their patent rights. They were told that Congress could strike a sensible compromise between the competing doctrines of contributory infringement and patent misuse if it eliminated the result of the *Mercoid* decisions yet preserved the result in *Carbice*. And they were told that the proposed legislation would achieve this effect by restricting contributory infringement to the sphere of nonstaple goods while exempting the control of such goods from the scope of patent misuse. These signals cannot be ignored. They fully support the conclusion that, by enacting §§ 271(c) and (d), Congress granted to patent holders a statutory right to control nonstaple goods that are capable only of infringing use in a patented invention, and that are essential to that invention's advance over prior art.

We find nothing in this legislative history to support the assertion that respondent's behavior falls outside the scope of § 271(d). To the contrary, respondent has done nothing that would extend its right of control over unpatented goods beyond the line that Congress drew. Respondent, to be sure, has licensed use of its patented process only in connection with purchases of propanil. But propanil is a *nonstaple* product, and its herbicidal property is the heart of respondent's invention. Respondent's method of doing business is thus essentially the same as the method condemned in the *Mercoid* decisions, and the legislative history reveals that § 271(d) was designed to retreat from *Mercoid* in this regard.

There is one factual difference between this case and *Mercoid*: the licensee in the *Mercoid* cases had offered a sublicense to the alleged contributory infringer, which offer had been refused. Seizing upon this difference, petitioners argue that respondent's unwillingness to offer similar licenses to its would-be competitors in the manufacture of propanil legally distinguishes this case and sets it outside § 271(d). To this argument there are at least three responses. First as we have noted, § 271(d) permits such licensing, but does not require it. Accordingly, petitioners' suggestion would import into the statute a requirement that simply is not there. Second, petitioners have failed to adduce any evidence from the legislative history that the offering of a license to the alleged contributory infringer was a critical factor in inducing Congress to retreat from the result of the *Mercoid* decisions. . . . Third, petitioners' argument runs contrary to the long-settled view that the essence of a patent grant is the right to exclude others from profiting by the patented invention. . . . If petitioners' argument were accepted, it would force patentees either to grant licenses or to forfeit their statutory protection against contributory infringement. Compulsory licensing is a rarity in our patent system,[7] and we decline to manufacture such a requirement out of § 271(d).

. . .

Since our present task is one of statutory construction, questions of public policy cannot be determinative of the outcome unless specific policy choices fairly can be attributed to Congress itself. In this instance, as we have already stated, Congress chose a compromise between competing policy interests. The policy of free competition runs deep in our law. It underlies both the doctrine of patent misuse and the general principle that the boundary of a patent monopoly is to be limited by the literal scope of the patent claims. But the policy of stimulating invention that underlies the entire patent system runs no less deep. And the doctrine of contributory infringement, which has been called "an expression both of law and morals," *Mercoid I*, 320 U.S., at 677, 64 S.Ct., at 277 (Frankfurter, J., dissenting), can be of crucial importance in ensuring that the endeavors and investments of the inventor do not go unrewarded.

It is perhaps noteworthy that holders of "new use" patents on chemical processes were among those designated to Congress as intended beneficiaries of the protection against contributory infringement that § 271 was designed to restore. See 1948 Hearings, at 4, 5, 18. We have been informed that the characteristics of practical

7. [Court's footnote 21.] Compulsory licensing of patents often has been proposed, but it has never been enacted on a broad scale. Although compulsory licensing provisions were considered for possible incorporation into the 1952 revision of the patent laws, they were dropped before the final bill was circulated.

chemical research are such that this form of patent protection is particularly important to inventors in that field. The number of chemicals either known to scientists or disclosed by existing research is
vast. It grows constantly, as those engaging in "pure" research publish their discoveries. The number of these chemicals that have
known uses of commercial or social value, in contrast, is small. Development of new uses for existing chemicals is thus a major component of practical chemical research. It is extraordinarily expensive.[8]
It may take years of unsuccessful testing before a chemical having a
desired property is identified, and it may take several years of further testing before a proper and safe method for using that chemical
is developed.

Under the construction of § 271(d) that petitioners advance, the
rewards available to those willing to undergo the time, expense, and
interim frustration of such practical research would provide at best a
dubious incentive. Others could await the results of the testing and
then jump on the profit bandwagon by demanding licenses to sell the
unpatented, nonstaple chemical used in the newly developed process.
Refusal to accede to such a demand, if accompanied by any attempt
to profit from the invention through sale of the unpatented chemical,
would risk forfeiture of any patent protection whatsoever on a finding of patent misuse. As a result, noninventors would be almost assured of an opportunity to share in the spoils, even though they had
contributed nothing to the discovery. The incentive to await the discoveries of others might well prove sweeter than the incentive to take
the initiative oneself.

Whether such a regime would prove workable, as petitioners urge,
or would lead to dire consequences, as respondent and several *amici*
insist, we need not predict. Nor do we need to determine whether
the principles of free competition could justify such a result. Congress' enactment of § 271(d) resolved these issues in favor of a
broader scope of patent protection. In accord with our understanding of that statute, we hold that Rohm & Haas has not engaged in
patent misuse, either by its method of selling propanil, or by its refusal to license others to sell that commodity. The judgment of the
Court of Appeals is therefore affirmed.

It is so ordered.

MR. JUSTICE WHITE, with whom MR. JUSTICE BRENNAN, MR. JUS-
TICE MARSHALL, and MR. JUSTICE STEVENS join, dissenting.

For decades this Court has denied relief from contributory infringement to patent holders who attempt to extend their patent monopolies to unpatented materials used in connection with patented inventions. The Court now refuses to apply this "patent misuse"
principle in the very area in which such attempts to restrain competition are most likely to be successful. The Court holds exempt from
the patent misuse doctrine a patent holder's refusal to license others

---

8. [Court's footnote 24.] For exam-
ple, the average cost of developing one   new pharmaceutical drug has been estimated to run as high as $54 million.

to use a patented process unless they purchase from him an unpatented product that has no substantial use except in the patented process. The Court's sole justification for this radical departure from our prior construction of the patent laws is its interpretation of 35 U.S.C. § 271, a provision that created exceptions to the misuse doctrine and that we have held must be strictly construed "in light of this nation's historical antipathy to monopoly" . . .

. . .

The plain language of § 271(d) indicates that respondent's conduct is not immunized from application of the patent misuse doctrine. The statute merely states that respondent may (1) derive revenue from sales of unpatented propanil, (2) license others to sell propanil, and (3) sue unauthorized sellers of propanil. While none of these acts can be deemed patent misuse if respondent is "otherwise entitled to relief," the statute does not state that respondent may exclude all competitors from the propanil market by refusing to license all those who do not purchase propanil from it. This is the very conduct that constitutes patent misuse under the traditional doctrine; thus the fact that respondent may have engaged in one or more of the acts enumerated in § 271(d) does not preclude its conduct from being deemed patent misuse.

. . .

The Court acknowledges that respondent refused to license others to sell propanil, but it observes that "nothing on the face of the statute requires it to do so." As much could be conceded but it would not follow that respondent is absolved from a finding of patent misuse. Section 271(d) does not define conduct that constitutes patent misuse; rather it simply outlines certain conduct that is not patent misuse. Because the terms of the statute are terms of exception, the absence of any express mention of a licensing requirement does not indicate that respondent's refusal to license others is protected by § 271(d). This much seems elementary.

. . .

. . . In *Mercoid*, as the patentee in that case emphasized in its brief here, the defendant-infringer had repeatedly refused licenses, but the Court nevertheless held that the misuse defense barred relief. To this extent, § 271 overturned *Mercoid* and intended to arm the patentee with the power to sue unlicensed contributory infringers selling nonstaple components used in connection with the patented process. . . .

The Court offers reasons of policy for its obvious extension of patent monopoly, but whether to stimulate research and development in the chemical field it is necessary to give patentees monopoly control over articles not covered by their patents is a question for Congress to decide, and I would wait for that body to speak more clearly than it has.

Accordingly, I respectfully dissent.

[The separate dissenting opinion of Justice Stevens is omitted.]

NOTES AND QUERIES

(1) *Queries.* Is *Morton Salt* still good law after *Dawson Chemical*? Would the answer turn on whether the specially configured salt tablets were considered "non-staples"? Justice Stevens wrote in a separate dissent in *Dawson Chemical*: "[I]t appears that the Court's decision would allow a manufacturer to condition a long-term lease of a patented piece of equipment on the lessee's agreement to purchase tailormade—i.e., nonstaple—supplies or components for use with the equipment exclusively from the patentee." [9] Is the answer to Justice Stevens that such a conditioned lease would still be a "misuse" because the sale of the salt tablets would not constitute contributory infringement under § 271(c) (unless the manufacturer had a patent on the process of using the tablets with the machine)?

Why did the patentees in *Morton Salt* and *Dawson Chemical* need to tie the unpatented products to the patent license? Are their economic problems quite different? Recall *Fortner II*, supra, p. 716, and the price discrimination problem. As for *Dawson Chemical*, is the problem inherent in the nature of the process patent (or, as in *Mercoid*, the combination patent). Justice Jackson, concurring in *Mercoid*, wrote:

> "A patent," said Mr. Justice Holmes, "is property carried to the highest degree of abstraction—a right in rem to exclude, without a physical object or content." Here the patent covers a combination—a system—a sequence—which is said to be new, although every element and factor in it is old and unpatentable. Thus we have an abstract right in an abstruse relationship between things in which individually there is no right—a legal concept which either is very profound or almost unintelligible, I cannot be quite sure which.
>
> . . .
>
> Of course the abstract right to the "sequence" has little economic importance unless its monopoly comprehends not only the arrangement but some, at least, of its components. If the patentee may not exclude competitors from making and vending strategic unpatented elements such as the thermostat, adapted to use in the combination, the patented system is so vulnerable to competition as to be almost worthless. On the other hand, if he may prohibit such competition, his system patent gathers up into its monopoly devices long known to the art and hence not themselves subject to any patent.

Have the policy considerations which favor patent protection over competition tipped the balance in *Dawson Chemical*? Compare the Court's result in *Dawson Chemical* to its decisions in other recent patent cases (*Chakrabarty*, supra p. 950; *Diehr*, supra p. 957). Has the Supreme Court reversed its historical stance with regard to the supremacy of antitrust principles over patent protection?

(2) *Grant-Backs.* Transwrap owned a patent on a machine that made transparent packages and filled them with candy. In 1937 it sold the machinery business to Stokes with an exclusive license to manufacture and sell the Transwrap machine, under patents owned by Transwrap or which it might acquire. The term of the agreement was ten years with an option to renew for five year periods during the life of any of the patents covered by the agreement. The agreement contained a formula for royalties. Stokes

---

9. 448 U.S., at 241, 100 S.Ct., at 2636, 65 L.Ed.2d, at 740.

covenanted to assign to Transwrap any improvement patents which it might acquire that were applicable to the Transwrap machine. Such improvement patents were included in the license agreement without payment of additional royalty. Transwrap sought to compel Stokes to assign improvement patents. Was the grant-back provision an unlawful attempt to extend Transwrap's patent monopoly to inventions not yet conceived? Would the obligation to assign improvement patents impair Stokes' incentive to research and invent?

In *Transparent-Wrap Machine Corp. v. Stokes & Smith Co.*, 329 U.S. 637, 67 S.Ct. 610, 91 L.Ed. 563 (1947), the Supreme Court (per Justice Douglas) held the grant-back provision "not per se illegal and unenforceable." Stressing that a patent is a "species of property" and that Congress has not made illegal the acquisition of improvement patents by the owner of a basic patent, the Court concluded that it made no difference whether the patentee "uses a license to obtain improvement patents or uses the wealth which he accumulates by exploiting his basic patent for that purpose."

(3) *Abuses of the Process—Fraud on the Patent Office.* Fraud on the patent office may result in nonenforcement of the patent in a suit against an infringer, on the ground of "unclean hands."[10] Such conduct may also open the patentee to treble damage suits under the antitrust laws for monopolizing the patented subject matter; i.e., the conduct eliminates the patent grant as a defense to a charge under Section 2 of the Sherman Act. But in *Walker Process Equipment, Inc. v. Food Machinery & Chemical Corp.*[11] the Supreme Court rejected as premature a contention that the assertion of an illegal patent "monopoly" should be treated as a *per se* violation of Section 2. The case was remanded for an appraisal of "the exclusionary power of the illegal patent claim in terms of the relevant market . . . It may be that the [patented] device . . . does not comprise a relevant market."[12]

Cf. *Charles Pfizer & Co. v. Federal Trade Commission,*[13] reviewing an FTC proceeding under Section 5 of the Federal Trade Commission Act in which the FTC found that the tetracycline patent had been issued on the basis of misrepresentations (possibly innocent) to the Patent Office and deliberate withholding of information that tetracycline was an incidental by-product of the production of earlier antibiotics. Without holding the patent invalid, the Commission ordered that it be generally licensed at reasonable royalty. The Court of Appeals sustained the order:

> The Patent Office, not having testing facilities of its own, must rely upon information furnished by applicants and their attorneys. Pfizer and Cy-

---

10. See Precision Instrument Manufacturing Co. v. Automotive Maintenance Machinery Co., 324 U.S. 806, 65 S.Ct. 993, 89 L.Ed. 1381 (1945).

11. 382 U.S. 172, 86 S.Ct. 347, 15 L.Ed.2d 247 (1965). For cases asserting fraud on the copyright office as grounds for a Section 2 claim, compare Wondura Products, Inc. v. Dart Industries, 1981-1 Trade Cas. ¶ 64,015 (N.D.Miss.1981) (rejecting analogy to Walker Process in copyright cases) with Vogue Ring Creations v. Hardman, 410 F.Supp. 609 (D.R.I.1976) (accepting analogy to Walker Process, but fraud on copyright office not proved). See Goldberg & Dannay, Fraud On The Copyright Office: Its Use And Misuse As A Defense In Copyright Infringement Actions, 44 N.Y.U.L.Rev. 540 (1969).

12. Compare Kearney & Trecker Corp. v. Cincinnati Milacron, Inc., 562 F.2d 365 (6th Cir. 1977) ("indefensible" conflict of interest on part of former patent office examiner leads to unenforceability and is grounds for Section 2 claim under Walker Process) with E. I. du Pont de Nemours & Co. v. Berkley & Co., Inc., 620 F.2d 1247 (8th Cir. 1980) ("inequitable conduct" which does not cause issuance of patent is insufficient for Section 2 claim under Walker Process).

13. 401 F.2d 574 (6th Cir. 1968), certiorari denied 394 U.S. 920, 89 S.Ct. 1195, 22 L.Ed.2d 453 (1969).

animid, like all other applicants, stood before the Patent Office in a confidential relationship and owed the obligation of frank and truthful disclosure.

ZENITH RADIO CORP. v. HAZELTINE RESEARCH, INC.

Supreme Court of the United States, 1969.
395 U.S. 100, 89 S.Ct. 1562, 23 L.Ed.2d 129.

MR. JUSTICE WHITE delivered the opinion of the Court.

Petitioner Zenith Radio Corporation (Zenith) is a Delaware Corporation which for many years has been successfully engaged in the business of manufacturing radio and television sets for sale in the United States and foreign countries. A necessary incident of Zenith's operations has been the acquisition of . . . licensing agreements with respondent Hazeltine Research, Inc. (HRI), an Illinois corporation which owns and licenses domestic patents, principally in the radio and television fields. . . .

Until 1959, Zenith had obtained the right to use all HRI domestic patents under HRI's so-called standard package license. In that year, however, with the expiration of Zenith's license imminent, Zenith declined to accept HRI's offer to renew, asserting that it no longer required a license from HRI. Negotiations proceeded to a stalemate, and in November 1959, HRI brought suit in the Northern District of Illinois, claiming that Zenith television sets infringed HRI's patents on a particular automatic control system. Zenith's answer alleged invalidity of the patent asserted and noninfringement, and further alleged that HRI's claim was unenforceable because of patent misuse as well as unclean hands through conspiracy with foreign patent pools. On May 22, 1963, more than three years after its answer had been filed, Zenith filed a counterclaim against HRI for treble damages and injunctive relief, alleging violations of the Sherman Act by misuse of HRI patents, including the one in suit, as well as by conspiracy among HRI, Hazeltine,* and patent pools in Canada, England, and Australia. Zenith contended that these three patent pools had refused to license the patents placed within their exlusive licensing authority, including Hazeltine patents to Zenith and others seeking to export American-made radios and televisions into those foreign markets.

The District Court, sitting without a jury, ruled for Zenith in the infringement action, 239 F.Supp., at 68–69, and its judgment in that respect, which was affirmed by the Court of Appeals, 388 F.2d at 30–33, is not in issue here. On the counterclaim, the District Court ruled, first, that HRI had misused its domestic patents by attempting to coerce Zenith's acceptance of a five-year package license, and by insisting on extracting royalties from unpatented products. Judgment was entered in Zenith's favor for treble the amount of its actual damages of approximately $50,000, and injunctive relief against fur-

---

* [Hazeltine, the parent corporation of HRI, had among its assets the foreign counterparts of HRI's U.S. patents, which it licensed for use in foreign countries.—Ed.]

ther patent misuse was awarded. Second, HRI and Hazeltine were found to have conspired with the foreign patent pools to exclude Zenith from the Canadian, English, and Australian markets. Hazeltine had granted the pools the exclusive right to license Hazeltine patents in their respective countries and had shared in the pools' profits, knowing that each pool refused to license its patents for importation and that each enforced its ban on imports with threats of infringement suits. HRI, along with its coconspirator, Hazeltine, was therefore held to have conspired with the pools to restrain the trade or commerce of the United States, in violation of § 1 of the Sherman Act, 15 U.S.C. § 1, and was liable for injury caused Zenith's foreign business by the operation of the pools. Total damages with respect to the three markets, when trebled, amounted to nearly $35,000,000.

. . .

Since the District Court's treble damage award for patent misuse was affirmed by the Court of Appeals, and HRI has not challenged that award in this Court, the only misuse issue we need consider at length is whether the Court of Appeals was correct in striking the last clause from Paragraph A of the injunction, which enjoined HRI from

> "A. Conditioning directly or indirectly the grant of a license to defendant-counterclaimant, Zenith Radio Corporation, or any of its subsidiaries under any domestic patent upon the taking of a license under any other patent *or upon the paying of royalties on the manufacture, use or sale of apparatus not covered by such patent.*" (Emphasis added.)

This paragraph of the injunction was directed at HRI's policy of insisting upon acceptance of its standard five-year package license agreement, covering the 500-odd patents within its domestic licensing portfolio and reserving royalties on the licensee's total radio and television sales, irrespective of whether the licensed patents were actually used in the products manufactured.

In striking the last clause of Paragraph A the Court of Appeals, in effect, made two determinations. First, under its view of Automatic Radio Mfg. Co. v. Hazeltine Research, Inc., 339 U.S. 827, 70 S.Ct. 894, 94 L.Ed. 1312 (1950), conditioning the grant of a patent license upon payment of royalties on unpatented products was not misuse of the patent. Second, since such conduct did not constitute patent misuse, neither could it be violative of the antitrust laws within the meaning of § 16 of the Clayton Act, under which Zenith had sought and the District Court had granted the injunction. With respect to the first determination, we reverse the Court of Appeals. We hold that conditioning the grant of a patent license upon payment of royalties on products which do not use the teaching of the patent does amount to patent misuse.

The trial court's injunction does not purport to prevent the parties from serving their mutual convenience by basing royalties on the sale of all radios and television sets, irrespective of the use of HRI's inventions. The injunction reaches only situations where the patentee directly or indirectly "conditions" his license upon the payment of royalties on unpatented products—that is, where the patentee refuses to license on any other basis and leaves the licensee with the choice between a license so providing and no license at all. Also, the injunction takes effect only if the license is conditioned upon the payment of royalties "on" merchandise not covered by the patent—where the express provisions of the license or their necessary effect is to employ the patent monopoly to collect royalties not for the use of the licensed invention, but for using, making, or selling an article not within the reach of the patent. . . .

Among other restrictions upon him, he may not condition the right to use his patent on the licensee's agreement to purchase, use, or sell, or not to purchase, use, or sell, another article of commerce not within the scope of his patent monopoly. His right to set the price for a license does not extend so far, whatever privilege he has "to exact royalties as high as he can negotiate." Brulotte v. Thys Co., 379 U.S. 29, 33, 85 S.Ct. 176, 179, 13 L.Ed.2d 99 (1964). And just as the patent's leverage may not be used to extract from the licensee a commitment to purchase, use, or sell other products according to the desires of the patentee, neither can that leverage be used to garner as royalties a percentage share of the licensee's receipts from sales of other products; in either case, the patentee seeks to extend the monopoly of his patent to derive a benefit not attributable to use of the patent's teachings.

In Brulotte v. Thys Co., supra, the patentee licensed the use of a patented machine, the license providing for the payment of a royalty for using the invention after, as well as before, the expiration date of the patent. Recognizing that the patentee could lawfully charge a royalty for practicing a patented invention prior to its expiration date and that the payment of this royalty could be postponed beyond that time, we noted that the post-expiration royalties were not for prior use but for current use, and were nothing less than an effort by the patentee to extend the term of his monopoly beyond that granted by law. *Brulotte* thus articulated in a particularized context the principle that a patentee may not use the power of his patent to levy a charge for making, using, or selling products not within the reach of the monopoly granted by the Government.

Automatic Radio is not to the contrary; it is not authority for the proposition that patentees have *carte blanche* authority to condition the grant of patent licenses upon the payment of royalties on unpatented articles. In that case, Automatic Radio acquired the privilege of using all present and future HRI patents by promising to pay a percentage royalty based on the selling price of its radio receivers, with a minimum royalty of $10,000 per year. HRI sued for the minimum royalty and other sums. Automatic Radio asserted patent misuse in that the agreement extracted royalties whether or not any of the patents were in any way used in Automatic Radio receivers. The District Court and the Court of Appeals approved the agreement as a convenient method designed by the parties to avoid determining

whether each radio receiver embodied an HRI patent. The percentage royalty was deemed an acceptable alternative to a lump sum payment for the privilege to use the patents. This Court affirmed.
. . . .

Nothing in the foregoing is inconsistent with the District Court's injunction against conditioning a license upon the payment of royalties on unpatented products or with the principle that patent leverge may not be employed to collect royalties for producing merchandise not employing the patented invention. The Court's opinion in *Automatic Radio* did not deal with the license negotiations which spawned the royalty formula at issue and did not indicate that HRI used its patent leverage to coerce a promise to pay royalties on radios not practicing the learning of the patent. No such inference follows from a mere license provision measuring royalties by the licensee's total sales even if, as things work out, only some or none of the merchandise employs the patented idea or process, or even if it was foreseeable that some undetermined portion would not contain the invention. It could easily be, as the Court indicated in *Automatic Radio*, that the licensee as well as the patentee would find it more convenient and efficient from several standpoints to base royalties on total sales than to face the burden of figuring royalties based on actual use. If convenience of the parties rather than patent power dictates the total-sales royalty provision, there are no misuse of the patents and no forbidden conditions attached to the license.

The Court also said in *Automatic Radio* that if the licensee bargains for the privilege of using the patent in all of his products and agrees to a lump sum or a percentage-of-total-sales royalty, he cannot escape payment on this basis by demonstrating that he is no longer using the invention disclosed by the patent. We neither disagree nor think such transactions are barred by the trial court's injunction. If the licensee negotiates for "the privilege to use any or all of the patents and developments as [he] desire[s] to use them," 339 U.S., at 834, 70 S.Ct., at 898, he cannot complain that he must pay royalties if he chooses to use none of them. He could not then charge that the patentee had refused to license except on the basis of a total-sales royalty.

But we do not read *Automatic Radio* to authorize the patentee to use the power of his patent to insist on a total-sales royalty and to override protestations of the licensee that some of his products are unsuited to the patent or that for some lines of his merchandise he has no need or desire to purchase the privileges of the patent. In such event, not only would royalties be collected on unpatented merchandise, but the obligation to pay for nonuse would clearly have its source in the leverage of the patent.

We also think patent misuse inheres in a patentee's insistence on a percentage-of-sales royalty, regardless of use, and his rejection of licensee proposals to pay only for actual use. Unquestionably, a licensee must pay if he uses the patent. Equally, however, he may insist upon paying only for use, and not on the basis of total sales, including products in which he may use a competing patent or in which no patented ideas are used at all. There is nothing in the right granted the patentee to keep others from using, selling, or manufacturing his invention which empowers him to insist on payment not only for use but for producing products which do not employ his discoveries at all.

Of course, a licensee cannot expect to obtain a license, giving him the privilege of use and insurance against infringement suits, without at least footing the patentee's expenses in dealing with him. He cannot insist upon paying on use alone and perhaps, as things turn out, pay absolutely nothing because he finds he can produce without using the patent. If the risks of infringement are real and he would avoid them, he must anticipate some minimum charge for the license—enough to insure the patentee against loss in negotiating and administering his monopoly, even if in fact the patent is not used at all. But we discern no basis in the statutory monopoly granted the patentee for his using that monopoly to coerce an agreement to pay a percentage royalty on merchandise not employing the discovery which the claims of the patent define.

. . .

MR. JUSTICE HARLAN, concurring in part and dissenting in part.

I concur in Parts I and II of the Court's opinion. However, I do not join Part III, in which the Court holds that a patent license provision which measures royalties by a percentage of the licensee's total sales is lawful if included for the "convenience" of both parties but unlawful if "insisted upon" by the patentee.

My first difficulty with this part of the opinion is that its test for validity of such royalty provisions is likely to prove exceedingly difficult to apply and consequently is apt to engender uncertainty in this area of business dealing, where certainty in the law is particularly desirable. In practice, it often will be very hard to tell whether a license provision was included at the instance of both parties or only at the will of the licensor. District courts will have the unenviable task of deciding whether the course of negotiations establishes "insistence" upon the suspect provision. Because of the uncertainty inherent in such determinations, parties to existing and future licenses will have little assurance that their agreements will be enforced. And it may be predicted that after today's decision the licensor will be careful to embellish the negotiations with an alternative proposal, making the court's unravelling of the situation that much more difficult.

Such considerations lead me to the view that any rule which causes the validity of percentage-of-sales royalty provisions to depend upon subsequent judicial examination of the parties' negotiations will disserve rather than further the interests of all concerned. Hence, I think that the Court has fallen short in failing to address itself to the question whether employment of such royalty provisions should invariably amount to patent misuse.

My second difficulty with this part of the Court's opinion is that in reality it overrules an aspect of a prior decision in this Court, Automatic Radio Co. v. Hazeltine Research, Inc., 339 U.S. 827, 70 S.Ct. 894, 94 L.Ed. 1312 (1950), without offering more than a shadow of a reason in law or economics for departing from that earlier ruling. Despite the Court's efforts to distinguish *Automatic Radio*, it cannot be denied that the Court there sustained a Hazeltine patent license of precisely the same tenor as the one involved here, on the ground that "[t]his royalty provision does not create another monopoly; it creates no restraint of competition beyond the legitimate grant of the patent." 339 U.S., at 833, 70 S.Ct., at 897.

In finding significance for present purposes in some of the qualifying language in *Automatic Radio*, I believe that the Court today has misconstrued that opinion. A reading of the opinion as a whole satisfies me that the *Automatic Radio* Court did not consider it relevant whether Hazeltine Research had "insisted" upon inclusion of the disputed provision, and that in emphasizing that the royalty terms had no "inherent" tendency to extend the patent monopoly and were not a *"per se"* misuse of patents, the Court was simply endeavoring to distinguish prior decisions in which patent misuse was found when the patent monopoly had been employed to "create *another* monopoly or restraint of competition". 339 U.S., at 832, 70 S.Ct., at 897 (Emphasis added.) Until now no subsequent decision has in any way impaired this aspect of *Automatic Radio*.

Since the Court's decision finds little if any support in the prior case law, one would expect from the Court an exposition of economic reasons for doing away with the *Automatic Radio* doctrine. However, the nearest thing to an economic rationale is the Court's declaration that:

"just as the patent's leverage may not be used to extract from the licensee a commitment to purchase, use, or sell other products according to the desires of the patentee, neither can that leverage be used to garner as royalties a percentage share of the licensee's receipts from sales of other products; in either case, the patentee seeks to extend the monopoly of his patent to derive a benefit not attributable to use of the patent's teachings."

The Court then finds in the patentee a heretofore nonexistent right to "insist upon paying only for use and not on the basis of total sales . . . ."

What the Court does not undertake to explain is *how* insistence upon a percentage-of-sales royalty enables a patentee to obtain an economic "benefit not attributable to the use of the patent's teachings," thereby involving himself in patent misuse. For it must be remembered that all the patentee has to license is the right to use his patent. It is solely for that right that a percentage-of-sales royalty is paid, and it is not apparent from the Court's opinion why this method of determining the *amount* of the royalty should be any less permissible than the other alternatives, whether or not it is "insisted" upon by the patentee.

One possible explanation for the Court's result, which seems especially likely in view of the Court's exception for cases where the provision was included for the "convenience" of both parties, is a desire to protect licensees against overreaching. But the Court does not cite, and the parties have not presented, any evidence that licensees as a class need such protection. Moreover, the Court does not explain why a royalty based simply upon use could not be equally overreaching.

Another possible justification for the Court's result might be that a royalty based directly upon use of the patent will tend to spur the licensee to "invent around" the patent or otherwise acquire a substitute which costs less, while a percentage-of-sales royalty can have no such effect because of the licensee's knowledge that he must pay the royalty regardless of actual patent use. No hint of such a rationale appears in the Court's opinion. Moreover, under this theory a percentage-of-sales royalty would be objectionable largely because of resulting damage to the rest of the economy, through less efficient allocation of resources, rather than because of possible harm to the licensee. Hence, the theory might not admit of the Court's exception for provisions included for the "convenience" of both parties.

Because of its failure to explain the reasons for the result reached in Part III, the Court's opinion is of little assistance in answering the question which I consider to be the crux of this part of the case: whether percentage-of-sales royalty provisions should be held without exception to constitute patent misuse. A recent economic analysis [14] argues that such provisions may have two undesirable consequences. First, as has already been noted, employment of such provisions may tend to reduce the licensee's incentive to substitute other, cheaper "inputs" for the patented item in producing an unpatented end-product. Failure of the licensee to substitute will, it is said, cause the price of the end-product to be higher and its output lower than would be the case if substitution had occurred. Second, it is suggested that under certain conditions a percentage-of-sales royalty arrangement may enable the patentee to garner for himself elements of profit, above the norm for the industry or economy, which are properly attributable not to the licensee's use of the patent but to other factors which cause the licensee's situation to differ from one of "perfect competition," and that this cannot occur when royalties are based upon use.

If accepted, this economic analysis would indicate that percentage-of-sales royalties should be entirely outlawed. However, so far as I have been able to find, there has as yet been little discussion of these matters either by lawyers or by economists. And I find scant illumination on this score in the briefs and arguments of the parties in this case. The Court has pointed out both today and in *Automatic Radio* that percentage-of-sales royalties may be administratively advantageous for both patentee and licensee. In these circumstances, confronted, as I believe we are, with the choice of holding such royalty provisions either valid or invalid across the board, I would, as an indi-

14. [Footnote number 5 in original] Baxter, Legal Restrictions on Exploita- tion of the Patent Monopoly: An Economic Analysis, 76 Yale L.J. 267 (1966).

vidual member of the Court, adhere for the present to the rule of
Automatic Radio.

NOTES AND QUERIES

(1) *Nondiminishing Royalty After Expiration of Some Patents in
Package.* See *Rocform Corp. v. Acitelli-Standard Concrete Wall, Inc.*, 367
F.2d 678 (6th Cir. 1966):

> The dissent also contends that a flat price for use of a number of pat-
> ents is permissible practice up to the termination date of "the last neces-
> sary patent." We believe this is too broad a contention. We do not deal
> here (as did the Supreme Court in Brulotte v. Thys Co.) with the sale of a
> piece of machinery which incorporated a number of patents. Rather we
> deal with a licensing arrangement where one important patent (about to
> expire) is grouped with others of longer duration for "leverage." Cf.
> American Security Co. v. Shatterproof Glass Corp. We believe such a
> contract, when it contains no diminution of license fee at the expiration of
> the most important patent and contains no termination clause at the will
> of the licensee, constitutes, in effect, an effort to continue to collect royal-
> ties on an expired patent.[15]

(2) *Discriminatory Royalty Rates.* A patentee is ordinarily free to
charge whatever royalty he pleases, and to set different royalty rates for
different licensees. Compare *Bela Seating Co. v. Poloron Product Co.*, 438
F.2d 733 (7th Cir. 1971) (patentee refused to license except at rate higher
than that paid by defendant's competitors; held: no abuse—patentee's desire
to get a higher return than on licenses previously granted under other circumstances, with no showing of intent to impair competition among licensees, is "valid reason" not "invidious discrimination") with *LaPeyre v. Federal Trade Commission*, 366 F.2d 117 (5th Cir. 1966) (rental rates on patented
shrimp peeling machines may not be set higher for Northwest canners than
for Gulf Coast canners; fact that savings in labor costs for Northwest canners was much greater, because their smaller shrimp were harder to peel by
hand, and desire of patentees to charge what traffic would bear unavailing
against "inately anticompetitive" effect on interregional competition among
shrimp canners).

Royalty rate discrimination in favor of licensees who purchase goods
from the patentee constitutes an abuse akin to the tying involved in the *Morton Salt* case.[16]

(3) *Coercive Bargaining as an Attempt to Monopolize.* In *W. L. Gore
& Associates, Inc. v. Carlisle Corp.*, 381 F.Supp. 680 (D.Del.1974), the district court held that Gore, the patentee, had overstepped the bounds of permissible bargaining when, in the negotiations with Carlisle over a license and
settlement of infringement suits, Gore threatened to cease purchasing from
a Carlisle subsidiary. Gore's behavior was held to be abuse of patent and a

15. Cf. McCullough Tool Co. v. Wells
Surveys, Inc., 343 F.2d 381, 409 (10th Cir.
1965) (no abuse in licensing a group of
patents at a flat rate which continued unchanged after expiration of some of the
patents).

16. See National Foam System, Inc. v.
Urquhart, 202 F.2d 659 (3d Cir. 1953);
Urquhart v. United States, 109 F.Supp.
409 (Ct.Cl.1953). But cf. United States

Gypsum Co. v. National Gypsum Co., 352
U.S. 457, 77 S.Ct. 490, 1 L.Ed.2d 465
(1957) upholding, 6–3, under peculiar circumstances, right of licensor to recover
on *quantum meruit* counts for use of
patent rights, while denying recovery on
the royalty provisions of the licenses,
which had been invalidated as instruments of misuse of patents.

violation of Section 2 of the Sherman Act. The Court of Appeals reversed,
529 F.2d 614 (3d Cir. 1976):

> . . . An effort by a patent holder to defend his valid patent monop-
> oly by exercising the right which he has in common with all others to do
> business with whom he pleases cannot rationally be regarded as a misuse
> of his patent. It surely cannot be the law that a patent holder must con-
> tinue to do business with a wilful infringer, thereby possibly contributing
> financially to the ability of the latter to defend against and possibly de-
> feat his infringement suit. To hold otherwise would be to require a plain-
> tiff to assist the defendant in its defense against the assertion of the
> plaintiff's valid patent claim.

[The following sentence is from footnote 2 of the Court's opinion.]

> This would be a different and more difficult case if we concluded, which
> we do not, that the plaintiff attempted to use its buying power in the wire
> market improperly to foreclose a challenge to the validity of its patents.

(4) *Comparison to Copyright—Block Booking and Blanket Licensing.*
In *United States v. Paramount Pictures, Inc.*, 334 U.S. 131, 68 S.Ct. 915, 92
L.Ed. 1260 (1948), the principal producers of moving pictures were found to
have monopolized first run exhibition of copyrighted feature films. Among
other practices forbidden by the decree was "block booking":

> Block-booking is the practice of licensing, or offering for license, one
> feature or group of features on condition that the exhibitor will also li-
> cense another feature or group of features released by the distributors
> during a given period. The films are licensed in blocks before they are
> actually produced. All the defendants, except United Artists, have en-
> gaged in the practice. Block-booking prevents competitors from bidding
> for single features on their individual merits. The District Court [66
> F.Supp. 349] held it illegal for that reason and for the reason that it "adds
> to the monopoly of a single copyrighted picture that of another copyright-
> ed picture which must be taken and exhibited in order to secure the
> first." That enlargement of the monopoly of the copyright was con-
> demned below in reliance on the principle which forbids the owner of a
> patent to condition its use on the purchase or use of patented or unpatent-
> ed materials. The court enjoined defendants from performing or enter-
> ing into any license in which the right to exhibit one feature is condi-
> tioned upon the licensee's taking one or more other features.[17]

As for the legality of blanket licensing arrangements, review *Broadcast
Music, Inc. v. Columbia Broadcasting System, Inc.*, supra p. 380. The majority in *BMI* only passed on the price fixing/*per se* question, but Justice
Stevens, in dissent, considered the question whether the blanket licensing
requirement was an unreasonable restraint of trade:[18]

> Under our prior cases, there would be no question about the illegality
> of the blanket-only licensing policy if ASCAP and BMI were the exclusive
> sources of all licenses. A copyright, like a patent, is a statutory grant of
> monopoly privileges. The rules which prohibit a patentee from enlarging
> his statutory monopoly by conditioning a license on the purchase of un-

---

17. See also United States v. Loew's,
Inc., 371 U.S. 38, 83 S.Ct. 97, 9 L.Ed.2d
11 (1962) (following Paramount Pictures,
Court holds block booking of copyrighted
feature motion pictures for television violates Section 1; even though feature
films were less than 8% of television programming, each copyrighted film booked
for television use "was in itself a unique
product").

18. 444 U.S. 1, 25, 28–38, 99 S.Ct.
1551, 1565, 1567–71, 60 L.Ed.2d 1, 20,
21–27 (1979).

patented goods, or by refusing to grant a license under one patent unless the licensee also takes a license under another, are equally applicable to copyrights.[19]

It is clear, however, that the mere fact that the holder of several patents has granted a single package license covering them all does not establish any illegality. This point was settled by Automatic Radio Manufacturing Co. v. Hazeltine Research, Inc., 339 U.S. 827, 834, 70 S.Ct. 894, 898, 94 L.Ed. 1312 and reconfirmed in Zenith Radio Corp. v. Hazeltine Research, Inc., 395 U.S. 100, 137–138, 89 S.Ct. 1562, 1583–1585, 23 L.Ed. 2d 129. The Court is therefore unquestionably correct in its conclusion that ASCAP's issuance of blanket licenses covering its entire inventory is not, standing alone, automatically unlawful. But both of those cases identify an important limitation on this rule. In the former, the Court was careful to point out that the record did not present the question whether the package license would have been unlawful if *Hazeltine* had refused to license on any other basis. 339 U.S., at 831, 70 S.Ct. at 896. And in the latter case, the Court held that the package license was illegal because of such a refusal. 395 U.S., at 140–141, 89 S.Ct., at 1585–1586.

Since ASCAP offers only blanket licenses, its licensing practices fall on the illegal side of the line drawn by the two *Hazeltine* cases. But there is a significant distinction: unlike *Hazeltine*, ASCAP does not have exclusive control of the copyrights in its portfolio, and it is perfectly possible—at least as a legal matter—for a user of music to negotiate directly with composers and publishers for whatever rights he may desire. The availability of a practical alternative alters what would otherwise be the competitive effect of a blockbooking or blanket licensing policy. ASCAP is therefore quite correct in its insistence that its blanket license cannot be categorically condemned on the authority of the blockbooking and package licensing cases. While these cases are instructive, they do not directly answer the question whether the ASCAP practice is unlawful.

[After evaluating the anticompetitive effect in the market for musical compositions—users who would buy less cannot; there is a disincentive to substitute less expensive music—Justice Stevens continued:]

Neither CBS nor any other user has been willing to assume the costs and risks associated with an attempt to purchase music on a competitive basis. The fact that an attempt by CBS to break down the ASCAP monopoly might well succeed does not preclude the conclusion that smaller and less powerful buyers are totally foreclosed from a competitive market. Despite its size, CBS itself may not obtain music on a competitive basis without incurring unprecedented costs and risks. The fear of unpredictable consequences, coupled with the certain and predictable costs and delays associated with a change in its method of purchasing music, unquestionably inhibits any CBS management decision to embark on a competitive crusade . . . .

   . . . Even without judicial intervention, the ASCAP monopoly might eventually be broken by CBS, if the benefits of doing so outweigh the significant costs and risks involved in commencing direct dealing. But that hardly means that the blanket licensing policy at issue here is lawful. An arrangement that produces marketwide price discrimination and significant barriers to entry unreasonably restrains trade even if the

19. [Footnote 12 from Justice Stevens' opinion.] Indeed, the leading cases condemning the practice of "blockbooking" involved copyrighted motion pictures, rather than patents.

discrimination and the barriers have only a limited life expectancy. History suggests, however, that these restraints have an enduring character.

Antitrust policy requires that great aggregations of economic power be closely scrutinized. That duty is especially important when the aggregation is composed of statutory monopoly privileges. Our cases have repeatedly stressed the need to limit the privileges conferred by patent and copyright strictly to the scope of the statutory grant. The record in this case plainly discloses that the limits have been exceeded and that ASCAP and BMI exercise monopoly powers that far exceed the sum of the privileges of the individual copyright holders. Indeed, ASCAP itself argues that its blanket license constitutes a product that is significantly different from the sum of its component parts. I agree with that premise, but I conclude that the aggregate is a monopolistic restraint of trade proscribed by the Sherman Act.

4. PATENT EXCHANGES: POOLS AND CROSS–LICENSING

THE GLASS CONTAINER PATENT POOL

Excerpt from Chapter VII of Hamilton, Patents and Free Enterprise, T.N.E.C. Mono, No. 31 (1941), pp. 109–115.

The gentlemen in the glass container industry have long been desirous of security. The raw material is to be found almost everywhere; the capital required is not excessive; labor which can be fitted to the task is widely available. And, in spite of the formidable appearance of the machine, the art of bottle-blowing is comparatively simple. All of the requisites, save one, are in easy reach of all comers. Were technology free, the industry would be wide open—and probably as chaotically competitive as women's dresses or bituminous coal. Yet, because of the closely guarded process of fabrication, a fence shuts in the industrial domain. A number of units—which once were inclined toward trade war—have found their places in an empire which bows to a single authority. Hartford, home of the Hartford Empire, is the capital; Corning, of the Houghton Associates, and Muncie, or "Middletown", of the Ball Brothers, are leading provincial cities. And Washington, D.C., the domicile of the Patent Office, is a kind of treasury, too remote to disturb with a will of its own, yet near enough to supply every necessary support to an entente cordial which runs on. . . .

As early as 1905—a point of time more than twice the life of a patent away—Owens had developed an automatic suction machine for making glassware; a little later Hartford-Fairmont patented a gob-feeding device which served the like purpose. At the same time Corning was perfecting a machine process for making glass bulbs. The three large concerns did not have to create a market for their products; they had only, with the rights which their patents gave, to go forward and possess it. They had little to fear from others; for the ancient art could not compete with the new technology. They did not, except to keep their grants alive, have to improve their methods. The only threat was a practical substitute; and it was slow in coming. The companies could—so long as basic patents were periodically refreshed—continue to supply a rapidly expanding market. If neighbors should attempt to barge in with the same process or product, the courts could be invoked to arrest the trespass. A stop was called to all competition from outsiders—in glass containers or in glass machinery. The field belonged to the three and, had they chosen, the Titans might have battled for possession.

Each cast longing eyes over the whole of the promised land—but in the end they did not so choose. A sharp boundary was drawn about a great empire by the series of patents; the companies had to appoint their own lines between provinces or leave them to the courts. In driving into the other fellow's territory the stakes were high but the costs and hazards were heavy. It was a game at which all could play; every foray was sure to be followed by reprisals; offense was certain to be the best defense. In 1915, Corning and Hartford bowed to the cost of litigation; a cross-licensing agreement gave to Hartford the field of glass containers and to Corning the realm of bulbs and specialty wares. The rapprochement presently led to an anschluss; and in 1922 the two concerns entered into a full-fledged pooling agreement. At the time, Hartford-Fairmont was reorganized as Hartford-Empire; a controlling interest, 59.5 percent, in the new venture went to the stockholders of the old Hartford-Fairmont Co.; 40.5 percent went to the Empire Co., a subsidiary of Corning, which in turn was controlled by the Houghton family. Their minority interest, however, received recognition in the right to name four of the nine directors of the new corporation. The common accord, in respect to production and price, was continued. The first act in the welding of the empire was complete.

Owens, however, had to be faced and Owens occupied strategic heights. It had found that Hartford's gob-feeding process was a menace to the sales of its suction machinery; so it had begun to buy up gob-feeding patents in preparation for an economic battle to be waged with legal weapons. In 1923 it instituted a suit for infringement against one of Hartford's licensees—the initial attack in an arduous and uncertain campaign. The parties took one long look at the hazardous way ahead, another at the richness of the prize to be won, and decided to divide the spoils. Except for the rights which Owens held in the suction process, each was licensed to make use of the patents of the others. As respects the suction process it was agreed that Owens should not assign its rights; Hartford should not license certain machinery without Owens' consent; Owens should not employ its patented process to manufacture products competing with Corning. As mutual consideration Owens was to pay royalties at Hartford's lowest rate; Hartford was to turn over 50 per cent of its divisible income less $600,000. The alliance was to be supported by equal contribution to a war chest which was to be drawn upon for the acquisition of patents and the prosecution of suits for infringement. The second act in the welding of the empire was complete.

Next a blitzkrieg was directed against the independents. They were harassed with suits for infringement, which kept them occupied, drained their resources, disorganized their markets. In the end they had to capitulate and accept the settlement dictated by the alliance. Their patents—not yet invalidated by litigation—were taken over by Hartford. Such as were left in business were compelled to accept licenses from Hartford and to pay a tribute of which Owens received a share. In instances, the threat of a bout at law was enough; in others independents or their customers had to have their days in court before they were willing to capitulate.

Along with these events went a move to domesticate the patents to the acquisitive arts. A research staff, widely publicized as an instrument of technical advance, was given the task of improving the processes of production. All innovations were duly patented, but not so promptly put into effect. As others came forward with inventions, Hartford intervened, and the proceedings were protracted until the resources of the applicant were completely exhausted. It caused its own novelties to linger around the Patent Office for years, thus deferring the date of issue and thus prolonging the life of the protection. One basic patent, for which application was made in 1910, did not emerge until 1937; thus a grant which should have run its course by 1927 retains its validity until 1944. A similar device, but fitted out with a narrowed claim, was in 1928 accorded letters patent which expire in 1945. Yet, although its life terminates then, protection runs on because of a longer grant. Thus far Hartford legal sanctions have been kept alive as the patent has been harnessed to the balance sheet.

The venture into imperialism was vigorously pushed by Hartford and associates. After a running fight of several years, Hazel-Atlas came into the entente. The runner-up to Owens lost its independence and was assigned its place in the empire. And Hartford's divisible income—which included royalty payments on the Hazel-Atlas patents by its former competitors—was now split three ways. Next Thatcher and Liberty, large manufacturers of milk bottles, came in; agreed to pay royalties; and received preferred treatment. Next their competitors were forced to take out licenses; and, in order that the market might not be spoiled, to accept production quotas fixed by Hartford. Last of all, a peremptory invitation was extended to Ball Bros. They had long been manufacturers of fruit jars, held the dominant position in the field, and lay entrenched behind their own patents. Ball continued to use their own process; agreed to pay royalties on inventions of which they made no use; and received assurance that no new licenses would be granted which encroached on their territory. The third act in the welding of the empire was now complete.

The monopoly had been fashioned; its lines stood sharply out. Concerns with power were accorded appropriate places; the small fry were treated as nuisances to be abated. An analysis of the total American production of glass containers reveals the design consciously wrought into the pattern of the industry. It shows Owens with 38.03 percent of the total output; Hazel-Atlas, 16.89; Anchor-Hocking, 8.01; Thatcher, 2.87; Ball Bros., 3.75; some 33 other licensees from Hartford, 27.05; and 3 independents with 3.40 percent. Thus of the total, Hartford is overlord to firms with 96.60 percent of the entire output. Of the 3 independents 2 are now being sued for infringement. And the authority of the sovereign, with its power to grant or deny access to the channels of trade, rests upon documents issued by the Federal Government.

Hartford has thus become benevolent despot to the glass container. Only by its leave can a firm come into the industry; the ticket of admission is to be had only upon its terms; and from its studied decision there is no appeal. The candidate must subscribe to its articles of faith; he must not be a price-cutter nor a troublemaker. So long as he lives up to its rules he may run his own business as he pleases. He may be as wasteful or as efficient as he pleases within his own establishment; but he may not make his customer the beneficiary of his efficiency. He enjoys a freedom under authority; the concerns are severally members one of another; independence must not go so far as to put a brother concern in financial jeopardy.

One who seeks induction into the mystery of bottle-making must present himself before "the character committee" of the sovereign company. He must persuade it that he is a man of integrity, that his financial position is secure, that his economic ideas are sound. But, however elegant his qualifications, he can scarcely hope to be accepted unless there is room for him in the trade. For admission does not depend upon probity and pecuniary competence alone; nor is it fixed by those automatic checks and balances of the market which are "the balance-wheel of capitalism". Rather the issue belongs to the politics of industry and turns upon how much competition is best for the competitors. The company prides iteslf upon its complete information, its ability to gauge the market, the neatness with which it accommodates its licenses to an increase in the demand for the product. Its avowed intent is, not the protection of vested interest against the newcomer, but doing nimbly and promptly what the market haltingly and clumsily would otherwise have to do for itself.

The empire is not opposed to competition; but it seeks to further normal, and to escape "ruinous competition". For that reason Hartford inserts restrictive provisions in its license. Whether concerns came in willingly or were conscripted, each was assigned its demesne. In general, the initial standard was the status quo. Each firm was permitted to manufacture the products and was accorded the share of the market to which it was accustomed. But it is not easy to arrange a number of parts which just grew into an orderly scheme, and in the process readjustments were necessary. A number of companies had to give up their minor wares; the overlapping of products was reduced to trimmer lines; and members too weak to dictate terms had to be content with what was offered. Rarely was a licensee permitted to extend his former domain. To such generosity "he has no right because he has never been in the habit of producing that ware" and his business was not "in that particular line". But no absolute ban was placed on expansion. If a licensee wished to take advantage of "some particular situation", Hartford could be depended upon to do the decent and reasonable thing.

The restrictions take a variety of forms. Limitation by type is universal; and containers of the same type may be distinguished by use. Fruit jars used for home canning and by commercial packers may look alike, but for purposes of the license they are distinct wares. The sale of the one for a purpose to which the other is ordinarily put would be a violation of the law of the industry. Such respect is accorded the division of labor that a concern is permitted to fabricate bottles for chocolate milk, with the condition that they are not to be sold to dairies. Precaution adds the postscript that under no circumstances are they to serve as containers to unchocolated milk. The Buck Glass Co. is authorized to manufacture wine bottles for sacramental purposes only. The operations of the Sayre Glass Works are to be restricted "to such bottles, jugs, and demijohns as are used for vinegar, ciders, sirups, bleaching fluids, hair tonics, barber supplies, and fluid extracts". Likewise Florida Glass Manufacturing Co. must fashion its containers so skillfully that they may be filled only with mayonnaise, peanut butter, preserves, sirup, and honey. Knox Glass Bottle Co. is allowed to make only amber ginger ale bottles; Mary Card Glass Co. only blue glass containers; Carr-Lowry Glass Co. only opal colored products. Hocking Glass Co. may not make products weighing more than 82 ounces; and Baurens Glass Works, Inc., is licensed to provide bottles for caster oil and turpentine, but none to exceed 4 ounces in capacity.

It is impossible to reduce such restrictions to a simple table. The criteria of classification are so numerous and so variable that an enumeration of all the instances is necessary to recite the story. Broad fields such as milk bottles, beer bottles, and fruit jars are not always left intact; narrow domains are often cut up into small holdings. A number of manufacturers are permitted to sell only to specified customers; one company may not ship his products outside the States of "Washington, Oregon, Idaho, and Montana, and the Territory of Alaska". Where a single concern has an exclusive license to manufacture a single type or for a specified use, output demands no formal control. Where two or more produce the same product, there must be an orderly sharing of the market. To such an accord a system of quotas is directed, which may be fixed either at a specific number of units or at a given fraction of the total output. But, no matter how devious the specifications, they hold no confusion and no source of discord. Each fief has its exact place in the pattern of the industry. The net result is a business despotism. The free play of the market has been replaced by the controls exerted from the directors' board. Hartford Empire is the creation of the dominant companies and represents their interest. The smaller concerns exist by its sufferance; and for them it establishes the conditions of business life. Its license—granted, revised, revoked at the pleasure of the corporation—is the right of its possessor to his trade. Its control runs out, through its affiliates, to comprehend all with whom they do business. In many instances it decrees that all who use a certain type of glass container must purchase from a single firm. In others it fixes the terms of ultimate sale and leaves to the processor of the product no option but to take or to refuse the bargain. The network of conditions attaching to license constitutes a scheme of arrangements under which the various firms carry on. If it is a "self-government for industry", it is an industry in which consumers, who must pay the bills, have little voice, and in which the various members share in proportion to their financial strength.

In Hartford-Empire the lines of a corporate estate appear in bold relief. As phial, fruit jar, beer bottle, the ware is the most ordinary device. Its raw materials are omnipresent; it demands little manual skill from labor; its technical process is easily mastered. Yet it has become a dominion unto itself, hedged off from invasion on all sides. An order, a government, a system of law has been constructed for the whole industry upon the grant of letters-patent from the Federal Government. In a series of moves, the corporation has made itself sovereign; usurped the operation of the market; made dependent provinces of each concern it has taken in. It appoints to each its product, decrees its price, limits its output. Its powers of police comprehend many fuedal estates; it levies toll upon every industry which must make use of its product. Its dominion extends to every aspect of the trade and its system of police is far more effective than that of any arm of the Government. Its authority—which rests upon a grant from the United States—is far broader than the Supreme Court has been willing to accord to a sovereign State of the Union.[20]

It is easy enough to recite a case for Hartford Empire. It has come into being in response to a demand for order within the industry and security to its firms. In glass containers, conditions do not invite a well-behaved competition; to allow the trade to remain open to all who wish to enter it is to invite chaos. Firms would rush in, capacity to produce would quickly outrun the capacity to absorb. A concern, met with a falling demand for its product, would seek to produce other wares. The advantages of specialization and quantity production, with their attending efficiencies, would presently be lost. As production fell back into a multiple process, costs would rise and higher bills would eventually be thrust upon the public. There would be a constant threat to solvency; the periodic epidemics of bankruptcy would fall upon all alike. In the end the plight of the glass container would become like that of textiles, dresses, or soft coal. All lines would fade from the trim design of the industry. All who have a stake in its operation would have to pay for an emergent disorder.

The scheme is a barrier against industrial confusion. The creation of a structure accommodated to the task to be done is affected with a public interest. As the modern system came into being, Statutes of the Realm repeatedly sought the well-ordering of particular trades. If somewhat later the whole matter was left to the market, it was

---

20. [Author's note 6.] New State Ice Co. v. Liebmann, 285 U.S. 262, 52 S.Ct. 371, 76 L.Ed. 747 (1932). If the activities of Hartford-Empire are legal, a grant of patent has an amplitude of authority in excess of the police power enjoyed by the several States.

because competition was regarded as competent to impose design and purpose. In glass containers it is no longer able to do so, and all that Hartford-Fairmont, Corning, Owens and others have done is to provide a substitute for its magic. For such an undertaking they need an official warrant, and letters patent are the best to be had. They have set up, as their creature, Hartford-Empire, whose office is to have and to hold patents. To it they have assigned their various rights and it has been charged to invent, to contrive, to improve, but at such a pace as to keep alive a few basic patents. If perchance it now and then strays from the promotion of the industrial arts, it is to serve the more important cause of an industry, whose trim lines makes it a model within the national economy.

It is idle to blame the architects for their industrial structure. Their concern was the pursuit of gain; they took the way of money-making; and if they made the road broader than legally it ought to have been, a public authority should appoint bounds. It may be that competition which served well enough an industrial system just hitting its stride is no longer appropriate—but the law of the land does not say so. It may be that a political should succeed an economic order in the conduct of trade; but if so, it should not ride roughshod over the little fellow, nor should it impose taxation without representation upon the consumer. If there is to be a government of industry, it should be a responsible one. Its task is to mediate between interests at stake, not to conduct the trade as if it were the property of a party. A sanction has been diverted from its accredited office to serve a private cause. A corporation has usurped the function of the market and has become sovereign of all that touches its product; as an authority, liable only to itself, it lords it over a gigantic domain. In glass containers, *l'état, c'est* Hartford Empire.

HARTFORD–EMPIRE CO. v. UNITED STATES

Supreme Court of the United States, 1945.
323 U.S. 386, 65 S.Ct. 373, 89 L.Ed. 322.

[Digest: The Supreme Court unanimously held the glass container pool in violation of Sections 1 and 2 of the Sherman Act. "It is clear that, by cooperative arrangements and binding agreements, the appellant corporations, over a period of years, regulated and suppressed competition in the use of glassmaking machinery and employed their joint patent position to allocate fields of manufacture and to maintain prices of unpatented glassware." (323 U.S. at 406–07, 65 S.Ct. at 384.)

Nevertheless, the Court was sharply divided on the scope of injunctive relief. The Court did approve provisions against patent license restrictions on production, use, markets, prices, etc., and defendants were limited to "reasonable" royalties on patents presently owned or acquired in the future on specified types of glassmaking machinery. Pending infringement suits were enjoined.

The majority, however, speaking through Justice Roberts, struck out a provision requiring defendants to license existing patents without payment of royalty. The government had justified this provision as necessary to open the field to new competitors against the entrenched position achieved by the pool participants through unlawful use of the patents. The Court answered that a patent is property and that the statutory jurisdiction to enjoin and prevent violations does not authorize forfeiture of property for past wrongs. (323 U.S. at 414–415, 65 S.Ct. 387–388)

The Court also deleted Paragraph 51 of the decree which forbade purchase of additional patents or exclusive licenses in the glass machinery field. The paragraph was said to be "inappropriate to restrain future violations of the antitrust statutes." (323 U.S. at 431, 65 S.Ct. 395)

With regard to defendants' practice of applying for patents to "block off" or "fence in" competing inventions, the government suggested an injunction against applications for patents "with the intention of never making commercial use of the inventions covered thereby, provided that failure to make such use within four years from the date of issuance of patents thereon shall be deemed *prima facie* proof of the presence of such intention at the time of the filing or prosecution of such applications". The Court responded that this proposal was "legislative rather than remedial . . . A patent owner is not in the position of a quasi-trustee for the public or under any obligation to see that the public acquires the free right to use the invention. He has no obligation either to use it or to grant its use to others. If he discloses the invention in his application so that it will come into the public domain at the end of the 17-year period of exclusive right he has fulfilled the only obligation imposed by the statute."

JUSTICES DOUGLAS, MURPHY and JACKSON did not participate in the decision. JUSTICES BLACK and RUTLEDGE dissented against modifications of the decree of the district court.]

MR. JUSTICE BLACK.

. . . The District Court found that these defendants started out in 1916 to acquire a monopoly on a large segment of the glass industry. Their efforts were rewarded by complete success. They have become absolute masters of that domain of our public economy. They achieved this result largely through the manipulation of patents and licensing agreements. They obtained patents for the express purpose of furthering their monopoly. They utilized various types of restrictions in connection with leasing those patents so as to retain their dominance in that industry. The history of this country has perhaps never witnessed a more completely successful economic tyranny over any field of industry than that accomplished by these appellants. They planned their monopolistic program on the basis of getting and keeping and using patents, which they dedicated to the destruction of free competition in the glass container industry. Their declared object was "To block the development of machines which might be constructed by others . . ." and "To secure patents on possible improvements of competing machines, so as to 'fence in' those and prevent their reaching an improved state." These patents were the major weapons in the campaign to subjugate the industry; they were also the fruits of appellant's victory. The restoration of competition in the glass container industry demands that appellants be deprived of these weapons. The most effective way to accomplish this end is to require, as the District Court did, that these patents be licensed royalty free.

MR. JUSTICE RUTLEDGE. . . . It seems to be implied from the number, character and detail of the revisions that it is the business of this Court to rewrite the decree, substituting its own judgment for that of the District Court when there is difference concerning the wisdom or need of a particular revision. A supporting notion, apparently, is that the "equity" procedure to enforce the Act is hedged with the same limitations non-statutory equity has placed about its action as a system of private remedial litigation. Both these ideas have backing in a third misconception, that men who have misused their property, and acquired much of it, by violating the Sherman Act, are free for the future to continue using it as are other owners who have committed no such offense; and that consequently the appropriate relief affecting such use is the least restriction which possibly will prevent repetition of past violations. . . .

The power, and much of the property, now aggregated in the combination's hands and those of its principal participants, was gathered by unlawful methods, at the expense of the public and competitors. Presumably neither power nor property could have been accumulated by lawful means. Nor can they now together be transferred legally to another. The loosened restrictions of this Court's revision may be sufficient to prevent, for the future, further acts of the character and having the effects of the past violations. But the pool has acquired more than 800 patents, which control the industry, of which Hartford alone holds more than 600. Its members, including Hartford, are not compelled to disgorge any of these, or prohibited to acquire others. Many of the patents, and certainly the cherished "patent position", were secured only by virtue of the illegal conduct. Whatever benefits may flow from these patents and the patent position thus created are inevitably the consequences of that conduct. Merely to throw off the illegal practices, such as restricted and discriminatory licensing, cannot reach those consequences. Every dollar hereafter, as well as heretofore, secured from licenses on the patents illegally aggregated in the combination's hands is money to which the participants are not entitled by virtue of the patent laws or others. It is the immediate product of the conspiracy. To permit these patents to remain in the guilty hands, as sources of continuing lucrative revenue, not only does not deprive their owners of the fruit of their misconduct. Rather it secures to them its continued benefits. The pool may no longer utilize illegal methods. It, and the constituent members, will continue to enjoy the preferred competitive position which their conduct has given them and to use both that position and the ill-gotten patents, together with the patent position, to derive trade advantage over rivals and gain from the public which the patent laws of themselves

never contemplated and the anti-trust laws, in my opinion, forbid.
. . .

The case presents again the fundamental problem of accommodating the provisions of the patent laws to those of the antitrust statutes. Basically these are opposed in policy, the one granting rights of monopoly, the other forbidding monopolistic activities. The patent legislation presents a special case, the anti-trust legislation the nation's general policy. Whether the one or the other is wise is not for us to determine. But their accommodation is one we must make, within the limits allowed to the judicial function, when the issue is presented.

The general policy has been to restrict the right of the patent-holder rigidly within the terms of his grant and, when he overreaches its boundary, to deny him the usual protections of the holder of property. That this ordinarily has been done in infringement suits or suits for cancellation does not qualify the fact or the policy. On the other hand, the antitrust statutes have received a broad construction and corresponding enforcement, where violation has been clearly shown. When the patent-holder so far overreaches his privilege as to intrude upon the rights of others and the public protected by the antitrust legislation, and does this in such a way that he cannot further exercise the privilege without also trespassing upon the rights thus protected, either his right or the other person's, and the public right, must give way. It is wholly incongruous in such circumstances to say that the privilege of the trespasser shall be preserved and the rights of all others which he has transgressed shall continue to give way to the consequences of his wrongdoing. . . .

The Court's major modifications, in my opinion, emasculate the decree.

NOTES AND QUERIES

(1) *Interchange of Patent Rights.* From the Report of the Attorney General's National Committee to Study the Antitrust Laws 242–247 (1955):

The term "patent pool" is not a term of art and it is both technically and semantically inadequate to describe the interchange of patent rights. Accordingly, we prefer the phrase "patent interchange" which for our purposes is defined as any arrangement for the interchange of patent rights where either one or more of the patent owners, or some separate entity, has the right to license others under the pooled patents. This definition, consistent with most cases involving patent interchange, excludes simple cross-license agreements.

The need for patent interchanges and conversely the antitrust risks which may accompany their use, has [sic] been judicially recognized. The technological interdependence of a vast number of patents and their legal mutual exclusiveness frequently necessitates exchange or waiver of patent rights. Patent interchanges may help resolve patent conflicts and thus make the assembled patents available to others. They may facilitate patent licensing of a multiplicity of patents; or make possible the use of mutually dependent or blocking patents. Patent interchange may thus promote rather than restrain competition.

On the other hand, the interchange of patents necessarily involves agreement and cooperation. If created with illicit purpose, or misused, it may lead to unreasonable restraints of trade and monopolization. Adjudicated cases demonstrate the manner in which entire industries may be regimented through misuse of the interchange. The patent is no shield for cooperative action outside the orbit of the patent grant, and those forming the interchange are subject to the prohibitions of the Sherman Act.

Separating a licit from an illicit purpose in inception, the courts emphasize an interchange's activities as evidence of intent underlying its formation.[21] An absence of restrictive practices evidences lack of improper intent.[22] Contrariwise, an interchange is unlawful if formed with the purpose of regimenting an industry,[23] fixing prices and eliminating competition, or threatening litigation with accompanying undue restraint of trade.[24]

Further emphasizing post-formation activities as revealing intent as to formation, interchanges of complementary [25] and of noncompeting [26] patents have been upheld as reasonable means of making the patents available for use. And the Cracking Process case held that, even in the field of competing patents, the existence of a bona fide patent dispute may justify an interchange arrangement "where the arrangement was found to have resulted in no monopoly, or restriction of competition in the business of licensing patented cracking processes or in the production of either ordinary or cracked gasoline." [27]

. . . Where monopoly over products or processes covered by the interchanged patents is found, then the question arises whether, in any case, such combined pool power violates Section 2 of the Sherman Act. The inevitable result of lawful use of the lawful patent monopoly is not to be penalized. To enable feasible patent use, however, it may be necessary to resolve patent conflicts or ambiguities by some interchange arrangement. Accordingly, should mere interchange be the sole means for commercial patent use, interchange which brings monopoly over products or processes covered by the interchanged patents, we believe, should not be held to violate Section 2.[28]   . . .

---

21. [This and the following seven footnotes are from the original Report, renumbered.] United States v. General Electric (Carboloy), 80 F.Supp. 989, 1015 (S.D.N.Y.1948).

22. Cutter Laboratories v. Lyophile-Cryochem Corp., 179 F.2d 80, 83 (9th Cir. 1949).

23. Hartford-Empire Co. v. United States, 323 U.S. 386, 406, 65 S.Ct. 373 (1945); United States v. National Lead Co., 63 F.Supp. 513 (S.D.N.Y.1945), aff'd 332 U.S. 319, 67 S.Ct. 1634 (1947); United States v. Vehicular Parking, Ltd., 54 F.Supp. 828, 834 (D.Del.1944); United States v. General Electric (lamps), 82 F.Supp. 753, 847 (D.N.J.1949).

24. Lynch v. Magnavox, 94 F.2d 883 (9th Cir. 1938); United States v. General

Instrument Corp., 87 F.Supp. 157, 191 (D.N.J.1949); United States v. Besser Mfg. Co., 96 F.Supp. 304 (E.D.Mich.1951), aff'd 343 U.S. 444, 72 S.Ct. 838 (1952).

25. Baker-Cammack Hosiery Mills v. Davis Co., 181 F.2d 550, 568 (4th Cir. 1950); Cutter Laboratories v. Lyophile-Cryochem Corp., 179 F.2d 80, 93, 94 (9th Cir. 1949).

26. United States v. Winslow, 227 U.S. 202, 33 S.Ct. 253 (1913).

27. Standard Oil Co. (Indiana) v. United States, 283 U.S. 163, 171, 175, 51 S.Ct. 421, 424, 425 (1931).

28. Cf. United States v. General Electric Co. (Carboloy), 80 F.Supp. 989, 1015 (S.D.N.Y.1948).

Regarding this conclusion, Louis B. Schwartz comments:

Everyone realizes that cases will occur where the owners of two patents must combine them by transfer or cross license in order to achieve a marketable product. But to transpose this simple solution to cases of "patent deadlocks" between giant firms whose combination will compel entire industries to pay non-competitive royalties is to ignore the crucial element of monopoly in the latter situation. When, as in the Cracking Patents case, several of the largest integrated petroleum companies develop and patent competing refining processes and are engaged in competitive licensing, we may be sure that none of them is going to abandon the field because of patent deadlock, even if we refuse to authorize them to pool their patents. If the Cracking Patents case had gone against the defendants a number of results might have followed, all preferable to the patent pool from the point of view of the public interest. The patent conflict between the companies might have been pressed to decision by the Supreme Court. Some or all of the patents might have been held invalid, thus opening the technology to general free use. Certainly the chance that a smaller licensee or infringer would be able successfully to challenge this combined array of patents was much reduced when the Big Four closed ranks. A second consequence of barring industry-dominating patent pools might be that one of the partners would ultimately establish its exclusive right to some or all of the process—but meanwhile there would have been a powerful incentive for research to produce other non-controlled processes. A third possibility would be independent competitive licensing. . . .

(2) *Research Joint Ventures.* Firms often collaborate on joint research projects. Such projects can avoid the costs of duplicate research as well as offer the usual risk-spreading advantage of joint ventures where high capital costs are required (see pp. 555–557, supra). Nevertheless, these joint ventures do pose competitive dangers. The Justice Department argues, for example: [29]

Industry-wide research projects that include many or all firms in a line of commerce, as well as projects involving the dominant firm or firms in an industry pose antitrust concerns. These are more likely to restrain competition in innovation than more limited projects involving a few firms with lesser market shares. A firm which knows that many or most of its competitors are not vigorously pursuing independent research because of a joint project may relax its own efforts and acquiesce in a slow-moving, passive, unimaginative joint research program. Hence, the danger arises that the joint project may become a device to retard rather than to stimulate innovative efforts. In these circumstances the pace of innovation pursued by the collective research project may be geared to that preferred by its least aggressive member.[30] There is danger, also, that a single project will produce less innovation than will a variety of single and joint efforts employing alternative approaches.

---

29. United States Department of Justice, Antitrust Guide Concerning Research Joint Ventures 11–12 (1980). This Guide was written in response to President Carter's direction that the Department clarify its position on collaborative research to make certain that the antitrust laws are not " 'mistakenly understood to prevent cooperative activity, even in circumstances where it would foster innovation without harming competition.' " Id., preface.

30. [Footnote from original.] Such a case was United States v. Automobile Mfgs. Assn., 307 F.Supp. 617 (C.D.Cal. 1969), aff'd sub nom. City of New York v. United States, 397 U.S. 248 (1970); [1969] TRADE CAS. (CCH) ¶ 72,907 (C.D. Cal.1969) (consent decree). See L. Sullivan, Antitrust, § 105 at 299–300 (1977).

Another problem posed by such joint ventures is the denial of access, either to the joint venture or the technology it develops. Recall those cases finding illegal a monopolist's refusal to grant competitors reasonable access to a limited "bottleneck" facility (e.g., a long-distance transmission line, a produce exchange, a cooperative news service, a railway line to a terminal). Should these precedents be applicable to research joint ventures where access is necessary for effective competition? [31] Or would such a result effectively require compulsory patent licensing, something the courts have not generally favored (see *SCM,* supra p. 982)?

(3) *Research Joint Ventures—Specific Industry Examples.* The Justice Department's Antitrust Guide cited the case against United States automobile manufacturers, alleging suppression of the development of emission control devices, as an example of a research joint venture which reduced incentives for innovation (see n. 30, supra). Although the Carter Administration had intended to seek a court extension of the consent decree previously entered into in that case, President Reagan instead requested the Justice Department to review the decree. The Antitrust Division subsequently sought modifications: [32] (1) to allow case-by-case review of (a) formerly barred agreements involving the cross-licensing of after-acquired patents, (b) publicity restrictions on research and development efforts, (c) joint assessment of the value of another's patent rights, and (d) licensing on a most-favored-purchaser basis; (2) to exempt totally from the decree otherwise lawful joint research projects, including those done with firms partially owned by one of the defendants; [33] (3) to end "outdated" provisions limiting exchange of information and the presentation of joint statements; and (4) to automatically terminate the decree in five years. Are the modifications simply a recognition of changes in auto industry structure since 1969, changes which suggest that one cannot confidently predict that information sharing of emissions technology by American manufacturers will always be anticompetitive? Or are the modifications a further reflection of a new Administration's general belief that private firms should be given more freedom to do what they want?

Consider also a New York Times report that Nippon Telegraph and Telephone (NTT) has signed an agreement with IBM to exchange patents on existing and future data processing technology. [34] The article points out that NTT is more advanced than IBM in the communications technology which will be included under the agreement (e.g., electronic switching equipment and semi-conductors), and that IBM wants that technology. The article also points out that IBM has a similar agreement with AT&T; and that NTT also has a technology sharing agreement with AT&T, whose details have not yet been worked out.

Queries. Are these companies not large enough to finance research individually? Should agreements with NTT be justified as providing otherwise unobtainable access to Japanese technology and markets (NTT purchases

31. Yes, says the Department of Justice's Research Joint Venture Guide, supra, at 21.

32. See "Justice, Major Auto Manufacturers Seek Modification of Emission Control Decree," ATRR No. 1039, Nov. 11, 1981, A–6–A–7. The proposed modifications were accepted by the district court. See United States v. Motor Vehicle Manufacturers Association, 1982–83

Trade Case ¶ 65,175 (C.D.Cal.1982); 1982–83 Trade Case ¶ 65,088 (text of consent decree).

33. For the further information on joint ventures in the automobile industry, see p. 582 supra.

34. N. Y. Times, Nov. 19, 1981, p. D. 5.

telecommunications equipment).[35] Should we be concerned about "spill-over" effects when NTT, IBM and AT&T are linked by similar agreements (see p. 582, supra)? Are the economic benefits from such patent licenses "reasonably within the reward" of the patent, or does the scope of the interchange render the agreement "unreasonable"?

(4) *Patent Exchanges to Settle Litigation; Settling Patent Office Interferences.* Patents may be cross-licensed in settlement of patent validity litigation; such cross-licensing agreements are subject to the antitrust laws.[36] Agreements may also be made to settle disputes over conflicting patent claims before such claims are resolved in a Patent and Trademark Office interference proceeding (see p. 937, supra). Collusive interference settlements were analyzed as follows by Justice White in a concurring opinion in *United States v. Singer Manufacturing Co.*[37] *Singer* dealt with a collaboration of American and European sewing machine interests, involving, inter alia, the transfer of European-held patent rights to the American partner who would be able more effectively to employ them against expanding Japanese sales in the United States. Justice Clark's opinion for the Court held that, whatever might be Singer's right to acquire a foreign patent for the purpose of excluding Japanese competition and reinforcing its own dominance of the American market, the whole sequence of transactions with the collaboration of European associates amounted to a conspiracy forbidden by Section 1 of the Sherman Act. Justice White wrote, in part:

> . . . There are two phases to the Government's case here: one, the conspiracy to exclude the Japanese from the market, and the other, the collusive termination of a Patent Office interference proceeding pursuant to an agreement between Singer and Gegauf to help one another to secure as broad a patent monopoly as possible, invalidity considerations notwithstanding. The Court finds a violation of § 1 of the Sherman Act in the totality of Singer's conduct, and intimates no views as to either phase of the Government's case standing alone. Since in my view either branch of the case is sufficient to warrant relief, I join the Court's opinion . . . .
>
> As to the conspiracy to exclude the Japanese, there is involved, as the Court points out, more than the transfer of the patent from one competitor to another; implicit in the arrangement is Singer's undertaking to enforce the patent on behalf of both itself and Gegauf. Moreover, Singer was the dominant manufacturer in the American sewing machine industry and was acquiring a patent which dominated the multicam field, an aspect of this case which in itself raises serious questions, in my view, and which is saved by the Court for future consideration. . . .
>
> More must be said about the interference settlement. In 1956, Singer's "Harris" multicam zigzag reissue-patent application was pending in the United States Patent Office; Gegauf had an application pending at the same time covering substantially the same subject matter, but enjoying a nine-day earlier priority date. In the circumstances, it appeared to Singer that, between Singer and Gegauf, Gegauf would have a better claim to a patent on the multicam zigzag, at least on the broad and thus more valuable claims. But it was by no means certain that either of them

35. For rejection of a similar justification, see Timken Roller Bearing Co. v. United States, discussed pp. 556, 581, supra.

36. See Duplan Corp. v. Deering Milliken, Inc., 444 F.Supp. 648 (D.S.C.1977),

affirmed in part 594 F.2d 979 (4th Cir. 1979), certiorari denied 444 U.S. 1015, 100 S.Ct. 666, 62 L.Ed.2d 645 (1980).

37. 374 U.S. 174, 83 S.Ct. 1773, 10 L.Ed.2d 823 (1963).

would get the patent. In cases where several applicants claim the same subject matter, the Patent Office declares an "interference." This is an adversary proceeding between the rival applicants, primarily for the purpose of determining relative priority. But a party to an interference also can, by drawing additional prior art to the attention of the Patent Office which will require the Office to issue no patent at all to anyone, prevent his rival from securing a patent which if granted might exclude him from the manufacture of the subject matter. Gegauf, after Singer approached it to negotiate an agreement before the Office declared an interference, feared that Singer might in self-defense draw to the attention of the Patent Office certain earlier patents the Office was unaware of, and which might cause the Gegauf claims to be limited or invalidated; Singer "let them know that we thought we could knock out their claims but that in so doing we were probably going to hurt both of us."

The result was that in April 1956 Singer and Gegauf entered a general cross-licensing agreement providing that the parties were not to attack one another's patent applications "directly or indirectly," not to do anything to restrict one another's claims in patents or applications, and to facilitate the allowance to one another of "claims as broad as possible." In August 1956 the Patent Office declared the anticipated interference. Singer and Gegauf settled the interference pursuant to their prior agreement: Singer withdrew its interfering claims and in April 1957 the Patent Office dissolved the interference proceeding before it had ever reached the litigation stage. Eventually the Gegauf patent issued and was sold to Singer as part of the concerted action to exclude the Japanese which is involved in the first branch of the case. . . .

In itself the desire to secure broad claims in a patent may well be unexceptionable—when purely unilateral action is involved. And the settlement of an interference in which the only interests at stake are those of the adversaries, as in the case of a dispute over relative priority only and where possible invalidity, because of known prior art, is not involved, may well be consistent with the general policy favoring settlement of litigation. But the present case involves a less innocuous setting. Singer and Gegauf agreed to settle an interference, at least in part, to prevent an open fight over validity. There is a public interest here, which the parties have subordinated to their private ends—the public interest in granting patent monopolies only when the progress of the useful arts and of science will be furthered because as the consideration for its grant the public is given a novel and useful invention. When there is no novelty and the public parts with the monopoly grant for no return, the public has been imposed upon and the patent clause subverted. . . . Whatever may be the duty of a single party to draw the prior art to the Office's attention, clearly collusion among applicants to prevent prior art from coming to or being drawn to the Office's attention is an inequitable imposition on the Office and on the public. . . . In my view, such collusion to secure a monopoly grant runs afoul of the Sherman Act's prohibitions against conspiracies in restraint of trade—if not bad *per se*, then such agreements are at least presumptively bad. The patent laws do not authorize, and the Sherman Act does not permit, such agreements between business rivals to encroach upon the public domain and usurp it to themselves.

35 U.S.C.A. § 135(c), enacted in 1962, requires parties to an agreement to terminate an interference proceeding to file such agreement with the Patent

Office. Failure to file makes the affected patents unenforceable.[38] Is this effective to reach the evil identified in the foregoing opinion? Would agreements to settle interferences disclose purpose, if there was one, "to prevent an open fight over validity"? Is the potential intervention of the antitrust agencies an adequate safeguard, or should they have power to veto such settlements?

(5) *Royalty Free Licensing Ordered. United States v. General Electric Co.,* 115 F.Supp. 835, 843–44 (D.N.J.1953). Forman, Chief Judge:

The defendants are each, jointly and severally, ordered and directed, forthwith upon entry of this Judgment, to dedicate [39] to the public any and all existing patents on lamps and lamp parts. . . .

There is a distinction between the application of the Supreme Court's ruling in the Hartford-Empire case as it addresses itself to the licensing of existing patents on lamps and lamp parts of the defendants and the licensing of patents on lamp making machinery. I have held that General Electric's attempt to maintain control over the lamp industry has been largely by way of extending its basic patents on lamps and lamp parts. To compel the completely free use of these patents is not to impose upon General Electric and other defendants penalties for misuse of patents and violation of the antitrust laws, but rather to check the intrusion of advantages thereby gained into the mechanics of competition in the lamp industry.

Where the profit margin on the production of lamps is as narrow as it is at the present time any licensing fees may prove an important factor in limiting or inhibiting the growth of competition. In view of the fact that General Electric achieved its dominant position in the industry and maintained it in great measure by its extension of patent control the requirement that it contribute its existing patents to the public is only a justified dilution of that control made necessary in the interest of free competition in the industry.

In another instance in the case of United States v. Imperial Chemical Industries, D.C.S.D.N.Y.1952, 105 F.Supp. 215, the court followed literally the language of the Hartford-Empire case and declined to order royalty free licensing. However, that case was based on violation of Section 1 of the Sherman Act. Violations of both Sections 1 and 2 have been found in this case.

General Electric and the other defendants are mounted upon an arsenal of a huge body of patents that can easily overwhelm and defeat competition by small firms desiring to stay in or gain a foothold in the industry. These operators may well be unequipped to engage in litigation on the validity of one patent after another at what could be incalculable expense. In order to avoid it they could be required to shoulder royalties

---

38. See, e.g., Moog, Inc. v. Pegasus Laboratories, Inc., 521 F.2d 501 (6th Cir. 1975) (holding patent unenforceable in private infringement action); United States v. FMC Corp., 514 F.Supp. 1166 (E.D.Pa.1981) (holding Justice Department has standing to seek declaratory judgment that patent is unenforceable where interference settlement agreement is not filed in accord with 135(c); Antitrust Division is intended beneficiary of the statute).

39. The distinction between dedication and compulsory licensing has importance insofar as persons desiring to use technology covered by compulsory licensing must negotiate with the patentee for the issuance of a license conforming to the terms of the decree; no such negotiations are necessary in respect to dedicated patents. 35 U.S.C.A. § 253 provides for dedication by writing recorded in the patent office.

which could prove to be the very factor that would push them out of the competitive circle of the market.

In the circumstances such as these it would appear that royalty free licensing of patents on lamps and lamp parts is an essential remedy as a preventive against a continuance of monopoly in this industry. It would appear to be no more objectionable as confiscatory than where compulsory licensing is ordered. In the latter case the owner admittedly is permitted to receive a royalty but he nevertheless loses a monopoly inherent in his ownership of the patent, and the royalty he is forced to accept at times is not one that he fixes. Royalty free licensing and dedication are but an extension of the same principle, not to be directed indiscriminately, of course, but well within the therapeutic measures to be administered under circumstances such as were made to appear in this case. . . .

(6) *Relief Against Market Division. United States v. National Lead Co.,* 63 F.Supp. 513 (S.D.N.Y.1945), affirmed 332 U.S. 319, 67 S.Ct. 1634, 91 L.Ed. 2077 (1947). By an elaborate system of cross-license agreements the dominant producers of titanium compounds, important paint ingredients, divided the world market into exclusive territories for each of the participants. The "licensed field" included all substances containing more than 2% titanium and "all apparatus, methods, and processes useful in the obtainment or manufacture or use" of titanium compounds. A simplification of basic elements of the scheme follows. There were a number of competing processes for producing titanium oxide, the most important of the compounds. Each process was patented in the country of the inventor and in other countries having patent systems. To prevent competition, each of the patentees licensed his process exclusively to the dominant producer or producers in any given country in exchange for a similar reciprocal license. Thus National Lead, having given a German firm exclusive licenses for Germany under NL patents, was itself excluded from the German market, but enjoyed a converse protection in the American market. Occasionally provision was made for joint exploitation of patent rights in a territory or country without a strong producer of its own, by means of a corporation whose stock was owned by several of the licensors. These private commercial treaties provided for exchange of technical information among the participants and included agreements for licensing on the same terms patents and inventions to be acquired by the parties in the future. The parties undertook to police their vendees to make sure that "illicit" traffic across the trade barriers set up by the agreements would be cut off. Rifkind, District Judge:

. . . The system of territorial allocation and suppression of transAtlantic traffic in titanium compounds and pigments cannot be justified as ancillary to the grant of a license under a patent. True, the network of agreements did involve cross-licensing of patents—but it was not limited thereto. The agreements applied to patents not yet issued and to inventions not yet imagined. They applied to commerce beyond the scope of any patents. They extended to a time beyond the duration of any then existing patent. They embraced acknowledgment of patent validity with respect to patents not yet issued, nor applied for, and concerning inventions not yet conceived. They extended to countries, such as China, where no system of patent monopolies exists . . . Where there is a refusal to license (or refusal to license except on specified conditions which would extend the patent monopoly) which is the product of agreement or conspiracy, on the part of the owners of competing patents, I believe, the law is offended to the same extent as the law is violated when several combine and agree not to do business with a particular customer or class of customers.

The Supreme Court affirmed a decree which, among other things, ordered defendants to license their titanium patents, presently owned or which might be acquired within five years, at reasonable royalty rates. Defendants were also required to supply, at a reasonable charge, "know-how", i.e., information on production techniques not embodied in patents.[40] Justices Douglas, Murphy and Rutledge, dissenting in part, would have made the licenses royalty-free and would have forbidden the defendants to include as a condition in their compulsory licenses that the licensees cross-license their own patents in the field. National Lead Company eventually signed a consent decree with a provision for royalty-free licensing, abandoning its opposition in part because of the difficulty of determining "reasonable" royalties. Many other consent decrees have incorporated royalty-free licensing.[41]

United States v. Aluminum Co. of America, 91 F.Supp. 333, 411 (S.D. N.Y.1950), distinguished the *National Lead* case, and ordered deletion of grant-back provisions from compulsory licenses.

In *United States v. Imperial Chemical Industries*, 105 F.Supp. 215 (S.D. N.Y.1952), another international cartel case involving market sharing through patent cross-licenses and jointly owned companies, the court refused to order the defendants to grant reasonable royalty licenses under patents which they might acquire subsequent to the decree, except in the case of improvements on patents which had been employed in the illegal scheme. It refused to compel licensing of existing patents, except within the precise technologies covering products common in manufacture to both ICI and DuPont. It refused to order royalty-free licensing. It refused to limit recovery against infringers to reasonable royalties, even where defendants were ordered to license on reasonable royalty, despite the argument that lengthy negotiations for a license on "reasonable" terms might prejudicially delay the entry of a new competitor into the market. (223–228)

ICI was ordered to grant immunities under British analogues of American patents, so as to permit Americans to export to England. DuPont was forbidden to collect royalties on nylon manufactured under its patents for export to England. (229–231) As to jointly owned enterprises, the decree gave the defendants alternatives. It required either split-up of physical assets among defendants or acquisition of entire ownership by one or another defendant. Use of common selling agents was enjoined. (242) But continued joint ownership of a Brazilian subsidiary was authorized on evidence

40. See Timberg, Equitable Relief Under the Sherman Act, 1950 U.Ill.L.Forum 629, 649. In United States v. American Can Co., 87 F.Supp. 18 (N.D.Cal.1949), 1950–51 Trade Cases ¶ 62,679, the know-how provisions included requirements that competitors be admitted to defendant's plant to observe production methods and that they be permitted to consult defendant's technicians and attend defendant's personnel training school.

41. See Timberg, supra n. 40. A consent decree requiring Western Electric Company and its parent, American Telephone and Telegraph Company, to license approximately 8700 Bell System equipment patents held at the time of the decree, royalty-free except to Radio Corp.

of America, General Electric Co., and Westinghouse Corp., was the subject of hearings before the Antitrust Subcommittee of the House Judiciary Committee, 85th Cong., 2d Sess. (1958), where the decree was criticized as inadequate to restore competition. See also In re Eli Lilly & Co., 95 F.T.C. 538 (1980) (relief for alleged monopolization of insulin market requires licensing of existing insulin patents and know-how to any U. S. company without royalties, and to foreign companies at "reasonable" royalties; licensing "without profit" of insulin technology acquired from others within next five years; and reasonable royalty licensing of insulin patents issued to it within next five years).

that Brazilian trade policy and other factors made it unlikely that there could be American exports of ammunition in the future. Remington was enjoined, however, from using this subsidiary as its Brazilian distributor while the joint membership continued. (245–246)

In *United States v. Holophane Co.*, 119 F.Supp. 114 (S.D.Ohio 1954), aff'd per curiam 352 U.S. 903, 77 S.Ct. 144, 1 L.Ed.2d 114 (1956) the court ordered the American member of the cartel to embark upon a specified marketing program designed to penetrate the territories from which the firm had excluded itself.

(7) *Collective Enforcement of Foreign Patents by American Firms to Exclude American Competitor From Foreign Market.* See *Zenith Radio Corp. v. Hazeltine Research, Inc.*, p. 1010 supra, sustaining liability notwithstanding the legality of the patent pool's operation under the law where the pool existed and the patents were issued.

(8) *Licensing of Government-Owned Patents.* For many years there has been debate over what the federal government should do with the many patents it has acquired as a result of inventions by its employees or under research contracts. In general it has followed a policy of licensing on a royalty-free, non-exclusive basis. It has been argued conceptually that the government's acquisition of a patent automatically extinguishes the monopoly, since there is no longer a private right to exclude, and there is no public advantage in the government's perpetuating a restraint of trade that came into existence solely to stimulate private invention. At the practical and political level, it is feared that the government would be in a position to play favorites if it undertook to license limited numbers of enterprises on a royalty basis. The administrative burden of policing patent rights through infringement suits would be heavy (the government has never instituted such a suit). Some believe it would be undesirable for the government to compete with private enterprise in licensing activities. Some believe it unfair to charge users for publicly-owned information.[42]

In 1980 Congress attempted to address these problems in the University and Small Business Patent Act.[43] Among its provisions are the following: Nonprofit organizations (e.g., universities) and small business firms may retain title to inventions made pursuant to a federal research grant. The patentee's right to grant exclusive licenses under such inventions is restricted in terms of time; royalties must be shared with the inventor; and the balance of any income earned after the payment of royalties and expenses must be utilized "for the support of scientific research or education." The federal agency which funded the research that produced the invention has the right to require the patentee to grant a nonexclusive, partially exclusive, or exclusive license in any field of use to a "responsible applicant" on "reasonable" terms. With regard to all other federally owned inventions, the Act gives the government the right to apply for and maintain patents, and to grant nonexclusive, exclusive, or partially exclusive licenses with or without royalties. Guidelines for licensing are set out, requiring, inter alia, that the prospective licensee provide a plan for developing or marketing the invention, that licenses should normally be granted only if the licensee agrees the in-

---

42. For a review and rebuttal of these arguments and a plea for "businesslike" administration of the government's patent property, see Forman, Patents—Their Ownership and Administration by the United States Government, 165 et seq. (1957); cf. Government Patent Policy Study (1968), arguing a need to confer exclusive private rights in order to encourage commercial exploitation of government patents.

43. 35 U.S.C.A. §§ 200–211.

vention will be "manufactured substantially" in the United States, and that exclusive or partially exclusive licenses be granted only after finding that such licensing is "a reasonable and necessary incentive" to call forth capital investment. Exclusive or partially exclusive licenses may not be granted if the grant will "tend substantially to lessen competition or result in undue concentration in any section of the country in any line of commerce to which the technology to be licensed relates, or to create or maintain other situations inconsistent with the antitrust laws."

This legislation was assailed as a "pure giveaway of rights that properly belong to the people." [44] On the other hand, it was lauded by universities. Would you favor extending to large corporations the ownership rights the legislation grants to nonprofit organizations and small business firms? Such legislation has already been proposed.[45]

May the government constitutionally vest exclusive rights in private firms in order to encourage *development*, as distinguished from *invention*? Is there a power to promote the general welfare or interstate commerce by conferring monopolies, apart from the patent and copyright power bestowed on Congress by Art. I, § 8, of the Constitution? (Recall the discussion of the innovation process, supra p. 972.)

(9) *Comparison to Copyright—Compulsory Licenses.* As previously noted, p. 960, the 1976 Copyright Act provides liability for cable television operators who retransmit television signals, but also provides for a compulsory license on the copyrighted works. In addition the Act provides that the exclusive rights to a nondramatic musical composition embodied in a phonograph record or tape are subject to compulsory licensing. Once there is an authorized distribution of a recording, other recording companies are entitled to make recordings, but licensees must pay a specified royalty.[46] The exclusive right to public performance of nondramatic musical works from phonorecords on coin-operated machines is also subject to compulsory licensing for an annual fee per jukebox, payable to the Register of Copyrights.[47] Finally, public broadcasting stations may transmit and record nondramatic musical, pictorial, graphic, and sculptural works, under a compulsory license.[48] The money collected from cable and jukebox compulsory licensees is distributed among copyright owners by a Copyright Royalty Tribunal.

C. THE CONFLICT BETWEEN FEDERAL AND STATE POLICIES

Conflicts between federal and state economic policies are not unusual. States frequently choose to engage in economic regulation; Constitutional provisions and the Sherman Act have then been interpreted to set broad limits on the state's power. In the area of pro-

44. H.R.Rep.No.96–1307, 96th Cong., 2nd Sess. 1, 29 (1980), reprinted in 1980 U.S.Code Cong. & Ad.News 6460, 6487 (dissent of Rep. Jack Brooks).

45. See "Universities, Researchers Challenge New Patent Rules," Nat'l L.J., Oct. 12, 1981, p. 46. Section 105 of the Copyright Act, 17 U.S.C.A. § 105, provides that copyright protection is unavailable for "any work of the United States Government." As for works produced under government commission, see H.R. Rep. No. 94–1476, 94th Cong., 2d Sess. 1,

59 (1976), reprinted in 1976 U.S.Code Cong. & Ad.News 5659, 5672 ("The bill deliberately avoids making any sort of outright, unqualified prohibition against copyright in works prepared under Government contract or grant."); Schnapper v. Foley, 667 F.2d 102 (D.C.Cir.1981) (Copyright Act permits registration of works commissioned by Government).

46. 17 U.S.C.A. § 115.

47. Id., § 116.

48. Id., § 118.

tecting rights to inventions (or to works of authorship) the courts have similarly been faced with resolving conflicts between state and federal law and economic policy. In these cases the states generally seek to give rights in excess of those accorded under federal patent or copyright law; and this consequently means that state law may not only conflict with patent and copyright law, but will likely be inconsistent with federal antitrust policy.

The cases in this section of the materials deal with these conflicts in the following settings: the enforcement of contracts under state law, the enforcement of state laws forbidding "unfair competition" and "passing off," and the enforcement of state trade secret laws. The question presented by these cases is how to pay adequate deference to state policies without at the same time providing avenues for undermining federal patent and antitrust policy, which place some limits on the economic power created by federal patent and copyright law.

SEARS, ROEBUCK & CO. v. STIFFEL CO.

Supreme Court of the United States, 1964.
376 U.S. 225, 84 S.Ct. 784, 11 L.Ed.2d 661.

MR. JUSTICE BLACK delivered the opinion of the Court.

The question in this case is whether a State's unfair competition law can, consistently with the federal patent laws, impose liability for or prohibit the copying of an article which is protected by neither a federal patent nor a copyright. The respondent, Stiffel Company, secured design and mechanical patents on a "pole lamp"—a vertical tube having lamp fixtures along the outside, the tube being made so that it will stand upright between the floor and ceiling of a room. Pole lamps proved a decided commercial success, and soon after Stiffel brought them on the market, Sears, Roebuck & Company put on the market a substantially identical lamp, which it sold more cheaply, Sears' retail price being about the same as Stiffel's wholesale price. Stiffel then brought this action against Sears in the United States District Court for the Northern District of Illinois, claiming in its first count that by copying its design Sears had infringed Stiffel's patents and in its second count that by selling copies of Stiffel's lamp Sears had caused confusion in the trade as to the source of the lamps and had thereby engaged in unfair competition under Illinois law. There was evidence that identifying tags were not attached to the Sears lamps although labels appeared on the cartons in which they were delivered to customers, that customers had asked Stiffel whether its lamps differed from Sears', and that in two cases customers who had bought Stiffel lamps had complained to Stiffel on learning that Sears was selling substantially identical lamps at a much lower price.

The District Court, after holding the patents invalid for want of invention, went on to find as a fact that Sears' lamp was "a substantially exact copy" of Stiffel's and that the two lamps were so much alike, both in appearance and in functional details, "that confusion between them is likely, and some confusion has already occurred." On these findings the court held Sears guilty of unfair competition, enjoined Sears "from unfairly competing with [Stiffel] by selling or attempting to sell pole lamps identical to or confusingly similar to" Stiffel's lamp, and ordered an accounting to fix profits and damages resulting from Sears' "unfair competition."

The Court of Appeals affirmed. That court held that, to make out a case of unfair competition under Illinois law, there was no need to show that Sears had been "palming off" its lamps as Stiffel lamps; Stiffel had only to prove that there was a "likelihood of confusion as to the source of the products"—that the two articles were sufficiently identical that customers could not tell who had made a particular one. Impressed by the "remarkable sameness of appearance" of the lamps, the Court of Appeals upheld the trial court's findings of likelihood of confusion and some actual confusion, findings which the appellate court construed to mean confusion "as to the source of the lamps." The Court of Appeals thought this enough under Illinois law to sustain the trial court's holding of unfair competition, and thus held Sears liable under Illinois law for doing no more than copying and marketing an unpatented article. We granted certiorari to consider whether this use of a State's law of unfair competition is compatible with the federal patent law.

Before the Constitution was adopted, some States had granted patents either by special act or by general statute, but when the Constitution was adopted provision for a federal patent law was made one of the enumerated powers of Congress because, as Madison put it in The Federalist No. 43, the States "cannot separately make effectual provision" for either patents or copyrights. That constitutional provision is Art. I, § 8, cl. 8, which empowers Congress "To promote the Progress of Science and useful Arts, by securing for limited Times to Authors and Inventors the exclusive Right to their respective Writings and Discoveries." Pursuant to this constitutional authority, Congress in 1790 enacted the first federal patent and copyright law, 1 Stat. 109, and ever since that time has fixed the conditions upon which patents and copyrights shall be granted. These laws, like other laws of the United States enacted pursuant to constitutional authority, are the supreme law of the land. When state law touches upon the area of these federal statutes, it is "familiar doctrine" that the federal policy "may not be set at naught, or its benefits denied" by the state law. This is true, of course, even if the state law is enacted in the exercise of otherwise undoubted state power.

The grant of a patent is the grant of a statutory monopoly; indeed, the grant of patents in England was an explicit exception to the statute of James I prohibiting monopolies. Patents are not given as favors, as was the case of monopolies given by the Tudor monarchs, see The Case of Monopolies (Darcy v. Allein), 11 Co.Rep. 84b., 77 Eng.Rep. 1260 (K.B.1602), but are meant to encourage invention by rewarding the inventor with the right, limited to a term of years fixed by the patent, to exclude others from the use of his invention. During that period of time no one may make use, or sell the patented product without the patentee's authority. But in rewarding useful invention, the "rights and welfare of the community must be fairly dealt with and effectually guarded." Kendall v. Winsor, 21 How. 322, 329, 16 L.Ed. 165 (1859). To that end the prerequisites to obtaining a patent are strictly observed, and when the patent has issued the limitations on its exercise are equally strictly enforced. To begin with, a genuine "invention" or "discovery" must be demonstrated "lest in the constant demand for new appliances the heavy hand of tribute be laid on each slight technological advance in an art." Once the patent issues, it is strictly construed; it cannot be used to secure any monopoly beyond that contained in the patent; the patentee's control over the product when it leaves his hands is sharply limited; and the patent monopoly may not be used in disregard of the antitrust laws. Finally, and especially relevant here, when the patent expires the monopoly created by it expires, too, and the right to make the article—including the right to make it in precisely the shape it carried when patented—passes to the public.

Thus the patent system is one in which uniform federal standards are carefully used to promote invention while at the same time preserving free competition. Obviously a State could not, consistently with the Supremacy Clause of the Constitution, extend the life of a patent beyond its expiration date or give a patent on an article which lacked the level of invention required for federal patents. To do either would run counter to the policy of Congress of granting patents only to true inventions, and then only for a limited time. Just as a State cannot encroach upon the federal patent laws directly, it cannot, under some other law, such as that forbidding unfair competition, give protection of a kind that clashes with the objectives of the federal patent laws.

In the present case the "pole lamp" sold by Stiffel has been held not to be entitled to the protection of either a mechanical or a design patent. An unpatentable article, like an article on which the patent has expired, is in the public domain and may be made and sold by whoever chooses to do so. What Sears did was to copy Stiffel's design and to sell lamps almost identical to those sold by Stiffel. This it had every right to do under the federal patent laws. That Stiffel originated the pole lamp and made it popular is immaterial. "Sharing in the goodwill of an article unprotected by patent or trademark is the exercise of a right possessed by all—and in the free exercise of which the consuming public is deeply interested." Kellogg Co. v. National Biscuit Co., supra, 305 U.S. at 122, 59 S.Ct. at 115. To allow a State by use of its law of unfair competition to prevent the copying of an article which represents too slight an advance to be patented would be to permit the State to block off from the public something which federal law has said belongs to the public. The result would be that while federal law grants only 14 or 17 years' protection to genuine inventions, see 35 U.S.C. §§ 154, 173, States could allow perpetual protection to articles too lacking in novelty to merit any patent at all under federal constitutional standards. This would be too great an encroachment on the federal patent system to be tolerated.

Sears has been held liable here for unfair competition because of a finding of likelihood of confusion based only on the fact that Sears' lamp was copied from Stiffel's unpatented lamp and that consequently the two looked exactly alike. Of course there could be "confusion" as to who had manufactured these nearly identical articles. But mere inability of the public to tell two identical articles apart is not enough to support an injunction against copying or an award of damages for copying that which the federal patent laws permit to be copied. Doubtless a State may, in appropriate circumstances, require that goods, whether patented or unpatented, be labeled or that other precautionary steps be taken to prevent customers from being misled as to the source, just as it may protect businesses in the use of their trademarks, labels, or distinctive dress in the packaging of goods so as to prevent others, by imitating such markings, from misleading purchasers as to the source of the goods. But because of the federal patent laws a State may not, when the article is unpatented and uncopyrighted, prohibit the copying of the article itself or award damages for such copying. Cf. G. Ricordi & Co. v. Haendler, 194 F.2d 914, 916 (C.A.2d Cir. 1952). The judgment below did both and in so doing gave Stiffel the equivalent of a patent monopoly on its unpatented lamp. That was error, and Sears is entitled to a judgment in its favor.

Reversed.

LEAR, INC. v. ADKINS

Supreme Court of the United States, 1969.

395 U.S. 653, 89 S.Ct. 1902, 23 L.Ed.2d 610.

[Adkins, an engineer employed by Lear, Inc., developed an improved aeronautical gyroscope. Adkins' employment contract provided that he was to own any ideas or inventions produced by him, but that Lear would be licensed at a mutually satisfactory rate. During the pendency of the gyroscope patent application, the parties entered into a licensing contract providing that Lear might terminate its obligations under the contract if the patent office refused to issue a patent or if the patent was later held invalid. A patent much narrower than the original application was eventually issued in 1960; but meanwhile in 1957, Lear decided that Adkins' patent was worthless because his invention had been anticipated by an earlier patent to someone else, and discontinued paying royalties. Upon issuance of the patent, Adkins sued on his contract in the California court, and secured a judgment of nearly $900,000. The California Supreme Court held that the contract was in force, since the patent had never been held invalid, and that Lear was foreclosed by estoppel from defending on the ground of invalidity of the patent.]

MR. JUSTICE HARLAN delivered the opinion of the Court.

Since the California Supreme Court's construction of the 1955 licensing agreement is solely a matter of state law, the only issue open to us is raised by the court's reliance upon the doctrine of estoppel to bar Lear from proving that Adkins' ideas were dedicated to the common welfare by federal law. In considering the propriety of the State Court's decision, we are well aware that we are not writing upon a clean slate. The doctrine of estoppel has been considered by this Court in a line of cases reaching back into the middle of the 19th century. Before deciding what the role of estoppel should be in the present case and in the future, it is, then, desirable to consider the role it has played in the past.

While the roots of the doctrine have often been celebrated in tradition, we have found only one 19th century case in this Court that invoked estoppel in a considered manner. And that case was decided before the Sherman Act made it clear that the grant of monopoly power to a patent owner constituted a limited exception to the general federal policy favoring free competition. Kinsman v. Parkhurst, 18 How. 289, 15 L.Ed. 385 (1856). Curiously, a second decision often cited as supporting the estoppel doctrine points clearly in the opposite direction. St. Paul Plow Works v. Starling, 140 U.S. 184, 11 S.Ct. 803, 35 L.Ed. 404 (1891), did not even question the right of the lower courts to admit the licensee's evidence showing that the patented device was not novel. A unanimous Court merely held that, where there was conflicting evidence as to an invention's novelty, it would not reverse the decision of the lower court upholding the patent's validity.

In the very next year, this Court found the doctrine of patent estoppel so inequitable that it refused to grant an injunction to enforce a licensee's promise never to contest the validity of the underlying patent. "It is as important to the public that competition should not be repressed by worthless patents, as that the patentee of a really valuable invention should be protected in his monopoly . . . ." Pope Manufacturing Co. v. Gormully, 144 U.S. 224, 234, 12 S.Ct. 632, 636, 36 L.Ed. 414 (1892).

Although this Court invoked an estoppel in 1905 without citing or considering *Pope's* powerful argument, United States v. Harvey Steel Co., 196 U.S. 310, 25 S.Ct. 240, 49 L.Ed. 492, the doctrine was not to be applied again in this Court until it was revived in Automatic Radio Manufacturing Co. v. Hazeltine Research, Inc., which declared, without prolonged analysis, that licensee estoppel was "the general rule." 339 U.S., at 836, 70 S.Ct., at 899. In so holding, the majority ignored the teachings of a series of decisions this Court had rendered during the 45 years since *Harvey* had been decided. During this period, each time a patentee sought to rely upon his estoppel privilege before this Court, the majority created a new exception to permit judicial scrutiny into the validity of the Patent Office's grant. Long before *Hazeltine* was decided, the estoppel doctrine had been so eroded that it could no longer be considered the "general rule," but was only to be invoked in an ever-narrowing set of circumstances.

The estoppel rule was first stringently limited in a situation in which the patentee's equities were far more compelling than those presented in the typical licensing arrangement. Westinghouse Electric & Manufacturing Co. v. Formica Insulation Co., 266 U.S. 342, 45 S.Ct. 117, 69 L.Ed. 316 (1924), framed a rule to govern the recurring problem which arises when the original patent owner, after assigning his patent to another for a substantial sum, claims that the patent is worthless because it contains no new ideas. The courts of appeals had traditionally refused to permit such a defense to an infringement action on the ground that it was improper both to "sell and keep the same thing," Faulks v. Kamp, 2 Cir., 3 F. 898, 902 (1880). Nevertheless, *Formica*, imposed a limitation upon estoppel which was radically inconsistent with the premises upon which the "general rule" is based. The Court held that while an assignor may not directly attack the validity of a patent by reference to the prior state of the art, he could introduce such evidence to *narrow* the claims made in the patent. "The distinction may be a nice one but seems to be workable." 266 U.S., at 351, 45 S.Ct., at 120. Workable or not, the result proved to be an anomaly: if a patent had *some* novelty *Formica* permitted the old owner to defend an infringement action by showing that the invention's novel aspects did not extend to the inclusion of the old owner's products; on the other hand, if a patent had *no* novelty at all, the old owner could not defend successfully since he would be obliged to launch the direct attack on the patent that *Formica* seemed to forbid. The incongruity of this position compelled at least one court of appeals to carry the reasoning of the *Formica* exception to its logical conclusion. In 1940 the Seventh Circuit held that a licensee could introduce evidence of the prior art to show that the licensor's claims were not novel at all and thus successfully defend an action for royalties. Casco Products Corp. v. Sinko Tool & Manufacturing Co., 116 F.2d 119.

In Scott Paper Co. v. Marcalus Manufacturing Co., 326 U.S. 249, 66 S.Ct. 101, 90 L.Ed. 47 (1945), this Court adopted a position similar to the Seventh Circuit's, undermining the basis of patent estoppel even more than *Formica* had done. In *Scott*, the original patent owner had attempted to defend an infringement suit brought by his assignee by proving that his product was a copy of an expired patent. The Court refused to permit the assignee to invoke an estoppel, finding that the policy of the patent laws would be frustrated if a manufacturer was required to pay for the use of information which under the patent statutes, was the property of all. Chief Justice Stone, for the Court, did not go beyond the precise question presented by a manufacturer who asserted that he was simply copying an expired patent. Nevertheless it was impossible to limit the *Scott* doctrine to such a narrow compass. If patent policy forbids estoppel when the old owner attempts to show that he did no more than copy an expired patent, why should not the old owner also be permitted to show that the invention lacked novelty because it could be found in a technical journal or because it was obvious to one knowledgeable in the art? As Justice Frankfurter's dissent indicated, id., at 258–264, 66 S.Ct., at 105–108, there were no satisfactory answers to these questions. The *Scott* exception had undermined the very basis of the "general rule."

At about the time *Scott* was decided, this Court developed yet another doctrine which was profoundly antithetic to the principles underlying estoppel. In Sola Electric Co. v. Jefferson Electric Co., 317 U.S. 173, 63 S.Ct. 172, 87 L.Ed. 165 (1942), the majority refused to permit a licensor to enforce the license's price-fixing provisions without permitting the licensee to contest the validity of the underlying patent. Since the price-fixing clause was *per se* illegal but for the existence of a valid patent, this narrow exception could be countenanced without compromising the general estoppel principle. But the *Sola* Court went further: it held that since the patentee had sought to enforce the price-fixing clause, the licensee could also avoid paying royalties if he could show that the patent was invalid. Five years later, the "antitrust exception" was given an even more extensive scope in the *Katzinger* and *MacGregor* cases. Here licensors were not permitted to invoke an estoppel despite the fact that they sought only to collect their royalties. The mere existence of a price-fixing clause in the license was held to be enough to bring the validity of the patent into question. Thus in the large number of cases in which licensing agreements contained restrictions that were arguably illegal under the antitrust laws, the doctrine of estoppel was a dead letter. Justice Frankfurter, in dissent, went even further, concluding that *Katzinger* and *MacGregor* had done all but repudiate the estoppel rule: "If a doctrine that was vital law for more than ninety years will be found to have now been deprived of life, we ought at least to give it decent public burial." 329 U.S., at 416, 67 S.Ct., at 428.

The lower courts, both state and federal, have also hedged the impact of estoppel by creating exceptions which have indicated a recognition of the broader policies pointing to a contrary approach. It is generally the rule that licensees may avoid further royalty payments, regardless of the provisions of their contract, once a third party proves that the patent is invalid. See, e.g., Drackett Chemical Co. v. Chamberlain Co., 63 F.2d 853 (6 Cir., 1933). Some courts have gone further to hold that a licensee may notify the patent owner that he is repudiating his agreement regardless of its terms, and may subsequently defend any action for royalties by proving patent invalidity. And even in the 19th century, state courts had held that if the licensee had not actually sold products incorporating the patent's ideas, he could challenge the validity of the patent.

The uncertain status of licensee estoppel in the case law is a product of judicial efforts to accommodate the competing demands of the common law of contracts and the federal law of patents. On the one hand, the law of contracts forbids a purchaser to repudiate his promises simply because he later becomes dissatisfied with the bargain he has made. On the other hand, federal law requires, that all ideas in general circulation be dedicated to the common good unless they are protected by a valid patent. When faced with this basic conflict in policy, both this Court and courts throughout the land have naturally sought to develop an intermediate position which somehow would remain responsive to the radically different concerns of the two different worlds of contract and patent. The result has been a failure. Rather than creative compromise, there has been a chaos of conflicting case law, proceeding on inconsistent premises. Before renewing the search for an acceptable middle ground, we must reconsider on their own merits the arguments which may properly be advanced on both sides of the estoppel question.

It will simplify matters greatly if we first consider the most typical situation in which patent licenses are negotiated. In contrast to the present case, most manufacturers obtain a license after a patent has issued. Since the Patent Office makes an inventor's ideas public when it issues its grant of a limited monopoly, a potential licensee has access to the inventor's ideas even if he does not enter into an agreement with the patent owner. Consequently, a manufacturer gains only two benefits if he chooses to enter a licensing agreement after the patent has issued. First, by accepting a license and paying royalties for a time, the licensee may have avoided the necessity of defending an expensive infringement action during the period when he may be least able to afford one. Second, the existence of an unchallenged patent may deter others from attempting to compete with the licensee.

Under ordinary contract principles the mere fact that some benefit is received is enough to require the enforcement of the contract, regardless of the validity of the underlying patent. Nevertheless, if one tests this result by the standard of good-faith commercial dealing, it seems far from satisfactory. For the simple contract approach entirely ignores the position of the licensor who is seeking to invoke the court's assistance on his behalf. Consider, for example, the equities of the licensor who has obtained his patent through a fraud on the Patent Office. It is difficult to perceive why good faith requires that courts should permit him to recover royalties despite his licensee's attempts to show that the patent is invalid.

Even in the more typical cases, not involving conscious wrongdoing, the licensor's equities are far from compelling. A patent, in the last analysis, simply represents a legal conclusion reached by the Patent Office. Moreover, the legal conclusion is predicated on factors as to which reasonable men can differ widely. Yet the Patent Office is often obliged to reach its decision in an *ex parte* proceeding, without the aid of the arguments which could be advanced by parties interested in proving patent invalidity. Consequently, it does not seem to us to be unfair to require a patentee to defend the Patent Office's judgment when his licensee places the question in issue, especially since the licensor's case is buttressed by the presumption of validity which attaches to his patent. Thus, although licensee estoppel may be consistent with the letter of contractual doctrine, we cannot say that it is compelled by the spirit of contract law, which seeks to balance the claims of promisor and promisee in accord with the requirements of good faith.

Surely the equities of the licensor do not weigh very heavily when they are balanced against the important public interest in permitting full and free competition in the use of ideas which are in reality a part of the public domain. Licensees may often be the only individuals with enough economic incentive to challenge the patentability of an inventor's discovery. If they are muzzled, the public may continually be required to pay tribute to would-be monopolists without need or justification. We think it plain that the technical requirements of contract doctrine must give way before the demands of the public interest in the typical situation involving the negotiation of a license after a patent has issued.

We are satisfied that Automatic Radio Manufacturing Co. v. Hazeltine Research, Inc., supra, itself the product of a clouded history, should no longer be regarded as sound law with respect to its "estoppel" holding, and that holding is now overruled.

The case before us, however, presents a far more complicated estoppel problem than the one which arises in the most common licensing context. The problem arises out of the fact that Lear obtained its license in 1955, more than four years before Adkins received his 1960 patent. Indeed, from the very outset of the relationship, Lear obtained special access to Adkins' ideas in return for its promise to pay satisfactory compensation.

Thus, during the lengthy period in which Adkins was attempting to obtain a patent, Lear gained an important benefit not generally obtained by the typical licensee. For until a patent issues, a potential licensee may not learn his licensor's ideas simply by requesting the information from the Patent Office. During the time the inventor is seeking patent protection, the governing federal statute requires the Patent Office to hold an inventor's patent application in confidence. If a potential licensee hopes to use the ideas contained in a secret patent application, he must deal with the inventor himself, unless the inventor chooses to publicize his ideas to the world at large. By promising to pay Adkins royalties from the very outset of their relationship, Lear gained immediate access to ideas which it may well not have learned until the Patent Office published the details of Adkins' invention in 1960. At the core of this case, then, is the difficult question whether federal patent policy bars a State from enforcing a contract regulating access to an unpatented secret idea.

Adkins takes an extreme position on this question. The inventor does not merely argue that since Lear obtained privileged access to his ideas *before 1960*, the company should be required to pay royalties accruing *before 1960* regardless of the validity of the patent which ultimately issued. He also argues that since Lear obtained special benefits before 1960, it should also pay royalties during the entire patent period (1960–1977), without regard to the validity of the Patent Office's grant. We cannot accept so broad an argument.

Adkins' position would permit inventors to negotiate all important licenses during the lengthy period while their applications were still pending at the Patent Office, thereby disabling entirely all those who have the strongest incentive to show that a patent is worthless. While the equities supporting Adkins' position are somewhat more appealing than those supporting the typical licensor, we cannot say that there is enough of a difference to justify such a substantial impairment of overriding federal policy.

Nor can we accept a second argument which may be advanced to support Adkins' claim to at least a portion of his post-patent royalties, regardless of the validity of the Patent Office grant. The terms of the 1955 agreement provide that royalties are to be paid until such time as the "patent . . . is held invalid," § 6, and the fact remains that the question of patent validity has not been finally determined in this case. Thus, it may be suggested that although Lear must be allowed to raise the question of patent validity in the present lawsuit, it must also be required to comply with its contract and continue to pay royalties until its claim is finally vindicated in the courts.

The parties' contract, however, is no more controlling on this issue than is the State's doctrine of estoppel, which is also rooted in contract principles. The decisive question is whether overriding federal policies would be significantly frustrated if licensees could be required to continue to pay royalties during the time they are challenging patent validity in the courts.

It seems to us that such a requirement would be inconsistent with the aims of federal patent policy. Enforcing this contractual provision would give the licensor an additional economic incentive to devise every conceivable dilatory tactic in an effort to postpone the day of final judicial reckoning. We can perceive no reason to encourage dilatory court tactics in this way. Moreover, the cost of prosecuting slow-moving trial proceedings and defending an inevitable appeal might well deter many licensees from attempting to prove patent invalidity in the courts. The deterrent effect would be particularly severe in the many scientific fields in which invention is proceeding at a rapid rate. In these areas, a patent may well become obsolete long before its 17-year term has expired. If a licensee has reason to believe that he will replace a patented idea with a new one in the near future, he will have little incentive to initiate lengthy court proceedings, unless he is freed from liability at least from the time he refuses to pay the contractual royalties. Lastly, enforcing this contractual provision would undermine the strong federal policy favoring the full and free use of ideas in the public domain. For all these reasons, we hold that Lear must be permitted to avoid the payment of all royalties accruing after Adkins' 1960 patent issued if Lear can prove patent invalidity.

Adkins' claim to contractual royalties accruing before the 1960 patent issued is, however, a much more difficult one, since it squarely raises the question whether, and to what extent, the States may protect the owners of *unpatented* inventions who are willing to disclose their ideas to manufacturers only upon payment of royalties. The California Supreme Court did not address itself to this issue with precision, for it believed that the venerable doctrine of estoppel provided a sufficient answer to all of Lear's claims based upon federal patent law. Thus, we do not know whether the Supreme Court would have awarded Adkins recovery even on his pre-patent royalties if it had recognized that previously established estoppel doctrine could no longer be properly invoked with regard to royalties accruing during the 17-year patent period. Our decision today will, of course, require the state courts to reconsider the theoretical basis of their decisions enforcing the contractual rights of inventors and it is impossible to predict the extent to which this re-evaluation may revolutionize the law of any particular State in this regard. Consequently, we have concluded, after much consideration, that even though an important question of federal law underlies this phase of the controversy, we should not now attempt to define in even a limited way the extent, if any, to which the States may properly act to enforce the contractual rights of inventors of unpatented secret ideas. Given the difficulty and importance of this task, it should be undertaken only after the state courts have, after fully focused inquiry, determined the extent to which they will respect the contractual rights of such inventors in the future. Indeed, on remand, the California courts may well reconcile the competing demands of patent and contract law in a way which would not warrant further review in this Court.

[Justices Black, Warren and Douglas concurred in the demise of estoppel, but would have gone further to state, on the authority of Sears, Roebuck & Co. v. Stiffel Co. [p. 1040 supra], that "no State has a right to authorize any kind of monopoly on what is claimed to be a new invention, except when a patent has been obtained . . . ." Mr. Justice White, concurring as to estoppel, would have limited the decision to that point, in the view that questions of contractual rights independent of validity of patent were for the State to decide.]

KEWANEE OIL CO. v. BICRON CORP.

Supreme Court of the United States, 1974.
416 U.S. 470, 94 S.Ct. 1879, 40 L.Ed.2d 315.

MR. CHIEF JUSTICE BURGER delivered the opinion of the Court.

We granted certiorari to resolve a question on which there is a conflict in the courts of appeals: whether state trade secret protection is pre-empted by operation of the federal patent law. In the instant case the Court of Appeals for the Sixth Circuit held that there was preemption. The Courts of Appeals for the Second, Fourth, Fifth, and Ninth Circuits have reached the opposite conclusion.

I

Harshaw Chemical Co., an unincorporated division of petitioner, is a leading manufacturer of a type of synthetic crystal which is useful in detection of ionizing radiation. In 1949 Harshaw commenced research into the growth of this type crystal and was able to produce one less than two inches in diameter. By 1966, as the result of expenditures in excess of $1 million, Harshaw was able to grow a 17-inch crystal, something no one else had done previously. Harshaw had developed many processes, procedures, and manufacturing techniques in the purification of raw materials and the growth and encapsulation of the crystals which enabled it to accomplish this feat. Some of these processes Harshaw considers to be trade secrets.

The individual respondents are former employees of Harshaw who formed or later joined respondent Bicron. While at Harshaw the individual respondents executed, as a condition of employment, at least one agreement each, requiring them not to disclose confidential information or trade secrets obtained as employees of Harshaw. Bicron was formed in August 1969 to compete with Harshaw in the production of the crystals, and by April 1970, had grown a 17-inch crystal.

Petitioner brought this diversity action in United States District Court for the Northern District of Ohio seeking injunctive relief and damages for the misappropriation of trade secrets. The District Court, applying Ohio trade secret law, granted a permanent injunction against the disclosure or use by respondents of 20 of the 40 claimed trade secrets until such time as the trade secrets had been released to the public, had otherwise generally become available to the public, or had been obtained by respondents from sources having the legal right to convey the information.

The Court of Appeals for the Sixth Circuit held that the findings of fact by the District Court were not clearly erroneous, and that it was evident from the record that the individual respondents appropriated to the benefit of Bicron secret information on processes obtained while they were employees at Harshaw. Further, the Court of Appeals held that the District Court properly applied Ohio law relating to trade secrets. Nevertheless, the Court of Appeals reversed the District Court, finding Ohio's trade secret law to be in conflict with the patent laws of the United States. The Court of Appeals reasoned that Ohio could not grant monopoly protection to processes and manufacturing techniques that were appropriate subjects for consideration under 35 U.S.C. § 101 for a federal patent but which had been in commercial use for over one year and so were no longer eligible for patent protection under 35 U.S.C. § 102(b).

We hold that Ohio's law of trade secrets is not preempted by the patent laws of the United States, and, accordingly, we reverse.

II

Ohio has adopted the widely relied-upon definition of a trade secret found at Restatement of Torts § 757, comment *b* (1939). According to the Restatement,

"[a] trade secret may consist of any formula, pattern, device or compilation of information which is used in one's business, and which gives him an opportunity to obtain an advantage over competitors who do not know or use it. It may be a formula for a chemical compound, a process of manufacturing, treating or preserving materials, a pattern for a machine or other device, or a list of customers."

The subject of a trade secret must be secret, and must not be of public knowledge or of a general knowledge in the trade or business. This necessary element of secrecy is not lost, however, if the holder of the trade secret reveals the trade secret to another "in confidence, and under an implied obligation not to use or disclose it." These others may include those of the holder's "employees to whom it is necessary to confide it, in order to apply it to the uses for which it is intended." Often the recipient of confidential knowledge of the subject of a trade secret is a licensee of its holder. See Lear, Inc. v. Adkins, 395 U.S. 653 (1969).

The protection accorded the trade secret holder is against the disclosure or unauthorized use of the trade secret by those to whom the secret has been confided under the express or implied restriction of nondisclosure or nonuse.[49] The law also protects the holder of a trade secret against disclosure or use when the knowledge is gained, not by the owner's volition, but by some "improper means," Restatement of Torts § 757(a), which may include theft, wiretapping, or even aerial reconnaissance. A trade secret law, however, does not offer protection against discovery by fair and honest means, such as by independent invention, accidental disclosure, or by so-called reverse engineering, that is by starting with the known product and working backward to divine the process which aided in its development or manufacture.

Novelty, in the patent law sense, is not required for a trade secret, . . . However, some novelty will be required if merely because that which does not possess novelty is usually known; secrecy, in the context of trade secrets, thus implies at least minimal novelty.

. . .

III

The first issue we deal with is whether the States are forbidden to act at all in the area of protection of the kinds of intellectual property which may make up the subject matter of trade secrets.

49. [Court's footnote 4.] Ohio Rev. Code Ann. § 1333.51(C) (Supp.1973) provides:

"No person, having obtained possession of an article representing a trade secret or access thereto with the owner's consent, shall convert such article to his own use or that of another person, or thereafter without the owner's consent make or cause to be made a copy of such article, or exhibit such article to another."

Ohio Rev.Code Ann. § 1333.99(E) (Supp.1973) provides:

"Whoever violates section 1333.51 of the Revised Code shall be fined not more than five thousand dollars, imprisoned not less than one nor more than ten years, or both."

Article I, § 8, cl. 8, of the Constitution grants to the Congress the power

> "[t]o promote the Progress of Science and useful Arts, by securing for limited Times to Authors and Inventors the exclusive Right to their respective Writings and Discoveries . . .."

In the 1972 Term, in Goldstein v. California, 412 U.S. 546 (1973), we held that the cl. 8 grant of power to Congress was not exclusive and that, at least in the case of writings, the States were not prohibited from encouraging and protecting the efforts of those within their borders by appropriate legislation. The States could, therefore, protect against the unauthorized rerecording for sale of performances fixed on records or tapes, even though those performances qualified as "writings" in the constitutional sense and Congress was empowered to legislate regarding such performances and could pre-empt the area if it chose to do so. This determination was premised on the great diversity of interests in our Nation—the essentially nonuniform character of the appreciation of intellectual achievements in the various States. Evidence for this came from patents granted by the States in the 18th century. 412 U.S., at 557.

Just as the States may exercise regulatory power over writings so may the States regulate with respect to discoveries. States may hold diverse viewpoints in protecting intellectual property relating to invention as they do in protecting the intellectual property relating to the subject matter of copyright. The only limitation on the States is that in regulating the area of patents and coyprights they do not conflict with the operation of the laws in this area passed by Congress, and it is to that more difficult question we now turn.

IV

The question of whether the trade secret law of Ohio is void under the Supremacy Clause involves a consideration of whether that law "stands as an obstacle to the accomplishment and execution of the full purposes and objectives of Congress." Hines v. Davidowitz, 312 U.S. 52, 67 (1941). . . .

The laws which the Court of Appeals in this case held to be in conflict with the Ohio law of trade secrets were the patent laws passed by the Congress in the unchallenged exercise of its clear power under Art. I, § 8, cl. 8 of the Constitution. The patent law does not explicitly endorse or forbid the operation of trade secret law. However, as we have noted, if the scheme of protection developed by Ohio respecting trade secrets "clashes with the objectives of the federal patent laws," Sears, Roebuck & Co. v. Stiffel Co., supra, at 231, then the state law must fall. To determine whether the Ohio law "clashes" with the federal law it is helpful to examine the objectives of both the patent and trade secret laws.

The stated objective of the Constitution in granting the power to Congress to legislate in the area of intellectual property is to "promote the Progress of Science and useful Arts." The patent laws pro-

mote this progress by offering a right of exclusion for a limited period as an incentive to inventors to risk the often enormous costs in
terms of time, research, and development. The productive effort
thereby fostered will have a positive effect on society through the
introduction of new products and processes of manufacture into the
economy, and the emanations by way of increased employment and
better lives for our citizens. In return for the right of exclusion—
this "reward for inventions," Universal Oil Co. v. Globe Co., 322 U.S.
471, 484 (1944)—the patent laws impose upon the inventor a requirement of disclosure. To insure adequate and full disclosure so that
upon the expiration of the 17-year period "the knowledge of the invention enures to the people, who are thus enabled without restriction to practice it and profit by its use," United States v. Dubilier
Condenser Corp., 289 U.S. 178, 187 (1933), the patent laws require
that the patent application shall include a full and clear description of
the invention and "of the manner and process of making and using
it" so that any person skilled in the art may make and use the invention. 35 U.S.C. § 112. When a patent is granted and the information
contained in it is circulated to the general public and those especially
skilled in the trade, such additions to the general store of knowledge
are of such importance to the public weal that the Federal Government is willing to pay the high price of 17 years of exclusive use for
its disclosure, which disclosure, it is assumed, will stimulate ideas and
the eventual development of further significant advances in the art.
The Court has also articulated another policy of the patent law: that
which is in the public domain cannot be removed therefrom by action
of the States.

"[F]ederal law requires that all ideas in general circulation be
dedicated to the common good unless they are protected by a valid
patent." Lear, Inc. v. Adkins, 395 U.S., at 668.

The maintenance of standards of commercial ethics and the encouragement of invention are the broadly stated policies behind trade
secret law. "The necessity of good faith and honest, fair dealing, is
the very life and spirit of the commercial world." National Tube Co.
v. Eastern Tube Co., 3 Ohio C.C.R. (n.s.), at 462. In A. O. Smith
Corp. v. Petroleum Iron Works Co., 73 F.2d, at 539, the Court emphasized that even though a discovery may not be patentable, that does
not

> "destroy the value of the discovery to one who makes it, or
> advantage the competitor who by unfair means, or as the benefici-
> ary of a broken faith, obtains the desired knowledge without him-
> self paying the price in labor, money, or machines expended by the
> discoverer."

In Wexler v. Greenberg, 399 Pa. 569, 578–579, 160 A.2d 430, 434–435
(1960), the Pennsylvania Supreme Court noted the importance of
trade secret protection to the subsidization of research and development and to increased economic efficiency within large companies
through the dispersion of responsibilities for creative developments.

Having now in mind the objectives of both the patent and trade secret law, we turn to an examination of the interaction of these systems of protection of intellectual property—one established by the Congress and the other by a State—to determine whether and under what circumstances the latter might constitute "too great an encroachment on the federal patent system to be tolerated." Sears, Roebuck & Co. v. Stiffel Co., 376 U.S., at 232.

As we noted earlier, trade secret law protects items which would not be proper subjects for consideration for patent protection under 35 U.S.C. § 101. As in the case of the recordings in Goldstein v. California, Congress, with respect to nonpatentable subject matter, "has drawn no balance; rather, it has left the area unattended, and no reason exists why the State should not be free to act." Goldstein v. California, supra, at 570 (footnote omitted).

Since no patent is available for a discovery, however useful, novel, and nonobvious, unless it falls within one of the express categories of patentable subject matter of 35 U.S.C. § 101, the holder of such a discovery would have no reason to apply for a patent whether trade secret protection existed or not. Abolition of trade secret protection would, therefore, not result in increased disclosure to the public of discoveries in the area of nonpatentable subject matter. Also, it is hard to see how the public would be benefited by disclosure of customer lists or advertising campaigns; in fact, keeping such items secret encourages businesses to initiate new and individualized plans of operation, and constructive competition results. This, in turn, leads to a greater variety of business methods than would otherwise be the case if privately developed marketing and other data were passed illicitly among firms involved in the same enterprise.

Congress has spoken in the area of those discoveries which fall within one of the categories of patentable subject matter of 35 U.S.C. § 101 and which are, therefore, of a nature that would be subject to consideration for a patent. Processes, machines, manufacturers, compositions of matter, and improvements thereof, which meet the tests of utility, novelty, and nonobviousness are entitled to be patented, but those which do not, are not. The question remains whether those items which are proper subjects for consideration for a patent may also have available the alternative protection accorded by trade secret law.

Certainly the patent policy of encouraging invention is not disturbed by the existence of another form of incentive to invention. In this respect the two systems are not and never would be in conflict. Similarly, the policy that matter once in the public domain must remain in the public domain is not incompatible with the existence of trade secret protection. By definition a trade secret has not been placed in the public domain.

The more difficult objective of the patent law to reconcile with trade secret law is that of disclosure, the *quid pro quo* of the right to exclude. We are helped in this stage of the analysis by Judge Henry Friendly's opinion in Painton & Co. v. Bourns, Inc., 442 F.2d 216 (CA2

1971). There the Court of Appeals thought it useful, in determining
whether inventors will refrain because of the existence of trade secret law from applying for patents, thereby depriving the public from
learning of the invention, to distinguish between three categories of
trade secrets:

> "(1) the trade secret believed by its owner to constitute a valid-
> ly patentable invention; (2) the trade secret known to its owner
> not to be so patentable; and (3) the trade secret whose valid pat-
> entability is considered dubious."

Trade secret protection in each of these categories would run against
breaches of confidence—the employee and licensee situations—and
theft and other forms of industrial espionage.

As to the trade secret known not to meet the standards of patentability, very little in the way of disclosure would be accomplished by
abolishing trade secret protection. With trade secrets of nonpatentable subject matter, the patent alternative would not reasonably be
available to the inventor. "There can be no public interest in stimulating developers of such [unpatentable] knowhow to flood an over-
burdened Patent Office with applications [for] what they do not consider patentable." Ibid. The mere filing of applications doomed to
be turned down by the Patent Office will bring forth no new public
knowledge or enlightenment, since under federal statute and regulation patent applications and abandoned patent applications are held
by the Patent Office in confidence and are not open to public inspection.

Even as the extension of trade secret protection to patentable subject matter that the owner knows will not meet the standards of patentability will not conflict with the patent policy of disclosure, it will
have a decidedly beneficial effect on society. Trade secret law will
encourage invention in areas where patent law does not reach, and
will prompt the independent innovator to proceed with the discovery
and exploitation of his invention. Competition is fostered and the
public is not deprived of the use of valuable, if not quite patentable,
invention.

Even if trade secret protection against the faithless employee
were abolished, inventive and exploitive effort in the area of patentable subject matter that did not meet the standards of patentability
would continue, although at a reduced level. Alternatively with the
effort that remained, however, would come an increase in the amount
of self-help that innovative companies would employ. Knowledge
would be widely dispersed among the employees of those still active
in research. Security precautions necessarily would be increased,
and salaries and fringe benefits of those few officers or employees
who had to know the whole of the secret invention would be fixed in
an amount thought sufficient to assure their loyalty. Smaller companies would be placed at a distinct economic disadvantage, since the
costs of this kind of self-help could be great, and the cost to the public of the use of this invention would be increased. The innovative
entrepreneur with limited resources would tend to confine his re-

search efforts to himself and those few he felt he could trust without the ultimate assurance of legal protection against breaches of confidence. As a result, organized scientific and technological research could become fragmented, and society, as a whole, would suffer.

Another problem that would arise if state trade secret protection were precluded is in the area of licensing others to exploit secret processes. The holder of a trade secret would not likely share his secret with a manufacturer who cannot be placed under binding legal obligation to pay a license fee or to protect the secret. The result would be to hoard rather than disseminate knowledge. Instead, then, of licensing others to use his invention and making the most efficient use of existing manufacturing and marketing structures within the industry, the trade secret holder would tend either to limit his utilization of the invention, thereby depriving the public of the maximum benefit of its use, or engage in the time-consuming and economically wasteful enterprise of constructing duplicative manufacturing and marketing mechanisms for the exploitation of the invention. The detrimental misallocation of resources and economic waste that would thus take place if trade secret protection were abolished with respect to employees or licensees cannot be justified by reference to any policy that the federal patent law seeks to advance.

Nothing in the patent law requires that States refrain from action to prevent industrial espionage. In addition to the increased costs for protection from burglary, wiretapping, bribery, and the other means used to misappropriate trade secrets, there is the inevitable cost to the basic decency of society when one firm steals from another. A most fundamental human right, that of privacy, is threatened when industrial espionage is condoned or is made profitable; the state interest in denying profit to such illegal ventures is unchallengeable.

The next category of patentable subject matter to deal with is the invention whose holder has a legitimate doubt as to its patentability. The risk of eventual patent invalidity by the courts and the costs associated with that risk may well impel some with a good-faith doubt as to patentability not to take the trouble to seek to obtain and defend patent protection for their discoveries, regardless of the existence of trade secret protection. Trade secret protection would assist those inventors in the more efficient exploitation of their discoveries and not conflict with the patent law. In most cases of genuine doubt as to patent validity the potential rewards of patent protection are so far superior to those accruing to holders of trade secrets, that the holders of such inventions will seek patent protection, ignoring the trade secret route. For those inventors "on the line" as to whether to seek patent protection, the abolition of trade secret protection might encourage some to apply for a patent who otherwise would not have done so. For some of those so encouraged, no patent will be granted and the result "will have been an unnecessary postponement in the divulging of the trade secret to persons willing to pay for it. If [the patent does issue], it may well be invalid, yet many will prefer to pay a modest royalty than to contest it, even though *Lear* allows them to accept a license and pursue the contest without paying royalties while the fight goes on. The result in such a case would be unjustified royalty payments from many who would prefer not to pay them rather than agreed fees from one or a few who are entirely willing to do so." Painton & Co. v. Bourns, Inc., 442 F.2d, at 225. The point is that those who might be encouraged to file for patents by the absence of trade secret law will include inventors possessing the chaff as well as the wheat. Some of the chaff—the nonpatentable discoveries—will be thrown out by the Patent Office, but in the meantime society will have been deprived of use of those discoveries through trade secret-protected licensing. Some of the chaff may not be thrown out. This Court has noted the difference between the standards used by the Patent Office and the courts to determine patentability. Graham v. John Deere Co., 383 U.S. 1, 18 (1966). In Lear, Inc. v. Adkins, 395 U.S. 653 (1969), the Court thought that an invalid patent was so serious a threat to the free use of ideas already in the public domain that the Court permitted licensees of the patent holder to challenge the validity of the patent. Better had the invalid patent never been issued. More of those patents would likely issue if trade secret law were abolished. Eliminating trade secret law for the doubtfully patentable invention is thus likely to have deleterious effects on society and patent policy which we cannot say are balanced out by the speculative gain which might result from the encouragement of some inventors with doubtfully patentable inventions which deserve patent protection to come forward and apply for patents. There is no conflict, then, between trade secret law and the patent law policy of disclosure, at least insofar as the first two categories of patentable subject matter are concerned.

The final category of patentable subject matter to deal with is the clearly patentable invention, i.e., that invention which the owner believes to meet the standards of patentability. It is here that the federal interest in disclosure is at its peak; these inventions, novel, useful and nonobvious, are " 'the things which are worth to the public the embarrassment of an exclusive patent.' " Graham v. John Deere Co., supra, at 9 (quoting Thomas Jefferson). The interest of the public is that the bargain of 17 years of exclusive use in return for disclosure be accepted. If a State, through a system of protection, were to cause a substantial risk that holders of patentable inventions would not seek patents, but rather would rely on the state protection, we would be compelled to hold that such a system could not constitutionally continue to exist. In the case of trade secret law no reasonable risk of deterrence from patent application by those who can reasonably expect to be granted patents exists.

Trade secret law provides far weaker protection in many respects than the patent law. While trade secret law does not forbid the discovery of the trade secret by fair and honest means, e.g., independent creation or reverse engineering, patent law operates "against the world," forbidding any use of the invention for whatever purpose for a significant length of time. The holder of a trade secret also takes a substantial risk that the secret will be passed on to his competitors, by theft or by breach of a confidential relationship, in a manner not easily susceptible of discovery or proof. Where patent law acts as a barrier, trade secret law functions relatively as a sieve. The possibility that an inventor who believes his invention meets the standards of patentability will sit back, rely on trade secret law, and after one year of use forfeit any right to patent protection, 35 U.S.C. § 102(b), is remote indeed.

Nor does society face much risk that scientific or technological progress will be impeded by the rare inventor with a patentable invention who chooses trade secret protection over patent protection. The ripeness-of-time concept of invention, developed from the study of the many independent multiple discoveries in history, predicts that if a particular individual had not made a particular discovery others would have, and in probably a relatively short period of time. If something is to be discovered at all very likely it will be discovered by more than one person. Singletons and Multiples in Science (1961), in R. Merton, The Sociology of Science 343 (1973); J. Cole & S. Cole, Social Stratification in Science 12–13, 229–230 (1973); Ogburn & Thomas, Are Inventions Inevitable?, 37 Pol.Sci.Q. 83 (1922). Even were an inventor to keep his discovery completely to himself, something that neither the patent nor trade secret laws forbid, there is a high probability that it will be soon independently developed. If the invention, though still a trade secret, is put into public use, the competition is alerted to the existence of the inventor's solution to the problem and may be encouraged to make an extra effort to independently find the solution thus known to be possible. The inventor faces pressures not only from private industry, but from the skilled scientists who work in our universities and our other great publicly supported centers of learning and research.

We conclude that the extension of trade secret protection to clearly patentable inventions does not conflict with the patent policy of disclosure. Perhaps because trade secret law does not produce any positive effects in the area of clearly patentable inventions, as opposed to the beneficial effects resulting from trade secret protection in the areas of the doubtfully patentable and the clearly unpatentable inventions, it has been suggested that partial pre-emption may be appropriate, and that courts should refuse to apply trade secret protection to inventions which the holder should have patented, and which would have been, thereby, disclosed.[50] However, since there is no real possibility that trade secret law will conflict with the federal policy favoring disclosure of clearly patentable inventions partial pre-emption is inappropriate. Partial pre-emption, furthermore, could well create serious problems for state courts in the administration of trade secret law. As a preliminary matter in trade secret actions,

50. [Court's footnote 20.] See Note, Patent Preemption of Trade Secret Protection of Inventions Meeting Judicial Standards of Patentability, 87 Harv. L.Rev. 807 (1974); Brief for the United States as *Amicus Curiae*, presenting the view within the Government favoring limited pre-emption (which view is not that of the United States, which believes that patent law does not pre-empt state trade secret law).

state courts would be obliged to distinguish between what a reasonable inventor would and would not correctly consider to be clearly patentable, with the holder of the trade secret arguing that the invention was not patentable and the misappropriator of the trade secret arguing its undoubted novelty, utility, and nonobviousness. Federal courts have a difficult enough time trying to determine whether an invention, narrowed by the patent application procedure and fixed in the specifications which describe the invention for which the patent has been granted, is patentable. Although state courts in some circumstances must join federal courts in judging whether an issued patent is valid, Lear, Inc. v. Adkins, supra, it would be undesirable to impose the almost impossible burden on state courts to determine the patentability—in fact and in the mind of a reasonable inventor—of a discovery which has not been patented and remains entirely uncircumscribed by expert analysis in the administrative process. Neither complete nor partial pre-emption of state trade secret law is justified.

. . . Trade secret law and patent law have co-existed in this country for over one hundred years. Each has its particular role to play, and the operation of one does not take away from the need for the other. Trade secret law encourages the development and exploitation of those items of lesser or different invention than might be accorded protection under the patent laws, but which items still have an important part to play in the technological and scientific advancement of the Nation. Trade secret law promotes the sharing of knowledge, and the efficient operation of industry; it permits the individual inventor to reap the rewards of his labor by contracting with a company large enough to develop and exploit it. Congress, by its silence over these many years, has seen the wisdom of allowing the States to enforce trade secret protection. Until Congress takes affirmative action to the contrary, States should be free to grant protection to trade secrets.

Since we hold that Ohio trade secret law is not preempted by the federal patent law, the judgment of the Court of Appeals for the Sixth Circuit is reversed, and the case is remanded to the Court of Appeals with directions to reinstate the judgment of the District Court.

It is so ordered.

MR. JUSTICE POWELL took no part in the decision of this case.

MR. JUSTICE MARSHALL, concurring in the result.

Unlike the Court, I do not believe that the possibility that an inventor with a patentable invention will rely on state trade secret law rather than apply for a patent is "remote indeed." State trade secret law provides substantial protection to the inventor who intends to use or sell the invention himself rather than license it to others, protection which in its unlimited duration is clearly superior to the 17-year monopoly afforded by the patent laws. I have no doubt that the existence of trade secret protection provides in some instances a substantial disincentive to entrance into the patent system, and thus deprives society of the benefits of public disclosure of the invention which it is the policy of the patent laws to encourage. This case may well be such an instance.

But my view of sound policy in this area does not dispose of this case. Rather, the question presented in this case is whether Congress, in enacting the patent laws, intended merely to offer inventors a limited monopoly in exchange for disclosure of their invention, or instead to exert pressure on inventors to enter into this exchange by withdrawing any alternative possibility of legal protection for their inventions. I am persuaded that the former is the case. State trade secret laws and the federal patent laws have co-existed for many, many years. During this time, Congress has repeatedly demonstrated its full awareness of the existence of the trade secret system, without any indication of disapproval. Indeed, Congress has in a number of instances given explicit federal protection to trade secret information provided to federal agencies. See, e.g., 5 U.S.C. § 552(b) (4); 18 U.S.C. § 1905; see generally Appendix to Brief for Petitioner. Because of this, I conclude that there is "neither such actual conflict between the two schemes of regulation that both cannot stand in the same area, nor evidence of a congressional design to preempt the field." Florida Avocado Growers v. Paul, 373 U.S. 132, 141 (1963). I therefore concur in the result reached by the majority of the Court.

MR. JUSTICE DOUGLAS, with whom MR. JUSTICE BRENNAN concurs, dissenting.

Today's decision is at war with the philosophy of Sears, Roebuck & Co. v. Stiffel Co., 376 U.S. 225, and Compco Corp. v. Day-Brite Lighting, Inc., 376 U.S. 234. . . . In *Sears,* as in the present case, an injunction against the unfair competitor issued. We said: "To allow a State by use of its law of unfair competition to prevent the copying of an article which represents too slight an advance to be patented would be to permit the State to block off from the public something which federal law has said belongs to the public. The result would be that while federal law grants only 14 or 17 years' protection to genuine inventions, see 35 U.S.C. §§ 154, 173, States could allow perpetual protection to articles too lacking in novelty to merit any patent at all under federal constitutional standards. This would be too great an encroachment on the federal patent system to be tolerated." 376 U.S., at 231–232.

The conflict with the patent laws is obvious. The decision of Congress to adopt a patent system was based on the idea that there will be much more innovation if discoveries are disclosed and patented than there will be when everyone works in secret. Society thus fosters a free exchange of technological information at the cost of a limited 17-year monopoly.[51]

51. [Footnote from Justice Douglas' opinion.] "The holding [of the Court of Appeals] in *Kewanee* seems correct. If it is permissible for an inventor to use the law of unfair competition as a substitute for patenting, certain categories of inventions would receive privileged protection under that law. Thus a new laser, television set, or airplane could not be protected because inventions which by their nature cannot be put into commercial use without disclosure, are not eligi-

A trade secret,[52] unlike a patent, has no property dimension. That was the view of the Court of Appeals, 478 F.2d 1074, 1081; and its decision is supported by what Mr. Justice Holmes said in Du Pont Powder Co. v. Masland, 244 U.S. 100, 102:

"The word property as applied to trade-marks and trade secrets is an unanalyzed expression of certain secondary consequences of the primary fact that the law makes some rudimentary requirements of good faith. Whether the plaintiffs have any valuable secret or not the defendant knows the facts, whatever they are, through a special confidence that he accepted. The property may be denied but the confidence cannot be. Therefore the starting point for the present matter is not property or due process of law, but that the defendant stood in confidential relations with the plaintiffs, or one of them. These have given place to hostility, and the first thing to be made sure of is that the defendant shall not fraudulently abuse the trust reposed in him. It is the usual incident of confidential relations. If there is any disadvantage in the fact that he knew the plaintiffs' secrets he must take the burden with the good."

A suit to redress theft of a trade secret is grounded in tort damages for breach of a contract—a historic remedy, Cataphote Corp. v. Hudson, 422 F.2d 1290. Damages for breach of a confidential relation are not pre-empted by this patent law, but an injunction against use is pre-empted because the patent law states the only monopoly over trade secrets that is enforceable by specific performance; and that monopoly exacts as a price full disclosure. A trade secret can be protected only by being kept secret. Damages for breach of a contract are one thing; an injunction barring disclosure does service for the protection accorded valid patents and is therefore pre-empted.

From the findings of fact of the lower courts, the process involved in this litigation was unique, such a great discovery as to make its patentability a virtual certainty. Yet the Court's opinion reflects a vigorous activist anti-patent philosophy. My objection is not because it is activist. This is a problem that involves no neutral principle.

ble for trade secret protection after they are put on the market. Those that can be maintained are eligible. But as the basic economic function of the patent system is to encourage the making and commercialization of inventions, there seems to be no justification for providing incentives beyond those provided by the patent law to discriminate between different categories of inventions, i.e., those that may inherently be kept secret and those that may not. Moreover, state rules which would grant such incentives seem to conflict with the economic *quid pro quo* underlying patent protection; i.e., a monopoly limited in time, in return for full disclosure of the invention. Thus federal law has struck a balance between incentives for inventors and the public's right to a competitive economy. In this sense, the patent law is an integral part of federal competitive policy." Adelman, Secrecy and Patenting: Some Proposals for Resolving the Conflict, 1 APLA Quarterly Journal 296, 298–299 (1973).

52. [Footnote from Justice Douglas' opinion.] Trade secrets often are unpatentable. In that event there is no federal policy which is contravened when an injunction to bar disclosure of a trade secret is issued. Moreover, insofar as foreign patents are involved our federal patent policy is obviously irrelevant. S. Oppenheim, Unfair Trade Practices 264–265 (2d ed. 1965). As respects further contrasts between patents and trade secrets see Milgrim, Trade Secret Protection and Licensing, 4 Pat.L.Rev. 375 (1972).

The Constitution in Art. I, § 8, cl. 8, expresses the activist policy which Congress has enforced by statutes. It is that constitutional policy which we should enforce, not our individual notions of the public good.

I would affirm the judgment below.

NOTES AND QUERIES

(1) *Queries.* Did the Court in *Kewanee*, in its consideration of the conflict between state and federal law, give adequate weight to federal antitrust policy? Isn't the point of *Sears* that Congress has struck the balance between the patent and antitrust systems in a way that will "promote invention while at the same time preserving free competition." *Sears*, supra p. 1040. Should the states be allowed to restrike that balance? [53] If an inventor is allowed the choice between patent and trade secret protection, which one will the inventor choose?

Suppose the Department of Justice had brought suit against Kewanee under Section 1 of the Sherman Act for entering into the secrecy agreements. Would it have been an absolute defense that such agreements were enforceable as a matter of state contract law? Were consistent with rights granted under state trade secret law? Review *Lear v. Adkins, FOGA v. FTC,* supra p. 532, and Judge Taft's analysis of covenants not to compete in *Addyston Pipe,* supra p. 329.

To what extent does the Court's finding of conformity between trade secret law and patent law depend on the Court's theory of invention? Do you agree with the "ripeness of time" theory (a/k/a "necessity is the mother of invention")? Is this theory consistent with the theory of invention underlying federal patent law?

(2) *Simulation as Lawful Competition.* See *Compco Corp. v. Day-Brite Lighting, Inc.,* 376 U.S. 234, 84 S.Ct. 779, 11 L.Ed.2d 669 (1964), decided on the same day as the *Sears* case, and Justice Harlan's special concurrence in both cases, 376 U.S. 239, 84 S.Ct. 782, reserving for the states the right to prohibit copying where the "dominant purpose and effect" is to palm one's goods off as another's. In *West Point Manufacturing Co. v. Detroit Stamping Co.,* 222 F.2d 581 (6th Cir. 1955), the court refused to enjoin defendant from selling under its own trademark clamps covered by plaintiff's expired patent, notwithstanding that defendant copied non-functional as well as functional features, and even used a photograph of plaintiff's clamp in promoting its own product. Cf. *Chas. D. Briddell v. Alglobe Trading Corp.,* 194 F.2d 416 (2d Cir. 1952), denying injunction against production and sale of cheap and inferior copies of plaintiff's high quality, distinctively styled, widely advertised steak knives.

Alexander, Honesty and Competition: Some Competitive Virtues in the False Naming of Goods, 39 S.Cal.L.Rev. 1 (1966), argued that excessive policing of "misrepresentation" may restrain rational consumer choice as well as freedom of competition. See also Symposium, Product Simulation: A Right or a Wrong? 64 Colum.L.Rev. 1178 (1964). Should American Producers be

---

53. See Goldstein, Kewanee Oil Co. v. Bicron Corp.: Notes on a Closing Circle, 1974 Supreme Court Review 81; Doerfer, The Limits on Trade Secret Law Imposed by Federal Patent and Antitrust Suprem- acy, 80 Harv.L.Rev. 1432, 1454 (1967); Wydick, Trade Secrets: Federal Preemption in Light of Goldstein and Kewanee (Part II—Conclusion), 56 J.Pat.Off.Soc'y 4, 23–24 (1974).

free to offer "Swiss" cheese and "Champagne" if they adequately disclose domestic origin?

Consider "Some Tales of 'Copycat' Products Are Best Left Untold, Sterling Drug Learns," Wall St. J., March 11, 1980, p. 18.* Is Sterling Drug's conduct "anti-innovative"? Or pro-competitive?

If you steal it, don't flaunt it.

That's marketing advice Steven W. Lapham would do well to remember. If he had heeded it last November, he might have kept himself and his employer out of court.

Mr. Lapham is new products director of Lehn & Fink Products Co., the Sterling Drug Inc. division that makes Lysol and other household cleansers. Four months ago he was a guest speaker at an American Marketing Association new products conference.

"Replicate, don't innovate," was Mr. Lapham's theme. "Trying to innovate as the only way to success is one of the greatest myths of new products ever created," he said.

Instead, he suggested, be a copycat. "Someone else has gone and done your homework for you," he said. "They have taken the risk, the time, and spent the dollars."

His example of successful mimicry: Lehn & Fink's own Love My Carpet rug and room deodorant, a copy of Airwick Industries Inc.'s Carpet Fresh.

Mr. Lapham told how Lehn & Fink was skeptical at first about Carpet Fresh, which was test-marketed by Airwick in mid-1977, and introduced nationally a year later. "We found it pretty hard to believe that Carpet Fresh had any potential at all," he said. "What housewife in her right mind would sprinkle white powder onto her carpeting before vacuuming? Who dirties their carpet first? The whole idea had to be wrong."

A Quick Copy

It wasn't. When Lehn & Fink monitored Airwick's test markets, it found that Carpet Fresh was "a terrific idea," Mr. Lapham explained. In December 1978, Lehn & Fink began a crash project to duplicate Carpet Fresh. A copy was on supermarket shelves within six months—far sooner than the two years or more it usually takes to develop a new product.

Mr. Lapham's candor may have startled his audience, but he didn't create much of a stir until a month later when Advertising Age, a trade publication, reported his remarks.

Then the harrumphing began. Marketing executives privately scorned Mr. Lapham's approach as one that did little to promote economic growth; some were surprised that such an important name in consumer products as Sterling Drug would stoop to mimicry. An Ad Age editorial said, "Where would the replicators be without the innovators? They wouldn't even have material on which to base their speeches."

Four weeks after the Ad Age story, Airwick finally spoke up—in federal district court in New Jersey. The company charged Lehn & Fink with patent infringement and asked for damages totaling triple the profits from Love My Carpet. Although Airwick officials say they had been contemplating litigation before Mr. Lapham's speech, the suit quotes his remarks extensively.

Imitation, of course, isn't unusual in marketing. Mr. Lapham's thesis had been put forth 13 years earlier in a Harvard Business Review article, "Innovative Imitation," by Harvard marketing theoretician Theodore Levitt. He urged companies to search for products they could copy through "reverse R&D—

working backwards from what others have done, and trying to do the same thing for oneself."

Ample Examples

Examples of successful copycats abound. International Business Machines Corp. wasn't first in computers nor RCA Corp. in television sets, Mr. Levitt noted. Mr. Lapham pointed to General Foods Corp.'s Jell-O pudding following R. J. Reynolds Industries Inc.'s My-T-Fine and Schick Inc. razor blades imitating Gillette Co.'s.

Even Airwick says it sometimes follows other companies' ideas. "When we see something successful, we try to put a unique twist on it," says Michael Sheets, president of Airwick's consumer products division. The company's new Air Wand room freshener, for example, is strikingly similar, except for its package shape and scent, to Clorox Co.'s Twice as Fresh.

Nonetheless, Airwick executives say that they were surprised by Lehn & Fink. "We were upset about the fact that they came in with an exact copy," says Frank Conkling, Airwick chairman. "If they had gone us one better in technology, we would have said, '*c'est la guerre*'."

Lehn & Fink's quick copy also stung Airwick's pride. Airwick, which had been acquired by Ciba-Geigy Ltd. in 1974, had only recently begun transforming itself from a stodgy one-product company into an innovator. And with Carpet Fresh, it had created more than a new product; it started an entirely new product type. Before, people simply vacuumed or shampooed their rugs. Carpet Fresh was a deodorizer; Airwick asserts that it removes smells from carpets, and as the powder passes through the vacuum's exhaust, perfumes the entire room.

It was also a rapid success, especially among households with infants, puppies and cigar smokers. Sales grew to about $60 million last year, and with other competitors jumping into the market, Carpet Fresh's market share was roughly 60%, Airwick says.

Airwick has also sued a manufacturer of store-brand versions of Carpet Fresh for patent infringement, but it is Lehn & Fink that has caused all the ruckus in the industry.

Did Mr. Lapham or Lehn & Fink anticipate such a strong reaction to the marketing association speech? Sterling has since silenced Mr. Lapham and says only that it has a "defensive case" against Airwick; Lehn & Fink's answer to the Airwick complaint is due soon.

To new product executives at other companies, though, the Lehn & Fink affair is mostly a case of indiscretion. "If you can imitate and get away with it, you should hide what you're doing," says a marketing expert versed in the law. "You don't win anything by shooting your mouth off in the marketplace."

(3) *Enforcement of Contract For Royalties.* In *Aronson v. Quick Point Pencil Co.*[54] the manufacturer sought a declaratory judgment that state contract law making enforceable its contract to pay royalties to the inventor was preempted by federal patent law. The contract, embodied in two documents, was entered into while the inventor's patent application was pending. The first document provided for royalties of 5% of sales; no duration was specified, although the licensee retained the right to cancel if sales did not meet expectations. The second provided that if the patent were not granted within five years, royalties would then be set at $2\frac{1}{2}\%$ of sales for as long as sales continued.

The Supreme Court, in an opinion by Chief Justice Burger, held the contract could be enforced. After stating that "[c]ommercial agreements tradi-

---

54. 440 U.S. 257, 99 S.Ct. 1096, 59 L.Ed.2d 296 (1979).

tionally are the domain of state law" (440 U.S. at 262, 99 S.Ct. at 1099), and that the enforcement of agreements licensing inventions "provides an additional incentive to invention" (id.), the Court continued:

No decision of this Court relating to patents justifies relieving Quick Point of its contract obligations. We have held that a state may not forbid the copying of an idea in the public domain which does not meet the requirements for federal patent protection. Compco Corp. v. Day-Brite Lighting, Inc., 376 U.S. 234, 84 S.Ct. 779, 11 L.Ed.2d 669 (1964); Sears Roebuck & Co. v. Stiffel Co., 376 U.S. 225, 84 S.Ct. 784, 11 L.Ed.2d 661 (1964). Enforcement of Quick Point's agreement, however, does not prevent anyone from copying the keyholder. It merely requires Quick Point to pay the consideration which it promised in return for the use of a novel device which enabled it to preempt the market.

In Lear, Inc. v. Adkins, 395 U.S. 653, 89 S.Ct. 1902, 23 L.Ed.2d 610 (1969), we held that a person licensed to use a patent may challenge the validity of the patent, and that a licensee who establishes that the patent is invalid need not pay the royalties accrued under the licensing agreement subsequent to the issuance of the patent. Both holdings relied on the desirability of encouraging licensees to challenge the validity of patents, to further the strong federal policy that only inventions which meet the rigorous requirements of patentability shall be withdrawn from the public domain. Accordingly, neither the holding nor the rationale of *Lear* controls when no patent has issued, and no ideas have been withdrawn from public use.

Enforcement of the royalty agreement here is also consistent with the principles treated in Brulotte v. Thys Co., 379 U.S. 29, 85 S.Ct. 176, 13 L.Ed.2d 99 (1964). There, we held that the obligation to pay royalties in return for the use of a patented device may not extend beyond the life of the patent. The principle underlying that holding was simply that the monopoly granted *under a patent* cannot lawfully be used to "negotiate with the leverage of that monopoly." The Court emphasized that to "use that leverage to project those royalty payments beyond the life of the patent is analogous to an effort to enlarge the monopoly of a patent . . . ." Here the reduced royalty which is challenged, far from being negotiated "with the leverage" of a patent, rested on the contingency that no patent would issue within five years.

No doubt a pending patent application gives the applicant some additional bargaining power for purposes of negotiating a royalty agreement. The pending application allows the inventor to hold out the hope of an exclusive right to exploit the idea, as well as the threat that the other party will be prevented from using the idea for 17 years. However, the amount of leverage arising from a patent application depends on how likely the parties consider it to be that a valid patent will issue. Here, where no patent ever issued, the record is entirely clear that the parties assigned a substantial likelihood to that contingency, since they specifically provided for a reduced royalty in the event no patent issued within five years.

This case does not require us to draw the line between what constitutes abuse of a pending application and what does not. It is clear that whatever role the pending application played in the negotiation of the 5% royalty, it played no part in the contract to pay the $2^{1}/_{2}\%$ royalty indefinitely.

. . .

Queries. (1) Suppose a patent had incorrectly been issued and the manufacturer successfully contested validity. Under *Lear,* would the agreement for royalties of 2½% of sales have still been enforceable? (2) Suppose a valid patent had been issued. At its expiration would the agreement for royalties of 2½% of sales have then been enforceable? After *Aronson,* is it now possible to draft an enforceable agreement for royalties which would extend payments past the 17 year limit of the patent? So long as the post-expiration agreement sets a lower rate?

In *Brulotte v. Thys Co.,*[55] discussed in *Zenith,* supra p. 1010, the Supreme Court reviewed a state court judgment awarding royalties under a patent license for the use of a patented machine after the patents expired. The Court held the "continuation" of royalties "unenforceable":[56]

> The present licenses draw no line between the term of the patent and the post-expiration period. The same provisions as respects both use and royalties are applicable to each. The contracts are, therefore, on their face a bald attempt to exact the same terms and conditions for the period after the patents have expired as they do for the monopoly period. We are, therefore, unable to conjecture what the bargaining position of the parties might have been and what resultant arrangement might have emerged had the provision for post-expiration royalties been divorced from the patent and nowise subject to its leverage.

> . . .

> A patent empowers the owner to exact royalties as high as he can negotiate with the leverage of that monopoly. But to use that leverage to project those royalty payments beyond the life of the patent is analogous to an effort to enlarge the monopoly of the patent by tying the sale or use of the patented article to the purchase or use of unpatented ones. The exaction of royalties for use of a machine after the patent has expired is an assertion of monopoly power in the post-expiration period when, as we have seen, the patent has entered the public domain. [A]fter expiration of the last of the patents incorporated in the machines "the grant of patent monopoly was spent" and . . . an attempt to project it into another term by continuation of the licensing agreement is unenforceable.

(4) *Comparison to Copyright.* In *Goldstein v. California,*[57] cited in *Kewanee,* the Supreme Court held that a California criminal prosecution for "tape piracy" (unauthorized copying of recorded popular musical performances) was not in conflict with the Copyright Clause of the Constitution or federal copyright law. State law forbade copying of a tape or record without the permission of the owner of the master recording. The ban on copying was not limited in time. Federal law when the copying in *Goldstein* occurred gave protection only to the underlying music and not to the performance; while the case was pending in state court Congress amended the Copyright Act to provide limited duration protection only for those sound recordings "fixed" between 1972 and 1975.[58] Chief Justice Burger, for the Court, wrote that the Constitution does not grant exclusive copyright power to the federal government, and that California could permissibly deal with

---

55. 379 U.S. 29, 85 S.Ct. 176, 13 L.Ed. 2d 99 (1964). Justice Harlan dissented.

56. 379 U.S. at 32–34, 85 S.Ct. at 179–80, 13 L.Ed.2d at 102–03.

57. 412 U.S. 546, 93 S.Ct. 2303, 37 L.Ed.2d 163 (1973).

58. This time limit was subsequently removed by Congress, and the 1976 Act now provides protection for subsequently produced sound recordings. See 17 U.S. C.A. §§ 102(a), 114.

"our modern technology" in the absence of coverage under federal legislation enacted in 1909. "No restraint" was placed on the use of an idea, because the statute did not forbid the performers from recording the songs anew; and the tape pirates' conduct "may adversely affect the continued production of new recordings, a large industry in California." *Sears* was distinguished on the ground that Congress intended the pole lamp to be unprotected from copying, because the lamp had not met the requirements for federal patent protection, but had left the area of sound recordings "unattended." Justices Douglas, Marshall, Brennan, and Blackmun dissented.

See also *International News Service v. Associated Press*,[59] in which the Supreme Court restrained one press association from using fresh news gathered by another, not on the grounds of copyright but as a matter of unfair competition:

> The news element—the information respecting current events contained in the literary production—is not the creation of the writer, but is a report of matters that ordinarily are publici juris. It is not to be supposed that the framers of the Constitution . . . intended to confer upon one who might happen to be the first to report a historic event the exclusive right for any period to spread the knowledge of it. . . .
>
> [But] although we may and do assume that neither party has any remaining property interest as against the public in uncopyrightable news matter after the moment of its first publication, it by no means follows that there is no remaining property interest in it as between themselves. For to both of them alike, news matter, however little susceptible of ownership or dominion in the absolute sense, is stock in trade, to be gathered at the cost of enterprise, organization, skill, labor, and money, and to be distributed and sold to those who will pay money for it, as for any other merchandise. Regarding the news, therefore, as but the material out of which both parties are seeking to make profits at the same time and in the same field, we hardly can fail to recognize that for this purpose, and as between them, it must be regarded as *quasi* property, irrespective of the rights of either as against the public.

Consider the California Resale Royalties Act, which provides that whenever a work of "fine art" is sold in California (or by a California resident) after the initial sale by the artist, the seller must pay 5 percent of the sale price to the artist. The statute does not apply to sales below $1000 or to resales after the artist's death; the right to payment is not transferable or waivable by the artist, although the artist can contract for a higher amount.[60] In *Morseburg v. Baylon*,[61] the Ninth Circuit Court of Appeals, relying on *Goldstein*, held that the 1909 Copyright Act did not preempt the statute.[62] The court did recognize the possibility, however, that the transferability of works of fine art could be adversely affected if other states sought to impose similar resale royalties. Nevertheless, the court found that the copyright laws manifest "no hostility" toward resale royalties and that the California and federal statutes "function harmoniously rather than discordantly."

59. 248 U.S. 215, 38 S.Ct. 68, 63 L.Ed. 211 (1918).

60. See Cal.Civil Code § 986 (West Supp.1980).

61. 621 F.2d 972 (9th Cir. 1980), certiorari denied 449 U.S. 983, 101 S.Ct. 399, 66 L.Ed.2d 245.

62. For the scope of statutory preemption of state law under the 1976 Act, see 17 U.S.C.A. § 301 (all rights "equivalent to" exclusive rights "within the general scope of copyright" are governed exclusively by the Copyright Act).

Query. Would you have voted for this statute? What might be its likely effect on the amount of art sold? To whom might its benefits accrue? [63]

63. See, e.g., Merryman & Elsen, Law, Ethics and the Visual Arts, ch. IV (1979); Emley, The Resale Royalties Act: Paintings, Preemption and Profit, 8 Gold- en Gate Univ.L.Rev. 239 (1978); Katz, Copyright Preemption Under the Copyright Act of 1976: The Case of Droit de Suite, 47 Geo.Wash.L.Rev. 200 (1978).

Chapter 10

MARKET RESTRAINTS AND THE
LABOR EXEMPTION

A.   INTRODUCTION AND LEGISLATIVE TEXTS

Joint action by employees to force an employer to pay higher wages was, at common law, a criminal conspiracy.[1] Nineteenth century legislators and courts legalized such joint activity. For a time it appeared that the Sherman Act prohibition against combinations in restraint of trade might reestablish the common law rule. But Twentieth Century legislation,[2] set forth below, ended this possibility and moved instead to promote labor organization by:

(1) declaring that labor is not an article of commerce under the antitrust laws, that unions are not illegal combinations, and that typical union activities like strikes and picketing should not be restrained or otherwise held to be violations of law;

(2) curtailing or eliminating the jurisdiction of courts to issue injunctions in labor disputes, especially preliminary restraining orders made without full hearing;

(3) forbidding employers to interfere with the self-organization of workers, and requiring employers to bargain with unions in good faith; and

(4) establishing the National Labor Relations Board (NLRB) with broad jurisdiction to regulate labor-management relations.

It is apparent, therefore, that the command to compete embodied in the Sherman Act has limited application in this area of economic activity.[3] This can be explained or rationalized in several ways. Some will see only an assertion by labor of class and political power at the expense of other groups. Some will see in labor organization only defensive or counter-organization, authorized or tolerated by the

---

1. See S. Perlman, History of Trade Unionism in the United States (1922); J. Commons et al., History of Labour in the United States (1918–1935); F. Frankfurter and N. Greene, The Labor Injunction (1930); Magruder, A Half Century of Legal Influence upon the Development of Collective Bargaining, 50 Harv.L.Rev. 1071 (1937).

2. National Labor Relations Act of 1935 (The Wagner Act) as amended by the Labor-Management Relations Act of 1947 (Taft-Hartley Act), 29 U.S.C.A. § 151 et seq.

3. See R. Gorman, Basic Text on Labor Law, chap. 27 (1976); L. Sullivan, Handbook on the Law of Antitrust, 723–31 (1977); Leslie, Principles of Labor Antitrust, 66 Va.L.Rev. 1183 (1980); Meltzer, Labor Unions, Collective Bargaining, and the Antitrust Laws, 32 U.Chi.L.Rev. 659 (1965); Winter, Collective Bargaining and Competition: The Application of Antitrust Standards to Union Activities, 73 Yale L.J. 14 (1963); Cox, Labor and the Antitrust Laws, 104 U.Pa.L.Rev. 252 (1955).

community to offset the bargaining power of great organizations of capital.[4] Some will argue that competition is an appropriate control mechanism for limiting returns on capital, but not workers' income. A return on capital is, almost by definition, income not earned by work; part of what the workers produce is withheld from them to give to investors (capitalists). This investment return is the incentive which causes some people to refrain from consuming all their income, i.e., to save, and so provide the capital equipment which multiplies the output of a given amount of labor. The argument proceeds that it is just to allow the return on capital to be governed by competition, since differences in the return direct the flow of capital into proper fields. When competition among capitalists drives down the rate of return, other capitalists take heed and no new plants are built in that business. Competition among capitalists can only reduce the amount of "unearned" income to the minimum necessary to attract needed investment. The capitalist so unfortunate or unwise as to invest in an overcrowded field will get no income and may fail to cover expenses, and so be retired by bankruptcy to the ranks of the workers.

Unrestricted competition among workers would have quite different consequences. Here, income that is "earned," in the sense of being worked for, is forced down to the lowest subsistence level which any group of human beings could tolerate. Unlike the retirement of the unsuccessful capitalist to the status of worker, there is no retreat but death from this competition among workers. All this is unpleasant to contemplate; capitalist class-interest, if it exists, could hardly ignore the social costs of marginal living for workers, or the possibility of violent revolution against a system which did not ameliorate the consequences of such a struggle.

It is possible therefore to regard the labor union's privileged position as another example of a "monopoly" (i.e., exemption from competition) conferred by law to promote certain community objectives, like the patent, the public utility certificate of convenience and necessity, and "reasonable" restraints of trade generally. The analogy suggests questions which may be borne in mind in reading this chapter:

1. What is the scope of the monopoly granted? Is it merely the right to eliminate competition among members of the union? Or may the union's collective power be exerted to restrain the activities of non-union workers?

2. To what extent does an "abuse of monopoly" doctrine exist here? Cf. material on abuse of patents in Chapter 9. May the labor "patent" be used to restrain trade in commodities competing with its product? May the labor patent be used not only to exact monopoly wages (cf. the patent royalty) but also to fix the price of the product manufactured by the employer (cf. patentee's control of manufacturing licensee's pricing)?

4. Compare the counter-organization rationale in Appalachian Coals, Inc. v. United States, p. 341 supra; Chicago Board of Trade v. United States, supra, p. 332; Aluminum Company of America v. United States, supra, p. 95; Broadcast Music, Inc. v. Columbia Broadcasting System, Inc., supra p. 380; Galbraith, American Capitalism—The Concept of Countervailing Power (1952).

3. Is it lawful for a union, not content with obtaining the maximum share of the gross income of an industry, to combine with employers to raise prices and thus increase the gross to be shared by labor?

4. What are the alternatives to market restraint as a means of achieving labor's legitimate objectives? Would a legal requirement of severance pay to take care of loss of employment due to introduction of machinery be a better solution for technological unemployment than a strike against the introduction of machinery? [5] Is it better public policy to encourage worker ownership in the firm which employs the worker? To what extent can minimum wage, social security and unemployment compensation laws reduce the occasion for private controls of the economy?

5. Is it lawful to assemble numerous unions (cf. patent pooling; public utility holding companies) into aggregations of power that can determine the rate of technological advance, or otherwise regiment an industry?

The statutory and case material which follows has been selected to illustrate aspects of labor and antitrust law defining union rights to exert pressure on persons other than employers or prospective employers, or to regulate commercial conditions in a trade. The material does not explore fully the intricacies of the antitrust-labor law conflict, a conflict with a unique history of judicial activism through antitrust injunctions and Congressional counter-activism limiting court jurisdiction over labor disputes and committing regulation of labor relations to collective bargaining and the administrative supervision of the N.L.R.B. [6] That conflict, one complicated by the specifics of labor legislation and the scope of the role of the N.L.R.B. as exclusive regulator of labor-management relations, is studied more fully in the course on labor law. In these materials we look generally at the interaction of antitrust and labor law policy, with emphasis upon recent trends suggesting a revival of judicial activism in the use of antitrust policy to regulate union activity—sometimes in spite of collective bargaining, N.L.R.B. regulation, and the statutes which follow.[7]

5. See Cox, Some Aspects of the Labor Management Relations Act, 61 Harv. L.Rev. 274, 288 (1948).

6. For a survey of the historical evolution of the judicial-Congressional conflict over the use of antitrust policy to regulate union activity, see, C. Summers, H. Wellington, & A. Hyde, Labor Law: Cases & Materials 174–282 (2d Ed. 1982).

7. For significant surveys of recent labor-antitrust litigation, see Casey & Cozzillio, Labor-Antitrust: The Problems

Of *Connell* And A Remedy That Follows Naturally, 1980 Duke L.J. 235; Handler & Zifchak, Collective Bargaining and the Antitrust Laws: The Emasculation of the Labor Exemption, 81 Colum.L.Rev. 459 (1981); Leslie, supra note 3; St. Antoine, *Connell*: Antitrust Law at the Expense of Labor Law, 62 Va.L.Rev. 603 (1976); Symposium, The Application of Antitrust Laws To Labor-Related Activities, 21 Duq.L.Rev. 331 (1983).

LABOR PROVISIONS OF THE CLAYTON ACT OF 1914

Sec. 6.[8] **The labor of a human being is not a commodity or article of commerce. Nothing contained in the antitrust laws shall be construed to forbid the existence and operation of labor, agricultural, or horticultural organizations,[9] instituted for the purposes of mutual help, and not having capital stock or conducted for profit, or to forbid or restrain individual members of such organizations from lawfully carrying out the legitimate objects thereof; nor shall such organizations, or the members thereof, be held or construed to be illegal combinations or conspiracies in restraint of trade, under the antitrust laws.**

. . .

Sec. 20.[10] **That no restraining order or injunction shall be granted by any court of the United States, or a judge or the judges thereof, in any case between an employer and employees, or between employers and employees, or between employees or between persons employed and persons seeking employment, involving, or growing out of, a dispute concerning terms or conditions of employment, unless necessary to prevent irreparable injury to property, or to a property right, of the party making the application** . . . .

And no such restraining order or injunction shall prohibit any person or persons, whether singly or in concert, from terminating any relation of employment, or from ceasing to perform any work or labor, or from recommending, advising or persuading others by peaceful means so to do; or from attending at any place where any such person or persons may lawfully be, for the purpose of peacefully obtaining or communicating information, or from peacefully persuading any person to work or to abstain from working; or from ceasing to patronize or to employ any party to such dispute, or from recommending, advising, or persuading others by peaceful and lawful means so to do; or from paying or giving to, or withholding from, any person engaged in such dispute, any strike benefits or other moneys or things of value; or from peaceably assembling in a lawful manner, and for lawful purposes; or from doing any act or thing which might lawfully be done in the absence of such dispute by any party thereto; nor shall any of the acts specified in this paragraph be considered or held to be violations of any law of the United States.

NORRIS–LAGUARDIA ACT OF 1932

Sec. 4.[11] **No court of the United States shall have jurisdiction to issue any restraining order or temporary or permanent injunction in any case involving or growing out of any labor dispute to prohibit any person or persons participating or interested in such dispute**

8. 15 U.S.C.A. § 17.

9. The exemption for agricultural and horticultural organizations raises issues similar to the labor exemption. See Report, National Commission for the Review of Antitrust Laws and Procedures, 253–272 (1979); Note, Trust Busting Down on the Farm: Narrowing the Scope of Antitrust Exemptions for Agricultural Cooperatives, 61 Va.L.Rev. 341 (1975).

10. 29 U.S.C.A. § 52.

11. 29 U.S.C.A. § 104.

(as these terms are herein defined) from doing, whether singly or in concert, any of the following acts:

(a) Ceasing or refusing to perform any work or to remain in any relation of employment;

(b) Becoming or remaining a member of any labor organization or of any employer organization . . .;

. . .

(e) Giving publicity to the existence of, or the facts involved in, any labor dispute, whether by advertising, speaking, patrolling, or by any other method not involving fraud or violence;

(f) Assembling peaceably to act or to organize to act in promotion of their interests in a labor dispute;

. . .

(h) Agreeing with other persons to do or not to do any of the acts heretofore specified;

. . .

NOTES

(1) *Restricting Regulation of Unions by Antitrust Injunctions.* Despite scholarly doubts about whether Congress ever intended the Sherman Act to be applied to unions,[12] many of the early Sherman Act cases were brought against labor unions rather than business combinations.[13] In the "Danbury Hatters Case," *Loewe v. Lawlor,*[14] the Supreme Court held unanimously that the Sherman Act applied to the activities of labor unions organizing a nationwide boycott of non-union hat manufacturers.

The use of antitrust policy to regulate union organizing, frustrating pressure for better wages and conditions by working people, became a major issue in the 1912 Presidential election. Wilson's promise of a "New Freedom" was fulfilled by the adoption of sections 6 and 14 of the Clayton Act, supra, in 1914.[15] The meaning and scope of these statutes was, however, ambiguous. Did they merely legitimize the right to form a union, immunize all union activities, or still leave room in particular cases for the application of antitrust policy to particular union activities?

In a series of cases, the Supreme Court narrowly interpreted these provisions of the Clayton Act, limiting the exemption to conduct directly related to the terms or conditions of employment.[16] The Court further limited the exemption to disputes between persons in a direct and current employer-employee relationship[17] and held the exemption was not intended to legalize

12. See E. Berman, Labor and The Sherman Act (1930); A. Mason, Organized Labor and The Law (1925); Boudin, The Sherman Act and Labor Disputes, 39 Colum.L.Rev. 1283 (1939), 40 Colum.L. Rev. 14 (1940); Shulman, Labor and The Antitrust Laws, 34 Ill.L.Rev. 769 (1940).

13. See C. Summers, H. Wellington & A. Hyde, Labor Law: Cases and Materials 207 (2d ed. 1982): "In the first seven years of the statute, the lower federal courts had found only one violation by a business combination, but had found the activities of labor unions to be violations twelve times."

14. 208 U.S. 274, 28 S.Ct. 301, 52 L.Ed. 488 (1908). A treble damage verdict of $252,000 against the union was upheld in Lawlor v. Loewe, 235 U.S. 522, 35 S.Ct. 170, 59 L.Ed. 341 (1915).

15. See Summers, Wellington & Hyde, supra note 13 at 208–09.

16. Duplex Printing Press Co. v. Deering, 254 U.S. 443, 41 S.Ct. 172, 65 L.Ed. 349 (1921); American Steel Foundries v. Tri-City Central Trades Council, 257 U.S. 184, 42 S.Ct. 72, 66 L.Ed. 189 (1921).

17. Id.

previously unlawful organizational activities like a secondary boycott [18] or nonpeaceful picketing.[19]

Congress responded by enacting the Norris-LaGuardia Act in 1932, further fencing in federal court jurisdiction over labor disputes and broadening labor's antitrust exemption. "Labor dispute" was defined to include disputes between "persons who are engaged in the same industry, trade, craft or occupation; or have direct or indirect interests therein," making it clear that the disputants need not "stand in the proximate relation of employer and employee." [20] The Act was especially intended to apply to "secondary boycotts," where strikers bring pressure against suppliers and customers of the employer, the Clayton Act having proved no obstacle to the issuance of injunctions in such cases.[21] The broadened restriction against federal antitrust injunctions enacted in the Norris-LaGuardia Act was not, however, accompanied by any declaration that the activity so immunized from injunction should be deemed lawful. Compare the final clause of section 20 of the Clayton Act, supra. Nevertheless, in *United States v. Hutcheson*,[22] the Supreme Court read the "interlacing statutes" and legislative history as evidencing a congressional intent to immunize from antitrust liability unions engaged in a "labor dispute" when the union acts in its self-interest and does not combine with non-labor groups.

Boys Markets, Inc. v. Retail Clerks Union [23] reinstated a limited injunctive power in the federal courts, notwithstanding Norris-LaGuardia, to enjoin strikes in breach of a no-strike agreement in a collective bargaining contract. This result was based on Congress' intent, expressed in labor legislation affirmatively regulating employer-union relations, discussed infra Note 2, to make collective bargaining agreements enforceable. In *Jacksonville Bulk Terminals, Inc. v. International Longshoremen's Association*,[24] however, the Supreme Court held that Norris-LaGuardia prohibited the issuance of an injunction against a union work stoppage that was politically motivated. The union had a collective bargaining agreement with a no-strike clause and requiring resolution of all disputes through a grievance procedure ending in arbitration. The union, expressing "moral outrage" over the Soviet invasion of Afghanistan, refused to allow members to load ships bound for the Soviet Union. Alleging the union's actions violated the no-strike clause, the employers sought an injunction pending arbitration. The Supreme Court held Section 4(a) of Norris-LaGuardia applied, finding politically motivated strikes were within the meaning of "labor dispute" and that a primary reason for adopting the Norris-LaGuardia Act was to exclude federal courts from making subjective judgments about the legitimacy of a union's activities when issuing labor injunctions. The Court also held that the *Boys Markets* exception (injunctions to enforce collective bargaining agreements) to Norris-La-

18. See Duplex Printing Press Co. v. Deering, supra note 16; Bedford Cut Stone Co. v. Journeymen Stone Cutters Association, 274 U.S. 37, 47 S.Ct. 522, 71 L.Ed. 916 (1927).

19. Coronado Coal Co. v. United Mine Workers, 268 U.S. 295, 45 S.Ct. 551, 69 L.Ed. 963 (1925). See also Truax v. Corrigan, 257 U.S. 312, 42 S.Ct. 124, 66 L.Ed. 254 (1921) (declaring all but informational picketing by a single union representative unlawful); Interface of National Labor and Antitrust Policies: When Antitrust Liability Attaches, 33 Lab.L.J. 115 (1982).

20. 29 U.S.C.A. § 113.

21. See Bedford Cut Stone Co. v. Journeymen Stone Cutter's Association, supra note 18; Duplex Printing Press Co. v. Deering, supra note 16.

22. 312 U.S. 219, 61 S.Ct. 463, 85 L.Ed. 788 (1941).

23. 398 U.S. 235, 90 S.Ct. 1583, 26 L.Ed.2d 199 (1970).

24. ___ U.S. ___, 102 S.Ct. 2673, 73 L.Ed.2d 327 (1982).

Guardia's prohibition on injunctions was inapplicable and no labor injunction could issue pending the arbitrator's ruling on the legality of the strike under the terms of the collective bargaining agreement.

(2) *Federal Legislation Affirmatively Regulating Labor-Management Relations.* A second era of labor legislation opened after adoption of the Norris-LaGuardia Act. Instead of focusing on limiting judicial intervention in labor disputes, the new era in Congress focused on encouraging unionism and collective bargaining, while also establishing a regime of administrative regulation under the N.L.R.B. In a series of major statutes, Congress extensively regulated labor-management relations, oscillating between guaranteeing union organizing and bargaining rights and then imposing limitations upon the exercise of those rights where abuse was manifested. In summary, those major statutes are:

The Wagner Act (National Labor Relations Act) (1935): [25] Granting employees the right to organize, bargain collectively and engage in concerted activity in aid of organizing and bargaining; restricting employer rights to obstruct the exercise of employee rights by refusing to bargain, coercing employees, favoring company unions, etc.; and, creating the N.L.R.B. to regulate activity under the Act by prohibiting "unfair labor practices" in violation of the Act.

The Taft Hartley Act (Labor Management Relations Act) (1947): [26] Curbing union abuses of rights granted under the Norris-LaGuardia Act and the Wagner Act by prohibiting union coercion of employees and coercing employers to discriminate; restricting union refusals to bargain; barring closed shop agreements and permitting agency shops; and restricting the use of secondary boycotts—coercing an employer through boycotts of third parties—in some but not all circumstances. The Act authorizes a damage action for newly prohibited secondary pressure.[27] The distinctions between various forms of secondary boycotts, distinctions not generally recognized in antitrust law, are significant in labor law. A complex jurisprudence has grown up about these distinctions and the scope of N.L.R.B. jurisdiction over them; issues of significance in subsequent cases discussed herein.

The Landrum-Griffin Act (Labor Management Reporting and Disclosure Act) (1959): [28] This Act, inter alia, further circumscribed the use of secondary boycotts designed to "threaten, restrain, or coerce" any person in furtherance of a proscribed objective defined as an unfair labor practice. Coercion of secondary employers as well as secondary employees to strike or not use or process a primary employer's goods or services were made unlawful,[29] as were "hot cargo" agreements. A "hot cargo" agreement is one which an employer agrees to cease dealing with a third party, usually an employer with which the union has a labor dispute.[30] Provisos to the hot cargo prohi-

25. 29 U.S.C.A. §§ 151 et seq. The Act was upheld in the famous case of National Labor Relations Board v. Jones & Laughlin Steel Corp., 301 U.S. 1, 57 S.Ct. 615, 81 L.Ed. 893 (1937), marking the end of the Court's activism in striking down state and federal social and labor legislation on substantive due process grounds.

26. 61 Stat. 136 (1947), codified in 29 U.S.C.A. §§ 141–97.

27. § 303(b), 61 Stat. 158 (1947), 29 U.S.C.A. § 187(b).

28. 73 Stat. 519 (1959), codified in 29 U.S.C.A. §§ 158–97 & §§ 401–531.

29. 29 U.S.C.A. § 158(b)(4). See generally Lesnick, The Gravaman of the Secondary Boycott, 62 Colum.L.Rev. 1363 (1962).

30. 29 U.S.C.A. § 158(e):

It shall be an unfair labor practice for any labor organization and any employer to enter into any contract or agreement, express or implied, whereby such employer ceases or refrains or agrees to cease or refrain from handling, using, selling, transporting or otherwise dealing in any of the products of any other employer, or to cease

bition exempt such agreements in the construction industry where related to contracting or subcontracting at the job site and hot cargo agreements generally in the garment industry.[31]

This detailed and complex regulation of labor union activity is generally enforced by N.L.R.B. cease and desist orders against forbidden union and management "unfair labor practices." In addition, limited authority to seek injunctions is granted to the N.L.R.B.[32] or the Attorney General where a strike or lockout "affects an entire industry or substantial part thereof" and "will imperil national health or safety." [33] With the addition of private damage actions for unlawful secondary boycott pressure and unlawful hot cargo agreements, as well as the Clayton and Norris-LaGuardia Act exemptions, it would appear a pervasive scheme of regulation had been established. The question is: What, if any, application of the antitrust laws exists in this significant and heavily regulated field?

B.   THE SCOPE OF THE LABOR EXEMPTION

ALLEN BRADLEY CO. v. LOCAL UNION NO. 3, INTERNATIONAL BROTHERHOOD OF ELECTRICAL WORKERS

Supreme Court of the United States, 1945.
325 U.S. 797, 65 S.Ct. 1533, 89 L.Ed. 1939.

MR. JUSTICE BLACK delivered the opinion of the Court.

The question presented is whether it is a violation of the Sherman Anti-Trust Act for labor unions and their members, prompted by a desire to get and hold jobs for themselves at good wages and under high working standards, to combine with employers and with manufacturers of goods to restrain competition in, and to monopolize the marketing of, such goods. . . .

Petitioners are manufacturers of electrical equipment. Their places of manufacture are outside of New York City, and most of them are outside of New York State as well. They have brought this action because of their desire to sell their products in New York City, a market area that has been closed to them through the activities of respondents and others.

Respondents are a labor union, its officials and its members. The union, Local No. 3 of the International Brotherhood of Electrical Workers, has jurisdiction only over the metropolitan area of New York City. It is therefore impossible for the union to enter into a collective bargaining agreement with petitioners. Some of petitioners do have collective bargaining agreements with other unions, and in some cases even with other locals of the I.B.E.W.

Some of the members of respondent union work for manufacturers who produce electrical equipment similar to that made by petition-

---

doing business with any other person, and any contract or agreement entered into heretofore or hereafter containing such an agreement shall be to such extent unenforcible and void. . . .

31. 29 U.S.C.A. § 158(e).

32. 29 U.S.C.A. § 160.

33. 29 U.S.C.A. § 178. See United Steelworkers of America v. United States, 361 U.S. 39, 80 S.Ct. 1, 4 L.Ed.2d 12 (1959).

ers; other members of respondent union are employed by contractors and work on the installation of electrical equipment, rather than in its production.

The union's consistent aim for many years has been to expand its membership, to obtain shorter hours and increased wages, and to enlarge employment opportunities for its members. To achieve this latter goal—that is, to make more work for its own members—the union realized that local manufacturers, employers of the local members, must have the widest possible outlets for their product. The union therefore waged aggressive campaigns to obtain closed shop agreements [34] with all local electrical equipment manufacturers and contractors. Using conventional labor union methods, such as strikes and boycotts, it gradually obtained more and more closed shop agreements in the New York City area. Under these agreements, contractors were obligated to purchase equipment from none but local manufacturers who also had closed shop agreements with Local No. 3; manufacturers obligated themselves to confine their New York City sales to contractors employing the Local's members. In the course of time, this type of individual employer-employee agreement expanded into industry-wide understandings, looking not merely to terms and conditions of employment but also to price and market control. Agencies were set up composed of representatives of all three groups to boycott recalcitrant local contractors and manufacturers and to bar from the area equipment manufactured outside its boundaries. The combination among the three groups, union, contractors, and manufacturers, became highly successful from the standpoint of all of them. The business of New York City manufacturers had a phenomenal growth, thereby multiplying the jobs available for the Local's members. Wages went up, hours were shortened, and the New York electrical equipment prices soared, to the decided financial profit of local contractors and manufacturers. The success is illustrated by the fact that some New York manufacturers sold their goods in the protected city market at one price and sold identical goods outside of New York at a far lower price. All of this took place, as the Circuit Court of Appeals declared, "through the stifling of competition", and because the three groups, in combination as "copartners", achieved "a complete monopoly which they used to boycott the equipment manufactured by the plaintiffs." Interstate sale of various types of electrical equipment has, by this powerful combination, been wholly suppressed.

Quite obviously, this combination of business men has violated both Sections (1) and (2) of the Sherman Act, unless its conduct is immunized by the participation of the union. For it intended to and did restrain trade in and monopolize the supply of electrical equip-

---

34. [This and the following footnote are from the Court's opinion.] Closed shop agreements require the employer to hire only members of the union. The Labor Management Relations Act, 1947 (Taft-Hartley Act), 29 U.S.C.A. § 158 made this an "unfair labor practice", but permitted "union shop" agreements, requiring non-union employees to join within 30 days after the beginning of employment.

ment in the New York City area to the exclusion of equipment manufactured in and shipped from other states, and did also control its price and discriminate between its would-be customers. Our problem in this case is therefore a very narrow one—do labor unions violate the Sherman Act when, in order to further their own interests as wage earners, they aid and abet business men to do the precise things which that Act prohibits?

The Sherman Act as originally passed contained no language expressly exempting any labor union activities. Sharp controversy soon arose as to whether the Act applied to unions. One viewpoint was that the only evil at which Congress had aimed was high consumer prices achieved through combinations looking to control of markets by powerful groups; that those who would have a great incentive for such combinations would be the business men who would be the direct beneficiaries of them; therefore, the argument proceeded, Congress drafted its law to apply only to business combinations, particularly the large trusts, and not to labor unions or any of their activities as such. Involved in this viewpoint were the following contentions: that the Sherman Act is a law to regulate trade, not labor, a law to prescribe the rules governing barter and sale, and not the personal relations of employers and employees; that good wages and working conditions helped and did not hinder trade, even though increased labor costs might be reflected in the cost of products; that labor was not a commodity; that laborers had an inherent right to accept or terminate employment at their own will, either separately or in concert; that to enforce their claims for better wages and working conditions, they had a right to refuse to buy goods from their employer or anybody else; that what they could do to aid their cause, they had a right to persuade others to do; and that the Antitrust laws designed to regulate trading were unsuitable to regulate employer-employee relations and controversies. The claim was that the history of the legislation supported this line of argument.

The contrary viewpoint was that the Act covered all classes of people and all types of combinations, including unions, if their activities even physically interrupted the free flow of trade or tended to create business monopolies, and that a combination of laborers to obtain a raise in wages was itself a prohibited monopoly. Federal courts adopted the latter view and soon applied the law to unions in a number of cases. Injunctions were used to enforce the Act against unions. At the same time employers invoked injunctions to restrain labor union activities even where no violation of the Sherman Act was charged.

Vigorous protests arose from employee groups. The unions urged congressional relief from what they considered to be two separate, but partially overlapping evils—application of the Sherman Act to unions, and issuance of injunctions against strikes, boycotts and other labor union weapons. Numerous bills to curb injunctions were offered. Other proposed legislation was intended to take labor unions wholly outside any possible application of the Sherman Act. All of this is a part of the well known history of the era between 1890 and 1914.

To amend, supplement and strengthen the Sherman Act against monopolistic business practices, and in response to the complaints of the unions against injunctions and application of the Act to them, Congress in 1914 passed the Clayton Act. Elimination of those "trade practices" which injuriously affected competition was its first objective. Each section of the measure prohibiting such trade practices contained language peculiarly appropriate to commercial transactions as distinguished from labor union activities, but there is no record indication in anything that was said or done in its passage which indicates that those engaged in business could escape its or the Sherman Act's prohibitions by obtaining the help of labor unions or others. That this bill was intended to make it all the more certain that competition should be the rule in all commercial transactions is clear from its language and history.

In its treatment of labor unions and their activities the Clayton Act pointed in an opposite direction. Congress in that Act responded to the prolonged complaints concerning application of the Sherman law to labor groups by adopting Section 6; for this purpose, and also drastically to restrict the general power of federal courts to issue labor injunctions, Section 20, 29 U.S.C.A. § 52 was adopted. Section 6 declared that labor was neither a commodity nor an article of commerce, and that the Sherman Act should not be "construed to forbid the existence and operation of labor, agricultural, or horticultural organizations, instituted for the purposes of mutual help . . . ." Section 20 limited the power of courts to issue injunctions in a case "involving, or growing out of, a [labor] dispute [over] terms or conditions of employment . . . ." It declared that no restraining order or injunction should prohibit certain specified acts, and further declared that no one of these specified acts should be "held to be violations of any law of the United States." This Act was broadly proclaimed by many as labor's "Magna Carta", wholly exempting labor from any possible inclusion in the Anti-trust legislation; others, however, strongly denied this.

This Court later declined to interpret the Clayton Act as manifesting a congressional purpose wholly to exempt labor unions from the Sherman Act. Duplex Printing Press Co. v. Deering, 254 U.S. 443, 41 S.Ct. 172, 65 L.Ed. 349, 16 A.L.R. 196; Bedford Cut Stone Co. v. Journeymen Stone Cutters' Ass'n, 274 U.S. 37, 47 S.Ct. 522, 71 L.Ed. 916, 54 A.L.R. 791. In those cases labor unions had engaged in a secondary boycott; they had boycotted dealers, by whom the union members were not employed, because those dealers insisted on selling goods produced by the employers with whom the unions had an existing controversy over terms and conditions of employment. This Court held that the Clayton Act exempted labor union activities only insofar as those activities were directed against the employees' immediate employers and that controversies over the sale of goods by other dealers did not constitute "labor disputes" within the meaning of the Clayton Act.

Again the unions went to Congress. They protested against this Court's interpretation, repeating the arguments they had made against application of the Sherman Act to them. Congress adopted their viewpoint, at least in large part, and in order to escape the effect of the Duplex and Bedford decisions, passed the Norris-LaGuardia Act, 47 Stat. 71, 29 U.S.C.A. § 101 et seq. That Act greatly broadened the meaning this Court had attributed to the words "labor dispute", further restricted the use of injunctions in such a dispute, and emphasized the public importance under modern economic conditions of protecting the rights of employees to organize into unions and to engage in "concerted activities for the purpose of collective bargaining or other mutual aid or protection." This congressional purpose found further expression in the Wagner Act, 49 Stat. 449, 29 U.S.C.A. § 151 et seq.

We said in Apex Hosiery Co. v. Leader, supra, that labor unions are still subject to the Sherman Act to "some extent not defined." The opinion in that case, however, went on to explain that the Sherman Act "was enacted in the era of 'trusts' and of 'combinations' of businesses and of capital organized and directed to control of the market by suppression of competition in the marketing of goods and services, the monopolistic tendency of which had become a matter of public concern"; that its purpose was to protect consumers from monopoly prices, and not to serve as a comprehensive code to regulate and police all kinds and types of interruptions and obstructions to the flow of trade. This was a recognition of the fact that Congress had accepted the arguments made continuously since 1890 by groups opposing application of the Sherman Act to unions. It was an interpretation commanded by a fair consideration of the full history of Antitrust and labor legislation.

United States v. Hutcheson, 312 U.S. 219, 61 S.Ct. 463, 85 L.Ed. 788, declared that the Sherman, Clayton and Norris-LaGuardia Acts must be jointly considered in arriving at a conclusion as to whether labor union activities run counter to the Antitrust legislation. Conduct which they permit is not to be declared a violation of federal law. That decision held that the doctrine of the Duplex and Bedford cases was inconsistent with the congressional policy set out in the three "interlacing statutes."

The result of all this is that we have two declared congressional policies which it is our responsibility to try to reconcile. The one seeks to preserve a competitive business economy; the other to preserve the rights of labor to organize to better its conditions through the agency of collective bargaining. We must determine here how far Congress intended activities under one of these policies to neutralize the results envisioned by the other.

Aside from the fact that the labor union here acted in combination with the contractors and manufacturers, the means it adopted to contribute to the combination's purpose fall squarely within the "specified acts" declared by Section 20 not to be violations of federal law. For the union's contribution to the trade boycott was accomplished through threats that unless their employers bought their goods from local manufacturers the union laborers would terminate the "relation of employment" with them and cease to perform "work or labor" for them; and through their "recommending, advising, or persuading others by peaceful and lawful means" not to "patronize" sellers of the boycotted electrical equipment. Consequently, under our holdings in the Hutcheson case and other cases which followed it, had there been no union-contractor-manufacturer combination the union's actions here, coming as they did within the exemptions of the Clayton and Norris-LaGuardia Acts, would not have been violations of the Sherman Act. We pass to the question of whether unions can with impunity aid and abet business men who are violating the Act.

On two occasions this Court has held that the Sherman Act was violated by a combination of labor unions and business men to restrain trade.[35] In neither of them was the Court's attention sharply called to the crucial questions here presented. Furthermore, both were decided before the passage of the Norris-LaGuardia Act, and prior to our holding in the Hutcheson case. It is correctly argued by respondents that these factors greatly detract from the weight which the two cases might otherwise have in the instant case. Without regard to these cases, however, we think Congress never intended that unions could, consistently with the Sherman Act, aid non-labor groups to create business monopolies and to control the marketing of goods and services.

Section 6 of the Clayton Act declares that the Sherman Act must not be so construed as to forbid the "existence and operation of labor, agricultural, or horticultural organizations, instituted for the purposes of mutual help . . . ." But "the purposes of mutual help" can hardly be thought to cover activities for the purpose of "employer-help" in controlling markets and prices. And in an analogous situation where an agricultural association joined with other groups to control the agricultural market, we said:

> "The right of these agricultural producers thus to unite in preparing for market and in marketing their products, and to make the contracts which are necessary for that collaboration, cannot be deemed to authorize any combination or conspiracy *with other persons* in restraint of trade that these producers may see fit to devise." United States v. Borden Co., 308 U.S. 188, 204, 205, 60 S.Ct. 182, 191, 84 L.Ed. 181. (Italics supplied.)

We have been pointed to no language in any act of Congress or in its reports or debates nor have we found any, which indicates that it was ever suggested, considered, or legislatively determined that labor unions should be granted an immunity such as is sought in the present case. It has been argued that this immunity can be inferred from a union's right to make bargaining agreements with its employ-

35. United States v. Brims, 272 U.S.   v. United States, 291 U.S. 293, 54 S.Ct.
549, 47 S.Ct. 169, 71 L.Ed. 403; Local 167   396, 78 L.Ed. 804.

er. Since union members can without violating the Sherman Act
strike to enforce a union boycott of goods, it is said they may settle
the strike by getting their employers to agree to refuse to buy the
goods. Employers and the union did here make bargaining agreements in which the employers agreed not to buy goods manufactured
by companies which did not employ the members of Local No. 3. We
may assume that such an agreement standing alone would not have
violated the Sherman Act. But it did not stand alone. It was but one
element in a far larger program in which contractors and manufacturers united with one another to monopolize all the business in New
York City, to bar all other business men from that area, and to
charge the public prices above a competitive level. It is true that
victory of the union in its disputes, even had the union acted alone,
might have added to the cost of goods, or might have resulted in individual refusals of all of their employers to buy electrical equipment
not made by Local No. 3. So far as the union might have achieved
this result acting alone, it would have been the natural consequence
of labor union activities exempted by the Clayton Act from the coverage of the Sherman Act. But when the unions participated with a
combination of business men who had complete power to eliminate all
competition among themselves and to prevent all competition from
others, a situation was created not included within the exemptions of
the Clayton and Norris-LaGuardia Acts.

It must be remembered that the exemptions granted the unions
were special exemptions to a general legislative plan. The primary
objective of all the Antitrust legislation has been to preserve business
competition and to proscribe business monopoly. It would be a surprising thing if Congress, in order to prevent a misapplication of that
legislation to labor unions, had bestowed upon such unions complete
and unreviewable authority to aid business groups to frustrate its primary objective. For if business groups, by combining with labor unions, can fix prices and divide up markets, it was little more than a
futile gesture for Congress to prohibit price fixing by business
groups themselves. Seldom, if ever, has it been claimed before, that
by permitting labor unions to carry on their own activities, Congress
intended completely to abdicate its constitutional power to regulate
interstate commerce and to empower interested business groups to
shift our society from a competitive to a monopolistic economy. Finding no purpose of Congress to immunize labor unions who aid and
abet manufacturers and traders in violating the Sherman Act, we
hold that the district court correctly concluded that the respondents
had violated the Act.

Our holding means that the same labor union activities may or
may not be in violation of the Sherman Act, dependent upon whether
the union acts alone or in combination with business groups. This, it
is argued, brings about a wholly undesirable result—one which leaves
labor unions free to engage in conduct which restrains trade. But
the desirability of such an exemption of labor unions is a question for
the determination of Congress. Apex Hosiery Co. v. Leader, supra.
It is true that many labor union activities do substantially interrupt

the course of trade and that these activities, lifted out of the prohibitions of the Sherman Act, include substantially all, if not all, of the normal peaceful activities of labor unions. It is also true that the Sherman Act "draws no distinction between the restraints effected by violence and those achieved by peaceful . . . means . . .," Apex Hosiery Co. v. Leader, supra, 310 U.S. 513, 60 S.Ct. 1002, 84 L.Ed. 1311, 128 A.L.R. 1044, and that a union's exemption from the Sherman Act is not to be determined by a judicial "judgment regarding the wisdom or unwisdom, the rightness or wrongness, the selfishness or unselfishness of the end of which the particular union activities are the means." United States v. Hutcheson, supra, 312 U.S. 232, 61 S.Ct. 466, 85 L.Ed. 788. Thus, these congressionally permitted union activities may restrain trade in and of themselves. There is no denying the fact that many of them do so, both directly and indirectly. Congress evidently concluded, however, that the chief objective of Antitrust legislation, preservation of business competition, could be accomplished by applying the legislation primarily only to those business groups which are directly interested in destroying competition. The difficulty of drawing legislation primarily aimed at trusts and monopolies so that it could also be applied to labor organizations without impairing the collective bargaining and related rights of those organizations has been emphasized both by congressional and judicial attempts to draw lines between permissible and prohibited union activities. There is, however, one line which we can draw with assurance that we follow the congressional purpose. We know that Congress feared the concentrated power of business organizations to dominate markets and prices. It intended to outlaw business monopolies. A business monopoly is no less such because a union participates, and such participation is a violation of the Act.

This brings us to a consideration of the scope of the declaratory judgment and the injunction granted by the district court. We cannot sustain the judgment or the injunction in the form in which they were entered. The judgment and the injunction apply only to the union, its members, and its agents, since they were the only parties against whom relief was asked. . . .

Respondents objected to the form of the injunction and specifically requested that it be amended so as to enjoin only those prohibited activities in which the union engaged in combination "with any person, firm or corporation which is a non-labor group . . . ." Without such a limitation, the injunction as issued runs directly counter to the Clayton and the Norris-LaGuardia Acts. The district court's refusal so to limit it was error.

The judgment of the Circuit Court of Appeals ordering the action dismissed is accordingly reversed and the cause is remanded to the district court for modification and clarification of the judgment and injunction, consistent with this opinion.

Reversed and remanded.

MR. JUSTICE MURPHY, dissenting.

My disagreement with the Court rests not so much with the legal principles announced as with the application of those principles to the facts of the case.

If the union in this instance had acted alone in its self-interest, resulting in a restraint of interstate trade, the Sherman Act concededly would be inapplicable. But if the union had aided and abetted manufacturers or traders in violating the Act, the union's statutory immunity would disappear. I cannot agree, however, that the circumstances of this case demand the invocation of the latter rule.

The union here has not in any true sense "aided" or "abetted" a primary violation of the Act by the employers. In the words of the union, it has been "the dynamic force which has driven the employer-group to enter into agreements" whereby trade has been affected. The fact that the union has expressed its self-interest with the aid of others rather than solely by its own activities should not be decisive of statutory liability. What is legal if done alone should not become illegal if done with the assistance of others and with the same purpose in mind. Otherwise a premium of unlawfulness is placed on collective bargaining.

Had the employers embarked upon a course of unreasonable trade restraints and had they sought to immunize themselves from the Sherman Act by using the union as a shield for their nefarious practices, we would have quite a different case. The union then could not be said to be acting in its self-interest in combining with the employers to carry out trade restraints primarily for the employers' interests, even though incidental benefits might accrue to the union. Under such conditions the union fairly could be said to be aiding and abetting a violation of the Act and its immunity would be lost. The facts of this case, however, do not allow such conclusions to be drawn.

I would therefore affirm the judgment of the court below.

MR. JUSTICE ROBERTS.

While I should reverse the judgment, I am unable to concur in the court's opinion. I think it conveys an incorrect impression of the genesis and character of the conspiracy charged in the complaint, and misapplies recent decisions of the court.

There is no doubt that the programme adopted by Local No. 3 envisaged the exclusion, from the entire New York City area, of any electrical workers, whether engaged in manufacturing or installing electrical devices and equipment, except members of the Local. The organization from time to time increased the classes of members, so as to add to its original membership of workers engaged in fabricating and installing electrical devices, equipment, and apparatus the additional categories of shop employes engaged in manufacturing electrical equipment and all workers employed in alterations, additions, and repairs involving electrical equipment. It succeeded in unionizing and imposing closed shops employing only members of Local

3, not only on all building contractors but on all repair contractors and their establishments and all manufacturers of electrical equipment. Membership in the union was closely restricted and the campaign eventuated in a situation where no electrical work could be done by persons other than members of the union, no building construction could be done by other than union men, no matter what their trade, and no manufactured electrical appliance or apparatus could be installed in the New York area without the consent of Local No. 3. That consent was given only if the device, appliance or apparatus was manufactured, or work done on it, by members of the Local. Complicated apparatus which had to be manufactured outside New York City, because no establishment making it existed within the city, had to be dismantled and rebuilt by members of the Local before it could be used in the New York area.

It is true that before Local No. 3 obtained this complete control of the industry in its area of operation certain associated building contractors dealt jointly as an association with the union. As respects certain manufacturers which came under the dominance of the union this is not true. Nor is it true of repair businesses. On the contrary, it is the fact that each one of these was individually coerced by the union's power to agree to its terms. It is, therefore, inaccurate to say that the employers used the union to aid and abet them to restrain interstate commerce. Some of the employers, notably the building contractors, did jointly cooperate with the union; other sorts of employers were forced individually to comply with the union's demands, until all of them had succumbed.

There can be no question of the purpose of the union. It was to exclude from use in the City of New York articles of commerce made outside the city and offered for sale to users within the city; it was completely to monopolize the manufacture and sale of all electrical equipment and devices within New York, and to exclude from use in the area every such article manufactured outside the city, whether in a closed union shop or not. The results of this programme are obvious. Interstate commerce between New York City and manufacturers having establishments outside the city was completely broken off, and the monopoly created, raised, standardized and fixed the prices of merchandise and apparatus.

As I understand the opinion of the court, such a programme, and such a result, is wholly within the law provided only that employers do not jointly agree to comply with the union's demands. Unless I misread the opinion, the union is at liberty to impose every term and condition as shown by the record in this case and to enforce those conditions and procure an agreement from each employer to such conditions by calling strikes, by lockout, and boycott, provided only such employer agrees for himself alone and not in concert with any other.

I point out again, as respects certain employers here concerned, that that is the situation, whereas, with respect to the building construction employers, there was mutual agreement with the union.

But the opinion takes no note of the distinction in fact. It seems to me that the law as announced by the court creates an impossible situation such as Congress never contemplated and leaves commerce paralyzed beyond escape.

Until Apex Hosiery Co. v. Leader was decided I had thought that a conspiracy by laborers to interrupt the free flow of commerce was a violation of the Sherman Act. That case, however, announced a narrower doctrine. Its teaching is that only activity of labor which harms the commercial competitive system through raising prices, restricting production, or otherwise controlling the market, falls within the proscription of the Sherman Act. In that case it was said:

> "Furthermore, successful union activity, as for example consummation of a wage agreement with employers, may have some influence on price competition by eliminating that part of such competition which is based on differences in labor standards. Since, in order to render a labor combination effective it must eliminate the competition from non-union made goods, see American Steel Foundries v. Tri-City Central Trades Council, 257 U.S. 184, 209, 42 S.Ct. 72, 78, 66 L.Ed. 189, 27 A.L.R. 360, an elimination of price competition based on differences in labor standards is the objective of any national labor organization. But this effect on competition has not been considered to be the kind of curtailment of price competition prohibited by the Sherman Act."

It was added that the restraint there under examination was not shown "to have any actual or intended effect on price or price competition." The decision indicated that, in some undefined circumstances, labor organizations might be subject to the statute.

In United States v. Hutcheson, secondary boycotts by labor unions to keep out of the market nonunion goods, or goods worked on by other unions, were held immune from liability, civil or criminal, under the Sherman Act. It was there said:

> "So long as a union acts in its self-interest and does not combine with non-labor groups, the licit and the illicit under § 20 are not to be distinguished by any judgment regarding the wisdom or unwisdom, the rightness or wrongness, the selfishness or unselfishness of the end of which the particular union activities are the means."

Thus, although a conspiracy between laborers is distinguished from one between them and employers, it is intimated, as I think, that a purpose on the part of a labor group to harm the commercial competitive system, to raise prices, to restrict production, or otherwise control the market, would not render the concerted action illegal, provided only that no employer participated. The reservation made in the Apex case was discarded in the Hutcheson case. This advance in the law was emphasized in United States v. Building & Construction Trades Council, 313 U.S. 539, 61 S.Ct. 839, 85 L.Ed. 1508, and United States v. United Brotherhood of Carpenters and Joiners, 313 U.S. 539, 61 S.Ct. 839, 85 L.Ed. 1508, but the court went even farther, in United States v. American Federation of Musicians, 318 U.S. 741, 63 S.Ct.

665, 87 L.Ed. 1120, and, as I think, rendered a decision contrary to that now announced. There a motion to dismiss a bill of complaint was granted and this court sustained that action. The complaint charged a conspiracy by the American Federation of Musicians, a nationwide organization, and its officers to obtain employment for its members by eliminating entirely from interstate commerce all phonograph records and electrical transcriptions of music and eliminating all competition between transcribed music and that produced by living musicians. The conspiracy charged was absolutely to prevent manufacture or sale of phonograph records and electrical transcriptions; to eliminate from the market all manufacturers, distributors, jobbers or retailers of the same, and to prevent the use of the articles, either in public places or private homes, and, of course, to prevent their sale. In the bill it was charged that the conspiracy did not grow out of or involve any dispute concerning terms or conditions of employment; that the purpose of the conspiracy was to eliminate from the market, manufacture, sale and use of mechanical recordings and records and transcriptions unless the persons engaged in this business should enter into agreements with the union, hiring useless and unnecessary labor, as the union would demand. The further purpose of the conspiracy charged was to exclude from the market competition by anyone who failed exclusively to employ members of the union. The complaint further charged that the purpose and effect of the conspiracy was unlawfully to destroy all manufacture and sale, in interstate commerce of phonograph records and electrical transcriptions, eliminate all competition between music produced by mechanical means and music produced by living musicians, to deprive the public of an inexpensive means of entertainment in public places and in the home.

This court's affirmance of the dismissal of this complaint can only mean that every business-man who desires to stay in business must if a union so demands enter into an agreement with the union eliminating certain articles from his manufacture, from his sales, or from his use. The decision must necessarily mean that it would not be unlawful to enter into such an agreement with the union, otherwise we should have the anomaly that the union's demand for such an agreement is impeccable but the employer's acquiescence is unlawful. As shown by the opinion of the District Court in that case, the Government contended that the Union's effort represented "an attempt by the union to force employers to combine with it for the purpose of restraining interstate trade . . . ." The District Court shortly answered this contention by saying: "In the court's opinion, United States v. Brims, 272 U.S. 549, 47 S.Ct. 169, 71 L.Ed. 403, and like cases, are not pertinent." This must mean that each employer, in the instant case, is at liberty to agree with the union on all the terms and conditions which create a complete monopoly, a complete boycott, a complete closing of the market, and a serious price fixing affecting competitive commercial transactions. This is what I understand the court now holds. This is what was accomplished with impunity by the Federation of Musicians. But the situation created by such a holding is unreal.

As I have pointed out, in two branches of the industry, the manufacturers and employers, one by one, succumbed to union pressure and entered into agreements. Was not such an action, in each instance, a conspiracy? Are more than two parties required to conspire, and did not each of those conspiracies, to some extent, hinder and restrain interstate commerce and affect the market and the competitive price situation? As each agreement was consummated the market was, to that extent, closed and the boycott against out-of-the-city manufacturers tightened.

But more. The union did not conduct its campaign in a corner. Albeit the findings are that manufacturers and repairers of electrical appliances violently resisted the unionization of their businesses, they, one by one, surrendered and signed. In doing so many must have had knowledge of what others were doing or had done. And, as the coverage became complete, each one was enabled to stifle out of town competition and to raise prices. In any action against them and the union charging conspiracy it would be urged that a conspiracy need not consist of a written or verbal agreement but might be inferred from similarity of action. And it would be little protection to the employers concerned that, in each instance, a separate agreement was signed between union and employer.

The course of decision in this court has now created a situation in which, by concerted action, unions may set up a wall around a municipality of millions of inhabitants against importation of any goods if the union is careful to make separate contracts with each employer, and if union and employers are able to convince the court that, while all employers have such agreements, each acted independently in making them,—this notwithstanding the avowed purpose to exclude goods not made in that city by the members of the union; notwithstanding the fact that the purpose and inevitable result is the stifling of competition in interstate trade and the creation of a monopoly.

The only answer I find in the opinion of the court is that Congress has so provided. I think it has not provided any such thing and that the figmentary difference between employers negotiating jointly with the only union with which they can deal,—which imposes like conditions on all employers—and each employer dealing separately with the same union is unrealistic and unworkable. And the language of § 20 of the Clayton Act, 29 U.S.C.A. § 52, makes no such distinction.

This court, as a result of its past decisions, is in the predicament that whatever it decides must entail disastrous results. I can understand that the Circuit Court of Appeals felt constrained by the prior decisions of this court to order the judgment of the District Court reversed and the action dismissed. If the present decision is, as I think, a retrogression from earlier holdings, I welcome it: if it is but a limitation of them I concur in the partial alleviation of an impossible situation. But I would not limit the injunction as the opinion directs.

NOTES AND QUERIES

(1) *APEX, HUTCHESON, AND ALLEN BRADLEY—The Pre-1965 Trilogy Defining The Boundaries of The Labor Exemption.* The Court's *Allen-Bradley* opinion discusses *Apex Hosiery Co. v. Leader* and *United States v. Hutcheson*, two post Norris-LaGuardia and Wagner Act cases spelling out a wide-ranging labor exemption from antitrust. Together the three cases have been read as having established a sensible and reliable test for defining the outer boundaries of the labor exemption:

> Together this trilogy of hallmark opinions teaches that the availability of the labor exemption turns on the answers to three questions: First, is the challenged conduct exempt under Norris-LaGuardia from the issuance of a labor injunction? Second, does the conduct substantially affect market competition? Third, is it unilaterally motivated? Thus, if union conduct is embraced by the permissive provisions of Norris-LaGuardia, or if it does not have the effect of restraining commercial competition (as opposed to competition based on differences in labor standards), and if it is pursued by the union solely in its own self-interest, it is exempt from antitrust liability. Conversely, if the challenged conduct is outside the protective ambit of Norris-LaGuardia, and if it directly affects market competition, or if it is the product of conspiracy with employer groups, then it is subject to the antitrust laws.
>
> Had the Supreme Court not tampered with this trilogy, it would stand today as the bedrock of labor-antitrust principles.[36]

Query. How solid a "bedrock" and clearcut a definition of the limits of the labor exemption did *Allen Bradley* create? Note that the Court's opinion recognizes that the union could have achieved lawfully the same goals of expanded membership, shorter hours and higher wages if it had "acted alone." Liability was premised upon the union's participation "with a combination of businessmen who had complete power to eliminate all competition among themselves and to prevent all competition from others. . . ." It has been pointed out that the difficulty with this test is that unions only "act alone" when "attempting to force some action upon an employer" and success in achieving their objective will frequently culminate in an agreement limiting competition with a firm or combination of firms.[37] Moreover, the agreement usually has an "effect on commercial competition." How can one tell the point at which a union's activity moves from the purely unilateral pursuit of its legitimate labor goals to unlawful collaboration with employers to restrain "commercial competition"?

(2) *Union Antitrust Suits Claiming Employer Activity Falls Outside the Exemption.* Joint action by employers outside the labor exemption may also be made the basis of antitrust claims by third parties or a union injured in its business or property. Courts confronted with such cases find an exemption where the collaboration is directed toward resisting union demands on issues within the purview of the labor laws.[38] Where, however, joint em-

---

36. Handler & Zifchak, Collective Bargaining and The Antitrust Laws: The Emasculation of the Labor Exemption, 81 Colum.L.Rev. 459, 482–83 (1981).

37. Leslie, Principles of Labor Antitrust, 66 Va.L.Rev. 1183, 1203 (1980). Despite these ambiguities in the Allen Bradley opinion, the Supreme Court "was rarely called upon to examine the labor exemption" for twenty years following the opinion. See Casey & Cozzellio, Labor-Antitrust: The Problems of Connell and a Remedy That Follows Naturally, 1980 Duke L.J. 235, 242.

38. See California State Council of Carpenters v. Associated General Contractors, Inc., infra note rev'd; Amalgamated Meat Cutters & Butchers Work-

ployer action is aimed at restraining trade, claims that the action is designed to benefit union members will not immunize the conduct: "[B]enefits to organized labor cannot be used as a cat's paw to pull an employer's chestnuts out of the antitrust fire." [39]   Employer collaborative effort to disadvantage a union, by boycotting those who deal with the union, may also give rise to antitrust liability.   In *California State Council of Carpenters v. Associated General Contractors of California, Inc.,*[40] a divided Ninth Circuit upheld jurisdiction over a union's antitrust complaint alleging that the defendant contractors (with whom it had a collective bargaining agreement) conspired to boycott subcontractors with whom the union had agreements in favor of non-union subcontractors.   Joint employer action coercing third parties not to deal with the union was held to be outside the labor exemption for employer activity involving collective bargaining activity over wages, hours and terms of employment.   An employer conspiracy to destroy a union by a boycott of firms the union had organized was further held not to be within the "pro-labor spirit" of the Clayton and Norris-LaGuardia exemptions from the antitrust laws.   The Supreme Court's reversal of the opinion acknowledged the Union stated a claim under the antitrust laws, but dismissed the claim because it was indirect (injury alleged was to boycotted employers) and proof of damages was speculative.   (___ U.S. at ___, 103 S.Ct. at 913):

> We conclude, therefore, that the Union's allegations of consequential harm resulting from a violation of the antitrust laws, although buttressed by an allegation of intent to harm the Union, are insufficient as a matter of law.   Other relevant factors—the nature of the Union's injury, the tenuous and speculative character of the relationship between the alleged antitrust violation and the Union's alleged injury, the potential for duplicative recovery or complex apportionment of damages, and the existence of more direct victims of the alleged conspiracy—weigh heavily against judicial enforcement of the Union's antitrust claim.   Accordingly, we hold that, based on the allegations of this complaint, the District Court was correct in concluding that the Union is not a person injured by reason of a violation of the antitrust laws within the meaning of § 4 of the Clayton Act.   The judgment of the Court of Appeals is reversed.

(3) *Union "Standing" in Antitrust Controversies Over Union Organization and Wage Levels.*   In *Tugboat, Inc. v. Mobile Towing Co.,*[41] the antitrust action grew out of a contest between Tugboat and Mobile to dominate tugging in Mobile Bay, Alabama.   Mobile Towing and the Seafarers International Union charged that Tugboat had conspired with its own union, allegedly company-dominated, to drive Mobile out of business by unfairly obtaining lower labor rates than were set in the Seafarers' contract.   Held: the Seafarers Union and its members had standing to seek treble damages and injunctive relief under section 4 of the Clayton Act, since they were the targets of the alleged antitrust violation as much as Mobile Towing.   "An employee who is deprived of a work opportunity has been injured in his commercial interests or enterprise, because the selling of one's labor is a commercial interest."   Similarly the union is in the business of attracting and represent-

---

men, Local No. 576 v. Wetterau Foods, Inc., 597 F.2d 133 (8th Cir. 1979); Amalgamated Clothing & Textile Workers Union v. J. P. Stevens & Co., Inc., 638 F.2d 7 (2d Cir. 1980).

39.   United States v. Women's Sportswear Manufacturers Association, 336

U.S. 460, 464, 69 S.Ct. 714, 716, 93 L.Ed. 2d 805, 811 (1949).

40.   648 F.2d 527 (9th Cir. 1980), reversed ___ U.S. ___, 103 S.Ct. 897, 74 L.Ed.2d 723 (1983).

41.   534 F.2d 1172 (5th Cir. 1976).

ing employees, and injury to that business is compensable under section 4 of the Clayton Act.

Queries. Does the language of the Court in *Tugboat* go beyond the issue directly before it, i.e. standing to sue? Is the opinion in *Tugboat* consistent with the holding in *California State Council*? On the substantive issue, how do both opinions square with the declaration in section 6 of the Clayton Act that labor is not an article of commerce?

(4) *Industry-Wide Bargaining and the Labor Exemption.* A union has significant incentives to unionize an entire industry and impose similar wage and working conditions upon all firms in the industry. Professor Leslie has described those incentives as follows:

> An industry's nonunion firms present a substantial threat to the industry's unionized firms. If a union-imposed wage bill increases the cost of production, the unionized firm will earn less profit than it could absent the union's intervention. A firm, therefore, often has an incentive to resist unionization and, once unionized, to seek to return to a nonunion status. The firm's current ownership of assets that cannot easily be sold or transferred to another industry may limit its opportunity to leave the industry for other investments. Ultimately, however, these impediments to the movement of capital will diminish. At the same time, opportunities in the industry's nonunion sector are enhanced by a rise in the price of the product and a decrease in the cost of labor. Because it enjoys a greater than average return on capital, the nonunion sector will draw more capital into the industry, driving down the product price and making the unionized sector's position more untenable. Consequently, a union has a considerable incentive to organize along product-market lines.

> Once it organizes the entire industry, the union will want to prevent entry by nonunion firms. An entrant with lower costs made possible by a nonunion wage rate may price its output below that of its unionized product-market competitors and, unless its size makes it relatively insignificant, threaten union gains. Because the fortunes of unionized employees rise and fall with those of their employer, substantial competition from a nonunion firm with a lower wage bill directly threatens the effectiveness and even the continued existence of the union. The more direct the competition between firms, the greater is the threat to unions. Moreover, nonunionized firms that have any competitive advantages, including those gained other than by a reduced wage bill, threaten unionized employees. Thus, the union has an incentive to prevent nonunion firms from competing.

> When nonunion competition threatens unionized firms, the union has three predictable responses: (1) organize the nonunion firm; (2) pressure the nonunion firm to match the union's wage package with the unionized firms; or (3) force the nonunion firm out of the market. The first response protects the union's wage bill and increases its membership; the second insures that any competitive advantage to the nonunion firm does not come from a lower wage bill, but it does not protect the unionized firms from other competitive disadvantages; the third completely protects the unionized firms. The third response has the added benefit of permitting the union to concentrate on fewer firms when negotiating and administering bargaining agreements. Although the unionized firms benefit from each of the union responses, they benefit most from the third response, which tends to concentrate the market.[42]

42. Leslie, supra note 37, at 1190–92.

As the following materials indicate, the union's interest may extend to the overall economic stability of the industry and deeply involve the union in securing industry-wide cooperation to cure problems normally within the province of the management of individual firms. Just how far unions may go in inducing industry-wide compliance with programs in the interests of the industry or union members, where there is a differential effect on the ability of firms to compete, is the question to be explored, infra, in the latest trilogy of labor exemption decisions, *Pennington, Jewel Tea* and *Connell.*

ROLE OF THE ILGWU IN STABILIZING THE WOMEN'S GARMENT INDUSTRY

Excerpts from article by Theresa Wolfson in 4 Ind. and
Labor Relations Rev. 33 (1950).

The history of the men's and women's garment industries is one replete with the evils of unbridled and uncontrolled competition. These industries were born in the sweatshops, and had a tradition of excessive exploitation, homework, and violence in industrial relations. The story has been familiar to most students of labor history. What is not so familiar is the fact that, out of the chaos of excessive competition, the industry has been compelled to evolve a program of stabilization in order to survive. Garment factories appeared and disappeared. Employers became workers and crossed the line back again into the employing class. Only the unions were able to forge themselves into powerful unified bodies, and through the years they hammered out a policy of stabilization which had unity of purpose and form. This stabilization program came into existence primarily through the initiative of the International Ladies' Garment Workers' Union and Amalgamated Clothing Workers Union, which, according to the statement of one of the outstanding labor leaders, recognized that "there is no security for workers in an insecure industry."

What was the nature of the competition which existed in the garment industry that bred economic insecurity?

The women's clothing industry, which includes the manufacture of dresses, cloaks and suits, underwear and nightwear, corsets and allied articles, infants' and children's wear, and such accessory industries as artificial-flower making, is primarily an industry in which capital investment is small. In fact, in comparison with similar industries responsible for a similar volume of production, the industry is outstanding in the fact that a loft, a few sewing machines, pressing machines, a style, and fabrics constitute the chief form of capital investment.

Economic Structure of Women's Clothing Industry

In 1939, the volume of business of all dress firms having contracts with the International Ladies' Garment Workers' Union was $349,482,204. This large volume of business on low capitalization can best be summed up in the fact that the capitalization per worker is approximately $400, whereas in most manufacturing industries it is from $2,450 to $6,000 per worker.

The industry is one in which labor, rather than the machine, is the dominant factor. There is comparatively easy entrance into the industry on the part of the entrepreneur. Financial success depends in the main not on the size of the plant but on the ingenuity of the manufacturer in devising and adopting new styles. . . .

A Study in Self-regulation

. . . Since 1910 the union has been concerned with the problem of industrial self-regulation. It was, as a matter of fact, compelled to do so in its efforts to combat the evils of homework and sweatshop. No other agency either in the government or in industry was created for the sole purpose of protecting and improving the conditions of workers at that time. In 1910 the union, in its first collective agreement, often referred to as the "Protocol of Peace," urged the Cloak Manufacturers' Association to cease sending out homework and to eliminate the subcontractor. The subcontractor was a worker in a shop who would contract for work with his employer and then hire other workers, recently arrived immigrants who were defenseless, to work for him at a wage that was less than a living wage. The subcontractor retained the difference between what he received from the employer and what he paid the workers. . . . This was but the first step in industry regulation.

A series of reforms was proposed by the New York Cloak Makers Union when it was seen that the Protocol was not effective in checking or controlling the number of contractors. The proposed reforms were:

(1) Registration of all contractors with the union at the beginning of each season. . . .

(4) No jobber or manufacturer to be permitted to take on additional contractors as long as his regular contractors were not fully supplied with work.

(5) Decisions of the Board of Arbitration to be rendered within 48 hours and disciplinary measures to be developed to ensure observance of the agreement.

These proposals were not accepted by the employers but they became the goals for which the union strove in order to stabilize the industry. . . .

Employers' Associations

The union recognized that stability of industrial relations depends upon a stable employer group as well as upon an organized worker group. The union, therefore, encouraged and even aided in the formation of employers' associations. . . . The depression of the 1930's seriously affected the women's garment industry. The number of firms engaged in the production of women's clothing declined by 43.7 percent from 1929 to 1933, while the total number of manufacturing establishments in the United States fell by 32.4 percent.

Competition was intensified during this depression and "retailers held a whip over the industry and exacted tribute in the form of special discounts, consignment buying, and agreements which permitted them to return merchandise they could not sell."

The National Industrial Recovery Act helped the industry through the (1) introduction of fair trade regulations curbing ruinous competition; (2) enforcement of nationwide uniform labor standards which added to industrial stability and benefited employers; and (3) the establishment of industrial codes providing for a 35-hour work week, the placement of the N.R.A. label on all garments, and substantial wage increases.

When the National Industrial Recovery Act was held unconstitutional in May 1935, the coat and suit division of the garment industry voluntarily set up a code of its own. The National Coat and Suit Recovery Board, as of July 1935, was composed of employer and union representatives from all markets and was designed to maintain voluntary supervision over work standards and establish fair practices in the industry. A Consumers' Protection label was placed upon all garments manufactured by employers who were members of the board. The sale of these labels became the source of income for the administration and enforcement of the regulations set up by the board.

The 1936 Agreement

Another principle of standardization for which the union fought was that of the *limitation and control of contractors*. The 1936 agreement between the ILGWU and the National Dress Manufacturers Association and the United Association of Dress Manufacturers (jobbers) specifically stated that the purpose of the agreement was "to remove existing disputes and differences between contractors on the one hand and jobbers and manufacturers on the other." Each association prepared on the first day of each month, a list of names of all its members and the location of their place of business and subsequently furnished a written notice of any additions or changes to the list. A copy of this list was filed with the Impartial Chairman of the industry. The agreement provided: (1) Contractors registered in this manner must operate union shops. (2) The administrative board created under the agreement could add additional contractors if and when jobbers and manufacturers increased their volume of business. No member of the National Association could have more than one *temporary* contractor at any time unless he obtains consent from the administrative board. (3) A member of the National Association who sent out his work to contractors and did not maintain an "inside" shop, when there was insufficient work for all his contractors, had to distribute his work equitably among his contractors, on the basis of the number of machine operators employed, with due regard to the ability of the contractor and the workers to produce and perform. Furthermore manufacturers were not permitted to establish "inside" shops without receiving the consent of the administrative board of the industry. Specifically this agreement set up a board of regulation and control to limit the number of competitors in the industry and also devise rules and regulations to govern these producers. The Association was to police its own membership and impose fines on those employers who were recalcitrant in living up to the regulations. Once a month representatives of the union and the Association had the right to examine the books and records of all members of the association to determine the degree of compliance with these regulations. Contractors might be discharged for poor workmanship or late deliveries. . . .

The 1936 agreement furthermore attempted to control the rate of technological innovation by stating that in shops employing less than six hand pressers, pressing machines could not be installed unless all the pressers were guaranteed employment. Other types of technological innovation had to be sanctioned by the administrative board, and the effect upon the workers' welfare had always to be considered. . . .

In the 1937 agreement with the Merchant Ladies Garment Association, representing 700 jobbers, the union was able to carry this industrial regulation program one step further by urging that all employers belonging to this association keep a uniform set of books and records relating to pay rolls, labor costs, and outside production; that a penalty be agreed upon by members of the Association, to be imposed upon any member who sent work to a nonunion contractor; and that such damages be sufficiently high to pay the costs of investigation and to offset any advantages gained by said manufacturer.
. . .

By 1939 the union recognized that, notwithstanding the fact that the wage scales in the New York dress industry were as high as the 1937 level, there was about $250,000 less in the pay envelopes of the workers each week. Union leaders felt that the New York market was losing ground, and they set to work to discover the factors responsible for this loss. Some employers declared that the high labor costs were driving the manufacturers out of the New York market. The union felt that perhaps antiquated business methods existing in the New York market made it difficult for these manufacturers to compete with the streamlined methods of production of newer markets elsewhere in the country.

The Problem of Inefficiency

The union undertook a six-months study of the industry, including a study of factory management, profits, labor costs, and trade practices. The study revealed that the industry was burdened with inexcusable waste and inefficiency. A study of five firms producing the same type of garment ($2.87 wholesale price) revealed that three firms had an average labor cost of 65 cents per dress, two firms averaged 67 cents. Profits, however, varied from a high of 19 cents per dress to a low of 3 cents. Profits were determined by a variation in every other single element except labor: fluctuations in cost of materials, shop overhead, administrative and sales expenses, and net selling price. Industrial engineers undertook to analyze the problems in greater detail. The New York market turned out 79,000,000 dresses a year in 125,000 different styles. Even though all factories had their hourly minimum wage rates established by contract, and their piece rates established by conference between workers and employers, it was found that workers lost much time and consequently suffered reduction in earning power because of inefficiency in factory management. Equipment was old and poor. There was no co-ordination between the cutting schedule and the operating schedule. There was a lack of machine maintenance. There was time wasted due to the high number of idle plant hours attributed to seasonality as well as to general inefficiency. There seemed to be a woeful lack of planning by employers, as well as a lack of satisfactory methods of cost accounting and budgetary control. New York retailers also complained because of late deliveries, improper sizing, and the substitution of materials.

The union urged an *efficiency clause* in its 1941 agreement, which would establish standards of efficiency, including adequate lighting, ventilation, proper supervisory facilities, and routing of goods to workers in order that they might not be kept waiting. It further urged a consolidation of contracting shops into units large enough to make good management profitable. It set up a management engineering department within the union with offices in New York, Chicago, and Los Angeles. . . .

The study further revealed that the employers had failed to use modern methods of promoting the industry—that they were backward in selling their dresses on a large scale.

Once industrial relations are firmly established in an industry, and the union does not have to spend all its energies fighting for the right to exist, it is then possible for the union leaders to think of the well-being of their members in terms of the entire industry. *When a union is the only force capable of industry consciousness and industry enforcement—then in the interests of its members that union can and must concern itself with industry problems.* . . .

UNITED MINE WORKERS OF AMERICA v. PENNINGTON

Supreme Court of the United States, 1965.
381 U.S. 657, 85 S.Ct. 1585, 14 L.Ed.2d 626.

MR. JUSTICE WHITE delivered the opinion of the Court.

This action began as a suit by the trustees of the United Mine Workers of America Welfare and Retirement Fund against the respondents individually and as owners of Phillips Brothers Coal Company, a partnership, seeking to recover some $55,000 in royalty payments alleged to be due and payable under the trust provisions of the National Bituminous Coal Wage Agreement of 1950, as amended, September 29, 1952, executed by Phillips and United Mine Workers of America on or about October 1, 1953, and re-executed with amendments on or about September 8, 1955, and October 22, 1956. Phillips filed an answer and a cross claim against UMW, alleging in both that the trustees, the UMW and certain large coal operators had conspired to restrain and to monopolize interstate commerce in violation of §§ 1 and 2 of the Sherman Antitrust Act. Actual damages in the amount of $100,000 were claimed for the period beginning February 14, 1954, and ending December 31, 1958.

The allegations of the cross claim were essentially as follows: Prior to the 1950 Wage Agreement between the operators and the union, severe controversy had existed in the industry, particularly over wages, the welfare fund and the union's efforts to control the working time of its members. Since 1950, however, relative peace has existed in the industry, all as the result of the 1950 wage agreement and its amendments and the additional understandings entered into between UMW and the large operators. Allegedly the parties considered overproduction to be the critical problem of the coal industry. The agreed solution was to be the elimination of the smaller companies, the larger companies thereby controlling the market. More specifically, the union abandoned its efforts to control the working time of the miners, agreed not to oppose the rapid mechanization of the mines which would substantially reduce mine employment, agreed to help finance such mechanization and agreed to impose the terms of the 1950 agreement on all operators without regard for their ability to pay. The benefit to the union was to be increased wages as productivity increased with mechanization, these increases to be demanded of the smaller companies whether mechanized or not. Royalty payments into the welfare fund were to be increased also, and the union was to have effective control over the Fund's use. The union and large companies agreed upon other steps to exclude the marketing, production, and sale of nonunion coal. Thus the companies agreed not to lease coal lands to nonunion operators, and in 1958 agreed not to sell or buy coal from such companies. The companies and the union jointly and successfully approached the Secretary of Labor to obtain establishment under the Walsh-Healy Act, 41 U.S.C. § 35 et seq. (1958 ed.), of a minimum wage for employees of contractors selling coal to the TVA, such minimum wage being much higher than in other industries and making it difficult for small companies to compete in the TVA term contract market. At a later time, at a meeting attended by both union and company representatives, the TVA was urged to curtail its spot market purchases, a substantial portion of which were exempt from the Walsh-Healy order. Thereafter four of the larger companies waged a destructive and collusive price-cutting campaign in the TVA spot market for coal, two of the companies, West Kentucky Coal Co. and its subsidiary Nashville Coal Co., being those in which the union had large investments and over which it was in position to exercise control.

The complaint survived motions to dismiss and after a five-week trial before a jury, a verdict was returned in favor of Phillips and against the trustees and the union, the damages against the union being fixed in the amount of $90,000, to be trebled under 15 U.S.C. § 15 (1958 ed.). The trial court set aside the verdict against the trustees but overruled the union's motion for judgment notwithstanding the verdict or in the alternative for a new trial. The Court of Appeals affirmed. 325 F.2d 804. It ruled that the union was not exempt from liability under the Sherman Act on the facts of this case, considered the instructions adequate and found the evidence generally sufficient to support the verdict. We granted certiorari. . . .

I.

We first consider UMW's contention that the trial court erred in denying its motion for directed verdict and for judgment notwithstanding the verdict, since a determination in UMW's favor on this issue would finally resolve the controversy. The question presented by this phase of the case is whether in the circumstances of this case the union is exempt from liability under the antitrust laws. We think the answer is clearly in the negative and that the union's motions were correctly denied.

The antitrust laws do not bar the existence and operation of labor unions as such. Moreover, § 20 of the Clayton Act and § 4 of the Norris-LaGuardia Act permit a union, acting alone, to engage in the conduct therein specified without violating the Sherman Act. United States v. Hutcheson, 312 U.S. 219, 61 S.Ct. 463, 85 L.Ed. 788. . . .

But neither § 20 nor § 4 expressly deals with arrangements or agreements between unions and employers. Neither section tells us whether any or all such arrangements or agreements are barred or permitted by the antitrust laws. Thus Hutcheson itself stated:

> "So long as a union acts in its self-interest *and does not combine with non-labor groups,* the licit and the illicit under § 20 are not to be distinguished by any judgment regarding the wisdom or unwisdom, the rightness or wrongness, the selfishness or unselfishness of the end of which the particular union activities are the means." 312 U.S., at 232, 61 S.Ct. at 466. (Emphasis added.)

And in Allen Bradley Co. v. Local Union No. 3, IBEW, 325 U.S. 797, 65 S.Ct. 1533, 89 L.Ed. 1939, this Court made explicit what had been merely a qualifying expression in Hutcheson and held that "when the unions participated with a combination of business men who had complete power to eliminate all competition among themselves and to prevent all competition from others, a situation was created not included with the exemptions of the Clayton and Norris-LaGuardia Acts." Id., 325 U.S. at 809, 65 S.Ct. at 1540. Subsequent cases have applied the Allen Bradley doctrine to such combinations without regard to whether they found expression in a collective bargaining agreement, and even though the mechanism for effectuating the purpose of the combination was an agreement on wages or on hours of work.

If the UMW in this case, in order to protect its wage scale by maintaining employer income, had presented a set of prices at which the mine operators would be required to sell their coal, the union and the employers who happened to agree could not successfully defend this contract provision if it were challenged under the antitrust laws by the United States or by some party injured by the arrangement. In such a case, the restraint on the product market is direct and immediate, is of the type characteristically deemed unreasonable under the Sherman Act and the union gets from the promise nothing more concrete than a hope for better wages to come.

Likewise, if as is alleged in this case, the union became a party to a collusive bidding arrangement designed to drive Phillips and others from the TVA spot market, we think any claim to exemption from antitrust liability would be frivolous at best. For this reason alone the motions of the unions were properly denied.

A major part of Phillips' case, however, was that the union entered into a conspiracy with the large operators to impose the agreed upon wage and royalty scales upon the smaller, nonunion operators, regardless of their ability to pay and regardless of whether or not the union represented the employees of these companies, all for the purpose of eliminating them from the industry, limiting production and pre-empting the market for the large, unionized operators. The UMW urges that since such an agreement concerned wage standards, it is exempt from the antitrust laws.

It is true that wages lie at the very heart of those subjects about which employers and unions must bargain and the law contemplates agreements on wages not only between individual employers and a union but agreements between the union and employers in a multi-employer bargaining unit. The union benefit from the wage scale agreed upon is direct and concrete and the effect on the product market, though clearly present, results from the elimination of competition based on wages among the employers in the bargaining unit, which is not the kind of restraint Congress intended the Sherman Act to proscribe. We think it beyond question that a union may conclude a wage agreement for the multi-employer bargaining union without violating the antitrust laws and that it may as a matter of its own policy, and not by agreement with all or part of the employers of that unit, seek the same wages from other employers.

This is not to say that an agreement resulting from union-employer negotiations is automatically exempt from Sherman Act scrutiny simply because the negotiations involve a compulsory subject of bargaining, regardless of the subject or the form and content of the agreement. Unquestionably the Board's demarcation of the bounds of the duty to bargain has great relevance to any consideration of the sweep of labor's antitrust immunity, for we are concerned here with harmonizing the Sherman Act with the national policy expressed in the National Labor Relations Act of promoting "the peaceful settlement of industrial disputes by subjecting labor-management controversies to the mediatory influence of negotiation." But there are limits to what a union or an employer may offer or extract in the name of wages, and because they must bargain does not mean that the agreement reached may disregard other laws.

We have said that a union may make wage agreements with a multi-employer bargaining unit and may in pursuance of its own union interests seek to obtain the same terms from other employers. No case under the antitrust laws could be made out on evidence limited to such union behavior.[43] But we think a union forfeits its exemption from the antitrust laws when it is clearly shown that it has agreed with one set of employers to impose a certain wage scale on other bargaining units. One group of employers may not conspire to eliminate competitors from the industry and the union is liable with the employers if it becomes a party to the conspiracy This is true even though the union's part in the scheme is an undertaking to secure the same wages, hours or other conditions of employment from the remaining employers in the industry.

We do not find anything in the national labor policy that conflicts with this conclusion. This Court has recognized that a legitimate aim of any national labor organization is to obtain uniformity of labor standards and that a consequence of such union activity may be to eliminate competition based on differences in such standards. But there is nothing in the labor policy indicating that the union and the employers in one bargaining unit are free to bargain about the wages, hours and working conditions of other bargaining units or to attempt to settle these matters for the entire industry. On the contrary, the duty to bargain unit by unit leads to a quite different conclusion. The union's obligation to its members would seem best served if the union retained the ability to respond to each bargaining situation as the individual circumstances might warrant, without being strait-jacketed by some prior agreement with the favored employers.

So far as the employer is concerned it has long been the Board's view that an employer may not condition the signing of a collective agreement on the union's organization of a majority of the industry. American Range Lines, Inc., 13 N.L.R.B. 139, 147 (1939); . . . Newton Chevrolet, Inc., 37 N.L.R.B. 334, 341 (1941). In such cases the obvious interest of the employer is to ensure that acceptance of the union's wage demands will not adversely affect his competitive position. In American Range Lines, Inc., supra, the Board rejected that employer interest as a justification for the demand. "[A]n employer cannot lawfully deny his employees the right to bargain collectively through their designated representative in an appropriate unit because he envisions competitive disadvantages accruing from such bargaining." Such an employer condition, if upheld, would clearly re-

---

43. [Court's footnote] Unilaterally and without agreement with any employer group to do so, a union may adopt a uniform wage policy and seek vigorously to implement it even though it may suspect that some employers cannot effectively compete if they are required to pay the wage scale demanded by the union. The union need not gear its wage demands to those which the weakest units in the industry can afford to pay. Such union conduct is not alone sufficient evidence to maintain a union-employer conspiracy charge under the Sherman Act. There must be additional direct or indirect evidence of the conspiracy. There was, of course, other evidence in this case, but we indicate no opinion as to its sufficiency.

duce the extent of collective bargaining. Thus, in Newton Chevrolet, Inc., supra, where it was held a refusal to bargain for the employer to insist on a provision that the agreed contract terms would not become effective until five competitors had signed substantially similar contracts, the Board stated that "[t]here is nothing in the Act to justify the imposition of a duty upon an exclusive bargaining representative to secure an agreement from a majority of an employer's competitors as a condition precedent to the negotiation of an agreement with the employer. To permit individual employers to refuse to bargain collectively until some or all of their competitors had done so clearly would lead to frustration of the fundamental purpose of the Act to encourage the practice of collective bargaining." Permitting insistence on an agreement by the union to attempt to impose a similar contract on other employers would likewise seem to impose a restraining influence on the extent of collective bargaining, for the union could avoid impasse only by surrendering its freedom to act in its own interest *vis-à-vis* other employers, something it will be unwilling to do in many instances. Once again, the employer's interest is a competitive interest rather than an interest in regulating its own labor relations, and the effect on the union of such an agreement would be to limit the free exercise of the employees' right to engage in concerted activities accordingly to their own views of their self-interest. In sum, we cannot conclude that the national labor policy provides any support for such agreements.

On the other hand, the policy of the antitrust laws is clearly set against employer-union agreements seeking to prescribe labor standards outside the bargaining unit. One could hardly contend, for example, that one group of employers could lawfully demand that the union impose on other employers wages that were significantly higher than those paid by the requesting employers, or a system of computing wages that, because of differences in methods of production, would be more costly to one set of employers than to another. The anticompetitive potential of such a combination is obvious, but is little more severe than what is alleged to have been the purpose and effect of the conspiracy in this case to establish wages at a level that marginal producers could not pay so that they would be driven from the industry. And if the conspiracy presently under attack were declared exempt it would hardly be possible to deny exemption to such avowedly discriminatory schemes.

From the viewpoint of antitrust policy, moreover, all such agreements between a group of employers and a union that the union will seek specified labor standards outside the bargaining unit suffer from a more basic defect, without regard to predatory intention or effect in the particular case. For the salient characteristic of such agreements is that the union surrenders its freedom of action with respect to its bargaining policy. Prior to the agreement the union might seek uniform standards in its own self-interest but would be required to assess in each case the probable costs and gains of a strike or other collective action to that end and thus might conclude that the objective of uniform standards should temporarily give way.

After the agreement the union's interest would be bound in each case to that of the favored employer group. It is just such restraints upon the freedom of economic units to act according to their own choice and discretion that run counter to antitrust policy.

Thus the relevant labor and antitrust policies compel us to conclude that the alleged agreement between UMW and the large operators to secure uniform labor standards throughout the industry, if proved, was not exempt from the antitrust laws.

[The opinion here considers the union's contention that the trial court erroneously permitted the jury to consider approaches to the Secretary of Labor and to TVA officials as part of the conspiracy. The verdict was set aside on this ground. This part of the opinion is discussed supra, pp. 837–838. JUSTICES DOUGLAS, BLACK, and CLARK, concurring, would have had the jury on retrial instructed that the union would be liable "if there were an industry-wide collective bargaining agreement whereby employers and the union agreed on a wage scale that exceeded the financial ability of some operators to pay and . . . if it was made for the purpose of forcing some employers out of business." Furthermore, an agreement "containing these features is prima facie evidence of a violation."]

MR. JUSTICE GOLDBERG, with whom MR. JUSTICE HARLAN and MR. JUSTICE STEWART join, dissenting from the opinion but concurring in the reversal in the Pennington case.

Stripped of all the pejorative adjectives and reduced to their essential facts, both Pennington and Jewel Tea represent refusals by judges to give full effect to congressional action designed to prohibit judicial intervention via the antitrust route in legitimate collective bargaining. The history of these cases furnishes fresh evidence of the observation that in this area, necessarily involving a determination of "what public policy in regard to the industrial struggle demands," Duplex Printing Press Co. v. Deering, 254 U.S. 443, 479, 485, 41 S.Ct. 172, 183, 65 L.Ed. 349 (dissenting opinion of Mr. Justice Brandeis), "courts have neither the aptitude nor the criteria for reaching sound decisions." Cox, Labor and Antitrust Laws—A Preliminary Analysis, 104 U.Pa.L.Rev. 252, 269–270 (1955); see Winter, Collective Bargaining and Competition: The Application of Antitrust Standards to Union Activities, 73 Yale L.J. 14 (1963).

[The opinion reviews the history of expanding exemption of union activity from the antitrust laws and the concurrent development of specific labor law controls of union abuses.]

In my view, this history shows a consistent congressional purpose to limit severely judicial intervention into collective bargaining under cover of the wide umbrella of the antitrust laws, and, rather, to deal with what Congress deemed to be specific abuses on the part of labor unions by specific proscriptions in the labor statutes. I believe that the Court should respect this history of congressional purpose and should reaffirm the Court's holdings in Apex and Hutcheson which, unlike earlier decisions, gave effect to rather than frustrated, the congressional design. The sound approach of Hutcheson is that the labor exemption from the antitrust laws derives from a synthesis of all pertinent congressional legislation—the nature of the Sherman Act itself, §§ 6 and 20 of the Clayton Act, the Norris-LaGuardia Act, the Fair Labor Standards Act, the Walsh-Healy and Davis-Bacon Acts, and the Wagner Act with its Taft-Hartley and Landrum-Griffin amendments. This last statute, in particular, provides that both employers and unions must bargain over "wages, hours, and other terms and conditions of employment." 29 U.S.C. § 158(a)(5), (b)(3), (d) (1958 ed.). Following the sound analysis of Hutcheson, the Court should hold that, in order to effectuate congressional intent, collective bargaining activity concerning mandatory subjects of bargaining under the Labor Act is not subject to the antitrust laws. This rule flows directly from the Hutcheson holding that a union acting as a union, in the interests of its members, and not acting to fix prices or allocate markets in aid of an employer conspiracy to accomplish these objects, with only indirect union benefits, is not subject to challenge under the antitrust laws. To hold that mandatory collective bargaining is completely protected would effectuate the congressional policies of encouraging free collective bargaining, subject only to specific restrictions contained in the labor laws, and of limiting judicial intervention in labor matters via the antitrust route—an intervention which necessarily under the Sherman Act places on judges and juries the determination of "what public policy in regard to the industrial struggle demands."

Section 6 of the Clayton Act made it clear half a century ago that it is not national policy to force workers to compete in the "sale" of their labor as if it were a commodity or article of commerce. The policy was confirmed and extended in the subsequent Norris-LaGuardia Act. Other federal legislation establishing minimum wages and maximum hours takes labor standards out of competition. The Fair Labor Standards Act, 52 Stat. 1060, as amended, 29 U.S.C. §§ 201–219 (1958 ed.), clearly states that the existence of "labor conditions" insufficient for a "minimum standard of living . . . constitutes an unfair method of competition in commerce." Id., at § 202(a). Moreover, this court has recognized that in the Walsh-Healy Act, 49 Stat. 2036, as amended, 41 U.S.C. § 35 et seq., Congress brought to bear the "leverage of the Government's immense purchasing power to raise labor standards" by eliminating substandard producers from eligibility for public contracts. Endicott-Johnson Corp. v. Perkins, 317 U.S. 501, 507, 63 S.Ct. 339, 342. See also Davis-Bacon Act, 46 Stat. 1494, 40 U.S.C. § 276a (1958 ed.). The National Labor Relations Act itself clearly expresses one of its purposes to be "the stabilization of competitive wage rates and working conditions within and between industries." 29 U.S.C. § 151. In short, business competition based on wage competition is not national policy and "the mere fact of such restrictions on competition does not . . . bring the parties . . . within the condemnation of the Sherman Act." Apex Hosiery Co. v. Leader, supra, 310 U.S. at 503, 60 S.Ct. at 997.

The National Labor Relations Act also declares it to be the policy of the United States to promote the establishment of wages, hours, and other terms and conditions of employment by free collective bargaining between employers and unions. The Act further provides that both employers and unions must bargain about such mandatory subjects of bargaining. This national scheme would be virtually destroyed by the imposition of Sherman Act criminal and civil penalties upon employers and unions engaged in such collective bargaining. To tell either side that they must bargain about a point but may be subject to antitrust penalties if they reach an agreement is to stultify the congressional scheme.

Moreover, mandatory subjects of bargaining are issues as to which union strikes may not be enjoined by either federal or state courts. To say that the Union can strike over such issues but that both it and the employer are subject to possible antitrust penalties for making collective bargaining agreements concerning them is to assert that Congress intended to permit the parties to collective bargaining to wage industrial warfare but to prohibit them from peacefully settling their disputes. This would not only be irrational but would fly in the face of the clear congressional intent of promoting "the peaceful settlement of industrial disputes by subjecting labor-management controversies to the mediatory influence of negotiation." . . .

The Court in Pennington today ignores this history of the discredited judicial attempt to apply the antitrust laws to legitimate collective bargaining activity, and it flouts the clearly expressed congressional intent that, since "[t]he labor of a human being is not a commodity or article of commerce," the antitrust laws do not proscribe, and the national labor policy affirmatively promotes, the "elimination of price competition based on differences in labor standards," Apex Hosiery Co. v. Leader, supra, 310 U.S. at 503, 60 S.Ct. at 997. While purporting to recognize the indisputable fact that the elimination of employer competition based on substandard labor conditions is a proper labor union objective endorsed by our national labor policy and that, therefore, "a union may make wage agreements with a multi-employer bargaining unit and may in the pursuance of its own interests seek to obtain the same terms from other employers," Pennington, 381 U.S., at 665, 85 S.Ct., at 1591, the Court holds that "a union forfeits its exemption from the antitrust laws when it is clearly shown that it has agreed with one set of employers to impose a certain wage scale on other bargaining units." Ibid.

This rule seems to me clearly contrary to the congressional purpose manifested by the labor statutes, and it will severely restrict free collective bargaining. Since collective bargaining inevitably involves and requires discussion of the impact of the wage agreement reached with a particular employer or group of employers upon competing employers, the effect of the Court's decision will be to bar a basic element of collective bargaining from the conference room. If a union and employer are prevented from discussing and agreeing

upon issues which are, in the great majority of cases, at the central
core of bargaining, unilateral force will inevitably be substituted for
rational discussion and agreement.   Plainly and simply, the Court
would subject both unions and employers to antitrust sanctions, criminal as well as civil, if in collective bargaining they concluded a wage
agreement and, as part of the agreement, the union has undertaken
to use its best efforts to have this wage accepted by other employers
in the industry.   Indeed, the decision today even goes beyond this.
Under settled antitrust principles which are accepted by the Court as
appropriate and applicable, which were the basis for jury instructions
in Pennington, and which will govern it upon remand, there need not
be direct evidence of an express agreement.   Rather the existence of
such an agreement, express or implied, may be inferred from the conduct of the parties.

Or, as my Brother Douglas would have it, conduct of the parties
could be prima facie evidence of an illegal agreement.   As the facts
of Pennington illustrate, the jury is therefore at large to infer such
an agreement from "clear" evidence that a union's philosophy that
high wages and mechanization are desirable has been accepted by a
group of employers and that the union has attempted to achieve like
acceptance from other employers.   For, as I have pointed out,
stripped of all adjectives, this is what Pennington presents.   Yet the
Court today holds "the alleged agreement between UMW and the
large operators to secure uniform labor standards throughout the industry, if proved, was not exempt from the antitrust laws."

The rational thing for an employer to do, when faced with union
demands he thinks he cannot meet, is to explain why, in economic
terms, he believes that he cannot agree to the union requests.   Indeed, the Labor Act's compulsion to bargain in good faith requires
that he meaningfully address himself to the union's requests.   A recurring and most understandable reason given by employers for their
resistance to union demands is that competitive factors prevent them
from accepting the union's proposed terms.   Under the Court's holding today, however, such a statement by an employer may start both
the employer and union on the road to antitrust sanctions, criminal
and civil.   For a jury may well interpret such discussion and subsequent union action as showing an implicit or secret agreement to impose uniform standards on other employers.   Nor does the Court's
requirement that there be "direct or indirect evidence of the conspiracy," whatever those undefined terms in the opinion may mean—provide any substantial safeguard for uninhibited collective bargaining
discussions.   In Pennington itself, the trial court instructed the jury
that a union's unilateral actions did not subject it to antitrust sanctions, and yet the jury readily inferred a "conspiracy" from the "direct or indirect evidence" of the union's publicly stated policy in favor
of high wages and mechanization, its collective bargaining agreement
with a group of employers establishing high wages, and its attempts
to obtain similar high wages from other employers.

Furthermore, in order to determine whether, under the Court's standard, a union is acting unilaterally or pursuant to an agreement with employers, judges and juries will inevitably be drawn to try to determine the purpose and motive of union and employer collective bargaining activities. . . .

In Pennington, central to the alleged conspiracy is the claim that hourly wage rates and fringe benefits were set at a level designed to eliminate the competition of the smaller nonunion companies by making the labor cost too high for them to pay. Indeed, the trial judge charged that there was no violation of the Sherman Act in the establishing of wages and welfare payments through the national contract, "provided" the mine workers and the major coal producers had not agreed to fix "high" rates "in order to drive the small coal operators out of business." Under such an instruction, if the jury found the wage scale too "high" it could impute the unlawful purpose of putting the nonunion operators out of business. It is clear that the effect of the instruction therefore, was to invite 12 jurymen to become arbiters of the economic desirability of the wage scale in the Nation's coal industry. The Court would sustain the judgment based on this charge and thereby put its stamp of approval on this role for courts and juries.

The Court's approval of judges and juries determining the permissible wage scale for working men in an industry is confirmed by the Court's express statement "there are limits to what a Union or an employer may offer or extract in the name of wages," Pennington, 381 U.S. at 665, 85 S.Ct. at 1591. To allow a jury to infer an illegal "conspiracy" from the agreed-upon wage scale means that the jury must determine at what level the wages could be fixed without impelling the parties into the ambit of the antitrust laws. Is this not another way of saying that, via the antitrust route, a judge or jury may determine, according to their own notions of what is economically sound, the amount of wages that a union can properly ask for or that an employer can pay? It is clear, as experience shows, that judges and juries neither have the aptitude nor possess the criteria for making this kind of judgment. In Pennington, absent the alleged conspiracy, would the wage rate and fringe benefits have been lower? Should they have been lower? If Pennington were an action for injunctive relief, what would be the appropriate remedy to reach the labor cost which is at the heart of the alleged antitrust violation? A judicial determination of the wage rate? A judicial nullification of the existing rate with a direction to negotiate a lower one? I cannot believe that Congress has sanctioned judicial wage control under the umbrella of the Sherman Act, for, absent a national emergency, Congress has never legislated wage control in our free enterprise economy.

The history I have set out makes clear that Congress intended to foreclose judges and juries from making essentially economic judgments in antitrust actions by determining whether unions or employers had good or bad motives for their agreements on subjects of mandatory bargaining. Moreover, an attempted inquiry into the motives of employers or unions for entering into collective bargaining agreements on subjects of mandatory bargaining is totally artificial. It is precisely in this area of wages, hours, and other working conditions that Congress has recognized that unions have a substantial, direct, and basic interest of their own to advance.

As I have discussed, the Court's test is not essentially different from the discredited purpose-motive approach. Only rarely will there be direct evidence of an express agreement between a union and an employer to impose a particular wage scale on other employers. In most cases, as was true of Pennington, the trial court will instruct the jury that such an illegal agreement may be inferred from the conduct—"indirect evidence"—of the union and employers. To allow a court or a jury to infer an illegal agreement from collective bargaining conduct inevitably requires courts and juries to analyze the terms of collective bargaining agreements and the purposes and motives of unions and employers in agreeing upon them. Moreover, the evidence most often available to sustain antitrust liability under the court's theory would show, as it did in Pennington, simply that the motives of the union and employer coincide—the union seeking high wages and protection from low-wage, nonunion competition and the employer who pays high wages seeking protection from competitors who pay lower wages. When there is this coincidence of motive, does the illegality of the "conspiracy" turn on whether the Union pursued its goal of a uniform wage policy through strikes and not negotiation? As I read the Court's opinion this is precisely what the result turns on and thus unions are forced, in order to show that they have not illegally "agreed" with employers, to pursue their aims through strikes and not negotiations. Yet, it is clear that such a result was precisely what the National Labor Relations Act was designed to prevent. The only alternative to resolution of collective bargaining issues by force available to the parties under the Court's holding is the encouragement of fraud and deceit. An employer will be forced to take a public stand against a union's wage demands, even if he is willing to accept them, lest a too ready acceptance be used by a jury to infer an agreement between the union and employer that the same wages will be sought from other employers. Yet, I have always thought that in collective bargaining, even more than in other areas of contractual agreement, the objective is open covenants openly arrived at.

Furthermore, I do not understand how an inquiry can be formulated in terms of whether the union action is unilateral or is a consequence of a "conspiracy" with employers independently of the economic terms of the collective bargaining agreement. The agreement must be admitted into evidence and the Court holds that its economic consequences are relevant. In the end, one way or another, the entire panoply of economic fact becomes involved, and judges and juries under the Court's view would then be allowed to speculate about why a union bargained for increased compensation, or any other labor standard within the scope of mandatory bargaining. It is precisely this type of speculation that Congress has rejected.

The plain fact is that it makes no sense to turn antitrust liability of employers and unions concerning subjects of mandatory bargaining on whether the union acted "unilaterally" or in "agreement" with employers. A union can never achieve substantial benefits for its members through unilateral action; I should have thought that the unsuccessful history of the Industrial Workers of the World, which eschewed collective bargaining and espoused a philosophy of winning benefits by unilateral action, proved this beyond question. See Dulles, Labor in America 208–223 (1949); Chaplin, Wobbly (1948). Furthermore, I cannot believe that Congress, by adopting the antitrust laws, put its stamp of approval on this discredited IWW philosophy of industrial relations; rather, in the Clayton Act and the labor statutes, Congress has repudiated such a philosophy. Our national labor policy is designed to encourage the peaceful settlement of industrial disputes through the negotiation of agreements between employers and unions. Unions cannot, as the history of the IWW shows, successfully retain employee benefits by unilateral action; nor can employers be assured of continuous operation without contractual safeguards. The history of labor relations in this country shows, as Congress has recognized, that progress and stability for both employers and employees can be achieved only through collective bargaining agreements involving mutual rights and responsibilities.

This history also shows that labor contracts establishing more or less standardized wages, hours, and other terms and conditions of employment in a given industry or market area are often secured either through bargaining with multi-employer associations or through bargaining with market leaders that sets a "pattern" for agreements on labor standards with other employers. These are two similar systems used to achieve the identical result of fostering labor peace through the negotiation of uniform labor standards in an industry. Yet the Court makes antitrust liability for both unions and employers turn on which of these two systems is used. It states that uniform wage agreements may be made with multi-employer units but an agreement cannot be made to affect employers outside the formal bargaining unit. I do not believe that the Court understands the effect of its ruling in terms of the practical realities of the automobile, steel, rubber, shipbuilding, and numerous other industries which follow the policy of pattern collective bargaining. See Chamberlain, Collective Bargaining 259–263 (1951). I also do not understand why antitrust liability should turn on the form of unit determination rather than the substance of the collective bargaining impact on the industry.

Finally, it seems clear that the essential error at the core of the Court's reasoning is that it ignores the express command of Congress that "[t]he labor of a human being is not a commodity or article of commerce," and therefore that the antitrust laws do not prohibit the "elimination of price competition based on differences in labor standards." Apex Hosiery Co. v. Leader, supra, 310 U.S. at 503, 60 S.Ct. at 997. This is made clear by a simple question that the Court does not face. Where there is an "agreement" to seek uniform wages in an industry, in what item is competition restrained? The answer to this question can only be that competition is restrained in employee wage standards. That is, the union has agreed to restrain the free competitive market for labor by refusing to provide labor to other employers below the uniform rate. Under such an analysis, it would seem to follow that the existence of a union itself constitutes a restraint of trade, for the object of a union is to band together the individual workers in an effort, by common action, to obtain better wages and working conditions—i.e., to obtain a higher price for their labor. The very purpose and effect of a labor union is to limit the power of an employer to use competition among workingmen to drive down wage rates and enforce substandard conditions of employment. If competition between workingmen to see who will work for the lowest wage is the ideal, all labor unions should be eliminated. . . .[44]

NOTES AND QUERIES

(1) *Kinks in the Line Demarking the Labor Exemption.* The *Pennington* case and its companion case, *Local 189, Amalgamated Meat Cutters v. Jewel Tea Co.*, discussed infra p. 1113, have been criticized for confusing the lines drawn by prior cases defining the labor exemption.[45] After *Pennington* and *Jewel Tea*, an agreement dealing with issues made mandatory subjects of collective bargaining by labor legislation—wages, hours, and conditions of employment—could be the basis of antitrust liability where the agreement is directed at restraining the trade of third parties. Such agreements are not unusual, because unions and employers are often interested in securing industry-wide uniformity to even-out competitive disparities in labor costs. The scope of the exemption appears to turn on the degree to which the union's aims are unilaterally arrived at, the directness of the union's concerns about the issues involved, the degree to which the issues are ones within areas of mandatory bargaining with the primary employer, and the degree to which the arrangement impinges the freedom of third parties. While *Allen Bradley* concerned conduct by employers and the union which imposed restraints on the commercial competition of third parties, the agreement in *Pennington* involved wages—a mandatory bargaining subject. *Pennington*, therefore, opened the possibility of an antitrust challenge to labor agreements concerned with mandatory bargaining subjects hitherto believed to be exempt and subject to regulation only under labor legislation.

The standards by which such an antitrust challenge would be measured were far from clear. *Pennington* appeared to permit a judicial balancing of

---

44. On the subsequent history of this and related litigation, involving among other issues the question whether the Clayton Act requirement of "clear proof" against a union applies only to the union officer's authority to act for the union or also to the factual basis of substantive liability, see Ramsey v. UMW, 401 U.S. 302, 91 S.Ct. 658, 28 L.Ed.2d 64 (1971); Tenn. Cons. Coal Co. v. UMW, 416 F.2d 1192 (6th Cir. 1969), cert. denied 397 U.S. 964, 90 S.Ct. 999, 25 L.Ed.2d 256 (1970).

45. See Casey & Cozzellio, Law-Antitrust: The Problems of Connell and A Remedy That Follows Naturally, 1980 Duke L.J. 235, 242–47; Cox, Labor and The Antitrust Laws: Pennington and Jewel Tea, 46 B.U.L.Rev. 317 (1966).

the union's labor objectives and the effect of the agreement in restraining trade. Allegations that the agreement was for the purpose of furthering an employer restraint of trade rather than to achieve a legitimate union objective, even without specific conduct beyond the collective bargaining agreement furthering the employer restraint as in *Allen Bradley,* appeared sufficient to forfeit the exemption. Left unclear was what the plaintiff would be required to prove to make out a violation of the antitrust laws.

This issue was addressed in *Smitty Baker Coal Co. v. United Mine Workers,*[46] where a small coal operator claimed the union was engaged in a conspiracy to impose a wage settlement on small operators and drive them out of business. The Fourth Circuit, thoroughly reviewing the cases interpreting *Pennington,* wrote:

> [I]t is not enough that the Union may have entered into a contract with a multi-employer unit in a national industry to establish an antitrust violation by the Union or, for that matter, the employer-group. That may in some cases take the action out of the exemption enjoyed by labor, but it will not *per se* amount to an antitrust violation. To amount to an antitrust violation the agreement must be rooted in an anti-competitive purpose, and must effect an anti-competitive result, as evidenced by action "ruining" a competitor's business or driving him "out of business." Unless there is such an agreement between the labor organization and the non-labor group and such an anti-competitive result, there is no conspiracy actionable under the antitrust laws.
>
> . . .
>
> It is thus manifest from this review of the pertinent authorities applying the *Pennington* doctrine, on which the plaintiff relies for an antitrust conspiracy, that such doctrine requires (a) an agreement between the Union and an employer-group consisting of a substantial number of the larger employers in an industry to establish a wage scale for the employees-of-the-group-members-of-the Union, (b) which wage scale the Union and the employer group knew that the marginal employers in the industry could not afford, and (c) which wage scale the Union undertook to impose on the marginal nonmember operators, (d) with the intent to drive these marginal operators out of business and to remove them as competitors of the employer-group. And this is the view of the *Pennington* model as taken in other decisions and as expressed by commentators. Were the rule otherwise, labor organizations would be subject to liabilities greater than and different from those to which businesses would be subjected. Such a result would mock the congressionally granted exemptions in favor of labor organizations.[47]

The Supreme Court has held the question of whether the exemption is forfeited is separate from the question of whether the collaboration violates the antitrust laws. In *Federal Maritime Commission v. Pacific Maritime Association,*[48] the Court stated:

> It is plain from our cases that an antitrust case need not be tried and a violation found before a determination can be made that a collective-bargaining agreement is not within the labor exemption, just as it is clear that denying the exemption does not mean that there is an antitrust violation.[49]

46. 620 F.2d 416 (4th Cir. 1980), certiorari denied, 449 U.S. 870, 101 S.Ct. 207, 66 L.Ed.2d 89.

47. 620 F.2d, at 431–433.

48. 435 U.S. 40, 98 S.Ct. 927, 55 L.Ed. 2d 96 (1978).

49. 435 U.S., at 61, 98 S.Ct., at 939, 55 L.Ed.2d at 113.

Subsequent lower court opinions have established a two part analysis; requiring, first, proof of an agreement by the union and the employer to impose the wages on a plaintiff not party to the collective bargaining agreement to prove the exemption forfeited; and second, requiring proof the agreement was entered into with the intent to injure the plaintiff's business, i.e., predatory intent, to prove the agreement is one to violate the antitrust laws.[50]

(2) *Multi-Employer or Industry-Wide Bargaining.* The issue whether a single union should be permitted to organize the employees of more than one employer has been resolved in favor of national industry-wide organization.[51] This solution has been criticized and defended.[52] It was criticized as extending labor's immunity for collective economic coercion beyond the rationale giving rise to the immunity (equalizing bargaining power between an employer and his employees). Critics viewed it also as creating monopolistic power to interrupt production processes on a national scale and to extort from the community wages in excess of those which would be forthcoming where competing entrepreneurs bargained separately with their own organized employees. Multi-employer bargaining has been defended as contributing to labor peace through central resolution of controversies that would otherwise reach impasse in numerous local bargaining arenas, and by eliminating "unfair competition" between employers in wage rates.

Given the national union, the question arises how the multiple employers may achieve a unified bargaining position. Collaboration of employers for collective bargaining with the giant union appears to be immunized from the antitrust laws by the declaration in section 6 of the Clayton Act that the "labor of a human being is not a commodity or article of commerce," even though that section was plainly designed to immunize collective economic pressure by *unions*, rather than collective wage depression by employers. Antitrust immunity for employer collaboration might arguably be implied from the labor legislation and policy favoring bargaining on a trans-firm basis. The degree to which employer collaboration has been pushed may be seen in cases such as the following:

National Labor Relations Board v. Truck Drivers Local Union No. 449,[53] held that a concerted lockout by employers in response to a strike directed at one member of the group was not an unfair interference with employees' rights, in the light of a history of multi-employer bargaining in the industry and the necessity of countering "whipsawing", i.e., striking one employer at a time.

Six Carrier Mutual Aid Pact,[54] approved, pursuant to section 412 of the Federal Aviation Act, an agreement among six major airlines that in case of a strike opposed to recommendations of a Presidential Emergency Board, or other "unlawful" strike, each line would pay to any struck line the extra

50. See James R. Snyder Co., Inc. v. Associated General Contractors, Detroit Chapter, Inc., 677 F.2d 1111 (6th Cir. 1982), certiorari denied __ U.S. __, 103 S.Ct. 374, 74 L.Ed.2d 508; Mid-America Regional Bargaining Association v. Will County Carpenters District Council, 675 F.2d 881 (7th Cir. 1982), certiorari denied __ U.S. __, 103 S.Ct. 132, 74 L.Ed.2d 114.

51. Multi-employer/multi-union bargaining has been enforced by the N.L.R.B. under section 8(b)(3) of the National Labor Relations Act, 29 U.S.C.A. 158(b)(3). See, Local 260 Wood, Wire and Metal Lathers International Union, 228 NLRB No. 179 (1977).

52. See Report of Comm. on Education and Labor, H. of Rep., 80th Cong., 1st Sess. (1947); Lewis, The Labor-Monopoly Problem: A Positive Program, 59 J.Pol.Econ. 277 (1951).

53. 353 U.S. 87, 77 S.Ct. 643, 1 L.Ed. 2d 676 (1957).

54. 29 C.A.B. 168 (1959).

revenues resulting from diversion of revenues to the operating lines. The Board approval, carrying with it exemption from antitrust laws, was conditioned on deletion of a provision binding the struck carrier to direct to the other parties as much of its normal traffic as possible: "The public interest is not served if the traveling public, unaware of alternative air services which might be preferable, is advised according to carrier obligation rather than passenger convenience." Member Minetti, dissenting, argued that the statutory finding that the agreement was not adverse to the public interest should not be made without affirmative evidence of promotion of transportation goals, where antitrust exemption follows approval, and that the majority decision imposed multi-employer bargaining without the consent of the employees, inasmuch as those who helped finance continued resistance by a struck carrier would influence the terms on which settlement could be reached.[55]   *Air Line Pilots' Association v. Civil Aeronautics Board,*[56] sustained an Airlines' Mutual Aid Pact against attacks under both the labor laws and the antitrust laws.

On multi-employer bargaining as a vehicle for imposing restraints on individual employees, see *Mackey v. National Football League,*[57] and *McCourt v. California Sports, Inc.*[58]

On multi-employer bargaining as a restraint on the freedom of employers to withdraw from the bargaining unit, see *Charles D. Bonanno Linen Service, Inc. v. National Labor Relations Board,*[59] upholding finding of an unfair labor practice in withdrawing from bargaining unit after impasse reached in bargaining.

LOCAL UNION NO. 189, AMALGAMATED MEAT CUTTERS v. JEWEL TEA CO.

Supreme Court of the United States, 1965.
381 U.S. 676, 85 S.Ct. 1596, 14 L.Ed.2d 640.

MR. JUSTICE WHITE announced the judgment of the Court and delivered an opinion, in which THE CHIEF JUSTICE and MR. JUSTICE BRENNAN join.

Like No. 48, United Mine Workers of America v. Pennington, 381 U.S. 657, 85 S.Ct. 1585 decided today, this case presents questions regarding the application of §§ 1 and 2 of the Sherman Antitrust Act, to activities of labor unions. In particular, it concerns the lawfulness of the following restriction on the operating hours of food store meat departments contained in a collective agreement executed after joint multi-employer, multi-union negotiations:

"Market operating hours shall be 9:00 a.m. to 6:00 p.m. Monday through Saturday, inclusive. No customer shall be served

55. See Note, Six Carrier Mutual Aid Pact, 60 Col.L.Rev. 205 (1960); Note, Six Carrier Mutual Aid Pact, 35 Ind.L.J. 491 (1960). A comparable program of joint strike insurance by the railroads was sustained against attack based on the antitrust laws. Kennedy v. Long Island Railroad, 319 F.2d 366 (2d Cir. 1963).

56. 163 U.S.App.D.C. 451, 502 F.2d 453 (1974), certiorari denied 402 U.S. 972, 95 S.Ct. 1391, 43 L.Ed.2d 652 (1975).

57. 543 F.2d 606 (8th Cir. 1976), certiorari dismissed 434 U.S. 801, 98 S.Ct. 28, 54 L.Ed.2d 59 (1977).

58. 600 F.2d 1193 (6th Cir. 1979).

59. 454 U.S. 404, 102 S.Ct. 720, 70 L.Ed.2d 656 (1982).

who comes into the market before or after the hours set forth above."

This litigation arose out of the 1957 contract negotiations between the representatives of 9,000 Chicago retailers of fresh meat and the seven union petitioners, who are local affiliates of the Amalgamated Meat Cutters and Butcher Workmen of North America, AFL–CIO, representing virtually all butchers in the Chicago area. During the 1957 bargaining sessions the employer group presented several requests for union consent to a relaxation of the existing contract restriction on marketing hours for fresh meat, which forbade the sale of meat before 9 a.m. and after 6 p.m. in both service and self-service markets.[60] The unions rejected all such suggestions, and their own proposal retaining the marketing hours restriction was ultimately accepted at the final bargaining session by all but two of the employers, National Tea Co. and Jewel Tea Co. (hereinafter "Jewel"). Associated Food Retailers of Greater Chicago, a trade association having about 1,000 individual and independent merchants as members and representing some 300 meat dealers in the negotiations, was among those who accepted. Jewel, however, asked the union negotiators to present to their membership, on behalf of it and National Tea, a counter-offer that included provision for Friday night operations. At the same time Jewel voiced its belief, as it had midway through the negotiations, that any marketing hours restriction was illegal. On the recommendation of the union negotiators the Jewel offer was rejected by the union membership, and a strike was authorized. Under the duress of the strike vote, Jewel decided to sign the contract previously approved by the rest of the industry.

In July 1958 Jewel brought suit against the unions, certain of their officers, Associated, and Charles H. Bromann, Secretary-Treasurer of Associated, seeking invalidation under §§ 1 and 2 of the Sherman Act of the contract provision that prohibited night meat market operations. The gist of the complaint was that the defendants and others had conspired together to prevent the retail sale of fresh meat before 9 a.m. and after 6 p.m. As evidence of the conspiracy Jewel relied in part on the events during the 1957 contract negotiations—the acceptance by Associated of the market hours restriction and the unions' imposition of the restriction on Jewel through a strike threat. Jewel also alleged that it was a part of the conspiracy that the unions would neither permit their members to work at times other than the hours specified nor allow any grocery firm to sell meat, with or without employment of their members, outside those hours; that the members of Associated, which had joined only one of the

60. [This and the following four footnotes are from the original opinions. They are renumbered.] The practice in the Chicago area is for the employers and the butchers to execute separate, but similar, collective agreements for self-service and service markets. A self-service market is "one in which fresh beef, veal, lamb, mutton or pork are available for sale on a prepackage self-service basis." Semi-self-service markets, those in which fresh meat is made available on a prepackaged basis but there is also a service counter offering custom cutting for those who prefer it, are governed by the self-service contract. Service markets are those in which no fresh meat is made available on a self-service basis.

1957 employer proposals for extended marketing hours, had agreed among themselves to insist on the inclusion of the marketing hours limitation in all collective agreements between the unions and any food store operator; that Associated, its members and officers had agreed with the other defendants that no firm was to be permitted to operate self-service meat markets between 6 p.m. and 9 p.m.; and that the unions, their officers and members had acted as the enforcing agent of the conspiracy.

The complaint stated that in recent years the prepackaged self-service system of marketing meat had come into vogue, that 174 of Jewel's 196 stores were equipped to vend meat in this manner, and that a butcher need not be on duty in a self-service market at the time meat purchases were actually made. The prohibition of night meat marketing, it was alleged, unlawfully impeded Jewel in the use of its property and adversely affected the general public in that many persons find it inconvenient to shop during the day. An injunction, treble damages and attorney's fees were demanded.

The trial judge held the allegations of the complaint sufficient to withstand a motion to dismiss made on the grounds, *inter alia*, that (a) the "alleged restraint [was] within the exclusive regulatory scope of the National Labor Relations Act and [was] therefore outside the jurisdiction of the Court" and (b) the controversy was within the labor exemption to the antitrust laws. That ruling was sustained on appeal. Jewel Tea Co. v. Local Unions Nos. 189, etc., Amalgamated Meat Cutters, AFL–CIO, 274 F.2d 271 (C.A.7th Cir. 1960), cert. denied, 362 U.S. 936, 80 S.Ct. 757, 4 L.Ed.2d 747. After trial, however, the District Judge ruled the "record was devoid of any evidence to support a finding of a conspiracy" between Associated and the unions to force the restrictive provision on Jewel. Testing the unions' action standing alone, the trial court found that even in self-service markets removal of the limitation on marketing hours either would inaugurate longer hours and night work for the butchers or would result in butchers' work being done by others unskilled in the trade. Thus, the court concluded, the unions had imposed the marketing hours limitation to serve their own interests respecting conditions of employment, and such action was clearly within the labor exemption of the Sherman Act established by Hunt v. Crumboch, 325 U.S. 821, 65 S.Ct. 1545, 89 L.Ed. 1954; United States v. Hutcheson, 312 U.S. 219, 61 S.Ct. 463, 85 L.Ed. 788; United States v. American Federation of Musicians, 318 U.S. 741, 63 S.Ct. 665, 87 L.Ed. 1120. Alternatively, the District Court ruled that even if this was not the case, the arrangement did not amount to an unreasonable restraint of trade in violation of the Sherman Act.

The Court of Appeals reversed the dismissal of the complaint as to both the unions and Associated. Without disturbing the District Court's finding that, apart from the contractual provision itself, there was no evidence of conspiracy, the Court of Appeals concluded that a conspiracy in restraint of trade had been shown. The court noted that "the rest of the industry agreed with the defendant local unions to continue the ban on night operations, while plaintiff resisted" and concluded that Associated and the unions "entered into a combination or agreement, which constituted a conspiracy, as charged in the complaint. . . . Whether it be called an agreement, contract or conspiracy, is immaterial."

Similarly, the Court of Appeals did not find it necessary to review the lower court's finding that night marketing would affect either the butchers' working hours or their jurisdiction, for the court held that an employer-union contract respecting working hours would be unlawful. "One of the proprietary functions is the determination of what days a week and what hours of the day the business will be open to supply its customers. . . . As long as all rights of employees are recognized and duly observed by the employer, including the number of hours per day that any one shall be required to work, any agreement by a labor union, acting in concert with business competitors of the employer, designed to interfere with his operation of a retail business . . . is a violation of the Sherman Act. . . . [T]he furnishing of a place and advantageous hours of employment for the butchers to supply meat to customers are the prerogatives of the employer."

We granted certiorari on the unions' petition,[61] and now reverse the Court of Appeals.

I.

We must first consider the unions' attack on the appropriateness of the District Court's exercise of jurisdiction, which is encompassed in their contention that this controversy is within the exclusive primary jurisdiction of the National Labor Relations Board. On this point, which is distinct from the unions' argument that the operating hours restriction is subject to regulation only by the Board and is thus wholly exempt from the antitrust laws, the unions' thesis is that the pivotal issue is whether the operating hours restriction is a "term or condition of employment" and that the District Court should have held the case on its docket pending a Board proceeding to resolve that issue, which is said to be peculiarly within the competence of the Board.

"The doctrine of primary jurisdiction . . . applies where a claim is originally cognizable in the courts, and comes into play whenever enforcement of the claim requires the resolution of issues which,

---

61. The grant of certiorari was limited to the following questions:

"1. Based on the District Court's undisturbed finding that the limitation 'was imposed after arm's length bargaining, . . . and was fashioned exclusively by the unions to serve their own interests—how long and what hours members shall work, what work they shall do, and what pay they shall receive,' whether the limitation upon market operating hours and the controversy concerning it are within the labor exemption of the Sherman Antitrust Act.

"2. Whether a claimed violation of the Sherman Antitrust Act which falls within the regulatory scope of the National Labor Relations Act is within the exclusive primary jurisdiction of the National Labor Relations Board."

under a regulatory scheme, have been placed within the special competence of an administrative body; in such a case the judicial process is suspended pending referral of such issues to the administrative body for its views." United States v. Western Pac. R. Co., 352 U.S. 59, 63–64, 77 S.Ct. 161, 165, 1 L.Ed.2d 126. The doctrine is based on the principle "that in cases raising issues of fact not within the conventional experiences of judges or cases requiring the exercise of administrative discretion, agencies created by Congress for regulating the subject matter should not be passed over," Far East Conference v. United States, 342 U.S. 570, 574, 72 S.Ct. 492, 494, 96 L.Ed. 576, and "requires judicial abstention in cases where protection of the integrity of a regulatory scheme dictates preliminary resort to the agency which administers the scheme," United States v. Philadelphia Nat. Bank, 374 U.S. 321, 353, 83 S.Ct. 1715, 1736, 10 L.Ed.2d 915.

Whether a proposed bargaining subject is a term or condition of employment is an issue that the Board frequently determines in considering charges that an employer or union has violated the duty to bargain in good faith concerning "wages, hours, and other terms and conditions of employment," the mandatory subjects of bargaining described in § 8(d) of the National Labor Relations Act. Such an issue may be raised by an unfair labor practice charge of violation of § 8(a) (5) or § 8(b)(3) through, for example, a refusal to bargain on a mandatory subject of bargaining, see National Labor Relations Board v. Katz, 369 U.S. 736, 82 S.Ct. 1107, 8 L.Ed.2d 230, or insistence on a nonmandatory subject, see National Labor Relations Board v. Wooster Division of Borg-Warner Corp., 356 U.S. 342, 78 S.Ct. 718, 2 L.Ed. 2d 823. Thus, the unions contend, Jewel could have filed an unfair labor practice charge with the board on the ground that the unions had insisted on a nonmandatory subject—the marketing hours restriction. Obviously classification of bargaining subjects as "terms or conditions of employment" is a matter concerning which the Board has special expertise. Nevertheless, for the reasons stated below we cannot conclude that this is a proper case for application of the doctrine of primary jurisdiction.

To begin with, courts are themselves not without experience in classifying bargaining subjects as terms or conditions of employment. Just such a determination must be frequently made when a court's jurisdiction to issue an injunction affecting a labor dispute is challenged under the Norris-LaGuardia Act, which defines "labor dispute" as including "any controversy concerning terms or conditions of employment." Norris-LaGuardia Act § 13(c).

Secondly, the doctrine of primary jurisdiction is not a doctrine of futility; it does not require resort to "an expensive and merely delaying administrative proceeding when the case must eventually be decided on a controlling legal issue wholly unrelated to determinations for the ascertainment of which the proceeding was sent to the agency." Federal Maritime Board v. Isbrandtsen Co., 356 U.S. 481, 521, 78 S.Ct. 851, 873, 2 L.Ed.2d 926 (Frankfurter, J., dissenting). It was only after commencement of trial that it became evident that a major issue in this case would be whether the marketing hours restriction was a term or condition of employment. Jewel's complaint alleged the existence of a conspiracy between Associated and the unions to impose the marketing-hours provision on Jewel—that is, it was alleged that the unions had agreed with a part of the bargaining unit to impose certain terms on the rest of the unit. We hold today in United Mine Workers of America v. Pennington with respect to allegations of a similar employer-union agreement to impose a particular scale of wages—indisputably at the core of "wages, hours, and other terms and conditions of employment"—that such an understanding is not exempt from the Sherman Act. At the stage when the decision whether to refer the parties to the board was made, therefore, the issues were so framed that a Board determination would have been of subsidiary importance at best.

Finally, we must reject the unions' primary jurisdiction contention because of the absence of an available procedure for obtaining a Board determination. The Board does not classify bargaining subjects in the abstract but only in connection with unfair labor practice charges of refusal to bargain. The typical antitrust suit, however, is brought by a stranger to the bargaining relationship, and the complaint is not that the parties have refused to bargain but, quite the contrary, that they have agreed. Jewel's conspiracy allegation in the present case was just such a complaint. Agreement is of course not a refusal to bargain, and in such cases the Board affords no mechanism for obtaining a classification of the subject matter of the agreement. Moreover, even in the few instances when the antitrust action could be framed as a refusal to bargain charge, there is no guarantee of Board action. It is the function of the Board's General Counsel rather than the Board or a private litigant to determine whether an unfair labor practice complaint will ultimately issue. National Labor Relations Act § 3(d). And the six-month limitation period of § 10(b) of the Act would preclude many litigants from even filing a charge with the General Counsel. Indeed, Jewel's complaint in this very case was filed more than six months after it signed the 1957 collective agreement. "[W]e know of no case where the court has ordered reference of an issue which the administrative body would not itself have jurisdiction to determine in a proceeding for that purpose." Montana-Dakota Utilities Co. v. Northwestern Public Serv. Co., 341 U.S. 246, 254, 71 S.Ct. 692, 696, 95 L.Ed. 912.[62]

II.

Here, as in United Mine Workers of America v. Pennington, the claim is made that the agreement under attack is exempt from the antitrust laws. We agree, but not on the broad grounds urged by the union.

---

62. To be distinguished are the preemption cases in which the possibility that the Board may not exercise jurisdiction renders state courts no less powerless to act, see San Diego Building Trades Council v. Garmon, 359 U.S. 236, 245–246, 79 S.Ct. 773, 3 L.Ed.2d 775. See generally, Local 20 Teamster v. Morton, 377 U.S. 252, 84 S.Ct. 1253, 12 L.Ed.2d 280.

It is well at the outset to emphasize that this case comes to us stripped of any claim of a union-employer conspiracy against Jewel. The trial court found no evidence to sustain Jewel's conspiracy claim and this finding was not disturbed by the Court of Appeals. We therefore have a situation where the unions, having obtained a marketing-hours agreement from one group of employers, has successfully sought the same terms from a single employer, Jewel, not as a result of a bargain between the unions and some employers directed against other employers, but pursuant to what the unions deemed to be in their own labor union interests.

Jewel does not allege that it has been injured by the elimination of competition among the other employers within the unit with respect to marketing hours; Jewel complains only of the unions' action in forcing it to accept the same restriction, the union acting not at the behest of any employer group but in pursuit of its own policies. It might be argued that absent any union-employer conspiracy against Jewel and absent any agreement between Jewel and any other employer, the Union-Jewel contract cannot be a violation of the Sherman Act. But the issue before us is not the broad substantive one of a violation of the antitrust laws—was there a conspiracy or combination which unreasonably restrained trade or an attempt to monopolize and was Jewel damaged in its business—but whether the agreement is immune from attack by reason of the labor exemption from the antitrust laws. The fact that the parties to the agreement are but a single employer and the unions representing its employees does not compel immunity for the agreement. We must consider the subject matter of the agreement in the light of the national labor policy.

We pointed out in Pennington that exemption for union-employer agreements is very much a matter of accommodating the coverage of the Sherman Act to the policy of the labor laws. Employers and unions are required to bargain about wages, hours and working conditions, and this fact weighs heavily in favor of antitrust exemption for agreements on these subjects. But neither party need bargain about other matters and either party commits an unfair labor practice if it conditions its bargaining upon discussions of a nonmandatory subject. Jewel, for example, need not have bargained about or agreed to a schedule of prices at which its meat would be sold and the union could not legally have insisted that it do so. But if the union had made such a demand, Jewel had agreed and the United States or an injured party had challenged the agreement under the antitrust laws, we seriously doubt that either the union or Jewel could claim immunity by reason of the labor exemption, whatever substantive questions of violation there might be.

Thus the issue in this case is whether the marketing-hours restriction, like wages, and unlike prices, is so intimately related to wages, hours and working conditions that the unions' successful attempt to obtain that provision through bona fide, arms-length bargaining in pursuit of its own labor union policies, and not at the behest of or in combination with nonlabor groups, falls within the protection of the national labor policy and is therefore exempt from the Sherman Act.[63] We think that it is.

The Court of Appeals would classify the marketing hours restriction with the product-pricing provision and place both within the reach of the Sherman Act. In its view, labor has a legitimate interest in the number of hours it must work but no interest in whether the hours fall in the daytime, in the nighttime or on Sundays. "[T]he furnishing of a place and advantageous hours of employment for the butchers to supply meat to customers are the prerogatives of the employer." 331 F.2d 547, 549. That reasoning would invalidate with respect to both service and self-service markets the 1957 provision that "eight hours shall constitute the basic work day, Monday through Saturday; *work to begin at 9:00 a.m. and stop at 6:00 p.m. . . .*" as well as the marketing hours restriction.

Contrary to the Court of Appeals, we think that the particular hours of the day and the particular days of the week during which employees shall be required to work are subjects well within the realm of "wages, hours, and other terms and conditions of employment" about which employers and unions must bargain. And, although the effect on competition is apparent and real, perhaps more so than in the case of the wage agreement, the concern of union members is immediate and direct. Weighing the respective interests involved, we think the national labor policy expressed in the National Labor Relations Act places beyond the reach of the Sherman Act union-employer agreements on when, as well as how long, employees must work. An agreement on these subjects between the union and the employers in a bargaining unit is not illegal under the Sherman Act, nor is the union's unilateral demand for the same contract of other employers in the industry.

Disposing of the case, as it did, on the broad grounds we have indicated, the Court of Appeals did not deal separately with the marketing hours provision, as distinguished from hours of work, in connection with either service or self-service markets. The dispute here pertains principally to self-service markets.

The unions argue that since night operations would be impossible without night employment of butchers, or an impairment of the butchers' jurisdiction, or a substantial effect on the butchers' workload, the marketing hours restriction is either little different in effect from the valid working hours provision that work shall stop at 6 p.m. or is necessary to protect other concerns of the union members. If

---

63. The crucial determinant is not the form of the agreement—e.g., prices or wages—but its relative impact on the product market and the interests of union members. Thus in Local 24 of Intern. Broth. of Teamsters Union v. Oliver, 358 U.S. 283, 79 S.Ct. 297, we held that federal labor policy precluded application of state antitrust laws to an employer-union agreement that when leased trucks were driven by their owners, such owner-drivers should receive, in addition to the union wage, not less than a prescribed minimum rental. Though in form a scheme fixing prices for the supply of leased vehicles, the agreement was designed "to protect the negotiated wage scale against the possible undermining through diminution of the owner's wages for driving which might result from a rental which did not cover his operating costs." Id., at 293–294, 79 S.Ct. at 303.

the unions' factual premises are true, we think the unions could impose a restriction on night operations without violation of the Sherman Act; for then operating hours, like working hours, would constitute a subject of immediate and legitimate concern to union members.

Jewel alleges on the other hand that the night operation of self-service markets requires no butcher to be in attendance and does not infringe any other legitimate union concern. Customers serve themselves; and if owners want to forego furnishing the services of a butcher to give advice or to make special cuts, this is not the unions' concern since their desire to avoid night work is fully satisfied and no other legitimate interest is being infringed. In short, the connection between working hours and operating hours in the case of the self-service market is said to be so attenuated as to bring the provision within the prohibition of the Sherman Act.

If it were true that self-service markets could actually operate without butchers, at least for a few hours after 6 p.m., that no encroachment on butchers' work would result and that the workload of butchers during normal working hours would not be substantially increased, Jewel's position would have considerable merit. For then the obvious restraint on the product market—the exclusion of self-service stores from the evening market for meat—would stand alone, unmitigated and unjustified by the vital interests of the union butchers which are relied upon in this case. In such event the limitation imposed by the union might well be reduced to nothing but an effort by the union to protect one group of employers from competition by another, which is conduct that is not exempt from the Sherman Act. Whether there would be a violation of §§ 1 and 2 would then depend on whether the elements of a conspiracy in restraint of trade or an attempt to monopolize had been proved.[64]

Thus the dispute between Jewel and the unions essentially concerns a narrow factual question: Are night operations without butchers, and without infringement of butchers' interests, feasible? The District Court resolved this factual dispute in favor of the unions. It found that "in stores where meat is sold at night it is impractical to operate without either butchers or other employees. Someone must

---

64. One issue, for example, would be whether the restraint was unreasonable. Judicial pronouncements regarding the reasonableness of restraints on hours of business are relatively few. Some cases appear to have viewed such restraints as tantamount to limits on hours of work and thus reasonable, even though contained in agreements among competitors. [Citing Chicago Board of Trade v. United States, 246 U.S. 231, 38 S.Ct. 242, 62 L.Ed. 683 (1918)].

. . . Other cases have upheld operating hours restraints in factual circumstances that make it seem likely that the agreement affected hours of operation and hours of work in equal measure but without stressing that fact.

Kold Kist, Inc. v. Amalgamated Meat Cutters, Local No. 421, 99 Cal.App.2d 191, 221 P.2d 724 (Cal.Ct.App.1950), held unreasonable a union-employer agreement limiting night sales of frozen poultry, which had previously been obtained from the plaintiff-distributor. The plaintiff alleged, however, that he had been severely affected, since many stores had stopped carrying its products entirely due to the lack of storage facilities in which to keep the poultry during hours in which sale was prohibited, and such effects may be atypical.

The decided cases thus do not appear to offer any easy answer to the question whether in a particular case an operating hours restraint is unreasonable.

arrange, replenish and clean the counters and supply customer services." Operating without butchers would mean that "their work would be done by others unskilled in the trade," and "would involve an increase in workload in preparing for the night work and cleaning the next morning." 215 F.Supp., at 846. Those findings were not disturbed by the Court of Appeals, which, as previously noted, proceeded on a broader ground. Our function is limited to reviewing the record to satisfy ourselves that the trial judge's findings are not clearly erroneous. Fed.Rules Civ.Proc., 52(a).

The trial court had before it evidence concerning the history of the unions' opposition to night work, the development of the provisions respecting night work and night operations, the course of collective negotiations in 1957 and 1959, and 1961 with regard to those provisions, and the characteristics of meat marketing insofar as they bore on the feasibility of night operations without butchers. . . .

The unions' evidence with regard to the practicability of night operations without butchers was accurately summarized by the trial judge as follows:

"[I]n most of plaintiff's stores outside Chicago, where night operations exist, meat cutters are on duty whenever a meat department is open after 6 P.M. . . . .. Even in self-service departments, ostensibly operated without employees on duty after 6 P.M., there was evidence that requisite customer services in connection with meat sales were performed by grocery clerks. In the same vein, defendants adduced evidence that in the sale of delicatessen items, which could be made after 6 P.M. from self-service cases under the contract, 'practically' always during the time the market was open the manager, or other employees, would be rearranging and restocking the cases. There was also evidence that even if it were practical to operate a self-service meat market after 6 P.M. without employees, the night operations would add to the workload in getting the meats prepared for night sales and in putting the counters in order the next day." 215 F.Supp., at 844.

Jewel challenges the unions' evidence on each of these points—arguing, for example, that its preference to have butchers on duty at night, where possible under the union contract, is not probative of the feasibility of not having butchers on duty and that the evidence that grocery clerks performed customer services within the butchers' jurisdiction was based on a single instance resulting from "entrapment" by union agents. But Jewel's argument—when considered against the historical background of union concern with working hours and operating hours and the virtually uniform recognition by employers of the intimate relationship between the two subjects, as manifested by bargaining proposals in 1957, 1959, and 1961—falls far short of a showing that the trial judge's ultimate findings were clearly erroneous.

Judgment reversed and case remanded to the United States District Court for the Northern District of Illinois for further proceedings in conformity with the judgment of this Court.

MR. JUSTICE DOUGLAS, with whom MR. JUSTICE BLACK and MR. JUSTICE CLARK concur, dissenting.

If we followed Allen Bradley Co. v. Local Union No. 3, 325 U.S. 797, 65 S.Ct. 1533, 89 L.Ed. 1939, we would hold with the Court of Appeals that this multi-employer agreement with the union not to sell meat between 6 p.m. and 9 a.m. was not immunized from the antitrust laws and that respondent's evidence made out a prima facie case that it was in fact a violation of the Sherman Act.

If, in the present case, the employers alone agreed not to sell meat from 6 p.m. to 9 a.m., they would be guilty of an anticompetitive practice, barred by the antitrust laws. Absent an agreement or conspiracy, a proprietor can keep his establishment open for such hours as he chooses. My Brother White recognizes, as he must, that the agreement in this case has an "effect on competition [that] is apparent and real" and that it is an "obvious restraint on the product market." That Jewel has been coerced by the unions into respecting this agreement means that Jewel cannot use convenience of shopping hours as a means of competition. . . .

At the conclusion of respondent's case, the District Court dismissed Associated and Bromann from the action, which was tried without a jury, on the ground that there was no evidence of a conspiracy between Associated and the unions. But in the circumstances of this case the collective agreement itself, of which the District Court said there was clear proof, was evidence of a conspiracy among the employers with the unions to impose the marketing hours restriction on Jewel via a strike threat by the unions. This tended to take from the merchants who agreed among themselves their freedom to work their own hours and to subject all who, like Jewel, wanted to sell meat after 6 p.m. to the coercion of threatened strikes, all of which if done in concert only by businessmen would violate the antitrust laws.

In saying that there was no conspiracy, the District Court failed to give any weight to the collective agreement itself as evidence of a conspiracy and to the context in which it was written. This Court makes the same mistake. We said in Allen Bradley Co. v. Local Union No. 3, supra, 325 U.S. at 808, 65 S.Ct. at 1539, ". . . we think Congress never intended that unions could, consistently with the Sherman Act, aid non-labor groups to create business monopolies and to control the marketing of goods and services." Here the contract of the unions with a large number of employers shows it was planned and designed not merely to control but entirely to prohibit "the marketing of goods and services" from 6 p.m. until 9 a.m. the next day. Some merchants relied chiefly on price competition to draw trade; others employed courtesy, quick service, and keeping their doors open long hours to meet the convenience of customers. The unions here induced a large group of merchants to use their collective strength to hurt others who wanted the competitive advantage of selling meat after 6 p.m. Unless Allen Bradley is either overruled or greatly impaired, the unions can no more aid a group of businessmen to force their competitors to follow uniform store marketing hours than to force them to sell at fixed prices. Both practices take away the freedom of traders to carry on their business in their own competitive fashion.

My Brother White's conclusion that the concern of the union members over *marketing* hours is "immediate and direct" depends upon there being a necessary connection between marketing hours and working hours. That connection is found in the District Court's finding that "in stores where meat is sold at night it is impractical to operate without either butchers or other employees." It is, however, undisputed that on some nights Jewel does so operate in some of its stores in Indiana, and even in Chicago it sometimes operates without butchers at night in the sale of fresh poultry and sausage, which are exempt from the union ban.

It is said that even if night self-service could be carried on without butchers, still the union interest in store hours would be immediate and direct because competitors would have to stay open too or be put at a disadvantage—and some of these competitors would be non-self-service stores that would have to employ union butchers at night. But Allen Bradley forecloses such an expansive view of the labor exemption to the antitrust laws.

MR. JUSTICE GOLDBERG concurred specially in an opinion joined by JUSTICES HARLAN and STEWART:

. . . The judicial expressions in Jewel Tea represent another example of the reluctance of judges to give full effect to congressional purpose in this area and the substitution by judges of their views for those of Congress as to how free collective bargaining should operate. In this case the Court of Appeals would have held the Union liable for the Sherman Act's criminal and civil penalties because in the court's social and economic judgment, the determination of the hours at which meat is to be sold is a "proprietory" matter within the exclusive control of management and thus the Union had no legitimate interest in bargaining over it. My Brother Douglas, joined by Mr. Justice Black and Mr. Justice Clark, would affirm this judgment apparently because the agreement was reached through a multi-employer bargaining unit. But, as I have demonstrated above, there is nothing even remotely illegal about such bargaining. Even if an independent conspiracy test were applicable to the Jewel Tea situation, the simple fact is that multi-employer bargaining conducted at arm's length does not constitute union abetment of a business combination. It is often a self-defense form of employer bargaining designed to match union strength.

My Brother White, joined by The Chief Justice and Mr. Justice Brennan, while not agreeing with my Brother Douglas, would reverse the Court of Appeals. He also, however, refuses to give full effect to the congressional intent that judges should not, under cover of the Sherman Act umbrella, substitute their economic and social policies for free collective bargaining. My Brother White recognizes that the issue of the hours of sale of meat concerns a mandatory subject of bargaining based on the trial court's findings that it directly affected the hours of work of the butchers in the self-service markets, and therefore, since there was a finding that the Union was not abetting an independent employer conspiracy, he joins in reversing the Court of Appeals. In doing so, however, he apparently draws lines among mandatory subjects of bargaining, presumably based on a judicial determination of their importance to the worker, and states that not all agreements resulting from collective bargaining based on mandatory subjects of bargaining are immune from the antitrust laws, even absent evidence of union abetment of an independent conspiracy of employers. Following this reasoning, my Brother White indicates that he would sustain a judgment here, even absent evidence of union abetment of an independent conspiracy of employers, if the trial court had found "that self-service markets could actually operate without butchers, at least for a few hours after 6 p.m., that no encroachment on butchers' work would result and that the workload of butchers during normal working hours would not be substantially increased . . . ." Such a view seems to me to be unsupportable. It represents a narrow, confining view of what labor unions have a legitimate interest in preserving and thus bargaining about. Even if the self-service markets could operate after 6 p.m., without their butchers and without increasing the work of their butchers at other times, the result of such operation can reasonably be expected to be either that the small, independent, service markets would have to remain open in order to compete, thus requiring their union butchers to work at night, or that the small, independent, service markets would not be able to operate at night and thus would be put at a competitive disadvantage. Since it is clear that the large, automated self-service markets employ less butchers per volume of sales than service markets do, the Union certainly has a legitimiate interest in keeping service markets competitive so as to preserve jobs. Job security of this kind has been recognized to be a legitimate subject of union interest. The direct interest of the union in not working undesirable hours by curtailing all business at those hours is, of course, a far cry from the indirect "interest" in Allen Bradley in fixing prices and allocating markets solely to increase the profits of favored employers. . . .

Moreover, while these cases involve suits against unions, we should not overlook the fact that if unions are held liable under the antitrust laws for collective bargaining activities concerning mandatory subjects, then the employer parties to this mandatory collective bargaining would also be subject to antitrust penalties, criminal and civil. It would seem the height of unfairness so to penalize employers for the discharge of their statutory duty to bargain on wages, hours, and other terms and conditions of employment, which duty, this Court has held, requires the employer to enter into a signed contract with the union embodying the collective bargaining terms agreed upon.

My view that Congress intended that collective bargaining activity on mandatory subjects of bargaining under the Labor Act not be subject to the antitrust laws does not mean that I believe that Congress intended that activity involving all nonmandatory subjects of bargaining be similarly exempt. That direct and overriding interests of unions in such subjects as wages, hours, and other working conditions, which Congress has recognized in making them subjects of mandatory bargaining is clearly lacking where the subject of the agreement is price-fixing and market allocation. Moreover, such activities are at the core of the type of anticompetitive commercial restraint at which the antitrust laws are directed.

Nor does my view mean that where a union operates as a businessman, exercising a proprietory or ownership function, that it is beyond the reach of the antitrust laws merely because it is a union. On the contrary, the labor exemption is inapplicable where the union acts not as a union but as an entrepreneur. See, e.g., Streiffer v. Seafarers Sea Chest Corp., 162 F.Supp. 602 (D.C.E.D.La.); United States v. Seafarers Sea Chest Corp., 1956 CCH Trade Cases ¶ 68,298 (D.C.E.D.N.Y.). Therefore, if a union is found by sufficient evidence and under proper instructions to have participated as a proprietor in actions violative of the antitrust laws, it is no more shielded from antitrust sanctions than any other business participant. . . .

NOTES AND QUERIES

(1) *Queries.* In *Jewel Tea*, might the butchers have insisted that their employers refrain from selling canned meats, fresh or canned fish, and other items which compete with fresh meat and so lower the demand for butchers' skills? Would agreement among employers as to hours of operation constitute a reasonable restraint of trade under the *Chicago Board of Trade* case, p. 332 supra, or would it be a *per se* violation of the Sherman Act as concerted control of production? Is the common-law favor towards shopkeepers' concerted limitation of their working hours to be extended to concert of grocery chains to avoid service at hours which a substantial body of the public finds convenient? Should these kinds of questions be decided by an administative agency like the N.L.R.B. applying labor law policy, or courts applying antitrust policy?

(2) *Price Control Justified to Protect Union Wages? American Federation of Musicians v. Carroll,*[65] dealt with rules of the Musicians Union concerning "club dates," usually single performance occasions like weddings or commencements. Since the musicians do not work regularly for a single employer, as in the case of a symphony orchestra, conventional collective bargaining agreements are not feasible. The band leader, who may or may not play himself, is the entrepreneur, seeking engagements, arranging transportation, bargaining with booking agents and caterers (a fruitful source of business). The leaders, being themselves performers and conductors, were members of the union, unless like plaintiff, Carroll, they were dropped from the union and thus excluded from the business for violation of the club-date rules.

These rules provided a "price list" according to which: (1) a band can be hired only at a price that includes union wages for the performers, double pay for the leader, and 8% more for social security and other expenses; (2) a band that goes outside the local union's territory must charge a 10% premi-

65. 391 U.S. 99, 88 S.Ct. 1562, 20 L.Ed.2d 460 (1968).

um; (3) no engagements can be accepted from caterers; and (4) no engagements can be accepted from a booking agent not licensed by the union.

The Court, speaking through Justice Brennan:

(i) rejected the argument that the presence of leader-entrepreneurs in
the union presented a situation where labor was combining with employers to restrain trade; since these "entrepreneurs" were themselves usually performing or conducting, and were thus at least potential competitors
for jobs.

(ii) held that establishment of price floors on orchestral engagements
did not constitute a *per se* violation of the Sherman Act. "[T]his overlooks the necessity of inquiry beyond form. . . .   The critical inquiry
is whether the price floors in actuality operate to protect . . .
wages." The opinion reviewed evidence showing that the pressure of unrestrained price competition among leaders caused them to evade union
wage scales in a business where wages constitute a very large element of
price, and to substitute a leader's performing in place of a potential additional musician.

(iii) declared that the booking agent and caterer restrictions were also
valid because "intimately bound up with the subject of wages," in view of
evidence that these intermediaries charged such exorbitant commissions
as to induce leaders to cut employment and pay, as in the case of price
competition.

From Justice Brennan's opinion:

The analyses of Mr. Justice White and Mr. Justice Goldberg in *Jewel
Tea* support our conclusion. *Jewel Tea* did not hold that an agreement
respecting marketing hours would always come within the labor exemption. Rather, that case held that such an agreement was lawful because
it was found that the marketing-hours restriction had a substantial effect
on hours worked by the union members. Similarly, the price-list requirement is brought within the labor exemption under the finding that the
requirement is necessary to assure that scale wages will be paid to the
sidemen and the leader. If the union may not require that the full-time
leader charge the purchaser of the music an amount sufficient to compensate him for the time he spends selecting musicians and performing the
other musical functions involved in leading, the full-time leader may compete with other union members who seek the same jobs through price
differentiation in the product market based on differences in a labor standard. His situation is identical to that of a truck owner in *Oliver I* who
does not charge an amount sufficient to compensate him for the value of
his labor services in driving the truck, and is a situation which the union
can prevent consistent with its antitrust exemption. There can be no differentiation between the leader who appears with his orchestra and the
one who on occasion hires a subleader. In either case part of the union-
prescribed "leader's fee" is attributable to service rendered in either conducting or playing and part to the service rendered in selecting musicians,
bookkeeping, etc. The only difference is that in the former situation the
leader keeps the entire fee while in the latter he is required to pay that
part of it attributable to playing or conducting to the subleader.[66]

66. 391 U.S., at 112–13, 88 S.Ct., at
1570–71, 20 L.Ed.2d, at 470.

From Mr. Justice White's dissent (concurred in by Mr. Justice Black):

Unions are, of course, not without interest in the prices at which employers sell. As the majority points out, by seeing that employers sell at prices covering all their costs, a union can insure employer solvency and make more certain employee collection of wages owed them. In addition, assuring that competing employers charge at least a minimum price prevents price competition from exerting downward pressure on wages. On the other hand, price competition, a significant aid to satisfactory resource allocation and a deterrent to inflation, would be substantially diminished if industry-wide unions were free to dictate uniform prices through agreements with employers. I have always thought that this strong policy outweighed the legitimate union interest in the prices at which employers sell, and until today I had thought that the Court agreed. Of course the lack of discussion of this question in the majority's opinion, and the failure to refer to the unanimous rejection in *Jewel Tea* of antitrust immunity for union efforts to fix industry-wide prices, suggest that the Court takes this step without full awareness of the implications and the likely consequences. The step is nonetheless disturbing, and I must record my dissent.[67]

Small entrepreneurs have sometimes been taken into the union, which then seeks to promote the common interest of entrepreneurs and employees in higher prices for the products. Although this avoids in form the *Allen-Bradley* ban on combination between union and separately identified employer organizations, the courts have usually held that price-fixing and market-allocating efforts of such unions are enjoinable as commercial restraints going beyond the bounds of labor's legitimate concerns with wages and terms and conditions of employment.[68]

(3) *Labor Panel Hits Milk Price Wars*, New York Times, May 6, 1964, p. 80M:

A special board of arbitration announced a ruling yesterday that could have far-reaching effects in mitigating price wars in the milk industry. The decision said the board should be authorized by the industry and the unions to afford relief when it found that a distribution practice or a policy of pricing at unreasonably low levels was undermining established methods of delivering milk and injuring the job security of milk drivers. The form of relief, the decision declared, should protect the legitimate concern of the unions without impairing the public interest or unduly infringing on the prerogatives of management. In its award the board set up an avenue of complaint and redress for milk drivers who believe that their jobs are being jeopardized by the spread of company stores and "unreasonably" low prices for milk. At the same time, however, the ruling gives employers the right to similar recourse if unions violate no-strike contracts in opposing innovations in the distribution of milk.

The decision, described as precedent-setting by the board chairman, Theodore W. Kheel, gives the three-man arbitration panel unusually broad powers with which to eliminate what it may consider to be abuses in the distribution and pricing of milk. The procedure for obtaining relief is through the board itself. If one of the unions determines that milk is

---

67. 391 U.S., at 119–20, 88 S.Ct., at 1574, 20 L.Ed.2d, at 473–74.

68. Columbia River Packers Association v. Hinton, 315 U.S. 143, 62 S.Ct. 520, 86 L.Ed. 750 (1942); Los Angeles Meat & Provision Drivers Union v. United States, 371 U.S. 94, 83 S.Ct. 162, 9 L.Ed.2d 150 (1962); United States Steel Corp. v. Fraternal Association of Steelhaulers, 431 F.2d 1046 (3d Cir. 1970).

being distributed or priced in a manner prejudicial to wages, working conditions and job security, it has the right to bring a complaint before the board. Employers likewise may go to the board to complain about contract violations by the unions in opposing new methods of distributing milk. The board, according to the decision, has the right to dismiss a complaint or to issue orders to protect the jobs and working conditions of the workers and also the interest of consumers in the continuing availability of services. To achieve the desired relief, the board may seek an injunction, authorize the union to resort to self help, that is, to strike, or to adopt other remedies.

In discussing the growing problem of company stores and outlets, the board said that price cutting had become so intense in some areas that milk was being sold far below cost.

"Not only were the wholesale dealers required as a result to subsidize these price wars," the board explained, "but the margins of the storekeepers were also reduced or eliminated in many cases. The decline in the number of retail routes and men employed thereon accelerated."

Compare *Milk Wagon Drivers' Union v. Lake Valley Farm Products, Inc.,*[69] (union pickets price-cutting retailers and dairies supplying them through independent "peddlers"; federal injunction held unavailable) with *United States v. Milk Drivers & Dairy Employees Union,*[70] (*Allen Bradley* applied as basis for federal injunction against union "combining" with dairies and stores in collective bargaining agreement to fix prices and exclude independent "peddlers").

(4) *Worker Censorship. I.P.C. Distributors v. Chicago Moving Picture Machine Operators Union.*[71] Motion to dismiss moving picture exhibitor's suit for treble damages and injunction against union which ordered operators not to exhibit film, entitled "Salt of the Earth", supposedly of communist inspiration. The district court held: (i) Allegation of injury to public is sufficient despite limited impact on one picture in two theaters, since it is alleged that:

the public has been and will continue to be deprived of seeing the motion picture . . . by the arbitrary censorship of the defendants. . . . Certainly the public has the same interest in being able to see motion pictures of its choice as it has in being able to read books and newspapers, and see plays and attend meetings of its choice. This interest is not always protected; but whether or not this is one of those occasions on which it must be limited is not properly before me on motion to dismiss.

(ii) A controversy between the exhibitor and the union "as to the kind of pictures the defendants should be required to project" is not so clearly a "labor dispute" as to require dismissal on the theory that the behavior is legalized under a "harmonizing" reading of the Sherman, Norris-LaGuardia, Clayton and Labor-Management Relations Acts. (iii) "The fact that it acts alone does not grant a union an unlimited license to escape the antitrust laws."

Compare the more recent decision, by the Supreme Court, in *Jacksonville Bulk Terminals v. International Longshoremen's Association,*[72] where a union with a no-strike clause in its collective bargaining agreement refused to load ships bound for Russia as a protest of the Russian invasion of Af-

69. 311 U.S. 91, 61 S.Ct. 122, 85 L.Ed. 63 (1940).

70. 153 F.Supp. 803 (D.Minn.1957).

71. 132 F.Supp. 294 (N.D.Ill.1955).

72. ___ U.S. ___, 102 S.Ct. 2673, 73 L.Ed.2d 327 (1982).

ghanistan. The employer sued for an injunction under Section 301(a) of the Labor Management Relations Act, to enforce the no-strike and arbitration clauses of the collective bargaining agreement. Held: Injunctive relief may be barred under Norris-LaGuardia because the union's non-economic motive does not "inevitably" mean that there is no "labor dispute":

> The critical element in determining whether the provisions of the Norris-LaGuardia Act apply is whether "the employer-employee relationship [is] the matrix of the controversy." *Columbia River Packers Association v. Hinton*, 315 U.S. 143, 147, 62 S.Ct. 520, 522, 86 L.Ed. 750 (1942). In this case, the Employer and the Union representing its employees are the disputants, and their dispute concerns the interpretation of the labor contract that defines their relationship. Thus, the employer-employee relationship is the matrix of this controversy.[73]

In a footnote to its opinion, the Court further defined "labor dispute":

> A labor dispute might be present under the facts of this case even in the absence of the dispute over the scope of the no-strike clause. Regardless of the political nature of the Union's objections to handling Soviet-bound cargo, these objections were expressed in a work stoppage by employees against their employer, which focused on particular work assignments. Thus, apart from the collective-bargaining agreement, the employer-employee relationship would be the matrix of the controversy. We need not decide this question, however, because this case does involve a dispute over the interpretation of the parties' collective-bargaining agreement.[74]

Compare "Censors in the Shop: Some Printers Refuse Controversial Copy," Wall Street Journal, December 10, 1970, p. 1:

> Last February John Verburg and a score of his fellow printers walked off the job at the University of Kansas Printing Service in Lawrence. But the workers didn't want more money, and they weren't asking for shorter hours. They weren't even seeking a longer coffee break. The work stoppage came after the editors of Harambee, a newspaper put out by black students at the college, presented an issue of their publication to the shop for printing. As Mr. Verburg, the foreman, saw it, the issue "contained so many revolutionary things and obscenities and profanities that it was against our good conscience to print it." And, indeed, the state-owned shop didn't print the paper until the Kansas attorney general ruled that the issue didn't violate obscenity laws.
>
> In more than a half-dozen other instances over the past year, print-shop employes have refused to work on material ranging from erotic books published by Grove Press and Olympia Press to a satirical prospectus attacking the Vietnam war. Some authorities believe the total of such cases may be much higher.

Is it not a legitimate concern of workers what "filth" they must handle? Does the *Jacksonville* case provide a sufficient remedy by barring federal court intervention for a work stoppage by a union? Is this sufficient protection for an individual worker offended by his job assignment? If, balancing that interest against the interest in free flow of information, worker censorship should be forbidden, can that result be reached under the Sherman Act, or must Congress amend Section 8(b)?

73. ___ U.S., at ___, 102 S.Ct., at 2681, 73 L.Ed.2d at 337.

74. ___ U.S., at ___, n. 12, 102 S.Ct., at 2681, n. 12, 73 L.Ed.2d, at 337, n. 12.

(5) *Labor Law Limits on Job Protection.   Order of Railroad Telegraphers v. Chicago & North Western Railway Co.,*[75] held 5–4 that "labor dispute" in the Norris-LaGuardia Act embraced a controversy between a railroad and its employees over whether the railroad might abandon certain unprofitable stations. The railroad took the position that it was willing to bargain about severance pay and other employment conditions, but that discontinuance of stations was in the first instance a management decision, subject to review by public regulatory agencies from whom authorizing certificates would be obtained and before whom the union would have the opportunity to present its views on public interest.

As to the legality of a union's insisting that the employer continue to retain and pay employees to do useless work ("featherbedding"), duplicating what the employer is having done mechanically, see *American Newspaper Publishers Association v. National Labor Relations Board,*[76] (such demand is not "for services which are not to be performed," within the meaning of section 8(b)(6) of the National Labor Relations Act); [77] *National Labor Relations Board v. Gamble Enterprises,*[78] (no violation of section 8(b)(6) where Musicians Union insists upon pay for its members during performance by visiting orchestra, where "the union was seeking actual employment . . . not merely standby pay," although employer made it clear that he did not need and would not use their services).

Drawing the line between valid work preservation demands and an illegal secondary boycott under § 8(b)(4)(B) of the National Labor Relations Act, or a "hot cargo" agreement under § 8(e) of the Act, remains a frequently litigated issue. The basic test requires a determination of whether the primary purpose of the work preservation demand is for the purpose of preserving work traditionally performed by union members or for some secondary purpose to satisfy union demands elsewhere.[79] For example, in *National Labor Relations Board v. International Longshoremen's Association,*[80] the Supreme Court reversed a Board finding of an unfair labor practice arising out of collectively bargained rules on containers which required longshoremen to strip and repack containers packed within a 50 mile radius of the dock. In determining whether the rules were valid work preservation rules—primary activity between an employer and the union and not invalid secondary activity aimed at others not party to the agreement—the Court required the Board to examine the traditional work patterns of longshoremen, the impact of the new technology of containerized shipping on those work patterns, and how the agreement sought to accomplish preservation of those work patterns. It was held that the Board erred by focusing on the impact of the rules on truckers and consolidators off the pier, rather that the effect of the rules on the traditional work patterns of longshoremen. The determination can have significant antitrust consequences, because a finding that a work preservation agreement is in reality an illegal secondary boycott or hot cargo agreement may provide the basis for an antitrust action against the parties to the

75. 362 U.S. 330, 80 S.Ct. 761, 4 L.Ed. 2d 774 (1960).

76. 345 U.S. 100, 73 S.Ct. 552, 97 L.Ed. 852 (1953).

77. Cf. The Lea Act, 47 U.S.C.A. § 506, making it a crime to attempt to compel a broadcasting station to employ persons "in excess of the number needed by such licensee to perform actual services;" United States v. Petrillo, 332 U.S. 1, 67 S.Ct. 1538, 91 L.Ed. 1877 (1947).

78. 345 U.S. 117, 73 S.Ct. 560, 97 L.Ed. 864 (1953).

79. National Labor Relations Board v. Pipefitters Union, 429 U.S. 507, 97 S.Ct. 891, 51 L.Ed.2d 1 (1977).

80. 447 U.S. 490, 100 S.Ct. 2305, 65 L.Ed.2d 289 (1980).

agreement. See *Consolidated Express, Inc. v. New York Shipping Association, Inc.*, discussed infra p. 1149.

(6) *State Law and Preemption. Opera on Tour v. Weber*,[81] enjoined a "conspiracy" between the Musicians Union and the Stagehands Union "to destroy" plaintiff's business by getting the stagehands to refuse to work for plaintiff so long as plaintiff used recorded orchestral accompaniment instead of live musicians. Plaintiff was a nonprofit organization engaged in performing opera in non-metropolitan areas, and would have been unable to continue in business if it had to transport a live orchestra. Elimination of mechanical substitutes for labor was held not "a lawful labor objective", so that the controversy was not a "labor dispute".[82]

In *International Brotherhood of Teamsters, Local 309 v. Hanke*,[83] Hanke and his three sons, as partners, ran a used car lot and service station in Seattle, Wash. Like 90% of the used car dealers in Seattle, the Hankes had no employees. An Automobile Drivers and Demonstrators Union, which included in its membership used car dealers as well as salesmen, negotiated an agreement with the Independent Automobile Dealers Association to keep used car lots closed evenings and weekends. The Hankes were not members of the Dealers Association, and refused to close evenings and weekends. The Drivers Union then enlisted the aid of its powerful affiliate, the Teamsters Union, which picketed the Hankes. As a result the Hankes lost patronage, and drivers for Hankes' suppliers refused to make deliveries to them. The state courts enjoined, and the United States Supreme Court affirmed, 5–3, holding that the state had not unconstitutionally abridged the union's freedom to communicate by peaceful picketing. The plurality, per Frankfurter, J.:

> Here we have a glaring instance of the interplay of competing social-economic interests and viewpoints. Unions obviously are concerned not to have union standards undermined by non-union shops. This interest penetrates into self-employer shops. On the other hand, some of our profoundest thinkers from Jefferson to Brandeis have stressed the importance to a democratic society of encouraging self-employer economic units as a counter-movement to what are deemed to be the dangers inherent in excessive concentration of economic power. . . .

> Washington here concluded that, even though the relief afforded the Hankes entailed restriction upon communication that the unions sought to convey through picketing, it was more important to safeguard the value which the State placed upon self-employers, leaving all other channels of communication open to the union. The relatively small interest of the unions considerably influenced the balance that was struck. Of 115 used car dealers in Seattle maintaining union standards all but ten were self-employers with no employees. "From this fact," so we are informed by the Supreme Court of Washington, "the conclusion seems irresistible that the union's interest in the welfare of a mere handful of members (of

81. 285 N.Y. 348, 34 N.E.2d 349, 136 A.L.R. 267 (1941).

82. Cf. Rochette & Parzini Corp. v. Campo, 301 N.Y. 228, 93 N.E.2d 652 (1950), (stone workers union refusal to work for plaintiff because "prices were getting too cheap in the industry" presents no "labor dispute", but state antitrust act is inapplicable as a basis for injunctive relief since it contains a provision like the Clayton Act excepting activ-

ites of a bona fide labor union); Bright v. Pittsburgh Musical Society, 379 Pa. 335, 108 A.2d 810 (1954) (musicians union refusal to play for plaintiff's comedy act, because plaintiff was interviewed on a "disc jockey" program, does not involve a "labor dispute" so the court has juridiction to enjoin).

83. 339 U.S. 470, 70 S.Ct. 773, 94 L.Ed. 995 (1950).

whose working conditions no complaint at all is made) is far outweighed by the interests of individual proprietors and the people of the community as a whole, to the end that little businessmen and property owners shall be free from dictation as to business policy by an outside group having but a relatively small and indirect interest in such policy." [84]

Although the prohibitions of the Clayton and Norris-LaGuardia Acts against injunctions are not directly applicable to state courts, the integral relationship between federal anti-injunction policy and paramount federal labor relations law may have the effect of preempting the state courts from issuing injunctions.[85] *Connell Construction Co., Inc. v. Plumbers & Steamfitters Local No. 100*, infra p. 1135, held state antitrust laws preempted even though federal antitrust policy was not necessarily preempted. The Court stated:

> In this area, the accommodation between federal labor and antitrust policy is delicate. Congress and this Court have carefully tailored the antitrust statutes to avoid conflict with the labor policy favoring lawful employee organization, not only by delineating exemptions from antitrust coverage but also by adjusting the scope of the antitrust remedies themselves. State antitrust laws generally have not been subjected to this process of accommodation. If they take account of labor goals at all, they may represent a totally different balance between labor and antitrust policies. Permitting state antitrust law to operate in this field could frustrate the basic federal policies favoring employee organization and allowing elimination of competition among wage earners, and interfere with the detailed system Congress has created for regulating organizational techniques.

> Because employee organization is central to federal labor policy and regulation of organizational procedures is comprehensive, federal law does not admit the use of state antitrust law to regulate union activity that is closely related to organizational goals. Of course, other agreements between unions and nonlabor parties may yet be subject to state antitrust laws. The governing factor is the risk of conflict with the NLRA or with federal labor policy.[86]

The Supreme Court has declined to hold that federal labor law preempts state law under which an American maritime union was enjoined from picketing foreign vessels with low-wage crews. *Windward Shipping (London) v. American Radio Association.*[87] The ground taken by Mr. Justice Rehnquist, speaking for the majority, was that the union's activity was not "in

84. 339 U.S., at 475–77, 70 S.Ct., at 776–77, 94 L.Ed., at 1002–03. See also Giboney v. Empire Storage & Ice Co., 336 U.S. 490, 69 S.Ct. 684, 93 L.Ed. 834 (1949), sustaining an injunction against a union under the Missouri antitrust act. The "union" of ice peddlers picketed Empire as part of a campaign to get all wholesale ice dealers to agree to refrain from selling to non-union peddlers. The statute made such agreements criminal. The constitutional protection of free speech as applied to peaceful picketing was held not applicable to attempts to force Empire into criminal conduct. The employees were said to be "exercising their economic power together with that of their allies to compel Empire to abide

by union rather than state regulation of trade".

85. See Lesnick, State-Court Injunctions and the Federal Common Law of Labor Contracts: Beyond Norris-LaGuardia, 79 Harv.L.Rev. 757 (1966). Cf. the history of removal of injunction actions from state to federal court, at the instigation of defendant unions, in order to preclude injunctions. See Boys Markets, Inc. v. Retail Clerks Union, 398 U.S. 235, 90 S.Ct. 1583, 26 L.Ed.2d 199 (1970).

86. 421 U.S., at 636-37, 95 S.Ct., at 1842, 44 L.Ed.2d, at 433–34.

87. 415 U.S. 104, 94 S.Ct. 959, 39 L.Ed.2d 195 (1974), on remand 524 S.W.2d 772 (Tex.Civ.App.1975).

commerce" within the meaning of the Labor Management Relations Act, which must be construed in the light of congressional intention to deal with *American* labor problems, and of a long history of "comity and accommodation" in international maritime trade. Could Windward Shipping prevail in a damage action under the antitrust laws?

(7) *Entrepreneurs' Unions.* It has been urged, usually unsuccessfully, that self-employed individuals with little bargaining power, whose prices for services represent essentially payment for labor, and who confront highly organized buyers, should be permitted to bargain collectively.[88] The principal legislative expression of this point of view is the exemption from the Sherman Act of "agricultural", "horticultural", and "fishery" cooperatives. See pp. 394–396 supra. To the extent that these are available to corporate and other capital-intensive organizations, they go beyond the rationale of protecting the return for labor.

Ring v. Spina,[89] held illegal under the Sherman Act the Minimum Basic Agreement required of all play producers by the Dramatists Guild of the Authors League of America. The agreement fixed minimum royalties, minimum advance payments, and minimum periods of performance. The defense that playwrights had constituted themselves a labor union, with the protections of the Clayton and Norris-LaGuardia Acts was rejected. But cf. *Inge v. Twentieth Century-Fox Film Corp.,*[90] enforcing a restriction in a copyright license despite defense that the clause was required by the Dramatists Guild.

(8) *The Labor Union in Business: Problems of Vertical Integration.* Unions with large funds at their disposal must invest. If the investment is in loans or other commitments in business enterprises for which union members work, problems of conflict of interest and unfair competition may arise. For example in order to protect the union's investment, its officers may have to refrain from demanding wages as high as other firms are required to pay. In *United States v. Seafarers Sea Chest Corp.,*[91] it was charged that a seamen's union set up a business in "slop chest" supplies, and compelled ship owners to patronize this firm, through provisions in the collective bargaining contract. A consent judgment required cancellation of these provisions and enjoined defendant from engaging in this business after five years unless, after three years, it proved that effective competition existed in the sale of

88. Taylor v. Local No. 7, International Union of Journeymen Horseshoers, 353 F.2d 593 (4th Cir. 1965), held 3–2 that no labor dispute but only illegal price-fixing was involved in a controversy between the horseshoers and owners racing horses in Maryland over the union-fixed minimum fee of $16 per horse, in view of the degree of independence of the farriers, who worked at many tracks for many owners and with their own equipment. See Jacobs, Are "Independent Contractors" Really Independent?, 3 DePaul L.Rev. 23 (1953); Gottesman, Restraint of Trade—Employees or Enterprisers?, 15 U.Chi.L.Rev. 638 (1948).

89. 148 F.2d 647 (2d Cir. 1945).

90. 143 F.Supp. 294 (S.D.N.Y.1956).

91. Civ. No. 14,674, E.D.N.Y.1954. Cf. Streiffer v. Seafarers Sea Chest Corp., 162 F.Supp. 602 (E.D.La.1958) (no

labor dispute and no immunity from treble damage action under Sherman Act: "The profits at which the Union's activities were aimed were not the employers' profits but those of independent businessmen outside the shipping trade. Moreover, the Union's object was not to reduce those profits but to divert them to Union coffers"); National Association of Women & Childrens Apparel Salesmen, Inc. v. Federal Trade Commission, 479 F.2d 139 (5th Cir.), certiorari denied 414 U.S. 1004, 94 S.Ct. 360, 38 L.Ed.2d 240 (1973) (association of salesmen was acting "for the protection and enhancement of its business interests" when it conducted an annual trade show, and so committed an unfair trade practice when it excluded from the show entitled manufacturers who refused to sign the association's standard employment contract).

slop chest supplies to vessel owners employing defendant's members.   Cf. *Bausch & Lomb Optical Co.*[92] (holding that an employer is exempt from the ordinary statutory duty to bargain with his employees' union, where the union operates a competing business).

Under what circumstances would a union's collaboration with an employer, whether by way of heavy financial aid or by participation in his commercial maneuvers, convert the employer's lawful effort to acquire trade ascendancy into an unlawful conspiracy to monopolize or restrain trade? [93]

(9) *Queries.*   May an industry-wide automobile workers' union bargain with an employer over the price which the manufacturer shall charge for the cars?   Consider the following report from The Wall Street Journal of Aug. 23, 1957, p. 2:

> Harlow Curtice, president of General Motors Corp., in effect turned down the proposal of Walter P. Reuther, president of the A.F.L.–C.I.O. United Auto Workers, that the company cut factory prices of its 1958 models by $100 from current levels.   Although he did not specifically mention Mr. Reuther's request, Mr. Curtice restated G.M.'s position that "prices of its products were not properly the subject of collective bargaining." . . . Mr. Reuther proposed in letters last weekend to G.M., Ford Motor Co. and Chrysler Corp. that the "big three" auto makers trim their prices and promised the union would soften its demands in bargaining on new labor contracts next year.

If Congress should require employers to bargain with the unions regarding hours of operation, innovation and abandonment of products or manufacturing techniques, maintenance or discontinuance of subcontracting relationships, pricing, etc., would it be irrational to retain the Sherman Act prohibition against some kinds of agreement that might otherwise emerge from the bargaining?   Does the objective of peaceful negotiation preclude opportunities for either side to advance illegality as a ground for resisting demands?   See *Kaiser Steel Corp. v. Mullins*, infra p. 800.   Should union leaders be invited to serve on the board of directors of firms they must bargain with? [94]

CONNELL CONSTRUCTION CO., INC. v. PLUMBERS AND STEAMFITTERS LOCAL UNION NO. 100

Supreme Court of the United States, 1975.
421 U.S. 616, 95 S.Ct. 1830, 44 L.Ed.2d 418.

Mr. Justice Powell delivered the opinion of the Court.

The building trades union in this case supported its efforts to organize mechanical subcontractors by picketing certain general contractors, including petitioner.   The union's sole objective was to com-

---

92.   108 N.L.R.B. 1955, 34 L.R.R.M. 1222 (1954).

93.   Cf. Scott Publishing Co. v. Columbia Basin Publishers, Inc., 293 F.2d 15 (9th Cir. 1961); Union Leader Corp. v. Newspapers of New England, Inc., 180 F.Supp. 125 (D.Mass.1960), affirmed 284 F.2d 582 (2d Cir. 1960); Note, Union Investment in Business, 46 Minn.L.Rev. 573 (1962).

94.   See "UAW Chief Is in an Awkward Spot, Advising Restraint in Chrysler Talks", Wall St. J., Aug. 12, 1982, p. 21 (describing UAW President Douglas A. Fraser's problem with persuading union members to "swallow some very distasteful wage and benefit concessions" given Chrysler by the Union; Fraser sits on the Board of Directors of Chrysler as the result of earlier union bargaining with Chrysler to help rehabilitate the company.)

pel the general contractors to agree that in letting subcontracts for mechanical work they would deal only with firms that were parties to the union's current collective-bargaining agreement. The union disclaimed any interest in representing the general contractors' employees. In this case the picketing succeeded, and petitioner seeks to annul the resulting agreement as an illegal restraint on competition under federal and state law. The union claims immunity from federal antitrust statutes and argues that federal labor regulation preempts state law.

I

Local 100 is the bargaining representative for workers in the plumbing and mechanical trades in Dallas. When this litigation began, it was party to a multiemployer bargaining agreement with the Mechanical Contractors Association of Dallas, a group of about 75 mechanical contractors. That contract contained a "most favored nation" clause, by which the union agreed that if it granted a more favorable contract to any other employer it would extend the same terms to all members of the Association.

Connell Construction Co. is a general building contractor in Dallas. It obtains jobs by competitive bidding and subcontracts all plumbing and mechanical work. Connell has followed a policy of awarding these subcontracts on the basis of competitive bids, and it has done business with both union and nonunion subcontractors. Connell's employees are represented by various building trade unions. Local 100 has never sought to represent them or to bargain with Connell on their behalf.

In November 1970, Local 100 asked Connell to agree that it would subcontract mechanical work only to firms that had a current contract with the union.

. . .

When Connell refused to sign this agreement, Local 100 stationed a single picket at one of Connell's major construction sites. About 150 workers walked off the job, and construction halted. Connell filed suit in state court to enjoin the picketing as a violation of Texas antitrust laws. Local 100 removed the case to federal court. Connell then signed the subcontracting agreement under protest. It amended its complaint to claim that the agreement violated §§ 1 and 2 of the Sherman Act, and was therefore invalid. Connell sought a declaration to this effect and an injunction against any further efforts to force it to sign such an agreement.

By the time the case went to trial, Local 100 had submitted identical agreements to a number of other general contractors in Dallas. Five others had signed, and the union was waging a selective picketing campaign against those who resisted.

The District Court held that the subcontracting agreement was exempt from federal antitrust laws because it was authorized by the construction industry proviso to § 8(e) of the National Labor Relations Act. The court also held that federal labor legislation pre-empted the State's antitrust laws. The Court of Appeals for the Fifth Circuit affirmed, 483 F.2d 1154 (1973), with one judge dissenting. It held that Local 100's goal of organizing nonunion subcontractors was a legitimate union interest and that its efforts toward that goal were therefore exempt from federal antitrust laws. On the second issue, it held that state law was pre-empted . . . We granted certiorari on Connell's petition. We reverse on the question of federal antitrust immunity and affirm the ruling on state law pre-emption.

II

The basic sources of organized labor's exemption from federal antitrust laws are §§ 6 and 20 of the Clayton Act, and the Norris-La-Guardia Act. These statutes declare that labor unions are not combinations or conspiracies in restraint of trade, and exempt specific union activities, including secondary picketing and boycotts, from the operation of the antitrust laws. They do not exempt concerted action or agreements between unions and nonlabor parties. Mine Workers v. Pennington, 381 U.S. 657, 662, 85 S.Ct. 1585, 1589, 14 L.Ed.2d 626 (1965). The Court has recognized, however, that a proper accommodation between the congressional policy favoring collective bargaining under the NLRA and the congressional policy favoring free competition in business markets requires that some union-employer agreements be accorded a limited nonstatutory exemption from antitrust sanctions. Meat Cutters v. Jewel Tea Co., 381 U.S. 676, 85 S.Ct. 1596, 14 L.Ed.2d 640 (1965).

The nonstatutory exemption has its source in the strong labor policy favoring the association of employees to eliminate competition over wages and working conditions. Union success in organizing workers and standardizing wages ultimately will affect price competition among employers, but the goals of federal labor law never could be achieved if this effect on business competition were held a violation of the antitrust laws. The Court therefore has acknowledged that labor policy requires tolerance for the lessening of business competition based on differences in wages and working conditions. See Mine Workers v. Pennington, supra, 381 U.S. at 666, 85 S.Ct. at 1591; Jewel Tea, supra, 381 U.S. at 692–693, 85 S.Ct. at 1603–1604 (opinion of White, J.). Labor policy clearly does not require, however, that a union have freedom to impose direct restraints on competition among those who employ its members. Thus, while the statutory exemption allows unions to accomplish some restraints by acting unilaterally, e.g., Federation of Musicians v. Carroll, 391 U.S. 99, 88 S.Ct. 1562, 20 L.Ed.2d 460 (1968), the nonstatutory exemption offers no similar protection when a union and a nonlabor party agree to restrain competition in a business market.

In this case Local 100 used direct restraints on the business market to support its organizing campaign. The agreements with Connell and other general contractors indiscriminately excluded nonunion subcontractors from a portion of the market, even if their competitive advantages were not derived from substandard wages and working conditions but rather from more efficient operating methods. Curtailment of competition based on efficiency is neither a goal of federal labor policy nor a necessary effect of the elimination of competition among workers. Moreover, competition based on efficiency is a positive value that the antitrust laws strive to protect.

The multiemployer bargaining agreement between Local 100 and the Association, though not challenged in this suit, is relevant in determining the effect that the agreement between Local 100 and Connell would have on the business market. The "most favored nation" clause in the multiemployer agreement promised to eliminate competition between members of the Association and any other subcontractors that Local 100 might organize. By giving members of the Association a contractual right to insist on terms as favorable as those given any competitor, it guaranteed that the union would make no agreement that would give an unaffiliated contractor a competitive advantage over members of the Association. Subcontractors in the Association thus stood to benefit from any extension of Local 100's organization, but the method Local 100 chose also had the effect of sheltering them from outside competition in that portion of the market covered by subcontracting agreements between general contractors and Local 100. In that portion of the market, the restriction on subcontracting would eliminate competition on all subjects covered by the multiemployer agreement, even on subjects unrelated to wages, hours, and working conditions.

Success in exacting agreements from general contractors would also give Local 100 power to control access to the market for mechanical subcontracting work. The agreements with general contractors did not simply prohibit subcontracting to any nonunion firm; they prohibited subcontracting to any firm that did not have a contract with Local 100. The union thus had complete control over subcontract work offered by general contractors that had signed these agreements. Such control could result in significant adverse effects on the market and on consumers—effects unrelated to the union's legitimate goals of organizing workers and standardizing working conditions. For example, if the union thought the interests of its members would be served by having fewer subcontractors competing for the available work, it could refuse to sign collective-bargaining agreements with marginal firms. Or, since Local 100 has a well-defined geographical jurisdiction, it could exclude "traveling" subcontractors by refusing to deal with them. Local 100 thus might be able to create a geographical enclave for local contractors, similar to the closed market in *Allen Bradley*, supra.

This record contains no evidence that the union's goal was anything other than organizing as many subcontractors as possible.[95]

95. [This and the following 3 footnotes are from the majority's opinion, renumbered.] There was no evidence that Local 100's organizing campaign was connected with any agreement with members of the multiemployer bargaining unit, and the only evidence of agreement among those subcontractors was the "most favored nation" clause in the collective-bargaining agreement. In fact,

This goal was legal, even though a successful organizing campaign ultimately would reduce the competition that unionized employers face from nonunion firms. But the methods the union chose are not immune from antitrust sanctions simply because the goal is legal. Here Local 100, by agreement with several contractors, made nonunion subcontractors ineligible to compete for a portion of the available work. This kind of direct restraint on the business market has substantial anticompetitive effects, both actual and potential, that would not follow naturally from the elimination of competition over wages and working conditions. It contravenes antitrust policies to a degree not justified by congressional labor policy, and therefore cannot claim a nonstatutory exemption from the antitrust laws.

There can be no argument in this case, whatever its force in other contexts, that a restraint of this magnitude might be entitled to an antitrust exemption if it were included in a lawful collective-bargaining agreement. In this case, Local 100 had no interest in representing Connell's employees. The federal policy favoring collective bargaining therefore can offer no shelter for the union's coercive action against Connell or its campaign to exclude nonunion firms from the subcontracting market.

III

Local 100 nonetheless contends that the kind of agreement it obtained from Connell is explicitly allowed by the construction-industry proviso to § 8(e) and that antitrust policy therefore must defer to the NLRA. The majority in the Court of Appeals declined to decide this issue, holding that it was subject to the "exclusive jurisdiction" of the NLRB. This Court has held, however, that the federal courts may decide labor law questions that emerge as collateral issues in suits brought under independent federal remedies, including the antitrust laws. We conclude that § 8(e) does not allow this type of agreement.

Local 100's argument is straightforward: the first proviso to § 8(e) allows "an agreement between a labor organization and an employer in the construction industry relating to the contracting or subcontracting of work to be done at the site of the construction, alteration, painting, or repair of a building, structure or other work." [96]

Connell has not argued the case on a theory of conspiracy between the union and unionized subcontractors. It has simply relied on the multiemployer agreement as a factor enhancing the restraint of trade implicit in the subcontracting agreement it signed.

96. Section 8(e) provides:

It shall be an unfair labor practice for any labor organization and any employer to enter into any contract or agreement, express or implied, whereby such employer ceases or refrains or agrees to cease or refrain from handling, using, selling, transporting or otherwise dealing in any of the products of any other employer, or to cease doing business with any other person, and any contract or agreement entered into heretofore or hereafter containing such an agreement shall be to such extent unenforcible and void: Provided, That nothing in this subsection shall apply to an agreement between a labor organization and an employer in the construction industry relating to the contracting or subcontracting of work to be done at the site of the construction, alteration, painting, or repair of a building, structure, or other work . . . .." 29 U.S.C.A. § 158(e).

Local 100 is a labor organization, Connell is an employer in the construction industry, and the agreement covers only work "to be done at the site of construction, alteration, painting or repair of any building, structure, or other works." Therefore, Local 100 says, the agreement comes within the proviso. Connell responds by arguing that despite the unqualified language of the proviso, Congress intended only to allow subcontracting agreements within the context of a collective-bargaining relationship; that is, Congress did not intend to permit a union to approach a "stranger" contractor and obtain a binding agreement not to deal with nonunion subcontractors. On its face, the proviso suggests no such limitation. This Court has held, however, that § 8(e) must be interpreted in light of the statutory setting and the circumstances surrounding its enactment . . .

Section 8(e) was part of a legislative program designed to plug technical loopholes in § 8(b)(4)'s general prohibition of secondary activities. In § 8(e) Congress broadly proscribed using contractual agreements to achieve the economic coercion prohibited by § 8(b)(4). The provisos exempting the construction and garment industries were added by the Conference Committee in an apparent compromise between the House bill which prohibited all "hot cargo" agreements, and the Senate bill, which prohibited them only in the trucking industry. Although the garment-industry proviso was supported by detailed explanations in both Houses, the construction-industry proviso was explained only by bare references to "the pattern of collective bargaining" in the industry. It seems, however, to have been adopted as a partial substitute for an attempt to overrule this Court's decision in NLRB v. Denver Building & Construction Trades Council, 341 U.S. 675, 71 S.Ct. 943, 95 L.Ed. 1284 (1951). Discussion of "special problems" in the construction industry, applicable to both the § 8(e) proviso and the attempt to overrule *Denver Building Trades,* focused on the problems of picketing a single nonunion subcontractor on a multiemployer building project, and the close relationship between contractors and subcontractors at the jobsite. Congress limited the construction-industry proviso to that single situation, allowing subcontracting agreements only in relation to work done on a jobsite. In contrast to the latitude it provided in the garment-industry proviso, Congress did not afford construction unions an exemption from § 8(b)(4)(B) or otherwise indicate that they were free to use subcontracting agreements as a broad organizational weapon. . . .

Local 100 does not suggest that its subcontracting agreement is related to any of these policies. It does not claim to be protecting Connell's employees from having to work alongside nonunion men. The agreement apparently was not designed to protect Local 100's members in that regard, since it was not limited to jobsites on which they were working. Moreover, the subcontracting restriction applied only to the work Local 100's members would perform themselves and allowed free subcontracting of all other work, thus leaving open a possibility that they would be employed alongside nonunion subcontractors. Nor was Local 100 trying to organize a nonunion subcontractor on the building project it picketed. The union admits that it sought the agreement solely as a way of pressuring mechanical sub-contractors in the Dallas area to recognize it as the representative of their employees.

If we agreed with Local 100 that the construction-industry proviso authorizes subcontracting agreements with "stranger" contractors, not limited to any particular jobsite, our ruling would give construction unions an almost unlimited organizational weapon. The unions would be free to enlist any general contractor to bring economic pressure on nonunion subcontractors, as long as the agreement recited that it only covered work to be performed on some jobsite somewhere. The proviso's jobsite restriction then would serve only to prohibit agreements relating to subcontractors that deliver their work complete to the jobsite.

It is highly improbable that Congress intended such a result. One of the major aims of the 1959 Act was to limit "top-down" organizing campaigns, in which unions used economic weapons to force recognition from an employer regardless of the wishes of his employees. Congress accomplished this goal by enacting § 8(b)(7), which restricts primary recognitional picketing, and by further tightening § 8(b)(4)(B), which prohibits the use of most secondary tactics in organizational campaigns. Construction unions are fully covered by these sections. The only special consideration given them in organizational campaigns is § 8(f), which allows "prehire" agreements in the construction industry, but only under careful safeguards preserving workers' rights to decline union representation. The legislative history accompanying § 8(f) also suggests that Congress may not have intended that strikes or picketing could be used to extract prehire agreements from unwilling employers.

These careful limits on the economic pressure unions may use in aid of their organizational campaigns would be undermined seriously if the proviso to § 8(e) were construed to allow unions to seek subcontracting agreements, at large, from any general contractor vulnerable to picketing. Absent a clear indication that Congress intended to leave such a glaring loophole in its restrictions on "top-down" organizing, we are unwilling to read the construction-industry proviso as broadly as Local 100 suggests. Instead, we think its authorization extends only to agreements in the context of collective-bargaining relationships and in light of congressional references to the *Denver Building Trades* problem, possibly to common-situs relationships on particular jobsites as well.

Finally, Local 100 contends that even if the subcontracting agreement is not sanctioned by the construction-industry proviso and therefore is illegal under § 8(e), it cannot be the basis for antitrust liability because the remedies in the NLRA are exclusive. This argument is grounded in the legislative history of the 1947 Taft-Hartley amendments. Congress rejected attempts to regulate secondary activities by repealing the antitrust exemptions in the Clayton and Norris-La-Guardia Acts, and created special remedies under the labor law instead. It made secondary activities unfair labor practices under

§ 8(b)(4), and drafted special provisions for preliminary injunctions at the suit of the NLRB and for recovery of actual damages in the district courts. § 10(*l*) of the NLRA, and § 303 of the Labor Management Relations Act. But whatever significance this legislative choice has for antitrust suits based on those secondary activities prohibited by § 8(b)(4), it has no relevance to the question whether Congress meant to preclude antitrust suits based on the "hot cargo" agreements that it outlawed in 1959. There is no legislative history in the 1959 Congress suggesting that labor-law remedies for § 8(e) violations were intended to be exclusive, or that Congress thought allowing antitrust remedies in cases like the present one would be inconsistent with the remedial scheme of the NLRA.[97]

We therefore hold that this agreement, which is outside the context of a collective-bargaining relationship and not restricted to a particular jobsite, but which nonetheless obligates Connell to subcontract work only to firms that have a contract with Local 100, may be the basis of a federal antitrust suit because it has a potential for restraining competition in the business market in ways that would not follow naturally from elimination of competition over wages and working conditions.

IV

[In this part of its opinion the Court held that state antitrust law, regulating union activities in aid of organization, is preempted because of "a substantial risk of conflict with policies central to federal labor law." See p. 1132, supra.]

V

Neither the District Court nor the Court of Appeals decided whether the agreement between Local 100 and Connell, if subject to the antitrust laws, would constitute an agreement that restrains trade within the meaning of the Sherman Act. The issue was not

---

97. The dissenting opinion of Mr. Justice Stewart argues that § 303 provides the exclusive remedy for violations of § 8(e), thereby precluding recourse to antitrust remedies. For that proposition the dissenting opinion relies upon "considerable evidence in the legislative materials." Post, at 1848. In our view, these materials are unpersuasive. In the first place, Congress did not amend § 303 expressly to provide a remedy for violations of § 8(e). See Labor-Management Reporting and Disclosure Act of 1959, §§ 704(d), (e), 73 Stat. 544–545. The House in 1959 did reject proposals by Representatives Hiestand, Alger, and Hoffman to repeal labor's antitrust immunity. Post, at 1848–1851. Those proposals, however, were much broader than

the issue in this case. The Hiestand-Alger proposal would have repealed antitrust immunity for any action in concert by two or more labor organizations. The Hoffman proposal apparently intended to repeal labor's antitrust immunity entirely. That the Congress rejected these extravagant proposals hardly furnishes proof that it intended to extend labor's antitrust immunity to include agreements with nonlabor parties, or that it thought antitrust liability under the existing statutes would be inconsistent with the NLRA. The bill introduced by Senator McClellan two years later provides even less support for that proposition. Like most bills introduced in Congress, it never reached a vote.

briefed and argued fully in this Court. Accordingly, we remand for consideration whether the agreement violated the Sherman Act.

Reversed in part, affirmed in part, and remanded.

[Mr. Justice Douglas dissented on the ground that the union's conduct is regulated solely by the labor laws in the absence of allegations of an *Allen Bradley*-type conspiracy by the union and employer to restrain trade.]

MR. JUSTICE STEWART, with whom MR. JUSTICE DOUGLAS, MR. JUSTICE BRENNAN, and MR. JUSTICE MARSHALL join, dissenting.

. . .

For a period of 15 years, from passage of the Norris-LaGuardia Act, in 1932 until enactment of the Labor Management Relations Act (the Taft-Hartley Act), in 1947, union economic pressure directed against a neutral, secondary employer was not subject to sanctions under either federal labor law or antitrust law, at least in the absence of proof that the union was coercing the secondary employer in furtherance of a conspiracy with a nonlabor group. "Congress abolished, for purposes of labor immunity, the distinction between primary activity between the 'immediate disputants' and secondary activity in which the employer disputants and the members of the union do not stand 'in the proximate relation of employer and employee. . . .'" National Woodwork Mfrs. Assn. v. NLRB, 386 U.S. 612, 623, 87 S.Ct. 1250, 1257, 18 L.Ed.2d 357.

. . .

Congressional concern over labor abuses of the broad immunity granted by the Norris-LaGuardia Act was one of the considerations that resulted in passage of the Taft-Hartley Act in 1947, which, among other things, prohibited specified union secondary activity. The central thrust of that statutory provision was to forbid "a union to induce employees to strike against or to refuse to handle goods for their employer when an object is to force him or another person to cease doing business with some third party." Carpenters' Union v. NLRB, 357 U.S. 93, 98, 78 S.Ct. 1011, 1015, 2 L.Ed.2d 1186.[98] In condeming "specific union conduct directed to specific objectives," ibid., however, Congress deliberately chose not to subject unions engaging in prohibited secondary activity to the sanctions of the antitrust laws.

. . .

[The opinion traces the legislative history of 8(b)(4).]

98. [Footnote 2 from Justice Stewart's opinion.] The Act added § 8(b)(4) to the National Labor Relations Act, making it an unfair labor practice for a labor organization or its agents "to engage in, or to induce or encourage the employees of any employer to engage in, a strike or a concerted refusal in the course of their employment to use, manufacture, process, transport, or otherwise handle or work on any goods, articles, materials, or commodities or to perform any services, where an object thereof is: (A) forcing or requiring any employer or self-employed person to join any labor or employer organization or any employer or other person to cease using, selling, handling, transporting, or otherwise dealing in the products of any other producer, processor, or manufacturer or to cease doing business with any other person . . . ." 61 Stat. 141.

With only "clarifying changes," the House-Senate Conferees and then both Houses of Congress agreed to regulate union secondary activity by making specified activity an unfair labor practice under § 8(b)(4) of the National Labor Relations Act, authorizing the Board to seek injunctions against such activity, 29 U.S.C. § 160(*l*), and providing for recovery of actual damages in a suit by a private party under Senator Taft's compromsie proposal, which became § 303 of the Labor Management Relations Act, 29 U.S.C. § 187. Congress in 1947 did not prohibit all secondary activity by labor unions, and those practices which it did outlaw were to be remedied only by seeking relief from the Board or by pursuing the newly created, exclusive federal damages remedy provided by § 303.

II

Contrary to the assertion in the Court's opinion, the deliberate congressional decision to make § 303 the exclusive private remedy for unlawful secondary activity is clearly relevant to the question of Local 100's antitrust liability in the case before us. The Court is correct, of course, in noting that § 8(e)'s prohibition of "hot cargo" agreements was not added to the Act until 1959, and that § 303 was not then amended to cover § 8(e) violations standing alone. But as part of the 1959 amendments designed to close "technical loopholes" perceived in the Taft-Hartley Act, Congress amended § 8(b)(4) to make it an unfair labor practice for a labor organization to threaten or coerce a neutral employer, either directly or through his employees, where an object of the secondary pressure is to force the employer to enter into an agreement prohibited by § 8(e). At the same time, Congress expanded the scope of the § 303 damages remedy to allow recovery of the actual damages sustained as a result of a union's engaging in secondary activity to force an employer to sign an agreement in violation of § 8(e).[99] In short, Congress has provided an employer like Connell with a fully effective private damages remedy for the allegedly unlawful union conduct involved in this case.

The essence of Connell's complaint is that it was coerced by Local 100's picketing into "conspiring" with the union by signing an agreement that limited its ability to subcontract mechanical work on a competitive basis. If, as the Court today holds, the subcontracting agreement is not within the construction-industry proviso to § 8(e), then Local 100's picketing to induce Connell to sign the agreement consti-

99. [Footnote 6 from Justice Stewart's opinion.] Section 303, as amended by the Labor-Management Reporting and Disclosure Act of 1959, 73 Stat. 519, 545, now provides:

"(a) It shall be unlawful, for the purpose of this section only, in an industry or activity affecting commerce, for any labor organization to engage in any activity or conduct defined as an unfair labor practice in section 158(b)(4) of this title.

"(b) Whoever shall be injured in his business or property by reason o[f] any violation of subsection (a) of this section may sue therefor in any district court of the United States subject to the limitations and provisions of section 185 of this title without respect to the amount in controversy, or in any other court having jurisdiction of the parties, and shall recover the damages by him sustained and the cost of the suit." 29 U.S.C. § 187.

tuted a § 8(b)(4) unfair labor practice, and was therefore also unlawful under § 303(a). Accordingly, Connell has the right to sue Local 100 for damages sustained as a result of Local 100's unlawful secondary activity pursuant to § 303(b), 29 U.S.C. § 187(b). Although "limited to actual, compensatory damges," Teamsters v. Morton, 377 U.S., at 260, 84 S.Ct. at 1258, Connell would be entitled under § 303 to recover all damages to its business that resulted from the union's coercive conduct, including any provable damage caused by Connell's inability to subcontract mechanical work to nonunion firms. Similarly, any nonunion mechanical contractor who believes his business has been harmed by Local 100's having coerced Connell into signing the subcontracting agreement is entitled to sue the union for compensatory damages; for § 303 broadly grants its damages action to "[w]hoever shall be injured in his business or property" by reason of a labor organization's engaging in a § 8(b)(4) unfair labor practice.[1]

. . .

In sum, the legislative history of the 1947 and 1959 amendments and additions to national labor law clearly demonstrates that Congress did not intend to restore antitrust sanctions for secondary boycott activity such as that engaged in by Local 100 in this case, but rather intended to subject such activity only to regulation under the National Labor Relations Act and § 303 of the Labor Management Relations Act. The judicial imposition of "independent federal remedies" not intended by Congress, no less than the application of state law to union conduct that is either protected or prohibited by federal labor law, threatens "to upset the balance of power between labor and management expressed in our national labor policy." Accordingly, the judgment before us should be affirmed.

1. [Footnote 9 from Justice Stewart's opinion.] If Connell and Local 100 had entered into a purely voluntary "hot cargo" agreement in violation of § 8(e), an injured nonunion mechanical subcontractor would have no § 303 remedy because the union would not have engaged in any § 8(b)(4) unfair labor practice. The subcontractor, however, would still be able to seek, the full range of Board remedies available for a § 8(e) unfair labor practice. Moreover, if Connell had truly agreed to limit its subcontracting without any coercion whatsoever on the part of Local 100, the affected subcontractor might well have a valid antitrust claim on the ground that Local 100 and Connell were engaged in the type of conspiracy aimed at third parties with which this Court dealt in Allen Bradley Co. v. Electrical Workers, 325 U.S. 797, 65 S.Ct. 1533, 89 L.Ed. 1939. At the very least, an antitrust suit by an injured subcontractor under circumstances in which Congress had failed to provide any form of private remedy for damage resulting from an illegal "hot cargo" agreement would present a very different question from the one before us—a question which it is not now necessary to answer. Cf. Meat Cutters v. Jewel Tea Co., 381 U.S. 676, 708 n. 9, 85 S.Ct. 1607, 1613, 14 L.Ed.2d 640 (opinion of Goldberg, J.).

On the other hand, the signatory of a purely voluntary agreement that violates § 8(e) is fully protected from any damage that might result from the illegal "hot cargo" agreement by his ability simply to ignore the contract provision that violates § 8(e). If the union should attempt to enforce the illicit "hot cargo" clause through any form of coercion, the employer may then bring a § 303 damages suit or may file an unfair labor practice charge with the Board. See 29 U.S.C. § 158(b)(4)(B). Since § 8(e) provides that any prohibited agreement is "unenforcible and void," any union effort to invoke legal processes to compel the neutral employer to comply with his purely voluntary agreement would obviously be unavailing.

NOTES AND QUERIES

(1) *The Distinction Between the Statutory and Non-Statutory Labor Exemption.* The distinction drawn in *Connell* between the "statutory" and "non-statutory" exemption has since become critical for analyzing labor-antitrust cases. The Court traces the non-statutory exemption to *Jewel Tea*, supra. Do you find it there? Review the language of Sections 6 and 20 of the Clayton Act, supra pp. 1072–1073. Do you find that language (the "statutory exemption"?) helpful in deciding any of the cases in this section? Is there any indication that the Court, in *any* of these cases, has paid particularly close attention to the statutory language? Or has the Court, in each case, been involved in balancing antitrust policy expressed in the Sherman Act against labor policy expressed in the Clayton Act and the labor laws?

Does the distinction drawn in *Connell* between a statutory and non-statutory exemption imply that the non-statutory exemption is weaker? If not, why draw the distinction? *Connell* indicates that the "non-statutory" exemption applies when there is agreement with a non-labor group. Does this mean that labor is safest when it is unsuccessful in obtaining the goals it seeks?

(2) *Using the Statutory Exemption—The Union as a Buyers' Cartel.* The statutory exemption was further explicated by the Supreme Court in *H.A. Artists & Associates, Inc. v. Actors' Equity Association.*[2] Defendant union represented the vast majority of stage actors and actresses in the United States. In addition to negotiating collective bargaining agreements with theatrical producers, the union established a "licensing" system for theatrical agents (who find jobs for actors) under which the union regulated the agents' commission rates. The agents were required to pay a yearly license fee to the union; under union rules, union members were forbidden from dealing with non-licensed agents. The district court and court of appeals had found the licensing system exempt from antitrust liability. The Supreme Court unanimously affirmed:[3]

> Labor unions are lawful combinations that serve the collective interests of workers, but they also possess the power to control the character of competition in an industry. Accordingly, there is an inherent tension between national antitrust policy, which seeks to maximize competition, and national labor policy, which encourages cooperation among workers to improve the conditions of employment. In the years immediately following passage of the Sherman Act, courts enjoined strikes as unlawful restraints of trade when a union's conduct or objectives were deemed "socially or economically harmful." *Duplex Printing Press Co. v. Deering*, 254 U.S. 443, 485, 41 S.Ct. 172, 183, 65 L.Ed. 349 (Brandeis, J., dissenting). In response to these practices, Congress acted, first in the Clayton Act and later in the Norris-LaGuardia Act, to immunize labor unions and labor disputes from challenge under the Sherman Act.

· · ·

In *United States v. Hutcheson*, 312 U.S. 219, 61 S.Ct. 463, 85 L.Ed. 788, the Court held that labor unions acting in their self-interest and not

2. 451 U.S. 704, 101 S.Ct. 2102, 68 L.Ed.2d 558 (1981).

3. 451 U.S., at 713–22, 101 S.Ct., at 2108–12, 68 L.Ed.2d at 566–73. The majority reversed the court of appeals decision that the licensing fees were a permissible component of the regulatory system, finding Equity's "cost-covering" justification "inadequate." Chief Justice Burger, and Justices Brennan and Marshall dissented on this point.

in combination with nonlabor groups enjoy a statutory exemption from Sherman Act liability. . . .

The statutory exemption does not apply when a union combines with a "non-labor group." *Hutcheson,* 312 U.S., at 232, 61 S.Ct., at 466. Accordingly, antitrust immunity is forfeited when a union combines with one or more employers in an effort to restrain trade. In *Allen Bradley v. Electrical Workers,* 325 U.S. 797, 65 S.Ct. 1533, 89 L.Ed. 1939, for example, the Court held that a union had violated the Sherman Act when it combined with manufacturers and contractors to erect a sheltered local business market in order "to bar all other businessmen from [the market], and to charge the public prices above a competitive level." Id., at 809, 65 S.Ct., at 1539. The Court indicated that the union efforts would, standing alone, be exempt from antitrust liability, ibid., but because the union had not acted unilaterally, the exemption was denied. Congress "intended to outlaw business monopolies. A business monopoly is no less such because a union participates, and such participation is a violation of the Act." Id., at 811, 65 S.Ct., at 1540.[4]

The Court of Appeals properly recognized that the threshold issue was to determine whether or not Equity's franchising of agents involved any combination between Equity and any "non-labor groups," or persons who are not "parties to a labor dispute."[5] And the court's conclusion that the trial court had not been clearly erroneous in its finding that there was no combination between Equity and the theatrical producers to create or maintain the franchise system is amply supported by the record.

The more difficult problem is whether the combination between Equity and the agents who agreed to become franchised was a combination with a "non-labor group." The answer to this question is best understood in light of *American Federation of Musicians v. Carroll,* 391 U.S. 99, 88 S.Ct. 1562, 20 L.Ed.2d 460. There, four orchestra leaders, members of the American Federation of Musicians, brought an action based on the Sherman Act challenging the union's unilateral system of regulating "club dates," or one-time musical engagements. These regulations, *inter alia,* enforced a closed shop; required orchestra leaders to engage a minimum number of "sidemen," or instrumentalists; prescribed minimum prices for local engagements; prescribed higher minimum prices for traveling orchestras; and permitted leaders to deal only with booking agents licensed by the union.

Without disturbing the finding of the Court of Appeals that the orchestra leaders were employers and independent contractors, the Court concluded that they were nonetheless a "labor group" and parties to a "labor dispute" within the meaning of the Norris-LaGuardia Act, and

---

4. [Court's footnote 19.] Even where there are union agreements with nonlabor groups that may have the effect of sheltering the nonlabor groups from competition in product markets, the Court has recognized a "nonstatutory" exemption to shield such agreements if they are intimately related to the union's vital concerns of wages, hours and working conditions. See, e.g., Meat Cutters v. Jewel Tea, 381 U.S. 676, 85 S.Ct. 1596, 14 L.Ed. 2d 640. This nonstatutory exemption was described . . . in Connell Construction Co. v. Plumbers & Steamfitters . . . .. Neither the District Court nor

the Court of Appeals in this case decided whether the nonstatutory exemption would independently shield the respondent from the petitioners' antitrust claims.

5. [Court's footnote 20.] Of course, a party seeking refuge in the statutory exemption must be a bona fide labor organization, and not an independent contractor or entrepreneur. There is no dispute about Equity's status as a bona fide labor organization. [Should there have been?—Ed.]

thus that their involvement in the union regulatory scheme was not an unlawful combination between "labor" and "non-labor" groups. The Court agreed with the trial court that the applicable test was whether there was "job or wage competition or some other economic interrelationship affecting legitimate union interests between the union members and the independent contractors."

The Court also upheld the restrictions on booking agents, who were *not* involved in job or wage competition with union members. Accordingly, these restrictions had to meet the "other economic interrelationship" branch of the disjunctive test quoted above. And the test was met because those restrictions were "at least as intimately bound up with the subject of wages ' . . . as the price floors.' " The Court noted that the booking agent restrictions had been adopted, in part, because agents had "charged exorbitant fees, and booked engagements for musicians at wages . . . below union scale."

The restrictions challenged by the petitioners in this case are very similar to the agent restrictions upheld in the *Carroll* case. The essential features of the regulatory scheme are identical: members are permitted to deal only with agents who have agreed (1) to honor their fiduciary obligations by avoiding conflicts of interest, (2) not to charge excessive commissions and (3) not to book members for jobs paying less than the union minimum. And as in *Carroll*, Equity's regulation of agents developed in response to abuses by employment agents who occupy a critical role in the relevant labor market. The agent stands directly between union members and jobs, and is in a powerful position to evade the union's negotiated wage structure.

The peculiar structure of the legitimate theater industry, where work is intermittent, where it is customary if not essential for union members to secure employment through agents, and where agents' fees are calculated as a percentage of a member's wage, makes it impossible for the union to defend even the integrity of the minimum wages it has negotiated without regulation of agency fees. The regulations are "brought within the labor exemption . . . [because they are] necessary to assure that scale wages will be paid. . . ." *Carroll*, 391 U.S., at 112, 88 S.Ct., at 1570. They "embody a direct frontal attack upon a problem thought to threaten the maintenance of the basic wage structure." *Teamsters Union v. Oliver*, 358 U.S. 283, at 294, 79 S.Ct. 297, at 303, 3 L.Ed.2d 312. Agents must, therefore, be considered a "labor group," and their controversy with Equity is plainly a "labor dispute" as defined in the Norris La-Guardia Act: "representation of persons in negotiating, fixing, maintaining, changing, or seeking to arrange terms or conditions of employment, regardless of whether or not the disputants stand in the proximate relation of employer and employee." 29 U.S.C. § 113.

Agents perform a function—the representation of union members in the sale of their labor—that in most nonentertainment industries is performed exclusively by unions. In effect, Equity's franchise system operates as a substitute for maintaining a hiring hall as the representative of its members seeking employment.

Finally, Equity's regulations are clearly designed to promote the union's legitimate self-interest. *Hutcheson*, 312 U.S., at 232, 61 S.Ct., at 466. In a case such as this, where there is no direct wage or job competition between the union and the group it regulates, the *Carroll* formulation to determine the presence of a nonlabor group—whether there is "some . . . economic interrelationship affecting legitimate union interests . . ."—necessarily resolves this issue.

Queries. Could the union, similarly, set the rates its members will pay lawyers involved in contract negotiations? [6] Does the test used by Justice White in *Jewel Tea* and *Pennington* help? Or is it irrelevant now, on the ground that those cases involved the non-statutory exemption? How would the union have fared had it been viewed as agreeing with "non-labor" groups and therefore entitled (only?) to the non-statutory exemption?

(3) *The Conflict Between Antitrust and Labor Law Remedies.* The history of applying the antitrust laws to labor unions illustrates a constant conflict between hostile courts imposing liability and Congress creating a more balanced system of labor law regulation designed to deal in an expert way with labor-management conflict. Does *Connell* give too little weight to this history? Should the Court have been more inclined to refer the parties to labor law remedies, particularly when Connell could either have sued for single-damages arising out of the union's *picketing* (but not the contract Connell "agreed" to),[7] or breached the resulting contract and avoided liability on a theory of illegality (see *Kaiser Steel v. Mullins*, discussed infra). Or is *Connell* properly part of the Supreme Court's more general critical approach to "special interest" antitrust exemptions—whether for lawyers, insurance company practices, or municipalities[8]—allowing liability for anticompetitive conduct unprotected by any labor policy, because the conduct occurred outside a collective bargaining agreement and constituted an unfair labor practice?

(4) *Labor-Antitrust Litigation and "Primary Jurisdiction".* Whether a dispute should be litigated before the N.L.R.B. as an unfair labor practice first, or can be litigated as an antitrust case independent of the N.L.R.B., can pose vexing jurisdictional and substantive questions. For example, the 1969 collective bargaining agreement between the International Longshoremen's Association and shippers, regulating the use of containers in the ocean shipping industry, provoked a spate of antitrust and labor law litigation. Longshoremen, concerned about the widespread use of giant containers and container ships taking work from them, negotiated work rules restricting the

6. The Court attempted to meet this argument as follows:

The petitioners argue that theatrical agents are indistinguishable from "numerous other groups of persons who merely supply products and services to union members" such as landlords, grocers, accountants and lawyers. But it is clear that agents differ from these groups in two critical respects: the agents control access to jobs and negotiation of the terms of employment. For the actor or actress, therefore, agent commissions are not merely a discretionary expenditure of disposable income, but a virtually inevitable concomitant of obtaining employment.

451 U.S., at 719 n. 25, 101 U.S., at 2111–12, n. 25, 68 L.Ed.2d, at 572 n. 25.

7. See Section 303 of the Taft-Hartley Act, amended by the Landrum-Griffin Act, which provides: (a) It shall be unlawful, for the purpose of this section only, in an industry or activity affecting commerce, for any labor organization to engage in any activity or conduct defined as an unfair labor practice in section 158(b)(4) of this title.

(b) Whoever shall be injured in his business or property by reason of any violation of subsection (a) may sue therefor in any district court of the United States subject to the limitations and provisions of section 185 of this title without respect to the amount in controversy, or in any other court having jurisdiction of the parties, and shall recover the damages by him sustained and the cost of the suit. 29 U.S.C.A. § 187.

8. E.g., Goldfarb v. Virginia State Bar, discussed supra pp. 413–414; Union Labor Life Insurance Co. v. Pireno, ___ U.S. ___, 102 S.Ct. 3002, 73 L.Ed.2d 647 (1982) (discussing other McCarran-Ferguson Act cases); Community Communications Co., Inc. v. City of Boulder, discussed supra pp. 820–834.

packing of containers away from dockside for cargoes less than container size. The rules required that containers that were filled by consolidating unrelated lots would be stripped and repacked at the dock by union members, if the containers had been packed within a fifty mile radius of the dock. Shippers and firms engaged in consolidating less-than-container loads challenged the rules through antitrust and labor law suits filed in several circuits and before the N.L.R.B.[9] The resulting procedural quagmire finally caused the Third Circuit to vacate an earlier antitrust decision that the Supreme Court remanded for reconsideration,[10] and to stay proceedings on the antitrust claims pending N.L.R.B. consideration of unfair labor practice charges remanded to the Board as a result of an appeal of the labor law cases in the Supreme Court.[11] Left unanswered, among other issues, was the ultimate collateral estoppel impact of the Board's decision on the labor law issues in the pending antitrust cases challenging the container rules on antitrust grounds.

Compare this history with the Supreme Court's willingness to decide the 8(e) issue in *Connell*. Consider also the subsequent decision in *Kaiser Steel Corp. v. Mullins*,[12] involving the National Coal Wage Agreement of 1974, a collectively bargained agreement requiring signatory coal producers to make payments to the United Mine Workers' health and retirement funds based on the amount of coal produced and the hours worked by covered employees. The Agreement also required the employers to make payments for coal purchased or acquired from other producers, if those producers had not made contributions to the UMW's funds. For a period of four years Kaiser failed to report or make payments on coal it purchased from non-signatories for use in its steel manufacturing, while paying on coal it produced itself. In a suit under federal law by the union to collect these royalties, Kaiser asserted a defense of illegality, claiming the agreement violated Sections 1 and 2 of the Sherman Act and Section 8(e) of the Labor Management Relations Act (the "hot cargo" provision discussed in *Connell*, supra). The Supreme Court held that contract illegality is a defense where enforcement compels conduct forbidden by the antitrust laws or where the clause violates Section 8(e). With regard to the argument that the 8(e) illegality defense could not be entertained in court because it was committed to the exclusive jurisdiction of the N.L.R.B., the Court wrote:

> The Court of Appeals [in *Connell*] refused to decide whether § 8(e) permitted the agreement or whether the agreement constituted an unfair labor practice under § 8(e), holding that the NLRB "has exclusive jurisdiction to decide in the first instance what Congress meant in 8(e) and 8(b) (4)." This Court reversed on the ground that "the federal courts may decide labor law questions that emerge as collateral issues in suits brought under independent federal remedies, including the antitrust laws." The Court then addressed the § 8(e) issue on the merits and found that § 8(e) did not allow the agreement at issue. As a result, the agreement was subject to the antitrust laws, for the majority was persuaded that the legislative history did not suggest "labor-law remedies for § 8(e) violations were intended to be exclusive, or that Congress

9. Consolidated Express, Inc. v. New York Shipping Association, 602 F.2d 494 (3d Cir. 1979), vacated and remanded 448 U.S. 902, 100 S.Ct. 3040, 65 L.Ed.2d 1131 (1980).

10. See Consolidated Express, Inc. v. New York Shipping Association, 641 F.2d 90 (3d Cir. 1981).

11. See National Labor Relations Board v. International Longshoremen's Association, 447 U.S. 490, 100 S.Ct. 2305, 65 L.Ed.2d 289 (1980).

12. 455 U.S. 72, 102 S.Ct. 851, 70 L.Ed.2d 833 (1982).

thought allowing antitrust remedies in cases like the present one would be inconsistent with the remedial scheme of the NLRA."

In *Connell*, we decided the § 8(e) issue in the first instance. It was necessary to do so to determine whether the agreement was immune from the antitrust laws. Here a court must decide whether the purchased coal clause violates § 8(e) in order to determine whether to enforce the clause. . . . [W]here a § 8(e) defense is raised by a party where the defense is not directed to a collateral matter but to the portion of the contract for which enforcement is sought, a court must entertain the defense. While only the Board may provide affirmative remedies for unfair labor practices, a court may not enforce a contract provision which violates § 8(e). Were the rule otherwise, parties could be compelled to comply with contract clauses, the lawfulness of which would be insulated from review by any court.[13]

Queries. What impact will the *Mullins* decision have on collective bargaining and the resolution of disputes arising under a collectively bargained contract? Might parties to labor negotiations make "concessions" in the course of labor negotiations which they intend later to back out of on the ground of antitrust or 8(e) illegality?

C.　DETERMINING THE APPROPRIATE ANTITRUST STANDARD TO BE APPLIED TO NON–EXEMPT ACTIVITY

LARRY V. MUKO, INC. v. SOUTHWESTERN PENNSYLVANIA BUILDING & CONSTRUCTION TRADES COUNCIL (MUKO II)

United States Court of Appeals for the Third Circuit, 1982.
670 F.2d 421, certiorari denied ___ U.S. ___, 103 S.Ct. 229, 74 L.Ed.2d 182 (1982).

ADAMS, CIRCUIT JUDGE.

This is the second time this case has come before us. In *Larry V. Muko, Inc. v. Southwestern Pennsylvania Building and Construction Trades Council,* 609 F.2d 1368 (3d Cir. 1979) [*Muko* I], this Court, sitting *in banc,* reversed a district court order granting defendant's motion for a directed verdict and remanded the case for a new trial. The second trial resulted in a jury verdict for the defendants, and the plaintiff once again has appealed to this Court. We affirm.

I.

Long John Silver's, Inc. ("Silver's"), a Delaware corporation headquartered in Lexington, Kentucky, operates fast food seafood restaurants in several markets across in the United States. In 1973, it decided to enter the Pittsburgh, Pennsylvania market, and contracted

---

13. 455 U.S., at 86, 102 S.Ct., at 860, 70 L.Ed.2d, at 844–45. See also Urban, The Antitrust Exemption for Labor Organizations in the Construction Industry—Application of the 8(e) Proviso after Connell Construction Co. v. Plumbers and Steamfitters Local 100, 2 Whitt.L. Rev. 285 (1980); Silbergeld, Hot Cargo Agreements After Connell Construction Company: Recent Decisions of the N.L. R.B., 5 Empl.Rel. L.J. 560 (1980).

with Larry V. Muko, Inc. ("Muko"), a non-union general contractor experienced in constructing fast food restaurants, to build its first outlet in Monroeville, a suburb of Pittsburgh. After completion of the Monroeville restaurant, Silver's president Jim Patterson met with Larry Muko and indicated his willingness to give future construction business to Muko if his prices remained competitive and the quality of his construction remained good. Muko was awarded a contract to build a second restaurant in Lower Burrell, Pennsylvania, but Silver's did not commit itself any further.

During construction of the Monroeville restaurant, two labor organizations, the Southwestern Pennsylvania Building and Construction Trades Council and the Building and Construction Trades Council of Pittsburgh (the "Councils"), picketed the site. After completion of construction, handbills were distributed to customers of the Monroeville restaurant urging them not to patronize Silver's because the chain used "contractors who are paying less than the established prevailing wages in the area." The handbill exhorted the customers "to protect the living and working standards established by the Building Trades Council."

Silver's management was alarmed when it was informed that customers were leaving the premises after reading the handbill. In response to the leafletting, Silver's arranged a meeting with the Building Trades Councils. After the meeting, Silver's vice-president sent a letter to the Councils emphasizing the company's "desire to establish good working relationships with the unions in the Greater Pittsburgh Area" and stating Silver's "intent . . . to use only union contractors certified by the [Councils]" in the future. The letter concluded: "In any relationship between two parties there must be mutual need and assistance . . .. It is . . . extremely important to both parties that our location at Monroeville, Pennsylvania and the one under construction in Lower Burrell Township, Pennsylvania not be subjected to any kind of informational picketing."

Subsequently, Silver's employed only unionized general contractors to build its Pittsburgh-area restaurants, although the general contractors were free to use non-union subcontractors. Silver's discussed with Muko the question whether Muko would be willing to bid on the construction of its restaurants as a union firm. Muko declined to build under such circumstances, however, and it was not awarded any of Silver's contracts after the construction of the Lower Burrell restaurant.

On August 12, 1975, Muko filed the present lawsuit against Silver's and the two Councils, alleging that the defendants had entered into an agreement to award contracts for the construction of Silver's restaurants in the Pittsburgh area only to union contractors. This, claimed Muko, was an unreasonable restraint of trade in violation of section 1 of the Sherman Act and sections 4 and 16 of the Clayton Act. After Muko presented its case at a jury trial held on July 19–20, 1977, the district court granted the defendants' motion for a directed verdict. The directed verdict apparently was granted "because the court believed the evidence could sustain no finding other than a unilateral decision on the part of Silver's to accept bids only from union contractors." 609 F.2d at 1372. On appeal, this Court, sitting *in banc*, reversed and remanded the case for a new trial. 609 F.2d 1368. We held that the jury could have found an agreement between Silver's and the Councils that was not exempt from antitrust scrutiny because, under the standards set forth in *Connell Construction Co. v. Plumbers & Steamfitters Local 100*, 421 U.S. 616, 95 S.Ct. 1830, 44 L.Ed.2d 418 (1975), such an agreement might have "actual or potential anticompetitive effects that would not flow naturally from the elimination of competition over wages and working conditions." 609 F.2d at 1373.

Upon remand, a bifurcated jury trial on issues of liability and damages took place. . . . The jury . . . found that the defendants had reached an agreement, outside the labor exemption, to exclude Muko as a competitor for Silver's construction work. Because the jury concluded that the agreement was not an unreasonable restraint of trade, however, the district court entered judgment for the defendants. The district court subsequently denied Muko's motion for a new trial and denied defendants' conditional motions for judgment n.o.v. This appeal followed.

II.

Muko challenges two aspects of the district court proceeding. First, it claims that the trial judge erred as a matter of law when he instructed the jury to apply the rule of reason, rather than the *per se* standard, to the agreement at issue. Second, it argues that, even if the district judge was correct in applying the rule of reason, he erred in his instructions on the relevant product market. We disagree with both contentions.

III.

A.

In the earlier *en banc* opinion in this case, we declined to decide the proper standard by which to measure any potential antitrust violation. We intimated, however, that traditional antitrust principles would govern such a determination by the district court:

> The jury might have found a concerted refusal to deal with a class of contractors of which Muko is a member. But whether the evidence here is viewed as capable of sustaining a finding of a group boycott, to which a *per se* rule would apply, or some lesser restraint to which a rule of reason analysis might apply, it was sufficient to take Muko's case to the jury. We have no occasion on this record to rule on whether, after hearing the defendants' evi-

dence as well, the court should instruct the jury that it should measure the agreement by rule of reason or *per se* standards.

609 F.2d at 1376 (footnote omitted).

In counseling that the level of antitrust inquiry depends upon the nature of the conduct alleged, even in the labor-antitrust context, *Muko* I reflected the approach taken by a panel of this Court in *Consolidated Express, Inc. v. New York Shipping Association*, 602 F.2d 494 (3d Cir. 1979), vacated and remanded on other grounds, 448 U.S. 902, 100 S.Ct. 3040, 65 L.Ed.2d 1131 (1980) [*"Conex"*], a case decided several months prior to *Muko* I. There, the plaintiff was a freight consolidator whose business was threatened after defendants New York Shipping Association (an association of employers) and the longshoremen's union negotiated "Rules on Containers" and the so-called "Dublin Supplement" in response to the perceived threat to waterfront labor posed by technological change in the shipping industry. Conex claimed, *inter alia*, that the defendants' enforcement of the rules constituted a group boycott of the plaintiffs that was illegal *per se* under the Sherman Act.[14] We held, as an initial matter, "that the proper method of analysis is to determine the issue of nonstatutory labor exemption separately, . . . and then to proceed with conventional antitrust scrutiny of the complaint." 602 F.2d at 522. In so holding, the *Conex* Court expressly rejected Professor Handler's view "that there be a full-scale rule of reason inquiry in every instance in which a non-exempt activity is claimed to be in violation of antitrust." Handler, *Labor and Antitrust: A Bit of History*, 40 Antitrust L.J. 233, 239–40 (1971). Pointing to *United Mineworkers v. Pennington*, 381 U.S. 657, 85 S.Ct. 1585, 14 L.Ed.2d 626 (1965), and its companion case, *Local 189, Amalgamated Meat Cutters v. Jewel Tea Co.*, 381 U.S. 676, 85 S.Ct. 1596, 14 L.Ed.2d 640 (1965), Judge Gibbons concluded: "[T]he three groups of Justices in those cases, while they diverged widely on other issues, appear to have agreed that 'settled antitrust principles' would be 'appropriate and applica-

---

14. [This and the following 4 footnotes are from the Court's opinion, renumbered.] The National Labor Relations Board had previously held the rules to be a violation of § 8(e) of the NLRA, 29 U.S.C. § 158(e). That section declares that it "shall be an unfair labor practice for any labor organization and any employer to enter into any contract or agreement, express or implied, whereby such employer ceases or refrains or agrees to cease or refrain from handling, using, selling, transporting or otherwise dealing in any of the products of any other employer, or to cease doing business with any other person. . . ." In NLRB v. International Longshoremen's Ass'n, 447 U.S. 490, 100 S.Ct. 2305, 65 L.Ed.2d 289 (1980), however, a related case on certiorari from the District of Columbia Circuit, the Supreme Court held

that, in determining that the agreement implementing the Rules on Containers violated § 8(e), the Board had applied an incorrect legal standard. The Court therefore remanded that case to the Board for further proceedings, and subsequently vacated and remanded our decision in Conex for further consideration in light of International Longshoremen's Ass'n, 448 U.S. at 902, 100 S.Ct. at 2305, 65 L.Ed.2d 289. On remand, we ordered Conex stayed pending disposition of the § 8(e) charge by the Board. 641 F.2d 90 (3d Cir. 1981). We noted, however, that those aspects of our earlier decision not predicated on a finding that § 8(e) had been violated—including, presumably, our discussion of the proper standard of antitrust scrutiny—were not affected by the vacation and stay. 641 F.2d at 94.

ble' to activity found to be nonexempt. . . . Those 'settled' principles include the *per se* rule, *where the facts warrant its application.*" 602 F.2d at 522–23 (emphasis added).

We take this opportunity explicitly to reaffirm the holding in *Conex,* as reflected implicitly in *Muko* I. In so doing we adopt a middle position between that advocated by Professor Handler and that proposed by the appellant in the case at hand. While we agree with Professor Handler that the "factors to be considered in determining the existence of an antitrust *exemption* are separate and distinct from those bearing on the presence of an antitrust *infraction,*" and that "once such conduct is deemed not exempt, it is incumbent upon the decisionmaker to consider the relative anticompetitiveness of the conduct before imposing antitrust liability," Handler & Zifchak, *Collective Bargaining and the Antitrust Laws: The Emasculation of the Labor Exemption,* 81 Colum.L.Rev. 459, 511 (1981), we do not share Professor Handler's view that union conduct necessarily "should be measured by the rule of reason in recognition of the peculiar labor relations context in which the restraint arises even if, in a nonlabor context, similar conduct might be per se unlawful." Id. at 510.[15] The mere fact that a labor union is one of the participants in an otherwise illegal combination should not preclude a determination that, in appropriate circumstances, the conduct is unreasonable *per se.* The *per se* rule is, essentially, a short cut employed by a court in determining unreasonableness; as Professor Sullivan has taught, "the *per se* doctrine is precisely a special case of rule of reason analysis." L. Sullivan, Handbook of the Law of Antitrust (1977). If, after extensive experience with a particular kind of union conduct, a court concludes that the conduct invariably restrains competition, it is unnecessary, in our view, for the court to engage in lengthy rule-of-reason analysis when the *per se* rule would yield identical results more efficiently and expeditiously.

It is important, however, to caution against mechanical or imprudent application of the *per se* rule in the labor context. A finding that particular union conduct has anticompetitive effects that do "not flow naturally from the elimination of competition over wages and working conditions," and hence is non-exempt under *Connell,* should not drive a court inexorably to the conclusion that the union has violated the antitrust laws. We thus cannot agree with Muko, who contends that every labor-antitrust case in which the labor exemption is found to be inapplicable should be held illegal under the *per se* standard.

---

15. Several commentators appear to share Professor Handler's view. See, e.g., Casey & Cozzillio, Labor-Antitrust: The Problems of *Connell* and a Remedy that Follows Naturally, 1980 Duke L.J. 235, 278; Comment, *Consolidated Express:* Antitrust Liability for Illegal Labor Activities, 80 Colum.L.Rev. 645, 660–63 (1980). Cf. Leslie, Principles of Labor Antitrust, 66 Va.L.Rev. 1183, 1222–24 (1980) (rejecting both the *per se* and the rule of reason standards and urging that union-imposed restrictions should be deemed unlawful "only if they involve price-fixing, output-restricting, or market-sharing arrangements").

In support of this proposition Muko points to the following language in the *Conex* opinion:

> [O]nce a court has concluded that the labor exemption does not shield anticompetitive conduct, application of the rule of reason is redundant. The justification offered for application of the rule of reason is the need to recognize, in the antitrust context, labor's legitimate interest in the collective bargaining process. That interest, however, is precisely the same one that must be taken into account in determining the scope of the nonstatutory labor exemption. A holding that the exemption does not apply embodies a judgment that considerations of labor policy are outweighed by the anticompetitive dangers posed by the challenged restraint. The proposed use of the rule of reason would, therefore, simply be an invitation to the court or jury to reweigh under a different label the question of the non-statutory exemption.

602 F.2d at 523–24.

Although this language appears to support Muko's contention, the actual holding in *Conex* is far narrower in scope. In *Conex*, in fact, this Court carefully analyzed the conduct in question before determining that it constituted a *per se* illegal group boycott. Indeed, the Court suggested that had procompetitive effects been shown, the boycott may have been removed from the category of *per se* violations. As the *Conex* majority points out, "public interest" considerations, such as the advancement of labor policy, are not proper subjects for examination under the rule of reason. *National Society of Professional Engineers v. United States,* 435 U.S. 679, 688, 98 S.Ct. 1355, 1363, 55 L.Ed.2d 637 (1978). The passage from *Conex* quoted above merely reflects the view that it is unnecessary, if not improper, to weigh "labor's legitimate interest in the collective bargaining process" twice—once in determining the labor exemption and again in deciding the antitrust liability question. There is no indication that the Court was prepared to find that the defendants' conduct was *per se* illegal merely because it was not exempt from the antitrust laws.[16] Moreover, in *Muko* I, Judge Gibbons—who earlier had written *Conex*—explicitly left open the possibility that a "lesser restraint," though nonexempt, might be judged under the rule of reason.

In short, a fair reading of both *Conex* and *Muko* I impels the conclusion that, once it is ascertained that union activity falls outside the protection of the labor exemption, a court must apply traditional antitrust principles in determining whether the activity in question vio-

---

16. We are thus unpersuaded by Muko's recitation of the legislative history of § 8(e) of the NLRA, (the so-called "hot cargo" provision) which indicates Congress' intent to make hot cargo agreements illegal *per se* under the labor laws. Brief for Appellant at 16–18. See note 2 supra. Even assuming that the defendants' conduct would be deemed illegal under § 8(e), we see no reason to presume that Congress intended the same conduct to be ipso facto violative of the antitrust laws, which were enacted at a different time, for a different purpose, and which provide for sharply different relief. See Connell Construction Co. v. Plumbers & Steamfitters Local 100, 421 U.S. 616, 634, 95 S.Ct. 1830, 1840, 44 L.Ed.2d 418 (1975).

lates the antitrust laws.[17] In most cases the rule of reason will supply the measure of illegality; the *per se* rule may, however, be invoked where appropriate. We turn now to this inquiry.

B.

Though framed in absolute terms, section 1 of the Sherman Act has been construed throughout its history to proscribe only *unreasonable* restraints of trade. . . . There are, however, "certain agreements or practices which because of their pernicious effect on competition and lack of any redeeming virtue are conclusively presumed to be unreasonable and therefore illegal without elaborate inquiry as to the precise harm they have caused or the business excuse for their use." *Northern Pacific Railway Co. v. United States*, 356 U.S. 1, 5, 78 S.Ct. 514, 518, 2 L.Ed.2d 545 (1958). Such determinations of *per se* illegality are not casually made. . . .

Group boycotts have typically been among those categories of conduct deemed unreasonable *per se*. In *Klor's*, [supra, p. 541] for example, the Supreme Court condemned as unlawful an agreement between a large chain department store and a group of manufacturers and distributors not to deal with a smaller, competing retail store.

. . .

Though *Klor's* appears flatly to proscribe group boycotts, whatever their form or function, courts and commentators alike continue to resist the notion that all concerted refusals to deal fall automatically as *per se* violations of the antitrust laws. Generally, the application of the *per se* rule has been limited to those "classic" boycotts in which a group of business competitors seek to benefit economically by excluding other competitors from the marketplace. "The crucial element" in such boycotts, according to Professor Sullivan, "is an effort to exclude or cause disadvantage to one or more competitors by

---

17. A number of other courts appear to have adopted a similar approach. See, e.g., Ackerman-Chillingworth v. Pacific Electrical Contractor Assoc., 579 F.2d 484, 490 n. 7 (9th Cir. 1978) (applying the rule of reason to the facts at issue, but noting: "in the absence of any of the competitive injuries wrought by the classic-type boycotts traditionally considered as unlawful *per se*, the district court properly rejected application of the *per se* rule"); Smith v. Pro Football, Inc., 593 F.2d 1173, 1177–82 (D.C.Cir. 1978) (applying the "traditional framework of analysis under § 1 of the Sherman Act," court concludes that the defendants' conduct should be tested under the rule of reason because it cannot be considered a classic group boycott, which would require invocation of the *per se* rule); Mackey v. National Football League, 543 F.2d 606, 618–19 (8th Cir. 1976), cert. dismissed, 434 U.S. 801, 98 S.Ct. 28, 54 L.Ed.2d 59 (1977) (same). But see Berman Enterprises Inc. v. Local 333, International Longshoremen's Assoc., 644 F.2d 930, 936 (2d Cir. 1981) (concluding without discussion that the rule of reason "would be applicable"); South-East Coal Company v. Consolidation Coal Company, 434 F.2d 767, 775 (6th Cir. 1970) (holding that "when a labor union and an employer enter into a plan or scheme of the type which results in the union closing its exemption from liability under the antitrust law, that plan or scheme is by definition an unreasonable restraint under the antitrust laws"). Cf. Commerce Tankers Corp. v. National Maritime Union of America, 553 F.2d 793, 802 (2d Cir. 1977) (court remands for consideration of antitrust claim without deciding which standard applies, but notes that there is "at least a substantial question whether a per se approach under the antitrust laws is applicable in the case of a non-exempt labor activity").

cutting them off from trade relationships which are necessary to any firm trying to compete. The classic boycott . . . also usually entails an effort to induce two or more suppliers or customers not to deal with firms being excluded from the protected level." L. Sullivan, *Handbook of the Law of Antitrust* 260 (1977).

While the Supreme Court has not confronted this issue directly, a survey of the Court's group boycott decisions in which the *per se* rule was invoked "confirms that it is attempts by competitors to exclude horizontal competitors which trigger the per se rule." Comment, *Protest Boycotts Under the Sherman Act*, 128 U.Pa.L.Rev. 1131, 1151 (1980). In *Klor's*, for example, the unlawful conduct was the attempt by one retailer to push a competitor out of the market. . . .

Our circuit is among those that have attempted to limit the application of the *per se* rule to the "classic" boycott. As we stated in *DeFilippo v. Ford Motor Co.*, 516 F.2d 1313, 1317 (3d Cir.) cert. denied, 423 U.S. 912, 96 S.Ct. 216, 46 L.Ed.2d 141 (1975):

> The inquiry in any case seeking to apply this rule of *per se* unreasonableness must be whether or not the activities of defendants properly fall within the "group boycott" categorization. . . . "The term 'group boycott' . . . is in reality a very broad label for divergent types of concerted activity. To outlaw certain types of business conduct merely by attaching the 'group boycott' and 'per se' labels obviously invites the chance that certain types of reasonable concerted activity will be proscribed."

Id. at 1317–18 . . .

In *DeFilippo*, we concluded, after surveying the relevant Supreme Court precedents, that a concerted activity constitutes a *per se* illegal "group boycott" only when " 'there [is] a purpose either to exclude a person or group from the market, or to accomplish some other anti-competitive objective, or both.' " 516 F.2d at 1318 . . . ..

In contrast, the Court indicated its willingness to apply the *per se* rule in *Cernuto, Inc. v. United Cabinet Corp.*, 595 F.2d 164 (3d Cir. 1979). There, the manufacturer of kitchen cabinets allegedly terminated its sales to a discount retailer at the urging of another competing retailer, who wished to maintain prices. Like *Klor's* and *General Motors*, the case involved the attempt of one competitor to squeeze out its direct competitor. "[A]lthough the termination in such a situation is, itself, a vertical restraint, the desired impact is horizontal and on the dealer, not the manufacturer, level." 595 F.2d at 168. Thus, we reversed the summary judgment entered in favor of the defendants on the ground that at trial a *per se* violation of the Sherman Act might be found. See Comment, *Vertical Agreement as Horizontal Restraint: Cernuto, Inc. v. United Cabinet Corp.*, 128 U.Pa.L.Rev. 622 (1980).

Finally, in *Conex*, discussed supra, we addressed the question whether a group boycott in the labor context was *per se* unreasonable. There, we outlined a "core group of situations" in which group boycotts have been deemed illegal *per se:*

> (1) horizontal combinations of traders at one level of distribution having the purpose of excluding direct competitors from the market; (2) vertical combinations, designed to exclude from the market direct competitors of some members of the combination; and (3) coercive combinations aimed at influencing the trade practices of boycott victims.

602 F.2d at 522.

In *Conex,* after holding that the Rules on Containers and the Dublin Supplement were not exempt from the antitrust laws, the Court concluded that the facts of the case did warrant the application of the *per se* rule. Specifically, we found that the rules had "horizontal, vertical, and coercive aspects": the goal of the union organization was "work acquisition" because the "union's efforts clearly were directed toward the elimination of teamster competition"; the rules "wholly bar" the plaintiffs from providing their services in the market in question; the "anticompetitive effect of [the] arrangement [was] clear"; nor was there "any suggestion in the record that the application of the Rules will in the long run have procompetitive rather than anticompetitive effects." In sum, the Court determined that the rules represented " 'agreements whose nature and necessary effect are so plainly anticompetitive that no elaborate study of the industry is needed to establish their illegality.' " *Conex* at 522–23, (quoting *National Society of Professional Engineers v. United States,* 435 U.S. 679, 98 S.Ct. 1355, 55 L.Ed.2d 637 (1978)).

C.

Applying the foregoing principles to the case at hand, we conclude that the agreement between Silver's and the Trade Councils should not be deemed unreasonable *per se.* A distillation of the facts at issue here makes it clear that this is not a classic group boycott; the defendants' conduct should not be proscribed until the factfinder has been given the opportunity to determine its reasonableness. Simply put, a small retailer has been picketed by a union. To preserve its business, the firm agrees to purchase union-made goods or services in the future. We cannot agree with Muko or the dissent that this is the kind of behavior against which the *per se* rule traditionally has been invoked. Unlike *Klor's* and *General Motors,* this is not a case in which one competitor, through concerted action with a supplier or customer, attempts to cut another, horizontal competitor out of the marketplace. Nor is there any suggestion of attempted price-fixing, as in *Cernuto.* Notwithstanding the dissent's assertion, which is not grounded on record evidence, that Muko "must be viewed as the representative of non-union labor," the fact remains that neither Silver's nor the Trades Councils was in competition with each other or with Muko. There is no evidence that Silver's goal was to affect Muko's business; rather, it is uncontradicted that Silver's sought only to retain the goodwill of its customers in a new market. The Councils' goal was to ensure payment of the prevailing union wage to Pittsburgh-area construction workers. The record is barren of anything to suggest that either of the defendants wished, through their concerted action, to gain an advantage over Muko in an *economic* or *competitive* sense. This fundamentally distinguishes the present case from *Conex*, which involved an agreement between the defendant longshoremen's union, common carriers, and stevedores to exclude from direct competition all the teamsters employed by the plaintiff freight consolidators.

We note, too, the limited nature of the restraint at issue here. Unlike *Conex*, in which the defendant union imposed a widespread restraint of trade, affecting the entire shipping industry, the "refusal to deal" in this case involved only one relatively small buyer: Silver's. Moreover, we fail to perceive the significant anticompetitive effects alleged by the appellant. Again, unlike *Conex*, the agreement did not have the necessary effect of destroying Muko's business; indeed, the evidence shows that Muko's profits increased during the time in question. Silver's also appeared prepared to give Muko the job of constructing future restaurants if Muko employed union labor. Finally, procompetitive effects were demonstrated—Silver's gained a position in the otherwise crowded Pittsburgh-area fast food market.

. . .

In sum, we have been referred to no case that suggests that the agreement at issue here is one "whose nature and necessary effect [is] so plainly anticompetitive that no elaborate study of the industry is needed. . . ." *Conex* at 522–23. Accordingly, we hold that the district court did not err in instructing the jury to apply the rule of reason, rather than the *per se* standard, to the conduct in question in this case.

[In part IV of its opinion, the Court rejected Muko's contention that the lower court had erroneously instructed the jury on relevant market standards. Muko, the trial court, and—apparently—the Court of Appeals all assumed relevant market analysis to be a necessary element of a rule of reason case. For criticism of this view, see Chapter 4, supra. p. 361.]

V.

To summarize, we hold that the district court correctly instructed the jury on the rule of reason standard as well as on the relevant product market. Accordingly, the order of the district court, entering judgment for the defendants, will be affirmed.

SLOVITER, CIRCUT JUDGE, dissenting.

My difference with the majority is narrow but fundamental. I agree with the majority that . . . "once it is ascertained that union activity falls outside the protection of the labor exemption, a court must apply traditional antitrust principles in determining whether the activity in question violates the antitrust laws." I disagree with the majority that the application of traditional antitrust principles to the agreement found by the jury in this case supports the trial court's instruction to the jury that the rule of reason rather than the *per se* standard must be applied.

Although the parties disagree on the inferences to be drawn from the evidence, the jury could have found that at the meeting on November 1, 1973, representatives of Silver's and the Trades Councils reached an agreement, the substance of which was reflected in the letter sent by Silver's Vice-President within a week thereafter, that Silver's would use only union contractors certified by the Trades Councils in the construction of the Silver's restaurants. . . .

The majority gives four reasons for its unwillingness to apply the *per se* standard usually applicable to concerted refusals to deal: (1) "neither Silver's nor the Trades Councils was in competition with each other or with Muko," and no evidence suggests that either defendant wished, through their concerted action, to gain an advantage over Muko in an economic or competitive sense; (2) "the 'refusal to deal' in this case involved only one relatively small buyer: Silver's", rather than the imposition of a "widespread restraint of trade"; (3) "the agreement did not have the necessary effect of destroying Muko's business," since his profits increased during the time in question and Silver's might have permitted Muko to construct future restaurants if Muko employed union labor; and (4) "procompetitive effects were demonstrated" because Silver's gained a position in the otherwise crowded Pittsburgh-area fast food market. I believe the grounds on which the majority bases its decision are either factually erroneous or legally irrelevant. Those grounds will be considered seriatim.

[As to reason # 1, the dissent, citing *St. Paul Fire & Marine Insurance Co. v. Barry*, 438 U.S. 531, 98 S.Ct. 2923, 57 L.Ed.2d 932 (1978), maintains that a *per se* unlawful "boycott" need not be one targeting competitors but includes concerted refusals to deal with a customer or to buy from a supplier. The competitive impact in this case is the exclusion of a non-union contractor in favor of unionized contractors. The agreement is a "classic boycott, one which entails exclusionary conduct for economic benefit."

As to reason # 2 the dissent points out that the restraint is not limited to "a single seller, a single buyer and a single transaction." The restraint involved a substantial building program by Silver's, a large geographic area, and a large number of non-union contractors. Moreover, citing *Klor's* and *Cernuto*, the dissent points out *per se* boycott analysis has not been waived simply because the victim is one small businessman. "Once the jury found 'a concerted refusal to deal with a class of contractors of which Muko is a member', it follows . . . that the agreement must be characterized as a group boycott and is one to which the *per se* rule applies."

As to reason # 3, the dissent characterizes the failure of the restraint to destroy Muko's business as "legally irrelevant" to the invocation of a *per se* rule. "The extent of injury, if any, suffered by Muko is evidence directed to the amount of damages to which he would be entitled rather than to the standard by which the conduct should be judged." Citing *National Society of Professional Engineers* the dissent concludes: "The 'necessary effect' of the agreement . . . is inevitably exclusionary" and it should therefore be declared *per se* unlawful without an "elaborate study of the industry."

As to reason # 4, the dissent disagreed with the majority's description of the restraint as providing "procompetitive effects" because it permitted Silver's to gain entry into the fast food market in Pittsburgh. "The self-interest of Silver's in avoiding union pickets and displeasure is hardly synonymous with a 'procompetitive effect.' Even if there were evidence of such an effect, antitrust cases have always rejected the premise that a procompetitive effect in one market will excuse an anticompetitive effect in another." The dissent concludes this portion of the opinion: "[T]he majority has proffered no legally cognizable basis for application of the rule of reason to an agreement not to use non-union contractors."]

Since I believe none of the reasons given by the majority to support the use of a rule of reason standard when unions conspire with business to exclude a non-union firm from the market withstands analysis, I conclude that the underlying rationale for the majority's approach must stem from its discomfort with the application of traditional antitrust rules in the labor context. Judge Adams candidly set forth his concern in his concurring opinion in *Muko I*, 609 F.2d at 1376–77. While there may be some merit in that position, it is, as Judge Adams recognized, one which we, as an inferior court, are not free to take in light of the Supreme Court's decision in *Connell*. Further, were we free to examine the issue anew, I have grave question whether the extension of labor's exemption from the antitrust laws should be accomplished by the courts or whether it should not be left to Congress.

For the aforesaid reasons, I would reverse the judgment of the district court, and remand for retrial so that the jury may apply a *per se* standard to the concerted refusal to deal which it already found existed and which it found extended beyond labor's nonstatutory exemption from the antitrust laws.

NOTES AND QUERIES

(1) *Manipulating Antitrust Standards of Per Se Illegality as a Device for Reconsidering the Question of Exemption.* *Muko I*[18] held (1) it was for the jury to determine whether the agreement's purpose was to exclude non-union contractors; and (2) if the jury so found, there was no statutory labor exemption from antitrust liability, citing *Pennington* and *Allen Bradley*. If there were no statutory exemption, immunity from the antitrust laws must "be found in the non-statutory exemption." In that regard, the opinion fur-

18. Larry V. Muko, Inc. v. Southwestern Pennsylvania Building & Construction Trades Council, 609 F.2d 1368 (3d Cir. 1979) (en banc).

ther held a jury could find that the non-statutory labor exemption was inapplicable:

> We understand *Connell* to hold, then, that an agreement between a union and a business organization, outside a collective bargaining relationship, which imposes a direct restraint upon a business market, and which is not justified by congressional labor policy because it has actual or potential anticompetitive effects that would not flow naturally from the elimination of competition over wages and working conditions, is not exempt from antitrust scrutiny.[19]

Judge Adams, author of the majority opinion in *Muko II*, wrote a concurring opinion in *Muko I* expressing misgivings about *Connell* and its application in *Muko I*:

> Were we in a position to decide this case on a clean slate, I would probably be inclined to hold that the union activity complained of here is not within the purview of the antitrust statutes but is instead solely a matter for scrutiny under labor law. I would subscribe to the view that unions ought to be subject to antitrust liability only when they combine with non-labor forces for the purpose of assisting those forces in suppressing commercial competition and in monopolizing the marketing of goods and services. When, however, unions are essentially pursuing traditional labor objectives, such as organizing employees or seeking to obtain higher wages and better working conditions for their members, it would appear logical to me that resort should be had primarily to labor law concepts to circumscribe the permissible scope of their conduct and to penalize them for their excesses.
>
> · · ·
>
> But whatever the merits of such an approach, the Supreme Court has rather clearly chosen to allow greater sway to the antitrust laws in the labor field. As the majority opinion points out, under the most recent Supreme Court pronouncement in *Connell* . . . it is immaterial for purposes of determining whether labor-related activity is exempt from possible antitrust scrutiny that the union has as its goal legitimate and legal objectives: "[T]he methods the union chose are not immune from antitrust sanctions simply because the goal is legal." So long as there is a "direct restraint on the busines market" having "substantial anticompetitive effects, both actual and potential, that would not flow naturally from the elimination of competition over wages and working conditions," *Connell* teaches, the union's activity "contravenes antitrust policies to a degree not justified by congressional labor policy, and therefore cannot claim a nonstatutory exemption from the antitrust laws." Given this explicit ruling by the Supreme Court, which I believe the majority has demonstrated is controlling as applied to the evidence introduced by the plaintiff in this case, I am constrained to join in the majority's opinion.[20]

Judge Aldisert, in a scholarly and far ranging dissent in *Muko I*, was more blunt in criticizing *Connell*:[21]

> Our late colleague Abraham Freedman was fond of saying at decision conferences, "The way you come out in this case depends on how you go in." Judge Freedman was expressing in a few words one of the most

---

19. 609 F.2d at 1373.

20. Id. at 1376–77.

21. Id. at 1377–87. The opinions are extensively analyzed in King & Moser,

Muko and Conex: The Third Circuit Responds to *Connell*, 8 Pepperdine L.Rev. 79 (1980).

important aspects of the judicial process—that in judicial decision making, value judgments inhere in the choosing of the controlling legal precept.

The majority has made a value judgment. They have decided that when a labor union is involved in litigation with a business firm other than one with which it has a collective bargaining agreement, the court is required to take as a starting point the body of antitrust laws. They ask whether the alleged agreement here was exempt from antitrust scrutiny or lawful under antitrust law, but do not ask what I perceive to be the real issue—does antitrust law apply to these facts at all, and if so, why. From the majority's initial premise, it follows that organized labor's activity is generally proscribed by antitrust laws unless labor can convince the court that its activity falls within some narrow exception to those laws. All labor exemptions rest on the meaning and interaction of the antitrust and the labor statutes. But these exceptions, which have been given the patronizing labels, "statutory" and "non-statutory" exemptions, have been carved out, not by Congress, but by the federal courts.

One who agrees with the majority's value judgment, and the political, sociological, and economic philosophies which influence it, will not fault the result it commands. But I disagree with their fundamental legal and philosophical premises. While I admit that their view is supported by a respectable body of federal decisions, I argue for a different set of fundamental values, values less antagonistic to the rights of organized labor and more reflective of the national labor policy judgments made by Congress.

I have a second disagreement with the majority which is more prosaic—I do not share their unabashed infatuation with the decision in *Connell* . . .. As a member of an inferior court in the federal judicial hierarchy, I must respect the precedential value of *Connell*. But I detect from it no inspirational philosophy or policy statements which persuade me to extend its holding, certainly not to the dissimilar, material facts of this case.

My starting point is a recognition that both the labor and the antitrust laws embody equally important congressional declarations of public policy. Unlike the majority, I do not think that either policy has a preferred status over the other. They must be viewed, in Justice Frankfurter's felicitous expression, "as a harmonizing text." . . . In order to harmonize these apparently divergent policies, and because of the legislatively enacted national labor policy, I think it proper to presume that labor activity does not come within the purview of the antitrust laws unless it is *clearly not* conduct for which the labor laws provide penalties and sanctions.

Queries. Does Judge Adams' majority opinion in *Muko II* reach the result he advocated in *Muko I*, by shifting the antitrust standard for labor boycotts from *per se* illegality to a rule of reason? Is the court re-litigating the issue of labor's antitrust immunity under the guise of defining the standard for antitrust illegality? Does the decision to apply a *per se* rule depend, as the majority opinion suggests, upon "extensive experience with a particular kind of *labor conduct*," or upon extensive experience with a particular type of commercial practice generally? Have the courts in other cases you have read examined whether *per se* rules are affected by the fact the restraint is one affecting gasoline marketing, the distribution of television sets, the services of professional engineers or doctors, etc.? Do you agree with Judge Aldisert's approach and would it require a reversal of *Connell* to implement?

(2) *Varying the Antitrust Standard of Proof in Non-Exempt Labor Restraints of Trade.* In *James R. Snyder Co., Inc. v. Associated General Contractors, Detroit Chapter, Inc.*[22] independent masonry contractors charged the union they bargained with had conspired with a general contractor's bargaining group to impose the general contractor's wage agreement on independent contractors. After recognizing that the issue of whether the exemption was forfeited was separate from the issue of whether the conduct violated the antitrust laws, the Court of Appeals held proof of a conspiracy to impose the defendant's wage settlement on other employers would, under *Pennington,* "eliminate any claim of a labor exemption under the antitrust laws."[23] On the question of the standard for proving an antitrust violation, the Court held the plaintiff must prove the union and employer agreement to impose wage rates on other employers was done with a "predatory intent"— an "intent to injure the plaintiff's business." An intent to preserve multi-employer bargaining on both the part of the union and the general contractors was held not sufficient evidence of predatory intent. Rather, the Court held the plaintiff must prove an intent to drive the plaintiffs out of business.

Queries. Is this approach consistent with *Muko II?* Should courts apply the same substantive standard of illegality as used elsewhere in antitrust, but vary the burden of proof to show a violation in light of the need to accommodate labor law and antitrust? (See discussion supra Chapter IV, B 3, "Sufficiency of the Evidence and Burdens of Proof"). Is part of the difficulty in *Muko II* a failure to recognize *per se* "rules" as evidentiary presumptions of illegality and "tools" of analysis rather than hard and fast rules with no exceptions? Is another part of the difficulty with *Muko II* a failure to recognize that the burden of proof might be varied to accommodate some overriding public policy (i.e., harmonize labor law and antitrust law) as in the *Snyder* case? Is a further difficulty with *Muko II,* the failure of the Supreme Court to appreciate fully the implications of their decision in *Connell* for cases like *Muko II?*

(3) *Picketing, The First Amendment and Antitrust.* The status of picketing as a form of "speech" protected by the First Amendment has had a checkered history. In *Thornhill v. Alabama,*[24] the Court held picketing aimed at organizing a beauty shop was a form of constitutionally protected free speech. Shortly thereafter, limitations began to be applied to the concept of picketing as a form of constitutionally protected speech in view of its potential for coercion and otherwise injuring the rights of third parties.[25] By 1957, the Court upheld a state court injunction against picketing designed to coerce an employer to coerce his employees.[26]

Federal labor legislation has now generally been held to preempt state labor regulation (see p. 1132 supra). Under the National Labor Relations Act's ban on coercion by secondary boycotts there is a proviso to § 8(b)(4)(ii)

22. 677 F.2d 1111 (6th Cir. 1982), certiorari denied ___ U.S. ___, 103 S.Ct. 374, 74 L.Ed.2d 508.

23. Id. at 1119.

24. 310 U.S. 88, 60 S.Ct. 736, 84 L.Ed. 1093 (1940).

25. The evolution of the picketing-free speech controversy is briefly traced in C. Summers, H. Wellington & A. Hyde, Labor Law: Cases and Materials,

pp. 467–68 (2d Ed. 1982). One of the more significant cases in this evolution from an antitrust viewpoint is Giboney v. Empire Storage & Ice Co., 336 U.S. 490, 69 S.Ct. 684, 93 L.Ed. 834 (1949).

26. International Brotherhood of Teamsters, Local 695 v. Vogt, Inc., 354 U.S. 284, 77 S.Ct. 1166, 1 L.Ed.2d 1347 (1957), rehearing denied 354 U.S. 945, 77 S.Ct. 1423, 1 L.Ed.2d 1558.

(B) exempting "publicity, other than by picketing, for the purpose of truthfully advising the public . . . that a product or products are produced by an employer with whom the labor organization has a primary dispute and are distributed by another employer, as long as such publicity does not have an effect of inducing any individual employed by any person other than the primary employer in the course of his employment to refuse to pick up, deliver, or transport any goods, or not to perform any services, at the establishment of the employer engaged in such distribution." [27]   In *National Labor Relations Board v. Fruit and Vegetable Packers and Warehousemen, Local 760*,[28] union informational picketing to inform consumers at grocery stores selling apples packed and warehoused by firms the union was striking was held an unfair labor practice by the N.L.R.B. The Board held the above quoted provision with the language "other than picketing" outlawed all picketing directed at customers at a secondary site. The Court of Appeals set aside the order on the grounds that the Board must show the picketing would "threaten, coerce or restrain" the grocery stores before the Board could find the conduct an unfair labor practice.[29]   The Supreme Court reversed the Court of Appeals, holding Congress did not intend to bar picketing aimed at informing consumers of a labor dispute even though the union picketing resulted in decreased purchases by the grocery stores. Where the picketing is aimed at persuading consumers not to trade at all with the secondary employers (the grocery stores), however, it can be found an unfair labor practice.

More recent decisions on picketing have tended to acknowledge first amendment concerns about regulating it, particularly where the picketing is informational and aimed at informing the public about a labor dispute.[30]   The Court has also been recognizing "commercial speech" as protected by the First Amendment and has defined the "persons" entitled to invoke First Amendment protections to include corporations. These developments, when considered together, may have significant implications for cases like *Muko II*.

Queries: What result in *Muko II* if the unions had simply picketed Silver's restaurants and had not "agreed" with Silver's to restrict Silver's use of non-union contractors? Could the union's "informational" picketing be characterized as protected First Amendment speech, thereby precluding N.L.R.B. or judicial action under the antitrust laws to restrain or punish the picketing? [31]

27. 29 U.S.C.A. § 158(b)(4)(ii)(B); Pleasure, Publicity Proviso to Section 8(b)(4) of the National Labor Relations Act and the Noerr-Pennington Doctrine: Protection for Labor's Voice to be Heard, 40 Fed. B. News & J. 213 (1981).

28. 377 U.S. 58, 84 S.Ct. 1063, 12 L.Ed.2d 129 (1964).

29. 308 F.2d 311 (D.C.Cir. 1962).

30. See, e.g., Hudgens v. National Labor Relations Board, 424 U.S. 507, 96 S.Ct. 1029, 47 L.Ed.2d 196 (1976).

31. See National Association for Advancement of Colored People v. Claiborne Hardware Co., discussed *supra* pp. 538–540.

INDEX

†